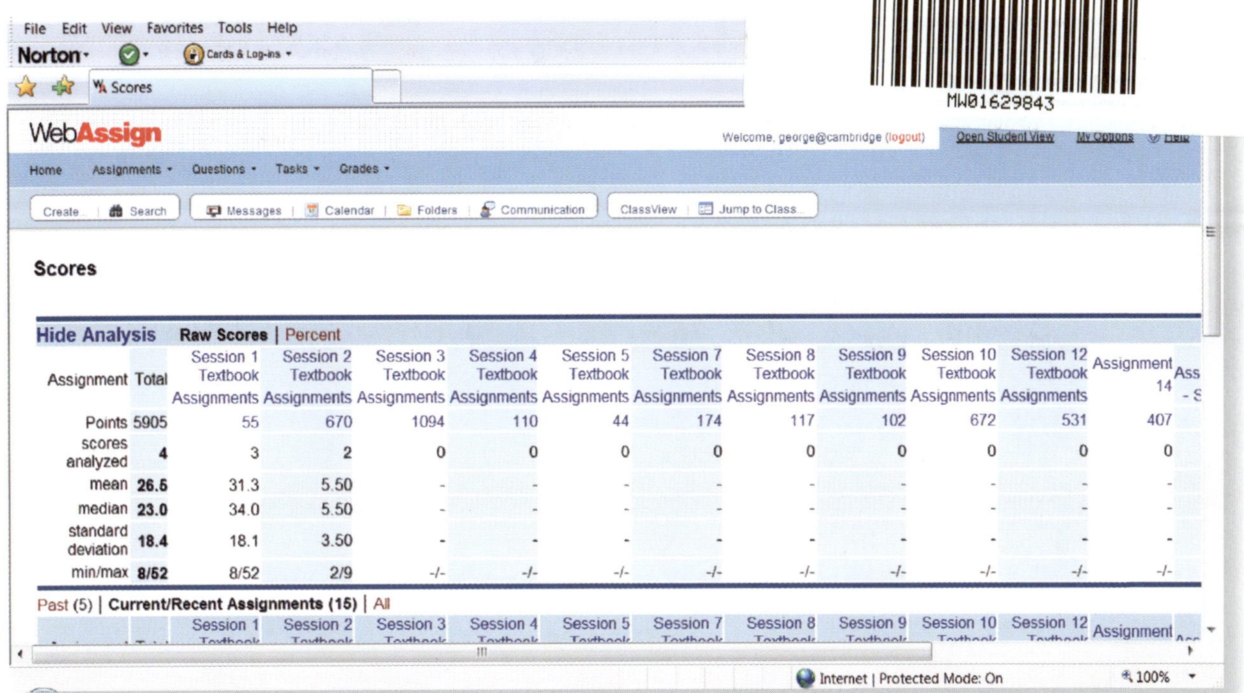

Make Instruction Needs-Based

- Identify where your students are struggling and customize your instruction to address their needs.
- Gauge how your entire class or individual students are doing by viewing the easy to use grade book.
- Ensure your MBAs are getting the additional reinforcement and direction they need between class meetings.

Provide Instruction and Practice When You Are Not Available

- With our eLectures, your students can revisit accounting topics as many times as they like or until they master the topic.
- You can create a set of practice problems that students can attempt and receive feedback on outside your class.

Want to learn more about WebAssign?

Contact your sales representative or email customerservice@cambridgepub.com

Cambridge Business Publishers Series in Accounting

Financial Accounting

- **Financial Accounting, 3e** by Dyckman, Magee, and Pfeiffer
- **Financial Accounting for MBAs, 4e** by Easton, Wild, Halsey, and McAnally
- **Financial Accounting for Executives & MBAs, 2e** by Ferris & Wallace
- **Cases in Financial Reporting and Analysis, 6e** by Engel, Hirst, and McAnally

Managerial Accounting

- **Managerial Accounting, 5e** by Hartgraves, Morse, and Davis
- **Cases in Managerial and Cost Accounting, 1e** by Allen, Brownlee, Haskins, and Lynch

Combined Financial & Managerial Accounting

- **Financial & Managerial Accounting for MBAs, 2e** by Easton, Halsey, McAnally, Hartgraves, and Morse

Intermediate Accounting

- **Cases in Financial Reporting and Analysis, 6e** by Engel, Hirst, and McAnally

Cost Accounting

- **Cases in Managerial and Cost Accounting, 1e** by Allen, Brownlee, Haskins, and Lynch

Financial Statement Analysis & Valuation

- **Financial Statement Analysis & Valuation, 2e** by Easton, McAnally, Fairfield, Zhang, and Halsey
- **Cases in Financial Reporting and Analysis, 6e** by Engel, Hirst, and McAnally

Advanced Accounting

- **Advanced Accounting, 1e** by Hamlen, Huefner, and Largay
- **Advanced Accounting, 1e** by Halsey & Hopkins

THIRD EDITION

Financial Accounting

THOMAS R. DYCKMAN
Cornell University

ROBERT P. MAGEE
Northwestern University

GLENN M. PFEIFFER
Chapman University

Cambridge
BUSINESS PUBLISHERS

To my wife, Ann, and children, Daniel, James, Linda, and David;
and to Pete Dukes, a friend who is always there.
    —TRD

To my wife, Peggy, and our family, Paul and Teisha, Michael and
Heather, and grandchildren Sage, Caillean, Rhiannon, Corin,
Connor, and Harrison.
    —RPM

To my wife, Kathie, and my daughter, Jaclyn
    —GMP

Cambridge Business Publishers

FINANCIAL ACCOUNTING, Third Edition, by Thomas R. Dyckman, Robert P. Magee, and Glenn M. Pfeiffer.

10 Digit ISBN 1-934319-60-0
13 Digit ISBN 978-1-934319-60-4

Bookstores & Faculty: To order this book, contact the company via email **customerservice@cambridgepub.com** or call 800-619-6473.

Students: To order this book, please visit the book's website and order directly online.

Printed in Canada 10 9 8 7 6 5 4 3 2 1

About the Authors

The combined skills and expertise of Tom Dyckman, Bob Magee, and Glenn Pfeiffer create the ideal team to author this exciting financial accounting textbook. Their combined experience in award-winning teaching, consulting, and research in the area of financial accounting and analysis provides a powerful foundation for this pioneering textbook.

Thomas R. Dyckman is Ann Whitney Olin Professor of Accounting and Quantitative Analysis and Associate Dean for Academic Affairs at Cornell University's Johnson Graduate School of Management. In addition to teaching accounting and quantitative analysis, he has taught in Cornell's Executive Development Program. He earned his doctorate degree from the University of Michigan. He is a former member of the Financial Accounting Standards Board Advisory Committee and the Financial Accounting Foundation, which oversees the FASB. He was president of the American Accounting Association in 1982 and received the association's *Outstanding Educator* Award for the year 1987. He also received the AICPA's *Notable Contributions to Accounting Literature Award* in 1966 and 1978.

Professor Dyckman has extensive industrial experience that includes work with the U.S. Navy and IBM. He has conducted seminars for Cornell Executive Development Program and Managing the Next Generation of Technology, as well as for Ocean Spray, Goodyear, Morgan Guaranty, GTE, Southern New England Telephone, and Goulds Pumps.

Professor Dyckman has coauthored eleven books and written over 50 journal articles on topics from financial markets to the application of quantitative and behavioral theory to administrative decision making. He has been a member of the editorial boards of *The Accounting Review, The Journal of Finance and Quantitative Analysis, The Journal of Accounting and Economics, The Journal of Management Accounting Research,* and *The Journal of Accounting Education.*

Robert P. Magee is Keith I. DeLashmutt Professor of Accounting Information and Management at the Kellogg School of Management at Northwestern University. He received his A.B., M.S. and Ph.D. from Cornell University. Prior to joining the Kellogg faculty in 1976, he was a faculty member at the University of Chicago's Graduate School of Business. For academic year 1980-81, he was a visiting faculty member at IMEDE (now IMD) in Lausanne, Switzerland.

Professor Magee's research focuses on the use of accounting information to facilitate decision-making and control within organizations. He has published articles in *The Accounting Review,* the *Journal of Accounting Research,* the *Journal of Accounting and Economics,* and a variety of other journals. He is the author of *Advanced Managerial Accounting* and co-author (with Thomas R. Dyckman and David H. Downes) of *Efficient Capital Markets and Accounting: A Critical Analysis.* The latter book received the Notable Contribution to the Accounting Literature Award from the AICPA in 1978. Professor Magee has served on the editorial boards of *The Accounting Review,* the *Journal of Accounting Research,* the *Journal of Accounting and Economics* and the *Journal of Accounting, Auditing and Finance.* From 1994–96, he served as Editor of *The Accounting Review,* the quarterly research journal of the American Accounting Association. He received the American Accounting Association's Outstanding Accounting Educator Award in 1999 and the Illinois CPA Society Outstanding Educator Award in 2000.

Professor Magee teaches financial accounting to MBA and Executive MBA students. He has received several teaching awards at the Kellogg School, including the Alumni Choice Outstanding Professor Award in 2003.

Glenn M. Pfeiffer is Professor of Accounting and Economics at the George L. Argyros School of Business and Economics at Chapman University. He received his M.S. and Ph.D. from Cornell University after he earned a bachelors degree from Hope College. Prior to joining the faculty at the Argyros School, he held appointments at the University of Washington, Cornell University, the University of Chicago, the University of Arizona, and San Diego State University.

Professor Pfeiffer's research focuses on financial reporting and capital markets. He has investigated issues relating to lease accounting, LIFO inventory liquidation, earnings per share, employee stock options, corporate reorganization, and technology investments. He has published articles in *The Accounting Review,* the *Financial Analysts Journal,* the *International Journal of Accounting Information Systems,* the *Journal of Applied Business Research,* the *Journal of High Technology Management Research,* the *Journal of Accounting Education,* and several other academic journals. In addition, he has published numerous case studies in financial accounting and reporting.

Professor Pfeiffer teaches financial accounting and financial analysis to undergraduate, MBA, and Executive students. He has also taught managerial accounting for MBAs. He has won several teaching awards at both the undergraduate and graduate levels.

Preface

Welcome to the third edition of *Financial Accounting* and, to adopters of the first and second editions, thank you for the great success those editions have enjoyed. We wrote this book to equip students with the accounting techniques and insights necessary to succeed in today's business environment. It reflects our combined experience in teaching financial accounting to college students at all levels. For anyone who pursues a career in business, the ability to read, analyze, and interpret published financial reports is an essential skill. *Financial Accounting* is written for future business leaders who want to understand how financial statements are prepared and how the information in published financial reports is used by investors, creditors, financial analysts, and managers. Our goal is to provide the most engaging, relevant, and accessible textbook available.

TARGET AUDIENCE

Financial Accounting is intended for use in the first financial accounting course at either the undergraduate or graduate level; one that balances the preparation of financial statements with their analysis and interpretation. This book accommodates mini-courses lasting only a few days as well as extended courses lasting a full semester.

Financial Accounting is real-world oriented and focuses on the most salient aspects of accounting. It teaches students how to read, analyze, and interpret financial accounting data to make informed business decisions. To that end, it consistently incorporates **real company data**, both in the body of each chapter and throughout the assignment material.

REAL DATA INCORPORATED THROUGHOUT

Today's business students must be skilled in using real financial statements to make business decisions. We feel strongly that the more exposure students get to real financial statements, the more comfortable they become with the variety in financial statements that exists across companies and industries. Through their exposure to various financial statements, students will learn that, while financial statements do not all look the same, they can readily understand and interpret them to make business decisions. Furthermore, today's students must have the skills to go beyond basic financial statements to interpret and apply nonfinancial disclosures, such as footnotes and supplementary reports. We expose students to the analysis and interpretation of real company data and nonfinancial disclosures through the use of focus companies in each chapter, the generous incorporation of footnotes, financial analysis discussions in nearly every chapter, and an abundance of assignments that draw on real company data and disclosures.

Focus Companies for Each Chapter

Each chapter's content is explained through the accounting and reporting activities of real companies. Each chapter incorporates a "focus company" for special emphasis and demonstration. The enhanced instructional value of focus companies comes from the way they engage students in real analysis and interpretation. Focus companies were selected based on student appeal and the diversity of industries.

Chapter 1	**Nike**	**Chapter 7**	**Home Depot**
Chapter 2	**Walgreens**	**Chapter 8**	**Procter & Gamble**
Chapter 3	**Walgreens**	**Chapter 9**	**Verizon**
Chapter 4	**Walgreens**	**Chapter 10**	**American Airlines**
Chapter 5	**PepsiCo**	**Chapter 11**	**Pfizer**
Chapter 6	**Cisco**	**Chapter 12**	**Google**

Footnotes and Management Disclosures

We incorporate footnote and other management disclosures, where appropriate, throughout the book. We explain the significance of the footnote and then demonstrate how to use the disclosed information to make managerial inferences and decisions. A representative sample follows.

Footnote Disclosures, and Interpretations

In its balance sheets, Cisco reports Accounts receivables, net of allowance for doubtful accounts of $3,177 million at July 25, 2009, and $3,821 at July 26, 2008. In its MD&A, the company provides the following information.

Allowances for Receivables and Sales Returns

The allowances for receivables were as follows (in millions, except percentages):

	July 25, 2009	July 26, 2008
Allowance for doubtful accounts	$216	$177
Percentage of gross accounts receivable	6.4%	4.4%

The allowances are based on our assessment of the collectability of customer accounts. We regularly review the allowances to ensure their adequacy by considering factors such as historical experience, credit quality, age of the receivable balances and economic conditions that may affect a customer's ability to pay. In addition, we perform credit reviews and statistical portfolio analysis to assess the credit quality of our receivables. We also consider the concentration of receivables outstanding with a particular customer in assessing the adequacy of our allowances . . .

Financial Analysis Discussions

Each chapter includes a financial analysis discussion that introduces key ratios and applies them to the financial statements of the chapter's focus company. By weaving some analysis into each chapter, we try to instill in students a deeper appreciation for the significance of the accounting methods being discussed. One such analysis discussion follows.

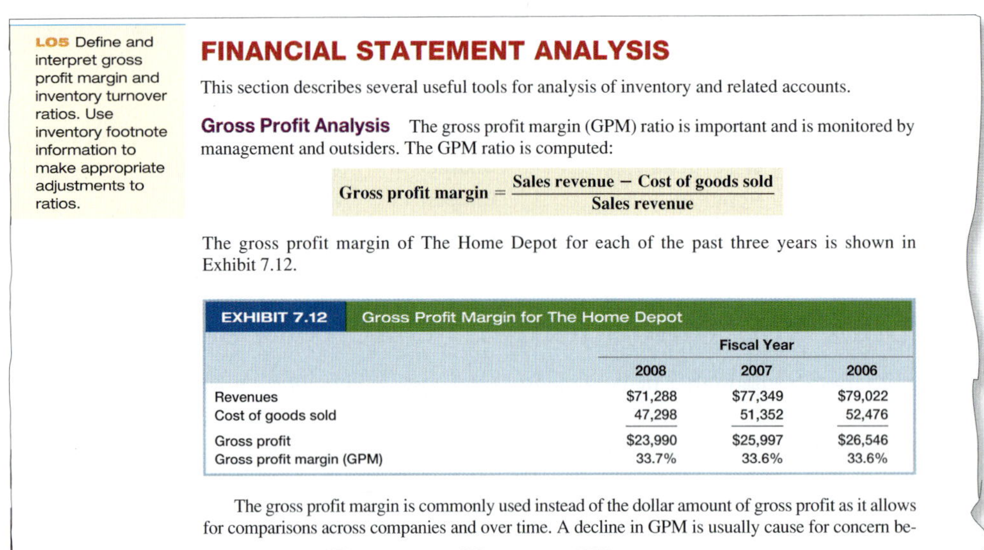

LO5 Define and interpret gross profit margin and inventory turnover ratios. Use inventory footnote information to make appropriate adjustments to ratios.

FINANCIAL STATEMENT ANALYSIS

This section describes several useful tools for analysis of inventory and related accounts.

Gross Profit Analysis   The gross profit margin (GPM) ratio is important and is monitored by management and outsiders. The GPM ratio is computed:

$$\text{Gross profit margin} = \frac{\text{Sales revenue} - \text{Cost of goods sold}}{\text{Sales revenue}}$$

The gross profit margin of The Home Depot for each of the past three years is shown in Exhibit 7.12.

EXHIBIT 7.12	Gross Profit Margin for The Home Depot		
	Fiscal Year		
	2008	**2007**	**2006**
Revenues	$71,288	$77,349	$79,022
Cost of goods sold	47,298	51,352	52,476
Gross profit	$23,990	$25,997	$26,546
Gross profit margin (GPM)	33.7%	33.6%	33.6%

The gross profit margin is commonly used instead of the dollar amount of gross profit as it allows for comparisons across companies and over time. A decline in GPM is usually cause for concern be-

Assignments that Draw on Real Data

It is essential for students to be able to apply what they have learned to real financial statements. Therefore, we have included an abundance of assignments in each chapter that draw on recent, real data and disclosures. These assignments are readily identified by an icon in the margin that usually includes the company's ticker symbol and the exchange on which the company's stock trades. A representative example follows.

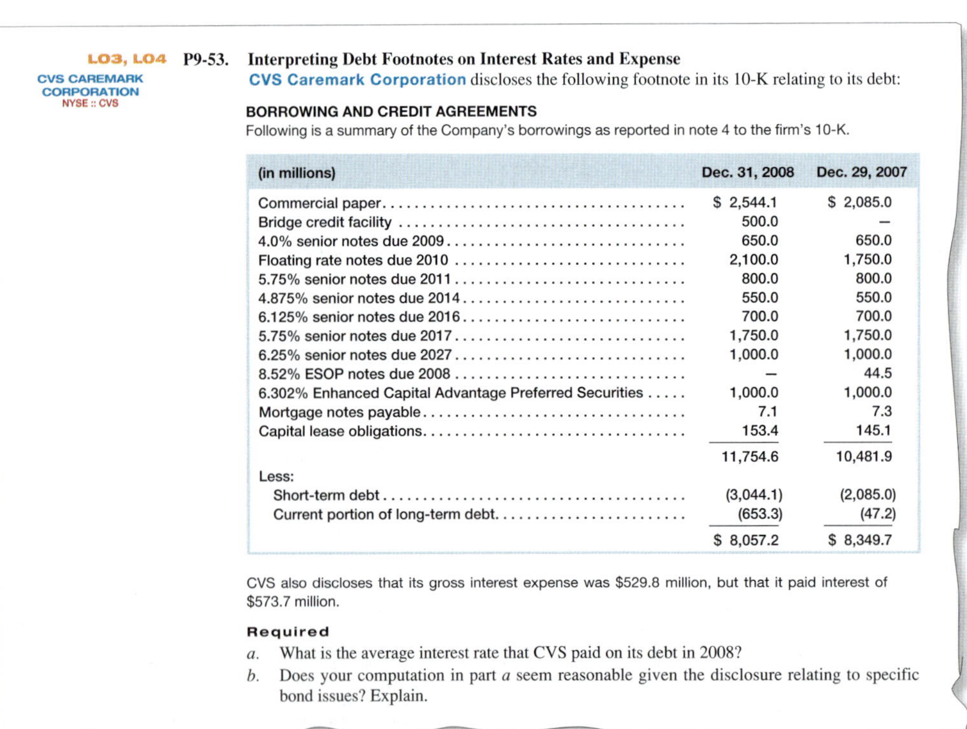

LO3, LO4

CVS CAREMARK CORPORATION
NYSE :: CVS

P9-53.   Interpreting Debt Footnotes on Interest Rates and Expense

CVS Caremark Corporation discloses the following footnote in its 10-K relating to its debt:

BORROWING AND CREDIT AGREEMENTS
Following is a summary of the Company's borrowings as reported in note 4 to the firm's 10-K.

(in millions)	Dec. 31, 2008	Dec. 29, 2007
Commercial paper	$ 2,544.1	$ 2,085.0
Bridge credit facility	500.0	—
4.0% senior notes due 2009	650.0	650.0
Floating rate notes due 2010	2,100.0	1,750.0
5.75% senior notes due 2011	800.0	800.0
4.875% senior notes due 2014	550.0	550.0
6.125% senior notes due 2016	700.0	700.0
5.75% senior notes due 2017	1,750.0	1,750.0
6.25% senior notes due 2027	1,000.0	1,000.0
8.52% ESOP notes due 2008	—	44.5
6.302% Enhanced Capital Advantage Preferred Securities	1,000.0	1,000.0
Mortgage notes payable	7.1	7.3
Capital lease obligations	153.4	145.1
	11,754.6	10,481.9
Less:		
Short-term debt	(3,044.1)	(2,085.0)
Current portion of long-term debt	(653.3)	(47.2)
	$ 8,057.2	$ 8,349.7

CVS also discloses that its gross interest expense was $529.8 million, but that it paid interest of $573.7 million.

Required

a.   What is the average interest rate that CVS paid on its debt in 2008?

b.   Does your computation in part *a* seem reasonable given the disclosure relating to specific bond issues? Explain.

BALANCED APPROACH

As instructors of introductory financial accounting, we recognize that the first financial accounting course serves the general business students as well as potential accounting majors. *Financial Accounting* embraces this reality. This book **balances financial reporting, analysis, interpretation**, and **decision making** with the more standard aspects of accounting such as **journal entries**, **T-accounts**, and the **preparation of financial statements**.

3-Step Process: Analyze, Journalize, Post

One technique we use throughout the book to maintain a balanced approach is the incorporation of a 3-step process to analyze and record transactions. **Step 1** analyzes the impact of various transactions on the financial statements using the financial statement effects template. **Step 2** records the transaction using journal entries and **Step 3** requires students to post the journal entries to T-accounts.

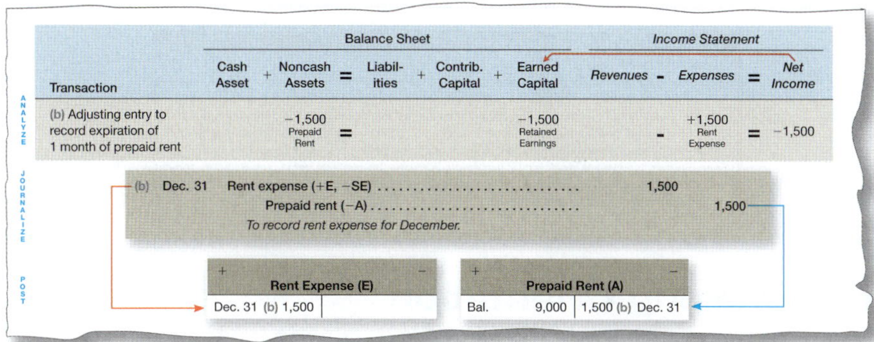

The template captures each transaction's effects on the four financial statements: the balance sheet, income statement, statement of stockholders' equity, and statement of cash flows. For the balance sheet, we differentiate between cash and noncash assets to identify the cash effects of transactions. Likewise, equity is separated into the contributed and earned capital components (the latter includes retained earnings as its major element). Finally, income statement effects are separated into revenues, expenses, and net income (the updating of retained earnings is denoted with an arrow line running from net income to earned capital). This template provides a convenient means to represent financial accounting transactions and events in a simple, concise manner for assessing their effects on financial statements.

INTERNATIONAL FINANCIAL REPORTING STANDARDS (IFRS)

The convergence of U.S. GAAP and International Financial Reporting Standards (IFRS) is in process. Our introductory students should be prepared for this eventuality with a basic understanding of the similarities and differences in the current reporting requirements and methods under U.S. GAAP and IFRS. Consequently, we incorporate discussions that examine these similarities and differences where appropriate throughout the book in IFRS Reporting Insight boxes, as illustrated here:

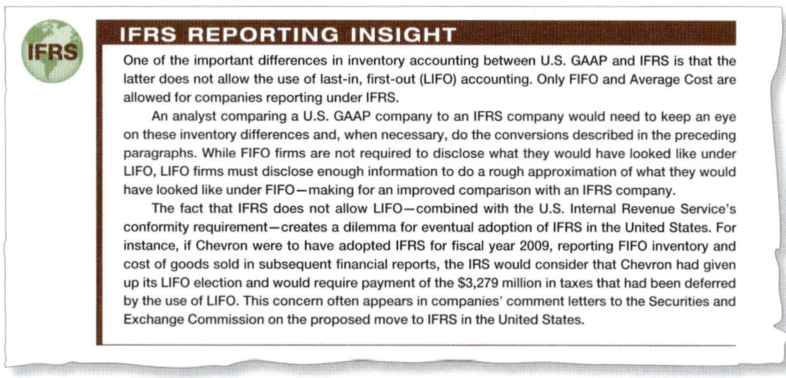

IFRS REPORTING INSIGHT

One of the important differences in inventory accounting between U.S. GAAP and IFRS is that the latter does not allow the use of last-in, first-out (LIFO) accounting. Only FIFO and Average Cost are allowed for companies reporting under IFRS.

An analyst comparing a U.S. GAAP company to an IFRS company would need to keep an eye on these inventory differences and, when necessary, do the conversions described in the preceding paragraphs. While FIFO firms are not required to disclose what they would have looked like under LIFO, LIFO firms must disclose enough information to do a rough approximation of what they would have looked like under FIFO—making for an improved comparison with an IFRS company.

The fact that IFRS does not allow LIFO—combined with the U.S. Internal Revenue Service's conformity requirement—creates a dilemma for eventual adoption of IFRS in the United States. For instance, if Chevron were to have adopted IFRS for fiscal year 2009, reporting FIFO inventory and cost of goods sold in subsequent financial reports, the IRS would consider that Chevron had given up its LIFO election and would require payment of the $3,279 million in taxes that had been deferred by the use of LIFO. This concern often appears in companies' comment letters to the Securities and Exchange Commission on the proposed move to IFRS in the United States.

We also include exercises and problems throughout the text, where appropriate, to stimulate a discussion of international reporting differences. Our approach is conceptual—we purposefully avoid the detailed mechanics that are more appropriate for an intermediate level accounting course at either the undergraduate or graduate level. We feel strongly that our IFRS coverage exposes students to the similarities and differences without overwhelming them.

INNOVATIVE PEDAGOGY

Financial Accounting includes special features specifically designed for the student.

Business Insights

Students appreciate and become more engaged when they can see the real world relevance of what they are learning in the classroom. We have included a generous number of current, real world examples throughout each chapter in Business Insight boxes. The following is a representative example:

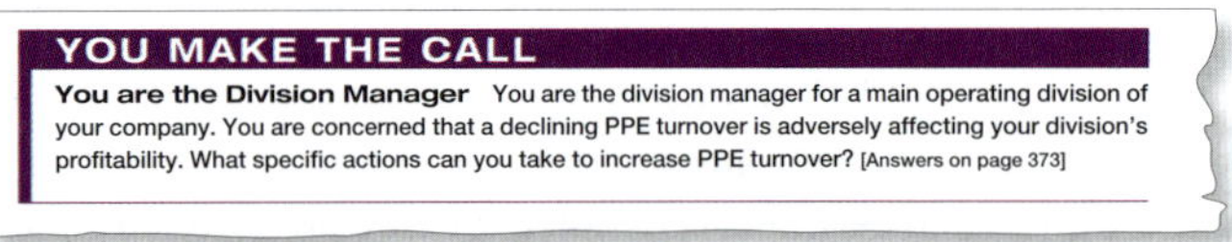

Decision Making Orientation

One primary goal of a financial accounting course is to teach students the skills needed to apply their accounting knowledge to solving real business problems. With that goal in mind, **You Make the Call** boxes in each chapter encourage students to apply the material presented to solving actual business scenarios.

Mid-Chapter and Chapter-End Reviews

Financial accounting can be challenging—especially for students lacking business experience or previous exposure to business courses. To reinforce concepts presented in each chapter and to ensure student comprehension, we include mid-chapter and chapter-end reviews that require students to recall and apply the financial accounting techniques and concepts described in each chapter.

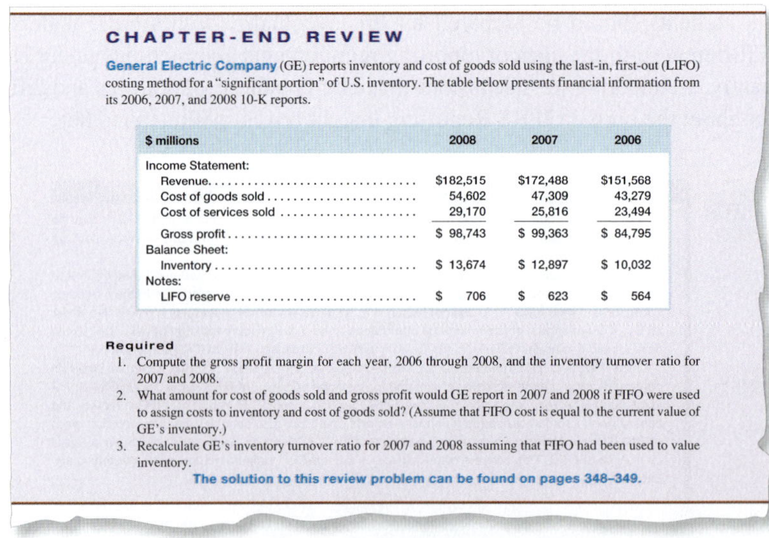

CHAPTER-END REVIEW

General Electric Company (GE) reports inventory and cost of goods sold using the last-in, first-out (LIFO) costing method for a "significant portion" of U.S. inventory. The table below presents financial information from its 2006, 2007, and 2008 10-K reports.

$ millions	2008	2007	2006
Income Statement:			
Revenue	$182,515	$172,488	$151,568
Cost of goods sold	54,602	47,309	43,279
Cost of services sold	29,170	25,816	23,494
Gross profit	$ 98,743	$ 99,363	$ 84,795
Balance Sheet:			
Inventory	$ 13,674	$ 12,897	$ 10,032
Notes:			
LIFO reserve	$ 706	$ 623	$ 564

Required

1. Compute the gross profit margin for each year, 2006 through 2008, and the inventory turnover ratio for 2007 and 2008.
2. What amount for cost of goods sold and gross profit would GE report in 2007 and 2008 if FIFO were used to assign costs to inventory and cost of goods sold? (Assume that FIFO cost is equal to the current value of GE's inventory.)
3. Recalculate GE's inventory turnover ratio for 2007 and 2008 assuming that FIFO had been used to value inventory.

The solution to this review problem can be found on pages 348–349.

Research Insights for Business Students

Academic research plays an important role in the way business is conducted, accounting is performed, and students are taught. It is important for students to recognize how modern research and modern business practice interact. Therefore, we periodically incorporate relevant research to help students understand the important relation between research and modern business.

> **RESEARCH INSIGHT**
>
> **LIFO and Stock Prices**   The value-relevance of inventory disclosures depends at least partly on whether investors rely more on the income statement or the balance sheet to assess future cash flows. Under LIFO, cost of goods sold reflects current costs, whereas FIFO ending inventory reflects current costs. This implies that LIFO enhances the usefulness of the income statement to the detriment of the balance sheet. This trade-off partly motivates the required LIFO reserve disclosure (the adjustment necessary to restate LIFO ending inventory and cost of good sold to FIFO).
>
> Research suggests that LIFO-based income statements better reflect stock prices than do pro forma FIFO income statements that are constructed using the LIFO reserve. Research also shows a negative relation between stock prices and LIFO reserve—meaning that higher magnitudes of LIFO reserve are associated with lower stock prices. This is consistent with the LIFO reserve being viewed as an inflation indicator (for either current or future inventory costs) detrimental to company value.

FLEXIBILITY FOR COURSES OF VARYING LENGTHS

Many instructors have approached us to ask about suggested chapter coverage based on courses of varying length. To that end, we provide the following table of possible course designs:

	15 Week Semester-Course	10 Week Quarter-Course	6 Week Mini-Course	1 Week Intensive-Course
Chapter 1	Week 1	Week 1	Week 1	Day 1
Chapter 2	Week 2 & 3	Week 2	Week 1 & 2	Day 1
Chapter 3	Week 3 & 4	Week 3 & 4	Week 2 & 3	Day 2
Chapter 4	Week 5 & 6	Week 4 & 5	Optional	Optional
Chapter 5	Week 6 & 7	Optional	Optional	Optional
Chapter 6	Week 7 & 8	Week 6	Week 3	Day 3
Chapter 7	Week 9	Week 7	Week 4	Day 4
Chapter 8	Week 10	Week 8	Week 5	Day 4
Chapter 9	Week 11 & 12	Week 9	Week 6	Day 5
Chapter 10	Week 12 & 13	Week 10	Week 6 (optional)	Skim
Chapter 11	Week 14	Optional	Optional	Optional
Chapter 12	Week 15	Optional	Optional	Optional

NEW TO THE 3RD EDITION

- Robert Magee of Northwestern University's Kellogg School of Management joined the author team this edition.
- We have expanded the discussion of **International Financial Reporting Standards (IFRS)** and incorporated new IFRS Reporting Insight boxes throughout the text to introduce students to the similarities and differences between U.S. GAAP and IFRS.

- Chapter 4 on Cash Flows now introduces the direct method before transitioning to the indirect method. The spreadsheet approach to preparing the SCF is now an appendix to the chapter.

- The chapter on financial statement analysis was rewritten and now presents a traditional approach to profitability analysis. It shows how return on equity (ROE) and its components reveal company profitability drivers. (The analysis of operating returns, which was the focus of this chapter in the 2nd edition, has been moved to an appendix.) This chapter was moved forward in the book—it is now Chapter 5—to emphasize the importance of analysis for business decisions.

- Pro forma financial statements are now covered in an appendix to Chapter 5.

- The tax discussion in Chapter 10 has been expanded to include examples that illustrate the temporary and permanent differences that exist between income reported to the IRS for tax purposes and that which is reported under accrual accounting.

- The real company data throughout the book has been updated to reflect the most current financial statements available at the time of publication.

- Walgreens is featured as the focus company for Chapters 2, 3, and 4.

- Chapter 5 features PepsiCo as the focus company. In addition, American Airlines replaces Southwest Airlines as the focus company in Chapter 10.

- Appendix A explains time value of money concepts and provides TVM tables. Calculations are also illustrated using a financial calculator. The use of a financial calculator to value liabilities is highlighted in Chapters 9 and 10. A representative example follows:

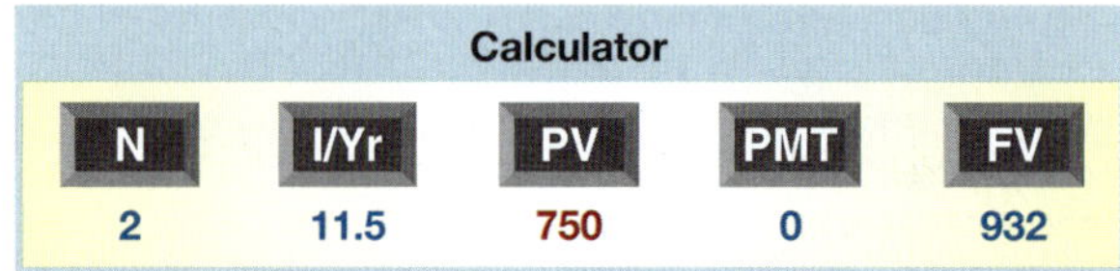

In addition to the chapter specific changes, there have been several changes that span the entire book. Some of these global changes include: updated numbers for examples, illustrations, and assignments that use real data; updated footnotes and other nonfinancial disclosures; updated excerpts from the business and popular press; numerous assignments in each chapter have been revised or replaced with new assignments; and a new, accessible design was created for the 3rd edition.

SUPPLEMENT PACKAGE

Homework Management System

WebAssign. This supplement is ideal for distance learning and for faculty responsible for large sections and/or courses requiring independent learning. Available for an additional fee, WebAssign is a Web-based homework management system that enables students to solve select assignments in each chapter and receive instant feedback. Assignments with the WebAssign logo (**WebAssign.**) in the margin next to them are available in WebAssign. Instructors can access the gradebook feature to track student progress throughout the term. For more information, contact your sales representative or try the WebAssign demo at **www.webassign.com/textbooks/accounting_textbooks.html**.

Companion Casebook

Cases in Financial Reporting, 6th edition by Ellen Engel (University of Chicago), D. Eric Hirst (University of Texas – Austin), and Mary Lea McAnally (Texas A&M University). This book comprises 28 cases and is a perfect companion book for faculty interested in exposing students to a wide range of real financial statements. The cases are current and cover companies from Canada, France, Austria, the Netherlands, the UK, India, as well as from the U.S. Each case deals with a specific financial accounting topic within the context of one (or more) corporation's financial statements. Each case contains financial statement information (a balance sheet, income statement, statement of cash flows, and footnotes) and a set of directed questions pertaining to one or two specific financial accounting issues. This is a separate, saleable casebook (**ISBN 978-1-934319-19-2**). Contact your sales representative to request a desk copy or email **customerservice@cambridgepub.com**.

For Instructors

Instructor CD-ROM: This convenient supplement provides the text's ancillary materials on a portable CD-ROM. All the faculty supplements that accompany the textbook are available, including PowerPoint, Solutions Manual, Test Bank, and Computerized Test Bank.

Solutions Manual: Created by the authors, the *Solutions Manual* contains complete solutions to all the assignment material in the text.

PowerPoint: The PowerPoint slides outline key elements of each chapter.

Test Bank: The test bank includes multiple-choice items, matching questions, short essay questions, and problems.

Website: All instructor materials are accessible via the book's Website (password protected) along with other useful links and marketing information. **www.cambridgepub.com**

Blackboard Cartridge: A full complement of online material is available for incorporation with your Blackboard course management system.

For Students

Student Solutions Manual: Created by the authors, the student solutions manual contains solutions to the even numbered assignments in the textbook. This is a restricted item that is only available to students after their instructor has authorized its purchase.

Website: Practice quizzes and other useful links are available to students free of charge on the book's Website.

ACKNOWLEDGMENTS

Special thanks to Mark DeFond, Jane Kennedy, and Pat Wilkie for there thoughtful contributions to the second edition. We also want to thank Stan Baiman, Dan Bens, Mary Ellen Carter, Craig Chapman, Tom Fields, Mark Finn, Ian Gow, Rebecca Hann, Ben Lansford, Barbara Lougee, Luann Lynch, and Sri Sridharan for their feedback on the various drafts of the new edition. This book also benefited greatly from the valuable feedback of focus group attendees, reviewers, students, and colleagues. We are extremely grateful to them for their help in making this project a success.

Hank Adler, *Chapman University*

Ashiq Ali, *University of Texas–Dallas*

Matthew J. Anderson, *Michigan State University*

Stan Baiman, *University of Pennsylvania*

Karthik Balakrishnan, *University of Pennsylvania*

Jan Barton, *Emory University*

Eli Bartov, *New York University*

James Benjamin, *Texas A&M University*

Dan Bens, *University of Arizona*

Anne Beyer, *Stanford University*

Charles Bokemeier, *Michigan State University*

Rada Brooks, *University of California–Berkeley*

Helen Brubeck, *San Jose State University*

Thomas Buchman, *University of Colorado–Boulder*

Richard J. Campbell, *University of Rio Grande*

Mary Ellen Carter, *Boston College*

Paul Chaney, *Vanderbilt University*

Craig Chapman, *Northwestern University*

Sean Chen, *Furman University*

Agnes Cheng, *Louisiana State University*

Hans Christensen, *University of Chicago*

Daniel Cohen, *New York University*

Mark DeFond, *University of Southern California*

Bruce Dehning, *Chapman University*

Doug DeJong, *University of Iowa*

Norris Dorsey, *California State University–Northridge*

Allan Drebin, *Northwestern University*

Ron Dye, *Northwestern University*

James Emig, *Villanova University*

Martin (Bud) Fennema, *Florida State University*

Tom Fields, *Washington University*

Mark Finn, *Northwestern University*

Lisa Gillespie, *Loyola University*

Rajul Gokarn, *Clark Atlanta University*

Ian Gow, *Northwestern University*

Wayne Guay, *University of Pennsylvania*

Karl Hackenbrack, *Vanderbilt University*

Rebecca Hann, *University of Maryland*

Al Hartgraves, *Emory University*

Rayford Harwell, *California State University–East Bay*

Susan Hass, *Simmons College*

Haihong He, *California State University–Los Angeles*

Leslie Hodder, *Indiana University*

Marsha Huber, *Otterbein College*

Ronald J. Huefner, *SUNY–Buffalo*

Richard E. Hurley, *University of Connecticut*

Robert L. Hurt, *California State University–Pomona*

Alan Jagolinzer, *Stanford University*

Marianne L. James, *California State University–Los Angeles*

Rick Johnston, *Ohio State University*

Chris Jones, *George Washington University*

Duane Kennedy, *University of Waterloo*

Jane Kennedy, *University of Washington*

Gopal Krishnan, *George Mason University*

William Kross, *University at Buffalo*

Benjamin Lansford, *Pennsylvania State University*

Elliot Levy, *Bentley College*

Xu Li, *University of Texas–Dallas*

Thomas Lin, *University of Southern California*

Barbara Lougee, *University of San Diego*

Andrew Luzi, *University of Pennsylvania*

Luann Lynch, *University of Virginia–Darden*

Bruce McClain, *Cleveland State University*

John McCauley, *San Diego State University*

Sara Melendy, *Gonzaga University*

Greg Miller, *University of Michigan*

Marilyn Misch, *Pepperdine University–Malibu*

Sandeep Nabar, *Oklahoma State University*

Walter O'Connor, *Fordham University*

Shailendra Pandit, *University of Illinois–Chicago*

Susan Parker, *Santa Clara University*

Marietta Peytcheva, *Lehigh University*

Morton Pincus, *University of California–Irvine*

S.E.C. Purvis, *University of Nevada–Reno*

Edward Riedl, *Harvard University*

Susan Riffe, *Southern Methodist University*

Leslie Robinson, *Dartmouth College*

Darren Roulstone, *Ohio State University*

Anwar Y. Salimi, *California State University–Pomona*

Robert Scharlach, *University of Southern California*

Steve Sefcik, *University of Washington*

Margaret Shackell-Dowell, *Ithaca College*

Devin Shanthikumar, *Harvard University*

Timothy Shields, *Chapman University*

Parveen Sinha, *Chapman University*

Kathleen Sobieralski, *University of Maryland*

Sri Sridharan, *Northwestern University*

Vic Stanton, *University of California–Berkeley*

Doug Stevens, *Florida State University*

Phillip Stocken, *Dartmouth College*

Robin Tarpley, *George Washington University*

Nicole Thibodeau, *Willamette University*

Wayne Thomas, *University of Oklahoma*

Ken Trotman, *University of New South Wales*

Howard Turetsky, *San Jose State University*

Mark Vargus, *University of Texas–Dallas*

Joseph Weintrop, *City University of New York*

Stephen Zeff, *Rice University*

In addition, we are extremely grateful to George Werthman, Jill Fischer, Jocelyn Mousel, Keith Chasse, Debbie Golden, Terry McQuade, and the entire team at Cambridge Business Publishers for their encouragement, enthusiasm, and guidance. We have had a very positive textbook authoring experience thanks, in large part, to our publisher.

Thomas R. Dyckman *Robert P. Magee* *Glenn M. Pfeiffer*

Ithaca, NY *Evanston, IL* *Orange, CA*

March 2010

Brief Contents

Index

Chapter 3

Adjusting Accounts for Financial Statements   95

Chapter 4

Reporting and Analyzing Cash Flows   151

Chapter **7**

Reporting and Analyzing Inventory 305

Chapter **8**

Reporting and Analyzing Long-Term Operating Assets 351

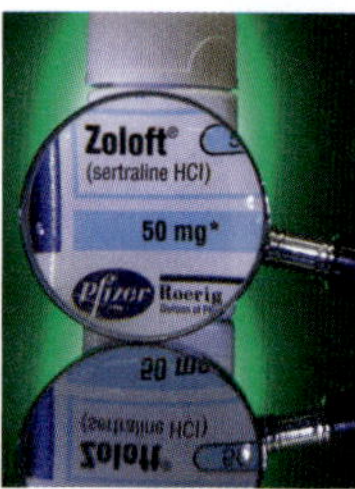

Chapter **12**

Reporting and Analyzing Intercorporate Investments   537

1. Identify the users of accounting information and discuss the costs and benefits of disclosure. (p. 4)

2. Describe a company's business activities and explain how these activities are represented by the accounting equation. (p. 7)

3. Introduce the four key financial statements including the balance sheet, income statement, statement of stockholders' equity, and statement of cash flows. (p. 11)

4. Describe the institutions that regulate financial accounting and their role in establishing generally accepted accounting principles. (p. 17)

5. Compute two key ratios that are commonly used to assess profitability and risk—return on equity and the debt-to-equity ratio. (p. 20)

6. Appendix 1A: Explain the conceptual framework for financial reporting. (p. 23)

© Getty Images

Introducing Financial Accounting

By 2009, **Nike** products were marketed on six continents and total company sales exceeded $19 billion. The company recently announced plans to open 100 new retail stores with a goal of reaching sales of $23 billion by 2011.

NIKE
www.Nike.com

Phil Knight majored in accounting and was a member of the track team at the University of Oregon. Today he is the chairman of the board of the largest sports and fitness company in the world.

A few years after graduation, Knight teamed up with his former track coach, Bill Bowerman, to form a business called Blue Ribbon Sports to import, sell, and distribute running shoes from Japan. Blue Ribbon Sports, or BRS as it came to be known, was started on a shoestring—Knight and Bowerman each contributed $500 to start the business. A few years later, BRS introduced its own line of running shoes called Nike, named for the Greek goddess of victory. It also unveiled a new logo, the now familiar Nike swoosh. Following the overwhelming success of the Nike shoe line, BRS officially changed its company name to Nike, Inc. Today, the company is worth more than $20 billion.

Nike is one of the premier marketing companies of the last 30 years. The swoosh along with advertising campaigns featuring taglines such as "just do it," have made the company and its products instantly recognizable to consumers all over the world. Endorsements by the most recognizable icons in sports, including Michael Jordan, Tiger Woods, Maria Sharapova, Alex Rodriguez, Mia Hamm, and Lance Armstrong, add to Nike's brand recognition.

Besides its marketing prowess, Nike owes much of its success to innovative design and development of products including athletic shoes, athletic apparel, sports equipment, eyewear, and watches. In recent years, Nike expanded its product offering by acquiring other companies such as Converse, an established athletic shoe company; Hurley International, a leading designer and distributor of surf, skate, and snowboarding apparel and footwear; and Umbro, specializing in soccer equipment, footwear, and apparel.

How does someone take a $1,000 investment and turn it into a company with sales of over $19 billion? Well, Nike's success is not an accident. Along the way, Nike management made countless decisions that ultimately led the company to where it is today. Each of these decisions involved identifying alternative courses of action and weighing their costs, benefits, and risks in light of the available information.

Accounting is the process of identifying, measuring, and communicating financial information to help people make *economic* decisions. People use financial accounting information to facilitate a wide variety of transactions, including assessing whether, and on what terms, they should invest in

(continued on next page)

a firm, seek employment in a business, or continue purchasing its products. Accounting information is crucial to any successful business, and without it, most businesses would not even exist.

This book explains how to create and analyze *financial statements*, an important source of accounting information prepared by companies to communicate with a variety of users. We begin by introducing transactions between the firm and its investors, creditors, suppliers, employees, and customers. We continue by demonstrating how accounting principles are applied to these transactions to create the financial statements. Then, we "invert" the process and learn how to analyze the firm's financial statements to assess the firm's underlying economic performance. Our philosophy is simple—we believe it is crucial to have a deep understanding of financial accounting to become critical readers and users of financial statements. Financial statements tell a story—a business story. Our goal is to understand that story, and apply the knowledge gleaned from financial statements to make good business decisions.

Sources: *Nike.com; Nike, Inc. 2009 10-K Report; Business Week (October 2007, August 2009); Portland Business Journal (October 2007).*

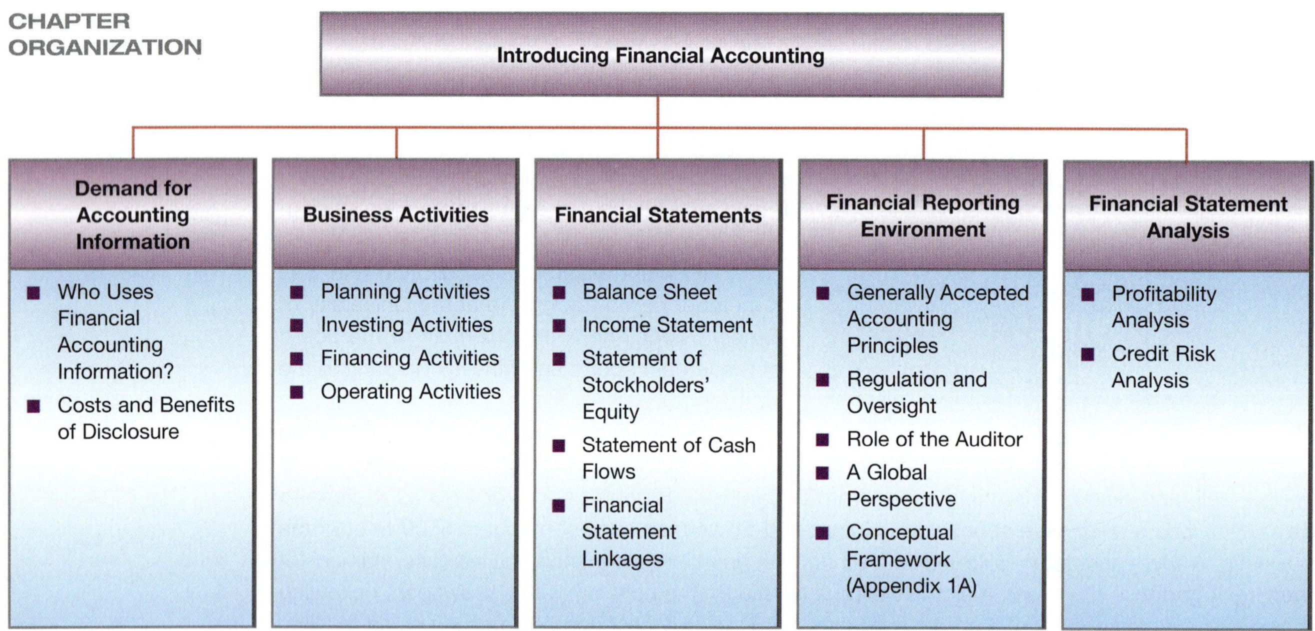

DEMAND FOR ACCOUNTING INFORMATION

LO1 Identify the users of accounting information and discuss the costs and benefits of disclosure.

Accounting can be defined as the process of recording, summarizing, and analyzing financial transactions. While accounting information attempts to satisfy the needs of a diverse set of users, the accounting information a company produces can be classified into two categories:

- **Financial accounting**—designed primarily for decision makers outside of the company
- **Managerial accounting**—designed primarily for decision makers within the company

Financial accounting reports include information about company profitability and financial health. This information is useful to various economic actors who wish to engage in contracts with the firm, including investors, creditors, employees, customers, and governments. Managerial accounting information is not reported outside of the company because it includes proprietary information about the profitability of specific products, divisions, or customers. Company managers use managerial accounting reports to make decisions such as whether to drop or add products or divisions, or whether to continue serving different types of customers. This text focuses on understanding and analyzing financial accounting information.

EXHIBIT 1.1	Information Needs of Decision Makers Who Use Financial and Managerial Accounting		
	Decision Makers	**Decisions**	**Information**
Financial Accounting	• Investors and analysts • Creditors • Suppliers and customers	• Buy or sell stock? • Lend or not? • Purchase/sell goods or not?	• Sales and costs • Cash in and out • Assets and liabilities
Managerial Accounting	• Top management • Marketing teams • Production and operations	• Develop new strategy? • Launch a new product or not? • Manage operations	• Product sales and costs • Department performance reports • Budgets and quality reports

Who Uses Financial Accounting Information?

Demand for financial accounting information derives from numerous users including:

- Shareholders and potential shareholders
- Creditors and suppliers
- Managers and directors
- Financial analysts
- Other users

Shareholders and Potential Shareholders

Corporations are the dominant form of business organization for large companies around the world, and corporate shareholders are one important group of decision makers that have an interest in financial accounting information. A **corporation** is a form of business organization that is characterized by a large number of owners who are not involved in managing the day-to-day operations of the company.[1] A corporation exists as a legal entity that issues **shares of stock** to its owners in exchange for cash and, therefore, the owners of a corporation are referred to as *shareholders* or **stockholders**.

Because the shareholders are not involved in the day-to-day operations of the business, they rely on the information in financial statements to evaluate management performance and assess the company's financial condition.

In addition to corporations, sole proprietorships and partnerships are also common forms of business ownership. A **sole proprietorship** has a single owner who typically manages the daily operations. Small family-run businesses, such as corner grocery stores, are commonly organized as sole proprietorships. A **partnership** has two or more owners who are also usually involved in managing the business. Many professionals, such as lawyers and CPAs, organize their businesses as partnerships.

Most corporations begin as small, privately held businesses (sole proprietorships or partnerships). As their operations expand, however, they require additional capital to finance their growth. One of the principle advantages of a corporation over sole proprietorships and partnerships is the ability to raise large amounts of cash by issuing (selling) stock. For example, as Nike grew from a small business with only two owners into a larger company, it raised the funds needed for expansion by selling shares of Nike stock to new shareholders. Large corporations can raise funds by issuing stock on organized exchanges, such as the **New York Stock Exchange (NYSE)** or **NASDAQ** (which is an acronym for the National Association of Securities Dealers Automated Quotations system). Corporations with stock traded on public exchanges are known as *publicly traded corporations* or simply *public corporations*.

---

[1] Most countries have business forms that are similar in structure to those of a U.S. corporation, though they are referred to by different names. For example, while firms that are incorporated in the United States have the extension, "Inc." appended to their names, similar firms in the United Kingdom are referred to as a Public Limited Company, which has the extension "PLC."

Financial statements and the accompanying footnotes provide information on the risk and return associated with owning shares of stock in the corporation, and they reveal how well management has performed. Financial statements also provide valuable insights into future performance by revealing management's plans for new products, new operating procedures, and new strategic directions for the company. Corporate management provides this information because the information reduces uncertainty about the company's future prospects which, in turn, increases the market price of its shares and helps the company raise the funds it needs to grow.

FYI Financial statements are typically required when a business requests a bank loan.

Creditors and Suppliers

Few businesses rely solely on shareholders for the cash needed to operate the company. Instead, most companies borrow from banks or other lenders known as **creditors**. Creditors use financial accounting information to help determine loan terms, loan amounts, interest rates, and collateral. In addition, creditors' loans often include contractual requirements based on information found in the financial statements.

Suppliers use financial information to establish credit sales terms and to determine their long-term commitment to supply-chain relations. Supplier companies often justify an expansion of *their* businesses based on the growth and financial health of their customers. Both creditors and suppliers rely on information in the financial statements to monitor and adjust their contracts and commitments with a company.

Managers and Directors

Financial statements can be thought of as a financial report card for management. A well-managed company earns a good return for its shareholders, and this is reflected in the financial statements. In most companies, management is compensated, at least in part, based on the financial performance of the company. That is, managers often receive cash bonuses, shares of stock, or other *incentive compensation* that is linked directly to the information in the financial statements.

FYI The Sarbanes-Oxley Act requires issuers of securities to disclose whether they have a code of ethics for the senior officers.

Publicly traded corporations are required by law to have a **board of directors**. Directors are elected by the shareholders to represent shareholder interests and oversee management. The board hires executive management and regularly reviews company operations. Directors use financial accounting information to review the results of operations, evaluate future strategy, and assess management performance.

Both managers and directors use the published financial statements of *other companies* to perform comparative analyses and establish performance benchmarks. For example, managers in some companies are paid a bonus for financial performance that exceeds the industry average.

Financial Analysts

Many decision makers lack the time, resources, or expertise to efficiently and effectively analyze financial statements. Instead, they rely on professional financial analysts, such as credit rating agencies like **Moody's** investment services, portfolio managers, and security analysts. Financial analysts play an important role in the dissemination of financial information and often specialize in specific industries. Their analysis helps to identify and assess risk, forecast performance, establish prices for new issues of stock, and make buy or sell recommendations to investors.

Other Users of Financial Accounting Information

External decision makers include many users of accounting information in addition to those listed above. For example, *prospective employees* often examine the financial statements of an employer to learn about the company before interviewing for or accepting a new job.

Labor unions examine financial statements in order to assess the financial health of firms prior to negotiating labor contracts on behalf of the firms' employees.

Customers use accounting information to assess the ability of a company to deliver products or services and to assess the company's long-term reliability. *Tax agencies* use financial accounting to help establish and implement tax policies. Other *government agencies* rely on accounting information to develop and enforce regulations, including public protection, price setting, import-export, and various other policies. Timely and reliable information is crucial to effective regulatory policy. Moreover, accounting information is often used to assess penalties for companies that violate various regulations.

Costs and Benefits of Disclosure

The act of providing financial information to external users is called **disclosure**. As with every decision, the benefits of disclosure must be weighed against the costs of providing the information.

One reason companies are motivated to disclose financial information to external decision makers is that it may lower financing and operating costs. For example, when a company applies for a loan, the bank uses the company's financial statements to help determine the appropriate interest rate. Without adequate financial disclosures in its financial statements, the bank is likely to demand a higher interest rate or perhaps not make the loan at all. Thus, in this setting, a benefit of financial disclosure is that it reduces the company's cost of borrowing.

While there are benefits from disclosing financial information, there are also costs. Besides the obvious cost of hiring accountants and preparing the financial statements, financial disclosures can also result in costs being imposed by competitors. It is common practice for managers to scrutinize the financial statements of competitors to learn about successful products, new strategies, innovative technologies, and changing market conditions. Thus, disclosing too much information can place a company at a competitive disadvantage. Disclosure may also raise investors' expectations about a company's future profitability. If those expectations are not met, they may bring litigation against the managers.

There are also political costs that are potentially associated with accounting disclosure. Highly visible companies, such as defense contractors and oil companies, are often the target of scrutiny by the public and by government officials. When these companies report unusually large accounting profits, they are often the target of additional regulation or increased taxes.

Stock market regulators impose disclosure standards for publicly traded corporations, but the nature and extent of the required disclosures vary substantially across countries. Further, since the requirements only set the minimum level of disclosure, the quantity and quality of information provided by firms can vary. This variation in disclosure ultimately reflects differences among companies in the benefits and costs of disclosing information to the public.

YOU MAKE THE CALL

You are a Product Manager   There is often friction between investors' needs for information and a company's desire to safeguard competitive advantages. Assume that you are the product manager for a key department at your company and you are asked for advice on the extent of information to disclose in the annual report on a potentially lucrative new product that your department has test marketed. What advice do you provide and why? [Answer on page 27]

BUSINESS ACTIVITIES

Businesses produce accounting information to help develop strategies, attract financing, evaluate investment opportunities, manage operations, and measure performance. Before we can attempt to understand the information provided in financial statements, we must understand these business activities. That is, what does a business actually do? For example:

LO2 Describe a company's business activities and explain how these activities are represented by the accounting equation.

- Where does a company such as Nike find the resources to develop new products and open new retail stores?

- What new products should Nike bring to market?

- How much should Nike spend on product development? On advertising? On executive compensation?

- How does Nike management determine if a product is a success?

Questions such as these define the activities of Nike and other companies.

Exhibit 1.2 illustrates the activities of a typical business. All businesses *plan* business activities, *finance* those activities, *invest* resources in those activities, and then engage in *operating* activities. Companies conduct all these activities while confronting a variety of *external forces,* including competition from other businesses, government regulation, economic conditions and market forces, and changing preferences of customers. The financial statements provide information that helps us understand and evaluate each of these activities.

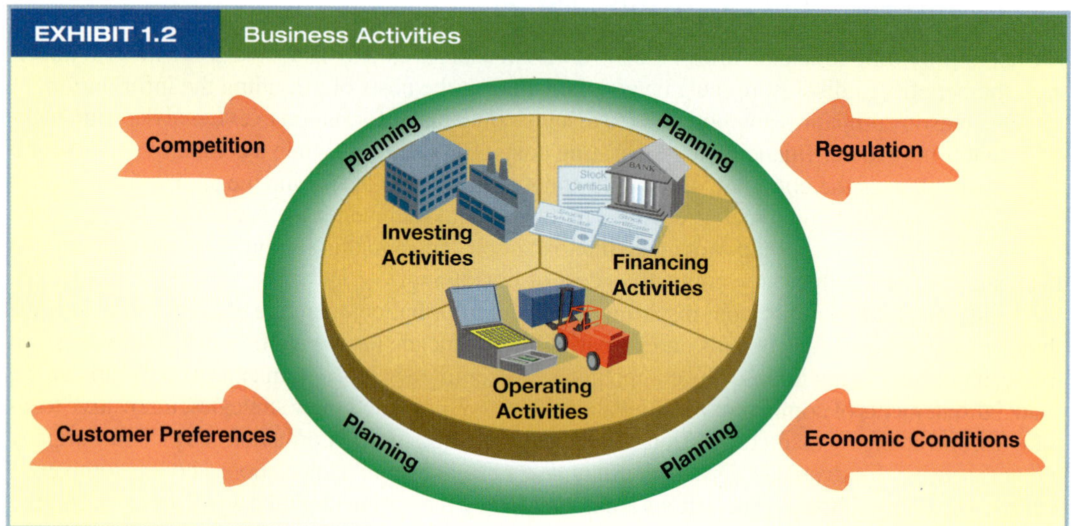

EXHIBIT 1.2   Business Activities

Planning Activities

A company's goals, and the strategies adopted to reach those goals, are the product of its **planning activities**. Nike, for example, states that its mission is "To bring inspiration and innovation to every athlete in the world" adding "If you have a body, you are an athlete." However, in its 2009 annual report to shareholders, **Nike** management suggests another goal that focuses on financial success and earning a return for the shareholders.

> Our goal is to deliver value to our shareholders by building a profitable global portfolio of branded footwear, apparel, equipment, and accessories businesses.

As is the case with most businesses, Nike's primary goal is to create value for its owners, the shareholders. How the company plans to do so is the company's **strategy**.

A company's *strategic (or business) plan* describes how it plans to achieve its goals. The plan's success depends on an effective review of market conditions. Specifically, the company must assess both the demand for its products and services, and the supply of its inputs (both labor and capital). The plan must also include competitive analyses, opportunity assessments, and consideration of business threats. The strategic plan specifies both broad management designs that generate company value and tactics to achieve those designs.

Most information in a strategic plan is proprietary and guarded closely by management. However, outsiders can gain insight into planning activities through various channels, including newspapers, magazines, and company publications. Understanding a company's planning activities helps focus accounting analysis and place it in context.

Investing Activities

Investing activities consist of acquiring and disposing of the resources needed to produce and sell a company's products and services. These resources, called **assets**, provide future benefits to the company. Companies differ on the amount and mix of these resources. Some companies require buildings and equipment while others have abandoned "bricks and mortar" to conduct business through the Internet.

Some assets that a company invests in are used quickly. For instance, a retail clothing store hopes to sell its spring and summer merchandise before purchasing more inventory for the fall and winter. Other assets are acquired for long-term use. Buildings are typically used for several decades. The relative proportion of short-term and long-term investments depends on the type of business and the strategic plan that the company adopts. For example, Nike has relatively few long-term assets because it outsources most of the production of its products to other companies.

The graph in Exhibit 1.3 compares the relative proportion of short-term and long-term assets held by **Nike** and nine other companies, several of which are featured in later chapters. **Apple** has adopted a business model that requires very little investment in long-term resources. A majority of its investments are short-term assets. In contrast, **Verizon**, **Southwest Airlines**, and **Procter & Gamble** all rely heavily on long-term investments. These companies hold relatively small proportions of short-term assets. This mix of long-term and short-term assets is described in more detail in Chapter 2.

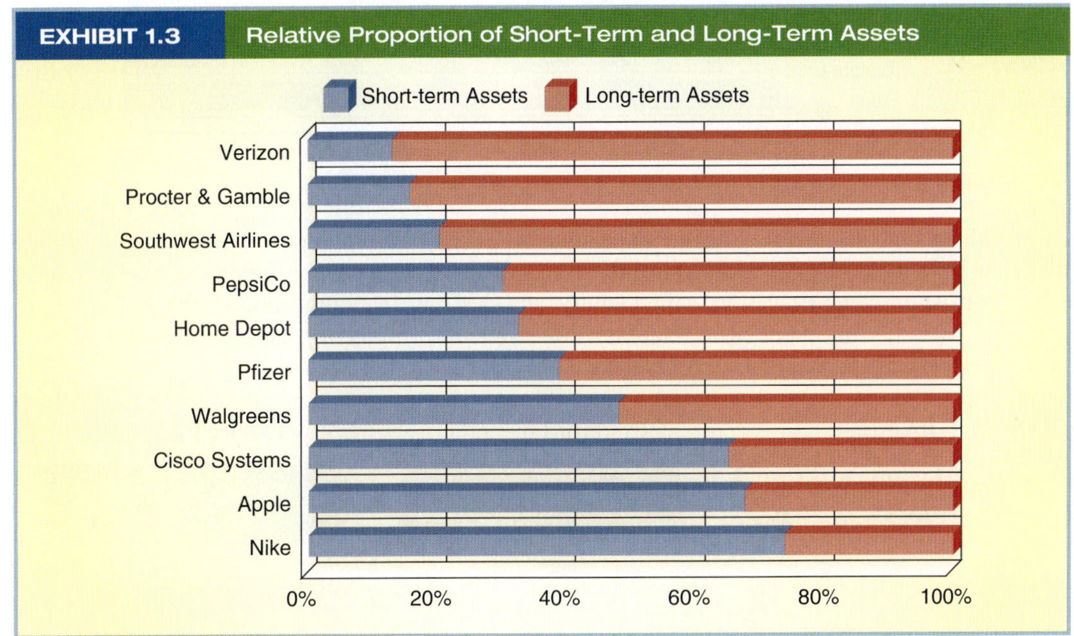

EXHIBIT 1.3   Relative Proportion of Short-Term and Long-Term Assets

Financing Activities

Investments in resources require funding, and **financing activities** refer to the methods companies use to fund those investments. *Financial management* is the planning of resource needs, including the proper mix of financing sources.

Companies obtain financing from two sources: equity (owner) financing and creditor (non-owner) financing. *Equity financing* refers to the funds contributed to the company by its owners along with any income retained by the company. One form of equity financing is the cash raised from the sale (or issuance) of stock by a corporation. *Creditor* (or debt) *financing* is funds contributed by non-owners, which create *liabilities*. **Liabilities** are obligations the company must repay in the future. One example of a liability is a bank loan. We draw a distinction between equity and creditor financing for an important reason: creditor financing imposes a legal obligation to repay, usually with interest, and failure to repay amounts borrowed can result in adverse legal consequences such as bankruptcy. In contrast, equity financing does not impose an obligation for repayment.

Exhibit 1.4 compares the relative proportion of creditor and equity financing for Nike and other companies. **Verizon** uses liabilities to finance 79% of its resources. In contrast, pharmaceutical company **Pfizer** relies more heavily on its equity financing, receiving 48% of its financing

FYI Creditors are those to whom a company owes money.

FYI It is useful to separate equity from creditor financing when analyzing a company's performance.

from creditors. **Nike** has the lowest proportion of creditor financing in this sample of companies with just 34% of its assets financed by nonowners.

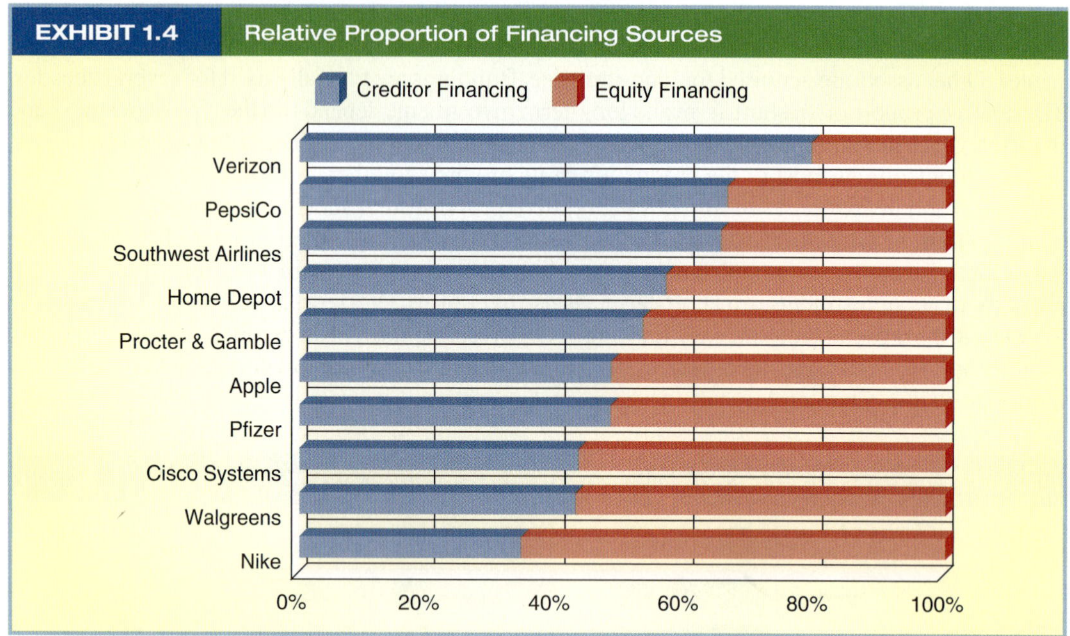

As discussed in the previous section, companies acquire resources, called assets, through investing activities. The cash to acquire these resources is obtained through financing activities, which consist of owner financing, called equity, and creditor financing, called liabilities (or debt). Thus, we have the following basic relation: *investing equals financing*. This equality is called the **accounting equation**, which is expressed as:

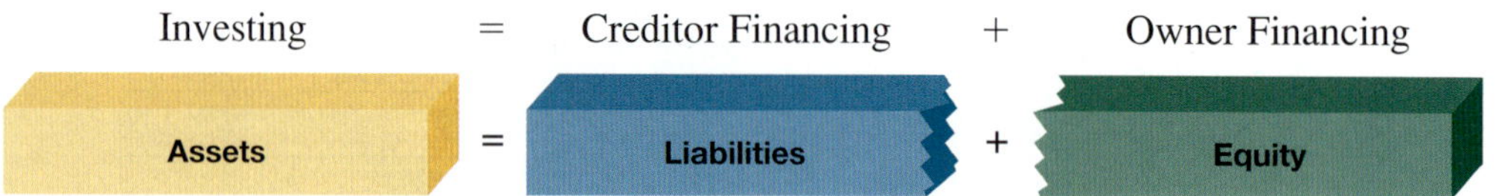

At fiscal year-end 2009, the accounting equation for **Nike** was as follows ($ millions):

$$\$13,249.6 = \$4,556.5 + \$8,693.1$$

By definition, the accounting equation holds for all companies at all times. This relation is a very powerful tool for analyzing and understanding companies, and we will use it often throughout the text.

Operating Activities

Operating activities refer to the production, promotion, and selling of a company's products and services. These activities extend from a company's input markets involving its suppliers to its output markets involving its customers. Input markets generate *operating expenses* (or *costs*) such as inventory, salaries, materials, and logistics. Output markets generate *operating revenues* (or *sales*) from customers. Output markets also generate some operating expenses such as marketing and distributing products and services to customers. When operating revenues exceed operating expenses, companies report *operating income,* also called *operating profit* or *operating earnings.* When operating expenses exceed operating revenues, companies report operating losses.

Revenue is the increase in equity resulting from the sale of goods and services to customers. The amount of revenue is determined *before* deducting expenses. An **expense** is the cost incurred to generate revenue, including the cost of the goods and services sold to customers as well as the cost of carrying out other business activities. **Income**, also called *net income*, equals revenue minus expense, and is the net increase in equity from the company's operating activities.

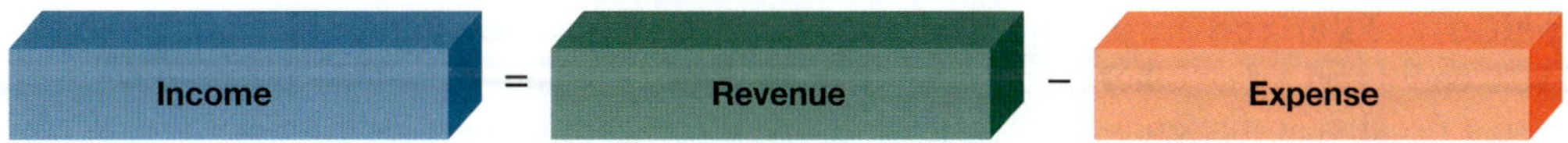

For fiscal year 2009, Nike reported revenues of over $19 billion, yet its reported income was a fraction of that amount—just under $1.5 billion.

BUSINESS INSIGHT

Each year, *Fortune* magazine ranks the 500 largest corporations in the United States based on total revenues. For fiscal year 2008, **Nike** ranked 136th on the *Fortune 500* list with revenues of just over $19 billion. The company also ranked 84th in profits, with net income of approximately $1.9 billion. For comparison, the largest corporation was **Exxon-Mobil**, with revenues of $442.8 billion and $45.2 billion in net income. *(Source: Fortune, May 2009)*

FINANCIAL STATEMENTS

Four financial statements are used to periodically report on a company's business activities. These statements are:

- **balance sheet**, which lists the company's investments and sources of financing using the accounting equation;
- **income statement**, which reports the results of operations;
- **statement of stockholders' equity**, which details changes in owner financing;
- **statement of cash flows**, which details the sources and uses of cash.

LO3 Introduce the four key financial statements including the balance sheet, income statement, statement of stockholders' equity, and statement of cash flows.

Exhibit 1.5 shows how these statements are linked across time. A balance sheet reports on a company's position at a *point in time*. The income statement, statement of stockholders' equity, and the statement of cash flows report on performance over a *period of time*. The three statements in the middle of Exhibit 1.5 (period-of-time statements) link the balance sheet from the beginning of a period to the balance sheet at the end of a period.

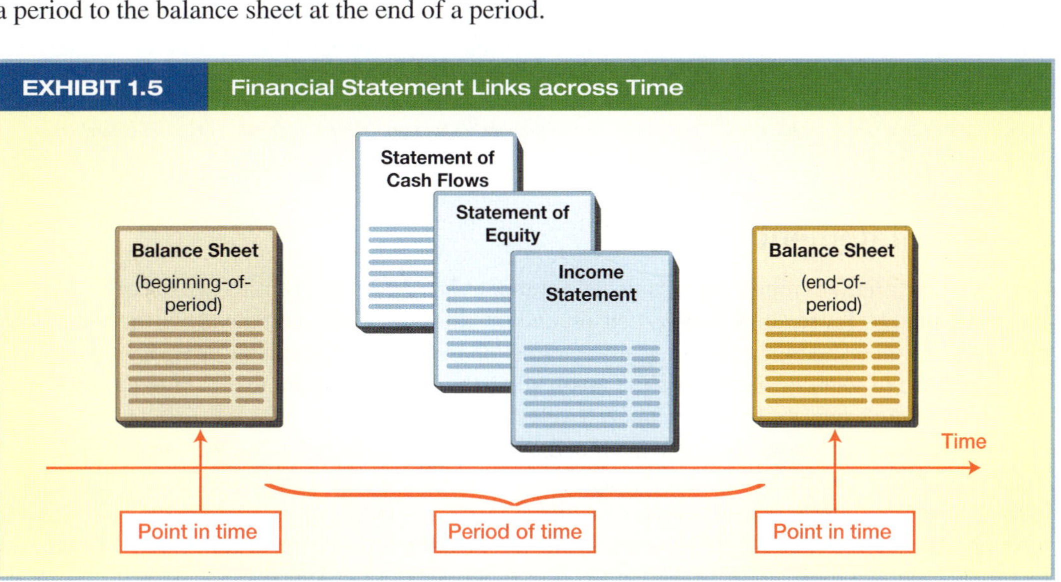

EXHIBIT 1.5   Financial Statement Links across Time

A one-year, or annual, reporting period is common, which is called the *accounting*, or *fiscal year*. Semiannual, quarterly, and monthly reporting periods are also common. *Calendar-year* companies have a reporting period that begins on January 1 and ends on December 31. **Pfizer**, **PepsiCo**, and **Verizon** are examples of calendar-year companies. Some companies choose a fiscal year ending on a date other than December 31. Seasonal businesses, such as retail stores, often choose a fiscal year that ends when sales and inventories are at their lowest level. For example, **Home Depot**, the retail home improvement store chain, ends its fiscal year on February 1, after the busy holiday season. **Nike** has a May 31 fiscal year. The heading of each statement identifies the: (1) company name, (2) statement title, and (3) date or time period of the statement.

> **FYI** The heading of each financial statement includes Who, What, and When.

Balance Sheet

> **FYI** The balance sheet is also known as the statement of financial position and the statement of financial condition.

A **balance sheet** reports a company's financial position at a point in time. It summarizes the result of the company's investing and financing activities by listing amounts for assets, liabilities, and equity. The balance sheet is based on the accounting equation, also called the *balance sheet equation*: Assets = Liabilities + Equity.

Nike's balance sheet for fiscal year 2009 is reproduced as Exhibit 1.6 and reports that assets are $13,249.6 million, liabilities are $4,556.5 million, and equity is $8,693.1 million, where owner financing is the sum of contributed capital of $2,874.2, retained earnings of $5,451.4, and other equity of $367.5. Thus, the balance sheet equation holds true for Nike's balance sheet: assets equal liabilities plus equity.

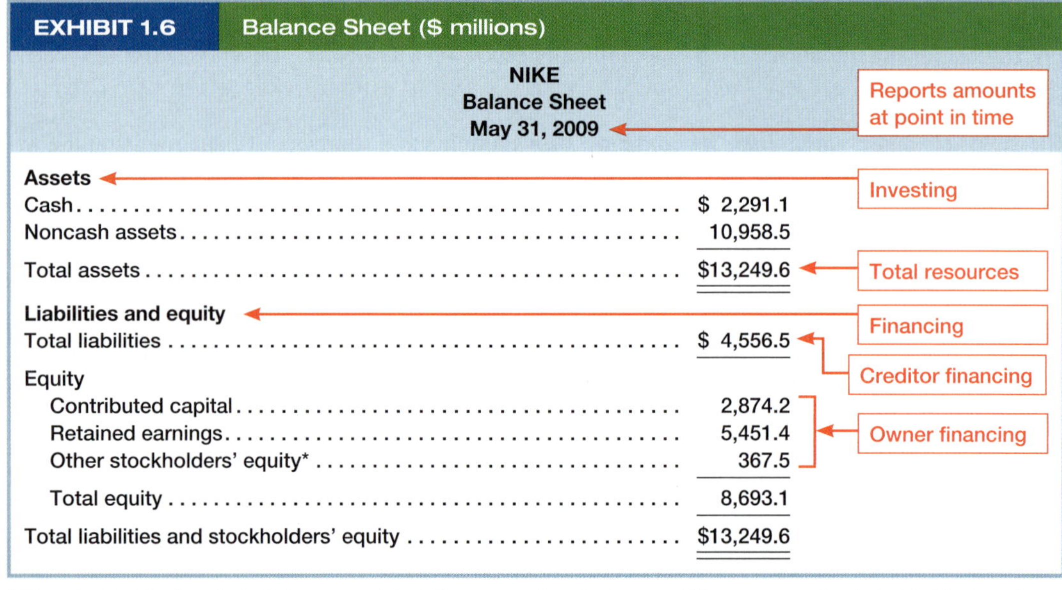

*Other stockholders' equity includes accumulated other comprehensive income. Other components of stockholders' equity are discussed in Chapter 11.

Income Statement

The **income statement** reports the results of a company's operating activities over a period of time. It details amounts for revenues and expenses, and the difference between these two amounts is net income. Revenue is the increase in equity that results from selling goods or providing services to customers and expense is the cost incurred to generate revenue. Net income is the increase in equity *after* subtracting expenses from revenues.

An important difference between the income statement and the balance sheet is that the balance sheet presents the company's position at a *point in time*, for instance December 31, 2010, while the income statement presents a summary of activity over a *period of time*, such as January 1, 2010, through December 31, 2010. Because of this difference, the balance sheet reflects the cumulative history of a company's activities. The amounts listed in the balance sheet carry over from the end of one fiscal year to the beginning of the next fiscal year, while the amounts listed in the income statement do not carry over from one year to the next.

Refer to Nike's income statement for the fiscal year ended May 31, 2009, shown as Exhibit 1.7. It reports that revenues = $19,176.1 million, expenses = $17,689.4 million, and net income = $1,486.7 million. Thus, revenues minus expenses equal net income for Nike.

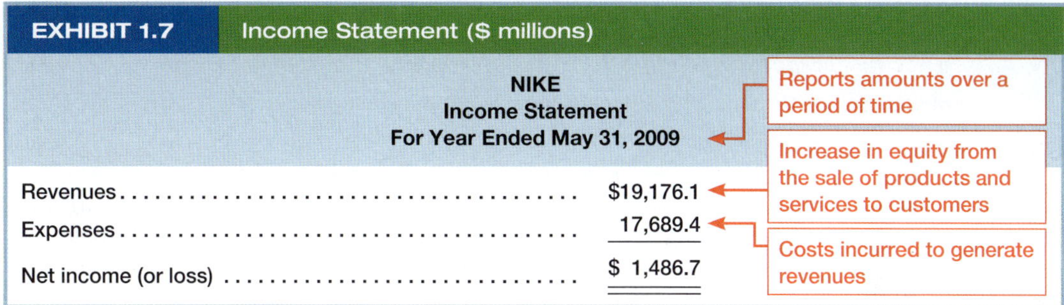

EXHIBIT 1.7   Income Statement ($ millions)

NIKE
Income Statement
For Year Ended May 31, 2009

Revenues	$19,176.1
Expenses	17,689.4
Net income (or loss)	$ 1,486.7

For manufacturing and merchandising companies, the **cost of goods sold** is an important expense that is typically disclosed separately in the income statement immediately following revenues. It is also common to report a subtotal for gross profit (also called gross margin), which is revenues less the cost of goods sold. The company's remaining expenses are then reported below gross profit. Nike's income statement is presented in this format in Exhibit 1.8:

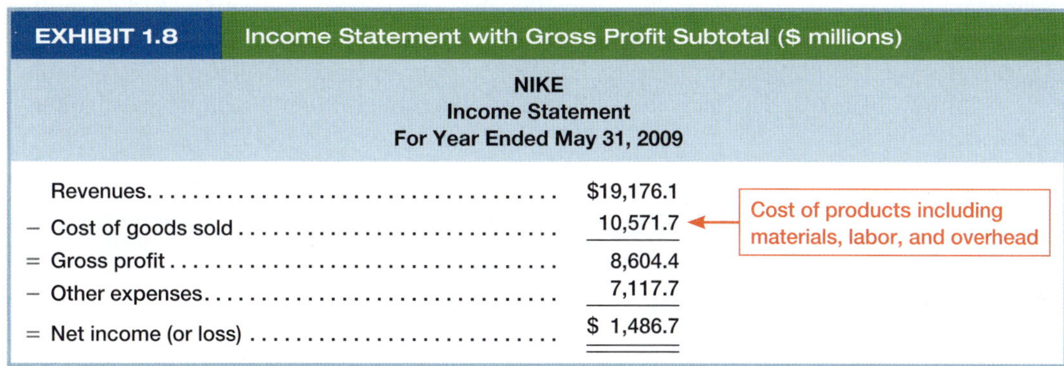

EXHIBIT 1.8   Income Statement with Gross Profit Subtotal ($ millions)

NIKE
Income Statement
For Year Ended May 31, 2009

Revenues	$19,176.1
− Cost of goods sold	10,571.7
= Gross profit	8,604.4
− Other expenses	7,117.7
= Net income (or loss)	$ 1,486.7

Statement of Stockholders' Equity

The **statement of stockholders' equity**, or simply *statement of equity,* reports the changes in the equity accounts over a period of time. Nike's statement of stockholders' equity for fiscal year ended May 31, 2009, is shown as Exhibit 1.9. During the year ended May 31, 2009, Nike's equity changed due to share issuance and income reinvestment. The exhibit details and classifies these changes into three categories:

- Contributed capital (includes common stock, and additional paid-in capital)
- Retained earnings (includes cumulative net income or loss, and deducts dividends)
- Other stockholders' equity

Contributed capital represents the net amount received from issuing stock to shareholders (owners). **Retained earnings** (also called *earned capital*) represents the income the company has earned since its inception, minus the dividends it has paid out to shareholders. Thus, retained earnings equals the amount of income retained in the company. The change in retained earnings links consecutive balance sheets through the income statement. Nike's retained earnings increased from $5,073.3 million at May 31, 2008, to $5,451.4 million at May 31, 2009. This increase is explained by net income of $1,486.7 million, less dividends of $475.2 million and other changes of $633.4 million.

The category titled "other changes" refers to changes in equity that are not recorded in income and is discussed in Chapter 11.

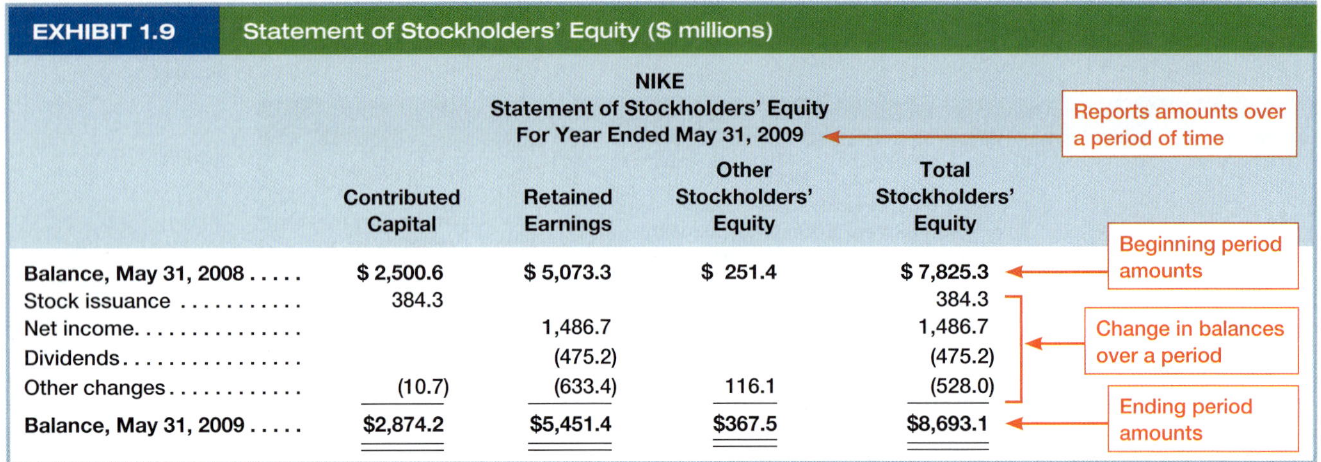

EXHIBIT 1.9   Statement of Stockholders' Equity ($ millions)

NIKE
Statement of Stockholders' Equity
For Year Ended May 31, 2009

	Contributed Capital	Retained Earnings	Other Stockholders' Equity	Total Stockholders' Equity
Balance, May 31, 2008	$ 2,500.6	$ 5,073.3	$ 251.4	$ 7,825.3
Stock issuance	384.3			384.3
Net income.		1,486.7		1,486.7
Dividends.		(475.2)		(475.2)
Other changes.	(10.7)	(633.4)	116.1	(528.0)
Balance, May 31, 2009	$2,874.2	$5,451.4	$367.5	$8,693.1

Statement of Cash Flows

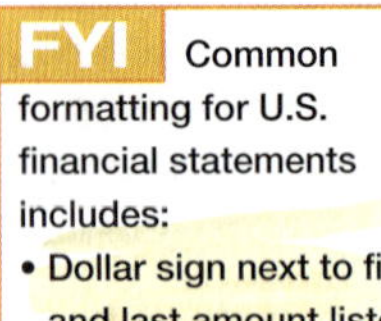

The **statement of cash flows** reports net cash flows from operating, investing, and financing activities over a period of time. Nike's statement of cash flows for fiscal year ended May 31, 2009, is shown in Exhibit 1.10. The statement reports that the cash balance increased by $157.2 million during the fiscal year. Operating activities provided $1,736.1 million (a cash inflow), investing activities used $798.1 million (a cash outflow), and financing activities used $780.8 million (a cash outflow). The resulting increase of $157.2 million brought Nike's ending balance of cash to $2,291.1 million.

EXHIBIT 1.10   Statement of Cash Flows ($ millions)

NIKE
Statement of Cash Flows
For Year Ended May 31, 2009

Operating cash flows	$1,736.1
Investing cash flows	(798.1)
Financing cash flows.	(780.8)
Net increase (decrease) in cash	157.2
Cash, May 31, 2008.	2,133.9
Cash, May 31, 2009.	$2,291.1

Operating cash flow is the amount of cash generated from operating activities. This amount usually differs from net income due to differences between the time that revenues and expenses are recorded, and the time that the related cash receipts and disbursements occur. For example, a company may report revenues for goods sold to customers this period, but not collect the payment until next period. Consistent with most companies, Nike's operating cash flows of $1,736.1 do not equal its net income of $1,486.7. Exhibit 1.11 compares net income and operating cash flows for Nike and several other companies. The exhibit shows that there is large variation across companies in the amount of net income and operating cash flows.

Both cash flow and net income are important for making business decisions. They each capture different aspects of firm performance and together help financial statement users better understand and assess a company's past, present, and future business activities.

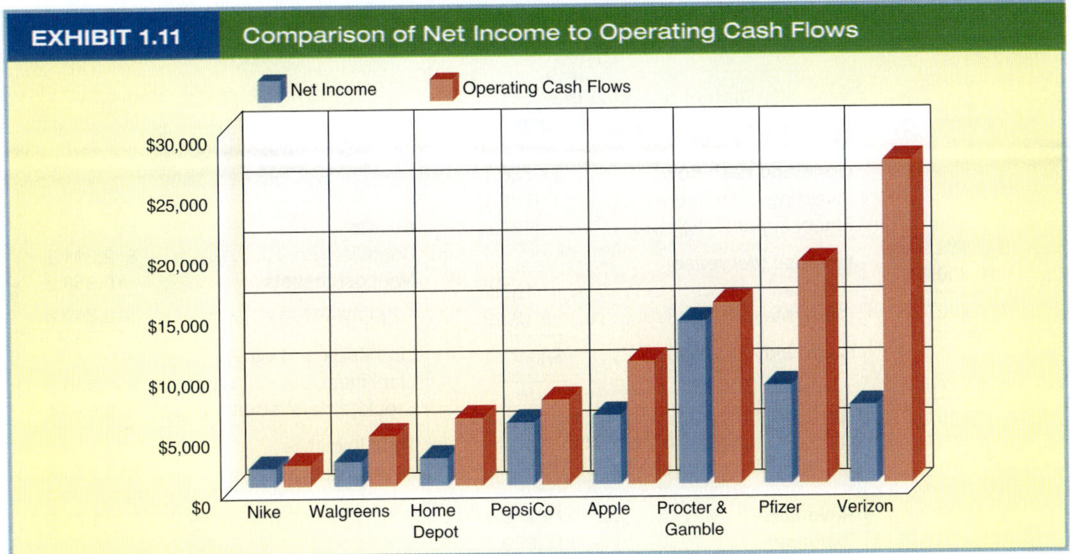

Financial Statement Linkages

A central feature of the accounting system is the linkage among the four primary statements, referred to as the *articulation* of the financial statements. Three of the key linkages are:

- The statement of cash flows links the beginning and ending cash in the balance sheet.
- The income statement links the beginning and ending retained earnings in the statement of stockholders' equity.
- The statement of stockholders' equity links the beginning and ending equity in the balance sheet.

Exhibit 1.12 demonstrates these links using Nike's financial statements from Exhibits 1.6 through 1.10. The left side of Exhibit 1.12 presents Nike's beginning-year balance sheet for fiscal year 2009 (which is the same as the balance sheet for the end of fiscal year 2008) and the right side presents Nike's year-end balance sheet for fiscal year 2009. These balance sheets report Nike's investing and financing activities at the beginning and end of fiscal year, two distinct points in time. The middle column of Exhibit 1.12 presents the three financial statements that report Nike's fiscal year 2009 business activities over time: the statement of cash flows, the income statement, and the statement of stockholders' equity. The three key linkages shown in Exhibit 1.12 are:

- The statement of cash flows explains how operating, financing, and investing activities increased the cash balance by $157.2 million, from the $2,133.9 million reported in the beginning-year balance sheet, to the $2,291.1 million reported in the year-end balance sheet.
- The net income of $1,486.7 million reported in the income statement is added to retained earnings in the statement of stockholders' equity.
- The statement of stockholders' equity explains how total equity of $7,825.3 million, reported in the beginning-year balance sheet, becomes total equity of $8,693.1 million, reported in the year-end balance sheet.

Information Beyond Financial Statements

Important information about a company is communicated to various decision makers through reports other than financial statements. These reports include the following:

- Management Discussion and Analysis (MD&A)
- Independent Auditor Report
- Financial statement footnotes
- Regulatory filings, including proxy statements and other SEC filings

We describe and explain the usefulness of these additional information sources throughout the book.

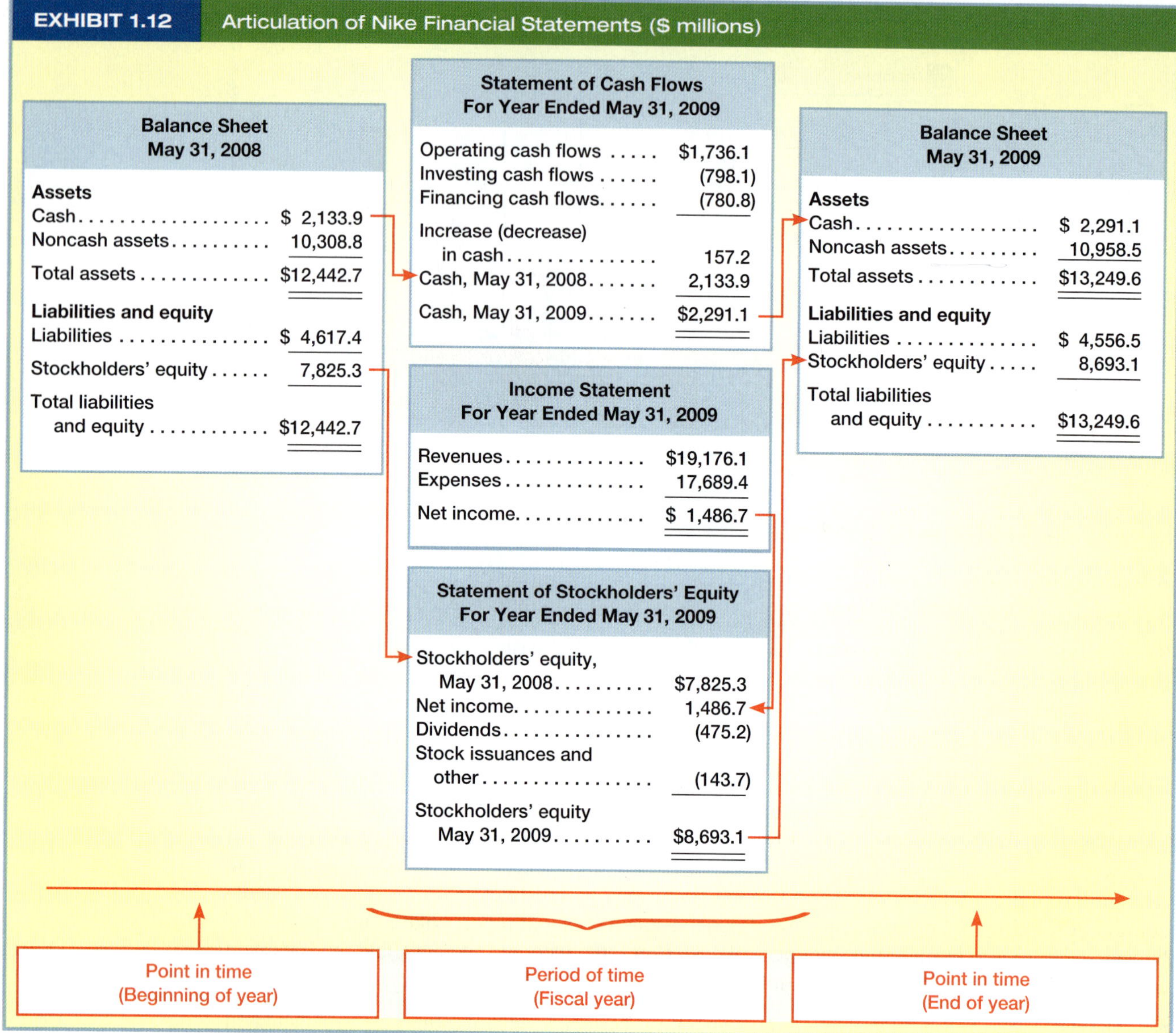

MID-CHAPTER REVIEW

Based in Germany, **Adidas** is one of **Nike**'s primary competitors. It markets athletic shoes and apparel under the Adidas and Reebok brands. It also sells Solomon ski equipment and TaylorMade golf equipment. Adidas's financial statements are reported in Euros; the currency of the European Union. The following information is from the company's December 31, 2008, financial statements (€ millions):

	2008
Cash...	€ 244
Cash flow from operations	497
Sales revenue	10,799
Stockholders' equity...	3,400
Cost of goods sold	5,543
Cash flow used for financing	(104)
Total liabilities	6,133
Other expenses...	4,612
Noncash assets...	9,289
Cash flow used for investing	(444)
Net income..	€ 644

FINANCIAL REPORTING ENVIRONMENT

Information presented in financial statements is of critical importance to external decision makers. Financial statements affect the prices paid for equity securities and interest rates attached to debt securities. To the extent that financial performance and condition are accurately communicated to business decision makers, debt and equity securities are more accurately priced. By extension, financial reporting plays a crucial role in efficient resource allocation within and across economies. Accounting information contributes to the efficient operation of securities markets, labor markets, commodity markets, and other markets.

LO4 Describe the institutions that regulate financial accounting and their role in establishing generally accepted accounting principles.

To illustrate, imagine the consequences of a breakdown in the integrity of financial reporting. The Enron scandal provides a case in point. At the beginning of 2001, **Enron** was one of the most innovative and respected companies in the United States. With revenues of over $100 billion and total company value of over $60 billion, it was the fifth largest U.S. corporation based on market value. In October 2001, the company released its third quarter earnings report to the public. Although operating earnings were higher than in previous years, the income statement contained a $1 billion "special charge." Financial analysts began investigating the cause of this charge and discovered that it was linked to related-party transactions and questionable accounting practices. Once it became clear to the capital markets that Enron had not faithfully and accurately reported its financial condition and performance, people became unwilling to purchase its securities. The value of its debt and equity securities dropped precipitously and the company was unable to obtain the cash needed for operating activities. By the end of 2001, Enron was bankrupt!

The Enron case illustrates the importance of reliable financial reporting. Accountants recognize the importance of the information that they produce and, as a profession, they agree to follow a set of standards for the presentation of financial statements and the disclosure of related financial information. In the following paragraphs, we discuss these standards, or *principles*, as well as the institutional and regulatory environment in which accountants operate.

Generally Accepted Accounting Principles

Decision makers who rely on audited financial statements expect that all companies follow similar procedures in preparing their statements. In response to these expectations, accountants have developed a set of standards and procedures called **generally accepted accounting principles (GAAP)**. GAAP is not a set of immutable laws. Instead, it is a set of standards and accepted practices, based on underlying principles, that are designed to guide the preparation of the financial statements. GAAP is subject to change as conditions warrant. As a result, specific rules are altered or new practices are formulated to fit changes in underlying economic circumstances or business transactions.

Some people mistakenly assume that financial accounting is an exact discipline—that is, companies select the proper standard to account for a transaction and then follow the rules. The reality is that GAAP allows companies considerable discretion in preparing financial statements. The choice of methods often yields financial statements that are markedly different from one company to another in terms of reported income, assets, liabilities, and equity amounts. In addition, financial statements depend on numerous estimates. Consequently, even though two companies may engage in the same transactions and choose the same accounting methods, their financial statements will differ because their managements have made different estimates about such things as the amount to be collected from customers who buy on credit, the length of time that buildings and equipment will be in use, and the future costs for product warranties.

Accounting standard setters walk a fine line regarding choice in accounting. On one hand, they are concerned that management discretion in preparing financial statements will lead to abuse by those seeking to influence the decisions of those who rely on the statements. On the other hand, they are concerned that companies are too diverse for a "one size fits all" financial accounting system. Ultimately, GAAP attempts to strike a balance by imposing constraints on the choice of accounting procedures, while allowing companies some flexibility within those constraints.

YOU MAKE THE CALL

You are a Financial Analyst   Accountants, business leaders, and politicians have long debated the importance of considering the **economic consequences** of accounting standards (GAAP). Should accounting standards be designed to influence behavior and effect social or economic change considered by, say, a government body or other interested group? Alternatively should such standards be designed simply to provide relevant and reliable information on which economic decisions can be made by others with a reasonable degree of confidence? What do you believe the objectives of financial reporting should be? [Answers on page 27]

Regulation and Oversight

Following the U.S. stock market crash of 1929, the United States Congress passed the Securities Acts of 1933 and 1934. These acts were passed to require disclosure of financial and other information about securities being offered for public sale and to prohibit deceit, misrepresentations, and other fraud in the sale of securities. The 1934 Act created the **Securities and Exchange Commission (SEC)** and gave it broad powers to regulate the issuance and trading of securities. The act also provided that companies with more than $10 million in assets and whose securities are held by more than 500 owners must file annual and other periodic reports, including a complete set of financial statements.

While the SEC has ultimate authority over financial reporting by companies in the United States, it has ceded the task of setting accounting standards to a professional body, the **American Institute of Certified Public Accountants (AICPA)**. Over the years, the AICPA has sponsored three standard-setting organizations.

Currently, accounting standards are established by the **Financial Accounting Standards Board (FASB)**. The FASB is a seven-member board that has the primary responsibility for setting financial accounting standards in the United States. It has published over 160 accounting statements governing the preparation of financial reports. These, along with numerous bulletins, interpretations, opinions, and earlier standards form the body of GAAP.

Besides setting standards for financial accounting, the FASB has developed a framework to form the basis for future discussion of proposed standards and serve as a guide to accountants for reporting information that is not governed by specific standards. A summary of this *Conceptual Framework* is presented in Appendix 1A at the end of this chapter.

In the wake of the Enron and other scandals, concerns over the quality of corporate financial reporting led Congress to pass the **Sarbanes-Oxley Act** in 2002. The goal of this Act—sometimes referred to as SOX—was to increase the level of confidence that external users, particularly investors, have in the financial statements. To accomplish this objective, SOX imposed a number of requirements to:

- Increase management's responsibility for accounting information
- Increase the independence of the auditors
- Increase the accountability of the board of directors
- Establish adequate **internal controls** to prevent fraud

SOX requires that the chief executive officer (CEO) and the chief financial officer (CFO) of a publicly traded corporation personally sign a statement attesting to the accuracy and completeness of financial statements. The prospect of severe penalties is designed to make these managers more vigilant in monitoring the financial accounting process. In addition, SOX established the **Public Company Accounting Oversight Board (PCAOB)** to approve auditing standards and monitor the quality of financial statements and audits.

SOX has had an impact on financial disclosures. One source reports that approximately nine percent of publicly traded corporations restated their financial statements within a recent two-year period. While this percentage may seem small, it represents more than 1,200 companies.

The Sarbanes-Oxley Act is not without critics. Many small companies complain that the additional reporting and auditing requirements established in the act are prohibitively costly. Of even greater concern is the criticism that the penalties imposed on management for misstatements or errors are too severe. Some argue that managers have become less forthcoming in their disclosures and more conservative in choosing accounting methods and making accrual estimates to avoid the possibility of heavy fines or criminal charges.

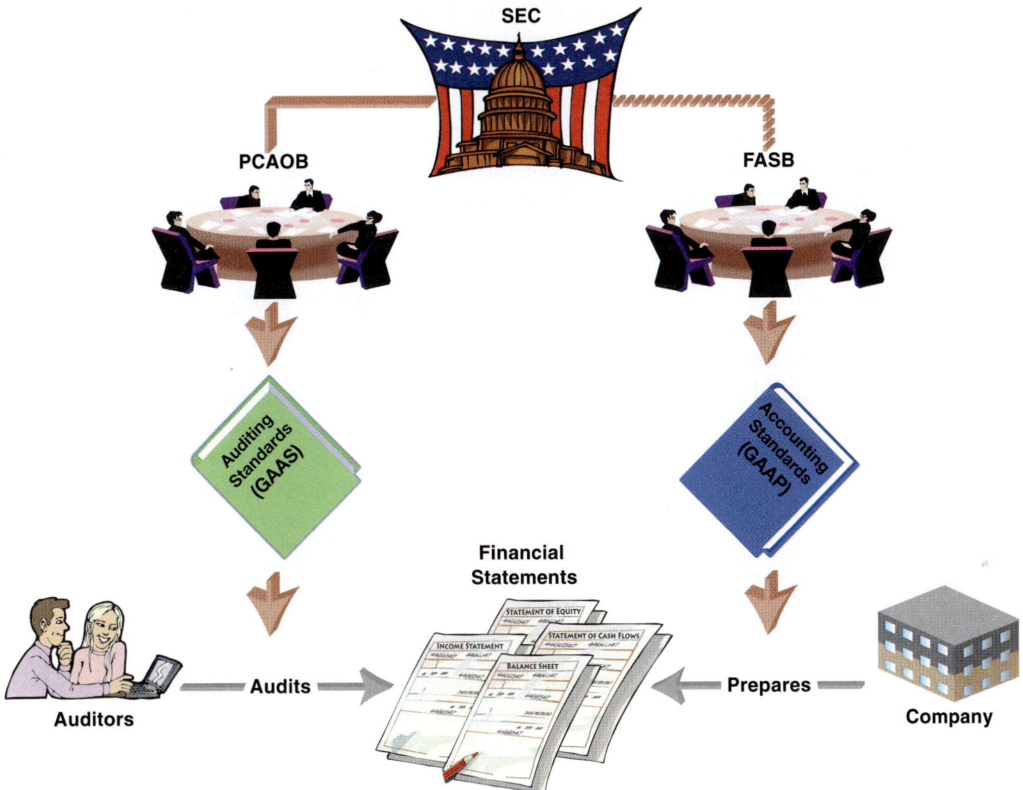

Role of the Auditor

What prevents a company from disclosing false or misleading information? For one thing, the financial statements are prepared by management, and management must take responsibility for what is disclosed. Management's reputation can be severely damaged by false disclosures when subsequent events unfold to refute the information. This situation can adversely affect the firm's ability to compete in capital, labor, and consumer markets. It can also lead to litigation and even criminal charges against management.

Even though management must personally attest to the accuracy and completeness of the financial statements, markets also demand assurances from independent parties. Therefore, the financial statements of publicly traded corporations must be **audited** by an *independent audit firm*. The auditors provide an opinion as to whether the statements *present fairly* and *in all material respects* a company's financial condition and the results of its operations.

The audit opinion is not a guarantee. Auditors only provide reasonable assurance that the financial statements are free of material misstatements. Even so, auditors provide a valuable service. Auditors effectively ensure that the information contained in the financial statements is reliable, thus increasing the confidence of outside decision makers in the information they use to make investment, credit, and other decisions. Therefore, creditors and shareholders of privately held corporations often demand that the financial statements be audited as well.

A Global Perspective

Businesses increasingly operate in global markets. Consumers and businesses with access to the Internet can purchase products and services from anywhere in the world. Products produced in one country are often made with parts and materials imported from many different countries. Businesses outsource parts of operations to other countries to take advantage of better labor markets in those countries. Capital markets are global as well. Corporations whose securities trade on the New York Stock Exchange may also trade on exchanges in London, Toronto, Tokyo, or Hong Kong.

Because countries have a variety of laws and customs, accounting principles and practices vary considerably from one country to the next. Many companies based in countries other than the United States choose to present financial statements that conform to U.S. GAAP because they believe that doing so provides them better access to investors in the U.S. capital markets. Many other companies prepare financial statements following GAAP of the country in which they are based.

The globalization of capital markets combined with the diversity of international accounting principles has led to an effort to increase comparability of financial information across countries. To this end, the **International Accounting Standards Board (IASB)** was established to develop acceptable accounting standards on a worldwide basis. The IASB is charged with creating **International Financial Reporting Standards (IFRS)** with the intention of unifying all public companies under one global set of reporting standards. Currently, over 12,000 companies in more than 100 countries report under IFRS. Worldwide, many stock exchanges now require that companies prepare financial statements consistent with IFRS as a prerequisite for listing their securities. U.S. companies are expected to report under IFRS by 2014, though many companies will likely choose to comply with the international standards as soon as 2010.

Because it is international in its scope, the IASB has no legal authority to impose accounting standards on any country. However, by working with standard setters within countries, such as the FASB within the United States, the IASB is working to reduce diversity in financial reporting practice. Despite the push for comparability, not everyone is convinced that IFRS will improve the usefulness of accounting information. As one observer put it, "There is a real risk of a veneer of comparability that hides a lot of differences." Countries—29 at last count—have typically reserved the right to adopt exceptions to IFRS when they deem them to be appropriate.

IFRS INSIGHT

Prior to 2007, foreign-based companies wishing to sell securities in the United States were required to reconcile their financial statements to be consistent with U.S. GAAP. However, in June 2007, the SEC adopted a rule that allows foreign companies using international accounting standards to stop reconciling their financial statements to American rules. While this change will make it easier for U.S. investors to purchase securities from around the world, a June 2007 *New York Times* article referred to a "Tower of Babel in Accounting." The article raises concerns about the difficulty of comparing companies when their financial statements are based on diverse reporting standards.

L05 Compute two key ratios that are commonly used to assess profitability and risk—return on equity and the debt-to-equity ratio.

FINANCIAL STATEMENT ANALYSIS

The financial statements provide insights into the financial health and performance of a company. However, the accounting data presented in these statements is difficult to interpret in its raw form. For example, knowing that Nike's net income was $1,486.7 million in 2009 is, by itself, not very useful. Similarly, knowing the dollar amount of liabilities does not tell us whether or not Nike relies too heavily on creditor financing.

Financial analysts use a number of tools to help interpret the information found in the financial statements. They look at trends over time and compare one company to another. They calculate ratios using financial statement information to summarize the data in a form that is easier to interpret. Ratios also allow us to compare the performance and condition of different companies even if the companies being compared are dramatically different in size. Ratios also help analysts spot trends or changes in performance over time.

Throughout the book, we introduce ratios that are commonly used by financial analysts and other users who rely on the financial statements. Our goal is to develop an understanding of how to effectively use the information in the financial statements, as well as to demonstrate how these statements are prepared. In this chapter we introduce one important measure of **profitability** and one measure of financial **risk**.

Profitability Analysis

There are many ways to measure company success. One crucial measure is profitability. Profitability reveals whether or not a company is able to bring its product or service to the market in an efficient manner, and whether the market values that product or service. Companies that are consistently unprofitable are unlikely to succeed in the long run.

A key profitability metric for stockholders and other decision makers is company return on equity. This metric compares the level of net income with the amount of equity financing used to generate that income. **Return on equity (ROE)** is computed as:

$$\text{Return on equity (ROE)} = \frac{\text{Net income}}{\text{Average stockholders' equity}}$$

The income number in the numerator of the return measure reflects performance for a specific period. This implies that the measure used in the denominator should reflect the *average* level of equity investment for that same period. Accordingly, we use the average equity level for ratio analysis in our examples and end-of-chapter assignments since it normally provides a better measure of capital utilization for a period and is the predominant method for analyst services, such as **S&P Compustat**.

Nike's ROE is calculated by dividing its 2009 net income of $1,486.7 million by its average stockholders' equity of $8,259.2 million:

$$\frac{\$1,486.7}{(\$7,825.3 + \$8,693.1)/2} = \frac{\$1,486.7}{\$8,259.2} = 0.180 \text{ or } 18.0\%$$

The average stockholders' equity was calculated by adding together the stockholders' equity at May 31, 2008, and at May 31, 2009, and dividing by 2: ($7,825.3 million + $8,693.1 million)/2. Thus, Nike's stockholders earned an accounting return of 18.0% on their investment in 2009.

While Nike's ROE seems reasonable, it is useful to compare this return with the ROE earned by other companies. Exhibit 1.13 presents ROE for several companies in graphical form.

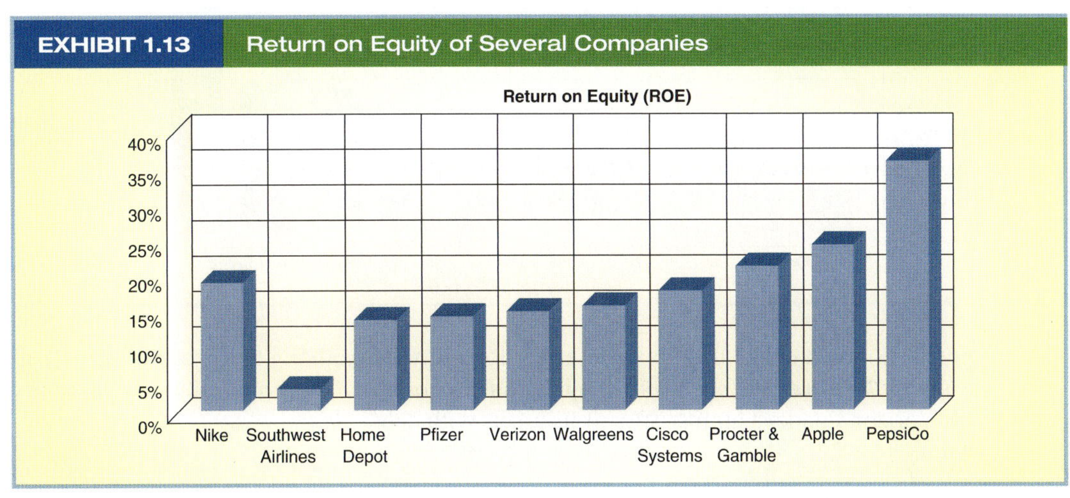

EXHIBIT 1.13   **Return on Equity of Several Companies**

From this exhibit we can see that Nike's ROE is somewhat lower than two companies—**Apple** and **PepsiCo**—while it was significantly higher than **Southwest Airlines**. It is also useful to make comparisons with companies in the same line of business or industry. As an illustration, the chapter-end review compares Nike with its chief competitor, **Adidas**.

Credit Risk Analysis

FYI Return cannot be evaluated without considering risk; the greater the risk of any decision, the greater the expected return.

In addition to measuring profitability, analysts also frequently analyze the level of risk associated with investing in or lending to a given company. The riskier an investment is, the greater the return demanded by investors. For example, a low-risk borrower is likely to be able to borrow money at a lower interest rate than would a high-risk borrower. Similarly, there is a risk-return trade-off in equity returns. Investments in risky stocks are expected to earn higher returns than investments in low-risk stocks, and stocks are priced accordingly. The higher expected rate of return is compensation for accepting greater uncertainty in returns.

Many factors contribute to the risk of an investment. One important factor is a company's *long-term solvency*. **Solvency** refers to the ability of a company to remain in business and avoid bankruptcy or financial distress. Solvency is closely related to the extent to which a company relies on creditor financing. As the amount of creditor financing increases, the possibility of bankruptcy also increases. Short of bankruptcy, a company that has borrowed too much will occasionally find that the required interest payments are hurting the company's cash flow. Analysts use measures of long-term solvency to assess a company's ability to make the necessary interest and principal payments on its debt. One such measure is the **debt-to-equity ratio**:

$$\text{Debt-to-equity ratio} = \frac{\text{Total liabilities}}{\text{Total stockholders' equity}}$$

This measure captures the extent to which a company relies on creditor versus owner financing to fund its investment in assets. The higher the ratio, the more the firm is financed with debt. Nike's debt-to-equity ratio was 0.524 at May 31, 2009, calculated as follows ($ millions):

$$\frac{\$4,556.5}{\$8,693.1} = 0.524$$

A debt-to-equity ratio equal to 1 indicates that the company is using equal parts debt and equity financing. Nike financed less than half of its assets with liabilities, so its debt-to-equity ratio is well below 1. To see how this compares with some other companies, consider Exhibit 1.14.

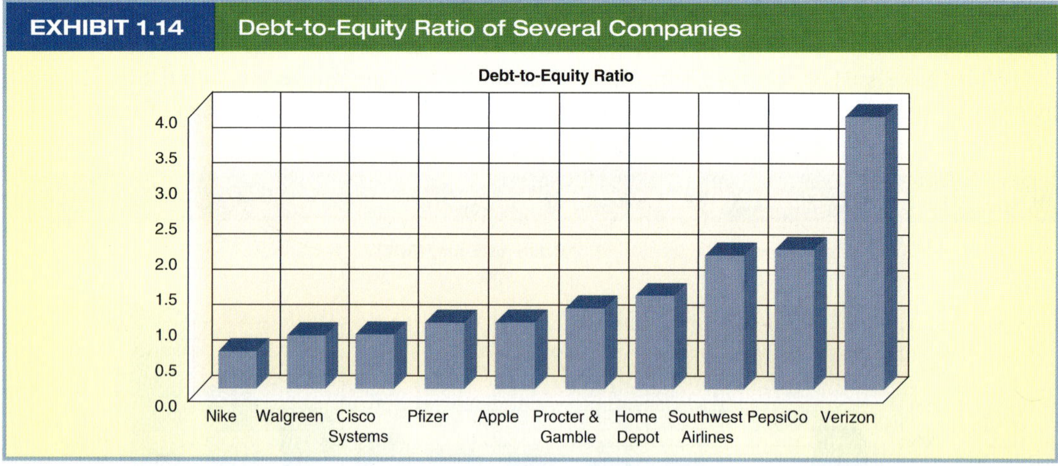

EXHIBIT 1.14 Debt-to-Equity Ratio of Several Companies

The graph shows that Nike had the lowest debt-to-equity ratio among this group of firms, followed closely by **Walgreens** and **Cisco Systems**. In contrast, **Verizon** had a debt-to-equity ratio of 3.9. Verizon financed almost 80% of its assets with debt.

There are other measures of profitability and risk that will be introduced in later chapters. Collectively, these ratios, when placed in the context of the company's business activities, help to provide a clear picture of the *drivers* of a company's financial performance and the factors affecting its financial condition. Understanding these performance drivers and their impact on the financial health of a company is key to effectively using the information presented in the financial statements.

CHAPTER-END REVIEW

Adidas, a major competitor of Nike, markets athletic shoes and apparel under the Adidas and Reebok brands. It also sells Solomon ski equipment and TaylorMade golf equipment. The following information is from Adidas's 2008 financial statements (Adidas's financial statements are reported in Euros, the currency of the European Union):

(millions)	Adidas
Net income (loss) (2008)	€ 644
Stockholders' equity (2008 year-end)	3,400
Stockholders' equity (2007 year-end)	3,034
Total liabilities (2008 year-end)	(6,133)

Required

a. Calculate the 2008 return on equity (ROE) ratio for Adidas.
b. Calculate the 2008 debt-to-equity ratio for Adidas.
c. Compare the profitability and risk of Adidas to that of Nike.

The solution to this review problem can be found on page 37.

APPENDIX 1A: Conceptual Framework for Financial Reporting

Accountants establish GAAP to ensure that the financial statements published by a company reflect its economic condition and performance. To meet this objective, the FASB sets accounting standards that reduce management discretion for reporting much of the information in the financial statements. To provide a structure for considering future standards, as well as to guide accountants in areas where standards do not currently exist, the FASB has developed a **conceptual framework**. This conceptual framework includes, among other things, a statement of the *objectives* of financial reporting along with a discussion of the *qualitative characteristics* of accounting information that are important to users. We discuss these objectives and characteristics in this appendix, along with some of the important assumptions underlying the preparation of financial statements.

LO6 Explain the conceptual framework for financial reporting.

Objectives of Financial Reporting

A fundamental goal of financial accounting is to provide information that promotes the efficient allocation and use of economic resources. To this end, the FASB established several objectives of financial reporting which are summarized here.

FYI The FASB and the IASB are currently working to create a common conceptual framework that will guide firms reporting under International Financial Reporting Standards (IFRS).

- Financial accounting should provide information that is useful to investors, creditors, and other decision makers who possess a reasonable knowledge of business activities and accounting.

- Financial accounting should provide information to help investors and creditors assess the amount, timing, and uncertainty of cash flows. This includes the information presented in the cash flow statement as well as other information that might help investors and creditors assess future dividend and debt payments.

- Financial accounting should provide information about economic resources and financial claims on those resources. This includes the information in the balance sheet and any supporting information that might help the user assess the value of the company's assets and future obligations.

- Financial accounting should provide information about a company's financial performance, including net income and its components (i.e., revenues and expenses).
- Financial accounting should provide information that allows decision makers to monitor company management to evaluate their effective, efficient, and ethical stewardship of company resources.

Qualitative Characteristics of Accounting Information

Qualitative characteristics of useful accounting information were developed to help managers, accountants, auditors, and standard setters make reasonable choices among accounting alternatives. These qualitative characteristics are depicted in Exhibit 1A.1 and discussed below.

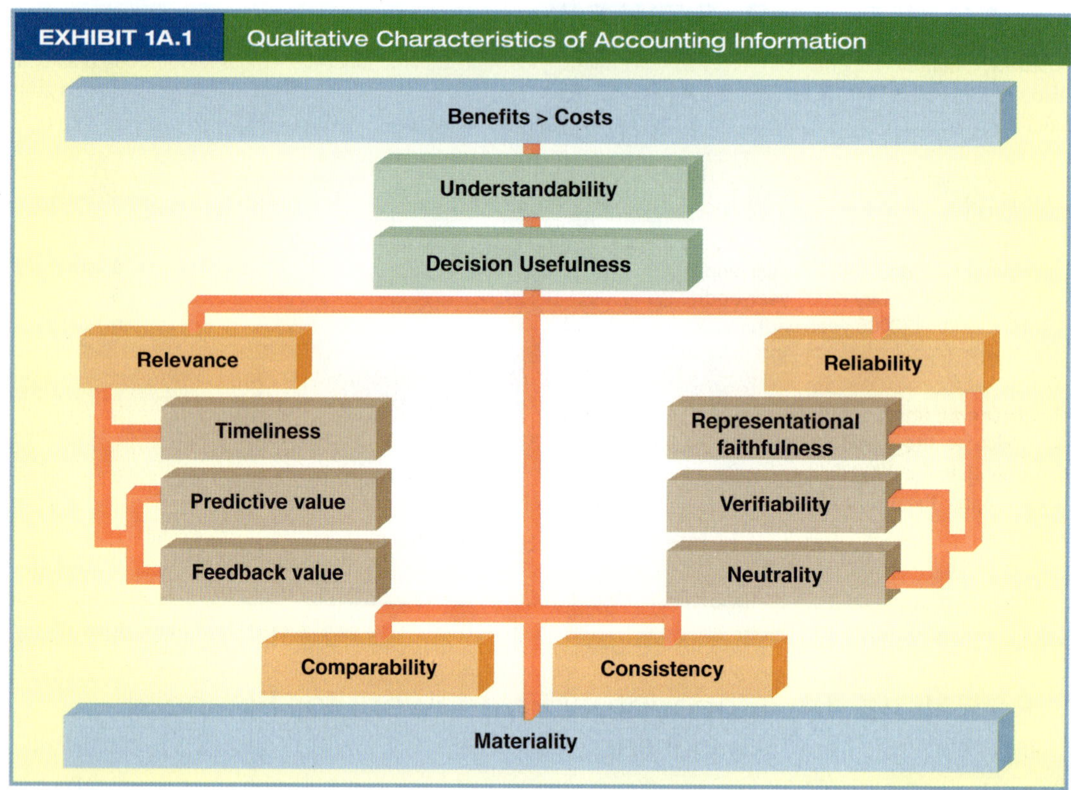

Exhibit 1A.1 neither distinguishes between primary and secondary qualities nor does it assign priorities among the qualities. It is an explanatory device and must be applied with consideration of the specific application intended. Each of the qualities is essential in some degree, but that degree will differ depending on the circumstances. We now expand briefly on each of the qualities delineated in the exhibit.

Benefits > Costs   Reported accounting information must be cost-effective. This characteristic implies that if the benefit to the economy does not exceed the cost, the information does not meet the test of usefulness. The operational difficulty with this information quality is that while the reporting cost can usually be ascertained, the benefit to information users is often difficult to quantify. Nevertheless, the need to weigh costs and benefits is seen as an overriding constraint on the financial reporting process.

Materiality   Materiality refers to whether or not a particular amount is large enough to affect a decision. Some items are not reported based on this constraint because they are considered *not material* in that the magnitude of the omission would not influence the judgment of a reasonable decision maker. In practice, materiality is typically judged by the relative size of an item related to a major reported variable such as total assets, sales revenues, or net income. However, some items are required to meet a lower threshold of materiality. The more critical an item is to understanding the condition and performance of the company, the finer the screen that should be used to determine whether or not it is material.

Understandability and Decision Usefulness   Accounting information should be presented so that a knowledgeable reader can understand how it relates to the decision problem at hand. Because different users will require different information, suppliers (standard setters) must tread a fine line between reporting (requiring) too much or too little information.

BUSINESS INSIGHT

What Is Material? *The Wall Street Journal* (August 26, 2005) reported that the SEC initiated an informal inquiry into **Pixar Animation Studios** concerning its disclosure of "heavier than expected returns of its *The Incredibles* DVD that forced the Emeryville, California-based studio to miss its second quarter earnings forecast." This inquiry follows an informal SEC investigation of **DreamWorks Animation**, the filmmaker that twice reduced earnings forecasts after substantial returns of its *Shrek 2* DVD. The issue in these two cases is whether companies are under obligation to inform market participants of material events affecting earnings. The *Journal* points out that "in the wave of recent corporate scandals some companies have been more conservative in assessing what constitutes a material event."

Relevance Accounting information must have the ability to make a difference in a decision. Such information may be useful in making *predictions* about future performance of the company or in providing *feedback* to evaluate past events. In either case, the *timeliness* of the disclosure is paramount to its relevance.

- **Timeliness**: The information must be available to decision makers before it loses its capacity to influence decisions. That is, information that is reported *after* a decision is made is not relevant to that decision.
- **Predictive value**: Refers to the ability of the information to increase the accuracy of a forecast.
- **Feedback value**: Refers to the quality of information that enables users to confirm or correct prior expectations.

RESEARCH INSIGHT

Research has documented a decline in the value relevance of accounting information, particularly earnings, over the past few decades. The decline has been attributed by some to conservatism in reporting. However, recent research has not been able to establish an association between this decrease in value relevance and conservatism despite using several alternative measures of conservative accounting. One explanation offered for the research finding is that conservatism favors more objective measures while avoiding additional estimation, thereby increasing reliability. If true, conservative accounting measurement could lead to greater relevance. The issue remains unresolved at this time and conservatism in reporting continues.

Reliability Accounting information should be accurate and free of misstatement or bias. It must be reasonably neutral, verifiable, and possess representational faithfulness.

- **Representational faithfulness**: Accounting information should reflect the underlying economic events it purports to measure.
- **Verifiability**: This characteristic implies that consensus among measures assures that the information is free of error. An independent DVD auditor should be able to examine the economic events and transactions underlying the financial statements and reach conclusions that are similar to those of management concerning how these events are measured and reported.
- **Neutrality**: Information must be free of any bias intended to attain a predetermined result or to induce a particular mode of behavior.

Comparability Accounting information should enable users to identify similarities and differences between sets of economic phenomena. For instance, the financial statements of different companies should be presented in a way that allows users to make comparisons across companies concerning their activities, financial condition, and performance. Although management has the flexibility to choose how events are measured and reported, this discretion should not be used to obscure the underlying economic substance of the event. One of the consequences of comparability is that firms in the same business (industry) should use the same, or similar, reporting techniques.

Consistency The information supplied to decision makers should exhibit conformity from one reporting period to the next with unchanging policies and procedures. Companies can choose to change accounting methods, and sometimes they are required to do so by standard setters. However, such changes make it difficult to evaluate financial performance over time. Accounting changes should be rare and supported as the better means of reporting the organization's financial condition and performance. Whenever possible, using the same accounting methods from one period to the next increases the quality of accounting information.

Underlying Assumptions

Four assumptions underlie the preparation of financial statements. Knowing these assumptions is helpful in understanding how the statements are prepared and in interpreting the information reported therein. These assumptions include:

Separate Economic Entity   For accounting purposes, the activities of a company are considered independent, distinct, and separate from the activities of its stockholders and from other companies.

Going Concern   Companies are assumed to have continuity in that they can be expected to continue in operation over time. This assumption is essential for valuing assets (future benefits) and liabilities (future obligations).

Accounting Period   While continuity is assumed, company operations must be reported periodically, normally each fiscal year. Interim reporting periods, such as quarterly or monthly reports, allow companies to supplement the annual financial statements with more timely information.

Measuring Unit   The unit of measure is the monetary unit of the country in which the firm's accounting reports are issued. The dollar is the monetary unit in the United States.

YOU MAKE THE CALL

You are the Bank Loan Officer   Hertz, the rental car firm, has a fleet of relatively new automobiles that it rents to customers for usually short periods. Suppose that Hertz applied to your bank for a loan and offered their fleet of cars as collateral. Would you, as the loan officer, be satisfied with the value shown on Hertz's balance sheet as a measure of the fleet's value? If not, what value would you prefer and how might you estimate that value? [Answers on page 28]

SUMMARY

LO1   Identify the users of accounting information and discuss the costs and benefits of disclosure. (p. 4)

- There are many diverse decision makers who use financial information.
- The benefits of disclosure of credible financial information must exceed the costs of providing the information.

LO2   Describe a company's business activities and explain how these activities are represented by the accounting equation. (p. 7)

- To effectively manage a company or infer whether it is well managed, we must understand its activities as well as the competitive and regulatory environment in which it operates.
- All corporations *plan* business activities, *finance* and *invest* in them, and then engage in *operations*.
- Financing is obtained partly from stockholders and partly from creditors, including suppliers and lenders.
- Investing activities involve the acquisition and disposition of the company's productive resources called assets.
- Operating activities include the production of goods or services that create operating revenues (sales) and expenses (costs). Operating profit (income) arises when operating revenues exceed operating expenses.

LO3   Introduce the four key financial statements including the balance sheet, income statement, statement of stockholders' equity, and statement of cash flows. (p. 11)

- The four basic financial statements used to periodically report the company's progress are the balance sheet, the income statement, the statement of stockholders' equity, and the statement of cash flows. These statements articulate with one another.
- The balance sheet reports the company's financial position *at a point* in time. It lists the company's asset, liability, and equity items, and it typically aggregates similar items.
- The income statement reports the firm's operating activities to determine income earned, and thereby the firm's performance *over a period* of time.
- The stockholders' equity statement reports the changes in the key equity accounts *over a period* of time.
- The statement of cash flows reports the cash flows into and out of the firm from its operating, investing, and financing sources *over a period* of time.

Describe the institutions that regulate financial accounting and their role in establishing generally accepted accounting principles. (p. 17)   **LO4**

- Generally Accepted Accounting Principles (GAAP) are established standards and accepted practices designed to guide the preparation of the financial statements.
- While the Securities and Exchange Commission (SEC) has ultimate authority over financial reporting by companies in the United States, it has ceded the task of setting accounting standards to the accounting profession.
- The Financial Accounting Standards Board (FASB) has the primary responsibility for setting financial accounting standards in the United States.
- The Sarbanes-Oxley Act established the Public Company Accounting Oversight Board (PCAOB) to approve auditing standards and monitor the quality of financial statements and audits.
- International financial reporting standards (IFRS) are set by the International Accounting Standards Board (IASB).
- IFRS are an attempt to achieve a greater degree of commonality in financial reporting across different countries. U.S. companies will likely be required to comply with IFRS by 2014.

Compute two key ratios that are commonly used to assess profitability and risk—return on equity and the debt-to-equity ratio. (p. 20)   **LO5**

- **Return on equity (ROE)**—a measure of profitability that assesses the performance of the firm relative to the investment made by stockholders (equity financing)
    - Return on equity (ROE) is an important profitability metric for stockholders.

$$ROE = \frac{Net\ income}{Average\ stockholders'\ equity}$$

- **Debt-to-equity ratio**—a measure of long-term solvency that relates the amount of creditor financing to the amount of equity financing
    - The debt-to-equity ratio is an important measure of long-term solvency, a determinant of overall company risk.

$$D/E = \frac{Total\ liabilities}{Total\ stockholders'\ equity}$$

Appendix 1A: Explain the conceptual framework for financial reporting. (p. 23)   **LO6**

- The conceptual framework includes, among other things, a statement of the *objectives* of financial reporting along with a discussion of the *qualitative characteristics* of accounting information that are important to users.

GUIDANCE ANSWERS . . . YOU MAKE THE CALL

You are a Product Manager   There are at least two considerations that must be balanced—namely, the disclosure requirements and your company's need to protect its competitive advantages. You must comply with all minimum required disclosures. The extent to which you offer additional disclosures depends on the sensitivity of the information; that is, how beneficial it is to your existing and potential competitors. Another consideration is how the information disclosed will impact your existing and potential investors. Disclosures such as this can be beneficial in that they convey the positive investments that are available to your company. Still, there are many stakeholders impacted by your decision and each must be given due consideration.

You are a Financial Analyst   This question has received a lot of discussion from both sides under the title "Economic Consequences." On one side are those who maintain that accounting rules should not only reflect a rule's economic consequences but should be designed to facilitate the attainment of a specific economic goal. A recent example is the case where the oil industry lobbied for an accounting rule that they and others believed would increase the incentive to explore and develop new oil deposits.

Those on the other side of the argument believe that accounting should try to provide data that is objective, reliable, and free from bias without considering the economic consequences of the decisions to be made. They believe that accounting rule makers have neither the insight nor the public mandate to attempt forecasts of the economic effects of financial reporting. Decisions that will affect the allocation of resources or that affect society's social structure should be made only by our elected representatives. While there are substantive points on both sides, we believe that it is the job of accounting rule makers to work toward the objective of financial reporting that reflects economic reality, subject to practical measurement limitations.

You are a Member of the Board of Directors   In order to perform a thorough audit, a company's auditors must gain an intimate knowledge of its operations, its internal controls, and its accounting system. Because of this familiarity, the accounting firm is in a position to provide insights and recommendations that another consulting firm might not be able to provide. However, the independence of the auditor is critical to the credibility of the audit and there is some concern that the desire to retain a profitable consulting engagement might lead the auditors to tailor their audit opinions to "satisfy the customer." Contrary to this concern, however, research finds that there is no evidence that auditors provide more optimistic audit reports for the companies they consult for. Rather, it appears that litigation and/or reputation concerns are reasonably effective in keeping auditors honest. Nevertheless, recent legislation in the United States now prohibits auditors from performing consulting services for their audit clients.

You are the Bank Loan Officer   The value shown on Hertz's books will be the purchase price, though perhaps reduced for the time the fleet has been in use. However, the bank would want to know the current market value of the fleet, not its book value, and the bank would then adjust this market value. The current market value of a single car can be found in used-car market quotes. If the bank ultimately becomes the owner of the fleet, it will need to sell the cars, probably a few at a time through wholesalers. Therefore, the adjusted market value and the book value are likely to differ for several reasons, including:

1. Hertz would have been able to buy the fleet at a reduced value due to buying in large volume regularly (market value lower than used-car quotes).
2. Hertz is likely to have kept the cars in better condition than would the average buyer (market value higher than used-car quotes).
3. The bank would reduce the value by some percentage due to the costs associated with disposing of the fleet (including the wholesaler's discount) and the length of the bank loan (reduction to the value as otherwise determined).

KEY RATIOS

$$\text{Return on equity (ROE)} = \frac{\text{Net income}}{\text{Average stockholders' equity}} \qquad \text{Debt-to-equity} = \frac{\text{Total liabilities}}{\text{Total stockholders' equity}}$$

KEY TERMS

Accounting (p. 4)

Accounting equation (p. 10)

American Institute of Certified Public Accountants (AICPA) (p. 18)

Assets (p. 8)

Audited (p. 19)

Balance sheet (pp. 11, 12)

Board of directors (p. 6)

Conceptual framework (p. 23)

Corporation (p. 5)

Cost of goods sold (p. 13)

Creditors (p. 6)

Debt-to-equity ratio (p. 22)

Disclosure (p. 7)

Economic consequences (p. 18)

Expense (p. 10)

Feedback value (p. 25)

Financial accounting (p. 4)

Financial Accounting Standards Board (FASB) (p. 18)

Financing activities (p. 9)

Generally accepted accounting principles (GAAP) (p. 17)

Income (p. 11)

Income statement (pp. 11, 12)

Internal controls (p. 18)

International Accounting Standards Board (IASB) (p. 20)

International Financial Reporting Standards (IFRS) (p. 20)

Investing activities (p. 8)

Liabilities (p. 9)

Managerial accounting (p. 4)

Neutrality (p. 25)

Operating activities (p. 10)

Partnership (p. 5)

Planning activities (p. 8)

Predictive value (p. 25)

Profitability (p. 21)

Public Company Accounting Oversight Board (PCAOB) (p. 19)

Representational faithfulness (p. 25)

Retained earnings (p. 13)

Return on equity (ROE) (p. 21)

Revenue (p. 10)

Risk (p. 21)

Sarbanes-Oxley Act (p. 18)

Securities and Exchange Commission (SEC) (p. 18)

Shares of stock (p. 5)

Sole proprietorship (p. 5)

Solvency (p. 22)

Statement of cash flows (pp. 11, 14)

Statement of stockholders' equity (pp. 11, 13)

Stockholders (p. 5)

Strategy (p. 8)

Suppliers (p. 6)

Timeliness (p. 25)

Verifiability (p. 25)

MULTIPLE CHOICE

1. Which of the following is a potential cost of the public disclosure of accounting information?
   a. Loss of competitive advantage caused by revealing information to competitors.
   b. Potential increased regulation and taxes due to reporting excessive profits in politically sensitive industries.
   c. Raising and then failing to meet the expectations of investors.
   d. All of the above are potential costs of disclosure.

2. Banks that lend money to corporations are considered
   a. creditors.
   b. stockholders.
   c. both *a* and *b* above.
   d. neither *a* nor *b* above.

3. Which of the following financial statements reports the financial condition of a company at a point in time?
   a. the balance sheet
   b. the income statement
   c. the statement of cash flows
   d. the statement of stockholders' equity

4. Which of the following is *not* one of the four basic financial reports?
   a. the balance sheet
   b. the income statement
   c. the statement of stockholders' equity
   d. the notes to the financial statements

5. Which of the following expressions is a correct statement of the accounting equation?
   a. Equity + Assets = Liability
   b. Assets − (Liabilities + Equity) = 0
   c. Liabilities − Equity = Assets
   d. Liabilities + Assets = Equity

Multiple Choice Answers
1. d 2. a 3. a 4. d 5. b

Superscript ^{A} denotes assignments based on Appendix 1A.

DISCUSSION QUESTIONS

Q1-1. What are the three major business activities of a company that are motivated and shaped by planning activities? Explain each activity.

Q1-2. The accounting equation (Assets = Liabilities + Equity) is a fundamental business concept. Explain what this equation reveals about a company's sources and uses of funds and the claims on company resources.

Q1-3. Companies prepare four primary financial statements. What are those financial statements and what information is typically conveyed in each?

Q1-4. Does a balance sheet report on a period of time or at a point in time? Also, explain the information conveyed in that report.

Q1-5. Does an income statement report on a period of time or at a point in time? Also, explain the information conveyed in that report.

Q1-6. Does a statement of cash flows report on a period of time or at a point in time? Also, explain the information and activities conveyed in that report.

Q1-7. Explain what is meant by the articulation of financial statements.

Q1-8. The trade-off between risk and return is a fundamental business concept. Briefly describe both risk and return and their trade-off. Provide some examples that demonstrate investments of varying risk and the approximate returns that you might expect to earn on those investments.

Q1-9. Why might a company voluntarily disclose more information than is required by GAAP?

Q1-10. Financial statements are used by several interested stakeholders. Develop a listing of three or more potential external users of financial statements and their applications.

Q1-11. What ethical issues might managers face in dealing with confidential information?

Q1-12. Return on equity (ROE) is an important summary measure of financial performance. How is it computed? Describe what this metric reveals about company performance.

Q1-13. Business decision makers external to the company increasingly demand more financial information on business activities of companies. Discuss the reasons why companies have traditionally opposed the efforts of regulatory agencies like the SEC to require more disclosure.

Q1-14. What are generally accepted accounting principles and what organization presently establishes them?

Q1-15. What are International Financial Reporting Standards (IFRS)? Why are IFRS needed? What potential issues can you see with requiring all public companies to prepare financial statements using IFRS?

Q1-16. What is the primary function of the auditor? To what does the auditor attest in its opinion?

Q1-17.[A] What are the objectives of financial accounting? Which of the financial statements satisfies each of these objectives?

Q1-18.[A] What are the four qualitative characteristics of accounting information? Explain how each characteristic improves the quality of accounting disclosures.

Assignments with the Web Assign**. logo in the margin are available in WebAssign.**
See the Preface of the book for details.

MINI EXERCISES

LO2 **M1-19.** **Financing and Investing Relations, and Financing Sources**

DELL INC.
NASDAQ :: DELL

Total assets of **Dell Inc.** equal $26,500 million and its equity is $4,721 million. What is the amount of its liabilities? Does Dell receive more financing from its owners or nonowners, and what percentage of financing is provided by its owners?

LO2 **M1-20.** **Financing and Investing Relations, and Financing Sources**

**COCA-COLA
COMPANY**
NYSE :: KO

Total assets of **The Coca-Cola Company** equal $40,519 million and its liabilities equal $20,047 million. What is the amount of its equity? Does Coke receive more financing from its owners or nonowners, and what percentage of financing is provided by its owners?

LO2 **M1-21.** **Applying the Accounting Equation and Computing Financing Proportions**

Use the accounting equation to compute the missing financial amounts (a), (b), and (c). Which of these companies is more owner-financed? Which of these companies is more nonowner-financed?

HEWLETT-PACKARD
NYSE :: HPQ
GENERAL MILLS
NYSE :: GIS
HARLEY-DAVIDSON
NYSE :: HOG

($ millions)	Assets	=	Liabilities	+	Equity
Hewlett-Packard...............	$113,331		$74,389		$ (a)
General Mills..................	$ 17,875		$ (b)		$ 5,175
Harley-Davidson...............	$ (c)		$ 5,713		$ 2,116

LO3 **M1-22.** **Identifying Key Numbers from Financial Statements**

APPLE INC.
NASDAQ :: AAPL

Access the most recent 10-K for **Apple Inc.**, at the SEC's EDGAR database for financial reports (www.sec.gov). What are Apple's dollar amounts for assets, liabilities, and equity at September 30, 2009? Confirm that the accounting equation holds in this case. What percent of Apple's assets is financed from creditor financing sources?

LO3 **M1-23.** **Verifying Articulation of Financial Statements**

DUPONT
NYSE :: DD

Access the 2008 10-K for **DuPont** at the SEC's EDGAR database of financial reports (www.sec.gov). Using its consolidated statement of stockholders' equity, prepare a table showing the articulation of its retained (reinvested) earnings.

LO3 **M1-24.** **Identifying Financial Statement Line Items and Accounts**

Several line items and account titles are listed below. For each, indicate in which of the following financial statement(s) you would likely find the item or account: income statement (IS), balance sheet (BS), statement of stockholders' equity (SE), or statement of cash flows (SCF).

a. Cash asset
b. Expenses
c. Noncash assets

d. Contributed capital
e. Cash outflow for land
f. Retained earnings

g. Cash inflow for stock issued
h. Cash outflow for dividends
i. Net income

M1-25. **Ethical Issues and Accounting Choices**
LO1

Assume that you are a technology services provider and you must decide whether to record revenue from the installation of computer software for one of your clients. Your contract calls for acceptance of the software by the client within six months of installation before payment is due. Although you have not yet received formal acceptance, you are confident that it is forthcoming. Failure to record these revenues will cause your company to miss Wall Street's earnings estimates. What stakeholders will be affected by your decision and how might they be affected?

M1-26. **Internal Controls and Their Importance**
LO4

The Sarbanes-Oxley legislation requires companies to report on the effectiveness of their internal controls. What are internal controls and their purpose? Why do you think Congress felt it to be such an important area to monitor and report on?

EXERCISES

E1-27. **Applying the Accounting Equation and Assessing Financing Contributions**
LO2

Determine the missing amount from each of the separate situations (a), (b), and (c) below. Which of these companies is more owner-financed? Which of these companies is more creditor-financed?

Web**Assign.**

($ millions)	Assets	=	Liabilities	+	Equity
a. Motorola, Inc.	$27,869		$?		$ 9,507
b. Kraft Foods Inc.	$?		$40,878		$22,200
c. Merck & Co., Inc.	$47,196		$28,437		$?

MOTOROLA
NYSE :: MOT

KRAFT FOODS
NYSE :: KFT

MERCK & CO.
NYSE :: MRK

E1-28. **Applying the Accounting Equation and Financial Statement Articulation**
LO2, LO3

Answer the following questions. (*Hint*: Apply the accounting equation.)

Web**Assign.**

a. **Intel Corporation** had assets equal to $50,715 million and liabilities equal to $11,627 million for a recent year-end. What was the total equity for Intel's business at year-end?

INTEL
NASDAQ :: INTC

b. At the beginning of a recent year, **JetBlue**'s assets were $6,023 million and its equity was $1,261 million. During the year, assets increased $425 million and liabilities increased $200 million. What was its equity at the end of the year?

JETBLUE
NASDAQ :: JBLU

c. At the beginning of a recent year, **The Walt Disney Company**'s liabilities equaled $30,175 million. During the year, assets increased by $1,569 million, and year-end assets equaled $62,497 million. Liabilities decreased $1 million during the year. What were its beginning and ending amounts for equity?

WALT DISNEY
COMPANY
NYSE :: DIS

E1-29. **Financial Information Users and Uses**
LO1

Financial statements have a wide audience of interested stakeholders. Identify two or more financial statement users that are external to the company. Specify two questions for each user identified that could be addressed or aided by use of financial statements.

E1-30. **Financial Statement Relations to Compute Dividends**
LO3

Colgate-Palmolive Company reports the following balances in its retained earnings.

WebAssign.

COLGATE-PALMOLIVE
NYSE :: CL

($ millions)	2008	2007
Retained earnings	$11,759.5	$10,627.5

During 2008, Colgate-Palmolive reported net income of $1,957.2 million.

a. Assume that the only changes affecting retained earnings were net income and dividends. What amount of dividends did Colgate-Palmolive pay to its shareholders in 2008?

b. This dividend amount constituted what percent of its net income?

E1-31. **Calculating Gross Profit and Preparing an Income Statement**
LO3

In 2008, **Colgate-Palmolive Company** reported sales revenue of $15,329.9 million and cost of goods sold of $6,703.5 million. Its net income was $1,957.2 million. Calculate gross profit and prepare an income statement using the format illustrated in Exhibit 1.8.

COLGATE-PALMOLIVE
NYSE :: CL

LO2, LO5   **E1-32.** **Applying the Accounting Equation and Calculating Return on Equity and Debt-to-Equity Ratio**

At the end of 2008, **Colgate-Palmolive Company** reported stockholders' equity of $1,922.1 million and total assets of $9,979.3. Its balance in stockholders' equity at the end of 2007 was $2,286.2 million. Net income in 2008 was $1,957.2 million.

a.   Calculate Colgate-Palmolive's return on equity ratio for 2008.

b.   Calculate its debt-to-equity ratio as of December 31, 2008. (Hint: Apply the accounting equation to determine total liabilities.)

LO1, LO4, LO6   **E1-33.**[A] **Accounting in Society**

Financial accounting plays an important role in modern society and business.

a.   What role does financial accounting play in the allocation of society's financial resources?

b.   What are three aspects of the accounting environment that can create ethical pressure on management?

PROBLEMS

LO2, LO5   **P1-34.** **Applying the Accounting Equation and Calculating Ratios**

The following table contains financial statement information for **The Procter & Gamble Company** ($ millions):

Year	Assets	Liabilities	Equity	Net Income
2007	$?	$71,254	$66,760	$10,340
2008	143,992	?	69,494	12,075
2009	134,833	71,734	?	13,436

Required

a.   Compute the missing amounts for assets, liabilities, and equity for each year.

b.   Compute return on equity for 2008 and 2009. The median ROE for Fortune 500 companies is about 15%. How does P&G compare with this median?

c.   Compute the debt-to-equity ratio for 2008 and 2009. The median debt-to-equity ratio for the Fortune 500 companies is 1.8. How does P&G compare to this median?

LO2, LO3   **P1-35.** **Formulating Financial Statements from Raw Data**

Following is selected financial information from **General Mills, Inc.**, for its fiscal year ended May 31, 2009 ($ millions):

Cash asset.	$ 749.8
Net cash from operations	1,828.2
Sales	14,691.3
Stockholders' equity	5,174.7
Cost of goods sold	9,457.8
Net cash from financing	(1,450.5)
Total liabilities	12,700.1
Other expenses	3,929.1
Noncash assets.	17,125.0
Net cash from investing	(288.9)
Net income.	1,304.4
Cash, beginning year	661.0

Required

a.   Prepare an income statement, balance sheet, and statement of cash flows for General Mills, Inc.

b.   What portion of the financing is contributed by owners?

LO2, LO3   **P1-36.** **Formulating Financial Statements from Raw Data**

Following is selected financial information from **Abercrombie & Fitch** for its fiscal year ended January 31, 2009 ($ millions):

Cash asset	$ 522
Cash flows from operations	491
Sales	3,540
Stockholders' equity	1,846
Cost of goods sold	1,179
Cash flows from financing	(113)
Total liabilities	1,002
Other expenses	2,089
Noncash assets	2,326
Cash flows from investing	26
Net income	272
Cash, beginning year	118

Required

a. Prepare an income statement, balance sheet, and statement of cash flows for Abercrombie & Fitch.

b. Determine the owner and creditor financing levels.

P1-37. Formulating Financial Statements from Raw Data   LO3

Following is selected financial information from **Cisco Systems, Inc.**, for the year ended July 25, 2009 ($ millions):

CISCO SYSTEMS
NASDAQ :: CSCO

Cash asset	$ 5,718
Cash flows from operations	9,897
Sales	36,117
Stockholders' equity	38,647
Cost of goods sold	13,023
Cash flows from financing	589
Total liabilities	29,481
Other expenses	16,960
Noncash assets	62,410
Cash flows from investing	(9,959)
Net income	6,134
Cash, beginning year	5,191

Required

Prepare an income statement, balance sheet, and statement of cash flows for Cisco Systems, Inc.

P1-38. Formulating a Statement of Stockholders' Equity from Raw Data   LO3

Crocker Corporation began calendar-year 2010 with stockholders' equity of $100,000, consisting of contributed capital of $70,000 and retained earnings of $30,000. During 2010, it issued additional stock for total cash proceeds of $30,000. It also reported $50,000 of net income, of which $25,000 was paid as a cash dividend to shareholders.

WebAssign.

Required

Prepare the 2010 statement of stockholders' equity for Crocker Corporation.

P1-39. Formulating a Statement of Stockholders' Equity from Raw Data   LO3

DP Systems, Inc., reports the following selected information at December 31, 2010 ($ millions):

Contributed capital, December 31, 2009 and 2010	$ 550
Retained earnings, December 31, 2009	2,437
Cash dividends, 2010	281
Net income, 2010	859

Required

Use this information to prepare its statement of stockholders' equity for 2010.

P1-40. Analyzing and Interpreting Return on Equity   LO3, LO5

Nokia Corp. manufactures, markets, and sells phones and other electronics. Stockholders' equity for Nokia are €16,510 in 2008 and €17,388 in 2007. In 2008, Nokia reported net income of €3,889 on sales of €50,710.

NOKIA
NYSE :: NOK

Required

a. What is Nokia's return on equity for 2008?

b. Nokia's total assets were €39,582 at the end of 2008. Compute its debt-to-equity ratio.

c. What are total expenses for Nokia in 2008?

LO3, LO5   **P1-41.**   **Presenting an Income Statement and Computing Key Ratios**

BEST BUY
NYSE :: BBY

Best Buy Co., Inc., reported the following amounts in its February 28, 2009, and March 1, 2008, financial statements.

($ millions)	2009	2008
Sales revenue	$45,015	$40,023
Cost of sales	34,017	30,477
Net income	1,003	1,407
Total assets	15,826	12,758
Stockholders' equity	4,643	4,484

Required

a. Prepare an income statement for Best Buy for the year ended February 28, 2009, using the format illustrated in Exhibit 1.8.

b. Calculate Best Buy's return on equity for the year ended February 28, 2009.

c. Compute Best Buy's debt-to-equity ratio as of February 28, 2009.

LO3, LO5   **P1-42.**   **Presenting an Income Statement and Computing Key Ratios**

WebAssign.

DELL INC.
NASDAQ :: DELL

Dell Inc. reported the following amounts in its January 30, 2009, and February 1, 2008, financial statements.

($ millions)	2009	2008
Sales revenue	$61,101	$61,133
Cost of sales	50,144	49,462
Other expenses	8,479	8,724
Total assets	26,500	27,561
Stockholders' equity	4,271	3,735

Required

a. Prepare an income statement for Dell as of January 30, 2009, using the format illustrated in Exhibit 1.8.

b. Calculate Dell's return on equity for the year ended January 30, 2009.

c. Compute Dell's debt-to-equity ratio as of January 30, 2009.

CASES AND PROJECTS

LO2, LO3, LO5   **C1-43.**   **Computing and Interpreting Key Ratios and Formulating an Income Statement**

THE GAP
NYSE :: GPS

NORDSTROM
NYSE :: JWN

Data from the financial statements of **The Gap, Inc.**, and **Nordstrom, Inc.**, are presented below.

($ millions)	The Gap	Nordstrom
Total liabilities, 2008	$ 3,177	$4,451
Total liabilities, 2007	3,564	4,485
Total assets, 2008	7,564	5,661
Total assets, 2007	7,838	5,600
Revenue, 2008	14,526	8,573
Cost of goods sold, 2008	9,079	5,417
Net income, 2008	967	401

Required

a. Compute the return on equity ratio for The Gap and Nordstrom for 2008. Which company earned the higher return for its shareholders?

b. Compute the debt-to-equity ratio for each company as of 2008. Which company relies more on creditor financing?

c. Prepare a 2008 income statement for each company using the format in Exhibit 1.8. For each firm, compute gross profit as a percentage of sales revenue.

d. Based on your answers to questions a, b, and c, compare these two retail companies. What might be the cause of any differences in the ratios that you computed?

C1-44. Computing and Interpreting Key Ratios

LO5

JETBLUE AIRWAYS
NASDAQ:: JBLU

SOUTHWEST AIRLINES
NYSE :: LUV

Data from the financial statements of **JetBlue Airways** and **Southwest Airlines** are presented below.

($ millions)	Jet Blue Airways	Southwest Airlines
Total liabilities, December 31, 2008	$4,762	$ 9,355
Total liabilities, December 31, 2007	4,562	9,831
Total assets, December 31, 2008	6,023	14,308
Total assets, December 31, 2007	5,598	16,772
Revenue, 2008	3,388	11,023
Net income, 2008	(76)	178

Required

a. Compute the return on equity ratio for JetBlue and Southwest for 2008. Which company earned the higher return for its shareholders?

b. Compute the debt-to-equity ratio for each company as of December 31, 2008. Which company relies more on creditor financing?

c. For each firm, compute net income as a percentage of revenue in 2008.

d. Based on your answers to questions *a*, *b*, and *c*, compare these two competitors. What might be the cause of any differences in the ratios that you computed?

C1-45. Interpreting Financial Statement Information

LO1, LO3, LO5

Paula Seale is negotiating the purchase of an extermination firm called Total Pest Control. Seale has been employed by a national pest control service and knows the technical side of the business. However, she knows little about accounting data and financial statements. The sole owner of the firm, Meg Krey, has provided Seale with income statements for the past three years, which show an average net income of $72,000 per year. The latest balance sheet shows total assets of $285,000 and liabilities of $45,000. Seale brings the following matters to your attention and requests advice.

1. Krey is asking $300,000 for the firm. She has told Seale that because the firm has been earning 30% on its investment, the price should be higher than the net assets on the balance sheet.

2. Seale has noticed no salary for Krey on the income statements, even though she worked half-time in the business. Krey explained that because she had other income, the firm only paid $18,000 in cash dividends to Krey (the sole shareholder). If she purchases the firm, Seale will hire a full-time manager for the firm at an annual salary of $36,000.

3. Krey's tax returns for the past 3 years report a lower net income for the firm than the amounts shown in the financial statements. Seale is skeptical about the accounting principles used in preparing the financial statements.

Required

a. How did Krey arrive at the 30% return figure in point 1? If Seale accepts Krey's average annual income figure of $72,000, what would Seale's percentage return be, assuming that the net income remained at the same level and that the firm was purchased for $300,000?

b. Should the dividend to Krey affect the net income reported in the financial statements? What will Seale's percentage return be if she takes into consideration the $36,000 salary she plans to pay a full-time manager?

c. Could there be legitimate reasons for the difference between net income shown in the financial statements and net income reported on the tax returns, as mentioned in point 3? How might Seale obtain additional assurance about the propriety of the financial statements?

C1-46. Management, Auditing, and Ethical Behavior

LO1, LO4

Jackie Hardy, CPA, has a brother, Ted, in the retail clothing business. Ted ran the business as its sole owner for 10 years. During this 10-year period, Jackie helped Ted with various accounting matters. For example, Jackie designed the accounting system for the company, prepared Ted's personal income tax returns (which included financial data about the clothing business), and recommended various cost control procedures. Ted paid Jackie for all these services. A year ago, Ted markedly expanded the business; Ted is president of the corporation and also chairs the corporation's board of directors. The board of directors has overall responsibility for corporate affairs. When the corporation was formed, Ted asked Jackie to serve on its board of directors. Jackie accepted. In addition, Jackie now prepares the corporation's income tax returns and continues to advise her brother on accounting matters.

Recently, the corporation applied for a large bank loan. The bank wants audited financial statements for the corporation before it will decide on the loan request. Ted asked Jackie to perform the audit. Jackie replied that she cannot do the audit because the code of ethics for CPAs requires that she be independent when providing audit services.

Required

a.   Why is it important that a CPA be independent when providing audit services?

b.   Which of Jackie's activities or relationships impair her independence?

SOLUTIONS TO REVIEW PROBLEMS

Mid-Chapter Review

a.

ADIDAS
Balance Sheet (€ millions)
December 31, 2008

Cash	€ 244	Total liabilities	€6,133
Noncash assets	9,289	Stockholders' equity	3,400
Total assets	€9,533	Total liabilities and stockholders' equity	€9,533

ADIDAS
Income Statement (€ millions)
For Year Ended December 31, 2008

Sales revenue	€10,799
Cost of goods sold	5,543
Gross profit	5,256
Other expenses	4,612
Net income (loss)	€ 644

ADIDAS
Statement of Cash Flows (€ millions)
For Year Ended December 31, 2008

Cash flow from operations	€497
Cash flow from investing	(444)
Cash flow from financing	(104)
Net increase (decrease) in cash	(51)
Cash, beginning of year	295
Cash, end of year	€244

b.   Adidas reported revenues of €10,799 million (which is approximately equivalent to $16,198 million) compared to Nike's $19,176.1 million. Adidas reported net income of €644 million ($966 million) compared to Nike's $1,486.7 million. Adidas's operations produced cash flow of €497 million ($745 million) while Nike's cash flow from operations was $1,736.1 million. Hence, based on revenues, Nike is a slightly larger company in that it reported greater sales for the year. Consistent with its larger size, Nike's operating cash flows and income are also larger than those of Adidas.

<u>**Chapter-End Review**</u>

   a. $\text{ROE} = \dfrac{\text{€644 million}}{(\text{€3,034 million} + \text{€3,400 million})/2} = 0.200 \text{ or } 20.0\%$

   b. $\text{Debt-to-equity} = \dfrac{\text{€6,133 million}}{\text{€3,400 million}} = 1.80$

   c.   One additional benefit to using ratios to analyze financial information is that ratios can be computed for amounts denominated in any currency. Thus, we can compare Adidas and Nike without translating Euros into Dollars. Adidas's ROE of 20.0% is slightly higher than Nike's of 18.0%. This means that Adidas is more profitable in that it earned a higher return for its stockholders in 2008.

       Adidas's debt-to-equity ratio is 1.80 compared to Nike's 0.524. This means that Adidas relies much more on debt financing than does Nike. The higher debt-to-equity ratio indicates a higher level of risk associated with an investment in Adidas than with an investment in Nike.

checkout
cigarettes
smoke busters
Value!

Constructing Financial Statements

2

More than a hundred years have passed since Charles R. Walgreen, Sr. purchased his first pharmacy in 1901. In that time, the company that bears his name—**Walgreen Co.**—has grown remarkably, opening its 7,000th drugstore in the fall of 2009. Walgreens operates drugstores in 50 states, the District of Columbia, Guam, and Puerto Rico; it has more than 238,000 employees; and it fills more than 18% of the retail prescriptions in the United States. The year 2009 marked the 16th consecutive time that Walgreens was named to *Fortune*'s list of Most Admired Companies in America.

WALGREENS
www.walgreens.com

Even with such a significant presence, Walgreens faces a number of challenges. The economic changes of the recent past have made consumers more cautious and cost-conscious. Pharmacy sales constitute 65 percent of Walgreens' sales, and it faces rising costs for pharmaceuticals and increasing competition from other drugstore chains like **CVS Caremark Corporation** and discount retailers like **Wal-Mart Stores, Inc.** Government health care reforms have the potential to reshape the landscape for providers of health products and services like Walgreens.

These factors contributed to a drop in profits in 2009, even though sales revenue increased by 7%. New Chief Executive Officer, Gregory D. Wasson, must find a strategy for profitable growth. The company has slowed the rate of new store openings and turned its focus to cost control and operating efficiencies.

As we discovered in Chapter 1, companies like Walgreens prepare financial statements annually. These financial statements allow investors and creditors to assess the impact of changing economic conditions on the company's financial health and performance.

This chapter will introduce and explain financial statements using Walgreens as its prime example. The chapter also introduces some key accounting procedures such as transaction analysis, journal entries, and posting. The general ledger, key accounting assumptions, and basic accounting definitions are also introduced.

Sources: "In the beginning…" Walgreens history on the corporate Web site; Walgreen Co. and Subsidiaries 2009 annual report; *Fortune* magazine Web site.

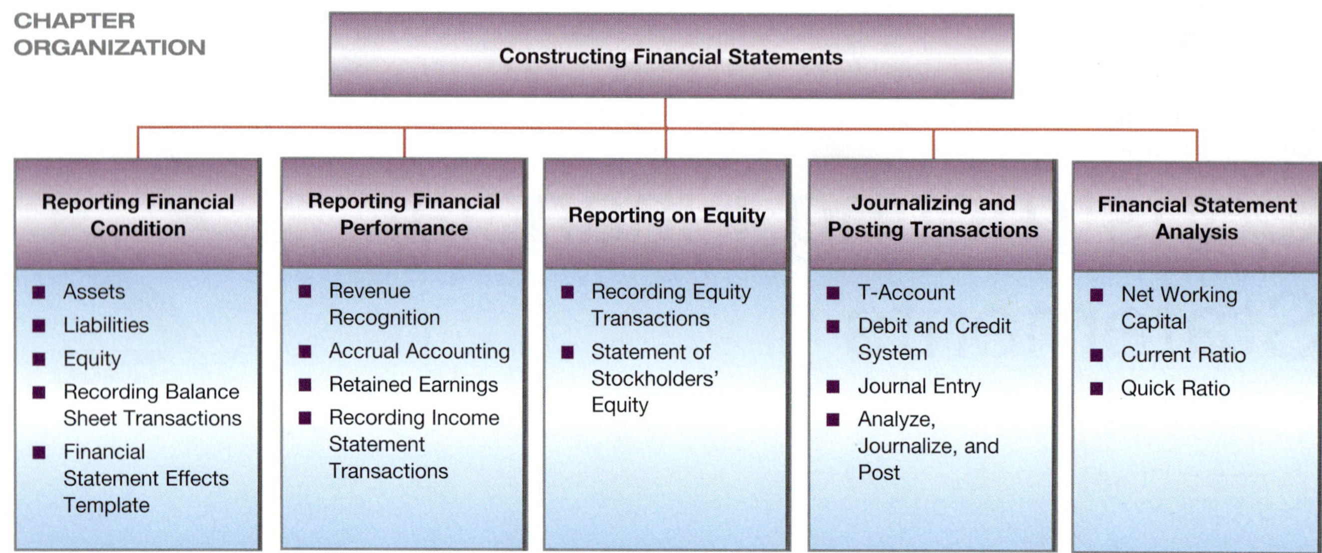

In Chapter 1, we introduced the four financial statements—the balance sheet, the income statement, the cash flow statement, and the statement of stockholders' equity. In this chapter and in Chapter 3, we turn our attention to how the balance sheet and income statement are prepared. The statement of cash flows is discussed in detail in Chapter 4, and the statement of stockholders' equity is discussed in detail in Chapter 11.

REPORTING FINANCIAL CONDITION

LO1 Describe and construct the balance sheet and understand how it can be used for analysis.

The balance sheet reports on a company's financial condition and is divided into three components: assets, liabilities, and stockholders' equity. It provides us with information about the resources available to management and the claims against those resources by creditors and shareholders. At the end of August 2009, **Walgreens** reports total assets of $25,142 million, total liabilities of $10,766 million, and equity of $14,376 million. Drawing on the **accounting equation**, Walgreens' balance sheet is summarized as follows ($ million).

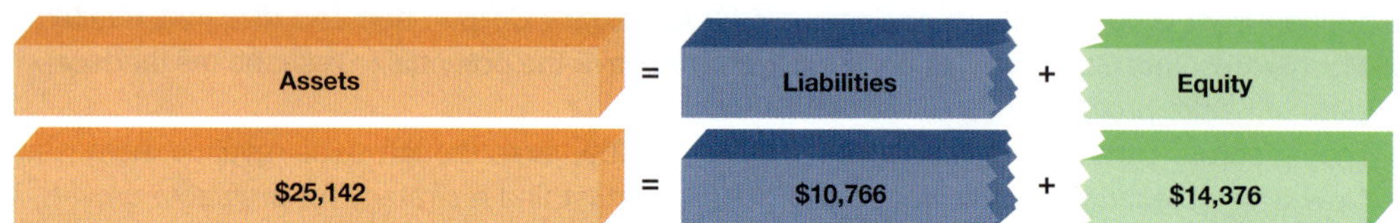

The balance sheet is prepared at a *point in time*. It is a snapshot of the financial condition of the company at that instant. For Walgreens, the above balance sheet amounts were reported at the close of business on August 31, 2009. Balance sheet accounts carry over from one period to the next; that is, the ending balance from one period becomes the beginning balance for the next period.

Walgreens' 2009 and 2008 balance sheets are shown in Exhibit 2.1. These balance sheets report the assets and the liabilities and shareholders' equity amounts as of August 31, the company's fiscal year-end. Walgreens had $25,142 million in assets at the end of August 31, 2009, with the same amount reported in liabilities and shareholders' equity. Companies report their audited financial results on a yearly basis.[1] Many companies use the calendar year as their fiscal year. Other companies prefer to prepare their yearly report at a time when business activity is at a low level. Walgreens is an example of the latter.

Assets

An **asset** is a resource that is expected to provide a company with future economic benefits. When a company incurs a cost to acquire future benefits, that cost is capitalized and an asset is recorded. An asset must possess two characteristics to be reported on the balance sheet:

---

[1] Companies also report quarterly financial statements, and these are reviewed by the independent accountant, but not audited.

1. It must be owned or controlled by the company.
2. It must possess expected future benefits that can be measured.

The first requirement, that the asset must be owned or controlled by the company, implies that the company has legal title to the asset or has the unrestricted right to use the asset. This requirement presumes that the cost to acquire the asset has been incurred, either by paying cash, by trading other assets, or by assuming an obligation to make future payments.

The second requirement indicates that the company expects to receive some future benefit from ownership of the asset. Benefits can be the expected cash receipts from selling the asset or from selling products produced by the asset. Benefits can also refer to the receipt of other noncash assets, such as accounts receivable or the reduction of a liability (e.g. when assets are given up to settle debts). It also requires that a monetary value can be assigned to the asset.

Companies acquire assets to yield a return for their shareholders. Assets are expected to produce revenues, either directly (e.g. inventory that is sold) or indirectly (e.g. a manufacturing plant that produces inventories for sale). To create shareholder value, assets must yield income that is in excess of the cost of the funds utilized to acquire the assets.

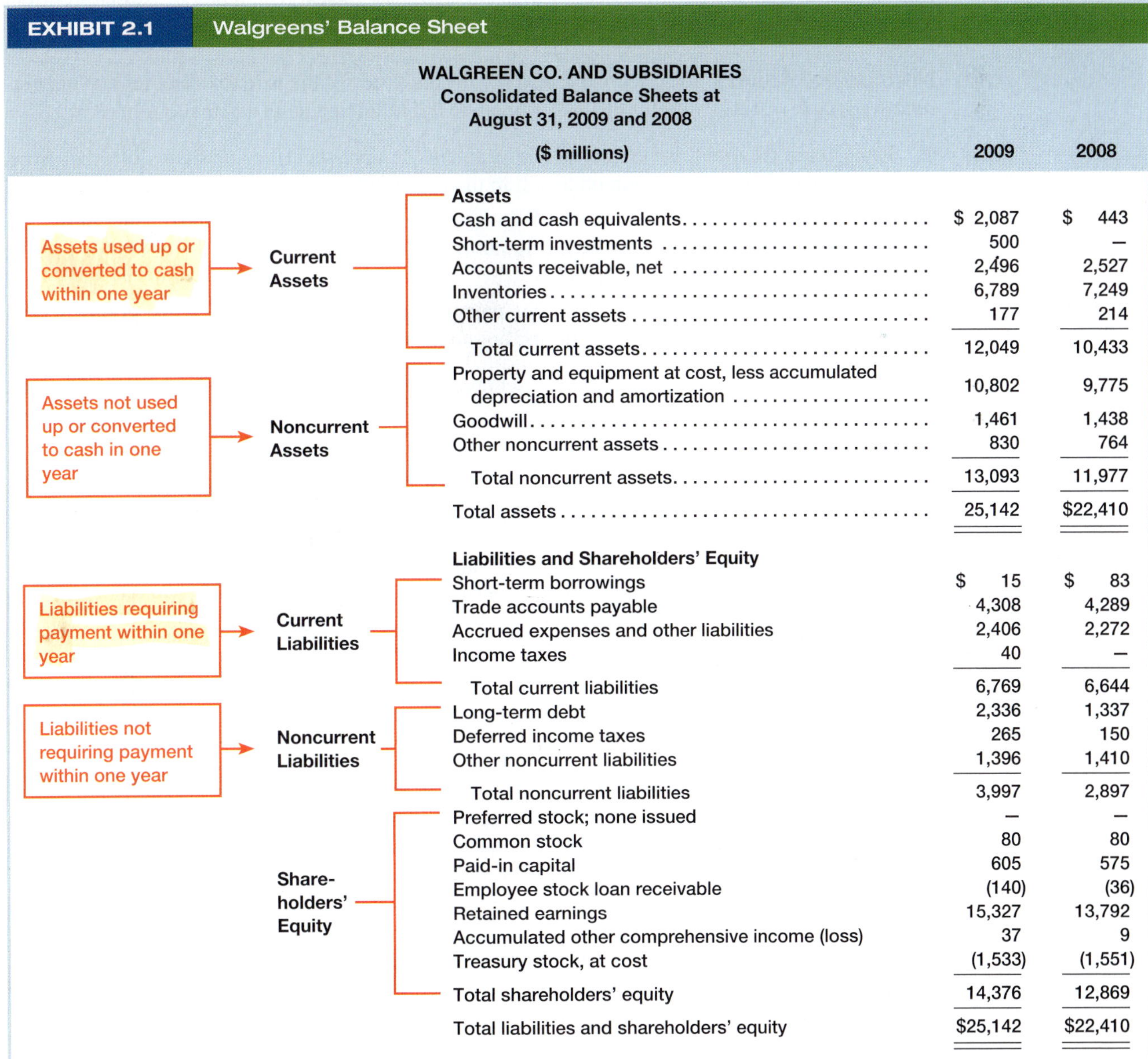

EXHIBIT 2.1   Walgreens' Balance Sheet

WALGREEN CO. AND SUBSIDIARIES
Consolidated Balance Sheets at
August 31, 2009 and 2008

($ millions)	2009	2008
Assets		
Cash and cash equivalents	$ 2,087	$ 443
Short-term investments	500	—
Accounts receivable, net	2,496	2,527
Inventories	6,789	7,249
Other current assets	177	214
Total current assets	12,049	10,433
Property and equipment at cost, less accumulated depreciation and amortization	10,802	9,775
Goodwill	1,461	1,438
Other noncurrent assets	830	764
Total noncurrent assets	13,093	11,977
Total assets	25,142	$22,410
Liabilities and Shareholders' Equity		
Short-term borrowings	$ 15	$ 83
Trade accounts payable	4,308	4,289
Accrued expenses and other liabilities	2,406	2,272
Income taxes	40	—
Total current liabilities	6,769	6,644
Long-term debt	2,336	1,337
Deferred income taxes	265	150
Other noncurrent liabilities	1,396	1,410
Total noncurrent liabilities	3,997	2,897
Preferred stock; none issued	—	—
Common stock	80	80
Paid-in capital	605	575
Employee stock loan receivable	(140)	(36)
Retained earnings	15,327	13,792
Accumulated other comprehensive income (loss)	37	9
Treasury stock, at cost	(1,533)	(1,551)
Total shareholders' equity	14,376	12,869
Total liabilities and shareholders' equity	$25,142	$22,410

Current Assets

In the United States, the assets section of a balance sheet is presented in order of **liquidity**, which refers to the ease of converting noncash assets into cash. The most liquid assets are called **current assets**. Current assets are assets expected to be converted into cash or used in operations within the next year, or within the next operating cycle. Some typical examples of current assets include the following accounts, which are listed in order of their liquidity:

FYI Cash equivalents are short-term, highly liquid investments that mature in three months or less and can be easily converted to cash.

- **Cash**—currency, bank deposits, certificates of deposit, and other *cash equivalents;*
- **Marketable securities**—short-term investments that can be quickly sold to raise cash;
- **Accounts receivable**—amounts due to the company from customers arising from the sale of products or services on credit;
- **Inventory**—goods purchased or produced for sale to customers;
- **Prepaid expenses**—costs paid in advance for rent, insurance, or other services.

The amount of current assets is an important measure of liquidity. Companies require a degree of liquidity to effectively operate on a daily basis. However, current assets are expensive to hold—they must be insured, monitored, financed, and so forth—and they typically generate returns that are less than those from noncurrent assets. As a result, companies seek to maintain just enough current assets to cover liquidity needs, but not so much so as to reduce income unnecessarily.

Noncurrent Assets

The second section of the asset side of the balance sheet reports noncurrent (long-term) assets. **Noncurrent assets** include the following asset accounts:

- **Long-term financial investments**—investments in debt securities or shares of other firms that management does not intend to sell in the near future;
- **Property, plant, and equipment (PPE)**—includes land, factory buildings, warehouses, office buildings, machinery, office equipment, and other items used in the operations of the company;
- **Intangible and other assets**—includes patents, trademarks, franchise rights, goodwill, and other items that provide future benefits, but do not possess physical substance.

Noncurrent assets are listed after current assets because they are not expected to expire or be converted into cash within one year.

Measuring Assets

Assets that are intended to be used, such as inventory and property, plant, and equipment, are reported on the balance sheet at their **historical cost** (with adjustments for depreciation in some cases). Historical cost refers to the original acquisition cost. The use of historical cost to report asset values has the advantage of **reliability**. Historical costs are reliable because the acquisition cost (the amount of cash paid to purchase the asset) can be objectively determined and accurately measured. The disadvantage of historical costs is that some assets can be significantly undervalued on the balance sheet. For example, the land in Anaheim, California, on which Disneyland was built more than 50 years ago, was purchased for a mere fraction of its current market value.

FYI Excluded assets often relate to self-developed, knowledge-based assets, like organizational effectiveness and technology. This is one reason that knowledge-based industries are so difficult to analyze. Yet, excluded assets are presumably reflected in company market values. This fact can explain why the firm's market capitalization (its share price multiplied by the number of shares) is often greater than the book value shown on the balance sheet.

Some assets, such as marketable securities, are reported at current market value or **fair market value**. The market value of these assets can be easily obtained from online price quotes or from reliable sources such as **The Wall Street Journal**. Reporting certain assets at fair market value increases the **relevance** of the information presented in the balance sheet. Relevance refers to how useful the information is to those who use the financial statements for decision making. For example, marketable securities are intended to be sold for cash when cash is needed by the company to pay its obligations. Therefore, the most relevant value for marketable securities is the amount of cash that the company expects to receive when the securities are sold.

Only those asset values that can be accurately measured are reported on the balance sheet. For this reason, some of a company's most important assets are often not reflected among the reported assets of the company. For example, the well-recognized Walgreens logo does not appear as an asset on the company's balance sheet. The image of Mickey Mouse and that of the Aflac Duck are also absent from **The Walt Disney Company**'s and **Aflac Incorporated**'s balance sheets. These items are referred to as an unrecognized intangible asset. These intangible assets and the Coke bottle silhouette, the Kleenex name, an excellent management team, or a well-designed supply chain, are measured and reported on the balance sheet only when they are purchased from a third party. As a result, *internally created* intangible assets, such as the Mickey Mouse image, are not reported on a balance sheet, even though many of these internally created intangible assets are of enormous value.

Liabilities and Equity

Liabilities and equity represent the sources of capital to the company that are used to finance the acquisition of assets. Liabilities represent the firm's obligations for borrowed funds from lenders or bond investors, as well as obligations to pay suppliers, employees, tax authorities, and other parties. These obligations can be interest-bearing or non-interest-bearing. Equity represents capital that has been invested by the shareholders, either directly via the purchase of stock, or indirectly in the form of earnings that are reinvested in the business and not paid out as dividends (retained earnings). We discuss liabilities and equity in this section.

The liabilities and equity sections of Walgreens' balance sheets for 2009 and 2008 are reproduced in the lower section of Exhibit 2.1. Walgreens reports $10,766 million of total liabilities and $14,376 million of equity as of its 2009 fiscal year-end. The total of liabilities and equity equals $25,142—the same as the total assets—because the shareholders have a residual claim on the company.

A **liability** is a probable future economic sacrifice resulting from a current or past event. The economic sacrifice can be a future cash payment to a creditor, or it can be an obligation to deliver goods or services to a customer at a future date. A liability must be reported in the balance sheet when each of the following three conditions is met:

1. The future sacrifice is probable.
2. The amount of the obligation is known or can be reasonably estimated.
3. The transaction or event that caused the obligation has occurred.

When conditions 1 and 2 are satisfied, but the transaction that caused the obligation has not occurred, the obligation is called an **executory contract** and no liability is reported. An example of such an obligation is a purchase order. When a company signs an agreement to purchase materials from a supplier, it commits to making a future cash payment of a known amount. However, the obligation to pay for the materials is not considered a liability until the materials are delivered. Therefore, even though the company is contractually obligated to make the cash payment to the supplier, a liability is not recorded on the balance sheet. However, information about purchase commitments and other executory contracts is useful to investors and creditors, and the obligations should be disclosed in the footnotes to the financial statements. In its annual report, Walgreens reports open inventory purchase orders of $1,477 million at the end of fiscal year 2009.

Current Liabilities   Liabilities on the balance sheet are listed according to maturity. Obligations that are due within one year or within one operating cycle are called **current liabilities**. Some examples of common current liabilities include:

- **Accounts payable**—amounts owed to suppliers for goods and services purchased on credit.
- **Accrued liabilities**—obligations for expenses that have been recorded but not yet paid. Examples include accrued compensation payable (wages earned by employees but not yet paid), accrued interest payable (interest on debt that has not been paid), and accrued taxes (taxes due).
- **Short-term borrowings**—short-term debt payable to banks or other creditors.
- **Deferred (unearned) revenues**—an obligation created when the company accepts payment in advance for goods or services it will deliver in the future. Sometimes also called advances from customers or customer deposits.

- **Current maturities of long-term debt**—the current portion of long-term debt that is due to be paid within one year.

Noncurrent Liabilities   **Noncurrent liabilities** are obligations to be paid after one year. Examples of noncurrent liabilities include:

- **Long-term debt**—amounts borrowed from creditors that are scheduled to be repaid more than one year in the future. Any portion of long-term debt that is due within one year is reclassified as a current liability called *current maturities of long-term debt*.
- **Other long-term liabilities**—various obligations, such as warranty and deferred compensation liabilities and long-term tax liabilities, that will be satisfied at least a year in the future. These items are discussed in later chapters.

Detailed information about a company's noncurrent liabilities, such as payment schedules, interest rates, and restrictive covenants, are provided in the footnotes to the financial statements.

BUSINESS INSIGHT

How Much Debt Is Reasonable?   **Walgreens** reports total assets of $25,142 million, liabilities of $10,766 million, and equity of $14,376 million. This means that Walgreens finances 43% of its assets with borrowed funds and 57% with shareholder investment. Liabilities represent claims for fixed amounts, while shareholders' equity represents a flexible claim (because shareholders have a residual claim). Companies must monitor their financing sources and amounts because borrowing too much increases risk, and investors must recognize that companies may have substantial obligations (like Walgreens' inventory purchase commitment) that do not appear on the balance sheet.

Stockholders' Equity   **Equity** reflects capital provided by the owners of the company. It is often referred to as a *residual interest*. That is, stockholders have a claim on any assets that are not needed to meet the company's obligations to creditors. The following are examples of items that are typically included in stockholders' equity:

- **Common stock**—the capital received from the primary owners of the company. Total common stock is divided into shares. One share of common stock represents the smallest fractional unit of ownership of a company.[2]
- **Additional paid-in capital**—amounts received from the primary owners in addition to the par value or stated value of the common stock.
- **Treasury stock**—the amount paid for its own common stock that the company has reacquired.
- **Retained earnings**—the accumulated earnings that have not been distributed to stockholders as dividends.
- **Accumulated other comprehensive income or loss**—accumulated changes in equity that are not reported in the income statement; discussed in Chapters 11 and 12.

The equity section of a balance sheet consists of two basic components: contributed capital and earned capital. **Contributed capital** is the net funding that a company has received from issuing and reacquiring its equity shares. That is, the funds received from issuing shares less any funds paid to repurchase such shares. Walgreens' equity section reports $14,376 million in equity. Its contributed capital is a negative $988 million ($80 million in common stock plus $605 million in [additional] paid-in capital minus $140 million in an employee stock loan receivable minus $1,533

---

[2] Many companies' common shares have a par value, but that value has little economic significance. For instance, Walgreens' shares have a par value of $.078125 per share, while the market price of the stock is about $39 at the time of this writing. In most cases, the sum of common stock (at par) and additional paid-in capital represents the value of stockholders' contributions to the business in exchange for shares.

million in treasury stock). The negative balance indicates that Walgreens has returned more cash to its shareholders (by buying its own stock) than it has received in cash from its shareholder capital contributions.

Earned capital is the cumulative net income (and losses) retained by the company (not paid out to shareholders as dividends). Earned capital typically includes retained earnings and accumulated other comprehensive income or loss. Walgreens' earned capital is $15,364 million ($15,327 million in retained earnings plus $37 million in accumulated other comprehensive income). Other comprehensive income is discussed in Chapters 11 and 12.

RETAINED EARNINGS   There is an important relation for retained earnings that reconciles its beginning and ending balances as follows:

> Beginning retained earnings
> + Net income (or − Net loss)
> − Dividends
> ___________________________
> = Ending retained earnings

This relation is useful to remember, even though there are other items that sometimes impact retained earnings. We revisit this relation after our discussion of the income statement and show how it links the balance sheet and income statement.

MID-CHAPTER REVIEW 1

Assume Schaefer's Pharmacy, Inc. has the following detailed accounts as part of its accounting system. Enter the letter of the balance sheet category A through E in the space next to the balance sheet items numbered 1 through 20. Enter an **X** in the space if the item is not reported on the balance sheet.

A.   Current assets
B.   Long-term assets
C.   Current liabilities
D.   Long-term liabilities
E.   Equity

1. Accounts receivable
2. Short-term notes payable
3. Land
4. Retained earnings
5. Intangible assets
6. Common stock
7. Repairs expense
8. Equipment
9. Treasury stock
10. Investments (noncurrent)
11. Rent expense
12. Cash
13. Buildings
14. Accounts payable
15. Prepaid rent
16. Borrowings (due in 25 years)
17. Marketable securities
18. Inventories
19. Additional paid-in capital
20. Unearned revenue

The solution to this review problem can be found on page 89.

Analyzing and Recording Transactions for the Balance Sheet

The balance sheet is the foundation of the accounting system. Every event, or transaction, that is recorded in the accounting system must be recorded so that the following accounting equation is maintained:

$$\text{Assets} = \text{Liabilities} + \text{Equity}$$

We use this fundamental relation throughout the book to help us assess the financial impact of transactions. This is our "step 1" when we encounter a transaction. Our "steps 2 and 3" are to journalize those financial impacts and then post them to individual accounts to emphasize the linkage from entries to accounts (steps 2 and 3 are explained later in this chapter).

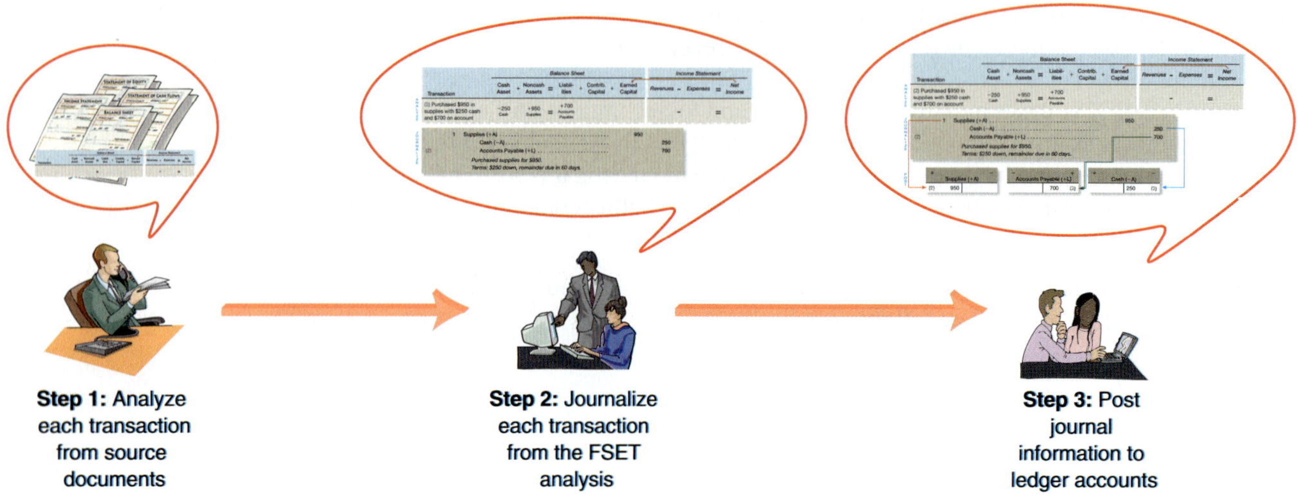

Step 1: Analyze each transaction from source documents

Step 2: Journalize each transaction from the FSET analysis

Step 3: Post journal information to ledger accounts

Financial Statement Effects Template   To analyze the financial impacts of transactions, we employ the following **financial statement effects template (FSET)**.

	Balance Sheet					Income Statement		
Transaction	Cash Asset	+ Noncash Assets	= Liabil- ities	+ Contrib. Capital	+ Earned Capital	Revenues	- Expenses	= Net Income
			=				-	=

The template accomplishes several things. First and foremost, it captures the transaction that must be recorded in the accounting system. That "recording" function will be our focus for the next few pages. But accounting is not just recording financial data; it is also the reporting of information that is useful to financial statement readers. So, the template also depicts the effects of the transaction on the four financial statements: balance sheet, income statement, statement of stockholders' equity, and statement of cash flows. For the balance sheet, we differentiate between cash and noncash assets so as to identify the cash effects of transactions. Likewise, equity is separated into the contributed and earned capital components (the latter includes retained earnings as its major element). Finally, income statement effects are separated into revenues, expenses, and net income (the updating of retained earnings is denoted with an arrow line running from net income to earned capital). This template provides a convenient means to represent financial accounting transactions and events in a simple, concise manner for analyzing, journalizing, and posting.

The Account   An **account** is a mechanism for accumulating the effects of an organization's transactions and events. For instance, an account labeled "Merchandise Inventory" allows a retailer's accounting system to accumulate information about the receipts of inventory from suppliers and the delivery of inventory to customers.

Before a transaction is recorded, we first analyze the effect of the transaction on the accounting equation by asking the following questions:

■ What accounts are affected by the transaction?

■ What is the direction and magnitude of each effect?

To maintain the equality of the accounting equation, each transaction must affect (at least) two accounts. For example, a transaction might increase assets and increase equity by equal amounts. Another transaction might increase one asset and decrease another asset, while yet another might decrease an asset and decrease a liability. These *dual effects* are what constitute the **double-entry accounting system**.

The account is a record of increases and decreases for each important asset, liability, equity, revenue, or expense item. The **chart of accounts** is a listing of the titles (and identification codes) of all accounts for a company.[3] Account titles are commonly grouped into five categories: assets, liabilities, equity, revenues, and expenses. The accounts for Natural Beauty Supply, Inc. (introduced below), follow:

	Assets		Equity
			310 Common Stock
	110 Cash		320 Retained Earnings
	120 Accounts Receivable		**Revenues and Income**
	130 Other Receivables		410 Sales Revenue
	140 Inventory		420 Interest Revenue

Assets

110 Cash
120 Accounts Receivable
130 Other Receivables
140 Inventory
150 Prepaid Insurance
160 Security Deposit
170 Fixtures and Equipment
175 Accumulated Depreciation—Fixtures and Equipment

Liabilities

210 Accounts Payable
220 Interest Payable
230 Wages Payable
240 Taxes Payable
250 Unearned Revenue
260 Notes Payable

Equity

310 Common Stock
320 Retained Earnings

Revenues and Income

410 Sales Revenue
420 Interest Revenue

Expenses

510 Cost of Goods Sold
520 Wages Expense
530 Rent Expense
540 Advertising Expense
550 Depreciation Expense—Fixtures and Equipment
560 Insurance Expense
570 Interest Expense
580 Tax Expense

Each transaction entered in the template must maintain the equality of the accounting equation, and the accounts cited must correspond to those in its chart of accounts.

Transaction Analysis Using FSET   To illustrate the effect of transactions on the accounting equation and, correspondingly, the financial statements, we consider the business activities of Natural Beauty Supply, Inc. Natural Beauty Supply was established to operate as a retailer of organic beauty and health care products, though the owners hoped that they also would become a wholesale provider of such products to local salons. The company began business on November 1, 2010. The following transactions occurred on the first day of business:

LO2 Use the financial statement effects template (FSET) to analyze transactions.

(1) Nov. 1   Investors contributed $20,000 cash to launch Natural Beauty Supply, Inc. (NBS), in exchange for 10,000 shares of NBS stock.

(2) Nov. 1   NBS borrowed $5,000 cash from a family member of the company's founders by signing a note. The $5,000 must be paid back on November 30 with interest of $50.

(3) Nov. 1   NBS arranged to rent a storefront location and began to use the property. The landlord requires payment of $1,500 at the end of each month. NBS paid a $2,000 security deposit that will be returned at the end of the lease.

(4) Nov. 1   NBS purchased, on account, and received $17,000 of inventory consisting of natural soaps and beauty products.

Let's begin by analyzing the financial statement effects of the first transaction. At the beginning of its life, Natural Beauty Supply has accounts that are empty of entries, so the financial statements would be filled with zeroes. In the company's very first transaction, shareholders invested $20,000 cash in Natural Beauty Supply, and the company issued 10,000 shares of common stock, increased equity (contributed capital). This transaction is reflected in the following financial ments effects template.

---

[3] Accounting systems at large organizations will have much more detail in their account structures than we will use here. The account structure's detail allows management to accumulate information by responsibility center or by product line or by customer.

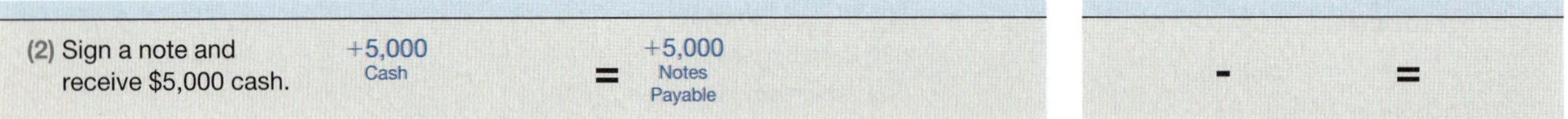

Assets (cash) and equity (common stock) increased by the same amount, and the accounting equation remains in balance (as it always must).

In the second transaction, Natural Beauty Supply borrowed cash by signing a note (loan agreement) with a family member. This transaction increased cash (an asset) and increased notes payable (a liability) by the same amount. The notes payable liability recognizes the obligation to repay the family member.

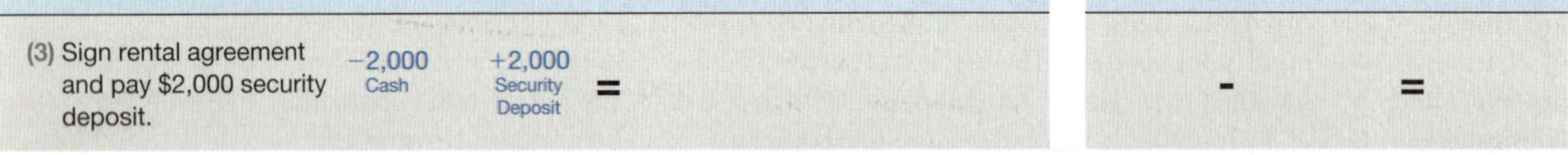

At this point, Natural Beauty Supply would not record anything for the interest that will eventually be paid. Interest expense occurs with the passage of time, and at the moment of borrowing on November 1, there is no interest obligation to be recognized.

Also on November 1, 2010, Natural Beauty Supply arranged for rental of a location and paid a security deposit which it expects to be returned at a future date. This transaction decreased cash (an asset) and increased security deposits (another asset). We'll assume that Natural Beauty Supply hopes to move to a more upscale location within a year, so the security deposit is considered a current asset.

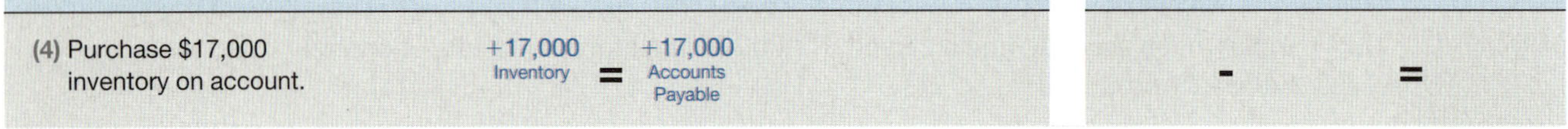

Like the case of interest expense, Natural Beauty Supply would make no entry for rent expense on November 1, because the obligation to pay for the use of the location occurs with the passage of time.

Finally, Natural Beauty Supply purchased and received $17,000 of inventory on credit. This transaction increased inventory (an asset) by $17,000 and increased accounts payable (a liability) by $17,000, recognizing the obligation to the supplier. This transaction is recorded as follows:

| (4) Purchase $17,000 inventory on account. | +17,000 Inventory | = | +17,000 Accounts Payable | | | – | = |

To summarize, the description of each transaction appears in the first column of the template. Then the financial statement effects of that transaction are recorded with a + or a – in the appropriate columns of the template. Under each number, the account title within that column of the balance sheet or income statement is entered. So far, Natural Beauty Supply's activities have not affected the revenue or expense accounts of the income statement.

After each transaction, the equality of the accounting equation is maintained. If we so choose, we can prepare a balance sheet at any time, reflecting the transactions up to that point in time. At the end of the day on November 1, 2010, Natural Beauty Supply's balance sheet appears as follows:

NATURAL BEAUTY SUPPLY, INC.
Balance Sheet
November 1, 2010

Assets		Liabilities and Equity	
Cash	$23,000	Notes payable	$ 5,000
Inventory	17,000	Accounts payable	17,000
Security deposit	2,000	Total current liabilities	22,000
Total current assets	42,000	**Equity**	
		Common stock	20,000
Total assets	$42,000	Total liabilities and equity	$42,000

MID-CHAPTER REVIEW 2

Assume that Schaefer's Pharmacy, Inc. enters into the following transactions. Record each of the following transactions in the financial statement effects template.

  a. Issued common stock for $20,000 cash.
  b. Purchased inventory costing $8,000 on credit.
  c. Purchased equipment costing $10,000 for cash.
  d. Paid suppliers $3,000 cash for part of the inventory purchased in *b*.

The solution to this review problem can be found on page 89.

REPORTING FINANCIAL PERFORMANCE

While balance sheets provide useful information about the structure of a company's resources and the claims on those resources at a point in time, they provide little sense of recent movement or trajectory. The retained earnings balance represents the amount earned (but not paid out in dividends) over the entire life of the company. Looking at the difference between points in time doesn't give a clear picture about what happened between those points in time. For that perspective, we need the income statement to see whether our business activities generated more resources than they used. For instance, Walgreens' retained earnings increased by $1,535 million over fiscal year 2009, but that amount does not convey the volume of activity that occurred to accomplish it.

LO3 Describe and construct the income statement and discuss how it can be used to evaluate management performance.

Walgreens' fiscal year 2009 Statement of Earnings is shown in Exhibit 2.2. Walgreens reported net income of $2,006 million on revenues of $63,335 million, or about $0.032 of each revenue dollar ($2,006 million/$63,335 million). The remaining $0.968 of that revenue dollar relates to costs incurred to generate the revenues, such as the costs of products sold and equipment used, wages, advertising and promotion, interest and taxes. Interpretation of this $0.032 amount requires further analysis, as shown in Chapter 5, but we can compare it to previous amounts of $0.037 in fiscal year 2008, and $0.038 in fiscal year 2007.

To analyze an income statement, we need to understand some terminology. **Revenues** result from increases in **net assets** (assets minus liabilities) that are caused by the company's operating activities. **Expenses** result from decreases in net assets (assets minus liabilities) that are caused by the company's revenue-generating activities, including costs of products and services sold, operating costs like depreciation, wages and advertising, nonoperating costs like interest on debt and, finally, taxes on income. The difference between revenues and expenses is **net income** when revenues exceed expenses, or **net loss** when expenses exceed revenues. The connection to the balance sheet can be seen in that reporting net income means that revenues exceeded expenses, which in turn means that the company's business activities increased its net assets.

Operating expenses are the usual and customary costs that a company incurs to support its main business activities. These include cost of goods sold, selling expenses, depreciation expense, amorti-

FYI The income statement is also called the statement of earnings or the statement of operations or the profit and loss statement. Walgreens uses all three terms (profit, income and earnings) in Exhibit 2.2.

FYI The terms revenues and sales are often used interchangeably.

EXHIBIT 2.2

WALGREEN CO. AND SUBSIDIARIES
Consolidated Statement of Earnings
Year ended August 31, 2009
($ millions)

Net sales	$63,335
Cost of sales	45,722
Gross profit	17,613
Selling, general and administrative expenses	14,366
Operating Income	3,247
Interest (expense) income, net	(83)
Earnings before income tax provision	3,164
Income tax provision	1,158
Net earnings	$ 2,006

zation expense, and research and development expense. Not all of these expenses are recognized in the period in which cash is disbursed. For example, depreciation expense is recognized in the time period during which the asset is used, not in the period when it was first acquired in exchange for cash. In contrast, other expenses, such as compensation expense, are recognized in the period when the services are performed, which is often before cash is actually paid to employees. Walgreens' operating expenses in 2009 were $60,088 million ($45,722 million + $14,366 million).

Nonoperating revenues and expenses relate to the company's financing and investing activities, and include interest revenue and interest expense. Business decision makers and analysts usually segregate operating and nonoperating activities as they offer different insights into company performance and condition. Walgreens' income statement reports net nonoperating expenses in 2009 of $83 million, followed by tax expense of $1,158 million.

It is helpful to distinguish income from continuing operations from nonrecurring items. Many readers of financial statements are interested in forecasting future company performance and focus their analysis on sources of operating income that are expected to *persist* into the future. Nonrecurring revenues and expenses are unlikely to arise in the future and are largely irrelevant to predictions of future performance. Consequently, many decision makers identify transactions and events that are unlikely to recur and separate them from operating income in the income statement. These nonrecurring items are described in greater detail in Chapter 6.

Accrual Accounting for Revenues and Expenses

LO4 Explain revenue recognition, accrual accounting, and their effects on retained earnings.

The income statement's ability to measure a company's periodic performance depends on the proper timing of revenues and expenses. Revenue should be recorded when it is earned, even if not yet received in cash. This is called **revenue recognition**. Similarly, expenses are recorded by **matching** them with revenues when incurred, even if not yet paid in cash, as assets are used or obligations created. **Accrual accounting** refers to this practice of recognizing revenues when earned and matching expenses when incurred.

An important consequence of accrual accounting for revenues and expenses is that the balance sheet depicts the resources of the company (besides cash) and the obligations which the company must fulfill in the future. Accrual accounting is required under U.S. GAAP and IFRS because it is considered to be the most useful information for making business decisions and evaluating business performance. (That is not to say that information on cash flows is not important—but it is conveyed by the statement of cash flows discussed in Chapter 4.)

Walgreens' total revenues in 2009 were $63,335 million. **Cost of goods sold** (cost of sales) is an expense item in the income statements of manufacturing and merchandising companies. It represents the cost of products that are delivered to customers during the period. The difference between revenues (at selling prices) and cost of goods sold (at purchase price or manufacturing cost) is called **gross profit**. Gross profit for merchandisers and manufacturers is an important number as it represents the remaining income available to cover all of the company's overhead and other expenses (selling, general and administrative expenses, interest, and so on). Walgreens' gross profit in 2009 is calculated as total net revenues less cost of sales, which equals $17,613 million ($63,335 million − $45,722 million).

The principles of revenue and expense recognition are crucial to income statement reporting. To illustrate, assume a company purchases inventories for $100,000 cash, which it sells later in that same period for $150,000 cash. The company would record $150,000 in revenue when the inventory is delivered to the customer, because at that point, we say that it has been earned. Also assume that the company pays $20,000 cash for sales employee wages during the period. The income statement is designed to tell how effective the company was at generating more resources than it used, and it would appear as follows:

Revenues	$150,000
Cost of goods sold	100,000
Gross profit	50,000
Wages expense	20,000
Net income (earnings)	$ 30,000

In this illustration, there is a correspondence between each of the revenues/expenses and a cash inflow/outflow. Net income was $30,000 and the increase in cash was $30,000.

However, that need not be the case under accrual accounting. Suppose that the company sells its product on **credit** (also called *on account*) rather than for cash. Does the seller still report sales revenue? The answer is yes. Under GAAP, revenues are reported when a company has earned those sales. Earned means that the company has done everything required under the sales agreement— no major contingencies remain—and cash is realized or realizable. The seller reports an accounts receivable asset on its balance sheet, and revenue can be recognized without cash collection.

Credit sales mean that companies can report substantial sales revenue and assets without receiving cash. When such receivables are ultimately collected, no further revenue is recorded because it was recorded earlier when the revenue recognition criteria were met. The collection of a receivable merely involves the decrease of one asset (accounts receivable) and the increase of another asset (cash), with no resulting increase in net assets.

Next consider a different situation. Assume that the company sells gift cards to customers for $9,500. Should the $9,500 received in cash be recognized as revenue? No. Even though the gift cards were sold and cash was collected, the revenue has not been earned. The revenue from gift cards is recognized when the product or service is provided. For example, revenue can be recognized when a customer purchases an item of merchandise using the gift card for payment. Hence, the $9,500 would be recorded as an increase in cash and an increase in *unearned revenue*, a liability, with no resulting increase in net assets.

The proper timing of revenue recognition suggests that the expenses incurred in earning that revenue be recognized in the same fiscal period. Thus, if merchandise inventory is purchased in one period and sold in another, the cost of the merchandise should be retained in the accounting records until the items are sold. It would not be proper to recognize expense when the inventory was purchased or the cash was paid. Accurate income determination requires the proper timing of revenue and expense recognition, and the exchange of cash is *not* the essential ingredient.

We have already seen that when a company incurs a cost to acquire a resource that will produce benefits in the future (for example, merchandise inventory for future sale), it recognizes an asset. That asset represents costs that are waiting to be recognized as expenses in the future, based on the matching principle. When inventory is delivered to a customer, we recognize that the asset no longer belongs to the selling company. The inventory asset is decreased, and cost of goods sold is recognized.

The same principle applies when employees earn wages for work in one period, but are paid in the next period. Wages expense must be recognized when the cost is incurred, regardless of when they are paid. If the company in the illustration doesn't pay its employees until the following reporting period, it would recognize a wages payable liability of $20,000 and, because this decreases net assets, a wage expense of the same amount.

When wages are paid in the next reporting period, both cash and the wages payable liability are decreased. No expense is reported when the wages are paid, because the expense was recognized when the employees worked to generate sales in the prior period.

Accrual accounting principles are crucial for reporting the income statement revenues and expenses in the proper period, and these revenues and expenses provide a more complete view of the inflows and outflows of cash for the firm. Was an outflow of cash supposed to produce benefits in the current period or in a future period? Was an inflow of cash the result of past operations or current operations? The accrual accounting model uses the balance sheet and income statement to answer such questions and to enable users of financial statements to make more timely assessments of the firm's economic performance.

However, accrual accounting's timeliness requires management to estimate future events in determining the amount of expenses incurred and revenue earned. The precise amount of cash to be received or disbursed cannot be known until a later date. In the case of wages, the amount of the accrual is known with certainty. In other cases (e.g., incentive bonuses), it may not.

Retained Earnings

Net income for the period is added to the company's retained earnings, which, in turn, is part of stockholders' equity. The linkage between the income statement and the beginning- and end-of-period balance sheets, which we called articulation in Chapter 1, is achieved by tying net income to retained earnings because Net Income is, by definition, the *change* in Retained Earnings resulting from business activities during an accounting period. This link is highlighted by the red arrow at the top of the financial statement effects template (FSET).[4] There are typically other adjustments to retained earnings. The most common adjustment is for dividend payments to stockholders. Exhibit 2.3 provides the annual adjustments to retained earnings for Walgreens.

EXHIBIT 2.3	Walgreens' Retained Earnings Reconciliation

WALGREEN CO. AND SUBSIDIARIES
Year Ended August 31, 2009
($ millions)

Retained earnings, August 31, 2008.	$13,792
Add: Net earnings	2,006
	15,798
Less: Cash dividends declared.	471
Retained earnings, August 31, 2009.	$15,327

Analyzing and Recording Transactions for the Income Statement

Earlier, we introduced the financial statement effects template as a tool to illustrate the effects of transactions on the balance sheet. In this section, we show how this template is used to analyze transactions that may affect the current period's income statement. To do so, we extend our illustration of Natural Beauty Supply (NBS) to reflect the following events:

(5) Nov. 2   NBS paid $670 to advertise in the local newspaper for November.

(6) Nov. 18   NBS paid $13,300 cash to its suppliers in partial payment for the earlier delivery of inventory.

(7) Nov. —   During the month of November, NBS sold products to retail customers. The customers paid $7,000 cash for products that had cost $4,000.

(8) Nov. —   During the month of November, sales to wholesale customers totaled $2,400 for merchandise that had cost $1,700. Instead of paying cash, wholesale customers are required to pay for the merchandise within ten working days.

---

[4] In the FSET, we show that each transaction that affects the income statement also impacts retained earnings. This is useful for *analyzing* the effect of the transaction on both the income statement and balance sheet. However, the impact of net income on retained earnings is *recorded* only once each accounting period, after all of the revenues and expenses have been recorded. This recording procedure is explained later in this chapter and in Chapter 3.

(9) Nov. — NBS employed a salesperson who earned $1,400 for the month of November and was paid that amount in cash.

(10) Nov. 24 NBS received an order from a wholesale customer to deliver products in December. The agreed price of the products to be delivered is $700 and the cost is $450.

(11) Nov. 25 NBS introduced holiday gift certificates, which entitle the recipient to a one-hour consultation on the use of NBS's products. $300 of gift certificates were sold for cash, but none were redeemed before the end of November.

(12) Nov. 30 NBS received $1,450 in partial payment from customers billed in (8).

(13) Nov. 30 NBS repaid the loan and interest in (2).

(14) Nov. 30 NBS paid $1,680 for a twelve-month fire insurance policy. Coverage begins on December 1.

(15) Nov. 30 NBS paid $1,500 to the landlord for November rent.

In the fifth transaction, Natural Beauty Supply gave cash in return for advertising for the month of November. This payment does not create a benefit for future periods, so it does not create an asset. Nor does the payment discharge an existing obligation. Therefore, it decreases NBS's net assets (assets minus liabilities). The purpose of this decrease in net assets is to generate revenues for the company, so it is matched by an expense in the income statement.

We begin by entering the decrease in cash and an increase in expenses. (The minus sign in front of expenses insures that the accounting equation still holds.) Recording the expense allows the income statement to keep track of the flows of assets and liabilities that result from the company's operations.

		Balance Sheet					Income Statement		
Transaction	Cash Asset	+ Noncash Assets	= Liabil- ities	+ Contrib. Capital	+ Earned Capital		Revenues -	Expenses =	Net Income
(5) Pay $670 cash for November advertising.	−670 Cash		=				-	+670 Advertising Expense	=

However, the FSET goes further than recording the accounting entry. It also depicts the effects of the expense on net income and of net income on retained earnings. So, the complete FSET description of transaction (5) is as follows. The FSET uses color to differentiate between the accounting entry (in blue) and the resulting effect on income and retained earnings (in black).

(5) Pay $670 cash for November advertising.	−670 Cash	=	−670 Retained Earnings	-	+670 Advertising Expense	=	−670

In the sixth transaction, Natural Beauty Supply made a partial payment of $13,300 in cash to the suppliers who delivered inventory on November 1. This transaction decreases cash by $13,300 and decreases the accounts payable liability by $13,300. The income statement is not affected by this payment. The cost of merchandise is reflected in the income statement when the merchandise is sold, not when it is paid for (as we will see shortly).

(6) Pay $13,300 cash in partial payment to suppliers from transaction 4.	−13,300 Cash	=	−13,300 Accounts Payable	-	=

In transaction seven, Natural Beauty Supply sold products to customers who paid $7,000 in cash. This cash receipt is an increase in net assets resulting from NBS's revenue-generating activities, so it results in revenue being recognized in the income statement. As in transaction 5, the FSET also depicts the impact of these sales on net income and on the retained earnings balance.

Transaction	Cash Asset	+	Noncash Assets	=	Liabil-ities	+	Contrib. Capital	+	Earned Capital		Revenues	−	Expenses	=	Net Income
(7a) Sell $7,000 of products for cash.	+7,000 Cash			=					+7,000 Retained Earnings		+7,000 Sales Revenue	−		=	+7,000

At the same time, NBS must recognize that these sales transactions involved an exchange, and cash was received while inventory costing $4,000 was delivered. Transaction (7b) recognizes that NBS no longer has this inventory and that this decrease in net assets produces an expense called cost of goods sold. In this way, the income statement portrays the increases in net assets (revenues) and the decreases in net assets (expenses like cost of goods sold and advertising) from the company's operating activities. (Again, the minus sign in front of all expenses insures that the accounting equation remains balanced.)

Transaction	Cash Asset	Noncash Assets	=	Liabil-ities	Contrib. Capital	Earned Capital	Revenues	−	Expenses	=	Net Income
(7b) Record $4,000 for the cost of merchandise sold in transaction 7a.		−4,000 Inventory	=			−4,000 Retained Earnings		−	+4,000 Cost of Goods Sold	=	−4,000

The eighth transaction is very similar to the previous one, except that Natural Beauty Supply's customers will pay for the products ten days after they were delivered. Should NBS recognize revenue on these sales? The products have been delivered, so the revenue has been earned.[5] Therefore, NBS should recognize that it has a new asset—accounts receivable—equal to $2,400, and that it has earned revenue in the same amount. As above, NBS would also record cost of goods sold to recognize the cost of inventory delivered to the customers.

Transaction	Cash Asset	Noncash Assets	=	Liabil-ities	Contrib. Capital	Earned Capital	Revenues	−	Expenses	=	Net Income
(8a) Sell $2,400 of products on account.		+2,400 Accounts Receivable	=			+2,400 Retained Earnings	+2,400 Sales Revenue	−		=	+2,400
(8b) Record $1,700 for the cost of merchandise sold in transaction 8a.		−1,700 Inventory	=			−1,700 Retained Earnings		−	+1,700 Cost of Goods Sold	=	−1,700

The ninth entry records wage expense. In this case, wages were paid in cash. Cash is decreased by $1,400, and this decrease in net assets results in a recognition of wages expense in the income statement (with resulting decreases in net income and retained earnings).

Transaction	Cash Asset	Noncash Assets	=	Liabil-ities	Contrib. Capital	Earned Capital	Revenues	−	Expenses	=	Net Income
(9) Record $1,400 in wages to employees.	−1,400 Cash		=			−1,400 Retained Earnings		−	+1,400 Wages Expense	=	−1,400

Transaction ten involves a customer order for products to be delivered in December. This is an example of an *executory contract*, which does not require a journal entry. NBS has not earned revenue, because it has not yet delivered the products.

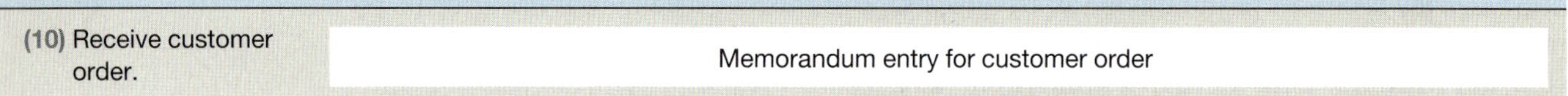

Transaction		
(10) Receive customer order.	Memorandum entry for customer order	

In transaction eleven, Natural Beauty Supply sold gift certificates for $300 cash, but none were redeemed. In this case, NBS has received cash, but revenue cannot be recognized because it has not yet been earned. Rather, NBS has accepted an obligation to provide services in the future when the gift certificates are redeemed. This obligation is recognized as a liability titled unearned revenue.

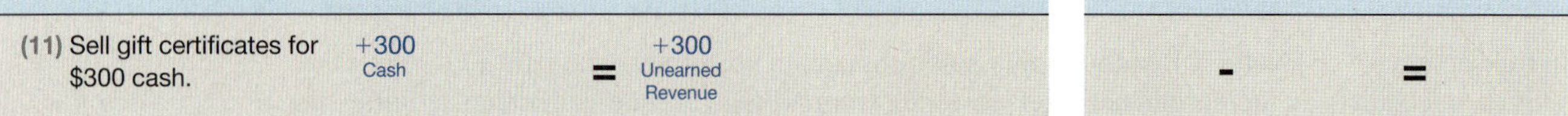

Transaction	Cash Asset	Noncash Assets	=	Liabil-ities	Contrib. Capital	Earned Capital	Revenues	−	Expenses	=	Net Income
(11) Sell gift certificates for $300 cash.	+300 Cash		=	+300 Unearned Revenue				−		=	

---

[5] In Chapter 6, we will consider the possibility that a customer might not pay the receivable. For the time being, we will assume that the receivables' collectability is assured.

In transaction twelve, NBS received $1,450 cash as partial payment from customers billed in transaction eight. Cash increases by $1,450 and accounts receivable decreases by $1,450. Recall that revenues are recorded when earned (transaction 8), not when cash is received.

Transaction	Cash Asset		Noncash Assets		Liabil- ities		Contrib. Capital		Earned Capital		Revenues		Expenses		Net Income
		+		=		+		+				−		=	
(12) Receive $1,450 cash as partial payment from customers billed in transaction 8.	+1,450 Cash		−1,450 Accounts Receivable	=								−		=	

In transaction thirteen on November 30, Natural Beauty Supply paid back the family member who had loaned money to the business. The cash payment was the agreed-upon $5,050 ($5,000 principal and $50 interest). The repayment of the principal does not change the net assets of NBS; cash goes down by $5,000 and the note payable liability goes down an equal amount. However, the payment of $50 interest does cause the net assets to decrease, and this net asset decrease creates an <u>interest expense</u> in the income statement.

Transaction	Cash Asset		Noncash Assets		Liabil- ities		Contrib. Capital		Earned Capital		Revenues		Expenses		Net Income
(13) Pay interest of $50 and repay principal of $5,000.	−5,050 Cash			=	−5,000 Notes Payable				−50 Retained Earnings				−	+50 Interest Expense	=	−50

In the fourteenth transaction, NBS paid an annual insurance premium of $1,680 for coverage beginning December 1. NBS will receive the benefits of the insurance coverage in the future, so insurance expense will be recognized in those future periods. At this time, a noncash asset titled prepaid insurance is increased by $1,680, and cash is decreased by the same amount.

Transaction	Cash Asset		Noncash Assets		Liabil- ities		Contrib. Capital		Earned Capital		Revenues		Expenses		Net Income
(14) Pay $1,680 for one-year insurance policy.	−1,680 Cash		+1,680 Prepaid Insurance	=								−		=	

In the last transaction of the month of November, Natural Beauty Supply paid $1,500 cash to the landlord for November's rent. This $1,500 reduction of net assets is balanced by rent expense in the income statement.

Transaction	Cash Asset		Noncash Assets		Liabil- ities		Contrib. Capital		Earned Capital		Revenues		Expenses		Net Income
(15) Pay $1,500 rent for November.	−1,500 Cash			=					−1,500 Retained Earnings				−	+1,500 Rent Expense	=	−1,500

We can summarize the revenue and expense entries of these transactions to prepare an income statement for Natural Beauty Supply for the month ended November 30, 2010.

NATURAL BEAUTY SUPPLY, INC.
Income Statement
For Month Ended November 30, 2010

Sales revenue	$ 9,400
Cost of goods sold	5,700
Gross profit	3,700
Wages expense	1,400
Rent expense	1,500
Advertising expense	670
Operating income	130
Interest expense	50
Net income	$ 80

REPORTING ON EQUITY

Analyzing and Recording Equity Transactions

LO5 Illustrate equity transactions and the statement of stockholders' equity.

Earlier we recorded the effect of issuing common stock on the balance sheet of Natural Beauty Supply. To complete our illustration, we illustrate one final equity transaction—a dividend payment.

(16) Nov. 30   Natural Beauty Supply paid $50 cash dividend to its shareholders.

To record the dividend payment, we decrease cash and decrease retained earnings.

		Balance Sheet					Income Statement		
Transaction	Cash Asset	+ Noncash Assets	= Liabil- ities	+ Contrib. Capital	+ Earned Capital		Revenues - Expenses	=	Net Income
(16) Pay $50 cash dividend to shareholders.	−50 Cash		=		−50 Retained Earnings		-	=	

No revenue or income is recorded from a stock issuance. Similarly, no expense is recorded from a dividend. This is always the case. Companies cannot report revenues and expenses from capital transactions (transactions with stockholders' relating to their investment in the company).

The FSET entries can be accumulated by account to determine the ending balances for assets, liabilities and equity. Natural Beauty Supply's balance sheet for November 30, 2010, appears in Exhibit 2.4. The balance in retained earnings is $30 (net income of $80 less the cash dividend of $50).

EXHIBIT 2.4	Natural Beauty Supply's Balance Sheet

NATURAL BEAUTY SUPPLY, INC.
Balance Sheet
November 30, 2010

Assets		Liabilities	
Cash	$ 8,100	Accounts payable	$ 3,700
Accounts receivable	950	Unearned revenue	300
Inventory	11,300	Total current liabilities	4,000
Prepaid insurance	1,680		
Security deposit	2,000	**Equity**	
Total current assets	24,030	Common stock	20,000
		Retained earnings	30
		Total equity	20,030
Total assets	$24,030	Total liabilities and equity	$24,030

Statement of Stockholders' Equity

The statement of stockholders' equity is a reconciliation of the beginning and ending balances of selected stockholders' equity accounts. The statement of stockholders' equity for Natural Beauty Supply for the month of November is in Exhibit 2.5.

This statement highlights three main changes to Natural Beauty Supply's equity during November.

1. Natural Beauty raised $20,000 in equity capital during the month.

2. Natural Beauty Supply earned net income of $80. That is, its business activities increased the company's net assets by $80 during the month.

3. Natural Beauty Supply declared a $50 cash dividend.

EXHIBIT 2.5	Natural Beauty Supply's Statement of Stockholders' Equity

NATURAL BEAUTY SUPPLY, INC.
Statement of Stockholders' Equity
For Month Ended November 30, 2010

	Contributed Capital	Earned Capital	Total Equity
Balance, November 1, 2010.................	$ 0	$ 0	$ 0
Common stock issued	20,000	—	20,000
Net income....................................	—	80	80
Cash dividends	—	(50)	(50)
Balance, November 30, 2010................	$20,000	$30	$20,030

YOU MAKE THE CALL

You are an Analyst **Callaway Golf Company** reported a balance in retained earnings of $518.9 million at December 31, 2008. This amount compares to $470.5 one year earlier at the end of 2007. In 2008, Callaway reported net income of $66.2 million. Why did the company's retained earnings go up by less than this amount? [Answer on page 70]

MID-CHAPTER REVIEW 3

Part 1. Assume that Schaefer's Pharmacy, Inc.'s records show the following amounts at December 31, 2011. Use this information, as necessary, to prepare its 2011 income statement (ignore income taxes).

Cash...........................	$ 3,000	Cash dividends	$ 1,000
Accounts receivable	12,000	Revenues.......................	25,000
Office equipment.................	32,250	Rent expense....................	5,000
Land...........................	36,000	Wages expense..................	8,000
Accounts payable	7,500	Utilities expense	2,000
Common stock	45,750	Other expenses	4,000

Part 2. Assume that Schaefer's Pharmacy, Inc. reports the following selected financial information for the year ended December 31, 2011.

Retained earnings, Dec. 31, 2011....	$30,000	Dividends.......................	$ 1,000
Net income.....................	$ 6,000	Retained earnings, Dec. 31, 2010....	$25,000

Prepare the 2011 calendar-year retained earnings reconciliation for this company.

Part 3. Use the listing of accounts and figures reported in part 1 along with the ending retained earnings from part 2 to prepare the December 31, 2011, balance sheet for Schaefer's Pharmacy, Inc.

The solution to this review problem can be found on pages 89–90.

JOURNALIZING AND POSTING TRANSACTIONS

The financial statement effects template is a useful tool for illustrating the effects of a transaction on the balance sheet, income statement, statement of stockholders' equity, and statement of cash flows. However, when representing individual transactions or analyzing individual accounts, the accounting system records information in journal entries (step 2) that are collected in individual accounts. This section introduces the basics of that system. It also introduces the T-account as a useful tool for learning debits and credits and for representing accounts in the ledger (step 3).

LO6 Use journal entries and T-accounts to analyze and record transactions.

T-Account

Accountants commonly use a graphic representation of an account called a **T-account**, so named because it looks like a large T. The typical form of a T-account is

Account Title	
Debits	Credits
(Dr.)	(Cr.)
Always the left side	Always the right side

One side of the T-account is used to record increases to the account and the other side is used to record decreases.

Accountants record individual transactions using the journal entry. A **journal entry** is an accounting entry in the financial records (journals) of a company. This is the *bookkeeping* aspect of accounting. Even if we never make a journal entry for a company, we will interact with accounting and finance professionals who do, and who will use this language. Further, journal entries and T-accounts can help in reconstructing transactions and interpreting their financial effects.

FYI Recall that an account is a record of increases and decreases in key asset, liability, equity, revenue or expense items.

Debit and Credit System

Accountants describe increases and decreases in accounts using the terms **debit** and **credit**. The left side of each account is the debit side (abbreviated Dr.) and the right side of each account is the credit side (abbreviated Cr.). In some accounts, increases are recorded on the debit (left) side of the account and decreases are recorded on the credit (right) side of the account. In other accounts, just the opposite is true—increases are credits and decreases are debits. An easy way to remember what the words debit and credit reflect is to visualize a balance sheet in "T" account form with assets on the left and liabilities and equity on the right as follows:

FYI Debit and credit are accounting terms meaning left and right, respectively.

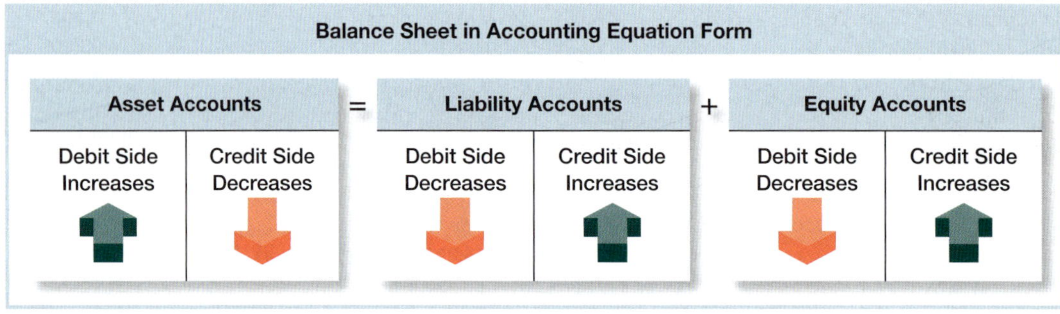

Thus, assets are assigned a *normal debit balance* because they are on the left side. Liabilities and equity are assigned a *normal credit balance* because they are on the right side. So, to reflect an increase in an asset, we debit the asset account. To reflect an increase in a liability or equity account we credit the account. Conversely, to reflect a decrease in an asset account, we credit it. To reflect a decrease in a liability or equity account we debit it. (There are exceptions to these normal balances; one case is accumulated depreciation, which is explained in Chapter 3.)

The balance sheet must always balance (assets = liabilities + equity). So too must total debits equal total credits in each journal entry. There can, however, be more than one debit and one credit in an entry. These so-called **compound entries** still adhere to the rule: *total debits equal total credits for each entry*. This important relation is extended below to show the *expanded accounting equation* in T-account form with the inclusion of debit (Dr.) and credit (Cr.) rules. Equity is expanded to reflect increases from stock issuances and revenues, and to reflect decreases from dividends and expenses.

FYI The rule that total debits equal total credits for each entry is known as double-entry accounting, or the duality of accounting.

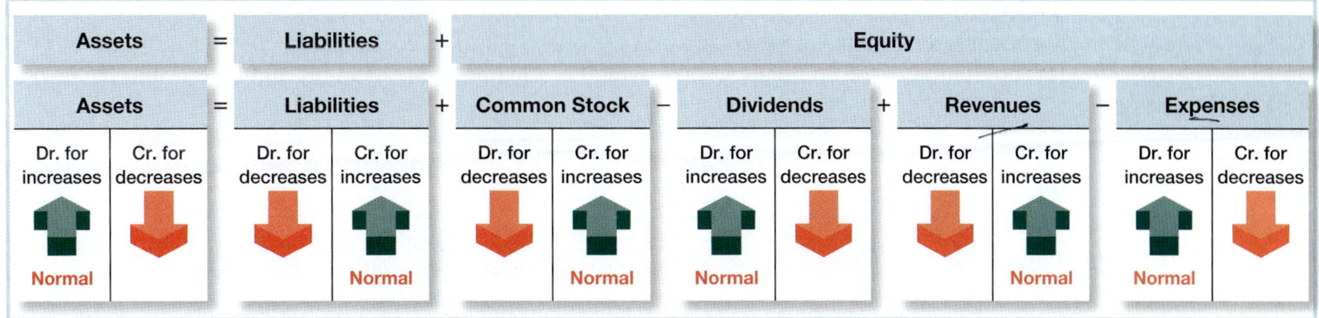

Income (revenues less expenses) feeds directly into retained earnings. Also, anything that increases equity is a credit and anything that decreases equity is a debit. So, to reflect an increase in revenues (which increases retained earnings and, therefore, equity), we credit the revenue account, and to reflect an increase in an expense account (which reduces retained earnings and, therefore, equity), we debit it.

> **FYI** The **normal balance** of any account is on the side on which increases are recorded.

To summarize, the following table reflects the use of the terms debit and credit to reflect increases and decreases to the usual balance sheet and the income statement relations.

Accounting Relation		Debit	Credit
Balance sheet	Assets (A).............................	Increase	Decrease
	Liabilities (L)...........................	Decrease	Increase
	Equity (SE)	Decrease	Increase
Income statement	Revenue (R)	Decrease	Increase
	Expense (E)	Increase	Decrease

T-Account with Debits and Credits

To illustrate use of debits and credits with a T-account, we use a Cash T-account shown below. There is a beginning balance of $2,500 on the left side (which is also the ending balance of the previous period). Increases in cash have been placed on the left side of the Cash T-account and the decreases have been placed on the right side. Transactions (a) and (d) increased the cash balance, while transactions (b), (c), and (e) decreased it.

The ending balance of cash is $3,700. An account balance is determined by totaling the left side and the right side money columns and entering the difference on the side with the larger total. The T-account is an extremely simple record that can be summarized in terms of four elements: (1) beginning balance, (2) additions, (3) deductions, and (4) ending balance.

+	Cash (A)		−
Beg. bal.	2,500		
(a)	4,000	1,500	(b)
(d)	200	500	(c)
		1,000	(e)
End. bal.	3,700		

Dates and other related data are usually omitted in T-accounts, but it is customary to *key* entries with a number or a letter to identify the similarly coded transaction. The number or letter is keyed to the journal entry (discussed next) that identifies the transaction involved. The type and number of accounts used by a business depend on the complexity of its operations and the degree of detail demanded by managers.

The Journal Entry

The journal entry records each transaction (step 2) by summarizing the debits and credits. To illustrate the use of journal entries and T-accounts (step 3), assume that Walgreens: (1) Paid employees $1,200 cash wages, and (2) Paid $9,500 cash to acquire equipment. The journal entries and T-accounts reflecting these two transactions follow. The T-accounts can be viewed as an abbreviated representation of the company *ledger,* which is a listing of all accounts and their dollar balances.

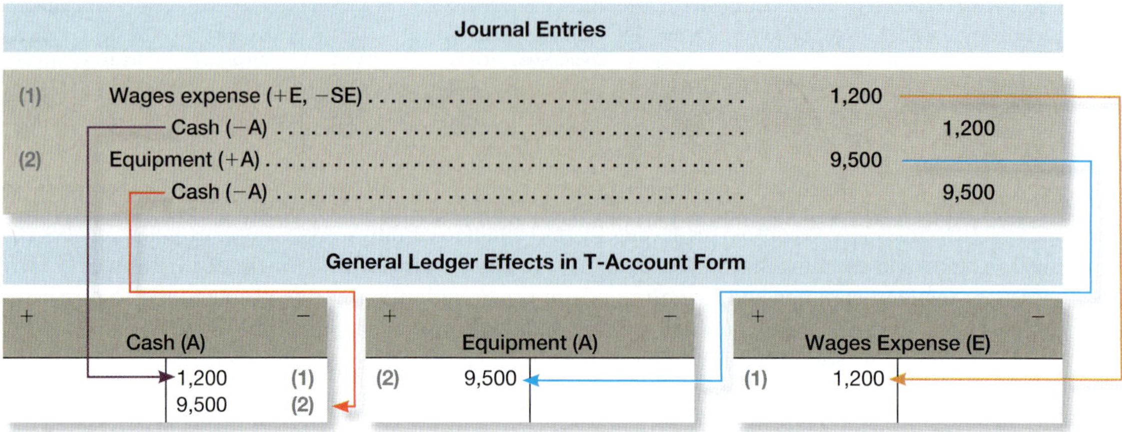

For journal entries, debits are recorded first followed by the credits. Credits are commonly indented. The dollar amounts are entered in both the debit (left) column and credit (right) column. In practice, recordkeepers also enter the date. An alternative presentation is to utilize the abbreviation *Dr* to denote debits and *Cr* to denote credits that precede the account title. We use the first approach in this book.

Analyze, Journalize, and Post

To illustrate the use of journal entries and T-accounts to record transactions, we return to Natural Beauty Supply and reexamine the same transactions recorded earlier in the financial statement effects template. The following layout illustrates our 3-step accounting process of analyzing, journalizing, and posting.

		Balance Sheet					Income Statement		
Transaction	**Cash Asset** $+$	**Noncash Assets** $=$	**Liabil- ities** $+$	**Contrib. Capital** $+$	**Earned Capital**	**Revenues** $-$	**Expenses** $=$	**Net Income**
(1) Issue stock for $20,000 cash.	+20,000 Cash	$=$		+20,000 Common Stock			$-$	$=$

(1) Cash (+A).   20,000
    Common stock (+SE).   20,000
    Issue 10,000 shares of common stock.

	+	Cash (A)	−		−	Common Stock (SE)	+
	(1)	20,000				20,000	(1)

		Balance Sheet					Income Statement		
(2) Sign a note and receive $5,000 cash.	+5,000 Cash	$=$	+5,000 Notes Payable				$-$	$=$

(2) Cash (+A).   5,000
    Notes payable (+L).   5,000
    Borrow $5,000 on a one-month, 12% (per annum) note.

	+	Cash (A)	−		−	Notes Payable (L)	+
	(2)	5,000				5,000	(2)

continued

continued from previous page

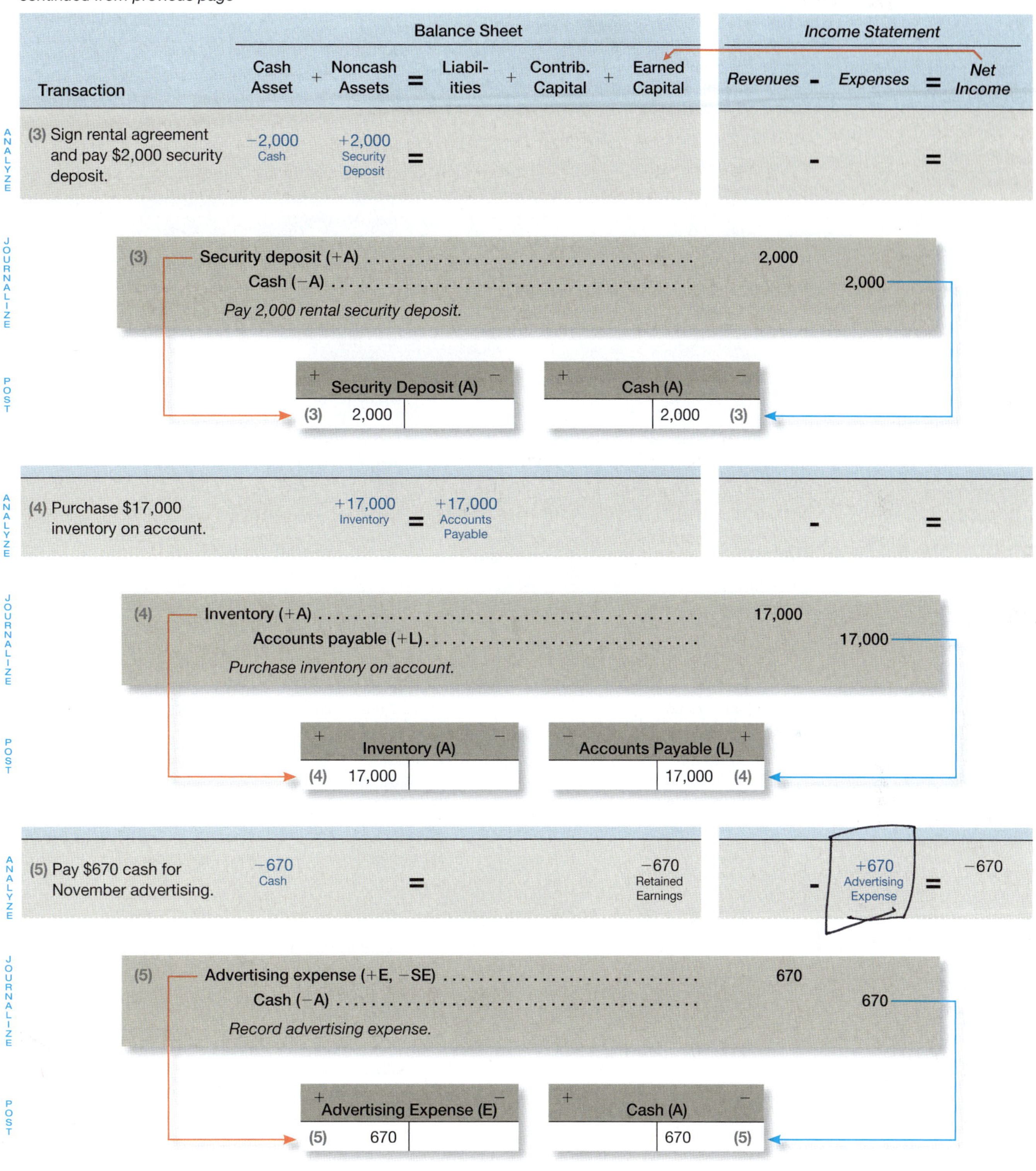

For entries involving income statement accounts, only the transaction itself (**blue type** in the FSET) is recorded in the journal entry and T-account posting. The resulting effects on income and retained earnings occur during the reporting process.

continued

continued from previous page

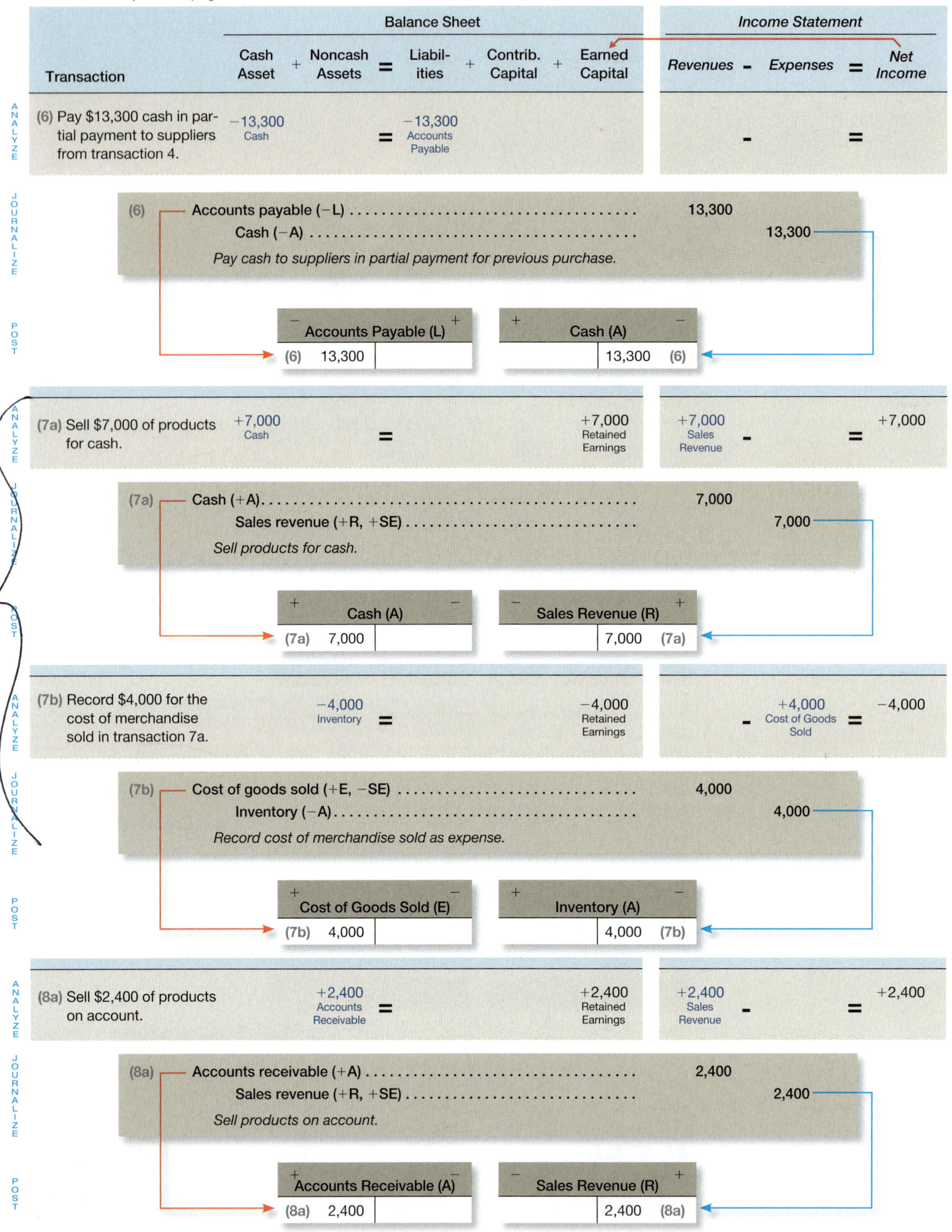

continued

continued from previous page

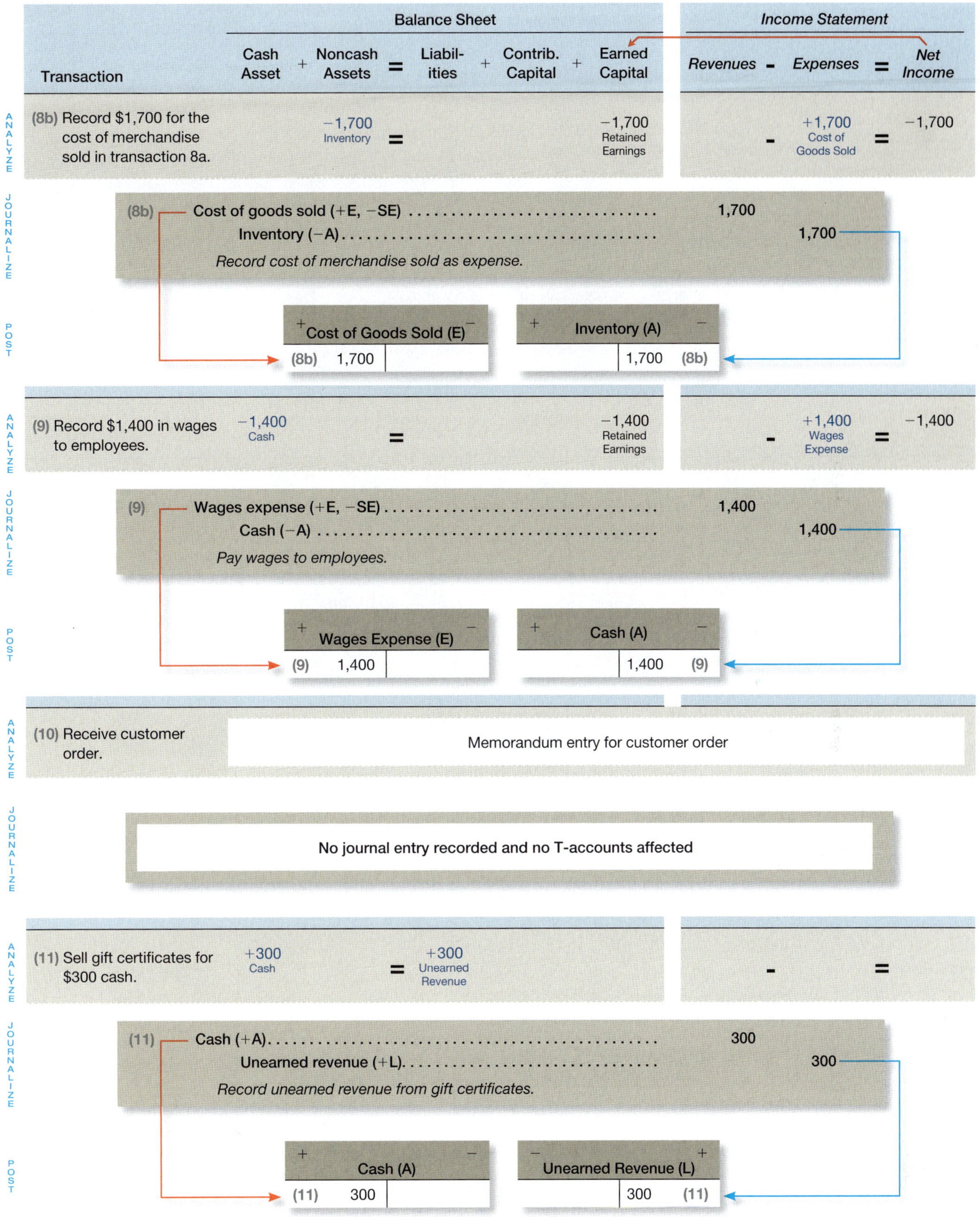

continued

continued from previous page

continued

continued from previous page

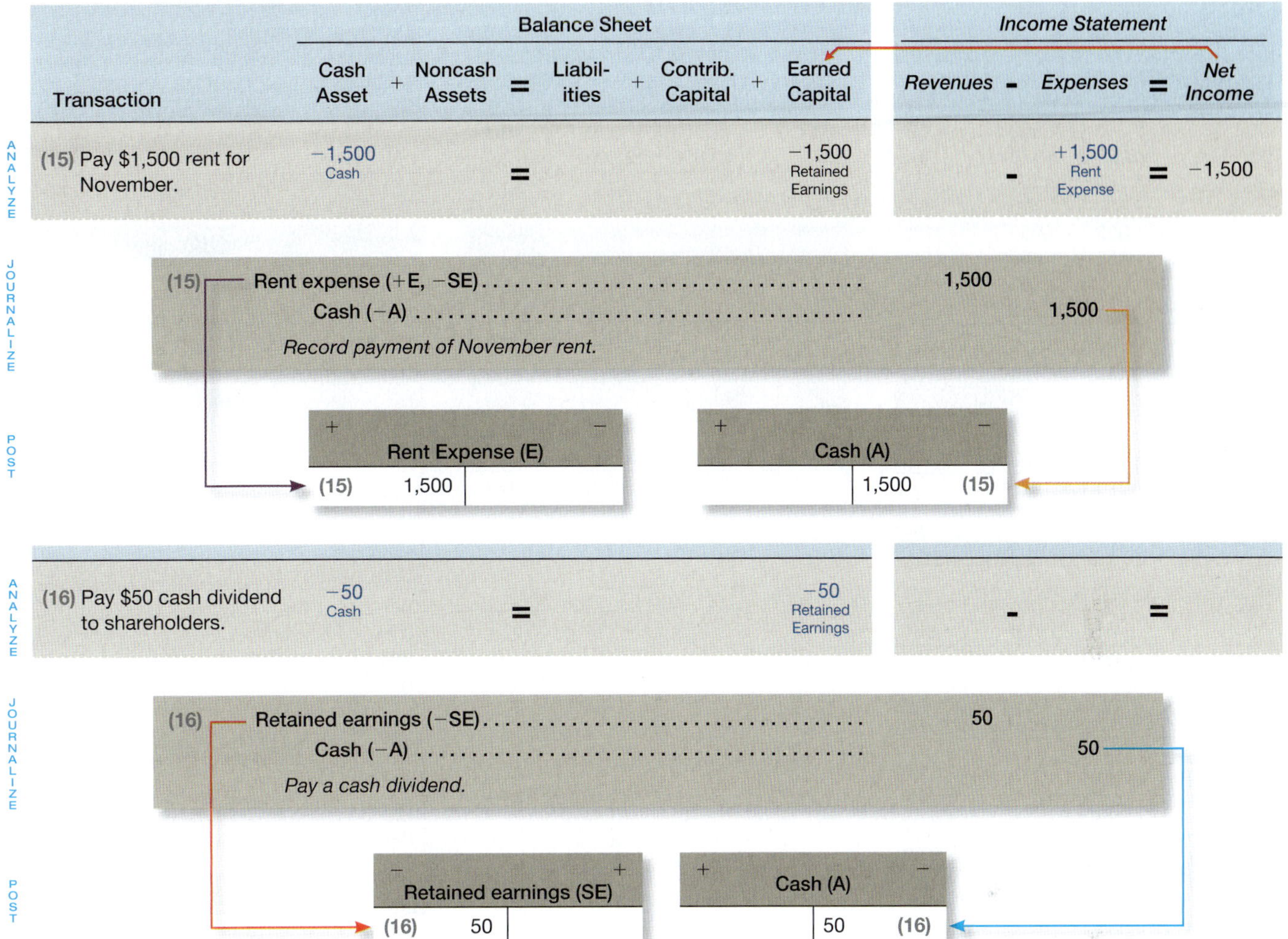

As shown above, each of the journal entries is posted to the appropriate T-accounts, which represent the general ledger. The complete general ledger reflecting each of these sixteen transactions follows. The dashed line around the six equity accounts indicates those that are reported in the income statement before becoming part of retained earnings. Each balance sheet T-account starts with an opening balance (zero in this case), and the ending balances will be the starting balances for December. Income statement T-accounts do not have an opening balance, for reasons we will explore in Chapter 3.

As always, we see that: Assets = Liabilities + Equity. Specifically, $24,030 assets ($8,100 + $950 + $11,300 + $1,680 + $2,000) = $4,000 liabilities ($3,700 + $300) + $20,030 equity ($20,000 − $50 + $9,400 − $5,700 − $1,400 − $1,500 − $670 − $50).

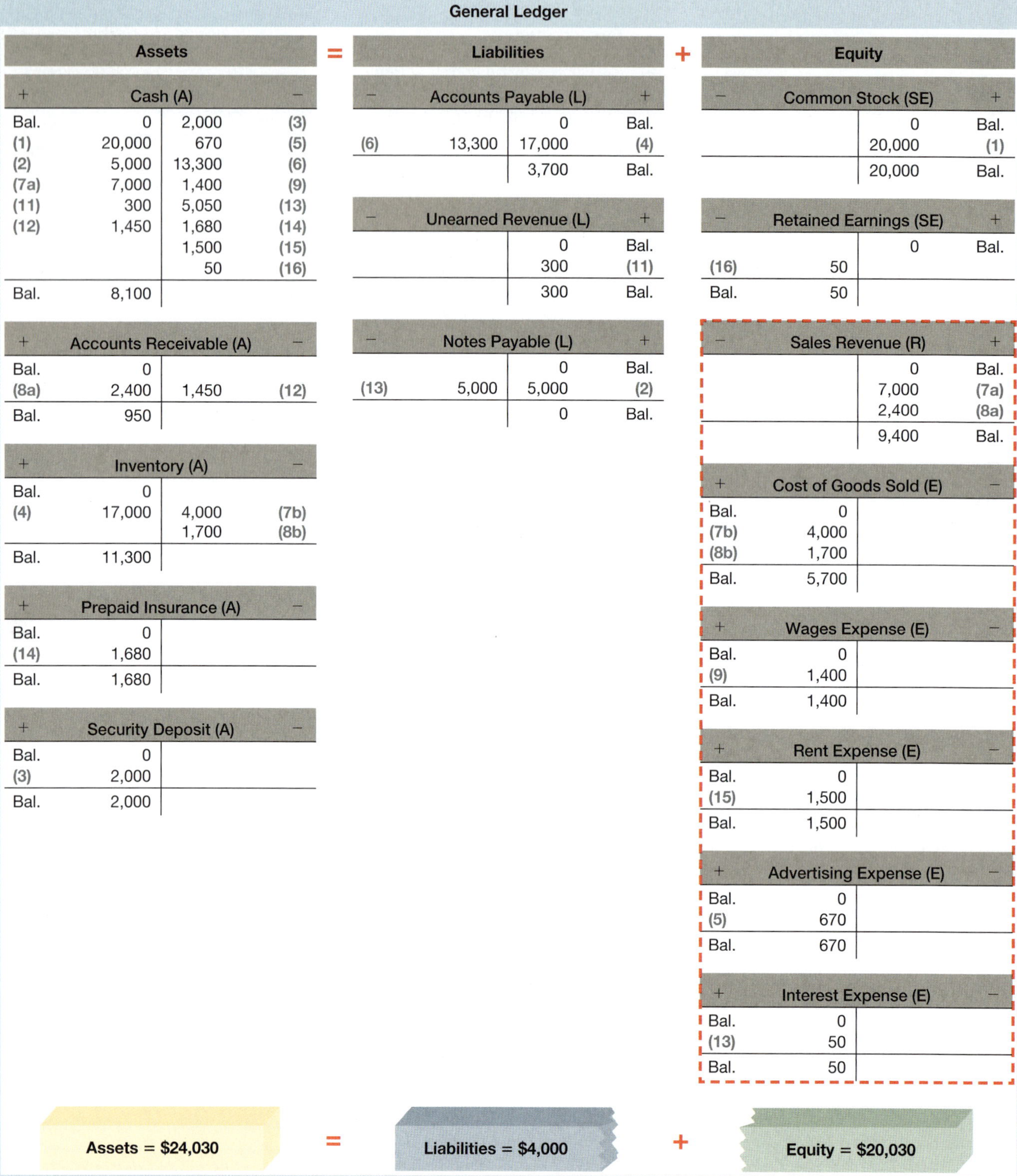

General Ledger

Assets = Liabilities + Equity

+ Cash (A) −
Bal. 0 | 2,000 (3)
(1) 20,000 | 670 (5)
(2) 5,000 | 13,300 (6)
(7a) 7,000 | 1,400 (9)
(11) 300 | 5,050 (13)
(12) 1,450 | 1,680 (14)
| 1,500 (15)
| 50 (16)
Bal. 8,100 |

+ Accounts Receivable (A) −
Bal. 0 |
(8a) 2,400 | 1,450 (12)
Bal. 950 |

+ Inventory (A) −
Bal. 0 |
(4) 17,000 | 4,000 (7b)
| 1,700 (8b)
Bal. 11,300 |

+ Prepaid Insurance (A) −
Bal. 0 |
(14) 1,680 |
Bal. 1,680 |

+ Security Deposit (A) −
Bal. 0 |
(3) 2,000 |
Bal. 2,000 |

− Accounts Payable (L) +
| 0 Bal.
(6) 13,300 | 17,000 (4)
| 3,700 Bal.

− Unearned Revenue (L) +
| 0 Bal.
| 300 (11)
| 300 Bal.

− Notes Payable (L) +
| 0 Bal.
(13) 5,000 | 5,000 (2)
| 0 Bal.

− Common Stock (SE) +
| 0 Bal.
| 20,000 (1)
| 20,000 Bal.

− Retained Earnings (SE) +
| 0 Bal.
(16) 50 |
Bal. 50 |

− Sales Revenue (R) +
| 0 Bal.
| 7,000 (7a)
| 2,400 (8a)
| 9,400 Bal.

+ Cost of Goods Sold (E) −
Bal. 0 |
(7b) 4,000 |
(8b) 1,700 |
Bal. 5,700 |

+ Wages Expense (E) −
Bal. 0 |
(9) 1,400 |
Bal. 1,400 |

+ Rent Expense (E) −
Bal. 0 |
(15) 1,500 |
Bal. 1,500 |

+ Advertising Expense (E) −
Bal. 0 |
(5) 670 |
Bal. 670 |

+ Interest Expense (E) −
Bal. 0 |
(13) 50 |
Bal. 50 |

Assets = $24,030 = Liabilities = $4,000 + Equity = $20,030

FINANCIAL STATEMENT ANALYSIS

Assessing Liquidity

Analysts often compare the level of current liabilities with that of current assets. We usually prefer more current assets than current liabilities to ensure that companies have sufficient liquidity to pay their short-term debts when they mature.

LO7 Compute net working capital, the current ratio, and the quick ratio, and explain how they reflect liquidity.

Net working capital, or simply working capital, reflects the difference between current assets and current liabilities and is defined as:

$$\text{Net working capital} = \text{Current assets} - \text{Current liabilities}$$

Walgreens' net working capital on August 31, 2009, is positive ($5,280 million = $12,049 million − $6,769 million) and represents an increase from 2008. The principal causes of this increase are higher balances in cash and short-term investments, so the company's liquidity position improved from 2008 to 2009.

A company's net working capital is one of several measures of a company's ability to pay its debts, a measure of its **liquidity**. The larger the current assets are when compared to its liabilities, the more liquid it is. Because net working capital is in dollars, using it to compare liquidity across firms, across industries, and over time is difficult. For this reason, the ratio of current assets to current liabilities, called the **current ratio**, is used and is defined as:

$$\text{Current ratio} = \frac{\text{Current assets}}{\text{Current liabilities}}$$

An even more conservative liquidity measure, called the **quick ratio**, replaces current assets with the most liquid of the current assets and is defined as:

$$\text{Quick ratio} = \frac{\text{Cash} + \text{Short-term securities} + \text{Accounts receivable}}{\text{Current liabilities}}$$

These two liquidity measures for Walgreens at its 2009 fiscal year-end are:

$$\text{Current ratio} = \frac{\$12,049}{\$6,769} = 1.78 \text{ or } 178\%$$

$$\text{Quick ratio} = \frac{(\$2,087 + \$500 + \$2,496)}{\$6,769} = 0.75 \text{ or } 75\%$$

Current ratios that exceed 1.0 are deemed to represent a strong current liquidity position. For firms with unpredictable sales and collections, an even greater ratio may be desirable. However, a current ratio below 1.0 is not always bad for at least two reasons:

1. Some firms, including grocery stores, consistently have large operating cash inflows (coupled with some other current assets) that can be used to settle their current liabilities.

2. A company can efficiently manage its working capital by minimizing receivables and inventories while maximizing payables, and still be liquid. **Dell Inc.** and **Wal-Mart Stores, Inc.**, for example, use their strong buying power to extract extended credit terms from suppliers.

The net working capital required to conduct business operations depends on the company's **operating cycle**, which is the time between paying cash for goods or employee services and receiving cash from customers—see Exhibit 2.6. The longer the operating cycle the more working capital is required. Walgreens' operating cycle is a little longer than one month.

Manufacturing companies begin with cash that is used to purchase materials and pay employees engaged in the manufacture of inventories held for resale. In contrast, wholesale and retail firms often purchase their inventory on credit (accounts payable) from other companies. This financing is called **trade credit**. When inventories are sold, they are often sold either on credit (accounts receivable) or for cash. When receivables are ultimately collected, a portion of the cash received is used to repay accounts payable and the remainder goes to the cash account for the next operating cycle.

EXHIBIT 2.6   Operating Cycle

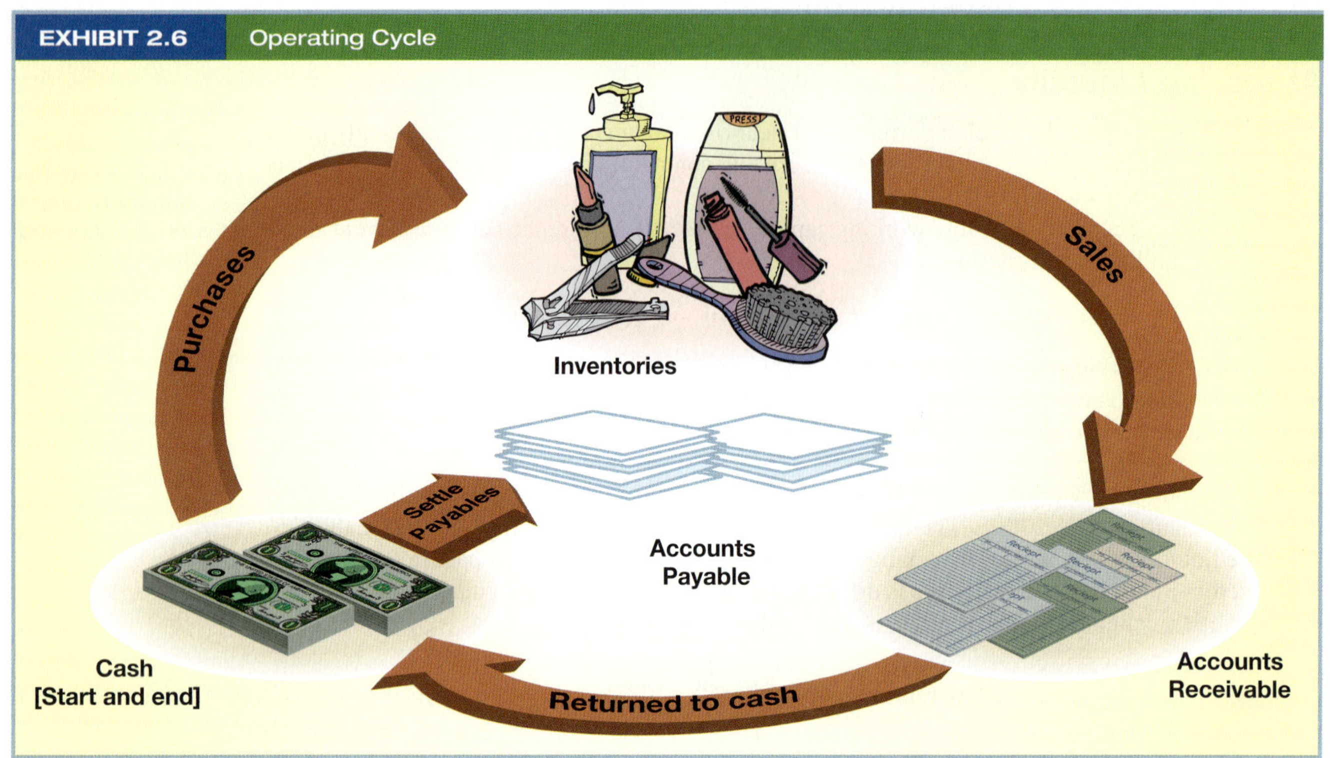

CHAPTER-END REVIEW

Assume that the following accounts appear in the ledger of M.E. Carter, a financial consultant to companies in the retail sector. Cash; Accounts Receivable; Office Equipment; Prepaid Subscriptions; Accounts Payable; Common Stock; Retained Earnings; Fees Earned; Salaries Expense; Rent Expense; and Utilities Expense. For each of the following 10 transactions: (a) analyze and enter each into the financial statement effects template, (b) prepare journal entries for each of the transactions, and (c) set up T-accounts for each of the ledger accounts and post the journal entries to those T-accounts—key all entries with the number identifying the transaction. Prepare the general ledger in T-account form, enter the financial effects of all transactions, and determine the ending balance for each account.

(1)   M.E. Carter started the firm by contributing $19,500 cash to the business in exchange for common stock.

(2)   The firm purchased $10,400 in office equipment on account.

(3)   Paid $700 cash for this period's office rent.

(4)   Paid $9,600 cash for subscriptions to online financial databases covering the next three periods.

(5)   Billed clients $11,300 for services rendered.

(6)   Made $6,000 cash payment on account for the equipment purchased in transaction 2.

(7)   Paid $2,800 cash for assistant's salary for this period.

(8)   Collected $9,400 cash from clients previously billed in transaction 5.

(9)   Received $180 invoice for this period's utilities; it is paid early in the next period.

(10) Paid $1,500 cash for dividends to shareholders.

The solution to this review problem can be found on pages 90–92.

SUMMARY

Describe and construct the balance sheet and understand how it can be used for analysis. (p. 40)　　LO1

- Assets, which reflect investment activities, are reported (in order of their liquidity) as current assets (expected to be used typically within a year) and long-term (or plant) assets.

- Assets are reported at their historical cost and not at market values (with few exceptions) and are restricted to those that can be reliably measured.

- Not all assets are reported on the balance sheet; a company's intellectual capital, often one of its more valuable assets, is one example.

- For an asset to be recorded, it must be owned or controlled by the company and carry future economic benefits.

- Liabilities and equity are the sources of company financing; ordered by maturity dates.

- Net working capital measured as current assets less current liabilities or in ratio form as current assets/ current liabilities, is an important measure of the company's liquidity, the ability of the firm to pay its current liabilities.

Use the financial statement effects template (FSET) to analyze transactions. (p. 47)　　LO2

- The FSET captures the effects of transactions on the balance sheet, income statement, statement of stockholders' equity, and the statement of cash flows.

- Income statement effects are separated into revenues, expenses, and net income. The updating of retained earnings is denoted with an arrow line running from net income to earned capital.

Describe and construct the income statement and discuss how it can be used to evaluate management performance. (p. 49)　　LO3

- The income statement presents the revenues, expenses, and net income recognized by the company during the accounting period.

- Net income (or loss) is the increase (decrease) in net assets that results from business activities.

- Net income is determined based on the use of accrual accounting.

Explain revenue recognition, accrual accounting, and their effects on retained earnings. (p. 50)　　LO4

- Revenues must be recognized only when they have been earned and realized (or realizable).

- Expenses incurred to generate revenues should be recognized in the same period as the revenues.

Illustrate equity transactions and the statement of stockholders' equity. (p. 56)　　LO5

- The statement of stockholders' equity reports transactions resulting in changes in equity accounts during the accounting period.

- Transactions between the company and its owners, such as dividend payments, are not reported in the income statement.

Use journal entries and T-accounts to analyze and record transactions. (p. 57)　　LO6

- Transactions are recorded in the accounting system using journal entries.

- Journal entries are posted to a general ledger, represented by "T-accounts."

- Accountants use "debits" and "credits" to record transactions in the accounts.

Compute net working capital, the current ratio, and the quick ratio, and explain how they reflect liquidity. (p. 67)　　LO7

- Net working capital: an indicator of a firm's ability to pay its short-term debts computed as the difference between current assets and current liabilities.

- Current ratio (CR): A measure of solvency indicating the degree of coverage of current liabilities by current assets.

- Quick ratio (QR): A measure of the ability to cover current liabilities using only cash and cash equivalents such as money market accounts.

GUIDANCE ANSWERS . . . YOU MAKE THE CALL

You are an Analyst   In 2008, Callaway paid cash dividends of $17.8 million. The net income and dividend payments account for the change in retained earnings ($518.9 − $470.5 = $66.2 − $17.8). On occasion, companies pay dividends in excess of their earnings (or pay dividends even when earning losses), resulting in a decrease in retained earnings over the period.

KEY RATIOS

$$\text{Net working capital} = \text{Current assets} - \text{Current liabilities}$$

$$\text{Current ratio} = \frac{\text{Current assets}}{\text{Current liabilities}} \qquad \text{Quick ratio} = \frac{\text{Cash and cash equivalents}}{\text{Current liabilities}}$$

KEY TERMS

Account (p. 46)

Accounting equation (p. 40)

Accounts payable (p. 43)

Accounts receivable (p. 42)

Accrual accounting (p. 50)

Accrued liabilities (p. 43)

Accumulated other comprehensive income or loss (p. 44)

Additional paid-in capital (p. 44)

Asset (p. 40)

Cash (p. 42)

Cash accounting (p. 51)

Chart of accounts (p. 47)

Common stock (p. 44)

Compound entries (p. 58)

Contributed capital (p. 44)

Cost of goods sold (p. 50)

Credit (p. 51, 58)

Current assets (p. 42)

Current liabilities (p. 43)

Current maturities of long-term debt (p. 44)

Current ratio (p. 67)

Debit (p. 58)

Deferred (unearned) revenues (p. 43)

Double-entry accounting system (p. 46)

Earned capital (p. 45)

Equity (p. 44, 45)

Executory contract (p. 43)

Expenses (p. 49)

Fair market value (p. 42)

Financial statement effects template (FSET) (p. 46)

Gross profit (p. 50)

Historical cost (p. 42)

Intangible and other assets (p. 42)

Inventory (p. 42)

Journal entry (p. 58)

Liability (p. 43)

Liquidity (p. 42, 67)

Long-term debt (p. 44)

Long-term financial investments (p. 42)

Marketable securities (p. 42)

Matching (p. 50)

Net assets (p. 49)

Net income (p. 49)

Net loss (p. 49)

Net working capital (p. 67)

Noncurrent assets (p. 42)

Noncurrent liabilities (p. 44)

Nonoperating revenues and expenses (p. 50)

Normal balance (p. 59)

Notes payable (p. 44)

Operating cycle (p. 67)

Operating expenses (p. 49)

Other long-term liabilities (p. 44)

Prepaid expenses (p. 42)

Property, plant, and equipment (PPE) (p. 42)

Quick ratio (p. 67)

Relevance (p. 42)

Reliability (p. 42)

Retained earnings (p. 44)

Revenue recognition (p. 50)

Revenues (p. 49)

Shareholders' equity (p. 45)

Short-term borrowings (p. 43)

Stockholders' equity (p. 45)

T-account (p. 58)

Trade credit (p. 67)

Treasury stock (p. 44)

MULTIPLE CHOICE

1. Which of the following conditions must exist for an item to be recorded as an asset?
   a. Item is not owned or controlled by the company.
   b. Future benefits from the item cannot be reliably measured.
   c. Item must be a tangible asset.
   d. Item must be expected to yield future benefits.

2. Company assets that are excluded from the company financial statements
   a. are presumably reflected in the company's stock price.
   b. include all of the company's intangible assets.
   c. are known as intangible assets.
   d. include investments in other companies.

3. If an asset declines in value, which of the following must be true?
   a. A liability also declines.
   b. Equity also declines.
   c. Either a liability or equity also declines or another asset increases in value.
   d. Neither *a* nor *b* can occur.

4. Which of the following is true about accrual accounting?
   a. Accrual accounting does not require matching.
   b. Accrual accounting is required under GAAP.
   c. Accrual accounting recognizes revenue only when cash is received.
   d. Recognition of a prepaid asset is not an example of accrual accounting.

5. Which of the following options accurately identifies the effects a cash sale of an iPhone has on Apple's accounts?
   a. Accounts receivable increases, sales revenue increases, cost of goods sold increases, and inventory decreases.
   b. Cash increases, sales revenue increases, cost of goods sold decreases, and inventory decreases.
   c. Accounts receivable increases, sales revenue increases, cost of goods sold decreases, and inventory decreases.
   d. Cash increases, sales revenue increases, cost of goods sold increases, and inventory decreases.

DISCUSSION QUESTIONS

Q2-1. The balance sheet consists of assets, liabilities, and equity. Define each category and provide two examples of accounts reported within each category.

Q2-2. Two important concepts that guide income statement reporting are the revenue recognition principle and the matching principle. Define and explain each of these two guiding principles.

Q2-3. GAAP is based on the concept of accrual accounting. Define and describe accrual accounting.

Q2-4. What is the statement of stockholders' equity? What information is conveyed in that statement?

Q2-5. What are the two essential characteristics of an asset?

Q2-6. What does the concept of liquidity refer to? Explain.

Q2-7. What does the term *current* denote when referring to assets?

Q2-8. Assets are recorded at historical costs even though current market values might, arguably, be more relevant to financial statement readers. Describe the reasoning behind historical cost usage.

Q2-9. Identify three intangible assets that are likely to be excluded from the balance sheet because they cannot be reliably measured.

Q2-10. How does the quick ratio differ from the current ratio?

Q2-11. What three conditions must be satisfied to require reporting of a liability on the balance sheet?

Q2-12. Define net working capital. Explain how increasing the amount of trade credit can reduce the net working capital for a company.

Q2-13. On December 31, 2010, Miller Company had $700,000 in total assets and owed $220,000 to creditors. If this corporation's common stock totaled $300,000, what amount of retained earnings is reported on its December 31, 2010, balance sheet?

Assignments with the WebAssign logo in the margin are available in WebAssign. See the Preface of the book for details.

MINI EXERCISES

LO1 **M2-14.** **Determining Retained Earnings and Net Income Using the Balance Sheet**
The following information is reported for Kinney Corporation at the end of 2010.

Accounts Receivable	$ 23,000	Retained Earnings	$?
Accounts Payable	11,000	Supplies Inventory	9,000
Cash	8,000	Equipment	138,000
Common Stock	110,000		

a. Compute the amount of retained earnings at the end of 2010.
b. If the amount of retained earnings at the beginning of 2010 was $30,000, and $12,000 in cash dividends were declared and paid during 2010, what was its net income for 2010?

LO1 **M2-15.** **Applying the Accounting Equation to the Balance Sheet**
Determine the missing amount in each of the following separate company cases.

	Assets	Liabilities	Equity
a.	$200,000	$85,000	$?
b.	?	32,000	28,000
c.	93,000	?	52,000

LO1 **M2-16.** **Applying the Accounting Equation to the Balance Sheet**
Determine the missing amount in each of the following separate company cases.

	Assets	Liabilities	Equity
a.	$375,000	$105,000	$?
b.	?	43,000	11,000
c.	878,000	?	422,000

LO1 **M2-17.** **Applying the Accounting Equation to Determine Unknown Values**
Determine the following for each separate company case:
a. The stockholders' equity of Jensen Corporation, which has assets of $450,000 and liabilities of $326,000.
b. The liabilities of Sloan & Dechow, Inc., which has assets of $618,000 and stockholders' equity of $165,000.
c. The assets of Clem Corporation, which has liabilities of $400,000, common stock of $200,000, and retained earnings of $185,000.

LO5 **M2-18.** **Analyzing Transaction Effects on Equity**
Would each of the following transactions increase, decrease, or have no effect on equity?
a. Paid cash to acquire supplies.
b. Paid cash for dividends to shareholders.
c. Paid cash for salaries.
d. Purchased equipment for cash.
e. Shareholders invested cash in business in exchange for common stock.
f. Rendered service to customers on account.
g. Rendered service to customers for cash.

M2-19. Identifying and Classifying Financial Statement Items   LO1, LO3, LO5

For each of the following items, identify whether they would most likely be reported in the balance sheet (B) or income statement (I).

a. Machinery _____   *e.* Common stock _____   *i.* Taxes expense _____
b. Supplies expense _____   *f.* Factory buildings _____   *j.* Cost of goods sold _____
c. Prepaid advertising _____   *g.* Receivables _____   *k.* Long-term debt _____
d. Advertising expense _____   *h.* Taxes payable _____   *l.* Treasury stock _____

M2-20. Computing Net Income   LO2, LO3, LO4

Healy Corporation recorded service revenues of $100,000 in 2010, of which $70,000 were for credit and $30,000 were for cash. Moreover, of the $70,000 credit sales for 2010, it collected $20,000 cash on those receivables before year-end 2010. The company also paid $60,000 cash for 2010 wages.

a. Compute the company's net income for 2010.
b. Suppose you discover that employees had earned an additional $10,000 in wages in 2010, but this amount had not been paid. Would 2010 net income change? If so, by how much?

M2-21. Classifying Items in Financial Statements   LO1, LO3, LO5

Next to each item, indicate whether it would most likely be reported: on the balance sheet (B), the income statement (I), or the statement of stockholders' equity (SE).

a. Liabilities _____   *d.* Revenues _____   *g.* Assets _____
b. Net income _____   *e.* Stock issuance _____   *h.* Expenses _____
c. Cash _____   *f.* Dividends _____   *i.* Equity _____

M2-22. Classifying Items in Financial Statements   LO1, LO3, LO4, LO5

For each of the following items, indicate whether it is most likely reported on the balance sheet (B), the income statement (I), or the statement of stockholders' equity (SE).

a. Accounts receivable _____   *e.* Notes payable _____
b. Prepaid rent _____   *f.* Supplies expense _____
c. Net income _____   *g.* Land _____
d. Stockholders' equity _____   *h.* Supplies _____

M2-23. Classifying Items in Financial Statements   LO1, LO3, LO4, LO5

For each of the following items, indicate whether it is most likely reported on the balance sheet (B), the income statement (I), or the statement of stockholders' equity (SE).

a. Cash (year-end balance) _____   *e.* Dividends _____
b. Advertising expense _____   *f.* Accounts payable _____
c. Common stock _____   *g.* Inventory _____
d. Printing fees earned _____   *h.* Equipment _____

M2-24. Determining Company Performance and Retained Earnings Using the Accounting Equation   LO4

Use your knowledge of accounting relations to complete the following table for **Limited Brands, Inc.** (All amounts in $ millions.)

LIMITED BRANDS, INC.
NYSE::LTD

Fiscal year ending	February 2, 2008	January 31, 2009
Beginning retained earnings (deficit)	$4,277	$4,758
Net income (loss).	718	?
Dividends paid.	?	201
Increases (decreases) from other retained earnings changes	(10)	—
Ending retained earnings (deficit).	?	$4,777

M2-25. Analyzing the Effect of Transactions on the Balance Sheet   LO1, LO6

Following the example in *a* below, indicate the effects of transactions *b* through *i* on assets, liabilities, and equity, including identifying the individual accounts affected.

a. Rendered legal services to clients for cash
ANSWER: Increase assets (Cash)
Increase equity (Service Revenues)

    b.   Purchased office supplies on account
    c.   Issued additional common stock in exchange for cash
    d.   Paid amount due on account for office supplies purchased in *b*
    e.   Borrowed cash (and signed a six-month note) from bank
    f.   Rendered legal services and billed clients
    g.   Paid cash to acquire a desk lamp for the office
    h.   Paid cash to cover interest on note payable to bank
    i.   Received invoice for this period's utilities

LO1, LO6   **M2-26.   Analyzing the Effect of Transactions on the Balance Sheet**

Following the example in *a* below, indicate the effects of transactions *b* through *i* on assets, liabilities, and equity, including identifying the individual accounts affected.

    a.   Paid cash to acquire a computer for use in office
        ANSWER: Increase assets (Office Equipment)
                  Decrease assets (Cash)
    b.   Rendered services and billed client
    c.   Paid cash to cover rent for this period
    d.   Rendered services to client for cash
    e.   Received amount due from client in *b*
    f.   Purchased an office desk on account
    g.   Paid cash to cover this period's employee salaries
    h.   Paid cash to cover desk purchased in *f*
    i.   Declared and paid a cash dividend

LO1, LO5   **M2-27.   Constructing a Retained Earnings Reconciliation from Financial Data**

JOHNSON &
JOHNSON
NYSE :: JNJ

Following is financial information from **Johnson & Johnson** for the year ended December 28, 2008. Prepare the 2008 fiscal-year retained earnings reconciliation for Johnson & Johnson ($ millions).

Retained earnings, Dec. 30, 2007....	$55,280	Dividends........................	$5,024
Net earnings	12,949	Retained earnings, Dec. 28, 2008....	?
Other retained earnings changes....	174		

LO3   **M2-28.   Analyzing Transactions to Compute Net Income**

Guay Corp., a start-up company, provided services that were acceptable to its customers and billed those customers for $350,000 in 2010. However, Guay collected only $280,000 cash in 2010, and the remaining $70,000 of 2010 revenues were collected in 2011. Guay employees earned $200,000 in 2010 wages that were not paid until the first week of 2011. How much net income does Guay report for 2010? For 2011 (assuming no new transactions)?

LO1, LO2, LO3,   **M2-29.   Analyzing Transactions Using the Financial Statement Effects Template**
LO4, LO5, LO6

Report the effects for each of the following independent transactions using the financial statement effects template provided.

Web**Assign**.

	Balance Sheet						Income Statement		
Transaction	Cash Asset	+ Noncash Assets	= Liabil- ities	+ Contrib. Capital	+ Earned Capital		Revenues -	Expenses =	Net Income
a. Issue stock for $1,000 cash.			=					-	=
b. Purchase inventory for $500 cash.			=					-	=
c. Sell inventory for $2,000 on credit.			=					-	=

continued

continued from previous page

Transaction	Balance Sheet							Income Statement		
	Cash Asset	+	Noncash Assets	=	Liabil- ities	+	Contrib. Capital	+ Earned Capital	Revenues -	Expenses = Net Income
d. Record $500 for cost of inventory sold in *c.*				=					-	=
e. Receive $2,000 cash on receivable from *c.*				=					-	=

M2-30. Journalizing Business Transactions   LO1, LO6

Refer to the transactions in M2-29. Prepare journal entries for each of the transactions *a* through *e.*   Web**Assign**.

M2-31. Posting to T-Accounts   LO1, LO6

Refer to the transactions in M2-29. Set up T-accounts for each of the accounts referenced by the transactions and post the amounts for each transaction to those T-accounts.   Web**Assign**.

EXERCISES

E2-32. Constructing Balance Sheets and Computing Working Capital   LO1, LO7

The following balance sheet data are reported for Beaver, Inc., at May 31, 2010.

Accounts Receivable	$18,300	Accounts Payable	$ 5,200
Notes Payable	20,000	Cash	12,200
Equipment	55,000	Common Stock	42,500
Supplies	16,400	Retained Earnings	?

Assume that on June 1, 2010, only the following two transactions occurred.

June 1   Purchased additional equipment costing $15,000, giving $2,000 cash and a $13,000 note payable.
Declared and paid a $7,000 cash dividend.

a.   Prepare its balance sheet at May 31, 2010.
b.   Prepare its balance sheet at June 1, 2010.
c.   Calculate its net working capital at June 1, 2010. (Assume that Notes Payable are noncurrent.)

E2-33. Applying the Accounting Equation to Determine Missing Data   LO1, LO2, LO3, LO5

For each of the four separate situations *1* through *4* below, compute the unknown amounts referenced by the letters *a* through *d* shown.

	1	2	3	4
Beginning				
Assets	$28,000	$12,000	$28,000	$ (d)
Liabilities	18,600	5,000	19,000	9,000
Ending				
Assets	30,000	26,000	34,000	40,000
Liabilities	17,300	(b)	15,000	19,000
During Year				
Common Stock Issued	2,000	4,500	(c)	3,500
Revenues	(a)	28,000	18,000	24,000
Expenses	8,500	21,000	11,000	17,000
Cash Dividends Paid	5,000	1,500	1,000	6,500

LO1, LO3, LO7 **E2-34.** **Preparing Balance Sheets, Computing Income, and Applying the Current and Quick Ratios**
Balance sheet information for Lang Services at the end of 2010 and 2011 is:

	December 31, 2011	December 31, 2010
Accounts Receivable	$22,800	$17,500
Notes Payable	1,800	1,600
Cash	10,000	8,000
Equipment	32,000	27,000
Supplies	4,700	4,200
Accounts Payable	25,000	25,000
Stockholders' Equity	?	?

a. Prepare its balance sheet for December 31 of each year.
b. Lang Services raised $5,000 cash through issuing additional common stock early in 2011, and it declared and paid a $17,000 cash dividend in December 2011. Compute its net income or loss for 2011.
c. Calculate the current ratio and quick ratio for 2011.
d. Assume the industry average is 1.5 for the current ratio and 1.0 for the quick ratio. Comment on Lang's current and quick ratios relative to the industry.

LO1, LO3 **E2-35.** **Constructing Balance Sheets and Determining Income**
WebAssign.
Following is balance sheet information for Lynch Services at the end of 2010 and 2011.

	December 31, 2011	December 31, 2010
Accounts Payable	$ 6,000	$ 9,000
Cash	23,000	20,000
Accounts Receivable	42,000	33,000
Land	40,000	40,000
Building	250,000	260,000
Equipment	43,000	45,000
Mortgage Payable	90,000	100,000
Supplies	20,000	18,000
Common Stock	220,000	220,000
Retained Earnings	?	?

a. Prepare balance sheets at December 31 of each year.
b. The firm declared and paid a cash dividend of $10,000 in December 2011. Compute its net income for 2011.

LO1, LO7 **E2-36.** **Constructing Balance Sheets and Applying the Current and Quick Ratios**
WebAssign.
The following balance sheet data are reported for Brownlee Catering at September 30, 2011.

Accounts Receivable	$17,000	Accounts Payable	$24,000
Notes Payable	12,000	Cash	10,000
Equipment	34,000	Common Stock	27,500
Supplies Inventory	9,000	Retained Earnings	?

Assume that on October 1, 2011, only the following two transactions occurred:

June 1   Purchased additional equipment costing $11,000, giving $3,000 cash and signing an $8,000 note payable.
       Declared and paid a cash dividend of $3,000.

Required
a. Prepare Brownlee Catering's balance sheet at September 30, 2011.
b. Prepare the company's balance sheet at the close of business on October 1, 2011.
c. Calculate Brownlee's current and quick ratios on September 30 and October 1. (Assume that Notes Payable are noncurrent.)

d. The October 1, 2011 transactions have decreased Brownlee's current and quick ratios, reflecting a decline in liquidity. Identify two transactions that would increase the company's liquidity.

E2-37. **Constructing Financial Statements from Transaction Data** LO1, LO3, LO4

Baiman Corporation commences operations at the beginning of January. It provides its services on credit and bills its customers $30,000 for January sales. Its employees also earn January wages of $12,000 that are not paid until the first of February. Complete the following statements for the month-end of January.

Income Statement		Balance Sheet	
Sales . . . . $		Cash. . . . . $ 8,000	
Wages expense.		Accounts receivable	
Net income (loss). . . . . $		Total assets . . . . $	
		Wages payable . . . . $	
		Common stock 8,000	
		Retained earnings	
		Total liabilities and equity . . . . $	

E2-38. **Classifying Balance Sheet and Income Statement Accounts and Computing Performance and Liquidity Measures** LO1, LO3, LO4, LO7

Following are selected accounts for **The Procter & Gamble Company** for 2008. PROCTER & GAMBLE NYSE :: PG

($ millions)	Amount	Classification
Net sales	$79,029	
Depreciation expense	1,358	
Retained earnings	57,309	
Net earnings	13,436	
Property, plant & equipment (net).	19,462	
Selling, general & administrative expense	24,008	
Accounts receivable	5,836	
Total liabilities	71,734	
Stockholders' equity	63,099	

a. Indicate the appropriate classification of each account as appearing in either its balance sheet (B) or its income statement (I).

b. Using the data, compute its amounts for total assets and for total expenses.

c. Estimate Procter & Gamble's return on equity (ROE) and its debt-to-equity ratio (ROE and debt-to-equity were defined in Chapter 1).

E2-39. **Classifying Balance Sheet and Income Statement Accounts and Computing ROE** LO1, LO3, LO5

Following are selected accounts for **Target Corporation** for 2008. TARGET NYSE :: TGT

($ millions)	Amount	Classification
Sales	$62,884	
Depreciation and amortization	1,826	
Retained earnings	11,443	
Net earnings	2,214	
Property, plant & equipment, net	25,756	
Selling, general & administrative expense	12,954	
Accounts payable	6,337	
Total liabilities and shareholders' investment	44,106	
Total shareholders' investment	13,712	

a. Indicate the appropriate classification of each account as appearing in either its balance sheet (B) or its income statement (I).

   b.   Using the data, compute Target's total assets and total expenses.

   c.   Estimate Target's return on equity. (ROE was defined in Chapter 1.)

LO1, LO3, LO7   **E2-40.**   **Classifying Balance Sheet and Income Statement Accounts and Computing Performance and Liquidity Measures**

BRIGGS & STRATTON
NYSE :: BGG

Following are selected accounts for **Briggs & Stratton Corporation** for June 28, 2009.

($ millions)	Amount	Classification
Net sales	$2,092	
Interest expense	31	
Retained earnings	1,076	
Net income	32	
Property, plant & equipment, net	364	
Engineering, selling, general & administrative expense	265	
Accounts receivable, net	263	
Total liabilities	924	
Shareholders' investment	695	

   a.   Indicate the appropriate classification of each account as appearing in either its balance sheet (B) or its income statement (I).

   b.   Using the data, compute its amounts for total assets and for total expenses.

   c.   Estimate BGG's return on equity and its debt-to-equity ratio (ROE and debt-to-equity were defined in Chapter 1.)

LO1, LO3, LO5   **E2-41.**   **Classifying Balance Sheet and Income Statement Accounts and Computing Debt-to-Equity**

KIMBERLY-CLARK
NYSE :: KMB

Following are selected accounts for **Kimberly-Clark Corporation** for 2008.

($ millions)	Amount	Classification
Net sales	$19,415	
Cost of goods sold	13,557	
Retained earnings	9,465	
Net income	1,690	
Property, plant & equipment, net	7,667	
Marketing research and selling, general expense	3,291	
Accounts receivable, net	2,492	
Total liabilities	14,211	
Total stockholders' equity	3,878	

   a.   Indicate the appropriate classification of each account as appearing in either its balance sheet (B) or its income statement (I).

   b.   Using the data, compute its amounts for total assets and for total expenses.

   c.   Compute Kimberly-Clark's debt-to-equity ratio. (Debt-to-equity was defined in Chapter 1.)

LO1, LO2   **E2-42.**   **Analyzing Transactions Using the Financial Statement Effects Template**

Record the effect of each of the following independent transactions using the financial statements effects template provided. Confirm that Assets = Liabilities + Equity for each transaction.

	Balance Sheet						Income Statement		
Transaction	Cash Asset	+ Noncash Assets	= Liabil- ities	+ Contrib. Capital	+ Earned Capital		Revenues -	Expenses =	Net Income
(1) Receive €50,000 in exchange for common stock.			=					-	=
(2) Borrow €10,000 from bank.			=					-	=

continued

		Balance Sheet						Income Statement		
Transaction	Cash Asset	+ Noncash Assets	= Liabilities	+ Contrib. Capital	+ Earned Capital		Revenues	− Expenses	= Net Income
(3) Purchase €2,000 of supplies inventory on credit.			=					−	=
(4) Receive €15,000 cash from customers for services provided.			=					−	=
(5) Pay €2,000 cash to supplier in transaction 3.			=					−	=
(6) Receive order for future services with €3,500 advance payment.			=					−	=
(7) Pay €5,000 cash dividend to shareholders.			=					−	=
(8) Pay employees €6,000 cash for compensation earned.			=					−	=
(9) Pay €500 cash for interest on loan in transaction 2.			=					−	=
Totals			=					−	=

E2-43. Recording Transactions Using Journal Entries and T-Accounts   LO1, LO6

Use the information in Exercise 2-42 to complete the following.

    a.   Prepare journal entries for each of the transactions (1) through (9).

    b.   Set up T-accounts for each of the accounts used in part *a* and post the journal entries to those T-accounts. (The T-accounts will not have opening balances.)

E2-44. Constructing Balance Sheets   LO1, LO6, LO7

The following balance sheet data are reported for Bettis Contractors at June 30, 2010.

Accounts Payable	$ 8,900	Common Stock	$100,000
Cash	14,700	Retained Earnings	?
Supplies	30,500	Notes Payable	30,000
Equipment	98,000	Accounts Receivable	9,200
Land	25,000		

Assume that during the next two days only the following three transactions occurred:

July 1   Paid $5,000 cash toward the notes payable owed.

    2   Purchased equipment for $10,000, paying $2,000 cash and an $8,000 note payable for the remaining balance.

    2   Declared and paid a $5,500 cash dividend.

    a.   Prepare a balance sheet at June 30, 2010.

    b.   Prepare a balance sheet at July 2, 2010.

    c.   Calculate its current and quick ratios at June 30, 2010. (Notes Payable is a noncurrent liability.)

    d.   Assume the industry average is 3.0 for the current ratio and 2.0 for the quick ratio. Comment on Bettis's current and quick ratios relative to the industry.

LO1, LO2 **E2-45.** **Analyzing Transactions Using the Financial Statement Effects Template**

Record the effect of each of the following independent transactions using the financial statement effects template provided. Confirm that Assets = Liabilities + Equity.

	Balance Sheet					Income Statement		
Transaction	Cash Asset	+ Noncash Assets	= Liabil- ities	+ Contrib. Capital	+ Earned Capital	Revenues	- Expenses	= Net Income
(1) Receive $20,000 cash in exchange for common stock.			=				-	=
(2) Purchase $2,000 of inventory on credit.			=				-	=
(3) Sell inventory for $3,000 on credit.			=				-	=
(4) Record $2,000 for cost of inventory sold in 3.			=				-	=
(5) Collect $3,000 cash from transaction 3.			=				-	=
(6) Acquire $5,000 of equipment by signing a note.			=				-	=
(7) Pay wages of $1,000 in cash.			=				-	=
(8) Pay $5,000 on a note payable that came due.			=				-	=
(9) Pay $2,000 cash dividend.			=				-	=
Totals			=				-	=

LO1, LO6 **E2-46.** **Recording Transactions Using Journal Entries and T-Accounts**

Use the information in Exercise 2-45 to complete the following.

a. Prepare journal entries for each of the transactions 1 through 9.

b. Set up T-accounts for each of the accounts used in part *a* and post the journal entries to those T-accounts. (The T-accounts will not have opening balances.)

PROBLEMS

LO1, LO3 **P2-47.** **Comparing Operating Characteristics Across Industries**

Review the following selected 2008–2009 income statement and balance sheet data.

($ millions)	Sales	Cost of Goods Sold	Gross Profit	Net Income	Assets	Liabilities	Equity
Comcast.....	$34,256	$13,472	$20,784	$2,547	$113,017	$72,567	$40,450
Apple........	36,537	23,397	13,140	5,704	53,851	26,019	27,832
Nike.........	19,176	10,572	8,604	1,487	13,250	4,557	8,693
Target.......	64,948	44,157	20,791	2,214	44,106	30,394	13,712
Harley-Davidson	5,594	3,663	1,931	655	7,829	5,713	2,116

COMCAST CORPORATION
NASDAQ :: CMCSA

APPLE INC.
NASDAQ :: AAPL

NIKE, INC.
NYSE :: NKE

TARGET CORPORATION
NYSE :: TGT

HARLEY-DAVIDSON, INC.
NYSE :: HOG

Required

a. Compare and discuss how these companies finance their operations.

b. Which company reports the highest ratio of income to assets (net income/total assets)? Suggest a reason for this result.

c. Which company has the highest estimated ROE? Is this result a surprise? Explain.

P2-48. Comparing Operating Characteristics Within an Industry

Selected data from **Dell, Inc.** follow.

($ millions)	Sales	Cost of Goods Sold	Gross Profit	Net Income	Assets	Liabilities	Equity
Dell..........	$61,101	$50,144	$10,957	$2,478	$26,500	$22,229	$4,271

Required

a. Using the data for **Apple Inc.** in P2-47, compare and discuss the two companies on the basis of how they finance their operations.

b. Which company reports the higher ratio of income to assets (net income/total assets)? Suggest a reason for this result.

c. Which firm has the higher gross margin (gross profit as a percentage of sales)? What factors might account for the difference?

P2-49. Comparing Operating Characteristics Within an Industry

Review the following selected income statement and balance sheet data for **Verizon Communications Inc.**

($ millions)	Sales	Cost of Goods Sold	Gross Profit	Net Income	Assets	Liabilities	Equity
Verizon........	$97,354	$39,007	$58,347	$6,428	$202,352	$160,646	$41,706

Required

a. Using the data for **Comcast Corporation** in P2-47, compare and discuss how Verizon and Comcast finance their operations.

b. Which company reports the higher ratio of income to assets (net income/total assets)? Suggest a reason for this result.

c. Which company is likely better able to raise capital? Explain.

P2-50. Comparing Operating Structure Across Industries

Review the following selected income statement and balance sheet data.

($ millions)	Current Assets	Long-term Assets	Total Assets	Current Liab.	Long-term Liab.	Total Liab.	Equity
3M*..................	$ 9,598	$15,949	$25,547	$ 5,839	$9,829	$15,668	$ 9,879
Abercrombie & Fitch**	1,085	1,763	2,848	450	553	1,003	1,845
Apple†	36,265	17,586	53,851	19,282	6,737	26,019	27,832

* Manufacturer of consumer and business products

** Retailer of name-brand apparel at premium prices

† Computer company

Required

a. Compare and discuss how these companies finance their operations.

b. Which company has the greatest net working capital? Do you have any concerns about any firm's net working capital position? Explain.

P2-51. Preparing a Balance Sheet, Computing Net Income, and Understanding Equity Transactions

At the beginning of 2010, Barth Company reported the following balance sheet.

Assets		Liabilities	
Cash	$ 4,800	Accounts payable	$12,000
Accounts receivable	14,700	**Equity**	
Equipment	10,000	Common stock	47,500
Land	50,000	Retained earnings	20,000
Total assets	$79,500	Total liabilities and equity	$79,500

Required

a. At the end of 2010, Barth Company reported the following assets and liabilities: Cash, $8,800; Accounts Receivable, $18,400; Equipment, $9,000; Land, $50,000; and Accounts Payable, $7,500. Prepare a year-end balance sheet for Barth. (*Hint:* Report equity as a single total.)

b. Assuming that Barth did not issue any common stock during the year but paid $12,000 cash in dividends, what was its net income or net loss for 2010?

c. Assuming that Barth issued an additional $13,500 common stock early in the year but paid $21,000 cash in dividends before the end of the year, what was its net income or net loss for 2010?

LO1, LO3 **P2-52.** **Analyzing and Interpreting the Financial Performance of Competitors**

Abercrombie & Fitch Co. and **Nordstrom, Inc.**, are major retailers that concentrate in the higher-end clothing lines. Following are selected data from their fiscal-year 2008 financial statements:

($ millions)	ANF	JWN
Total liabilities and equity	$2,848	$5,661
Net income	272	401
Net sales	3,540	8,272
Total liabilities	1,003	4,451

Required

a. What is the total amount of assets invested in (1) ANF and (2) JWN? What are the total expenses for each company (1) in dollars and (2) as a percentage of sales?

b. What is the return on equity (ROE) for (1) ANF and (2) JWN? ANF's total equity at the beginning of 2008 is $1,618 million and JWN's beginning 2008 equity is $1,115 million. (ROE was defined in Chapter 1.)

P2-53. **Analyzing Balance Sheet Numbers from Incomplete Data and Interpreting Liquidity Measures**

LO1, LO3, LO4, LO6, LO7

Selected balance sheet amounts for **3M Company**, a manufacturer of consumer and business products, for six recent years follow:

($ millions)	Current Assets	Long-term Assets	Total Assets	Current Liabilities	Long-term Liabilities	Total Liabilities	Stockholders' Equity
2003	?	9,880	17,600	5,082	4,633	9,715	?
2004	8,720	11,988	?	6,071	4,259	?	10,378
2005	?	13,398	20,513	5,238	5,175	10,413	?
2006	?	12,348	21,294	7,323	4,012	11,335	?
2007	9,838	14,856	?	?	7,585	12,947	11,747
2008	9,598	15,949	?	5,839	9,829	?	9,879

Required

a. Compute the missing balance sheet amounts for each of the six years shown.

b. What types of accounts would you expect to be included in current assets? In long-term assets?

c. Calculate the current ratio for 2003 and 2008.

d. Assume the industry average is 2.0 for the current ratio. Comment on 3M's current ratio relative to the industry.

LO1, LO3, LO7 **P2-54.** **Analyzing and Interpreting Balance Sheet Data and Interpreting Liquidity Measures**

Selected balance sheet amounts for **Abercrombie & Fitch Co.**, a retailer of name-brand apparel at premium prices, for seven recent fiscal years follow.

($ millions)	Current Assets	Long-term Assets	Total Assets	Current Liabilities	Long-term Liabilities	Total Liabilities	Stockholders' Equity
2002	$ 405	$?	$ 771	$?	$ 12	$ 176	$ 595
2003	601	394	?	211	?	245	750
2004	753	?	1,199	?	48	328	871
2005	671	718	?	429	?	?	889
2006	947	?	1,790	?	303	795	?
2007	?	1,156	2,248	511	?	843	1,405
2008	1,140	1,428	?	543	406	949	?

Required

a. Compute the missing balance sheet amounts for each of the seven years shown.

b. What asset category would you expect to constitute the majority of its current assets?

c. Has the proportion of current and long-term assets changed markedly over the past seven years? Explain.

d. Does the company appear to be conservatively financed; that is, financed by a greater proportion of equity than of debt? Explain.

e. Calculate the current ratio for 2002 and 2008.

f. Assume the industry average is 2.25 for the current ratio. Comment on Abercrombie's current ratio relative to the industry.

P2-55. Analyzing Transactions Using the Financial Statement Effects Template and Preparing an Income Statement

LO1, LO2, LO3, LO4

WebAssign.

On December 1, 2010, R. Lambert formed Lambert Services, which provides career and vocational counseling services to graduating college students. The following transactions took place during December, and company accounts include the following: Cash, Accounts Receivable, Land, Accounts Payable, Notes Payable, Common Stock, Retained Earnings, Counseling Services Revenue, Rent Expense, Advertising Expense, Interest Expense, Salary Expense, and Utilities Expense.

1. Raised $7,000 cash through common stock issuance.
2. Paid $750 cash for December rent on its furnished office space.
3. Received $500 invoice for December advertising expenses.
4. Borrowed $15,000 cash from bank and signed note payable for that amount.
5. Received $1,200 cash for counseling services rendered.
6. Billed clients $6,800 for counseling services rendered.
7. Paid $2,200 cash for secretary salary.
8. Paid $370 cash for December utilities.
9. Declared and paid a $900 cash dividend.
10. Purchased land for $13,000 cash to use for its own facilities.
11. Paid $100 cash to bank as December interest expense on note payable.

Required

a. Report the effects for each of the separate transactions 1 through 11 using the financial statement effects template. Total all columns and prove that (1) assets equal liabilities plus equity at December 31, and (2) revenues less expenses equal net income for December.

b. Prepare an income statement for the month of December.

P2-56. Recording Transactions in Journal Entries and T-Accounts

LO6

WebAssign.

Use the information in Problem 2-55 to complete the following requirements.

Required

a. Prepare journal entries for each of the transactions 1 through 11.

b. Set up T-accounts for each of the accounts used in part *a* and post the journal entries to those T-accounts.

P2-57. Analyzing and Interpreting Balance Sheet Data and Interpreting Liquidity Measures

LO1, LO3, LO4, LO6, LO7

Selected balance sheet amounts for **Apple Inc.**, a computer company, for seven recent fiscal years follow.

APPLE INC.
NYSE:: AAPL

($ millions)	Current Assets	Long-term Assets	Total Assets	Current Liabilities	Long-term Liabilities	Total Liabilities	Stockholders' Equity
2004	$?	$ 995	$ 8,050	$ 2,651	$?	$ 2,974	$?
2005	10,300	1,251	?	3,484	?	?	7,466
2006	?	2,696	17,205	6,471	?	7,221	?
2007	21,956	?	25,347	?	1,535	10,815	14,532
2008	32,311	7,261	?	14,092	?	18,542	21,030
2009	36,265	?	53,851	19,282	?	26,019	27,832

Required

a.   Compute the missing balance sheet amounts for each of the six years shown.

b.   What asset category would you expect to constitute the majority of Apple's current assets? Of its long-term assets?

c.   Is the company conservatively financed; that is, is it financed by a greater proportion of equity than of debt?

d.   Calculate the current ratio for 2004 and 2009.

e.   Assume the industry average is 2.0 for the current ratio. Comment on Apple's current ratio relative to the industry.

LO1, LO3, LO4,
LO6, LO7

HARLEY-DAVIDSON,
INC.
NYSE :: HOG

P2-58.   Analyzing Balance Sheet Numbers from Incomplete Data and Calculating Working Capital

Selected balance sheet amounts for **Harley-Davidson, Inc.**, a motorcycle manufacturer, for six recent years follow.

($ millions)	Current Assets	Long-term Assets	Total Assets	Current Liabilities	Long-term Liabilities	Total Liabilities	Stockholders' Equity
2003	2,729	2,194	?	956	1,010	?	2,958
2004	?	1,800	5,483	?	1,092	2,265	?
2005	3,145	?	?	873	2,211	?	3,083
2006	3,551	1,981	5,532	1,596	?	?	2,757
2007	3,467	2,190	?	1,905	?	3,282	2,375
2008	5,378	?	7,829	?	3,110	5,713	2,116

Required

a.   Compute the missing amounts for each of the six years shown.

b.   What asset categories would you expect to be included in its current assets? In its long-term assets?

c.   Is the company conservatively financed; that is, is it financed by a greater proportion of equity than of debt? Explain.

d.   Calculate net working capital for 2003 and 2008.

LO1, LO3

NIKE, INC.
NYSE :: NKE

P2-59.   Analyzing and Interpreting Income Statement Data

Selected income statement information for **Nike, Inc.**, a manufacturer of athletic footwear, for seven recent fiscal years follows.

($ millions)	Revenues	Cost of Goods Sold	Gross Profit	Operating Expenses	Operating Income	Other Expenses	Net Income
2002	$?	$ 6,005	$3,888	$2,820	$1,068	$405	$?
2003	10,697	6,313	?	?	1,246	772	474
2004	?	7,001	5,252	?	1,550	604	?
2005	13,740	?	?	4,222	?	682	1,211
2006	14,955	?	6,587	?	?	717	1,392
2007	16,326	9,165	?	5,029	2,132	640	?
2008	18,627	?	8,387	5,954	2,433	?	1,883

Required

a.   Compute the missing amounts for each of the seven years shown.

b.   Compute the gross profit margin (gross profit/sales) for each of the seven years and comment on its level and any trends that are evident.

c.   What would you expect to be the major cost categories constituting its operating expenses?

P2-60. **Analyzing Transactions Using the Financial Statement Effects Template and Preparing an Income Statement**   LO1, LO2, LO3, LO4

On June 1, 2010, a group of pilots in Melbourne, Australia, formed Outback Flights by issuing common stock for $50,000 cash. The group then leased several amphibious aircraft and docking facilities, equipping them to transport campers and hunters to outpost camps owned by various resorts in remote parts of Australia. The following transactions occurred during June 2010, and company accounts include the following: Cash, Accounts Receivable, Prepaid Insurance, Accounts Payable, Common Stock, Retained Earnings, Flight Services Revenue, Rent Expense, Entertainment Expense, Advertising Expense, Insurance Expense, Wages Expense, and Fuel Expense.

1. Issued common stock for $50,000 cash.
2. Paid $4,800 cash for June rent of aircraft, dockage, and dockside office.
3. Received $1,600 invoice for the cost of a reception to entertain resort owners in June.
4. Paid $900 cash for June advertising in various sport magazines.
5. Paid $1,800 cash for insurance premium for July.
6. Rendered flight services for various groups for $22,700 cash.
7. Billed client $2,900 for transporting personnel, and billed various firms for $13,000 in flight services.
8. Paid $1,500 cash to cover accounts payable.
9. Received $13,200 on account from clients in transaction 7.
10. Paid $16,000 cash to cover June wages.
11. Received $3,500 invoice for the cost of fuel used during June.
12. Declared and paid a $3,000 cash dividend.

Required

a. Report the effects for each of the separate transactions 1 through 12 using the financial statement effects template. Total all columns and prove that (1) assets equal liabilities plus equity at June 30, and (2) revenues less expenses equal net income for June.

b. Prepare an income statement for the month of June.

P2-61. **Recording Transactions in Journal Entries and T-Accounts**   LO6

Use the information in Problem 2-60 to complete the following requirements.

Required

a. Prepare journal entries for each of the transactions 1 through 12.

b. Set up T-accounts for each of the accounts used in part *a* and post the journal entries to those T-accounts.

P2-62. **Analyzing and Interpreting Income Statement Numbers from Incomplete Data**   LO1, LO3

Selected income statement information for **Starbucks Corporation**, a coffee-related restaurant chain, for seven recent fiscal years follows.

STARBUCKS CORPORATION
NASDAQ :: SBUX

($ millions)	Sales	Cost of Goods Sold	Gross Profit	Operating Expenses	Operating Income	Other Expenses	Net Income
2003	$ 4,076	$?	$2,390	$1,965	$?	$157	$268
2004	5,294	2,191	?	?	606	?	389
2005	?	2,605	3,764	?	781	287	?
2006	7,787	?	4,608	?	?	329	564
2007	9,412	3,999	?	4,359	1,054	?	673
2008	10,383	?	5,738	?	504	188	316
2009	?	4,325	5,450	4,888	562	171	?

Required

a. Compute the missing amounts for each of the seven years shown.

b. Compute the gross profit margin (gross profit/sales) for each of the seven years and comment on its level and any trends that are evident.

c. What would you expect to be the major cost categories constituting its operating expenses?

P2-63. **Analyzing, Reconstructing, and Interpreting Income Statement Data**   LO3

Selected income statement information for **Target Corporation**, a department store chain, for seven recent fiscal years follows:

TARGET CORPORATION
NYSE :: TGT

($ millions)	Revenues	Cost of Goods Sold	Gross Profit	Operating Expenses	Operating Income	Other Expenses	Net Income
2002	$42,722	$?	$13,462	$?	$3,264	$1,610	$1,654
2003	?	31,790	14,991	11,472	3,519	1,678	?
2004	45,682	31,445	?	10,636	3,601	?	3,198
2005	?	34,927	16,344	?	?	1,915	2,408
2006	57,878	39,399	?	?	5,069	?	2,787
2007	?	41,895	19,576	14,304	5,272	2,423	?
2008	62,884	44,157	?	14,325	4,402	?	2,214

Required

a. Compute the missing amounts for each of the seven years shown.

b. Compute the gross profit margin (gross profit/sales) for each of the seven years and comment on its level and any trends that are evident.

c. What would we expect to be the major cost categories constituting its operating expenses?

LO1, LO3, LO4, LO5 **P2-64.** **Preparing the Income Statement, Statement of Stockholders' Equity, and the Balance Sheet**
The records of Geyer, Inc., show the following information after all transactions are recorded for 2011.

Notes Payable	$ 4,000	Supplies.	$ 6,100
Service Fees Earned	67,600	Cash	14,800
Supplies Expense	9,700	Advertising Expense	1,700
Insurance Expense	1,500	Salaries Expense.	30,000
Miscellaneous Expense	200	Rent Expense	7,500
Common Stock (beg. year).	4,000	Retained Earnings (beg. year).	6,200
Accounts Payable	1,800		

Geyer, Inc., raised $1,400 cash through the issuance of additional common stock during this year and it declared and paid a $13,500 cash dividend near year-end.

Required

a. Prepare its income statement for 2011.

b. Prepare its statement of stockholders' equity for 2011.

c. Prepare its balance sheet at December 31, 2011.

P2-65. **Analyzing Transactions Using the Financial Statement Effects Template and Preparing Financial Statements**

LO1, LO2, LO3, LO4, LO5

Schrand Aerobics, Inc., rents studio space (including a sound system) and specializes in offering aerobics classes. On January 1, 2011, its beginning account balances are as follows: Cash, $5,000; Accounts Receivable, $5,200; Equipment, $0; Notes Payable, $2,500; Accounts Payable, $1,000; Common Stock, $5,500; Retained Earnings, $1,200; Services Revenue, $0; Rent Expense, $0; Advertising Expense, $0; Wages Expense, $0; Utilities Expense, $0; Interest Expense, $0. The following transactions occurred during January.

1. Paid $600 cash toward accounts payable.
2. Paid $3,600 cash for January rent.
3. Billed clients $11,500 for January classes.
4. Received $500 invoice from supplier for T-shirts given to January class members as an advertising promotion.
5. Collected $10,000 cash from clients previously billed for services rendered.
6. Paid $2,400 cash for employee wages.
7. Received $680 invoice for January utilities expense.
8. Paid $20 cash to bank as January interest on notes payable.
9. Declared and paid $900 cash dividend to stockholders.
10. Paid $4,000 cash on January 31 to purchase sound equipment to replace the rental system.

Required

a. Using the financial statement effects template, enter January 1 beginning amounts in the appropriate columns of the first row. (*Hint:* Beginning balances for columns can include amounts from more than one account.)

b. Report the effects for each of the separate transactions *1* through *10* in the financial statement effects template set up in part *a*. Total all columns and prove that (1) assets equal liabilities plus equity at January 31, and (2) revenues less expenses equal net income for January.

c. Prepare its income statement for January 2011.

d. Prepare its statement of stockholders' equity for January 2011.

e. Prepare its balance sheet at January 31, 2011.

P2-66. **Recording Transactions in Journal Entries and T-Accounts**
Use the information in Problem 2-65 to complete the following requirements.

LO6

Required

a. Prepare journal entries for each of the transactions 1 through 10.

b. Set up T-accounts, including beginning balances, for each of the accounts used in part *a*. Post the journal entries to those T-accounts.

P2-67. **Analyzing Transactions Using the Financial Statement Effects Template and Preparing Financial Statements**

LO1, LO2, LO3, LO4, LO5

Kross, Inc., provides appraisals and feasibility studies. On January 1, 2011, its beginning account balances are as follows: Cash, $6,700; Accounts Receivable, $14,800; Notes Payable, $2,500; Accounts Payable, $600; Retained Earnings, $12,400; and Common Stock, $6,000. The following transactions occurred during January, and company accounts include the following: Cash, Accounts Receivable, Vehicles, Accounts Payable, Notes Payable, Services Revenue, Rent Expense, Interest Expense, Salary Expense, Utilities Expense, Common Stock, and Retained Earnings.

1. Paid $950 cash for January rent.
2. Received $8,800 cash on customers' accounts.
3. Paid $500 cash toward accounts payable.
4. Received $1,600 cash for services performed for customers.
5. Borrowed $5,000 cash from bank and signed note payable for that amount.
6. Billed the city $6,200 for services performed, and billed other credit customers for $1,900 in services.
7. Paid $4,000 cash for salary of assistant.
8. Received $410 invoice for January utilities expense.
9. Declared and paid a $6,000 cash dividend.
10. Paid $9,800 cash to acquire a vehicle (on January 31) for business use.
11. Paid $50 cash to bank for January interest on notes payable.

Required

a. Using the financial statement effects template, enter January 1 beginning amounts in the appropriate columns of the first row. (*Hint:* Beginning balances for columns can include amounts from more than one account.)

b. Report the effects for each of the separate transactions 1 through 11 in the financial statement effects template set up in part *a*. Total all columns and prove that (1) assets equal liabilities plus equity at January 31, and (2) revenues less expenses equal net income for January.

c. Prepare its income statement for January 2011.

d. Prepare its statement of stockholders' equity for January 2011.

e. Prepare its balance sheet at January 31, 2011.

P2-68. **Recording Transactions in Journal Entries and T-Accounts**
Use the information in Problem 2-67 to complete the following requirements.

LO6

Required

a. Prepare journal entries for each of the transactions 1 through 11.

b. Set up T-accounts, including beginning balances, for each of the accounts used in part *a*. Post the journal entries to those T-accounts.

CASES AND PROJECTS

LO1, LO3, LO4, LO5, LO6

C2-69. Constructing Financial Statements from Cash Data

Sarah Penney operates the Wildlife Picture Gallery, selling original art and signed prints received on consignment (rather than purchased) from recognized wildlife artists throughout the country. The firm receives a 30% commission on all art sold and remits 70% of the sales price to the artists. All art is sold on a strictly cash basis.

Sarah began the business on March 1, 2011. The business received a $10,000 loan from a relative of Sarah to help her get started; it took on a note payable agreeing to pay the loan back in one year. No interest is being charged on the loan, but the relative does want to receive a set of financial statements each month. On April 1, 2011, Sarah asks for your help in preparing the statements for the first month.

Sarah has carefully kept the firm's checking account up to date and provides you with the following complete listing of the cash receipts and cash disbursements for March 2011.

Cash Receipts	
Original investment by Sarah Penney	$ 6,500
Loan from relative	10,000
Sales of art	95,000
Total cash receipts	111,500
Cash Disbursements	
Payments to artists for sales made	54,000
Payment of March rent for gallery space	900
Payment of March wages to staff	4,900
Payment of airfare for personal vacation of Sarah (vacation will be in April)	500
Total cash disbursements	60,300
Cash balance, March 31, 2011	$ 51,200

Sarah also gives you the following documents she has received:

1. A $350 invoice for March utilities; payment is due by April 15, 2011.
2. A $1,700 invoice from Careful Express for the shipping of artwork sold in March; payment is due by April 10, 2011.
3. Sarah signed a one-year lease for the gallery space; as an incentive to sign the lease, the landlord reduced the first month's rent by 25%; the monthly rent starting in April is $1,200.

In your discussions with Sarah, she tells you that she has been so busy that she is behind in sending artists their share of the sales proceeds. She plans to catch up within the next week.

Required

From the above information, prepare the following financial statements for Wildlife Picture Gallery: (*a*) income statement for the month of March 2011; (*b*) statement of stockholders' equity for the month of March 2011; and (*c*) balance sheet as of March 31, 2011.

LO3

C2-70. Financial Records and Ethical Behavior

Andrea Frame and her supervisor are sent on an out-of-town assignment by their employer. At the supervisor's suggestion, they stay at the Spartan Inn (across the street from the Luxury Inn). After three days of work, they settle their lodging bills and leave. On the return trip, the supervisor gives Andrea what appears to be a copy of a receipt from the Luxury Inn for three nights of lodging. Actually, the supervisor indicates that he prepared the Luxury Inn receipt on his office computer and plans to complete his expense reimbursement request using the higher lodging costs from the Luxury Inn.

Required

What are the ethical considerations that Andrea faces when she prepares her expense reimbursement request?

SOLUTIONS TO REVIEW PROBLEMS

Mid-Chapter Review 1

1. A	2. C	3. B	4. E	5. B	6. E	7. X	8. B	9. E	10. B
11. X	12. A	13. B	14. C	15. A	16. D	17. A	18. A	19. E	20. C

Mid-Chapter Review 2

	Balance Sheet						Income Statement		
Transaction	Cash Asset	+ Noncash Assets	= Liabil- ities	+ Contrib. Capital	+ Earned Capital		Revenues −	Expenses	= Net Income
(a) Issue common stock for $20,000.	+20,000 Cash		=	+20,000 Common Stock			−		=
(b) Purchase $8,000 of inventory on credit.		+8,000 Inventory	= +8,000 Accounts Payable				−		=
(c) Purchase equipment for $10,000 cash.	−10,000 Cash	+10,000 Equipment	=				−		=
(d) Pay suppliers $3,000 cash.	−3,000 Cash		= −3,000 Accounts Payable				−		=
Totals	+7,000	+18,000	= +5,000	+20,000					
	Assets		= Liabilities +	Equity					

Mid-Chapter Review 3

Solution to Part 1.

SCHAEFER'S PHARMACY, INC.
Income Statement
For Year Ended December 31, 2011

Revenues		$25,000
Expenses		
Wages expense	$8,000	
Rent expense	5,000	
Utilities expense	2,000	
Other expenses	4,000	
Total expenses		19,000
Net income		$ 6,000

Solution to Part 2.

SCHAEFER'S PHARMACY, INC.
Retained Earnings Reconciliation
For Year Ended December 31, 2011

Retained earnings, Dec. 31, 2010	$25,000
Add: Net income	6,000
Less: Dividends	(1,000)
Retained earnings, Dec. 31, 2011	$30,000

Solution to Part 3.

SCHAEFER'S PHARMACY, INC.
Balance Sheet
December 31, 2011

Cash..........................	$ 3,000		Accounts payable	$ 7,500
Accounts receivable	12,000			
Office equipment...............	32,250		Common stock	45,750
Land........................	36,000		Retained earnings	30,000
Total assets	$83,250		Total liabilities and equity	$83,250

Chapter-End Review

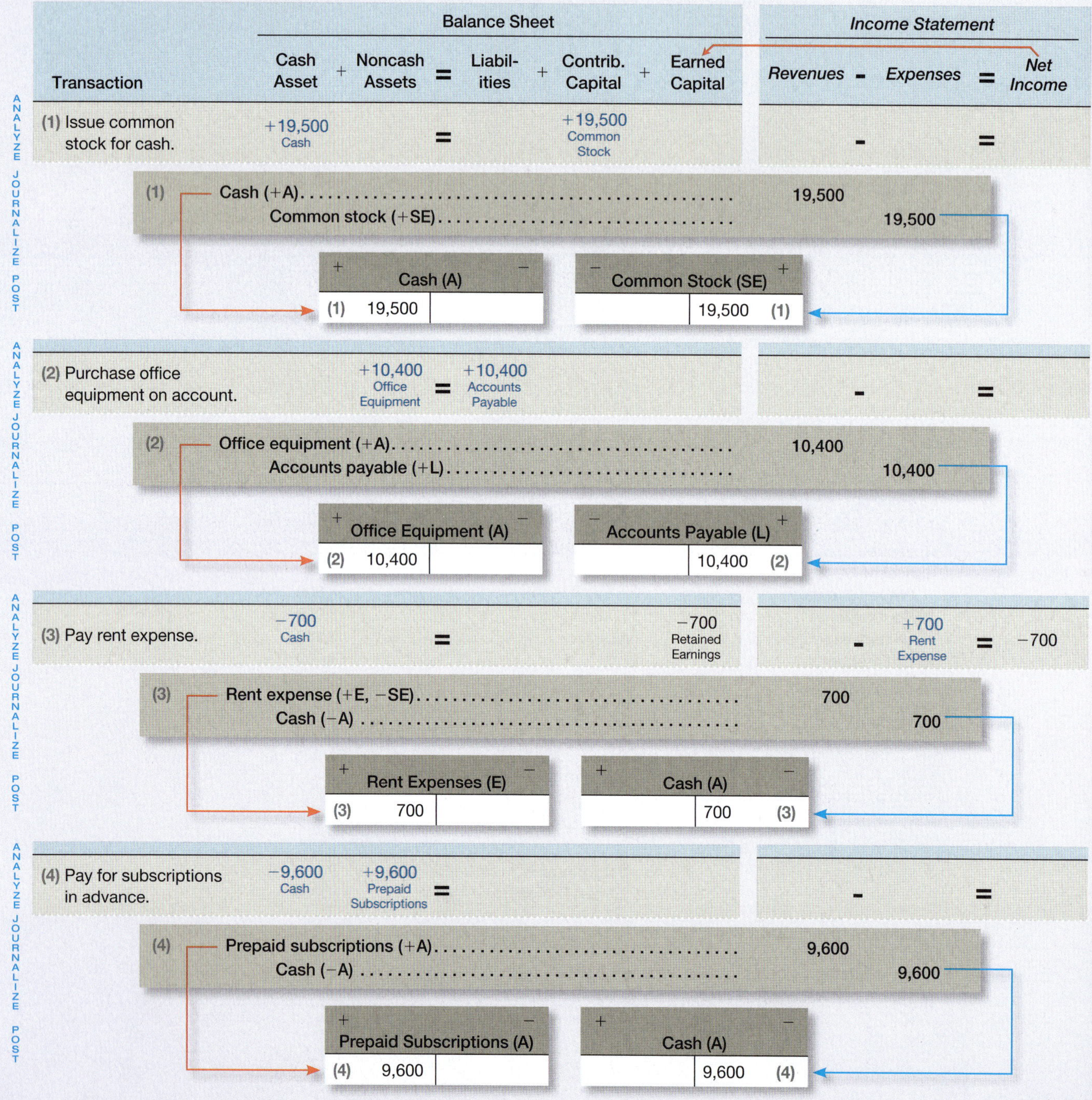

continued

continued from previous page

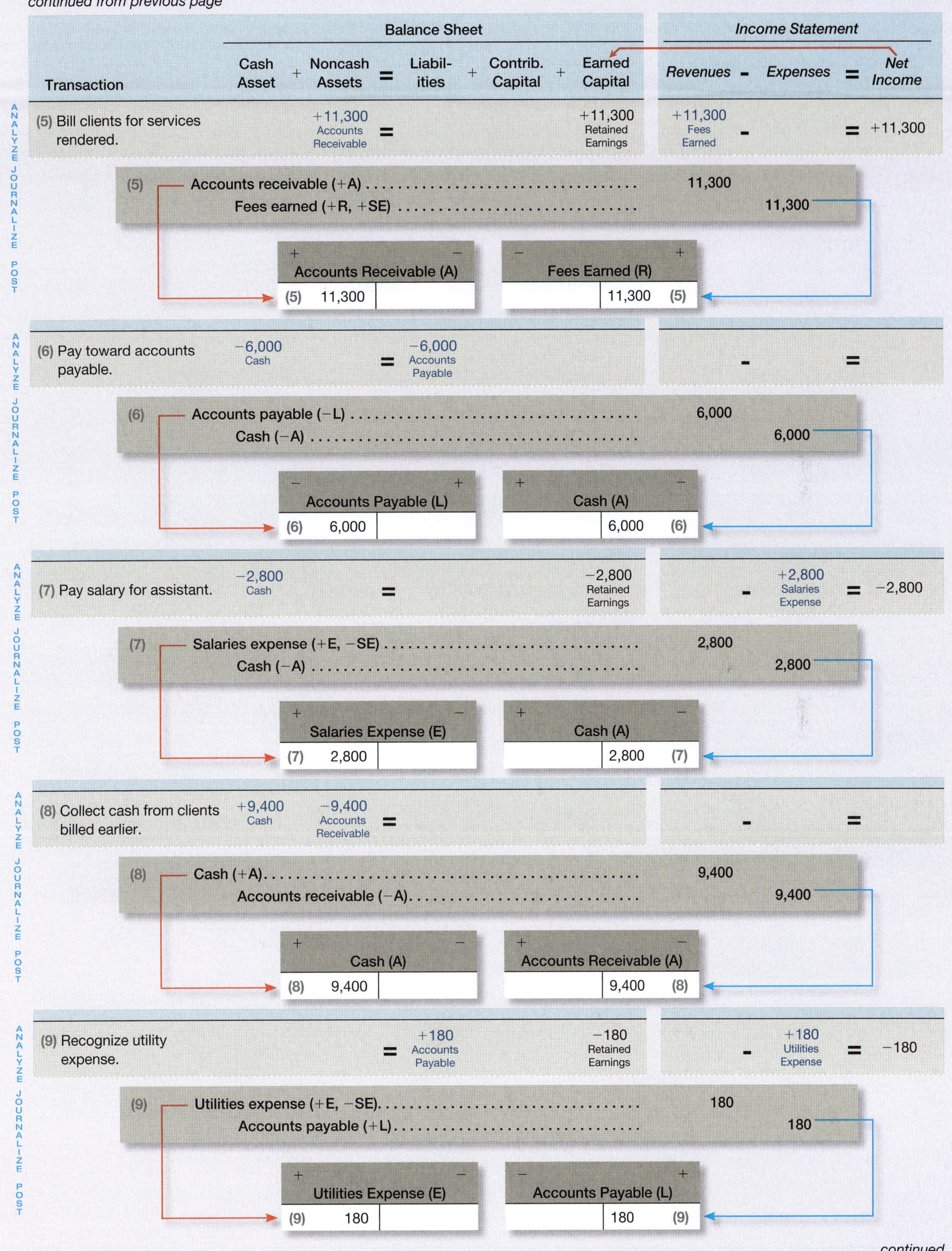

continued

continued from previous page

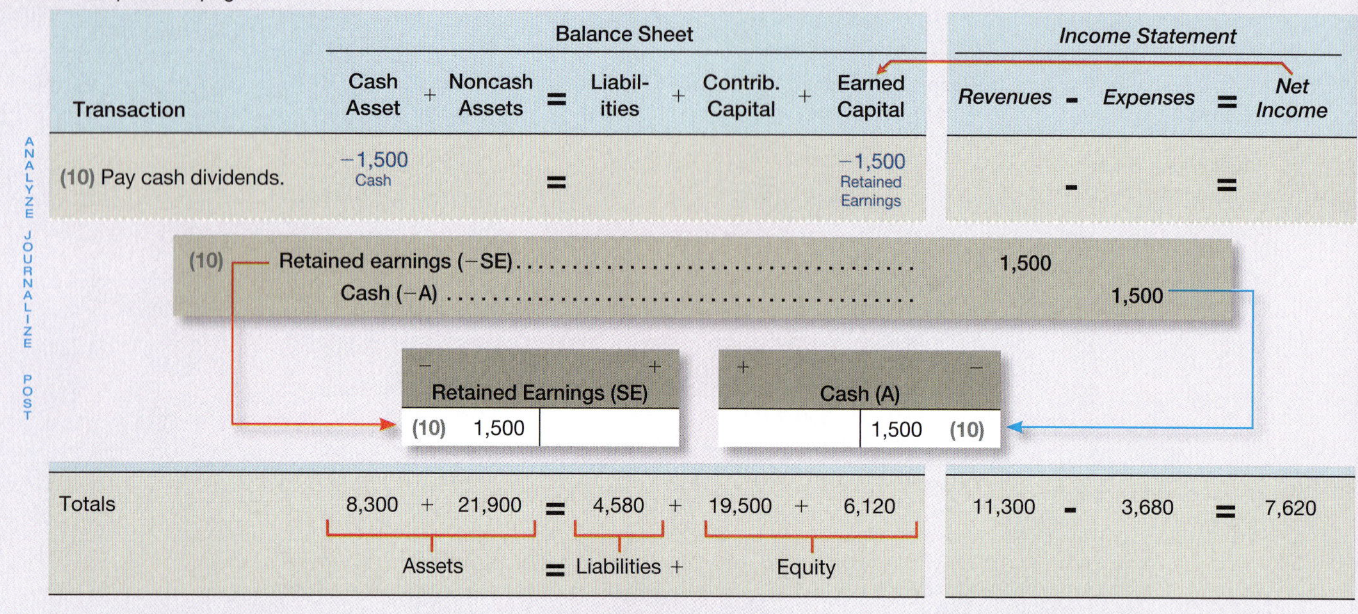

| Totals | 8,300 + 21,900 = 4,580 + 19,500 + 6,120 | 11,300 − 3,680 = 7,620 |

Assets   = Liabilities +   Equity

General Ledger

| **Assets** | = | **Liabilities** | + | **Equity** |

Cash (A)

+			−
(1)	19,500	700	(3)
(8)	9,400	9,600	(4)
		6,000	(6)
		2,800	(7)
		1,500	(10)
End. bal:	8,300		

Accounts Receivable (A)

+			−
(5)	11,300	9,400	(8)
End. bal:	1,900		

Prepaid Subscriptions (A)

+			−
(4)	9,600		
End. bal:	9,600		

Office Equipment (A)

+			−
(2)	10,400		
End. bal:	10,400		

Accounts Payable (L)

−			+
(6)	6,000	10,400	(2)
		180	(9)
		4,580	End. bal.

Common Stock (SE)

−			+
		19,500	(1)
		19,500	End. Bal.

Retained Earnings (SE)

−			+
(10)	1,500		
End. bal:	1,500		

Fees Earned (R)

−			+
		11,300	(5)
		11,300	End. Bal.

Salaries Expense (E)

+			−
(7)	2,800		
End. bal:	2,800		

Rent Expense (E)

+			−
(3)	700		
End. bal:	700		

Utilities Expense (E)

+			−
(9)	180		
End. bal:	180		

Assets = $30,200   =   Liabilities = $4,580   +   Equity = $25,620

1. Identify the major steps in the accounting cycle. (p. 96)

2. Review the process of journalizing and posting transactions. (p. 97)

3. Describe the adjusting process and illustrate adjusting entries. (p. 103)

4. Prepare financial statements from adjusted accounts. (p. 112)

5. Describe the process of closing temporary accounts. (p. 116)

6. Analyze changes in balance sheet accounts. (p. 119)

© Getty Images

Adjusting Accounts for Financial Statements

Walgreen Co.'s traditional method of growing sales and net income has been adding drugstores, either through store openings or acquisitions of other drugstore companies. But with 7000 existing stores, that strategy has a diminishing impact on financial performance.

WALGREENS
www.walgreens.com

Chief Executive Officer Gregory Wasson has charted a new approach to achieving profit growth by slowing store growth, cutting costs, and leveraging the existing store network. A "Rewiring for Growth" initiative should reduce operating costs by $1 billion annually by fiscal year 2011. The number of items offered in drug stores is being reduced to give shoppers a more pleasant experience and to reduce the company's investment in slow-moving products. The number of in-store clinics will increase. Stated differently, Walgreen's management is "adjusting" or "updating" its business plan in light of the changing environment. Financial analysts are waiting to see how these changes will impact Walgreen's financial results.

Since the financial statements should reflect the firm's underlying economic reality, Walgreen's management will need to "adjust" or "update" its financial statements to reflect the changes in its strategy and outlook.

Accounting adjustments are a key part of creating the financial statements, and they are central to the difference between accrual and cash accounting. While cash accounting only records transactions that involve cash receipts and disbursements, accrual accounting records revenues when they are earned (even if cash has not yet been received) and expenses as they are incurred (regardless of when the cash disbursement associated with that expense is made). The quality, or lack thereof, of the financial statements often hinges on the quality of those adjustments. Thus, understanding how and why accounting adjustments occur is fundamentally important to those who wish to analyze and interpret the financial statements.

This chapter will describe the need for adjustments, how they are prepared, their financial statement effect, and the need for ethics and oversight in this process. We illustrate how financial statements are prepared from those adjusted accounts. Then, we end the chapter with the closing process for the financial statements. Such "closing of the books" enables firms to report their performance for the year and then "open the books" anew for the next period.

Sources: Crain's Chicago Business, "Walgreen Plans Mac-like Attack" August 3, 2009; Walgreen Co. and Subsidiaries 2009 annual report.

CHAPTER ORGANIZATION

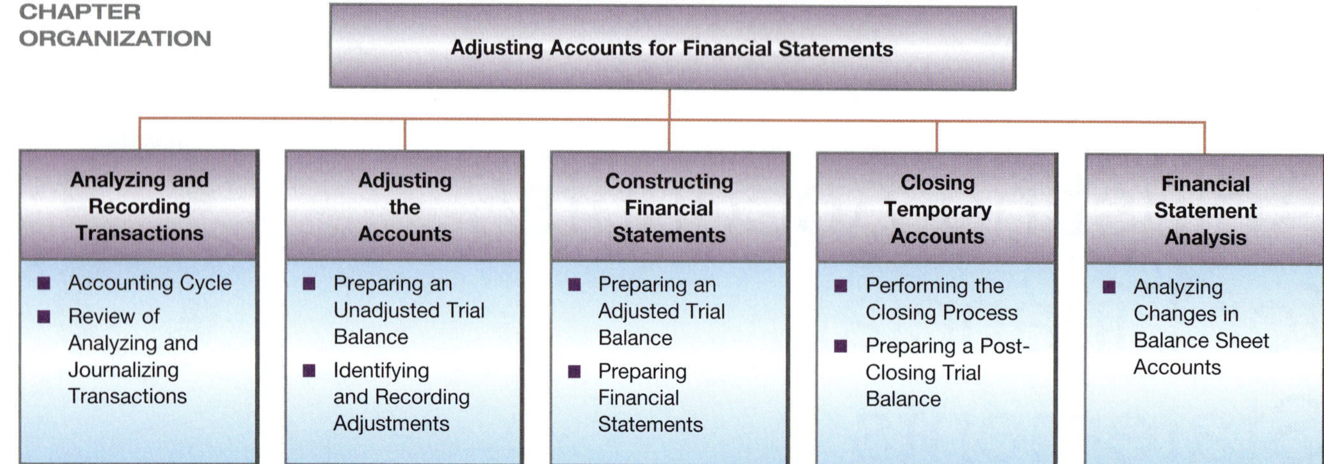

The double-entry accounting system introduced in Chapter 2 provides us with a framework for the analysis of business activities, and we used that framework to record transactions and create financial reports. This chapter describes more fully the procedures companies use to account for the operations of a business during a specific time period. All companies, regardless of size or complexity, perform accounting steps, known as the *accounting cycle*, to accumulate and report their financial information. An important step in the accounting cycle is the *adjusting* process that occurs at the end of every reporting period. This chapter focuses on the accounting cycle with emphasis on the adjusting process.

ACCOUNTING CYCLE

LO1 Identify the major steps in the accounting cycle.

Companies engage in business activities. These activities are analyzed for their financial impact, and the results from that analysis are entered into the accounting information system. When management and others want to know where the company stands financially, and what its recent performance tells about future prospects, the financial data often require adjustment prior to financial statements being prepared. At the end of the accounting period, the company *closes the books*. This closing process prepares accounts for the next accounting period.

The process described constitutes the major steps in the **accounting cycle**—a sequence of activities to accumulate and report financial statements. The steps are: analyze, record, adjust, report, and close. Exhibit 3.1 shows the sequence of major steps in the accounting cycle.

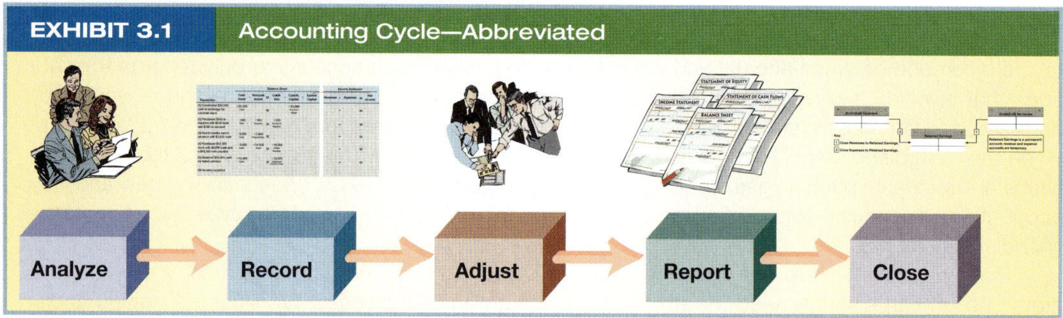

EXHIBIT 3.1 Accounting Cycle—Abbreviated

The steps in the accounting cycle do not occur with equal frequency. That is, companies analyze and record daily transactions throughout the accounting period, but they adjust and report only when management requires financial statements, often monthly or quarterly, but at least annually. Closing occurs once during the accounting cycle, at the period-end.

The annual (one-year) accounting period adopted by a company is known as its **fiscal year**. Companies with fiscal year-ends on December 31 are said to be on a **calendar year**. About 60% of U.S. companies are on a calendar-year basis. Many companies prefer to have their accounting year coincide with their "natural" year; that is, the fiscal year ends when business is slow. For example,

Limited Brands Inc., a specialty retailer, ends its fiscal year on the Friday nearest January 31. **Starbucks Corporation** ends its fiscal year on the Sunday nearest to October 1. The **Boston Celtics**, a professional basketball team, ends its fiscal year on June 30, during its off-season.

ANALYZING AND RECORDING TRANSACTIONS

The purpose of this section is to (1) review the analysis and recording of transactions as described in Chapter 2, and (2) to extend the Natural Beauty Supply example to illustrate the process of adjusting and closing accounts in the next section. Natural Beauty Supply's fiscal year-end is December 31.

LO2 Review the process of journalizing and posting transactions.

Review of Accounting Procedures

The **chart of accounts** for Natural Beauty Supply is in Exhibit 3.2, and lists the titles and numbers of all accounts found in its general ledger. The account titles are grouped into the five major sections of the general ledger (assets, liabilities, equity, revenues, and expenses). Recall from Chapter 2 that the recording process involves analyzing, journalizing, and posting. Also recall that the **general journal**, or *book of original entry*, is a tabular record where business activities are captured in debits and credits and recorded in chronological order before they are posted to the general ledger. The word *journalize* means to record a transaction in a **journal**. Each transaction entered in the journal must be stated in terms of equal dollar amounts of debits and credits—the double-entry system at work. The account titles cited must correspond to those in the general ledger (per the chart of accounts).

EXHIBIT 3.2	Chart of Accounts for Natural Beauty Supply

Assets	**Equity**
110 Cash	310 Common Stock
120 Accounts Receivable	320 Retained Earnings
130 Other Receivables	
140 Inventory	**Revenues and Income**
150 Prepaid Insurance	410 Sales Revenue
160 Security Deposit	420 Interest Income
170 Fixtures and Equipment	
175 Accumulated Depreciation—	**Expenses**
Fixtures and Equipment	510 Cost of Goods Sold
	520 Wages Expense
Liabilities	530 Rent Expense
210 Accounts Payable	540 Advertising Expense
220 Interest Payable	550 Depreciation Expense—
230 Wages Payable	Fixtures and Equipment
240 Taxes Payable	560 Insurance Expense
250 Unearned Revenue	570 Interest Expense
260 Notes Payable	580 Tax Expense

After transactions are journalized, the debits and credits in each journal entry are transferred to their related general ledger accounts. This transcribing process is called posting to the general ledger, or simply **posting**. Journalizing and posting occur simultaneously when recordkeeping is automated. When records are kept manually, posting from the general journal can be done daily, every few days, or at the end of a month. Today, computers are used extensively to perform mechanical accounting tasks such as posting.

FYI Demand for information is often immediate in our fast-paced economy. Accordingly, electronic files of the ledger usually contain up-to-date account balances.

Review of Recording Transactions

In Chapter 2, we recorded the November activities of Natural Beauty Supply (NBS) and created the end-of-November financial statements. As NBS continues its activities into the next month, the end-of-November balance sheet provides the starting point for December. Exhibit 3.3 provides a summary of Natural Beauty Supply's December transactions

EXHIBIT 3.3		Transactions for Natural Beauty Supply for December 2010
Event	**Date**	**Description**
(17)	Dec. 1	NBS signed a three-year note to borrow $11,000 cash from a financial institution. NBS will pay interest on the first day of every month at the rate of 12% per year or 1% per month. The $11,000 principal is due at the end of three years.
(18)	Dec. 1	NBS purchased and installed improved fixtures and equipment for $18,000 cash.
(19)	Dec. 10	NBS paid $700 to advertise in the local newspaper for December.
(20)	Dec. 20	NBS paid $3,300 cash to its suppliers in partial payment for the delivery of inventory in November.
(21)	Dec. —	During the month of December, NBS sold products costing $5,000 to retail customers for $8,500 cash.
(22)	Dec. —	During the month of December, sales to wholesale customers totaled $4,500 for merchandise that had cost $3,000. Instead of paying cash, wholesale customers are required to pay for the merchandise within ten working days.
(23)	Dec. —	$1,200 of gift certificates were sold during the month of December. Each gift certificate entitles the recipient to a one-hour consultation on the use of NBS' products.
(24)	Dec. —	NBS employed salespersons who were paid $1,625 in cash in December.
(25)	Dec. —	During the month of December, NBS received $3,200 in cash from wholesale customers for products that had been delivered earlier.
(26)	Dec. 28	NBS purchased and received $4,000 of inventory on account.
(27)	Dec. 31	NBS paid $1,500 to the landlord for December rent.
(28)	Dec. 31	NBS paid $50 cash dividend to its shareholders.

Most of these transactions are similar to those that we analyzed in Chapter 2. Each of the transactions involves an exchange of some kind. Suppliers provide inventory and employees provide labor services in exchange for cash or the promise of future cash payments. Customers receive products in exchange for cash or a promise to pay cash in the future. For each of these items, we analyze, journalize, and post as shown in Chapter 2.

NBS has the opportunity to secure long-term financing from a financial institution, and signs a note that must be paid back at the end of three years. Cash increases, and a noncurrent liability increases. Interest payments are made at the start of every month, beginning on January 2, 2011, but no entry is made for interest until time passes and an interest obligation is created.

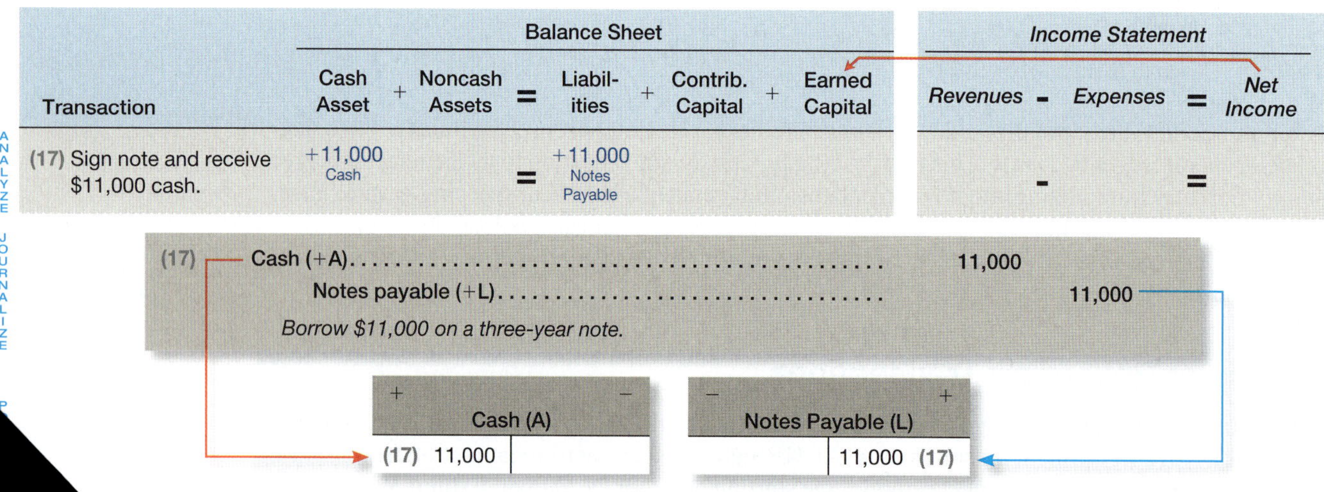

NBS pays $18,000 cash to purchase improved fixtures and equipment for its store location. One asset (cash) decreases, while a noncurrent asset (Fixtures and Equipment) goes up.

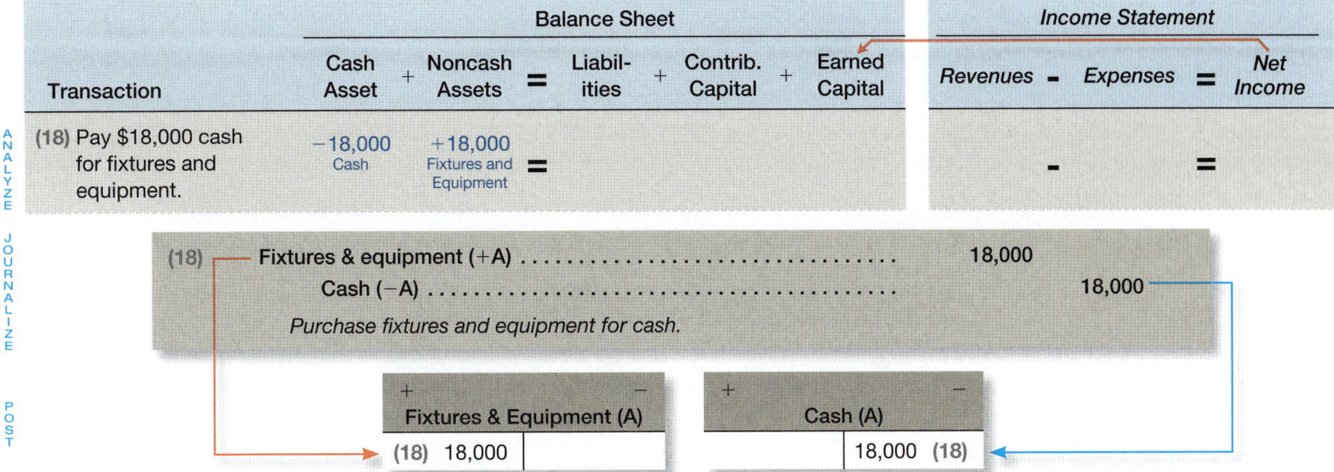

Transactions (19) and (20) are similar to ones that we saw in Chapter 2. The expenditure for advertising results in an expense that decreases net income and ultimately, retained earnings. The payment to suppliers fulfills (in part) an obligation that appeared in the November 30 balance sheet.

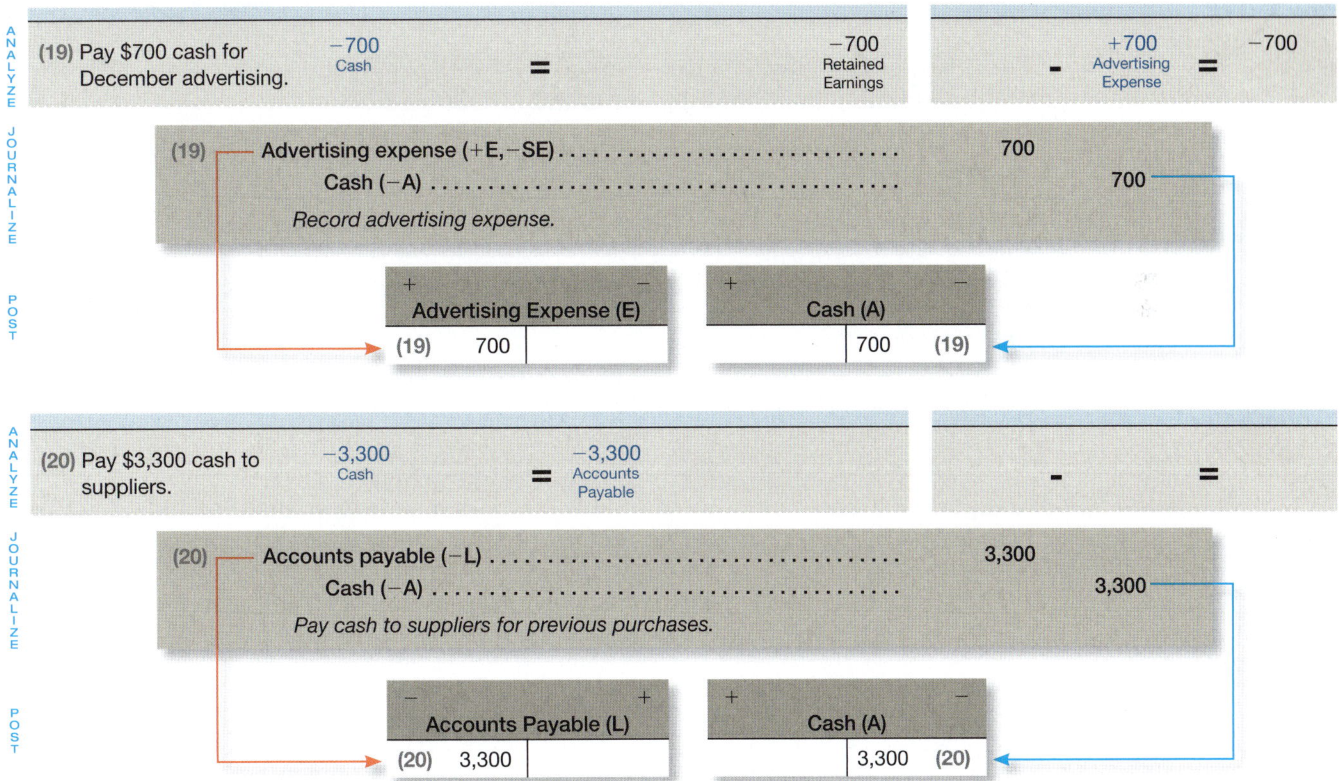

Sales to customers in (21), (22), and (23) are also similar to transactions in Chapter 2, and they are accounted for in similar fashion. Revenue is recognized when products are delivered to customers, rather than when cash is received. When cash is received after delivery, an accounts receivable asset is recognized; when cash is received before delivery, an unearned revenue liability is recognized. Cost of goods sold expense is recognized when the associated revenue is recognized.

Balance Sheet
Income Statement
Transaction
Cash Asset + Noncash Assets = Liabil-ities + Contrib. Capital + Earned Capital
Revenues - Expenses = Net Income
(21a) Sell $8,500 of products for cash.
+8,500 Cash
=
+8,500 Retained Earnings
+8,500 Sales Revenue
-
=
+8,500
(21a) Cash (+A).................................... 8,500
Sales revenue (+R,+SE)............................ 8,500
Sell products for cash.
+
Cash (A)
-
(21a) 8,500
-
Sales Revenue (R)
+
8,500 (21a)
(21b) Record $5,000 for the cost of merchandise sold in transaction 21a.
-5,000 Inventory =
-5,000 Retained Earnings
+5,000 Cost of Goods Sold = -5,000
(21b) Cost of goods sold (+E,-SE).......................... 5,000
Inventory (-A)................................. 5,000
Record cost of merchandise sold as expense.
+
Cost of Goods Sold (E)
-
(21b) 5,000
+
Inventory (A)
-
5,000 (21b)
(22a) Sell $4,500 of products on account.
+4,500 Accounts Receivable =
+4,500 Retained Earnings
+4,500 Sales Revenue
-
=
+4,500
(22a) Accounts receivable (+A)...................... 4,500
Sales revenue (+R,+SE)............................ 4,500
Sell products on account.
+
Accounts Receivable (A)
-
(22a) 4,500
-
Sales Revenue (R)
+
4,500 (22a)
(22b) Record $3,000 for the cost of merchandise sold in transaction 22a.
-3,000 Inventory =
-3,000 Retained Earnings
+3,000 Cost of Goods Sold = -3,000
(22b) Cost of goods sold (+E,-SE).......................... 3,000
Inventory (-A)................................. 3,000
Record cost of merchandise sold as expense.
+
Cost of Goods Sold (E)
-
(22b) 3,000
+
Inventory (A)
-
3,000 (22b)
ANALYZE JOURNALIZE POST

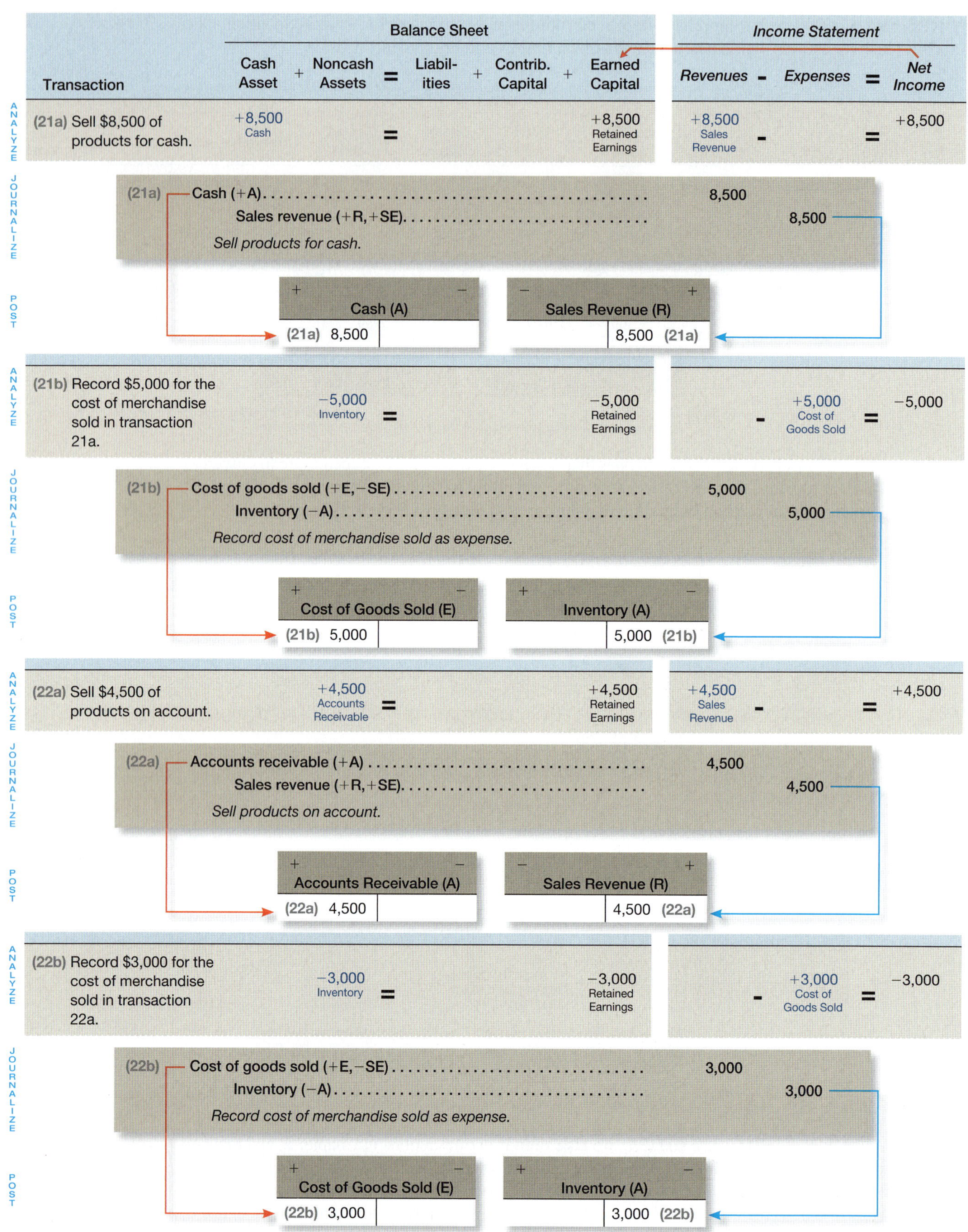

continued

continued from previous page

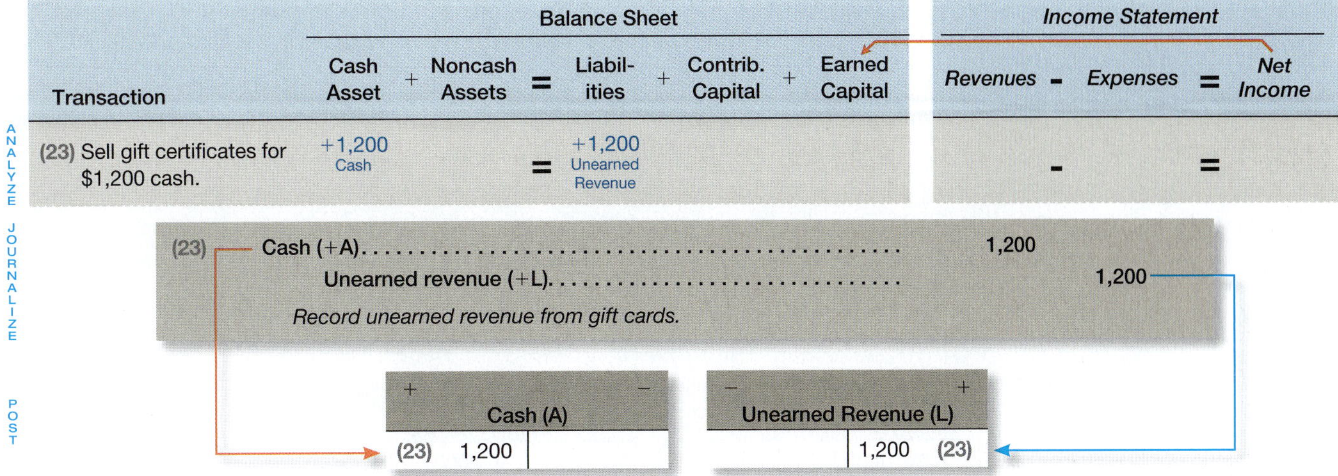

The final five transactions in December also are similar to transactions that NBS had in November. Payment of wages to the employee is reflected in a wage expense. Cash received from wholesale (credit) customers does not cause revenue; rather the increase in cash is balanced by a decrease in accounts receivable. Purchase of inventory on account does not create an expense—the cost of the inventory is held in the inventory asset account until it is purchased by a customer. Payments to the landlord are balanced by a rent expense in the income statement. The cash dividend to shareholders decreases an asset (cash) and shareholders' equity (retained earnings), but does not affect the income statement.

continued

continued from previous page

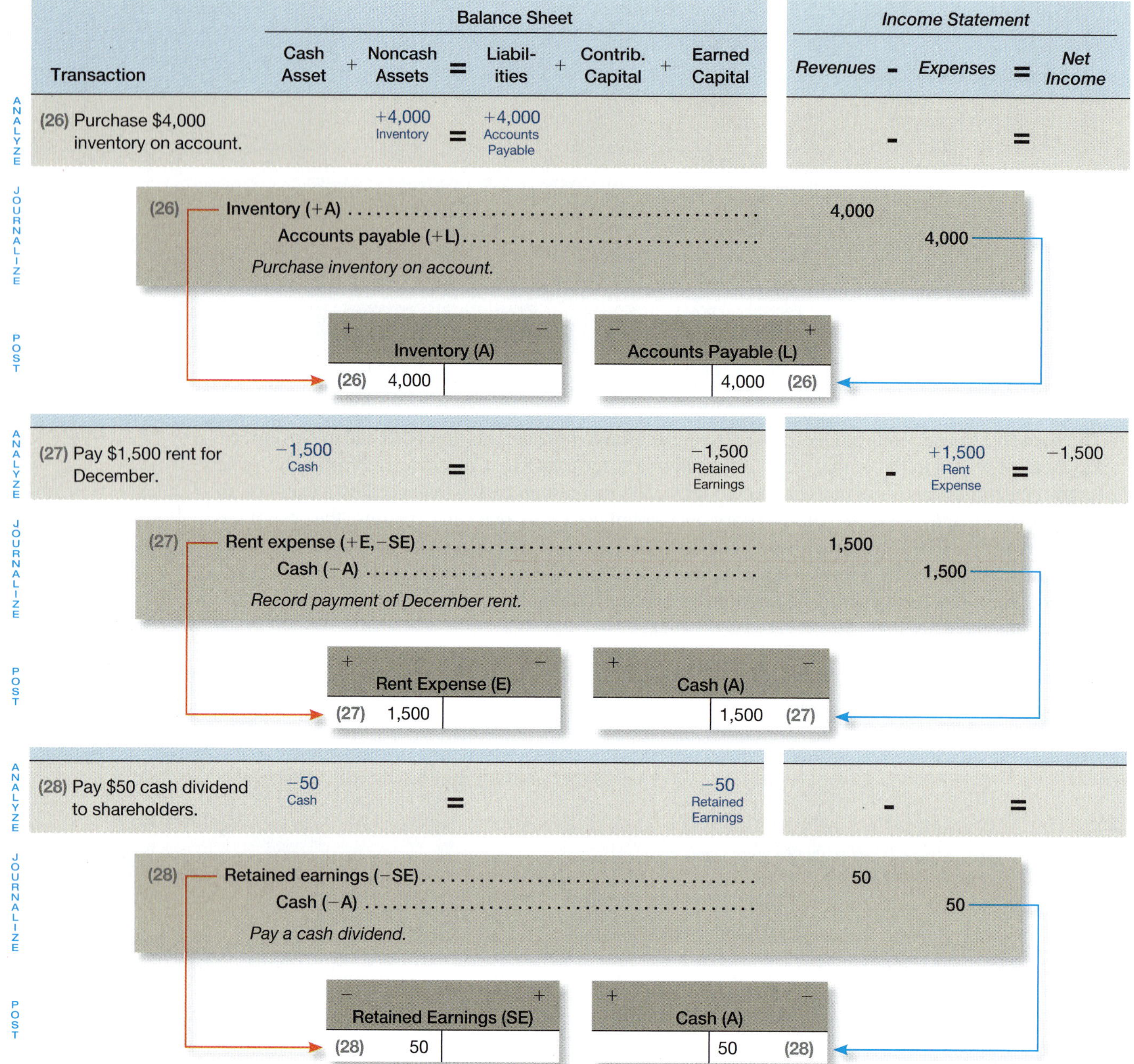

Exhibit 3.4 presents the general ledger accounts of Natural Beauty Supply in T-account form for December. Each balance sheet account has an opening balance equal to the end-of-November balance, and each income statement account starts with a zero balance so it records only the events of the current period. The December transactions (17–28) have been posted. You can trace each of the postings from the transactions above to these ledger accounts.

But the amounts in these accounts are not ready to be assembled into financial reports. There are revenues and expenses and changes in assets and liabilities that occur with the passage of time.[1] Accounting for these items is essential for us to determine how well a company has performed in an accounting period and to assess its financial standing.

---

[1] Natural Beauty Supply's November activities in Chapter 2 were carefully chosen so we could produce financial statements without adjusting entries. But, as Exhibit 3.1 depicts, the adjusting process is an essential part of the accounting cycle.

EXHIBIT 3.4	General Ledger for Natural Beauty Supply before Adjustments

General Ledger

| Assets | | | = | Liabilities | | + | Equity | |

Cash (A) (+ / −)

Bal.	8,100		
(17)	11,000	18,000	(18)
(21a)	8,500	700	(19)
(23)	1,200	3,300	(20)
(25)	3,200	1,625	(24)
		1,500	(27)
		50	(28)
Bal.	6,825		

Accounts Receivable (A) (+ / −)

Bal.	950		
(22a)	4,500	3,200	(25)
Bal.	2,250		

Inventory (A) (+ / −)

Bal.	11,300		
(26)	4,000	5,000	(21b)
		3,000	(22b)
Bal.	7,300		

Prepaid Insurance (A) (+ / −)

Bal.	1,680	
Bal.	1,680	

Security Deposit (A) (+ / −)

Bal.	2,000	
Bal.	2,000	

Fixtures and Equipment (A) (+ / −)

Bal.	0	
(18)	18,000	
Bal.	18,000	

Accounts Payable (L) (− / +)

		3,700	Bal.
(20)	3,300	4,000	(26)
		4,400	Bal.

Unearned Revenue (L) (− / +)

	300	Bal.
	1,200	(23)
	1,500	Bal.

Notes Payable (L) (− / +)

	0	Bal.
	11,000	(17)
	11,000	Bal.

Common Stock (SE) (− / +)

	20,000	Bal.
	20,000	Bal.

Retained Earnings (SE) (− / +)

		30	Bal.
(28)	50		
Bal.	20		

Sales Revenue (R) (− / +)

		8,500	(21a)
		4,500	(22a)
		13,000	Bal.

Cost of Goods Sold (E) (+ / −)

(21b)	5,000	
(22b)	3,000	
Bal.	8,000	

Wages Expense (E) (+ / −)

(24)	1,625	
Bal.	1,625	

Rent Expense (E) (+ / −)

(27)	1,500	
Bal.	1,500	

Advertising Expense (E) (+ / −)

(19)	700	
Bal.	700	

Assets = $37,570 = **Liabilities = $16,940** + **Equity = $20,630**

ADJUSTING THE ACCOUNTS

It is important that accounts in financial statements be properly reported. For many accounts, the balances shown in the general ledger after all transactions are posted are not the proper balances for financial statements. Thus, when it is time to prepare financial statements, management must review account balances and make proper adjustments to these balances. The adjustments required are based on accrual accounting and generally accepted accounting principles. This section focuses on these issues.

LO3 Describe the adjusting process and illustrate adjusting entries.

Preparing an Unadjusted Trial Balance

The T-accounts in Exhibit 3.4 show balances for each account after recording all transactions, and this set of balances is called an **unadjusted trial balance** because it shows account balances before any adjustments are made. The purpose of an unadjusted trial balance is to be sure the general ledger is in balance before management adjusts the accounts. Showing all general ledger account balances in one place also makes it easier to review accounts and determine which account balances require adjusting. Natural Beauty Supply's unadjusted trial balance at December 31 is in Exhibit 3.5.

EXHIBIT 3.5	Unadjusted Trial Balance		
NATURAL BEAUTY SUPPLY **Unadjusted Trial Balance** **December 31, 2010**			
		Debit	**Credit**
Cash		$ 6,825	
Accounts Receivable		2,250	
Inventory		7,300	
Prepaid Insurance		1,680	
Security Deposit		2,000	
Fixtures & Equipment		18,000	
Accounts Payable			$ 4,400
Unearned Revenue			1,500
Notes Payable			11,000
Common Stock			20,000
Retained Earnings		20	
Sales Revenue			13,000
Cost of Goods Sold		8,000	
Wages Expense		1,625	
Rent Expense		1,500	
Advertising Expense		700	
Totals		$49,900	$49,900

Types of Adjustments

Accrual adjustments are caused by a variety of accounting practices. There are some revenues and expenses that arise with the passage of time, rather than in a transaction. There are asset and liability values that change over time or that require estimation based on recent events. All of these require adjustments before proper financial statements can be produced.

Adjusting entries have two common characteristics. First, they occur at the end of a reporting period, just before the construction of financial statements. Second, they (almost) never involve cash. Changes in cash require a transaction, and adjusting entries are not transactions.

Through the course of this book, we will encounter quite a few required adjusting entries, but we will start with four general types of adjustments made at the end of an accounting period.

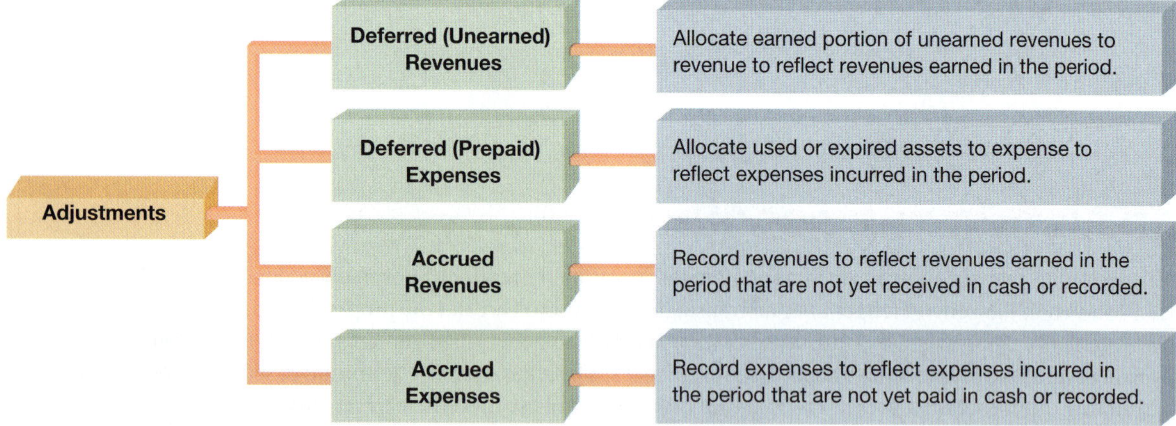

Journal entries made to reflect these adjustments are known as **adjusting entries**. Each adjusting entry usually affects a balance sheet account (an asset or liability account) and an income statement account (an expense or revenue account). The first two types of adjustments—allocating assets to expense and allocating unearned revenues to revenue—are often referred to as **deferrals**. The distinguishing characteristic of a deferral is that the adjustment deals with an amount previously recorded in a balance sheet account; the adjusting entry decreases the balance sheet account and increases an income statement account. The last two types of adjustments—accruing expenses and accruing revenues—are often referred to as **accruals**. The unique characteristic of an accrual is that the adjustment deals with an amount not previously recorded in any account; the type of adjusting entry increases both a balance sheet account and an income statement account. Both accruals and deferrals allow revenue to be recognized when it is earned and realizable and the expenses of the period to be matched against the revenues from that period's operations. Let's consider each of these adjustments in more detail.

Type 1: Deferred Revenue—Allocating Unearned Revenue to Revenue

Companies often receive fees for services before services are rendered. Such transactions are recorded by debiting Cash and crediting a liability account for the **unearned revenue**—also referred to as **deferred revenue**. This account reflects the obligation for performing future services. As services are performed, revenue is earned. At period-end, an adjusting entry records the revenue that was earned in the current accounting period and the liability amount that was reduced.

DEFERRED REVENUE   During November and December, Natural Beauty Supply sold gift certificates that entitled the recipient to a one-hour consultation with a salesperson on the use of natural and organic health and beauty products. When the gift certificates were purchased, NBS recognized an unearned revenue liability that reflected the obligation to provide these services. During the month of December, gift certificates totaling $900 were redeemed. On December 31, Natural Beauty Supply made the adjustment (a) in the following template, journal entry, and T-accounts to recognize the (partial) fulfillment of the obligation and to recognize that $900 of revenue has now been earned. The $900 increase in sales revenue is reflected in net income and carried over to retained earnings.

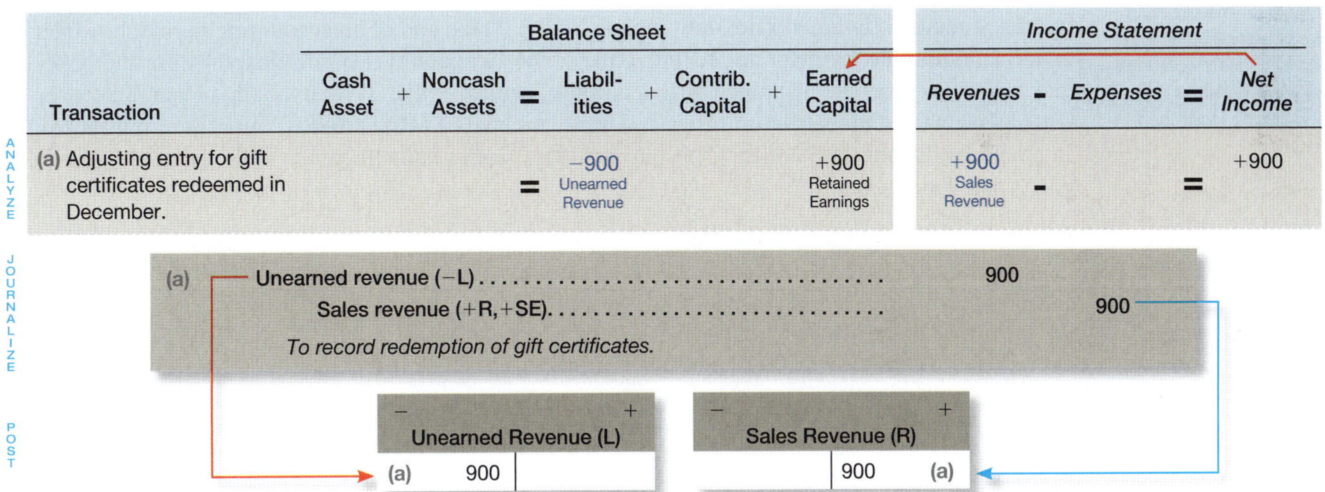

After this entry (a) is posted, the unearned revenue liability account has a balance of $600 for the remaining gift certificates outstanding, and the sales revenue account reflects the $900 earned in December.

In this case, the cost of the salesperson's time has already been recognized as an expense. If Natural Beauty Supply's gift certificates had been redeemable for products, then we would have had to recognize a cost of goods sold expense for the items purchased with the redeemed certificates.

Other examples of revenues received in advance include gift cards, rental payments received in advance by real estate management companies, insurance premiums received in advance by insurance companies, subscription revenues received in advance by magazine and newspaper publishers, and membership fees received in advance by health clubs. In each case, a liability account is set up when the advance payment is received. Later, an adjusting entry is made to reflect the revenues earned from the services provided or products delivered during the period.

YOU MAKE THE CALL

You are the Chief Accountant   REI requires customers of its travel-vacation business to make an initial deposit equal to $400 when the trip is reserved and to make full payment two months before departure. REI's refunding policy is to return the entire deposit if the customer informs REI of the trip's cancellation three or more months in advance of the trip. REI will refund all but $400 of the deposit if the customer cancels between 60 and 90 days prior to the trip or 50% of the deposit if a customer cancels between 30 and 60 days prior to the trip. There is no refund if notification occurs within 30 days of the trip. REI's cancellation rate is very low. How should you account for deposits, and when should revenue be recorded? [Answers on page 122]

Type 2: Prepaid Expenses—Allocating Assets to Expenses

Many cash outlays benefit several accounting periods. Examples are purchases of buildings, equipment, and supplies; prepayments of rent and advertising; and payments of insurance premiums covering several periods. These outlays are debited to an asset account when the expenditure occurs. Then at the end of each accounting period, the estimated portion of the outlay that has expired in that period or has benefited that period, is transferred to an expense account.

We can usually see when adjustments of this type are needed by inspecting the unadjusted trial balance for costs that benefit several periods. Looking at the December 31 trial balance of Natural Beauty Supply (Exhibit 3.5), for example, adjustments are required to record the costs of prepaid insurance and the fixtures and equipment for the month of December.

PREPAID INSURANCE   On November 30, Natural Beauty Supply paid one year's insurance premium in advance and debited the $1,680 payment to Prepaid Insurance, an asset account. As each day passes and the insurance coverage is being used, insurance expense is being incurred, and the prepaid insurance is decreasing. It is not necessary to record insurance expense on a daily basis because financial statements are not prepared daily. At the end of an accounting period, however, an adjustment must be made to recognize the proper amount of insurance expense for the period and to decrease prepaid insurance by that amount. On December 31, one month's insurance coverage has been used up, so Natural Beauty Supply transfers $140 ($1,680/12 months) from Prepaid Insurance to Insurance Expense. This entry is identified as adjustment (b) in the template, journal entry, and T-accounts.

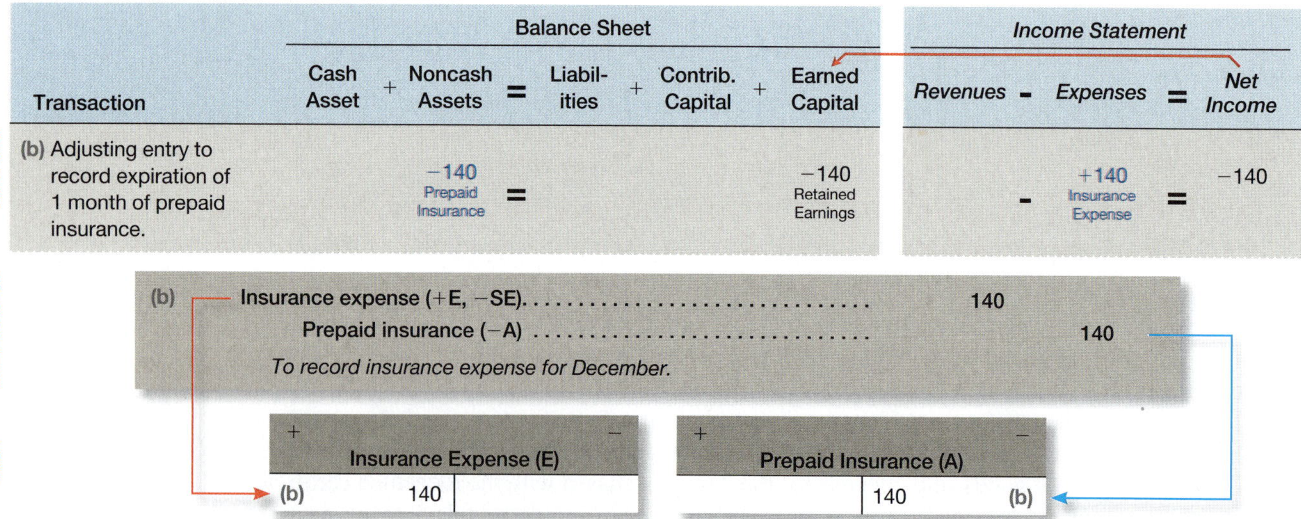

The posting of this adjusting entry creates the proper insurance expense of $140 for December in the Insurance Expense ledger account and reduces the Prepaid Insurance balance to the (eleven-month) amount that is prepaid as of December 31, which is $1,540.

Examples of other prepaid expenses for which similar adjustments are made include prepaid rent and prepaid advertising. When rent payments are made in advance, the amount is debited to a Prepaid Rent asset. At the end of an accounting period, the adjusting entry to record the portion of occupancy or usage that expired during the period must debit Rent Expense and credit Prepaid Rent. Similarly, when advertising services are purchased in advance, the payment is debited to Prepaid Advertising. At the end of an accounting period, an adjustment is needed to recognize the cost of any of the prepaid advertising used during the period. The adjusting entry debits Advertising Expense and credits Prepaid Advertising.

DEPRECIATION   The process of allocating the costs of equipment, vehicles, and buildings to the periods benefiting from their use is called **depreciation**. Each accounting period in which such assets are used must reflect a portion of their cost as expense because these assets helped generate revenue for those periods. This periodic expense is known as *depreciation expense*. Periodic depreciation expense is an estimate. The procedure we use here estimates the annual amount of depreciation expense by dividing the asset cost by its estimated useful life. (We assume that the entire asset cost is depreciated—so-called zero salvage value; later in the book we consider salvage values other than zero.) This method is called **straight-line depreciation** (used by the great majority of companies).

Expenses are recorded when business activities reduce net assets. But when we record depreciation expense, the asset amount is not reduced directly. Instead, the reduction is recorded in a contra account (labeled XA in the journal entries and T-accounts) called *Accumulated Depreciation*. **Contra accounts** are so named because they are used to record reductions in or offsets against a related account. The Accumulated Depreciation account normally has a credit balance and appears in the balance sheet as a deduction from the related asset amount. Use of the contra asset Accumulated Depreciation allows the original cost of the asset to be reported in the balance sheet, followed (and reduced) by the accumulated depreciation.

The fixtures and equipment purchased by Natural Beauty Supply for $18,000 are expected to last for four years. Straight-line depreciation recorded on the equipment is $4,500 per year ($18,000/4 years), or $375 per month ($18,000/48 months). At December 31, Natural Beauty Supply makes adjustment (c), as shown in the following template, journal entry, and T-accounts.

The introduction of contra assets requires a new column in the FSET for these accounts.[2] Increases in a contra asset decrease the net balance of the company's long-term assets. The new column is preceded by a minus sign to indicate that increases in contra assets create a decrease in the asset side of the accounting equation.

> **FYI**   Contra accounts are used to provide more information to users of financial statements. For example, Accumulated Depreciation is a contra asset reported in the balance sheet, which enables users to estimate asset age. For Natural Beauty Supply, the December 31 balance sheet reveals that its Fixtures and Equipment is nearly new as its accumulated depreciation is only $375, which is 1/48th of the $18,000 original cost.

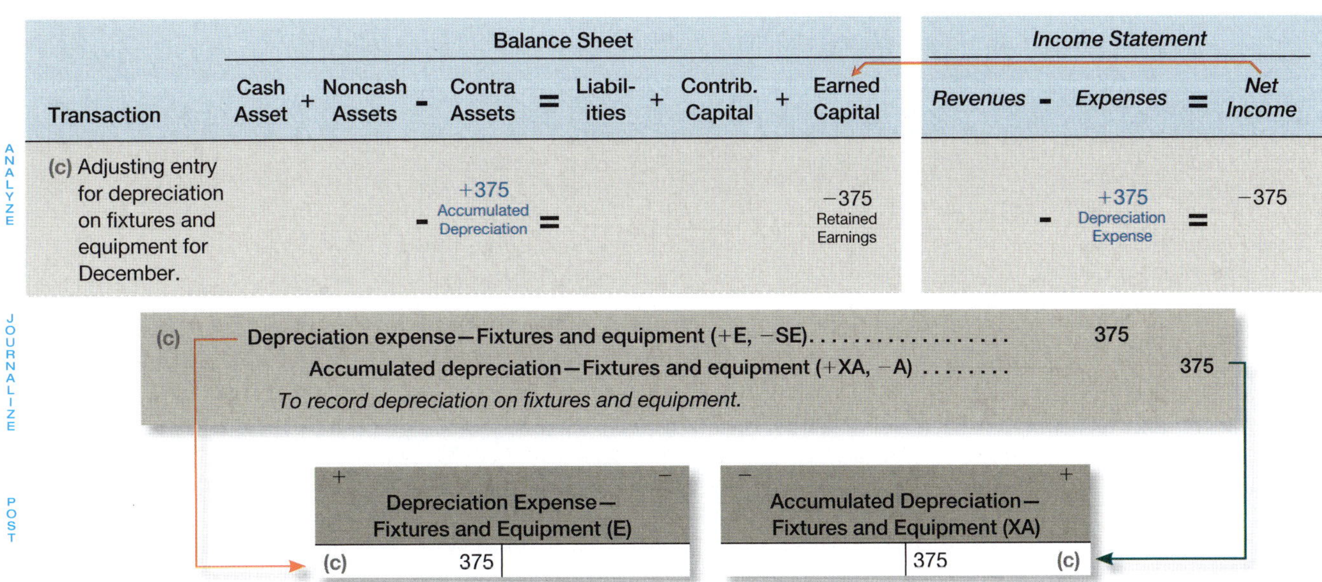

---

[2] Our practice will be to include a separate FSET column where contra assets are required, but not to do so all the time. As we progress through the topics in this text, we will also see examples of contra liability accounts and contra equity accounts.

When this entry is posted, it properly reflects the cost of using this asset during December, and the $375 depreciation appears in the December income statement. On the balance sheet, the accumulated depreciation is subtracted from the asset amount. The resulting balance (cost less accumulated depreciation), which is the asset's **book value**, represents the unexpired asset cost to be allocated as an expense in future periods. For example, the December 31, 2010, balance sheet reports the equipment with a book value of $17,625, as follows.

Fixtures and Equipment	$18,000
Less: Accumulated depreciation	375
Fixtures and Equipment, net..	$17,625 (book value)

In each subsequent month, $375 will be recognized as depreciation expense, and the accumulated depreciation contra asset will increase by the same amount (from $375 to $750 to $1,125 and so on). As a result, the book value of the fixtures and equipment will decrease by $375 each month.

Type 3: Accrued Revenues

Revenues should be recognized in the period in which they are earned and realizable. Yet a company may provide services or earn income during a period that are neither paid for by clients or customers nor billed at the end of the period. Such values should be included in the firm's current period income statement. To accomplish this, end-of-period adjusting entries are made to reflect any revenues or income for the period that have been earned and realized, but are not received or billed. Such accumulated revenue is often called **accrued revenue** or **accrued income**.

ACCRUED SALES REVENUE/INCOME   At the end of December, Natural Beauty Supply learns that its bank has decided to provide interest on checking accounts for small businesses like NBS. Each month, NBS earns interest income based on the average balance in its checking account. The interest will be paid into NBS's checking account on the fifth business day of the following month. Based on its average daily balance, NBS earned $30 in interest during December.

In this instance, Natural Beauty Supply will not receive the interest payment until January. Nevertheless, the company has earned interest during the month of December, and it is sure to collect the amount owed. Therefore, it should recognize an interest receivable (or "other receivables") asset and an interest income in the income statement. (We might also call this interest revenue, but the term interest income is more commonly used for nonfinancial companies.) The entry in the FSET, the journal entry, and the T-account posting would be as follows.

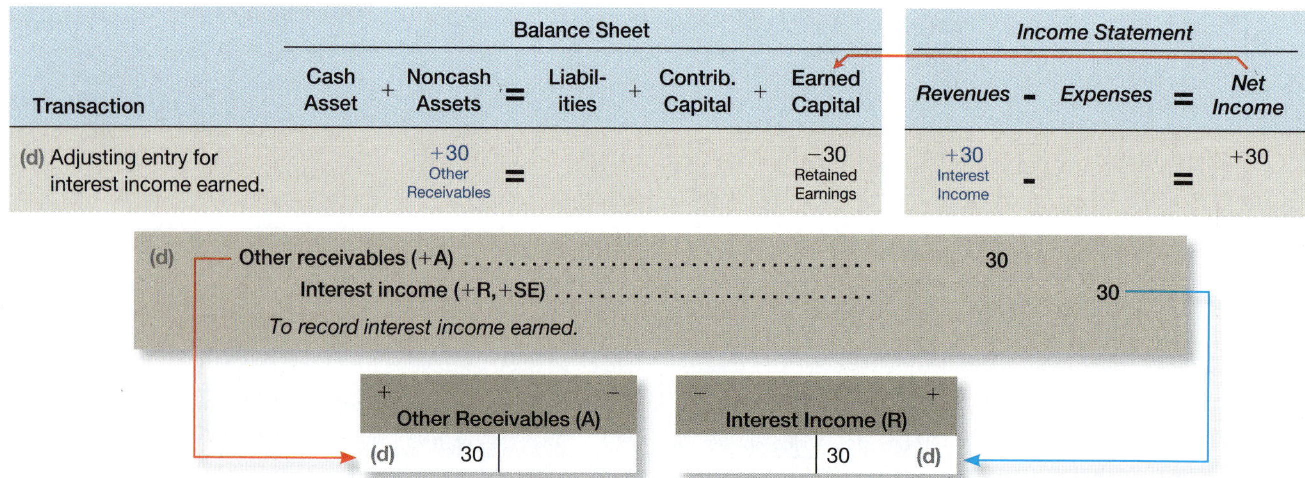

Revenue accruals also occur for landlords who receive rent payments after they are earned and for companies who engage in long-term projects in construction or consulting. In all these cases, revenue has been earned over time without a transaction in which a finished product is delivered to a customer. We will look into these issues more closely in Chapter 6.

Type 4: Accrued Expenses   Companies often incur expenses before paying for them. Wages, interest, utilities, and taxes are examples of expenses that are incurred before cash payment is made. Usually the payments are made at regular intervals of time, such as weekly, monthly, quarterly, or annually. If the accounting period ends on a date that does not coincide with a scheduled cash payment date, an adjusting entry is required to reflect the expense incurred since the last cash payment. Such an expense is referred to as an **accrued expense**. Natural Beauty Supply has three such required adjustments for December 31; one for wages, one for interest and one for income tax.

ACCRUED WAGES   Natural Beauty Supply employees are paid on a weekly basis. Recall that wages of $1,625 were paid during December in transaction 24. However, as of December 31, the company's employees have earned wages of $480 that will be paid in January. Wages expense of $480 must be recorded in the income statement for December because the employees earned those wages, which helped generate revenues for December.

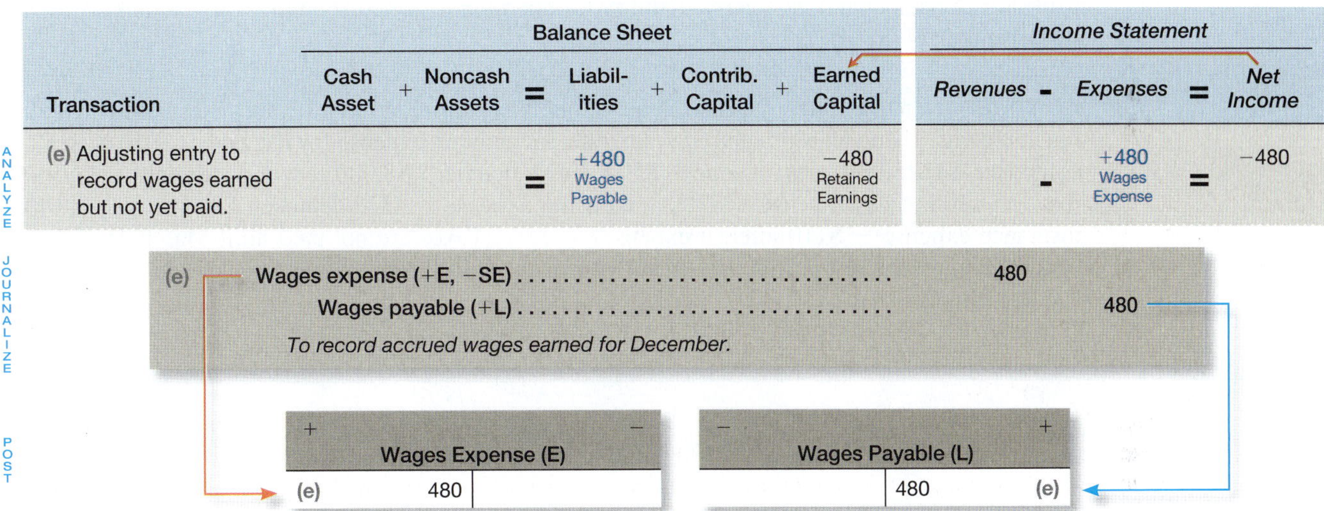

This adjustment enables the firm to reflect as December expense the cost of all wages *incurred* during the month rather than just the wages *paid*. In addition, the balance sheet shows the liability for unpaid wages at the end of the period.

When the employees are paid in January, the following entry is made.

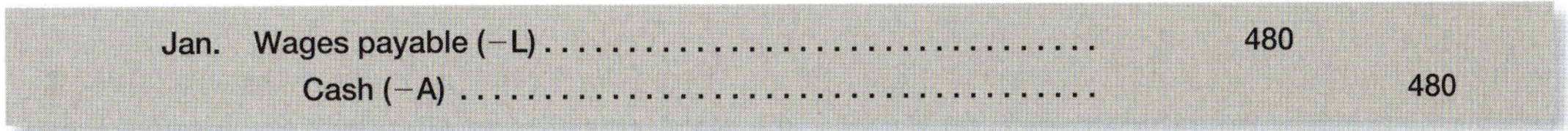

This entry eliminates the liability recorded in Wages Payable at the end of December and reduces Cash for the wages paid.

ACCRUED INTEREST   On December 1, 2010, Natural Beauty Supply signed a three-year note payable for $11,000. This note has a 12% annual interest rate and requires monthly (interest-only) payments (1% per month), payable on the first day of the following month. (The interest payment for the month of December is due on January 1.) The $11,000 principal on the note is due at the end of three years. An adjusting entry is required at December 31, 2010, to record interest expense for December. December's interest is $110[$11,000 $\times$ (12%/12 months)], and at December 31 NBS makes adjustment (f) in the following template, journal entry, and T-accounts.

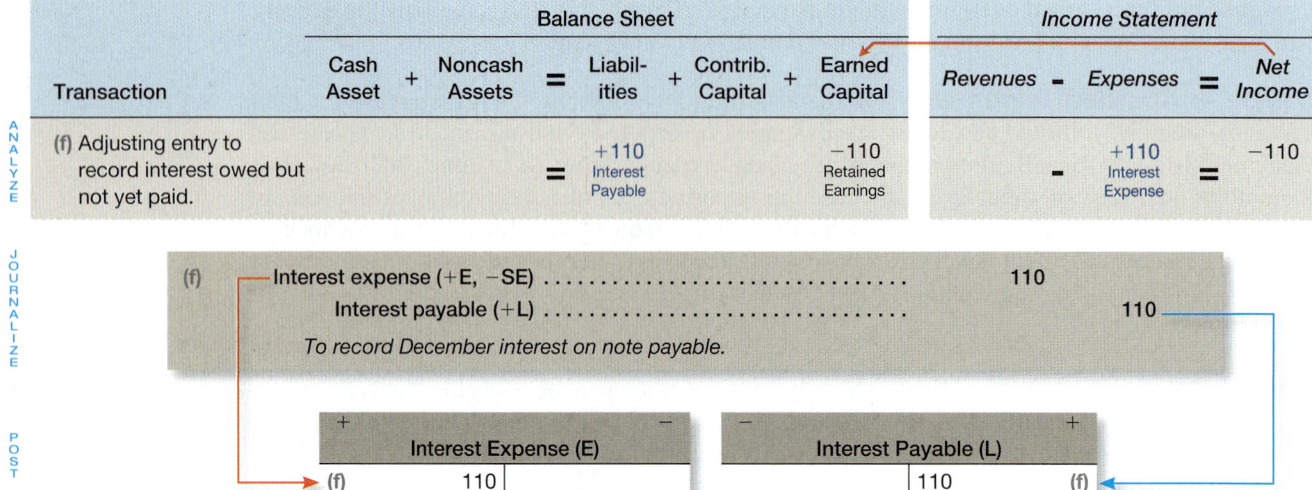

When these entries are posted to the general ledger, the accounts show the correct interest expense for December and the interest liability for one month's interest on the note that has accrued by December 31.

ACCRUED INCOME TAX   Natural Beauty Supply is required to pay income taxes based on how much it earns. Using an estimated 35% tax rate, income tax expense for December 2010 is $350, computed as ($13,900 sales revenue + $30 interest income − $8,000 cost of goods sold − $1,500 rent − $2,105 wages expense − $700 advertising expense − $375 depreciation expense − $140 insurance expense − $110 interest expense) × 35%. Taxes are not paid until March 15, 2011. Natural Beauty Supply makes adjustment (g) for taxes in the following template, journal entry, and T-accounts.

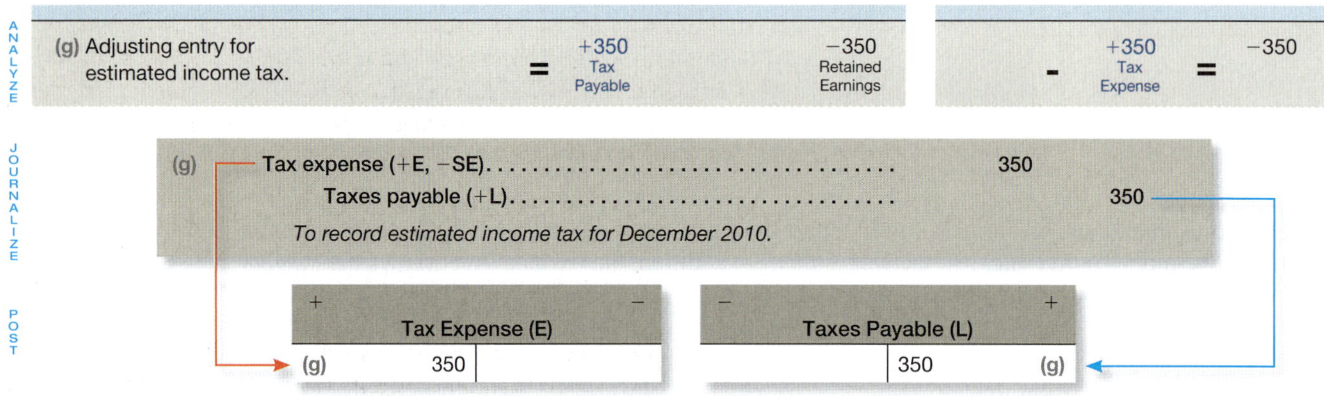

Exhibit 3.6 summarizes the four types of accounting adjustments, the usual journal entries required for each, and their financial impacts on the balance sheet and income statements.

Ethics and Adjusting Entries

When companies engage in transactions, there is some evidence of the exchange. Cash increases or decreases; asset and liability levels change. Adjusting entries are much more dependent on estimation processes. What was the value of service provided to customers, but not yet billed? What obligations have arisen in the past period without a transaction? What is their value? What is the expected useful life of our depreciable assets?

The usefulness of financial performance measures such as net income depends on these questions being answered to the best of management's ability. However, there may be pressures not to

EXHIBIT 3.6	Summary of Accounting Adjustments			
			Financial Effects If Not Adjusted	
Accounting Adjustment	**Examples**	**Adjusting Entry**	**Balance Sheet**	**Income Statement**
Deferrals:				
Unearned revenues	Delivery on advances from clients, gift cards, and subscribers	Dr. Liability Cr. Revenue	Liability overstated Equity understated	Revenue understated
Prepaid expenses	Expiration of prepaid rent, insurance, and advertising ; depreciation of buildings and equipment	Dr. Expense Cr. Asset (or Contra asset)	Asset overstated Equity overstated	Expense understated
Accruals:				
Accrued revenues	Earned but not received service, sales, and interest revenues	Dr. Asset Cr. Revenue	Asset understated Equity understated	Revenue understated
Accrued expenses	Incurred but unpaid wages, interest, and tax expenses	Dr. Expense Cr. Liability	Liabilty understated Equity overstated	Expense understated

provide the most accurate information. For instance, an estimate might convey information about management's strategy that could be used by competitors. Or, the financial community may have set expectations for performance that management cannot meet by executing its current business plan. In these circumstances, a manager may be pressured to use the discretion inherent in the reporting process to meet analysts' expectations or to disguise a planned course of action.

The financial reporting environment described in Chapter 1 imposes significant controls on financial reporting, because that reporting process is so important to the health of the economy. Managers who do not report accurately and completely may be subject to severe penalties. Moreover, adjusting entry estimates have a "self-correcting" character. Underestimating expenses today means greater expenses tomorrow; overestimating revenues today means lower revenues tomorrow.

MID-CHAPTER REVIEW

The following transactions relate to Lundholm Transport Company.

a. The Supplies and Parts balance on September 30, 2010, the company's accounting year-end, reveals $100,000 available. This amount reflects its beginning-year balance and all purchases for the year. A physical inventory indicates that much of this balance has been used in service operations, leaving supplies valued at $9,000 remaining at year-end September 30, 2010.

b. A $5,000 bill for September and October rent on the warehouse was received on September 29, but has not yet been paid or recorded.

c. A building holding its offices was purchased for $400,000 five years ago. The building's life was estimated at 8 years. Assume the entire asset cost is depreciated over its useful life. No depreciation has been recorded for this fiscal year.

d. An executive was hired on September 15 with an annual $120,000 salary. Payment and work are to start on October 15. No entry has yet been made to record this event.

e. A services contract is signed with the local university on September 1. Lundholm Transport Company received $1,200 cash on September 1 as a retainer for the months of September and October, but it has not yet been recorded. Lundholm Transport Company retains the money whether the university requires its services or not.

f. Employees are paid on the first day of the month following the month in which work is performed. Wages earned in September, but not yet paid or recorded as of September 30, amount to $25,000.

Required

1. For each of the 6 transactions described: (1) enter their effects in the financial statement effects template, and (2) prepare the related journal entries. Lundholm Transport's ledger includes the following ledger accounts and unadjusted normal balances at September 30: Cash $80,000; Accounts Receivable $95,000;

Supplies and Parts $100,000; Building $400,000; Accumulated Depreciation—Building $200,000; Land $257,500; Accounts Payable $20,000; Wages Payable $0; Unearned Revenue $0; Common Stock $80,000; Retained Earnings $380,000; Services Revenue $720,000; Rent Expense $27,500; Depreciation Expense $0; Wages Expense $440,000; Supplies and Parts Expense $0.

2. Set up T-accounts for all ledger accounts in part 1 and enter the beginning unadjusted balance, the adjustments from part 1, and the adjusted ending balance.

The solution to this review problem can be found on pages 141–143.

CONSTRUCTING FINANCIAL STATEMENTS FROM ADJUSTED ACCOUNTS

LO4 Prepare financial statements from adjusted accounts.

This section explains the preparation of financial statements from the adjusted financial accounts.

Preparing an Adjusted Trial Balance

After adjustments are recorded and posted, the company prepares an adjusted trial balance. The **adjusted trial balance** lists all the general ledger account balances after adjustments. Much of the content for company financial statements is taken from an adjusted trial balance. Exhibit 3.7 shows the general ledger accounts for Natural Beauty Supply after adjustments, in T-account form.

The adjusted trial balance at December 31 for Natural Beauty Supply is prepared from its general ledger accounts and is in the right-hand two columns of Exhibit 3.8. We show the unadjusted balances along with the adjustments to highlight the adjustment process.

Preparing Financial Statements

A company prepares its financial statements from the adjusted trial balance (and sometimes other supporting information). The set of financial statements consists of (and is prepared in the order of) the income statement, statement of stockholders' equity, balance sheet, and statement of cash flows. The following diagram summarizes this process.

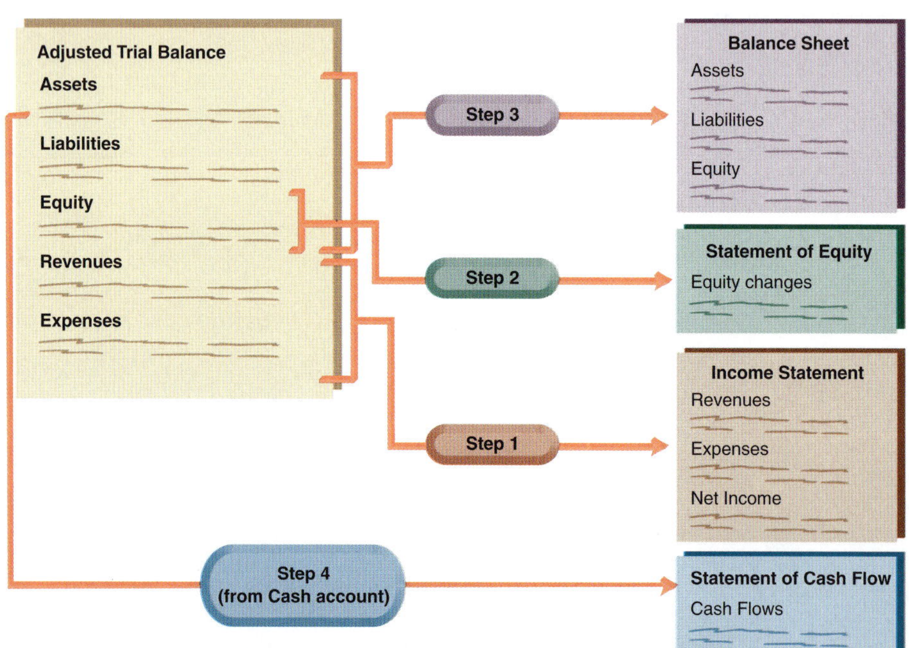

Income Statement   The income statement reports a company's revenues and expenses. Natural Beauty Supply's adjusted trial balance contains two revenue/income accounts and eight

EXHIBIT 3.7 — General Ledger for Natural Beauty Supply after Adjustments

General Ledger

Assets = Liabilities + Equity

Assets

+ Cash (A) −

Bal.	8,100		
(17)	11,000	18,000	(18)
(21a)	8,500	700	(19)
(23)	1,200	3,300	(20)
(25)	3,200	1,625	(24)
		1,500	(27)
		50	(28)
Bal.	6,825		

+ Accounts Receivable (A) −

Bal.	950		
(22a)	4,500	3,200	(25)
Bal.	2,250		

+ Other Receivables (A) −

Bal.	0		
(d)	30		
Bal.	30		

+ Inventory (A) −

Bal.	11,300		
(26)	4,000	5,000	(21b)
		3,000	(22b)
Bal.	7,300		

+ Prepaid Insurance (A) −

Bal.	1,680	140	(b)
Bal.	1,540		

+ Security Deposit (A) −

Bal.	2,000		
Bal.	2,000		

+ Fixtures and Equipment (A) −

Bal.	0		
(18)	18,000		
Bal.	18,000		

− Accumulated Depreciation—Fixtures and Equipment (XA) +

		0	Bal.
		375	(c)
		375	Bal.

Liabilities

− Accounts Payable (L) +

		3,700	Bal.
(20)	3,300	4,000	(26)
		4,400	Bal.

− Interest Payable (L) +

		0	Bal.
		110	(f)
		110	Bal.

− Wages Payable (L) +

		0	Bal.
		480	(e)
		480	Bal.

− Taxes Payable (L) +

		0	Bal.
		350	(g)
		350	Bal.

− Unearned Revenue (L) +

		300	Bal.
(a)	900	1,200	(23)
		600	Bal.

− Notes Payable (L) +

		0	Bal.
		11,000	(17)
		11,000	Bal.

Equity

− Common Stock (SE) +

		20,000	Bal.
		20,000	Bal.

− Retained Earnings (SE) +

		30	Bal.
(28)	50		
Bal.	20		

− Sales Revenue (R) +

		8,500	(21a)
		4,500	(22a)
		900	(a)
		13,900	Bal.

− Interest Income (R) +

		30	(d)
		30	Bal.

+ Cost of Goods Sold (E) −

(21b)	5,000		
(22b)	3,000		
Bal.	8,000		

+ Wages Expense (E) −

(24)	1,625		
(e)	480		
Bal.	2,105		

+ Rent Expense (E) −

(27)	1,500		
Bal.	1,500		

+ Advertising Expense (E) −

(19)	700		
Bal.	700		

+ Depreciation Expense—Fixtures and Equipment (E) −

(c)	375		
Bal.	375		

+ Insurance Expense (E) −

(b)	140		
Bal.	140		

+ Interest Expense (E) −

(f)	110		
Bal.	110		

+ Tax Expense (E) −

(g)	350		
Bal.	350		

Assets = $37,570 = Liabilities = $16,940 + Equity = $20,630

EXHIBIT 3.8	Unadjusted and Adjusted Trial Balances

NATURAL BEAUTY SUPPLY, INC.
Trial Balance
December 31, 2010

	Unadjusted Trial Balance		Adjustments				Adjusted Trial Balance	
	Debit	Credit	Debit		Credit		Debit	Credit
Cash.................................	$ 6,825						$ 6,825	
Accounts Receivable	2,250						2,250	
Other Receivables.....................			(d) $ 30				30	
Inventory	7,300						7,300	
Prepaid Insurance.....................	1,680				(b) $ 140		1,540	
Security Deposit	2,000						2,000	
Fixtures and Equipment	18,000						18,000	
Accumulated Depreciation					(c) 375			$ 375
Accounts Payable		$ 4,400						4,400
Interest Payable.......................					(f) 110			110
Wages Payable					(e) 480			480
Taxes Payable........................					(g) 350			350
Unearned Revenue		1,500	(a) 900					600
Notes Payable........................		11,000						11,000
Common Stock		20,000						20,000
Retained Earnings.....................	20						20	
Sales Revenue........................		13,000			(a) 900			13,900
Interest Income					(d) 30			30
Cost of Goods Sold....................	8,000						8,000	
Wages Expense.......................	1,625		(e) 480				2,105	
Rent Expense	1,500						1,500	
Advertising Expense...................	700						700	
Depreciation Expense..................			(c) 375				375	
Insurance Expense			(b) 140				140	
Interest Expense			(f) 110				110	
Tax Expense			(g) 350				350	
Totals................................	$49,900	$49,900	$2,385		$2,385		$51,245	$51,245

expense accounts. The revenues and expenses are reported in Natural Beauty Supply's income statement for December as shown in Exhibit 3.9. Its net income for December is $650.

EXHIBIT 3.9	Income Statement

NATURAL BEAUTY SUPPLY, INC.
Income Statement
For Month Ended December 31, 2010

Sales revenue	$13,900
Cost of goods sold	8,000
Gross profit..	5,900
Wage expense..	2,105
Rent expense...	1,500
Advertising expense	700
Depreciation expense..	375
Insurance expense	140
Operating income...	1,080
Interest income	30
Interest expense	(110)
Income before tax expense	1,000
Tax expense	350
Net income	$ 650

Statement of Stockholders' Equity   The statement of stockholders' equity reports the events causing the major equity components to change during the accounting period. Exhibit 3.10 shows Natural Beauty Supply's statement of stockholders' equity for December. A review of its common stock account in the general ledger provides some of the information for this statement; namely, its balance at the beginning of the period and stock issuances during the period. The net income (or net loss) amount comes from the income statement. Dividends during the period are reflected in the retained earnings balance from the adjusted trial balance.

EXHIBIT 3.10	Statement of Stockholders' Equity

NATURAL BEAUTY SUPPLY, INC.
Statement of Stockholders' Equity
For Month Ended December 31, 2010

	Contributed Capital	Earned Capital	Total Equity
Balance, November 30, 2010	$20,000	$ 30	$20,030
Net income.	—	650	650
Common stock issued	—	—	—
Cash dividends	—	(50)	(50)
Balances, December 31, 2010	$20,000	$630	$20,630

Balance Sheet   The balance sheet reports a company's assets, liabilities, and equity. The assets and liabilities for **Natural Beauty Supply**'s balance sheet at December 31, 2010, shown in Exhibit 3.11, come from the adjusted trial balance in Exhibit 3.8. The amounts reported for Common Stock and Retained Earnings in the balance sheet are taken from the statement of stockholders' equity for December (Exhibit 3.10).

EXHIBIT 3.11	Balance Sheet

NATURAL BEAUTY SUPPLY, INC.
Balance Sheet
December 31, 2010

Assets			Liabilities		
Cash.		$ 6,825	Accounts payable		$ 4,400
Accounts receivable		2,250	Interest payable.		110
Other receivables		30	Wages payable		480
Inventory		7,300	Taxes payable		350
Prepaid insurance		1,540	Unearned revenue.		600
Security deposit		2,000	Current liabilities		5,940
Current assets		19,945	Notes payable		11,000
Fixtures and Equipment	$18,000		Total liabilities		16,940
Less: Accumulated depreciation . . .	375		**Equity**		
Fixtures and Equipment, net.		17,625	Common stock		20,000
			Retained earnings		630
Total assets		$37,570	Total liabilities and equity		$37,570

Statement of Cash Flows   The statement of cash flows is formatted to report cash inflows and outflows by the three primary business activities:

- *Cash flows from operating activities*   Cash flows from the company's transactions and events that relate to its primary operations.
- *Cash flows from investing activities*   Cash flows from acquisitions and divestitures of investments and long-term assets.
- *Cash flows from financing activities*   Cash flows from issuances of and payments toward equity, borrowings, and long-term liabilities.

The net cash flows from these three sections yield the change in cash for the period.

In analyzing the statement of cash flows, we should not necessarily conclude that the company is better off if cash increases and worse off if cash decreases. It is not the cash change that is most important, but the reasons for the change. For example, what are the sources of the cash inflows? Are these sources mainly from operating activities? To what uses have cash inflows been put? Such questions (and their answers) are key to properly using the statement of cash flows. In Chapter 4, we examine the statement of cash flows more closely, and we answer these questions. The procedures for preparing a statement of cash flows are discussed in the next chapter. For completeness, we present Natural Beauty Supply's statement of cash flows for December in Exhibit 3.12.

EXHIBIT 3.12	Statement of Cash Flows

NATURAL BEAUTY SUPPLY, INC.
Statement of Cash Flows
For Month Ended December 31, 2010

Cash Flows from Operating Activities	
Cash received from customers	$12,900
Cash paid for inventory	(3,300)
Cash paid for wages	(1,625)
Cash paid for rent	(1,500)
Cash paid for advertising	(700)
Net cash provided by operating activities	5,775
Cash Flows from Investing Activities	
Cash paid for fixtures and equipment	(18,000)
Net cash used for investing activities	(18,000)
Cash Flows from Financing Activities	
Cash received from loans	11,000
Cash paid for dividends	(50)
Net cash provided by financing activities	10,950
Net change in cash	(1,275)
Cash balance, November 30, 2010	8,100
Cash balance, December 31, 2010	$ 6,825

CLOSING TEMPORARY ACCOUNTS

LO5 Describe the process of closing temporary accounts.

Temporary accounts consist of revenues and expenses. These accounts accumulate data that relate to a specific accounting period. As such, their balances are reported in period financial statements—the income statement, cash flow statement, and statement of stockholders' equity. At the end of each accounting period, the balances of these temporary accounts are transferred to a permanent account—the Retained Earnings account. This part of the accounting cycle is referred to as the **closing process**.

A temporary account is *closed* when an entry is made that changes its balance to zero. The entry is equal in amount to the account's balance but is opposite to the balance as a debit or credit. An account that is closed is said to be closed *to* the account that receives the offsetting debit or credit. Thus, a closing entry simply transfers the balance of one account to another account. When closing entries bring temporary account balances to zero, the temporary accounts are then ready to accumulate data for the next accounting period.

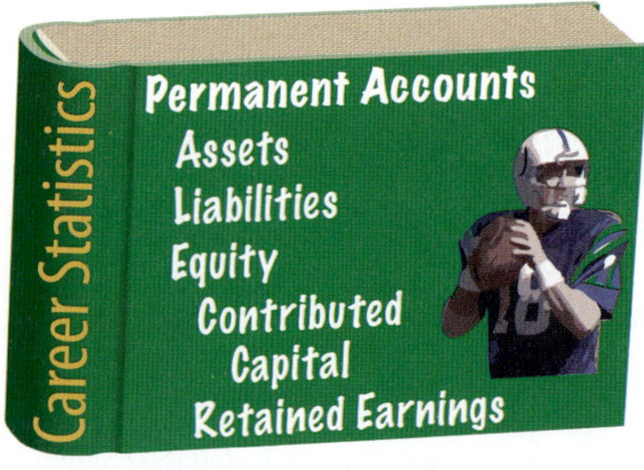

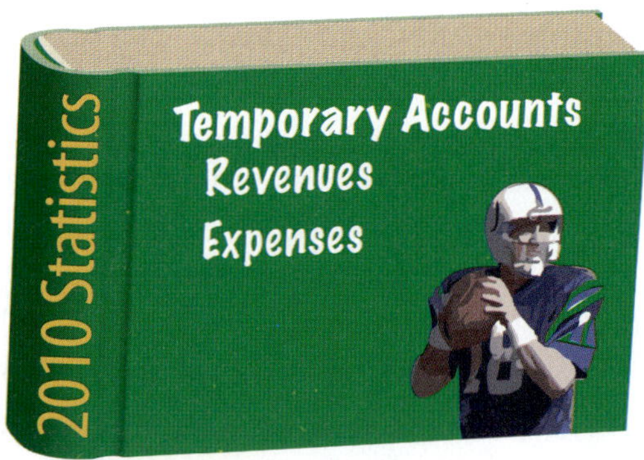

Closing Process

The Retained Earnings account can be used to close the temporary revenue and expense accounts.[3]
The entries to close temporary accounts are:

1. **Close revenue accounts**. Debit each revenue account for an amount equal to its balance, and credit Retained Earnings for the total of revenues.
2. **Close expense accounts**. Credit each expense account for an amount equal to its balance, and debit Retained Earnings for the total of expenses.

After these temporary accounts are closed, the difference equals the period's net income (if revenues exceed expenses) or net loss (if expenses exceed revenues) and that difference is now included in Retained Earnings. The closing process is graphically portrayed as follows.

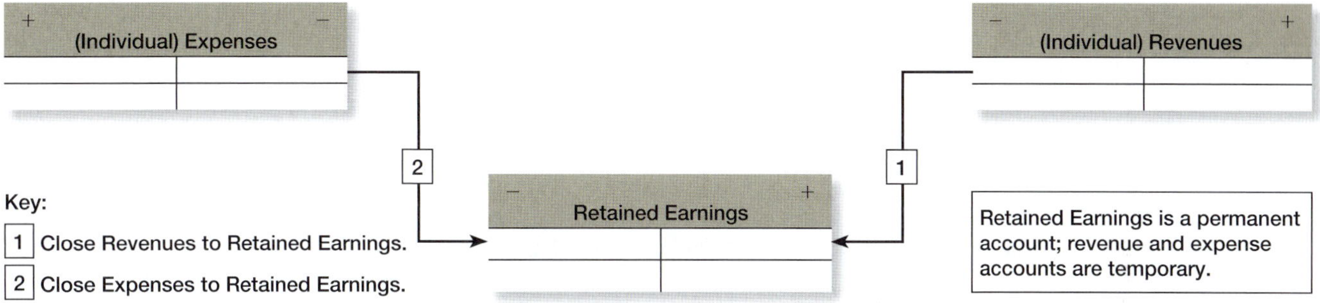

Closing Steps Illustrated

Exhibit 3.13 illustrates the entries for closing revenues and expenses for Natural Beauty Supply. The effects of these entries in T-accounts are shown after the journal entries. (We do not show the financial statement effects template for closing entries; **the template automatically closes revenues and expenses to the Retained Earnings account whenever they occur**—see earlier transactions for examples.)

EXHIBIT 3.13	Closing Revenues and Expenses*		
1	Dec. 31	Sales revenue (−R).....................................	13,900	
		Interest income (−R).....................................	30	
		Retained earnings (+SE).........................		13,930
2	Dec. 31	Retained earnings (−SE).............................	13,280	
		Cost of goods sold (−E)...........................		8,000
		Wages expense (−E)...............................		2,105
		Rent expense (−E)................................		1,500
		Advertising expense (−E).........................		700
		Depreciation expense (−E).......................		375
		Insurance expense (−E)..........................		140
		Interest expense (−E)............................		110
		Tax expense (−E)................................		350

* The two entries in this exhibit can be combined into a single entry where the credit (debit) to retained earnings would be net income (loss).

___
[3] *All* revenue and expense accounts are temporary accounts, so all revenue and expense accounts are closed to retained earnings at the end of the reporting period. In addition, a company may use a temporary account entitled Dividends Declared to record the amount of shareholder dividends declared during a reporting period. This account would accumulate a debit balance (because it reduces equity), and it would be closed to retained earnings at the end of the reporting period.

After these two steps, the net adjustment to the Retained Earnings account is a credit equal to the company's net income of $650, computed as $13,930 less $13,280. The Retained Earnings account in this case is increased by $650. Recall that Natural Beauty Supply paid a cash dividend of $50 (transaction 28), which reduces retained earnings and results in the ending balance of $630.

Preparing a Post-Closing Trial Balance

After closing entries are recorded and posted to the general ledger, all temporary accounts have zero balances. At this point, a **post-closing trial balance** is prepared. A balancing of this trial balance is evidence that an equality of debits and credits has been maintained in the general ledger throughout the adjusting and closing process and that the general ledger is in balance to start the next accounting period. Only balance sheet accounts appear in a post-closing trial balance. The post-closing trial balance for Natural Beauty Supply is in Exhibit 3.14.

EXHIBIT 3.14	Post-Closing Trial Balance

NATURAL BEAUTY SUPPLY, INC.
Post-Closing Trial Balance
December 31, 2010

	Debit	Credit
Cash	$ 6,825	
Accounts Receivable	2,250	
Other Receivables	30	
Inventory	7,300	
Prepaid Insurance	1,540	
Security Deposit	2,000	
Fixtures and Equipment	18,000	
Accumulated Depreciation		$ 375
Accounts Payable		4,400
Interest Payable		110
Wages Payable		480
Taxes Payable		350
Unearned Revenue		600
Notes Payable		11,000
Common Stock		20,000
Retained Earnings		630
Totals	$37,945	$37,945

SUMMARIZING THE ACCOUNTING CYCLE

The sequence of accounting procedures known as the accounting cycle occurs each fiscal year (period) and represents a systematic process for accumulating and reporting financial data of a company. Exhibit 3.15 expands on Exhibit 3.1 to include descriptions of the five major steps in the accounting cycle.

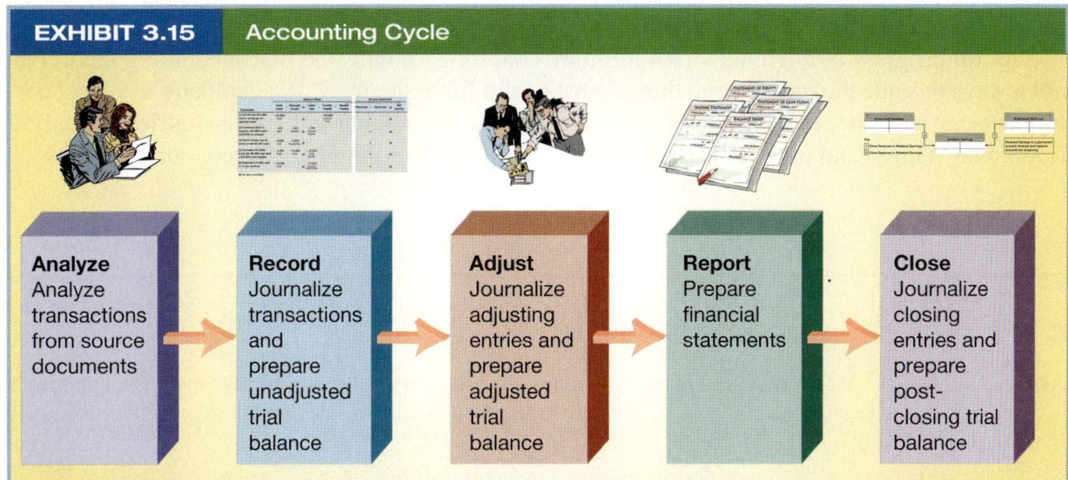

EXHIBIT 3.15 Accounting Cycle

FINANCIAL STATEMENT ANALYSIS

Using Information on Levels and Flows

A careful reader of financial statements must differentiate between those things that depict *levels* and those that depict *flows* or *changes*. The balance sheet portrays levels of resources and claims on those resources at a point in time, and the income statement portrays changes in those levels over a period of time. Knowing how the levels and flows relate to each other can be a very useful tool for analysis.

LO6 Analyze changes in balance sheet accounts.

For instance, suppose that a service business has an inventory of office supplies. On July 1, an inventory count determined that the business had $2,400 of supplies inventory on hand. During the third calendar quarter, there were deliveries of office supplies with a cost of $5,700. And, at the end of the third quarter—on September 30—an inventory count found $1,900 of supplies on hand. What amount of supplies expense should be recognized for the quarter?

Finding the answer to this question is easier if one remembers the transactions that can affect the supplies inventory account, and that these transactions (changes) must lead from the beginning inventory level to the ending inventory level. At present, we know of two such transactions: the purchase of supplies inventory and the usage of supplies inventory.

(a)	Supplies inventory (+A).	5,700	
	Cash (−A) or Accounts payable (+L).		5,700
	Purchase supplies inventory.		
(b)	Supplies expense (+E, −SE)	?	
	Supplies inventory (−A)		?
	Record expense for supplies used.		

The supplies inventory T-account must look like the following:

+	Supplies Inventory (A)	−
Bal.	2,400	
(a)	5,700	? (b)
Bal.	1,900	

Balancing the account requires that $2,400 + $5,700 - ? = $1,900$, and the value that satisfies this condition is $6,200. That amount would be recorded as supplies expense for the quarter.

This application of the T-account structure is a simple one—in fact, it is used in part *a* of the Mid-Chapter Review. But, suppose that a separate source of information told us that $5,900 in supplies had been taken from inventory for client service activities. When put into the T-account analysis above, that would imply that an additional $300 in supplies had been removed for reasons such as breakage, obsolescence, or pilferage.

As we progress through the topics in future chapters, we will find that accounting reports do not always provide the information that is most useful for assessment of a company's current performance or standing. In those cases, we can often use T-accounts and journal entries to analyze levels and changes and to develop the numbers that do a better job of answering our questions.

CHAPTER-END REVIEW

Assume that Atwell Laboratories, Inc., operates with an accounting fiscal year ending June 30. The company's accounts are adjusted annually and closed on that date. Its unadjusted trial balance ($ millions) as of June 30, 2010, is as follows.

ATWELL LABORATORIES, INC.
Unadjusted Trial Balance
June 30, 2010

	Debit	Credit
Cash.	$ 1,000	
Accounts Receivable	9,200	
Prepaid Insurance.	6,000	
Supplies.	31,300	
Equipment	270,000	
Accumulated Depreciation—Equipment		$ 60,000
Accounts Payable.		3,100
Unearned Fees		4,000
Fees Revenue		150,000
Wages Expense.	58,000	
Rent Expense	22,000	
Common Stock		120,400
Retained Earnings.		60,000
Totals	$397,500	$397,500

Additional Information

1. Atwell acquired a two-year insurance policy on January 1, 2010. The policy covers fire and casualty; Atwell had no coverage prior to January 1, 2010.

2. An inventory of supplies was taken on June 30 and the amount available was $6,300.

3. All equipment was purchased on July 1, 2007, for $270,000. The equipment's life is estimated at 9 years. Assume the entire asset cost is depreciated over its useful life.

4. Atwell received a $4,000 cash payment on April 1, 2010, from Beave Clinic for diagnostic work to be provided uniformly over the next 4 months, beginning April 1, 2010. The amount was credited to Unearned Fees. The service was provided per the agreement.

5. Unpaid and unrecorded wages at June 30, 2010, were $600.

6. Atwell rents facilities for $2,000 per month. Atwell has not yet made or recorded the payment for June 2010.

Required

1. Show the impact of the adjustments using the FSET, prepare the necessary adjusting journal entries, and enter them in T-accounts. Atwell's ledger includes the following ledger accounts and unadjusted normal balances at June 30: Cash $1,000; Accounts Receivable $9,200; Supplies $31,300; Prepaid Insurance $6,000; Equipment $270,000; Accumulated Depreciation—Equipment $60,000; Accounts Payable $3,100; Wages Payable $0; Rent Payable $0; Unearned Fees $4,000; Common Stock $120,400; Retained Earnings $60,000; Fees Revenue $150,000; Rent Expense $22,000; Insurance Expense $0; Depreciation Expense $0; Wages Expense $58,000; Supplies Expense $0. Use "Unadj. bal." to denote the unadjusted balance in each account when such a balance exists, and use "Adj. bal." to denote the adjusted balance.

2. Prepare its adjusted trial balance.

3. Prepare its closing journal entries and post them to the T-accounts (key the entries).

4. Prepare its balance sheet as of June 30, 2010, and its income statement and statement of stockholders' equity for the year ended June 30, 2010.

The solution to this review problem can be found on pages 144–148.

SUMMARY

Identify the major steps in the accounting cycle (in order). (p. 96) **LO1**

- The major steps in the accounting cycle are

    a. Analyze   *b.* Record   *c.* Adjust   *d.* Report   *e.* Close

Review the process of journalizing and posting transactions. (p. 97) **LO2**

- Transactions are initially recorded in a journal; the entries are in chronological order, and the journal shows the total effect of each transaction or adjustment.
- Posting is the transfer of information from a journal to the general ledger accounts.

Describe the adjusting process and illustrate adjusting entries. (p. 103) **LO3**

- Adjusting entries achieve the proper recognition of revenues and the proper matching of expenses with those revenues; adjustments are summarized as follows.

Adjustment	Adjusting Entry
Adjusting prepaid expenses	Increase expense Decrease asset
Adjusting unearned revenues	Decrease liability Increase revenue
Accruing expenses	Increase expense Increase liability
Accruing revenues	Increase asset Increase revenue

Prepare financial statements from adjusted accounts. (p. 112) **LO4**

- An income statement, statement of stockholders' equity, balance sheet, and statement of cash flows are prepared from an adjusted trial balance and other information.

LO5 **Describe the process of closing temporary accounts. (p. 116)**

- *Closing the books* means closing (yielding zero balances) revenues and expenses—that is, all temporary accounts. Revenue and expense account balances are transferred (closed) to the Retained Earnings account.

LO6 **Analyze changes in balance sheet accounts. (p. 119)**

- The combination of balance sheet levels and income statement flows allows a financial statement reader to infer the effects of transactions and adjustments that are not disclosed directly.

GUIDANCE ANSWERS . . . YOU MAKE THE CALL

You are the Chief Accountant Deposits represent a liability and should be included in REI's current liabilities at the time the cash or check is received. The account that would be used may have several names, including advances, trip deposits, and unearned revenues. Revenue should not be recognized until the trip has been completed. It is not unusual for events to occur that result in a refund of some portion or even all of the traveler's total payment. In the present case involving a low cancellation rate, waiting until the trip is over is not only conservative reporting, but is likely more efficient bookkeeping as well.

KEY TERMS

Accounting cycle (p. 96)	Chart of accounts (p. 97)	General journal (p. 97)
Accruals (p. 105)	Close expense accounts (p. 117)	Journal (p. 97)
Accrued expense (p. 109)	Close revenue accounts (p. 117)	Post-closing trial balance (p. 118)
Accrued income (p. 108)	Closing process (p. 116)	
Accrued revenue (p. 108)	Contra accounts (p. 107)	Posting (p. 97)
Adjusted trial balance (p. 112)	Deferrals (p. 105)	Straight-line depreciation (p. 107)
Adjusting entries (p. 105)	Deferred revenue (p. 105)	
Book value (p. 108)	Depreciation (p. 107)	Unadjusted trial balance (p. 104)
Calendar year (p. 96)	Fiscal year (p. 96)	Unearned revenue (p. 105)

MULTIPLE CHOICE

1. A journal entry that contains more than two accounts is called
   a. a posted journal entry.
   b. an adjusting journal entry.
   c. an erroneous journal entry.
   d. a compound journal entry.

2. Posting refers to the process whereby journal entry information is transferred from
   a. journal to general ledger accounts.
   b. general ledger accounts to a journal.
   c. source documents to a journal.
   d. a journal to source documents.

3. Which of the following is an example of an adjusting entry?
   a. Recording the purchase of supplies on account
   b. Recording depreciation expense on a truck
   c. Recording cash received from customers for services rendered
   d. Recording the cash payment of wages to employees

4. A piece of equipment was placed in service on January 1, 2008. The cost of the equipment was $20,000, and it is expected to have no value at the end of its eight-year life. Using straight-line depreciation, what amounts will be seen for depreciation expense and accumulated depreciation for fiscal (and calendar) year 2010?

	Fiscal Year 2010 Depreciation Expense	Fiscal Year-end 2010 Accumulated Depreciation
a.	$2,500	$ 2,000
b.	–0–	$20,000
c.	$2,500	$ 7,500
d.	$7,500	$ 7,500

5. When a customer places an order, Custom Cakes requires a deposit equal to the full purchase price. However, Custom Cakes does not recognize revenue until the completed cake is delivered. During the month of November 2010, Custom Cakes received $24,000 in customer deposits. The balance in its unearned revenue liability was $4,000 at the beginning of November and $6,000 at the end of November. How much revenue did Custom Cakes recognize during the month of November?
   a. $26,000
   b. $24,000
   c. $22,000
   d. $4,000

DISCUSSION QUESTIONS

Q3-1. What are the five major steps in the accounting cycle? List them in their proper order.

Q3-2. What does the term *fiscal year* mean?

Q3-3. What are three examples of source documents that underlie business transactions?

Q3-4. What is the nature and purpose of a general journal?

Q3-5. Explain the process of posting.

Q3-6. What is a compound journal entry?

Q3-7. What is a chart of accounts? Give an example of a coding system for identifying different types of accounts.

Q3-8. Why is the adjusting step of the accounting cycle necessary?

Q3-9. What four different types of adjustments are frequently necessary at the close of an accounting period? Give examples of each type.

Q3-10. On January 1, Prepaid Insurance was debited with the cost of a two-year premium, $1,872. What adjusting entry should be made on January 31 before financial statements are prepared for the month?

Q3-11. What is a contra account? What contra account is used in reporting the book value of a depreciable asset?

Q3-12. A building was acquired on January 1, 2007, at a cost of $4,000,000, and its depreciation is calculated using the straight-line method. At the end of 2011, the accumulated depreciation contra asset for the building is $800,000. What will be the balance in the building's accumulated depreciation contra asset at the end of 2018? What is the building's book value at that date?

Q3-13. The publisher of *International View*, a monthly magazine, received two-year subscriptions totaling $9,720 on January 1. (a) What entry should be made to record the receipt of the $9,720? (b) What entry should be made at the end of January before financial statements are prepared for the month?

Q3-14. Globe Travel Agency pays an employee $475 in wages each Friday for the five-day workweek ending on that day. The last Friday of January falls on January 27. What adjusting entry should be made on January 31, the fiscal year-end?

Q3-15. The Bayou Company earns interest amounting to $360 per month on its investments. The company receives the interest every six months, on December 31 and June 30. Monthly financial statements are prepared. What adjusting entry should be made on January 31?

Q3-16. Which groups of accounts are closed at the end of the accounting year?

Q3-17. What are the two major steps in the closing process?

Q3-18. What is the purpose of a post-closing trial balance? Which of the following accounts should *not* appear in the post-closing trial balance: Cash; Unearned Revenue; Prepaid Rent; Depreciation Expense; Utilities Payable; Supplies Expense; and Retained Earnings?

Q3-19. Dehning Corporation is an international manufacturer of films and industrial identification products. Included among its prepaid expenses is an account titled Prepaid Catalog Costs; in recent years, this account's size has ranged between $2,500,000 and $4,000,000. The company states that catalog costs are initially capitalized and then written off over the estimated useful lives of the publications (generally eight months). Identify and briefly discuss the accounting principles that support Dehning Corporation's handling of its catalog costs.

Q3-20. At the beginning of January, the first month of the accounting year, the Supplies account had a debit balance of $825. During January, purchases of $260 worth of supplies were debited to the account. Although only $630 of supplies were still available at the end of January, the necessary adjusting entry was omitted. How will the omission affect (a) the income statement for January, and (b) the balance sheet prepared at January 31?

Assignments with the WebAssign logo in the margin are available in WebAssign.
See the Preface of the book for details.

MINI EXERCISES

LO2   M3-21.   Journalizing Transactions in Template, Journal Entry Form, and T-Accounts
Creative Designs, a firm providing art services for advertisers, began business on June 1, 2010. The following accounts in its general ledger are needed to record the transactions for June: Cash; Accounts Receivable; Supplies; Office Equipment; Accounts Payable; Common Stock; Retained Earnings; Service Fees Earned; Rent Expense; Utilities Expense; and Salaries Expense. Record the following transactions for June (a) using the financial statement effects template and (b) in journal entry form. (c) Set up T-accounts for each of the ledger accounts and post the entries to them (key the numbers in T-accounts by date).

June 1 Anne Clem invested $12,000 cash to begin the business in exchange for common stock.
  2 Paid $950 cash for June rent.
  3 Purchased $6,400 of office equipment on account.
  6 Purchased $3,800 of art materials and other supplies; paid $1,800 cash with the remainder due within 30 days.
  11 Billed clients $4,700 for services rendered.
  17 Collected $3,250 cash from clients on their accounts.
  19 Paid $3,000 cash toward the account for office equipment suppliers (see June 3).
  25 Paid $900 cash for dividends.
  30 Paid $350 cash for June utilities.
  30 Paid $2,500 cash for June salaries.

LO2   M3-22.   Journalizing and Posting Transactions
Minute Maid, a firm providing housecleaning services, began business on April 1, 2010. The following accounts in its general ledger are *needed* to record the transactions for April: Cash; Accounts Receivable; Supplies; Prepaid Van Lease; Equipment; Notes Payable; Accounts Payable; Common Stock; Retained Earnings; Cleaning Fees Earned; Wages Expense; Advertising Expense; and Van Fuel Expense. Record the following transactions for April (a) using the financial statement effects template and (b) in journal entry form. (c) Set up T-accounts for each of the ledger accounts and post the entries to them (key the numbers in T-accounts by date).

April 1 A. Falcon invested $9,000 cash to begin the business in exchange for common stock.
  2 Paid $2,850 cash for six months' lease on van for the business.
  3 Borrowed $10,000 cash from bank and signed note payable agreeing to repay it in 1 year plus 10% interest.
  3 Purchased $5,500 of cleaning equipment; paid $2,500 cash with the remainder due within 30 days.
  4 Paid $4,300 cash for cleaning supplies.
  7 Paid $350 cash for advertisements to run in newspaper during April.

21 Billed customers $3,500 for services performed.
23 Paid $3,000 cash on account to cleaning equipment suppliers (see April 3).
28 Collected $2,300 cash from customers on their accounts.
29 Paid $1,000 cash for dividends.
30 Paid $1,750 cash for April wages.
30 Paid $995 cash to service station for gasoline used during April.

M3-23. Journalizing Transactions and Adjusting Accounts

Deluxe Building Services offers custodial services on both a contract basis and an hourly basis. On January 1, 2010, Deluxe collected $20,100 in advance on a six-month contract for work to be performed evenly during the next six months.

a. Prepare the entry on January 1 to record the receipt of $20,100 cash for contract work (1) using the financial statements effect template and (2) in journal entry form.

b. Prepare the adjusting entry to be made on January 31, 2010, for the contract work done during January (1) using the financial statements effect template and (2) in journal entry form.

c. At January 31, a total of 30 hours of hourly rate custodial work was unbilled. The billing rate is $19 per hour. Prepare the adjusting entry needed on January 31, 2010, (1) using the financial statements effect template and (2) in journal entry form. (The firm uses the account Fees Receivable to reflect amounts due but not yet billed.)

M3-24. Adjusting Accounts

Selected accounts of Ideal Properties, a real estate management firm, are shown below as of January 31, 2010, before any adjusting entries have been made.

Unadjusted Account Balances	Debits	Credits
Prepaid Insurance	$6,660	
Supplies	1,930	
Office Equipment	5,952	
Unearned Rent Revenue		$ 5,250
Salaries Expense	3,100	
Rent Revenue		15,000

Monthly financial statements are prepared. Using the following information, record the adjusting entries necessary on January 31 (a) using the financial statements effect template and (b) in journal entry form.

1. Prepaid Insurance represents a three-year premium paid on January 1, 2010.
2. Supplies of $850 were still available on January 31.
3. Office equipment is expected to last eight years.
4. On January 1, 2010, Ideal Properties collected six months' rent in advance from a tenant renting space for $875 per month.
5. Accrued employee salaries of $490 are not recorded as of January 31.

M3-25. Inferring Transactions from Financial Statements

Dick's Sporting Goods, Inc., a retailer of sporting goods equipment, apparel, and footwear, operates more than 380 stores in 39 states. For the fiscal year ended January 31, 2009, Dick's purchased merchandise inventory costing $2,913.49 ($ millions). Assume that all purchases were made on account. The following T-accounts reflect information contained in the company's 2008 and 2009 balance sheets (in $ millions).

+	Inventories (A)		−
2/2/2008 Bal.	887.36		
1/31/2009 Bal.	854.77		

−	Accounts Payable (L)		+
		365.75	2/2/2008 Bal.
		299.11	1/31/2009 Bal.

a. Prepare the entry, using the financial statement effects template and in journal entry form, to record its purchases for the 2009 fiscal year.

b. What amount did Dick's pay in cash to its suppliers for fiscal year ended January 31, 2009? Explain. Assume that Accounts Payable is affected only by transactions related to inventory.

c. Prepare the entry, using the financial statement effects template and in journal entry form, to record cost of goods sold for the year ended January 31, 2009.

LO4 **M3-26. Preparing a Statement of Stockholders' Equity**

On December 31, 2010, the credit balances of the Common Stock and Retained Earnings accounts were $30,000 and $18,000, respectively, for Architect Services Company. Its stock issuances for 2011 totaled $6,000, and it paid $9,700 cash toward dividends in 2011. For the year ended December 31, 2011, the company had net income of $29,900. Prepare a 2011 statement of stockholders' equity for Architect Services.

LO5 **M3-27. Applying Closing Procedures**

Assume you are in the process of closing procedures for Echo Corporation. You have already closed all revenue and expense accounts to the Retained Earnings account. The total debits equal $308,800 and total credits equal $347,400. The Retained Earnings account had a credit balance of $99,000 at the start of this current year. What is the post-closing ending balance of Retained Earnings at the end of this current year?

LO5 **M3-28. Preparing Closing Entries Using Journal Entries and T-Accounts**

The adjusted trial balance at December 31, 2010, for Smith Company includes the following selected accounts.

Adjusted Account Balances	Debit	Credit
Commissions Revenue		$84,900
Wages Expense	$36,000	
Insurance Expense	1,900	
Utilities Expense	8,200	
Depreciation Expense	9,800	
Retained Earnings		72,100

a. Prepare entries to close these accounts in journal entry form.

b. Set up T-accounts for each of these ledger accounts, enter the balances above, and post the closing entries to them. After these entries are posted, what is the post-closing balance of the Retained Earnings account?

LO2, LO3, LO6 **M3-29. Inferring Transactions from Financial Statements**

Barnes & Noble, Inc., sells books through its Barnes & Noble bookstores and superstores, through B. Dalton Booksellers, and through the Internet. For the year ended January 31, 2009, Barnes & Noble purchased merchandise inventory at a cost of $3,385.90 ($ millions). Assume that all purchases were made on account. The following T-accounts reflect information contained in the company's 2008 and 2009 balance sheets (in millions).

+	Merchandise Inventories (A)	−		−	Accounts Payable (L)	+
2/2/2008 Bal. 1,358.17					831.67	2/2/2008 Bal.
1/31/2009 Bal. 1,203.47					746.60	1/31/2009 Bal.

a. Prepare the entry, using the financial statement effects template and in journal entry form, to record its purchases.

b. What amount did Barnes & Noble pay in cash to its suppliers for the year ended January 31, 2009? Explain.

c. Prepare the entry, using the financial statement effects template and in journal entry form, to record cost of goods sold for the year ended January 31, 2009.

LO2, LO3, LO5 **M3-30. Preparing Entries Across Two Periods**

Hatcher Company closes its accounts on December 31 each year. On December 31, 2010, Hatcher accrued $600 of interest income that was earned on an investment but not yet received or recorded (the investment will pay interest of $900 cash on January 31, 2011). On January 31, 2011, the company received the $900 cash as interest on the investment. Prepare journal entries to:

a. Accrue the interest earned on December 31;

b. Close the Interest Income account on December 31 (the account has a year-end balance of $2,400 after adjustments); and

c. Record the cash receipt of interest on January 31, 2011.

EXERCISES

E3-31. Journalizing and Posting Closing Entries
The adjusted trial balance as of December 31, 2010, for Brooks Consulting Company contains the following selected accounts.

Adjusted Account Balances	Debit	Credit
Service Fees Earned		$80,300
Rent Expense	$20,800	
Salaries Expense	45,700	
Supplies Expense	5,600	
Depreciation Expense	10,200	
Retained Earnings		67,000

a. Prepare entries to close these accounts in journal entry form.
b. Set up T-accounts for each of the ledger accounts, enter the balances above, and post the closing entries to them. After these entries are posted, what is the post-closing balance of the Retained Earnings account?

E3-32. Preparing and Journalizing Adjusting Entries
For each of the following separate situations, prepare the necessary adjustments (a) using the financial statement effects template, and (b) in journal entry form.

1. Unrecorded depreciation on equipment is $610.
2. The Supplies account has an unadjusted balance of $2,990. Supplies still available at the end of the period total $1,100.
3. On the date for preparing financial statements, an estimated utilities expense of $390 has been incurred, but no utility bill has yet been received or paid.
4. On the first day of the current period, rent for four periods was paid and recorded as a $2,800 debit to Prepaid Rent and a $2,800 credit to Cash.
5. Nine months ago, the **Hartford Insurance Company** sold a one-year policy to a customer and recorded the receipt of the premium by debiting Cash for $624 and crediting Unearned Premium Revenue for $624. No adjusting entries have been prepared during the nine-month period. Hartford's annual financial statements are now being prepared.
6. At the end of the period, employee wages of $965 have been incurred but not yet paid or recorded.
7. At the end of the period, $300 of interest income has been earned but not yet received or recorded.

E3-33. Preparing Adjusting and Closing Entries Across Two Periods
Norton Company closes its accounts on December 31 each year. The company works a five-day work week and pays its employees every two weeks. On December 31, 2010, Norton accrued $4,700 of salaries payable. On January 7, 2011, the company paid salaries of $12,000 cash to employees. Prepare journal entries to:

a. Accrue the salaries payable on December 31;
b. Close the Salaries Expense account on December 31 (the account has a year-end balance of $250,000 after adjustments); and
c. Record the salary payment on January 7.

E3-34. Analyzing Accounts Using Adjusted Data
Selected T-account balances for Fields Company are shown below as of January 31, 2011; adjusting entries have already been posted. The firm uses a calendar-year accounting period but prepares *monthly* adjustments.

+	Supplies (A)	−		+	Supplies Expense (E)	−
Jan. 31 Bal.	800			Jan. 31 Bal.	960	

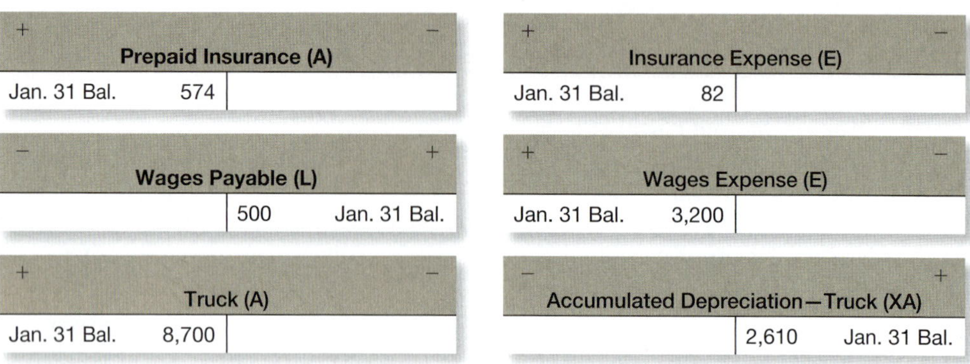

a.   If the amount in Supplies Expense represents the January 31 adjustment for the supplies used in January, and $620 worth of supplies were purchased during January, what was the January 1 beginning balance of Supplies?

b.   The amount in the Insurance Expense account represents the adjustment made at January 31 for January insurance expense. If the original insurance premium was for one year, what was the amount of the premium and on what date did the insurance policy start?

c.   If we assume that no beginning balance existed in Wages Payable or Wages Expense on January 1, how much cash was paid as wages during January?

d.   If the truck has a useful life of five years, what is the monthly amount of depreciation expense and how many months has Fields owned the truck?

LO2, LO3, LO6   E3-35.   Preparing Adjusting Entries

Jake Thomas began Thomas Refinishing Service on July 1, 2010. Selected accounts are shown below as of July 31, before any adjusting entries have been made.

Unadjusted Account Balances	Debit	Credit
Prepaid Rent	$5,700	
Prepaid Advertising.	630	
Supplies.	3,000	
Unearned Refinishing Fees.		$ 600
Refinishing Fees Revenue.		2,500

Using the following information, prepare the adjusting entries necessary on July 31 (a) using the financial statement effects template and (b) in journal entry form. (c) Set up T-accounts for each of the ledger accounts, enter the balances above, and post the adjusting entries to them.

1.   On July 1, the firm paid one year's advance rent of $5,700 in cash.

2.   On July 1, $630 cash was paid to the local newspaper for an advertisement to run daily for the months of July, August, and September.

3.   Supplies still available at July 31 total $1,100.

4.   At July 31, refinishing services of $800 have been performed but not yet recorded or billed to customers. The firm uses the account Fees Receivable to reflect amounts due but not yet billed.

5.   A customer paid $600 in advance for a refinishing project. At July 31, the project is one-half complete.

LO2, LO3, LO6   E3-36.   Inferring Transactions from Financial Statements

WINNEBAGO INDUSTRIES
NYSE :: WGO

Winnebago Industries Inc. manufactures and sells motor homes as well as retail parts and accessories, throughout the United States and Canada. The following information is taken from Winnebago's fiscal 2009 10-K report. (All amounts in $ thousands.)

Selected Balance Sheet Data	2008	2009
Inventories.	$110,596	$46,850
Accrued Compensation Liability.	10,070	10,204

a. Winnebago spent $178,519 to purchase and manufacture inventories for its fiscal year 2009. Prepare the entry, using the financial statement effects template and in journal entry form, to record cost of goods sold for its fiscal year 2009.

b. Assume that Winnebago reported compensation expense of $40,000 for its fiscal year 2009. What amount of compensation was paid to its employees for fiscal year 2009?

E3-37.   Preparing Closing Procedures   LO5

The adjusted trial balance of Parker Corporation, prepared December 31, 2011, contains the following selected accounts.

Adjusted Account Balances	Debit	Credit
Service Fees Earned		$92,500
Interest Income		2,200
Salaries Expense	$41,800	
Advertising Expense	4,300	
Depreciation Expense	8,700	
Income Tax Expense	9,900	
Retained Earnings		42,700

a. Prepare entries to close these accounts in journal entry form.

b. Set up T-accounts for each of the ledger accounts, enter the balances above, and post the closing entries to them. After these entries are posted, what is the post-closing balance of the Retained Earnings account?

E3-38.   Inferring Transactions from Financial Statements   LO2, LO3, LO6

Ethan Allen Interiors Inc., a leading manufacturer and retailer of home furnishings and accessories, sells products through an exclusive network of more than 150 retail stores. All of Ethan Allen's products are sold by special order. Customers generally place a deposit equal to 25% to 50% of the purchase price when ordering. Orders take 4 to 12 weeks to be delivered. Selected fiscal-year information from the company's balance sheets is as follows ($ thousands):

Selected Balance Sheet Data	2008	2009
Inventories	$186,265	$156,519
Customer Deposits Liability	47,297	31,691

a. In fiscal 2009, Ethan Allen reported total sales revenue of $674,277. Assume that the company collected customer deposits equal to $200,000 over the year. Prepare entries, using the financial statement effects template and in journal entry form, to record customer deposits and its sales revenue for fiscal year 2009.

b. During fiscal 2009, Ethan Allen purchased or manufactured inventory at a cost of $297,189. Prepare the adjusting entry, using the financial statement effects template and in journal entry form, that it made to record cost of sales.

E3-39.   Preparing Financial Statements and Closing Procedures   LO4, LO5

Solomon Corporation's adjusted trial balance for the year ending December 31, 2011, is:

SOLOMON CORPORATION
Adjusted Trial Balance
December 31, 2011

	Debit	Credit
Cash	$ 4,000	
Accounts Receivable	6,500	
Equipment	78,000	
Accumulated Depreciation		$ 14,000
Notes Payable		10,000
Common Stock		43,000
Retained Earnings		12,600
Service Fees Earned		71,000
Rent Expense	18,000	
Salaries Expense	37,100	
Depreciation Expense	7,000	
Totals	$150,600	$150,600

a. Prepare its income statement and statement of stockholders' equity for the current year, and its balance sheet for the current year-end. Cash dividends were $8,000 and there were no stock issuances or repurchases.

b. Prepare entries to close its temporary accounts in journal entry form.

c. Set up T-accounts for each of the ledger accounts, enter the balances above, and post the closing entries to them. After these entries are posted, what is the post-closing balance of the Retained Earnings account?

PROBLEMS

LO2, LO3, LO4 **P3-40.** **Journalizing and Posting Transactions, and Preparing a Trial Balance and Adjustments**
B. Lougee opened Lougee Roofing Service on April 1, 2010. Transactions for April are as follows:

Apr. 1 Lougee contributed $11,500 cash to the business in exchange for common stock.

  1 Paid $2,880 cash for two-year premium toward liability insurance effective immediately.

  2 Paid $6,100 cash for the purchase of a used truck.

  2 Purchased $3,100 of ladders and other equipment; paid $1,000 cash, with the balance due in 30 days.

  5 Purchased $1,200 of supplies on account.

  5 Received an advance of $1,800 cash from a customer for roof repairs to be done during April and May.

  12 Billed customers $5,500 for roofing services performed.

  18 Collected $4,900 cash from customers on their accounts.

  29 Paid $675 cash for truck fuel used in April.

  30 Paid $100 cash for April newspaper advertising.

  30 Paid $2,500 cash for assistants' wages.

  30 Billed customers $4,000 for roofing services performed.

Required

a. Set up a general ledger in T-account form for the following accounts: Cash; Accounts Receivable; Supplies; Prepaid Insurance; Trucks; Accumulated Depreciation—Trucks; Equipment; Accumulated Depreciation—Equipment; Accounts Payable; Unearned Roofing Fees; Common Stock; Roofing Fees Earned; Fuel Expense; Advertising Expense; Wages Expense; Insurance Expense; Supplies Expense; Depreciation Expense—Trucks; and Depreciation Expense—Equipment.

b. Record these transactions for April (1) using the financial statement effects template and (2) in journal entry form. (3) Post these entries to their T-accounts (key numbers in T-accounts by date).

c. Prepare an unadjusted trial balance as of April 30, 2010.

d. Supplies still available on April 30 amount to $400; and depreciation for April was $125 on the truck and $35 on equipment; and one-fourth of the roofing fee received in advance was earned by April 30. Prepare entries to adjust the books for Insurance Expense, Supplies Expense, Depreciation Expense—Trucks, Depreciation Expense—Equipment, and Roofing Fees Earned (1) using the financial statement effects template and (2) in journal entry form. (3) Post adjusting entries to their T-accounts.

P3-41. Preparing an Unadjusted Trial Balance and Adjustments   LO2, LO3, LO4

SnapShot Company, a commercial photography studio, has just completed its first full year of operations on December 31, 2010. General ledger account balances *before* year-end adjustments follow; no adjusting entries have been made to the accounts at any time during the year. Assume that all balances are normal.

Cash.........................	$ 2,150	Accounts Payable...............	$ 1,910
Accounts Receivable	3,800	Unearned Photography Fees	2,600
Prepaid Rent	12,600	Common Stock	24,000
Prepaid Insurance..............	2,970	Photography Fees Earned	34,480
Supplies......................	4,250	Wages Expense.................	11,000
Equipment....................	22,800	Utilities Expense	3,420

An analysis of the firm's records discloses the following.

1. Photography services of $925 have been rendered, but customers have not yet paid or been billed. The firm uses the account Fees Receivable to reflect amounts due but not yet billed.
2. Equipment, purchased January 1, 2010, has an estimated life of 10 years.
3. Utilities expense for December is estimated to be $400, but the bill will not arrive or be paid until January of next year.
4. The balance in Prepaid Rent represents the amount paid on January 1, 2010, for a 2-year lease on the studio.
5. In November, customers paid $2,600 cash in advance for photos to be taken for the holiday season. When received, these fees were credited to Unearned Photography Fees. By December 31, all of these fees are earned.
6. A 3-year insurance premium paid on January 1, 2010, was debited to Prepaid Insurance.
7. Supplies available at December 31 are $1,520.
8. At December 31, wages expense of $375 has been incurred but not paid or recorded.

Required

a. Prove that debits equal credits for SnapShot's unadjusted account balances by preparing its unadjusted trial balance at December 31, 2010.
b. Prepare its adjusting entries: (1) using the financial statement effects template, and (2) in journal entry form.
c. Set up T-accounts, enter the balances above, and post the adjusting entries to them.

P3-42. Preparing Adjusting Entries, Financial Statements, and Closing Entries   LO2, LO3, LO4, LO5

Murdock Carpet Cleaners ended its first month of operations on June 30, 2011. Monthly financial statements will be prepared. The unadjusted account balances are as follows.

MURDOCK CARPET CLEANERS Unadjusted Trial Balance June 30, 2011	Debit	Credit
Cash..	$ 1,180	
Accounts Receivable	450	
Prepaid Rent	3,100	
Supplies...	2,520	
Equipment...	4,440	
Accounts Payable...		$ 760
Common Stock		2,000
Retained Earnings..		5,300
Service Fees Earned		4,650
Wages Expense...	1,020	
	$12,710	$12,710

The following information is available.

1. The balance in Prepaid Rent was the amount paid on June 1 for the first four months' rent.
2. Supplies available at June 30 were $820.
3. Equipment, purchased June 1, has an estimated life of five years.
4. Unpaid and unrecorded employee wages at June 30 were $210.
5. Utility services used during June were estimated at $300. A bill is expected early in July.
6. Fees earned for services performed but not yet billed on June 30 were $380. The company uses the account Accounts Receivable to reflect amounts due but not yet billed.

Required

a. Prepare its adjusting entries at June 30, 2011: (1) using the financial statement effects template, and (2) in journal entry form.
b. Set up T-accounts, enter the balances above, and post the adjusting entries to them.
c. Prepare its income statement for June and its balance sheet at June 30, 2011.
d. Prepare entries to close its temporary accounts in journal entry form and post the closing entries to the T-accounts.

LO3 **P3-43.** **Preparing Adjusting Entries**

The following information relates to the December 31 adjustments for Kwik Print Company. The firm's fiscal year ends on December 31.

1. Weekly employee salaries for a five-day week total $1,800, payable on Fridays. December 31 of the current year is a Tuesday.
2. Kwik Print has $20,000 of notes payable outstanding at December 31. Interest of $200 has accrued on these notes by December 31, but will not be paid until the notes mature next year.
3. During December, Kwik Print provided $900 of printing services to clients who will be billed on January 2. The firm uses the account Fees Receivable to reflect amounts due but not yet billed.
4. Starting December 1, all maintenance work on Kwik Print's equipment is handled by Richardson Repair Company under an agreement whereby Kwik Print pays a fixed monthly charge of $400. Kwik Print paid six months' service charge in advance on December 1, debiting Prepaid Maintenance for $2,400.
5. The firm paid $900 cash on December 15 for a series of radio commercials to run during December and January. One-third of the commercials have aired by December 31. The $900 payment was debited to Prepaid Advertising.
6. Starting December 16, Kwik Print rented 400 square feet of storage space from a neighboring business. The monthly rent of $0.80 per square foot is due in advance on the first of each month. Nothing was paid in December, however, because the neighbor agreed to add the rent for the one-half of December to the January 1 payment.
7. Kwik Print invested $5,000 cash in securities on December 1 and earned interest of $38 on these securities by December 31. No interest payment will be received until January.
8. Annual depreciation on the firm's equipment is $2,175. No depreciation has been recorded during the year.

Required

Prepare its adjusting entries required at December 31:

a. using the financial statement effects template, and
b. in journal entry form.

LO4, LO5 **P3-44.** **Preparing Financial Statements and Closing Entries**

The following adjusted trial balance is for Trueman Consulting Inc. at December 31, 2010. The company had no stock issuances or repurchases during 2010.

	Debit	Credit
Cash..	$ 2,700	
Accounts Receivable	3,270	
Supplies...	3,060	
Prepaid Insurance...................................	1,500	
Equipment...	6,400	
Accumulated Depreciation—Equipment		$ 1,080
Accounts Payable....................................		845
Long-Term Notes Payable		7,000
Common Stock		1,000
Retained Earnings...................................		3,305
Service Fees Earned................................		58,400
Rent Expense	12,000	
Salaries Expense.....................................	33,400	
Supplies Expense	4,700	
Insurance Expense	3,250	
Depreciation Expense—Equipment................	720	
Interest Expense	630	
	$71,630	$71,630

Required

a. Prepare its income statement and statement of stockholders' equity for 2010 and its balance sheet at December 31, 2010.

b. Prepare entries to close its accounts in journal entry form.

P3-45. Preparing Closing Entries LO5

The following adjusted trial balance is for Wilson Company at December 31, 2010.

	Debit	Credit
Cash..	$ 8,500	
Accounts Receivable	8,000	
Prepaid Insurance...................................	3,600	
Equipment...	72,000	
Accumulated Depreciation..........................		$ 12,000
Accounts Payable....................................		600
Common Stock		25,000
Retained Earnings...................................		19,100
Service Fees Earned................................		97,200
Miscellaneous Income		4,200
Salaries Expense.....................................	42,800	
Rent Expense	13,400	
Insurance Expense	1,800	
Depreciation Expense...............................	8,000	
Income Tax Expense.................................	8,800	
Income Tax Payable		8,800
	$166,900	$166,900

Required

a. Prepare closing entries in journal entry form.

b. After the firm's closing entries are posted, what is the post-closing balance for the Retained Earnings account?

c. Prepare its post-closing trial balance.

P3-46. Preparing Entries Across Two Periods LO2, LO3, LO5

The following selected accounts appear in Shaw Company's unadjusted trial balance at December 31, 2010, the end of its fiscal year (all accounts have normal balances).

Prepaid Advertising.............	$ 1,200	Unearned Service Fees..........	$ 5,400
Wages Expense.................	43,800	Service Fees Earned............	87,000
Prepaid Insurance..............	3,420	Rental Income	4,900

Required

a. Prepare its adjusting entries at December 31, 2010, (1) using the financial statement effects template, and (2) in journal entry form using the following additional information.

1. Prepaid advertising at December 31 is $800.
2. Unpaid and unrecorded wages earned by employees in December are $1,300.
3. Prepaid insurance at December 31 is $2,280.
4. Unearned service fees at December 31 are $3,000.
5. Rent revenue of $1,000 owed by a tenant is not recorded at December 31.

b. Prepare entries on January 4, 2011, using the financial statement effects template and in journal entry form, to record (1) payment of $2,400 cash in wages, which includes the $1,300 accrued at December 31 and (2) cash receipt of the $1,000 rent revenue owed from the tenant.

LO2, LO3, LO4   **P3-47.   Journalizing and Posting Transactions, and Preparing a Trial Balance and Adjustments**
Market-Probe, a market research firm, had the following transactions in June 2010, its first month of operations.

June 1 B. May invested $24,000 cash in the firm in exchange for common stock.

     1 The firm purchased the following: office equipment, $11,040; office supplies, $2,840. Terms are $4,400 cash with the remainder due in 60 days. (Make a compound entry requiring two credits.)

     2 Paid $875 cash for June rent owed to the landlord.

     2 Contracted for 3 months' advertising in a local newspaper at $310 per month and paid for the advertising in advance.

     2 Signed a 6-month contract with a customer to provide research consulting services at a rate of $3,200 per month. Received two months' fees in advance. Work on the contract started immediately.

   10 Billed various customers $5,800 for services rendered.

   12 Paid $3,600 cash for two weeks' salaries (5-day week) to employees.

   15 Paid $1,240 cash to employee for travel expenses to conference.

   18 Paid $520 cash to post office for bulk mailing of research questionnaire (postage expense).

   26 Paid $3,600 cash for two weeks' salaries to employees.

   28 Billed various customers $5,200 for services rendered.

   30 Collected $7,800 cash from customers on their accounts.

   30 Paid $1,500 cash for dividends.

Required

a. Set up a general ledger in T-account form for the following accounts: Cash; Accounts Receivable; Office Supplies; Prepaid Advertising; Office Equipment; Accumulated Depreciation—Office Equipment; Accounts Payable; Salaries Payable; Unearned Service Fees; Common Stock; Retained Earnings; Service Fees Earned; Salaries Expense; Advertising Expense; Supplies Expense; Rent Expense; Travel Expense; Depreciation Expense—Office Equipment; and Postage Expense.

b. Record these transactions (1) using the financial statement effects template, and (2) in journal entry form. (3) Post these entries to their T-accounts (key numbers in T-accounts by date).

c. Prepare an unadjusted trial balance at June 30, 2010.

d. Prepare adjusting entries (1) using the financial statement effects template and (2) in journal entry form, that reflect the following information at June 30, 2010:

- Office supplies available, $1,530
- Accrued employee salaries, $725
- Estimated life of office equipment is 8 years

Adjusting entries must also be prepared for advertising and service fees per information in the June transactions. (3) Post adjusting entries to their T-accounts.

LO3   **P3-48.   Preparing an Unadjusted Trial Balance and Adjusting Entries**
DeliverAll, a mailing service, has just completed its first full year of operations on December 31, 2010. Its general ledger account balances *before* year-end adjustments follow; no adjusting entries have been made to the accounts at any time during the year. Assume that all balances are normal.

Cash..........................	$ 2,300	Accounts Payable..............	$ 2,700
Accounts Receivable	5,120	Common Stock	9,530
Prepaid Advertising.............	1,680	Mailing Fees Earned	86,000
Supplies......................	6,270	Wages Expense.................	38,800
Equipment....................	42,240	Rent Expense	6,300
Notes Payable.................	7,500	Utilities Expense	3,020

An analysis of the firm's records reveals the following.

1. The balance in Prepaid Advertising represents the amount paid for newspaper advertising for one year. The agreement, which calls for the same amount of space and cost each month, covers the period from February 1, 2010, to January 31, 2011. DeliverAll did not advertise during its first month of operations.
2. Equipment, purchased January 1, has an estimated life of eight years.
3. Utilities expense does not include expense for December, estimated at $325. The bill will not arrive until January 2011.
4. At year-end, employees have earned an additional $1,200 in wages that will not be paid or recorded until January.
5. Supplies available at year-end amount to $1,520.
6. At year-end, unpaid interest of $450 has accrued on the notes payable.
7. The firm's lease calls for rent of $525 per month payable on the first of each month, plus an amount equal to 1/2% of annual mailing fees earned. The rental percentage is payable within 15 days after the end of the year.

Required

a. Prove that debits equal credits for its unadjusted account balances by preparing its unadjusted trial balance at December 31, 2010.
b. Prepare its adjusting entries: (1) using the financial statement effects template, and (2) in journal entry form.
c. Set up T-accounts, enter the balances above, and post the adjusting entries to them.

P3-49. Preparing Adjusting Entries   L03, L04, L05

Wheel Place Company began operations on March 1, 2010, to provide automotive wheel alignment and balancing services. On March 31, 2010, the unadjusted balances of the firm's accounts are as follows.

WHEEL PLACE COMPANY **Unadjusted Trial Balance** **March 31, 2010**		
	Debit	**Credit**
Cash..	$ 1,900	
Accounts Receivable	3,820	
Prepaid Rent	4,770	
Supplies..	3,700	
Equipment..	36,180	
Accounts Payable...		$ 2,510
Unearned Service Revenue		1,000
Common Stock		38,400
Service Revenue		12,360
Wages Expense...	3,900	
Totals..	$54,270	$54,270

The following information is available.

1. The balance in Prepaid Rent was the amount paid on March 1 to cover the first 6 months' rent.
2. Supplies available on March 31 amount to $1,720.
3. Equipment has an estimated life of nine years and a zero salvage value.
4. Unpaid and unrecorded wages at March 31 were $560.
5. Utility services used during March were estimated at $390; a bill is expected early in April.

6. The balance in Unearned Service Revenue was the amount received on March 1 from a car dealer to cover alignment and balancing services on cars sold by the dealer in March and April. The Wheel Place agreed to provide the services at a fixed fee of $500 each month.

Required

a. Prepare its adjusting entries at March 31, 2010, (1) using the financial statement effects template, and (2) in journal entry form.

b. Set up T-accounts, enter the balances above, and post the adjusting entries to them.

c. Prepare its income statement for March and its balance sheet at March 31, 2010.

d. Prepare entries to close its temporary accounts in journal entry form and post the closing entries to the T-accounts.

LO4, LO5 **P3-50.** **Preparing Financial Statements and Closing Entries**

Trails, Inc., publishes magazines for skiers and hikers. The company's adjusted trial balance for the year ending December 31, 2010, is:

	Debit	Credit
Cash.	$ 3,400	
Accounts Receivable	8,600	
Supplies.	4,200	
Prepaid Insurance.	930	
Office Equipment.	66,000	
Accumulated Depreciation.		$ 11,000
Accounts Payable.		2,100
Unearned Subscription Revenue		10,000
Salaries Payable		3,500
Common Stock.		25,000
Retained Earnings.		23,220
Subscription Revenue.		168,300
Advertising Revenue.		49,700
Salaries Expense.	100,230	
Printing and Mailing Expense.	85,600	
Rent Expense	8,800	
Supplies Expense	6,100	
Insurance Expense	1,860	
Depreciation Expense.	5,500	
Income Tax Expense.	1,600	
Totals.	$292,820	$292,820

Required

a. Prepare its income statement and statement of stockholders' equity for 2010, and its balance sheet at December 31, 2010. There were no cash dividends and no stock issuances or repurchases during the year.

b. Prepare entries to close its accounts in journal entry form.

LO5 **P3-51.** **Preparing Closing Entries**

The following adjusted trial balance is for Mayflower Moving Service at December 31, 2010.

	Debit	Credit
Cash.	$ 3,800	
Accounts Receivable	5,250	
Supplies.	2,300	
Prepaid Advertising.	3,000	
Trucks	28,300	
Accumulated Depreciation—Trucks.		$ 10,000
Equipment.	7,600	
Accumulated Depreciation—Equipment		2,100
Accounts Payable.		1,200
Unearned Service Fees.		2,700
Common Stock		5,000
Retained Earnings.		15,550
Service Fees Earned.		72,500
Wages Expense.	29,800	

continued

continued from previous page

	Debit	Credit
Rent Expense	10,200	
Insurance Expense	2,900	
Supplies Expense	5,100	
Advertising Expense	6,000	
Depreciation Expense—Trucks	4,000	
Depreciation Expense—Equipment	800	
Totals	$109,050	$109,050

Required

a. Prepare closing entries in journal entry form.

b. After its closing entries are posted, what is the post-closing balance for the Retained Earnings account?

c. Prepare Mayflower's post-closing trial balance.

P3-52. Preparing Entries Across Two Periods

LO2, LO3, LO5

The following selected accounts appear in Zimmerman Company's unadjusted trial balance at December 31, 2010, the end of its fiscal year (all accounts have normal balances).

Prepaid Maintenance	$2,700	Commission Fees Earned	$84,000
Supplies	8,400	Rent Expense	10,800
Unearned Commission Fees	8,500		

Required

a. Prepare its adjusting entries at December 31, 2010 (1) using the financial statement effects template, and (2) in journal entry form. Additional information is as follows.

   1. On September 1, 2010, the company entered into a prepaid equipment maintenance contract. Zimmerman Company paid $2,700 to cover maintenance service for 6 months, beginning September 1, 2010. The $2,700 payment was debited to Prepaid Maintenance.

   2. Supplies available on December 31 are $3,200.

   3. Unearned commission fees at December 31 are $4,000.

   4. Commission fees earned but not yet billed at December 31 are $2,800. (*Hint:* Debit Fees Receivable.)

   5. Zimmerman Company's lease calls for rent of $900 per month payable on the first of each month, plus an annual amount equal to 1% of annual commissions earned. This additional rent is payable on January 10 of the following year. (*Hint:* Use the adjusted amount of commissions earned in computing the additional rent.)

b. Prepare entries on January 10, 2011, using both the financial statement effects template and in journal entry form, to record (1) the billing of $4,600 in commissions earned (which includes the $2,800 of commissions earned but not billed at December 31) and (2) the cash payment of the additional rent owed for 2010.

P3-53. Preparing Adjusting Entries, Financial Statements, and Closing Entries

LO3, LO4, LO5, LO6

Fischer Card Shop is a small retail shop. Fischer's balance sheet at year-end 2010 is as follows. The following information details transactions and adjustments that occurred during 2011.

   1. Sales total $145,850 in 2011; all sales were cash sales.

   2. Inventory purchases total $76,200 in 2011; at December 31, 2011, inventory totals $14,500.

   3. Accounts payable totals $4,100 at December 31, 2011.

   4. Annual store rent for 2011 totals $24,000 and was paid on March 1, 2011, covering the next 12 months. The balance in prepaid rent at December 31, 2010, was the balance remaining from the advance rent payment in 2010.

   5. Wages are paid every other week on Friday; during 2011, Fischer paid $12,500 cash for wages. At December 31, 2011 (a Saturday), Fischer owed employees unpaid and unrecorded wages of $350.

   6. Depreciation on equipment totals $1,700 in 2011.

<table>
<tr><td colspan="4" align="center">**FISCHER CARD SHOP**
Balance Sheet
December 31, 2010</td></tr>
<tr><td>Cash.........................</td><td align="right">$ 8,500</td><td>Accounts payable ....</td><td align="right">$ 5,200</td></tr>
<tr><td>Inventories..................</td><td align="right">12,000</td><td>Wages payable ....</td><td align="right">100</td></tr>
<tr><td>Prepaid rent.................</td><td align="right">3,800</td><td>Total current liabilities.................</td><td align="right">5,300</td></tr>
<tr><td>Total current assets...........</td><td align="right">24,300</td><td>Total equity (includes retained earnings)..</td><td align="right">23,500</td></tr>
<tr><td>Equipment ....$7,500</td><td></td><td>Total liabilities and equity..............</td><td align="right">$28,800</td></tr>
<tr><td>Less accumulated depreciation.. 3,000</td><td></td><td></td><td></td></tr>
<tr><td>Equipment, net ....</td><td align="right">4,500</td><td></td><td></td></tr>
<tr><td>Total Assets.................</td><td align="right">$28,800</td><td></td><td></td></tr>
</table>

Required

a. Prepare any necessary journal entries for 2011 and adjusting entries at December 31, 2011, (1) using the financial statement effects template, and (2) in journal entry form.
b. Set up T-accounts, enter the balances above, and post the adjusting entries to them.
c. Prepare its income statement for 2011, and its balance sheet at December 31, 2011.
d. Prepare entries to close its temporary accounts in journal entry form and post the closing entries to the T-accounts.

LO2, LO3, LO4, LO5   **P3-54.**   **Applying the Entire Accounting Cycle**

WebAssign

Rhoades Tax Services began business on December 1, 2010. Its December transactions are as follows.

Dec. 1 Rhoades invested $20,000 in the business in exchange for common stock.
  2 Paid $1,200 cash for December rent to Bomba Realty.
  2 Purchased $1,080 of supplies on account.
  3 Purchased $9,500 of office equipment; paying $4,700 cash with the balance due in 30 days.
  8 Paid $1,080 cash on account for supplies purchased December 2.
 14 Paid $900 cash for assistant's wages for 2 weeks' work.
 20 Performed consulting services for $3,000 cash.
 28 Paid $900 cash for assistant's wages for 2 weeks' work.
 30 Billed clients $7,200 for December consulting services.
 31 Paid $1,800 cash for dividends.

Required

a. Set up a general ledger in T-account form for the following accounts: Cash; Fees Receivable; Supplies; Office Equipment; Accumulated Depreciation—Office Equipment; Accounts Payable; Wages Payable; Common Stock; Retained Earnings; Consulting Revenue; Supplies Expense; Wages Expense; Rent Expense; and Depreciation Expense.
b. Record these transactions (1) using the financial statement effects template, and (2) in journal entry form. (3) Post these entries to their T-accounts (key numbers in T-accounts by date).
c. Prepare an unadjusted trial balance at December 31, 2010.
d. Journalize the adjusting entries at December 31 (using both the financial statement effects template and journal entry form), drawing on the following information.
  1. Supplies available at December 31 are $710.
  2. Accrued wages payable at December 31 are $270.
  3. Depreciation for December is $120.
  4. Rhoades has spent 30 hours on an involved tax fraud case during December. When completed in January, his work will be billed at $75 per hour. (It uses the account Fees Receivable to reflect amounts earned but not yet billed.)

  Then post adjusting entries to their T-accounts.
e. Prepare an adjusted trial balance at December 31, 2010.
f. Prepare a December 2010 income statement and statement of stockholders' equity, and a December 31, 2010, balance sheet.
g. Record its closing entries (1) using the financial statement effects template and (2) in journal entry form. Post these entries to their T-accounts.
h. Prepare a post-closing trial balance at December 31, 2010.

CASES AND PROJECTS

C3-55. Preparing Adjusting Entries, Financial Statements, and Closing Entries   LO2, LO3, LO4, LO5
Seaside Surf Shop began operations on July 1, 2010, with an initial investment of $50,000. During the initial 3 months of operations, the following cash transactions were recorded in the firm's checking account.

Cash receipts		Cash payments	
Initial investment by owner	$ 50,000	Rent	$ 24,000
Collected from customers	81,000	Fixtures and equipment	25,000
Borrowed from bank 7/1/2010	10,000	Merchandise inventory	62,000
Total cash receipts	$141,000	Salaries	6,000
		Other expenses	13,000
		Total cash payments	$130,000

Additional information

1. Most sales were for cash, however, the store accepted a limited amount of credit sales; at September 30, 2010, customers owed the store $9,000.
2. Rent was paid on July 1 for six months.
3. Salaries of $3,000 per month are paid on the 1st of each month for salaries earned in the month prior.
4. Inventories are purchased for cash; at September 30, 2010, inventory worth $21,000 was available.
5. Fixtures and equipment were expected to last five years with zero salvage value.
6. The bank charges 12% annual interest (1% per month) on its bank loan.

Required

a. Prepare any necessary adjusting entries at September 30, 2010, (1) using the financial statement effects template, and (2) in journal entry form.
b. Set up T-accounts and post the adjusting entries to them.
c. Prepare its initial three-month income statement for 2010 and its balance sheet at September 30, 2010. (Ignore taxes.)
d. Analyze the statements from part c and assess the company's performance over its initial 3 months.

C3-56. Analyzing Transactions, Impacts on Financial Ratios, and Loan Covenants   LO2, LO3, LO6
Wyland Consulting, a firm started three years ago by Reyna Wyland, offers consulting services for material handling and plant layout. Its balance sheet at the close of 2010 is as follows.

<table>
<tr><td colspan="7" align="center">WYLAND CONSULTING
Balance Sheet
December 31, 2010</td></tr>
<tr><td colspan="3" align="center">Assets</td><td colspan="4" align="center">Liabilities</td></tr>
<tr><td>Cash</td><td></td><td>$ 3,400</td><td>Notes payable</td><td></td><td></td><td>$30,000</td></tr>
<tr><td>Accounts receivable</td><td></td><td>22,875</td><td>Accounts payable</td><td></td><td></td><td>4,200</td></tr>
<tr><td>Supplies</td><td></td><td>13,200</td><td>Unearned consulting fees</td><td></td><td></td><td>11,300</td></tr>
<tr><td>Prepaid insurance</td><td></td><td>4,500</td><td>Wages payable</td><td></td><td></td><td>400</td></tr>
<tr><td>Equipment</td><td>$68,500</td><td></td><td>Total liabilities</td><td></td><td></td><td>45,900</td></tr>
<tr><td>Less: accumulated depreciation</td><td>23,975</td><td>44,525</td><td colspan="4" align="center">Equity</td></tr>
<tr><td></td><td></td><td></td><td>Common stock</td><td></td><td></td><td>8,000</td></tr>
<tr><td></td><td></td><td></td><td>Retained earnings</td><td></td><td></td><td>34,600</td></tr>
<tr><td>Total assets</td><td></td><td>$88,500</td><td>Total liabilities and equity</td><td></td><td></td><td>$88,500</td></tr>
</table>

Earlier in the year Wyland obtained a bank loan of $30,000 cash for the firm. One of the provisions of the loan is that the year-end debt-to-equity ratio (ratio of total liabilities to total equity) cannot exceed 1.0. Based on the above balance sheet, the ratio at the end of 2010 is 1.08. Wyland is concerned about being in violation of the loan agreement and requests assistance in reviewing the situation. Wyland believes that she might have overlooked some items at year-end. Discussions with Wyland reveal the following.

1. On January 1, 2010, the firm paid a $4,500 insurance premium for 2 years of coverage; the amount in Prepaid Insurance has not yet been adjusted.
2. Depreciation on the equipment should be 10% of cost per year; the company inadvertently recorded 15% for 2010.
3. Interest on the bank loan has been paid through the end of 2010.
4. The firm concluded a major consulting engagement in December, doing a plant layout analysis for a new factory. The $6,000 fee has not been billed or recorded in the accounts.
5. On December 1, 2010, the firm received an $11,300 advance payment from Croy Corporation for consulting services to be rendered over a 2-month period. This payment was credited to the Unearned Consulting Fees account. One-half of this fee was earned by December 31, 2010.
6. Supplies costing $4,800 were available on December 31; the company has made no entry in the accounts.

Required

a. What portion of the company is financed by debt versus equity (called the debt-to-equity ratio and defined in Chapter 1) at December 31, 2010?

b. Is the firm in violation of its loan agreement? Prepare computations to support the correct total liabilities and total equity figures at December 31, 2010.

LO2, LO3 **C3-57.** **Ethics, Accounting Adjustments, and Auditors**

It is the end of the accounting year for Juliet Javetz, controller of a medium-sized, publicly held corporation specializing in toxic waste cleanup. Within the corporation, only Javetz and the president know that the firm has been negotiating for several months to land a large contract for waste cleanup in Western Europe. The president has hired another firm with excellent contacts in Western Europe to help with negotiations. The outside firm will charge an hourly fee plus expenses, but has agreed not to submit a bill until the negotiations are in their final stages (expected to occur in another 3 to 4 months). Even if the contract falls through, the outside firm is entitled to receive payment for its services. Based upon her discussion with a member of the outside firm, Javetz knows that its charge for services provided to date will be $150,000. This is a material amount for the company.

Javetz knows that the president wants negotiations to remain as secret as possible so that competitors will not learn of the contract the company is pursuing in Europe. In fact, the president recently stated to her, "This is not the time to reveal our actions in Western Europe to other staff members, our auditors, or the readers of our financial statements; securing this contract is crucial to our future growth." No entry has been made in the accounting records for the cost of contract negotiations. Javetz now faces an uncomfortable situation. The company's outside auditor has just asked her if she knows of any year-end adjustments that have not yet been recorded.

Required

a. What are the ethical considerations that Javetz faces in answering the auditor's question?

b. How should Javetz respond to the auditor's question?

LO2, LO3, LO4 **C3-58.** **Inferring Adjusting Entries from Financial Statements**

J. Jill Group, Inc., a specialty retailer of women's apparel, markets its products through retail stores and catalogs. Selected information from its 2005 and 2004 balance sheets is as follows.

Selected Balance Sheet Data ($ thousands)	2004	2005
Prepaid catalog expenses (asset)	$3,894	$4,306
Advertising credits receivable	21	534
Unearned gift certificate revenue	6,108	7,053

The following excerpts are from J. Jill's 2005 10-K report.

- Catalog costs in the direct segment are considered direct response advertising and as such are capitalized as incurred and amortized over the expected sales life of each catalog, which is generally a period not exceeding six months.

- The Company periodically enters into arrangements with certain national magazine publishers whereby the Company includes magazine subscription cards in its catalog mailings in exchange for advertising credits or discounts on advertising.

Required

a. Assume that J. Jill spent $62,550 to design, print, and mail catalogs in 2005. Also assume that it received advertising credits of $849. Prepare the entry, using the financial statement effects template and in journal entry form, that J. Jill would have recorded when these costs were incurred.

b. Prepare the adjusting entry, using the financial statement effects template and in journal entry form, that would be necessary to record its amortization of prepaid catalog costs.

c. How do advertising credits expire? Prepare the adjusting entry, using both the financial statement effects template and in journal entry form, that J. Jill would record to reflect the change in advertising credits.

d. Assume that J. Jill sold gift certificates valued at $19,175 in 2005. Prepare the entry, using the financial statement effects template and in journal entry form, that J. Jill would make to record these sales. Next, prepare the entry, using the financial statement effects template and in journal entry form, that it makes to record merchandise sales to customers who pay with gift certificates.

SOLUTIONS TO REVIEW PROBLEMS

Mid-Chapter Review

Part 1 Solution

a.

Transaction		Balance Sheet						Income Statement		
	Cash Asset +	Noncash Assets -	Contra Assets =	Liabilities +	Contrib. Capital +	Earned Capital		Revenues -	Expenses =	Net Income
(a) Adjusting entry to record supplies and parts used.		−91,000 Supplies and Parts				−91,000 Retained Earnings			−91,000 Supplies and Parts Expenses	−91,000

(a)	Supplies and parts expense (+E, −SE)	91,000	
	Supplies and parts (−A)		91,000

b.

Transaction		Balance Sheet						Income Statement		
	Cash Asset +	Noncash Assets -	Contra Assets =	Liabilities +	Contrib. Capital +	Earned Capital		Revenues -	Expenses =	Net Income
(b) Adjusting entry to record rent expense accrued but not yet paid.				+2,500 Accounts Payable		−2,500 Retained Earnings			+2,500 Rent Expense	−2,500

(b)	Rent expense (+E, −SE)	2,500	
	Accounts payable (+L)		2,500

The $2,500 expense for October is not recorded because it is not yet incurred as of September 30.

c.

Transaction	Balance Sheet						Income Statement		
	Cash Asset +	Noncash Assets −	Contra Assets =	Liabil- ities +	Contrib. Capital +	Earned Capital	Revenues −	Expenses =	Net Income
(c) Adjusting entry to record depreciation on building.			+50,000 Accumulated Depreciation —Building =			−50,000 Retained Earnings		+50,000 Depreciation Expense =	−50,000

(c)			
	Depreciation expense (+E, −SE)	50,000	
	Accumulated depreciation—Building (+XA, −A)		50,000

d. No entry required; the executive has not yet begun work and thus no expense is incurred.

e.

Transaction	Balance Sheet						Income Statement		
(e) Adjusting entry to record cash advance, of which a part is earned.	+1,200 Cash	−	=	+600 Unearned Revenue	+600 Retained Earnings		+600 Services Revenue −	=	+600

(e)			
	Cash (+A)...	1,200	
	Unearned revenue (+L)...................................		600
	Services revenue (+R, +SE)		600

f.

Transaction	Balance Sheet						Income Statement		
(f) Adjusting entry to record wages earned but not yet paid.	−	=		+25,000 Wages Payable	−25,000 Retained Earnings		−	+25,000 Wages Expense =	−25,000

(f)			
	Wages expense (+E, −SE)	25,000	
	Wages payable (+L).......................................		25,000

Part 2 Solution

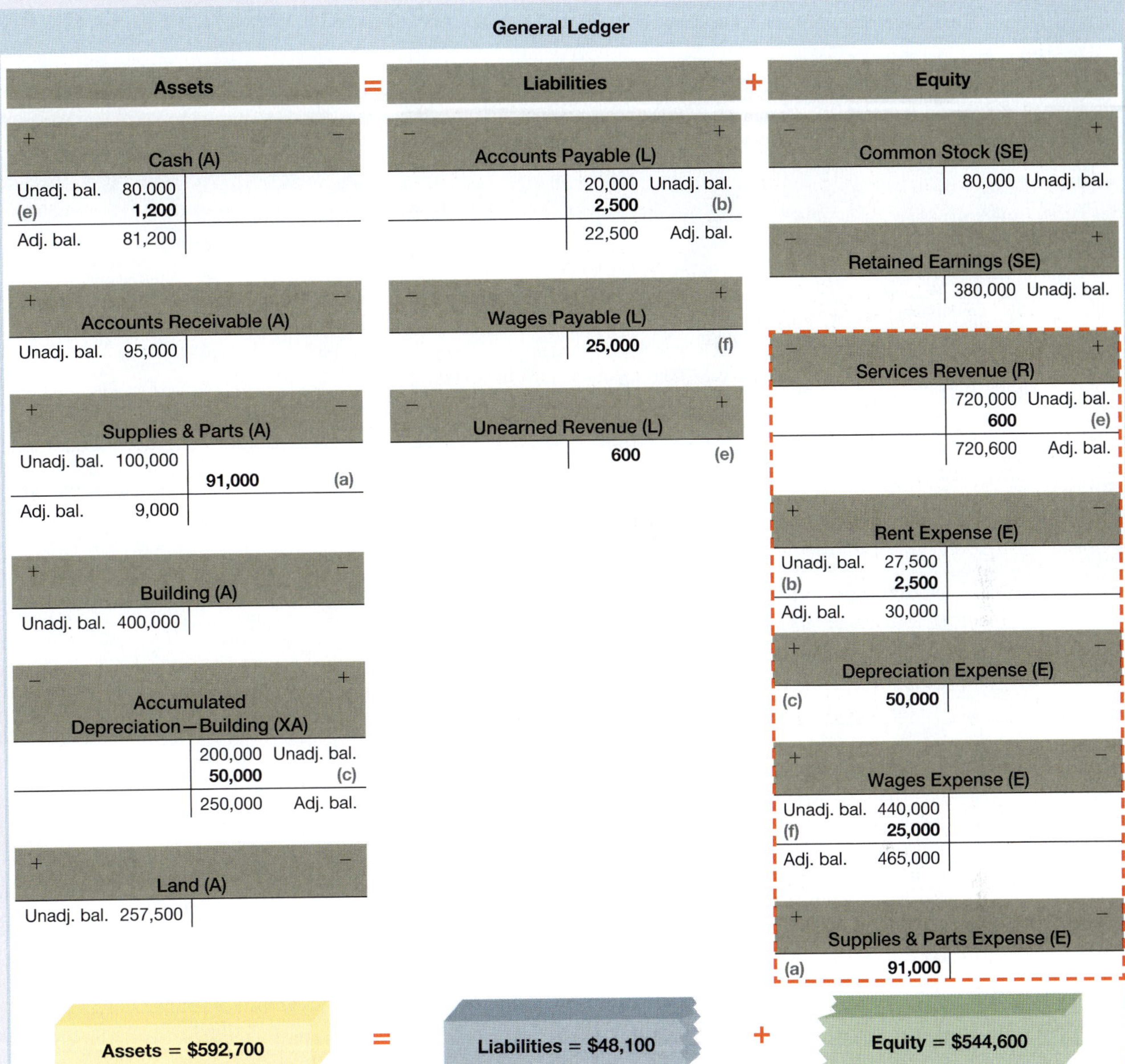

Chapter-End Review

Solutions
Part 1

Transaction	Cash Asset	+	Noncash Assets	−	Contra Assets	=	Liabil- ities	+	Contrib. Capital	+	Earned Capital		Revenues	−	Expenses	=	Net Income
					Balance Sheet										**Income Statement**		
(1) Adjustment to record insurance expense.			−1,500 Prepaid Insurance	−		=					−1,500 Retained Earnings			−	+1,500 Insurance Expense	=	−1,500

(1)	Insurance expense (+E, −SE)...............................	1,500	
	Prepaid insurance (−A)		1,500
	Record insurance expired $6,000 × (6 months/24 months).		

Transaction	Cash Asset	+	Noncash Assets	−	Contra Assets	=	Liabil- ities	+	Contrib. Capital	+	Earned Capital		Revenues	−	Expenses	=	Net Income
(2) Adjustment to record supplies expense.			−25,000 Supplies	−		=					−25,000 Retained Earnings			−	+25,000 Supplies Expense	=	−25,000

(2)	Supplies expense (+E, −SE)	25,000	
	Supplies (−A)		25,000
	Record supplies used ($31,300 − $6,300).		

Transaction	Cash Asset	+	Noncash Assets	−	Contra Assets	=	Liabil- ities	+	Contrib. Capital	+	Earned Capital		Revenues	−	Expenses	=	Net Income
(3) Adjustment to record depreciation expense.				−	+30,000 Accumulated Depreciation —Equipment	=					−30,000 Retained Earnings			−	+30,000 Depreciation Expense	=	−30,000

(3)	Depreciation expense (+E, −SE)	30,000	
	Accumulated depreciation—Equipment (+XA, −A)		30,000
	Record depreciation [($270,000 − $0) ÷ 9 years].		

Transaction	Cash Asset	+	Noncash Assets	−	Contra Assets	=	Liabil- ities	+	Contrib. Capital	+	Earned Capital		Revenues	−	Expenses	=	Net Income
(4) Adjustment to record fees revenue.				−		=	−3,000 Unearned Fees	+		+	+3,000 Retained Earnings		+3,000 Fees Revenue	−		=	+3,000

(4)	Unearned fees (−L)	3,000	
	Fees revenue (+R, +SE).............................		3,000
	Record fees earned.		

Transaction	Cash Asset	+	Noncash Assets	−	Contra Assets	=	Liabil- ities	+	Contrib. Capital	+	Earned Capital		Revenues	−	Expenses	=	Net Income
(5) Adjustment to record wages expense.				−		=	+600 Wages Payable	+		+	−600 Retained Earnings			−	+600 Wages Expense	=	−600

(5)	Wages expense (+E, −SE)	600	
	Wages payable (+L)		600
	Record employee wages incurred.		

continued

continued from previous page

Transaction	Balance Sheet						Income Statement		
	Cash Asset +	Noncash Assets −	Contra Assets =	Liabil-ities +	Contrib. Capital +	Earned Capital	Revenues −	Expenses =	Net Income
(6) Adjustment to record rent expense.	−	=		+2,000 Rent Payable		−2,000 Retained Earnings	−	+2,000 Rent Expense =	−2,000

(6)	Rent expense (+E, −SE)	2,000	
	Rent payable (+L)		2,000
	Record rent owed.		

General Ledger

Assets = Liabilities + Equity

+ Cash (A) −

Unadj. bal.	1,000	
Adj. bal.	1,000	

+ Accounts Receivable (A) −

Unadj. bal.	9,200	
Adj. bal.	9,200	

+ Prepaid Insurance (A) −

Unadj. bal.	6,000	1,500	(1)
Adj. bal.	4,500		

+ Supplies (A) −

Unadj. bal.	31,300	25,000	(2)
Adj. bal.	6,300		

+ Equipment (A) −

Unadj. bal.	270,000	
Adj. bal.	270,000	

− Accumulated Depreciation—Equipment (XA) +

		60,000	Unadj. bal.
		30,000	(3)
		90,000	Adj. bal.

− Accounts Payable (L) +

		3,100	Unadj. bal.
		3,100	Adj. bal.

− Unearned Fees (L) +

(4)	3,000	4,000	Unadj. bal.
		1,000	Adj. bal.

− Wages Payable (L) +

		600	(5)
		600	Adj. bal.

− Rent Payable (L) +

		2,000	(6)
		2,000	Adj. bal.

− Common Stock (SE) +

		120,400	Unadj. bal.
		120,400	Adj. bal.

− Retained Earnings (SE) +

		60,000	Unadj. bal.
		60,000	Adj. bal.

− Fees Revenue (R) +

		150,000	Unadj. bal.
		3,000	(4)
		153,000	Adj. bal.

+ Insurance Expense (E) −

(1)	1,500	

+ Supplies Expenses (E) −

(2)	25,000	
Adj. bal.	25,000	

+ Depreciation Expense (E) −

(3)	30,000	
Adj. bal.	30,000	

+ Rent Expense (E) −

Unadj. bal.	22,000	
(6)	2,000	
Adj. bal.	24,000	

+ Wages Expense (E) −

Unadj. bal.	58,000	
(5)	600	
Adj. bal.	58,600	

Assets = $201,000 = Liabilities = $6,700 + Equity = $194,300

Part 2

ATWELL LABORATORIES, INC.
Adjusted Trial Balance
June 30, 2010

	Debits	Credits
Cash	$ 1,000	
Accounts Receivable	9,200	
Prepaid Insurance	4,500	
Supplies	6,300	
Equipment	270,000	
Accumulated Depreciation—Equipment		$ 90,000
Accounts Payable		3,100
Rent Payable		2,000
Wages Payable		600
Unearned Fees		1,000
Fees Revenue		153,000
Wages Expense	58,600	
Rent Expense	24,000	
Insurance Expense	1,500	
Supplies Expense	25,000	
Depreciation Expense	30,000	
Common Stock		120,400
Retained Earnings		60,000
Totals	$430,100	$430,100

Part 3

a.	Retained earnings (−SE)	139,100	
	Insurance expense (−E)		1,500
	Supplies expense (−E)		25,000
	Depreciation expense (−E)		30,000
	Rent expense (−E)		24,000
	Wages expense (−E)		58,600

b.	Fees revenue (−R)	153,000	
	Retained earnings (+SE)		153,000

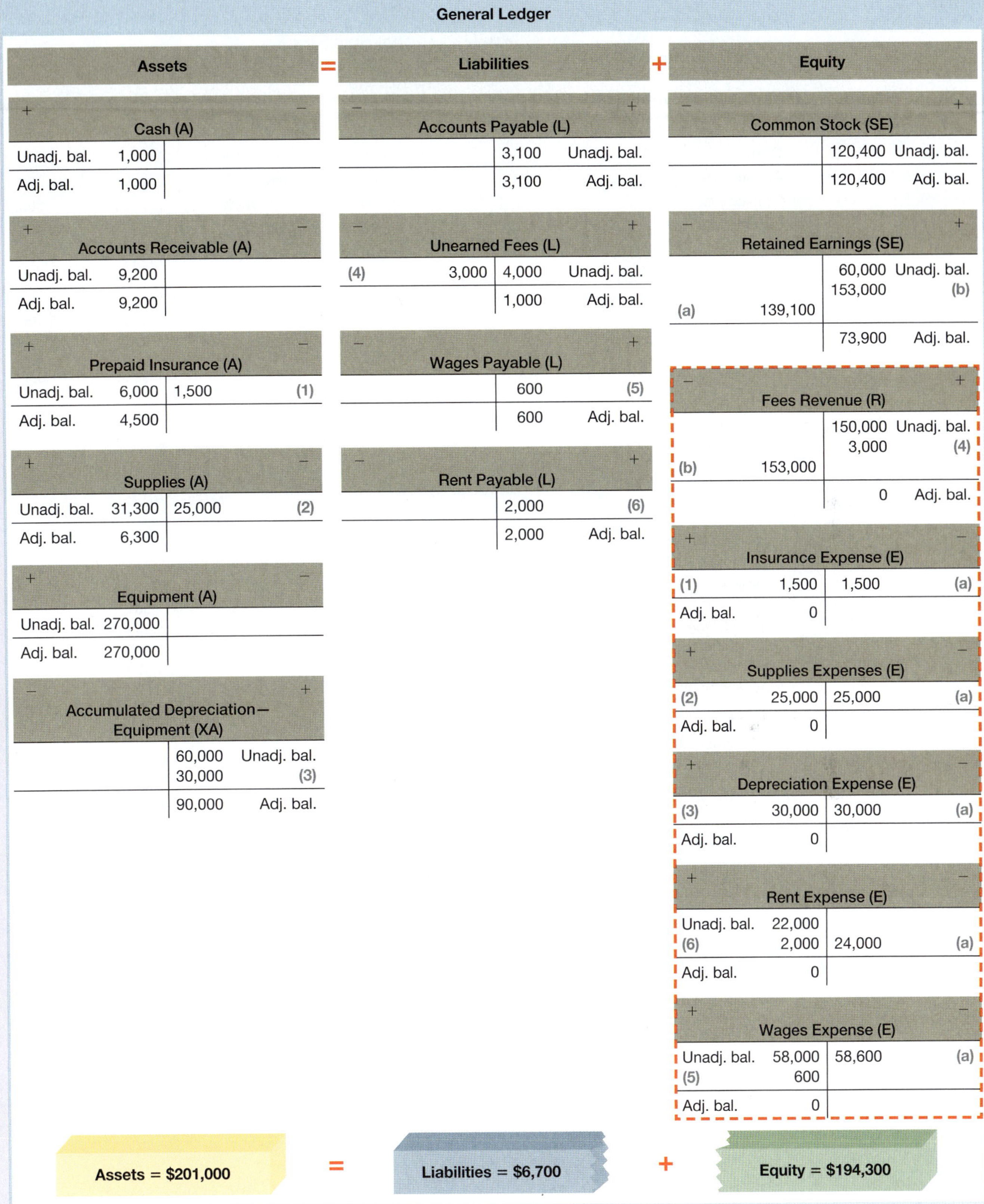

General Ledger

Assets = Liabilities + Equity

Cash (A)
Unadj. bal. 1,000
Adj. bal. 1,000

Accounts Receivable (A)
Unadj. bal. 9,200
Adj. bal. 9,200

Prepaid Insurance (A)
Unadj. bal. 6,000   1,500   (1)
Adj. bal. 4,500

Supplies (A)
Unadj. bal. 31,300   25,000   (2)
Adj. bal. 6,300

Equipment (A)
Unadj. bal. 270,000
Adj. bal. 270,000

Accumulated Depreciation—Equipment (XA)
60,000   Unadj. bal.
30,000   (3)
90,000   Adj. bal.

Accounts Payable (L)
3,100   Unadj. bal.
3,100   Adj. bal.

Unearned Fees (L)
(4)   3,000   4,000   Unadj. bal.
1,000   Adj. bal.

Wages Payable (L)
600   (5)
600   Adj. bal.

Rent Payable (L)
2,000   (6)
2,000   Adj. bal.

Common Stock (SE)
120,400   Unadj. bal.
120,400   Adj. bal.

Retained Earnings (SE)
60,000   Unadj. bal.
153,000   (b)
(a)   139,100
73,900   Adj. bal.

Fees Revenue (R)
150,000   Unadj. bal.
3,000   (4)
(b)   153,000
0   Adj. bal.

Insurance Expense (E)
(1)   1,500   1,500   (a)
Adj. bal.   0

Supplies Expenses (E)
(2)   25,000   25,000   (a)
Adj. bal.   0

Depreciation Expense (E)
(3)   30,000   30,000   (a)
Adj. bal.   0

Rent Expense (E)
Unadj. bal.   22,000
(6)   2,000   24,000   (a)
Adj. bal.   0

Wages Expense (E)
Unadj. bal.   58,000   58,600   (a)
(5)   600
Adj. bal.   0

Assets = $201,000   =   Liabilities = $6,700   +   Equity = $194,300

Part 4

ATWELL LABORATORIES, INC.
Balance Sheet
June 30, 2010

Assets			Liabilities		
Cash.		$ 1,000	Accounts payable	$	3,100
Accounts receivable		9,200	Unearned fees		1,000
Prepaid insurance		4,500	Wages payable		600
Supplies		6,300	Rent payable		2,000
Total current assets.		21,000	Total current liabilities.		6,700
Equipment, original cost	$270,000				
Less accumulated depreciation	90,000	180,000	**Equity**		
			Common stock		120,400
			Retained earnings		73,900
Total assets		$201,000	Totals liabilities and equity		$201,000

ATWELL LABORATORIES, INC.
Income Statement
For Year Ended June 30, 2010

Fees revenue		$153,000
Expenses		
Insurance expense	$ 1,500	
Supplies expense	25,000	
Depreciation expense	30,000	
Rent expense.	24,000	
Wages expense	58,600	
Total expense		139,100
Net income.		$ 13,900

ATWELL LABORATORIES, INC.
Statement of Stockholders' Equity
For Year Ended June 30, 2010

	Common Stock	Retained Earnings	Total
Balance at June 30, 2009	$120,400	$60,000	$180,400
Net Income	—	13,900	13,900
Balance at June 30, 2010	$120,400	$73,900	$194,300

Atwell's statement of stockholders' equity is much simpler than the usual statement because we have focused on the adjustment and closing process. In doing so, we did not consider additional activities in which corporations commonly engage, such as paying dividends, issuing stock, and repurchasing stock. (Requirements did not ask for a statement of cash flows. The next chapter is devoted to the statement of cash flows.)

LEARNING OBJECTIVES

1. Explain the purpose of the statement of cash flows and how it complements the income statement and the balance sheet. (p. 152)

2. Construct and explain the statement of cash flows. (p. 157)

3. Compute and interpret ratios that reflect a company's liquidity and solvency. (p. 173)

4. Appendix 4A: Use a spreadsheet to construct the statement of cash flows. (p. 175)

© Getty Images

Reporting and Analyzing Cash Flows

The year 2009 was challenging for **Walgreen Co.** Although revenue grew by 7.3%, earnings declined by more than $150 million. Despite the drop in earnings, Walgreen's stock price climbed from just over $21 per share early in 2009 to more than $40 late in the year.

WALGREENS
www.walgreens.com

Walgreen operates 6,997 drugstores. In 2009 it opened 626 new stores and closed 72 stores. As we noted in the opening to Chapter 3, Walgreen plans to slow its new store growth in response to the recession. As CEO Gregory Wasson put it "This allows us to put about a half billion dollars of capital expenditures back into the stores." Nevertheless, opening new stores requires cash.

In addition to new stores, the company began its "Customer Centric Retailing" initiative in 2009. The purpose of this program is to redesign existing stores to ensure optimal layouts, shelf height and sight lines, and improve product assortment and brand offerings. The initiative is expected to cost $30 thousand to $50 thousand per store and be completed by 2011. This cost, along with the cost of opening new stores, is listed in Walgreen's cash flow statement under *investing activities*. During 2009, Walgreen spent almost $2 billion on new property and equipment, and an additional $405 million acquiring other businesses and intangible assets.

Also in 2009, Walgreen's board of directors announced a plan to repurchase up to $2 billion of the company's common stock while maintaining its policy of paying out 30% to 35% of net income to stockholders as dividends. In 2009, stock purchases totaled $279 million and cash dividends paid totaled $446 million. These cash outflows are reported in Walgreen's statement of cash flows under *financing activities*.

New stores, redesigned stores, stock repurchases and dividends all require cash outflows. Where does this cash come from? In order to maintain store growth and improvement while enhancing stockholder returns, Walgreen must generate positive cash flow from *operating activities*. In 2009, Walgreen's operating activities produced cash inflows of $4,111 million, which is more than double its net income. In fact, Walgreen's cash flow from operating activities has exceeded net income each year for the past four years.

(continued on next page)

(continued from previous page)

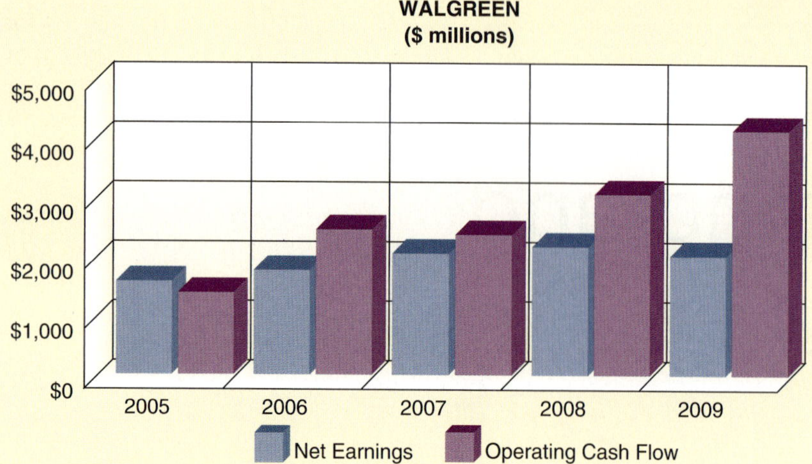

As we will discover in this chapter, a business must make sure that its cash inflows are adequate to fund new investments, meet obligations to creditors as they come due, and pay dividends to shareholders. Even a profitable company can fail if it does not have a healthy cash flow. We will also discover why it is important to look at the cash flow statement along with the income statement and balance sheet when trying to assess the financial health of a company.

Sources: The *New York Times*, January 2, 2009; *Chicago Tribune*, January 9, 2009; Walgreen Company 2009, 2008 and 2007 annual reports.

CHAPTER ORGANIZATION

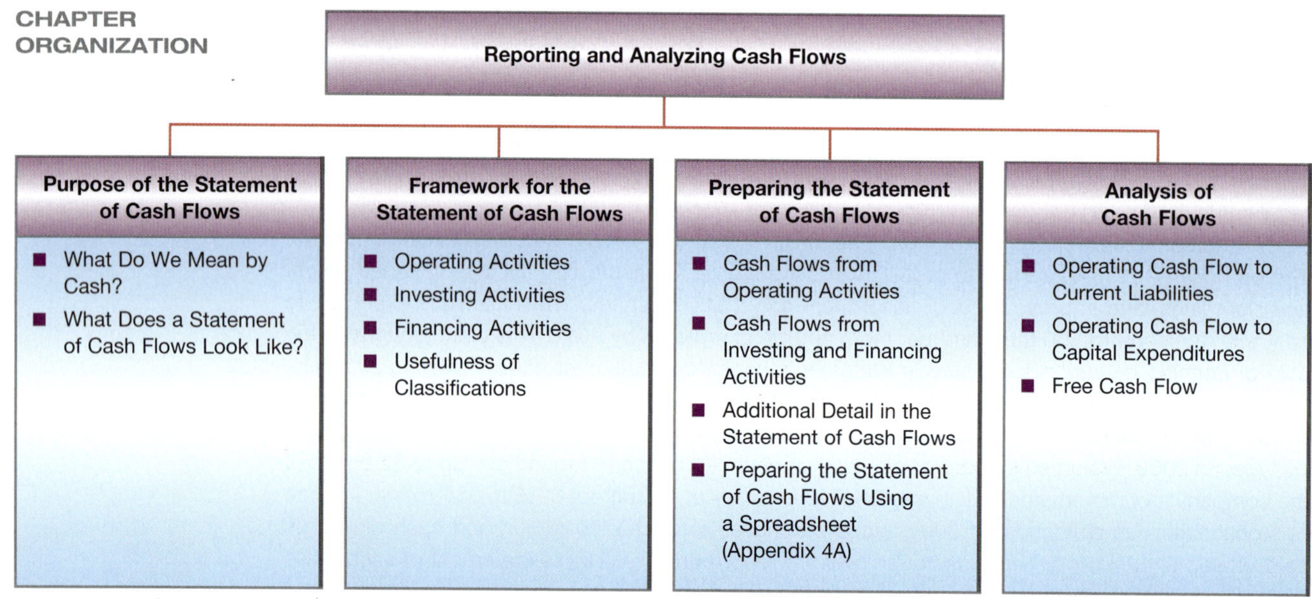

PURPOSE OF THE STATEMENT OF CASH FLOWS

LO1 Explain the purpose of the statement of cash flows and how it complements the income statement and the balance sheet.

In addition to the balance sheet and the income statement, corporations are required to report a statement of cash flows. The **statement of cash flows** tells us how a company generated cash (cash inflows) and how it used cash (cash outflows). The statement of cash flows complements the income statement and the balance sheet by providing answers to questions that neither the income statement nor the balance sheet can provide.

Understanding the statement of cash flows helps us understand a firm's liquidity (ability to pay near-term liabilities), and it helps us assess a firm's solvency (ability to pay long-term liabilities). With information about how cash was generated or used, creditors and investors are better able to assess a firm's ability to settle its liabilities and pay dividends to shareholders. A firm's need for outside financing is also better evaluated when using cash flow data. Over time, the statement of cash flows permits users to observe and assess management's investing and financing policies. For example, a business that is not generating enough cash flow internally, i.e., from operations, must get cash from borrowing, issuing shares, or selling off its assets.

The statement of cash flows also provides information about a firm's ability to generate sufficient amounts of cash to respond to unanticipated needs and opportunities. Information about past cash flows, particularly cash flows from operations, helps in assessing a company's financial flexibility. An evaluation of a firm's ability to survive an unexpected drop in demand, for example, should include a review of its past cash flows from operations. The larger these cash flows, the greater is the firm's ability to withstand adverse changes in economic conditions.

So, whether we are a potential investor, loan officer, future employee, supplier, or customer, we greatly benefit from an understanding of the cash inflows and outflows of a company.

What Do We Mean by "CASH"?

The statement of cash flows explains the change in a firm's cash *and* cash equivalents. **Cash equivalents** are short-term, highly liquid investments that are (1) easily convertible into a known cash amount and (2) close enough to maturity that their market value is not sensitive to interest rate changes (generally, investments with initial maturities of three months or less). Treasury bills, commercial paper (short-term notes issued by corporations), and money market funds are typical examples of cash equivalents.

When preparing a statement of cash flows, the cash and cash equivalents are added together and treated as a single sum. The addition is done because the purchase and sale of investments in cash equivalents are considered to be part of a firm's overall management of cash rather than a source or use of cash. As statement users evaluate and project cash flows, for example, it should not matter whether the cash is readily available in a cash register or safe, deposited in a bank account, or invested in cash equivalents. Consequently, transfers back and forth between a firm's cash on hand, its bank accounts, and its investments in cash equivalents, are not treated as cash inflows and cash outflows in its statement of cash flows. When discussing the statement of cash flows, managers generally use the word *cash* rather than the phrase *cash and cash equivalents*. We will follow the same practice.

What Does a Statement of Cash Flows Look Like?

Exhibit 4.1 reproduces Walgreen's cash flow statement (in $ millions) for 2009. During 2009, Walgreen reported net income of $2,006 million and an increase of $4,111 million in cash from operating activities. Investing activities used $2,776 million in cash but financing activities provided $309 million of cash. In sum, Walgreen's cash increased by $1,644 million, from $443 million at September 1, 2008, to $2,087 million at August 31, 2009.

FRAMEWORK FOR THE STATEMENT OF CASH FLOWS

In analyzing the statement of cash flows, it is not always correct to conclude that the company is better off if cash increases and worse off if cash decreases. It is not the cash change that is most important, but the reasons for that change. For example, what are the sources of cash inflows? Are these sources transitory, i.e., one-time cash inflow or outflows, or are they likely to persist into the future? Are these sources mainly from operating activities, or did cash increase because of short-term borrowing or additional owner investment?

We must also review the uses of cash. Has the company invested its cash in operating areas to strengthen its competitive position? Is it able to comfortably meet its debt obligations? Has it sold important operating assets to meet its debt obligations? Such questions, and the answers to them, are key to properly evaluating the business and its managers. The statement of cash flows is extremely useful in this regard.

EXHIBIT 4.1	Walgreen Cash Flow Statement

WALGREEN CO. AND SUBSIDIARIES
Consolidated Statements of Cash Flows
For the year ended August 31, 2009

(in millions)

Cash Flows from Operating Activities	
Net earnings	$2,006
Adjustments to reconcile net earnings to net cash provided by operating activities—	
Depreciation and amortization	975
Deferred income taxes	260
Stock compensation expense	85
Other	12
Changes in operating assets and liabilities—	
Accounts receivable, net	6
Inventories	533
Other assets	7
Trade accounts payable	11
Accrued expenses and other liabilities	66
Income taxes	105
Other non-current liabilities	45
Net cash flow provided by operating activities	4,111
Cash Flows from Investing Activities	
Purchases of short-term investments	(2,600)
Proceeds from sale of short-term investments	2,100
Additions to property and equipment	(1,927)
Proceeds from sale of assets	51
Business and intangible asset acquisitions, net	(405)
Net proceeds from corporate-owned life insurance policies	5
Net cash used for investing activities	(2,776)
Cash Flows from Financing Activities	
Net (payment) proceeds from short-term borrowings	(70)
Net proceeds from issuance of long-term debt	987
Stock purchases	(279)
Proceeds related to employee stock plans	138
Cash dividends paid	(446)
Other	(21)
Net cash provided by (used for) financing activities	309
Changes in Cash and Cash Equivalents	
Net increase (decrease) in cash and cash equivalents	1,644
Cash and cash equivalents, September 1, 2008	443
Cash and cash equivalents, August 31, 2009	$2,087

The statement of cash flows classifies cash receipts and payments into one of three categories: operating activities, investing activities, or financing activities. Classifying cash flows into these categories identifies the effects on cash of each of the major activities of a firm. The combined effects on cash of all three categories explain the net change in cash for the period. The period's net change in cash is then reconciled with the beginning and ending amounts of cash.

Operating Activities

A company's income statement mainly reflects the transactions and events that constitute its operating activities. The cash effects of these operating transactions and events determine the net cash flow from operating activities. The usual focus of a firm's **operating activities** is on selling goods or rendering services, but the activities are defined broadly enough to include any cash receipts or payments that are not classified as investing or financing activities. For example, cash received from collection of receivables and cash payments to purchase inventories are treated as cash flows from operating activities. The following are examples of cash inflows and outflows relating to operating activities.

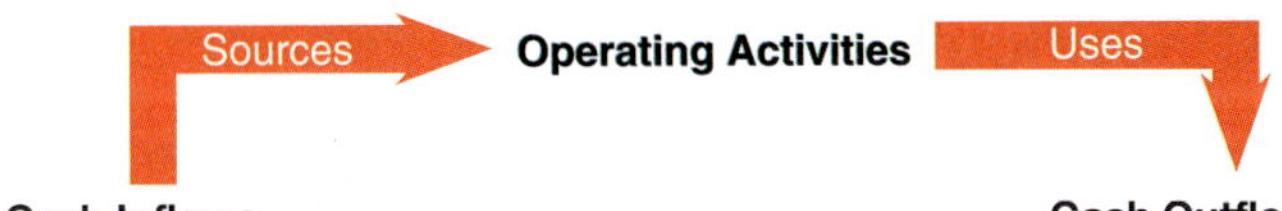

Cash Inflows

1. Cash receipts from customers for sales made or services rendered.
2. Cash receipts of interest and dividends.
3. Other cash receipts that are not related to investing or financing activities, such as lawsuit settlements, and refunds received from suppliers.

Cash Outflows

1. Cash payments to employees or suppliers.
2. Cash payments to purchase inventories.
3. Cash payments of interest to creditors.
4. Cash payments of taxes to government.
5. Other cash payments that are not related to investing or financing activities, such as contributions to charity and lawsuit settlements.

Investing Activities

A firm's transactions involving (1) the acquisition and disposal of property, plant, and equipment (PPE) assets and intangible assets, (2) the purchase and sale of government securities and securities of other companies, including stocks, bonds, and other securities that are not classified as cash equivalents, and (3) the lending and subsequent collection of money constitute the basic components of its **investing activities**. The related cash receipts and payments appear in the investing activities section of the statement of cash flows. Examples of these cash flows follow:

> **FYI** Cash flows from investing activities are cash inflows and outflows related to acquiring or selling productive assets and the investments in securities of other companies.

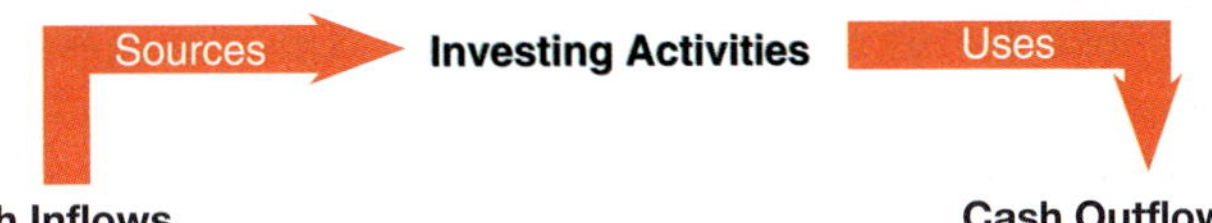

Cash Inflows

1. Cash receipts from sales of property, plant, and equipment (PPE) assets and intangible assets.
2. Cash receipts from sales of investments in government securities and securities of other companies.
3. Cash receipts from repayments of loans by borrowers.

Cash Outflows

1. Cash payments to purchase property, plant, and equipment (PPE) assets and intangible assets.
2. Cash payments to purchase government securities and securities of other companies.
3. Cash payments made to lend money to borrowers.

Financing Activities

A firm engages in **financing activities** when it receives capital from owners, returns capital to owners, borrows from creditors, and repays amounts borrowed. Cash flows related to these transactions are reported in the financing activities section of the statement of cash flows. Examples of these cash flows follow:

> **FYI** Cash flows from financing activities are cash inflows and outflows related to external sources of financing (owners and nonowners).

Cash Inflows

1. Cash receipts from issuances of common stock and preferred stock and from sales of treasury stock.
2. Cash receipts from issuances of bonds payable, mortgage notes payable, and other notes payable.

Cash Outflows

1. Cash payments to acquire treasury stock.
2. Cash payments of dividends.
3. Cash payments to settle outstanding bonds payable, mortgage notes payable, and other notes payable.

Paying cash to settle such obligations as accounts payable, wages payable, interest payable, and income tax payable are operating activities, not financing activities because they are related to the daily operations of the company such as buying and selling inventory. Also, cash received as interest and dividends and cash paid as interest (not dividends) are classified as cash flows from operating activities. However, cash paid to shareholders as dividends is classified as cash flows from financing activities.

> **FYI** **Treasury stock** refers to the amount paid by a company to purchase its own common stock.

Usefulness of Classifications

The classification of cash flows into three categories of activities helps financial statement users interpret cash flow data. To illustrate, assume that **Walgreen**, **CVS**, and **Rite Aid** each reports a $100,000 cash increase during the current year. Information from their current-year statements of cash flows is summarized in Exhibit 4.2.

EXHIBIT 4.2	Summary Information for Three Competitors		
	Walgreen	**CVS**	**Rite Aid**
Net cash provided by operating activities	$100,000	$ 0	$ 0
Cash flows from investing activities			
Sale of property, plant, and equipment	0	100,000	0
Cash flows from financing activities			
Issuance of notes payable	0	0	100,000
Net increase in cash	$100,000	$100,000	$100,000

Although each company's net cash increase was the same, the source of the increase varied by company. This variation affects the analysis of the cash flow data, particularly for potential short-term creditors who must evaluate the likelihood of obtaining repayment in the future for any funds loaned to the company. Based only on these cash flow data, a potential creditor would feel more comfortable lending money to Walgreen than to either CVS or Rite Aid. This choice is because Walgreen's cash increase came from its operating activities, whereas both CVS and Rite Aid could only break even on their cash flows from operations. Also, CVS's cash increase came from the sale of property, plant, and equipment (PPE) assets—a source of cash that is not likely to recur regularly. Rite Aid's cash increase came entirely from borrowed funds. This means Rite Aid faces additional cash burdens in the future when the interest and principal payments on the note payable become due.

BUSINESS INSIGHT

Objectivity of Cash Usefulness of financial statements is enhanced when the underlying data are objective and verifiable. Measuring cash and the changes in cash are among the most objective measurements that accountants make. Thus, the statement of cash flows is arguably the most objective financial statement. This characteristic of the statement of cash flows is welcomed by those investors and creditors interested in evaluating the quality of a firm's income.

MID-CHAPTER REVIEW 1

Assume **Walgreen** executed the following transactions during 2010. Indicate whether the transaction creates a cash inflow (In) or outflow (Out). Next, determine how each item should be classified in the statement of cash flows: an operating activity (O), an investing activity (I), or a financing activity (F). For example: $50 cash received for the sale of non-prescription drugs. Answer: In/O

1. ____ $250,000 cash paid to purchase a warehouse
2. ____ $120,000 cash paid for interest on a loan
3. ____ $850,000 cash paid to employees as wages
4. ____ $20,000,000 cash raised through the issuance of stock
5. ____ $450,000 cash paid to the government for taxes
6. ____ $350,000 cash received as part of a settlement of a legal case
7. ____ $630,000 cash received from the sale of long-term securities
8. ____ $75,000 cash received from the sale of used office equipment
9. ____ $500,000 cash dividend paid to shareholders
10. ____ $90,000 cash received as interest earned on a government bond

The solution to this review problem can be found on page 201.

PREPARING THE STATEMENT OF CASH FLOWS—OPERATING ACTIVITIES

In Chapter 3, we presented a statement of cash flows for Natural Beauty Supply (hereafter, NBS) for the month of December, 2010. This statement is reproduced in Exhibit 4.3. The statement details how NBS's cash balance decreases by $1,275 in December, from $8,100 to $6,825. The statement was prepared by examining all of the cash transactions that occurred during the month, and then grouping them according to the type of activity each represents—operating, investing, or financing. These cash transactions can be taken directly from the cash T-account, which is reproduced here:

LO2 Construct and explain the statement of cash flows.

+	Cash (A)		−
Beg. Bal.	8,100		
(17)	11,000	18,000	(18)
(21)	8,500	700	(19)
(23)	1,200	3,300	(20)
(25)	3,200	1,625	(24)
		1,500	(27)
		50	(28)
End. Bal.	6,825		

This approach to preparing the statement of cash flows is straightforward and doesn't require any additional bookkeeping steps, other than those introduced in Chapters 2 and 3.

EXHIBIT 4.3	NBS Statement of Cash Flows (Direct Method)

NATURAL BEAUTY SUPPLY, INC.
Statement of Cash Flows
For the Month of December, 2010

Cash Flows from Operating Activities		
Cash received from customers	$12,900	
Cash paid for inventory	(3,300)	
Cash paid for wages	(1,625)	
Cash paid for rent	(1,500)	
Cash paid for advertising	(700)	
Net cash provided by operating activities		$ 5,775
Cash Flows from Investing Activities		
Cash paid for fixtures and equipment	(18,000)	
Net cash used for investing activities		(18,000)
Cash Flows from Financing Activities		
Cash received from loans	11,000	
Cash paid for dividends	(50)	
Net cash provided by financing activities		10,950
Net change in cash		(1,275)
Cash balance, November 30, 2010		8,100
Cash balance, December 31, 2010		$ 6,825

However, for many companies, the number and variety of cash transactions that occur each period is so large that such an approach is often impractical. A company the size of Walgreen, for example, has thousands of cash transactions each day. It has accounts with several different banks in numerous locations, and regularly transfers cash from one account to another or back and forth between cash accounts and cash equivalents, as needed. Consequently for Walgreen, simply listing the cash transactions is not practical.

An alternative to this approach of compiling a list of cash flows is to reconcile the information in the income statement and balance sheet to prepare the cash flow statement. The statement of cash flows complements the balance sheet and the income statement. The balance sheet details the financial position of the company at a given point in time. Comparing two balance sheets prepared at the beginning and at the end of a period reveals changes that transpired during the accounting period. These changes are explained by the income statement and the statement of cash flows. Both the income statement and the cash flow statement summarize the events and transactions of the business during the accounting period, and as such, provide complementary descriptions of a company's activities. While the cash flow statement provides information that is not explicitly found in either of the other two statements, it must articulate with the balance sheet and income statement to present a complete picture of company activities. Thus, we can rely on income statement and balance sheet data to provide the raw material for the preparation of the statement of cash flows. Exhibit 4.4 presents the income statement and comparative balance sheets for NBS. We will use this data to prepare NBS's cash flow statement.

EXHIBIT 4.4	NBS Income Statement and Comparative Balance Sheet

NATURAL BEAUTY SUPPLY
Income Statement
For the month of December, 2010

Sales revenue		$13,900
Cost of goods sold		8,000
Gross profit		5,900
Operating expenses:		
Rent	$1,500	
Wages	2,105	
Advertising	700	
Depreciation	375	
Insurance	140	
Total operating expenses		4,820
Operating income		1,080
Interest income		30
Interest expense		(110)
Income before taxes		1,000
Income tax expense		350
Net income		$ 650

NATURAL BEAUTY SUPPLY
Comparative Balance Sheets

	12/31/10	11/30/10
Assets:		
Cash	$ 6,825	$ 8,100
Interest receivable	30	
Accounts receivable	2,250	950
Inventory	7,300	11,300
Prepaid insurance	1,540	1,680
Security deposit	2,000	2,000
Fixtures and equipment	18,000	
Accumulated depreciation	(375)	
Total assets	$37,570	$24,030
Liabilities:		
Accounts payable	$ 4,400	$ 3,700
Unearned revenue	600	300
Wages payable	480	
Interest payable	110	
Income taxes payable	350	
Notes payable	11,000	
Stockholders' equity:		
Common stock	20,000	20,000
Retained earnings	630	30
Total liabilities and equity	$37,570	$24,030

Converting Revenues and Expenses to Cash Flows from Operating Activities

We know from Chapter 3 that net income consists of revenues and expenses, gains and losses. We also know that these are often not cash transactions. For example, sales on account will be considered revenue but are not cash flows (until collected). Depreciation is an expense but is not a current-period cash flow (the cash flow presumably occurred when the underlying asset was acquired). Therefore, we can compute cash flow from operating activities by making adjustments to the revenues and expenses presented in the income statement. The adjustment amounts represent differences between revenues, expenses, gains, and losses recorded under accrual accounting and the related operating cash inflows and outflows. The adjustments are added to or subtracted from net income, depending on whether the related cash flow is more or less than the accrual amount.

To illustrate this adjustment procedure, consider the following transactions that occurred for NBS in December, 2010:

(22) During the month of December, sales to wholesale customers totaled $4,500 for merchandise that had cost $3,000. Instead of paying cash, wholesale customers are required to pay for the merchandise within ten working days.

(25)   During the month of December, NBS received $3,200 in cash from wholesale customers for products that had been delivered earlier.

For this illustration, we focus on the revenue side of this transaction. To record the sale of merchandise to wholesale customers (transaction 22a), NBS recorded an increase to accounts receivable (a noncash asset) and an increase to sales revenue in the amount of $4,500. The subsequent collection of cash from wholesale customers as payment on accounts receivable (transaction 25) was recorded as an increase to cash and a decrease to accounts receivable of $3,200.

+ Cash (A) −		− Accounts Receivable (A) −		− Sales Revenue (R) +	
(25) 3,200		Beg. Bal. 950			4,500 (22a)
		(22a) 4,500	3,200 (25)		
		End Bal. 2,250			

These two transactions resulted in the following changes in the financial statements:

- Cash increased by $3,200; this cash flow should be included in operating activities in the cash flow statement.
- Revenue increased by $4,500; this income flow is included in the income statement.
- Accounts receivable increased by $1,300 ($2,250 − $950); this change in the balance of accounts receivable is revealed by comparing the balance sheet prepared at the beginning of the month to one prepared at month-end.

The difference between the income flow (revenue of $4,500) and the cash flow (cash receipts of $3,200) is equal to the increase in accounts receivable ($1,300 = $4,500 − $3,200). This result is not a mere coincidence. The portion of the sales revenue that has not yet been collected as cash is held in accounts receivable. That is, to the extent that the sales revenue exceeds the cash collected, accounts receivable is increased. Similarly, if more cash had been collected on accounts receivable than revenues recorded as sales on account, the accounts receivable balance would have decreased. In general, the difference between sales on account and cash collected is equal to the change in accounts receivable.

As a second illustration, let's examine the cost of merchandise purchased and sold. To do so, we must work backwards to reconstruct the transactions affecting two balance sheet accounts—inventory and accounts payable. Cost of goods sold totaled $8,000 in December ($5,000 for retail customers—transaction 21—and $3,000 for wholesale customers—transaction 22). The summary journal entry to record cost of goods sold (COGS) is recorded as a debit to COGS and a credit to inventory.

Next, we can balance the inventory T-account to compute purchases, which were recorded in entry 26 as a debit to inventory and a credit to accounts payable.

$$\textbf{Beginning inventory + Purchases − COGS } = \textbf{ Ending inventory}$$
$$\textbf{\$11,300 + Purchases − \$8,000 } = \textbf{ \$7,300}$$
$$\textbf{Purchases } = \textbf{ \$4,000}$$

Finally, we balance the T-account for accounts payable to solve for the amount of cash paid to suppliers during December (transaction 20). The entry to record this payment is a debit to accounts payable and a credit to cash.

$$\textbf{Beginning accounts payable + Purchases − Payments } = \textbf{ Ending accounts payable}$$
$$\textbf{\$3,700 + \$4,000 − Payments } = \textbf{ \$4,400}$$
$$\textbf{Payments } = \textbf{ \$3,300}$$

Posting the three entries for COGS, purchases, and cash payments to the T-accounts reveals the reconstructed accounts for inventory and accounts payable.

+ Cash (A) −		+ Inventory (A) −		− Accounts Payable (L) +		+ Cost of Goods Sold (E) −
		Beg. Bal. 11,300			3,700 Beg. Bal.	
		(26) 4,000			4,000 (26)	
	3,300 (20)		8,000 (21, 22)	(20) 3,300		(21, 22) 8,000
		End. Bal. 7,300			4,400 End Bal.	

These transactions had the following effect on the financial statements:

- Cost of goods sold was $8,000; this amount was subtracted in the income statement.
- Cash paid to suppliers for merchandise was $3,300; this amount is listed as a cash outflow in the cash flow statement.
- Inventory decreased by $4,000 and accounts payable increased by $700; the changes are determined by comparing the beginning and ending balances in the comparative balance sheets.

The expense reported in the income statement (cost of goods sold of $8,000) exceeded the cash paid to suppliers ($3,300) by $4,700. When we examine the balance sheet, we see that inventory decreased by $4,000 and accounts payable increased by $700. Thus, the difference between the income flow (cost of goods sold) and the cash flow (cash paid for merchandise) is equal to the combined changes in two balance sheet accounts (inventory and accounts payable).

The relationships illustrated in the above examples suggest a general rule that we can use to prepare the cash flow statement:

> The difference between a revenue or an expense reported in the income statement and a related cash receipt or expenditure reported in the statement of cash flows will be reflected in the balance sheet as a change in one or more balance sheet accounts.

Put another way, to convert an income flow to a cash flow, we adjust the income flow by the change in a balance sheet account:

$$\textbf{Income flow} \quad \pm \quad \textbf{Adjustment} \quad = \quad \textbf{Cash flow}$$
or, equivalently,

$$\textbf{Revenue or expense} \quad \pm \quad \textbf{Change in balance sheet account(s)} \quad = \quad \textbf{Cash receipt or payment}$$

Exhibit 4.5 summarizes the adjustments needed to convert the revenues, expenses, gains and losses presented in the income statement to cash receipts and payments presented in the statement of cash flows.

Natural Beauty Supply Case Illustration

We next illustrate the process of converting NBS's December revenues and expenses to corresponding cash flows from operating activities.

Convert Sales to Cash Received from Customers   The conversion of sales to cash received from customers is a two-step process. First, sales revenue is adjusted for the change in

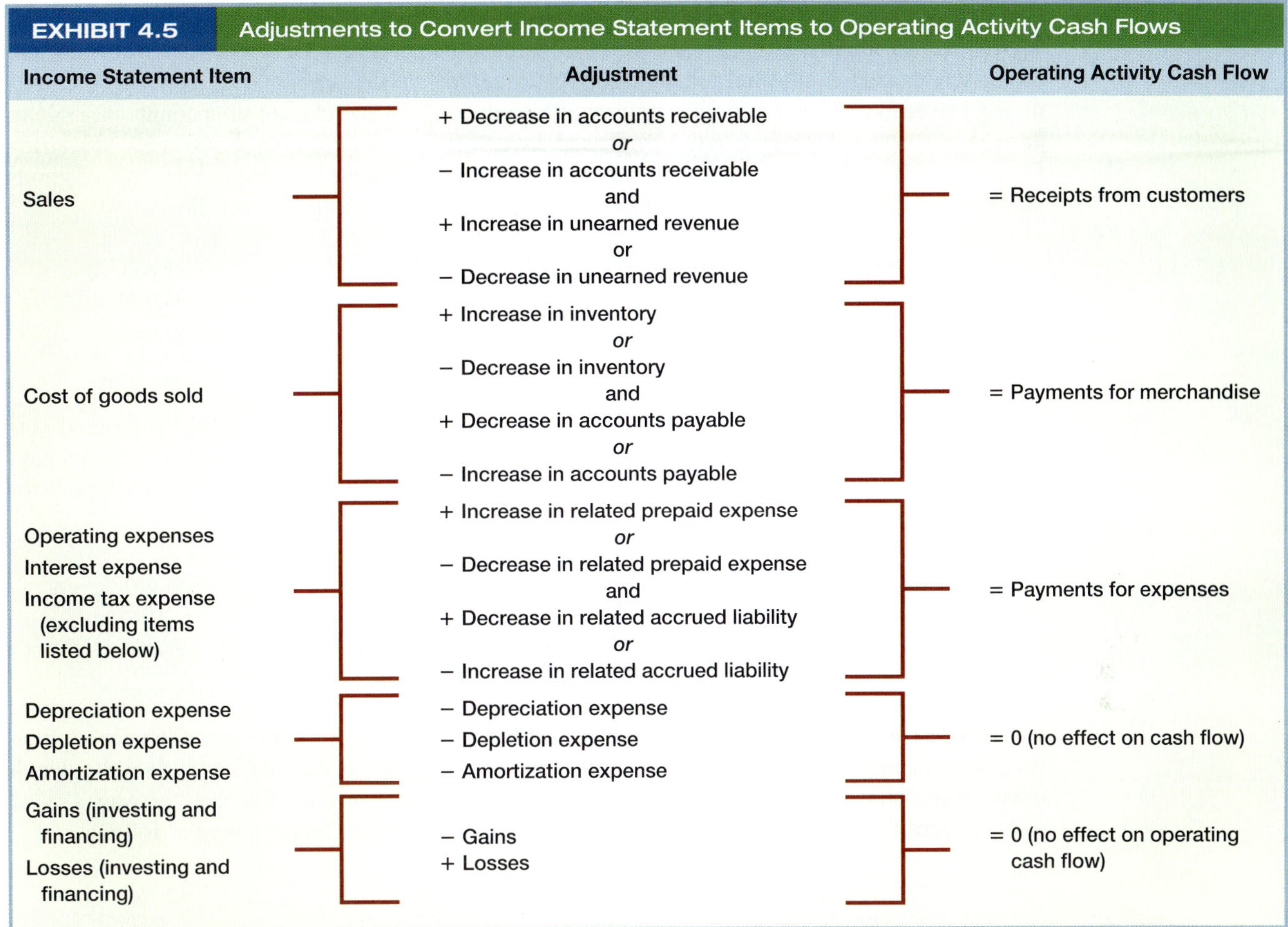

EXHIBIT 4.5 — Adjustments to Convert Income Statement Items to Operating Activity Cash Flows

accounts receivable to determine the amount of cash received for earned revenue during December. Then the cash received for earned revenue amount is adjusted for the change in cash received as unearned revenue for the period.

During December, accounts receivable increased $1,300 ($2,250 − $950). This increase means that during December, cash collections on account (which decrease accounts receivable) were less than credit sales (which increase accounts receivable). We compute cash received from customers for earned revenue as follows.

	Sales revenue	$13,900
−	Increase in accounts receivable	(1,300)
=	Cash received from customers for earned revenue	$12,600

During December, unearned revenue increased $300 ($600 − $300). This increase means that during December, cash collections in advance on sales of gift certificates (which increase unearned revenue) were more than earned revenue from gift certificates redeemed (which decreases unearned revenue). We compute cash received from customers as follows.

	Cash received from customers for earned revenue	$12,600
+	Increase in unearned revenue	300
=	Cash received from customers	$12,900

Convert Cost of Goods Sold to Cash Paid for Merchandise Purchased   The conversion of cost of goods sold to cash paid for merchandise purchased is a two-step process. First, cost of goods sold is adjusted for the change in inventory to determine the amount of purchases during December. Then the purchases amount is adjusted for the change in accounts payable to derive the cash paid for merchandise purchased. Inventory decreased from $11,300 to $7,300 during December. This $4,000 decrease indicates that the cost of goods sold exceeded the cost of goods purchased during December. The month's purchases amount is computed as follows.

	Cost of goods sold	$8,000
−	Decrease in inventory	(4,000)
=	Purchases	$4,000

During December, accounts payable increased $700 ($4,400 − $3,700). This increase reflects the fact that cash payments for merchandise purchased on account (which decrease accounts payable) were less than purchases on account (which increase accounts payable). The cash paid for merchandise purchased, therefore, is computed as follows.

	Purchases	$4,000
−	Increase in accounts payable	(700)
=	Cash paid for merchandise	$3,300

Convert Wages Expense to Cash Paid to Employees   An adjustment to wages expense is needed because the ending accrued liability for wages payable increased from $0 to $480, which means that cash paid to employees as wages during December was $480 less than the wages owed to employees for the period. The cash paid to employees, therefore, is computed as follows.

	Wages expense	$2,105
−	Increase in wages payable	(480)
=	Wages paid	$1,625

Convert Rent Expense to Cash Paid for Rent   No adjustment to rent expense is needed. NBS pays rent each month at the end of the month. As a consequence, there is no balance in prepaid rent (or accrued rent payable) in the balance sheet at the beginning or at the end of December. This means that rent expense and cash paid for rent are the same amount: $1,500.

Convert Advertising Expense to Cash Paid for Advertising   No adjustment to advertising expense is needed. The absence of any beginning or ending prepaid advertising or accrued liability for advertising payable means that advertising expense and cash paid for advertising are the same amount: $700.

Convert Insurance Expense to Cash Paid for Insurance   Prepaid insurance decreased $140 during December. The $140 decrease reflects the excess of the insurance expense during December (which decreases prepaid insurance) over the cash paid for insurance during the period (which increases prepaid insurance). Starting with insurance expense the cash paid for insurance is computed as follows.

	Insurance expense	$140
−	Decrease in prepaid insurance	(140)
=	Insurance paid	$ 0

Convert Interest Expense to Cash Paid for Interest   An adjustment to interest expense is needed because the ending accrued liability for interest payable increased from $0 to $110, which means that cash paid as interest during December was $110 less than the interest owed for the period. The cash paid for interest, therefore, is computed as follows.

	Interest expense	$110
−	Increase in interest payable	(110)
=	Interest paid	$ 0

Convert Interest Income to Interest Received in Cash

NBS earned interest income of $30 in December. However this interest will not be received until January of 2011. As a result, interest receivable increased from $0 on November 30, 2010, to $30 on December 31, 2010. The increase in interest receivable means that the amount of interest income earned was greater than the amount of interest received in cash. Thus, the increase in interest receivable is subtracted from interest income to get interest collected in cash.

	Interest income	$30
−	Increase in interest receivable	(30)
=	Interest received in cash	$ 0

Eliminate Depreciation Expense and Other Noncash Operating Expenses

Depreciation expense is a noncash expense. Because it does not represent a cash payment, depreciation expense is eliminated as we convert accrual expense amounts to the corresponding amounts of cash payments.

	Depreciation expense	$375
−	Depreciation expense	(375)
=	Cash paid for depreciation	$ 0

Convert Income Tax Expense to Cash Paid for Income Taxes

The increase in income tax payable from $0 at November 30, to $350 at December 31, means that December's income tax expense (which increases income tax payable) was $350 more than December's tax payments (which decrease income tax payable). If we start with income tax expense, then we calculate cash paid for income taxes as follows.

	Income tax expense	$350
−	Increase in income tax payable	(350)
=	Cash paid for income taxes	$ 0

Omit Gains and Losses Related to Investing and Financing Activities

The income statement may contain gains and losses related to investing or financing activities. Examples include gains and losses from the sale of plant assets and gains and losses from the retirement of bonds payable. Because these gains and losses are not related to operating activities, we omit them as we convert income statement items to various cash flows from operating activities. The cash flows relating to these gains and losses are reported in the investing activities or financing activities sections of the statement of cash flows. NBS had no gains or losses in December.

We have now applied the adjustments to convert each accrual revenue and expense to the corresponding operating cash flow. We use these individual cash inflows and outflows to prepare the operating activities section of the statement of cash flows. The adjustments to convert revenues and expenses to operating cash flows are summarized in Exhibit 4.6.

EXHIBIT 4.6	Converting Revenues and Expenses to Cash Flows from Operating Activities (Direct Method)		
	A **Revenue or** **Expense**	**B** **Adjustments**	**C** **Operating** **Cash Flow**
Revenues/Cash Receipts:			
Sales revenue	$13,900		
− Increase in accounts receivable		$(1,300)	
+ Increase in unearned revenue		300	
Cash received from customers			$12,900
Interest income	30		
− Increase in interest receivable		(30)	
Cash received for interest			0
	13,930	(1,030)	12,900
Less Expenses/Cash Payments:			
Cost of goods sold	8,000		
− Decrease in inventory		(4,000)	
− Increase in accounts payable		(700)	
Cash paid for merchandise			3,300
Wages expense	2,105		
− Increase in wages payable		(480)	
Cash paid for wages			1,625
Rent expense	1,500		
Cash paid for rent			1,500
Advertising expense	700		
Cash paid for advertising			700
Insurance expense	140		
− Decrease in prepaid insurance		(140)	
Cash paid for insurance			0
Interest expense	110		
− Increase in interest payable		(110)	
Cash paid for interest			0
Depreciation expense	375		
− Depreciation expense		(375)	
Cash paid for deprecation			0
Income tax expense	350		
− Increase in income tax payable		(350)	
Cash paid for income taxes			0
	13,280	(6,155)	7,125
Net income	$ 650		
Total adjustments		$5,125	
Cash flow from operating activities			$ 5,775

MID-CHAPTER REVIEW 2

The income statement and comparative balance sheets for Mug Shots, Inc., (a photography studio) are presented below. Use the information in these financial statements to compute Mug Shots' cash flow from operating activities.

MUG SHOTS, INC.
Income Statement
For Month Ended December 31, 2010

Revenue		
Sales revenue		$31,000
Expenses		
Cost of goods sold	$16,700	
Wages expense	4,700	
Interest expense	300	
Advertising expense	1,800	
Rent expense	1,500	
Depreciation expense	700	
Total expenses		25,700
Income before taxes		5,300
Income tax expense		1,855
Net income		$ 3,445

MUG SHOTS, INC.
Comparative Balance Sheets

	12/31/10	11/30/10
Assets		
Cash	$10,700	$ 5,000
Accounts receivable	2,500	
Inventory	32,300	24,000
Prepaid rent	7,500	9,000
Equipment	30,000	18,000
Accumulated depreciation	(700)	
Total assets	$82,300	$56,000
Liabilities		
Accounts payable	$25,000	$24,000
Interest payable	300	
Wages payable	2,200	
Income tax payable	1,855	
Unearned revenue	500	
Notes payable	30,000	12,000
Equity		
Common stock	20,000	20,000
Retained earnings	2,445	
Total liabilities and equity	$82,300	$56,000

The solution to this review problem can be found on page 201.

Cash Flow from Operating Activities Using the Indirect Method

Two alternative formats are used to report the net cash flow from operating activities: the direct method and the indirect method. *Both methods report the same amount of net cash flow from operating activities*. Net cash flows from investing and financing activities are prepared in the same manner under both the indirect and direct methods; only the format for cash flows from operating activities differs.

In the previous section, we computed cash flow from operating activities using the direct method. The **direct method** presents the components of cash flow from operating activities as a list of gross cash receipts and gross cash payments. This format is illustrated in Exhibit 4.3. The direct method is logical and relatively easy to follow. In practice, however, nearly all statements of cash flows are presented using what is called the **indirect method**. Under this method, the cash flow from operations section begins with net income and applies a series of adjustments to net income to convert it to net cash flow from operating activities. However, the adjustments to net income are not cash flows themselves, so the indirect method does not report any detail concerning individual operating cash inflows and outflows. In other words, there are no cash flows in the operating section of the cash flow statement, except the subtotal—cash flow from operations.

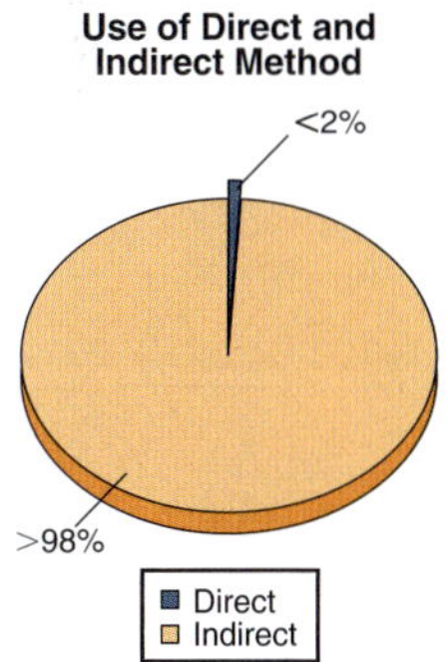

Accountants estimate that *more than 98% of companies preparing the statement of cash flows use the indirect method*. The indirect method is popular because (1) it is easier and less expensive to prepare than the direct method and (2) companies that use the direct method are required to present a supplemental disclosure showing the indirect method (thus, essentially requiring the company to report both methods).

The procedure for computing cash flow from operations using the indirect method is very similar to the procedure we used for the direct method. In fact, the indirect method can be viewed as a "shortcut" calculation. That is:

Net income ± Adjustments = Cash flow from operating activities

In Exhibit 4.6, revenue and expense components of the income statement are presented in column A. This column totals to net income. Column B lists the adjustments, and cash receipts and payments are listed in column C. The total of Column C is cash flow from operating activities. The indirect method skips the listing of individual revenues and expenses and starts with net income. After adjustments, we have total cash flow from operating activities, but not individual receipts and payments.

Exhibit 4.7 identifies several specific adjustments to convert net income to net cash flow from operating activities under the indirect method. The first several adjustments cover depreciation expense, amortization expense, and gains and losses from investing and financing activities. The remaining adjustments relate to the effects on cash flow of changes in assets and liabilities related to operations. It is possible to adjust from a positive net income to a negative cash flow from operations and from a negative income to a positive cash flow from operations. It all depends on the noncash components of income and the operating cash flows that are not included in net income.

EXHIBIT 4.7	Detailed Adjustments to Convert Net Income to Operating Cash Flows
Add to Net Income	**Deduct from Net Income**
Depreciation expense	—
Amortization expense	—
Depletion expense	—
Losses (investing and financing)	Gains (investing and financing)
Decrease in accounts receivable	Increase in accounts receivable
Decrease in inventory	Increase in inventory
Decrease in prepaid expenses	Increase in prepaid expenses
Increase in accounts payable	Decrease in accounts payable
Increase in unearned revenue	Decrease in unearned revenue
Increase in accrued liabilities	Decrease in accrued liabilities
Increase in deferred tax liabilities	Decrease in deferred tax liabilities

These adjustments are essentially the same as those used to prepare cash flow from operating activities using the direct method. For example, an increase in accounts receivable represents sales that have not yet been collected in cash. Sales on account have the effect of increasing net income without increasing cash flow. Thus we must subtract this increase in receivables from net income to get cash flow from operating activities. Similarly, an increase in wages payable represents wages that are reported as an expense in the income statement but, as yet, not paid in cash. Accrued expenses such as wages payable reduce net income, but have no effect on cash flow. Thus we add back this noncash expense to net income to get operating cash flow. In general, an increase in a noncash asset reduces cash flow while a decrease will result in an increase in cash flow. Conversely, an increase in a liability is a positive adjustment to cash flow, while a decrease reduces cash flow.

Many of these adjustments are not cash inflows or outflows. Instead, positive adjustments represent a non-use of cash while negative adjustments are a non-source of cash. A good example is the adjustment for depreciation. We add depreciation to get cash flow from operations because depreciation is an expense (subtracted to produce net income) that does not reduce cash. However, depreciation is not a source of cash. Instead, it is a non-cash expense. When we add depreciation to net income, we are simply adding back an expense that did not require a cash outlay.

Cash flow from operating activities for NBS is computed using the indirect method in Exhibit 4.8. The calculation begins with the December net income of $650 and ends with cash flow from operating activities ($5,775). The total cash flow from operating activities is the same amount as was computed in Exhibit 4.6 using the direct method. If we compare Exhibit 4.6 and Exhibit 4.8, we see that the two exhibits are very similar. The only difference is that all of the revenues and expenses are listed in the first column of Exhibit 4.6, while exhibit 4.8 only lists the total—net income. Similarly, the right-hand column of exhibit 4.6 lists all of the cash inflows and outflows, while the right-hand column of Exhibit 4.8 only lists the net cash flow from operating activities. In both exhibits, the center column lists the adjustments.

EXHIBIT 4.8	NBS Cash Flow from Operating Activities—Indirect Method

Net income.	$650	
Adjustments:		
+ Depreciation expense	375	
− Increase in accounts receivable	(1,300)	
− Increase in interest receivable	(30)	
+ Decrease in inventory	4,000	
+ Decrease in prepaid insurance	140	
+ Increase in unearned revenue	300	
+ Increase in accounts payable	700	
+ Increase in wages payable	480	
+ Increase in interest payable	110	
+ Increase in income tax payable	350	
Total adjustments	5,125	
Cash flow from operating activities		$5,775

MID-CHAPTER REVIEW 3

Refer to the financial statements for the Mug Shots, Inc. presented in Mid-Chapter Review 2. Compute cash flows from operating activities for Mug Shots, Inc. using the indirect method.

The solution to this review problem can be found on page 202.

PREPARING THE STATEMENT OF CASH FLOWS— INVESTING AND FINANCING ACTIVITIES

The remaining sections of the statement of cash flows focus on investing and financing activities. Investing activities are concerned with transactions affecting noncurrent (and some current) non-cash assets. Financing activities are concerned with raising capital from owners and creditors. The presentation of the cash effects of investing and financing transactions is not affected by the method of presentation (direct or indirect) of cash flows from operating activities.

Cash Flows from Investing Activities

Investing activities cause changes in noncash asset accounts. Usually the accounts affected (other than cash) are noncurrent asset accounts such as property, plant and equipment assets and long-term investments, although short-term investment accounts can also be affected. To determine the cash flows from investing activities, *we analyze changes in all noncash asset accounts not used in computing net cash flow from operating activities.* Our objective is to identify any investing cash flows related to these changes.

Increases in noncash assets cause cash outflow. Conversely, a decrease in a noncash asset results in cash inflow. This relationship is highlighted in the following decision guide:

Cash flows increase due to:	Cash flows decrease due to:
A **decrease** in assets	An **increase** in assets

NBS had only one investing transaction during December—the purchase of fixtures and equipment for $18,000. Any change in the fixtures and equipment account in the balance sheet is usually the result one or both of the following transactions: (1) buying assets, or (2) selling assets. Buying and selling assets are classified as investing transactions. NBS's journal entry to record the purchase of fixtures and equipment for cash reproduced as follows:

(18)	Fixtures and equipment (+A)	18,000	
	Cash (−A)		18,000

The resulting $18,000 cash outflow is listed in the statement of cash flows under cash flow used for investing activities.

Cash Flows from Financing Activities

Financing activities cause changes in liability and stockholders' equity accounts. Usually the accounts affected are noncurrent accounts such as bonds payable and common stock, although a current liability such as short-term notes payable, or the short-term portion of long-term debt due in the next year, can also be affected. To determine the cash flows from financing activities, *we analyze changes in all liability and stockholders' equity accounts that were not used in computing net cash flow from operating activities.* Our objective is to identify any financing cash flows related to these changes.

Increases in liabilities and stockholders' equity accounts cause cash inflows. Conversely, a decrease in a liability or stockholders' equity account usually results in cash outflows. This relationship is highlighted in the following decision guide:

Cash flows increase due to:	Cash flows decrease due to:
An **increase** in liabilities or stockholders' equity	A **decrease** in liabilities or stockholders' equity

NBS had two financing transactions during December. It borrowed $11,000 on a three-year note, resulting in an increase in cash, and it paid $50 in cash dividends to shareholders. The journal entry to record the $11,000 note and the corresponding T-account is illustrated as:

The resulting $11,000 cash inflow is listed in the statement of cash flows under cash flow from financing activities.

The journal entry to record dividends and the corresponding T-account for retained earnings is illustrated as follows:

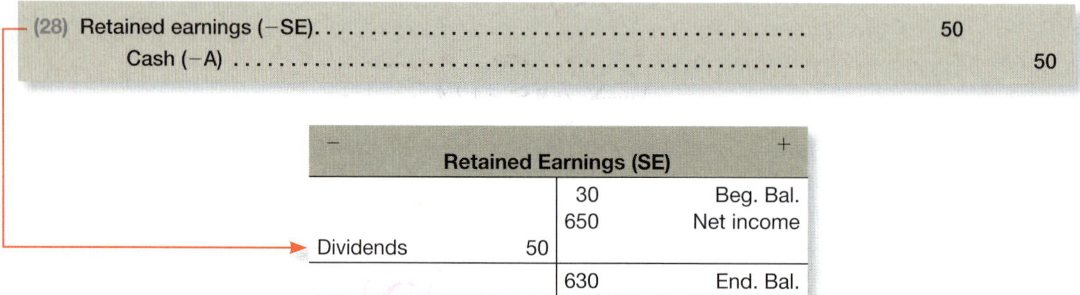

The increase in retained earnings due to net income is listed under cash flows from operating activities. The dividend payment, however, is a financing cash outflow. It would be deducted from cash flow from financing activities.

The statement of cash flows lists cash flows from operating activities first (using either the direct or the indirect method), followed by cash flows from investing activities, then cash flows from financing activities. Once all three categories of cash flows have been listed, we total the three amounts to arrive at net cash flow for the period. The final step is to reconcile the cash balance from the beginning of the period to the ending balance. The completed statement of cash flows for NBS using the indirect method for operating cash flows is presented in Exhibit 4.9. We see from this statement that operating activities produced a cash inflow of $5,775, while investing activities resulted in a cash outflow of $18,000, and financing activities resulted in a cash inflow of $10,950. The sum of these three amounts ($5,775 − $18,000 + $10,950) equals the change in cash for December of $1,275 ($6,825 − $8,100).

EXHIBIT 4.9	NBS Statement of Cash Flows—Indirect Method

NATURAL BEAUTY SUPPLY
Statement of Cash Flows
For the Month of December, 2010

Operating activities:		
Net income	$ 650	
Adjustments:		
+ Depreciation expense	375	
− Increase in accounts receivable	(1,300)	
− Increase in interest receivable	(30)	
+ Decrease in inventory	4,000	
+ Decrease in prepaid insurance	140	
+ Increase in unearned revenue	300	
+ Increase in accounts payable	700	
+ Increase in wages payable	480	
+ Increase in interest payable	110	
+ Increase in income tax payable	350	
Total adjustments	5,125	
Cash flow from operating activities		$5,775
Investing activities:		
Purchase of fixtures and equipment	(18,000)	
Cash flow used for investing activities		(18,000)
Financing activities:		
Bank note	11,000	
Dividends paid	(50)	
Cash flow from financing activities		10,950
Net decrease in cash		(1,275)
Cash, November 30, 2010		8,100
Cash, December 31, 2010		$ 6,825

FYI The net cash inflow or outflow for the period is the same amount as the increase or decrease in cash and cash equivalents for the period from the balance sheet.

MID-CHAPTER REVIEW 4

Refer to the financial statements for Mug Shots, Inc. in Mid-Chapter Review 2. Prepare a complete statement of cash flows for December using the indirect method for cash flows from operating activities. Follow the format used in Exhibit 4.9.

The solution to this review problem can be found on page 202.

YOU MAKE THE CALL

You are the Chief Accountant   The July 27, 2005, *Wall Street Journal* reported that Cendant has "agreed to sell its marketing services division for $1.83 million, ending ownership of a business that staggered the company with a $500 million accounting fraud." How would the sale be reflected in Cendant's cash flow statement? [Answer on page 178]

ADDITIONAL DETAIL IN THE STATEMENT OF CASH FLOWS

The FASB requires that financing and investing items be presented in the statement of cash flows using gross amounts instead of net amounts. For example, assume Walgreen decided to sell property for $2 million and bought other property for $3 million. Because the FASB requires firms to show gross amounts for investing and financing activities, it would not be acceptable to show the net change of $1 million in its statement of cash flows. Walgreen must show the gross amounts from the $2 million sale and the $3 million purchase.

Case Illustration   Natural Beauty Supply did not have any disposals of assets or repayments of debt in December 2010, so there is no adjustment to make in this case. However, let's consider the financial statements of One World Café, a coffee shop that is located next door to NBS. The income statement and comparative balance sheet for One World Café are presented in Exhibit 4.10. The cash flow statement is presented in Exhibit 4.11.

EXHIBIT 4.10	One World Café Income Statement and Comparative Balance Sheets

ONE WORLD CAFÉ, INC.
Income Statement
For Year Ended December 31, 2010

Revenue		
Sales revenue		$390,000
Expenses		
Cost of goods sold	$227,000	
Wages expense.	82,000	
Advertising expense	9,800	
Depreciation expense.	17,000	
Interest expense	200	
Loss on sale of plant assets. . .	2,000	
Total expenses		338,000
Income before taxes		52,000
Income tax expense		17,000
Net income.		$ 35,000

ONE WORLD CAFÉ, INC.
Comparative Balance Sheets
At December 31

	2010	2009
Assets		
Cash.	$ 8,000	$ 12,000
Accounts receivable	22,000	28,000
Inventory	94,000	66,000
Prepaid advertising	12,000	9,000
Plant assets	208,000	170,000
Less accumulated depreciation	(72,000)	(61,000)
Total assets	$272,000	$224,000
Liabilities		
Accounts payable	$ 27,000	$ 14,000
Wages payable	6,000	2,500
Income tax payable.	3,000	4,500
Notes payable	5,000	—
Equity		
Common stock	134,000	125,000
Retained earnings	97,000	78,000
Total liabilities and equity	$272,000	$224,000

From the footnotes of One World Café's annual report, we see that plant assets were purchased for cash in 2010, and obsolete plant assets that originally cost $12,000, with accumulated depreciation of $6,000, were sold for $4,000 cash, which netted a $2,000 loss [Book value = Original cost ($12,000) − Accumulated depreciation ($6,000)]. In addition, the footnotes to One World Café indicate additional common stock was issued for cash in 2010 and that cash dividends of $16,000 were declared and paid during the year. In addition, One World Café purchased $5,000 of plant assets by issuing notes payable in 2010.

From the cash flow statement, we see that plant assets were both sold and purchased during the year. Reviewing One World Café's comparative balance sheet, we see that plant assets increased from $170,000 to $208,000, an increase of $38,000. We also determine that accumulated depreciation has increased $11,000 from $61,000 to $72,000. However, the $38,000 increase in plant assets and the $11,000 increase in accumulated depreciation are **net** increases, not gross increases. Consequently, we need to determine the gross amounts to ensure the statement of cash flows we create properly presents the gross amounts in the investing activities section.

In addition to the changes in plant assets and accumulated depreciation, notes payable increased by $5,000 in 2010. The best way to fully understand what happened to cause the changes in balance sheet accounts during the year, and the impact of these changes on cash flows, is to "work backwards" to reconstruct the investing and financing transactions using journal entries and T-accounts, especially the plant assets account.

EXHIBIT 4.11	Cash Flow Statement for One World Café

ONE WORLD CAFÉ, INC.
Statement of Cash Flows
For Year Ended December 31, 2010

Cash provided by operating activities		
Net income	$35,000	
Add (deduct) items to convert net income to cash basis		
Depreciation	17,000	
Loss on sale of plant assets	2,000	
Accounts receivable	6,000	
Inventory	(28,000)	
Prepaid advertising	(3,000)	
Accounts payable	13,000	
Wages payable	3,500	
Income tax payable	(1,500)	
Net cash provided by operating activities		$44,000
Cash flows from investing activities		
Plant assets	(45,000)	
Proceeds from sale of plant assets	4,000	
Net cash used for investing activities		(41,000)
Cash flows from financing activities		
Issuance of common stock	9,000	
Payment of dividends	(16,000)	
Net cash flows used for financing activities		(7,000)
Net cash decrease		(4,000)
Cash at beginning of year		12,000
Cash at end of year		$ 8,000

Gains and Losses on Investing and Financing Activities

If the income statement contains gains and losses that relate to investing or financing activities, these gains (losses) must be subtracted from (added back to) net income in computing cash flows from operations. Gains and losses from the sale of investments, PPE assets, or intangible assets illustrate gains and losses from investing (not operating) activities. A gain or loss from the retirement of bonds payable is an example of a financing gain or loss. The full cash flow effect from these types of events is reported in the investing or financing sections of the statement of cash flows.

To illustrate, we record the sale of plant assets at a loss with the following journal entry:

(1)	Cash (+A)	4,000	
	Accumulated depreciation (−XA, +A)	6,000	
	Loss on sale of plant assets (+E, −SE)	2,000	
	Plant assets (−A)		12,000

+	Plant Assets (A)	−		−	Accumulated Depreciation (XA)	+
Beg. Bal. 170,000					61,000	Beg. Bal.
	12,000	(1)		(1)	6,000 | 17,000	Depreciation
					72,000	End. bal.

The $4,000 of cash received from this sale should be listed as a cash inflow under cash flows from investing activities. The $4,000 cash flow is equal to the $6,000 net book value of the plant assets that were sold ($12,000 − $6,000) less the $2,000 loss on the sale. The loss must be added as an adjustment to net income under operating activities.

Why is the loss on the sale added in the operating section of the statement of cash flows? Recall that net income is presented in the operating section of the statement of cash flows and that net income is determined by deducting expenses and losses from revenues. In this case, One World Café's net income reflects a deduction for the $2,000 loss on the sale. However, the loss must be recorded in the investing section, not the operating section. Consequently, we must add back the $2,000 to the operating section to avoid double-counting.

Therefore, these gains or losses must be eliminated as we convert net income to net cash flow from operating activities. To eliminate their impact on net income, gains are subtracted and losses are added to net income.

YOU MAKE THE CALL

You are the Securities Analyst You are analyzing a company's statement of cash flows. The company has two items relating to its accounts receivable. First, the company finances the sale of its products to some customers with notes receivable; the increase to notes receivable is classified as an investing activity. Second, the company sells its accounts receivable to another company. As a result, the sale of receivables is reported as an asset sale, which reduces receivables and yields a gain or loss on sale. This action increases its operating cash flows. How should you interpret these items in the cash flow statement? [Answer on pp. 178–179]

Noncash Investing and Financing Activities

In addition to reporting how cash changed from one balance sheet to the next, cash flow reporting is intended to present summary information about a firm's investing and financing activities. Many of these activities affect cash and are therefore already included in the investing and financing sections of the statement of cash flows. Some significant investing and financing events, however, do not affect current cash flows. Examples of **noncash investing and financing activities** are the issuance of stocks, bonds, or leases in exchange for property, plant, and equipment (PPE) assets or intangible assets; the exchange of long-term assets for other long-term assets; and the conversion of long-term debt into common stock.

To illustrate the effect of noncash transactions on the preparation of the cash flow statement, consider One World Café's purchase of $5,000 of plant assets that was financed with notes payable. The journal entry to record the purchase is as follows:

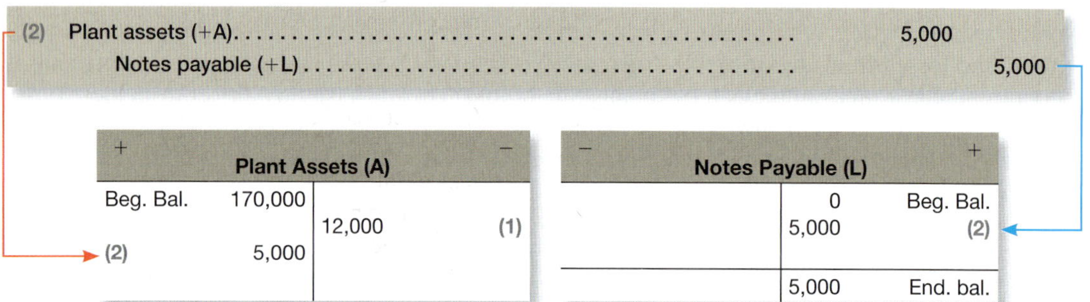

Because this purchase did not use any cash, it is not presented in the statement of cash flows. Only those capital expenditures that use cash are listed as cash flows from investing activities. That is, cash flows from investing activities should reflect the actual amount of cash spent to purchase plant assets.

Noncash investing and financing transactions generally do affect *future* cash flows. Issuing notes payable to acquire equipment, for example, requires future cash payments for interest and principal on the notes. Alternatively, converting bonds payable into common stock eliminates future cash payments related to the bonds. Knowledge of these types of events, therefore, is helpful to users of cash flow data who wish to assess a firm's future cash flows.

Information on noncash investing and financing transactions is disclosed in a schedule that is separate from the statement of cash flows. The separate schedule is reported either immediately below the statement of cash flows or among the notes to the financial statements.

Solving for purchases of plant assets.   The remaining entry affecting plant assets is the purchase of plant assets for cash. The amount of plant assets purchased can be determined by solving for the missing amount in the plant assets T-account:

+	Plant Assets (A)		−
Beg. Bal.	170,000		
		12,000	(1)
(2)	5,000		
(3)	X		
End. Bal.	208,000		

Balancing the account requires that we solve for the unknown amount:

$$\$170{,}000 + \$5{,}000 + X - \$12{,}000 \;=\; \$208{,}000$$
$$X \;=\; \$45{,}000$$

Thus, plant assets costing $45,000 were purchased for cash. This amount is listed as a cash outflow under cash flows for investing activities.

Examining the cash flow statement for One World Café in Exhibit 4.11, we see that two cash flows are listed under investing activities: (1) a $45,000 cash outflow for the purchase of plant assets, and (2) a $4,000 cash inflow from the sale of plant assets. The purchase of plant assets costing $5,000 by issuing notes payable is not listed; nor is the increase in notes payable listed under financing activities.

Appendix 4A at the end of this chapter introduces a spreadsheet approach that can be used to prepare the statement of cash flows. The appendix uses the One World Café financial statements as the illustration.

Supplemental Disclosures

When the indirect method is used in the statement of cash flows, three separate supplemental disclosures are required: (1) two specific operating cash outflows—cash paid for interest and cash paid for income taxes, (2) a schedule or description of all noncash investing and financing transactions, and (3) the firm's policy for determining which highly liquid, short-term investments are treated as cash equivalents. If the direct method is used, a reconciliation of net income to cash flows from operating activities is also required. A firm's policy regarding cash equivalents is placed in the financial statement notes. The other disclosures are reported either in the notes or at the bottom of the statement of cash flows.

One World Café Case Illustration   One World Café incurred $200 of interest expense which was paid in cash. It also reported income tax expense of $17,000 and reported a decrease in income taxes payable of $1,500 ($4,500 − $3,000). Thus, One World Café paid $18,500 ($17,000 + $1,500) in income taxes during 2010. It also had the noncash investment in plant assets costing $5,000, which was financed with notes payable. One World Café would provide the following disclosure:

Supplemental cash flow information
Cash payments for interest	$ 200
Cash payments for income taxes	18,500
Noncash transaction—investment in plant assets financed with notes payable	5,000

ANALYSIS OF CASH FLOWS

Data from the statement of cash flows enter into various financial ratios. Two such ratios are:

1. Operating cash flow to current liabilities
2. Operating cash flow to capital expenditures.

These ratios complement the liquidity and solvency ratios introduced in Chapters 1 and 2.

LO3 Compute and interpret ratios that reflect a company's liquidity and solvency.

Operating Cash Flow to Current Liabilities

The **operating cash flow to current liabilities (OCFCL) ratio** is a measure of the ability to liquidate current liabilities and is calculated as:

$$\text{Operating cash flow to current liabilities} = \frac{\text{Operating cash flow}}{\text{Average current liabilities}}$$

Operating cash flow is obtained from the statement of cash flows; it represents the excess amount of cash derived from operations during the year. The denominator is the average of the beginning and ending current liabilities for the year. For 2009, Walgreen's cash flow from operations was $4,111 million and its current liabilities averaged $6,706.5 million [($6,769 + $6,644)/2], yielding OCFCL ratio of 0.61, computed as $4,111/$6,706.5. The higher this ratio, the stronger is a firm's ability to settle current liabilities as they come due. For 2008, this ratio was 0.45. The increase in Walgreen's OCFCL ratio from 0.45 to 0.61 means that the company is in a stronger liquidity position in 2009 than it was in 2008.

Operating Cash Flow to Capital Expenditures

To remain competitive, an entity must be able to replace, and expand when appropriate, its property, plant, and equipment. A ratio that helps assess a firm's ability to do so from internally generated cash flow is the **operating cash flow to capital expenditures (OCFCX) ratio**, which is computed as follows.

$$\text{Operating cash flow to capital expenditures} = \frac{\text{Operating cash flow}}{\text{Annual capital expenditures}}$$

The numerator in this ratio comes from the first section of the statement of cash flows—the section reporting the net cash flow from operating activities. Information for the denominator can be found in one or more places in the financial statements or in the Management Discussion and Analysis section of the 10-K report. Capital expenditures are shown in the investing activities section of the statement of cash flows. Also, capital expenditures often appear in the comparative selected financial data presented as supplementary information to the financial statements.

A ratio in excess of 1.0 means that the firm's current operating activities are providing cash in excess of the amount needed to provide the desired level of plant capacity and would normally be considered a sign of financial strength. This ratio is also viewed as an indicator of long-term solvency—a ratio exceeding 1.0 means that there is operating cash flow in excess of capital needs that can then be used to repay outstanding long-term debt. Walgreen spent $1,927 million to purchase property and equipment in 2009 and $405 million to acquire other businesses and intangible assets. Thus total capital expenditures was $2,332 million, yielding an OCFCX ratio of 1.76 ($4,111/$2,332). The same ratio was 1.07 in 2008.

The interpretation of this ratio for a firm is influenced by its trend in recent years, the ratio size being achieved by other firms in the same industry, and the stage of the firm's life cycle. A firm in the early stages of its life cycle when periods of rapid expansion occur, is expected to experience a lower ratio than a firm in the mature stage of its life cycle when maintenance of plant capacity is more likely than expansion of capacity.

Following are recent OCFCX ratios for several companies:

Colgate-Palmolive Company (consumer grocery products)	3.27
Lockheed Martin Corporation (aerospace)	3.81
Verizon Communications Inc. (telecommunications)	0.80
Google (Internet services)	1.55
The Home Depot Inc. (home products)	2.99

Free Cash Flow

Free cash flow is a measure of a company's ability to apply its resources to new endeavors. Free cash flow is defined in several ways; one of the more common definitions follows:

> **Free cash flow = Cash flow from operations − Net capital expenditures**

Net capital expenditures is defined as capital expenditures less the cash proceeds from selling or disposing of property, plant and equipment. In 2009, Walgreen sold assets for $51 million in cash. Its net capital expenditures was $2,281 million ($2,332 − $51). Thus, its free cash flow was $1,830 million ($4,111 million − $2,281 million). Free cash flow reflects on the funds available for investing in new ventures, buying back stock, paying down debt, or returning funds to stockholders in the form of dividends. The concept is also used in mergers and acquisitions to indicate cash that would be available to the acquirer for investment.

RESEARCH INSIGHT

Is the Cash Flow Statement Useful?   Some analysts rely on cash flow forecasts to value common stock. Research shows that both net income and operating cash flows are correlated with stock prices, but that stock prices are more highly correlated with net income than with cash flows. So, do we need both statements? Evidence suggests that by using *both* net income and cash flow information, we can improve our forecasts of *future* cash flows. Also, net income and cash flow together are more highly correlated with stock prices than either net income or cash flow alone. This result suggests that, for purposes of stock valuation, information from the cash flow statement complements information from the income statement.

CHAPTER-END REVIEW

Refer to One World Café's statement of cash flows and comparative balance sheets from Exhibits 4.10 and 4.11 to complete the following.

Required

1. Calculate the operating cash flow to current liabilities (OCFCL) ratio for One World Café and interpret your findings.
2. Calculate One World Café's operating cash flow to capital expenditures (OCFCX) ratio. What observations can you make about your findings?
3. Calculate the free cash flow for One World Café.

The solution to this review problem can be found on page 202.

APPENDIX 4A: A Spreadsheet Approach to Preparing the Statement of Cash Flows

Preparing the statement of cash flows is aided by the use of a spreadsheet. The procedure is somewhat mechanical and is quite easy once someone has mastered the material in the chapter. We illustrate this procedure using the data for One World Café presented in the chapter in Exhibit 4.10. By following the steps presented below, we are able to readily prepare One World Café's cash flow statement for 2010.

LO4 Use a spreadsheet to construct the statement of cash flows.

To set up the spreadsheet, we list all of the accounts in the balance sheet in the first column of the spreadsheet. We list depreciable assets net of accumulated depreciation. In the next column, we list the most recent balance sheet (the ending balances) followed by the earlier balance sheet (beginning balances). There is no need to list totals such as total assets or total current liabilities. See Exhibit 4A.1.

Step 1: compute the changes in the balance sheet accounts.   Subtract the beginning balances in each account from the ending balances and record these in column D. We highlight the change in the cash balance, because this is the amount that we are trying to explain. At this point it is useful to verify that the change in cash is equal to the changes in liabilities plus the changes in stockholders' equity minus the changes in noncash assets:

$$\Delta\text{Cash} = \Delta\text{Liabilities} + \Delta\text{Stockholders' Equity} - \Delta\text{Noncash Assets}$$

Step 2: analyze the changes to determine the effect of each on cash flow.   For each account except cash, we determine whether the change in the account balance affected

EXHIBIT 4A.1   Cash Flow Spreadsheet for One World Café

A	B	C	D	E	F	G	H
				Effect of change on cash flow			No effect
	2010	2009	Change	Operating	Investing	Financing	on cash
Assets							
Cash...................	8,000	12,000	(4,000)				
Accounts receivable	22,000	28,000	(6,000)	6,000			
Inventory	94,000	66,000	28,000	(28,000)			
Prepaid advertising........	12,000	9,000	3,000	(3,000)			
Plant assets, net	136,000	109,000	27,000				
Depreciation............				17,000			
Plant assets purchased...					(45,000)		(5,000)
Plant assets, sold:				2,000	4,000		
Liabilities							
Accounts payable	27,000	14,000	13,000	13,000			
Wages payable	6,000	2,500	3,500	3,500			
Income tax payable........	3,000	4,500	(1,500)	(1,500)			
Notes payable	5,000	0	5,000				5,000
Equity							
Common stock	134,000	125,000	9,000			9,000	
Retained earnings.........	97,000	78,000	19,000				
Net income.............				35,000			
Dividends						(16,000)	
Totals..................				44,000	(41,000)	(7,000)	0

operating activities, investing activities or financing activities. Columns E, F, and G list the effects on cash flow for operating, investing and financing, respectively.

For changes in liabilities and stockholders' equity, the effect on cash is equal to the amount of the change. For example, the $13,000 increase in accounts payable is listed as a positive $13,000 cash flow adjustment under operations, while the $1,500 decrease in income tax payable results in a corresponding negative adjustment to operating cash flow. Changes in assets have the opposite effect on cash. Increases in assets have a negative effect on cash while decreases in assets lead to positive adjustments to cash. For example, the $6,000 decrease in accounts receivable resulted in a $6,000 increase in operating cash flow (positive adjustment) while the $3,000 increase in prepaid advertising caused a decrease in operating cash flow (negative adjustment).

Step 3: analyze the change in retained earnings.   Some accounts require special attention because the change in the account balance involves two types of cash flow effects. For example, the change in retained earnings is actually two changes—net income, which is related to operations, and dividends, which is a financing cash flow.

One World Café's retained earnings increased by $19,000. It reported net income of $35,000, which is listed as an operating inflow, and paid dividends of $16,000, a cash outflow listed under financing activities. For clarity, it is helpful to list each of these changes on a separate line. Thus, we insert two lines into the spreadsheet immediately below retained earnings—the first for net income and the second for dividends. The $35,000 inflow and the $16,000 outflow net to $19,000.

Step 4: analyze the change in plant assets.   A change in depreciable assets is actually the result of both operating and investing transactions. The change in plant assets can be explained by looking at the individual transactions that caused the change. As was the case with retained earnings, it is helpful to list each of these transactions in a separate row in the spreadsheet. Thus, we insert three rows into the spreadsheet immediately below the change in plant assets. First, we recall that One World Café reported depreciation expense of $17,000. This is listed in the first row under plant assets as a positive adjustment to cash flow from operations.

In the next row, we list purchases of plant assets. One World Café purchased plant assets for $45,000 in cash, which is listed under investing as a cash outflow. There was also the $5,000 purchase of plant assets that was financed with notes payable. This transaction did not affect cash. We create one final column (column H) to hold the effect of balance sheet changes that have no effect on cash flow. Here, we list −$5,000 in the row labeled "plant assets purchased," and +$5,000 in the notes payable row.

In the third row below plant assets, we list the sale of plant assets. One World Café sold plant assets for $4,000 cash, recognizing a loss of $2,000. The loss is listed under operations (as a positive adjustment to operating cash flow) and the proceeds from the sale are listed under investing as a cash inflow.

When all of the balance sheet changes have been analyzed, the change for each account should add up to the sum of the effect on operating, investing, and financing cash flows, plus the amount in the "no effect" column. That is, for each change listed in the spreadsheet, we can add columns E, F, G, and H to get the change in the balance sheet account. For retained earnings: $35,000 − $16,000 = $19,000. For assets, the total will be the negative of the change. Adding up entries for plant assets: $17,000 − $45,000 − $5,000 + $2,000 + $4,000 = −$27,000.

Step 5: total the columns.   We add up the effects listed in columns E, F, G, and H to get the cash flow subtotals. One World Café had cash flow from operations of $44,000, investing cash flows of −$41,000 and financing cash flows of −$7,000. The total for the "no effect" column (column H) should be $0, because the entries in this column had no effect on cash flow. Finally, we add up these totals to make sure that the cash flow effects equal the change in cash: $44,000 − $41,000 − $7,000 − $0 = −$4,000. If the totals do not add up to the change in cash, then there must be an error in analyzing one or more of the balance sheet changes. For example, if we had forgotten to subtract dividends, then the cash flow effects in columns E, F, and G would not add up to the change in retained earnings listed in column D. Likewise, if we had mistakenly omitted the sale of plant assets, then the change in plant assets would not add up correctly. Totaling the columns and rows is a check to verify that our analysis is complete and correct.

Step 6: prepare the cash flow statement.   Starting with operating cash flows (column E), we list each of the items in the statement of cash flows. We start with net income, and then add depreciation and the loss on the sale of plant assets, then we list the remaining adjustments, starting with the change in accounts receivable and working down the column. Next, we do the same for the items listed in the investing (column F) and financing (column G) sections of the cash flow statement. The resulting statement is identical to the statement presented in Exhibit 4.11.

APPENDIX-END REVIEW

The comparative balance sheets and income statement for Rocky Road Bicycles, Inc., are as follows.

ROCKY ROAD BICYCLES, INC. Comparative Balance Sheets		
At December 31	**2010**	**2009**
Assets		
Cash	$ 106,000	$ 96,000
Accounts receivable	156,000	224,000
Inventory	752,000	528,000
Prepaid rent	68,000	72,000
Plant assets	1,692,000	1,360,000
Less accumulated depreciation	(562,000)	(488,000)
Total assets	$2,212,000	$1,792,000
Liabilities		
Accounts payable	$ 216,000	$ 112,000
Wages payable	18,000	20,000
Income tax payable	44,000	36,000
Equity		
Common stock	1,142,000	1,000,000
Retained earnings	792,000	624,000
Total liabilities and equity	$2,212,000	$1,792,000

Additional Information:

- Rocky Road reported net income of $326,000 in 2010.
- Depreciation expense was $122,000 in 2010.
- Rocky Road sold plant assets during 2010. The plant assets originally cost $88,000, with accumulated depreciation of $48,000, and were sold for a gain of $16,000.
- Rocky Road declared and paid a $158,000 cash dividend in 2010.

Required
Use a spreadsheet to create a statement of cash flows for Rocky Road Bicycles, Inc.

The solution to this review problem can be found on pages 203.

SUMMARY

LO1 **Explain the purpose of the statement of cash flows and how it complements the income statement and the balance sheet. (p. 152)**

- The statement of cash flows summarizes information about the flow of cash into and out of the business.
- The statement of cash flows classifies the cash flows into three categories: cash flows from operations, cash flows from investing, and cash flows from financing activities.

LO2 **Construct and explain the statement of cash flows. (p. 157)**

- The direct method presents net cash flow from operating activities by showing the major categories of operating cash receipts and payments.
- The operating cash receipts and payments are usually determined by converting the accrual revenues and expenses to corresponding cash amounts.
- Cash investment outlays are captured in the investing section along with any cash receipts from asset disposals. Because cash receipts include any gain on sale (or reflect any loss), the gain (loss) must be subtracted from (added to) net income in the operating section to avoid double-counting.
- Cash obtained from the issuance of securities or borrowings, and any repayments of debt, are disclosed in the financing section. Cash dividends are also included in this section. Interest payments are included in the operating section of the statement.
- Some events, for example assets donated to the firm, provide resources to the business that are important but which do not involve cash outlays. These events are disclosed separately, along with the statement of cash flows as supplementary disclosures or in the notes.

LO3 **Compute and interpret ratios that reflect a company's liquidity and solvency. (p. 173)**

- Two ratios of importance that are based on cash flows include:
  - Operating cash flow to current liabilities—a measure of the adequacy of current operations to cover current liability payments.
  - Operating cash flow to capital expenditures—a reflection of a company's ability to replace or expand its activities based on the level of current operations.
- Free cash flow is defined as: Cash flow from operations − Net capital expenditures.
- Free cash flow is a measure of a company's ability to apply its resources to new endeavors.

LO4 **Appendix 4A: Use a spreadsheet to construct the statement of cash flows. (p. 175)**

- A spreadsheet helps to prepare the statement of cash flows by classifying the effect of each change in the balance sheet as operating, investing, financing, or not affecting cash.
- The spreadsheet approach relies on the key relationship:
  Cash = Liabilities + Stockholders' equity − Noncash assets

GUIDANCE ANSWERS . . . YOU MAKE THE CALL

You are the Chief Accountant   The transaction's effect will appear in the investing section of the cash flow statement in the amount of a positive $1.83 million.

You are the Securities Analyst   Many companies, but not all, treat customers' notes receivable as an investing activity. In 2005, the SEC became concerned with this practice and issued letters to a number of companies objecting to this accounting classification. "Presenting cash receipts from receivables generated by the sale of inventory as investing activities in the company's consolidated statements of cash flows is not in accordance with GAAP," wrote the chief accountant for the SEC's division of corporation finance, in her letter to the companies ("Little Campus Lab Shakes Big Firms—Georgia Tech Crew's Report Spurs Change in Accounting for Operating Cash Flow," March 1, 2005, *The Wall Street Journal*). The SEC's position is that these notes receivable are an operating activity and analysts are certainly justified in treating them likewise. Concerning the sale of receivables, the transaction can be treated as a sale with a consequent reduction in receivables and a gain or loss on the sale recorded in the income statement. Many analysts treat this as a financing activity and argue that the cash inflow should not be regarded as an increase in operating cash flows. Bottom line: many argue that operating cash flows do not increase as a result of these two transactions and analysts should adjust the statement of cash flows to properly classify the financing of notes receivable as an operating activity and the sale of receivables as a financing activity.

KEY RATIOS

$$\text{Operating cash flow to current liabilities} = \frac{\text{Operating cash flow}}{\text{Average current liabilities}}$$

$$\text{Operating cash flow to capital expenditures} = \frac{\text{Operating cash flow}}{\text{Annual capital expenditures}}$$

$$\text{Free cash flow} = \text{Cash flow from operations} - \text{Net capital expenditures}$$

KEY TERMS

Cash equivalents (p. 153)

Financing activities (p. 155)

Free cash flow (p. 174)

Indirect method (p. 165)

Investing activities (p. 155)

Net (p. 170)

Noncash investing and financing activities (p. 172)

Operating cash flow to capital expenditures ratio (OCFCX) (p. 174)

Operating cash flow to current liabilities ratio (OCFCL) (p. 174)

Operating activities (p. 154)

Statement of cash flows (p. 152)

Treasury stock (p. 155)

MULTIPLE CHOICE

1. Which of the following is not disclosed in a statement of cash flows?
   a. a transfer of cash to a cash equivalent investment
   b. the amount of cash at year-end
   c. cash outflows from investing activities during the period
   d. cash inflows from financing activities during the period

2. Which of the following events appears in the cash flows from investing activities section of the statement of cash flows?
   a. cash received as interest
   b. cash received from issuance of common stock
   c. cash purchase of equipment
   d. cash payment of dividends

3. Which of the following events appears in the cash flows from financing activities section of the statement of cash flows?
   a. cash purchase of equipment
   b. cash purchase of bonds issued by another company
   c. cash received as repayment for funds loaned
   d. cash purchase of treasury stock

4. Tyler Company has a net income of $49,000 and the following related items:

Depreciation expense	$ 5,000
Accounts receivable increase	2,000
Inventory decrease	10,000
Accounts payable decrease	4,000

Using the indirect method, what is Tyler's net cash flow from operations?
   a. $42,000
   b. $46,000
   c. $58,000
   d. $38,000

5. Refer to information in Mid-Chapter Review 2. The operating cash flow to current liabilities ratio for Mug Shots, Inc. in December is
   a. 6.4%.
   b. 2.9%.
   c. 2.6%.
   d. impossible to determined from the data provided.

Superscript ^{A} denotes assignments based on Appendix 4A.

DISCUSSION QUESTIONS

Q4-1. What is the definition of *cash equivalents*? Give three examples of cash equivalents.

Q4-2. Why are cash equivalents included with cash in a statement of cash flows?

Q4-3. What are the three major types of activities classified on a statement of cash flows? Give an example of a cash inflow and a cash outflow in each classification.

Q4-4. In which of the three activity categories of a statement of cash flows would each of the following items appear? Indicate for each item whether it represents a cash inflow or a cash outflow:
   a. Cash purchase of equipment.
   b. Cash collection on loans.
   c. Cash dividends paid.
   d. Cash dividends received.
   e. Cash proceeds from issuing stock.
   f. Cash receipts from customers.
   g. Cash interest paid.
   h. Cash interest received.

Q4-5. Traverse Company acquired a $3,000,000 building by issuing $3,000,000 worth of bonds payable. In terms of cash flow reporting, what type of transaction is this? What special disclosure requirements apply to a transaction of this type?

Q4-6. Why are noncash investing and financing transactions disclosed as supplemental information to a statement of cash flows?

Q4-7. Why is a statement of cash flows a useful financial statement?

Q4-8. What is the difference between the direct method and the indirect method of presenting net cash flow from operating activities?

Q4-9. In determining net cash flow from operating activities using the indirect method, why must we add depreciation back to net income? Give an example of another item that is added back to net income under the indirect method.

Q4-10. Vista Company sold for $98,000 cash land originally costing $70,000. The company recorded a gain on the sale of $28,000. How is this event reported in a statement of cash flows using the indirect method?

Q4-11. A firm uses the indirect method. Using the following information, what is its net cash flow from operating activities?

Net income.	$88,000
Accounts receivable decrease	13,000
Inventory increase.	9,000
Accounts payable decrease	3,500
Income tax payable increase	1,500
Depreciation expense	6,000

Q4-12. What separate disclosures are required for a company that reports a statement of cash flows using the indirect method?

Q4-13. If a business had a net loss for the year, under what circumstances would the statement of cash flows show a positive net cash flow from operating activities?

Q4-14. A firm is converting its accrual revenues to corresponding cash amounts using the direct method. Sales on the income statement are $925,000. Beginning and ending accounts receivable on the balance sheet are $58,000 and $44,000, respectively. What is the amount of cash received from customers?

Q4-15. A firm reports $86,000 wages expense in its income statement. If beginning and ending wages payable are $3,900 and $2,800, respectively, what is the amount of cash paid to employees?

Q4-16. A firm reports $43,000 advertising expense in its income statement. If beginning and ending prepaid advertising are $6,000 and $7,600, respectively, what is the amount of cash paid for advertising?

Q4-17. Rusk Company sold equipment for $5,100 cash that had cost $35,000 and had $29,000 of accumulated depreciation. How is this event reported in a statement of cash flows using the direct method?

Q4-18. What separate disclosures are required for a company that reports a statement of cash flows using the direct method?

Q4-19. How is the operating-cash-flow-to-current-liabilities ratio calculated? Explain its use.

Q4-20. How is the operating-cash-flow-to-capital-expenditures ratio calculated? Explain its use.

**Assignments with the WebAssign. logo in the margin are available in WebAssign.
See the Preface of the book for details.**

MINI EXERCISES

M4-21. Identifying the Impact of Account Changes on Cash Flow from Operating Activities (Indirect Method)   **LO1, LO2**

The following account changes were presented in a recent balance sheet for **Target Corporation**. Determine whether the amount of change would be added to (+) or subtracted from (−) Target's net income for the period when calculating cash flow from operations ($ millions).

TARGET NYSE :: TGT

a. ______$823 increase in accounts payable
b. ______$319 increase in accrued liabilities
c. ______$853 decrease in inventory
d. ______$448 decrease in accounts receivable
e. ______$1,259 increase in depreciation and amortization

M4-22. Classifying of Cash Flows   **LO1, LO2**

For each of the items below, indicate whether the cash flow relates to an operating activity, an investing activity, or a financing activity.

a. Cash receipts from customers for services rendered.
b. Sale of long-term investments for cash.
c. Acquisition of plant assets for cash.
d. Payment of income taxes.
e. Bonds payable issued for cash.
f. Payment of cash dividends declared in previous year.
g. Purchase of short-term investments (not cash equivalents) for cash.

M4-23. Classifying Cash Flow Statement Components   **LO2**

The following table presents selected items from a recent cash flow statement of **Dole Food Company, Inc.** For each item, determine whether the amount would be disclosed in the cash flow statement under operating activities, investing activities, or financing activities. (Dole uses the indirect method of reporting.)

DOLE FOOD COMPANY, INC. NYSE :: DOLE

DOLE FOOD COMPANY, INC.
Selected Items from Its Cash Flow Statement

1	Cash dividends paid
2	Change in inventories
3	Depreciation and amortization
4	Long-term debt repayments
5	Change in accounts payable and accrued liabilities
6	Net income
7	Proceeds from sales of assets
8	Change in provision for deferred income taxes
9	Change in prepaid expenses and other assets
10	Short-term debt borrowings
11	Capital additions

LO1, LO2   **M4-24. Classifying Cash Flows**

For each of the items below, indicate whether it is (1) a cash flow from an operating activity, (2) a cash flow from an investing activity, (3) a cash flow from a financing activity, (4) a noncash investing and financing activity, or (5) none of the above.

a.   Paid cash to retire bonds payable at a loss.
b.   Received cash as settlement of a lawsuit.
c.   Acquired a patent in exchange for common stock.
d.   Received advance payments from customers on orders for custom-made goods.
e.   Gave large cash contribution to local university.
f.   Invested cash in 60-day commercial paper (a cash equivalent).

LO1, LO2   **M4-25. Classifying Cash Flow Statement Components**

PACIFIC SUNWEAR
NASDAQ :: PSUN

The following table presents selected items from the cash flow statement of **Pacific Sunwear of California, Inc.** For each item determine whether the amount would be disclosed in the cash flow statement under operating activities, investing activities, or financing activities. (Pacific Sunwear uses the indirect method of reporting.)

PACIFIC SUNWEAR OF CALIFORNIA, INC.
Selected Items from its Cash Flow Statement

1	Depreciation and amortization
2	Proceeds from the sale of common stock and exercise of stock options
3	Loss on disposal of equipment
4	Change in accrued liabilities
5	Repayments of long-term debt obligations
6	Changes in income taxes payable and deferred income taxes
7	Change in accounts receivable
8	Purchases of property and equipment
9	Repurchase and retirement of common stock
10	Purchases of short-term investments

LO2   **M4-26. Calculating Net Cash Flow from Operating Activities (Indirect Method)**

The following information was obtained from Galena Company's comparative balance sheets. Assume that Galena Company's 2010 income statement showed depreciation expense of $8,000, a gain on sale of investments of $9,000, and a net income of $45,000. Calculate the net cash flow from operating activities using the indirect method.

	Dec 31, 2010	Dec 31, 2009
Cash.	$ 19,000	$ 9,000
Accounts receivable	44,000	35,000
Inventory	55,000	49,000
Prepaid rent.	6,000	8,000
Long-term investments.	21,000	34,000
Plant assets	150,000	106,000
Accumulated depreciation	40,000	32,000
Accounts payable	24,000	20,000
Income tax payable.	4,000	6,000
Common stock	121,000	92,000
Retained earnings	106,000	91,000

LO2   **M4-27. Classifying Cash Flow Statement Components and Determining Their Effects**

ETHAN ALLEN
INTERIORS
NYSE :: ETH

The following table presents selected items from a recent cash flow statement of **Ethan Allen Interiors Inc.**

a.   For each item determine whether the amount would be disclosed in the cash flow statement under operating activities, investing activities, or financing activities. (Assume it uses the indirect method of reporting.)
b.   For each item, determine whether the effect on cash flow is positive, negative, or indeterminate.

ETHAN ALLEN INTERIORS INC. AND SUBSIDIARIES
Consolidated Statements of Cash Flows—Selected Items

1	Purchases of short-term investments
2	Payment of cash dividends
3	Depreciation and amortization
4	Increase in deferred income tax liability
5	Decrease in customer deposits
6	Capital expenditures
7	Increase in income taxes and accounts payable
8	Payments on long-term debt and capital leases
9	Gain on disposal of property, plant, and equipment
10	Increase in prepaid and other current assets
11	Net proceeds from issuance of common stock
12	Proceeds from the disposal of property, plant, and equipment
13	Net income
14	Decrease in inventories
15	Borrowings on revolving credit facility

M4-28. Calculating Net Cash Flow from Operating Activities (Indirect Method) **LO2**

Cairo Company had a $21,000 net loss from operations for 2010. Depreciation expense for 2010 was $8,600 and a 2010 cash dividend of $6,000 was declared and paid. Balances of the current asset and current liability accounts at the beginning and end of 2010 follow. Did Cairo Company's 2010 operating activities provide or use cash? Use the indirect method to determine your answer.

	Ending	Beginning
Cash...	$ 3,500	$ 7,000
Accounts receivable	16,000	25,000
Inventory	50,000	53,000
Prepaid expenses	6,000	9,000
Accounts payable	12,000	8,000
Accrued liabilities	5,000	7,600

M4-29. Classifying Cash Flow Statement Components and Determining Their Effects **LO2**

The following table presents selected items from a recent cash flow statement of **Nordstrom, Inc.** **NORDSTROM, INC.**
NYSE :: JWN

a. For each item, determine whether the amount would be disclosed in the cash flow statement under operating activities, investing activities, or financing activities. (Nordstrom uses the indirect method of reporting.)

b. For each item, determine whether the effect on cash flow is positive, negative, or indeterminate.

NORDSTROM, INC.
Consolidated Statement of Cash Flows—Selected Items

1	Increase in accounts receivable
2	Capital expenditures
3	Purchases of short-term investments
4	Increase in deferred income tax liability
5	Principal payments on long-term debt
6	Increase in merchandise inventories
7	Decrease in income taxes payable
8	Proceeds from employee stock purchase plan
9	Increase in accounts payable
10	Net earnings
11	Repurchase of common stock
12	Increase in accrued salaries, wages, and related benefits
13	Proceeds from sale of assets
14	Cash dividends paid
15	Depreciation and amortization of buildings and equipment

LO2 **M4-30.** **Calculating Operating Cash Flows (Direct Method)**
Calculate the cash flow for each of the following cases.

a. Cash paid for rent:

Rent expense.	$60,000
Prepaid rent, beginning year.	10,000
Prepaid rent, end of year	8,000

b. Cash received as interest:

Interest income	$16,000
Interest receivable, beginning year	3,000
Interest receivable, end of year	3,700

c. Cash paid for merchandise purchased:

Cost of goods sold	$98,000
Inventory, beginning year	19,000
Inventory, end of year	22,000
Accounts payable, beginning year	11,000
Accounts payable, end of year	7,000

LO2 **M4-31.** **Calculating Operating Cash Flows (Direct Method)**
Howell Company's current year income statement reports the following:

Sales	$825,000
Cost of goods sold	550,000
Gross profit	$275,000

Howell's comparative balance sheets show the following (accounts payable relate to merchandise purchases):

	End of Year	Beginning of Year
Accounts receivable	$ 71,000	$60,000
Inventory	109,000	96,000
Prepaid expenses	3,000	8,000
Accounts payable	31,000	37,000

Compute Howell's current-year cash received from customers and cash paid for merchandise purchased.

EXERCISES

LO3 **E4-32.** **Comparing Firms Using Ratio Analysis**
Consider the following 2008 data for several pharmaceutical firms ($ millions):

	Average current liabilities	Cash from operations	Expenditures on PPE	Proceeds from the sale of PPE
Merck & Co., Inc.	$ 5,618	$ 3,364	$ 747	$44
Pfizer Inc.	24,422	18,238	1,701	0
Abbott Laboratories	10,347	6,995	1,288	0

a. Compute the operating cash flow to current liabilities (OCFCL) ratio for each firm.
b. Compute the free cash flow for each firm.
c. Comment on the results of your computations.

E4-33. Comparing Firms Using Ratio Analysis   **LO3**

Consider the following data for several firms from 2008 ($ millions):

	Average current liabilities	Cash from operations	Expenditures on PPE	Proceeds from the sale of PPE
Wal-Mart Stores, Inc..........	$ 56,934	$23,147	$11,499	$ 714
General Electric Company.....	246,925	48,601	16,010	10,975
Exxon Mobil Corporation......	53,706	59,725	19,318	5,985

WAL-MART
NYSE :: WMT

GENERAL ELECTRIC
NYSE :: GE

EXXON MOBIL CORP.
NYSE :: XOM

a. Compute the operating cash flow to current liabilities (OCFCL) ratio for each firm.

b. Compute the free cash flow for each firm.

c. Comment on the results of your computations.

E4-34. Classifying Cash Flow Statement Components and Preparing the Statement of Cash Flow   **LO1, LO2**

The table below contains data from a recent cash flow statement of **Target Corporation**.

WebAssign.

TARGET
NYSE :: TGT

TARGET CORPORATION	
Data from the Consolidated Statement of Cash Flows ($ millions)	
Additions to long-term debt	$3,557
Cash balance at the beginning of the year	2,450
Net earnings	2,214
Depreciation and amortization	1,826
Decrease in accounts receivable, net	793
Deferred income taxes	91
Decrease in inventory	77
Proceeds from disposal of property and equipment.	39
Stock issued and other	35
Loss on disposal of property and equipment	33
Stock based compensation (non-cash)	72
Other operating adjustments	(57)
Decrease in accrued liabilities	(230)
Decrease in accounts payable	(389)
Dividends paid.	(465)
Reduction of short-term debt.	(500)
Other investments	(865)
Reductions of long-term debt.	(1,455)
Repurchase of common stock	(2,815)
Expenditures for property and equipment.	(3,547)

a. For each item, indicate whether the item is operating, investing, or financing.

b. Prepare the cash flow statement (indirect method) using the data from the table.

c. Compute Target's cash balance at the end of the period.

E4-35. Calculating Net Cash Flow from Operating Activities (Indirect Method)   **LO2, LO3**

Lincoln Company owns no plant assets and reported the following income statement for the current year:

WebAssign.

Sales		$750,000
Cost of goods sold	$470,000	
Wages expense.................................	110,000	
Rent expense.................................	42,000	
Insurance expense	15,000	637,000
Net income.		$113,000

Additional balance sheet information about the company follows:

	End of Year	Beginning of Year
Accounts receivable	$54,000	$49,000
Inventory	60,000	66,000
Prepaid insurance	8,000	7,000
Accounts payable	22,000	18,000
Wages payable	9,000	11,000

Use the information to (a) calculate the net cash flow from operating activities under the indirect method. Also, compute its (b) operating cash flow to current liabilities (OCFCL) ratio. (Assume current liabilities consist of accounts payable and wages payable.)

LO1, LO2 E4-36. Classifying Cash Flow Statement Components and Preparing the Statement of Cash Flow

OAKLEY, INC.
NYSE :: OO

The table below contains data from a cash flow statement of **Oakley, Inc.**

OAKLEY, INC. AND SUBSIDIARIES Data from the Consolidated Statements of Cash Flows ($ thousands)	
Proceeds from bank borrowings	$254,211
Cash balance at the beginning of the year	82,157
Net income	44,788
Depreciation and amortization	37,571
Increase in accrued expenses and other current liabilities	14,886
Increase in accounts payable	10,135
Stock issued and other	5,774
Increase in accrued income taxes	4,937
Loss on investments	4,329
Noncash compensation	3,081
Loss on sale of equipment	460
Proceeds from the sale of property and equipment	221
Purchases of investments	(705)
Increase in accounts receivable	(1,611)
Increase in prepaid expenses and other current assets	(2,268)
Repurchase of common stock	(10,351)
Payment of cash dividends	(10,952)
Deferred income taxes	(11,222)
Increase in inventories	(23,177)
Purchases of property and equipment	(52,527)
Acquisitions of other businesses	(86,751)
Repayment of bank borrowings	(231,673)

a. For each item, indicate whether the item is operating, investing, or financing.

b. Prepare the cash flow statement (indirect method) using the data from the table.

c. Compute Oakley's cash balance as of the end of the period.

d. Oakley's cash flow statement reports "Proceeds from bank borrowings" and "Repayments of bank borrowings." Why might both have occurred in the same period? Compute its net change in bank borrowings. Why does Oakley present both amounts in the cash flow statement rather than simply showing the net change?

LO2 E4-37. Preparing a Statement of Cash Flows (Indirect Method)

Use the following information about Lund Corporation for 2010 to prepare a statement of cash flows under the indirect method.

Accounts payable increase.	$ 9,000
Accounts receivable increase.	4,000
Accrued liabilities decrease	3,000
Amortization expense	6,000
Cash balance, beginning of 2010	22,000
Cash balance, end of 2010	15,000
Cash paid as dividends.	29,000
Cash paid to purchase land	90,000
Cash paid to retire bonds payable at par.	60,000
Cash received from issuance of common stock	35,000
Cash received from sale of equipment	17,000
Depreciation expense	29,000
Gain on sale of equipment	4,000
Inventory decrease	13,000
Net income.	76,000
Prepaid expenses increase.	2,000

E4-38. Reconciling Changes in Balance Sheet Accounts

The following table presents selected items from the 2008 and 2007 balance sheets and income statement of **Lowe's Companies, Inc.**

LO1, LO2

Web Assign.

LOWE'S COMPANIES, INC.
NYSE :: LOW

LOWE'S COMPANIES, INC. ($ millions)

	Selected Balance Sheet Data			Selected Income Statement Data	
	2008	**2007**			**2008**
Merchandise inventories.	$ 8,209	$ 7,611	Cost of merchandise sold.		$31,729
Property, net of depreciation . . .	22,722	21,361	Depreciation expense .		1,539
Accounts payable	4,109	3,713	Net income.		2,195
Retained earnings	17,049	15,345			

   a. Compute the cash paid for merchandise inventories in 2008. Assume all merchandise was purchased on account.

   b. Compute the net cost of property acquired in 2008.

   c. Compute the cash dividends paid in 2008.

E4-39. Analyzing Investing and Financing Cash Flows

During 2010, Paxon Corporation's long-term investments account (at cost) increased $15,000, which was the net result of purchasing stocks costing $80,000 and selling stocks costing $65,000 at a $6,000 loss. Also, its bonds payable account decreased $10,000, the net result of issuing $130,000 of bonds and retiring bonds with a book value of $140,000 at a $9,000 gain. What items and amounts appear in the (a) cash flows from investing activities and (b) cash flows from financing activities sections of its 2010 statement of cash flows?

LO1, LO2

Web Assign.

E4-40. Reconciling Changes in Balance Sheet Accounts

The following table presents selected items from the 2008 and 2007 balance sheets and 2008 income statement of **Borders Group, Inc.**

LO2

BORDERS GROUP, INC.
NYSE :: BGP

BORDERS GROUP, INC. ($ millions)

	Selected Balance Sheet Data			Selected Income Statement Data	
	2008	**2007**			**2008**
Merchandise inventories.	$915.2	$1,242.0	Cost of merchandise sold.		$2,484.8
Property and Equipment, (net) . .	494.2	592.8	Depreciation expense		107.1
Trade accounts payable	350.0	511.9	Loss on property and equipment . . .		57.1
Retained earnings	63.8	250.5	Net loss		186.7

   a. Compute the cash paid for merchandise inventories in 2008. Assume all merchandise was purchased on account.

    b.   Borders reported expenditures for property and equipment of $79.9 million in 2008. Compute the cash proceeds from the sale of property and equipment in 2008.

    c.   Determine the cash dividends paid in 2008.

    d.   For each part *a, b,* and *c,* prepare journal entries to record the cash transactions.

LO2 **E4-41.** **Calculating Operating Cash Flows (Direct Method)**

Calculate the cash flow for each of the following cases.

    a.   Cash paid for advertising:

Advertising expense	$62,000
Prepaid advertising, beginning of year	11,000
Prepaid advertising, end of year	15,000

    b.   Cash paid for income taxes:

Income tax expense	$29,000
Income tax payable, beginning of year	7,100
Income tax payable, end of year	4,900

    c.   Cash paid for merchandise purchased:

Cost of goods sold	$180,000
Inventory, beginning of year	30,000
Inventory, end of year	25,000
Accounts payable, beginning of year	10,000
Accounts payable, end of year	12,000

LO2 **E4-42.** **Preparing a Statement of Cash Flows (Direct Method)**

Use the following information about the 2010 cash flows of Mason Corporation to prepare a statement of cash flows under the direct method. Refer to Exhibit 4.3 for the appropriate format.

Cash balance, end of 2010	$12,000
Cash paid to employees and suppliers	148,000
Cash received from sale of land	40,000
Cash paid to acquire treasury stock	10,000
Cash balance, beginning of 2010	16,000
Cash received as interest	6,000
Cash paid as income taxes	11,000
Cash paid to purchase equipment	89,000
Cash received from customers	194,000
Cash received from issuing bonds payable	30,000
Cash paid as dividends	16,000

LO2, LO3 **E4-43.** **Analyzing Operating Cash Flows (Direct Method)**

Refer to the information in Exercise 4-35. Calculate the net cash flow from operating activities using the direct method. Show a related cash flow for each revenue and expense. Also, compute its (1) operating cash flow to current liabilities (OCFCL) ratio and (2) operating cash flow to capital expenditures (OCFCX) ratio. (Assume current liabilities consist of accounts payable and wages payable.)

LO1, LO2 **E4-44.** **Interpreting Cash Flow from Operating Activities**

Carter Company's income statement and cash flow from operating activities (indirect method) are provided as follows ($ thousands):

Income statement		Cash flow from operating activities	
Revenue.	$400	Net income.	$35
Cost of goods sold	215	Plus depreciation expense	70
Gross profit	185	Operating asset adjustments	
Operating expenses	110	Less increase in accounts receivable.	(25)
Operating income	75	Less increase in inventories	(50)
Interest expense	25	Less increase in prepaid rent	(5)
Income before taxes	50	Plus increase in accounts payable	65
Income tax expense	15	Plus increase in income tax payable	5
Net income.	$ 35	Cash flow from operating activities	$95

a.   For each of the four statements below, determine whether the statement is true or false.
b.   If the statement is false, provide the (underlined) dollar amount that would make it true.
   1.   Carter collected $375 from customers in the current period.
   2.   Carter paid $0 interest in the current period.
   3.   Carter paid $20 in income taxes in the current period.
   4.   If Carter increased the depreciation expense by $50, it would increase its cash from operations by $50.

PROBLEMS

P4-45.   Reconciling and Computing Operating Cash Flows from Net Income   LO2
Petroni Company reports the following selected results for its calendar year 2010.

Net income.	$135,000
Depreciation expense	25,000
Gain on sale of assets.	5,000
Accounts receivable increase.	10,000
Accounts payable increase.	6,000
Prepaid expenses decrease	3,000
Wages payable decrease	4,000

Required
Prepare the operating section only of Petroni Company's statement of cash flows for 2010 under the indirect method of reporting.

P4-46.   Preparing a Statement of Cash Flows (Indirect Method)   LO2, LO3
Wolff Company's income statement and comparative balance sheets follow.   WebAssign.

WOLFF COMPANY		
Income Statement		
For Year Ended December 31, 2010		
Sales		$635,000
Cost of goods sold	$430,000	
Wages expense.	86,000	
Insurance expense	8,000	
Depreciation expense	17,000	
Interest expense	9,000	
Income tax expense	29,000	579,000
Net income.		$ 56,000

WOLFF COMPANY Balance Sheets	Dec. 31, 2010	Dec. 31, 2009
Assets		
Cash..	$ 11,000	$ 5,000
Accounts receivable	41,000	32,000
Inventory	90,000	60,000
Prepaid insurance..	5,000	7,000
Plant assets..	250,000	195,000
Accumulated depreciation	(68,000)	(51,000)
Total assets...	$329,000	$248,000
Liabilities and Stockholders' Equity		
Accounts payable	$ 7,000	$ 10,000
Wages payable	9,000	6,000
Income tax payable......................................	7,000	8,000
Bonds payable...	130,000	75,000
Common stock	90,000	90,000
Retained earnings	86,000	59,000
Total liabilities and equity.............................	$329,000	$248,000

Cash dividends of $29,000 were declared and paid during 2010. Also in 2010, plant assets were purchased for cash, and bonds payable were issued for cash. Bond interest is paid semiannually on June 30 and December 31. Accounts payable relate to merchandise purchases.

Required

a. Compute the change in cash that occurred during 2010.

b. Prepare a 2010 statement of cash flows using the indirect method.

c. Compute and interpret Wolff's (1) operating cash flow to current liabilities ratio, and (2) operating cash flow to capital expenditures ratio.

LO1, LO2   **P4-47.**   **Computing Cash Flow from Operating Activities (Direct Method)**
Refer to the income statement and comparative balance sheets for Wolff Company presented in P4-46.

Required

a. Compute Wolff Company's cash flow from operating activities using the direct method. Use the format illustrated in Exhibit 4.6 in the chapter.

b. What can we learn from the direct method that may not be readily apparent when reviewing a cash flow statement prepared using the indirect method?

LO2, LO3   **P4-48.**   **Preparing a Statement of Cash Flows (Indirect Method)**
Arctic Company's income statement and comparative balance sheets follow.

ARCTIC COMPANY Income Statement For Year Ended December 31, 2010		
Sales		$728,000
Cost of goods sold	$534,000	
Wages expense...	190,000	
Advertising expense	31,000	
Depreciation expense...................................	22,000	
Interest expense	18,000	
Gain on sale of land....................................	(25,000)	770,000
Net loss		$ (42,000)

ARCTIC COMPANY Balance Sheets		
	Dec. 31, 2010	**Dec. 31, 2009**
Assets		
Cash	$ 49,000	$ 28,000
Accounts receivable	42,000	50,000
Inventory	107,000	113,000
Prepaid advertising	10,000	13,000
Plant assets	360,000	222,000
Accumulated depreciation	(78,000)	(56,000)
Total assets	$490,000	$370,000
Liabilities and Stockholders' Equity		
Accounts payable	$ 17,000	$ 31,000
Interest payable	6,000	—
Bonds payable	200,000	—
Common stock	245,000	245,000
Retained earnings	52,000	94,000
Treasury stock	(30,000)	—
Total liabilities and equity	$490,000	$370,000

During 2010, Arctic sold land for $70,000 cash that had originally cost $45,000. Arctic also purchased equipment for cash, acquired treasury stock for cash, and issued bonds payable for cash in 2010. Accounts payable relate to merchandise purchases.

Required

a. Compute the change in cash that occurred during 2010.

b. Prepare a 2010 statement of cash flows using the indirect method.

c. Compute and interpret Arctic's (1) operating cash flow to current liabilities ratio, and (2) operating cash flow to capital expenditures ratio.

P4-49. **Computing Cash Flow from Operating Activities (Direct Method)**   LO2
Refer to the income statement and comparative balance sheets for Arctic Company presented in P4-48.

Required

a. Compute Arctic Company's cash flow from operating activities using the direct method. Use the format illustrated in Exhibit 4.6 in the chapter.

b. What can we learn from the direct method that may not be readily apparent when reviewing a cash flow statement prepared using the indirect method?

P4-50. **Preparing a Statement of Cash Flows (Indirect Method)**   LO2, LO3
Dair Company's income statement and comparative balance sheets follow.

DAIR COMPANY Income Statement For Year Ended December 31, 2010		
Sales		$700,000
Cost of goods sold	$440,000	
Wages and other operating expenses	95,000	
Depreciation expense	22,000	
Amortization expense	7,000	
Interest expense	10,000	
Income tax expense	36,000	
Loss on bond retirement	5,000	615,000
Net income		$ 85,000

	DAIR COMPANY	
	Balance Sheets	
	Dec. 31, 2010	**Dec. 31, 2009**
Assets		
Cash.	$ 27,000	$ 18,000
Accounts receivable	53,000	48,000
Inventory	103,000	109,000
Prepaid expenses	12,000	10,000
Plant assets.	360,000	336,000
Accumulated depreciation	(87,000)	(84,000)
Intangible assets	43,000	50,000
Total assets	$511,000	$487,000
Liabilities and Shareholders' Equity		
Accounts payable	$ 32,000	$ 26,000
Interest payable.	4,000	7,000
Income tax payable.	6,000	8,000
Bonds payable.	60,000	120,000
Common stock	252,000	228,000
Retained earnings	157,000	98,000
Total liabilities and equity	$511,000	$487,000

During 2010, the company sold for $17,000 cash old equipment that had cost $36,000 and had $19,000 accumulated depreciation. Also in 2010, new equipment worth $60,000 was acquired in exchange for $60,000 of bonds payable, and bonds payable of $120,000 were retired for cash at a loss. A $26,000 cash dividend was declared and paid in 2010. Any stock issuances were for cash.

Required

a. Compute the change in cash that occurred in 2010.

b. Prepare a 2010 statement of cash flows using the indirect method.

c. Prepare separate schedules showing (1) cash paid for interest and for income taxes and (2) noncash investing and financing transactions.

d. Compute its (1) operating cash flow to current liabilities ratio, (2) operating cash flow to capital expenditures ratio, and (3) free cash flow.

LO1, LO2   **P4-51.**   **Interpreting the Statement of Cash Flows**

STAPLES, INC.
NASDAQ :: SPLS

Following is the statement of cash flows of **Staples, Inc.**

	STAPLES, INC.
	Statement of Cash Flows
($ thousands)	**Year Ended** **January 31, 2009**
Operating activities	
Net income.	$ 805,264
Adjustments to reconcile net income to cash provided by operating activities:	
Depreciation and amortization	548,911
Noncash loss on write-down of assets	150,081
Amortization of deferred financing costs.	13,496
Stock-based compensation	174,803
Deferred income taxes	33,370
Decrease in receivables	131,474
Decrease in merchandise inventories	177,163
Increase in prepaid expenses and other current assets.	(43,915)
Decrease in accounts payable	(212,414)
Decrease in accrued expenses and other current liabilities.	(149,351)

continued

continued from previous page

STAPLES, INC. Statement of Cash Flows	
($ thousands)	**Year Ended January 31, 2009**
Increase in other liabilities	56,948
Cash provided by operating activities	1,685,830
Investing activities:	
Acquisition of property and equipment	(378,329)
Acquisition of businesses and other long-term investments	(4,381,811)
Proceeds from the sale of short-term investments	27,016
Cash used for investing activities	(4,733,124)
Financing activities:	
Proceeds from borrowings, net	3,653,029
Payments on borrowings	(2,180,296)
Proceeds from issuance of commercial paper	1,195,557
Proceeds from the exercise of stock options and the sale of common stock	154,178
Cash dividends paid	(231,465)
Common stock repurchased for treasury stock	(84,961)
Cash provided by financing activities	2,506,042
Effect of exchange rate changes on cash and cash equivalents	(70,422)
Net decrease in cash and cash equivalents	(611,674)
Cash and cash equivalents at the beginning of the year	1,245,448
Cash and cash equivalents at year-end	$ 633,774

Required

a. Explain why Staples adds $548,911,000 of depreciation and amortization to net income to calculate cash flows from operating activities.

b. Staples lists a positive amount of $177,163,000 relating to merchandise inventories. What does this suggest about the change in inventories during the year? Under what circumstances might this positive cash inflow be of some concern? Explain.

c. Staples reports a cash outflow of over $4.7 billion for investing activities. Is this cash outflow a cause for concern? Explain.

d. Why does Staples list the "effect of exchange rate changes on cash and cash equivalents" in its cash flow statement? What does this amount represent?

e. Staples' cash balance decreased by $633,774,000 during the year. Does Staples present a "healthy" cash flow picture for the year? Explain.

P4-52. **Preparing a Statement of Cash Flows (Indirect Method)**
Rainbow Company's income statement and comparative balance sheets follow.

RAINBOW COMPANY Income Statement For Year Ended December 31, 2010		
Sales		$750,000
Dividend income		15,000
Total revenue		765,000
Cost of goods sold	$440,000	
Wages and other operating expenses	130,000	
Depreciation expense	39,000	
Patent amortization expense	7,000	
Interest expense	13,000	
Income tax expense	44,000	
Loss on sale of equipment	5,000	
Gain on sale of investments	(3,000)	675,000
Net income		$ 90,000

RAINBOW COMPANY Balance Sheets		
	Dec. 31, 2010	**Dec. 31, 2009**
Assets		
Cash and cash equivalents.	$ 19,000	$ 25,000
Accounts receivable	40,000	30,000
Inventory	103,000	77,000
Prepaid expenses	10,000	6,000
Long-term investments.	—	57,000
Land.	190,000	100,000
Buildings	445,000	350,000
Accumulated depreciation—Buildings.	(91,000)	(75,000)
Equipment	179,000	225,000
Accumulated depreciation—Equipment	(42,000)	(46,000)
Patents.	50,000	32,000
Total assets	$903,000	$781,000
Liabilities and Stockholders' Equity		
Accounts payable	$ 20,000	$ 16,000
Interest payable.	6,000	5,000
Income tax payable.	8,000	10,000
Bonds payable.	155,000	125,000
Preferred stock ($100 par value).	100,000	75,000
Common stock ($5 par value).	379,000	364,000
Paid-in capital in excess of par value—Common	133,000	124,000
Retained earnings	102,000	62,000
Total liabilities and equity	$903,000	$781,000

During 2010, the following transactions and events occurred:

1. Sold long-term investments costing $57,000 for $60,000 cash.
2. Purchased land for cash.
3. Capitalized an expenditure made to improve the building.
4. Sold equipment for $14,000 cash that originally cost $46,000 and had $27,000 accumulated depreciation.
5. Issued bonds payable at face value for cash.
6. Acquired a patent with a fair value of $25,000 by issuing 250 shares of preferred stock at par value.
7. Declared and paid a $50,000 cash dividend.
8. Issued 3,000 shares of common stock for cash at $8 per share.
9. Recorded depreciation of $16,000 on buildings and $23,000 on equipment.

Required

a. Compute the change in cash and cash equivalents that occurred during 2010.
b. Prepare a 2010 statement of cash flows using the indirect method.
c. Prepare separate schedules showing (1) cash paid for interest and for income taxes and (2) noncash investing and financing transactions.
d. Compute its (1) operating cash flow to current liabilities ratio, (2) operating cash flow to capital expenditures ratio, and (3) free cash flow.

LO2 **P4-53.** **Preparing a Statement of Cash Flows (Direct Method)**

WebAssign.

Refer to the data for Rainbow Company in Problem 4-52.

Required

a. Compute the change in cash that occurred in 2010.
b. Prepare a 2010 statement of cash flows using the direct method. Use one cash outflow for "cash paid for wages and other operating expenses." Accounts payable relate to inventory purchases only.
c. Prepare separate schedules showing (1) a reconciliation of net income to net cash flow from operating activities and (2) noncash investing and financing transactions.

P4-54. **Interpreting Cash Flow Information**

The 2009 cash flow statement for **Apple Inc.** is presented below (all $ amounts in millions):

LO1, LO2

APPLE INC.
NASDAQ :: AAPL

APPLE INC. Consolidated Statement of Cash Flows Year ended September 26, 2009	
Cash and cash equivalents, beginning of the year	$11,875
Operating activities:	
Net income	5,704
Adjustments to reconcile net income to operating cash flow:	
Depreciation of property, plant and equipment	577
Amortization of intangible assets and other	126
Stock-based compensation	710
Loss on disposal of property, plant and equipment	26
Deferred income tax benefit	(519)
Changes in operating assets and liabilities:	
Accounts receivable	(939)
Inventories	54
Other current assets	(1,050)
Other assets	(1,346)
Accounts payable	92
Deferred revenue	6,908
Other liabilities	(184)
Cash generated by operating activities	10,159
Investing activities:	
Purchases of property, plant and equipment	(1,144)
Proceeds from the disposal of property, plant and equipment	42
Purchases of intangible assets	(69)
Purchase of marketable securities	(46,724)
Proceeds from sales and maturities of marketable securities	30,678
Purchases of long-term investments and other	(217)
Cash used for investing activities	(17,434)
Financing activities:	
Proceeds from issuance of common stock	475
Cash proceeds from stock-based compensation, including tax benefits	188
Cash generated from financing activities	663
Decrease in cash and cash equivalents	(6,612)
Cash and cash equivalents, end of the year	$ 5,263

Required

a. Apple reported net sales of $36,537 in its fiscal 2009 income statement. What amount of cash did Apple collect from customers during the year?

b. Apple's cost of goods sold was $23,397 in 2009. Assuming that accounts payable applies only to the purchase of inventory, what amount did Apple pay to purchase inventory in 2009?

c. At September 26, 2009, Apple reported a balance of $2,954 in property, plant and equipment, net of accumulated depreciation. What was the balance in this account at the end of fiscal 2008?

d. Apple lists stock-based compensation as a positive amount ($710) under cash flow from operating activities. Why is this amount listed here? Explain how this amount increases cash flow from operating activities.

P4-55. **Reconstructing Transactions from Financial Statements**

The comparative balance sheets of **The Home Depot, Inc.**, are presented below (all $ amounts in millions):

LO1, LO2

THE HOME DEPOT,
INC.
NYSE :: HD

THE HOME DEPOT, INC. AND SUBSIDIARIES
Consolidated Balance Sheets
February 1, 2009 and February 3, 2008

	2009	2008
Assets		
Cash and cash equivalents	$ 519	$ 445
Short-term investments	6	12
Accounts receivable	972	1,259
Merchandise inventories	10,673	11,731
Other current assets	1,192	1,227
Total current assets	13,362	14,674
Property and equipment, at cost	36,477	36,412
Less accumulated depreciation	10,243	8,936
Net property and equipment	26,234	27,476
Goodwill and other assets	1,568	2,174
Total assets	$41,164	$44,324
Liabilities and Stockholders' Equity		
Current installments of long-term debt	$ 1,767	$ 300
Short-term debt	—	1,747
Accounts payable	4,822	5,732
Accrued salaries and related expenses	1,129	1,094
Deferred revenue	1,165	1,474
Sales taxes payable	337	445
Income taxes payable	289	60
Other accrued expenses	1,644	1,854
Total current liabilities	11,153	12,706
Long-term debt, excluding current installments	9,667	11,383
Other long-term liabilities	2,198	1,833
Deferred income taxes	369	688
Total liabilities	23,387	26,610
Common stock, including additional paid-in capital	6,133	5,885
Treasury stock, at cost	(372)	(314)
Retained earnings	12,093	11,388
Accumulated other comprehensive income (loss)	(77)	755
Total liabilities and stockholders' equity	$41,164	$44,324

Required

a. The Home Depot reported sales revenue of $71,288 in fiscal 2009. What amount of cash was collected from customers during the year?

b. Cost of sales totaled $47,298 in 2009. If all merchandise inventories were purchased on accounts payable, what amount of cash did Home Depot pay to purchase inventories in 2009?

c. The Home Depot purchased property and equipment costing $1,884 in fiscal 2009. Of this amount, $1,847 was purchased with cash, and the remaining amount was financed with long-term debt. Compute the original cost of the property and equipment that Home Depot sold or disposed of in 2009.

d. Prepare a journal entry to record the purchase of property and equipment financed with long-term debt described in c.

e. What amount did Home Depot pay to repay long-term debt, including current installments, in 2009?

f. The Home Depot reported a provision for income taxes (income tax expense) of $1,278 in 2009. What amount of income taxes did Home Depot pay in cash in 2009?

g. Net income was $2,260 in 2009. Assume that net income and dividends are the only changes recorded to retained earnings. Compute the amount dividends declared and paid in 2009.

P4-56.[A] **Preparing the Statement of Cash Flows Using a Spreadsheet**

LO2, LO3, LO4

THE HOME DEPOT, INC.
NYSE :: HD

Refer to the comparative balance sheets for **The Home Depot** presented in Problem 4-55. In addition, assume that the following information is available (all $ amounts in millions):

- Net income totaled $2,260 in fiscal 2009.
- Depreciation was $1,785.
- Home Depot reported a loss on property and equipment of $580 during the year.
- Stock-based compensation expense (a noncash expense) was $176 in 2009.
- Home Depot purchased property and equipment costing $1,884 in 2009. Of that amount, $1,847 was purchased for cash and the remainder was financed with long-term debt.
- Home Depot purchased short-term investments costing $168 in 2009.

Required

a. Set up a spreadsheet to analyze the changes in Home Depot's comparative balance sheets. Use the format illustrated in Exhibit 4A.1.

b. Prepare a statement of cash flows for The Home Depot for 2009 using the indirect method. For the purpose of this exercise, classify changes in "goodwill and other assets," "other long-term liabilities," and "accumulated other comprehensive income" as relating to operating activities.

c. Using information in the statement of cash flows prepared in part b, compute (1) the operating cash flow to current liabilities ratio and (2) the operating cash flow to capital expenditures ratio.

CASES AND PROJECTS

C4-57. **Analyzing a Projected Statement of Cash Flows and Loan Covenants**

LO1, LO2

The President and CFO of Lambert Co. will be meeting with their bankers next week to discuss the short-term financing needs of the company for the next six months. Lambert's controller has provided a projected income statement for the next six-month period, and a current balance sheet along with a projected balance sheet for the end of that six-month period. These statements are presented below ($ millions).

LAMBERT CO.
Projected Six-Month Income Statement

Revenues	$400
Cost of goods sold	200
Gross profit	200
Selling and administrative expense	50
Depreciation expense	120
Income before income taxes	30
Income taxes	12
Net income	$ 18

LAMBERT CO.
Current and Projected Six-Month Balance Sheets

	Current	6-month projected
Cash	$ 50	$???
Accounts receivable	180	220
Inventory	200	180
Total current assets	430	???
Property, plant & equipment, cost	400	500
Less accumulated depreciation	(150)	(220)
Property, plant & equipment, net	250	280
Total assets	$680	???

continued

continued from previous page

<table>
<tr><td colspan="3" align="center">LAMBERT CO.
Current and Projected Six-Month Balance Sheets</td></tr>
<tr><td></td><td align="center">Current</td><td align="center">6-month
projected</td></tr>
<tr><td>Accounts payable</td><td>$150</td><td>$180</td></tr>
<tr><td>Income taxes payable</td><td>20</td><td>10</td></tr>
<tr><td>Short-term borrowing</td><td>50</td><td>???</td></tr>
<tr><td>Long-term debt</td><td>200</td><td>180</td></tr>
<tr><td>Total liabilities</td><td>420</td><td>???</td></tr>
<tr><td>Common stock at par</td><td>100</td><td>125</td></tr>
<tr><td>Retained earnings</td><td>160</td><td>148</td></tr>
<tr><td>Total liabilities and shareholders' equity</td><td>$680</td><td>???</td></tr>
</table>

Additional Information (already reflected in the projected income statement and balance sheet):

- Lambert's current long-term debt includes $100 that is due within the next six months. During the next six months, the company plans to take advantage of lower interest rates by issuing new long-term debt that will provide $80 in cash proceeds.
- During the next six months, the company plans to dispose of equipment with an original cost of $125 and accumulated depreciation of $50. An appraisal by an equipment broker indicates that Lambert should be able to get $75 in cash for the equipment. In addition, Lambert plans to acquire new equipment at a cost of $225.
- A small issue of common stock for cash ($25) and a cash dividend to shareholders ($30) are planned in the next six months.
- Lambert's outstanding long-term debt imposes a restrictive loan covenant on the company that requires Lambert to maintain a debt-to-equity ratio below 1.75.

Required

The CFO says, "I would like a clear estimate of the amount of short-term borrowing that we will need six months from now. I want you to prepare a forecasted statement of cash flows that we can take to the meeting next week."

Prepare the required statement of cash flows, using the indirect method to compute cash flow from operating activities. The forecasted statement should include the needed amount of short-term borrowing and should be consistent with the projected balance sheet and income statement, as well as the loan covenant restriction.

LO1, LO2   C4-58.   Reconstructing Journal Entries and T-Accounts from Completed Financial Statements

Lundholm Company's comparative balance sheets, income statement, and statement of cash flows for July are presented below:

<table>
<tr><td colspan="3" align="center">LUNDHOLM COMPANY
Comparative Balance Sheets</td></tr>
<tr><td></td><td align="center">July 1</td><td align="center">July 31</td></tr>
<tr><td>Cash</td><td>$ 600</td><td>$ 1,184</td></tr>
<tr><td>Accounts receivable</td><td>6,500</td><td>6,800</td></tr>
<tr><td>Inventory</td><td>2,400</td><td>1,800</td></tr>
<tr><td>Prepaid rent</td><td>—</td><td>400</td></tr>
<tr><td>Current assets</td><td>9,500</td><td>10,184</td></tr>
<tr><td>Fixtures and equipment at cost</td><td>1,900</td><td>2,620</td></tr>
<tr><td>Accumulated depreciation</td><td>(800)</td><td>(880)</td></tr>
<tr><td>Plant and equipment, net</td><td>1,100</td><td>1,740</td></tr>
<tr><td>Total assets</td><td>$10,600</td><td>$11,924</td></tr>
</table>

continued

continued from previous page

LUNDHOLM COMPANY
Comparative Balance Sheets

	July 1	July 31
Accounts payable	$ 3,000	$ 3,100
Salaries and wages payable	100	70
Taxes payable	—	374
Bank loan payable	1,600	—
Current liabilities	4,700	3,544
Long-term loan	—	2,000
Common stock	4,600	4,600
Retained earnings	1,300	1,780
Total liabilities and shareholders' equity	$10,600	$11,924

LUNDHOLM COMPANY
Income Statement
Month ended July 31

Revenue		$3,800
Operating expenses:		
Cost of goods sold	$1,800	
Salaries and wages	700	
Rent	200	
Depreciation	150	
Total operating expenses		2,850
Operating income		950
Interest expense		16
Income before taxes		934
Income taxes		374
Net income		$ 560

LUNDHOLM COMPANY
Statement of Cash Flows
Month ended July 31

Operating activities:	
Net income	$ 560
Adjustments:	
Depreciation	150
Increase in accounts receivable	(300)
Decrease in inventory	600
Increase in prepaid rent	(400)
Increase in accounts payable	100
Decrease in salaries and wages payable	(30)
Increase in taxes payable	374
Total adjustments	494
Cash flow from operating activities	1054
Investing activities:	
Proceeds from disposal of fixtures and equipment	10
Purchases of fixtures and equipment	(800)
Cash flow used for investing activities	(790)
Financing activities:	
Loan repayment	(1,600)
Proceeds from new loan	2,000
Dividends paid to shareholders	(80)
Cash flow from financing activities	320
Net increase in cash	584
Cash balance, July 1	600
Cash balance, July 31	$1,184

Required

a. Set up T-accounts and enter beginning and ending balances for each account in Lundholm Company's balance sheet.

b. Provide a set of *summary journal entries* for July that would produce the financial statements presented above. For simplicity, you may assume that all of Lundholm Company's sales are made on account and that all of its purchases are made on account. One such entry is provided as an example.

(1)	Accounts receivable (+A)	3,800	
	Sales revenue (+R, +SE)		3,800

c. Post the journal entries from part *a* to T-accounts and verify ending balances.

LO1, LO3 **C4-59.** **Interpreting the Statement of Cash Flows**

SOUTHWEST AIRLINES
NYSE :: LUV

The statement of cash flows for **Southwest Airlines Co.** is presented below:

SOUTHWEST AIRLINES CO. Consolidated Statement of Cash Flows	
($ millions)	**Year ended December 31, 2008**
Cash flows from operating activities:	
Net income	$ 178
Adjustments to reconcile net income to operating cash flow:	
Depreciation and amortization	599
Deferred income taxes	56
Gains on sale and leaseback of aircraft	(12)
Share based compensation expense	18
Decrease in accounts and other receivables	71
Increase in other current assets	(384)
Decrease in accounts payable and accrued liabilities	(1,853)
Increase in air traffic liability	32
Other, net	(226)
Cash flows used in operating activities	(1,521)
Cash flows from investing activities:	
Purchases of property and equipment	(923)
Purchases of short-term investments	(5,886)
Proceeds from the sale of short-term investments	5,831
Cash used in investing activities	(978)
Cash flows from financing activities:	
Issuance of long-term debt	1,000
Proceeds from credit line borrowing	91
Proceeds from revolving credit agreement	400
Proceeds from sale leaseback transactions	173
Proceeds from stock issued through employee stock plans	117
Payments on long-term debt and capital lease obligations	(55)
Payments of cash dividends	(13)
Repurchase of common stock	(54)
Other, net	(5)
Cash provided by financing activities	1,654
Net decrease in cash and cash equivalents	(845)
Cash and cash equivalents at beginning of period	2,213
Cash and cash equivalents at end of period	$1,368

Required

a. Southwest begins its cash flow statement with net income of $178 million, then adds $599 million for depreciation and amortization. Why is Southwest adding depreciation and amortization to net income in this computation?

b. Southwest reports $18 million related to share based compensation expense as part of cash flow from operating activities. How does this expense increase cash flows?

c. Southwest reported gains from sale leaseback transactions of $12 million as a cash outflow and proceeds from sale leaseback transactions of $173 million as a cash inflow. Explain, if you can, the nature of this transaction and why it is presented in this way.

d. Compute Southwest's free cash flow.

e. Southwest reports a cash outflow from operating activities of $1,521 million, despite reporting net income of $178 million. Does this raise concerns about the health of Southwest Airlines?

SOLUTIONS TO REVIEW PROBLEMS

Mid-Chapter Review 1

Solution

1. Out/I; 2. Out/O; 3. Out/O; 4. In/F; 5. Out/O; 6. In/O; 7. In/I; 8. In/I; 9. Out/F; 10. In/O

Mid-Chapter Review 2

Solution

a.

MUG SHOTS, INC.
Computation of Cash Flow from Operating Activities

	Revenue or Expense	Adjustments	Operating Cash Flow
Revenues/Cash Receipts:			
Sales revenue	$31,000		
− Increase in accounts receivable		$(2,500)	
+ Increase in unearned revenue		500	
Cash received from customers			$29,000
Less Expenses/Cash Payments:			
Cost of goods sold	16,700		
+ Increase in inventory		8,300	
− Increase in accounts payable		(1,000)	
Cash paid for merchandise			24,000
Wages expense	4,700		
− Increase in wages payable		(2,200)	
Cash paid for wages			2,500
Rent expense	1,500		
− Decrease in prepaid rent		(1,500)	
Cash paid for rent			0
Advertising expense	1,800		
Cash paid for advertising			1,800
Interest expense	300		
− Increase in interest payable		(300)	
Cash paid for interest			0
Depreciation expense	700		
− Depreciation expense		(700)	
Cash paid for deprecation			0
Income tax expense	1,855		
− Increase in income tax payable		(1,855)	
Cash paid for income taxes			0
	27,555	745	28,300
Net income	$ 3,445		
Total adjustments		$(2,745)	
Cash flow from operating activities			$ 700

Mid-Chapter Review 3

Solution

MUG SHOTS, INC.		
Cash Flow from Operating Activities—Indirect Method		
Net income.	$3,445	
Adjustments:		
+ Depreciation expense		$ 700
− Increase in accounts receivable		(2,500)
+ Increase in inventory		(8,300)
+ Decrease in prepaid rent		1,500
+ Increase in unearned revenue		500
+ Increase in accounts payable		1,000
+ Increase in wages payable		2,200
+ Increase in interest payable		300
+ Increase in income tax payable		1,855
Total adjustments		(2,745)
Cash flow from operating activities		$700

Mid-Chapter Review 4

Solution

MUG SHOTS, INC.		
Statement of Cash Flows		
For Month Ended December 31, 2010		
Cash flow from operating activities		
Net income.		$ 3,445
Depreciation		700
Accounts receivable increase		(2,500)
Inventory increase.		(8,300)
Prepaid rent decrease		1,500
Accounts payable increase		1,000
Unearned revenue increase		500
Income tax payable increase		1,855
Wages payable increase		2,200
Interest payable increase		300
Net cash provided by operating activities		$700
Cash flow from investing activities		
Purchase of equipment	(12,000)	
Net cash used by investing activities.		(12,000)
Cash flow from financing activities		
Bank loan	18,000	
Payment of dividend.	(1,000)	
Net cash provided by financing activities		17,000
		5,700
Cash, beginning of period.		5,000
Cash, end of period.		$10,700

Chapter-End Review

Solution

1. We assume that One World Café's notes payable are classified as current liabilities. If so, current liabilities are $41,000 ($27,000+$6,000+$3,000+$5,000) in 2010 and $21,000 ($14,000+$2,500+$4,500) in 2009.

   $44,000 / [($41,000 + $21,000)/2] = 1.42

   One World Café is generating cash flows from operations in excess of its current liabilities. Assuming that this continues, it should have no difficulty meeting its obligations.

2. $44,000 / $45,000 = 0.98

   One World Café spent a little more on plant capacity than it generated through operations. However, for a small business, capital expenditures are often irregular. Thus, this ratio is not alarmingly low.

3. $44,000 − ($45,000 − $4,000) = $3,000.

Appendix-End Review

Solution

a.

Cash Flow Spreadsheet for Rocky Road Bicycles, Inc.							
A	B	C	D	E	F	G	H
				Effect of change on cash flow			No effect
	2010	2009	Change	Operating	Investing	Financing	on cash
Assets:							
Cash	106,000	96,000	10,000				
Accounts receivable	156,000	224,000	(68,000)	68,000			
Inventory	752,000	528,000	224,000	(224,000)			
Prepaid rent	68,000	72,000	(4,000)	4,000			
Plant assets, net	1,130,000	872,000	258,000				
Depreciation				122,000			
Plant assets purchased					(420,000)		
Plant assets sold:				(16,000)	56,000		
Liabilities:							
Accounts payable	216,000	112,000	104,000	104,000			
Wages payable	18,000	20,000	(2,000)	(2,000)			
Income tax payable	44,000	36,000	8,000	8,000			
Equity:							
Common stock	1,142,000	1,000,000	142,000			142,000	
Retained earnings	792,000	624,000	168,000				
Net income				326,000			
Dividends						(158,000)	
Totals				390,000	(364,000)	(16,000)	0

$$\$390{,}000 - \$364{,}000 - \$16{,}000 = \$10{,}000.$$

b.

ROCKY ROAD BICYCLES, INC.
Statement of Cash Flows
For Year Ended December 31, 2010

Cash provided by operating activities		
Net income		$326,000
Add (deduct) items to convert net income to cash basis		
Depreciation	122,000	
Gain on sale of plant assets	(16,000)	
Accounts receivable	68,000	
Inventory	(224,000)	
Prepaid rent	4,000	
Accounts payable	104,000	
Wages payable	(2,000)	
Income tax payable	8,000	
Net cash provided by operating activities		$390,000
Cash flows from Investing activities		
Plant assets	(420,000)	
Proceeds from sale of plant assets	56,000	
Net cash used for investing activities		(364,000)
Cash flows from financing activities		
Issuance of common stock	142,000	
Payment of dividends	(158,000)	
Net cash used for financing activities		(16,000)
Net cash increase		10,000
Cash at beginning of year		96,000
Cash at end of year		$106,000

1. Prepare and analyze common-size financial statements. (p. 206)

2. Compute and interpret measures of return on investment, including return on equity (ROE), return on assets (ROA), and return on financial leverage (ROFL). (p. 211)

3. Disaggregate ROA into profitability (profit margin) and efficiency (asset turnover) components. (p. 213)

4. Compute and interpret measures of liquidity and solvency. (p. 218)

5. Appendix 5A: Measure and analyze the effect of operating activities on ROE. (p. 225)

6. Appendix 5B: Prepare *pro forma* financial statements. (p. 227)

© Getty Images

Analyzing and Interpreting Financial Statements

5

In 2008, **PepsiCo** CEO Indra K. Nooyi wrestled with a dilemma. As she reviewed the performance of the company's three operating divisions, it became clear that the company's flagship brand, Pepsi, was losing market share and profitability. The food products division, including Frito-Lay and Quaker Oats, was performing well. So was PepsiCo's international operation, which was expanding in markets such as China and Russia. However, demand for Pepsi had declined 29% since 2000 as consumer preferences shifted away from soft drinks toward juices and bottled water. The North American beverage division was relying on sales of noncarbonated products to maintain revenue and earnings growth and, as the recession deepened, she expected that sales of those products would decline along with soft drink revenues.

PEPSICO
www.pepsico.com

PepsiCo was created by the merger of Pepsi-Cola and the Frito-Lay Company. Since then, the company has grown through selective acquisitions and creative marketing of its products. By 2008, its sales topped $43.25 billion and the company ranked 52nd in the Fortune 500 ranking of the largest companies based on revenues. Between 2003 and 2008, PepsiCo's stock price outperformed that of its chief competitor, Coca-Cola, as well as the S&P 500.

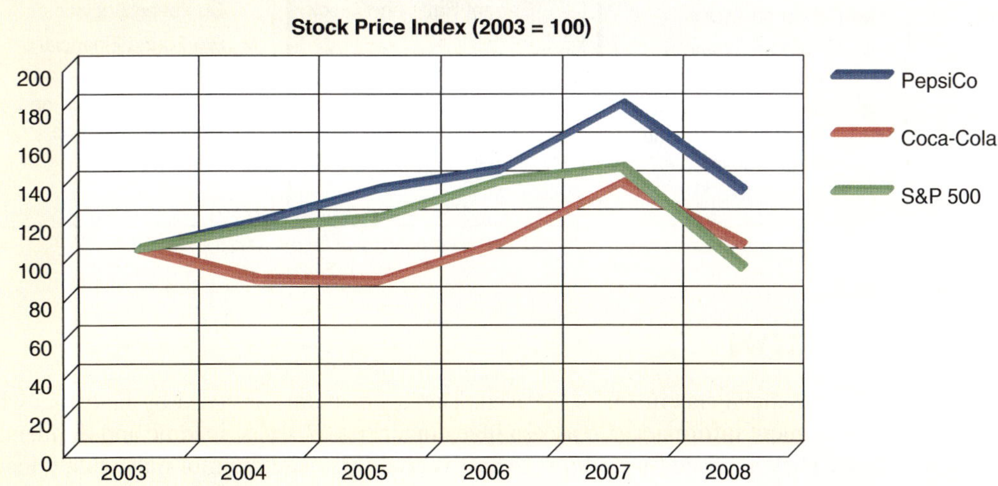

(continued on next page)

(continued from previous page)

As is the case in most companies, PepsiCo's management employs a number of financial measures to assess the performance and financial condition of its operating units. These measures include ratios related to profitability and asset utilization as well as return on investment. Outside stakeholders—investors, creditors and financial analysts—use similar measures to evaluate company performance, assess credit risk, and estimate share value.

This chapter focuses on the analysis of information reported in the financial statements. We discuss a variety of measures that provide insights into a company's performance to answer questions such as: Is it managed efficiently and profitably? Does it use assets efficiently? Is the performance achieved with an optimal amount of debt? We pay especially close attention to measures of return. Although profitability is important, it is only part of the story. More meaningful insights are gained by comparing the level of profitability with the amount of investment. All return metrics follow the same basic formula—they divide some measure of profit by a measure of investment. In Chapter 1, we introduced one such return metric, namely return on equity (ROE). In this chapter, we review ROE and add another return metric—return on assets (ROA)—which measures the return produced by the company's investment in its assets.

ROE and ROA differ by the use of debt financing, or financial leverage. Companies can increase ROE by borrowing money and using these funds to finance investment in operating assets. However, debt financing can increase company risk and, if not used judiciously, is likely to have a detrimental effect on ROE and even lead to financial distress. In the latter part of this chapter, we examine metrics that measure liquidity and solvency that allow us to assess that risk.

PepsiCo tackled its sluggish beverage sales by launching a major "rebranding" program for all of its beverage product lines, including Pepsi, Gatorade, Tropicana, SoBe Lifewater, Sierra Mist, and others. Rebranding requires creating new product logos, new packaging, new slogans and, most importantly, new advertising campaigns. The new packaging reached grocery store shelves in mid-January of 2009 and new ads were launched to coincide with the 2009 Super Bowl. The result? It is too soon to tell. Rebranding strategies can breathe new life into sluggish product sales, but such efforts can also backfire. Ultimately, we will be able to assess the success of this initiative by looking at specific measures of PepsiCo's performance. In doing so, we seek the answer to the root question: Can the company achieve a high return on investment and, if so, is that return sustainable?

Sources: PepsiCo 10-K, 2004, 2005, 2006, 2007, 2008; *BusinessWeek*, March 2, 2009, April 27, 2009; *Barrons*, July 8, 2009; *The Wall Street Journal*, March 31, 2009.

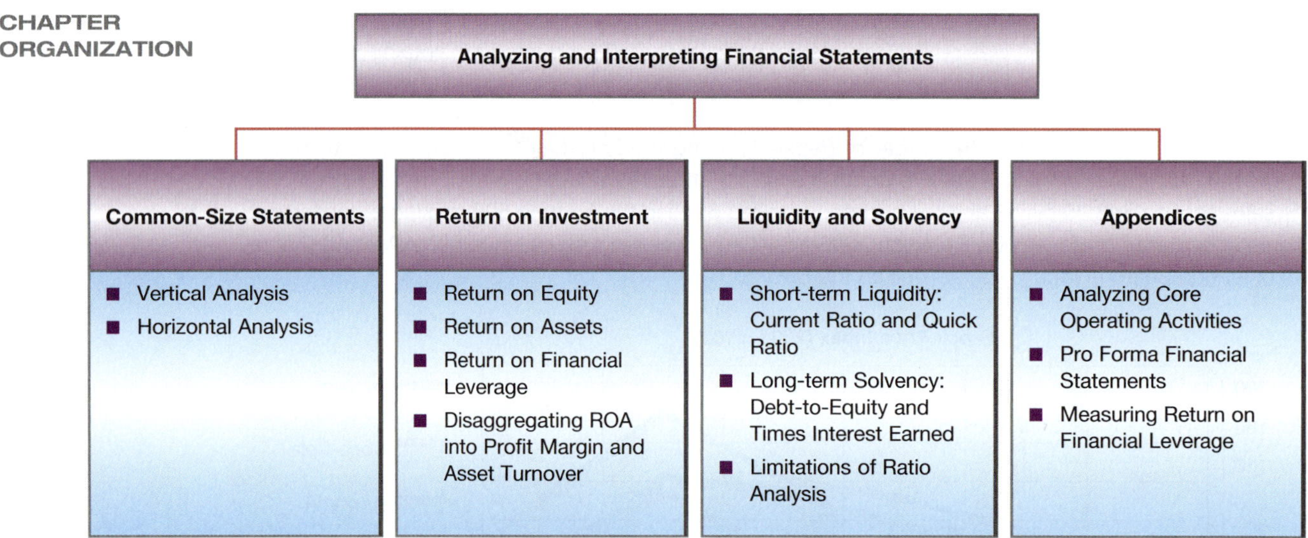

INTRODUCTION

LO1 Prepare and analyze common-size financial statements.

Companies prepare financial statements to be used. These statements are used by investors who rely on financial statement information to assess investment risk, forecast income and dividends, and estimate value. They are used by creditors to assess credit risk and monitor outstanding loans for compliance with debt covenants. And, as the PepsiCo example illustrates, they are used by management to evaluate the performance of operating units. **Financial statement analysis** identifies relationships between numbers within the financial statements and trends in these relationships from one period to the next. The goal is to help users such as investors, creditors, and managers interpret the information presented in the financial statements.

Financial statement analysis is all about making comparisons. Accounting information is difficult to interpret when the numbers are viewed in isolation. For example, a company that reports net income of $7 million may have had a good year or a bad year. However, if we know that total sales were $100 million, assets total $90 million, and that the previous year's net income was $6 million, we have a better idea about how well the company performed. If we go a step further and compare these numbers to those of a competing company or to an industry average, we begin to make an assessment about the relative quality of management, the prospects for future growth, overall company risk, and the potential to earn sustainable returns.

Assessing the Business Environment

Financial statement analysis cannot be undertaken in a vacuum. A meaningful interpretation of financial information requires an understanding of the business, its operations, and the environment in which it operates. That is, before we begin crunching the numbers, we must consider the broader business context in which the company operates. This requires that the analyst ask questions about the company and its business environment, including:

- *Life cycle*—At what stage in its life is this company? Is it a start-up, experiencing the growing pains that often result from rapid growth? Is it a mature company, reaping the benefits of its competitive advantages? Is it in decline?

- *Outputs*—What products does it sell? Are its products new, established, or dated? Do its products have substitutes? Are its products protected by patents? How complicated are its products to produce?

- *Customers*—Who are its customers? How often do customers purchase the company's products? What demographic trends are likely to have an effect on future sales?

- *Competition*—Who are the company's competitors? How is it positioned in the market relative to its competition? Is it easy for new competitors to enter the market for its products? Are its products differentiated from competitors' products? Does it have any cost advantages over its competitors?

- *Inputs*—Who are the company's suppliers? Are there multiple supply sources? Does the company depend on one (or a few) key supply sources creating the potential for high input costs?

- *Labor*—Who are the company's managers? How effective are they? Is the company unionized? Does it depend on a skilled or educated workforce?

- *Technology*—What technology does the company employ to produce its products? Does the company outsource production? What transport systems does the company rely on to deliver its products?

- *Capital*—To what extent does the company rely on public markets to raise needed capital? Has it recently gone public? Does it have expansion plans that require large sums of cash to carry out? Is it planning to acquire another company? Is it in danger of defaulting on its debt?

- *Political*—How does the company interact with the communities, states, and countries in which it operates? What government regulations affect the company's operations? Are any proposed regulations likely to have a significant impact on the company?

These are just a few of the questions that we should ask before we begin analyzing a company's financial statements. Ultimately, the answers will help us place our numerical analysis in the proper context, so that we can effectively interpret the accounting numbers.

In this chapter, we introduce the tools that are used to analyze and interpret financial statements. These tools include common-size financial statements that are used in vertical and horizontal analysis and ratios that measure return on investment and help to assess liquidity and solvency.

VERTICAL AND HORIZONTAL ANALYSIS

Companies come in all sizes, a fact that presents difficulties when making comparisons between firms and over time. **Vertical analysis** is a method that attempts to overcome this obstacle by restating financial statement information in ratio (or percentage) form. Specifically, it is common to express components of the income statement as a percent of net sales, and balance sheet items as a percent of total assets. This restatement is often referred to as **common-size financial statements** and it facilitates comparisons across companies of different sizes as well as comparisons of accounts within a set of financial statements.

Exhibit 5.1 presents PepsiCo's comparative balance sheets for 2008 and 2007. Next to the comparative balance sheets are common-size balance sheets for the same two years. Vertical analysis helps us interpret the composition of the balance sheet. For example, as of the end of 2008, 30% of PepsiCo's assets were current assets and 32.4% were property, plant and equipment. In addition, 66.4% of PepsiCo's total assets were financed with liabilities—up from 50.2% in 2007. This change was largely due to an increase in long-term debt obligations from 12.1% of total assets in 2007 to 21.8% in 2008. New production facilities overseas were financed with long-term debt in 2008. It is not uncommon for companies to use lower-cost debt financing to finance expansion, especially if management believes that low stock prices prevent them from issuing common stock. However, increasing debt levels are a concern if profits and cash flows are not growing fast enough to cover the rising debt payments.

EXHIBIT 5.1	PepsiCo Comparative Balance Sheets			
PEPSICO, INC. Balance Sheets and Common-Size Balance Sheets December 27, 2008 and December 29, 2007				
	as reported ($ millions)		**as a percentage of Total Assets**	
	2008	**2007**	**2008**	**2007**
ASSETS				
Cash and cash equivalents.	$ 2,064	$ 910	5.7%	2.6%
Short-term investments	213	1,571	0.6	4.5
Accounts and notes receivable, net.	4,683	4,389	13.0	12.7
Inventories.	2,522	2,290	7.0	6.6
Prepaid expenses and other current assets	1,324	991	3.7	2.9
Total current assets.	10,806	10,151	30.0	29.3
Property, plant and equipment, net	11,663	11,228	32.4	32.4
Amortizable intangible assets, net	732	796	2.0	2.3
Goodwill and other intangible assets.	6,252	6,417	17.4	18.5
Investments in noncontrolled affiliates	3,883	4,354	10.8	12.6
Other assets	2,658	1,682	7.4	4.9
Total assets.	$35,994	$34,628	100.0%	100.0%
LIABILITIES AND SHAREHOLDERS' EQUITY				
Short-term obligations	$ 369	$ —	1.0%	0.0%
Accounts payable and other current liabilities	8,273	7,602	23.0	22.0
Income taxes payable.	145	151	0.4	0.4
Total current liabilities.	8,787	7,753	24.4	22.4
Long-term debt obligations	7,858	4,203	21.8	12.1
Other liabilities.	7,017	4,792	19.5	13.8
Deferred income taxes	226	646	0.6	1.9
Total liabilities	23,888	17,394	66.4	50.2
Shareholders' equity.	12,106	17,234	33.6	49.8
Total liabilities and shareholders' equity	$35,994	$34,628	100.0%	100.0%

In Exhibit 5.2, we present PepsiCo's comparative income statements for 2008 and 2007, along with common-size income statements for the same years. Vertical analysis reveals that cost of sales is 47.1% of net revenue, up from 45.7% in 2007, while operating profit is 16% of net revenue, down from 18.2% the year before. The change in cost of sales represents more than half of the drop in operating profit from 2007 to 2008. The increase in cost of sales could be due to a number of causes, including unexpected increases in the cost of raw materials, supply chain problems, or production inefficiencies. While further analysis would be necessary to determine the exact cause of this change, common-size financial statements reveal the primary source of the drop in operating profits to be the rising cost of sales as a percentage of net revenue.

EXHIBIT 5.2	PepsiCo Comparative Income Statements

PEPSICO, INC.
Income Statements and Common-Size Income Statements
Fiscal years ended December 27, 2008 and December 29, 2007

	as reported ($ millions)		as a percentage of Net Revenue	
	2008	2007	2008	2007
Net revenue	$43,251	$39,474	100.0%	100.0%
Cost of sales	20,351	18,038	47.1	45.7
Selling, general and administrative expenses	15,901	14,208	36.8	36.0
Amortization of intangible assets	64	58	0.1	0.1
Operating profit	6,935	7,170	16.0	18.2
Bottling equity income	374	560	0.9	1.4
Interest expense	(329)	(224)	0.8	0.6
Interest income	41	125	0.1	0.3
Income before income taxes	7,021	7,631	16.2	19.3
Provision for income taxes	1,879	1,973	4.3	5.0
Net income.	$ 5,142	$ 5,658	11.9%	14.3%

Horizontal analysis examines changes in financial data across time. Comparing data across two or more consecutive periods is helpful in analyzing company performance and in predicting future performance. Exhibit 5.3 presents a horizontal analysis of a few selected items from Pep-siCo's income statement—revenue, operating income, and net income. The dollar amounts reported in each year from 2004 through 2008 are shown for each item along with a percentage change for each item. The amount of the change for a given year is computed by subtracting the amount for the prior year from the amount for the current year. The change is then divided by the reported amount for the prior year to get the percentage change. For example, PepsiCo's percentage change in net revenue was 11.3% in 2005, computed as follows:

$$11.3\% = \frac{\$32{,}562 \text{ million} - \$29{,}261 \text{ million}}{\$29{,}261 \text{ million}}$$

Exhibit 5.3 highlights some important changes in PepsiCo's income statement. During the 5-year period, revenues have shown steady growth, increasing by an average of just over 10% per year. On the other hand, net income has fluctuated more erratically during the half-decade, with large increases in some years and decreases in others. In 2008, revenues increased by 9.6%, yet net income declined by 9.1%. Only part of the decrease in net income was due to operations, as operating income decreased by only 3.3%.

EXHIBIT 5.3	Horizontal Analysis of Selected Income Statement Items

PEPSICO, INC.
Revenue, Operating Income and Net Income
($ millions and percent changes)

	2004	2005	2006	2007	2008
Revenue.	$29,261	$32,562	$35,137	$39,474	$43,251
		11.3%	7.9%	12.3%	9.6%
Operating income	5,259	5,922	6,502	7,170	6,935
		12.6%	9.8%	10.3%	−3.3%
Net income.	$ 4,212	$ 4,078	$ 5,642	$ 5,658	$ 5,142
		−3.2%	38.4%	0.3%	−9.1%

Horizontal analysis is useful in identifying unusual changes that might not be obvious when looking at the reported numbers alone. At the same time, it is important to look at both the percentage change and the reported dollar amount. If a reported amount is close to $0 in one year, the percentage change will likely be very large the following year, even if the amount reported in that year is small. Similarly, if reported earnings is negative one year and positive the next, the percentage change will be negative even though the earnings increased. Horizontal analysis that is based on a denominator that is negative or zero is not meaningful.

MID-CHAPTER REVIEW 1

Following are the 2008 and 2007 income statements and balance sheets for **The Coca-Cola Company**.

Required

Prepare common-size income statements and balance sheets for Coca-Cola.

THE COCA-COLA COMPANY AND SUBSIDIARIES
Consolidated Statements of Income
($ millions)

Year ended December 31	2008	2007
Net operating revenues.	$31,944	$28,857
Cost of goods sold	11,374	10,406
Gross profit	20,570	18,451
Selling, general and administrative expenses	11,774	10,945
Other operating charges.	350	254
Operating income	8,446	7,252
Interest income	333	236
Interest expense	(438)	(456)
Other income (loss)—net	(902)	841
Income before income taxes	7,439	7,873
Income taxes.	1,632	1,892
Net income.	$ 5,807	$ 5,981

THE COCA-COLA COMPANY AND SUBSIDIARIES
Consolidated Balance Sheets
($ millions)

December 31,	2008	2007
ASSETS		
Cash and cash equivalents.	$ 4,701	$ 4,093
Marketable securities	278	215
Trade accounts receivable	3,090	3,317
Inventories.	2,187	2,220
Prepaid expenses and other current assets	1,920	2,260
Total current assets.	12,176	12,105
Investments.	5,779	7,777
Property, plant and equipment, net	8,326	8,493
Goodwill and other intangible assets.	12,505	12,219
Other assets	1,733	2,675
Total assets .	$40,519	$43,269
LIABILITIES AND STOCKHOLDERS' EQUITY		
Accounts payable and accrued expenses.	$ 6,205	$ 6,915
Loans and notes payable	6,066	5,919
Current maturities of long-term debt	465	133
Accrued income taxes	252	258
Total current liabilities.	12,988	13,225
Long-term debt.	2,781	3,277
Other liabilities.	3,401	3,133
Deferred income taxes	877	1,890
Total liabilities .	20,047	21,525
Stockholders' equity.	20,472	21,744
Total liabilities and stockholders' equity	$40,519	$43,269

The solution to this review problem can be found on page 251.

RETURN ON INVESTMENT

Common-size financial statements and percentage changes are useful, but there is a limit to what we can learn from this type of analysis. While vertical and horizontal analysis focuses on relationships within a particular financial statement, either the income statement or the balance sheet, many of the questions that we might ask about a company can be answered only by comparing amounts between statements. For example, return on investment measures are ratios that divide some measure of performance—typically reported in the income statement—by the average amount of investment as reported in the balance sheet.

In this section, we discuss three important return metrics—return on equity (ROE), return on assets (ROA), and return on financial leverage (ROFL). In addition we will examine return on investment in detail by disaggregating ROA into performance drivers that capture profitability and efficiency.

LO2 Compute and interpret measures of return on investment, including return on equity (ROE), return on assets (ROA), and return on financial leverage (ROFL).

Return on Equity (ROE)

Return on equity (ROE) is the primary summary measure of company performance and is defined as:

$$ROE = \frac{\text{Net income}}{\text{Average stockholders' equity}}$$

ROE relates net income to the average investment by shareholders as measured by total stockholders' equity from the balance sheet. The net income number in the numerator measures the performance of the firm for a specific period (typically a fiscal year). Therefore, in order to accurately capture the return for that period, we use the average level of stockholders' equity for the same period as the denominator. The average is computed by adding the beginning and ending stockholders' equity balances and then dividing by two.

FYI Whenever we compare an income statement amount with a balance sheet amount, the balance sheet amount should be the *average* balance for the period (beginning balance plus ending balance divided by 2) rather than the year-end balance.

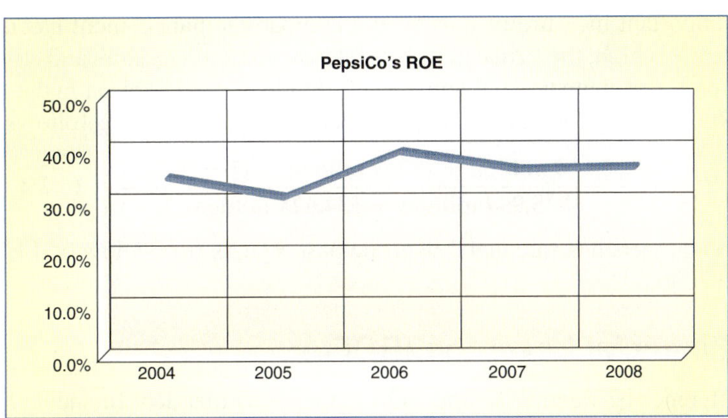

PepsiCo's ROE was 35.1% in 2008. This return is computed as $5,142 million/[($12,106 million + $17,234 million)/2]. PepsiCo's ROE has been consistently high over the past 5 years, ranging from a low of 29.4% in 2005 to a high of 38.1% in 2006.

ROE is widely used by analysts, investors, and managers as a key overall measure of company performance. Billionaire investor Warren Buffett highlights ROE as part of his acquisition criteria: "businesses earning good returns on equity while employing little or no debt." Companies can use debt to increase their return on equity, but too much debt increases risk as the failure to make required debt payments is likely to yield many legal consequences, including bankruptcy. This is one reason why many analysts focus on returns generated by assets used in operations, rather than on returns produced by increasing the amount of debt financing. Next, we discuss each of these sources of return in more detail.

Return on Assets (ROA)

ROE measures the return on the investment made by the firm's stockholders. In contrast, **return on assets (ROA)** measures the return earned on each dollar that the firm invests in assets. By focusing on the asset side of the balance sheet, ROA captures the returns generated by the firm's operating and investing activities, without regard for how those activities are financed. ROA is defined as:

$$\text{Return on assets (ROA)} = \frac{\text{Earnings before interest (EBI)}}{\text{Average total assets}}$$

Average total assets is computed in much the same way that we calculated average stockholders' equity for ROE. We add the beginning and ending balances in total assets and then divide by two. The numerator in this ratio, **earnings before interest (EBI)**, is defined to be:

$$\text{Earnings before interest (EBI)} = \text{Net income} + [\text{Interest expense} \times (1 - \text{Statutory tax rate})]$$

EBI measures the income generated by the firm before taking into account any of its financing costs. Interest costs should be excluded from the ROA calculation so that return is measured without the effect of debt financing. Because interest expense is subtracted when net income is calculated, it must be added back to net income when we compute EBI. However, interest expense is tax deductible and, as such, it reduces the firm's tax obligation. That is, interest expense produces a tax *savings* for the firm. This tax savings is equal to the interest expense times the statutory tax rate. In order to eliminate the full effect of interest cost on EBI, we must add back the interest expense *net* of the resulting tax savings. To accomplish this, we multiply the interest expense by $(1 -$ the statutory tax rate). This amount is then added to net income to get EBI. Thus, we can compute ROA as follows:

$$\text{Return on assets (ROA)} = \frac{\text{Net income} + [\text{Interest expense} \times (1 - \text{Statutory tax rate})]}{(\text{Beginning total assets} + \text{Ending total assets})/2}$$

ROA is an important measure of how well a company's management has utilized assets to earn a profit. If ROA is high, the firm can pay its interest costs to creditors and still have sufficient resources left over to distribute to stockholders as a dividend or to reinvest in the firm.

PepsiCo's ROA was 15.2% in 2008. PepsiCo's return is computed as follows: [1]

$$\text{ROA} = \frac{\$5{,}142 \text{ million} + [\$329 \text{ million} \times (1 - 35\%)]}{(\$35{,}994 \text{ million} + \$34{,}628 \text{ million})/2} = 15.2\%$$

PepsiCo's return on assets has fluctuated over the past 5 years from a low of 14.2% in 2005 to a high of 18.8% in 2006.

Return on Financial Leverage (ROFL)

The principal difference between ROE and ROA is the effect that debt financing has on the return measure. ROA is calculated so that it is independent of financing costs, whereas ROE is computed net of the cost of debt financing. **Financial leverage** refers to the effect that debt financing has on ROE. A firm's management can increase the return to shareholders (ROE) by effectively using financial leverage. On the other hand, too much financial leverage can be risky. To help gauge the effect that financial leverage has on a firm, the **return on financial leverage (ROFL)** is defined as:

$$\text{ROFL} = \text{ROE} - \text{ROA}$$

This return metric captures the amount of ROE that can be attributed to financial leverage. In the case of PepsiCo, the ROFL is 19.9% (35.1% − 15.2%). Over the past 5 years, financial lever-

---

[1] The statutory federal tax rate for corporations is 35% (per U.S. tax code). In addition, many states tax corporate income, and those state taxes are deductible for federal tax purposes. Consequently, the net state tax rate is the statutory state tax rate less the federal tax benefit. Most companies provide both the federal tax rate and the state tax rate (net of the federal tax deduction) as percentages in the income tax footnote. If this information is available, the statutory tax rate is the sum of the two percentages. However, state tax rates (net of the federal tax deduction) vary from one company to the next and are typically small. Therefore, for purposes of illustration, we ignore state income taxes and use the federal statutory tax rate of 35% in these ratio calculations.

age has had a significant impact on PepsiCo's performance. The impact of financial leverage on PepsiCo's ROE is illustrated in Exhibit 5.4. The height of each bar in the graph reflects PepsiCo's ROE for that year. Each bar is split into two components—ROA for the same year (the lower portion of each bar) and ROFL (the upper portion of each bar).

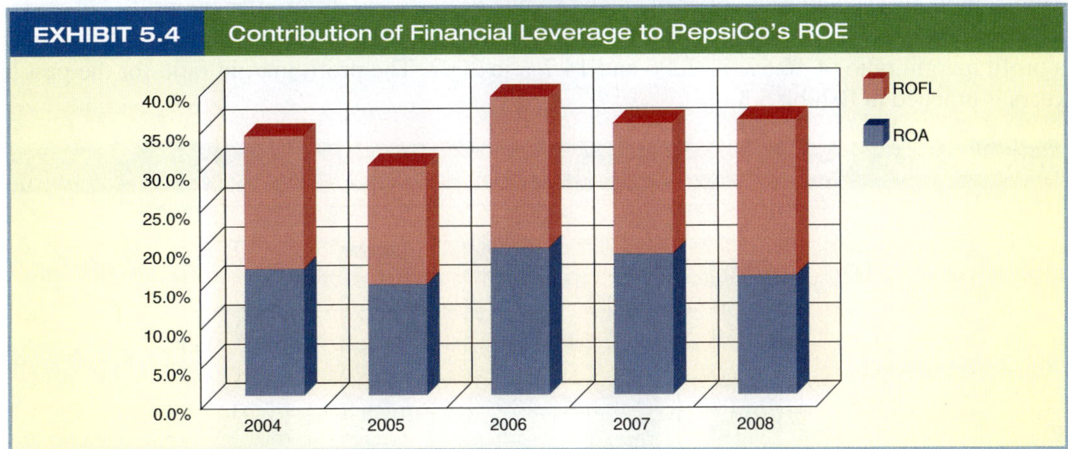

EXHIBIT 5.4 Contribution of Financial Leverage to PepsiCo's ROE

Later in this chapter, we examine the effects of financial leverage more closely and discuss several ratios that measure liquidity and solvency. These ratios help us to evaluate the risk associated with using financial leverage. In Appendix 5C, we present an alternative derivation of ROFL.

MID-CHAPTER REVIEW 2

Required

Refer to the financial statements for the **Coca-Cola Company** presented in Mid-Chapter Review 1 earlier in this chapter. Calculate Coca-Cola's ROE, ROA and ROFL for 2008.

The solution to this review problem can be found on page 252.

Disaggregating ROA

We can gain further insights into return on investment by disaggregating ROA into performance drivers that capture profitability and efficiency. ROA can be restated as the product of two ratios—profit margin and asset turnover—by simultaneously multiplying and dividing ROA by sales revenue:

LO3 Disaggregate ROA into profitability (profit margin) and efficiency (asset turnover) components.

$$\text{ROA} = \frac{\text{Earnings before interest}}{\text{Average total assets}} = \frac{\text{Earnings before interest}}{\text{Sales revenue}} \times \frac{\text{Sales revenue}}{\text{Average total assets}}$$

| Profit Margin | Asset Turnover |

The first ratio on the right-hand side of the above relationship is the **profit margin (PM)**. This ratio measures the profit, before interest expense, that is generated from each dollar of sales revenue. All other things being equal, a higher profit margin is preferable. Profit margin is affected by the level of gross profit that the company earns on its sales (sales revenue minus cost of goods sold), which depends on product prices and the cost of manufacturing or purchasing its product. It is also affected by operating expenses that are required to support sales of products or services. These include wages and salaries, marketing, research and development, as well as depreciation and other **capacity costs**. Finally, profit margin is affected by the level of competition, which affects product pricing, and by the company's operating strategy, which affects operating costs, especially discretionary costs such as advertising and research and development.

PepsiCo's profit margin ratio was 12.4% in 2008, computed as follows ($ millions):

$$\text{Profit margin (PM)} = \frac{\text{Earnings before interest (EBI)}}{\text{Sales revenue}} = \frac{\$5,142 + \$329 \times (1 - 35\%)}{\$43,251} = 12.4\%$$

This ratio indicates that each dollar of sales revenue produces 12.4¢ of after-tax profit before financing costs. PepsiCo's profit margin for 2008 is down somewhat from recent years. It reported a profit margin ratio of 16.5% in 2006 and 14.7% in 2007. The profit margin ratio for the past 5 years is graphed in Exhibit 5.5.

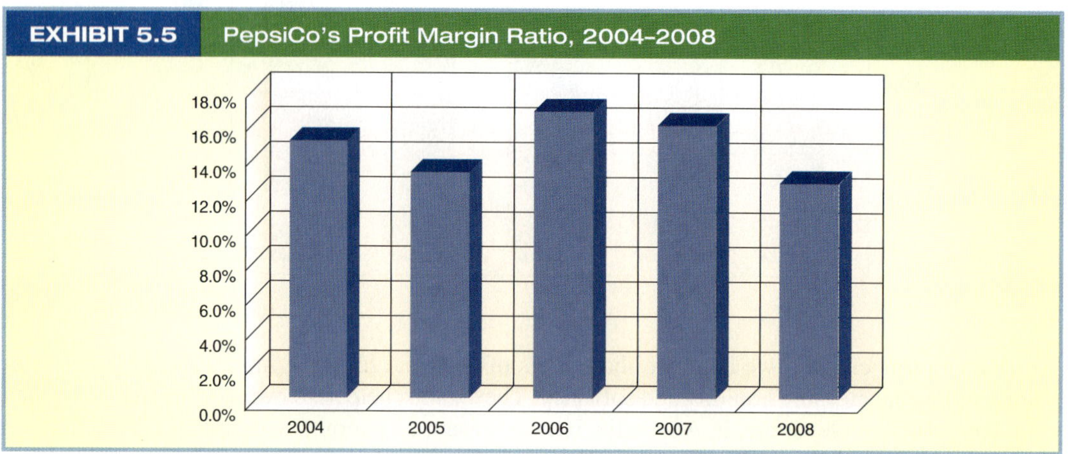

The **asset turnover (AT)** ratio reveals insights into a company's productivity and efficiency. This metric measures the level of sales generated by each dollar that a company invests in assets. A high asset turnover ratio suggests that assets are being used efficiently so, all other things being equal, a high asset turnover ratio is preferable. The ratio is affected by inventory management practices, credit policies, and most of all, the technology employed to produce a company's products or deliver its services.

The asset turnover ratio can be improved by increasing the level of sales for a given level of assets, or by efficiently managing assets. For many companies, efficiently managing working capital—primarily inventories and receivables—is the easiest way to limit investment in assets and increase turnover. On the other hand, it is usually more difficult to increase asset turnover by managing investment in long-term assets. Capital intensive companies, such as those in the communications or energy production industries, tend to have lower asset turnover ratios (often less than 1.0) because the production technology employed by these firms requires a large investment in property, plant and equipment. Retail companies, on the other hand, tend to have a relatively small investment in plant assets. As a result, they tend to have higher asset turnover ratios (sometimes over 3.0). These ratios are also affected by leasing and other methods of using assets that do not appear on the balance sheet. Leasing and other off-balance-sheet financing methods are discussed in Chapter 10.

PepsiCo's asset turnover ratio is computed as follows ($ millions):

$$\text{Asset turnover (AT)} = \frac{\text{Sales revenue}}{\text{Average total assets}} = \frac{\$43,251}{(\$35,994 + \$34,628)/2} = 1.225$$

The ratio indicates that each dollar of assets generates $1.225 in sales revenue each year. This is the highest asset turnover ratio that PepsiCo has reported in the past 5 years as illustrated by the graphic in Exhibit 5.6.

YOU MAKE THE CALL

You are the Entrepreneur   You are analyzing the performance of your start-up company. Your analysis of ROA reveals the following (industry benchmarks in parentheses): ROA is 16% (10%), PM is 18% (17%), and AT is 0.89 (0.59). What interpretations do you draw that are useful for managing your company?

[Answer, page 236]

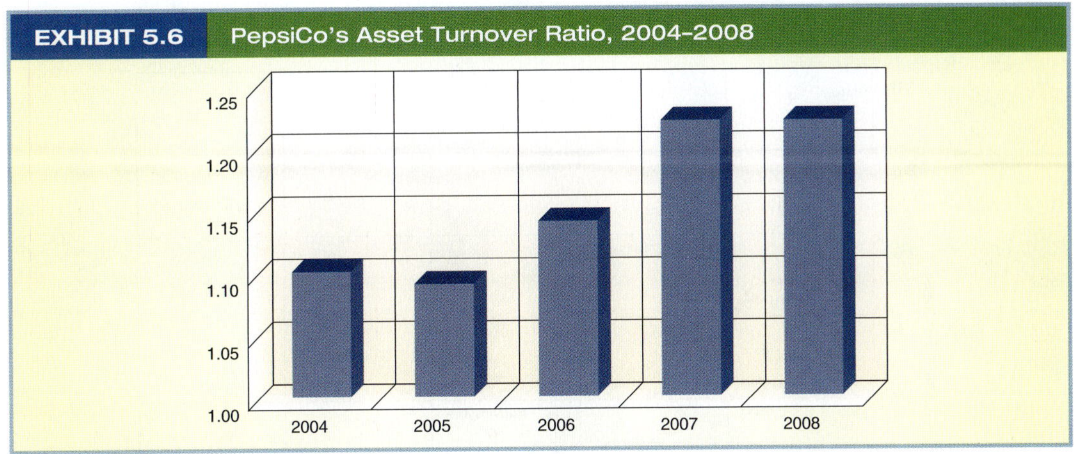

EXHIBIT 5.6   PepsiCo's Asset Turnover Ratio, 2004–2008

Trade-Off Between Profit Margin and Asset Turnover

ROA is the product of profit margin and asset turnover. By decomposing ROA in this way, we can identify the source of PepsiCo's decline in ROA between 2007 and 2008:

	ROA	=	Profit Margin	×	Asset Turnover
2007:	18.0%	=	14.7%	×	1.224
2008:	15.2%	=	12.4%	×	1.225

Between 2007 and 2008, PepsiCo's profit margin declined from 14.7% to 12.4% while, at the same time, asset turnover remained virtually unchanged. Thus the decline in ROA can be attributed to a declining profit margin. As we saw earlier in the chapter when we examined PepsiCo's common-size income statement, a major cause of this decline was the increase in cost of sales as a percentage of sales revenue. Because asset turnover is already high relative to years prior to 2007 (see Exhibit 5.6), it is likely that management's best opportunity to increase ROA in the future would be to focus its efforts on increasing profitability.

Basic economics tells us that any successful business must earn an acceptable return on investment if it wants to attract capital from investors and survive. Yet, there are an infinite number of combinations of asset turnover and profit margin that will yield a given ROA. The trade-off between profit margin and asset turnover is heavily influenced by a company's business model. A company can attempt to increase its ROA by targeting higher profit margins, or by increasing its asset turnover. To an extent, this trade-off is the result of strategic decisions made by management. However, to a greater extent, the relative mix of margin and turnover is dictated by the industry in which the company operates. As mentioned earlier, one determinant of a company's profit margin is its competitive environment, while asset turnover is heavily influenced by the production technology employed. For this reason, companies in the same industry tend to exhibit similar combinations of margin and turnover while comparisons between industries can exhibit much greater variation. That is, within a given industry, differences in the mix of profit margin and asset turnover often reflect the specific strategy employed by each individual firm, while variations between industries are caused by differences in the competitive environment and production technology of each industry.

This trade-off is illustrated in Exhibit 5.7. The solid curved line represents the average ROA for all companies over the period from 2006 through 2008. Each point along that curve represents a combination of asset turnover and profit margin that yields the average ROA. Industries that are plotted near the upper left side of the graph are those that achieve their ROA targets by maintaining a high asset turnover. These industries are often characterized by intense competition and low profit margins. On the other hand, industries in the lower right-hand portion of the graph have lower asset turnover ratios because they typically employ capital-intensive production technologies. At the same time, the competitive environment within these industries allows companies to achieve higher profit margins to offset the lower turnover ratios.

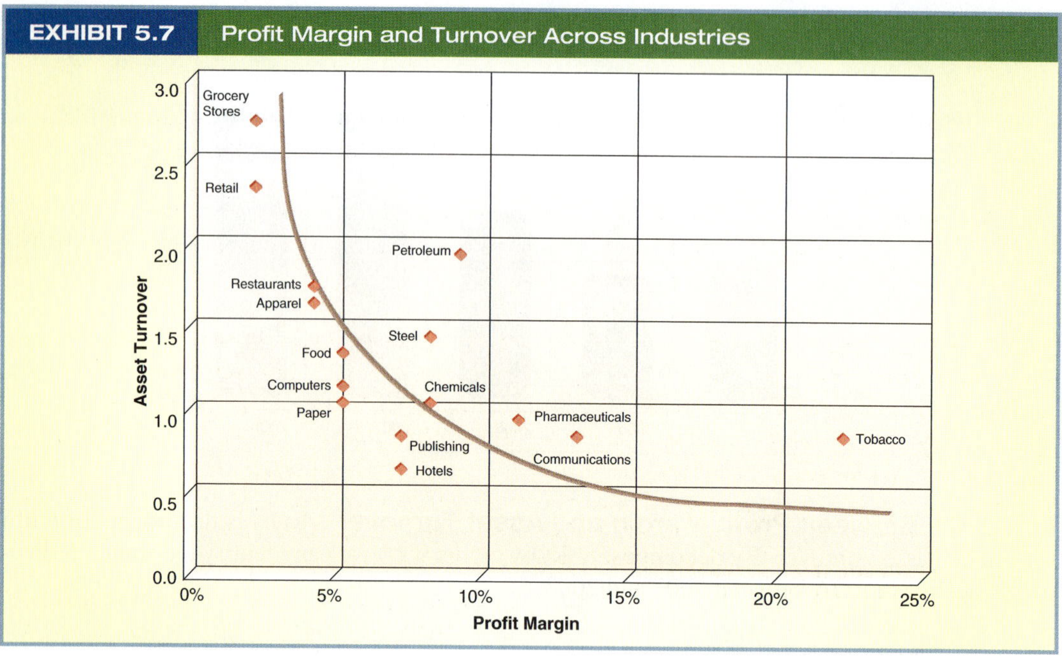

EXHIBIT 5.7 Profit Margin and Turnover Across Industries

BUSINESS INSIGHT

The DuPont Model Disaggregation of return on equity (ROE) into three components—profitability, turnover, and financial leverage—was initially introduced by the **E.I. DuPont de Nemours and Company** to aid its managers in performance evaluation. DuPont realized that management's focus on profit alone was insufficient because profit can be increased simply by adding investments in low-yielding, but safe, assets. Further, DuPont wanted managers to think like investors and to manage their portfolio of activities using investment principles that allocate scarce investment capital to competing projects based on a goal of maximizing return on investment.

The basic DuPont model disaggregates ROE as the product of three ratios as follows:

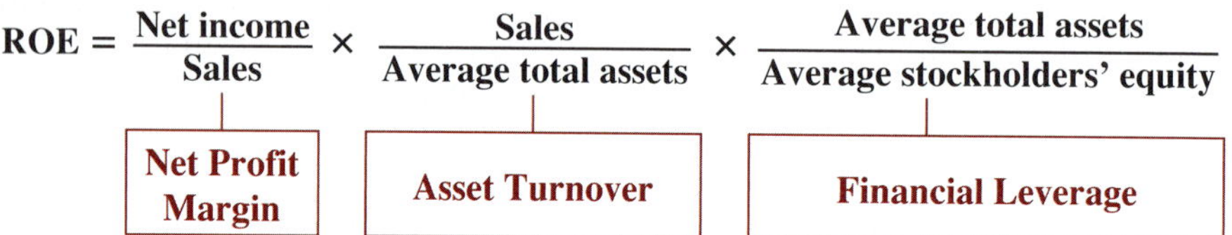

$$ROE = \frac{Net\ income}{Sales} \times \frac{Sales}{Average\ total\ assets} \times \frac{Average\ total\ assets}{Average\ stockholders'\ equity}$$

An important limitation of the DuPont model is that net profit margin is measured using net income in the numerator rather than earnings before interest (EBI). This means that this measure of profitability is affected by financial leverage—as financial leverage increases, interest expense increases and the net profit margin decreases. As a consequence, the model fails to adequately separate the effects of operating profitability on ROE from the effects of financial leverage. Despite this limitation, the DuPont model is widely used as a simple, straightforward way to disaggregate ROE.

Further Disaggregation of Profit Margin and Asset Turnover

While disaggregation of ROA into profit margin and asset turnover yields useful insights into the factors driving company performance, analysts, investors, creditors, and managers often disaggregate these measures even further. The purpose of this analysis is to be more precise about the specific determinants of profitability and efficiency.

To disaggregate profit margin (PM), we examine gross profit on products sold and individual expense accounts that contribute to the total cost of operations. The key ratios include the gross profit margin and expense-to-sales ratios. **Gross profit margin (GPM)** is defined as:

$$\text{Gross profit margin (GPM)} = \frac{\text{Sales revenue} - \text{Cost of goods sold}}{\text{Sales revenue}}$$

PepsiCo's GPM is 52.9% ([$43,251 million − $20,351 million]/$43,251 million). That is, just over half (52.9%) of every sales dollar is gross profit while slightly less than half (47.1%) goes to cover the cost of products sold.

Gross profit margin measures the percentage of each sales dollar that is left over after product costs are subtracted. It is easily determined by looking at the common-size income statement. This ratio is discussed in more detail in Chapter 7.

An **expense-to-sales (ETS)** ratio measures the percentage of each sales dollar that goes to cover a specific expense item and is computed by dividing the expense by sales revenue. Expense items that might be examined with ETS ratios include selling, general and administrative (SG&A) expenses, advertising expense, or research and development (R&D) expense, among others. Which specific ETS ratio is appropriate depends on the company being analyzed. For instance, advertising expense is an important expense item for a consumer products company, such as PepsiCo, while R&D expense is important for an R&D intensive pharmaceutical company, such as **Pfizer**. Analysts study trends in ETS ratios over time in an effort to uncover clues that might explain changes in profit margin and make predictions about future profitability.

PepsiCo's SG&A ETS ratio is computed by dividing selling, general and administrative expenses by net revenue. The resulting ETS ratio is 36.8% ($15,901 million/$43,251 million). This ratio indicates that 36.8% of every sales dollar goes to pay marketing and administrative costs. This ETS ratio is relatively high because this expense item includes PepsiCo's advertising expenditures.

To disaggregate asset turnover (AT), we examine individual asset accounts and compare them to sales or cost of goods sold. We focus on three specific turnover ratios—accounts receivable turnover (ART), inventory turnover (INVT), and property, plant and equipment turnover (PPET).

Accounts receivable turnover (ART) is defined as follows:

$$\text{Accounts receivable turnover (ART)} = \frac{\text{Sales revenue}}{\text{Average accounts receivable}}$$

ART measures how many times receivables have been turned (collected) during the period. More turns indicate that accounts receivable are being collected more quickly, while low turnover often indicates difficulty with a company's credit policies. PepsiCo's ART is 9.5 times ($43,251 million / [$4,683 million + $4,389 million]/2). ART is discussed in Chapter 6.

Inventory turnover (INVT) is defined as:

$$\text{Inventory turnover (INVT)} = \frac{\text{Cost of goods sold}}{\text{Average inventory}}$$

INVT measures the number of times during a period that total inventory is turned (sold). A high INVT indicates that inventory is managed efficiently. Retail companies, such as **Wal-Mart** and **Home Depot** focus a great deal of management attention on maintaining a high INVT ratio. PepsiCo's INVT is 8.5 times ($20,351 million/[$2,522 million + $2,290 million]/2). This ratio is discussed further in Chapter 7.

Property, plant and equipment turnover (PPET) measures the sales revenue produced for each dollar of investment in PP&E. It is computed as the ratio of sales to average PP&E assets:

$$\text{Property, plant \& equipment turnover (PPET)} = \frac{\text{Sales revenue}}{\text{Average PP\&E}}$$

PPET provides insights into asset utilization and how efficiently a company operates given its production technology. PepsiCo's PPET is 3.8 times ($43,251 million/[$11,663 million + $11,228 million]/2). This ratio is revisited in Chapter 8.

In the next section, we examine ratios that focus on liquidity and solvency. These ratios help us evaluate the risk associated with debt financing and weigh the costs and benefits of financial leverage. Exhibit 5.8 presents a schematic summary of the disaggregation of ROE. It identifies the two primary components of ROE—ROA and ROFL—and highlights the disaggregation of ROA into profit margin and asset turnover, along with the drivers of these ratios. In addition, the link between ROFL and liquidity and solvency analysis is highlighted.

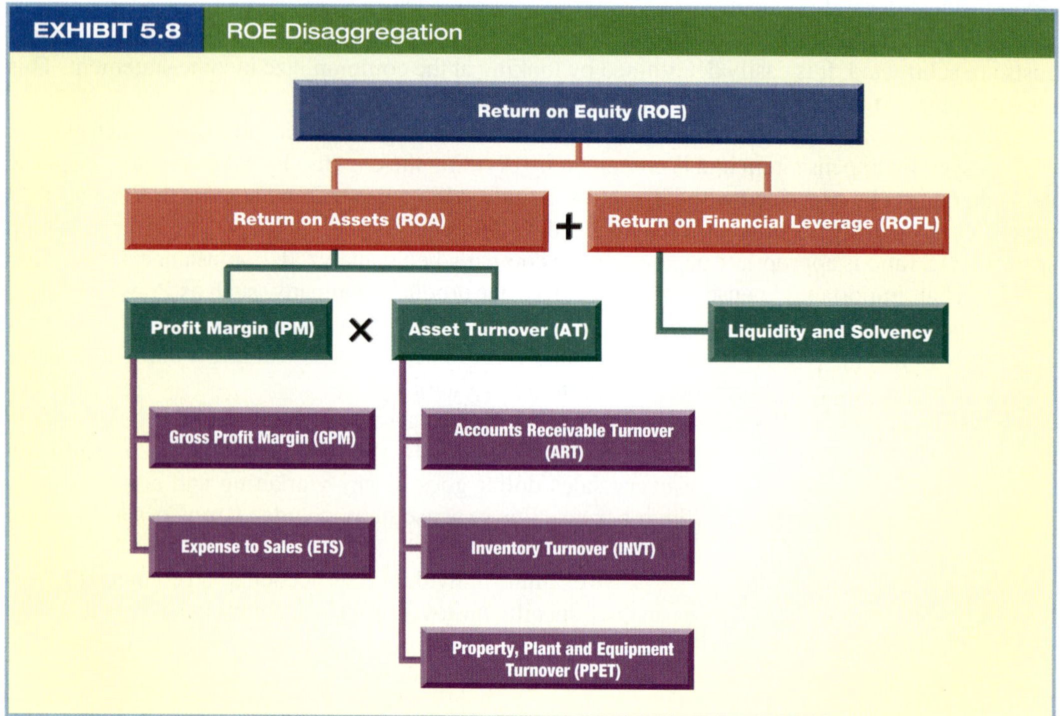

MID-CHAPTER REVIEW 3

Required

Refer to the financial statements for the **Coca-Cola Company** presented in Mid-Chapter Review 1 earlier in this chapter.

1. Calculate Coca-Cola's profit margin (PM) and asset turnover (AT) ratios for 2008.
2. Show that ROA = PM × AT using Coca-Cola's financial data.
3. Calculate Coca-Cola's gross profit margin (GPM), accounts receivable turnover (ART), inventory turnover (INVT), and property, plant and equipment turnover (PPET) ratios for 2008.
4. Evaluate Coca-Cola's ratios in comparison to those of PepsiCo.

The solution to this review problem can be found on page 252.

LIQUIDITY AND SOLVENCY

LO4 Compute and interpret measures of liquidity and solvency.

Companies can use debt to increase financial leverage and boost ROE. The increase in ROE due to the use of debt is called *return on financial leverage (ROFL)*. The primary advantage of debt financing is that it is typically less costly than equity financing; the cost of debt financing is currently about 4%, while equity financing averages about 12%.[2]

Exhibit 5.9 illustrates a comparison between two companies—one (Company A) is financed with 100% equity and the other (Company B) is financed with 50% debt and 50% equity. Both companies have $1,000 in (average) assets and EBI of $100, producing an ROA of 10% ($100/$1,000).

---

[2] Equity financing is more costly than debt because, in the event that the firm fails, creditors collect their investment first, while stockholders collect the residual. Stockholders, therefore, demand a greater return on investment to compensate for assuming greater risk.

Because Company A does not use debt financing, average equity equals average total assets. Also, it reports no interest expense in its income statement so net income equals EBI. Therefore, for Company A, ROE = ROA, and its ROFL = 0%.

EXHIBIT 5.9	The Effect of Debt Financing on ROE (ROA > interest rate)		
		Company A	Company B
Assets (average)		$1,000	$1,000
EBI		100	100
ROA (EBI/Assets)		10%	10%
Equity (average)		$1,000	$ 500
Debt		0	500
Interest expense (4% of debt)		0	20
Net income (EBI − interest)		100	80
ROE (Net income/equity)		10%	16%
ROFL (ROE − ROA)		0%	6%

In contrast, Company B has $500 of equity financing and $500 of debt financing. It reports interest expense of $20 ($500 × 4%) leaving net income of $80 ($100 − $20). Company B's ROE is 16% ($80/$500), which means that its ROFL is 6% (16% − 10%). Company B has made effective use of debt financing to increase its ROE. As long as a company's ROA is greater than its cost of debt, its ROFL will be positive.[3]

We might further ask: If a higher ROE is desirable, why don't companies use as much debt financing as possible? The answer is that there are risks associated with debt financing. As the amount of debt in a company's balance sheet increases, so does the burden of interest costs on income and debt payments on cash flows. In the best of times, financial leverage increases returns to stockholders (ROE). In contrast, when earnings are depressed, financial leverage has the effect of making a bad year even worse. In the worst case, too much debt can lead to financial distress and even bankruptcy.

To illustrate how debt financing can reduce shareholder returns, Exhibit 5.10 compares Company A and Company B in a year when reported profits are lower than in the previous example. Both companies have $1,000 in (average) assets and both report EBI of $30, producing an ROA of 3% ($30/$1,000). Company A does not use debt financing, so its ROE = 3%, and its ROFL = 0%. Because Company B has $500 of equity and $500 of debt, it reports interest expense of $20 ($500 × 4%) leaving net income of $10 ($30 − $20). Company B's ROE is 2% ($10/$500), which means that its ROFL is −1% (2% − 3%). That is, for Company B, the use of financial leverage has a negative effect on ROE. As this example illustrates, whenever ROA is less than the interest rate on the debt, debt financing reduces the return to shareholders.

EXHIBIT 5.10	The Effect of Debt Financing on ROE (ROA < interest rate)		
		Company A	Company B
Assets (average)		$1,000	$1,000
EBI		30	30
ROA (EBI/Assets)		3%	3%
Equity (average)		$1,000	$ 500
Debt		0	500
Interest expense (4% of debt)		0	20
Net income (EBI − interest)		30	10
ROE (Net income/equity)		3%	2%
ROFL (ROE − ROA)		0%	−1%

As a general rule, shareholders benefit from increased use of debt financing provided that the assets financed with the debt earn a return that exceeds the cost of the debt. However, increasing levels of debt result in successively higher interest rates charged by creditors. At some point, the cost of debt exceeds the return on assets that a company can expect from the debt financing. Thereafter,

---

[3] The interest cost on debt is tax deductable. Therefore, the relevant cost of debt to use to compare to ROA is the after-tax interest rate.

further debt financing does not make economic sense. The market, in essence, places a limit on the amount that a company can borrow.

In addition, creditors usually require a company to execute a loan agreement that places various restrictions on its operating activities. These restrictions, called **covenants**, help safeguard debtholders in the face of increased risk. This occurs because debtholders do not have a voice on the board of directors like stockholders do. These debt covenants impose a "cost" on the company beyond that of the interest rate, and these covenants are more stringent as a company increases its reliance on debt financing.

The median ratio of total liabilities to stockholders' equity, which measures the relative use of debt versus equity in a company's capital structure, is just over 1.0 for all publicly traded companies. This means that the typical company relies more on debt financing than on equity. However, the relative use of debt varies considerably across industries as illustrated in Exhibit 5.11.

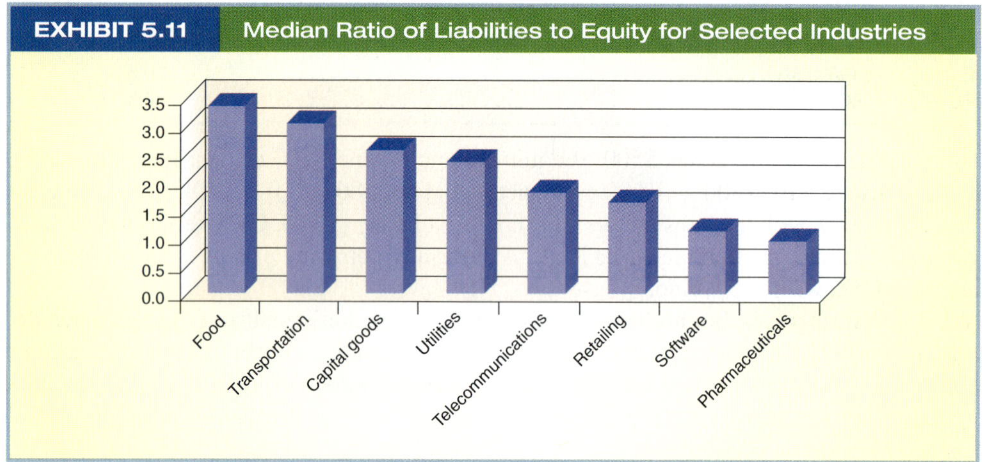

Companies in the utilities industry have relatively high proportions of debt. Because the utilities industry is regulated, profits and cash flows are relatively certain and stable and, as a result, utility companies can support a higher debt level. The transportation and food industries also utilize a relatively high proportion of debt. However, these industries are not regulated; they operate in more competitive and volatile markets and, consequently, the use of debt carries more risk. At the lower end of debt financing are pharmaceuticals and software companies. Historically, these industries have been characterized by relatively uncertain profits and cash flows. In addition, success in these industries depends heavily on intellectual property and human resources devoted to research and product development. These "assets" do not appear on the balance sheet and cannot be used as collateral when borrowing funds. Consequently, they use less debt in their capital structures.

To summarize, companies can effectively use debt to increase ROE. Although it reduces financing costs, debt increases **default risk**: the risk that the company will be unable to repay debt when it comes due. Because of this risk, analysts carefully examine a company's financial statements to determine if it is using debt financing effectively and judiciously.

The core of our analysis relating to debt is the examination of a company's ability to generate cash to *service* its debt (that is, to make required debt payments of both interest and principal). Analysts, investors, and creditors are primarily concerned about whether the company has sufficient cash available or, alternatively, whether it is able to generate the required cash in the future to cover its debt obligations. The analysis of available cash is called **liquidity analysis**. The analysis of the company's ability to generate sufficient cash in the future is called **solvency analysis** (so named because a bankrupt company is said to be "insolvent").

Liquidity Analysis

Liquidity refers to cash availability: how much cash a company has, and how much it can raise on short notice. The most common ratios used to assess the degree of liquidity are the current ratio and the quick ratio, which were first introduced in Chapter 2, as well as the operating cash flow to current liabilities ratio, which was introduced in Chapter 4. Each of these ratios links required near-term payments to cash available in the near term.

Current Ratio   *Current assets* are those assets that a company expects to convert into cash within the next operating cycle, which is typically a year. *Current liabilities* are those liabilities that come due within the next year. An excess of current assets over current liabilities (Current assets − Current liabilities), is known as *net working capital* or simply **working capital**. Positive working capital implies more expected cash inflows than cash outflows in the short run. The **current ratio** expresses working capital as a ratio and is computed as follows:

$$\text{Current ratio} = \frac{\text{Current assets}}{\text{Current liabilities}}$$

A current ratio greater than 1.0 implies positive working capital. Both working capital and the current ratio consider existing balance sheet data only and ignore cash inflows from future sales or other sources. The current ratio is more commonly used than working capital because ratios allow comparisons across companies of different size. Generally, companies prefer a higher current ratio; however, an excessively high current ratio indicates inefficient asset use. Furthermore, a current ratio less than 1.0 is not always problematic for at least two reasons:

1. A cash-and-carry company (like a grocery store) can have little or no receivables (and a low current ratio), but consistently large operating cash inflows ensure the company will be sufficiently liquid. A company can efficiently manage its working capital by minimizing receivables and inventories and maximizing payables. **Dell** and **Wal-Mart**, for example, use their buying power to exact extended credit terms from suppliers. Consequently, because both companies are essentially cash-and-carry companies, their current ratios are less than 1.0 and both are sufficiently liquid.

2. A service company will typically report little or no inventories among its current assets. In addition, some service companies do not report significant accounts receivable. If short-term borrowings and accrued expenses exceed cash and temporary investments, a current ratio of less than 1.0 would result. **Southwest Airlines** is an example of such a firm.

The aim of current-ratio analysis is to discern if a company is having, or is likely to have, difficulty meeting its short-term obligations. If a company cannot cover its short-term debts with cash provided by operations, it may need to liquidate current assets to meet its obligations. **PepsiCo**'s current ratio was 1.23 ($10,806 million/$8,787 million) at December 31, 2008. At the end of 2007, its current ratio was 1.31 ($10,151 million/$7,753 million).

Quick Ratio   The **quick ratio** is a variant of the current ratio. It focuses on quick assets, which are those assets likely to be converted to cash within a relatively short period of time, usually less than 90 days. Specifically, quick assets include cash, marketable securities, and accounts receivable; they exclude inventories and prepaid assets. The quick ratio is defined as follows:

$$\text{Quick ratio} = \frac{\text{Cash + Short-term securities + Accounts receivable}}{\text{Current liabilities}}$$

The quick ratio reflects on a company's ability to meet its current liabilities without liquidating inventories that could require markdowns. It is a more stringent test of liquidity than the current ratio and may provide more insight into company liquidity in some cases.

In 2008, PepsiCo's quick ratio was 0.79 ([$2,064 million + $213 million + $4,683 million]/$8,787 million), which was down from 0.89 in 2007 ([$910 million + $1,571 million + $4,389 million]/$7,753 million). While it is not uncommon for a company to report a quick ratio less than 1.0, PepsiCo's quick ratio has declined along with its current ratio.

Operating Cash Flow to Current Liabilities   The **operating cash flow to current liabilities (OCFCL)** ratio was introduced in Chapter 4 and is defined as follows:

$$\text{Operating cash flow to current liabilities (OCFCL)} = \frac{\text{Cash flow from operations}}{\text{Average current liabilities}}$$

Cash flow from operations is taken directly from the statement of cash flows. It represents the net amount of cash derived from operating activities during the year. Ultimately the ability of a company to pay its debts is determined by whether its operations can generate enough cash to cover debt payments. Thus, a higher OCFCL ratio is generally preferred by analysts.

PepsiCo reported an OCFCL ratio of 0.85 in 2008 ($6,999 million/[($8,787 million + $7,753 million)/2]). Its 2007 OCFCL ratio was 0.95 ($6,934 million/[($7,753 million + $6,860 million)/2]). As was the case with the current and quick ratios, PepsiCo's OCFCL ratio has decreased from 2007 to 2008. The change exhibited by these three measures suggests a decline in liquidity that should be examined further. Exhibit 5.12 provides a plot of all three ratios over the past 5 years. While the quick ratio reached a 5-year low in 2008, the current and OCFCL ratios are at or above their respective 5-year averages. It does not appear that PepsiCo has any liquidity issues at this time. However, analysts might become concerned if the current trend continues.

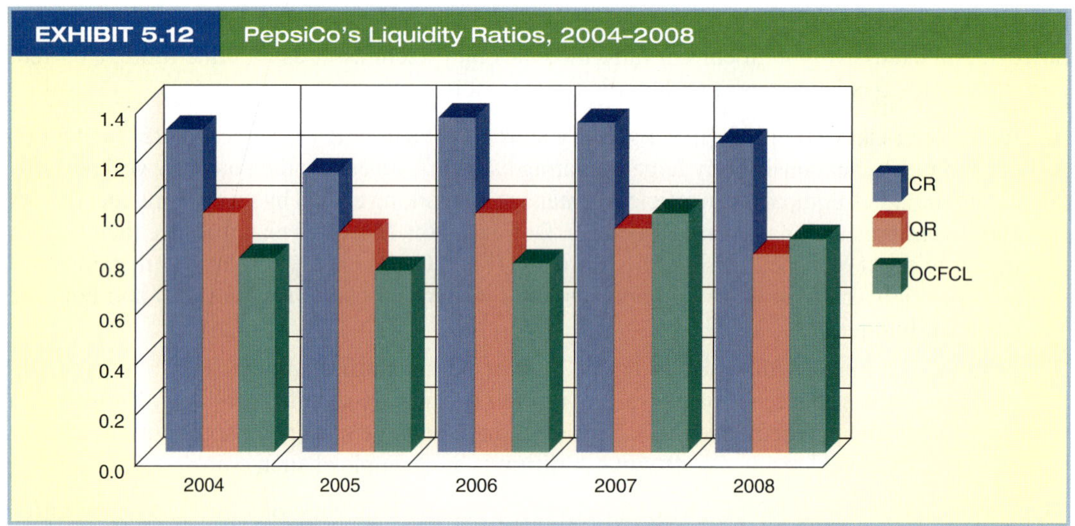

EXHIBIT 5.12 PepsiCo's Liquidity Ratios, 2004–2008

Solvency Analysis

Solvency refers to a company's ability to meet its debt obligations, including both periodic interest payments and the repayment of the principal amount borrowed. Solvency is crucial because an insolvent company is a failed company. There are two general approaches to measuring solvency. The first approach uses balance sheet data and assesses the proportion of capital raised from creditors. The second approach uses income statement data and assesses the profit generated relative to debt payment obligations. We discuss each approach in turn.

Debt-to-Equity The **debt-to-equity ratio**, which was introduced in Chapter 1, is a useful tool for the first type of solvency analysis. It is defined as follows:

$$\text{Debt-to-equity ratio} = \frac{\text{Total liabilities}}{\text{Stockholders' equity}}$$

This ratio conveys how reliant a company is on creditor financing compared with equity financing. A higher ratio indicates less solvency, and more risk. PepsiCo's debt-to-equity ratio is 1.97 for 2008 ($23,888 million/$12,106 million). In 2007, its ratio was 1.01 ($17,394 million/$17,234 million). The dramatic increase in the debt-to-equity ratio (see graph) was the result of a $6.5 billion increase in total liabilities and a $5.1 billion *decrease* in stockholders' equity. During 2008, PepsiCo increased its long-term debt as it expanded international operations. At the same time, stock repurchases and other factors reduced stockholders' equity even though the company reported net income for the year. PepsiCo's debt-to-equity ratio is well over the average of 1.0 for all public companies and raises questions about the company's long-term financing strategy.

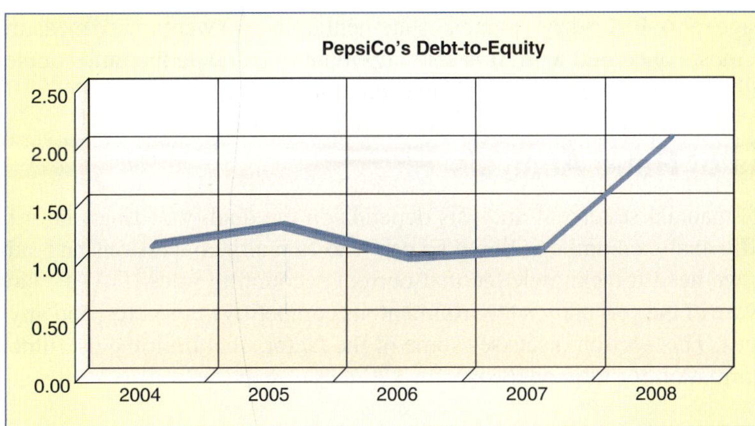

In practice, analysts use a variety of solvency measures that are similar to the debt-to-equity ratio. One variant of this ratio considers a company's *long-term* debt divided by equity. This approach assumes that current liabilities are repaid from current assets (so-called self-liquidating). Thus, it assumes that creditors and stockholders need only focus on the relative proportion of long-term capital.

Times Interest Earned   The second type of solvency analysis compares profits to liabilities. This approach assesses how much operating profit is available to cover debt obligations. A common measure for this type of solvency analysis is the **times interest earned (TIE)** ratio (see Chapter 9) defined as follows:

$$\text{Times interest earned} = \frac{\text{Earnings before interest expense and taxes}}{\text{Interest expense}}$$

The times interest earned ratio reflects the operating income available to pay interest expense. The underlying assumption is that only interest needs to be paid because the principal will be refinanced. This ratio is sometimes abbreviated as EBIT/I. The numerator is similar to earnings before interest (EBI), but it is *pretax* instead of after tax.

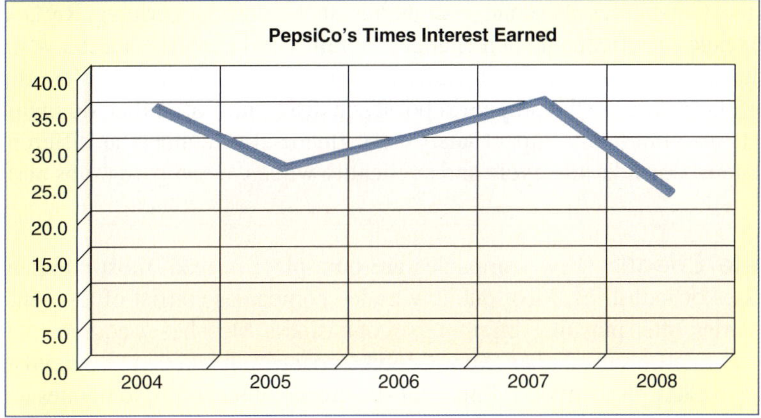

Management wants this ratio to be sufficiently high so that there is little risk of default. PepsiCo's times interest earned (TIE) ratio declined from 35.1 times in 2007 ([$7,631 million + $224 million]/$224 million) to 22.3 times in 2008 ([$7,021 million + $329 million]/$329 million). The large decline in TIE is consistent with the increase in the debt-to-equity ratio for the same period. Nevertheless, the current level of this ratio is not alarmingly low, suggesting that PepsiCo is more than capable of earning income that is sufficient to cover its financing costs.

There are many variations of solvency and liquidity analysis and the ratios used. The basic idea is to construct measures that reflect a company's credit risk exposure. There is not one "best" financial leverage ratio. Instead, as financial statement users, we want to use measures that capture the risk we are most concerned with. It is also important to compute the ratios ourselves to ensure we know what is included and excluded from each ratio.

Limitations of Ratio Analysis

The quality of financial statement analysis depends on the quality of financial information. We ought not blindly analyze numbers; doing so can lead to faulty conclusions and suboptimal decisions. Instead, we need to acknowledge that current accounting rules (GAAP) have limitations, and be fully aware of the company's environment, its competitive pressures, and any structural and strategic changes. This section discusses some of the factors that limit the usefulness of financial accounting information for ratio analysis.

GAAP Limitations   Several limitations in GAAP can distort financial ratios. Limitations include:

1. **Measurability**. Financial statements reflect what can be reliably measured. This results in nonrecognition of certain assets, often internally developed assets, the very assets that are most likely to confer a competitive advantage and create value. Examples are brand name, a superior management team, employee skills, and a reliable supply chain.

2. **Non-capitalized costs**. Related to the concept of measurability is the expensing of costs relating to "assets" that cannot be identified with enough precision to warrant capitalization. Examples are brand equity costs from advertising and other promotional activities, and research and development costs relating to future products.

3. **Historical costs**. Assets and liabilities are usually recorded at original acquisition or issuance costs. Subsequent increases in value are not recorded until realized, and declines in value are recognized only if deemed permanent.

Thus, GAAP balance sheets omit important and valuable assets. Our analysis of ROE, including that of liquidity and solvency, must consider that assets can be underreported and that ratios can be distorted. We discuss many of these limitations in more detail in later chapters.

Company Changes   Many companies regularly undertake mergers, acquire new companies, and divest subsidiaries. Such major operational changes can impair the comparability of company ratios across time. Companies also change strategies, such as product pricing, R&D, and financing. We must understand the effects of such changes on ratios and exercise caution when we compare ratios from one period to the next. Companies also behave differently at different points in their life cycles. For instance, growth companies possess a different profile than do mature companies. Seasonal effects also markedly impact analysis of financial statements at different times of the year. Thus, we must consider life cycle and cyclicality when we compare ratios across companies and over time.

Conglomerate Effects   Few companies are pure-play; instead, most companies operate in several businesses or industries. Most publicly traded companies consist of a parent company and multiple subsidiaries, often pursuing different lines of business. Most heavy equipment manufacturers, for example, have finance subsidiaries (**Ford Credit Corporation** and **Cat Financial** are subsidiaries of **Ford** and **Caterpillar** respectively). Financial statements of such conglomerates are consolidated and include the financial statements of the parent and its subsidiaries. Consequently, such consolidated statements are challenging to analyze. Typically, analysts break the financials apart into their component businesses and separately analyze each component. Fortunately, companies must report financial information (albeit limited) for major business segments in their 10-Ks.

Means to an End   Ratios reduce, to a single number, the myriad complexities of a company's operations. No one number can accurately capture the qualitative aspect of a company. Ratios cannot hope to capture the innumerable transactions and events that occur each day between a company and various parties. Ratios cannot meaningfully convey a company's marketing and management philosophies, its human resource activities, its financing activities, its strategic initiatives, and its product management. In our analysis we must learn to look through the numbers and ratios to better understand the operational factors that drive financial results. Successful analysis seeks to gain insight into what a company is really about and what the future portends. Our overriding purpose in analysis is to understand the past and present to better predict the future. Computing and examining ratios is just one step in that process.

CHAPTER-END REVIEW

Refer to the income statements and balance sheets for the **Coca-Cola Company** presented in Mid-Chapter Review 1 earlier in this chapter.

Required

Compute the following liquidity and solvency ratios for Coca-Cola and interpret your results in comparison to those of PepsiCo.

1. Current ratio
2. Quick ratio.
3. Debt-to-equity ratio.
4. Times interest earned.

The solution to this review problem can be found on page 252.

APPENDIX 5A: Analyzing and Interpreting Core Operating Activities

In Chapter 4, we analyzed cash flows by grouping them into three categories—operating, investing, and financing. Similarly, the income statement and balance sheet can be formatted to distinguish between operating and nonoperating (investing and financing) activities. In this appendix, we consider the effect of operating activities on the return on investment. The distinction between returns earned from operating activities and those generated by nonoperating activities is important. Operations provide the primary value drivers for stockholders. It is for this reason that many analysts argue that operating activities must be executed successfully if a company expects to remain profitable in the long run.

LO5 Measure and analyze the effect of operating activities on ROE.

Operating activities refer to the core transactions and events of a company. They consist of those activities required to deliver a company's products and services to its customers. A company is engaged in operating activities when it conducts research and development, establishes supply chains, assembles administrative support, produces and markets its products, and follows up with after-sale customer service. Although nonoperating activities, namely investing and financing activities, are important and must be managed well, they are not the primary value drivers for investors and creditors.

Operating returns are measured by the **return on net operating assets (RNOA)**. This return metric is defined as follows:

$$\text{RNOA} = \frac{\text{Net operating profit after taxes (NOPAT)}}{\text{Average net operating assets (NOA)}}$$

In order to calculate this ratio, we must first classify the income statement and balance sheet accounts into operating and nonoperating components so that we can assess each separately. First we will consider operating components of the income statement and the calculation of NOPAT. Then we consider operating and nonoperating components of the balance sheet and the calculation of NOA.

Reporting Operating Activities in the Income Statement

The income statement reports operating activities through accounts such as sales revenue, cost of goods sold, selling, general and administrative (SG&A) expenses, depreciation, rent, insurance, wages, advertising, and R&D expenses. These activities create the most long-lasting effects on profitability and cash flows. Nonoperating items in the income statement include interest expense on borrowed funds and interest and dividend income on investments as well as gains and losses on those investments.

A commonly used measure of operating income is **net operating profit after taxes (NOPAT)**. NOPAT is calculated as:

$$\textbf{NOPAT = Net income} - \textbf{[(Nonoperating revenues} - \textbf{Nonoperating expenses)} \times \textbf{(1} - \textbf{Marginal tax rate)]}$$

NOPAT is an important measure of profitability. It is similar to net income except that NOPAT focuses exclusively on after-tax *operating* performance.

Computation of NOPAT requires that we separate nonoperating revenues and expenses from operating sources of income. Companies often report income from operations as a subtotal (before income taxes) within the income statement. These numbers should be interpreted with caution. Currently, there are no requirements within GAAP that specify which revenue and expense items should be included in operating income.[4] As a consequence, some nonoperating items may be included (as part of SG&A expense, for example) while some operating items may be excluded. PepsiCo's income statement provides a good illustration. It reports operating profit of $6,935 million in its 2008 income statement. Yet, immediately below that amount is $374 million of income that is labeled "Bottling equity income" (see Exhibit 5.2). This is PepsiCo's share of the income earned by Pepsi bottling companies of which PepsiCo is part owner. Most analysts would argue that this amount should be included in the calculation of NOPAT for PepsiCo, because Pepsi bottling operations are clearly part of the core operating activities of the business.

The tax rate used to compute NOPAT is the **marginal tax rate**. This rate is the effective tax rate on nonoperating revenues and expenses. As we have done throughout this chapter, we use the federal statutory tax rate of 35% to approximate the marginal tax rate.[5] PepsiCo's NOPAT can be computed using this tax rate:

$$\textbf{NOPAT} = \textbf{\$5,142 million} - \textbf{[(\$41 million} - \textbf{\$329 million)} \times \textbf{(1} - \textbf{0.35)]} = \textbf{\$5,329.2 million}$$

PepsiCo's NOPAT is greater than its net income of $5,142 million in 2008. The difference between net income and NOPAT is the interest expense on its debt and interest income on its investments.

Reporting Operating Activities in the Balance Sheet

The balance sheet also reflects both operating and nonoperating activities. The asset side of the balance sheet reports resources devoted to operating activities in accounts such as cash, receivables, inventories, property, plant and equipment, and intangible assets. Among liabilities, accounts payable, accrued expenses, and some long-term liabilities such as deferred compensation and pension benefits arise out of operating activities. In addition, accrued and deferred income taxes are generally considered operating liabilities.

Investments in securities of other companies are usually considered nonoperating. The exception is that some equity-type investments are related to operations. PepsiCo's investment in several Pepsi bottling companies is an example of this type of investment. Equity investments are discussed further in Chapter 12. Among a company's liabilities, short-term and long-term debt accounts are classified as nonoperating. These include accounts such as notes payable, interest payable, current maturities of long-term debt, capital leases, and long-term debt.

PepsiCo reports short-term investments of $213 million in 2008 ($1,571 million in 2007), which are nonoperating. It also reports long-term investments of $3,883 in 2008 ($4,354 in 2007). However, some of these long-term investments are the aforementioned equity investments in Pepsi bottling companies. Equity investments total $2,429 million in 2008 and $3,140 million in 2007. Thus, the nonoperating portion of its long-term investments is $1,454 million in 2008 ($3,883 million − $2,429 million) and $1,214 million in 2007 ($4,354 million − $3,140 million). Its nonoperating liabilities include short-term debt obligations of $369 million in 2008 and long-term debt obligations of $7,858 in 2008 ($4,203 in 2007).

By subtracting total operating liabilities from total operating assets, we get **net operating assets (NOA)**.[6] PepsiCo's NOA for 2008 and 2007 is calculated as follows ($ millions):

	2008	2007
Operating assets	\$35,994 − \$213 − \$1,454 = \$34,327	\$34,628 − \$1,571 − \$1,214 = \$31,843
Operating liabilities	\$23,888 − \$7,858 − \$369 = \$15,661	\$17,394 − \$4,203 = \$13,191
NOA	\$18,666	\$18,652

---

[4] The FASB recently released a preliminary draft of a proposal for presenting financial statements in a new format. Among other things, the objective is to better distinguish operating and nonoperating activities.

[5] As we argued earlier in this chapter, the federal statutory tax rate is a reasonable approximation of the marginal tax rate in many instances, including our analysis of PepsiCo. However, some nonoperating sources of revenue and expense are not taxed at this 35% rate. For example, most dividend income received from investments in the stock of other corporations is excluded from taxable income. A detailed analysis of marginal tax rates is beyond the scope of this text. Nevertheless, a thorough analysis of operating return would normally include a close examination of a company's income taxes.

[6] Total operating assets can be computed by subtracting nonoperating assets from total assets. Similarly, we can determine operating liabilities either by adding up the operating items or by subtracting the nonoperating items from total liabilities.

Given NOPAT and NOA we can compute PepsiCo's RNOA as follows:

$$\text{RNOA} = \frac{\text{NOPAT}}{\text{Average NOA}} = \frac{\$5,329.2 \text{ million}}{(\$18,666 \text{ million} + \$18,652 \text{ million})/2} = 28.6\%$$

PepsiCo's ROE is 35.1% in 2008. Its RNOA is 28.7%, which represents about 82% of the total return earned by stockholders. The average publicly traded company derives 84% of its ROE from RNOA. Thus, PepsiCo is in line with other companies in that it derives the vast majority of its returns from operations.

Disaggregating RNOA

We gain further insights into operating returns by disaggregating RNOA into operating profit margin and asset turnover. RNOA can be presented as the product of net operating profit margin (NOPM) and net operating asset turnover (NOAT). We define **net operating profit margin (NOPM)** as the amount of operating profit produced as a percentage of each sales dollar. NOPM is similar to the profit margin (PM) ratio defined in the chapter, except that it excludes all nonoperating revenues and expenses from the calculation. PepsiCo's NOPM was 12.3% in 2008, computed as:

$$\text{NOPM} = \frac{\text{NOPAT}}{\text{Sales revenue}} = \frac{\$5,329.2 \text{ million}}{\$43,251 \text{ million}} = 12.3\%$$

The ratio indicates that each dollar of sales revenue generated 12.3¢ of after-tax operating profit. PepsiCo's NOPAT is very close to PepsiCo's EBI because the primary nonoperating item in the company's income statement is interest expense. Thus its NOPM is almost identical to its profit margin of 12.4%.

Net operating asset turnover (NOAT) is defined as the ratio of sales revenue to average net operating assets (NOA). NOAT captures the amount of sales revenue generated by each dollar of net investment in operating assets. PepsiCo's NOAT is 2.32 times, computed as:

$$\text{NOAT} = \frac{\text{Sales revenue}}{\text{Average NOA}} = \frac{\$43,251 \text{ million}}{(\$18,666 \text{ million} + \$18,652 \text{ million})/2} = 2.32$$

This ratio suggests that each dollar of investment in net operating assets generates $2.32 of sales revenue. This ratio is considerably higher than PepsiCo's asset turnover (AT) ratio of 1.225. This difference is caused by the difference between net operating assets (NOA) and total assets. NOAT is computed using average NOA in the denominator rather than average total assets. Thus, nonoperating assets are excluded, and operating assets are presented net of operating liabilities. The resulting denominator is, therefore, considerably smaller.

PepsiCo's RNOA is 28.6%. This return can be disaggregated into the product of NOPM and NOAT as follows:

$$\text{RNOA} = \text{NOPM} \times \text{NOAT}$$
$$28.6\% = 12.3\% \times 2.32$$

APPENDIX-END REVIEW A

Refer to the financial statements of the Coca-Cola Company presented in Mid-Chapter Review 1. Calculate Coca-Cola's return on net operating assets (RNOA) and then disaggregate RNOA into net operating profit margin (NOPM) and net operating asset turnover (NOAT).

The solution to this review problem can be found on page 253.

APPENDIX 5B: Pro Forma Financial Statements

The ability to forecast future financial activities is an important aspect of many business decisions. We might, for example, wish to estimate the value of a company's common stock before purchasing its shares. Or, we might want to evaluate the creditworthiness of a prospective borrower. We might also be interested in comparing the financial impact of alternative business strategies or tactics. For each of these decision contexts, a forecast of future earnings and cash flows would be relevant to such an evaluation.

Pro forma financial statements are hypothetical statements prepared to reflect specific assumptions about the company and its transactions. The most common type of pro forma statements are those prepared for

LO6 Prepare *pro forma* financial statements.

future periods based on assumptions about the future activities of a business.[7] By varying the assumptions, pro forma statements allow us to ask "what if" questions about the future activities of the company, the answers to which provide the necessary inputs underlying most business decisions.

In this appendix, we present a common, yet simple method for preparing pro forma financial statements. This method proceeds in seven steps:

1. Forecast sales revenue.

2. Forecast operating expenses, such as cost of goods sold and SG&A expenses.

3. Forecast operating assets and liabilities, including accounts receivable, inventory, property, plant and equipment, accounts payable, and prepaid and accrued expenses.

4. Forecast nonoperating assets, liabilities, contributed capital, revenues and expenses.

5. Forecast net income, dividends and retained earnings.

6. Forecast the amount of cash required to balance the balance sheet.

7. Prepare a pro forma cash flow statement based on the pro forma income statement and balance sheet.

Step 1. Forecast Sales Revenue

The sales forecast is the crucial first step in the preparation of pro forma financial statements, because many of the accounts in the pro forma income statement and balance sheet depend on their relation to the sales forecast. The general method for forecasting sales is to assume a revenue growth rate and apply that rate to the current sales revenue amount:

$$\textbf{Forecasted revenues} = \textbf{Current revenues} \times (1 + \textbf{Revenue growth rate})$$

A good starting point for estimating the revenue growth rate is the historical rate of sales growth. This is obtained by using data from the horizontal analysis discussed earlier in the chapter. For example, over the past four years, PepsiCo has experienced an average sales growth rate of 10.3%. Once we have this historical rate as a starting point, we can then adjust the growth rate up or down based on other relevant information. For example, we might attempt to answer the following questions:

- How will future sales be affected by economic conditions? What will happen in the economy in the coming year? Do we expect economic growth or a recession? How will economic growth vary in various markets, such as the United States, Europe, Asia, and Latin America?

- What changes are expected from the company? Are there any new strategic initiatives planned? Is the company planning to open new stores, launch new products, new advertising campaigns, or new pricing tactics? Do we expect any acquisitions of other businesses?

- What changes in the competitive environment do we expect? Are new competitors entering the market? How will existing competitors respond to changes in the company's strategy? How will substitute products affect sales?

To answer each of the above questions, we rely on a variety of information sources, not the least of which is the management's discussion and analysis (MD&A) section of the company's 10-K report. We can also use publicly available information from competitors, suppliers, customers, industry organizations and government agencies to provide some insight into trends that can have an effect on future revenues. Our objective is to be able to adjust the historical growth rate up or down to reflect the insights we gain from reviewing this additional information.

For the purpose of illustration, we assume PepsiCo's historical sales growth of 10.3% will continue into 2009. The resulting forecast of sales revenue is $47,706 million ($43,251 million × 1.103).

Step 2. Forecast Operating Expenses

Given our forecast of sales revenue, we then turn to forecasting operating expenses. We rely on the common-size income statement as a starting point to identify the relationship between operating expense items and sales revenue. That is, we use the expense-to-sales (ETS) ratio for each operating expense item to compute the forecasted expense:

$$\textbf{Forecasted operating expense} = \textbf{Forecasted revenues} \times \textbf{ETS ratio}$$

---

[7] The term "pro forma financial statements" is a term that is also used to describe *current* period financial statements prepared under alternative assumptions. For example, management might use the term pro forma earnings when referring to earnings computed after excluding a major revenue or expense item, such as restructuring charges or income from discontinued operations. The term can also be used to describe financial statements prepared under a different set of accounting principles.

While historical ETS ratios provide a good place to start, we may want to adjust these ratios up or down based on observed trends or any additional information that we might have. For example, when we examined PepsiCo's common-size income statements, we learned that cost of goods sold increased to 47.1% of sales in 2008, up from 45.7% in 2007. Will this trend continue into 2009? Or, alternatively, do we anticipate that this expense item will revert to historical levels in relation to sales? Has the company taken any steps to alter the trend in this ETS ratio? As was the case with the sales forecast, there are numerous sources of information that are potentially useful for making adjustments to the historical relationships.

For the purpose of illustration, we assume that the ETS ratios for all operating expense items remain the same in 2009 as they were in 2008. For example, we forecast PepsiCo's 2009 SG&A expense to be $17,556 million ($47,706 $\times$ 36.8%).

Step 3. Forecast Operating Assets and Liabilities

The sales forecast can also be used to forecast operating assets and liabilities. The relationship between operating assets and revenues is based on asset turnover analysis. For example, when we compute accounts receivable turnover (ART), sales revenue is divided by average accounts receivable. When forecasting accounts receivable, we assume a relationship between sales revenue and year-end accounts receivable:

$$\text{Forecasted accounts receivable} = \text{Forecasted sales revenue} \times \frac{\textbf{Reported accounts receivable}}{\textbf{Reported sales revenue}}$$

PepsiCo reports accounts and notes receivable of $4,683 million in 2008, which is 10.8% of the reported sales revenue of $43,251 million. The forecasted accounts receivable for 2009 is, therefore, $5,152 million ($47,706 $\times$ 10.8%).

The same procedure can be used to forecast other operating assets, such as inventories, prepaid expenses and property, plant and equipment, as well as operating liabilities such as accounts payable and accrued expenses.

Step 4. Forecast Nonoperating Assets, Liabilities, Revenues and Expenses

While operating expenses, assets, and liabilities tend to be related to sales revenue, this is typically not the case for nonoperating items. Instead, nonoperating revenues, such as interest and dividend income, tend to be related to investments, while nonoperating expense, namely interest expense, is related to debt financing. As a starting point, we forecast each of these items by assuming no change from the current amounts. For example, PepsiCo reported long-term debt of $7,858 million in 2008 along with short-term obligations of $369 million. We forecast the same level of debt financing in 2009. Likewise, interest expense should remain the same at $329 million.

There may be information in the notes or in the MD&A section of the 10-K report to suggest other assumptions. For example, the notes typically reveal the amount of long-term debt that will come due in each of the next five years. This information can be used to adjust the balance in short-term obligations, because current maturities of long-term debt would be included under this item. Nevertheless, an assumption of no change is a good place to start.

Step 5. Forecast Net Income, Dividends, and Retained Earnings

Once we have forecasts of sales revenue (from step 1), operating expenses (step 2), and nonoperating revenues and expenses (step 4), we can calculate pretax earnings, income tax expense, and net income. Income tax expense is forecasted by multiplying pretax income by the effective tax rate:

$$\text{Forecasted income tax expense} = \text{Forecasted pretax income} \times \text{Effective tax rate}$$

The **effective tax rate** is the average tax rate applied to pretax earnings, and is computed by dividing reported income tax expense by reported pretax earnings. PepsiCo's effective tax rate was 26.8% in 2008 ($1,879 million / $7,021 million). Although this rate can be adjusted up or down based on additional information, we apply the 2008 effective tax rate to compute 2009 forecasted income taxes. This assumption results in forecasted income taxes of $2,062 million ($7,694 million $\times$ 26.8%) and forecasted net income of $5,632 million ($7,694 million $-$ $2,062 million). PepsiCo's 2009 pro forma income statement is presented in Exhibit 5B.1 alongside its 2008 reported income statement.

Our forecast of dividends relies on the **dividend payout ratio**, defined as dividend payments divided by net income.

$$\text{Forecasted dividends} = \text{Forecasted net income} \times \text{Dividend payout ratio}$$

PepsiCo paid cash dividends of $2,541 million in 2008, which is 49.4% of its net income of $5,142 million. Using this dividend payout ratio, we forecast 2009 dividends to be $2,782 million ($5,632 million $\times$ 49.4%).

EXHIBIT 5B.1	PepsiCo Pro Forma Income Statement

PEPSICO, INC.
2008 Income Statement and 2009 Pro Forma Income Statement

($ millions)	pro forma 2009	as reported 2008
Net revenue ($43,251 × 1 + 10.3%)	$47,706	$43,251
Cost of sales ($47,706 × 47.1%)	22,470	20,351
Selling, general and administrative expenses ($47,706 × 36.8%)	17,556	15,901
Amortization of intangible assets ($47,706 × 0.15%)	72	64
Operating profit	7,608	6,935
Bottling equity income (no change)	374	374
Interest expense (no change)	(329)	(329)
Interest income (no change)	41	41
Income before income taxes	7,694	7,021
Provision for income taxes (26.8% × pretax income)	2,062	1,879
Net income	$ 5,632	$ 5,142

Next, we can forecast retained earnings using the forecasts of net income and dividends:

$$\text{Forecasted retained earnings} = \text{Beginning retained earnings} + \text{Forecasted net income} - \text{Forecasted dividends}$$

Throughout this chapter, we have presented PepsiCo's stockholders' equity as a single amount, without separating retained earnings from contributed capital. If we assume no change in contributed capital for 2009, we can forecast total stockholders' equity using the same method as would normally be used to forecast retained earnings. Thus, PepsiCo's forecasted 2009 stockholders' equity is $14,956 million ($12,106 million + $5,632 million − $2,782 million).

Step 6. Forecast Cash

If the forecasts of all other components of the balance sheet are in place, we can then forecast the cash balance. This forecast is simply a "plug" amount that makes the balance sheet balance:

$$\text{Forecasted cash} = \text{Forecasted liabilities} + \text{Forecasted stockholders' equity} - \text{Forecasted noncash assets}$$

It is possible that the resulting forecast of cash will be negative or unreasonably small or large. If this occurs, we then revisit steps 4 and 5. If the cash forecast is negative or too low, we adjust our forecast of short-term debt and interest expense to reflect increased borrowing to cover cash needs. If the cash forecast is too large, we can assume that excess cash is invested in marketable securities and increase the amount of interest income. In either case, we then modify our forecast of income taxes, net income, dividends and retained earnings, before recalculating the cash forecast.

PepsiCo's 2009 pro forma balance sheet is presented in Exhibit 5B.2, alongside the company's 2008 actual balance sheet. The cash balance is forecasted to increase by 97% (from $2,064 million in 2008 to $4,071 million in 2009). This increase is significant, and excess cash could be used to increase short-term investments, though we do not do so here.

Step 7. Prepare the Pro Forma Cash Flow Statement

Once we have a pro forma income statement and balance sheet, we can prepare a pro forma cash flow statement using the methods illustrated in Chapter 4. To do so, we need a forecast of depreciation expense (if that item is not explicitly listed as an operating expense in the income statement). The procedure for forecasting depreciation expense is the same as was used for other operating expenses—we simply use the depreciation ETS ratio.

PepsiCo reported depreciation expense of $1,479 million in 2008, which was 3.4% of sales revenue. Using this ETS ratio, we can forecast depreciation expense of $1,622 million in 2009 ($47,706 million × 3.4%). Using this forecast, along with other items forecasted earlier, we can prepare the pro forma cash flow statement, which is presented in Exhibit 5B.3.

Additional Considerations

Pro forma financial statements are based on a set of assumptions about the future. Any decisions that are based on pro forma statements are only as good as the quality of these assumptions. Therefore it is important that we appreciate the effect that each assumption has on the forecasted amounts. To this end, it is often helpful to use **sensitivity analysis** to examine the effect of alternative assumptions on the pro forma statements. For

EXHIBIT 5B.2	PepsiCo Pro Forma Balance Sheet

PEPSICO, INC.
2008 Balance Sheet and 2009 Pro Forma Balance Sheet

($ millions)	pro forma 2009	as reported 2008
ASSETS		
Cash and cash equivalents (plug to balance)	$ 4,071	$ 2,064
Short-term investments (no change)	213	213
Accounts and notes receivable, net ($47,706 × 10.8%)	5,152	4,683
Inventories ($47,706 × 5.8%)	2,767	2,522
Prepaid expenses and other current assets ($47,706 × 3.1%)	1,479	1,324
Total current assets	13,682	10,806
Property, plant and equipment, net ($47,706 × 27.0%)	12,881	11,663
Amortizable intangible assets, net ($47,706 × 1.7%)	811	732
Goodwill and other intangible assets (no change)	6,252	6,252
Investments in noncontrolled affiliates (no change)	3,883	3,883
Other assets ($47,706 × 6.1%)	2,910	2,658
Total assets	$40,419	$35,994
LIABILITIES AND SHAREHOLDERS' EQUITY		
Short-term obligations (no change)	$ 369	$ 369
Accounts payable and other current liabilities ($47,706 × 19.1%)	9,112	8,273
Income taxes payable ($47,706 × 0.33%)	157	145
Total current liabilities	9,638	8,787
Long-term debt obligations (no change)	7,858	7,858
Other liabilities ($47,706 × 16.2%)	7,728	7,017
Deferred income taxes ($47,706 × 0.5%)	239	226
Total liabilities	25,463	23,888
Shareholders' equity ($12,106 + $5,632 − $2,782*)	14,956	12,106
Total liabilities and shareholders' equity	$40,419	$35,994

* $2,782 = $5,632 × 49.4%

EXHIBIT 5B.3	PepsiCo Pro Forma Cash Flow Statement

PEPSICO, INC.
2009 Pro Forma Cash Flow Statement

($ millions)	pro forma 2009
Operations:	
Net income	$5,632
Adjustments:	
Depreciation ($47,706 × 3.4%)	1,622
Amortization of intangible assets	72
Increase in accounts and notes receivable	(469)
Increase in inventories	(245)
Increase in prepaid expenses and other current assets	(155)
Increase in other assets	(252)
Increase in accounts payable and other current liabilities	839
Increase in other liabilities	711
Increase in income taxes payable and deferred income taxes	25
Cash flow from operations	7,780
Investing activities:	
Investment in property, plant and equipment, net	(2,840)
Investment in amortizable intangible assets	(151)
Cash used for investing activities	(2,991)
Financing activities:	
Cash dividends paid	(2,782)
Cash used for financing activities	(2,782)
Net increase in cash (7,780 − 2,991 − 2,782)	2,007
Cash and cash equivalents, 2008	2,064
Cash and cash equivalents, 2009	$4,071

example, we might prepare three different pro forma income statements, one using our "most-likely" assumption for the sales forecast, and one each for the "best-case" and "worst-case" scenarios. In some situations, a change in the sales forecast can have a dramatic effect on net income and cash flows. Sensitivity analysis helps to identify these effects before a decision is made so that costly mistakes can be avoided.

It is also important to remember that these statements are predictions about the future and, as such, are bound to be wrong. That is, we expect that there will be **forecast errors**—differences between the forecasted and the actual amounts. The goal of a good forecast is accuracy, which means that we want the forecast errors to be as small as possible. Generating pro forma statements using a computer is relatively easy and the efficiency and precision of spreadsheet software can provide a false sense of confidence in the numbers. Spreadsheets routinely calculate forecasted amounts to the "nth" decimal place whether or not such precision is justified. However, an amount forecasted to the nearest penny may not be very useful if the forecast is off by millions of dollars. Remember: it is better to be imprecisely accurate then to be precisely inaccurate.

APPENDIX-END REVIEW B

Refer to the income statements and balance sheets of the Coca-Cola Company presented in Mid-Chapter Review 1.

Required
Make the following assumptions:

- 2009 sales revenue is $34,000 million.
- Operating expenses increase in 2009 in proportion to sales revenue.
- Operating assets and liabilities increase based on their 2008 relation to sales revenue. Classify "Goodwill and other intangible assets," "Other assets," and "Other liabilities" as operating.
- Assume that nonoperating revenues, expenses, assets and liabilities do not change from 2008 to 2009.
- Dividend payout is 60% of net income.

Prepare a pro forma income statement and balance sheet for 2009.

The solution to this review problem can be found on pages 253–254.

APPENDIX 5C: Measuring Return on Financial Leverage

In this appendix, we present an alternative method for calculating the return on financial leverage (ROFL). ROFL is the effect that debt financing has on ROE. In the chapter, we define ROFL as the difference between ROE and ROA. ROFL can also be computed directly. In order to do so, we first define the **net interest rate (NIR)**, which is the average interest rate after taxes on total liabilities, as follows:[8]

$$\text{Net interest rate (NIR)} = \frac{\text{Interest expense} \times (1 - \text{Statutory tax rate})}{\text{Average total liabilities}}$$

The net interest rate (NIR) is the ratio of annual net interest expense to average total liabilities. Because some liabilities, such as accounts payable and accrued expenses, are non-interest-bearing, the NIR is typically lower than prevailing interest rates. Nevertheless, NIR is an important variable that helps us understand the effects of financial leverage. Specifically, whenever ROA is greater than NIR, leverage will increase ROE, thus benefiting the firm. On the other hand, whenever ROA is less than NIR, debt financing will be harmful to the firm as it has the effect of reducing ROE.

Given our definition of the NIR, ROFL can be computed directly, as follows:

$$\text{ROFL} = \frac{\text{Average total liabilities}}{\text{Average stockholders' equity}} \times (\text{ROA} - \text{NIR})$$

The first term on the right-hand side of this equality is the ratio of average total liabilities to average stockholders' equity. This ratio is similar to the debt-to-equity ratio that was discussed earlier in the chapter except that the debt-to-equity ratio is computed using liabilities and stockholders' equity at a point in time (e.g., year-end) while the averages are used here.

---

[8] The net interest rate (NIR) should not be confused with *net interest* which is a term that is sometimes used in the income statement to refer to interest expense minus interest income.

The second term on the right-hand side of the equality is the aforementioned difference between ROA and NIR. This difference is called the **spread**. When the spread is positive (ROA > NIR), ROFL is positive and ROE is greater than ROA. When the spread is negative (ROA < NIR), ROFL is negative, which implies that ROE < ROA.

PepsiCo's ROFL is 19.9%, which is the difference between ROE and ROA (35.1% − 15.2%). We obtain the same value for ROFL when it is calculated directly. PepsiCo's NIR is 1.04%, which is computed as follows ($ millions):

$$\text{NIR} = \frac{\$329 \times (1 - 0.35)}{(\$23,888 + \$17,394)/2} = 1.04\%$$

Using the NIR, we can compute PepsiCo's ROFL as ($ millions):

$$\text{ROFL} = \frac{(\$23,888 + \$17,394)/2}{(\$12,106 + \$17,234)/2} \times (15.2\% - 1.04\%) = 19.9\%$$

APPENDIX-END REVIEW C

Refer to the financial statements for Coca-Cola presented in Mid-Chapter Review 1. Calculate Coca-Cola's NIR and ROFL for 2008.

The solution to this review problem can be found on page 254.

SUMMARY

Prepare and analyze common-size financial statements. (p. 206)   **LO1**

- Vertical analysis restates items in the income statement as a percentage of sales revenue and items in the balance sheet as a percentage of total assets.
- Horizontal analysis examines the percentage change from one year to the next for specific items in the income statement and balance sheet.

Compute and interpret measures of return on investment, including return on equity (ROE), return on assets (ROA), and return on financial leverage (ROFL). (p. 211)   **LO2**

- ROE is the primary measure of company performance. It captures the return earned by shareholder investment in the firm.
- ROA measures the return earned on the firm's investment in assets. It is not affected by the way those assets are financed.
- ROFL is the difference between ROE and ROA and measures the effect that financial leverage has on ROE.

Disaggregate ROA into profitability (profit margin) and efficiency (asset turnover) components. (p. 213)   **LO3**

- ROA can be disaggregated as the product of profit margin (PM) and asset turnover (AT).
- PM can be analyzed further by examining the gross profit margin and expense-to-sales ratios.
- AT can be analyzed further by examining accounts receivable turnover (ART), inventory turnover (INVT), and property, plant and equipment turnover (PPET).
- The trade-off between PM and AT is determined by the company's strategy and its competitive environment.

Compute and interpret measures of liquidity and solvency. (p. 218)   **LO4**

- The current ratio (CR) and quick ratio (QR) measure short-term liquidity by comparing liquid assets to short-term obligations.
- The debt-to-equity ratio (D/E) and times interest earned ratio (TIE) measure long-term solvency by comparing sources of financing and the level of earnings to the cost of debt (interest).

Appendix 5A: Measure and analyze the effect of operating activities on ROE. (p. 225)   **LO5**

- Net operating profit after taxes (NOPAT) measures the portion of income that results from a business' core operating activities.
- Return on net operating assets (RNOA), defined as NOPAT/average net operating assets, measures the return on a company's net investment in operating assets.

LO6 **Appendix 5B: Prepare *pro forma* financial statements. (p. 227)**
- *Pro forma* financial statements are statements prepared for future periods based on assumptions about the future activities of the business.
- *Pro forma* statements can be used to evaluate the effects of alternative actions or assumptions on the financial statements.

KEY RATIOS

RETURN MEASURES

$$\text{Return on equity (ROE)} = \frac{\text{Net income}}{\text{Average stockholders' equity}}$$

$$\text{Earnings before interest (EBI)} = \text{Net income} + \text{Interest} \times (1 - \text{Statutory tax rate})$$

$$\text{Return on assets (ROA)} = \frac{\text{Earnings before interest (EBI)}}{\text{Average total assets}}$$

$$\text{Return on financial leverage (ROFL)} = \text{ROE} - \text{ROA}$$

PROFITABILITY RATIOS

$$\text{Profit margin (PM)} = \frac{\text{EBI}}{\text{Sales revenue}}$$

$$\text{Gross profit margin (GPM)} = \frac{\text{Sales revenue} - \text{Cost of goods sold}}{\text{Sales revenue}}$$

$$\text{Expense-to-sales (ETS)} = \frac{\text{Individual expense items}}{\text{Sales revenue}}$$

TURNOVER RATIOS

$$\text{Asset turnover (AT)} = \frac{\text{Sales revenue}}{\text{Average total assets}}$$

$$\text{Accounts receivable turnover (ART)} = \frac{\text{Sales revenue}}{\text{Average accounts receivable}}$$

$$\text{Inventory turnover (INVT)} = \frac{\text{Cost of goods sold}}{\text{Average inventory}}$$

$$\text{Property, plant and equipment turnover (PPET)} = \frac{\text{Sales revenue}}{\text{Average PP\&E}}$$

LIQUIDITY RATIOS

$$\text{Current ratio (CR)} = \frac{\text{Current assets}}{\text{Current liabilities}}$$

$$\text{Quick ratio (QR)} = \frac{\text{Cash} + \text{ST investments} + \text{Receivables}}{\text{Current liabilities}}$$

$$\text{Operating cash flow to current liabilities (OCFCL)} = \frac{\text{Operating cash flow}}{\text{Average current liabilities}}$$

SOLVENCY RATIOS

$$\text{Times interest earned (TIE)} = \frac{\text{Earnings before interest expense and taxes (EBIT)}}{\text{Interest expense}}$$

$$\text{Debt-to-equity (DE)} = \frac{\text{Total liabilities}}{\text{Total stockholders' equity}}$$

KEY TERMS

Accounts receivable turnover (ART) (p. 217)

Asset turnover (AT) (p. 214)

Capacity costs (p. 213)

Common-size financial statements (p. 208)

Covenants (p. 220)

Current ratio (p. 221)

Debt-to-equity ratio (p. 222)

Default risk (p. 220)

Dividend payout ratio (p. 229)

Earnings before interest (EBI) (p. 212)

Effective tax rate (p. 229)

Expense-to-sales (ETS) (p. 217)

Financial leverage (p. 212)

Financial statement analysis (p. 206)

Forecast error (p. 232)

Gross profit margin (GPM) (p. 216)

Horizontal analysis (p. 209)

Inventory turnover (INVT) (p. 217)

Liquidity (p. 220)

Liquidity analysis (p. 220)

Marginal tax rate (p. 226)

Net interest rate (NIR) (p. 232)

Net operating assets (NOA) (p. 226)

Net operating asset turnover (NOAT) (p. 227)

Net operating profit after taxes (NOPAT) (p. 226)

Net operating profit margin (NOPM) (p. 227)

Operating cash flow to current liabilities (OCFCL) (p. 221)

Profit margin (PM) (p. 213)

Pro forma financial statements (p. 227)

Property, plant and equipment turnover (PPET) (p. 217)

Quick ratio (p. 221)

Return on assets (ROA) (p. 211)

Return on equity (ROE) (p. 211)

Return on financial leverage (ROFL) (p. 212)

Return on net operating assets (RNOA) (p. 225)

Sensitivity analysis (p. 230)

Solvency (p. 222)

Solvency analysis (p. 220)

Spread (p. 233)

Times interest earned (TIE) (p. 223)

Vertical analysis (p. 208)

Working capital (p. 221)

MULTIPLE CHOICE QUESTIONS

1. Which of the following ratios would not be affected by an increase in cost of goods sold?
   a. ROA
   b. INVT
   c. Quick ratio
   d. PM

2. A company has the following values: PM = 0.07; EBI = $1,885; Average total assets = $37,400. AT equals
   a. 0.05.
   b. 0.72.
   c. 0.36.
   d. AT is not determinable because its sales are not reported.

3. A company's current ratio is 2 and its quick ratio is 1. What can be said about the sum of the company's cash + marketable securities + accounts receivable?
   a. The sum exceeds the current liabilities.
   b. The sum is equal to the sum of the current liabilities.
   c. The sum is equal to 1/2 of the total current liabilities.
   d. None of the above is correct.

4. A company's interest expense is $500,000 and its net income is $14 million. If the company's effective tax rate is 30%, what is the company's times interest earned (TIE) ratio?
   a. 90
   b. 41
   c. 32
   d. 16

5. If a company's ROFL is negative, which of the following is *not* true?
   a. ROA > ROE
   b. The DE ratio is negative
   c. ROA < net interest rate
   d. The company likely has a low TIE ratio

GUIDANCE ANSWERS . . . YOU MAKE THE CALL

You are the Entrepreneur Your company is performing substantially better than its competitors. Namely, your ROA of 16% is markedly superior to competitors' ROA of 10%. However, ROA disaggregation shows that this is mainly attributed to your AT of 0.89 versus competitors' AT of 0.59. Your PM of 18% is essentially identical to competitors' PM of 17%. Accordingly, you will want to maintain your AT as further improvements are probably difficult to achieve. Importantly, you are likely to achieve the greatest benefit with efforts at improving your PM of 18%, which is only marginally better than the industry norm of 17%.

Superscript [A(B, C)] denotes assignments based on Appendix 5A (5B, 5C).

DISCUSSION QUESTIONS

Q5-1. Explain in general terms the concept of return on investment. Why is this concept important in the analysis of financial performance?

Q5-2. (a) Explain how an increase in financial leverage can increase a company's ROE. (b) Given the potentially positive relation between financial leverage and ROE, why don't we see companies with 100% financial leverage (entirely nonowner financed)?

Q5-3. Gross profit margin (Gross profit/Sales) is an important determinant of profit margin. Identify two factors that can cause gross profit margin to decline. Is a reduction in the gross profit margin always bad news? Explain.

Q5-4. Explain how a reduction in operating expenses as a percentage of sales can produce a short-term gain at the cost of long-term performance.

Q5-5. Describe the concept of asset turnover. What does the concept mean and why is it so important to understanding and interpreting financial performance?

Q5-6. Explain what it means when a company's ROE exceeds its ROA.

Q5-7. What are common-size financial statements? What role do they play in financial statement analysis?

Q5-8. How does a firm go about increasing its AT ratio? What strategies are likely to be most effective?

Q5-9.[A] What is meant by the term "net" in net operating assets (NOA)?

Q5-10. Why is it important to disaggregate ROA into profit margin (PM) and asset turnover (AT)?

Q5-11. What insights do we gain from the graphical relation between profit margin and asset turnover?

Q5-12. Explain the concept of liquidity and why it is crucial to company survival.

Q5-13. Identify at least two factors that limit the usefulness of ratio analysis.

Assignments with the Web**Assign**. logo in the margin are available in WebAssign.
See the Preface of the book for details.

MINI EXERCISES

LO2, LO3 **M5-14** **Return on Investment, DuPont Analysis and Financial Leverage**
The following table presents selected 2009 financial information for Sunder Company.

<table>
<tr><td colspan="2" align="center">SUNDER COMPANY
Selected 2009 Financial Data</td></tr>
<tr><td colspan="2">Balance Sheet:</td></tr>
<tr><td>Average total assets</td><td>$1,000,000</td></tr>
<tr><td>Average total liabilities</td><td>500,000</td></tr>
<tr><td>Average stockholders' equity</td><td>500,000</td></tr>
<tr><td colspan="2">Income statement:</td></tr>
<tr><td>Sales revenue</td><td>$1,000,000</td></tr>
<tr><td>Earnings before interest (net of tax)</td><td>20,000</td></tr>
<tr><td>Interest expense (net of tax)</td><td>15,000</td></tr>
<tr><td>Net income</td><td>5,000</td></tr>
</table>

a. Compute Sunder's ROE, ROA and ROFL for 2009.

b. Use the DuPont analysis described in the Business Insight on page 216 to disaggregate ROE.

c. How did the use of financial leverage affect Sunder's ROE in 2009? Explain.

M5-15. Common-Size Balance Sheets

Following is the balance sheet for **Target Corporation**. Prepare Target's common-size balance sheets as of January 31, 2009, and February 2, 2008.

($ millions)	January 31, 2009	February 2, 2008
Assets		
Cash and cash equivalents	$ 864	$ 2,450
Accounts receivable, net	8,084	8,054
Inventory	6,705	6,780
Other current assets	1,835	1,622
Total current assets	17,488	18,906
Property and equipment, net	25,756	24,095
Other noncurrent assets	862	1,559
Total assets	$44,106	$44,560
Liabilities and shareholders' investment		
Accounts payable	$ 6,337	$ 6,721
Accrued liabilities	2,913	3,097
Current portion of long-term debt and notes payable	1,262	1,964
Total current liabilities	10,512	11,782
Long-term debt	17,490	15,126
Deferred income taxes	455	470
Other noncurrent liabilities	1,937	1,875
Total shareholders' investment	13,712	15,307
Total liabilities and shareholders' investment	$44,106	$44,560

M5-16. Common-Size Income Statements

Following is the income statement for **Target Corporation**. Prepare Target's common-size income statement for the fiscal year ended January 31, 2009.

($ millions)	Fiscal year ended January 31, 2009
Sales	$62,884
Net credit card revenues	2,064
Total revenues	64,948
Cost of sales	44,157
Selling, general and administrative expenses	12,954
Credit card expenses	1,609
Depreciation and amortization	1,826
Earnings before interest expense and income taxes	4,402
Net interest expense	866
Earnings before income taxes	3,536
Provision for income taxes	1,322
Net earnings	$ 2,214

LO2, LO3

Web**Assign**.

TARGET
CORPORATION
NYSE :: TGT

M5-17. Compute ROA, Profit Margin, and Asset Turnover

Refer to the financial information for **Target Corporation**, presented in M5-15 and M5-16.

a. Compute its 2009 return on assets (ROA).

b. Disaggregate ROA into profit margin (PM) and net operating asset turnover (AT). Confirm that $ROA = PM \times AT$.

LO4

WebWeb**Assign**.

TARGET
CORPORATION
NYSE :: TGT

M5-18. Analysis and Interpretation of Liquidity and Solvency

Refer to the financial information of **Target Corporation (TGT)** in M5-15 and M5-16 to answer the following.

a. Compute Target's current ratio and quick ratio for 2009 and 2008. Comment on any observed trends.

b. Compute Target's times interest earned for 2009 and its debt-to-equity ratios for 2009 and 2008. Comment on any trends observed.

c. Summarize your findings in a conclusion about the company's liquidity and solvency. Do you have any concerns about Target's ability to meet its debt obligations?

LO1

3M COMPANY
NYSE :: MMM

M5-19. Common-Size Balance Sheets

Following is the balance sheet for **3M Company**. Prepare common-size balance sheets for 2008 and 2007.

3M COMPANY AND SUBSIDIARIES		
December 31 ($ millions, except per share amount)	2008	2007
Assets		
Cash and cash equivalents	$ 2,222	$ 2,475
Accounts receivable	3,195	3,362
Total inventories	3,013	2,852
Other current assets	1,168	1,149
Total current assets	9,598	9,838
Investments	638	778
Property, plant and equipment—net	6,886	6,582
Goodwill	5,753	4,589
Intangible assets—net	1,398	801
Prepaid pension and postretirement benefits	36	1,378
Other assets	1,238	728
Total assets	$25,547	$24,694
Liabilities and Stockholders' Equity		
Short-term borrowings and current portion of long-term debt	$ 1,552	$ 901
Accounts payable	1,301	1,505
Accrued payroll	644	580
Accrued income taxes	350	543
Other current liabilities	1,992	1,833
Total current liabilities	5,839	5,362
Long-term debt	5,166	4,019
Other liabilities	4,663	3,566
Total liabilities	15,668	12,947
Stockholders' equity—net	9,879	11,747
Total liabilities and stockholders' equity	$25,547	$24,694

LO1

3M COMPANY
NYSE :: MMM

M5-20. Common-Size Income Statements

Following is the income statement for **3M Company**. Prepare common-size income statements for 2008 and 2007.

3M COMPANY AND SUBSIDIARIES		
Year ended December 31 ($ millions)	2008	2007
Net sales	$25,269	$24,462
Operating expenses		
Cost of sales	13,379	12,735
Selling, general and administrative expenses	5,245	5,015
Research, development and related expenses	1,404	1,368
(Gain)/loss on sale of businesses	23	(849)
Total	20,051	18,269
Operating income	5,218	6,193
Interest expense and income		
Interest expense	215	210
Interest income	(105)	(132)
Total	110	78
Income before income taxes and minority interest	5,108	6,115
Provision for income taxes	1,588	1,964
Minority interest	60	55
Net income	$ 3,460	$ 4,096

M5-21. Compute ROA, Profit Margin, and Asset Turnover

Refer to the balance sheet and income statement information for **3M Company**, presented in M5-19 and M5-20.

a. Compute 3M's 2008 return on assets (ROA).

b. Disaggregate ROA into profit margin (PM) and asset turnover (AT). Confirm that ROA = PM × AT.

LO2, LO3
3M COMPANY
NYSE :: MMM

M5-22. Compute ROA, Profit Margin and Asset Turnover for Competitors

Selected balance sheet and income statement information from **Abercrombie & Fitch Co.** and **TJX Companies**, clothing retailers in the high-end and value-priced segments, respectively, follows.

LO2, LO3
ABERCROMBIE & FITCH CO.
NYSE :: ANF
TJX COMPANIES
NYSE :: TJX

Company ($ millions)	2008 Sales	2008 Earnings Before Interest	2008 Total Assets	2007 Total Assets
Abercrombie & Fitch	$ 3,540.3	$272.3	$2,848.1	$2,567.6
TJX Companies	18,999.5	889.9	6,178.2	6,599.9

a. Compute the 2008 return on assets (ROA) for both companies.

b. Disaggregate ROA into profit margin (PM) and asset turnover (AT) for each company. Confirm that ROA = PM × AT.

c. Discuss differences observed with respect to PM and AT and interpret these differences in light of each company's business model.

M5-23. Compute and Interpret Liquidity and Solvency Ratios

Selected balance sheet and income statement information from **Verizon Communications, Inc.**, follows.

LO4
VERIZON COMMUNICATIONS, INC.
NYSE :: VZ

($ millions)	2008	2007
Current assets	$ 26,075	$ 18,698
Current liabilities	25,906	24,741
Total liabilities	160,646	136,378
Equity	41,706	50,581
Earnings before interest and taxes	11,578	11,321
Interest expense	1,819	1,829
Net cash flow from operating activities	26,620	25,739

a. Compute the current ratio for each year and discuss any trend in liquidity. What additional information about the numbers used to calculate this ratio might be useful in helping us assess liquidity? Explain.

b. Compute times interest earned, the debt-to-equity, and the operating cash flow to total liabilities ratios for each year and discuss any trends for each. (The median total-liabilities-to-equity ratio for the telecommunications industry is 1.13.) Do you have any concerns about the extent of Verizon's financial leverage and the company's ability to meet interest obligations? Explain.

c. Verizon's capital expenditures are expected to increase substantially as it seeks to respond to competitive pressures to upgrade the quality of its communication infrastructure. Assess Verizon's liquidity and solvency in light of this strategic direction.

LO2, LO3

WebAssign.

THE PROCTER & GAMBLE COMPANY
NYSE :: PG

MCDONALD'S CORPORATION
NYSE :: MCD

VALERO ENERGY COPORATION
NYSE :: VLO

M5-24. Computing Turnover Ratios for Companies in Different Industries

Selected data from the 2008 financial statements of **The Procter & Gamble Company**, **McDonald's Corporation**, and **Valero Energy Corporation** are presented below:

($ millions)	Procter & Gamble	McDonald's	Valero Energy
Sales	$ 79,029	$23,522.4	$119,114
Cost of sales	38,898	5,586.1	107,429
Average receivables	6,299	992.5	5,294
Average inventories	7,648	118.4	4,355
Average PP&E	20,051	20,619.6	22,387
Average total assets	139,413	28,926.6	38,570

a. Compute the asset turnover (AT) ratio for each company.

b. Compute the accounts receivable turnover (ART), inventory turnover (INVT), and PP&E turnover (PPET) for each company.

c. Discuss any differences across these three companies in the turnover ratios computed in *a* and *b*.

EXERCISES

LO2, LO3

TARGET CORPORATION
NYSE :: TGT

WAL-MART STORES, INC.
NYSE :: WMT

E5-25. Compute and Interpret ROA, Profit Margin, and Asset Turnover of Competitors

Selected balance sheet and income statement information for department store retailers **Target Corporation** and **Wal-Mart Stores, Inc.**, follows.

($ millions)	Sales Revenue	Interest Expense	Net Income	Average Total Assets
Target	$ 62,884	$ 866	$ 2,214	$ 44,333
Wal-Mart	405,607	1,900	13,400	163,472

a. Compute the return on assets (ROA) for each company.

b. Disaggregate ROA into profit margin (PM) and asset turnover (AT) for each company.

c. Discuss any differences in these ratios for each company. Your interpretation should reflect the distinct business strategies of each company.

LO2, LO3

DELL INC.
NASDAQ :: DELL

APPLE INC.
NASDAQ :: AAPL

E5-26. Compute, Disaggregate, and Interpret Return on Investment of Competitors

Selected balance sheet and income statement information for the computer retailers, **Dell Inc.** and **Apple Inc.** follows.

($ millions)	Dell, Inc.	Apple, Inc.
Sales Revenue—2009	$61,101	$36,537
Interest Expense—2009	74	0
Net Income—2009	2,478	5,704
Total Assets—2009	26,500	53,851
Total Assets—2008	27,561	39,572
Stockholders' Equity—2009	4,271	27,832
Stockholders' Equity—2008	3,735	21,030

a. Compute the 2009 return on assets (ROA) for each company.

b. Disaggregate ROA into profit margin (PM) and asset turnover (AT) for each company.

c. Compute the 2009 return on equity (ROE) and return on financial leverage (ROFL) for each company.

d. Discuss any differences in these ratios for each company. Your interpretation should reflect the distinct business strategies of each company.

E5-27. Compute, Disaggregate, and Interpret RNOA of Competitors

Selected balance sheet and income statement information for the drug retailers **CVS Caremark Corporation** and **Walgreen Co.** follows.

LO2, LO3

CVS CAREMARK CORPORATION
NYSE :: CVS

WALGREEN CO.
NYSE :: WAG

($ millions)	CVS Caremark	Walgreen
Sales Revenue—2008	$87,471.9	$63,335
Interest Expense—2008	509.5	83
Net Income—2008	3,212.1	2,006
Total Assets—2008	60,959.9	25,142
Total Assets—2007	54,721.9	22,410
Stockholders' Equity—2008	34,574.4	14,376
Stockholders' Equity—2007	31,321.9	12,869

a. Compute the 2008 return on assets (ROA) for each company.

b. Disaggregate ROA into profit margin (PM) and asset turnover (AT) for each company.

c. Compute the 2008 return on equity (ROE) and return on financial leverage (ROFL) for each company.

d. Discuss any differences in these ratios for each company. Identify the factor(s) that drives the differences in ROA observed from your analyses in parts *a* through *c*.

E5-28. Compute, Disaggregate, and Interpret ROE

Selected fiscal year balance sheet and income statement information for the computer chip maker, **Intel Corporation**, follows ($ millions).

LO2, LO3

INTEL CORPORATION
NASDAQ :: INTC

Balance sheets ($ millions)	2008	2007	2006
Total assets	$50,715	$55,651	$48,368
Total liabilities	11,627	12,889	11,616
Total shareholders' equity	39,088	42,762	36,752

Income statements	2008	2007	2006
Sales revenue	$37,586	$38,334	$35,382
Earnings before interest and income taxes	8,174	9,959	8,270
Interest expense, net	488	793	1,202
Earnings before income taxes	7,686	9,166	7,068
Income tax expense	2,394	2,190	2,024
Net earnings	$ 5,292	$ 6,976	$ 5,044

a. Calculate Intel's return on equity (ROE) for fiscal years 2008 and 2007.

b. Calculate Intel's return on assets (ROA) and return on financial leverage (ROFL) for each year. Is financial leverage working to the advantage of Intel's shareholders?

c. Use the DuPont formulation in the Business Insight on page 216 to analyze the variations in Intel's ROE over this period. How does this analysis differ from your answers to *a* and *b* above?

E5-29. Return on Investment, Financial Leverage, and DuPont Analysis

The following tables provide information from the recent annual reports of **Nordstrom, Inc.** (Nordstrom's fiscal year ends on the Saturday closest to January 31st of the following calendar year, so fiscal year 2008 ended on January 31, 2009.)

LO2, LO3

NORDSTROM, INC.
NYSE :: JWN

Balance sheets ($ millions)	Jan. 31, 2009	Feb. 2, 2008	Feb. 3, 2007	Jan. 28, 2006
Total assets	$5,661	$5,600	$4,822	$4,921
Total liabilities	4,451	4,485	2,653	2,828
Total shareholders' equity	1,210	1,115	2,169	2,093

Income statements ($ millions) 52 weeks ended	Jan. 31, 2009	Feb. 2, 2008	Feb. 3, 2007
Sales revenue	$8,272	$8,828	$8,561
Earnings before interest and income taxes	779	1,247	1,149
Interest expense, net	131	74	43
Earnings before income taxes	648	1,173	1,106
Income tax expense	247	458	428
Net earnings	$ 401	$ 715	$ 678

a. Calculate Nordstrom's return on equity (ROE) for fiscal years 2008, 2007, and 2006.

b. Calculate Nordstrom's return on assets (ROA) and return on financial leverage (ROFL) for each year. Is financial leverage working to the advantage of Nordstrom's shareholders?

c. Nordstrom's fiscal year is normally 52 weeks long, but, occasionally, the fiscal year is 53 weeks long. Fiscal year 2007 had 53 weeks, while 2006 and 2008 had 52 weeks each. How would this difference affect your interpretation of ROE and ROA?

d. Use the DuPont formulation in the Business Insight on page 216 to analyze the variations in Nordstrom's ROE over this period. How does this analysis differ from your answers to a and b above?

LO2, LO3 **E5-30.** **Compute, Disaggregate and Interpret ROE and ROA**

STAPLES, INC.
NASDAQ :: SPLS

Selected balance sheet and income statement information from **Staples, Inc.**, follows ($ millions).

Sales 2008	Interest Expense 2008	Net Income 2008	Total Assets 2008	Total Assets 2007	Stockholders' Equity 2008	Stockholders' Equity 2007
$23,083.8	$149.8	$805.2	$13,006.0	$9,036.3	$5,564.2	$5,718.0

a. Compute the 2008 return on equity (ROE), return on assets (ROA), and return on financial leverage (ROFL).

b. Disaggregate ROA into profit margin (PM) and asset turnover (AT).

c. What inferences do we draw from PM compared to AT?

LO2, LO3 **E5-31.** **Compute, Disaggregate and Interpret ROE and ROA**

INTUIT INC.
NASDAQ :: INTU

Selected balance sheet and income statement information from the software company, **Intuit Inc.**, follows ($ millions).

Sales 2009	Interest Expense 2009	Net Income 2009	Total Assets 2009	Total Assets 2008	Stockholders' Equity 2009	Stockholders' Equity 2008
$3,182.5	$51.2	$447.0	$4,826.3	$4,666.6	$2,555.8	$2,073.0

a. Compute the 2009 return on equity (ROE), return on assets (ROA), and return on financial leverage (ROFL).

b. Disaggregate the ROA from part a into profit margin (PM) and asset turnover (AT).

c. What can we learn by comparing PM to AT? What explanation can we offer for the relation between ROE and ROA observed and for Intuit's use of financial leverage?

LO4 **E5-32.** **Compute and Interpret Liquidity and Solvency Ratios**

COMCAST
CORPORATION
NASDAQ :: CMCSA

Selected balance sheet and income statement information from **Comcast Corporation** for 2006 through 2008 follows ($ millions).

	Total Current Assets	Total Current Liabilities	Pretax Income	Interest Expense	Total Liabilities	Stockholders' Equity
2006	$5,202	$7,191	$3,594	$2,064	$69,238	$41,167
2007	3,667	7,952	4,349	2,289	72,077	41,340
2008	3,716	8,939	4,058	2,439	72,567	40,450

a. Compute the current ratio for each year and discuss any trend in liquidity. Do you believe the company is sufficiently liquid? Explain. What additional information about the accounting numbers comprising this ratio might be useful in helping you assess liquidity? Explain.

b. Compute times interest earned and the debt-to-equity ratio for each year and discuss any trends for each.

   c. What is your overall assessment of the company's liquidity and solvency from the analyses in (*a*) and (*b*)? Explain.

E5-33. **Compute and Interpret Liquidity and Solvency Ratios**   **LO4**

Selected balance sheet and income statement information from **Siemens, AG**, for 2006 through 2008 follows (€ millions).   **SIEMENS AG** OTC :: SMAWF

	Total Current Assets	Total Current Liabilities	Cash Flow from Operations	Pretax Income	Interest Expense	Total Liabilities	Stockholders' Equity
2006	€50,014	€38,964	€5,003	€3,418	€525	€61,633	€25,895
2007	47,932	43,894	9,822	5,101	897	61,928	29,627
2008	43,242	42,451	9,281	2,874	834	67,083	27,380

   a. Compute the current ratio for each year and discuss any trend in liquidity. Also compute the operating cash flow to current liabilities (OCFCL) ratio for each year. (In 2005, current liabilities totaled €39,833 million.) Do you believe the company is sufficiently liquid? Explain. What additional information about the accounting numbers comprising this ratio might be useful in helping you assess liquidity? Explain.

   b. Compute times interest earned and the debt-to-equity ratio for each year and discuss any trends for each.

   c. What is your overall assessment of the company's liquidity and solvency from the analyses in (*a*) and (*b*)? Explain.

E5-34. **Compute, Disaggregate and Interpret ROE and ROA**   **LO2, LO3**

Income statements for **The Gap, Inc.**, follow, along with selected balance sheet information ($ millions).   **THE GAP, INC.** NYSE :: GPS

THE GAP, INC.
Consolidated Statement of Earnings

Fiscal year ended	Jan. 31, 2009	Feb. 2, 2008
Net sales	$14,526	$15,763
Cost of goods sold and occupancy expenses	9,079	10,071
Gross profit	5,447	5,692
Operating expenses	3,899	4,377
Operating income	1,548	1,315
Interest income	37	117
Interest expense	1	26
Earnings from continuing operations before income taxes	1,584	1,406
Income taxes	617	539
Earnings from continuing operations	967	867
Loss from discontinued operations, net of income taxes	—	34
Net earnings	$ 967	$ 833

THE GAP, INC.
Selected Balance Sheet Data

	Jan. 31, 2009	Feb. 2, 2008
Merchandise inventories	$1,506	$1,575
Total assets	7,564	7,838
Total stockholders' equity	4,387	4,274

   a. Compute the return on equity (ROE), return on assets (ROA), and return on financial leverage (ROFL) for the fiscal year ended January 31, 2009.

   b. Disaggregate ROA into profit margin (PM) and asset turnover (AT).

   c. Compute the gross profit margin (GPM) and inventory turnover (INVT) ratios for the fiscal year ended January 31, 2009.

   d. Assess the Gap's performance. What are the most important drivers of the Gap's success?

LO1, LO6
THE GAP, INC.
NYSE :: GPS

E5-35.[B] **Common-Size and Pro Forma Income Statements**

Refer to the income statements for **The Gap, Inc.**, presented in E5-34.

a. Prepare common-size income statements for fiscal years ended January 31, 2009, and February 2, 2008. What are the most significant changes between these two income statements?

b. Prepare a pro forma income statement for the fiscal year ended January 30, 2010, based on the following assumptions:

- Net sales total $15,000 million.
- Cost of goods sold and occupancy expenses are 63% of sales.
- Operating expenses total 27% of sales.
- Interest income and interest expense are unchanged from the 2009 amounts.
- There are no discontinued operations.
- The Gap's effective tax rate is 38%.

c. Given the Gap's business strategy, what are the factors that ultimately determine the accuracy of the pro forma statement prepared in *b*?

PROBLEMS

LO2, LO3
NIKE, INC.
NYSE :: NKE

ADIDAS GROUP, AG
OTC :: ADDDF

P5-36. **Analysis and Interpretation of Return on Investment for Competitors**

Balance sheets and income statements for **Nike, Inc.**, and **Adidas Group** follow. Refer to these financial statements to answer the requirements.

	NIKE, INC. Balance Sheets ($ millions)		ADIDAS GROUP, AG Balance Sheets (€ millions)	
	May 31,		December 31,	
	2009	**2008**	**2008**	**2007**
Assets:				
Cash and cash equivalents..................	$ 2,291.1	$ 2,133.9	€ 244	€ 295
Short-term investments	1,164.0	642.2	141	86
Accounts receivable	2,883.9	2,795.3	1,624	1,459
Inventories...............................	2,357.0	2,438.4	1,995	1,629
Other current assets	1,038.0	829.5	930	669
Total current assets.......................	9,734.0	8,839.3	4,934	4,138
Property, plant and equipment, net	1,957.7	1,891.1	886	702
Intangible assets and goodwill..............	660.9	1,191.9	3,093	2,921
Long-term investments.....................	—	—	96	103
Other noncurrent assets	897.0	520.4	524	461
Total assets..............................	$13,249.6	$12,442.7	€9,533	€8,325
Liabilities and shareholders' equity:				
Short-term debt..........................	$ 374.9	$ 184.0	€ 797	€ 186
Accounts payable	1,031.9	1,287.6	1,218	849
Accrued liabilities	1,783.9	1,761.9	1,008	1,025
Income taxes payable.....................	86.3	88.0	321	285
Other current liabilities	—	—	301	270
Total current liabilities.....................	3,277.0	3,321.5	3,645	2,615
Long-term debt	437.2	441.1	1,776	1,960
Other noncurrent liabilities	842.3	854.8	712	716
Total liabilities	4,556.5	4,617.4	6,133	5,291
Shareholders' equity......................	8,693.1	7,825.3	3,400	3,034
Total liabilities and shareholders' equity	$13,249.6	$12,442.7	€9,533	€8,325

	NIKE, INC. Income Sheets ($ millions)		ADIDAS GROUP, AG Income Sheets (€ millions)	
	Year ended May 31,		Year ended December 31,	
	2009	**2008**	**2008**	**2007**
Net sales	$19,176.1	$18,627.0	€10,799	€10,299
Cost of sales	10,571.7	10,239.6	5,543	5,417
Gross profit	8,604.4	8,387.4	5,256	4,882
Operating expenses, net...............	6,149.6	5,953.7	4,186	3,933
Operating profit......................	2,454.8	2,433.7	1,070	949
Interest and other income..............	144.7	113.3	37	36
Interest expense	46.7	44.1	203	170
Restructuring and impairment charges	596.3	–	–	–
Income before income taxes	1,956.5	2,502.9	904	815
Income taxes........................	469.8	619.5	260	260
Net income..........................	$ 1,486.7	$ 1,883.4	€ 644	€ 555

Required

a. Compute return on equity (ROE), return on assets (ROA), and return on financial leverage (ROFL) for Nike in 2009 and for Adidas in 2008.

b. Disaggregate the ROA's computed into profit margin (PM) and asset turnover (AT) components. Which of these factors drives ROA for each company?

c. Compute the gross profit margin (GPM) and operating expense-to-sales ratios for each company. How do these companies' profitability measures compare?

d. Compute the accounts receivable turnover (ART), inventory turnover (INVT), and property, plant and equipment turnover (PPET) for each company. How do these companies' turnover measures compare?

e. Nike's fiscal year ends on May 31, 2009, while Adidas's fiscal year ends on December 31, 2008 (a difference of five months). How does this difference affect your analysis of ROE and ROA for these two companies?

f. Nike's financial statements are prepared in accordance with U.S. GAAP, while Adidas, a German company, follows IFRS rules. How does this difference in financial reporting standards affect your comparison of these companies' financial statements?

P5-37. Analysis and Interpretation of Liquidity and Solvency for Competitors

Refer to the financial statements of **Nike** and **Adidas** presented in P5-36.

LO4

NIKE, INC.
NYSE :: NKE

ADIDAS GROUP, AG
OTC :: ADDDF

Required

a. Compute each company's current ratio and quick ratio for each year. Comment on any changes that you observe.

b. Compute each company's times interest earned ratio and debt-to-equity ratio for each year. Comment on any observed changes.

c. Compare these two companies on the basis of liquidity and solvency. Do you have any concerns about either company's ability to meet its debt obligations?

P5-38. Analysis and Interpretation of Return on Investment for Competitors

Balance sheets and income statements for **The Home Depot, Inc.**, and **Lowe's Companies, Inc.**, follow. Refer to these financial statements to answer the requirements.

LO2, LO3

THE HOME DEPOT, INC.
NYSE :: HD

LOWE'S COMPANIES, INC.
NYSE :: LOW

($ millions)	HOME DEPOT, INC Balance Sheets		LOWE'S COMPANIES Balance Sheets	
	2008	2007	2008	2007
Assets:				
Cash and cash equivalents	$ 519	$ 445	$ 245	$ 281
Short-term investments	6	12	416	249
Accounts receivable	972	1,259	–	–
Inventories	10,673	11,731	8,209	7,611
Other current assets	1,192	1,227	381	545
Total current assets	13,362	14,674	9,251	8,686
Property, plant and equipment, net	26,234	27,476	22,722	21,361
Intangible assets and goodwill	1,134	1,209	–	–
Long-term investments	36	342	253	509
Other noncurrent assets	398	623	460	313
Total assets	$41,164	$44,324	$32,686	$30,869
Liabilities and shareholders' equity:				
Short-term debt	$ 1,767	$ 2,047	$ 1,021	$ 1,104
Accounts payable	4,822	5,732	4,109	3,713
Accrued liabilities	2,773	2,948	1,185	1,138
Deferred revenue	1,165	1,474	674	717
Income taxes payable	289	60	–	–
Other current liabilities	337	445	1,033	1,079
Total current liabilities	11,153	12,706	8,022	7,751
Long-term debt	9,667	11,383	5,039	5,576
Deferred income taxes	369	688	660	670
Other noncurrent liabilities	2,198	1,833	910	774
Total liabilities	23,387	26,610	14,631	14,771
Shareholders' equity	17,777	17,714	18,055	16,098
Total liabilities and shareholders' equity	$41,164	$44,324	$32,686	$30,869

($ millions)	HOME DEPOT, INC. Income Statements		LOWE'S COMPANIES Income Statements	
	2008	2007	2008	2007
Net sales	$71,288	$77,349	$48,230	$48,283
Cost of sales	47,298	51,352	31,729	31,556
Gross profit	23,990	25,997	16,501	16,727
Operating expenses	19,631	18,755	12,715	12,022
Operating income	4,359	7,242	3,786	4,705
Investment income and other	(145)	74	–	–
Interest expense	(624)	(696)	(280)	(194)
Income before income taxes	3,590	6,620	3,506	4,511
Income taxes	1,278	2,410	1,311	1,702
Income before discontinued operations	2,312	4,210		
Discontinued operations	(52)	185		
Net income	$ 2,260	$ 4,395	$ 2,195	$ 2,809

Required

a. Compute return on equity (ROE), return on assets (ROA), and return on financial leverage (ROFL) for each company in 2008.

b. Disaggregate the ROA's computed into profit margin (PM) and asset turnover (AT) components. Which of these factors drives ROA for each company?

c. Compute the gross profit margin (GPM) and operating expense-to-sales ratios for each company. How do these companies' profitability measures compare?

   d.   Compute the accounts receivable turnover (ART), inventory turnover (INVT), and property, plant and equipment turnover (PPET) for each company. How do these companies' turnover measures compare?

   e.   Compare and evaluate these competitors' performance in 2008.

P5-39. **Analysis and Interpretation of Liquidity and Solvency for Competitors**   **LO4**

Refer to the financial statements of **Home Depot** and **Lowe's** presented in P5-38.

HOME DEPOT, INC.
NYSE :: HD

LOWE'S COMPANIES, INC.
NYSE :: LOW

Required

   a.   Compute each company's current ratio and quick ratio for each year. Comment on any changes that you observe.

   b.   Compute each company's times interest earned ratio and debt-to-equity ratio for each year. Comment on any observed changes.

   c.   Compare these two companies on the basis of liquidity and solvency. Do you have any concerns about either company's ability to meet its debt obligations?

P5-40.[A] **Analysis of the Effect of Operations on ROE**   **LO5**

Refer to the financial statements of **Home Depot** and **Lowe's** presented in P5-38.

HOME DEPOT, INC.
NYSE :: HD

LOWE'S COMPANIES, INC.
NYSE :: LOW

Required

   a.   Compute each company's net operating profit after taxes (NOPAT) for 2008 and net operating assets (NOA) for 2008 and 2007. For purposes of this requirement, classify Home Depot's discontinued operations as nonoperating. Also, classify other assets and other liabilities (both current and noncurrent) as operating assets and liabilities in the balance sheet.

   b.   Compute each company's return on net operating assets (RNOA) for 2008.

   c.   Compute the 2008 net operating profit margin (NOPM) and net operating asset turnover (NOAT) for each company.

   d.   Compare operating returns for these two companies. How does RNOA compare to ROA? What insights are gained by focusing on operating returns?

P5-41. **Analysis and Interpretation of Profitability**   **LO2, LO3**

Balance sheets and income statements for **United Parcel Service, Inc., (UPS)** follow. Refer to these financial statements to answer the following requirements.

UNITED PARCEL SERVICE, INC.

UNITED PARCEL SERVICE, INC.
Income Statement

Years Ended December 31 ($ millions)	2008	2007
Revenue	$51,486	$49,692
Operating expenses		
Compensation and benefits	26,063	31,745
Other	20,041	17,369
	46,104	49,114
Operating profit	5,382	578
Other income and (expense)		
Investment income	75	99
Interest expense	(442)	(246)
	(367)	(147)
Income before income taxes	5,015	431
Income taxes	2,012	49
Net income	$ 3,003	$ 382

UNITED PARCEL SERVICE, INC.
Balance Sheet

December 31 ($ millions)	2008	2007
Assets		
Cash & cash equivalents	$ 507	$ 2,027
Marketable securities & short-term investments	542	577
Accounts receivable, net	5,547	6,084
Finance receivables, net	480	468
Income tax receivable	167	1,256
Deferred income taxes	494	606
Other current assets	1,108	742
Total current assets	8,845	11,760
Property, plant & equipment—net	18,265	17,663
Pension and postretirement benefit assets	10	4,421
Goodwill	1,986	2,577
Intangible assets, net	511	628
Other assets	2,262	1,993
Total assets	$31,879	$39,042
Liabilities and shareowners' equity		
Current maturities of long-term debt and commercial paper	$ 2,074	$ 3,512
Accounts payable	1,855	1,819
Accrued wages & withholdings	1,436	1,414
Dividends payable	—	440
Other current liabilities	2,452	2,655
Total current liabilities	7,817	9,840
Long-term debt	7,797	7,506
Accumulated postretirement benefit obligation	6,323	4,438
Deferred taxes & other liabilities	3,162	5,075
Total liabilities	25,099	26,859
Shareowners' equity	6,780	12,183
Total liabilities and shareowners' equity	$31,879	$39,042

Required

a. Compute ROA and disaggregate it into profit margin (PM) and asset turnover (AT) for 2008 and 2007; total assets is $33,210 million in 2006. Comment on the drivers of the ROA.

b. Compute any expense to sales (ETS) ratios that you think might help explain UPS's profitability.

c. Compute return on equity (ROE) for 2008 and 2007; the 2006 stockholders' equity is $15,482 million.

d. Comment on the difference between ROE and ROA. What does this relation suggest about UPS's use of debt?

LO4 P5-42. Analysis and Interpretation of Liquidity and Solvency

UNITED PARCEL
SERVICE
NYSE :: UPS

Refer to the financial information of **United Parcel Service** in P5-41 to answer the following requirements.

Required

a. Compute its current ratio and quick ratio for 2008 and 2007. Comment on any observed trends.

b. Compute its times interest earned and its debt-to-equity ratios for 2008 and 2007. Comment on any trends observed.

c. Summarize your findings in a conclusion about the company's liquidity and solvency. Do you have any concerns about its ability to meet its debt obligations?

LO5 P5-43.^A Computing and Analyzing Operating Returns

UNITED PARCEL
SERVICE
NYSE :: UPS

Refer to the financial statements of **United Parcel Service** in P5-41 to answer the following requirements.

Required

a. Compute net operating profit after taxes (NOPAT) for 2008 and net operating assets (NOA) for 2007 and 2008.

b. Compute the return on net operating assets (RNOA) for 2008. What percentage of UPS's ROE is generated by operations?

c. Decompose RNOA by computing net operating profit margin (NOPM) and net operating asset turnover (NOAT) for 2008.

d. What can be inferred about UPS from these ratios?

P5-44.[B] **Preparing Pro Forma Financial Statements**

Refer to the financial statements of **United Parcel Service** in P5-41 to answer the following requirements. The following assumptions should be useful:

- UPS's sales forecast for 2009 is $55,000 million.
- Operating expenses and operating profits increase in proportion to sales.
- Depreciation and amortization expense (which is included in other operating expenses) is 3.5% of sales.
- Investment income and interest expense are unchanged in 2009.
- Income taxes are 40% of pretax earnings.
- Marketable securities and short-term investments are unchanged in 2009; all other assets (except cash) increase in proportion to sales.
- Long-term debt and current maturities of long-term debt are unchanged in 2009; all other liabilities increase in proportion to sales.
- Dividends are 50% of net income. Income and dividends are the only changes to stockholders' equity in 2009.

Required

a. Prepare a pro forma income statement and pro forma balance sheet for 2009.

b. Prepare a pro forma cash flow statement for 2009.

P5-45.[C] **Direct Computation of ROFL**

Refer to the financial information of **United Parcel Service** in P5-41 to answer the following requirements.

Required

a. Compute its net interest rate (NIR) and Spread for 2008.

b. Compute UPS's ROFL using the NIR and spread you computed in question *a*.

c. What do your computations in parts *a* and *b* suggest about the company's use of borrowed funds?

P5-46. **Comparing Profitability Ratios for Competitors**

Selected income statement data for **Abbott Laboratories**, **Bristol-Myers Squibb Company**, **Johnson & Johnson**, **Merck & Co., Inc.**, and **Pfizer, Inc.** is presented in the following table:

($ millions)	Abbott Laboratories	Bristol-Myers Squibb	Johnson & Johnson	Merck	Pfizer
Sales revenue	$29,527.6	$20,527	$63,747	$23,850.3	$48,296
Cost of sales	12,612.0	6,396	18,511	5,582.5	8,112
SG&A expense.	8,435.6	6,342	21,490	7,377.0	14,537
R&D expense...................	2,786.0	3,585	7,758	4,805.3	7,945
Interest expense	528.5	310	435	251.3	782
Net income.	4,880.7	5,247	12,949	7,808.4	8,104

Required

a. Compute the profit margin (PM) and gross profit margin (GPM) ratios for each company.

b. Compute the research and development (R&D) expense to sales ratio and the selling, general and administrative (SG&A) expense to sales ratio for each company.

c. Compare the relative profitability of these pharmaceutical companies.

P5-47. **Comparing Profitability and Turnover Ratios for Retail Companies**

Selected financial statement data for **Best Buy Co., Inc.**, **The Kroger Co.**, **Nordstrom, Inc.**, **Staples, Inc.**, and **Walgreen Co.** is presented in the following table:

($ millions)	Best Buy	Kroger	Nordstrom	Staples	Walgreen
Sales revenue	$45,015	$76,000	$8,573	$23,084	$63,335
Cost of sales	34,017	58,564	5,417	16,837	45,722
Interest expense	94	485	131	28	83
Net income	1,003	1,249	401	805	2,006
Average receivables	1,209	865	1,865	1,344	2,512
Average inventories	4,731	4,854	928	2,229	7,019
Average PP&E	3,740	12,830	2,102	2,226	10,289
Average total assets	14,292	22,752	5,631	11,021	23,776

Required

a. Compute return on assets (ROA) profit margin (PM) and asset turnover (AT) for each company. Discuss the relative importance of PM and AT for each company.

b. Compute accounts receivable turnover (ART), inventory turnover (INVT) and property, plant and equipment turnover (PPET) for each company. Discuss any difference that you observe.

c. Compute the gross profit margin (GPM) for each company. How does the GPM differ across companies? Does this difference seem to correlate with differences in ART or INVT? Explain.

CASES AND PROJECTS

LO3 **C5-48.** **Management Application: Gross Profit and Strategic Management**

One way to increase overall profitability is to increase gross profit. This can be accomplished by raising prices and/or by reducing manufacturing costs.

Required

a. Will raising prices and/or reducing manufacturing costs unambiguously increase gross profit? Explain.

b. What strategy might you develop as a manager to (i) yield a price increase for your product, or (ii) reduce product manufacturing cost?

LO3 **C5-49.** **Management Application: Asset Turnover and Strategic Management**

Increasing net operating asset turnover requires some combination of increasing sales and/or decreasing net operating assets. For the latter, many companies consider ways to reduce their investment in working capital (current assets less current liabilities). This can be accomplished by reducing the level of accounts receivable and inventories, or by increasing the level of accounts payable.

Required

a. Develop a list of suggested actions to achieve all three of these objectives as manager.

b. Examine the implications of each. That is, describe the marketing implications of reducing receivables and inventories, and the supplier implications of delaying payment. How can a company achieve working capital reduction without negatively impacting its performance?

LO2, LO3, LO4 **C5-50.** **Ethics and Governance: Earnings Management**

Companies are aware that analysts focus on profitability in evaluating financial performance. Managers have historically utilized a number of methods to improve reported profitability that are cosmetic in nature and do not affect "real" operating performance. These are typically subsumed under the general heading of "earnings management." Justification for such actions typically includes the following arguments:

- Increasing stock price by managing earnings benefits shareholders; thus, no one is hurt by these actions.
- Earnings management is a temporary fix; such actions will be curtailed once "real" profitability improves, as managers expect.

Required

a. Identify the affected parties in any scheme to manage profits to prop up stock price.

b. Do the ends (of earnings management) justify the means? Explain.

c. To what extent are the objectives of managers different from those of shareholders?

d. What governance structure can you envision that might prohibit earnings management?

SOLUTIONS TO REVIEW PROBLEMS

Mid-Chapter Review 1

Solution

THE COCA-COLA COMPANY AND SUBSIDIARIES
Common Size Balance Sheets

December 31,	2008	2007
Assets		
Cash and cash equivalents	11.6%	9.5%
Marketable securities	0.7%	0.5%
Trade accounts receivable	7.6%	7.7%
Inventories	5.4%	5.1%
Prepaid expenses and other current assets	4.7%	5.2%
Total current assets	30.1%	28.0%
Investments	14.3%	18.0%
Property, plant and equipment, net	20.5%	19.6%
Goodwill and other intangible assets	30.9%	28.2%
Other assets	4.3%	6.2%
Total assets	100.0%	100.0%
Liabilities and Stockholders' Equity		
Accounts payable and accrued expenses	15.3%	16.0%
Loans and notes payable	15.0%	13.7%
Current maturities of long-term debt	1.1%	0.3%
Accrued income taxes	0.6%	0.6%
Total current liabilities	32.1%	30.6%
Long-term debt	6.9%	7.6%
Other liabilities	8.4%	7.2%
Deferred income taxes	2.2%	4.4%
Total liabilities	49.5%	49.7%
Stockholders' equity	50.5%	50.3%
Total liabilities and stockholders' equity	100.0%	100.0%

THE COCA-COLA COMPANY AND SUBSIDIARIES
Consolidated Statements of Income
($ millions)

Year ended December 31	2008	2007
Net operating revenues	100.0%	100.0%
Cost of goods sold	35.6%	36.1%
Gross profit	64.4%	63.9%
Selling, general and administrative expenses	36.9%	37.9%
Other operating charges	1.1%	0.9%
Operating income	26.4%	25.1%
Interest income	1.0%	0.8%
Interest expense	−1.4%	−1.6%
Other income (loss)—net	−2.8%	2.9%
Income before income taxes	23.3%	27.3%
Income taxes	5.1%	6.6%
Net income	18.2%	20.7%

Mid-Chapter Review 2

Solution ($ millions)

$$ROE = \frac{\$5,807}{(\$20,472 + \$21,744)/2} = 27.51\%$$

$$ROA = \frac{\$5,807 + \$438 \times (1 - .35)}{(\$40,519 + \$43,269)/2} = 14.54\%$$

$$ROFL = 27.51\% - 14.54\% = 12.97\%$$

Mid-Chapter Review 3

Solution ($ millions):

$$PM = \frac{\$5,807 + \$438 \times (1 - .35)}{\$31,944} = 19.07\%$$

$$AT = \frac{\$31,944}{(\$40,519 + \$43,269)/2} = 0.762$$

$$19.07\% \times 0.762 = 14.53\% \text{ (rounding difference)}$$

$$GPM = \frac{\$20,570}{\$31,944} = 64.4\%$$

$$ART = \frac{\$31,944}{(\$3,090 + \$3,317)/2} = 9.97$$

$$INVT = \frac{\$11,374}{(\$2,187 + \$2,220)/2} = 5.16$$

$$PPET = \frac{\$31,944}{(\$8,326 + \$8,493)/2} = 3.80$$

Although both PepsiCo and Coca-Cola have similar business models, PepsiCo is more profitable. PepsiCo's ROE is 35.1% compared to 27.5% for Coca-Cola. PepsiCo's ROA is only slightly higher than Coca-Cola's (15.2% vs. 14.5%), suggesting that PepsiCo relies more on financial leverage to boost overall returns to shareholders.

Coca-Cola has a higher profit margin (PM = 19.1%; GPM = 64.4%) than PepsiCo (PM = 12.4%; GPM = 52.9%). However, PepsiCo utilizes assets more efficiently, with AT = 1.225 compared to 0.762 for Coke. Closer analysis of turnover ratios reveals that ART and PPET are about the same for both companies, suggesting that they employ similar credit policies and production technologies. However, the difference in AT can be largely attributed to PepsiCo's efficient management of inventories. PepsiCo's INVT is 8.46 compared to Coke's 5.16 times.

Chapter-End Review

Solution ($ millions):

$$\text{Current ratio} = \frac{\$12,176}{\$12,988} = 0.94$$

$$\text{Quick ratio} = \frac{\$4,701 + \$278 + \$3,090}{\$12,988} = 0.62$$

$$\text{Debt-to-equity ratio} = \frac{\$20,047}{\$20,472} = 0.98$$

$$\text{Times interest earned} = \frac{\$7,439 + \$438}{\$438} = 17.98$$

PepsiCo is more liquid than Coca-Cola as indicated by a higher current ratio (1.23 vs. 0.94) and a higher quick ratio (0.79 vs. 0.62). However, PepsiCo has a much higher debt-to-equity ratio than Coke (1.97 vs. 0.98) suggesting that PepsiCo is relying more on debt financing. This is consistent with the higher ROFL ratio computed in Mid-Chapter Review 2. Nevertheless, neither company has significant issues related to solvency. Both report reasonably high times interest earned ratios (22.3 for PepsiCo and 17.98 for Coca-Cola).

Appendix-End Review A

Solution ($ millions):

Operating assets:
2008: $40,519 - $5,779 - $278 = $34,462$
2007: $43,269 - $7,777 - $215 = $35,277$

Operating liabilities:
2008: $6,205 + $252 + $3,401 + $877 = $10,735$
2007: $6,915 + $258 + $3,133 + $1,890 = $12,196$

Net operating assets (NOA):
2008: $34,462 - $10,735 = $23,727$
2007: $35,277 - $12,196 = $23,081$

$$\text{NOPAT} = \$8,446 \times (1 - .35) = \$5,489.9$$

$$\text{RNOA} = \frac{\$5,489.9}{(\$23,727 + \$23,081)/2} = 23.46\%$$

$$\text{NOPM} = \frac{\$5,489.9}{\$31,944} = 17.19\%$$

$$\text{NOAT} = \frac{\$31,944}{(\$23,727 + \$23,081)/2} = 1.365$$

Appendix-End Review B

Solution ($ millions):

THE COCA-COLA COMPANY AND SUBSIDIARIES Pro Forma Statements of Income ($ millions)	
Year ended December 31	**2009**
Net operating revenues	$34,000
Cost of goods sold ($34,000 × 35.6%)	12,104
Gross profit	21,896
Selling, general and administrative expenses ($34,000 × 36.9%)	12,546
Other operating charges ($34,000 × 1.1%)	374
Operating income	8,976
Interest income	333
Interest expense	(438)
Other income (loss)—net	(902)
Income before income taxes	7,969
Income taxes ($7,969 × 21.9%)	1,745
Net income	$ 6,224

THE COCA-COLA COMPANY AND SUBSIDIARIES
Pro Forma Balance Sheet
($ millions)

December 31,	2009
Assets	
Cash and cash equivalents	$ 5,953
Marketable securities	278
Trade accounts receivable ($34,000 × 9.7%)	3,298
Inventories ($34,000 × 6.8%)	2,312
Prepaid expenses and other current assets ($34,000 × 6.0%)	2,040
Total current assets	13,881
Investments	5,779
Property, plant and equipment, net ($34,000 × 26.1%)	8,874
Goodwill and other intangible assets ($34,000 × 39.1%)	13,294
Other assets ($34,000 × 5.4%)	1,836
Total assets	$43,664
Liabilities and Shareowners' Equity	
Accounts payable and accrued expenses ($34,000 × 19.4%)	$ 6,596
Loans and notes payable	6,066
Current maturities of long-term debt	465
Accrued income taxes ($34,000 × 0.8%)	272
Total current liabilities	13,399
Long-term debt	2,781
Other liabilities ($34,000 × 10.6%)	3,604
Deferred income taxes ($34,000 × 2.7%)	918
Total liabilities	20,702
Shareowners' equity ($20,472 + $6,224 − $3,734)	22,962
Total liabilities and shareowners' equity	$43,664

Appendix-End Review C

Solution ($ millions):

$$\text{NIR} = \frac{\$438\,(1 - .35)}{(\$20,047 + \$21,525)/2} = 1.37\%$$

$$\text{ROFL} = \frac{(\$20,047 + \$21,525)/2}{(\$20,472 + \$21,744)/2} \times (14.54\% - 1.37\%) = 12.97\%$$

CISCO

Reporting and Analyzing Revenues and Receivables

6

Cisco Systems, Inc., manufactures and sells networking and communication products for transporting data, voice, and video. It is the worldwide leader in networking for the Internet.

CISCO SYSTEMS
www.cisco.com

Its engineers have been prominent in the development of Internet Protocol (IP)-based networking technologies in the core areas of routing and switching, along with advancing technologies in areas such as IP telephony, wireless LAN, storage networking, and home networking. Its products are seemingly everywhere:

- Cisco routers and switches are a crucial component of all networks, including the Internet.
- Cisco wireless network and IP telephony products allow people to communicate freely and reduce the cost of long distance communications.
- Cisco wireless technology allows employees to connect to corporate networks over a virtual private network (VPN), and it has medical applications such as telerobotics that aid in surgery. Commercial applications include wireless displays on shopping carts, targeted advertisements, and quick checkout.
- Virtual classrooms, powered by Cisco's switching technology and web collaboration software, are part of the distance learning revolution.
- Cisco kiosks allow airline passengers to check flight information, purchase tickets, and print boarding passes.

After a decade of rapid annual growth, Cisco ran smack into the tech decline in 2001. The company reported a $1 billion loss after taking a massive $2.2 billion restructuring charge. The restructuring led to inventory write-downs and the severance of 6,000 employees and seemed to undermine Cisco's claims of cutting-edge e-efficiency (*Business Week* 2003). In short, Cisco restructured its business from the ground up.

Cisco's CEO, John Chambers, recently commented to *BusinessWeek*, "success in the 1990s was often based on how fast you could get to market and how fast you could blow a product through your distribution [channels]. Our market changed dramatically in terms of what customers expected; we needed to have engineering and manufacturing and professional services and [sales] and customer support working together in a way that wasn't required before."

(continued on next page)

(continued from previous page)

Fast forward six years, and Cisco reported fiscal 2008 net income of $8,052 million on net sales of $39,540 million, with net sales increasing almost 60% in three years. But then, like almost all companies, Cisco was affected by the economic downturn with 2009 net income of $6,134 million on net sales of $36,117 million. This downturn has not changed the company's long-term strategy, and Cisco is using its experience in prior downturns to expand its share of its customers' information technology spending, with focuses on areas like video and collaboration tools in network environments.

Profitability is the primary measure by which financial statement users gauge a company's success in efficiently offering products and services that receive a favorable response from customers. In this chapter, we focus on how companies report operating income. Operating income is determined by decisions about how and when to recognize revenues and how expenses are matched against revenues. In addition, the income statement also includes *transitory items*, such as restructuring charges. Transitory items are often important events reflecting very large dollar amounts and are distinguished by the fact that they are unlikely to recur in subsequent years. Understanding how such nonrecurring items are reported is crucial to interpreting a company's profitability.

Cisco's performance cannot be measured by profits alone. In order to control costs and improve operating profits, Cisco had to effectively manage operating assets. These assets include receivables, inventories, and plant assets. For example, accounts receivable is an important operating asset at Cisco because all of its sales are on account. By extending credit to customers on favorable credit terms, Cisco stimulates sales. However, extending credit exposes the company to collectibility risk—the risk that some customers will not pay the amounts owed. In addition, accounts receivable do not earn interest, and involve administrative costs associated with billing and collection. Hence, management of receivables is critical to financial success. In addition to discussing operating income, this chapter describes the reporting of receivables. The reporting of other operating assets is covered in subsequent chapters.

Cisco's performance is remarkable. It survived the bursting of the tech bubble and is reporting impressive profits even in the current economic climate. To ensure future success, however, it must continue to manage operating income and operating assets.

Sources: *Cisco Systems, Inc.*, 10-K Reports; *The Wall Street Journal*, February 7, 2005; *BusinessWeek*, November/December 2003; *USA Today*, August 7, 2007.

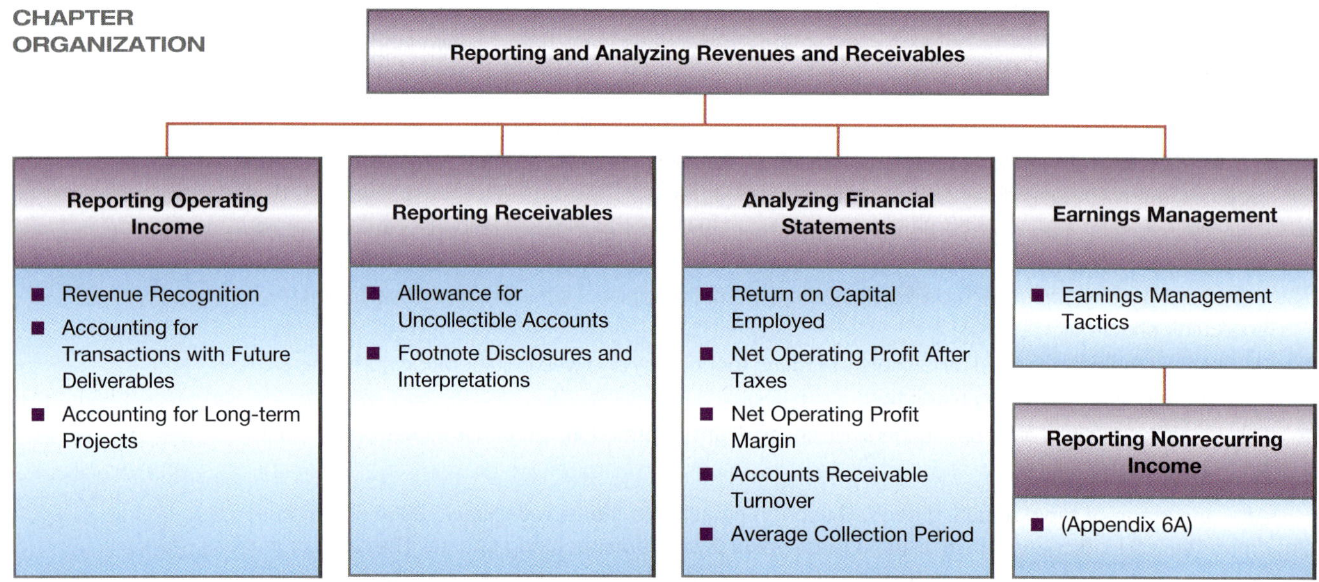

REPORTING OPERATING INCOME

The income statement is the primary source of information about recent company performance. This information is used to predict future performance for investment purposes and to assess the creditworthiness of a company. The income statement is also used to evaluate the quality of management.

This section describes the information reported in the income statement and its analysis implications. The central questions that the income statement attempts to answer are

- How profitable has the company been recently?

- How did it achieve that profitability?
- Will the current profitability level persist?

To answer these three profitability questions, it is not enough to focus on a company's net income. Rather, we must use the various classifications within the income statement to see how profits were achieved and what the future prospects look like. Exhibit 6.1 provides a schematic of the primary income statement classifications.

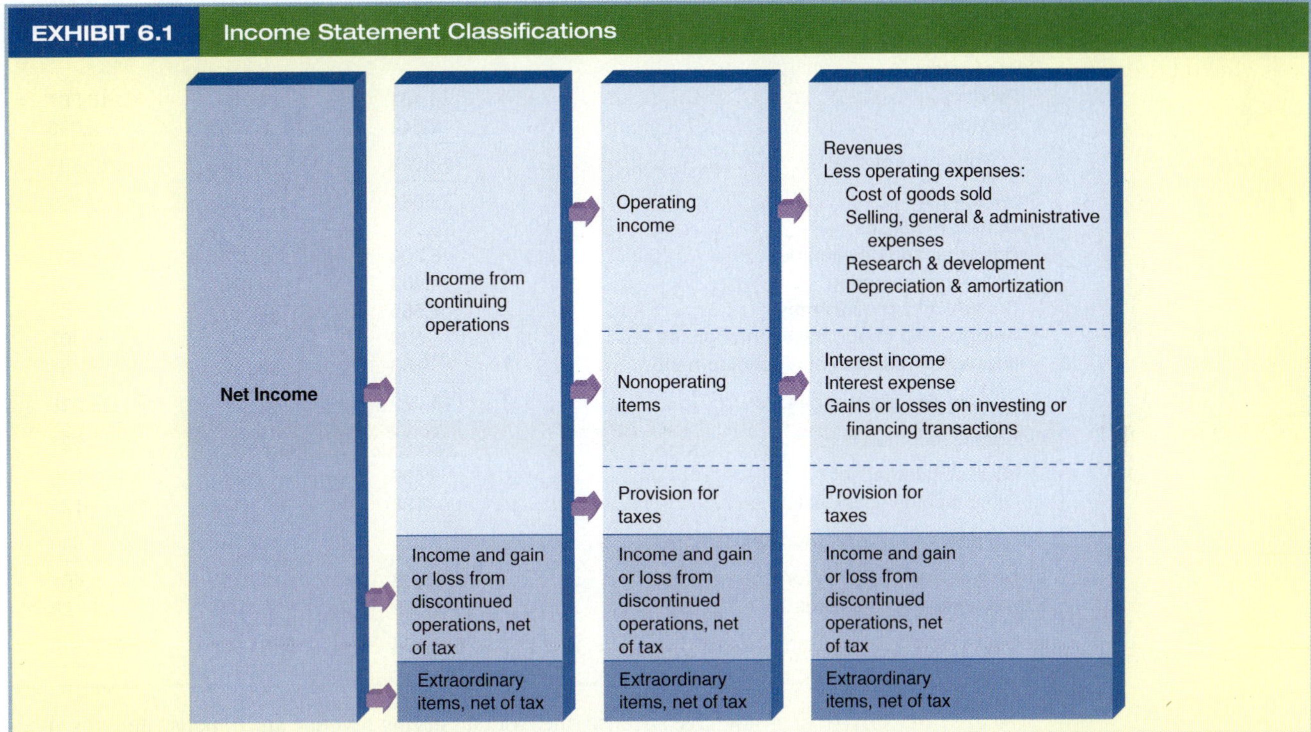

Operating activities refer to the primary transactions and events of a company. These include the purchase of goods from suppliers, the conversion of materials into finished products, the promotion and distribution of goods, the sale of goods and services to customers, and post-sale customer support. Operating activities are reported in the income statement under items such as sales, cost of goods sold, and selling, general, and administrative expenses. They represent a company's primary activities, which must be executed successfully for a company to remain consistently profitable.

Nonoperating activities relate to the financial (borrowing) and securities investment activities of a company. These activities are typically reported in the income statement under items such as interest income and expenses, dividend revenues, and gains and losses on sales of securities. Distinguishing income components by operating versus nonoperating is an important part of effective financial statement analysis because operating activities drive company performance. It is of interest, for example, to know whether company profitability results from operating activities, or whether poorly performing operating activities are being masked by income from nonoperating activities.

All the line items in income from continuing operations are presented before taxes, with the final line item being provision for income taxes, or tax expense. The accounting for income taxes is discussed more fully in Chapter 10.

Exhibit 6.2 presents the 2009, 2008, and 2007 income statements (also called statements of operations) for **Cisco Systems**. Cisco has no discontinued operations or extraordinary items during this time period, so income from continuing operations is the same as net income. Like many companies, Cisco presents operating income as a subtotal in its income statement. Cisco's operating income is computed by subtracting its total operating expenses (including cost of sales, research and development, sales and marketing, general and administrative, and amortization) from total sales revenues. Nonoperating income and expenses, such as interest income and expense, and other income and expense, are added to or deducted from the subtotal for operating income.

FYI When analyzing a company's income statement, it is important to distinguish operating activities from nonoperating activities and recurring activities from nonrecurring activities.

EXHIBIT 6.2	Distinguishing Operating and Nonoperating Sources of Income

CISCO SYSTEMS, INC.
Consolidated Statements of Operations
($ millions)

Year ended	July 25, 2009	July 26, 2008	July 28, 2007
Net sales:			
Product	$29,131	$33,099	$29,462
Service	6,986	6,441	5,460
Total net sales	36,117	39,540	34,922
Cost of sales:			
Product	10,481	11,660	10,567
Service	2,542	2,534	2,096
Total cost of sales	13,023	14,194	12,663
Gross Margin	23,094	25,346	22,259
Operating expenses:			
Research and development	5,208	5,325	4,598
Sales and marketing	8,403	8,690	7,401
General and administrative	1,565	1,387	1,151
Amortization of purchased intangibles	533	499	407
In-process research and development	63	3	81
Total operating expenses	15,772	15,904	13,638
Operating income	7,322	9,442	8,621
Interest income, net	499	824	715
Other income (loss), net	(128)	(11)	125
Interest and other income (loss), net	371	813	840
Income before provision for income taxes	7,693	10,255	9,461
Provision for income taxes	1,559	2,203	2,128
Net Income	$ 6,134	$ 8,052	$ 7,333

At this time, GAAP does not have specific rules for classifying revenue and expense items as either operating or nonoperating, so financial statement users must be careful to examine each revenue and expense item to determine if it is appropriately listed as part of operating income. Specifically, sales, cost of goods sold, and most selling, general, and administrative expenses are categorized as operating activities. Alternatively, investment-related income from dividends and interest is nonoperating, as is interest expense. Gains and losses on debt retirements and sales of investments are also nonoperating.[1]

While we think of Cisco as a networking and communications company, it has more than $29 billion (42% of its assets) invested in financial instruments (mostly government and government-backed securities) at 2009 fiscal year-end. And these assets provided $845 million in interest income for 2009. So, making predictions about Cisco's profitability for 2010 would be improved by separating the results of its product and service operations from those of its investing activities. In addition, operating income is the normal focus of business unit managers in a company—financing activities and investments in financial instruments and tax administration are usually determined at the central corporate level.

Revenue Recognition

Revenue is one of the most important metrics of a company's operating success. The objective of almost all operating activities is to obtain a favorable response from customers, and revenue is a primary indicator of how customers view the company's product and service offerings. Companies can improve profits by reducing costs, but the effects of those improvements are limited unless revenues are increasing. Accordingly, growth in revenue is carefully monitored by management and by investors, as exemplified by the attention given to "same-store sales growth" in the retail industry.

Revenue recognition refers to the timing and amount of revenue reported by the company. The decision of when to recognize revenue depends on relatively simple criteria. Despite their simplic-

---

[1] Of course, the distinction between operating and nonoperating items depends on the company's business. For Cisco Systems, interest income and expense would be classified as nonoperating, but for a financial institution (e.g., a bank), those same items would be considered part of their operations. Purchases and sales of production equipment would be considered nonoperating for Cisco, but operating for a company in the business of buying and selling used equipment.

ity, most SEC enforcement actions against companies for inaccurate, and sometimes fraudulent, financial reporting are for improper (usually premature) revenue recognition. Determining whether the criteria for revenue recognition are met is often subjective and requires judgment. Therefore, financial statement readers should pay careful attention to companies' revenue recognition, particularly when companies face market pressures to meet income targets.

GAAP dictates two **revenue recognition criteria** that must be met for revenue to be recognized (and reported) on the income statement. Revenue must be (1) **realized or realizable**, and (2) **earned**. *Realized or realizable* means that the company's net assets increase. That is, it receives an asset or satisfies a liability as a result of a transaction or event. *Earned* means that the seller has executed its duties under the terms of the sales agreement and that the title has passed to the buyer.

The SEC is so concerned about proper revenue recognition that it issued *Staff Accounting Bulletin (SAB) 101* to address this issue. *SAB 101* states that revenue is earned and realized, or realizable, when all of the following criteria have been met: (1) there is persuasive evidence that a sales agreement exists; (2) delivery has occurred or services have been rendered; (3) the seller's price is fixed or determinable; and (4) collectibility is reasonably assured.

Many companies recognize revenues when the product or service is delivered to the customer. For these companies, delivery occurs at the same time, or shortly after, the sale takes place. Complications arise if there is uncertainty about collectibility or when the sale is contingent on product performance, product approval, or similar contingencies. In some industries, it is standard practice to allow customers to return the product within a specified period of time. When the customer retains a **right of return**, it is sometimes inappropriate to recognize revenue at the time of delivery. For many companies, returns are either immaterial in amount or relatively easy to predict based on history of a large number of similar transactions. For these companies, revenue can be recognized when the product is delivered to the customer. The expected returns are estimated and deducted from revenue when reporting the sale in the income statement. However, if the return period is long or the amount of returns is difficult to estimate, revenues should not be recognized until the return period expires.

BUSINESS INSIGHT

Product Returns at Pfizer Following is an excerpt from **Pfizer Inc.**'s accounting policies as reported in its annual report.

> We record revenues from product sales when the goods are shipped and title passes to the customer. At the time of sale, we also record estimates for a variety of sales deductions, such as sales rebates, discounts and incentives, and product returns. When we cannot reasonably estimate the amount of future product returns, we record revenues when the risk of product return has been substantially eliminated.

Pfizer's policy regarding product returns is consistent with GAAP in that expected returns are estimated and deducted from sales at the time that the sale is recorded. If returns cannot be estimated, the sales revenue is deferred until the company is relatively certain that the product will not be returned.

The term "delivery" does not refer only to transportation to the customer's location, but also the transfer of title and the risks and rewards of ownership. In a **consignment** sale, a *consignor* delivers product to a *consignee*, but retains ownership until the consignee sells the product to the ultimate customer. As long as ownership remains with the consignor, a sale has not taken place. Only when the consignee sells the product should the consignor record the sales revenue.

INSTALLMENT METHOD Although rare, there are circumstances where collectibility cannot be reasonably assured, even though all other revenue recognition criteria are met. In these situations, GAAP requires that revenue recognition must be delayed until cash is collected. The **installment method** recognizes revenue when cash is collected, and records costs and gross profit in proportion to the amount of cash collected.

To illustrate, assume that inventory costing $65,000 is sold on credit for $100,000, yielding an expected gross profit of $35,000. Under normal conditions, we would recognize revenue and accounts receivable of $100,000, cost of goods sold expense and an inventory reduction of $65,000, and the resulting $35,000 gross profit all at the time of delivery. When the customer pays, cash increases and the accounts receivable decreases. All of the "value-added" from this transaction is recognized at the time of delivery.

However, suppose that we are uncertain of the collectibility of the $100,000 at the time of the delivery. Ultimately, the customer makes a $20,000 cash payment in the first year, a $50,000 cash payment in the second year, and the remaining $30,000 cash is paid in year three. Using the installment method delays revenue recognition (and gross profit) until cash is received. The gross profit percentage is 35% ($35,000/$100,000). The revenue, expense, and gross profit recognized each year are shown in Exhibit 6.3.

EXHIBIT 6.3	Revenue Recognition Using the Installment Method		
Year	Revenue recognized (cash collected)	Expense recognized (cash collected × 65%)	Gross profit (cash collected × 35%)
1.	$ 20,000	$13,000	20,000 × 35% = $ 7,000
2.	50,000	32,500	50,000 × 35% = 17,500
3.	30,000	19,500	30,000 × 35% = 10,500
Totals	$100,000	$65,000	$35,000

In the installment method, revenue is not recorded until it has been collected in cash. Expenses and gross profit are then matched in proportion to the revenues. In the event that the customer defaults on the sales contract, the product would be repossessed and returned to inventory. A loss would be recorded if the value of the repossessed inventory is less than the outstanding (unpaid) receivable.

Revenue Recognition Subsequent to Customer Purchase

Revenue Recognition Subsequent to Customer Purchase   There are many businesses in which customers purchase a product or a service prior to its delivery. For instance, a customer may pay for a year's subscription to a periodical. The publisher receives the cash at the start of the subscription, but it earns revenue when it delivers the periodical to the subscriber. Or, a homeowner may pay for the upcoming year's casualty insurance, but the insurance company can only recognize revenue as it provides insurance coverage.

In settings where a company's customers pay for the product or service prior to its delivery, the company must recognize a liability (usually called **unearned revenue** or **deferred revenue**)[2] at the time of the customer's payment. Then this liability is reduced, and revenue recognized, as the product or service is delivered.

Suppose that on January 1, a subscriber pays $36 for an annual subscription to a monthly magazine. At the time of payment, the publisher would make the following entry:

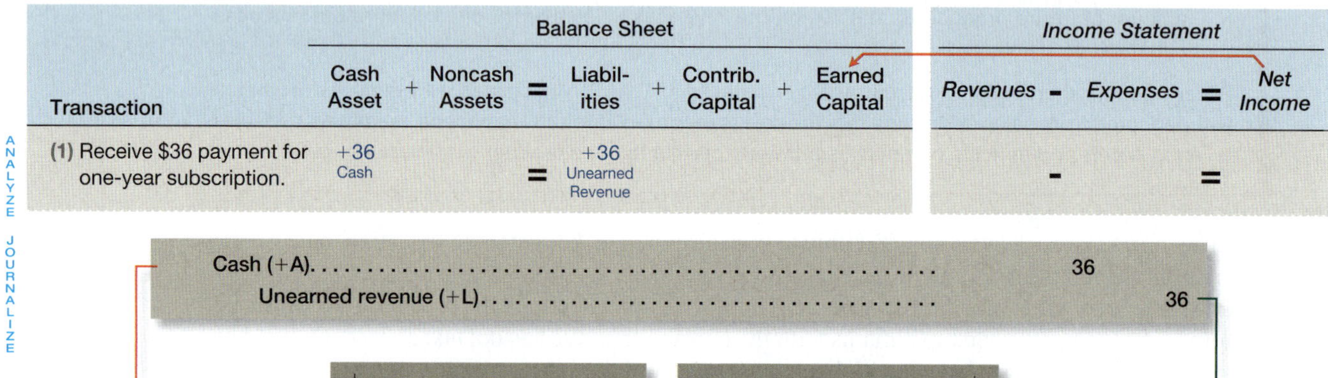

The unearned revenue liability represents the publisher's obligation—not to make a payment, but to provide the promised publication. Most liabilities reflect obligations to make a future payment, but unearned revenue is one of a handful of liabilities that represent an obligation for future performance.

---

[2] The term used for unearned revenue may be particular to the company's business. For instance, **AMR Corporation** (parent of American Airlines) shows an Air Traffic Liability of $3,708 million at the end of 2008 which represents customers' purchases of tickets in advance of their flights. **The Allstate Corporation** uses the term Unearned Premiums.

On March 31, at the end of its first quarter, the publisher would recognize that three magazines had been delivered to the subscriber, and the publisher has earned three times the monthly revenue of $3, or $9. The entry to recognize this revenue is the following.

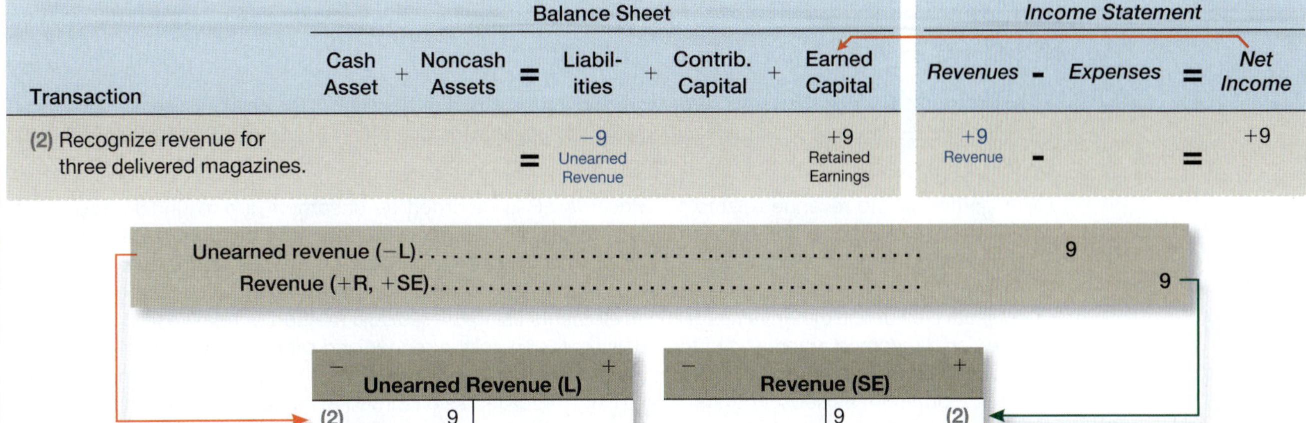

The same entries would be made until the subscription expired. In the March 31 balance sheet, the publisher would have a deferred revenue liability of $27, reflecting the remaining obligation for nine months of subscription delivery. And, the quarter's indirect method operating cash flows would include $9 in revenue (in net income) and the $27 increase in unearned revenue liability which, in total, reflect the $36 received from the customer.

A revenue recognition complication arises when two or more products or services are sold under the same sales agreement for one lump-sum price. **Bundled sales** such as this are commonplace in the software industry, where developers sell software, training, maintenance, and customer support in one transaction. In these circumstances, GAAP requires that the sales price be allocated among the various elements of the sale in proportion to their fair value. Revenue allocated to the elements that have not been delivered (such as maintenance and customer support) must be deferred and recognized as the service is rendered in future periods.

BUSINESS INSIGHT

Cisco's Revenue Recognition   Following is an excerpt from Cisco Systems' policies on revenue recognition as reported in footnotes to its recent annual report.

> The Company recognizes revenue when persuasive evidence of an arrangement exists, delivery has occurred, the fee is fixed or determinable, and collectibility is reasonably assured. In instances where final acceptance of the product, system, or solution is specified by the customer, revenue is deferred until all acceptance criteria have been met. Technical support services revenue is deferred and recognized ratably over the period during which the services are to be performed, which is typically from one to three years. Advanced services revenue is recognized upon delivery or completion of performance . . . When a sale involves multiple elements, such as sales of products that include services, the entire fee from the arrangement is allocated to each respective element based on its relative fair value and recognized when revenue recognition criteria for each element are met. Fair value for each element is established based on the sales price charged when the same element is sold separately based on vendor-specific objective evidence.

Cisco's criteria for revenue recognition mirror SEC guidance. The key components are that revenue is earned and that proceeds are realized or realizable. For Cisco, earned means that delivery to and acceptance by the customer occurs, or that Cisco is available to perform service commitments, even if not called upon.

Unearned revenue is seen in a growing number of financial statements as companies increase their promises of future deliveries of products and service in an effort to build a continuing relationship with their customers. From the point of view of a financial analyst, one implication of revenue deferral is that the change in revenue from one period to the next is not equal to the change in customer purchases over the same period. In the case of our publisher with one-year subscriptions, quarterly revenue is actually a composite of subscriber purchases over the current quarter plus the last three quarters and, therefore, not an ideal indicator of the how current customers are responding to the publisher's offerings.

MID-CHAPTER REVIEW 1

When **Microsoft Corporation** sells software, it recognizes part of the revenue at the time of customer purchase and defers the rest because it will deliver support and upgrades in the future. For instance, in its 2009 annual report, it states

> A portion of the revenue related to Windows XP is recorded as unearned due to undelivered elements including, in some cases, free post-delivery telephone support and the right to receive unspecified upgrades/enhancements of Microsoft Internet Explorer on a when-and-if-available basis. The amount of revenue allocated to undelivered elements is based on the vendor-specific objective evidence of fair value for those elements using the residual method or relative fair value method. Unearned revenue due to undelivered elements is recognized ratably on a straight-line basis over the related products' life cycles . . . Revenue from multi-year licensing arrangements is accounted for as subscriptions, with billings recorded as unearned revenue and recognized as revenue ratably over the billing coverage period.

In its income statement, Microsoft reports revenues for the past three years.

(in millions)	2009	2008	2007
Revenue	$58,437	$60,420	$51,122

In its indirect-method operating cash flows, Microsoft makes many adjustments to its net income in arriving at cash from operations. Two of the adjustments are the following:

(in millions)	2009	2008	2007
Deferral of unearned revenue	$24,409	$24,532	$21,032
Recognition of unearned revenue	(25,426)	(21,944)	(19,382)

"Deferral of unearned revenue" provides the amount of customer purchases made during a year that were not recognized as revenue at the time of customer purchase. That is the amount that was put into the unearned revenue liability during the year. "Recognition of unearned revenue" refers to the amounts of revenue recognized during the year that derived from customer purchases made in earlier periods. This amount was taken out of the unearned revenue liability during the year and recognized as revenue on the income statement.

Required
1. Calculate the revenue growth rates for fiscal years 2008 and 2009.
2. From the information on revenues and on changes in the unearned revenue liability, determine the amount of customer purchases for fiscal years 2007, 2008, and 2009.
3. Calculate the growth rates in customer purchases for fiscal years 2008 and 2009. Why do these differ from those calculated in part 1?

The solution to this review problem can be found on pages 299–300.

LO3 Illustrate revenue and expense recognition for long-term projects.

Revenue Recognition for Long-term Projects
Challenges arise in determining revenue recognition for companies with long-term production processes (spanning more than one reporting period) such as consulting firms, construction companies, and defense contractors. For these companies, revenue is often recognized using the **percentage-of-completion method**, which recognizes revenue based on the costs incurred under the contract relative to its total expected costs.[3] In addition to determining when to recognize revenues to properly measure and report a company's performance, we must also decide when to recognize expenses. The **matching principle** was introduced in Chapter 2 and requires that expenses be recognized in the same period that the associated revenue is recognized. The following illustration demonstrates the appropriate recognition of revenues and expenses using the percentage-of-completion method.

---

[3] In some circumstances, a company may use some other indicator of progress, like employee time or the achievement of customer-specified milestones.

PERCENTAGE-OF-COMPLETION METHOD   To illustrate the percentage-of-completion method, assume that Built-Rite Construction signs a $10 million contract to construct a building. The company estimates $7.5 million in construction costs, yielding an expected gross profit of $2.5 million. Further assume that Built-Rite incurs $4.5 million in construction costs during the first year of construction, and the remaining $3 million in costs during the second year. The amount of revenue and gross profit that Built-Rite would report each year is illustrated in Exhibit 6.4.

EXHIBIT 6.4	Revenue Recognition Using the Percentage-of-Completion Method			
Year	**Percentage completed**	**Revenue recognized**	**Expense recognized**	**Gross profit**
1...............	$4,500,000/$7,500,000 = 60%	$10,000,000 × 60% = $ 6,000,000	$4,500,000	$1,500,000
2...............	$3,000,000/$7,500,000 = 40%	$10,000,000 × 40% = $ 4,000,000	$3,000,000	$1,000,000
Totals............	100%	$10,000,000	$7,500,000	$2,500,000

Using the percentage-of-completion method, Built-Rite would report $1.5 million in gross profit from this project in the first year and $1.0 million in the second year. The timing of revenue and gross profit coincides with the amount of work completed.

The percentage-of-completion method of revenue recognition requires an estimate of total costs. This estimate is made at the beginning of the contract and is typically the one used to initially bid the contract. However, estimates are inherently inaccurate. If total construction costs are underestimated, the percentage of completion is overestimated (the denominator is too low) and too much revenue and gross profit are recognized in the early years of the project. The estimation process used in this method has the potential for inaccurate or, even, improper revenue recognition. Estimates of costs to complete projects are also difficult to verify for auditors. This uncertainty adds additional risk to financial statement analysis.

> **FYI** GAAP requires use of the percentage-of-completion method for long-term contracts whenever management can reasonably estimate revenues and expenses.

To justify use of the percentage-of-completion method, a company must have a signed contract with the customer that specifies a fixed or determinable price. In addition, project costs must be reasonably estimable. When a long-term project fails to meet these criteria, all revenue should be deferred until the contract is complete. This approach is known as the **completed contract method**. Exhibit 6.5 provides a comparison of the gross profit calculations using each of these two accounting methods for the Built-Rite Construction contract described earlier.

> **FYI** Application of percentage-of-completion enhances earnings timeliness relative to the completed contract method. However, poor or biased estimates for applying percentage-of-completion can reduce or reverse the benefits of that more timely reporting.

EXHIBIT 6.5	Comparison of the Percentage-of-Completion and Completed Contract Methods					
Percentage-of-Completion Method			**Completed Contract Method**			
	Year 1	**Year 2**		**Year 1**	**Year 2**	
Revenues.........	$6,000,000	$4,000,000	Revenues.........	$0	$10,000,000	
Expenses.........	4,500,000	3,000,000	Expenses.........	0	7,500,000	
Gross profit	$1,500,000	$1,000,000	Gross profit	$0	$ 2,500,000	

The total revenue and gross profit are the same under either revenue recognition method. Likewise, there is no difference in the costs incurred to construct the building. The only difference between the percentage-of-completion method and the completed contract method is *when* the revenue and gross profit are reported in the income statement.

It is very likely that Built-Rite would have received some cash payments from the customer during the construction period. However, neither the percentage-of-completion method nor the completed contract method is affected by the schedule of cash payments from the customer. It would

IFRS REPORTING INSIGHT

International Financial Reporting Standards do not allow the completed contract method to be used for long-term contracts when percentage-of-completion is not appropriate. Instead, companies are required to use the **cost-recovery method**, in which revenues are recognized in an amount equal to the cost incurred (and expensed) in each period. The pattern of profit recognition is the same as (or very similar to) completed contract, but the revenues and expenses occur differently.

not make sense for Built-Rite to enter into this contract unless it had a high degree of confidence in the customer's ability and willingness to pay.

MID-CHAPTER REVIEW 2

Following is a footnote from the 2010 annual report of Adler Corporation.

Note 2: Revenue Recognition
Revenue from long-term government contracts is recognized using the percentage of completion method of accounting. Production costs are capitalized by project and are expensed based on the ratio of current period costs to estimated total contract costs. Revenue from contracts with private organizations is recognized using the completed contract method.

Required
1. Speculate as to possible reasons why Adler Corporation uses different revenue recognition policies for long-term government contracts and for contracts with private organizations.
2. Assume that Adler signed a contract in 2010 for a long-term project at a contract price of $40,000,000. The project is estimated to take three years to complete and cost $30,000,000. The cost incurred in 2010 was $12,000,000, and projected costs in 2011 and 2012 are $13,500,000 and $4,500,000 respectively. Compute gross profit for each year assuming that the contract is reported using the
   a. percentage-of-completion method
   b. completed contract method
3. Assume that Adler Corporation overestimated the cost of the contract in question 2, such that the actual cost incurred in 2012 was $1,500,000 instead of $4,500,000. What effect would this overestimate have on income in each year?

The solution to this review problem can be found on page 300.

REPORTING ACCOUNTS RECEIVABLE

Receivables are usually a major part of operating working capital. They must be carefully managed as they represent a substantial asset for most companies. GAAP requires companies to report receivables at the amount they expect to collect, necessitating an estimation of uncollectible accounts. These estimates determine the receivables reported on the balance sheet and expenses reported on the income statement. Accordingly, it is important that companies accurately assess uncollectible accounts and report them. It is also necessary that readers of financial reports understand management's accounting choices and the effects of those choices on reported balance sheets and income statements.

When companies sell to other companies, they usually do not expect cash upon delivery as is common with retail customers. Instead, they offer credit terms, and the resulting sales are called **credit sales** or *sales on account*.

Companies establish credit policies (to determine which customers receive credit) by weighing the expected losses from uncollectible accounts against the expected profits generated by offering credit. Sellers know that some buyers will be unable to pay their accounts when they become due. Buyers, for example, can suffer business downturns that are beyond their control and which limit their cash available to meet liabilities. They must, then, make choices concerning which of their liabilities to pay. Liabilities to the IRS, to banks, and to bondholders are usually paid, as those creditors have enforcement powers and can quickly seize assets and disrupt operations, leading to bankruptcy and eventual liquidation. Buyers also try to cover their payroll, as they cannot exist without employees. Then, if there is cash remaining, these customers will pay suppliers to ensure a continued flow of goods.

When a customer faces financial difficulties, suppliers are often the last creditors to receive payment and are often not paid in full. Consequently, there is risk in the collectibility of accounts receivable. This *collectibility risk* is crucial to analysis of accounts receivable.

Accounts receivable are reported on the balance sheet of the seller at **net realizable value**, which is the net amount that the seller expects to collect. Cisco reports $3,177 million of accounts receivable in the current asset section of its 2009 balance sheet. Its receivables are reported net of allowances for doubtful accounts of $216 million. This means that the total amount owed to Cisco by customers is $3,393 million ($3,177 million + $216 million), but the company *estimates* that $216 million of these receivables will be uncollectible. Thus, only the net amount that Cisco expects to collect is reported on the balance sheet.

We might ask why Cisco would sell to companies from whom they do not expect to collect the amounts owed. The answer is they would not *if* they knew beforehand who those companies were. That is, Cisco probably cannot identify those companies that constitute the $216 million in uncollectible accounts as of its statement date. Yet, Cisco knows from past experience that a certain portion of its receivables will prove uncollectible. GAAP requires a company to estimate the dollar amount of uncollectible accounts each time it issues its financial statements (even if it cannot identify specific accounts that are uncollectible), and to report its accounts receivable at the resulting *net realizable value* (total receivables less an **allowance for uncollectible accounts**).

Determining the Allowance for Uncollectible Accounts

The amount of expected uncollectible accounts is usually estimated based on an **aging analysis**. When aging the accounts, an analysis of receivables is performed as of the balance sheet date. Specifically, each customer's account balance is categorized by the number of days or months that the related invoices are outstanding. Based on prior experience, assessment of current economic conditions, or on other available statistics, uncollectible (bad debt) percentages are applied to each of these categorized amounts, with larger percentages applied to older accounts. The result of this analysis is a dollar amount for the allowance for uncollectible accounts (also called allowance for doubtful accounts) at the balance sheet date.

LO4 Estimate and account for uncollectible accounts receivable.

To illustrate, Exhibit 6.6 shows an aging analysis for a seller that began operations this year and is owed $100,000 of accounts receivable at year-end. Those accounts listed as current consist of those outstanding that are still within their original credit period. Accounts listed as 1–60 days past due are those 1 to 60 days past their due date. This classification would include an account that is 45 days outstanding for a net 30-day invoice. This same logic applies to all aged categories.

EXHIBIT 6.6	Aging of Accounts Receivable		
Age of Accounts Receivable	**Receivable Balance**	**Estimated Percent Uncollectible**	**Accounts Estimated Uncollectible**
Current...............................	$ 50,000	2%	$1,000
1–60 days past due....................	30,000	3	900
61–90 days past due...................	15,000	4	600
Over 90 days past due	5,000	8	400
Total...............................	$100,000		$2,900

The calculation illustrated in Exhibit 6.6 also reflects the seller's experience with uncollectible accounts, which manifests itself in the uncollectible percentages for each aged category. For example, on average, 3% of buyers' accounts that are 1–60 days past due prove uncollectible for this seller. Hence, it estimates a potential loss of $900 for those $30,000 in receivables for that aged category.

Another means of estimating uncollectible accounts is to use the **percentage of sales**. To illustrate, if our seller reports sales of $100,000 and estimates the uncollectible accounts at 3% of sales, estimated uncollectible accounts would be $3,000. The percentage of sales approach focuses on the amount of potentially uncollectible accounts among current-period sales, whereas the aging analysis is based on the current balance in accounts receivable. Thus, these two methods nearly always result in different estimates of uncollectible accounts. While the percentage of sales method is arguably simpler, an aging analysis generally provides more accurate estimates.

Reporting the Allowance for Uncollectible Accounts

How does the accounting system record this estimate? The amount that appears in the balance sheet as accounts receivable represents a collection of individual accounts—one or more receivables for each customer. Because we need to keep track of exactly how much each customer owes us, we cannot simply subtract estimated uncollectibles from accounts receivable.

In Chapter 3, we introduced contra-asset accounts to record accumulated depreciation. A contra-asset account is directly associated with an asset account, but serves to offset the balance of the asset account. To record the estimated uncollectible accounts without disturbing the balance in accounts receivable, we use another contra-asset—the allowance for uncollectible accounts.

To illustrate, we use the data from Exhibit 6.6. First the summary journal entry to reflect credit sales follows.

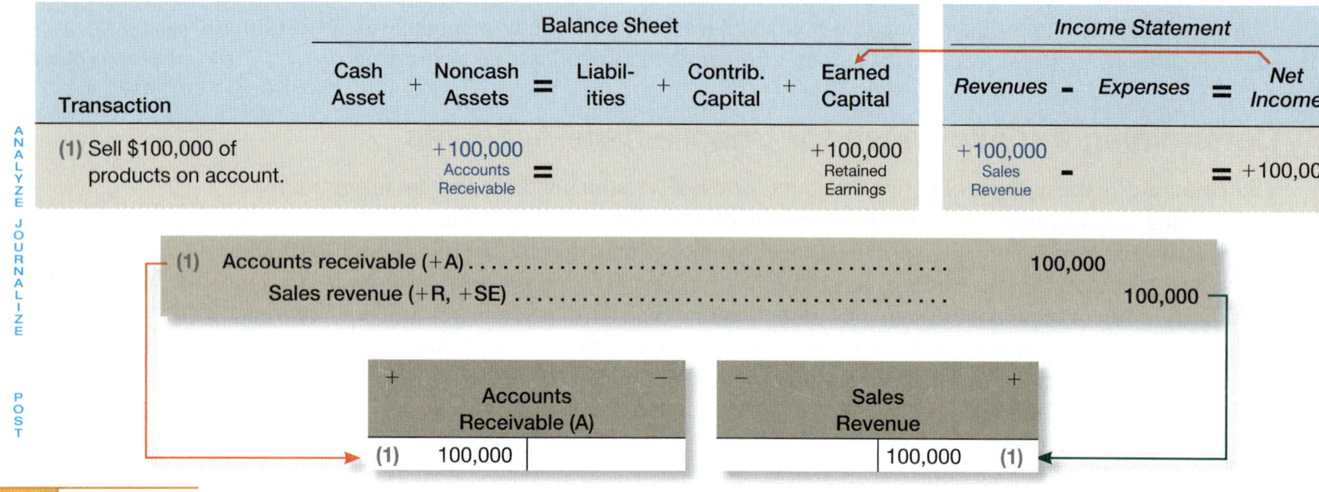

FYI The term *provision* is sometimes used as a substitute for expense; often when the reported expense is an estimate.

For an adjusting entry at year-end, uncollectible accounts are estimated and recorded as follows as **bad debts expense** (also called *provision for uncollectible accounts*). The allowance for uncollectible accounts is a contra-asset account. It offsets (reduces) accounts receivable.

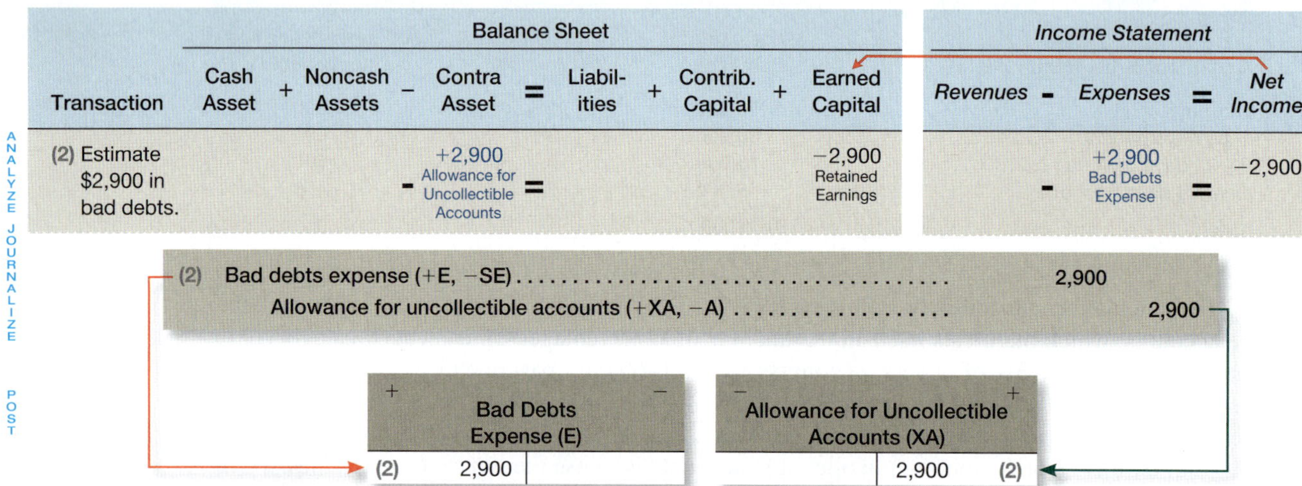

This accounting treatment serves three purposes. First, the balance in accounts receivable is reported in the balance sheet net of estimated uncollectible accounts as follows:

Accounts receivable, net of $2,900 in allowances. $97,100

The $97,100 is the net realizable value of the accounts receivable. Second, the original value of accounts receivable is preserved. The individual accounts that add up to the $100,000 in accounts receivable have not been altered. Third, bad debts expense of $2,900, which is part of the cost of offering credit to customers, is matched against the $100,000 sales generated on credit and reported in the income statement. Bad debts expense is usually included in SG&A expenses.[4]

The allowance for uncollectible accounts is increased by bad debts expense (estimated provision for uncollectibles) and decreased when an account is written off. Because the allowance for uncollectible accounts is a contra-asset account, credit entries increase its balance. The greater the balance in the contra-asset account, the more the corresponding asset account is offset.

Recording Write-offs of Uncollectible Accounts

Companies have collection processes and policies to determine when an overdue receivable should be classified as uncollectible. When an individual account reaches that classification, it is written off. To illustrate a write-off, assume that in the next period (Year 2), the company described above receives notice that one of its customers, owing $500 at the time, has declared bankruptcy. The seller's attorneys believe that the legal costs necessary to collect the amount would exceed the $500 owed. The seller could then decide to write off the account with the following entry.

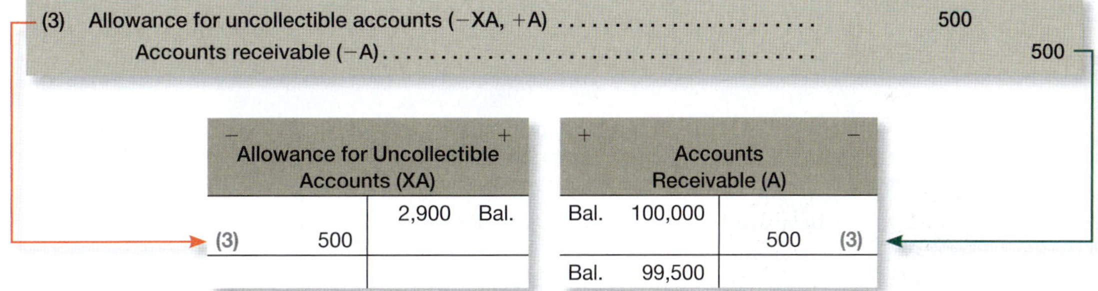

	Balance Sheet						Income Statement		
Transaction	Cash Asset	+ Noncash Assets	− Contra Asset	= Liabil- ities	+ Contrib. Capital	+ Earned Capital	Revenues −	Expenses	= Net Income
(3) Write off $500 in accounts receivable.*		−500 Accounts Receivable −	−500 Allowance for Uncollectible Accounts =				−		=

*There is no effect on accounts receivable, net of the allowance for uncollectible accounts. Consequently, there is no *net* effect on the balance sheet.

(3) Allowance for uncollectible accounts (−XA, +A)   500
         Accounts receivable (−A).   500

− Allowance for Uncollectible Accounts (XA) +		+ Accounts Receivable (A) −	
	2,900 Bal.	Bal. 100,000	
(3) 500			500 (3)
		Bal. 99,500	

Exhibit 6.7 summarizes the effects of this write-off on the individual accounts.

EXHIBIT 6.7	Effects of an Accounts Receivable Write-Off		
	Before Write-Off	Effects of Write-Off	After Account Write-Off
Accounts receivable	$100,000	$ (500)	$99,500
Less: Allowance for uncollectible accounts.	2,900	500	2,400
Accounts receivable, net of allowance	$ 97,100		$97,100

The net amount of accounts receivable that is reported in the balance sheet after the write-off is the same amount that was reported before the write-off. This is always the case. The individual account receivable was reduced and the contra-asset was reduced by the same amount. Also no entry was made

---

[4] Technically speaking, bad debts expense is not really an expense. It is, instead, a reduction of sales revenue. Although it is correct to record this item as a reduction of net sales, companies commonly record bad debt expense as part of selling expenses to emphasize that this amount is a cost of offering credit to customers.

to the income statement. The expense was estimated and recorded in the period when the credit sales were recorded.[5]

To complete the illustration, assume that management's aging of accounts at the end of Year 2 shows that the ending balance in the allowance account should be $3,000, so another $600 should be added to the allowance account at the end of Year 2. This $600 amount would reflect sales made in Year 2, as well as the seller's experience with collections during Year 2. The entry to record the Year 2 provision follows.

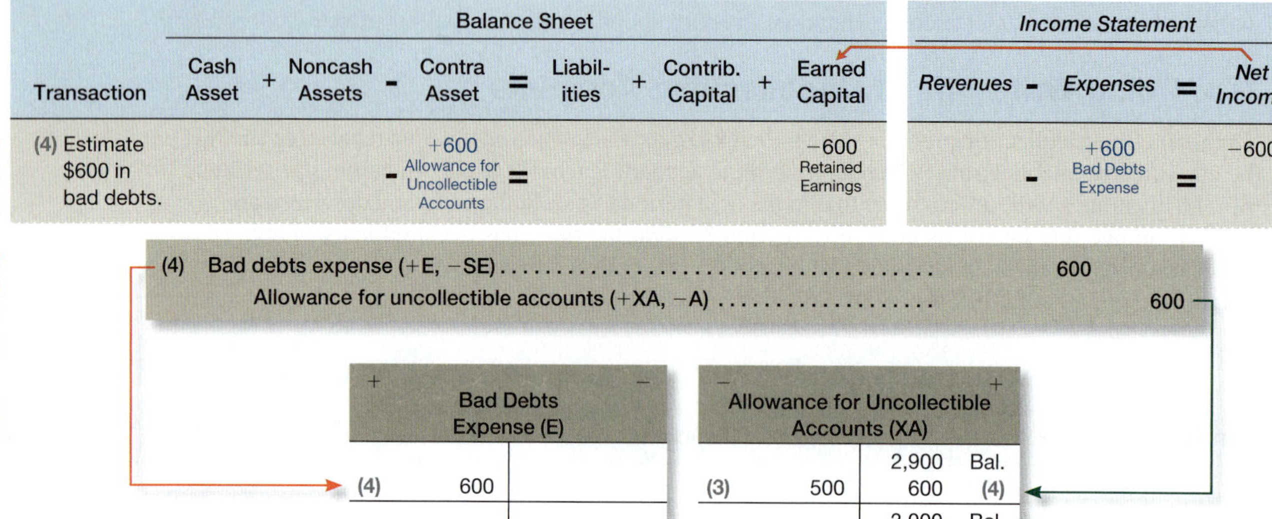

This entry is the same (albeit with a different dollar amount) as the entry made to record the estimate in Year 1. A reconciliation of allowance for uncollectible accounts for the two years follows.

	Year 1	Year 2
Allowance for uncollectible accounts, beginning balance	$ 0	$2,900
Add: provision for uncollectible accounts (bad debts expense estimate)	2,900	600
Subtract: write-offs of uncollectible accounts receivable.	0	500
Allowance for uncollectible accounts, ending balance.	$2,900	$3,000

To summarize, the *main balance sheet and income statement effects occur when the provision is made to the allowance for uncollectible accounts.* Accounts receivable (net) is reduced, and that reduction is reflected in the income statement as bad debts expense (usually part of selling, general, and administrative expenses). The net income reduction yields a corresponding equity reduction (via reduced retained earnings). Importantly, the main financial statement effects are at the point of *estimation*, not upon the event of *write-off*. In this way, the net accounts receivable reflects the most up-to-date judgments about future customer payments, and bad debts expense matches the current period's sales and incorporates any changes in management's assessment of the likelihood that customers will pay.

Footnote Disclosures, and Interpretations

In its balance sheets, Cisco reports Accounts receivables, net of allowance for doubtful accounts of $3,177 million at July 25, 2009, and $3,821 at July 26, 2008. In its MD&A, the company provides the following information.

---

[5] Suppose a previously written off account is unexpectedly paid. If that occurs, the write-off entry (3) is reversed (reinstating the receivable and increasing the allowance), and the payment of this reinstated receivable is accounted for in the usual fashion.

Allowances for Receivables and Sales Returns

The allowances for receivables were as follows (in millions, except percentages):

	July 25, 2009	July 26, 2008
Allowance for doubtful accounts	$216	$177
Percentage of gross accounts receivable	6.4%	4.4%

The allowances are based on our assessment of the collectability of customer accounts. We regularly review the allowances to ensure their adequacy by considering factors such as historical experience, credit quality, age of the receivable balances and economic conditions that may affect a customer's ability to pay. In addition, we perform credit reviews and statistical portfolio analysis to assess the credit quality of our receivables. We also consider the concentration of receivables outstanding with a particular customer in assessing the adequacy of our allowances . . .

In Cisco's 10-K report filed with the Securities and Exchange Commission, it discloses that its provision for doubtful accounts (bad debts expense) was $54 million, $34 million, and $6 million in fiscal years 2009, 2008, and 2007, respectively. Based on this information, we could construct a reconciliation of Cisco's allowance for doubtful accounts as presented in Exhibit 6.8.

EXHIBIT 6.8	Reconciliation of Cisco's Allowance for Doubtful Accounts

Allowance for Doubtful Accounts ($ millions)

Balance at July 26, 2008	$177
Provision for doubtful accounts	54
Write-offs	(15)
Balance at July 25, 2009	$216

The footnotes may also disclose whether or not a company has *pledged* its accounts receivable as collateral for a short-term loan. If this is the case, a short-term loan is presented in the liabilities section of the balance sheet and a footnote explains the arrangement. As an alternative to borrowing, a company may *factor* (or sell) its accounts receivable to a bank or other financial institution. If the receivables have been factored, the bank or other financial institution accepts all responsibility for collection. Consequently, the receivables do not appear on the balance sheet of the selling company because they have been sold.

The reconciliation of Cisco's allowance account provides insight into the level of its annual provision (bad debts expense) relative to its write-offs. In 2009, Cisco wrote off $15 million in uncollectible accounts while recording a provision for doubtful accounts (bad debts expense) of $54 million. Because the provision exceeded the write-offs, the total allowance increased from $177 million in 2008 to $216 million in 2009. After a pattern of steady decline in recent years, the 2009 allowance increased to 6.4% of gross accounts receivable from 4.4% of accounts receivable in 2008 and 4.0% of accounts receivable in 2007.

This change in Cisco's allowance as a percentage of receivables could be caused by a number of factors. First, the creditworthiness of Cisco's customers may have declined. This decline can be caused by changing economic conditions or a change in Cisco's credit policies (including collection efforts). Alternatively, perhaps the company's customer mix has changed, and it is now selling to less creditworthy customers.

The magnitude of Cisco's uncollectible accounts relative to the company's overall size and profitability makes it an unlikely place for earnings management. But companies in other industries (banking, publishing, retail) often have receivables that require substantial adjustments for expected returns or uncollectible accounts. For instance, the publisher **John Wiley & Sons, Inc.**, reports accounts receivable of $178.6 million in its April 30, 2009, balance sheet, but this amount is net of an allowance for doubtful accounts of $5.7 million and an allowance for sales returns of $55.2 million. So, Wiley only expects to collect about 75% of the amounts it has billed customers. For such companies, modest changes in expectations of returns or collections can have a material effect on reported income.

Experience tells us that many companies have used the allowance for uncollectible accounts to shift income from one period into another. For instance, a company may overestimate its allowance in some years. Such an overestimation may have been unintentional, or it may have been an intentional attempt to manage earnings by building up a reserve (during good years) that can be drawn down in subsequent periods. Such a reserve is sometimes called a **cookie jar reserve**. Alternatively, a company may underestimate its provision in some years. This underestimation may be unintentional, or it may be an attempt to boost earnings to achieve some desired target. Looking at the patterns in the reconciliation of the allowance for uncollectible accounts may provide some indicators of this behavior.

The MD&A section of a company's 10-K report often provides insights into changes in company policies, customers, or economic conditions to help explain changes in the allowance account. Further, the amount and timing of the uncollectible provision is largely controlled by management. Although external auditors assess the reasonableness of the allowance for uncollectible accounts, auditors do not possess the inside knowledge of management and are, therefore, at an information disadvantage, particularly if a dispute arises.

Some insight can be gained by comparing Cisco's allowance to those of its competitors. Exhibit 6.9 illustrates that Cisco's allowance as a percentage of total receivables is slightly greater than two of its competitors, **Alcatel-Lucent** and **Juniper Networks, Inc.**, while significantly below that of a third competitor, **3Com Corporation**. This result suggests that Cisco's policies are in line with those of its competitors. In addition, two of these three competitors have increased the allowance as a percentage of receivables over this period. These changes are consistent with a deterioration in overall economic conditions for the industry.

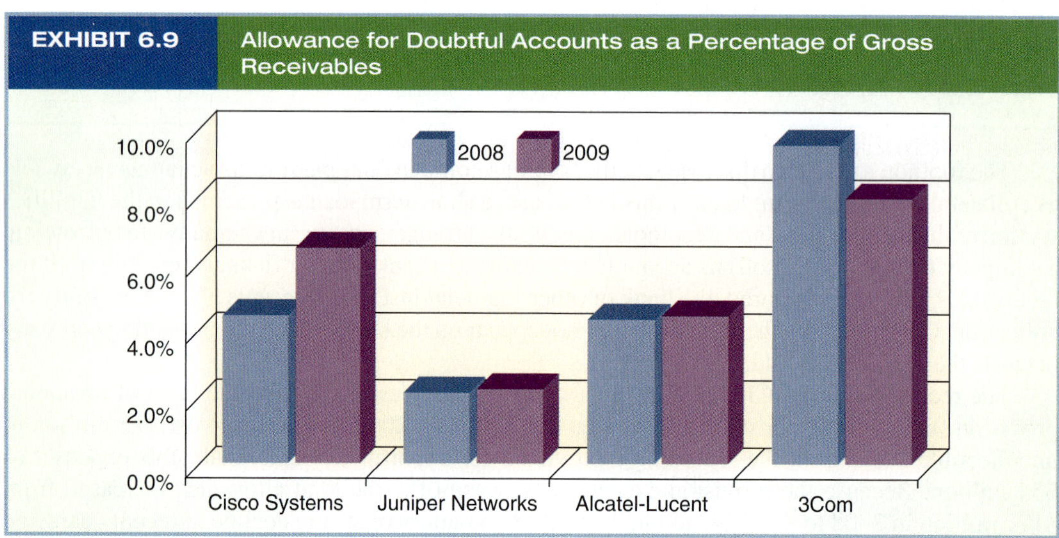

EXHIBIT 6.9 Allowance for Doubtful Accounts as a Percentage of Gross Receivables

These companies do not have identical fiscal year-ends. Cisco's fiscal year ends in late July, 3Com on May 31, and Juniper Networks and Alcatel-Lucent on December 31. The comparisons in this exhibit (and in those following) are based on the most recent financial statements for each company available prior to Cisco's statements.

Ultimately, a company makes two representations when reporting accounts receivable (net) in the current asset section of its balance sheet:

1. It expects to collect the asset amount reported on the balance sheet (remember, accounts receivable are reported net of allowance for uncollectible accounts).

2. It expects to collect the asset amount within the next year (implied from its classification as a current asset).

From an analysis viewpoint, we scrutinize the adequacy of a company's provision for its uncollectible accounts. If the provision is inadequate, the cash ultimately collected will be less than what the company is reporting as net receivables.

The financial statement effects of uncollectible accounts are at the point of estimation, not at the time of a write-off. Nevertheless, it is important to remember that management sets the size of the allowance, albeit with auditor assurances.

MID-CHAPTER REVIEW 3

At December 31, 2010, Engel Company had a balance of $770,000 in its Accounts Receivable account and an unused balance of $7,000 in its Allowance for Uncollectible Accounts. The company then analyzed and aged its accounts receivable as follows:

Current.	$468,000
1–60 days past due	244,000
61–180 days past due	38,000
Over 180 days past due	20,000
Total accounts receivable.	$770,000

In the past, the company experienced losses as follows: 1% of current balances, 5% of balances 1–60 days past due, 15% of balances 61–180 days past due, and 40% of balances over 180 days past due. The company bases its provision for credit losses on the aging analysis.

Required

1. What amount of uncollectible accounts (bad debts) expense will Engel report in its 2010 income statement?
2. Show how Accounts Receivable and the Allowance for Uncollectible Accounts appear in its December 31, 2010, balance sheet.
3. Assume that Engel's allowance for uncollectible accounts has maintained a historical average of 2% of gross accounts receivable. How do you interpret the level of the current allowance percentage?
4. Report the effects for each of the following summary transactions in the financial statement effects template, prepare journal entries, and then post the amounts to the appropriate T-accounts.
   a. Bad debts expense estimated at $23,580.
   b. Write off $5,000 in customer accounts.

The solution to this review problem can be found on pages 300–301.

ANALYZING FINANCIAL STATEMENTS

We began this chapter with a discussion of operating income and revenues and proceeded to introduce receivables. We now introduce five ratios that will aid in our analysis of income, revenue, and receivables. The first ratio is a commonly-used measure of business unit performance that relates the business unit's operating achievements to the resources that it was given. The next two ratios address important measures of operating profitability—net operating profit after taxes and net operating profit margin. The last two ratios, accounts receivable turnover ratio and the average collection period, aid in the analysis of receivables.

LO5 Calculate return on capital employed, net operating profit after taxes, net operating profit margin, accounts receivable turnover, and average collection period.

Return on Capital Employed (ROCE)

Return on capital employed (ROCE) is a common performance measure for business unit managers operating in large organizations. ROCE is calculated as follows:

$$\text{ROCE} = \frac{\text{Income from operations before taxes}}{\text{Average net operating assets}}$$

Operating managers do not have responsibility for taxes or for financing their operations. Those functions are performed by central administrators. So pretax operating income measures the revenues and expenses for which the business unit has responsibility. Net operating assets equals total operating assets minus current operating liabilities and represents the investment that has been made in the business unit by the larger organization.

Cisco Systems does not provide enough information in its annual report to calculate ROCE for different business units, but we can do it for the company as a whole. From Exhibit 6.2, we see that Cisco's pretax operating income is $7,322 million for 2009. Its average total assets for the year equal $63,431 million ([$68,128 million + $58,734 million] ÷ 2), but $25,164 million of this amount is invested in government securities. So, average operating assets are $38,267 over fiscal year 2009. Average current operating liabilities (excluding financial liabilities) are $13,507 million ([$13,655 million + $13,358 million] ÷ 2), so ROCE for 2009 is 29.6% ($7,322 million ÷ [$38,267 million − $13,507 million]).

Net Operating Profit After Taxes (NOPAT)

Net operating profit after taxes (NOPAT) is a widely used performance measure of operating profitability. NOPAT is calculated as follows:

$$\text{NOPAT} = \text{Net income} - [(\text{Nonoperating revenues} - \text{Nonoperating expenses}) \times (1 - \text{Marginal tax rate})]$$

As described in Appendix A of Chapter 5, we assume that the marginal tax rate on nonoperating revenues and expenses is equal to the federal statutory tax rate of 35%. To illustrate the calculation of NOPAT, refer to Cisco's income statement presented in Exhibit 6.2. Cisco reported net income of $6,134 million in 2009. It also reported net interest income of $499 million and an other net loss of $128 million. Therefore, Cisco's NOPAT for 2009 is $5,893 million [$6,134 million − ($499 million − $128 million) × (1 − 0.35)]. In 2008, Cisco's NOPAT was $7,524 million [$8,052 million − ($824 million − $11 million) × (1 − 0.35)].

NOPAT is an important measure of profitability. It is similar to net income except that NOPAT focuses exclusively on after-tax operating performance, while net income measures the overall performance of the company and includes both operating and nonoperating components. NOPAT is used as a performance measure by management and analysts alike and it is also used in a number of ratios, such as the Net operating profit margin.

Net Operating Profit Margin (NOPM)

The analysis of operating profit margin is important to interpreting the income statement. Profit margins are commonly used to compare a company to its competitors and to evaluate the performance of business segments. **Net operating profit margin (NOPM)** is a useful summary measure that focuses on the overall operating profitability of the company relative to its sales revenue. It is computed as follows:

$$\text{Net operating profit margin (NOPM)} = \frac{\text{NOPAT}}{\text{Sales revenue}}$$

Cisco's NOPM was 16.3% in 2009 ($5,893 million/$36,117 million). This compares with a NOPM of 19.0% in 2008 ($7,524 million/$39,540 million). Further analysis is required to explain this decrease in NOPM from 2008 to 2009. The decrease in NOPM may be due to changes in the economic environment, competitive pressures, changes in the product or customer mix, changes in cost structure and efficiency, or increases in research and development. It may also be that one of the years' results included nonrecurring items that might be included in operating income, such as restructuring costs. Such analysis is detailed later in this chapter. However, a casual examination of Cisco's income statement reveals that operating expenses decreased by a lower percentage than gross margin (revenues less cost of sales) in 2009. General and administrative expenses increased significantly, but sales and marketing expenses and research and development expenses experienced slight decreases.

Besides comparing current NOPM to past performance, it is useful to compare Cisco to other companies. To appreciate how NOPM varies by industry, Exhibit 6.10 compares Cisco's 2009 NOPM to that of several companies in other industries. While **Pfizer** had the highest NOPM in this group, Cisco reported a higher NOPM than the other companies in the comparison.

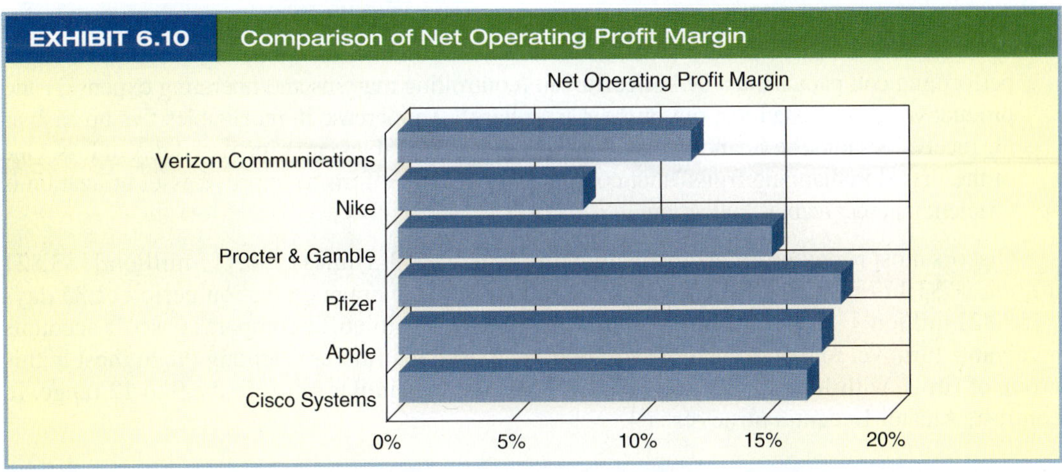

Accounts Receivable Turnover and Average Collection Period

Total asset turnover is computed as sales divided by average total assets. An important complement to this measure is the **accounts receivables turnover (ART)**, which is defined as:

$$\text{Accounts receivable turnover} = \frac{\text{Sales revenue}}{\text{Average accounts receivable}}$$

Accounts receivable turnover reveals how many times receivables have turned (been collected) during the period. More turns indicate that receivables are being collected more quickly. The denominator is the average of beginning receivables and ending receivables to recognize growth (or decline) in the company's investment in receivables over the period. (In a seasonal business, it would make sense to average the quarterly receivable balances.)

A companion measure to accounts receivable turnover is the **average collection period (ACP)** for accounts receivable, also called *days sales outstanding (DSO)*, which is defined as:

$$\text{Average collection period} = \frac{\text{Average accounts receivable}}{\text{Average daily sales}}$$

where average daily sales equals annual sales divided by the number of days in the period (for example, 365 for a year). The average collection period indicates how long, on average, the receivables are outstanding before being collected.

To illustrate, assume that annual sales are $1,000, and the average accounts receivable is $200. The accounts receivable turnover is 5, computed as $1,000/$200, and the average collection period (days sales outstanding) is 73 days, computed as $200/($1,000/365).

The accounts receivable turnover and the average collection period yield valuable insights on at least two dimensions:

1. *Receivables quality* A change in receivables turnover (and collection period) provides insight into accounts receivable quality. If turnover slows (collection period lengthens), the reason could be deterioration in collectibility of receivables. However, before reaching this conclusion, consider at least three alternative explanations:

   a. A seller can extend its credit terms. If the seller is attempting to enter new markets or take market share from competitors, it may extend credit terms to attract buyers.

   b. A seller can take on longer-paying customers. For example, facing increased competition, many computer and automobile companies began leasing their products, thus reducing the cash outlay for customers and stimulating sales. The change in mix away from cash sales and toward leasing had the effect of reducing receivables turnover and increasing the collection period.

   c. The seller can increase the allowance provision. Receivables turnover is often computed using net receivables (after the allowance for uncollectible accounts). Overestimating the provision reduces net receivables and increases turnover.

2. *Asset utilization* Asset turnover is an important measure of financial performance, both by managers for internal performance goals, as well as by the market in evaluating companies. High-performing companies must be both efficient (controlling margins and operating expenses) and productive (getting the most out of their asset base). An increase in receivables ties up cash as the receivables must be financed, and slower-turning receivables carry increased risk of loss. One of the first "low-hanging fruits" that companies pursue in efforts to improve asset utilization is efficiency in receivables collection.

Cisco's most recent accounts receivable turnover was 10.3 times ($36,117 million/[{$3,821 million + $3,177 million}/2]) in 2009. This equates to an average collection period of 35 days ([{$3,821 million + $3,177 million}/2] /[$36,117/365]). Exhibit 6.11 compares Cisco's accounts receivable turnover to that of its three competitors. Cisco's turnover is among the highest in this group of firms, with Juniper Network's and 3COM having similar ratios in the 9 to 12 range. In contrast, Alcatel-Lucent's turnover is 4.

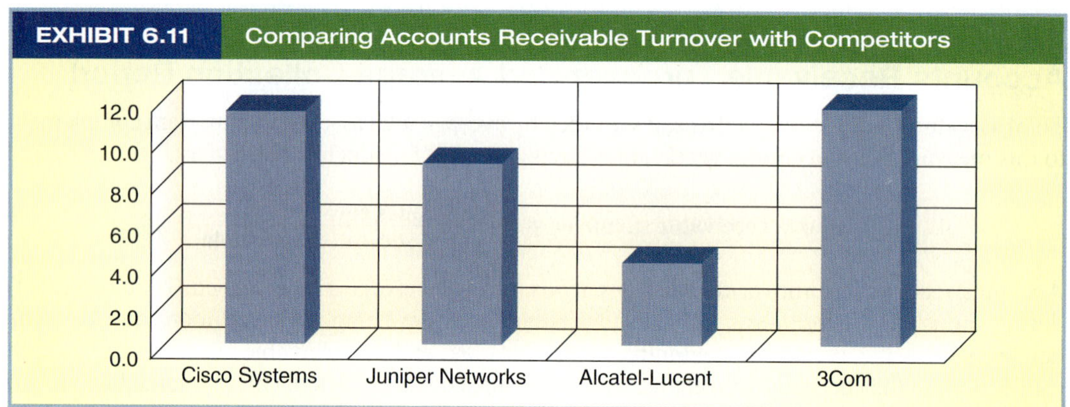

EXHIBIT 6.11   Comparing Accounts Receivable Turnover with Competitors

Comparing Cisco's accounts receivable turnover to several companies in other industries reveals a significant range of values, from **Apple**'s 23 days to Pfizer's 71 days (Exhibit 6.12). This variation likely reflects differences in the business model of each company. That is, variations across industries in accounts receivable turnover reflect differences in customers, products and services, competitive pressures, and credit policies that are specific to the individual firm.

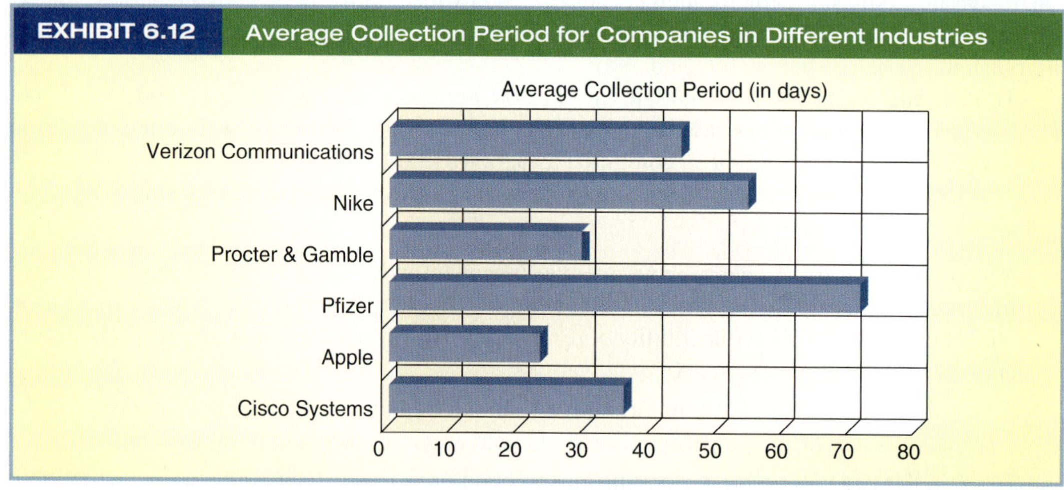

EXHIBIT 6.12   Average Collection Period for Companies in Different Industries

YOU MAKE THE CALL

You are the Receivables Manager   You are analyzing your receivables turnover report for the period, and you are concerned that the average collection period is lengthening, causing a drop in cash flow from operations. What specific actions can you take to reduce the average collection period?
[Answers on page 282]

EARNINGS MANAGEMENT

Management choices about transactions, accounting principles, estimates, disclosure, and presentation of income components are an inevitable part of financial reporting. Earnings management occurs when management uses this discretion to mask the underlying economic performance of a company.

There are many motives for earnings management, but these motives generally fall into one of two categories:

1. A desire to mislead some financial statement users about the financial performance of the company to gain economic advantage, or

2. A desire to influence legal contracts that use reported accounting numbers to specify contractual obligations and outcomes.[6]

Most earnings management practices relate to aggressive revenue or expense recognition practices. However, financial statement presentation can also be a concern. Below, we identify several examples of potentially misleading reporting.

- *Overly optimistic (or overly pessimistic) estimates.* The use of estimates in accrual accounting is extensive. For instance, revenue recognition based on percentage of completion requires estimates of future construction costs. Depreciation expense depends on estimates of useful life, and bad debts expense depends on estimates of future customer payments. Although changes in estimates may be warranted by changes in business conditions, they can have a significant effect on reported net income and, thereby, may provide opportunities for managers to report income that is better (or worse) than it should be.

- *Channel stuffing.* **Channel stuffing** arises when a company uses its market power over customers or distributors to induce them to purchase more goods than necessary to meet their normal needs. Or, the seller may offer significant price reductions to encourage buyers to stock up on their products. Channel stuffing usually occurs immediately before the end of an accounting period and boosts the seller's revenue for that period (while increasing the buyer's inventory). The practice is not illegal and revenue may be recorded, as long as the transactions meet the necessary criteria for a sale.

- *Strategic timing and disclosure of transactions and nonrecurring gains and losses.* Management has some discretion over the timing of transactions that can affect financial statements. If management has an asset (e.g., a tract of land) with book value less than market value, it can choose when to sell the asset to recognize a gain and maintain steady improvements in net income. This practice is known as **income smoothing**. In some cases, these smoothing effects are reported in combination with other items, making it more difficult to separate recurring amounts from nonrecurring amounts. Or, a company could take a **big bath** by recording a nonrecurring loss in a period of already depressed income. Concentrating bad news in a single period reduces the amount of bad news recognized in other periods. Given adequate disclosure, the astute reader of the financial statements will separate nonrecurring income items from persistent operating income, making these income management tactics transparent.

- *Mischaracterizing transactions as arm's-length.* Transfers of inventories or other assets to related entities typically are not recorded until later **arm's-length** sales occur. Sometimes sales are disguised as being sold to unrelated entities to inflate income when (1) the buyer is a related party to the seller, or (2) financing is provided or guaranteed by the seller, or (3) the buyer is a special-purpose entity that fails to meet independence requirements. This financial reporting practice is not consistent with GAAP and may be fraudulent.

The consequence of earnings management is that the usefulness of the information presented in the income statement is compromised. **Quality of earnings** is a term that analysts often use to describe the extent to which reported income reflects the underlying economic performance of a company. Financial statement users must be careful to examine the quality of a company's earnings before using that information to evaluate performance or value its securities.

---

[6] See Healy, Paul M., and James M. Wahlen, "A Review of Earnings Management Literature and Its Implications for Standard Setting." *Accounting Horizons*, December 1999.

BUSINESS INSIGHT

Sell-through Accounting at Cisco   Following is an excerpt from Cisco System's revenue recognition policies from its annual report.

> The Company uses distributors that stock inventory and typically sell to systems integrators, service providers, and other resellers. In addition, certain products are sold through retail partners. The Company refers to these sales through distributors and retail partners as its two-tier system of sales to the end customer. Revenue from distributors and retail partners is recognized based on a sell-through method using information provided by them.

> The "sell-through" method is essentially the same as the accounting for consignment arrangements. By not recognizing revenue until its distributors and retail partners sell its products to the final customer, Cisco greatly reduces the likelihood of any channel stuffing behavior.

YOU MAKE THE CALL

You are the Controller   While evaluating the performance of your sales staff, you notice that one of the salespeople consistently meets his quarterly sales quotas but never surpasses his goals by very much. You also discover that his customers often return an unusually large amount of product at the beginning of each quarter. What might be happening here? How would you investigate for potential abuse? [Answer on pages 282–283]

RESEARCH INSIGHT

Pro Forma Income   Nonrecurring items in income such as discontinued operations, restructuring charges and extraordinary items make it difficult for investors to determine what portion of income is sustainable into the future. The past decade has seen more companies reporting **pro forma income**, which purportedly excludes the effects of nonrecurring or noncash items that companies feel are unimportant for valuation purposes. Research, however, provides no evidence that more exclusions via pro forma income leads to more predictable future cash flows. More important, investors appear to be misled by the exclusions at the time of the pro forma income release. Research also finds that companies issuing pro forma income are more likely to be young companies concentrated in technology and business services. Too often, these companies are characterized by below-average sales and income when they choose to report pro forma income. Evidence also shows that the pro forma income can exceed GAAP income by as much as 20 percent.

Critics of pro forma income argue that the items excluded by managers from GAAP income are inconsistent across companies and time. They contend that a major motive for pro forma income is to mislead stakeholders. Legendary investor Warren Buffet puts pro forma in context (Berkshire Hathaway, Annual Report): "When companies or investment professionals use terms such as 'EBITDA' and 'pro forma,' they want you to unthinkingly accept concepts that are dangerously flawed."

CHAPTER-END REVIEW

The following data were taken from the fiscal year 2008 10-K reports of **Dell Inc.** and **Hewlett-Packard Company**:

($ millions)	Dell	HP
Sales revenue	$61,101	$118,364
Net income	2,478	8,329
Nonoperating revenues	134	—
Nonoperating expenses	—	—
Accounts receivable, net (end-of-year)	4,731	16,928
Accounts receivable, net (beginning-of-year))	5,961	13,420
Operating assets (end-of-year)	25,306	113,238
Operating assets (beginning-of-year)	25,793	88,547
Current operating liabilities (end-of-year)	14,746	42,763
Current operating liabilities (beginning-of-year)	18,301	36,074

Required

1. Compute the following for each company:
   a. Return on capital employed (ROCE).
   b. Net operating profit after taxes (NOPAT). Assume a 35% marginal tax rate.
   c. Net operating profit margin (NOPM).
   d. Accounts receivable turnover (ART).
   e. Average collection period (ACP).
2. Compare these two companies based on the ratios computed in (1). What inferences can you make about these competitors?

The solution to this review problem can be found on page 302.

APPENDIX 6A: Reporting Nonrecurring Items

In addition to categorizing income statement elements as either operating or nonoperating, it is also useful to separate **recurring** sources of income from those sources that are **nonrecurring**. Isolating nonrecurring earnings is useful for two reasons. First, to evaluate company performance or management quality, it is helpful to make comparisons of current performance with prior years and with other companies facing similar economic circumstances. It is easier to make these comparisons if we focus on recurring income components. Nonrecurring income components are likely to be specific to one company and one accounting period, making them irrelevant for comparative purposes. Second, estimation of company value involves forecasts of income and cash flows. Such forecasts are better when we can identify any nonrecurring effects in income and cash flows and then eliminate them from projections. Recurring earnings and cash flows are more **persistent** and, therefore, more useful in estimating company value.

LO7 Describe and illustrate the reporting for nonrecurring items.

Accounting standards attempt to distinguish some nonrecurring income components. Three of the most common nonrecurring items are:

- **Restructuring charges**—expenses and losses related to significant reorganization of a company's operations.
- **Discontinued operations**—income related to business units that the company has discontinued and sold or plans to sell.
- **Extraordinary items**—material gains or losses that are not related to normal business operations; extraordinary items must be both unusual in nature and infrequent in occurrence.

Discontinued Operations

Discontinued operations refer to any separately identifiable component of the company that management sells or intends to sell. The income or loss of the discontinued operations (net of tax), and the after-tax gain or loss on sale of the unit, are reported in the income statement below income from continuing operations. The segregation of discontinued operations means that its revenues and expenses are *not* reported with revenues and expenses from continuing operations.

To illustrate, assume that Chapman Company's income statement results were the following.

	Continuing Operations	Discontinued Operations	Total
Revenues........................	$10,000	$3,000	$13,000
Expenses........................	7,000	2,000	9,000
Pretax income	3,000	1,000	4,000
Tax expense (40%)	1,200	400	1,600
Net income......................	$ 1,800	$ 600	$ 2,400

The reported income statement would then appear with the separate disclosure for discontinued operations (shown in bold, separately net of any related taxes) as follows.

Revenues..	$10,000
Expenses..	7,000
Pretax income	3,000
Tax expense (40%)	1,200
Income from continuing operations	1,800
Income from discontinued operations, net of income taxes	600
Net income..	$ 2,400

Revenues and expenses reflect the continuing operations only, and the (persistent) income from continuing operations is reported after deducting the related tax expense. Results from the (transitory) discontinued operations are collapsed into one line item and reported separately net of any related taxes. The same is true for any gain or loss from sale of the discontinued operation's net assets. The net income figure is unchanged by this presentation, but our ability to evaluate and interpret income information is greatly improved.

Extraordinary Items

Extraordinary items refer to **transitory** events that are both unusual *and* infrequent. Their effects are segregated and reported separately in the income statement following income from continuing operations (and discontinued operations, if any). Management makes the determination of whether an event is unusual and infrequent for reporting purposes. GAAP provides the following guidance in determining whether or not an item is extraordinary:

- *Unusual nature.* The underlying event or transaction must possess a high degree of abnormality and be clearly unrelated to, or only incidentally related to, the ordinary activities of the entity, taking into account the entity's operating environment.
- *Infrequency of occurrence.* The underlying event or transaction must be of a type that would not reasonably be expected to recur in the foreseeable future, taking into account the entity's operating environment.

  The following items are generally *excluded* from extraordinary items:

- Write-down or write-off of assets
- Foreign currency gains and losses
- Gains and losses from disposal of specific assets or business segment
- Effects of a strike
- Accrual adjustments related to long-term contracts
- Costs of defense against a takeover
- Costs incurred as a result of the September 11, 2001, events

As with discontinued operations, extraordinary items are reported separately, net of income taxes, to facilitate forecasting of future income.

Restructuring Costs

Restructuring costs are similar to discontinued operations, except that they do not involve the sale of a component of the company with separately identifiable operations and cash flows. These costs typically involve activities such as consolidating production facilities, reorganizing sales operations, outsourcing some activities, or discontinuing product lines within a business unit. Restructuring costs are a substantial expense item in many companies' income statements. They tend to be large in magnitude and, as a result, GAAP requires enhanced disclosure, either as a separate line item in the income statement (as a "special item") or in a footnote. These costs are considered transitory because companies do not engage in restructuring activities every year. As such, these costs should be reclassified to a transitory category for analysis purposes even though companies include them in income from continuing operations. The reporting of restructuring costs in the income statement typically consists of two parts:

1. Employee severance costs
2. Asset write-downs

The first of these, **employee severance costs**, represent accrued (estimated) costs for termination of employees as part of a restructuring program. The second part of restructuring costs consists of **asset write-downs**, also called *write-offs* or *charge-offs*. Restructuring activities usually involve closure or relocation of manufacturing or administrative facilities. This process can require the write-down of long-term assets (such as plant assets), and the write-down of inventories that are no longer salable at current carrying costs.

RESEARCH INSIGHT

Restructuring Costs and Managerial Incentives Research has investigated the circumstances and effects of restructuring costs. Some research finds that stock prices increase upon announcement of a restructuring as if the market appreciates the company's candor. Research also finds that many companies that reduce income through restructuring costs later reverse those costs, resulting in a substantial income boost for the period of reversal. These reversals often occur when their absence would have yielded an earnings decline. Whether or not the market responds favorably to trimming the fat or simply disregards such transitory items as uninformative, managers have incentives to exclude such income-decreasing items from operating income. These incentives are contractually-based, extending from debt covenants and restrictions to managerial bonuses.

YOU MAKE THE CALL

You are the Financial Analyst You are analyzing the financial statements of a company that has reported a large restructuring cost, involving both employee severance and asset write-downs, in its income statement. How do you interpret and treat this cost in your analysis of its current and future period profitability? [Answer on page 283]

BUSINESS INSIGHT

Transitory Items at Pfizer Pfizer, Inc., reported net income of $8.1 billion in its 2008 income statement. This amount included two transitory items—a restructuring charge and income from discontinued operations. The restructuring charges were related to Pfizer's "initiatives to increase efficiency and streamline decision-making" and also to the integration of two significant acquisitions (Warner-Lambert and Pharmacia). The components of their restructuring charges were detailed in the following table in the footnotes.

(Millions of Dollars)	Costs Incurred				Activity through December 31, 2008	Accrual as of December 31, 2008
	2008	2007	2006	2005–2008		
Employee termination costs....	$2,004	$2,034	$ 809	$5,150	$3,045	$2,105
Asset impairments............	543	260	368	1,293	1,293	—
Other	79	229	119	440	390	50
Total.....................	$2,626	$2,523	$1,296	$6,883	$4,728	$2,155

This table also provides information on the fulfillment of employee termination costs; as of the end of fiscal year 2008, Pfizer has paid a little over $3 billion of the more than $5 billion in promised benefits to terminated employees.

The income and gains from discontinued operations relate to transitional activities from Pfizer's 2006 sale of its Consumer Healthcare business. For 2008, this item breaks down as follows:

Components of income from discontinued operations ($ millions)	Income reported in 2008
Income (loss) from operations of discontinued business (net of tax)....	$ (2)
Gain (loss) on sale of discontinued business (net of tax)	80
Total income from discontinued operations	$78

Transitory items can have a huge effect on reported net income. In 2008, restructuring charges were about 27% of Pfizer's income from continuing operations.

APPENDIX 6A REVIEW

On April 30, 2010, Singh Corporation decided to close its operations in Fiji. During the first four months of the year (January through April) these operations had reported a loss of $120,000. Singh paid its employees $12,000 in severance pay. The assets of this operation were sold at a loss of $18,000. The tax rate in Fiji is 30%.

Required

a. If this closure is recorded as discontinued operations, how should it be presented in Singh's income statement?
b. If this closure is classified as a restructuring charge, how would it be presented in Singh's income statement?
c. What would determine whether this event should be reported as discontinued operations or a restructuring charge?

The solution to this review problem can be found on page 302.

SUMMARY

LO1 **Describe and apply the criteria for determining when revenue is recognized. (p. 260)**
- Revenue is recognized when it is earned and realized (or realizable).

LO2 **Illustrate revenue and expense recognition when the transaction involves future deliverables. (p. 262)**
- When customers pay prior to the delivery of all elements of the product (or service) package, an unearned revenue liability must be recognized.
- When a company recognizes an unearned revenue liability, its reported revenue for a period does not coincide with the purchases made by customers in that period.

LO3 **Illustrate revenue and expense recognition for long-term projects. (p. 264)**
- Long-term contracts are recorded using the percentage-of-completion (POC) method when a signed contract exists with a fixed or determinable price, collection is reasonably assured, and the cost of completing the contract can be estimated.
- The completed contract method is used when the conditions for using POC are not met.
- The installment method is used for long-term sales contracts when collection of cash is not assured.

LO4 **Estimate and account for uncollectible accounts receivable. (p. 267)**
- Uncollectible accounts are usually estimated by aging the accounts receivable.
- Estimated uncollectible accounts are recorded as a contra-asset called allowance for uncollectible accounts.
- Write-offs of uncollectible accounts are deducted from accounts receivable and from the allowance account.

LO5 **Calculate return on capital employed, net operating profit after taxes, net operating profit margin, accounts receivable turnover, and average collection period. (p. 273)**
- Return on capital employed (ROCE) is a commonly used measure of business unit performance.
- Net operating profit after taxes (NOPAT) and the net operating profit margin (NOPM) are measures of the profitability of operating activities.
- Accounts receivable turnover (ART) and average collection period (ACP) measure the ability of the company to convert receivables into cash through collection.

LO6 **Discuss earnings management and explain how it affects analysis and interpretation of financial statements. (p. 277)**
- Earnings management occurs when management uses its discretion to mask the underlying economic performance of a company.
- The consequence of earnings management is that the usefulness of the information presented in the income statement is compromised.

LO7 **Appendix 6A: Describe and illustrate the reporting for nonrecurring items. (p. 279)**
- Extraordinary items and income from discontinued operations are transitory (nonrecurring) items that are reported net of income taxes after earnings from continuing operations.
- Restructuring charges include asset write-downs and employee severance costs. Even though these charges are typically reported among earnings from continuing operations, they are classified as transitory for analysis purposes.

GUIDANCE ANSWERS . . . YOU MAKE THE CALL

You are the Receivables Manager First, you must realize that the extension of credit is an important tool in the marketing of your products, often as important as advertising and promotion. Given that receivables are necessary, there are some methods we can use to speed their collection. (1) We can better screen the customers to whom we extend credit. (2) We can negotiate advance or progress payments from customers. (3) We can use bank letters of credit or other automatic drafting prcedures so that billings must not be sent. (4) We can make sure products are sent as ordered to reduce disputes. (5) We can improve administration of past due accounts to provide for more timely notices of delinquencies and better collection procedures.

You are the Controller The salesperson may be channel stuffing or recording sales without a confirmed sales order. The unusual amount of returns suggests that sales revenues are most likely being recognized prematurely. To investigate, you could examine specific sales orders from customers who returned goods early in the following quarter, or contact customers directly. Most companies delay bonuses until after an appropriate return period expires and only credit the sales staff with net sales.

You are the Financial Analyst   There are two usual components to a restructuring charge: asset write-downs (such as inventories, property, plant, and goodwill) and severance costs. Write-downs occur when the cash flow generating ability of an asset declines, thus reducing its current market value below its book value reported on the balance sheet. Arguably, this decline in cash flow generating ability did not occur solely in the current year and, most likely, has developed over several periods. Delays in loss recognition, such as write-downs of assets, are not uncommon. Thus, prior period income is arguably not as high as reported, and the current period loss is not as great as is reported. Turning to severance costs, their recognition can be viewed as an investment decision by the company that is expected to increase future cash flows (through decreased wages). If this cost accrual is capitalized on the balance sheet, current period income is increased and future period income would bear the amortization of this "asset" to match against future cash flow benefits from severance. This implies that current period income is not as low as reported; however, this adjustment is not GAAP as such severance costs cannot be capitalized. Yet, we can make such an adjustment in our analysis.

KEY RATIOS

Net operating profit after taxes (NOPAT)

$$\text{NOPAT} = \text{Net income} - [(\text{Nonoperating revenues} - \text{Nonoperating expenses}) \times (1 - \text{Marginal tax rate})]$$

Net operating profit margin (NOPM)

$$\text{NOPM} = \frac{\text{Net operating profit after taxes (NOPAT)}}{\text{Sales revenue}}$$

Accounts receivable turnover (ART)

$$\text{ART} = \frac{\text{Sales revenue}}{\text{Average accounts receivable}}$$

Average collection period (ACP)

$$\text{ACP} = \frac{\text{Average accounts receivable}}{\text{Average daily sales}}$$

Return on capital employed (ROCE)

$$\text{ROCE} = \frac{\text{Income from operations before taxes}}{\text{Average net operating assets}}$$

KEY TERMS

Accounts receivables turnover (ART) (p. 275)

Aging analysis (p. 267)

Allowance for uncollectible accounts (p. 267)

Arm's-length (p. 277)

Asset write-downs (p. 280)

Average collection period (ACP) (p. 275)

Bad debts expense (p. 268)

Big bath (p. 277)

Bundled sales (p. 263)

Channel stuffing (p. 277)

Completed contract method (p. 265)

Consignment (p. 261)

Cookie jar reserve (p. 272)

Cost-recovery method (p. 265)

Credit sales (p. 266)

Deferred revenue (p. 262)

Discontinued operations (p. 279)

Earned (p. 261)

Employee severance costs (p. 280)

Extraordinary items (pp. 279, 280)

Income smoothing (p. 277)

Installment method (p. 261)

Matching principle (p. 264)

Net operating profit after taxes (NOPAT) (p. 274)

Net operating profit margin (NOPM) (p. 274)

Net realizable value (p. 267)

Nonrecurring (p. 279)

Notes payable (p. 267)

Notes receivable (p. 267)

Percentage-of-completion method (p. 264)

Percentage of sales (p. 267)

Persistent (p. 279)

Pro forma income (p. 278)

Quality of earnings (p. 277)

Realized or realizable (p. 261)

Recurring (p. 279)

Restructuring charges (p. 279)

Restructuring costs (p. 280)

Return on capital employed (ROCE) (p. 273)

Revenue recognition (p. 260)

Revenue recognition criteria (p. 261)

Right of return (p. 261)

Transitory (p. 280)

Unearned revenue (p. 262)

MULTIPLE CHOICE

1. Which of the following best describes the condition(s) that must be present for the recognition of revenue?
   a. Revenue must be earned and collected.
   b. There are no uncertainties in measurement of income.
   c. Revenue must be earned and realizable.
   d. Expenses must be measurable and directly associated with the revenues.

2. A company's projects extend over several years and collection of receivables is reasonably certain. Each of its projects has a contract that specifies a price, and reliable estimates can be made of the extent of progress and cost to complete each project. The method that the company should use to account for construction revenue is the
   a. installment method.
   b. percentage-of-completion method.
   c. completed contract method.
   d. sales method.

3. The installment method of recognizing revenue
   a. is used only in cases in which no reasonable basis exists for estimating the collectibility of receivables.
   b. is not a generally accepted accounting method under any circumstances.
   c. is used for book purposes only if it is also used for tax purposes.
   d. is used by most firms that make installment sales.

4. When management selectively excludes some revenues, expenses, gains, and losses from earnings calculated using generally accepted accounting principles, it is an example of
   a. income smoothing.
   b. big bath accounting.
   c. cookie jar accounting.
   d. pro forma earnings.

5. If bad debts expense is determined by estimating uncollectible accounts receivable, the entry to record the write-off of a specific uncollectible account would decrease
   a. allowance for uncollectible accounts.
   b. net income.
   c. net book value of accounts receivable.
   d. bad debts expense.

6. If management intentionally underestimates bad debts expense, then net income is
   a. overstated and assets are understated.
   b. understated and assets are overstated.
   c. understated and asset are understated.
   d. overstated and assets are overstated.

Superscript [A] denotes assignments based on Appendix 6A

DISCUSSION QUESTIONS

Q6-1. What are the criteria that guide firms in recognition of revenue? What does each of the criteria mean? How are the criteria met for a company like **Abercrombie & Fitch Co.**, a clothing retailer? How are the criteria met for a construction company that builds offices under long-term contracts with developers?

Q6-2. Why are discontinued operations reported separately from continuing operations in the income statement?

Q6-3. What are the criteria for categorizing an event as an extraordinary item? Provide an example of an event that would properly be categorized as an extraordinary item and one that would not.

Q6-4. Identify the two typical categories of restructuring costs and their effects on the balance sheet and the income statement. Explain the concept of a *big bath* and why restructuring costs are often identified with this event.

Q6-5. Why might companies want to manage earnings? Describe some of the tactics that some companies use to manage earnings.

Q6-6. What is the concept of *pro forma income* and why has this income measure been criticized?

Q6-7. Why does GAAP allow management to make estimates of amounts that are included in financial statements? Does this improve the usefulness of financial statements? Explain.

Q6-8. How might earnings forecasts that are published by financial analysts encourage companies to manage earnings?

Q6-9. Explain how management can shift income from one period into another by its estimation of uncollectible accounts.

Q6-10. During an examination of Wallace Company's financial statements, you notice that the allowance for uncollectible accounts has decreased as a percentage of accounts receivable. What are the possible explanations for this change?

Q6-11. Under what circumstances would it be correct to say that a company would be better off with more uncollectible accounts?

Q6-12. Estimating the bad debts expense by aging accounts receivable generally results in smaller errors than the percentage of credit sales approach. Can you explain why?

**Assignments with the WebAssign logo in the margin are available in WebAssign.
See the Preface of the book for details.**

MINI EXERCISES

M6-13. Computing Percentage-of-Completion Revenues   LO3
Bartov Corporation agreed to build a warehouse for $2,500,000. Expected (and actual) costs for the warehouse follow: 2009, $400,000; 2010, $1,000,000; and 2011, $500,000. The company completed the warehouse in 2011. Compute revenues, expenses, and income for each year 2009 through 2011 using the percentage-of-completion method.

M6-14. Assessing Revenue Recognition of Companies   LO1
Identify and explain when each of the following companies should recognize revenue.
  a. **The GAP Inc.:** The GAP is a retailer of clothing items for all ages.
  b. **Merck & Company Inc.:** Merck engages in the development, manufacturing, and marketing of pharmaceutical products. It sells its drugs to retailers like **CVS Caremark Corporation** and **Walgreen Co.**
  c. **Deere & Company:** Deere manufactures heavy equipment. It sells equipment to a network of independent distributors, who in turn sell the equipment to customers. Deere provides financing and insurance services both to distributors and customers.
  d. **Bank of America Corporation:** Bank of America is a banking institution. It lends money to individuals and corporations and invests excess funds in marketable securities.
  e. **Johnson Controls Inc.:** Johnson Controls manufactures products for the U.S. Government under long-term contracts.

THE GAP INC.
NYSE :: GPS

MERCK & COMPANY
INC.
NYSE :: MRK

DEERE & COMPANY
NYSE :: DE

BANK OF AMERICA
CORPORATION
NYSE :: BAC

JOHNSON CONTROLS,
INC.
NYSE :: JCI

M6-15. Estimating Revenue Recognition with Right of Return   LO1
The Unlimited Company offers an unconditional return policy for its retail clothing business. It normally expects 2% of sales at retail selling prices to be returned at some point prior to the expiration of the return period, and returned items cannot be resold. Assuming that it records total sales of $5 million for the current period, how much net revenue would it report for this period?

M6-16. Using Percentage-of-Completion and Completed Contract Methods   LO3
Halsey Building Company signed a contract to build an office building for $40,000,000. The scheduled construction costs follow.

Year	Cost
2009	$ 9,000,000
2010	15,000,000
2011	6,000,000
Total	$30,000,000

The building is completed in 2011.

For each year, compute the revenue, expense, and gross profit reported for this construction project using each of the following methods.

a. Percentage-of-completion method
b. Completed contract method

LO1, LO2 **M6-17.** **Explaining Revenue Recognition and Bundled Sales**

A.J. Smith Electronics is a retail consumer electronics company that also sells extended warranty contracts for many of the products that it carries. The extended warranty provides coverage for three years beyond expiration of the manufacturer's warranty. In 2009, A.J. Smith sold extended warranties amounting to $1,700,000. The warranty coverage for all of these begins in 2010 and runs through 2012. The total expected cost of providing warranty services on these contracts is $500,000.

a. How should A.J. Smith recognize revenue on the extended warranty contracts?
b. Estimate the revenue, expense, and gross profit reported from these contracts in the year(s) that the revenue is recognized.
c. In 2010, as a special promotion, A.J. Smith sold a digital camera (retail price $300), a digital photograph printer (retail price $125), and an extended warranty contract for each (total retail price $75) as a package for a special price of $399. The extended warranty covers the period from 2011 through 2013. The company sold 200 of these camera-printer packages. Compute the revenue that A.J. Smith should recognize in each year from 2010 through 2013.

LO4 **M6-18.** **Reporting Uncollectible Accounts and Accounts Receivables**

Mohan Company estimates its uncollectible accounts by aging its accounts receivable and applying percentages to various aged categories of accounts. Mohan computes a total of $2,100 in estimated losses as of December 31, 2010. Its Accounts Receivable has a balance of $98,000, and its Allowance for Uncollectible Accounts has an unused balance of $500 before adjustment at December 31, 2010.

a. What is the amount of bad debts expense that Mohan will report in 2010?
b. Determine the net amount of accounts receivable reported in current assets at December 31, 2010.
c. Set up T-accounts for both Bad Debt Expense and for Allowance for Uncollectible Accounts. Enter any beginning balances and effects from the information above (including your results from parts a and b). Explain the numbers for each of your T-accounts.

LO4 **M6-19.** **Explaining the Allowance Method for Accounts Receivable**

At a recent board of directors meeting of Ascot, Inc., one of the directors expressed concern over the allowance for uncollectible accounts appearing in the company's balance sheet. "I don't understand this account," he said. "Why don't we just show accounts receivable at the amount owed to us and get rid of that allowance?" Respond to that director's question, include in your response (a) an explanation of why the company has an allowance account, (b) what the balance sheet presentation of accounts receivable is intended to show, and (c) how the matching principle relates to the analysis and presentation of accounts receivable.

LO4 **M6-20.** **Analyzing the Allowance for Uncollectible Accounts**

Following is the current asset section from **Kraft Foods, Inc.**, balance sheet:

At December 31 ($ millions)	2008	2007
Cash and cash equivalents.	$ 1,244	$ 567
Receivables (less allowances of $129 in 2008 and $94 in 2007). . . .	4,704	5,197
Inventories, net	3,729	4,096
Deferred income taxes	861	575
Other current assets	828	302
Total current assets	$11,366	$10,737

a. Compute the gross amount of accounts receivable for both 2008 and 2007. Compute the percentage of the allowance for uncollectible accounts relative to the gross amount of accounts receivable for each of these years.
b. How do you interpret the change in the percentage of the allowance for uncollectible accounts relative to total accounts receivable computed in part a?

M6-21.   Analyzing Accounts Receivable Changes   LO4

The comparative balance sheets of Sloan Company reveal that accounts receivable (before deducting allowances) increased by $15,000 in 2010. During the same time period, the allowance for uncollectible accounts increased by $2,100. If sales revenue was $120,000 in 2010 and bad debts expense was 2% of sales, how much cash was collected from customers during the year?

M6-22.   Evaluating Accounts Receivable Turnover for Competitors   LO5

The Procter & Gamble Company (PG) and **Colgate-Palmolive Company (CL)** report the following sales and accounts receivable balances ($ millions):

THE PROCTER & GAMBLE COMPANY
NYSE :: PG

COLGATE-PALMOLIVE COMPANY
NYSE :: CL

	PROCTER & GAMBLE			COLGATE-PALMOLIVE	
Fiscal year	Sales	Accounts Receivable	Fiscal year	Sales	Accounts Receivable
June 30, 2009	$76,029	$5,836	December 31, 2008....	$15,330	$1,592
June 30, 2008	81,748	6,761	December 31, 2008....	13,790	1,681

a.   Compute the 2009 accounts receivable turnover for both companies.

b.   Identify and discuss a potential explanation for the difference between these competitors' accounts receivable turnover.

M6-23.   Analyzing Accounts Receivable Changes   LO4

In 2010, Grant Corporation recorded credit sales of $3,200,000 and bad debts expense of $42,000. Write-offs of uncollectible accounts totaled $39,000 and one account, worth $12,000, that had been written off in an earlier year was collected in 2010.

a.   Prepare journal entries to record each of these transactions.

b.   If net accounts receivable increased by $220,000, how much cash was collected from credit customers during the year? Prepare a journal entry to record cash collections.

c.   Set up T-accounts and post each of the transactions in parts *a* and *b* to them.

d.   Record each of the above transactions in a financial statement effects template to show the effect of these entries on the balance sheet and income statement.

M6-24.   Analyzing Unearned Revenue Changes   LO2

Finn Publishing Corp. produces a monthly publication aimed at competitive swimmers, with articles profiling current stars of the sport, advice from coaches, and advertising by swimwear companies, training organizations and others. The magazine is distributed through newsstands and bookstores, and by mail to subscribers. The most common subscription is for twelve months. When Finn Publishing receives payment of an annual subscription, it recognizes an Unearned Revenue liability that is reduced by 1/12th each month as publications are provided.

The table below provides four years of revenues from the income statement and unearned revenue from the balance sheet. (All amounts in $ thousands.)

Fiscal year	Revenue	Unearned revenue liability (end of year)
2007	48,000	20,000
2008	55,000	24,000
2009	62,000	26,000
2010	62,000	25,000

a.   Calculate the growth in revenue from 2008 to 2009 and from 2009 to 2010.

b.   Calculate the amount of customer purchases in 2008, 2009, and 2010. Customer purchases are defined as sales made at newsstands and bookstores, plus the amount paid for new or renewal subscriptions. Again, calculate the growth rates from 2008 to 2009 and from 2009 to 2010.

c.   Explain the differences in growth rates between parts *a* and *b* above.

M6-25.   Applying Revenue Recognition Criteria   LO2

Commtech, Inc., designs and sells cellular phones. The company creates the technical specifications and the software for its products, though it outsources the production of the phones to an overseas contract manufacturer. Commtech has arrangements to sell its phones to the major wireless communications companies who, in turn, sell the phones to end customers packaged with calling plans.

The product life cycle for a phone model is about six months, and Commtech recognizes revenue at the time of delivery to the wireless communications company. The product team for the CD924 model has met to consider a possible modification to the phone. The software team has developed an improved global positioning application for a new phone model, and this application works in the CD924. It could be uploaded to existing phones through the wireless networks.

Marketing's analysis of focus groups and customer feedback is that further sales of the CD924 would be enhanced significantly if the new application were made available. The software engineers have demonstrated that the new GPS application can be successfully sent wirelessly to the CD924.

However, the finance manager points out that Commtech's financial statements have been based on the assumption that the company's phones do not involve "multiple deliverables," like upgrades. All revenue is recognized at the point of sale to the wireless communications companies. Like many communications hardware companies, Commtech has been under pressure to demonstrate its financial performance. Offering an upgrade to the CD924's navigation capabilities would probably be viewed as a significant deliverable in terms of customer value, and the finance manager says that "the accounting won't let us do it."

How should the product team proceed?

EXERCISES

LO1 **E6-26.** **Assessing Revenue Recognition Timing**
Discuss and justify when each of the following businesses should recognize revenues:

LIMITED BRANDS, INC.
NYSE :: LTD
BOEING COMPANY
NYSE :: BA
SUPERVALU, INC.
NYSE :: SVU
WELLS FARGO & COMPANY
NYSE :: WFC
HARLEY-DAVIDSON, INC.
NYSE ::HOG
TIME-WARNER INC.
NYSE :: TWX

a. A clothing retailer like **Limited Brands, Inc.**
b. A contractor like **The Boeing Company** that performs work under long-term government contracts.
c. An operator of grocery stores like **SUPERVALU, INC.**
d. A producer of television shows, such as **MTV** that syndicates its content to television stations.
e. A residential real estate developer who constructs only speculative houses and later sells these houses to buyers.
f. A banking institution like **Wells Fargo & Company** that lends money for home mortgages.
g. A manufacturer like **Harley-Davidson, Inc.**
h. A publisher of magazines such as **Time-Warner Inc.**

LO1, LO6 **E6-27.** **Assessing Revenue Recognition Timing and Income Measurement**
Discuss and justify when each of the following businesses should recognize revenue and identify any income measurement issues that are likely to arise.

a. **RealMoney.Com**, a division of **TheStreet.Com** provides investment advice to customers for an up-front fee. It provides these customers with password-protected access to its Web site where customers can download certain investment reports. Real Money has an obligation to provide updates on its Web site.

ORACLE CORPORATION
NASDAQ :: ORCL

b. **Oracle Corporation** develops general ledger and other business application software that it sells to its customers. The customer pays an up-front fee to gain the right to use the software and a monthly fee for support services.

INTUIT INC.
NASDAQ :: INTU

c. **Intuit Inc.** develops tax preparation software that it sells to its customers for a flat fee. No further payment is required and the software cannot be returned, only exchanged if defective.

d. A developer of computer games sells its software with a 10-day right of return period during which the software can be returned for a full refund. After the 10-day period has expired, the software cannot be returned.

LO3 **E6-28.** **Constructing and Assessing Income Statements Using Percentage of Completion**

GENERAL ELECTRIC COMPANY
NYSE :: GE
NSTAR
NYSE :: NST

Assume that **General Electric Company** agreed in February 2010 to construct an electricity generating facility for **NSTAR**, a utility serving the Boston area. The contract price of $500 million is to be paid as follows: $200 million at the time of signing; $100 million on December 31, 2010; and $200 million at completion in May 2011. General Electric incurred the following costs in constructing the power plant: $100 million in 2010, and $300 million in 2011.

    a.   Compute the amount of General Electric's revenue, expense, and income for both 2010 and 2011 under the percentage-of-completion revenue recognition method.

    b.   Compute the amount of GE's revenue, expense, and income for both 2010 and 2011 using the installment method.

    c.   Discuss whether you believe that the percentage of completion method or the installment method provides a good measure of GE's performance under the contract.

E6-29. Constructing and Assessing Income Statements Using Percentage of Completion

On March 15, 2010, Frankel Construction contracted to build a shopping center at a contract price of $120 million. The schedule of expected (equals actual) cash collections and contract costs follows:

Year	Cash Collections	Cost Incurred
2010	$ 30 million	$15 million
2011	50 million	40 million
2012	40 million	30 million
Total	$120 million	$85 million

    a.   Calculate the amount of revenue, expense, and income for each of the three years 2010 through 2012 using (1) the percentage-of-completion method, (2) the completed contract method, and (3) the installment method.

    b.   Discuss which method you believe provides the best measure of the construction company's performance under this contract.

E6-30. Revenue Recognition and the Installment Method

Bryant Company sold a software license to Cheng, Inc., for $2,500,000. The sales price is to be paid in installments, with $1,000,000 due in 2010, $750,000 due in 2011, $500,000 due in 2012, and $250,000 due in 2013. The cost of the software is $450,000. Cheng, Inc., is a start-up company that has been struggling to make a profit. As a result, there is some concern that Cheng, Inc., may be unable to meet its payment demands.

    a.   Compute the revenue, expense, and gross profit that would be reported each year using the installment method.

    b.   Assume that Cheng, Inc., defaults on this contract in 2012 before that year's payment is collected. What effect would this event have on Bryant's financial statements?

E6-31.[A] **Reporting Restructuring Charges**

PepsiCo Inc., reported restructuring charges of $543 million in its 2008 income statement. The following additional details were disclosed in its footnotes.

Restructuring charges included the following (in millions)	2008
Severance and other employee costs	$212
Asset impairments	149
Other costs	183
Total	$543

The severance and other employee costs reflect the costs of terminating approximately 3,500 employees. The asset impairments reflect the closure of six plants, and the other costs include, for example, the cost to buy out the remaining years on lease agreements, or penalties paid for canceling purchase contracts.

    In the same footnote, PepsiCo reports that $159 million has been paid out in cash by the end of 2008, and approximately $186 million has been noncash charges. The remaining liability at the end of 2008 is $198 million.

    PepsiCo's contract termination costs include, for example, the cost to buy out the remaining years on lease agreements, or penalties paid for canceling purchase contracts.

    a.   Summarize the effects of these restructuring entries in journal entry form. Post the entry to T-accounts.

    b.   Should restructuring charges be classified as discontinued operations? Why or why not?

LO1, LO6 **E6-32.** **Applying Revenue Recognition Criteria**

Simpyl Technologies, Inc., manufactures electronic equipment used to facilitate control of production processes and tracking of assets using RFID and other technologies. Since its initial public offering in 1996, the company has shown consistent growth in revenue and earnings, and the stock price has reflected that impressive performance.

Operating in a very competitive environment, Simpyl Technologies provides significant bonus incentives to its sales representatives. These representatives sell the company's products directly to end customers, to value-added resellers, and to distributers.

Consider the four situations below. In each case, determine whether Simpyl Technologies can recognize revenue at this time. Describe the reasons for your judgment.

a. When selling directly to the end customer, Simpyl Technologies requires a sales contract with authorized signatures from the customer company. At the end Simpyl's fiscal year, sales representative A asks to book revenue from a customer. The customer's purchasing manager has confirmed the intention to complete the purchase, but the contract has only one of the two required signatures. The second person is traveling and will return to the office in a few days (but after the end of Simpyl's fiscal year). The inventory to fulfill the order is sitting in Simpyl's warehouse. Can Simpyl recognize revenue at this time?

b. Sales representative B has an approved contract to deliver units that must be customized to meet the customer's specifications. Just prior to the end of the fiscal year, the uncustomized units are shipped to an intermediate staging area where they will be reconfigured to meet the customer's requirements. Can the sales representative recognize revenue on the basic, uncustomized units at this time?

c. Sales representative C has finalized an order from a value-added reseller who regularly purchases significant volumes of Simpyl's products. The products have been delivered to the customer at the beginning of the fiscal year, and Simpyl Technologies has no further responsibilities for the items. However, the sales representative (with the regional sales manager) is still conducting negotiations with the value-added reseller as to the volume discounts that will be offered for the current year. Can the sales representative recognize revenue on the items delivered to the customer?

d. Sales representative D has finalized an order from a distributor, and the items have been delivered. However, an examination of the distributor's financial condition shows that it does not have the resources to pay Simpyl for the items it has purchased. It needs to sell those items, so the resulting proceeds can be used to pay Simpyl. Can the sales representative recognize revenue on the items delivered to the distributor?

LO4 **E6-33.** **Reporting Uncollectible Accounts and Accounts Receivable**

LaFond Company analyzes its accounts receivable at December 31, 2010, and arrives at the aged categories below along with the percentages that are estimated as uncollectible.

Age Group	Accounts Receivable	Estimated Loss %
Current (not past due).........................	$250,000	0.5%
1–30 days past due...........................	90,000	1
31–60 days past due..........................	20,000	2
61–120 days past due.........................	11,000	5
121–180 days past due........................	6,000	10
Over 180 days past due	4,000	25
Total accounts receivable.....................	$381,000	

At the beginning of the fourth quarter of 2010, there was a credit balance of $4,350 in the Allowance for Uncollectible Accounts. During the fourth quarter, LaFond Company wrote off $3,830 in receivables as uncollectible.

a. What amount of bad debts expense will LaFond report for 2010?

b. What is the balance of accounts receivable that it reports on its December 31, 2010, balance sheet?

c. Set up T-accounts for both Bad Debts Expense and for the Allowance for Uncollectible Accounts. Enter any unadjusted balances along with the dollar effects of the information described (including your results from parts *a* and *b*). Explain the numbers in each of the T-accounts.

E6-34. Analysis of Accounts Receivable and Allowance for Doubtful Accounts

LO4, LO5, LO6

Ethan Allen Interiors Inc. reported the following amounts in its 2009 and 2008 10-K report.

Web**Assign**.

ETHAN ALLEN
INTERIORS INC.
NYSE::ETH

($ thousands)	2009	2008	2007
From the income statement:			
Net sales....................................	$674,277	$980,045	$1,005,312
From the balance sheet:			
Accounts receivable, net.........................	13,086	12,672	14,602
From the disclosure on Allowance for doubtful accounts:			
Balance at beginning of period......................	2,535	2,042	2,074
Additions (reductions) charged to income.............	(773)	493	10
Adjustments or deductions.........................	(400)	–	(42)
Balance at end of period...........................	1,362	2,535	2,042

   a. Prepare the journal entry to record accounts receivable written off as uncollectible in 2009. Also prepare the entry to record the provision for doubtful accounts (bad debts expense) for 2009. What effect did this entry have on Ethan Allen's income for 2009?

   b. Calculate Ethan Allen's gross receivables for the years given, and then determine the allowance for doubtful accounts as a percentage of the gross receivables. How much higher would Ethan Allen's 2009 bad debts expense have been if it had maintained the 2008 allowance as a percentage of gross accounts receivable?

   c. Calculate Ethan Allen's accounts receivable turnover for 2009 and 2008. (Use Accounts receivable, net for the calculation.)

   d. How much cash did Ethan Allen receive from customers in 2009?

   e. What might account for the patterns that are evident from the answers above?

E6-35. Analyzing and Reporting Receivable Transactions and Uncollectible Accounts (Using Percentage-of-Sales Method)

LO4

At the beginning of 2010, Penman Company had the following (normal) account balances in its financial records:

WebAssign.

Accounts Receivable	$122,000
Allowance for Uncollectible Accounts	7,900

During 2010, its credit sales were $1,173,000 and collections on credit sales were $1,150,000. The following additional transactions occurred during the year:

Feb. 17	Wrote off Nissim's account, $3,600.
May 28	Wrote off Weiss's account, $2,400.
Dec. 15	Wrote off Ohlson's account, $900.
Dec. 31	Recorded the provision for uncollectible accounts at 0.8% of credit sales for the year. (*Hint*: The allowance account is increased by 0.8% of credit sales regardless of any prior write-offs.)

Compute and show how accounts receivable and the allowance for uncollectible accounts are reported in its December 31, 2010, balance sheet.

E6-36. Estimating Bad Debts Expense and Reporting of Receivables

LO4

At December 31, 2010, Sunil Company had a balance of $375,000 in its accounts receivable and an unused balance of $4,200 in its allowance for uncollectible accounts. The company then aged its accounts as follows:

Current...	$304,000
0–60 days past due................................	44,000
61–180 days past due.............................	18,000
Over 180 days past due	9,000
Total accounts receivable.........................	$375,000

The company has experienced losses as follows: 1% of current balances, 5% of balances 0–60 days past due, 15% of balances 61–180 days past due, and 40% of balances over 180 days past due. The company continues to base its provision for credit losses on this aging analysis and percentages.

a. What amount of bad debts expense does Sunil report on its 2010 income statement?

b. Show how accounts receivable and the allowance for uncollectible accounts are reported in its December 31, 2010, balance sheet.

c. Set up T-accounts for both Bad Debts Expense and for the Allowance for Uncollectible Accounts. Enter any unadjusted balances along with the dollar effects of the information described (including your results from parts a and b). Explain the numbers in each of the T-accounts.

LO4   E6-37.   Estimating Uncollectible Accounts and Reporting Receivables over Multiple Periods

Barth Company, which has been in business for three years, makes all of its sales on credit and does not offer cash discounts. Its credit sales, customer collections, and write-offs of uncollectible accounts for its first three years follow:

Year	Sales	Collections	Accounts Written Off
2009	$751,000	$733,000	$5,300
2010	876,000	864,000	5,800
2011	972,000	938,000	6,500

a. Barth uses the allowance method of recognizing credit losses that provides for such losses at the rate of 1% of sales. (This means the allowance account is increased by 1% of credit sales regardless of any write-offs and unused balances.) What amounts for accounts receivable and the allowance for uncollectible accounts are reported on its balance sheet at the end of 2011? What total amount of bad debts expense appears on its income statement for each of the three years?

b. Comment on the appropriateness of the 1% rate used to provide for bad debts based on your results in part a. (*Hint*: T-accounts can help with this analysis.)

LO5   E6-38.   Evaluating Business Segment Information

Hewlett-Packard Company reports that its "organizational structure is based on a number of factors that management uses to evaluate, view and run its business operations." In its disclosures of segment information, there are four operating groups—the Technology Solutions Group (which includes the newly-acquired EDS), the Personal Systems Group, the Imaging and Printing Group, and HP Financial Services. The company provides the following information about these business segments:

	2008	2007	2006
Total net revenue:			
Technology Solutions Group	$44,826	$37,740	$34,226
Personal Systems Group	42,295	36,409	29,166
Imaging and Printing Group	29,385	28,465	26,786
HP Financial Services	2,698	2,336	2,078
Earnings from operations:			
Technology Solutions Group	$ 5,529	$ 4,156	$ 3,038
Personal Systems Group	2,375	1,939	1,152
Imaging and Printing Group	4,590	4,315	3,978
HP Financial Services	192	155	147
Total assets:			
Technology Solutions Group	$63,008	$39,116	$31,268
Personal Systems Group	16,451	14,153	12,237
Imaging and Printing Group	14,203	14,573	13,889
HP Financial Services	9,174	9,001	7,927

a. Calculate the 2008 Return on Capital Employed (ROCE) for each segment. (Base the calculation on total assets instead of net operating assets in the denominator—HP does not disclose operating liabilities by segment.)

b. Which segments are more profitable? Which are growing more quickly?

E6-39. **Analyzing Unearned Revenue Liabilities**   **LO1, LO2**

The Lyric Opera of Chicago was founded in 1954 and is widely regarded as one of the world's greatest opera companies. Each year, The Lyric has an eight-opera season that extends from September to March, and its loyal subscribers (numbering more than 30,000 in 2008–2009) eagerly reserve their seats for coming performances. In fact, many subscribers purchase their tickets for the upcoming year before the April 30 close of The Lyric's fiscal year. For these ticket purchases, The Lyric recognizes a liability entitled Deferred Ticket and Other Revenue and defined in their footnotes as "Deferred ticket revenue relates to ticket sales for the following opera season."

Information about The Lyric Opera's ticket revenue and deferred ticket revenue liability is given below ($ thousands). Assume that the "Other" portion of deferred revenue is negligible.

Fiscal year ended April 30	Ticket Sales (Revenue)	Deferred Ticket and Other Revenue (Year-end Liability)
2009	$28,051	$13,103
2008	27,432	17,246
2007	26,978	17,664
2006	27,297	16,882

a. What revenue recognition principle(s) drive The Lyric's deferral of advance ticket purchases?

b. Recreate the summary journal entries to recognize Ticket Sales revenue for The Lyric's fiscal year 2009 and advance sales for the fiscal year 2010 season.

c. What are possible causes for the decline in the Deferred Ticket and Other Revenue liability in 2009?

d. The Lyric Opera's season changes every year, with a mixture of classical and contemporary operas. At the end of each fiscal year, management of The Lyric can observe the revenue generated by the season just concluded and also its subscribers' enthusiasm for the upcoming season. How might that information be used in managing the organization?

PROBLEMS

P6-40.[A] **Identifying Operating and Nonrecurring Income Components**   **LO7**
Following is the The Dow Chemical Company income statement.

Required

a. Identify the components in its statement that you would consider operating.

b. Identify those components that you would consider transitory.

(In millions, except per share amount) For Year Ended December 31	2008
Net sales	$57,514
Cost of sales	52,019
Research and development expenses	1,310
Selling, general, and administrative expenses	1,969
Amortization of intangibles	92
Goodwill impairment losses	239
Restructuring charges	839
Purchased in-process research and development charges	44
Acquisition-related expenses	49
Asbestos-related credit	54
Equity in earnings of nonconsolidated affiliates	787
Sundry income—net	89
Interest income	86
Interest expense and amortization of debt discount	648
Income before income taxes and minority interests	1,321
Provision for income taxes	667
Minority interests' share in income	75
Net income available for common stockholders	$ 579

LO3   P6-41.   Percentage-of-Completion and Completed Contract Methods

WebAssign.

Philbrick Company signed a three-year contract to provide sales training to the employees of Elliot Company. The contract price is $1,200 per employee and the estimated number of employees to be trained is 400. The expected number to be trained in each year and the expected training costs follow.

	Number of employees	Training costs incurred
2010	125	$ 60,000
2011	200	75,000
2012	75	40,000
Total	400	$175,000

Required

a. For each year, compute the revenue, expense, and gross profit reported assuming revenue is recognized using the following method.

 1. Percentage-of-completion method, where percentage-of-completion is determined by the number of employees trained.

 2. Percentage-of-completion method, where percentage-of-completion is determined by the costs incurred.

 3. Completed contract method.

b. Which method do you believe is most appropriate in this situation? Explain.

LO6   P6-42.   Incentives for Earnings Management

Harris Corporation pays senior management an annual bonus from a bonus pool. The size of the bonus pool is determined as follows.

Reported net income	Bonus pool
Less than or equal to $10 million	$0
Greater than $10 million, but less than or equal to $20 million.	10% of income in excess of $10 million
Greater than $20 million	$1 million

Required

a. Assume that senior management expects current earnings to be $21 million and next year's earnings to be $18 million. What incentive does management of Harris Corporation have for managing earnings?

b. Assume that senior management expects current earnings to be $17 million and next year's earnings to be $24 million. What incentive does management of Harris Corporation have for managing earnings?

c. Assume that senior management expects current earnings to be $9.5 million and next year's earnings to be $12 million. What incentive does management of Harris Corporation have for managing earnings?

d. How might the bonus plan be structured to minimize the incentives for earnings management?

LO4, LO6   P6-43.   Interpreting the Accounts Receivable Footnote

TARGET CORPORATION
NYSE :: TGT

In its fiscal year 2007 annual report, **Target Corporation** reported the following information about its credit card receivables. Target has a policy of writing off receivables that are more than 180 days past due.

Receivables (millions)	2007	2006	2005
Year-end receivables	$8,624	$6,711	$6,117
Average receivables	$7,275	$6,161	$5,544
Accounts with three or more payments (60+ days) past due as a percentage of year-end receivables.	4.0%	3.5%	2.8%
Accounts with four or more payments (90+ days) past due as a percentage of year-end receivables.	2.7%	2.4%	1.9%

Allowance for Doubtful Accounts (millions)	2007	2006	2005
Allowance at beginning of year	$517	$451	$387
Bad debts provision	481	380	466
Net write-offs	(428)	(314)	(402)
Allowance at end of year	$570	$517	$451
As a percentage of year-end receivables	6.6%	7.7%	7.4%
Net write-offs as a percentage of average receivables	5.9%	5.1%	7.2%

a. A significant portion of Target's credit card receivables arise from purchases at the company's stores. Target's reported revenue from product sales was $61,471 million in 2007 and $57,878 million in 2006. Calculate Target's accounts receivable turnover for each year using gross receivables. Are customers paying more quickly in 2007?

b. What amount did Target report as accounts receivable, net on its ending 2007 balance sheet?

c. Reconstruct the entries (as summary journal entries) that Target made in its allowance for doubtful accounts in 2007.

d. As a percentage of year-end receivables, Target's allowance for doubtful accounts declined from 7.7% at the end of 2006 to 6.6% at the end of 2007. Does that seem consistent with the information given about the company's accounts receivable collection experience?

e. What are possible reasons for any inconsistencies?

P6-44. Analyzing and Interpreting Receivables and Its Related Ratios

Following is the current asset section from **Time-Warner Inc.**'s balance sheet ($ millions):

December 31	2002	2001
Current assets		
Cash and equivalents	$ 1,730	$ 719
Receivables, less allowances of $2,379 and $1,889 million	5,667	6,054
Inventories	1,896	1,791
Prepaid expenses and other current assets	1,862	1,687
Total current assets	$11,155	$10,251

During 2002, Time-Warner reported a $98,700 million net loss, all of which was attributed to the write-off of goodwill that it recognized in the merger of AOL and Time-Warner. Sales were $40,961 million in 2002 and $37,166 million in 2001.

Required

a. What is Time-Warner's gross amount of receivables at the end of (1) 2002 and (2) 2001?

b. For both 2002 and 2001, compute the ratio of (1) the allowance for uncollectible accounts to gross receivables and (2) gross receivables to sales. Identify and interpret the changes in these ratios over these two years.

c. Compute both the receivables turnover and the average collection period for 2002. Does the collection period (days sales in receivables) appear reasonable given Time-Warner's lines of business? Explain.

d. Given the large loss reported in 2002, it is reasonable to consider whether Time-Warner took a big bath by writing off other assets or padding reserves such as the allowance for uncollectible accounts. Do your results from part *b* suggest that this might be the case? Explain. What might be another explanation for the relative increase in the allowance for uncollectible accounts?

P6-45. Accounting for Product Returns

In its income statement for fiscal year 2008, **The Gap, Inc.**, reported net sales of $14,526 million and cost of goods sold and occupancy expenses of $9,079 million, resulting in a Gross Profit of $5,447 million. In its footnotes, The Gap reports that "Allowances for estimated returns are recorded based on estimated gross profit using our historical return patterns."

When The Gap accounts for estimated sales returns, it reduces sales revenue by the returns' expected sales price, reduces cost of goods sold by the returns' expected cost and recognizes a sales return allowance as a liability equal to the returns' expected gross profit.

A sales returns allowance of $21 million was reported among The Gap's liabilities at the end of fiscal year 2008, and the footnotes report that $700 million in allowance for returns was added to this liability during fiscal year 2008. Actual returns were reported at $701 million and subtracted from the liability.

Required

a. What was the balance in The Gap's sales returns allowance liability at the beginning of fiscal year 2008?

b. Suppose The Gap sells 100 units of an item for $50 each, and its gross profit on each unit is $20. Further, suppose The Gap expects that 10 of the units will be returned. What entries will be made to record the sale of 100 units (for cash) and the expected returns? What entry is made when ten customers subsequently return the items and receive a cash refund? Assume that the units are undamaged and can be sold to other customers.

c. Assume that the gross profit margin (gross profit divided by sales revenue) for returned items is the same as that for those that are not returned. Reconstruct the entry The Gap made to account for expected product returns in 2008. What were the 2008 gross sales for The Gap? What percentage of its sales does The Gap expect to be returned?

d. Suppose The Gap entered a new market in which it did not have the ability to predict product returns. How should it deal with the prospect of returns when it sells products to customers?

LO2 **P6-46.** **Analyzing Unearned Revenue Changes**

ELECTRONIC ARTS INC.
NASDAQ::ERTS

Electronic Arts Inc. (EA) is a developer, marketer, publisher and distributor of video game software and content to be played on a variety of platforms. There is an increasing demand for the ability to play these games in an online environment, and EA has developed this capability in many of its products. In addition, EA maintains servers (or arranges for servers) for the online activities of its customers. When customers purchase online subscriptions, revenue is recognized ratably over the subscription period.

EA treats a significant portion of its software sales as "multiple element arrangements" and—through fiscal 2007—deferred a portion of customer purchases based on the estimated value of the online services offered. Beginning in fiscal 2008, it was not possible to estimate the separate value of the software and the online services, so EA began to defer all such revenue over a six-month period. In addition, EA's 2009 10-K states that the company uses the Internet to provide post-purchase updates or additional content to customers, again treating such situations as "multiple element arrangements."

Information from Electronic Arts' financial statements is given below. Prior to fiscal year 2006, no revenue was deferred. All amounts are in $ millions.

Fiscal year ending March 31	Net revenue	Deferred net revenue (liability)
2005	$3,129	$ 0
2006	2,951	9
2007	3,091	32
2008	3,665	387
2009	4,212	261

Required

a. Calculate the growth rates in net revenue over the years in the table.

b. What are the purchases by customers in each of these years? What are the growth rates? Why do you think they differ from the growth rates in net revenue?

c. Would you predict a growth in 2010 revenue equal to that in 2009? Why?

CASES AND PROJECTS

LO1, LO6, LO7 **C6-47.**[A] **Analyzing and Interpreting Income Components and Disclosures**

XEROX CORPORATION
NYSE :: XRX

The income statement for **Xerox Corporation** follows.

XEROX CORPORATION
Consolidated Statements of Income

(in millions, except per-share data)	Year ended December 31,		
	2008	2007	2006
Revenues			
Sales	$ 8,325	$ 8,192	$ 7,464
Service, outsourcing and rentals	8,485	8,214	7,591
Finance income	798	822	840
Total Revenues	17,608	17,228	15,895
Costs and Expenses			
Cost of sales	5,519	5,254	4,803
Cost of service, outsourcing and rentals	4,929	4,707	4,328
Equipment financing interest	305	316	305
Research, development and engineering expenses	884	912	922
Selling, administrative and general expenses	4,534	4,312	4,008
Restructuring and asset impairment charges	429	(6)	385
Other expenses, net	1,122	295	336
Total Costs and Expenses	17,722	15,790	15,087
(Loss) Income before Income Taxes and Equity Income	(114)	1,438	808
Income tax (benefits) expenses	(231)	400	(288)
Equity in net income of unconsolidated affiliates	113	97	114
Net Income	$ 230	$ 1,135	$ 1,210

Required

a. Xerox reports three main sources of income: sales, services, and finance income. Describe the usual and proper revenue recognition policy for each of these sources.

b. Xerox reports restructuring costs of $429 million in 2008. It also reports restructuring costs in 2006. (1) Describe the two typical categories of restructuring costs and the accounting for each. (2) How do you recommend treating these costs for analysis purposes? (3) Should regular recurring restructuring costs be treated differently than isolated occurrences of such costs for analysis purposes?

c. Xerox reports $1,122 million in expenses labeled as "Other expenses, net." How can a company use the concept of materiality to minimize the disclosure relating to such items and, therefore, to potentially obscure its actual financial performance?

d. Which of the items in Xerox's income statement should be classified as operating? Which are transitory?

C6-48. Interpreting Revenue Recognition Policies and Earnings Management

A *Wall Street Journal* article dated October 31, 2007, reported that an internal investigation at **Dell Inc.** had uncovered evidence of earnings management. The article states:

An internal investigation found that senior executives and other employees manipulated the company's financial statements to give the appearance of hitting quarterly performance goals.

One of the biggest problems uncovered in the investigation was the way Dell recognized revenue on software products it sells. Dell, a large reseller of other companies' software products, said it historically recognized revenue from software licenses at the time that the products were sold. . . . Based on its internal review, it should have deferred more revenue from software sales.

Another issue was product warranties. In some cases, Dell said it improperly recognized revenue associated with [extended] warranties over a shorter period of time than the duration of the contract.

The income statements from Dell's 2007 10-K report are presented below, along with the footnote outlining Dell's revenue recognition policies:

	Fiscal Year Ended		
	February 2, 2007	February 3, 2006 As Restated	January 28, 2005 As Restated
Net revenue	$57,420	$55,788	$49,121
Cost of net revenue.	47,904	45,897	40,103
Gross margin	9,516	9,891	9,018
Operating expenses:			
Selling, general, and administrative	5,948	5,051	4,352
Research, development, and engineering . .	498	458	460
Total operating expenses	6,446	5,509	4,812
Operating income	3,070	4,382	4,206
Investment and other income, net	275	226	197
Income before income taxes	3,345	4,608	4,403
Income tax provision.	762	1,006	1,385
Net income.	$ 2,583	$ 3,602	$ 3,018

Revenue Recognition Net revenue includes sales of hardware, software and peripherals, and services (including extended service contracts and professional services). These products and services are sold either separately or as part of a multiple-element arrangement. Dell allocates revenue from multiple-element arrangements to the elements based on the relative fair value of each element, which is generally based on the relative sales price of each element when sold separately. The allocation of fair value for a multiple-element arrangement involving software is based on vendor specific objective evidence ("VSOE"), or in the absence of VSOE for delivered elements, the residual method. Under the residual method, Dell allocates revenue to software licenses at the inception of the license term when VSOE for all undelivered elements, such as Post Contract Customer Support ("PCS"), exists and all other revenue recognition criteria have been satisfied. In the absence of VSOE for undelivered elements, revenue is deferred and subsequently recognized over the term of the arrangement. For sales of extended warranties with a separate contract price, Dell defers revenue equal to the separately stated price. Revenue associated with undelivered elements is deferred and recorded when delivery occurs. Product revenue is recognized, net of an allowance for estimated returns, when both title and risk of loss transfer to the customer, provided that no significant obligations remain. Revenue from extended warranty and service contracts, for which Dell is obligated to perform, is recorded as deferred revenue and subsequently recognized over the term of the contract or when the service is completed. Revenue from sales of third-party extended warranty and service contracts or software PCS, for which Dell is not obligated to perform, and for which Dell does not meet the criteria for gross revenue recognition under EITF 99-19 is recognized on a net basis. All other revenue is recognized on a gross basis.

Required:

a. Explain how Dell accounts for sales of other companies' software products. What are the potential risks of abuse of these accounting policies as a means to manage earnings?

b. Explain how Dell accounts for sales of extended warranty contracts. How did Dell employees manipulate these policies to manage earnings?

c. Discuss the incentives that exist to manage earnings to "give the appearance of hitting quarterly performance goals." How can a company such as Dell prevent earnings management in circumstances such as this?

LO1, LO4, LO5 **C6-49.** **Analysis of Accounts Receivable Allowances and Turnover Ratios.**

OAKLEY, INC.
NYSE :: OO

Oakley, Inc., manufactures and markets fashion eyewear, apparel, footwear, and watches. The current asset section of the company's consolidated balance sheet and portions of the income statements for 2005 and 2006 are presented below. The following footnote provides details on Oakley's accounting for uncollectible accounts, and sales returns.

Accounts Receivable Valuation Allowances

($ thousands)	Balance at beginning of period	Additions charged to cost and expense	Deductions	Balance at end of period
For the year ended December 31, 2006:				
Allowance for doubtful accounts	$3,609	$2,095	$(?,???)	$4,142
Sales return reserve	$6,683	$7,547	$(?,???)	$7,237
Other allowances.	$ 347	$4,651	$(1,115)	$3,883

OAKLEY, INC. AND SUBSIDIARIES
Consolidated Balance Sheets

(in thousands, except share and per share data)	December 31, 2006	December 31, 2005
Assets		
Cash and cash equivalents	$ 31,313	$ 82,157
Accounts receivable, less allowances		
of $15,262 (2006) and $10,639 (2005).	109,168	99,430
Inventories, net	155,377	119,035
Other receivables	6,375	4,656
Deferred income taxes	17,933	14,766
Prepaid expenses and other assets	13,947	14,132
Total current assets	$334,113	$334,176

OAKLEY, INC. AND SUBSIDIARIES
Consolidated Statements of Income

Year Ended December 31 ($ thousands)	2006	2005	2004
Net sales	$761,865	$648,131	$585,468
Cost of goods sold	349,114	277,230	262,483
Gross profit	$412,751	$370,901	$322,985

Required

a. Prepare journal entries (and related T-accounts) to record bad debts expense and accounts receivable write-offs for 2006.

b. Oakley has also established an allowance for returns. How do returns differ from doubtful accounts? Under what circumstances might this difference affect the accounting for returns?

c. Calculate the accounts receivable turnover ratio for 2006.

SOLUTIONS TO REVIEW PROBLEMS

Mid-Chapter Review 1

Solution (all dollar amounts in millions)

1.

	2009	2008
Revenue growth rates. . .	($58,437 − $60,420)/$60,420	($60,420 − $51,122)/$51,122
	= −3.3%	= +18.2%

2. To determine the customer purchases during the year, we start with the revenue, then add the "Deferral of unearned revenue," then subtract the "Recognition of unearned revenue."

	2009	2008	2007
Revenue.	$58,437	$60,420	$51,122
Plus "Deferral of unearned revenue"	24,409	24,532	21,032
Less "Recognition of unearned revenue"	−25,426	−21,944	−19,382
Purchases made by customers	$57,420	$63,008	$52,772

3.

	2009	2008
Purchase growth rates	($57,420 − $63,008)/$63,008 = −8.9%	($63,008 − $52,772)/$52,772 = +19.4%

When a customer makes a purchase, Microsoft defers a substantial portion of the amount received and recognizes that portion over future periods. Therefore, revenue reported on the income statement is a combination of customer purchases in the current period, plus customer purchases in previous periods (up to three years ago). This has the effect of smoothing Microsoft's revenues over time. The revenue decline of 3.3% in 2009 is less than the decline in customer purchases (8.9%) because the revenue includes the effects of growth from previous periods.

Mid-Chapter Review 2

Solution

1. The terms of the contract are likely different for government contracts and contracts with private organizations. To justify the use of the percentage-of-completion method, there must be a contract that specifies a fixed or determinable price. The contracts for private organizations might have more ambiguity as far as the pricing is concerned. Alternatively, Adler most likely has experience that would indicate that government contracts are less likely to be cancelled.

2. The percentage completed in each year is 40% in 2010 ($12,000,000/$30,000,000), 45% in 2011 ($13,500,000/$30,000,000), and 15% in 2012 ($4,500,000/$30,000,000).

   a.   Percentage-of-completion method

	2010	2011	2012
Percentage completed	40%	45%	15%
Contract revenue.	$16,000,000	$18,000,000	$ 6,000,000
(Percentage completed × $40,000,000)			
Contract expense	12,000,000	13,500,000	4,500,000
Gross profit	$ 4,000,000	$ 4,500,000	$ 1,500,000

   b.   Completed contract method

	2010	2011	2012
Contract revenue.	$ 0	$ 0	$40,000,000
Contract expense	0	0	$30,000,000
Gross profit	$ 0	$ 0	$10,000,000

3. Income would be understated in 2010 and 2011, but the difference would be made up in 2012 with higher than expected earnings. The gross profit in 2012 would be $6,000,000 − $1,500,000 = $4,500,000.

Mid-Chapter Review 3

Solution

1. As of December 31, 2010,

Current.	$468,000	×	1%	=	$ 4,680
1–60 days past due	244,000	×	5%	=	12,200
61–180 days past due	38,000	×	15%	=	5,700
Over 180 days past due	20,000	×	40%	=	8,000
Amount required					$30,580
Unused allowance balance. . .					7,000
Provision					$23,580 2010 bad debts expense

2. Current assets section of balance sheet.

Accounts receivable, net of $30,580 in allowances.	$739,420

3. Engel Company has markedly increased the percentage of the allowance for uncollectible accounts to gross accounts receivable—from the historical 2% to the current 4% ($30,580/$770,000). There are at least two possible interpretations:

   a. The quality of Engel Company's receivables has declined. Possible causes include the following: (1) sales can stagnate and the company can feel compelled to sell to lower-quality accounts to maintain sales volume; (2) it may have introduced new products for which average credit losses are higher; and (3) its administration of accounts receivable can become lax.

   b. The company has intentionally increased its allowance account above the level needed for expected future losses so as to reduce current period income and "bank" that income for future periods (income shifting).

4. Transaction effects shown in the financial statement effects template.

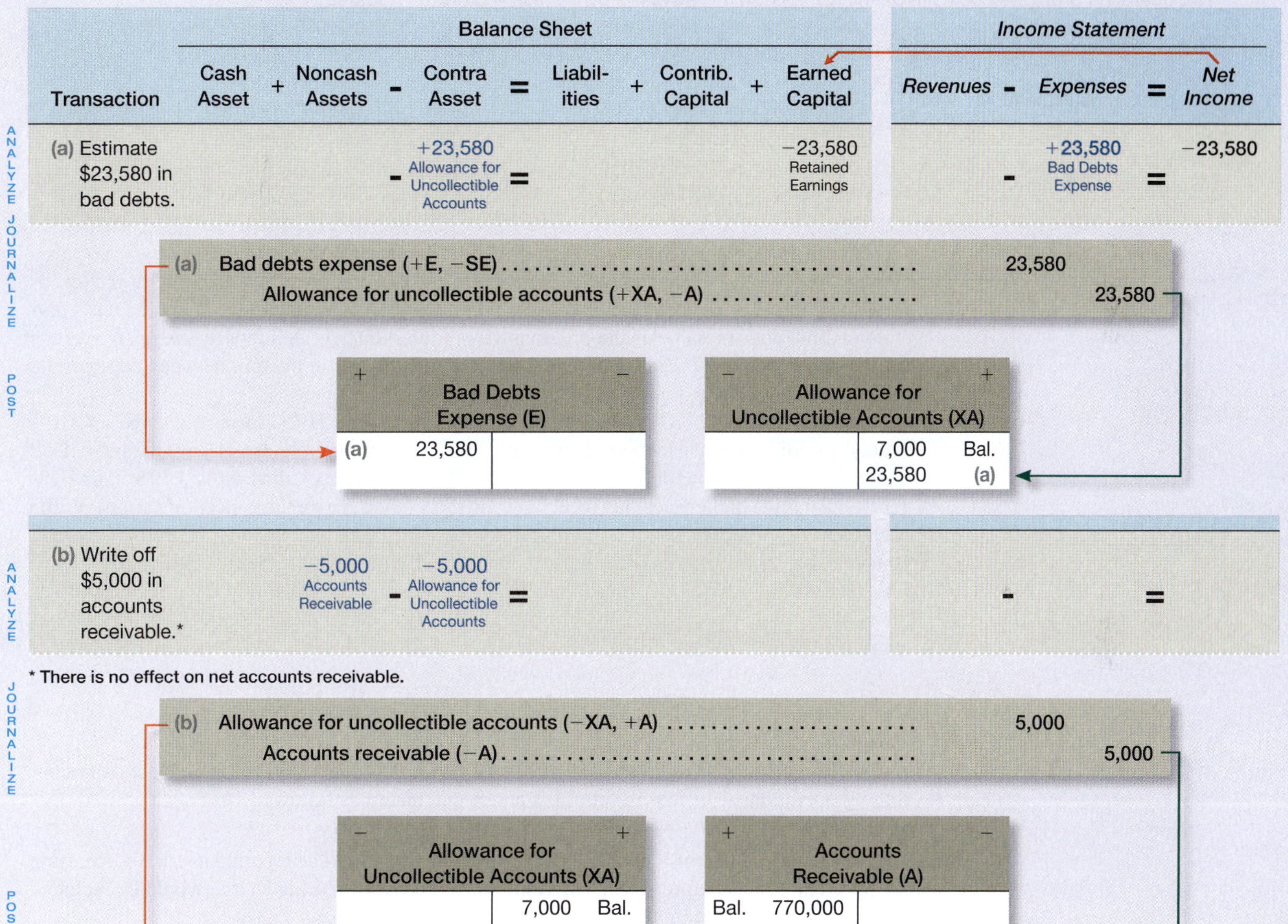

Chapter-End Review

Solution:

1.

($ millions)	Dell	HP
Average operating assets...............	$\dfrac{(\$25,306 + \$25,793)}{2} = \$25,549.5$	$\dfrac{(\$113,238 + \$88,547)}{2} = \$100,892.5$
Average current operating liabilities........	$\dfrac{(\$14,746 + \$18,301)}{2} = \$16,523.5$	$\dfrac{(\$42,763 + \$36,074)}{2} = \$39,418.5$
Return on capital employed (ROCE)........	$\dfrac{\$3,190}{(\$25,549.5 - \$16,523.5)} = 35.3\%$	$\dfrac{\$10,473}{(\$100,892.50 - \$39,418.5)} = 17.0\%$
Net operating profit after taxes (NOPAT)....	$\$2,478 - [(\$134) \times (1 - 0.35)] = \$2,391$	$\$8,329$
Net operating profit margin (NOPM)........	$\dfrac{\$2,391}{\$61,101} = 3.9\%$	$\dfrac{\$8,329}{\$118,364} = 7.0\%$
Accounts receivable turnover (ART)........	$\dfrac{\$61,101}{([\$5,961 + \$4,731]/2)}$ $= 11.4$ times	$\dfrac{\$118,364}{([\$13,420 + \$16,928]/2)}$ $= 7.8$ times
Average collection period (ACP)...........	$\dfrac{([\$5,961+\$4,731]/2)}{(\$61,101/365)}$ $= 32$ days	$\dfrac{([\$13,420+\$16,928]/2)}{(\$118,364/365)}$ $= 47$ days

2. HP has higher total sales and NOPAT. In addition, HP's net operating profit margin exceeds Dell's. HP has experienced growing revenue and operations in recent years, while Dell's revenue in 2008 was the same as the previous year. In its MD&A, Dell reports that their average selling price declined 7% in fiscal year 2008 due to a change in the mix between commercial and consumer business.

   However, Dell's ROCE was significantly higher than HP's, in part because of HP's acquisition of EDS that increased its assets (including intangible assets) significantly. Dell generates more sales per dollar of assets than HP—its total asset turnover is 2.39 versus HP's 1.17. Dell has the higher accounts receivable turnover (shorter average collection period). While each company likely has similar credit terms to business customers, they differ in their retail consumer sales strategy. Dell's retail sales are directly to the consumer and a large portion of these sales are for cash. HP, on the other hand, relies more on traditional retail sales outlets than does Dell. Hence, we are not surprised that the collection period on Dell's retail sales is significantly shorter than HP's.

Appendix Review

Solution:

a. A loss from discontinued operations of $105,000 would be reported below income from continuing operations. The loss is net of tax and is calculated as follows:
   $\$105,000 = (\$120,000 + \$12,000 + \$18,000) \times (1 - 30\%)$.

b. A restructuring charge of $30,000 ($12,000 + $18,000) would be reported as part of operating income. The loss is before taxes. The tax effect of the restructuring charge would be included in the provision for income taxes (income tax expense).

c. Singh could report this loss as discontinued operations only if the closure represented a separate business unit within the company. Otherwise, it must be reported as a restructuring charge.

1. Interpret disclosures of information concerning operating expenses, including manufacturing and retail inventory costs. (p. 307)

2. Account for inventory and cost of goods sold using different costing methods. (p. 312)

3. Apply the lower of cost or market rule to value inventory. (p. 317)

4. Evaluate how inventory costing affects management decisions and outsiders' interpretations of financial statements. (p. 321)

5. Define and interpret gross profit margin and inventory turnover ratios. Use inventory footnote information to make appropriate adjustments to ratios. (p. 324)

6. Appendix 7A: Analyze LIFO liquidations and the impact they have on the financial statements. (p. 330)

© Getty Images

Reporting and Analyzing Inventory

The Home Depot, Inc. is the world's largest home improvement retailer and the fourth largest retailer in the United States. By January 2009, the company operated more than 2,200 retail stores worldwide, and reported sales of more than $71 billion. The Home Depot prospered during the housing market boom between 1997 and 2005. Sales revenue increased, in part, due to the rapid increase in the number of stores. However, the housing slowdown and difficult economy of the past few years have caused The Home Depot to report stable or falling sales revenue. Store locations have grown at a slower pace, and specialty stores have been closed to allow a focus on the company's core business.

HOME DEPOT
www.HomeDepot.com

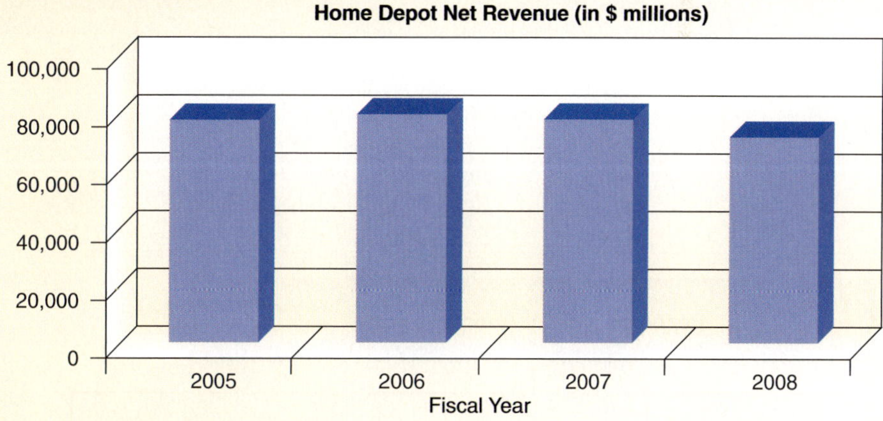

In this climate, the management of The Home Depot is focusing its attention on "improving the performance of our existing stores,"[1] with less emphasis on expansion. Accomplishing this improvement requires reversing a downward trend in same-store sales and effectively controlling the costs of operations. The Home Depot's net operating profit margin (net operating profit divided by sales revenue) increased steadily between 2001 and 2005, but that trend has reversed in recent years.

---

[1] Home Depot CEO Frank Blake in an interview with Rachel Tobin Blake published in *The Atlantic Journal-Constitution*, February 1, 2009.

(continued on next page)

(continued from previous page)

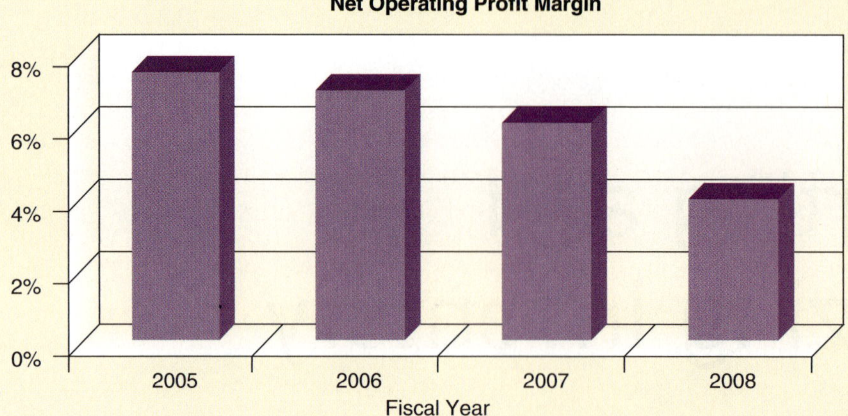

A key element of Home Depot's operating strategy is inventory management. Inventory represents one of the largest assets on Home Depot's balance sheet. A typical Home Depot store carries 30,000 to 40,000 products during the year, ranging from garden supplies to hardware and lumber to household appliances. These stores are stocked through a sophisticated logistics program designed to ensure product availability for customers and low supply chain costs. As of January 2009, the company operated 45 conventional distribution centers, 30 lumber distribution centers, 5 transit facilities, and 5 Rapid Deployment Centers where merchandise from manufacturers is received and prepared for immediate delivery to stores.

In this chapter, we examine the reporting of inventory and cost of goods sold. For most retail and manufacturing businesses, cost of goods sold and the related inventory management costs represent the largest source of expenses in the income statement. Carrying large stocks of inventory is costly for any business. The more that a business can minimize the amount of resources tied up in merchandise or materials, while still meeting customer demand, the more profitable it will be. Moreover, excessive inventory balances can indicate poor inventory management, obsolete products, and weakening sales. We will explore accounting methods designed to measure inventory costs and determine cost of goods sold. We will also look at measures that will help us assess the effectiveness of inventory management practices for companies such as The Home Depot.

Sources: The Home Depot, Inc. 2008-2009 10-K reports; The Home Depot does not end its fiscal year on December 31, but rather on the Sunday closest to January 31. So, "Fiscal Year 2008" actually ended on February 1, 2009. One interesting aspect of this practice is that most of The Home Depot's fiscal years have 52 weeks, but periodically a fiscal year will have 53 weeks. (Fiscal Year 2007 was one such year.)

CHAPTER ORGANIZATION

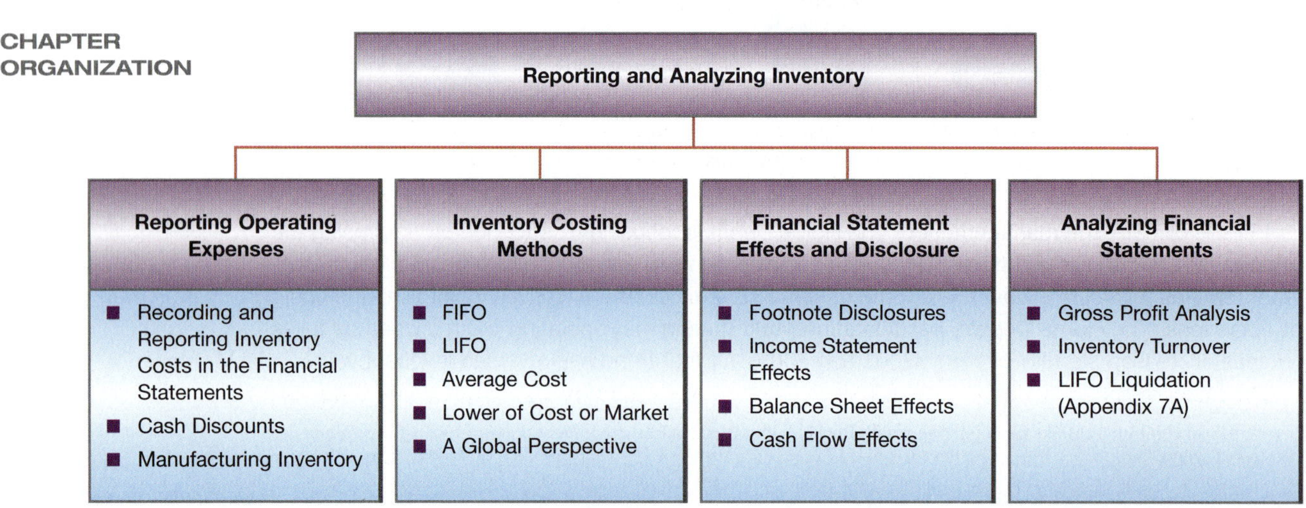

REPORTING OPERATING EXPENSES

In Chapter 6, we introduced the concept of operating income and discussed issues surrounding revenue recognition and how best to measure and report a company's performance. But the amount of revenue from customers must be interpreted relative to the resources that were required to achieve it. Operating expenses include the costs of acquiring the products (and services) that customers purchase, plus the costs of selling efforts, administrative functions, and any other activities that support the operations of the company. Careful examination of these costs allows financial statement users to judge management's performance, to identify emerging problems, and to make predictions of future performance. For instance, we may address the following questions.

LO1 Interpret disclosures of information concerning operating expenses, including manufacturing and retail inventory costs.

- Are the company's costs of providing products increasing or decreasing?

- Is the company able to maintain its margins in the face of changes in costs or competition?

- Does management's ability to judge customer tastes and preferences allow it to avoid overstocks of unpopular inventory and the resulting price discounts that reduce margins?

In this chapter, we begin our examination of operating expenses by studying inventory and cost of goods sold. The reporting of inventory and cost of goods sold is important for three reasons. First, cost of goods sold is often the largest single expense in a company's income statement, and inventory may be one of the largest assets in the balance sheet. Consequently, information about inventory and cost of goods sold is critical for interpreting the financial statements. Second, in order to effectively manage operations and resources, management needs accurate and timely information about inventory quantities and costs. Finally, alternative methods of accounting for inventory and cost of goods sold can distort interpretations of margins and turnovers unless the information in the financial statement footnotes is used.

Expense Recognition Principles

In addition to determining when to recognize revenues to properly measure and report a company's performance, we must also determine when to recognize expenses. The matching principle requires that expenses be recognized in the same period that the associated revenue is recognized. Expense recognition can be generally divided into the following three approaches.

- **Direct association.** Any cost that can be *directly* associated with a specific source of revenue should be recognized as an expense at the same time that the related revenue is recognized. For a merchandising company (a retailer or a wholesaler), an example of direct association is matching cost of goods sold with sales revenue when the product is delivered to the customer. The cost of acquiring the inventory is recorded in the inventory asset account until the item is sold; at that point, the inventory cost is removed from the inventory asset and transferred to expenses. The future costs of any obligations arising from current revenues should also be estimated and recognized as liabilities and matched as expenses against those revenues. An example of such an expense is expected warranty costs, which are covered in Chapter 9.

    For a manufacturing company, the accounting system distinguishes between *product costs* and *period costs*. Product costs are incurred to benefit the company's manufacturing activities and include raw materials, production workers and supervisors, depreciation on equipment and facilities, utilities, and so on. Even though some of these costs cannot be directly associated with a unit of production, the accounting system accumulates product costs and assigns them to inventory assets until the unit is sold. All costs not classified as product costs would be considered period costs.

- **Immediate recognition.** Many period costs are necessary for generating revenues and income but cannot be directly associated with specific revenues. Some costs can be associated with all of the revenues of an accounting period, but not with any specific sales transaction that occurred during that period. Examples include most administrative and marketing costs, and these costs are recognized as expenses in the period when the costs are incurred. Other expense items, such as research and development (R&D) expense, are recognized immediately because of U.S. GAAP requirements.

- **Systematic allocation.**   Costs that benefit more than one accounting period and cannot be associated with specific revenues or assigned to a specific period must be allocated across all of the periods benefited. The most common example is depreciation expense. When an asset is purchased, it is capitalized (recorded in an asset account) and then converted into an expense over the duration of its useful life according to a depreciation formula or schedule established by management. Depreciation of long-term assets is discussed in Chapter 8.

Inventory and cost of goods sold expense are important for product companies—manufacturers, wholesalers, and retailers. But before turning to an examination of these accounts at The Home Depot, we should recognize that cost of sales expense is also a critical performance component for many service companies, particularly those who engage in projects for their clients and customers. For fiscal 2008, the consulting firm **Accenture PLC** reports revenues of $25.3 billion and cost of services of $18.2 billion, and the professional staffing company **Robert Half International Inc.** reported net service revenues of $4.6 billion and direct costs of services of $2.7 billion, with a resulting gross profit of $1.9 billion. While these companies report no inventory, the relationship of revenues to costs of revenues remains important.

Reporting Inventory Costs in the Financial Statements

To help frame our discussion of inventory, Exhibits 7.1 and 7.2 present information from the current asset section of the balance sheet and the continuing operations section of the income statement for The Home Depot. We highlight merchandise inventories in the balance sheet as well as cost of goods sold in the income statement.

EXHIBIT 7.1	**Balance Sheets (Current Assets Only)**	
THE HOME DEPOT, INC.		
Consolidated Balance Sheets		
$ millions	**February 1, 2009**	**February 3, 2008**
ASSETS		
Current assets:		
Cash and cash equivalents...............................	$ 519	$ 445
Short-term investments	6	12
Receivables, net	972	1,259
Merchandise inventories...............................	10,673	11,731
Other current assets	1,192	1,227
Total current assets...................................	$13,362	$14,674

EXHIBIT 7.2	**Income Statement (Continuing Operations Only)**
THE HOME DEPOT, INC.	
Consolidated Statement of Earnings	
$ millions	**Fiscal year 2008**
NET SALES	$71,288
Cost of sales	47,298
GROSS PROFIT..	23,990
Total operating expenses	19,631
OPERATING INCOME	4,359
Other income and expense, net	(769)
EARNINGS FROM CONTINUING OPERATIONS BEFORE PROVISION FOR INCOME TAXES...	3,590
Provision for income taxes	1,278
EARNINGS FROM CONTINUING OPERATIONS	$ 2,312

When inventory is purchased or produced, it is capitalized and carried on the balance sheet as an asset until it is sold, at which time its cost is transferred from the balance sheet to the income statement as an expense (cost of goods sold). Cost of goods sold (COGS) is then subtracted from sales revenue to yield **gross profit**:

$$\textbf{Gross profit} = \textbf{Sales revenue} - \textbf{Cost of goods sold}$$

The manner in which inventory costs are transferred from the balance sheet to the income statement affects both the level of inventories reported on the balance sheet and the amount of gross profit (and net income) reported on the income statement.

Recording Inventory Costs in the Financial Statements

To illustrate the inventory purchasing and selling cycle, assume that a start-up company purchases 800 units of merchandise inventory at a cost of $4 cash per unit. We account for this transaction as follows:

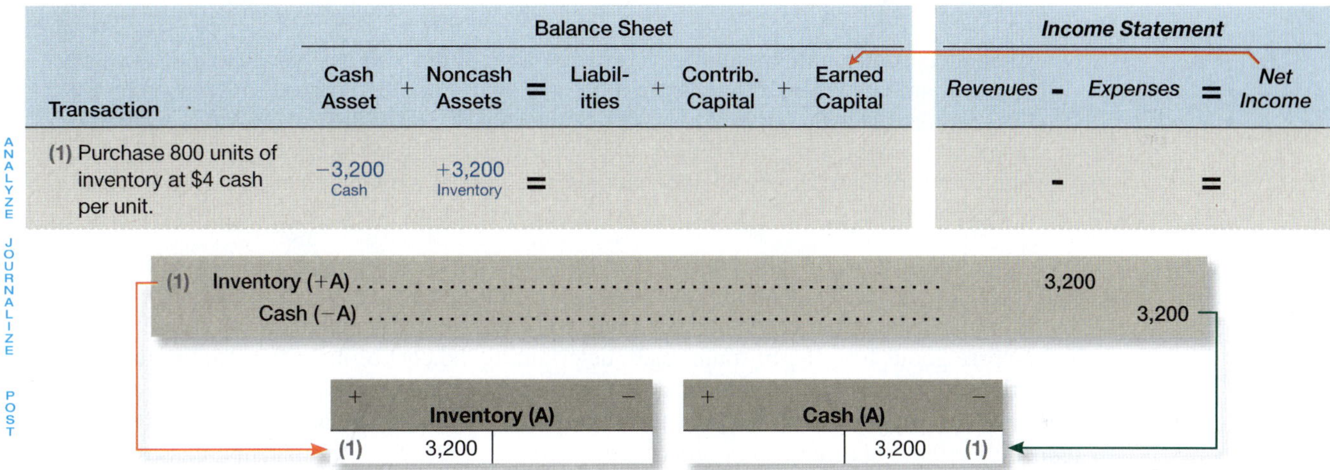

Next, assume this company sells 500 of those units for $7 cash per unit. The two following entries are required to record (a) the sales revenue and (b) the expense for the cost of the inventory sold.

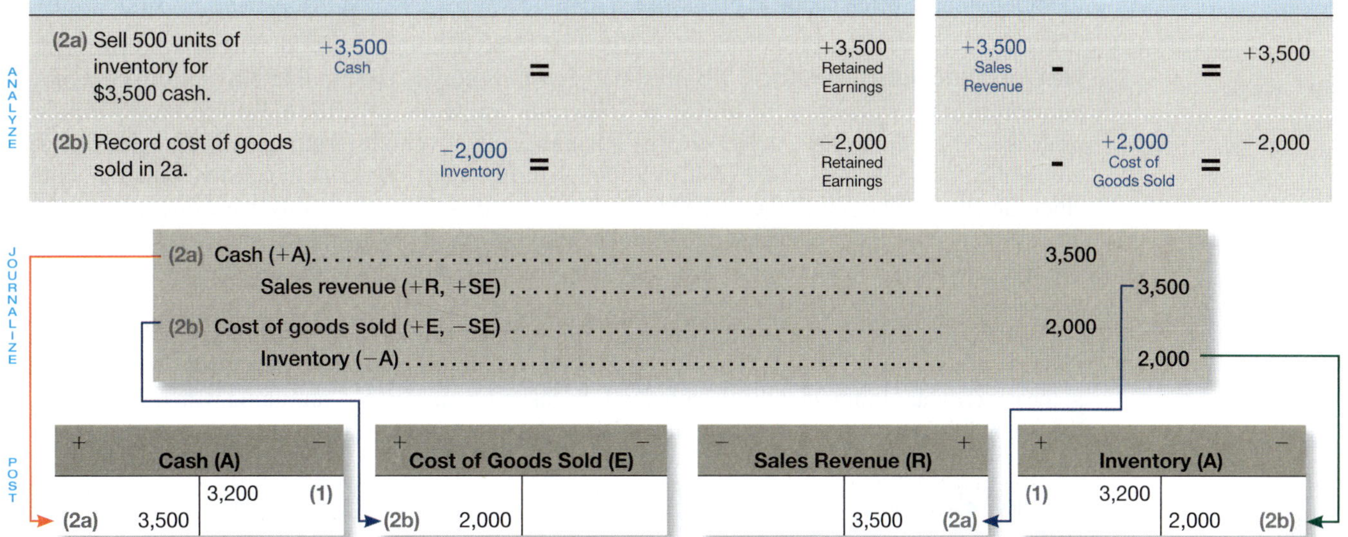

The gross profit from this sale is $1,500 ($3,500 − $2,000). Also, $1,200 worth of merchandise remains in inventory (300 units × $4 per unit).

Inventory and the Cost of Acquisition

In general, a company should recognize all inventories to which it holds legal title, and that inventory should be recognized at the cost of acquiring the inventory. On occasion, that means that the company will recognize items in inventory that are not on its premises. For instance, it may purchase inventory from a supplier on an "FOB shipping point" basis, meaning that the purchasing company receives title to the goods as soon as they are shipped by the supplier. The purchasing company should recognize the inventory as soon as it receives notice that the goods have been shipped. A similar situation may occur when a company has shipped its own products to a customer, but has not yet fulfilled the requirements for recognizing revenue on the shipment. In this case, the cost of the products will remain in the selling company's inventory account until revenue (and cost of goods sold) can be recognized.

It is also possible for a company to have physical possession of inventory items, but not to have legal title. **Target Corporation** reports the following in its fiscal year 2008 10-K report (p. 34).

> We routinely enter into arrangements with certain vendors whereby we do not purchase or pay for merchandise until the merchandise is ultimately sold to a guest. Revenues under this program are included in sales in the Consolidated Statements of Operations, but the merchandise received under the program is not included in inventory in our Consolidated Statements of Financial Position because of the virtually simultaneous purchase and sale of this inventory.

Inventory is reported in the balance sheet at its cost, including any cost to acquire, transport, and prepare goods for sale. In some cases, determining the cost of inventory requires accounting for various incentives that suppliers may offer to purchase more or to pay promptly. If a company qualifies for a supplier's volume discount or rebate, it should immediately recognize the effective reduction in the cost of inventory and cost of goods sold. Or, if the company purchases inventory on credit, suppliers often grant **cash discounts** to buyers if payment is made within a specified time period. Cash discounts are usually established as part of the credit terms and stated as a percentage of the purchase price. For example, credit terms of 1/10, n/30 (one-ten, net-thirty) indicate that a 1% cash discount is allowed if the payment is made within 10 days. If the cash discount is not taken, the full purchase price is due in 30 days.

Net-of-Discount Method   To illustrate a cash discount, assume that our start-up company purchases 1,000 units of merchandise at $4 per unit on terms of 1/10, n/30. The total purchase price is 1,000 × $4 = $4,000. However, if payment is made within 10 days, the net purchase price would then be $3,960 ($4,000 − $40). While this difference may seem like a small amount, consider the cost of not taking the discount. If the discount is missed, the buyer is afforded an extra 20 days to pay for the merchandise, for which it pays a penalty of $40, or $2 per day. $2 per day is the equivalent of $730 dollars per year which, in turn, is equivalent to paying interest at an annual rate of 18.4% ($730/$3,960).[2]

When cash discounts are offered, the inventory purchase should be recorded at its cost using the **net-of-discount method**. When the net-of-discount method is used, inventory is capitalized at the net cost, assuming that the discount will be taken by the buyer. Continuing with our example, the following journal entry would be recorded at the time of purchase:

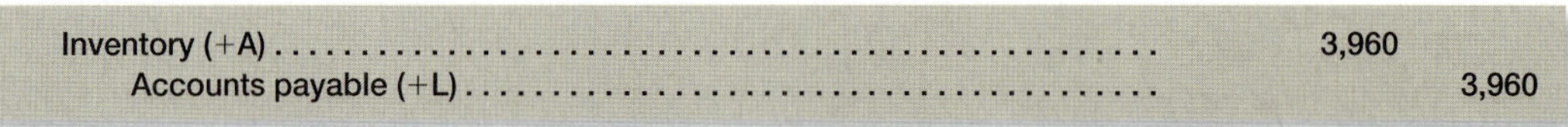

Inventory (+A)	3,960	
Accounts payable (+L)		3,960

---

[2] Compound interest methods (introduced in Chapter 9) would arrive at a slightly different annual rate of interest.

When payment is made within the 10-day discount period, accounts payable is debited and cash is credited. That is, no explicit entry is made to recognize the discount taken.

Accounts payable (−L)	3,960	
Cash (−A)		3,960

However, when a discount is missed, the lost discount must be recorded. To illustrate, if full payment is made within 30 days, the following journal entry would be recorded:

Accounts payable (−L)	3,960	
Interest expense, discounts lost (+E, −SE).	40	
Cash (−A)		4,000

Note that the missed discount is an expense in the period when the discount is lost. This serves two purposes. First, discounts lost are not treated as an inventory cost or as part of cost of goods sold, but rather like a finance charge. Second, the net-of-discount method highlights late payments by keeping an explicit record of lost discounts. Given the high cost of missed cash discounts, most businesses would want to minimize the amount of discounts lost. Thus, keeping a record of discounts lost is useful when it comes to managing cash and accounts payable.

Inventory Reporting by Manufacturing Firms

Retail and wholesale businesses purchase merchandise for resale to customers. In contrast, a manufacturing firm produces the goods it sells. Its inventory reporting is designed to reflect this difference in the nature of its operations.

Manufacturing firms typically report three categories of inventory account:

- **Raw materials inventory**—the cost of parts and materials purchased from suppliers for use in the production process. When raw materials are used in the production process, the cost of the materials used is transferred from raw materials inventory into the work-in-process inventory account.

- **Work-in-process inventory**—the cost of the inventory of partially completed goods. Work-in-process (abbreviated WIP) includes the materials used in the production of the product as well as labor cost and overhead cost. (Methods by which labor and overhead costs are assigned to products in the WIP account is a *managerial accounting* topic.) When the production process is completed, the cost of goods produced is transferred from WIP into the finished goods inventory account.

- **Finished goods inventory**—the cost of the stock of completed product ready for delivery to customers. When finished goods are sold, Cost of Goods Sold is debited and finished goods inventory is credited, much the same as in a retail business.

> **FYI** Only one inventory account appears in the financial statements of a merchandiser. A manufacturer normally has three inventory accounts: Raw Materials, Work-in-Process, and Finished Goods.

EXHIBIT 7.3	Components of Inventory for Cisco Systems, Inc.

Inventories ($ millions):	
Raw materials	$ 165
Work in process.	33
Finished goods	
Distributor inventory and deferred cost of sales	382
Manufactured finished goods	310
Total finished goods	692
Service-related spares	151
Demonstration systems	33
Total	$1,074

A complete illustration of the accounting process for a manufacturing business is beyond the scope of this text. However, it is useful to understand how these inventory accounts are presented in the financial statements of manufacturing firms. In some cases, each of the three categories of inventory is presented in the balance sheet. Often, however, the balance sheet only presents the combined total of the three accounts, leaving the detail to be presented in the footnotes. **Cisco Systems** reported inventory of $1,074 million in its balance sheet dated July 25, 2009. Exhibit 7.3 details the components of Cisco's inventory balance as presented in its 10-K report. It shows that finished goods inventory represented the largest portion of the total inventory balance and that more than half of these finished goods are held by Cisco's distributors. (Recall Cisco's "sell-through" revenue recognition described in Chapter 6.) Cisco reports two additional categories of inventory—spare parts and systems used in product demonstrations. Exhibit 7.3 is representative of the footnote disclosure provided by many manufacturing companies.

BUSINESS INSIGHT

If a manufacturing company has an unexpected buildup of inventory, the interpretation depends on the type of inventory. A larger-than-normal buildup of finished goods would imply that the company was having difficulty getting customers to purchase its products. However, if the buildup is in work-in-process inventory, it might imply a problem with manufacturing processes, particularly if accompanied by a decrease in finished goods inventory.

INVENTORY COSTING METHODS

LO2 Account for inventory and cost of goods sold using different costing methods.

The computation of cost of goods sold is important and is shown in Exhibit 7.4.

EXHIBIT 7.4	Cost of Goods Sold Computation
	Beginning inventory value (prior period ending balance sheet)
	+ Cost of inventory purchases and/or production
	Cost of goods available for sale
	− Ending inventory value (current period balance sheet)
	Cost of goods sold (current income statement)

The cost of inventory available at the beginning of a period is a carryover from the ending inventory balance of the prior period. The costs of current period purchases of inventory (or costs of newly manufactured inventories) are added to the costs of beginning inventory on the balance sheet, yielding the total cost of goods (inventory) available for sale. Then, the total cost of goods available either ends up in cost of goods sold for the period (reported on the income statement) or is carried forward as inventory to start the next period (reported on the ending balance sheet). This cost flow is schematically shown in Exhibit 7.5.

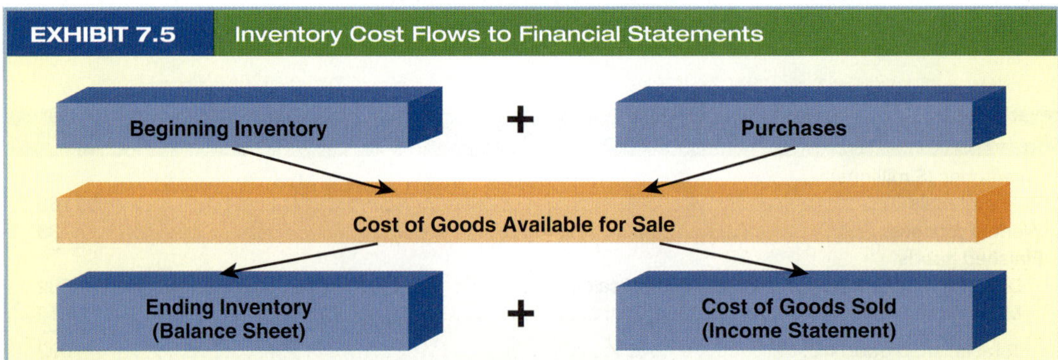

Understanding the flow of inventory costs is important. If the beginning inventory plus all inventory purchased or manufactured during the period is sold, then COGS is equal to the cost of the goods available for sale. However, when inventory remains at the end of a period, companies must identify the cost of those inventories that have been sold and the cost of those inventories that remain.

Most companies will organize the physical flow of their inventories to keep the cost of inventory management low, while minimizing the likelihood of spoilage or obsolescence. However, the accounting for inventory and cost of goods sold does not have to follow the physical flow of the units of inventory, so companies may report using a **cost flow assumption** that does not conform to the actual movement of product through the firm. (For instance, many grocery chains use last-in, first-out to account for inventory costs, but that doesn't mean that they put the newest produce out to sell while keeping the older produce back in the storeroom.)

Illustration   To illustrate the possible cost flow assumptions that companies can adopt, assume that Exhibit 7.6 reflects the inventory records of Butler Company.

EXHIBIT 7.6	Summary Inventory Records for Butler Company						
		Number of Units	Cost per Unit	Total Cost	Number of Units	Price per Unit	Total Revenue
January 1, 2010	Beginning inventory	500	$100	$ 50,000			
2010	Inventory purchased	200	170	34,000			
	Inventory sold				450	$250	$112,500
2011	Inventory purchased	600	180	108,000			
	Inventory sold				500	255	127,500

Butler Company began the period with inventory consisting of 500 units it purchased at a total cost of $50,000 ($100 each). During the two-year period, the company purchased additional 200 units costing $34,000 and 600 units costing $108,000. The total cost of goods available for sale for this two-year period equals $192,000.

Tracking the number of units available for sale each year and in inventory at the end of each year is simple. However, the changing cost per unit makes it more complicated to determine the cost of goods sold and the ending inventory. The relationships depicted in Exhibit 7.5 can hold in multiple ways, depending on the cost flow assumption chosen. Three inventory costing methods are acceptable under U.S. GAAP (though only two may be used under IFRS, as we will discuss later).[3]

First-In, First-Out (FIFO)

The **first-in, first-out (FIFO)** inventory costing method transfers costs from inventory in the order that they were initially recorded. That is, FIFO assumes that the first costs recorded in inventory (first-in) are the first costs transferred from inventory (first-out) to cost of goods sold. Conversely, the costs of the last units purchased are the costs that remain in inventory at year-end. Applying FIFO to the data in Exhibit 7.6 means that the costs relating to the 450 units sold are all taken from its *beginning* inventory, which consists of 500 units. The company's 2010 cost of goods sold and gross profit, using FIFO, is computed as follows:

FYI First-in, first-out (FIFO) assumes that goods are used in the order in which they are purchased; the inventory remaining represents the most recent purchases.

Sales	$112,500
COGS (450 @ $100 each)	45,000
Gross profit	$ 67,500

The cost remaining in inventory and reported on its 2010 year-end balance sheet is $39,000 ($50,000 + $34,000 − $45,000; also computed 50 × $100 + 200 × $170).

The same process can be used for 2011, and Exhibit 7.7 depicts the FIFO costing method and shows the resulting financial statement items using FIFO for 2010 and 2011. FIFO cost of goods sold

---

[3] *Accounting Trends & Techniques—2009*, published by the American Institute of Certified Public Accountants, reports the results of a survey of 500 companies' accounting practices. In 2008, 179 (36%) of those companies reported the use of LIFO cost for at least some inventories. FIFO cost was most common, used by 323 companies (65%), and average cost was used by 146 companies (29%). The numbers add to more than 100% because many companies use more than one inventory costing method.

for 2011 is 50 units at $100 each plus 200 units at $170 each plus 250 units at $180 each, or $84,000. Ending inventory for 2011 is 350 units at $180 each, or $63,000. Over the two-year period, the total cost of goods available for sale of $192,000 has either been recognized as cost of goods sold ($45,000 + $84,000 = $129,000) or remains in ending inventory ($63,000).

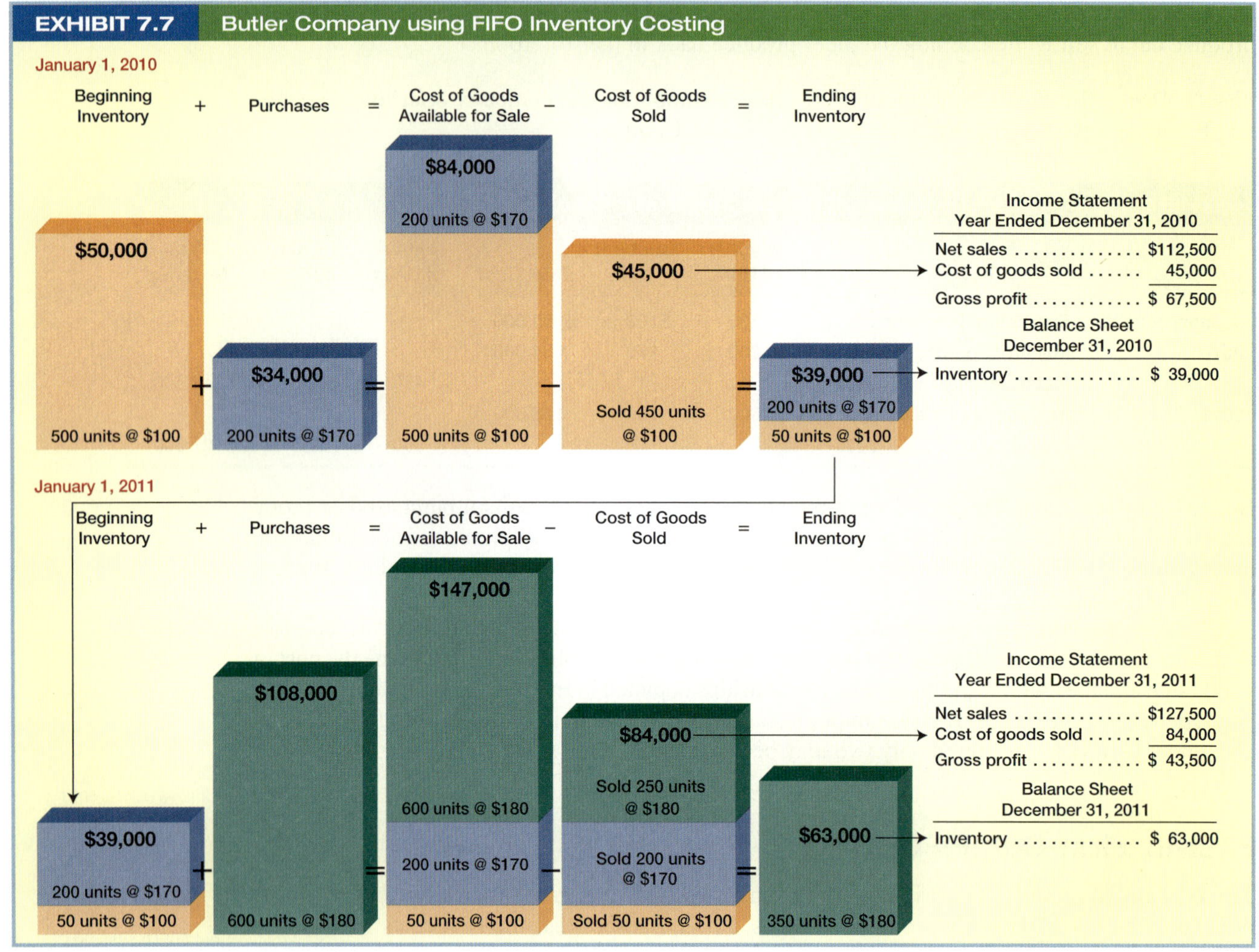

Last-In, First-Out (LIFO)

FYI Last-in, first-out (LIFO) matches the cost of the last goods purchased against revenue.

The **last-in, first-out (LIFO)** inventory costing method transfers to cost of goods sold the most recent costs that were recorded in inventory. That is, we assume that the most recent costs recorded in inventory (last-in) are the first costs transferred from inventory (first-out). Conversely, the costs of the first units purchased are the costs that remain in inventory at year-end. Butler Company's 2010 cost of goods sold and gross profit, using LIFO, is computed as follows:

Sales		$112,500
COGS: (200 @ $170 each = $34,000)		
(250 @ $100 each = $25,000)		59,000
Gross profit		$ 53,500

The cost remaining in inventory and reported on its 2010 balance sheet is $25,000 ($50,000 + $34,000 − $59,000; also computed 250 × $100).

The same process can be used for 2011, and Exhibit 7.8 depicts the LIFO costing method and shows the resulting financial statement values using LIFO for both years. LIFO cost of goods sold for 2011 is 500 units at $180 each, or $90,000. Ending inventory is 250 units at $100 each plus 100 units at $180 each, or $43,000. Again, the two-year total cost of goods available for sale of $192,000 has either been recognized as cost of goods sold ($59,000 + $90,000 = $149,000) or remains in inventory ($43,000).

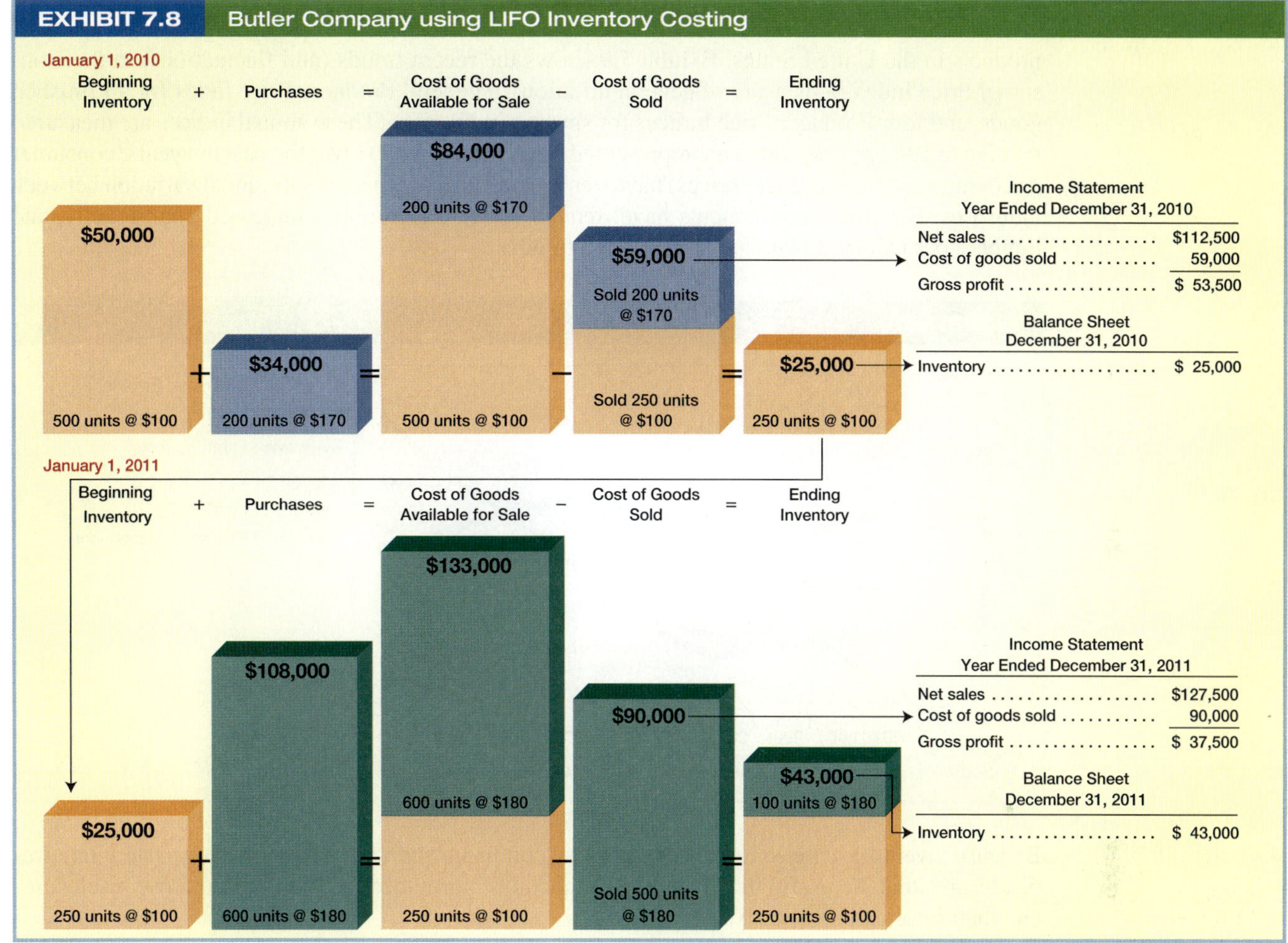

The exhibit shows that **LIFO layers** of inventories added in each year are kept separately. So, the ending inventory in 2011 consists of a pre-2010 layer of 250 units at $100 each plus a 2011 layer of 100 units at $180 each. When unit sales exceed purchases (as we will discuss in the appendix), the first costs carried to cost of goods sold are those purchased in the current year, followed by the most recent layer of LIFO inventory and working down to the oldest layers. So, the 2010 beginning inventory values of $100 per unit will remain in LIFO inventory as long as there are 250 units remaining at the end of the year. One aspect of this flow assumption is that reported LIFO inventory values can be significantly lower than the current cost of acquiring the same inventory.

LIFO inventory costing is always applied on a periodic, annual basis. This means that Butler's cost of goods sold and ending inventory for 2011 do not depend on the timing of the sales and purchases within the year. Inventory levels might be drawn down below 250 units *during* the year, but the 250 unit LIFO layer at $100 each will remain in ending inventory as long as inventory is built up to 250 units by the *end* of the year.

Inventory Costing and Price Changes

There are several important aspects of inventory costing that are illustrated by the Butler Company example. First, both LIFO and FIFO are historical cost methods, though they allocate the costs of inventory differently. All costs are accounted for, but in different ways.

Second, the differences between LIFO and FIFO arise when the costs of inventory change over time. In general, LIFO puts more recent costs into cost of goods sold expense, so LIFO cost of goods sold will be higher than FIFO cost of goods sold (and gross profit correspondingly lower) when the costs of inventory are rising over time. This phenomenon can be seen in years 2010 and 2011 for Butler Company. If the costs of inventory are falling, then FIFO cost of goods sold will exceed LIFO cost of goods sold.

One place where you can observe the cost trends of acquiring inventory is in the U.S. Bureau of Labor Statistics' Producer Price Indices. These track the costs of producing a wide variety of products in the United States. Exhibit 7.9 shows the recent trends (and fluctuations) in the Consumer Price Index (a measure of general inflation), a general Producer Price Index for all finished goods, and four Producer Price Indices for specific industries. (These annual indices are measured relative to 1982 prices, which are represented by a value of 100.) Over the past ten years, consumer prices (and average producer prices) have trended upward, but there is substantial variation between industries. Electronic components have trended down, gasoline has increased significantly, and lumber goes up and down with construction trends.

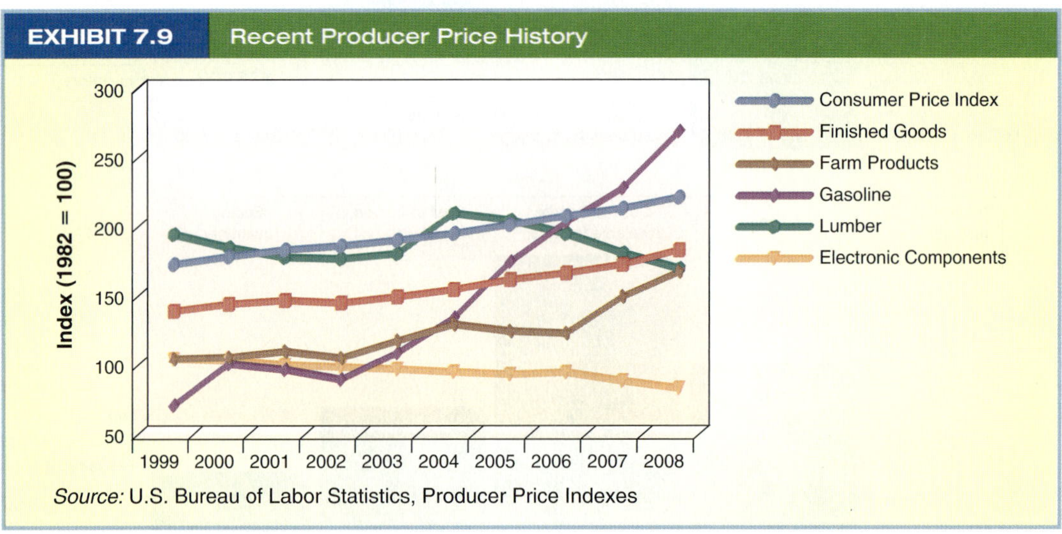

Source: U.S. Bureau of Labor Statistics, Producer Price Indexes

Because inventories are so important for many companies, the financial reporting system requires disclosures that are useful in interpreting financial performance. We will turn to those disclosures and their implications shortly.

Average Cost (AC)

The **average cost (AC)** method computes the 2010 cost of goods sold as an average of the cost to purchase all of the inventories that were available for sale during the period as follows:

Sales	$112,500
COGS (450 @ $120 [{$50,00 + $34,000}/700 units] each)	54,000
Gross profit	$ 58,500

The average cost of $120 per unit is determined from the total cost of goods available for sale divided by the number of units available for sale ($84,000/700 units). The cost remaining in inventory and reported on its 2010 balance sheet is $30,000 ($84,000 − $54,000; also computed 250 × $120).

When average cost is applied to the future years, the beginning inventory balance's average cost is again averaged with the inventory acquisitions made during the year. This new average is used to assign costs to that year's ending inventory and cost of goods sold. For the Butler Company, the average cost is $120 for 2010 and $162.35 (rounded) for 2011. The average cost for 2011 is the opening inventory balance plus the period's purchases ($30,000 + $108,000) divided by the total number of units available for sale (250 + 600). So, 2011 cost of goods sold is 500 units at $162.35 each, and ending inventory is 350 units at that same average cost. Exhibit 7.10 depicts the average cost method and shows the resulting financial statement values using average cost for both years.

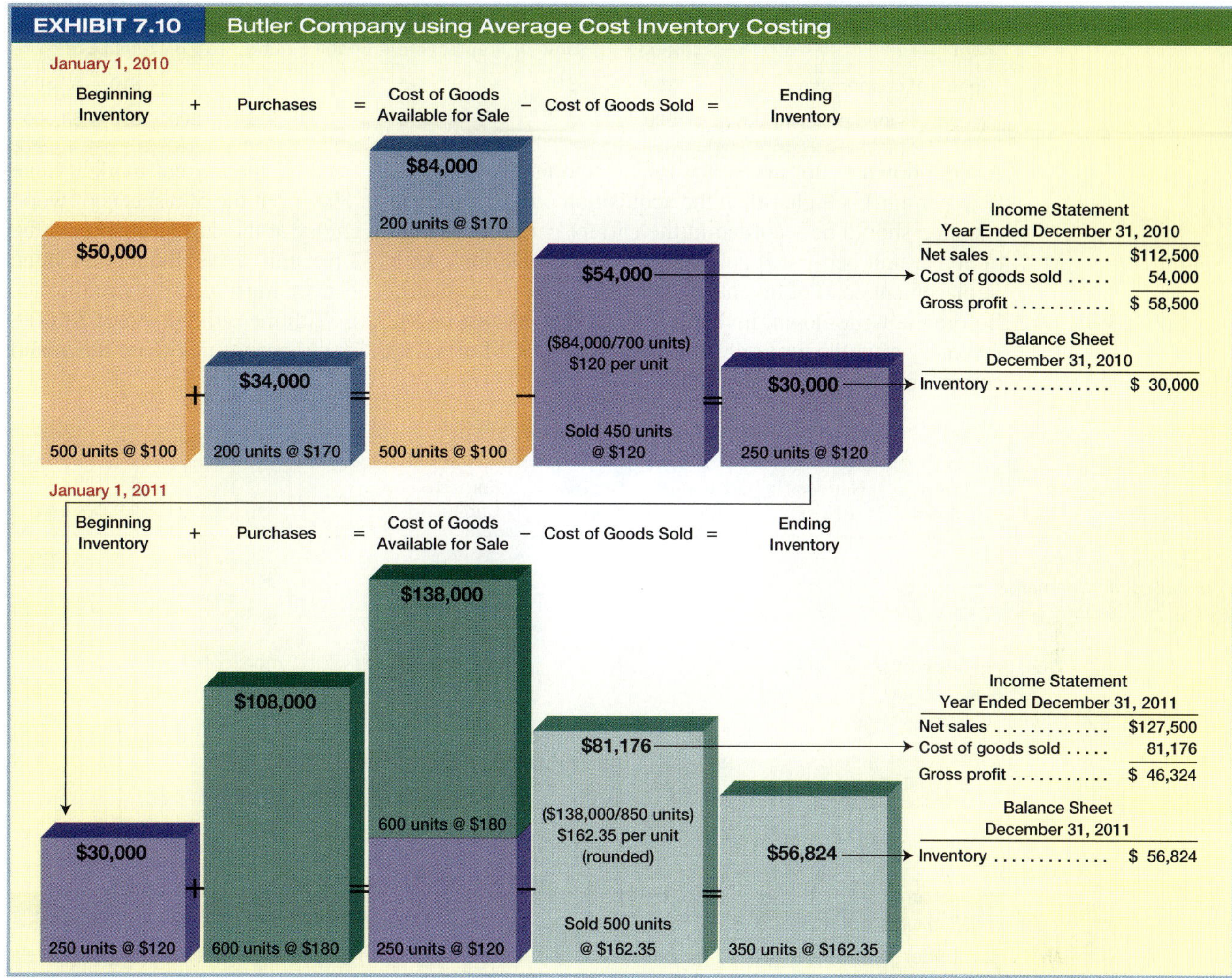

Lower of Cost or Market

Companies are required to write down the carrying amount of inventories on the balance sheet, *if* the reported cost (using FIFO, for example) exceeds the market value (determined by current replacement cost). This process is called reporting inventories at the **lower of cost or market (LCM)**. Should the replacement cost (market value) be less than reported cost, the inventories must be written down from cost to market value, resulting in the following financial statement effects.

LO3 Apply the lower of cost or market rule to value inventory.

- Inventory book value is written down to current market value (replacement cost), reducing total assets.
- Inventory write-down is reflected as an expense (part of cost of goods sold) on the income statement, reducing current period gross profit, income, and equity.

The most common occurrence of inventory write-downs is in connection with restructuring activities. These write-downs are included in cost of goods sold or on a separate line in the income statement.

FYI If inventory declines in value below its original cost, for whatever reason, the inventory is written down to reflect this loss.

The write-down of inventories can potentially shift income from one period to another. If, for example, inventories were written down below current replacement cost (too conservative), future gross profit would be increased as lower future costs would be reflected in cost of goods sold. GAAP anticipates this possibility by requiring that inventories not be written down below a floor that is equal to net realizable value less a normal markup. Although this does allow some discretion (and the ability to manage income), the net realizable value and markup values must be substantiated by auditors.

FYI Standards require the consistent application of costing methods from one period to another.

Illustration   To illustrate the lower of cost or market rule, assume Home Depot has the following items in its current period ending inventory:

Item	Quantity	Cost per Unit	Market Value (replacement cost)	LCM per unit	Total LCM
Spools of copper wire........	250	$10	$15	$10	250 × $10 = $2,500
Sheets of wood paneling	500	$ 8	$ 6	$ 6	500 × $ 6 = $3,000

A write-down is not necessary for the spools of copper wire because the current market value ($15 per unit) is higher than the acquisition cost ($10 per unit). However, the 500 sheets of wood paneling should be recorded in the current period's ending inventory at the current market value of $6 per unit because it is lower than the acquisition cost of $8 per unit. When the market value (replacement cost) of inventory declines below its acquisition cost, we must record a write-down. Before the write-down, inventory is recorded at cost of $6,500. With the write-down of $1,000, inventory after the write-down is recorded at LCM of $5,500. The effects of this write-down and corresponding journal entries follow:

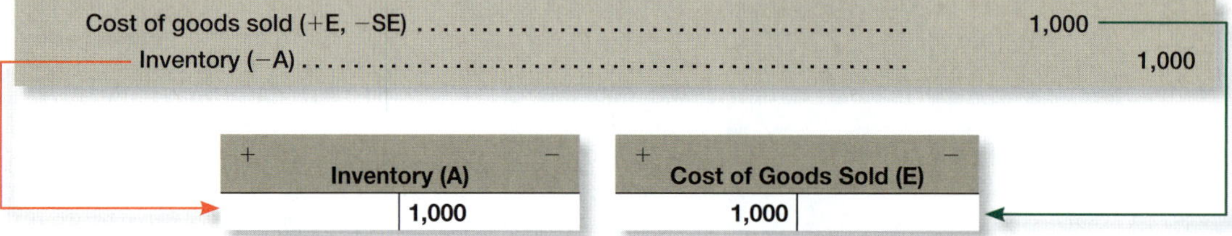

IFRS REPORTING INSIGHT

Under U.S. GAAP, inventory that has been written down cannot be revalued later at higher levels even if the market value of that inventory increases. IFRS, on the other hand, does allow companies to reverse the write-down of the inventory up to the acquisition cost if market values warrant. The revaluation results in a debit to Inventory and a credit to Cost of Goods Sold.

MID-CHAPTER REVIEW

Part 1

At the beginning of the current period, Hutton Company holds 1,000 units of its only product with a per-unit cost of $18. A summary of purchases during the current period follows:

	Units	Unit Cost	Cost
Beginning Inventory	1,000	$18.00	$18,000
Purchases: #1	1,800	18.25	32,850
#2	800	18.50	14,800
#3	1,200	19.00	22,800
Goods available for sale	4,800		$88,450

During the current period, Hutton sells 2,800 units.

Required

1. Assume that Hutton uses the first-in, first-out (FIFO) method. Compute the cost of goods sold for the current period and the ending inventory balance.

2. Assume that Hutton uses the last-in, first-out (LIFO) method. Compute the cost of goods sold for the current period and the ending inventory balance.
3. Assume that Hutton uses the average cost (AC) method. Compute the cost of goods sold for the current period and the ending inventory balance.
4. As manager, which one of these three inventory costing methods would you choose:
    a.   To reflect what is probably the physical flow of goods? Explain.
    b.   To minimize income taxes for the period? Explain.
5. Assume that Hutton utilizes the LIFO method and instead of purchasing lot #3, the company allows its inventory level to decline and delays purchasing lot #3 until the next period. Compute cost of goods sold under this scenario and discuss the effect of end-of-year purchases under LIFO.
6. Record the effects of each of the following summary transactions *a* and *b* in the financial statement effects template, prepare journal entries, set up T-accounts for each of the accounts used, and post the journal entries to those T-accounts.
    a.   Purchased inventory for $70,450 cash.
    b.   Sold $50,850 of inventory for $85,000 cash.

Part 2

Venner Company had the following inventory at December 31, 2010.

		Unit Price	
	Quantity	Cost	Market
Fans			
Model X1	300	$18	$19
Model X2	250	22	24
Model X3	400	29	26
Heaters			
Model B7	500	24	28
Model B8	290	35	32
Model B9	100	41	38

Required

1. Determine ending inventory by applying the lower of cost or market rule to
    a.   Each item of inventory.
    b.   Each major category of inventory.
    c.   Total inventory.
2. Which of the LCM procedures from requirement *a* results in the lowest net income for 2010? Explain.

The solution to this review problem can be found on pages 346–348.

FINANCIAL STATEMENT EFFECTS AND DISCLOSURE

The notes to the financial statements describe, at least in general terms, the inventory accounting method used by a company. To illustrate, The Home Depot reports $10,673 million in merchandise inventory on its February 1, 2009, balance sheet as a current asset. The following note was taken from that 10-K report:

Merchandise Inventories

The majority of the Company's Merchandise Inventories are stated at the lower of cost (first-in, first-out) or market. . . . The Company evaluates the inventory valued using the [FIFO] cost method at the end of each quarter to ensure that it is carried at the lower of cost or market. The valuation allowance for Merchandise Inventories valued under the cost method was not material to the Consolidated Financial Statements of the Company as of the end of fiscal 2008 and fiscal 2007.

FYI Standards require financial statement disclosure of (1) the composition of the inventory (in the balance sheet or a separate schedule in the notes), (2) significant or unusual inventory financing arrangements, and (3) inventory costing methods employed (which can differ for different types of inventory).

continued

continued from previous page

> Independent physical inventory counts or cycle counts are taken on a regular basis in each store and distribution center to ensure that amounts reflected in the accompanying Consolidated Financial Statements for Merchandise Inventories are properly stated. During the period between physical inventory counts in stores, the Company accrues for estimated losses related to shrink on a store-by-store basis based on historical shrink results and current trends in the business. Shrink (or in the case of excess inventory, "swell") is the difference between the recorded amount of inventory and the physical inventory. Shrink may occur due to theft, loss, inaccurate records for the receipt of inventory or deterioration of goods, among other things.

This note includes several items that would be of interest to financial statement users:

1. The Home Depot uses the FIFO method to determine the cost of its inventory.
2. Inventory is reported at the lower of cost or market value, and the amount of write-down (the valuation allowance) was not material at the financial statement date.
3. The company periodically takes a physical count of inventory to identify "shrink." Shrink refers to the loss of inventory due to theft, breakage or damage, spoilage (for perishable goods), or other losses, as well as inaccurate records.

When businesses adjust inventory balances for shrink, the loss is debited to cost of goods sold. Hence, cost of goods sold expense on the income statement includes the actual cost of products sold during the period plus the loss due to shrink as well as losses resulting from lower of cost or market adjustments and discounts lost.

Another illustration of inventory disclosure is taken from the notes of **Chevron Corporation**. Chevron reports an inventory of $6,854 million on its December 31, 2008, balance sheet. The following note was taken from its 2008 10-K report ($ millions):

> Crude oil, petroleum products and chemicals are generally stated at cost, using a Last-In, First-Out (LIFO) method. In the aggregate, these costs are below market. "Materials, supplies and other" inventories generally are stated at average cost.
>
> The excess of replacement cost over the carrying value of inventories for which the Last-In, First-Out (LIFO) method is used was $9,368 and $6,958 at December 31, 2008 and 2007, respectively. Replacement cost is generally based on average acquisition costs for the year. LIFO profits of $210, $113, and $82 were included in net income for the years 2008, 2007, and 2006, respectively.

There are several interesting items disclosed in Chevron's note:

1. Chevron uses LIFO to report the cost of its crude oil and petroleum products inventory, but uses average cost for materials, supplies and other. Neither U.S. GAAP nor tax authorities such as the IRS require the use of a single inventory costing method. That is, companies are allowed to, and frequently do, use different inventory costing methods for different categories of inventory. In addition, multinational companies may use one costing method in the United States and a different method for foreign inventory stocks.
2. Although Chevron reports inventory costs at the lower of cost or market, the market value of its inventory is significantly higher than its cost based on LIFO accounting. In fact, the note reports that replacement cost exceeded the $6,854 million LIFO cost by $9,368 million. That means that the replacement cost of its inventory was $16,222 million ($6,854 + $9,368). Companies using LIFO are required to report the difference between the LIFO cost and current value—determined either as market value or replacement cost or as the FIFO cost. The difference between the ending inventory's FIFO cost (or current cost) and its LIFO cost is called the **LIFO reserve**.

3. Chevron refers to "LIFO profits" of $210 million in 2008. LIFO profit is the amount of net income that results from **LIFO liquidation**, which we discuss in the appendix to this chapter. Like the LIFO reserve, companies using LIFO must disclose the existence and magnitude of any profits arising from the use of LIFO during the period.

Why do companies disclose such details on inventory, and why is so much attention paid to inventory in financial statement analysis? First, the magnitude of a company's investment in inventory is often large—impacting both balance sheets and income statements. Second, risks of inventory losses are often high, as they are tied to technical obsolescence and consumer tastes. Third, it can provide insight into future performance—both good and bad. Fourth, high inventory levels result in substantial costs for the company, such as:

- Financing costs to purchase inventories (when not purchased on credit)
- Storage costs of inventories (such as warehousing and related facilities)
- Handling costs of inventories (including wages)
- Insurance costs of inventories

Consequently, companies seek to keep inventories at levels that balance these costs against the cost of insufficient inventory (stock-out and resulting lost sales and delays in production, as machines and employees sit idle awaiting inventories to process).

Next we turn our focus on the effects of the different inventory costing assumptions on the financial statements.

Financial Statement Effects of Inventory Costing

The three inventory costing methods described above yield differing levels of gross profit for our illustrative example, as shown in Exhibit 7.11.

It is important to understand that, even though the various methods produce different financial statements, the underlying events are the same. That is, different accounting methods can make similar situations seem more different than they really are.

LO4 Evaluate how inventory costing affects management decisions and outsiders' interpretations of financial statements.

LIFO Reserve   Exhibit 7.11 demonstrates one of the income statement/balance sheet links that will prove useful in analyzing financial statements. In the beginning inventory for 2010, LIFO and FIFO start from the same point—500 units at $100 each. But during 2010, FIFO would record cost of goods sold that is $14,000 less than LIFO ($45,000 versus $59,000). During 2010, LIFO put $14,000 more into cost of goods sold than FIFO did, but that also means that LIFO put $14,000 less into ending inventory. We can see that the LIFO reserve has grown from zero to $14,000, the same amount. This relationship continues in 2011: the LIFO reserve increased by $6,000 (from $14,000 to $20,000), and the LIFO cost of goods sold was $6,000 greater than the FIFO cost of goods sold ($90,000 versus $84,000). The LIFO reserve equals the ending inventory's FIFO cost less LIFO cost, but it is also the *cumulative* difference between LIFO and FIFO cost of goods sold. The *change* in the LIFO reserve is the difference between LIFO and FIFO cost of goods sold for the current period.

So, if Butler Company chose to report using LIFO, we could estimate what the company's FIFO cost of goods sold would have been by seeing how the LIFO reserve changed.

FYI   If ending inventory is misstated, then (1) the inventory, retained earnings, working capital, and current ratio in the balance sheet are misstated, and (2) the cost of goods sold and net income in the income statement are misstated.

> **FIFO cost of goods sold = LIFO cost of goods sold − Change in the LIFO reserve**

That relationship could prove useful if we wanted to compare Butler Company's gross profit to that of another company using FIFO. Changes in the LIFO reserve can also give a rough indication of how a company's inventory costs changed over the period. If costs went up, the LIFO reserve will go up; if costs went down, the LIFO reserve will go down.

Income Statement Effects   The income differences between inventory accounting methods are a function of two factors. First is the speed and direction of inventory cost changes. For Butler Company, inventory costs have gone from $100 per unit to $180 per unit in a two-year period. If

EXHIBIT 7.11	Financial Statement Effects of Inventory Costing Methods			
		FIFO	**LIFO**	**Average Cost**
January 1, 2010	**Balance Sheet**			
	Beginning inventory	$ 50,000	$ 50,000	$ 50,000
	LIFO Reserve	—	—	—
Year Ended 2010	**Income Statement**			
	Revenue	$112,500	$112,500	$112,500
	Cost of Goods Sold:			
	Beginning inventory	50,000	50,000	50,000
	Add: Purchases	34,000	34,000	34,000
	Goods available for sale	84,000	84,000	84,000
	Subtract: Ending inventory	39,000	25,000	30,000
	Cost of goods sold	45,000	59,000	54,000
	Gross profit	67,500	53,500	58,500
	Selling, general and administrative expenses (assumed number)	10,000	10,000	10,000
	Income before income taxes	57,500	43,500	48,500
	Income tax expense (35%)	20,125	15,225	16,975
	Net income	$ 37,375	$ 28,275	$ 31,525
December 31, 2010	**Balance Sheet**			
	Ending inventory	$ 39,000	$ 25,000	$ 30,000
	LIFO Reserve	—	$ 14,000	—
Year Ended 2011	**Income Statement**			
	Revenue	$127,500	$127,500	$127,500
	Cost of Goods Sold:			
	Beginning inventory	39,000	25,000	30,000
	Add: Purchases	108,000	108,000	108,000
	Goods available for sale	147,000	133,000	138,000
	Subtract: Ending inventory	63,000	43,000	56,824
	Cost of goods sold	84,000	90,000	81,176
	Gross profit	43,500	37,500	46,324
	Selling, general and administrative expenses (assumed number)	10,000	10,000	10,000
	Income before income taxes	33,500	27,500	36,324
	Income tax expense (35%)	11,725	9,625	12,713
	Net income	$ 21,775	$ 17,875	$ 23,611
December 31, 2011	**Balance Sheet**			
	Ending inventory	63,000	43,000	56,824
	LIFO Reserve	—	20,000	—

costs increased more slowly, the difference between LIFO and FIFO would decrease. And, if costs decreased, the differences would reverse: FIFO cost of goods sold would be greater than LIFO cost of goods sold.

The second factor determining the differences is the length of time inventory is held by the company. If Butler Company were able to operate with zero inventory (or at least begin and end the reporting period with zero inventory), the three inventory accounting methods would yield exactly the same cost of goods sold. On the other hand, if inventory must be held for a long period, the differences would increase.

EFFECTS OF CHANGING COSTS When the cost of a company's products is changing, management will usually make corresponding changes in the prices it charges for those products. If costs are declining, competitive pressures will push down the prices customers are willing to pay. If costs are increasing, the company will try to increase prices to recover at least some of the greater cost. When costs fluctuate (for example, for a commodity), management may also cause its prices to fluctuate in an effort to maintain its target profit margin.[4]

If costs and prices are rising, then FIFO will report a higher gross margin, because the costs of older, lower-cost inventory are being matched against current selling prices. For tax purposes, the company would prefer to use LIFO because it would decrease gross profit and decrease taxable income. If Butler Company were subject to a 35% income tax rate, the use of LIFO rather than FIFO would have reduced taxes by $4,900 in 2010 ($20,125 − $15,225 in Exhibit 7.11, or 35% of the $14,000 difference in 2010 cost of goods sold) and by $2,100 in 2011 ($11,725 − $9,625 in Exhibit 7.11, or 35% of the $6,000 difference in 2011 cost of goods sold). In total over the two years, using LIFO (rather than FIFO) would have reduced Butler's tax bill by $7,000 (which equals 35% of the $20,000 LIFO reserve at the end of 2011).

In the United States, LIFO is a popular tax method for accounting for inventories that have an upward trend in costs. But, the Internal Revenue Service has imposed a LIFO conformity requirement. If Butler Company is using LIFO for tax reporting, it must use LIFO for reporting to its shareholders. For inventories with a decreasing trend in costs, FIFO will reduce the amount of taxes paid. FIFO is allowed by the Internal Revenue Service, but there is no corresponding conformity requirement for firms that use FIFO.

> **FYI** When a company adopts LIFO in its tax filings, the IRS requires it to use LIFO for reporting to its shareholders (in its 10-K). This requirement is known as the LIFO conformity rule.

Balance Sheet Effects   The ending inventory using LIFO for our illustration is less than that reported using FIFO. In prolonged periods of rising costs, using LIFO yields ending inventories that are markedly lower than FIFO. As a result, balance sheets using LIFO do not accurately represent the cost that a company would incur to replace its current investment in inventories.

Chevron, for example, reported that the current value of its inventory was $9,368 million higher than the LIFO cost at the end of 2008. That is, the amount presented in its balance sheet was understated (relative to current value) by more than $9 billion. For purposes of analysis, the value of the LIFO reserve can be viewed as an **unrealized holding gain**—a gain resulting from holding inventory as prices are rising. That is, there is a holding gain due to rising inventory costs that has not been recorded in the financial statements. This gain is not recognized until the inventory is sold. In its December 31, 2008, balance sheet, Chevron reported current assets of $36,470 million and current liabilities of $32,023 million, for a current ratio of $36,470 ÷ $32,023, or about 1.14. However, Chevron's inventory is not reported at an up-to-date amount, while the accounts payable would reflect the current prices owed to suppliers. Therefore, an improved measure of the current ratio would be [$36,470 + $9,368] ÷ $32,023, or about 1.43.

In contrast, by assigning the most recently purchased inventory items to ending inventory, FIFO costing tends to approximate current value in the balance sheet. Hence, companies using FIFO tend not to have large unrealized inventory holding gains. However, if prices fall, companies using FIFO are more likely to adjust inventory values to the lower of cost or market.

Cash Flow Effects   The increased gross profit using FIFO results in higher pretax income and, consequently, higher taxes payable (assuming FIFO is also used for tax reporting). Conversely, the use of LIFO in an inflationary environment results in a reduced tax liability.

Use of LIFO has reduced the dollar amount of Chevron inventories by $9,368 million, resulting in a cumulative increase in cost of goods sold and a cumulative decrease in gross profit and pretax profit of that same amount.[5] The decrease in cumulative pretax profits reduces Chevron's tax bill by $3,279 million ($9,368 million × 35% assumed corporate tax rate), which increases Chevron's cumulative operating cash flow by that same amount. The increased cash flow from tax savings is often cited as a compelling reason for management to adopt LIFO.

Adjusting the Balance Sheet to FIFO   For analysis purposes, we can use the LIFO reserve to adjust the balance sheet and income statement to achieve comparability between companies that

---

[4] LIFO has a reporting advantage when inventory costs fluctuate, in that it matches current period costs against current period revenues. For a company that holds one quarter's worth of inventory, FIFO would match the costs from three months ago against current period revenues. Such a "mismatch" might make it difficult for management to convey its success in maintaining its current profit margin.

[5] Recall: Cost of Goods Sold = Beginning Inventories + Purchases − Ending Inventories. Thus, as ending inventories decrease, cost of goods sold increases.

utilize different inventory costing methods. For example, if we wanted to compare Chevron with another company using FIFO, we can add the LIFO reserve to its LIFO inventory. As explained above, this $9,368 million increase in 2008 inventories would have increased its cumulative pretax profits by $9,368 million and taxes by $3,279 million. Thus, the balance sheet adjustments involve increasing inventories by $9,368 million, tax liabilities by $3,279 million, and retained earnings by the remaining after-tax amount of $6,089 million (computed as $9,368 − $3,279).

IFRS REPORTING INSIGHT

One of the important differences in inventory accounting between U.S. GAAP and IFRS is that the latter does not allow the use of last-in, first-out (LIFO) accounting. Only FIFO and Average Cost are allowed for companies reporting under IFRS.

An analyst comparing a U.S. GAAP company to an IFRS company would need to keep an eye on these inventory differences and, when necessary, do the conversions described in the preceding paragraphs. While FIFO firms are not required to disclose what they would have looked like under LIFO, LIFO firms must disclose enough information to do a rough approximation of what they would have looked like under FIFO—making for an improved comparison with an IFRS company.

The fact that IFRS does not allow LIFO—combined with the U.S. Internal Revenue Service's conformity requirement—creates a dilemma for eventual adoption of IFRS in the United States. For instance, if Chevron were to have adopted IFRS for fiscal year 2009, reporting FIFO inventory and cost of goods sold in subsequent financial reports, the IRS would consider that Chevron had given up its LIFO election and would require payment of the $3,279 million in taxes that had been deferred by the use of LIFO. This concern often appears in companies' comment letters to the Securities and Exchange Commission on the proposed move to IFRS in the United States.

Adjusting the Income Statement to FIFO

To adjust the income statement from LIFO to FIFO, we use the *change* in the LIFO reserve. For Chevron, the LIFO reserve changed from $6,958 million in 2007 to $9,368 million in 2008, an increase of $2,410 million. To adjust the income statement to FIFO, we would subtract $2,410 from the cost of goods sold (reported using LIFO) and add the same amount to gross profit and pretax income. To estimate net income, we need to adjust for income taxes. Assuming a corporate tax rate of 35%, the use of LIFO provides Chevron with a tax savings of $843.5 million ($2,410 million × .35). Thus, 2008 net income using FIFO would be higher by $1,566.5 million ($2,410 million − $843.5 million).

RESEARCH INSIGHT

LIFO and Stock Prices   The value-relevance of inventory disclosures depends at least partly on whether investors rely more on the income statement or the balance sheet to assess future cash flows. Under LIFO, cost of goods sold reflects current costs, whereas FIFO ending inventory reflects current costs. This implies that LIFO enhances the usefulness of the income statement to the detriment of the balance sheet. This trade-off partly motivates the required LIFO reserve disclosure (the adjustment necessary to restate LIFO ending inventory and cost of good sold to FIFO).

Research suggests that LIFO-based income statements better reflect stock prices than do pro forma FIFO income statements that are constructed using the LIFO reserve. Research also shows a negative relation between stock prices and LIFO reserve—meaning that higher magnitudes of LIFO reserve are associated with lower stock prices. This is consistent with the LIFO reserve being viewed as an inflation indicator (for either current or future inventory costs) detrimental to company value.

FINANCIAL STATEMENT ANALYSIS

This section describes several useful tools for analysis of inventory and related accounts.

Gross Profit Analysis   The gross profit margin (GPM) ratio is important and is monitored by management and outsiders. The GPM ratio is computed:

$$\text{Gross profit margin} = \frac{\text{Sales revenue} - \text{Cost of goods sold}}{\text{Sales revenue}}$$

The gross profit margin of The Home Depot for each of the past three years is shown in Exhibit 7.12.

EXHIBIT 7.12	Gross Profit Margin for The Home Depot		
		Fiscal Year	
	2008	**2007**	**2006**
Revenues	$71,288	$77,349	$79,022
Cost of goods sold	47,298	51,352	52,476
Gross profit	$23,990	$25,997	$26,546
Gross profit margin (GPM)	33.7%	33.6%	33.6%

The gross profit margin is commonly used instead of the dollar amount of gross profit as it allows for comparisons across companies and over time. A decline in GPM is usually cause for concern because it indicates that the company has less ability to pass on to customers increased costs in its products. Since companies try to charge the highest price the market will bear, a decline in GPM is often the result of market forces beyond the company's control. Some possible reasons for a GPM decline are:

- Product line is stale. Perhaps it is out of fashion and the company must resort to markdowns to reduce overstocked inventories. Or, perhaps the product lines have lost their technological edge, yielding reduced demand.

- A change in product mix resulting from a change in buyers' behavior (more generic brands, more necessities, fewer big-ticket items).

- New competitors enter the market. Perhaps substitute products or new technologies are now available from competitors, yielding increased pressure to reduce selling prices.

- General decline in economic activity. Perhaps an economic downturn reduces product demand. The weak housing market during the latter half of the decade likely affected the gross profits of home improvement companies.

- Inventory is overstocked. Perhaps the company overproduced goods and finds itself in an overstock position. This can require reduced selling prices to move inventory.

While the weakened housing market and the general economic conditions caused The Home Depot's sales revenue to decline from fiscal year 2006 to fiscal year 2008, the company was successful in maintaining its gross profit margin. In order to properly evaluate gross profit margin, it is useful to make comparisons with other companies in the same industry. Exhibit 7.13 graphically compares The Home Depot's gross profit margin with that of its largest competitor, **Lowe's Companies, Inc.**

EXHIBIT 7.13	Gross Profit Margin Comparison

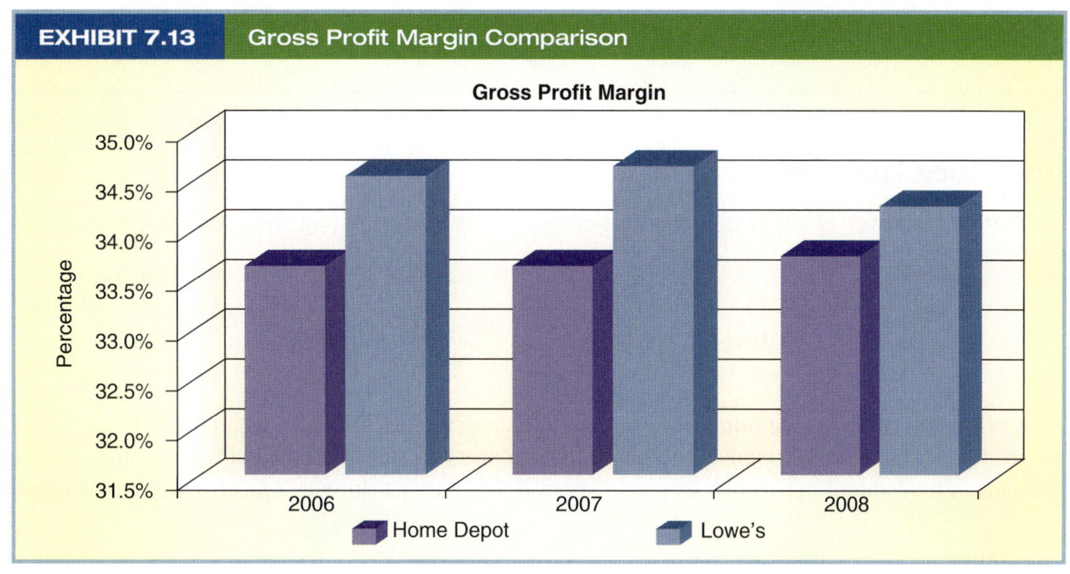

As the bar graph illustrates, Lowe's has reported a higher gross profit margin than The Home Depot over the last three years. In fiscal year 2008, Lowe's gross profit margin went down slightly, while The Home Depot's gross profit margin increased slightly.[6] However, The Home Depot's sales revenue declined by 7.8%, while Lowe's revenues declined by only 0.1%. As a result, Lowe's gross profit declined only marginally, whereas The Home Depot's gross profit declined by almost 8%. Further analysis is needed before we can draw any conclusions regarding the cause for this one-year change. However, a persistent decline in gross profit margin, especially relative to the competition, would signal problems for any company.

To gain further insights, Exhibit 7.14 compares the gross profit margin of The Home Depot with that of several other retailers: **Target Corporation**, a national chain of retail variety stores: **Best Buy Co., Inc.**, retail consumer electronics: and **Whole Foods Market Inc.**, a retail specialty grocery store chain. The graph illustrates that the highest gross profit margin belongs to Whole Foods, the specialty grocery store, while the lowest was that of Best Buy. Also, while the percentages fluctuate slightly from year to year, the *relative* level of gross profit percentage remains the same over time, reflecting the fact that the industry or type of business is a major determinant of gross profit margin.

Because of competitive pressures, companies rarely have the opportunity to affect gross margin with price increases. (Of course, an astute choice of product offerings may reduce pricing discounts and improve the gross profit margin.) Most improvements in gross margin that we witness are the result of better management of supply chains, production processes, or distribution networks. Similarly, a decline in gross profit margin may indicate problems or inefficiencies in these processes. Companies that succeed typically do so because of better performance on basic business processes. This is one of The Home Depot's primary objectives.

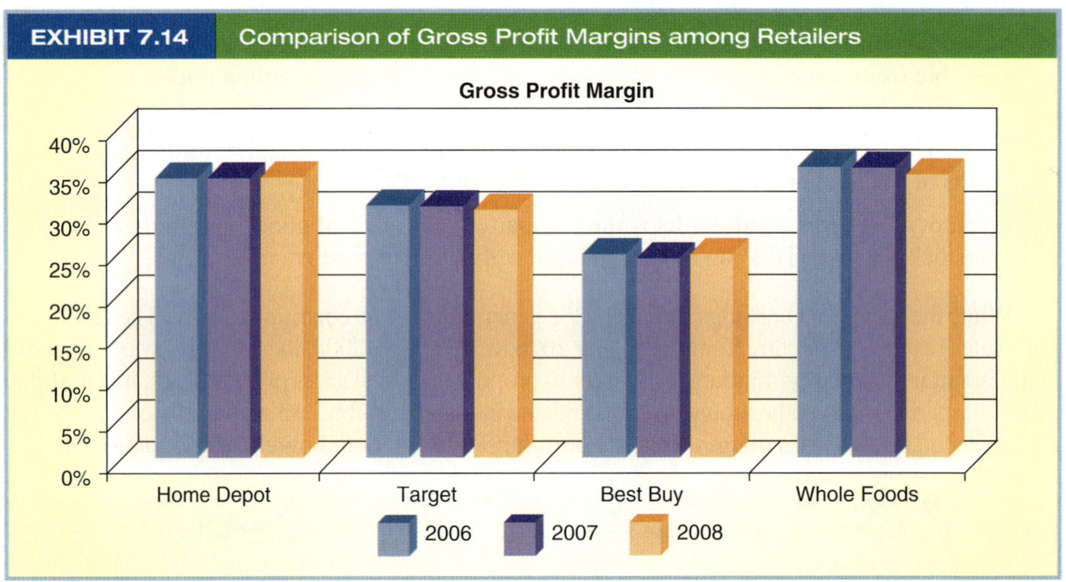

| EXHIBIT 7.14 | Comparison of Gross Profit Margins among Retailers |

Inventory Turnover

Inventory turnover (INVT) is a useful measure of inventory management and is computed as follows:

$$\text{Inventory turnover} = \frac{\text{Cost of goods sold}}{\text{Average inventory}}$$

Cost of goods sold is in the numerator because inventory is reported at cost. The denominator is the average of beginning inventory and ending inventory to recognize growth (or decline) in the company's investment in inventory over the period. Inventory turnover indicates how many times

---

[6] With $70,000 million in sales revenue, a 0.1% increase in gross margin increases gross profit (and pretax income) by $70 million.

inventory turns (is sold) during a period. More turns indicate that inventory is being sold more quickly.

Average inventory days outstanding (AIDO), also called *days inventory outstanding,* is a companion measure to inventory turnover and is computed as follows:

$$\text{Average inventory days outstanding} = \frac{\text{Average inventory}}{\text{Average daily cost of goods sold}}$$

where average daily cost of goods sold equals cost of goods sold divided by the number of days in the period (for example, 365 for a year).

Average inventory days outstanding indicates how long, on average, inventories are on the shelves or in production before being sold. For example, if a retailer's annual cost of goods sold is \$1,200 and average inventories are \$300, inventories are turning four times and are on the shelves 91.25 days [\$300/(\$1,200/365)] on average. This performance might be an acceptable turnover for the retail fashion industry where it needs to sell out its inventories each retail selling season, but it would not be acceptable for the grocery industry.

Analysis of inventory turnover is important for at least two reasons:

1. *Inventory quality.* Inventory turnover can be compared with those of prior periods and competitors. Higher turnover is viewed favorably, implying that products are salable, preferably without undue discounting of selling prices, or that production processes are functioning smoothly. Conversely, lower turnover implies that inventory is on the shelves for a longer period of time, perhaps from excessive purchases or production, missed fashion trends or technological advances, increased competition, and so forth. Our conclusions about higher or lower turnover must consider alternative explanations including:

   a. Company product mix can change to higher-margin, slower-turning inventories or vice-versa. This can occur from business acquisitions and the resulting consolidated inventories.

   b. A company can change its promotion policies. Increased, effective advertising is likely to increase inventory turnover. Advertising expense is in SG&A, not COGS. This means the cost is in operating expenses, but the benefit is in gross profit and turnover. If the promotion campaign is successful, the positive effects in margin and turnover should offset the promotion cost in SG&A.

   c. A company can realize improvements in manufacturing efficiency and lower investments in direct materials and work-in-process inventories. Such improvements reduce inventory and, consequently, increase inventory turnover. Although positive, it does not yield any information about the desirability of a company's product line.

2. *Asset utilization.* Companies strive to optimize their inventory investment. Carrying too much inventory is expensive, and too little inventory risks stock-outs and lost sales (current and future). There are operational changes that companies can make to reduce inventory:

   a. Improved manufacturing processes can eliminate bottlenecks and the consequent build-up of work-in-process inventories.

   b. Just-in-time (JIT) deliveries from suppliers that provide raw materials to the production line when needed can reduce the level of raw materials required.

   c. Demand-pull production, in which raw materials are released into the production process when final goods are demanded by customers instead of producing for estimated demand, can reduce inventory levels. **Dell Inc.** was founded on a business model that produced for actual, rather than estimated, demand; many of its computers are manufactured after the customer order is received.

Reducing inventories reduces inventory carrying costs, thus improving profitability and increasing cash flow (asset reduction is reflected as a cash inflow adjustment in the statement of cash flows). However, if inventories get too low, production can be interrupted and sales lost.

There is normal tension between the sales side of a company that argues for depth and breadth of inventory and the finance side that monitors inventory carrying costs and seeks to maximize cash flow. Companies, therefore, seek to *optimize* inventory investment, not *minimize* it.

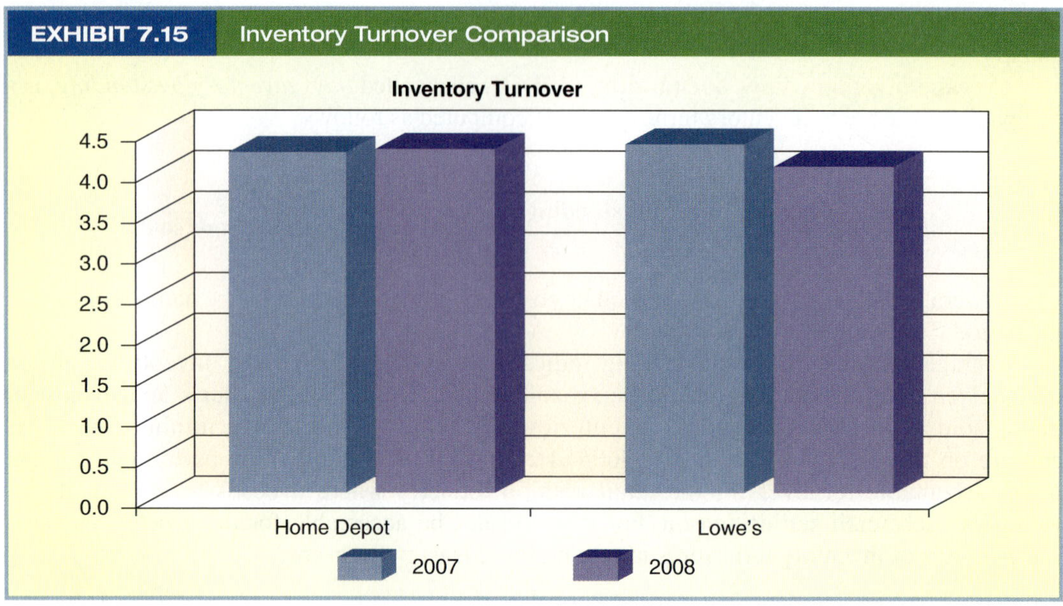

Exhibit 7.15 compares inventory turnover for The Home Depot with that of its chief rival, Lowe's Companies. The Home Depot's inventory turnover improved slightly in fiscal year 2008, as it reduced inventories in response to the economic downturn. Lowe's inventory turnover decreased, but these greater inventories may have allowed it to maintain revenues and gross profit in the changing economic climate.

It is also instructive to compare the home improvement retail industry, represented by The Home Depot, with other retailers as illustrated in Exhibit 7.16.

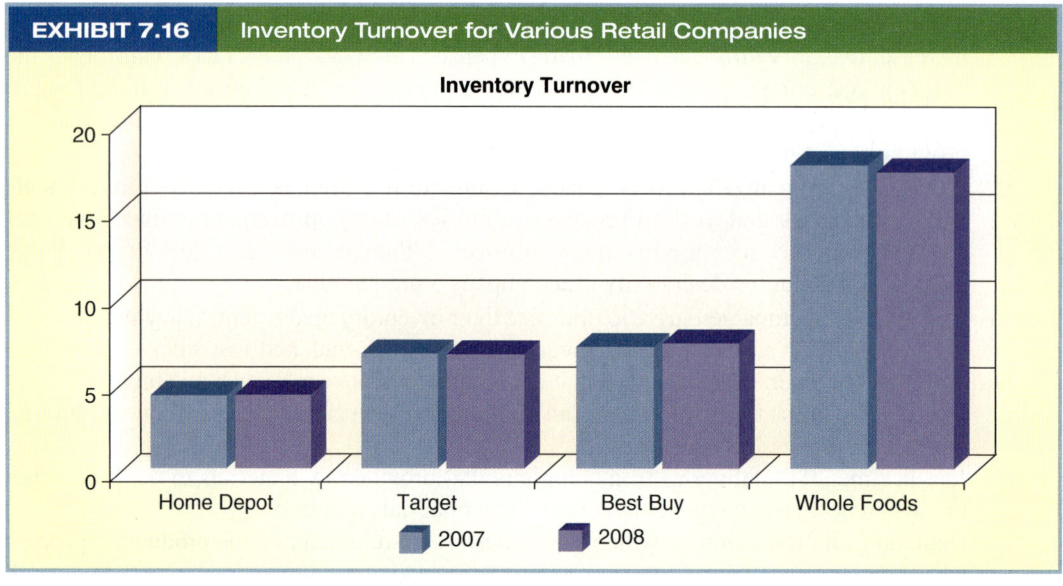

In the retail grocery industry, high inventory turnover is a necessity given that a significant portion of a grocer's inventory is perishable. Whole Foods' high turnover is typical of what we might expect from retail grocers. The Home Depot's turnover is lower than any of the comparison companies. Target's turnover is lower than that of Best Buy, the consumer electronics retailer, despite the fact that part of Target's sales is food related. The small portion of food product sales as a percentage of total sales explains why Target's turnover is not comparable to that of Whole Foods.

Adjusting Turnover Ratios For a company using the last-in, first-out (LIFO) inventory method, it is advisable to make an adjustment before calculating the inventory turnover ratio. LIFO

YOU MAKE THE CALL

You are the Plant Manager   You are analyzing your inventory turnover report for the month and are concerned that the average inventory days outstanding is lengthening. What actions can you take to reduce average inventory days outstanding? [Answer on page 334]

is most commonly used when management has experienced a trend of rising inventory costs. As a result, LIFO puts higher (newer) costs into cost of goods sold and leaves lower (older) costs in inventory. This creates a potential mismatch between the numerator and denominator of the inventory turnover ratio.

For instance, consider Butler Company's 2011 financial information in Exhibit 7.11. Measured in physical terms, Butler started 2011 with 250 units, sold 500 units during 2011, and ended 2011 with 350 units. So, the physical inventory turnover would be

$$\text{Physical inventory turnover} = \frac{\text{Units sold}}{\text{Average units held}} = \frac{500}{(250 + 350)/2} = 1.67 \text{ times}$$

However, the 2011 inventory turnover calculated using the LIFO reported numbers does not agree with the physical inventory turnover.

$$\text{LIFO inventory turnover} = \frac{\text{Cost of goods sold}}{\text{Average inventory}} = \frac{\$90,000}{(\$25,000 + \$43,000)/2} = 2.65 \text{ times}$$

Why is the LIFO inventory turnover higher? The distortion occurs because the LIFO cost of goods sold is 500 units valued at $180 each, while the beginning inventory is 250 units valued at $100 each and the ending inventory is 250 units valued at $100 each plus 100 units valued at $180 each. The difference between 1.67 and 2.65 comes about because LIFO causes the value per unit to be higher in the numerator than in the denominator.

A quick fix would be to use the LIFO reserve information to put the beginning and ending inventory values on a more up-to-date basis. LIFO puts the newer costs in cost of goods sold, while FIFO puts the newer costs in inventory. If Butler were using LIFO, we could use the reported inventory balances and the LIFO reserve information to determine that the beginning FIFO inventory would have been $39,000 ($25,000 + $14,000) and the ending FIFO inventory would have been $63,000 ($43,000 + $20,000).

$$\text{Adjusted inventory turnover} = \frac{\text{LIFO cost of goods sold}}{\text{Average FIFO inventory}} = \frac{\$90,000}{(\$39,000 + \$63,000)/2} = 1.76 \text{ times}$$

This adjusted ratio is much closer to what's actually happening to the inventories at Butler Company.

The magnitude of this adjustment can be significant. For instance, Chevron reports that its 2008 expense for "Purchased crude oil and products" was $171,397 million. Chevron's balance sheet totals for inventories were $5,310 at the end of 2007 and $6,854 million at the end of 2008, for an average of $6,082 million. These numbers would give an inventory turnover ratio of $171,397 ÷ $6,082, or 28.18 times, implying that inventory is held less than 13 days on average.

However, we know that the LIFO inventory balances are out of date. Chevron's LIFO reserve disclosure says that the replacement cost of inventories was higher than the reported amounts by $6,958 million at the end of 2007 and $9,368 million at the end of 2008, making the replacement cost of inventories equal to $12,268 million at the end of 2007 and $16,222 million at the end of 2008. The adjusted inventory turnover ratio would be $171,397 ÷ [($12,268 + $16,222)/2] = 12.03, implying that inventory is held just a little more than 30 days.

Following a similar line of analysis, it would be possible to construct a FIFO inventory turnover for Chevron, which could be useful in making comparisons to another company that uses IFRS in its financial reports.

CHAPTER-END REVIEW

General Electric Company (GE) reports inventory and cost of goods sold using the last-in, first-out (LIFO) costing method for a "significant portion" of U.S. inventory. The table below presents financial information from its 2006, 2007, and 2008 10-K reports.

$ millions	2008	2007	2006
Income Statement:			
Revenue.	$182,515	$172,488	$151,568
Cost of goods sold	54,602	47,309	43,279
Cost of services sold	29,170	25,816	23,494
Gross profit	$ 98,743	$ 99,363	$ 84,795
Balance Sheet:			
Inventory	$ 13,674	$ 12,897	$ 10,032
Notes:			
LIFO reserve	$ 706	$ 623	$ 564

Required

1. Compute the gross profit margin for each year, 2006 through 2008, and the inventory turnover ratio for 2007 and 2008.
2. What amount for cost of goods sold and gross profit would GE report in 2007 and 2008 if FIFO were used to assign costs to inventory and cost of goods sold? (Assume that FIFO cost is equal to the current value of GE's inventory.)
3. Recalculate GE's inventory turnover ratio for 2007 and 2008 assuming that FIFO had been used to value inventory.

The solution to this review problem can be found on pages 348–349.

APPENDIX 7A: LIFO Liquidation

When companies use LIFO inventory costing, the most recent costs of purchasing inventory are transferred to cost of goods sold, while older costs remain in ending inventory. Each time inventory is purchased at a different price, a new *layer* (also called a LIFO layer) is added to the inventory balance. As long as a year's purchases equal or exceed the quantity sold, older cost layers remain in inventory—sometimes for several years. On the other hand, when the quantity sold exceeds the quantity purchased, inventory costs from these older cost layers are transferred to cost of goods sold. This situation is called LIFO liquidation. Because these older costs are usually much lower than current replacement costs, LIFO liquidation normally yields a boost to current gross profit as these older costs are matched against current revenues.

To illustrate the effects of LIFO liquidation, we return to the example of Butler Company in Exhibit 7.6 and add an additional year. At the end of 2011, Butler has 350 units in inventory, 250 at $100 each and 100 at $180 each. Suppose that during 2012, the company purchases 500 units at $190 and sells 650 units. At the end of 2012, Butler will have only 200 units remaining in inventory and, under LIFO, those units will be assigned a cost of $100 each. The determination of cost of goods sold and ending inventory for 2012 can be seen in Exhibit 7A.1.

EXHIBIT 7A.1	Calculation of 2012 LIFO Inventory and Cost of Goods Sold	
Beginning Inventory	250 units at $100 each plus 100 units at $180 each	$ 43,000
Purchases	500 units at $190 each	95,000
Cost of goods available for sale		138,000
Ending inventory	200 units at $100 each	20,000
Cost of goods sold	500 units at $190 each plus 100 units at $180 each plus 50 units at $100 each	$118,000

Exhibit 7A.2 portrays graphically that the inventory reduction in 2012 eliminated the LIFO layer added in 2011 and reduced the original LIFO layer from the start of 2010.

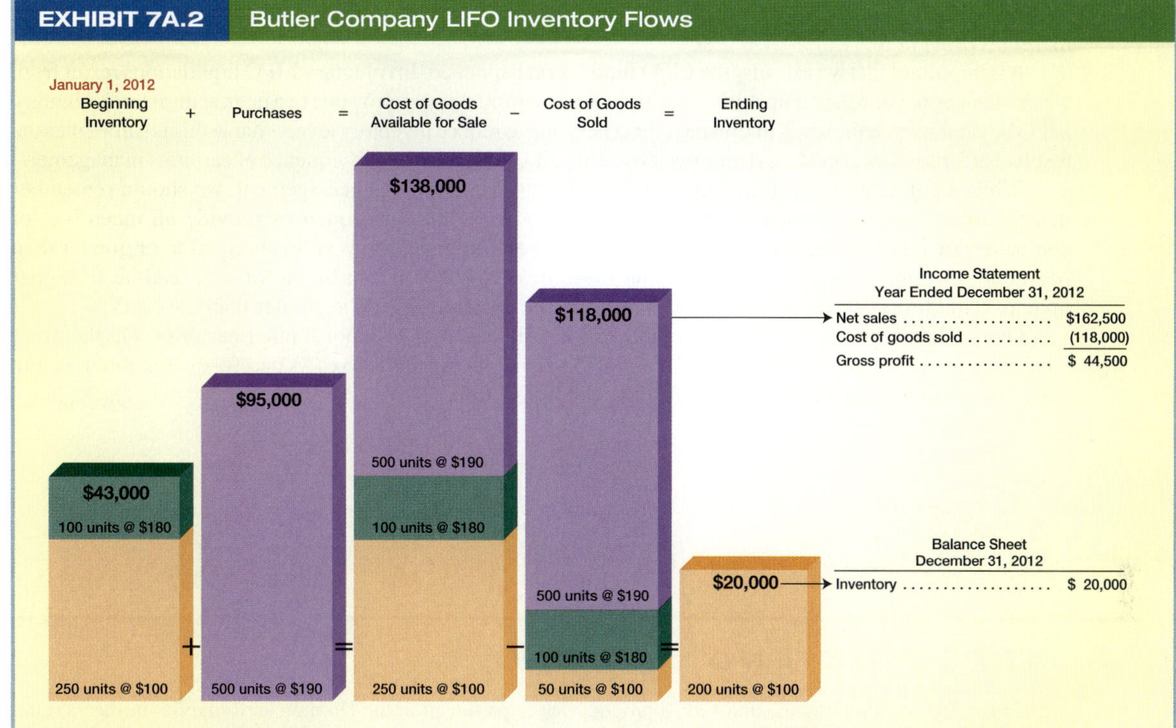

What would have happened if Butler had purchased 650 units at $190 in 2012? The ending inventory would have been identical to the beginning inventory. And, the cost of goods sold would have been $123,500 (650 units at $190 each), higher than the $118,000 cost of goods sold in Exhibit 7A.1. This difference can be attributed to the differences between the current unit cost of inventory ($190) and the old unit costs ($180 and $100) that had been in inventory but are now in cost of goods sold.

So, Butler's cost of goods sold has been *reduced* by $5,500 due to the LIFO liquidation, and its gross profit and income before tax have been *increased* by the same amount. If Butler's tax rate were 35%, the net income would be increased by $3,575. This **LIFO liquidation gain** must be disclosed in the company's footnotes.

The effect of LIFO liquidation is evident in the following footnote information from **Ford Motor Company**'s 2008 annual report.

All inventories are stated at the lower of cost or market. Cost for a substantial portion of U.S. inventories is determined on a last-in, first-out ("LIFO") basis. LIFO was used for approximately 23% and 25% of inventories at December 31, 2008 and 2007, respectively. Cost of other inventories is determined on a first-in, first-out ("FIFO") basis.

. . .

At December 31, 2008, inventory quantities were reduced, resulting in a liquidation of LIFO inventory quantities carried at lower costs prevailing in prior years as compared with the cost of 2008 purchases, the effect of which decreased *Automotive cost of sales* by about $209 million.

Ford reports that reductions in inventory quantities led to the sale (at current selling prices) of products that carried costs from prior years that were less than current costs. As a result of these inventory reductions, pretax income increased by $209 million from lower COGS. In this case, the LIFO inventory liquidation yielded a profit increase.

Analysis Implications

LIFO liquidation boosts gross profit when older, lower costs are matched against revenues based on current sales prices. This increase in gross profit is transitory. Once an old LIFO layer is liquidated, it can only be replaced at current prices. The transitory boost in gross profit temporarily distorts the gross profit margin (GPM) ratio.

It is important that we ask why the LIFO liquidation happened. Involuntary LIFO liquidations result from circumstances beyond the company's control, such as disruptions in supply due to a natural disaster. Voluntary LIFO liquidations are the result of a management decision to reduce inventory levels. While this is sometimes the result of efforts to lower costs and improve efficiency, it can also be the consequence of earnings management.

While a voluntary LIFO liquidation may be the result of earnings management, we should remember that the extra gross profit that is reported is taxable. These tax consequences provide an incentive for companies to *avoid* LIFO liquidations by maintaining ending inventories at levels equal to or greater than beginning inventory quantities. Maintaining these inventory levels can be inefficient, leading to higher inventory holding costs. However, in the short run, the tax savings can be greater than the costs.

On one hand, management could liquidate LIFO inventories to report higher earnings. On the other hand, management may hold too much inventory to avoid paying extra taxes. A careful evaluation of future cash flows will usually identify the preferred course of action.

APPENDIX-END REVIEW

Dickhaut Corporation imports and sells a product that is produced in the Dominican Republic. In the summer of 2010, a hurricane disrupted production and affected Dickhaut's supply of this product. Dickhaut uses LIFO to determine the cost of its inventory and cost of goods sold. On January 1, 2010, Dickhaut's inventory of this product consisted of the following:

Year Purchased	Quantity (units)	Cost Per Unit	Total Cost
2008	2,000	$20	$ 40,000
2009	3,000	30	90,000
Total	5,000		$130,000

Through mid-December, purchases were limited to 7,000 units, because the cost had increased to $70 per unit. Dickhaut sold 11,500 units during 2010 at a price of $65 per unit, which significantly depleted its inventory. However, the cost was expected to drop to $55 per unit by early January 2011.

Required

a. Assume that Dickhaut makes no further purchases during 2010. Compute its gross profit for 2010.
b. Assume that Dickhaut purchases 4,500 units before the end of December 2010, so that it maintains its balance of inventory at 5,000 units. Compute its gross profit for 2010.
c. How should Dickhaut disclose the LIFO liquidation if it chooses not to make a year-end purchase?
d. If Dickhaut's corporate tax rate is 35%, should it make a year-end purchase? If so, how many units should the company purchase before December 31, 2010? Assume that the management of Dickhaut believes it is efficient (in the long run) to carry 5,000 units in inventory.

The solution to this review problem can be found on page 349.

SUMMARY

Interpret disclosures of information concerning operating expenses, including manufacturing and retail inventory costs. (p. 307)   **LO1**

- Inventory is reported in the balance sheet at its cost, including any cost to acquire, transport and prepare goods for sale.
- Manufacturing inventory consists of raw materials, work in process and finished goods. The cost of manufacturing inventory includes the cost of materials and labor used to produce goods, as well as overhead cost.

Account for inventory and cost of goods sold using different costing methods. (p. 312)   **LO2**

- FIFO places the cost of the most recent purchases in ending inventory and older costs in the cost of goods sold.
- LIFO places the cost of the most recent purchases in cost of goods sold and older costs in inventory.
- The average cost method computes an average unit cost, which is used to value inventories *and* cost of goods sold.

Apply the lower of cost or market rule to value inventory. (p. 317)   **LO3**

- If the market value of inventory falls below its cost, the inventory is written down to market value, thereby reducing total assets.
- The loss is added to cost of goods sold and reported in the income statement (unless it is large enough to warrant separate disclosure).

Evaluate how inventory costing affects management decisions and outsiders' interpretations of financial statements. (p. 321)   **LO4**

- When inventory costs are rising, LIFO costing reports higher cost of goods sold and lower income than either FIFO or average costing.
- If LIFO is used for tax reporting, it must be used for financial reporting.
- Companies that use LIFO have an incentive to hold inventories to avoid LIFO *liquidation* and the resulting higher income taxes.
- LIFO distorts the inventory turnover ratio because inventories are often severely undervalued (relative to current cost of goods sold). Management can boost earnings by liquidating these undervalued inventories.
- International Financial Reporting Standards (IFRS) allows FIFO and average costing methods. LIFO is not permitted.

Define and interpret gross profit margin and inventory turnover ratios. Use inventory footnote information to make appropriate adjustments to ratios. (p. 324)   **LO5**

- Gross profit margin (GPM)—a measure of profitability that focuses on the amount of revenue in excess of cost of goods sold as a percentage of revenue
- Gross profit margin is defined as Gross profit/Sales revenue.
- Inventory turnover (INVT)—a measure of the frequency at which the average balance in inventory is sold each year
- Inventory turnover is defined as Cost of goods sold/Average inventory.
- These ratios provide insight into how efficiently the company is managing inventory.
- Footnote disclosures enable a financial statement reader to determine the up-to-date costs of LIFO inventories, to estimate what cost of goods sold would have been under FIFO, and to compute an inventory turnover ratio that is not subject to the distortions noted in LO4 above.

Appendix 7A: Analyze LIFO liquidations and the impact they have on the financial statements. (p. 330)   **LO6**

- LIFO liquidation is the result of selling and not replenishing inventory stocks purchased in previous accounting periods.
- When inventory costs are increasing, LIFO liquidation results in higher net income as the unrealized holding gains from LIFO are realized.

GUIDANCE ANSWERS . . . YOU MAKE THE CALL

You are the Plant Manager   Companies need inventories to avoid lost sales opportunities; however, there are several ways to minimize inventory needs. (1) We can reduce product costs by improving product design to eliminate costly features not valued by customers. (2) We can use more cost-efficient suppliers; possibly including production in lower wage-rate parts of the world. (3) We can reduce raw material inventories with just-in-time delivery from suppliers. (4) We can eliminate bottlenecks in the production process that increase work-in-process inventories. (5) We can manufacture for orders rather than for estimates of demand to reduce finished goods inventories. (6) We can improve warehousing and distribution to reduce duplicate inventories. (7) We can monitor product sales and adjust product mix as demand changes to reduce finished goods inventories.

KEY RATIOS

Gross profit (GP)

$$GP = \text{Sales revenue} - \text{Cost of goods sold}$$

Inventory turnover (INVT)

$$INVT = \frac{\text{Cost of goods sold}}{\text{Average inventory}}$$

Gross profit margin (GPM)

$$\text{Gross profit margin} = \frac{\text{Sales revenue} - \text{Cost of goods sold}}{\text{Sales revenue}}$$

Average inventory days outstanding (AIDO)

$$AIDO = \frac{\text{Average inventory}}{\text{Average daily cost of goods sold}}$$

KEY TERMS

Average cost (AC) (p. 316)

Average inventory days outstanding (AIDO) (p. 327)

Cash discounts (p. 310)

Cost flow assumption (p. 313)

Direct association (p. 307)

Finished goods inventory (p. 311)

First-in, first-out (FIFO) (p. 313)

FOB destination (p. 310)

FOB shipping point (p. 310)

Gross profit (p. 309)

Immediate recognition (p. 307)

Inventory turnover (INVT) (p. 326)

Last-in, first-out (LIFO) (p. 314)

LIFO layer (p. 330)

LIFO layers (p. 315)

LIFO liquidation (p. 321)

LIFO liquidation gain (p. 331)

LIFO reserve (p. 320)

Lower of cost or market (LCM) (p. 317)

Net-of-discount method (p. 310)

Raw materials inventory (p. 311)

Systematic allocation (p. 308)

Unrealized holding gain (p. 323)

Work-in-process inventory (p. 311)

MULTIPLE CHOICE

1.   Which of the following is not normally reported as part of total manufacturing inventory cost?
   a.   work-in-process
   b.   finished goods
   c.   property, plant and equipment
   d.   raw materials

2.   When the current year's ending inventory amount is overstated, then the
   a.   current year's cost of goods sold is overstated.
   b.   current year's total assets are understated.
   c.   current year's net income is overstated.
   d.   next year's income is overstated.

3.   In a period of rising prices, the inventory cost allocation method that tends to result in the lowest reported net income is
   a.   LIFO.
   b.   FIFO.
   c.   average cost.
   d.   specific identification.

4. Assume that Beyer Corporation has the following initial balance and subsequent purchase of inventory:

Beginning inventory, 2011...................	2,000 units @ $50 each	$100,000
Inventory purchased in 2011................	5,000 units @ $75 each	$375,000
Cost of goods available for sale in 2011	7,000 units	$475,000

During 2011, Beyer Corporation sold 6,000 units. Which of the following is not true?
   a. FIFO cost of goods sold would be $400,000.
   b. FIFO ending inventory would be $75,000.
   c. LIFO cost of goods sold would be $425,000.
   d. LIFO ending inventory would be $75,000.

5. Sletten Industries uses the last-in, first-out (LIFO) method of accounting for the inventories of its single product. For fiscal year 2011, the company reported sales revenue of $200 million and cost of goods sold of $135 million. The following table was reported in the financial statement footnotes.

$ millions	January 1, 2011	December 31, 2011
Inventory value at LIFO....................	$25	$28
LIFO Reserve...........................	14	22
Inventory value at FIFO....................	$39	$50

If Sletten Industries had used FIFO to account for its inventory, its 2011 gross profit would have been
   a. $87 million.
   b. $73 million.
   c. $57 million.
   d. $65 million.

DISCUSSION QUESTIONS

Q7-1. What is the justification for using the net-of-discount method to record inventory purchases when cash discounts are offered?

Q7-2. Why do relatively stable inventory costs reduce the importance of management's choice of an inventory costing method?

Q7-3. What is one explanation for increased gross profit during periods of rising inventory costs when FIFO is used?

Q7-4. If inventory costs are rising, which inventory costing method—first-in, first-out; last-in, first-out; or average cost—yields the (a) lowest ending inventory? (b) lowest net income? (c) largest ending inventory? (d) largest net income? (e) greatest cash flow assuming that method is used for tax purposes?

Q7-5. Even though it may not reflect their physical flow of goods, why might companies adopt last-in, first-out inventory costing in periods when costs are consistently rising?

Q7-6. In a recent annual report, **Kaiser Aluminum Corporation** made the following statement in reference to its inventories: "The Company recorded pretax charges of approximately $19.4 million because of a reduction in the carrying values of its inventories caused principally by prevailing lower prices for alumina, primary aluminum, and fabricated products." What basic accounting principle caused Kaiser Aluminum to record this $19.4 million pretax charge? Briefly describe the rationale for this principle.

Q7-7. Under what conditions would each of the inventory costing methods discussed in the chapter produce the same results?

Q7-8. What is inventory "shrink?" How does a company determine the amount of inventory shrink that may have occurred?

Q7-9. What is a LIFO reserve? How is the LIFO reserve related to unrealized holding gains?

Q7-10. Analysts claim that it is more difficult to forecast net income for a company that uses LIFO. Why might this be true?

Q7-11.[A] LIFO liquidation may be involuntary—that is beyond the control of management. Suggest two situations that might lead to involuntary LIFO liquidation.

Q7-12.[A] LIFO liquidation is often discretionary. What motives might management have to liquidate LIFO inventory?

Assignments with the WebAssign. logo in the margin are available in WebAssign. See the Preface of the book for details.

MINI EXERCISES

LO1 **M7-13. Recording Cash Discounts**

On November 15, 2010, Shields Company purchased inventory costing $6,200 on credit. The credit terms were 2/10, n/30.

a. Assume that Shields Company paid the invoice on November 23, 2010. Prepare journal entries to record the purchase of this inventory and the cash payment to the supplier using the net-of-discount method.

b. Set up the necessary T-accounts and post the journal entries from question *a* to the accounts

c. Compute the cost of a lost discount as an annual percentage rate.

LO1 **M7-14. Recording Cash Discounts**

Schrand Corporation purchases materials from a supplier that offers credit terms of 2/15, n/60. It purchased $12,500 of merchandise inventory from that supplier on January 20, 2011.

a. Assume that Schrand Corporation paid the invoice on February 15, 2011. Prepare journal entries to record the purchase of this inventory and the cash payment to the supplier using the net-of-discount method.

b. Set up the necessary T-accounts and post the journal entries from question *a* to the accounts.

c. Compute the cost of a lost discount as an annual percentage rate.

LO1 **M7-15. Determining Cost of Goods Sold for a Manufacturing Company**

Ybarra Products began operations in 2010. During its first year, the company purchased raw materials costing $84,000 and used $63,000 of those materials in the production of its products. The company's manufacturing operations also incurred labor costs of $58,000 and overhead costs of $28,000. At year end 2010, Ybarra had $19,000 of partially completed product in work-in-process inventory and $35,000 in finished goods inventory. What was Ybarra Company's cost of goods sold in 2010?

LO5 **M7-16. Calculating Gross Profit Margin**

JOHNSON & JOHNSON
NYSE :: JNJ

Johnson & Johnson reported the following revenue and cost of goods sold information in its 10-K report for 2006, 2007, and 2008:

$ millions	2008	2007	2006
Sales to customers	$63,747	$61,095	$53,324
Cost of products sold	18,511	17,751	15,057

Compute Johnson & Johnson's gross profit margin for each year.

LO1 **M7-17. Calculating Effect of Inventory Errors**

For each of the following scenarios, determine the effect of the error on income in the current period and in the subsequent period. To answer these questions, rely on the inventory equation:

Beginning inventory + Purchases − Cost of goods sold = Ending inventory

a. Porter Company received a shipment of merchandise costing $32,000 near the end of the fiscal year. The shipment was mistakenly recorded at a cost of $23,000.

b. Chiu, Inc., purchased merchandise costing $16,000. When the shipment was received, it was determined that the merchandise was damaged in shipment. The goods were returned to the supplier, but the accounting department was not notified and the invoice was paid.

c. After taking a physical count of its inventory, Murray Corporation determined that it had "shrink" of $12,500. However, inventory costing $5,000 was never counted.

M7-18. Calculating LIFO, FIFO, Income and Cash Flows   LO2, LO4

An acquaintance has proposed the following business plan to you. A local company requires a consistent quantity of a commodity and is looking for a reliable supplier. You could become that reliable supplier.

The cost of the commodity is expected to rise steadily over the foreseeable future, but the company is willing to pay more than the price that is current at the time. All you would need to do is make an investment, purchase the inventory and then deliver inventory to the company over the following year. One complication is that the commodity is available for purchase only seasonally, so at the end of every year you would need to purchase the supply for the following year. The customer pays promptly on delivery.

An initial cash investment of $62,000 would be used to purchase $50,000 of inventory in December 2010. The remaining cash would be held for liquidity needs. In the following year, you would deliver this inventory to the customer. Inventory costs are expected to increase by $10,000 per year, and the customer agrees to pay $15,000 more than the current cost of inventory. So, during 2011, you would deliver inventory that originally cost $50,000, receive payment of $75,000 and pay $60,000 to purchase inventory for the current year. This pattern would continue in future years, but with annually increasing costs of inventory and corresponding increases in the price charged the customer.

If you accept this proposal, your objective would be to receive $9,000 in dividends (about a 15% return on the $62,000 investment) at the end of each year. Assume your business would have an income tax rate of 40%.

a. Construct a projected balance sheet as of the end of December 2010.
b. Construct financial forecasts of income statements, cash flows (direct method) and balance sheets for the next three years (through 2013). Assume that your business would operate in a tax jurisdiction that requires the use of FIFO for inventory. Would this opportunity meet your financial objective?
c. Suppose that your business would operate in a tax jurisdiction that allowed the use of LIFO for inventory. Would this opportunity meet your financial objective? Why?

M7-19. Computing Cost of Goods Sold and Ending Inventory under FIFO, LIFO, and Average Cost   LO2

Assume that Gode Company reports the following initial balance and subsequent purchase of inventory:

Beginning inventory, 2010..................	1,000 units @ $100 each	$100,000
Inventory purchased in 2010.................	2,000 units @ $150 each	300,000
Cost of goods available for sale in 2010	3,000 units	$400,000

Assume that 1,700 units are sold during 2010. Compute the cost of goods sold for 2010 and the balance reported as ending inventory on its 2010 balance sheet under the following inventory costing methods:

a. FIFO
b. LIFO
c. Average Cost

M7-20. Inferring Purchases Using Cost of Goods Sold and Inventory Balances.   LO2

Geiger Corporation, a retail company, reported inventories of $1,320,000 in 2010 and $1,460,000 in 2011. The 2011 income statement reported cost of goods sold of $6,980,000.

a. Compute the amount of inventory purchased during 2011.
b. Prepare journal entries to record (1) purchases, and (2) cost of goods sold.
c. Post the journal entries in part *b* to their respective T-accounts.
d. Record each of the transactions in part *b* in the financial statement effects template to show the effect of these entries on the balance sheet and income statement.

M7-21. Computing Cost of Goods Sold and Ending Inventory   LO2

Bartov Corporation reports the following beginning inventory and purchases for 2010:

Beginning inventory, 2010..................	400 units @ $10 each	$ 4,000
Inventory purchased in 2010.................	700 units @ $12 each	8,400
Cost of goods available for sale in 2010	1,100 units	$12,400

Bartov sells 600 of these units in 2010. Compute its cost of goods sold for 2010 and the ending inventory reported on its 2010 balance sheet under each of the following inventory costing methods:

a.   FIFO

b.   LIFO

c.   Average Cost

LO5 M7-22. Computing and Evaluating Inventory Turnover

Wal-Mart Stores, Inc., and **Target Corporation** reported the following in their financial reports:

	Wal-Mart			**Target**		
Fiscal Year	**Sales**	**COGS**	**Inventory**	**Sales**	**COGS**	**Inventory**
2008	$405,607	$306,158	$34,511	$64,948	$45,766	$6,705
2007	378,476	286,350	35,159	63,367	43,766	6,780
2006	348,368	263,979	33,685	59,490	41,073	6,254

a.   Compute the 2008 and 2007 inventory turnovers for each of these two retailers.

b.   Discuss any changes that are evident in inventory turnover across years and companies from part *a*.

c.   Describe ways in which a retailer can improve its inventory turnover. Are there ways to increase inventory turnover that are not beneficial to the company's long-term interests?

LO2 M7-23. Inferring Purchases Using Cost of Goods Sold and Inventory Balances

Penno Company reported ending inventories of $23,560,000 in 2011 and $25,790,000 in 2010. Cost of goods sold totaled $142,790,000 in 2011.

a.   Prepare the journal entry to record cost of goods sold.

b.   Set up a T-account for inventory and post the cost of goods sold entry from part *a* to this account.

c.   Using the T-account from *b*, determine the amount of inventory that was purchased in 2011. Prepare a journal entry to record those purchases.

d.   Using the financial statement effects template, show the effects of the entries in parts *a* and *c* on the balance sheet and income statement.

LO3 M7-24. Determining Lower of Cost or Market

The following data refer to Froning Company's ending inventory.

Item Code	**Quantity**	**Unit Cost**	**Unit Market**
LXC.	60	$45	$48
KWT	210	38	34
MOR.	300	22	20
NES	100	27	32

Determine the ending inventory amount by applying the lower of cost or market rule to (*a*) each item of inventory and (*b*) the total inventory.

EXERCISES

LO5 E7-25. Analyzing Inventory and Margin in a Seasonal Business

West Marine, Inc., opened its first boating supply store in 1975. Since that time, the company has grown to be one of the largest boating supply companies in the world, with fiscal year 2008 revenues in excess of $630 million. The accompanying table provides financial information for two recent years. West Marine's fiscal year is closely aligned with the calendar year. All amounts are in thousands.

Time Period	Net Revenues	Cost of Goods Sold	Ending Inventory
Fiscal year 2006	—	—	$253,063
First quarter 2007.	$125,783	$ 98,693	279,500
Second quarter 2007	247,091	161,185	280,596
Third quarter 2007	188,391	130,475	254,736
Fourth quarter 2007	118,296	94,323	248,307
Fiscal year 2007	679,561	484,676	248,307
First quarter 2008.	113,263	90,778	286,899
Second quarter 2008	226,681	148,270	277,063
Third quarter 2008	180,249	130,518	245,069
Fourth quarter 2008.	111,065	94,246	222,601
Fiscal year 2008	631,258	463,812	222,601

a. Using the fiscal year (annual) information for 2007 and 2008, calculate the gross profit margin and the inventory turnover ratio.

b. West Marine is in a seasonal business, in which the sales total for the second and third quarters is about 80% higher than the sales total for the first and fourth quarters. Calculate the company's gross profit margin by quarter. What do you learn from the seasonal pattern in the gross profit margin?

c. What is the seasonal pattern in inventory balances? What effect does West Marine's choice of fiscal year-end have on the inventory turnover ratio calculated in *a*?

d. Recalculate West Marine's inventory turnover ratios for 2007 and 2008 using a weighted average of the company's inventory investment over the year.

E7-26. Applying and Analyzing Inventory Costing Methods

LO2, LO4

At the beginning of the current period, Chen carried 1,000 units of its product with a unit cost of $20. A summary of purchases during the current period follows:

	Units	Unit Cost	Cost
Beginning Inventory	1,000	$20	$20,000
Purchases: #1	1,800	22	39,600
#2	800	26	20,800
#3	1,200	29	34,800

During the current period, Chen sold 2,800 units.

a. Assume that Chen uses the first-in, first-out method. Compute its cost of goods sold for the current period and the ending inventory balance.

b. Assume that Chen uses the last-in, first-out method. Compute its cost of goods sold for the current period and the ending inventory balance.

c. Assume that Chen uses the average cost method. Compute its cost of goods sold for the current period and the ending inventory balance.

d. Which of these three inventory costing methods would you choose to:
   1. Reflect what is probably the physical flow of goods? Explain.
   2. Minimize income taxes for the period? Explain.
   3. Report the largest amount of income for the period? Explain.

E7-27. Computing Cost of Sales and Ending Inventory

LO2

Stocken Company has the following financial records for the current period:

	Units	Unit Cost
Beginning inventory	100	$46
Purchases: #1	650	42
#2	550	38
#3	200	36

Ending inventory at the end of this period is 350 units. Compute the ending inventory and the cost of goods sold for the current period using (*a*) first-in, first-out, (*b*) average cost, and (*c*) last-in, first-out.

LO3 **E7-28. Determining Lower of Cost or Market**

Crane Company had the following inventory at December 31, 2011.

		Unit Price	
	Quantity	Cost	Market
Desks			
Model 9001	70	$190	$210
Model 9002	45	280	268
Model 9003	20	350	360
Cabinets			
Model 7001	120	60	64
Model 7002	80	95	88
Model 7003	50	130	126

a. Determine the ending inventory amount by applying the lower of cost or market rule to
  1. Each item of inventory.
  2. Each major category of inventory.
  3. Total inventory.
b. Which of the LCM procedures from requirement *a* results in the lowest net income for 2011? Explain.

LO2, LO4 **E7-29. Analyzing Inventory Footnote Disclosure**

GENERAL MOTORS
NYSE :: GM

General Motors Corporation reported the following information in its 10-K report:

Inventories at December 31 ($ millions)	2008	2007
Productive material, work in process, and supplies	$ 4,849	$ 6,267
Finished product, service parts, etc.	9,426	10,095
Total inventories at FIFO	14,275	16,362
Less LIFO allowance	(1,233)	(1,423)
Total automotive and Other inventories, less allowances	$13,042	$14,939

The company reports its inventory using the LIFO costing method.

a. At what dollar amount are inventories reported on its 2008 balance sheet?
b. At what dollar amount would inventories have been reported in 2008 if FIFO inventory costing had been used?
c. What cumulative effect has the use of LIFO had, as of year-end 2008, on GM's pretax income, compared to the pretax income that would have been reported using the FIFO costing method?
d. Assuming a 35% income tax rate, what is the cumulative effect on GM's tax liability as of year-end 2008?

LO2, LO4 **E7-30. Analyzing of Inventory and Footnote Disclosure**

KRAFT FOODS
NYSE :: KFT

The current asset section of the **Kraft Foods Inc.** balance sheet follows ($ millions):

At December 31	2006	2005
Cash and cash equivalents	$ 239	$ 316
Receivables (less allowances of $114 and $119)	3,869	3,385
Inventories		
Raw materials	1,389	1,363
Finished product	2,117	1,980
	3,506	3,343
Deferred income taxes	387	879
Other current assets	253	230
Total current assets	$8,254	$8,153

Kraft also reports the following footnote to its 2006 10-K report:

Note 7. Inventories
The cost of approximately 41% and 40% of inventories in 2006 and 2005, respectively, was determined using the LIFO method. The stated LIFO amounts of inventories were approximately $70 million and $71 million higher than the current cost of inventories at December 31, 2006 and 2005, respectively.

Notice that not all of Kraft's inventories are reported using the same inventory costing method (companies can use different inventory costing methods for different inventory pools).

a. At what dollar amount are Kraft's inventories reported on its 2006 balance sheet?

b. At what dollar amount would inventories have been reported on Kraft's 2006 balance sheet had it used FIFO inventory costing?

c. What *cumulative* effect has the use of LIFO inventory costing had, as of year-end 2006, on its pretax income compared with the pretax income it would have reported had it used FIFO inventory costing? Explain.

d. Assuming a 35% income tax rate, by what *cumulative* dollar amount has Kraft's tax liability been affected by use of LIFO inventory costing as of year-end 2006? Has the use of LIFO inventory costing increased or decreased its cumulative tax liability?

e. What effect has the use of LIFO inventory costing had on Kraft's pretax income and tax liability for 2006 (assume a 35% income tax rate)?

E7-31. **Analyzing Inventories Using LIFO Inventory Footnote**   LO2, LO4, LO5

WHOLE FOODS
NASDAQ :: WFMI

The footnote below is from the 2008 10-K report of **Whole Foods Market, Inc.**, a Texas-based retail grocery chain.

Inventories   We value our inventories at the lower of cost or market. Cost was determined using the last-in, first-out ("LIFO") method for approximately 94.0% and 81.7% of inventories in fiscal years 2008 and 2007, respectively. Under the LIFO method, the cost assigned to items sold is based on the cost of the most recent items purchased. As a result, the costs of the first items purchased remain in inventory and are used to value ending inventory. The excess of estimated current costs over LIFO carrying value, or LIFO reserve, was approximately $32.7 million and $20.0 million at September 30, 2008 and September 29, 2007, respectively. Costs for the balance of inventories are determined by the first-in, first-out ("FIFO") method.

Whole Foods operates the world's largest chain of natural and organic food stores. In 2008, Whole Foods reported sales revenue of $7,954 million and cost of goods sold of $5,247 million. The following information was extracted from the company's 2008 and 2007 balance sheets:

$ millions	2008	2007
Merchandise inventories.....................	327	288

a. Calculate the amount of inventories purchased by Whole Foods in 2008.

b. What amount of gross profit would Whole Foods have reported if the FIFO method had been used to value all inventories?

c. Calculate the gross profit margin (GPM) as reported and assuming that the FIFO method had been used to value all inventories.

E7-32. **Calculating Gross Profit Margin and Inventory Turnover**   LO5

TIFFANY & CO.
NYSE :: TIF

ZALE CORPORATION
NYSE :: ZLC

BLUE NILE, INC.
NASDAQ :: NILE

The following table presents sales revenue, cost of goods sold, and inventory amounts for three retailers of fine jewelry, **Tiffany & Co.**, **Zale Corporation**, and **Blue Nile, Inc.** (an Internet retailer).

$ millions	2008	2007
Tiffany & Co.		
Revenues...............................	$2,860	$2,939
Cost of goods sold......................	1,215	1,282
Inventory..............................	1,601	1,372
Zale Corporation		
Revenues...............................	$2,138	$2,153
Cost of goods sold......................	1,090	1,030
Inventory..............................	780	1,021
Blue Nile, Inc.		
Revenues...............................	$ 295	$ 319
Cost of goods sold......................	235	254
Inventory..............................	19	21

a. Compute the gross profit margin (GPM) for each of these companies for 2008 and 2007.

b. Compute the inventory turnover ratios for 2008 and 2007, using the end-of-year inventory rather than the average inventory in the denominator.

c. What factors might determine the differences among these three companies' ratios?

d. In fiscal year 2008, Tiffany switched from the LIFO inventory method to the average cost method. (2007 inventory levels have been restated to average cost in the table on previous page.) In explaining the change in its 2008 10-K, Tiffany reports "The Company believes that the average cost method is preferable on the basis that it conforms to the manner in which the Company operationally manages its inventories and evaluates retail pricing." What are the advantages and disadvantages of Tiffany's using average costs to influence its retail pricing?

PROBLEMS

LO2, LO4, LO5

CATERPILLAR, INC.
NYSE :: CAT

KOMATSU LTD. (ADR)
OTC :: KMTUY

P7-33. **Analyzing Inventory and Its Footnote Disclosure**

Caterpillar Inc. and Komatsu Ltd. are international manufacturers of industrial and construction equipment. Caterpillar's headquarters is in the United States, while Komatsu's headquarters is in Japan. The following information comes from their recent financial statements.

Caterpillar—fiscal year ending December 31, 2008 ($ millions)

Cost of goods sold	$38,415
Beginning inventory	7,503
Ending inventory	8,781

Komatsu—fiscal year ending March 31, 2008 (¥ millions)

Cost of goods sold	¥1,590,963
Beginning inventory	518,441
Ending inventory	437,894

In its footnotes, Caterpillar also provides the following information:

Inventories are stated at the lower of cost or market. Cost is principally determined using the last-in, first-out (LIFO) method. The value of inventories on the LIFO basis represented about 70% of total inventories at December 31, 2008, and about 75% of total inventories at December 31, 2007 and 2006.

If the FIFO (first-in, first-out) method had been in use, inventories would have been $3,183 million, $2,617 million and $2,403 million higher than reported at December 31, 2008, 2007, and 2006 respectively.

Required:

a. Calculate the inventory turnover ratios for Caterpillar and Komatsu using the information reported in their financial statements. Describe some operational reasons that companies might have differing inventory turnover ratios, even if they are in the same industry.

b. Did the cost of Caterpillar's acquiring (i.e., producing) products go up or down in 2008?

c. Assuming a 35% income tax rate, by what *cumulative* dollar amount has Caterpillar's tax liability been affected by use of LIFO inventory costing as of fiscal year-end 2008? Has the use of LIFO inventory costing increased or decreased its cumulative tax liability?

d. What effect has the use of LIFO inventory costing had on Caterpillar's pretax income and tax liability for fiscal year 2008? (Assume a 35% tax rate.)

e. In its footnotes, Komatsu reports that it "determines cost of work in process and finished products using the specific identification method based on actual costs accumulated under a job-order cost system. The cost of finished parts is determined principally using the first-in, first-out method, with certain immaterial amounts using the last-in, first-out method." What effect does this footnote have on your interpretation in question *a* above? Use the information available to make a more appropriate comparison of the two companies' inventory turnover.

LO2, LO4, LO5

WebAssign.

KROGER
NYSE :: KR

P7-34 **Analyzing Inventory Disclosure Comparing LIFO and FIFO**

The current asset section of the 2008 and 2007 fiscal year end balance sheets of The Kroger Co. are presented in the accompanying table:

$ millions	January 1, 2009	February 2, 2008
Current assets		
Cash and temporary cash investments	$ 263	$ 242
Deposits in-transit	631	676
Receivables	944	786
FIFO inventory	5,659	5,453
LIFO credit	(800)	(604)
Prefunded employee benefits	300	300
Prepaid and other current assets	209	255
Total current assets	$7,206	$7,108

In addition, Kroger provides the following footnote describing its inventory accounting policy:

Inventories are stated at the lower of cost (principally on a last-in, first-out "LIFO" basis) or market. In total, approximately 98% and 97% of inventories for (fiscal year) 2008 and 2007, respectively, were valued using the LIFO method. Cost for the balance of the inventories, including substantially all fuel inventories, was determined using the first-in, first-out ("FIFO") method. Replacement cost was higher than the carrying amount by $800 at January 31, 2009, and $604 at February 2, 2008.

Required:

a. At what dollar amount does Kroger report its inventory in its January 31, 2009, balance sheet?

b. What is the cumulative effect (through January 31, 2009) of the use of LIFO on Kroger's pretax earnings?

c. Assuming a 35% tax rate, what is the cumulative (through January 31, 2009) tax effect of the use of LIFO to determine inventory costs?

d. Kroger reported net earnings of $1,249 million in its fiscal year 2008 income statement. Assuming a 35% tax rate, what amount of net earnings would Kroger report if the company used the FIFO inventory costing method?

e. Kroger reported merchandise costs (cost of goods sold) of $58,564 million in fiscal year 2008. Compute its inventory turnover for the year.

f. How would the inventory turnover ratio differ if the FIFO costing method had been used?

P7-35. Calculating Gross Profit and Inventory Turnover   **LO5**
The following table presents sales revenue, cost of goods sold, and inventory amounts for three computer/electronics companies, **Dell Inc., Hewlett-Packard Company**, and **Apple Inc.**

DELL INC.
NASDAQ :: DELL

HEWLETT-PACKARD AND COMPANY
NYSE :: HPQ

APPLE INC.
NASDAQ :: AAPL

$ millions	Fiscal year ending		
Dell Inc.	Jan. 30, 2009	Feb. 1, 2008	Feb. 2, 2007
Revenues	$61,101	$61,133	$57,420
Cost of goods sold	50,144	49,462	47,904
Inventory	867	1,180	660
Hewlett-Packard Company	Oct. 31, 2008	Oct. 31, 2007	Oct. 31, 2006
Revenues (Products only)	$91,697	$84,229	$73,557
Cost of goods sold	69,342	63,435	55,248
Inventory	7,879	8,033	7,750
Apple Inc.	Sep. 27, 2008	Sep. 29, 2007	Sep. 30, 2006
Revenues	$32,479	$24,006	$19,315
Cost of goods sold	21,334	15,852	13,717
Inventory	509	346	270

Required:

a. Compute the gross profit margin (GPM) for each of these companies for fiscal years 2008, 2007, and 2006.

b. Compute the inventory turnover ratios for fiscal years 2008 and 2007. (All three firms use FIFO inventory costing.)

c. What factors might determine the differences among these three companies' ratios?

P7-36.[A] **Analyzing and Interpreting Inventories and Its Related Ratios and Disclosures**   **LO2, LO4, LO6**
The current asset section from **The Stride Rite Corporation**'s annual report follows:

STRIDE RITE CORPORATION
NYSE :: SRR

$ thousands	November 28, 2003	November 29, 2002
Current Assets		
Cash and cash equivalents.	$103,272	$ 73,105
Accounts and notes receivable, less allowances of $9,406 in 2003 and $12,250 in 2002.	51,058	48,075
Inventories.	81,925	98,213
Deferred income taxes	14,393	20,588
Prepaid expenses and other current assets	19,452	14,131
Total current assets	$270,100	$254,112

Stride Rite reports the following related to its gross profit:

		Years Ended
$ thousands	2003	2002
Net sales	$550,124	$532,400
Cost of sales	340,614	337,951
Gross profit	$209,510	$194,449

Stride Rite further reports the following footnote related to its inventories:

Inventories   The cost of inventories, which consist primarily of finished product, at November 28, 2003, and November 29, 2002, was determined on a last-in, first-out (LIFO) basis. During 2003, the LIFO reserve decreased by $1,610,000 to $10,875,000 at November 28, 2003. If all inventories had been valued on a first-in, first-out (FIFO) basis, net income would have been lower by $1,019,000 ($.03 per share) in 2003. The LIFO reserve decreased in 2002 and increased in 2001, by $758,000 and $314,000, respectively. If all inventories had been valued on a FIFO basis, net income would have been lower by $516,000 ($.01 per share) in 2002 and would have been higher by $223,000 (less than $.01 per share) in 2001.

During 2003 and 2002, reductions in certain inventory quantities resulted in the sale of products carried at costs prevailing in prior years, which were different from current costs. As a result of these inventory reductions, net income was increased by $141,000 (less than $.01 per share) and decreased by $120,000 (less than $.01 per share) in 2003 and 2002, respectively.

a.   Compute the ratio of inventories to total current assets for both 2003 and 2002. Is the change you observe for the ratio a positive development for a company such as Stride Rite? Explain.

b.   Compute inventory turnover for both 2003 and 2002 (2001 ending inventories were $112,481). Interpret and explain the change in inventory turnover as positive or negative for the company.

c.   What inventory costing method does Stride Rite use? What effect has the use of this method (relative to FIFO or LIFO) had on its reported income over the three years, 2001–2003? Explain.

d.   Stride Rite reports that it decreased certain inventory quantities. Why do you believe Stride Rite reduced its inventory quantities? Is this development positive or negative for a company such as Stride Rite? Explain.

e.   What effect did reductions in inventory quantities have on Stride Rite's reported income for 2003 and for 2002? Explain.

CASES AND PROJECTS

LO2, LO4,
LO5, LO6

EXXON MOBIL CORP.
NYSE :: XOM
BP, P.L.C.
NYSE :: BP

C7-37.[A]   **Analyzing Effects of LIFO on Inventory Turnover Ratios**
The current assets of **Exxon Mobil Corporation** follow:

$ millions	2008	2007
Current assets		
Cash and cash equivalents.	$31,437	$33,981
Marketable securities	570	519
Notes and accounts receivable, less estimated doubtful amounts . . .	24,702	36,450
Inventories:		
Crude oil, products and merchandise	9,331	8,863
Materials and supplies	2,315	2,226
Other current assets	3,911	3,924
Total current assets	$72,266	$85,963

In addition, the following note was provided in its 2008 10-K report:

Inventories. Crude oil, products and merchandise inventories are carried at the lower of current market value or cost (generally determined under the last-in, first-out method—LIFO). Inventory costs include expenditures and other charges (including depreciation) directly and indirectly incurred in bringing the inventory to its existing condition and location. Selling expenses and general and administrative expenses are reported as period costs and excluded from inventory cost. Inventories of materials and supplies are valued at cost or less.

In 2008, 2007, and 2006, net income included gains of $341 million, $327 million, and $401 million, respectively, attributable to the combined effects of LIFO inventory accumulations and draw-downs. The aggregate replacement cost of inventories was estimated to exceed their LIFO carrying values by $10.0 billion and $25.4 billion at December 31, 2008 and 2007, respectively.

Required:

a. Exxon Mobil reported pretax earnings of $81,750 million in 2008. What amount of earnings would have been reported by the company if inventory had been reported using the FIFO costing method?

b. Exxon Mobil reported cost of goods sold of $249,454 million in 2008. Compute its inventory turnover ratio for 2008 using total inventories.

c. **BP, p.l.c.** (BP) reports its financial information using IFRS. For fiscal year 2008, BP reported cost of goods sold of $266,982 million, beginning inventory of $24,557 million and ending inventory of $15,409 million. Compute BP's inventory turnover ratio for fiscal year 2008.

d. Compare your answers in parts *b* and *c*. If that comparison is not appropriate, revise your calculations in such a way as to find out which company has faster inventory turnover.

e. What is meant by the statement that "2008 net income included gains of $341 million attributable to the combined effects of LIFO inventory accumulations and draw-downs"?

C7-38. Analyzing Effects of Change from LIFO to FIFO Inventory Costing

LO2, LO4

HORMEL FOODS
NYSE :: HRL

Hormel Foods Corporation provided the following footnote in its 2006 10-K report:

Change in Accounting Principle: In the first quarter of fiscal 2006, the company changed its method of accounting for the materials portion of turkey products and substantially all inventoriable expenses, packages, and supplies that had previously been accounted for utilizing the last-in first-out (LIFO) method to the first-in first-out (FIFO) method. As a result, all inventories are now stated at the lower of cost, determined on a FIFO basis, or market. The change is preferable because it provides a more meaningful presentation of the company's financial position as it values inventory in a manner that more closely approximates current cost; it provides a consistent and uniform costing method across the company's operations; FIFO inventory values better represent the underlying commercial substance of selling the oldest products first; it is the prevalent method used by other entities within the company's industry; and it enhances the comparability of the financial statements with those of our industry peers. As required by U.S. generally accepted accounting principles, the change has been reflected in the consolidated statements of financial position, consolidated statements of operations, and consolidated statements of cash flows through retrospective application of the FIFO method. Inventories as of the beginning of fiscal 2005 were increased by the LIFO reserve ($36.7 million), and shareholders' investment was increased by the after-tax effect ($23.0 million). Previously reported net earnings for fiscal years 2005 and 2004 were increased by $1.1 million and $1.9 million, respectively.

Required:

a. Hormel's 2005 10-K reports a LIFO reserve in the amount of $38.5 million. What dollar effect did this accounting method change have on total assets? retained earnings? income tax liabilities?

b. What were Hormel's stated reasons for the change?

c. What effect did this change likely have on 2006 net income?

d. Can you think of any possible motivations for this change in accounting method other than those provided by management?

SOLUTIONS TO REVIEW PROBLEMS

Mid-Chapter Review Part 1

Solution

Preliminary computation: Units in ending inventory = 4,800 available − 2,800 sold = 2,000

1. First-in, first-out (FIFO)

Cost of goods sold computation:	Units		Cost		Total
	1,000	@	$18.00	=	$18,000
	1,800	@	$18.25	=	32,850
	2,800				$50,850
Cost of goods available for sale....................		$88,450			
Less: Cost of goods sold		50,850			
Ending inventory ($22,800 + $14,800)		$37,600			

2. Last-in, first-out (LIFO)

Cost of goods sold computation:	Units		Cost		Total
	1,200	@	$19.00	=	$22,800
	800	@	$18.50	=	14,800
	800	@	$18.25	=	14,600
	2,800				$52,200
Cost of goods available for sale....................		$88,450			
Less: Cost of goods sold		52,200			
Ending inventory [$18,000 + (1,000 × $18.25)]		$36,250			

3. Average cost (AC)

Average unit cost	= $88,450/4,800	= $18.427	
Cost of goods sold	= 2,800 × $18.427	= $51,596	
Ending inventory	= 2,000 × $18.427	= $36,854	

4.   *a.* FIFO in most circumstances reflects physical flow. For example, FIFO would apply to the physical flow of perishables and to situations where the earlier items acquired are moved out first because of risk of deterioration or obsolescence.

    b. LIFO results in the lowest ending inventory amount during periods of rising costs, which in turn yields the lowest net income and the lowest income taxes.

5. Last-in, first-out with LIFO liquidation

Cost of goods sold computation:	Units		Cost		Total
	800	@	$18.50	=	$14,800
	1,800	@	$18.25	=	32,850
	200	@	$18.00	=	3,600
	2,800				$51,250
Cost of goods available for sale....................		$65,650			
Less: Cost of goods sold		51,250			
Ending inventory (800 × $18)		$14,400			

The company's LIFO gross profit has increased by $950 ($52,200 − $51,250). This increase is from LIFO liquidation, which is the reduction of inventory quantities that results in matching older (lower) cost layers against current selling prices. The company has, in effect, dipped into lower-cost layers to boost current period profit—all from a simple delay of inventory purchases.

6. Transaction effects shown in the financial statement effects template, journal entries, and T-accounts.

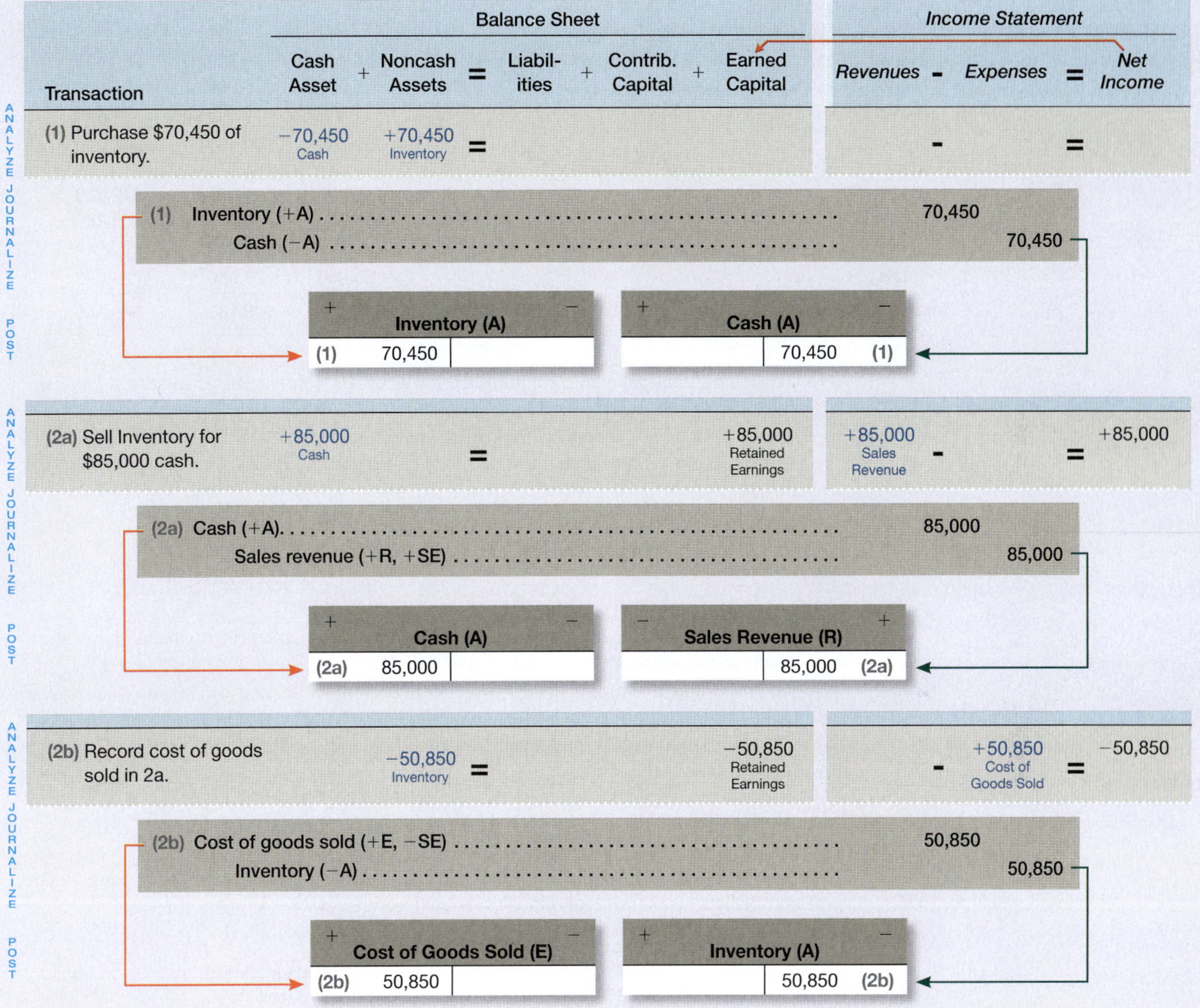

Mid-Chapter Review Part 2

Solution

1.

Item	Quantity	Cost	Market	Inventory Amounts		
				Cost	Market	LCM (by Item)
Fans						
Model X1	300	$18	$19	$ 5,400	$ 5,700	$ 5,400
Model X2	250	22	24	5,500	6,000	5,500
Model X3	400	29	26	11,600	10,400	10,400
Totals				$22,500	$22,100	$21,300
Heaters						
Model B7	500	24	28	$12,000	$14,000	$12,000
Model B8	290	35	32	10,150	9,280	9,280
Model B9	100	41	38	4,100	3,800	3,800
Totals				26,250	27,080	25,080
Totals				$48,750	$49,180	$46,380

a. As shown in this schedule, applying the lower of cost or market rule to each item of the inventory results in an ending inventory amount of $46,380.

b. Applying the lower of cost or market rule to each major category of the inventory results in an ending inventory amount of $48,350, calculated as follows:

Fans	$22,100
Heaters	26,250
	$48,350

c. As shown in this schedule, applying the lower of cost or market rule to the total inventory results in an ending inventory amount of $48,750.

2. The LCM procedure that results in the lowest ending inventory amount also results in the lowest net income for the year (the lower the ending inventory amount, the higher the cost of goods sold). Applying the lower of cost or market rule to each item of the inventory results in the lowest net income for the year.

Chapter-End Review

Solution:

1. Note that GE presents the cost of services sold as a separate expense item in the calculation of gross profit. The gross profit margin is calculated as follows:

Gross profit margin:		
2006:	$84,795/$151,568 =	0.559 (or 55.9%)
2007:	$99,363/$172,488 =	0.576 (or 57.6%)
2008:	$98,743/$182,515 =	0.541 (or 54.1%)
Inventory turnover:		
2007:	$47,309/[($12,897 + $10,032)/2] =	4.13 turns
2008:	$54,602/[($13,674 + $12,897)/2] =	4.11 turns

2. Cost of goods sold and gross profit must be adjusted by the change in the LIFO reserve to convert to FIFO.

Cost of goods sold		
2007:	$47,309 − ($623 − $564) =	$47,250
2008:	$54,602 − ($706 − $623) =	$54,519
Gross profit		
2007:	$99,363 + ($623 − $564) =	$99,422
2008:	$98,743 + ($706 − $623) =	$98,826

Note that the use of LIFO resulted in slightly higher cost of goods sold and lower gross profit in 2007 and 2008. The likely cause of this result is that GE's input costs increased slightly in both years.

3. Restated inventory turnover calculations:

$$2007: \quad \$47,250/[(\$13,520 + \$10,596)/2] = \quad 3.92 \text{ turns}$$
$$2008: \quad \$54,519/[(\$14,380 + \$13,520)/2] = \quad 3.91 \text{ turns}$$

Because inventory values are higher and cost of goods sold is lower under FIFO, the inventory turnover ratio is slightly lower when FIFO numbers are used.

Appendix-End Review

Solution:

a.

Sales revenue	
(11,500 × $65)	$747,500
Cost of goods sold	
(7,000 × $70) + (3,000 × $30) + (1,500 × $20)	610,000
Gross profit	$137,500

b.

Sales revenue	
(11,500 × $65)	$747,500
Cost of goods sold	
(11,500 × $70)	805,000
Gross profit	($ 57,500)

c. Dickhaut should report in its footnotes that gross profit was increased by $195,000 [$137,500 − ($57,500)] due to LIFO liquidation. It's worth noting that Dickhaut could report any gross profit between ($57,500) and $137,500 by adjusting its end-of-year purchases.

d. The replenishment decision should depend on the cash flows from each alternative over the planning period (until the point where inventory could be replenished next year at $55). The following table looks at three alternatives—no year-end purchase, a year-end purchase of 4,500 units, and a year-end purchase of 1,500 units. The second alternative would retain all the LIFO layers that were in the beginning inventory, while the third alternative would retain only the 2008 layer at $20 per unit. For this last alternative, cost of goods sold would be $685,000 (8,500 units at $70 each plus 3,000 units at $30 each).

As the table shows, the second alternative is preferred to the first, but the third alternative is preferred over the other two. (Of course, this analysis is based on the assumption that 5,000 units will be held in inventory for the entire planning horizon. If Dickhaut anticipates future inventory reductions, e.g., due to product changes, end-of-year purchases would only defer the payment of taxes and their relative advantage would decrease.)

	No purchase		Purchase 4,500 units		Purchase 1,500 units	
	Income	Cash Flows	Income	Cash Flows	Income	Cash Flows
Revenue	$747,500	$747,500	$747,500	$747,500	$747,500	$747,500
COGS	610,000		805,000		685,000	
Gross profit	137,500		(57,500)		62,500	
Tax (35%)	(48,125)	(48,125)	20,125	20,125	(21,875)	(21,875)
Year-end purchases				(315,000)		(105,000)
2011 purchases		(247,500)				(165,000)
Total cash flows		$451,875		$452,625		$455,625

1. Describe and distinguish between tangible and intangible assets. (p. 352)

2. Determine which costs to capitalize and report as assets and which costs to expense. (p. 354)

3. Apply different depreciation methods to allocate the cost of assets over time. (p. 356)

4. Determine the effects of asset sales and impairments on financial statements. (p. 359)

5. Describe the accounting and reporting for intangible assets. (p. 364)

6. Analyze the effects of tangible and intangible assets on key performance measures. (p. 370)

7. Explain the accounting for acquisition and depletion of natural resources. (p. 370)

Reporting and Analyzing Long-Term Operating Assets

Head and Shoulders Above Competitors

The Procter & Gamble Company (P&G) has successfully reinvented itself . . . again. Founded in 1837 by William Procter and James Gamble, P&G is the largest consumer products company in the world today. P&G markets its products in more than 180 countries and its annual sales now are in excess of $79 billion, which far exceeds competitors such as **Colgate-Palmolive Company** and

PROCTER & GAMBLE
www.pg.com

Kimberly-Clark Corporation. P&G has focused on its higher-margin products such as those in beauty care. This strategy has improved its profit margin and provided much needed dollars for marketing activities. Its advertising budget is almost 9.6% of sales, which is nearly double the budget of some of its key competitors.

Procter & Gamble's 5-year cumulative returns are graphed below:

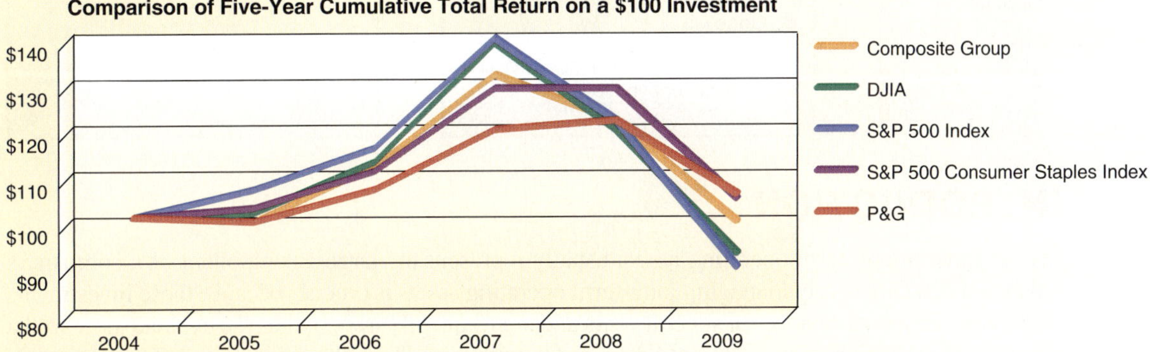

P&G's financial performance has been equally impressive. Its return on equity (ROE) in 2009 was 20%. Although more financially leveraged than the average publicly traded company, there is little need for concern because P&G generates almost $15 billion in operating cash flow, which is more than sufficient to cover its $1.2 billion in interest payments. P&G also generates sufficient cash to allow it to pay dividends in excess of $5 billion annually to shareholders.

P&G's product stable continues to be impressive. It consists of numerous well-recognized household brands—a partial listing follows by business segment:

(continued on next page)

(continued from previous page)

- **Fabric and Home Care**—Tide, Downy, Joy, Cascade, Mr. Clean, Bounce, Swiffer, and Febreze
- **Beauty Care**—Head & Shoulders, Pantene, Olay, Clairol, Max Factor, Old Spice, Ivory, Gillette, Braun, and Mach 3
- **Baby and Family Care**—Pampers, Charmin, Bounty, and Puffs
- **Health Care**—Crest, Vicks, Fixodent, PUR, and Pepto-Bismol
- **Snacks and Pet Care**—Pringles and Iams

Procter and Gamble's impressive performance, ranked 9th in profitability, 6th in market value and the firm was the 6th most admired company by *Fortune* in 2008. The company was severely impacted by the economic collapse during its 2008–2009 fiscal year. P&G's stock price, which had risen consistently over the 2000–2008 period to a high above $75, declined to a 55-week low of $54.77 by June 30, 2009, wiping out P&G's entire price increase since 2000. The immediate future will be difficult. P&G does not expect its earnings per share to improve in 2010 from its 2009 level. The new CEO, Robert McDonald, is likely to oversee substantial changes as P&G tries to exert greater control over its extensive empire.

In this chapter, we explore the reporting and analysis of long-term operating assets. In order to maintain growth in sales, income, and cash flows, capital-intensive companies like P&G must be diligent in managing long-term operating assets. As is the case with P&G, many companies have made large investments in innovation. These investments are not always reflected adequately in the balance sheet. Management's choices and GAAP rules concerning the reporting of long-term operating assets can have a marked impact on the analysis and interpretation of financial statements.

Sources: *Procter & Gamble* 2005, 2006, 2007, 2008 and 2009 10-K Reports; *BusinessWeek,* 13 April 2009; *The Wall Street Journal,* 10 March, 29 May and 11 June 2009; Fortune,16 and 27 March,13 April and 4 May 2009.

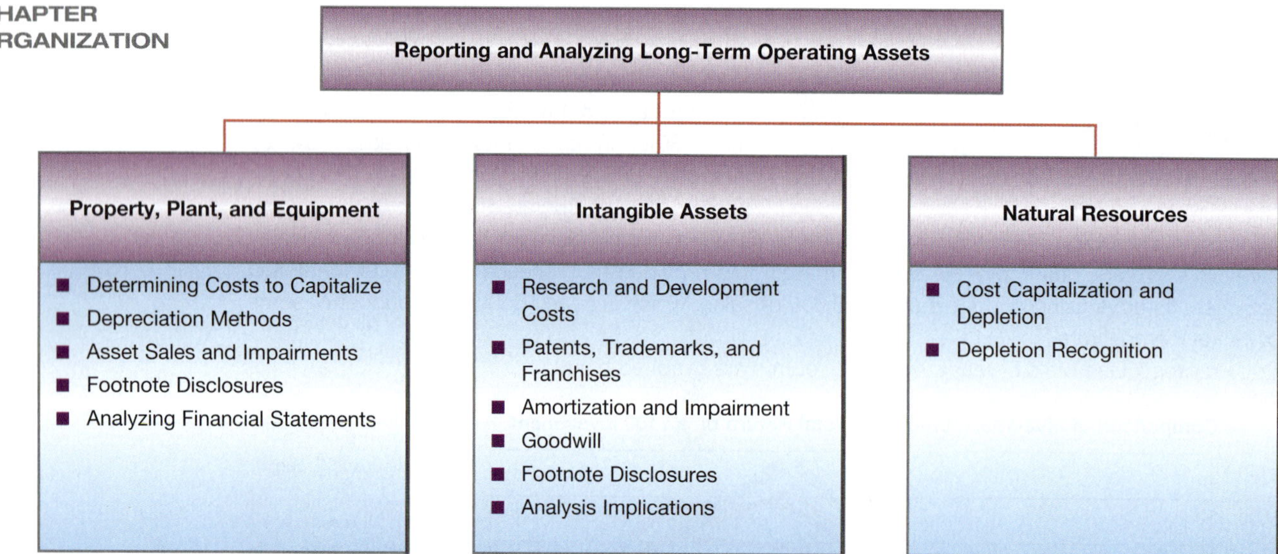

INTRODUCTION

Investments in long-term operating assets usually represent the largest component of a company's balance sheet. Effectively managing long-term operating assets is crucial, because these investments affect company performance for several years and are frequently irreversible. To evaluate how well a company is managing operating assets, we need to understand how they are measured and reported.

LO1 Describe and distinguish between tangible and intangible assets.

This chapter describes the accounting, reporting, and analysis of long-term operating assets including tangible and intangible assets. **Tangible assets** are assets that have physical substance. They are frequently included in the balance sheet as *property, plant and equipment*, and include land, buildings, machinery, fixtures, and equipment. **Intangible assets**, such as trademarks and patents, do not have physical substance, but provide the owner with specific rights and privileges.

Long-term operating assets have two common characteristics. First, unlike inventory, these assets are not acquired for resale. Instead, they are necessary to produce and deliver the products and services that generate revenues for the company. Second, these assets help produce revenues for multiple accounting periods. Consequently, accountants focus considerable attention on how they are reported in the balance sheet and how these costs are transferred over time to the income statement as expenses.

To illustrate the size and importance of long-term operating assets, the asset section (only) of P&G's balance sheet is reproduced in Exhibit 8.1. We can see as of June 30, 2009, the end of P&G's fiscal year, P&G's net investment in property, plant and equipment totaled approximately $19.5 billion and its intangible assets represent an $89.1 billion investment. Together, these two categories of assets make up over three-fourths of P&G's total assets.

EXHIBIT 8.1	Procter & Gamble Balance Sheet (assets only)	
	June 30	
Amounts in millions	**2009**	**2008**
Assets		
Current Assets		
Cash and cash equivalents	$ 4,781	$ 3,313
Accounts receivable	5,836	6,761
Inventories		
Materials and supplies	1,557	2,262
Work in process	672	765
Finished goods	4,651	5,389
Total inventories	6,880	8,416
Deferred income taxes	1,209	2,012
Prepaid expenses and other current assets	3,199	4,013
Total current assets	21,905	24,515
Property, Plant, and Equipment		
Buildings	6,724	7,052
Machinery and equipment	29,042	30,145
Land	885	889
	36,651	38,086
Accumulated depreciation	(17,189)	(17,446)
Net property, plant, and equipment	19,462	20,640
Goodwill and Other Intangible Assets		
Goodwill	56,512	59,767
Trademarks and other intangible assets, net	32,606	34,233
Net Goodwill and Other Intangible Assets	89,118	94,000
Other Noncurrent Assets	4,348	4,837
Total Assets	$134,833	$143,992

This chapter is divided into two main sections. The first section focuses on accounting for tangible property, plant, and equipment and the related depreciation expense that is reported each period in the income statement. The second section examines the measurement and reporting of intangible assets and natural resources.

PROPERTY, PLANT, AND EQUIPMENT (PPE)

For many companies, the largest category of operating assets is its long-term property, plant, and equipment (PPE) assets. The size and duration of this asset category raises several important questions, including:

- Which costs should be **capitalized** on the balance sheet as assets, and which should be expensed?
- How should capitalized costs be allocated to the accounting periods that benefited from the asset?
- How should asset sales or significant declines in market value be reported?

This section explains the accounting, reporting, and analysis of PPE assets and related items.

Determining Costs to Capitalize

LO2 Determine which costs to capitalize and report as assets and which costs to expense.

When a company acquires an asset, it must first decide which portion of the cost should be included among the expenses of the current period and which costs should be capitalized as part of the asset and reported in the balance sheet. Outlays to acquire PPE are called **capital expenditures**. Expenditures that are recorded as an asset must possess each of the following two characteristics:

1. The asset is owned or controlled by the company.
2. The asset is expected to provide future benefits.

All costs incurred to acquire an asset and prepare it for its intended use should be capitalized and reported in the balance sheet. These costs would include the purchase price of the asset plus any of the following: installation costs, taxes, shipping costs, legal fees, and setup or calibration costs.

Determining the specific costs that should be capitalized requires judgment. There are two important considerations to address when deciding which costs to capitalize. First, companies can only capitalize costs that are *directly linked* to future benefits. Incidental costs or costs that would be incurred regardless of whether the asset is purchased should not be capitalized. Second, the costs capitalized as an asset can be no greater than the expected future benefits to be derived from use of the asset. This requirement means that if a company reports a $200 asset, we can reasonably expect that it will derive at least $200 in expected future cash inflows from the use and ultimate disposition of the asset.

Sometimes, companies construct assets for their own use rather than purchasing a similar asset from another company. In this case, all of the costs incurred to construct the asset—including materials, labor, and a reasonable amount of overhead—should be included in the cost that is capitalized. In addition, in many cases, a portion of the interest expense incurred during the construction period should also be capitalized as part of the asset's cost. This interest is called **capitalized interest**. Capitalizing some of a company's interest cost as part of the cost of a self-constructed asset reduces interest expense in the current period and increases depreciation expense in future periods when the asset is placed in service.

Once an asset is placed in service, additional costs are often incurred to maintain and improve the asset. Routine repairs and maintenance costs are necessary to realize the full potential benefits of ownership of the asset and should be treated as expenses of the period in which the maintenance is performed. However, if the cost can be considered an *improvement or betterment* of the asset, the cost should be capitalized. An improvement or betterment is an outlay that either enhances the usefulness of the asset or extends the asset's useful life beyond the original expectation.

YOU MAKE THE CALL

You are the Company Accountant   Your company has just purchased a plot of land as a building site for an office building. After the purchase, you discover that the building site was once the site of an oil well. Before construction can commence, your company must spend $40,000 to properly cap the oil well and prepare the site to meet current environmental standards. How should you account for the $40,000 cleanup cost? [Answers on page 373]

Depreciation

FYI Depreciation is a systematic allocation of asset cost over the useful life—not a measure of the change in market value.

Once an asset has been recorded in the balance sheet, the cost must be transferred over time from the balance sheet to the income statement and reported as an expense. The *matching principle* requires that we match the cost of the asset with the revenues that it helped to generate. The nature of long-term operating assets is that they benefit more than one period. As a consequence, it is impossible to match a specific portion of the cost *directly* to the revenues of a particular period. Instead, we rely on a *systematic allocation* to assign a portion of the asset's cost to each period benefited. This systematic allocation of cost is called **depreciation**.

The concept of systematic allocation of an asset's cost is important. When depreciation expense is recorded, the reported value of the asset (also called the *book value* or *carrying value*) is reduced. Naturally, it is tempting to infer that the market value of the asset is lower as a result. However, this reported value does not reflect the market value of the asset. The market value of the asset may decline by more or less than the amount of depreciation expense, and can even increase in some periods. Depreciation expense should only be interpreted as an assignment of costs to an accounting period and not a measure of the decline in market value of the asset.

The amount of cost that is allocated to a given period is recorded as depreciation expense in the income statement and **accumulated depreciation** in the balance sheet. Accumulated depreciation is a contra-asset account (denoted "XA" in the journal entry). Like all contra-asset accounts, it offsets the balance in the corresponding asset account. To illustrate, assume that Dehning Company purchases a heavy-duty delivery truck for $100,000 and decides to record $18,000 of depreciation expense in the first year of operation. The following entries would be recorded.

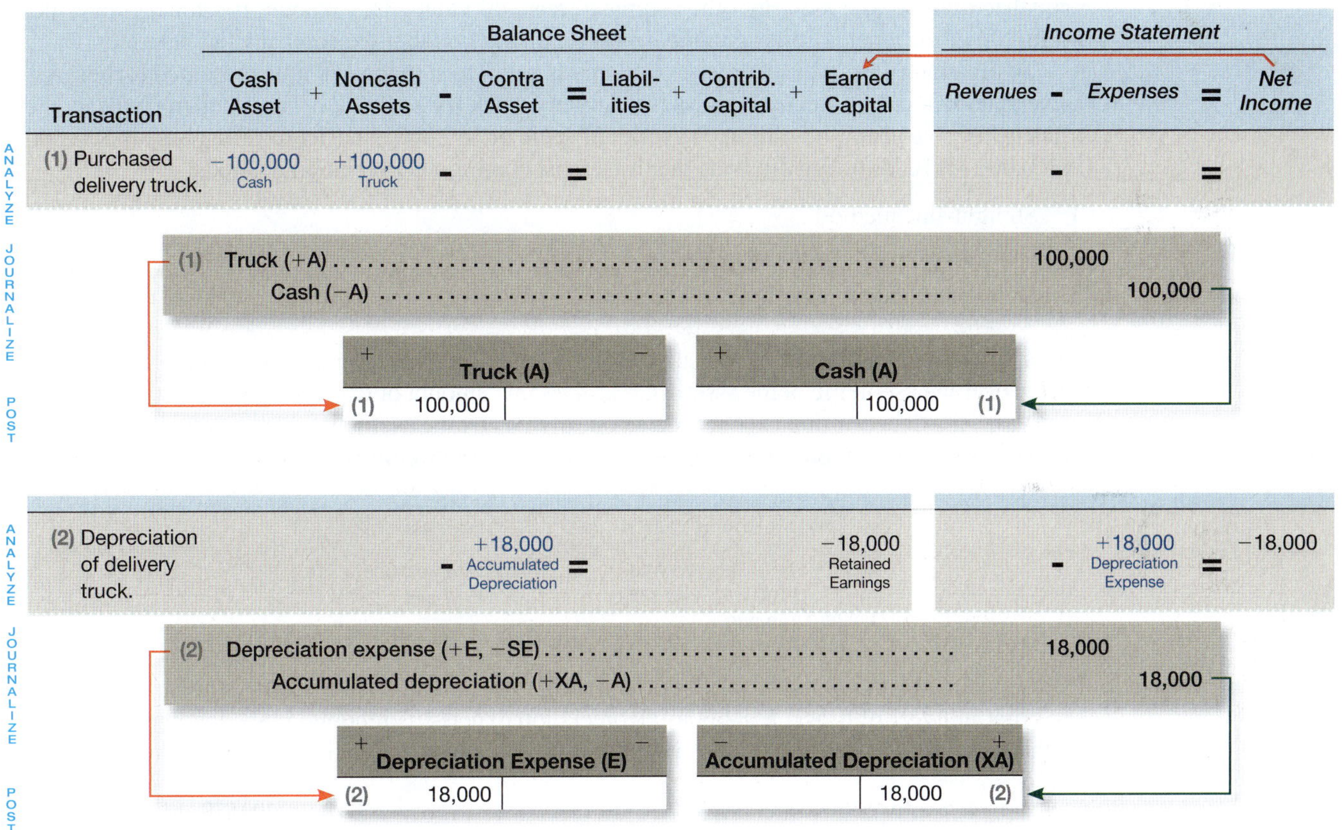

The asset would be presented in the balance sheet at period-end at its net book value.

Delivery truck, at cost	$100,000	
Less accumulated depreciation	18,000	
Delivery truck, net	$ 82,000	(Book Value)

By presenting the information using a contra-asset account, the original acquisition cost of the asset is preserved in the asset account. The net book value of the asset reflects the acquisition cost less the balance in the accumulated depreciation account. The balance in the accumulated depreciation account is the sum of the depreciation expense that has been recorded to date.

Depreciation Methods

Two estimates are required to compute the amount of depreciation expense to record each period.

1. **Useful life**. The useful life is the period of time over which the asset is expected to provide economic benefits to the company. The useful life is not the same as the physical life of the asset. An asset may or may not provide economic benefits to the company for its entire physical life. This useful life should not exceed the period of time that the company intends to use the asset. For example, if a company has a policy of replacing automobiles every two years, the useful life should be set at no longer than two years, even if the automobiles physically last three years or more.

2. **Residual (or salvage) value**. The residual value is the expected realizable value of the asset at the end of its useful life. This value may be the disposal or scrap value, or it may be an estimated resale value for a used asset.

These factors must be estimated when the asset is acquired. The **depreciation base**, also called the *nonrecoverable cost*, is the portion of the cost that is depreciated. The depreciation base is the capitalized cost of the asset less the estimated residual value. This amount is allocated over the useful life of the asset according to the *depreciation method* that the company has selected.

To illustrate alternative depreciation methods, we return to the example presented earlier. Assume that Dehning Company purchases a delivery truck for $100,000. The company expects the truck to last five years and estimates a residual value of $10,000. The depreciation base is $90,000 ($100,000 − $10,000). We illustrate the three most common depreciation methods:

1. Straight-line method
2. Double-declining-balance method
3. Units-of-production method

Straight-Line Method   Under the **straight-line method**, depreciation expense is recorded evenly over the useful life of the asset. That is, the same amount of depreciation expense is recorded each year. The **depreciation rate** is equal to one divided by the useful life. In our example, 1/5 = 0.2 or 20% per year. The depreciation base and depreciation rate follow.

Depreciation Base	Depreciation Rate
Cost − Salvage value = $100,000 − $10,000 = $90,000	1/Estimated useful life = 1/5 years = 20%

Depreciation expense per year for this asset is $18,000, computed as $90,000 × 20%. For the asset's first full year of usage, $18,000 of depreciation expense is reported in the income statement. At the end of that first year the asset is reported on the balance sheet as follows:

Truck, at cost.	$100,000
Less accumulated depreciation	18,000
Truck, net.	$ 82,000

Accumulated depreciation is the sum of all depreciation expense that has been recorded to date. The asset **book value (BV)**, or *net book value* or *carrying value,* is cost less accumulated depreciation. Although the word "value" is used here, it does not refer to market value. Depreciation is a cost allocation concept (transfer of costs from the balance sheet to the income statement), not a valuation concept.

In the second year of usage, another $18,000 of depreciation expense is recorded in the income statement and the net book value of the asset on the balance sheet follows:

Truck, at cost.	$100,000
Less accumulated depreciation	36,000
Truck, net.	$ 64,000

Accumulated depreciation now includes the sum of the first and second years' depreciation ($36,000), and the net book value of the asset is now reduced to $64,000. After the fifth year, a total of $90,000 of accumulated depreciation will be recorded, yielding a net book value for the truck of $10,000, its estimated salvage value.

Double-Declining-Balance Method   GAAP allows companies to use **accelerated depreciation** methods. Accelerated depreciation methods record more depreciation expense in the early years of an asset's useful life and less expense in the later years. The total depreciation expense recorded *over the entire useful life* of the asset is the same as with straight-line depreciation. The only difference is in the amount of depreciation recorded for *any given year*.

The **double-declining-balance (DDB) method** is an accelerated depreciation method that computes the depreciation rate as twice the straight-line rate. This double rate is then multiplied by the net book value of the asset, which declines each period as accumulated depreciation increases. For Dehning Company, the depreciation base and the depreciation rate are computed as follows:

Depreciation Base	Depreciation Rate
Net Book Value = Cost − Accumulated Depreciation	2 × SL rate = 2 × 20% = 40%

The depreciation expense for the first year of usage for this asset is $40,000, computed as $100,000 × 40%. At the end of the first full year, $40,000 of depreciation expense is reported on the income statement (compared with $18,000 under the SL method), and the asset is reported on the balance sheet as follows:

Truck, at cost.	$100,000
Less accumulated depreciation	40,000
Truck, net.	$ 60,000

> **FYI** When calculating DDB depreciation, the depreciation rate is multiplied by the book value; residual value is not subtracted from book value.

In the second year, $24,000 ($60,000 × 40%) of depreciation expense is reported in the income statement and the net book value of the asset on the balance sheet follows:

Truck, at cost.	$100,000
Less accumulated depreciation	64,000
Truck, net.	$ 36,000

The double-declining-balance method continues to record depreciation expense in this manner until the salvage amount is reached, at which point the depreciation process is discontinued. This leaves a net book value equal to the salvage value as with the straight-line method. The DDB depreciation schedule for the life of this asset is illustrated in Exhibit 8.2.

EXHIBIT 8.2	Double-Declining-Balance Depreciation Schedule		
Year	**Book Value at Beginning of Year**	**Depreciation Expense**	**Book Value at End of Year**
1.	$100,000	100,000 × 40% = $40,000	$60,000
2.	60,000	60,000 × 40% = 24,000	36,000
3.	36,000	36,000 × 40% = 14,400	21,600
4.	21,600	21,600 × 40% = 8,640	12,960
5.	12,960	12,960 − 10,000 = 2,960*	10,000

*The depreciation expense in the fifth year is not calculated as 40% × $12,960 because the resulting depreciation would reduce the net book value below the $10,000 residual value. Instead, the residual value ($10,000) is subtracted from the remaining book value ($12,960), resulting in depreciation expense of $2,960.

Exhibit 8.3 compares the depreciation expense and net book value for both the SL and DDB methods. During the first two years, the DDB method yields higher depreciation expense in comparison with the SL method. Beginning in the third year, this pattern reverses and the SL method produces higher depreciation expense. Over the asset's life, the same $90,000 in total depreciation expense is recorded, leaving a residual value of $10,000 on the balance sheet under both methods.

| EXHIBIT 8.3 | Comparison of Straight-Line and Double-Declining-Balance Depreciation | | | |

| | Straight-Line | | Double-Declining-Balance | |
Year	Depreciation Expense	Book Value at End of Year	Depreciation Expense	Book Value at End of Year
1	$18,000	$82,000	$40,000	$60,000
2	18,000	64,000	24,000	36,000
3	18,000	46,000	14,400	21,600
4	18,000	28,000	8,640	12,960
5	18,000	10,000	2,960	10,000
	$90,000		$90,000	

All depreciation methods yield the same salvage value

Total depreciation over asset life is identical for all methods

Units-of-Production Method   Under the **units-of-production method**, the useful life of the asset is defined in terms of the number of units of service provided by the asset. For instance, this could be the number of units produced, the number of hours that a machine is operated, or, as with Dehning Company's delivery truck, the number of miles driven. To illustrate, assume that Dehning Company estimates that the delivery truck will provide 150,000 miles of service before it is sold for its residual value of $10,000. The depreciation rate is expressed in terms of a cost per mile driven, computed as follows:

$$\frac{\$100,000 - \$10,000}{150,000 \text{ miles}} = \$0.60 \text{ per mile}$$

If the delivery truck is driven 35,000 miles in year 1, the depreciation expense for that year would be $21,000 (35,000 × $0.60). This method produces an amount of depreciation that varies from year to year as the use of the asset varies.

    Most companies use the straight-line method for financial reporting purposes and an accelerated depreciation method for tax returns.[1] The reason is that in the early years of the asset's useful life, straight-line depreciation yields higher income on shareholder reports, whereas accelerated depreciation yields lower taxable income. Even though this difference reverses in later years, companies prefer to defer the tax payments so that the cash savings can be invested to produce earnings. Further, even with the reversal in the later years of an asset's life, if total depreciable assets are growing at a fast enough rate, the additional first-year depreciation on newly acquired assets more than offsets the lower depreciation expense on older assets, yielding an indefinite deferral of taxable income and taxes paid.

Changes in Accounting Estimates

The estimates required in the depreciation process are made when the asset is acquired. When necessary, companies can, and do, change these estimates during the useful lives of assets. When either the useful life or residual value estimates change, the change is applied prospectively. That is, companies use the new estimates from the date of the change going forward and do not restate the financial statements of prior periods.

    To illustrate, assume that, after three years of straight-line depreciation, Dehning Company decided to extend the useful life of its truck from 5 years to 6 years. From Exhibit 8.3, the book value of the delivery truck at the end of the third year is $46,000. The change in estimated useful life

---

[1] The IRS mandates the use of MACRS (Modified Accelerated Cost Recovery System) for tax purposes. This method fixes the useful life for various classes of assets, assumes no salvage value, and generally produces depreciation amounts consistent with the double-declining-balance method.

would not require a formal accounting entry. Instead, depreciation expense would be recalculated for the remaining three years of the truck's useful life:

$$\frac{\$46,000 - \$10,000}{3 \text{ years}} = \$12,000 \text{ per year}$$

Thus, beginning in year four, depreciation expense of $12,000 (instead of $18,000) would be recorded each year.

Asset Sales and Impairments

This section discusses gains and losses from asset sales and computation and disclosure of asset impairments.

Gains and Losses on Asset Sales   The gain or loss on the sale (disposition) of a long-term asset is computed as follows:

> **Gain or loss on asset sale = Proceeds from sale − Book value of asset sold**

LO4 Determine the effects of asset sales and impairments on financial statements.

The book (carrying) value of an asset is its acquisition cost less accumulated depreciation. When an asset is sold, its acquisition cost and related accumulated depreciation are removed from the balance sheet and any gain or loss is reported in income from continuing operations. To illustrate such a transaction, assume that Dehning Company decided to sell the delivery truck after four years of straight-line depreciation. From Exhibit 8.3, we know that the book value of the truck is $28,000 ($100,000 − $72,000). If the truck is sold for $30,000, the entry to record the sale follows.

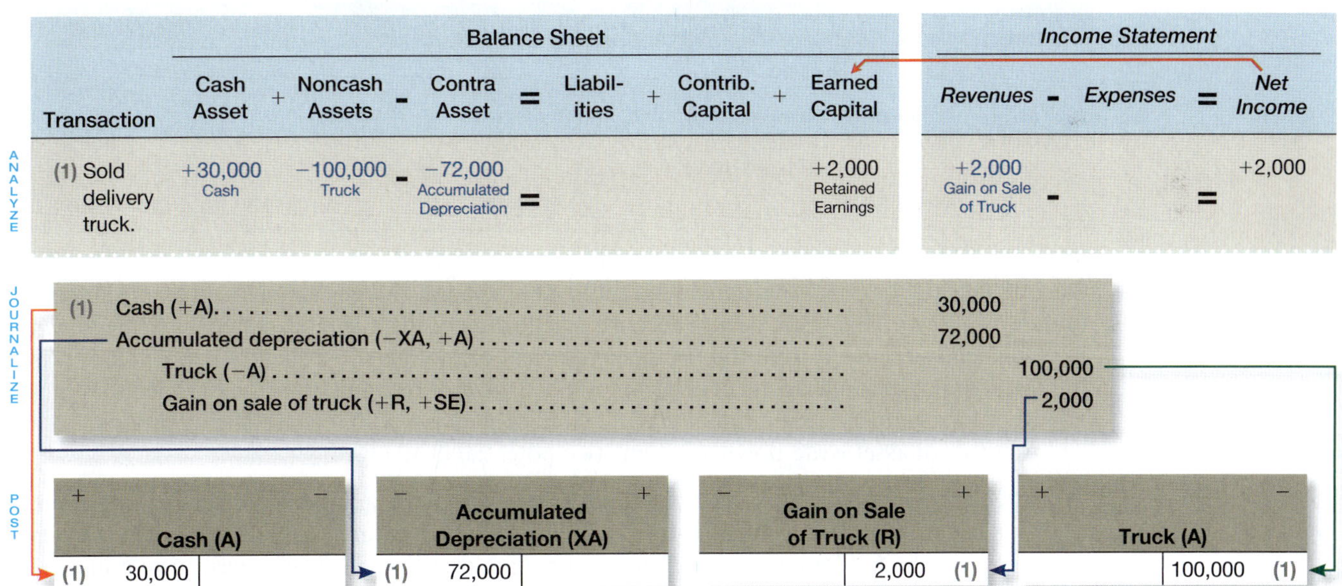

Gains and losses on asset sales can be large, and analysts must be aware of these nonrecurring operating income components. Further, if the gains are deemed immaterial, companies often include such gains and losses in general line items of the income statement—often as a component of selling, general and administrative expenses.

Asset Impairments   Property, plant, and equipment (PPE) assets are reported at their net book values (original cost less accumulated depreciation). This is the case even if market values of these assets increase subsequent to acquisition. As a result, there can be unrecognized gains hidden in the balance sheet.

However, if market values of PPE assets subsequently decrease—and it can be determined that the asset value is permanently impaired—then companies must recognize losses on those assets. **Impairment** of PPE assets is determined by comparing the sum of *expected* future (undiscounted) cash flows from the asset with its net book value. If these expected cash flows are greater than net book value, no impairment is deemed to exist. However, if the sum of expected cash flows is less than net book value, the asset is deemed impaired and it is written down to its current market value (generally, the discounted present value of those expected cash flows). Exhibit 8.4 depicts this impairment analysis.

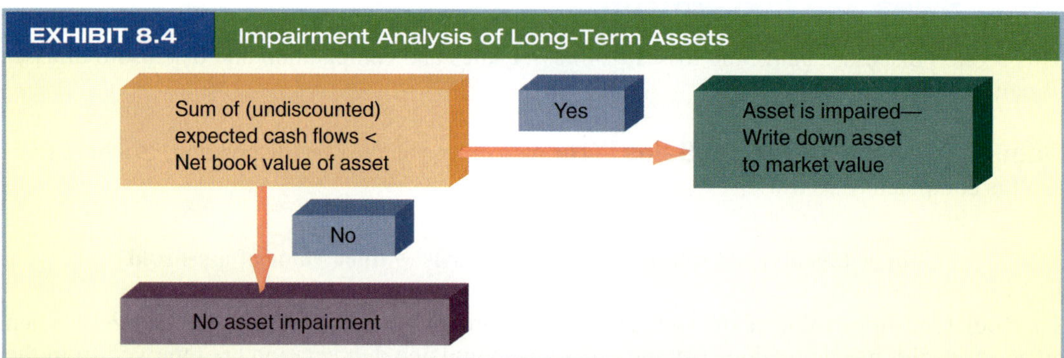

When a company records an impairment charge, assets are reduced by the amount of the write-down and the loss is recognized in the income statement, which reduces current period income. These effects are illustrated in Exhibit 8.5.

EXHIBIT 8.5   Financial Statement Effects of Asset Impairment

Balance Sheet					Income Statement		
Cash Asset	+ Noncash Assets	= Liabil-ities	+ Contrib. Capital	+ Earned Capital	Revenues −	Expenses	= Net Income
Decrease =				Decrease	−	Increase	= Decrease

Once a depreciable asset is written down, future depreciation charges are reduced by the amount of the writedown. This result occurs because that portion of the asset's cost that is written down is permanently removed from the balance sheet and cannot be subsequently depreciated. It is important to note that management determines if and when to recognize asset impairments. Write-downs of long-term assets are often recognized in connection with a restructuring program.

Analysis of asset write-downs presents two potential challenges:

1. *Insufficient write-down.* Assets sometimes are impaired to a larger degree than is recognized. This can arise if management is overly optimistic about future prospects or is reluctant to recognize the full loss in income. Underestimation of an impairment causes current income to be overstated and income in future years to be lower.

2. *Aggressive write-down.* This *big bath* scenario can arise if income is currently and severely depressed. Management's view is that the market will not penalize the firm for an extra write-off, and that doing so purges the balance sheet of costs that would otherwise reduce future years' income. This leads to income being overstated for several years after the write-down.

Neither of these cases is condoned under GAAP. Yet, because management is estimating future cash flows for the impairment test and such estimates are difficult to verify, it has some degree of latitude over the timing and amount of the write-off and can use that discretion to manage reported income.

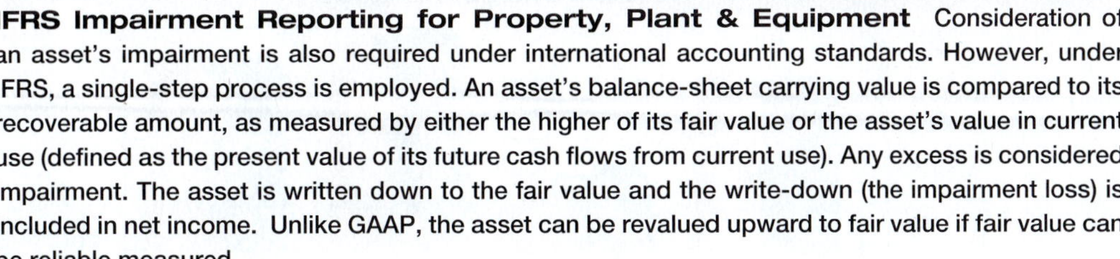

IFRS Impairment Reporting for Property, Plant & Equipment Consideration of an asset's impairment is also required under international accounting standards. However, under IFRS, a single-step process is employed. An asset's balance-sheet carrying value is compared to its recoverable amount, as measured by either the higher of its fair value or the asset's value in current use (defined as the present value of its future cash flows from current use). Any excess is considered impairment. The asset is written down to the fair value and the write-down (the impairment loss) is included in net income. Unlike GAAP, the asset can be revalued upward to fair value if fair value can be reliable measured.

Footnote Disclosure

Procter & Gamble provides the following information in footnote 1 of its 2009 Annual Report to describe its accounting for PPE assets.

Property, Plant and Equipment
Property, plant and equipment is recorded at cost reduced by accumulated depreciation. Depreciation expense is recognized over the assets' estimated useful lives using the straight-line method.

Machinery and equipment includes office furniture and fixtures (15-year life), computer equipment and capitalized software (3- to 5-year lives) and manufacturing equipment (3- to 20-year lives). Buildings are depreciated over an estimated useful life of 40 years. Estimated useful lives are periodically reviewed and, where appropriate, changes are made prospectively. Where certain events or changes in operating conditions occur, asset lives may be adjusted and an impairment assessment may be performed on the recoverability of the carrying amounts.

The note details P&G's depreciation method (straight-line) and the estimated useful lives of various classes of PPE assets. From this note, we can also infer that there was no material asset impairment recorded during the period covered by the report. If asset values were impaired, it would have been disclosed in this note or in a separate note.

ANALYZING FINANCIAL STATEMENTS

This section considers two measures useful for analysis of long-term asset utilization and age.

PPE Turnover

A crucial issue in analysis of PPE assets is their productivity (or efficient utilization). For example, what level of plant assets is necessary to generate a dollar of revenues? How capital intensive is the company and its competitors? PPE turnover is often used for insights into asset utilization and to address these and similar questions. It is defined as follows:

$$\text{PPE Turnover (PPET)} = \frac{\text{Sales revenue}}{\text{Average PPE, net}}$$

P&G's fiscal 2009 PPE asset turnover is 3.94 times, down from 4.07 in 2008. Its turnover remains in the middle range among companies that P&G competes with, as shown in the following chart. (The chart data are for 2008 for comparison purposes. P&G's fiscal year ends on June 30. The other firms end December 31.)

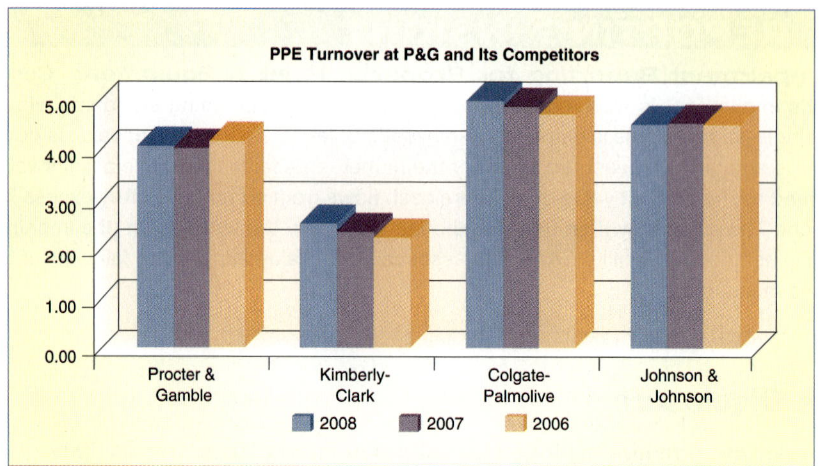

Companies prefer that PPE turnover be higher rather than lower. A higher PPE turnover implies a lower capital investment for a given level of sales. The result is an increase in profitability (as asset carrying costs are less) and an increase in cash flow.

PPE turnover is lower for *capital-intensive* manufacturing companies like P&G than it is for companies in service or knowledge-based industries. To this point, consider the following chart of plant asset turnover for companies from different industries.

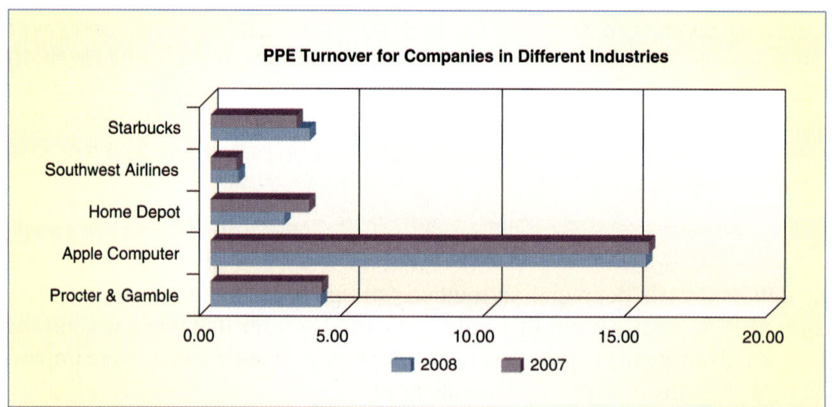

Apple Inc.'s PPE turnover is much higher than the turnover ratios of the other companies in this comparison because it outsources most of its component manufacturing. Typical of the airline industry, **Southwest Airlines Co.** has a low PPE turnover. P&G's PPE turnover of 3.9 times compares favorably with the other firms in this comparison (**The Home Depot**'s is 2.7 and **Starbucks Corporation**'s is 3.6). Nevertheless, P&G must constantly strive to improve its PPE asset utilization to remain competitive.

Percent Depreciated

P&G reports that the useful lives of its depreciable assets range from 3 to 5 years for computer equipment and software to 40 years for buildings. It is often useful to know whether a company's assets are relatively old or new.

We can estimate the percent of a company's depreciable assets that have been depreciated, reflecting the portion of depreciable assets that are no longer productive as of June 30, 2009, as follows:

$$\text{Percent depreciated} = \frac{\text{Accumulated depreciation}}{\text{Cost of depreciable asset}}$$

Using this ratio, we can calculate that P&G's assets are 48.1% depreciated, computed as follows:

$$48.1\% = \frac{\$17,189 \text{ million}}{(\$6,724 \text{ million} + \$29,042 \text{ million})}$$

BUSINESS INSIGHT

Federal authorities arrested WorldCom, Inc.'s CEO, Bernie Ebbers, and chief financial officer, Scott Sullivan, in August 2002 for allegedly conspiring to alter the telecommunications giant's financial statements to meet analyst expectations. They were accused of *cooking the books* so the company would not show a loss for 2001 and subsequent quarters.

Specifically, WorldCom incurred large costs in anticipation of an increase in Internet-related business that did not materialize. The executives shifted these costs to the balance sheet and recorded them as PPE, thereby inflating current profitability. By capitalizing these costs (moving them from the income statement to the balance sheet), WorldCom was able to disguise these costs as an asset to be allocated as future costs. Contrary to WorldCom's usual practices and prevailing accounting principles, no support existed for capitalization.

Although the WorldCom case also involved alleged fraud, an astute analyst would have suspected something was amiss from analysis of WorldCom's long-term asset turnover (Sales/Average long-term assets) as shown below. The decline in turnover reveals that its assets constituted an ever-increasing percent of total sales during 1995 to 2002, by quarter. This finding does not, in itself, imply fraud. It does, however, raise serious questions that should have been answered by WorldCom executives in meetings with analysts.

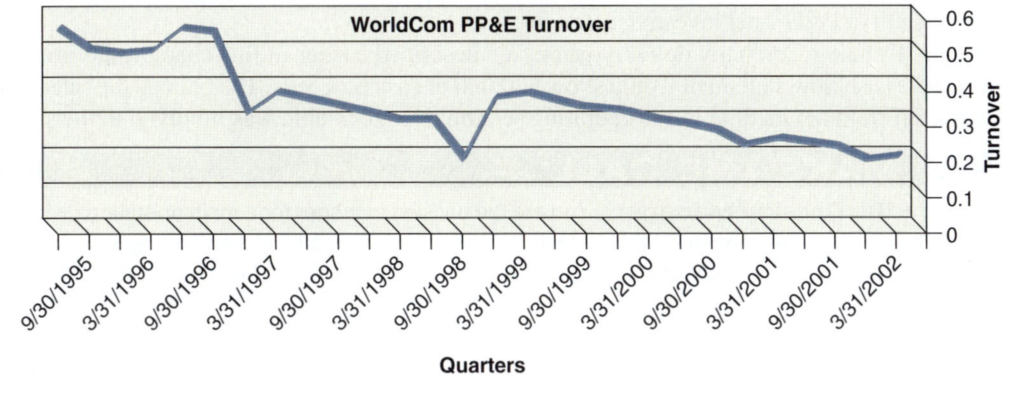

In this computation, $885 million in land cost is not included in the denominator because it is not a depreciable asset.

If assets were replaced evenly each year, the average asset would be 50% depreciated. P&G's depreciable assets are slightly younger than this benchmark. If, for example, depreciable assets are 80% depreciated, we might need to project a higher level of capital expenditures to replace assets in the near future. On the other hand, a low percent depreciated implies that a company is utilizing newer assets. If the cost of purchasing assets is generally increasing, we would expect that owning newer assets would result in higher depreciation charges than would owning older assets. We also expect that older assets are less efficient and require higher maintenance costs.

Examining the ratios of P&G's competitors shows that all have percent depreciated ratios that are essentially the same. (The data for P&G are again for the fiscal year ended June 30, 2008.)

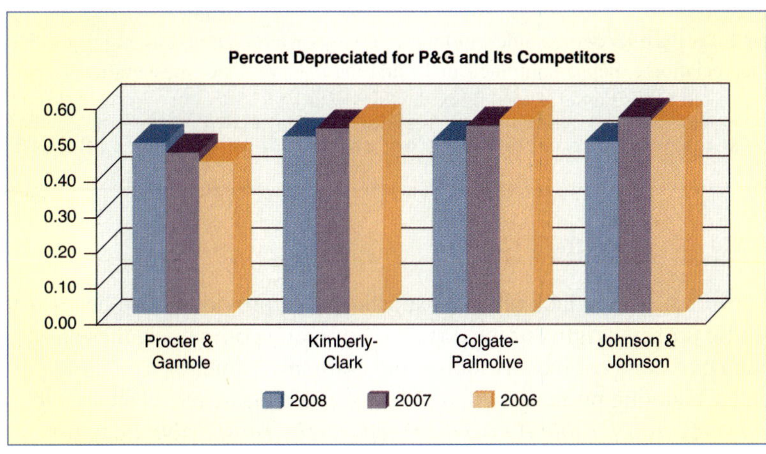

Cash Flow Effects

When cash is involved in the acquisition of plant or equipment, the cash amount is reported as a use of cash in the investment section of the statement of cash flows as discussed in Chapter 4. Any cash received from asset sales is reported as a source of cash. The investing section of Procter & Gamble's 2009 annual report is shown below.

	2009	2008	2007
INVESTING ACTIVITIES			
Capital expenditures.	(3,238)	(3,046)	(2,945)
Proceeds from asset sales	1,087	928	281
Acquisitions, net of cash acquired.	(368)	(381)	(492)
Change in investments	166	(50)	673
TOTAL INVESTING ACTIVITIES	(2,353)	(2,549)	(2,483)

In 2009, P&G paid cash of $3,238 million to acquire plant assets and received cash of $1,087 million on the disposal of plant and equipment. Losses (gains) on these disposal transactions would be added (subtracted) as adjustments in the operating section. Acquisitions of other companies amounted to about one-sixth of P&G's net investing activities.

For the Dehning Company delivery truck sale described earlier in this chapter, the investing section of the cash flow statement would show $30,000 of cash proceeds. The gain on the sale would be subtracted from net income in the operating section. No receivable was involved in the sale.

YOU MAKE THE CALL

You are the Division Manager   You are the division manager for a main operating division of your company. You are concerned that a declining PPE turnover is adversely affecting your division's profitability. What specific actions can you take to increase PPE turnover? [Answers on page 373]

MID-CHAPTER REVIEW

On January 2, Lev Company purchases equipment for use in fabrication of a part for one of its key products. The equipment costs $95,000, and its estimated useful life is five years, after which it is expected to be sold for $10,000.

Required
1. Compute depreciation expense for each year of the equipment's useful life for each of the following depreciation methods:
   a.   Straight-line
   b.   Double-declining-balance
2. Assume that Lev Company uses the straight-line depreciation method. Show the effects of these entries on the balance sheet and the income statement using the financial statement effects template. Prepare journal entries to record the initial purchase of the equipment on January 2 and the year-end depreciation adjustment on December 31, and post the journal entries to T-accounts.
3. Show how the equipment is reported on Lev's balance sheet at the end of the third year assuming straight-line depreciation.
4. Assume that this is the only depreciable asset the company owns and that it uses straight-line depreciation. Using the depreciation expense computed in *1a* and the balance sheet presentation from *3*, estimate the percent depreciated for this asset at the end of the third year.

The solution to this review problem can be found on pages 384–385.

INTANGIBLE ASSETS

LO5 Describe the accounting and reporting for intangible assets.

Intangible assets are assets that lack physical substance but provide future benefits to the owner in the form of specific property rights or legal rights. For many companies, these assets have become an important source of competitive advantage and company value.

For financial accounting purposes, intangible assets are classified as either *separately transferable or not separately transferable (Goodwill). Separately transferable* intangible assets generally fall into one of two categories. The first category is assets that are the product of contractual or other legal rights. These intangibles include patents, trademarks, copyrights, franchises, license agreements, broadcast rights, mineral rights, and noncompetition agreements. The second category of intangible assets includes benefits that are not contractually or legally defined, but can be separated from the company and sold, transferred, or exchanged. Examples include customer lists, unpatented technology, formulas, processes, and databases. Procter & Gamble reports its intangible assets on its 2009 balance sheet in just two categories ($ in millions): Goodwill $56,512; Trademarks and Other Intangible Assets $32,606. The majority of these assets resulted from the acquisition of **The Gillette Company**. Goodwill, which can not be separately transferred, is discussed later in this chapter.

The issues involved in reporting intangible assets are conceptually similar to those of accounting for property, plant and equipment. We must first decide which costs to capitalize and then we need to determine how and when those costs will be transferred to the income statement. However, intangible assets often pose a particularly difficult problem for accountants. This problem arises because the benefits provided by these assets are uncertain and difficult to quantify. In addition, the useful life of an intangible asset is often impossible to estimate with confidence.

As was the case with property, plant and equipment, intangible assets are either purchased from another individual or company or internally developed. Like PPE assets, the cost of purchased intangible assets is capitalized. Unlike PPE assets, though, we generally do not capitalize the cost of internally developed intangible assets. Research and development (R&D) costs, and the patents and technologies that are created as a result of R&D, serve as useful examples.

Research and Development Costs

R&D activities are a major expenditure for most companies, especially for those in technology and pharmaceutical industries where R&D expenses can exceed 10% of revenues. These expenses include employment costs for R&D personnel, R&D-related contract services, and R&D plant asset costs.

Companies invest millions of dollars in R&D because they expect that the future benefits resulting from these activities will eventually exceed the costs. Successful R&D activities create new products that can be sold and new technologies that can be utilized to create and sustain a competitive advantage. Unfortunately, only a fraction of R&D projects reach commercial production and it is difficult to predict which projects will be successful. Moreover, it is often difficult to predict when the benefits will be realized, even if the project is successful.

Because of the uncertainty surrounding the benefits of R&D, accounting for R&D activities follows a uniform method—*immediate recognition as an expense*, as described in Chapter 7. This approach applies to all R&D costs incurred prior to the start of commercial production, including the salaries and wages of personnel engaged in R&D activities, the cost of materials and supplies, and the equipment and facilities used in the project. Should any of the R&D activities prove successful, the benefits should result in higher net income in future periods. Costs incurred internally to develop new software products do not satisfy the capitalization requirement of providing expected future profits until the technological feasibility of the product is established. Therefore, until the feasibility requirement can be met, these costs are expensed.

IFRS REPORTING INSIGHT

IFRS Recognition of Internally-Developed Intangibles   Under International Financial Reporting Standards, development costs can be capitalized as intangible assets when specific criteria are met. For instance, the company must be able to demonstrate that it has the ability and the intention to complete the development process and to produce an intangible asset that will generate future benefits through use or sale.

If equipment and facilities are purchased for a specific R&D project, their cost is expensed immediately even though their useful life would typically extend beyond the current period. The expensing of R&D equipment and facilities is in stark contrast to the capitalization-and-depreciation of non-R&D plant assets. The expensing of R&D plant assets is mandated unless those assets have alternative future uses (in other R&D projects or otherwise). For example, a general research facility housing multi-use lab equipment should be capitalized and depreciated like any other depreciable asset. However, project-directed research buildings and equipment with no alternate uses must be expensed.

Patents

Successful research and development activity often leads a company to obtain a **patent** for its discoveries. A patent is an exclusive right to produce a product or use a technology. Patents are granted to protect the inventor of the new product or technology by preventing other companies from copying the innovation. The market value of a patent depends on the commercial success of the product or technology. For example, a patent on the formula for a new drug to treat diabetes could be worth billions of dollars.

If a patent is purchased from the inventor, the purchase price is capitalized and reported in the balance sheet as an intangible asset. On the other hand, if the patent is developed internally, only the legal costs and registration fees are capitalized. The R&D cost to develop the new product or technology is expensed as incurred. This accounting illustrates the marked difference between purchased and internally created intangible assets.

Copyrights

A copyright is an exclusive right granted by the government to an individual author, composer, play writer, or similar individual for the life of the creator plus 70 years. Corporations can also obtain a copyright for varying periods set by law. Copyrights, like patents, can be acquired. The acquisition cost would be capitalized and amortized over the expected remaining economic life.

Trademarks

A **trademark** is a registered name, logo, package design, image, jingle, or slogan that is associated with a product. Many trademarks are easily recognizable, such as the **Nike** "swoosh," the shape of a **Coca-Cola** bottle, **McDonald's** golden arches, and the musical tones played in computer advertisements featuring **Intel** computer chips. Companies spend millions of dollars developing and protecting trademarks and their value is enhanced by advertising programs that increase their recognition. If a trademark is purchased from another company, the purchase price is capitalized. However, the cost of internally developed trademarks is expensed as incurred. Likewise, all advertising costs are expensed immediately, even if the value of a trademark is enhanced by the advertisement. For this reason, many trademarks are not presented in the balance sheet.

Franchise Rights

A **franchise** is a contractual agreement that gives a company the right to operate a particular business in an area for a particular period of time. For example, a franchise may give the owner the right to operate a number of fast-food restaurants in a particular geographic region for twenty years. *Operating rights* and *licenses* are similar to franchise rights, except that they are typically granted by government agencies. Most franchise rights are purchased and, as a result, the purchase price should be capitalized and presented as an intangible asset in the balance sheet.

Amortization and Impairment of Identifiable Intangible Assets

When intangible assets are acquired and capitalized, a determination must be made as to whether the asset has a **definite life**. Examples of intangible assets with definite lives include patents and franchise rights. An intangible asset with a definite life must be *amortized* over the expected useful life of the asset. **Amortization** is the systematic allocation of the cost of an intangible asset to the periods benefited. Like the depreciation of tangible assets, amortization is motivated by the matching principle.

Amortization expense is generally recorded using the straight-line method. The expense is included in the income statement as a component of operating income, and is often included among selling, general and administrative expenses. The cost of the intangible asset is presented in the balance sheet net of accumulated amortization.

Amortization   To illustrate, assume that Landsman Company spent $100,000 in early 2010 to purchase a patent. The entry to record the capitalization of this cost follows.

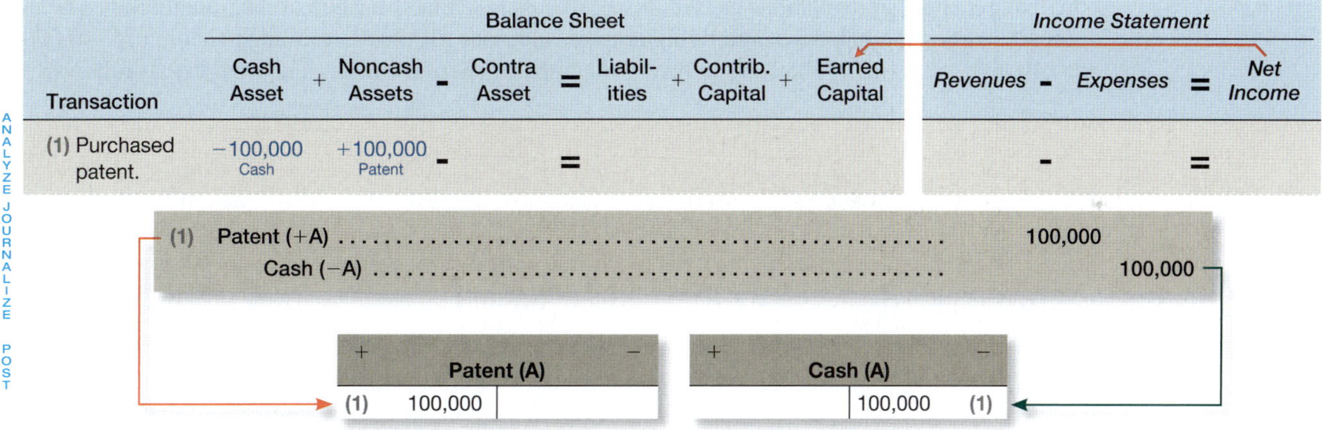

Although the patent had a remaining legal life of 12 years, Landsman estimated that the useful life of the patent was 5 years. Thus the intangible asset has a definite life. The entry to record the annual amortization expense at the end of 2010 follows.

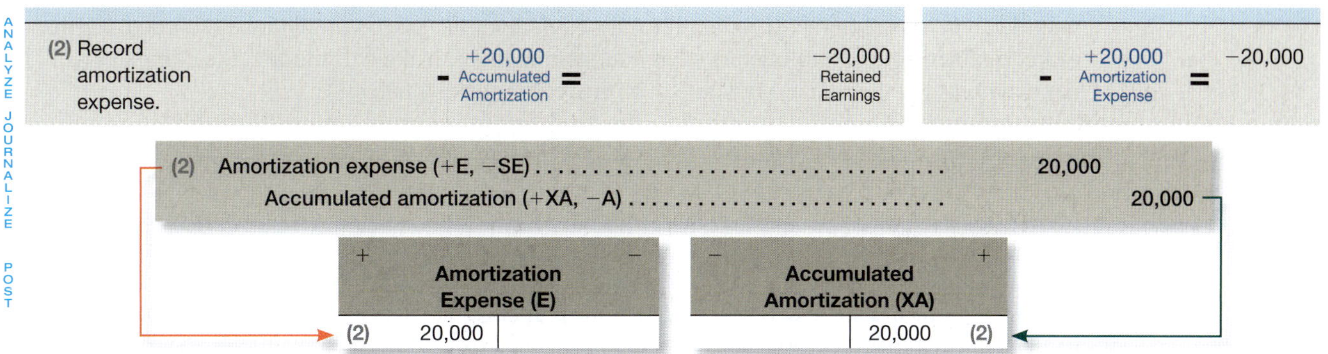

Impairment   Some transferable intangible assets, such as some trademarks, have indefinite lives. For these assets, the expected useful life extends far enough into the future that it is impossible for management to estimate a useful life. An intangible asset with an indefinite life should not be amortized until the useful life of the asset can be specified. That is, no expense is recorded until management can reasonably estimate the useful life of the asset.

Although intangible assets with indefinite lives are not subject to amortization, they must be tested annually to determine if their value has been impaired. The impairment test for intangibles is slightly different from the impairment test used to evaluate PPE assets. The intangible asset is impaired if the book value of the asset exceeds its fair market value and the write-down is equal to the difference between the book value and the market value.

To illustrate, assume that Norell Company purchased a trademark in 2006 for $240,000 and determined that the intangible asset had an indefinite life. The entry to record the purchase of the trademark follows.

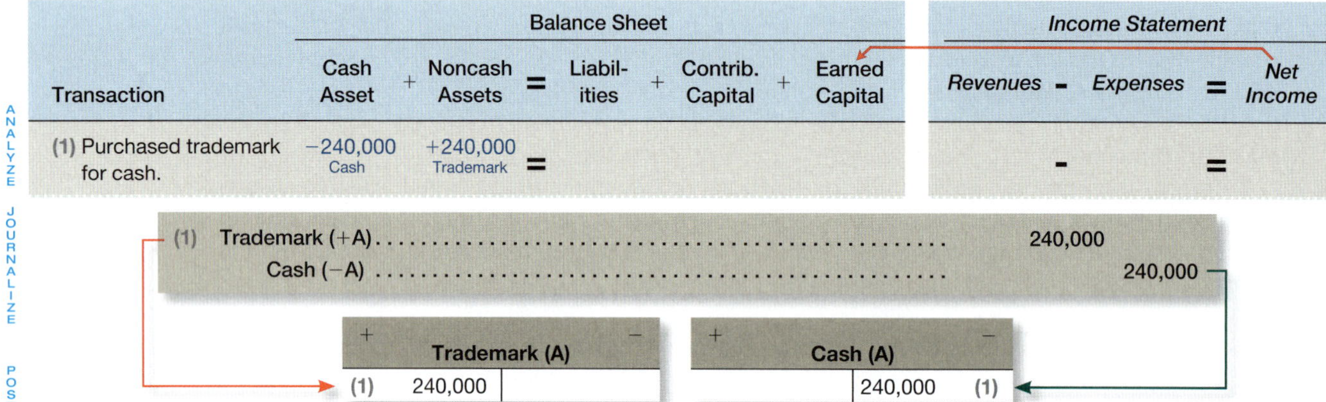

In 2010, changes in regulations caused Norell to conclude that the value of the trademark had been impaired. They estimated the current fair market value was $100,000, resulting in a loss of $140,000 ($240,000 – $100,000). The entry to record the impairment of the trademark would be as follows.

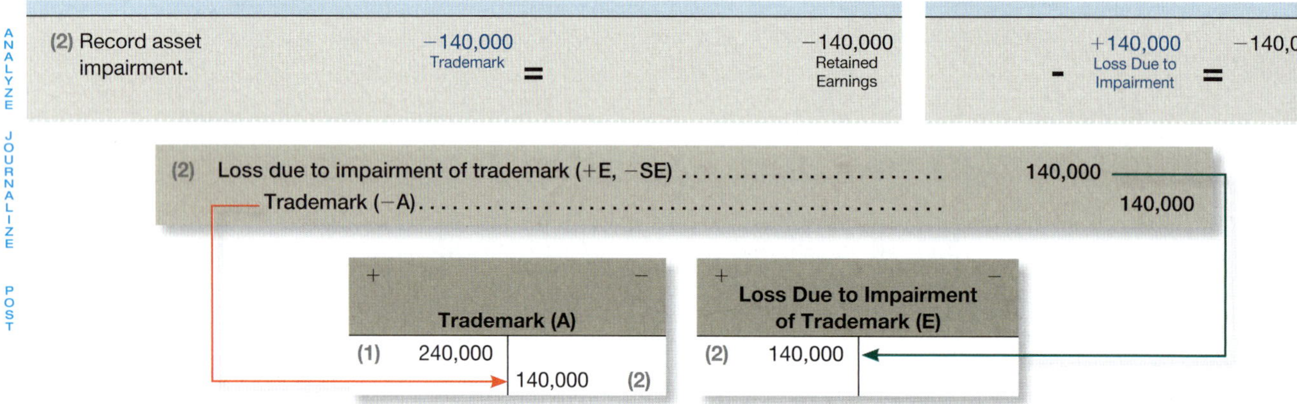

If the value of the trademark subsequently decreases further, additional impairment losses would be recorded. However, increases in the fair market value of the asset would not be recorded. Furthermore, if, at any time, Norell determined that the trademark had a definite life, the company would begin amortizing the remaining value over the remaining estimated life.

Goodwill

Goodwill is an intangible asset that is recorded only when one company acquires another company. **Goodwill** is defined as the excess of the purchase price paid for a company over the fair market value of its *identifiable* net assets (assets minus the liabilities assumed). The identifiable net assets include any *identifiable intangible assets* acquired in the purchase. Therefore, goodwill can neither be linked to any identifiable source, nor can it be sold or separated from the company. It represents the value of the acquired company above and beyond the specific identifiable assets listed on the balance sheet.

By definition, goodwill has an indefinite life. Once it is recorded in the balance sheet, it is not amortized. Instead, it is subject to an annual impairment test. Goodwill is impaired when the market value of the acquired business is less than the recorded book value. If this occurs, goodwill is written down to an imputed value. The goodwill write-down (also called a goodwill write-off) results in the immediate transfer of some or all of a company's goodwill book value from the balance sheet to the income statement as an expense. The book value of the intangible assets is immediately reduced and a corresponding expense is reported in the income statement. Like the impairment write-down of tangible assets, the write-down of goodwill is a discretionary expense whose amount and timing are largely determined by management (with auditor acceptance).

It is commonplace to see goodwill impairment write-downs related to unsuccessful acquisitions, particularly those from the acquisition boom of the late 1990s and the recent recession of 2008–2009. Goodwill write-downs usually represent material amounts. For example, **Time Warner Inc.** wrote off $54 billion of goodwill in the second quarter of 2002, which arose from the $106 billion merger of AOL and Time-Warner. This write-off exceeded the *total revenues* of 483 of the Fortune 500 companies (*Fortune*, 2002). Goodwill write-downs are usually nonrecurring, but are typically reported by companies in income from continuing operations. For analysis purpose we normally classify them as operating and nonrecurring.

IFRS REPORTING INSIGHT

Goodwill Impairment   Goodwill, similar to property, plant and equipment, must be periodically evaluated for impairment. However, once impaired, it can not be revalued upward.

Footnote Disclosures

The book value of P&G intangible assets exceeded 66% of its total asset value in 2009 (refer to Exhibit 8.1). In addition to the amount reported in the balance sheet, P&G provides the following in footnotes 1 and 2 that more fully describes its intangible asset accounting.

Note 1: Summary of Significant Accounting Policies—Goodwill and Other Intangible Assets

Goodwill and indefinite-lived brands are not amortized, but are evaluated for impairment annually or when indicators of a potential impairment are present. Our impairment testing of goodwill is performed separately from our impairment testing of individual indefinite-lived intangibles. The annual evaluation for impairment of goodwill and indefinite-lived intangibles is based on valuation models that incorporate assumptions and internal projections of expected future cash flows and operating plans. We believe such assumptions are also comparable to those that would be used by other marketplace participants.

We have a number of acquired brands that have been determined to have indefinite lives due to the nature of our business. We evaluate a number of factors to determine whether an indefinite life is appropriate, including the competitive environment, market share, brand history, product life cycles, operating plans, and the macroeconomic environment of the countries in which the brands are sold. When certain events or changes in operating conditions occur, an impairment assessment is performed and indefinite-lived brands may be adjusted to a determinable life.

The cost of intangible assets with determinable useful lives is amortized to reflect the pattern of economic benefits consumed, either on a straight-line or accelerated basis over the estimated periods benefited. Patents, technology and other intangibles with contractual terms are generally amortized over their respective legal or contractual lives. Customer relationships and other noncontractual intangible assets with determinable lives are amortized over periods generally ranging from 5 to 40 years. When certain events or changes in operating conditions occur, an impairment assessment is performed and lives of intangible assets with determinable lives may be adjusted.

Procter & Gamble's largest intangible is goodwill ($56.5 billion). The acquisition of Gillette in 2006 resulted in the recognition of $35.3 billion of goodwill, more than currently reported in 2009. Because goodwill is not amortized, we know that some assets involving goodwill have been sold or were impaired. Furthermore, P&G actually paid $53.4 billion for Gillette, and allocated $29.7 billion to other intangibles.

Note 2: Goodwill and Intangible Assets
Identifiable intangible assets were comprised of:

	2009		2008	
	Gross Carrying Amount	Accumulated Amortization	Gross Carrying Amount	Accumulated Amortization
Intangible assets with determinable lives				
Brands	$ 3,580	$1,253	$ 3,564	$1,032
Patents and technology	3,168	1,332	3,188	1,077
Customer relationships	1,853	411	1,947	353
Other	320	210	333	209
Total	8,921	3,206	9,032	2,671
Brands with indefinite lives	26,891	–	27,872	–
Total	$35,812	$3,206	$36,904	$2,671

There are two observations that we can make from the above disclosures. First, P&G has purchased a significant amount of intangible assets by acquiring other companies. We can infer this from the large amount of goodwill assets reported in the balance sheet ($56.5 billion). The major acquisition was Gillette in 2006. Second, most of P&G's identifiable intangible assets are trademarks and most have indefinite lives. Hence, we might expect that the amount of amortization expense in any given year would be small, as indicated by the total in the above table. However, goodwill impairment write-offs could be substantial in any given year.

Analysis Implications

LO6 Analyze the effects of tangible and intangible assets on key performance measures.

Because internally generated intangible assets are not capitalized, an important component of a company's assets is potentially hidden from users of the financial statements. Moreover, differential treatment of purchased and internally created assets makes it difficult to compare companies. If one company generates its patents and trademarks internally, while another company purchases these intangibles, their balance sheets can differ dramatically, even if the two companies are otherwise very similar.

These hidden intangible assets can distort our analysis of the financial statements. For example, when a company expenses R&D costs, especially R&D equipment and facilities that can potentially benefit more than one period, both the income statement and balance sheet are distorted. Net income, assets, and stockholders' equity are all understated.

The income statement effects may be small if a company regularly purchases R&D assets and the amount of purchases is relatively constant from year to year. Specifically, after the average useful life is reached, say in 5 to 10 years, the expensing of current-year purchases will be approximately the same as the depreciation that would have been reported had the assets been capitalized. Thus, the income statement effect is mitigated. However, the recorded assets and equity are still understated. This accounting produces an upward bias in asset turnover ratios and ROE.

NATURAL RESOURCES

LO7 Explain the accounting for acquisition and depletion of natural resources.

An important asset for some companies consists of natural resources such as oil reserves, mineral deposits, or timberlands. These assets are often referred to as **wasting assets**, because the asset is consumed as it is used.

Cost Capitalization and Depletion

The acquisition cost of a natural resource, plus any costs incurred to prepare the asset for its intended use, should be capitalized and reported among PPE assets in the balance sheet.

When the natural resource is used or extracted, inventory is created. The cost of the resource is transferred from the long-term asset account into inventory and, once the inventory is sold, to the income statement as cost of goods sold. The process of transferring costs from the resource account into inventory is called **depletion**.

Depletion is very much like depreciation of tangible operating assets, except that the amount of depletion recorded each period should reflect the amount of the resource that was actually extracted or used up during that period. As a result, depletion is usually calculated using the units-of-production method. The depletion rate is calculated as follows:

$$\text{Depletion rate per unit consumed} = \frac{\text{Acquisition cost} - \text{Residual value}}{\text{Estimated quantity of resource available}}$$

The calculation requires an estimate of the quantity of the resource available, which usually requires the assistance of experts, such as geologists or engineers, who are trained to make these determinations.

Depletion Recognition

Once the depletion rate is determined, the annual depletion is calculated by multiplying the depletion rate times the quantity of resource depleted during the period. This amount is subtracted from the natural resource asset account and added to inventory. Ultimately, the depletion becomes part of the cost of goods sold when the inventory is sold.

Illustration   To illustrate accounting for natural resources, assume that Nichols Company acquired property for $3,000,000 for the development of a copper mine. Nichols estimated that the mine would produce 1,500,000 tons of ore, and once mining is completed, the property could be sold for $600,000. The entry to record the purchase of the property follows.

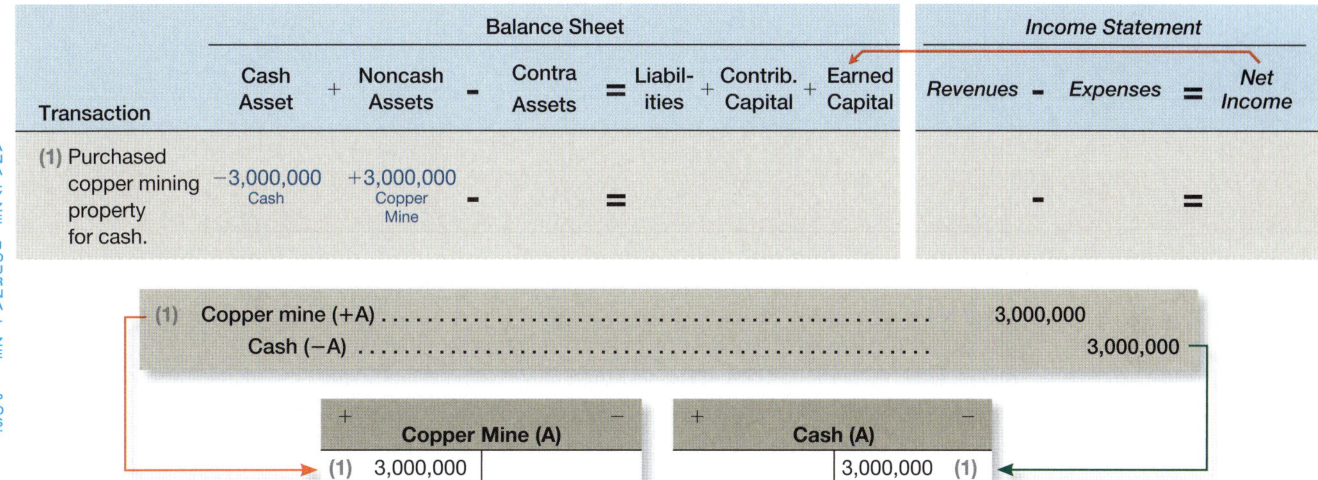

The depletion expense per ton of ore would be calculated as follows:

$$\frac{\$3,000,000 - \$600,000}{1,500,000 \text{ tons}} = 1.60 \text{ per ton}$$

If Nichols were to recover 250,000 tons of ore in 2010, the entry to record depletion of the copper mine would be as follows:

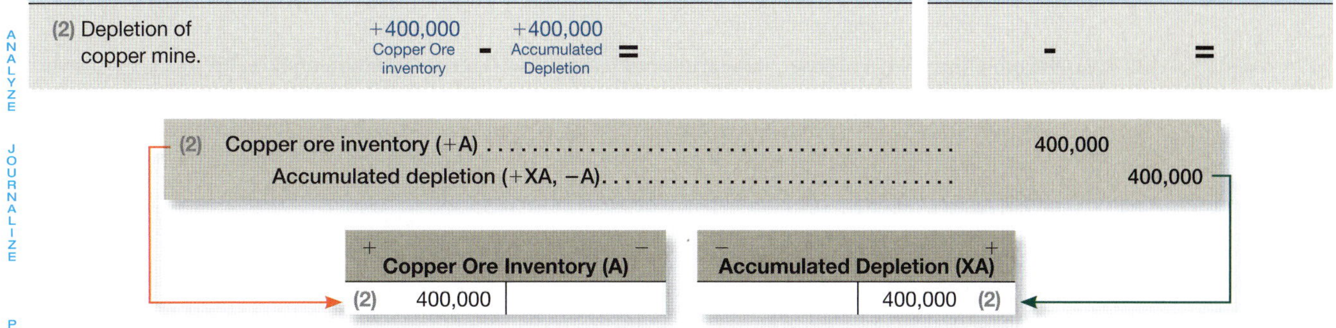

The depletion would remain in the inventory account until the copper ore is sold.

CHAPTER-END REVIEW

In 2010, Bowen Company's R&D department developed a new production process that significantly reduced the time and cost required to manufacture its product. R&D costs were $120,000. The process was patented on July 1, 2010. Legal costs and fees to acquire the patent totalled $12,500. Bowen estimated the useful life of the patent at 10 years.

On July 1, 2012, Bowen sold the nonexclusive right to use the new process to Kennedy Company for $90,000. Because Bowen retained the patent, the agreement allows Kennedy to use, but not sell, the new technology for a period of 5 years. Both Bowen Company and Kennedy Company have December 31 fiscal years.

On July 1, 2014, another competitor obtained a patent on a new process that made Bowen's patent obsolete.

Required

1. How should Bowen Company account for the R&D costs and legal costs incurred to obtain the patent? Show the effects of these entries using the financial statement effects template, prepare the appropriate journal entries necessary to account for the costs incurred in 2010, and post the entries to T-accounts.
2. What amount of amortization expense would Bowen record each year? Show the effects of these transactions using the financial statement effects template, prepare a journal entry to record amortization expense on December 31, 2010, and post the entries to T-accounts.
3. How would Kennedy Company record the acquisition of the rights to use the new technology? Show the effects of this transaction using the financial statement effects template, prepare a journal entry to record the purchase of the technology rights, and post the entry to T-accounts.
4. What effect would the new patent registered by the other competitor have on Bowen Company? On Kennedy Company? Show the effects of this transaction using the financial statement effects template, prepare a journal entry to record the impairment loss for Kennedy Company, and post the entry to T-accounts.

The solution to this review problem can be found on pages 385–387.

SUMMARY

LO1 **Describe and distinguish between tangible and intangible assets. (p. 352)**
- Tangible assets, including land, buildings, machinery, and equipment are assets with physical substance and are usually classified as property, plant and equipment.
- Intangible assets are long-term assets lacking in physical substance, such as patents, trademarks, franchise rights and goodwill.

LO2 **Determine which costs to capitalize and report as assets and which costs to expense. (p. 354)**
- All costs incurred to acquire an asset and prepare it for its intended use should be capitalized and reported in the balance sheet.
- The cost of self-constructed assets should include all costs incurred during construction, including the interest cost of financing the construction.

LO3 **Apply different depreciation methods to allocate the cost of assets over time. (p. 356)**
- Depreciation methods generally fall into three categories:
  (1) Straight-line depreciation
  (2) Accelerated depreciation, such as the double-declining-balance method
  (3) Units-of-production method

LO4 **Determine the effects of asset sales and impairments on financial statements. (p. 359)**
- The sale of a long-term asset will result in a gain or loss if the proceeds from the sale are greater than or less than the book value of the asset.
- If the expected benefits (undiscounted cash flows) derived from an asset fall below its book value, the asset is impaired and should be written down to fair market value.

LO5 **Describe the accounting and reporting for intangible assets. (p. 364)**
- For the most part, internally generated intangible asserts are not recognized in the balance sheet.
- Intangible assets purchased from other companies are capitalized and presented separately in the balance sheet.
- Intangible assets with definite lives are amortized using the straight-line method.
- Intangible assets with indefinite lives are not amortized.

Analyze the effects of tangible and intangible assets on key performance measures. (p. 370)　　**LO6**

- PPE turnover and long-term asset turnover ratios provide insights into the capital intensity of a company and how efficiently the company is utilizing these investments.
- The ratio of accumulated depreciation divided by the cost of depreciable assets measures the percent depreciated.

Explain the accounting for acquisition and depletion of natural resources. (p. 370)　　**LO7**

- Natural resources are valued at acquisition cost plus the cost to develop the resource.
- Natural resources are depleted using a method similar to the units-of-production method.

GUIDANCE ANSWERS . . . YOU MAKE THE CALL

You are the Company Accountant　Any cost that is necessary in order to bring an asset into service should be capitalized as a part of the cost of the asset. In this case, your company cannot build an office building on this property until the oil well is properly capped. Therefore, the $40,000 cost of capping the oil well should be capitalized as part of the cost of the land.

You are the Division Manager　To increase PPE turnover one must either increase sales or reduce PPE assets. The first step is to identify unproductive or inefficiently utilized assets. Unnecessary assets can be sold, and some processes can be outsourced. Also, by reducing down time, effective maintenance practices will increase asset productivity.

KEY RATIOS

$$\text{PPE Turnover (PPET)} = \frac{\text{Sales revenue}}{\text{Average PP\&E}} \qquad \text{Percent depreciated} = \frac{\text{Accumulated depreciation}}{\text{Cost of depreciable asset}}$$

KEY TERMS

Accelerated depreciation (p. 357)

Accumulated depreciation (pp. 355, 356)

Amortization (p. 367)

Book value (BV) (p. 356)

Capital expenditures (p. 354)

Capitalized (p. 353)

Capitalized interest (p. 354)

Definite life (p. 367)

Depletion (p. 370)

Depreciation (p. 354)

Depreciation base (p. 356)

Depreciation rate (p. 356)

Double-declining-balance (DDB) method (p. 357)

Franchise (p. 367)

Goodwill (p. 368)

Impairment (p. 360)

Intangible assets (p. 352)

Patent (p. 366)

Residual (or salvage) value (p. 356)

Straight-line method (p. 356)

Tangible assets (p. 352)

Trademark (p. 366)

Units-of-production method (p. 358)

Useful life (p. 356)

Wasting assets (p. 370)

MULTIPLE CHOICE

1. Burgstahler Corporation bought a lot to construct a new corporate office building. An older building on the lot was razed immediately so that the office building could be constructed. The cost of razing the older building should be
   a. recorded as part of the cost of the land.
   b. written off as a loss in the year of purchase.
   c. written off as an extraordinary item in the year of purchase.
   d. recorded as part of the cost of the new building.

2. The purpose of recording periodic depreciation of long-term PPE assets is to
   a. report declining asset values on the balance sheet.
   b. allocate asset costs over the periods benefited by use of the assets.
   c. account for costs to reflect the change in general price levels.
   d. set aside funds to replace assets when their economic usefulness expires.

3. When the estimate of an asset's useful life is changed,
   a. depreciation expense for all past periods must be recalculated.
   b. there is no change in the amount of depreciation expense recorded for future years.
   c. only depreciation expense for current and future years is affected.
   d. only depreciation expense in the current year is affected.

4. If the sale of a depreciable asset results in a loss, the proceeds from the sale were
   a. less than current market value.
   b. greater than cost.
   c. greater than book value.
   d. less than book value.

5. Which of the following principles best describes the current method of accounting for research and development costs?
   a. Revenue recognition method
   b. Systematic and rational allocation
   c. Immediate recognition as an expense
   d. Income tax minimization

6. Goodwill should be recorded in the balance sheet as an intangible asset only when
   a. it is sold to another company.
   b. it is acquired through the purchase of another business.
   c. a company reports above-normal earnings for five or more consecutive years.
   d. it can be established that a definite benefit or advantage has resulted from some item such as an excellent reputation for service.

DISCUSSION QUESTIONS

Q8-1. How should companies account for costs, such as maintenance or improvements, which are incurred after an asset is acquired?

Q8-2. What is the effect of capitalized interest on the income statement in the period that an asset is constructed? What is the effect in future periods?

Q8-3. Why is the recognition of depreciation expense necessary to properly match revenues and expenses?

Q8-4. Why do companies use accelerated depreciation for income tax purposes, when the total depreciation taken over the asset's useful life is identical to straight-line depreciation?

Q8-5. How should a company treat a change in an asset's estimated useful life or residual value? Which period(s)—past, present, or future—is affected by this change?

Q8-6. What factors determine the gain or loss from the sale of a long-term operating asset?

Q8-7. When is a PPE asset considered to be impaired? How is the impairment loss determined?

Q8-8. What is the proper accounting treatment for research and development costs? Why are R&D costs not capitalized under GAAP?

Q8-9. Why are some intangible assets amortized while others are not? What is meant by an intangible asset with an "indefinite life"?

Q8-10. Under what circumstances should a company report goodwill in its balance sheet? What is the effect of goodwill on the income statement?

**Assignments with the WebAssign. logo in the margin are available in WebAssign.
See the Preface of the book for details.**

MINI EXERCISES

LO2 **M8-11. Determining Whether to Capitalize or Expense**
For each of the following items, indicate whether the cost should be capitalized or expensed immediately:
   a. Paid $1,200 for routine maintenance of machinery
   b. Paid $5,400 to rent equipment for two years
   c. Paid $2,000 to equip the production line with new instruments that measure quality

    d.   Paid $20,000 to repair the roof on the building
    e.   Paid $1,600 to refurbish a machine, thereby extending its useful life
    f.   Purchased a patent for $5,000

M8-12. Computing Depreciation under Straight-Line and Double-Declining-Balance   LO3
A delivery van costing $18,000 is expected to have a $1,500 salvage value at the end of its useful life of 5 years. Assume that the truck was purchased on January 1, 2010. Compute the depreciation expense for 2011 (its second year) under each of the following depreciation methods:
    a.   Straight-line
    b.   Double-declining-balance

M8-13. Computing Depreciation under Alternative Methods   LO3
Equipment costing $130,000 is expected to have a residual value of $10,000 at the end of its six-year useful life. The equipment is metered so that the number of units processed is counted. The equipment is designed to process 1,000,000 units in its lifetime. In 2010 and 2011, the equipment processed 180,000 units and 140,000 units respectively. Calculate the depreciation expense for 2010 and 2011 using each of the following methods:
    a.   Straight-line
    b.   Double-declining-balance
    c.   Units of production

M8-14. Recording the Sale of PPE Assets   LO4
As part of a renovation of its showroom, O'Keefe Auto Dealership sold furniture and fixtures that were eight years old for $3,500 in cash. The assets had been purchased for $40,000 and had been depreciated using the straight-line method with no residual value and a useful life of ten years.
    a.   Prepare a journal entry to record this transaction.
    b.   Show how the sale of the furniture and fixtures affects the balance sheet and income statement using the financial statement effects template.

M8-15. Recording the Sale of PPE Assets   LO4
Gaver Company sold machinery that had originally cost $75,000 for $25,000 in cash. The machinery was three years old and had been depreciated using the double-declining-balance method assuming a five-year useful life and a residual value of $5,000.
    a.   Prepare a journal entry to record this sale.
    b.   Using the financial statement effects template, show how the sale of the machinery affects the balance sheet and income statement.

M8-16. Computing Depreciation under Straight-Line and Double-Declining-Balance for Partial Years   LO3
A machine costing $145,800 is purchased on May 1, 2010. The machine is expected to be obsolete after three years (36 months) and, thereafter, no longer useful to the company. The estimated salvage value is $5,400. Compute depreciation expense for both 2010 and 2011 under each of the following depreciation methods:
    a.   Straight-line
    b.   Double-declining-balance

M8-17. Accounting for Research and Development under IFRS   LO1, LO2, LO5
The following information on **Nokia Corp.**'s treatment of research and development is extracted from its 2008 financial statements. Nokia Corporation is a public limited liability company incorporated under the laws of the Republic of Finland. The company produces and markets mobile telecommunication equipment and reports under IFRS.

   NOKIA CORP.
   NYSE :: NOK

    a.   How does the reporting under IFRS differ from reporting under U.S. GAAP for research and development?
    b.   Can you suggest several specific R&D costs that would always be expensed under IFRS?
    c.   Should the amounts capitalized be tested annually for impairment?

Research and development
Research and development costs are expensed as they are incurred, except for certain development costs, which are capitalized when it is probable that a development project will generate future economic benefits, and certain criteria, including commercial and technological feasibility, have been met. Capitalized development costs, comprising direct labor and related overhead, are amortized on a systematic basis over their expected useful lives between two and five years.

During 2007, Nokia Siemens Networks recorded an impairment charge on capitalized development costs of €27 million. The impairment loss was determined as the full carrying amount of the capitalized development programs costs related to products that will not be included in future product portfolios. This impairment amount is included within research and development expenses in the consolidated profit and loss statement.

Capitalized development costs are subject to regular assessments of recoverability based on anticipated future revenues, including the impact of changes in technology. Unamortized capitalized development costs determined to be in excess of their recoverable amounts are expensed immediately.

LO3 M8-18. Computing Double-Declining-Balance Depreciation

DeFond Company purchased equipment for $50,000. For each of the following sets of assumptions, prepare a depreciation schedule (all years) for this equipment assuming that DeFond uses the double-declining-balance depreciation method.

Useful life	Residual value
a. Four years	$8,000
b. Five years	$3,000
c. Ten years	$1,000

LO7 M8-19. Computing and Recording Depletion Expense

The Nelson Oil Company estimated that the oil reserve that it acquired would produce 4 million barrels of oil. The company extracted 300,000 barrels the first year, 500,000 barrels in 2011, and 600,000 barrels in 2012. Nelson paid $32,000,000 for the oil reserve.

a. Compute the depletion expense for each year—2010, 2011, and 2012.

b. Prepare the journal entries to record (i) the acquisition of the oil reserve, and (ii) the depletion for 2010.

c. Open T-accounts and post the entries from part *b* in the accounts.

LO6 M8-20. Computing and Comparing PPE Turnover for Two Companies

TEXAS INSTRUMENTS INCORPORATED
NYSE :: TXN

INTEL CORPORATION
NASDAQ :: INTC

Texas Instruments Incorporated and **Intel Corporation** report the following information:

($ millions)	Texas Instruments		Intel Corp	
	Sales	PPE, net	Sales	PPE, net
2008	$12,501	$3,304	$37,586	$17,544
2007	13,835	3,609	38,334	16,918

a. Compute the 2008 PPE turnover for both companies. Comment on any difference you observe.

b. Discuss ways in which high-tech manufacturing companies like these can increase their PPE turnover.

LO5, LO6 M8-21. Assessing Research and Development Expenses

ABBOTT LABORATORIES
NYSE :: ABT

Abbott Laboratories reports the following income statement (in partial form):

Year Ended December 31 ($ 000s)	2008
Net sales	$29,527,552
Cost of products sold	12,612,022
Research and development*	2,786,067
Selling, general and administrative	8,435,624
Total operating cost and expenses	23,833,713
Operating earnings	$ 5,693,839

* including acquired in-process and collaborations R&D

a. Compute the percent of net sales that Abbott Laboratories spends on research and development (R&D). How would you assess the appropriateness of its R&D expense level?

b. Using the financial statement effects template, describe how the accounting for R&D expenditures affects Abbot Laboratories' balance sheet and income statement.

EXERCISES

E8-22. Recording Asset Acquisition, Depreciation, and Disposal
LO2, LO3, LO4

On January 2, 2011, Hutton Company acquired a machine for $85,000. In addition to the purchase price, Hutton spent $2,000 for shipping and installation, and $2,500 to calibrate the machine prior to use. The company estimates that the machine has a useful life of five years and residual value of $7,000.

a. Prepare journal entries to record the acquisition costs.

b. Calculate the annual depreciation expense using straight-line depreciation and prepare a journal entry to record depreciation expense for 2011.

c. On December 31, 2014, Hutton sold the machine to another company for $12,000. Prepare the necessary journal entry to record the sale.

E8-23. Computing Straight-Line and Double-Declining-Balance Depreciation
LO3

On January 2, Haskins Company purchases a laser cutting machine for use in fabrication of a part for one of its key products. The machine cost $80,000, and its estimated useful life is five years, after which the expected salvage value is $5,000. Compute depreciation expense for each year of the machine's useful life under each of the following depreciation methods:

a. Straight-line

b. Double-declining-balance

E8-24. Computing Depreciation, Asset Book Value, and Gain or Loss on Asset Sale
LO3, LO4

Sloan Company uses its own executive charter plane that originally cost $800,000. It has recorded straight-line depreciation on the plane for six full years, with an $80,000 expected salvage value at the end of its estimated 10-year useful life. Sloan disposes of the plane at the end of the sixth year.

a. At the disposal date, what is the (1) cumulative depreciation expense and (2) net book value of the plane?

b. Prepare a journal entry to record the disposal of the plane assuming that the sales price is
1. Cash equal to the book value of the plane.
2. $195,000 cash.
3. $600,000 cash.

E8-25. Computing Straight-Line and Double-Declining-Balance Depreciation
LO3

On January 2, 2010, Dechow Company purchases a machine to help manufacture a part for one of its key products. The machine cost $218,700 and is estimated to have a useful life of six years, with an expected salvage value of $23,400.

Compute each year's depreciation expense for 2010 and 2011 for each of the following depreciation methods.

a. Straight-line

b. Double-declining-balance

E8-26. Computing Depreciation, Asset Book Value, and Gain or Loss on Asset Sale
LO3, LO4

Palepu Company owns and operates a delivery van that originally cost $27,200. Straight-line depreciation on the van has been recorded for three years, with a $2,000 expected salvage value at the end of its estimated six-year useful life. Depreciation was last recorded at the end of the third year, at which time Palepu disposes of this van.

a. Compute the net book value of the van on the sale date.

b. Compute the gain or loss on sale of the van if its sales price is for:
1. Cash equal to book value (of van).
2. $15,000 cash.
3. $12,000 cash.

E8-27. Computing Depreciation and Accounting for a Change of Estimate
LO3

Lambert Company acquired machinery costing $110,000 on January 2, 2010. At that time, Lambert estimated that the useful life of the equipment was 6 years and that the residual value would be $15,000 at the end of its useful life. Compute depreciation expense for this asset for 2010, 2011, and 2012 using the

a. straight-line method.

b. double-declining-balance method.

c. Assume that on January 2, 2012, Lambert revised its estimate of the useful life to 7 years and changed its estimate of the residual value to $10,000. What effect would this have on depreciation expense in 2012 for each of the above depreciation methods?

LO3 E8-28. Computing Depreciation and Accounting for a Change of Estimate

In January 2010, Rankine Company paid $8,500,000 for land and a building. An appraisal estimated that the land had a fair market value of $2,500,000 and the building was worth $6,000,000. Rankine estimated that the useful life of the building was 30 years, with no residual value.

    a.   Calculate annual depreciation expense using the straight-line method.

    b.   Calculate depreciation for 2010 and 2011 using the double-declining-balance method.

    c.   Assume that in 2012, Rankine changed its estimate of the useful life of the building to 25 years. If the company is using the double-declining-balance method of depreciation, what amount of depreciation expense would Rankine record in 2012?

LO6 E8-29. Estimating the Percent Depreciated

Web**Assign**.

DEERE & COMPANY
NYSE :: DE

The property and equipment footnote from the **Deere & Company** balance sheet follows ($ millions):

PROPERTY AND DEPRECIATION

A summary of property and equipment at October 31, 2008, in millions of dollars follows:

	Useful Lives (Years)	2008
Land		$ 95
Buildings and building equipment	25	1,880
Machinery and equipment	11	4,147
Dies, patterns, tools, etc.	7	933
All other	5	651
Construction in progress		833
Total at cost		8,539
Less accumulated depreciation		4,411
Property and equipment—net		$4,128

During 2008, the company reported $467 million of depreciation expense.

    Estimate the percent depreciated of Deere's depreciable assets. How do you interpret this figure?

LO6 E8-30. Computing and Evaluating Receivables, Inventory, and PPE Turnovers

Web**Assign**.

3M COMPANY
NYSE :: MMM

3M Company reports the following financial statement amounts in its 10-K report:

($ millions)	Sales	Cost of Sales	Receivables	Inventories	PPE, net
2008	$25,269	$13,379	$3,195	$3,013	$6,886
2007	24,462	12,735	3,362	2,852	6,582
2006	22,923	11,713	3,102	2,601	5,907

    a.   Compute the receivables, inventory, and PPE turnover ratios for both 2008 and 2007.

    b.   What changes are evident in the turnover rates of 3M for these years? Discuss ways in which a company such as 3M can improve its turnover within each of these three areas.

LO1, LO5 E8-31. Identifying and Accounting for Intangible Assets

Web**Assign**.

In 2011, Holthausen Company acquired the assets of Leftwich Company including several intangible assets. These include a patent on Leftwich's primary product, a device called a plentiscope. Leftwich carried the patent on its books for $1,500, but Holthausen believes that the fair market value is $200,000. The patent expires in seven years, but competitors can be expected to develop competing patents within three years. Holthausen believes that, with expected technological improvements, the product is marketable for at least 20 years.

    The registration of the trademark for the Leftwich name is scheduled to expire in 15 years. However, the Leftwich brand name, which Holthausen believes is worth $500,000, could be applied to related products for many years beyond that.

    As part of the acquisition, Leftwich's principal researcher left the company. As part of the acquisition, he signed a five-year noncompetition agreement that prevents him from developing competing products. Holthausen paid the scientist $300,000 to sign the agreement.

    a.   What amount should be capitalized for each of the identifiable intangible assets?

    b.   What amount of amortization expense should Holthausen record in 2011 for each asset?

E8-32. **Computing and Recording Depletion Expense**   LO7

In 2010, Eldenburg Mining Company purchased land for $7,200,000 that had a natural resource reserve estimated to be 500,000 tons. Development and road construction costs on the land were $420,000, and a building was constructed at a cost of $50,000. When the natural resources are completely extracted, the land has an estimated residual value of $1,200,000. In addition, the cost to restore the property to comply with environmental regulations is estimated to be $800,000. Production in 2010 and 2011 was 60,000 tons and 85,000 tons, respectively.

a.   Compute the depletion charge for 2010 and 2011. (You should include depreciation on the building, if any, as part of the depletion charge.)

b.   Prepare a journal entry to record each year's depletion expense as determined in part *a*.

E8-33. **Computing and Interpreting Percent Depreciated and PPE Turnover**   LO6

The following footnote is from Note 4 to the 2008 10-K of **Adams Golf, Inc.**, a Texas-based   **ADAMS GOLF, INC.**
manufacturer of golf equipment ($ thousands):   NASDAQ :: ADGF

Property and Equipment, net
Property and equipment consist of the following at December 31, 2008 and 2007:

	2008	2007
Equipment	$ 2,442	$ 2,296
Computers and software	7,716	7,924
Furniture and fixtures	940	770
Leaseholds improvements	182	188
Accumulated depreciation and amortization	(10,070)	(10,132)
	$ 1,210	$ 1,046

a.   Calculate the percent depreciated ratio for each year.

b.   Sales revenue totaled $91,451 in 2008 (all values are in $ thousands). Calculate the PPE turnover ratio (PPET).

c.   Comment on these ratios. Do you notice anything unusual?

E8-34. **Evaluating R&D Expenditures of Companies**   LO5

R&D intensity is measured by the ratio of research and development expense to sales revenue. The   **ADAMS GOLF, INC.**
following table compares the R&D intensity for various companies.   NASDAQ :: ADGF

**CALLAWAY GOLF
COMPANY**
NYSE :: ELY

Company	R&D Intensity
Adams Golf, Inc.	4.11%
Callaway Golf Company.	2.63%
Apple Inc.	3.41%
Dell Inc.	1.09%
Intel Corporation	15.22%
Motorola, Inc.	13.63%
Baxter International Inc.	7.03%
Advanced Medical Optics, Inc.	6.41%
Pfizer Inc.	16.45%
Merck & Co.	20.15%

APPLE INC.
NASDAQ :: AAPL

DELL INC.
NASDAQ :: DELL

INTEL CORPORATION
NASDAQ :: INTC

MOTOROLA, INC.
NYSE :: MOT

**BAXTER
INTERNATIONAL INC.**
NYSE :: BAX

**ADVANCED MEDICAL
OPTICS, INC.**
NYSE :: EYE

PFIZER INC.
NYSE :: PFE

MERCK & CO.
NYSE :: MRK

a.   Comment on the differences among these companies. To what extent are the differences related to industry affiliation?

b.   What other factors (besides industry affiliation) might determine a company's R&D intensity?

E8-35. **Computing and Assessing Plant Asset Impairment**   LO4

Zeibart Company purchases equipment for $225,000 on July 1, 2006, with an estimated useful life   
of 10 years and expected salvage value of $25,000. Straight-line depreciation is used. On July 1,
2010, economic factors cause the market value of the equipment to decline to $90,000. On this
date, Zeibart examines the equipment for impairment and estimates $125,000 in future cash inflows
related to use of this equipment.

a.   Is the equipment impaired at July 1, 2010? Explain.

b.   If the equipment is impaired on July 1, 2010, compute the impairment loss and prepare a journal entry to record the loss.

c.   What amount of depreciation expense would Zeibart record for the 12 months from July 1, 2010 through June 30, 2011? Prepare a journal entry to record this depreciation expense.

    d.   Using the financial statement effects template, show how the entries in parts *b* and *c* affect Zeibart Company's balance sheet and income statement.

PROBLEMS

LO4 **P8-36.** **Computing and Recording Gain or Loss on Asset Sale**

WebAssign.

NORDSTROM INC.
NYSE :: JWN

The following information was provided in a footnote to the 2005 10-K report of **Nordstrom, Inc.**.

Note 10: Land, Buildings and Equipment

($ thousands)	January 29, 2005	January 31, 2004
Total land, buildings and equipment, at cost	$4,090,973	$3,928,936
Less accumulated depreciation and amortization	(2,310,607)	(2,121,158)
Land, buildings and equipment, net	$1,780,366	$1,807,778

Also, its cash flow statement revealed the following information ($ thousands):

- Depreciation expense was $264,769.
- Capital expenditures totaled $246,851.
- Proceeds from the sale of land, buildings and equipment totaled $5,473.

Required

Using this information, prepare a journal entry to record the sale of land, buildings and equipment.

LO5 **P8-37.** **Analyzing and Assessing Research and Development Expenses**

WebAssign.

AGILENT TECHNOLOGIES, INC.
NYSE :: A

HEWLETT-PACKARD COMPANY
NYSE :: HPQ

Agilent Technologies, Inc., the high-tech spin-off from **Hewlett-Packard Company**, reports the following operating profit for 2008 in its 10-K ($ millions):

Net revenue	
Products	$4,804
Services and other	970
Total net revenue	5,774
Costs and expenses	
Cost of products	2,030
Cost of services and other	548
Total costs	2,578
Research and development	704
Selling, general and administrative	1,697
Total costs and expenses	4,979
Income from operations	$ 795

Required

a.   What percentage of its total net revenue is Agilent spending on research and development?

b.   How are its balance sheet and income statement affected by the accounting for R&D costs?

c.   Agilent has reduced spending on research and development by over $300 million since 2003. What impact has this reduction had on operating profits? What are the potential long-term implications of this reduction in R&D?

LO1, LO2, LO4, LO5 **P8-38.** **Analyzing PPE Accounts and Recording PPE Transactions, Including Discontinued Operations**

TARGET CORPORATION
NYSE :: TGT

The 2008 and 2007 income statements and balance sheets (asset section only) for **Target Corporation** follow, along with its footnote describing Target's accounting for property and equipment. Target's cash flow statement for fiscal 2008 reported capital expenditures of $3,547 million and a loss on disposal of property and equipment of $33 million net.

Required

Prepare journal entries to record the following for 2008:

a.   Depreciation expense

b.   Amortization expense

c.   Capital expenditures

d.   Disposal of property, plant and equipment

e.   Repair and maintenance costs

Property and Equipment

Property and equipment are recorded at cost, less accumulated depreciation. Depreciation is computed using the straight-line method over estimated useful lives or lease term if shorter. We amortize leasehold improvements purchased after the beginning of the initial lease term over the shorter of the assets' useful lives or a term that includes the original lease term, plus any renewals that are reasonably assured at the date the leasehold improvements are acquired. Depreciation expense for 2008, 2007, and 2006 was $1,804 million, $1,644 million, and $1,509 million, respectively. For income tax purposes, accelerated depreciation methods are generally used. Repair and maintenance costs are expensed as incurred and were $609 million in 2008, $592 million in 2007, and $532 million in 2006. Facility pre-opening costs, including supplies and payroll, are expensed as incurred.

TARGET CORPORATION
Consolidated Income Statements

(in millions)	2008	2007
Sales	$62,884	$61,471
Net credit card revenues	2,064	1,896
Total revenues	64,948	63,367
Cost of sales	44,157	42,929
Selling, general and administrative expenses	12,954	12,670
Credit card expenses	1,609	837
Depreciation and amortization	1,826	1,659
Earnings before interest and taxes	4,402	5,272
Net interest expense	866	647
Earnings before income taxes	3,536	4,625
Provision for income taxes	1,322	1,776
Net earnings	$ 2,214	$ 2,849

TARGET CORPORATION
Consolidated Balance Sheets (Asset Section Only)

(in millions)	January 31, 2009	February 2, 2008
Assets		
Cash and cash equivalents	$ 864	$ 2,450
Credit card receivables, net	8,084	8,054
Inventory	6,705	6,780
Other current assets	1,835	1,622
Total current assets	17,488	18,906
Property and equipment		
Land	5,767	5,522
Buildings and improvements	20,430	18,329
Fixtures and equipment	4,270	3,858
Computer hardware and software	2,586	2,421
Construction-in-progress	1,763	1,852
Accumulated depreciation	(9,060)	(7,887)
Property and equipment, net	25,756	24,095
Other noncurrent assets	862	1,559
Total assets	$44,106	$44,560

P8-39. Reporting PPE Transactions and Asset Impairment

LO1, LO2, LO4

WILLIAMS-SONOMA
NYSE :: WSM

Note B from the fiscal 2008 10-K report of **Williams-Sonoma, Inc.**, (February 1, 2009) follows. Its cash flow statement reported that the company made capital expenditures of $191,789,000 during fiscal 2008 and recorded depreciation of $148,083,000. In addition, the company reported a loss on the disposal of property and equipment of $39,317,000.

Required

Prepare journal entries to record the following for fiscal 2008:

a. Depreciation expense
b. Capital expenditures
c. Impairment of property and equipment
d. Disposal of property and equipment

Note B: Property and Equipment
Property and equipment consists of the following:

Dollars in thousands	Feb. 1, 2009	Feb. 3, 2008
Leasehold improvements	$ 828,414	$ 800,658
Fixtures and equipment	578,259	544,152
Capitalized software	247,613	196,311
Land and buildings	133,406	133,435
Corporate systems projects in progress	66,469	96,493
Construction in progress	25,866	23,384
Corporate aircraft	11,503	48,668
Total	1,891,530	1,843,101
Accumulated depreciation and amortization	(949,311)	(862,026)
Property and equipment—net	$ 942,219	$ 981,075

We review the carrying value of all long-lived assets for impairment whenever events or changes in circumstances indicate that the carrying value of an asset may not be recoverable. We review for impairment all stores for which current or projected cash flows from operations are either negative or nominal, or the construction costs are significantly in excess of the amount originally expected. Impairment results when the carrying value of the assets exceeds the undiscounted future cash flows over the remaining life of the lease. Our estimate of undiscounted future cash flows over the lease term (typically 5 to 22 years) is based upon our experience, historical operations of the stores, and estimates of future store profitability and economic conditions. The future estimates of store profitability and economic conditions require estimating such factors as sales growth, gross margin, employment rates, lease escalations, inflation on operating expenses and the overall economics of the retail industry for up to 20 years in the future, and are therefore subject to variability and difficult to predict. If a long-lived asset is found to be impaired, the amount recognized for impairment is equal to the difference between the net carrying value and the asset's fair value. The fair value is estimated based upon future cash flows (discounted at a rate that is commensurate with the risk and approximates our weighted average cost of capital). We recorded impairment charges related to our underperforming retail stores of $33,995,000, $1,082,000, and $5,629,000 in selling, general and administrative expenses in fiscal 2008, fiscal 2007, and fiscal 2006, respectively.

CASES AND PROJECTS

LO4   **C8-40.**   **Interpreting and Reporting Property, Plant, and Equipment (PPE) Expenditures and Impairments**

ROHM AND HAAS COMPANY
NYSE :: ROH

Rohm and Haas Company is a global specialty materials company. The firm concentrates in three industry technology segments: circuit boards (e.g., flat panel display), packaging, and semiconductors. The following data is taken from the company's 2008 10-K.

Note 15: Land, Buildings, and Equipment, net

(in millions)	2008	2007	Estimated Life (Years)
Land	$ 154	$ 146	
Buildings and improvements	1,863	1,855	10–50
Machinery and equipment	6,278	6,155	3–20
Capitalized interest	367	352	11
Construction in progress	231	271	
Land, buildings, and equipment, gross	8,893	8,779	
Less: Accumulated depreciation	6,040	5,908	
Total	$2,853	$2,871	

In 2008, 2007, and 2006, respectively, interest costs of $15 million, $12 million, and $11 million were capitalized. Amortization of such capitalized costs included in depreciation expense was $14 million in 2008, 2007, and 2006, respectively.

Depreciation expense was $467 million, $412 million, and $403 million in 2008, 2007, and 2006, respectively.

Rohm and Haas reports asset impairments net of gains on sale of $42 million in 2008.

Land, Buildings, and Equipment, and Accumulated Depreciation

The value of our land, buildings, and equipment is carried at cost less accumulated depreciation. The principal lives (in years) used in determining depreciation rates of various assets are: buildings and improvements (10–50); machinery and equipment (5–20); automobiles, trucks and tank cars (3–10); furniture and fixtures, laboratory equipment and other assets (5–10); capitalized software (5–7); capitalized interest (11). The principle life used in determining the depreciation rate for leasehold improvements is the years remaining in the lease term or the useful life (in years) of the asset, whichever is shorter. These assets are depreciated over their estimated useful lives using straight-line methods. Construction costs, labor, and applicable overhead related to construction and installation of these assets are capitalized. Expenditures for additions and improvements that extend the lives or increase the capacity of plant assets are capitalized. Maintenance and repair costs for these assets are expensed as incurred. Repair and maintenance costs associated with planned major maintenance activities are expensed as incurred and are included in cost of goods sold. Replacements and betterment costs are capitalized. The cost and related accumulated depreciation of our assets are removed from the accounting records when they are retired or disposed.

Rohm and Haas reports the following additional information in their 2008 income statement and balance sheet ($ millions).

	2008	2007
Net sales	$9,575	$8,897
Cost of goods sold	7,165	6,430
Inventories	1,099	1,024

Required

a. Compute the turnover for PPE and inventory for 2008. Given an average PPE turnover of around 5 for the industry, does Rohm and Haas appear to be capital intensive? Justify. Why might an observer with just this limited information conclude that the company has additional operating assets?

b. Calculate the percentage depreciation of its operational assets. What implications does the result suggest for the company's future cash flows?

c. Rohm and Haas reports depreciation expense of $467 million in 2008. Estimate the average useful life of its depreciable assets.

d. Rohm and Haas purchased $520 million of PPE for cash, and sold PPE for cash of $15 million while recording a gain of $4 million. Create the necessary journal entries to reflect the asset purchases, this year's depreciation charge and the impairment of $42 million noted in requirement *e*.

e. Rohm and Haas reports asset impairments of $42 million in 2008. What impact does this charge have on Rohm and Haas's operating income and its cash flows for 2008? What implications do these impairments suggest for the future?

C8-41. **Managing Operating Assets to Improve Performance. A Management Application**   LO6
Return on a company's net operating assets is commonly used to evaluate financial performance. One way to increase performance is to focus on operating assets.

Required

Indicate how this might be done in relation to the following asset categories. Indicate also any potential problems a given action might create.

a. Receivables

b. Inventories

c. Property, plant, and equipment

d. Intangibles

LO4, LO5, LO6   **C8-42.   Determining the Effects of Capitalizing Versus Expensing Software Development Costs**

TAKE-TWO INTERACTIVE SOFTWARE, INC.
NASDAQ::TTWO

The following excerpts are taken from the 2008 annual report of **Take-Two Interactive Software, Inc.**, a maker and distributor of video games. All amounts are in thousands of U.S dollars.

Income Statement Information:	2008	2007
Net sales	$1,537,530	$ 981,791
Cost of goods sold	988,695	735,034
Operating expenses	432,982	374,455
Income from operations	$ 115,853	$(127,698)

Information from the Management Discussion, Balance Sheet and Note 5 :

Software Development Costs

The Company capitalizes internal software development costs including third-party production and other costs, subsequent to establishing technological feasibility of a title. Amortization of such costs as a component of cost of goods sold is recorded on a title-by-title basis commencing when the product is released and is based on the greater of the proportion of the current year's revenues to the total expected revenues to be recorded over the life of the title or the straight-line method over the remaining estimated useful life of the title, whichever is greater. At each balance sheet date, the Company evaluates the recoverability of capitalized software costs based on undiscounted future cash flows and charges to cost of goods sold any amounts that are deemed unrecoverable.

Capitalized Software Development Costs	2008	2007
Beginning balance	$175,906	$116,561
Additions	145,623	166,020
Amortization and write-downs	(146,102)	(106,675)
Ending balance	$108,428	$ 64,332

Assume an income tax rate of 35% where necessary.

Required:

a.   You wish to compare the performance of Take-Two with one of its competitors, **Electronic Arts, Inc.** However, Electronic Arts does not capitalize any significant amounts of its software development costs. Estimate Take-Two's 2008 Income from operations if it did not capitalize any software development costs. *Briefly* explain your adjustment(s).

b.   Is there any indication that Take-Two might have changed its software amortization estimates from 2007 to 2008? Explain *briefly*.

SOLUTIONS TO REVIEW PROBLEMS

Mid-Chapter Review

Solution

1*a.* Straight-line Depreciation expense = ($95,000 − $10,000)/5 years = $17,000 per year

1*b.* Double-declining-balance (twice straight-line rate = 2 × (100%/5) = 40%

Year	Book Value × Rate	Depreciation Expense
1	$95,000 × 0.40 =	$38,000
2	($95,000 − $38,000) × 0.40 =	22,800
3	($95,000 − $60,800) × 0.40 =	13,680
4	($95,000 − $74,480) × 0.40 =	8,208
5	($95,000 − $82,688) × 0.40	2,312*

*The formula value of $4,925 is not reported because it would depreciate the asset below residual value. Only the $2,312 needed to reach residual value is depreciated.

2a.

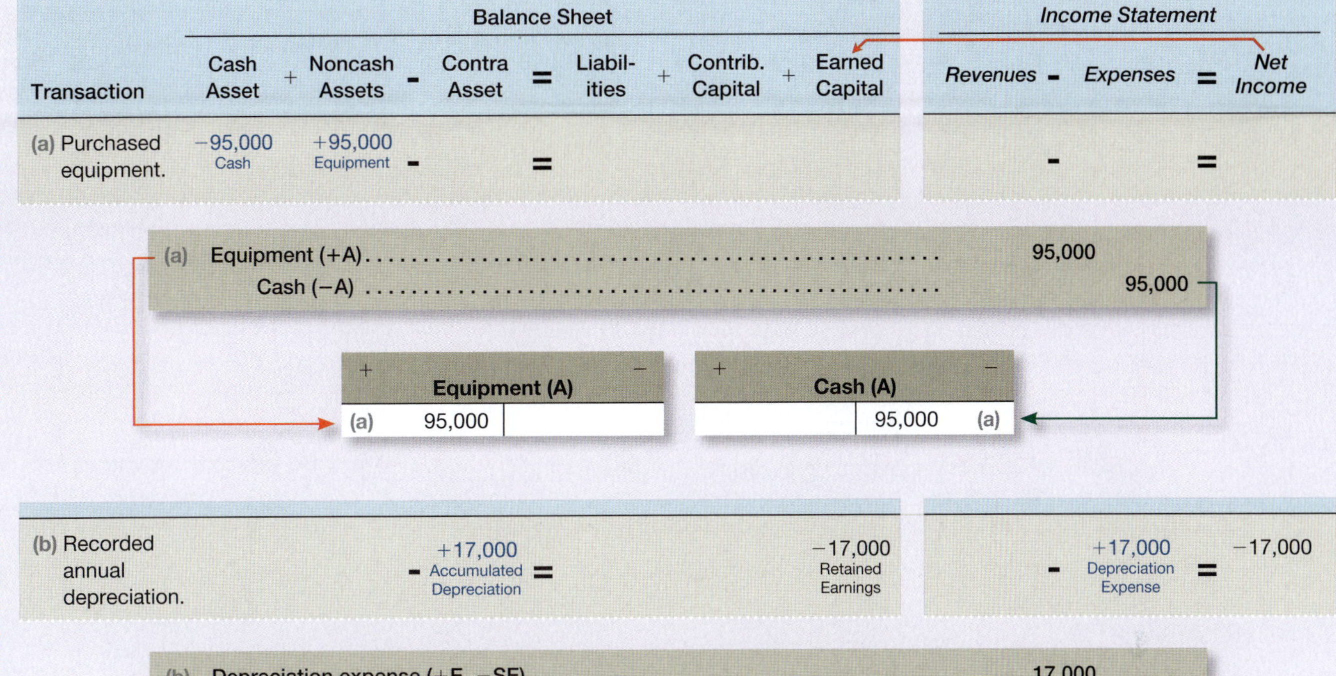

3.

Equipment, cost	$95,000
Less accumulated depreciation	51,000
Equipment, net	$44,000

Equipment is reported on Lev's balance sheet at its net book value of $44,000.

4. The percent depreciated is computed as: Accumulated Depreciation/Depreciable Asset Cost = $51,000/$95,000=53.7%. The equipment is more than one-half depreciated at the end of the third year. Again, the lack of knowledge of salvage value has resulted in an underestimate of the percent depreciated. Still, this estimate is useful in that we know that the company's asset is over one-half depreciated and is likely to require replacement in about 2 years (less than one-half of its useful life of 5 years). This replacement will become a cash outflow or financing need when it arises and should be considered in our projections of future cash flows.

Chapter-End Review

Solution

1. Bowen Company would expense the $120,000 in R&D costs in 2010. The $12,500 in legal fees to obtain the patent would be capitalized. As a result, the book value of the patent would be $12,500 on July 1, 2010. The entries to record these costs would be:

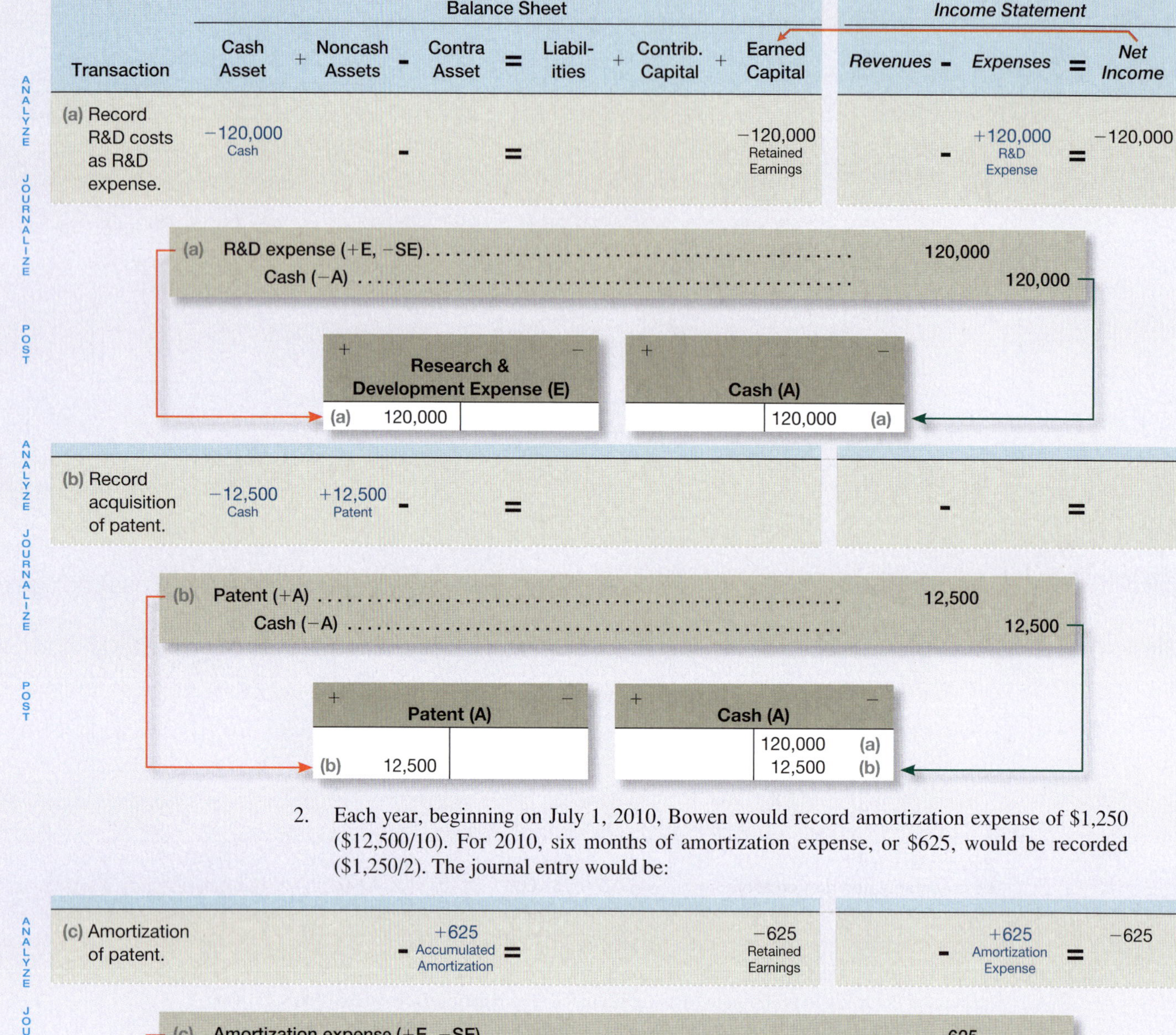

2. Each year, beginning on July 1, 2010, Bowen would record amortization expense of $1,250 ($12,500/10). For 2010, six months of amortization expense, or $625, would be recorded ($1,250/2). The journal entry would be:

3. Because Kennedy purchased the right to use the technology, the purchase price can be capitalized as an intangible asset and amortized over the five-year length of the agreement. Kennedy would record amortization expense of $18,000 ($90,000/5) each year, beginning July 1, 2012. (Bowen would recognize the $90,000 as revenue.) The journal entry that Kennedy Company would need to record the acquisition of the technology rights would be as follows:

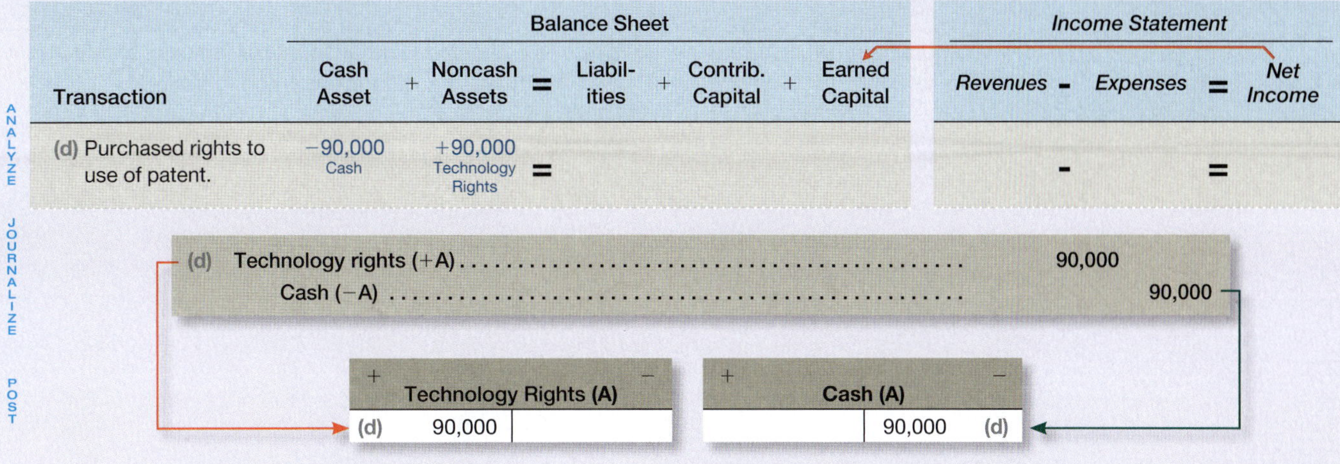

4. Given that the patent is obsolete, both Bowen Company and Kennedy Company would record impairment losses. Bowen would write off the unamortized balance in the patent account, resulting in a loss of $7,500 [$12,500 − ($1,250 × 4)]. Kennedy Company would write off the remaining value of the technology agreement, recording an impairment loss of $54,000 [$90,000 − ($18,000 × 2)]. Kennedy's journal entry would be:

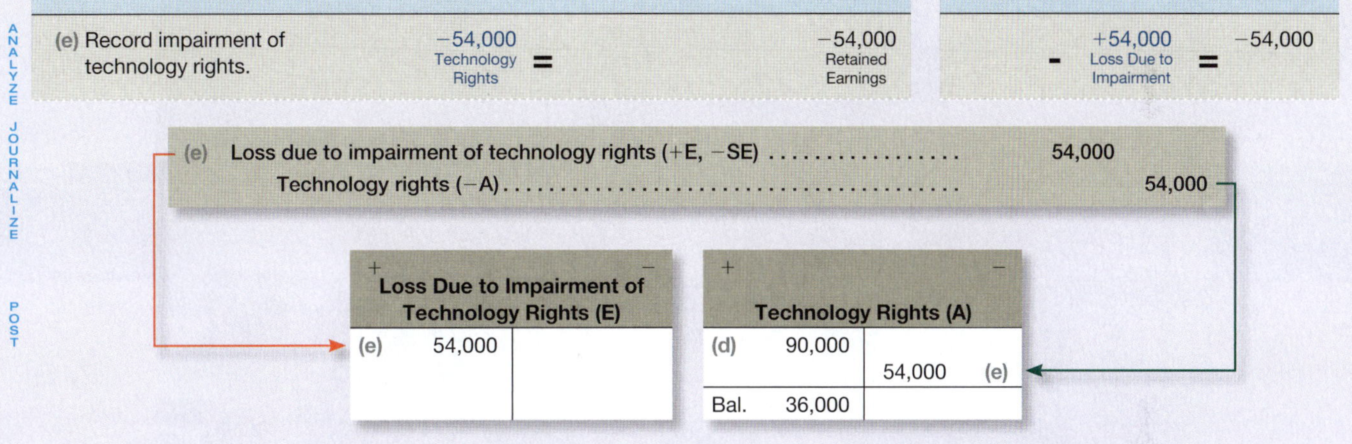

© Getty Images

Reporting and Analyzing Liabilities

In 2000, **Bell Atlantic Corporation** merged with **GTE** to form **Verizon Communications**. After its 2006 acquisition of **MCI Communications Corp.** and subsequent acquisition of **Alltel Corporation** in 2008, the corporation has become the world's largest provider of communications services. The firm recently ranked 17th in the United States and 1st in the telecommunications industry by revenues.

VERIZON
www.verizon.com

While revenues and operating profits have grown by 48% and 55%, respectively, since 2004, the company's stock price has not kept pace. The firm's stock price, which traded as high as $70 in late 1999, has recently traded at under $30 per share. The industry is experiencing increased competition fueled by **AT&T**'s acquisition of **Bell South**. Ivan Seidenberg, Verizon's CEO since mid-2002, has one of the toughest jobs in business as he attempts to fend off a host of competitors including **Comcast**, **Qwest**, **Sprint Nextel**, **DirecTV Group**, **AT&T**, and a host of others.

Seidenberg will be betting the firm on extending its fiber-optic service (FiOS) to 18 million homes—one-half its market—by 2010 at a cost of $23 billion. The firm is also faced with $55.1 billion of long-term debt not including $6.1 billion maturing in 2010, and $32.5 billion in accumulated employee benefit obligations. Fortunately, the firm's cash flow from operations remains strong at $26.6 billion. Seidenberg will need it all and more as he attempts to reposition the firm in the face of increased competition and mounting cash needs.

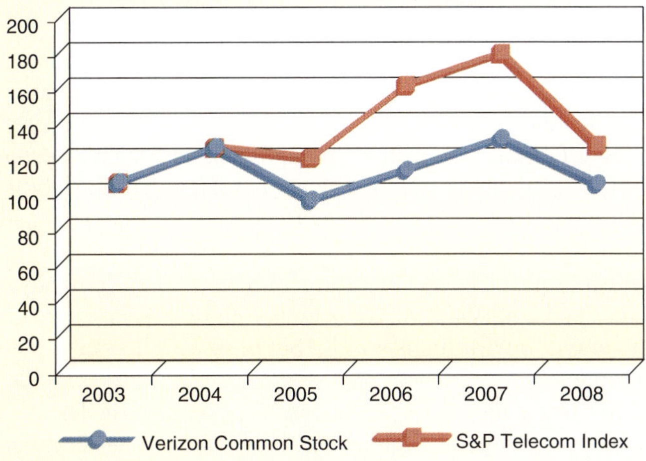

(continued on next page)

(continued from previous page)

This chapter focuses on liabilities—that is, short-term and long-term obligations. Liabilities (including debt) are one of two financing sources for a company. The other source is shareholder financing. Bonds and notes are a major part of most companies' liabilities. In this chapter, we show how to price liabilities and how the issuance and subsequent payment of the principal and interest on them affect financial statements. We also discuss the required disclosures that enable us to effectively analyze a company's ability to make its liability payments as they mature.

As Verizon faces increased competition from other telecom companies, cable, and Internet providers, it must continue to innovate in order to maintain its position as the industry leader. This objective will require large investments in technology and infrastructure, only part of which will come from its operating cash flow. To be successful, Seidenberg will need to manage Verizon's growing debt burden and efficiently allocate cash resources between strategic investments and debt payments.

Sources: *Fortune* 3/2007, 4/2007 and 2/2006; *Forbes* 4/2007; *Verizon* 2007, 2006, 2005, 2004 and 2003 Annual Reports; *Verizon* 2008, 2007, 2006, 2005, 2004 and 2003 10-Ks.

CHAPTER ORGANIZATION

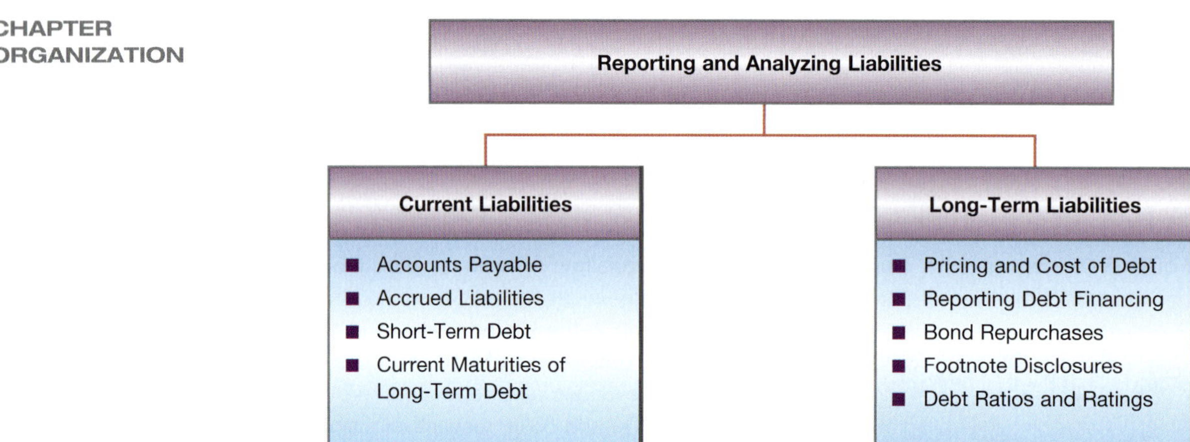

INTRODUCTION

The accounting equation (Assets = Liabilities + Equity) is a useful tool in helping us think about how the balance sheet and income statement are constructed, the linkages between the financial statements, and the effects of transactions on financial statements. The accounting equation is also useful in helping us think about the statements from another perspective, namely, how the business is financed (sources of funds) and how those resources are utilized (uses of funds). Consider the following representation of the accounting equation:

$$\textbf{Assets} \ = \ \textbf{Liabilities} + \textbf{Equity}$$
$$\textbf{Uses} \ = \ \textbf{Sources}$$

Assets represent investments that management has made. They include current assets such as cash, accounts receivable, and inventories. They also include long-term assets such as manufacturing and administrative facilities, as well as intangible assets, such as patents and trademarks. Most companies also invest a portion of funds in assets such as Treasury bills and money market funds that provide the liquidity a company needs to conduct transactions and to react to market opportunities and changes.

Just as asset disclosures provide us with information on where a company invests its funds, the disclosures on liabilities and equity inform us as to how those assets are financed. To be successful, a company must not only invest funds wisely, but must also be astute in the manner in which it finances those investments.

Companies hope to finance their assets at the lowest possible cost. The cost of financing assets with liabilities is the interest charged by the lender. While most long-term liabilities bear explicit interest rates, many current liabilities (such as accounts payable and accrued liabilities) are non-interest-bearing. This does not mean that these liabilities are cost-free. For example, while a supplier may offer interest-free credit terms, the cost of that credit is implicitly included in the price it charges for the goods or services it sells.

Current liabilities, as the name implies, are short-term in nature, generally requiring payment within the coming year. As a result, they are not a suitable source of funding for long-term assets that generate cash flows over several years. Instead, companies often finance long-term assets with long-term liabilities that require payments over several years, so that the cash outflows of the financing source match the cash inflows of the assets to which they relate.

When a company acquires assets, and finances them with liabilities, its **financial leverage** increases. Because the magnitude of required liability payments increases with the level of liability financing, those larger payments increase the chance of default should a downturn in business occur. Increasing levels of liabilities, then, make the company riskier to creditors who, consequently, demand a higher return on the financing they provide to the company. The assessment of default risk is part of liquidity and solvency analysis.

This chapter, along with Chapter 10, focuses on liabilities that are reported on the balance sheet and the corresponding interest costs reported in the income statement. All such liabilities represent probable, nondiscretionary, future obligations that are the result of events that have already occurred. Chapter 10 also addresses *off-balance sheet financing*, which encompasses future obligations that are reported in the notes, but not on the face of the balance sheet. An understanding of both on-balance sheet and off-balance sheet financing is central to evaluating a company's financial condition and assessing its risk of default.

CURRENT LIABILITIES

Liabilities are separated into current and long-term. Current liabilities are due within 1 year. Long-term liabilities are due beyond 1 year. The focus of this section is on current liabilities. Most current liabilities such as those related to utilities, wages, insurance, rent, and taxes, generate a corresponding impact on operating expenses. **Verizon**'s current liabilities as taken from its 2008 balance sheet follow.

At December 31 ($ millions)	2008	2007
Current liabilities		
Debt maturing within one year	$ 4,993	$ 2,954
Accounts payable and accrued liabilities	13,814	14,462
Other	7,099	7,325
Total current liabilities	$25,906	$24,741

Verizon reports three categories of current liabilities: (1) long-term liability (debt) obligations that are scheduled for payment in the upcoming year, (2) accounts payable and accrued liabilities, and (3) other current liabilities, which consist mainly of customer deposits, dividends declared but not yet paid, and miscellaneous short-term obligations too small to list separately.

It is helpful to separate current liabilities into operating and nonoperating components. These two components primarily consist of:

1. Current operating liabilities

    ■ **Accounts payable** Obligations to others for amounts owed on purchases of goods and services. These are usually non-interest-bearing.

    ■ **Accrued liabilities** Obligations for expenses incurred that have not been paid as of the end of the current period. These include, for example, accruals for employee wages earned but yet unpaid, accruals for taxes (usually quarterly) on payroll and current-period profits, and accruals for other liabilities such as rent, utilities, and insurance. Accruals are made to properly reflect the liabilities owed as of the statement date and the expenses incurred in the period. Each one is journalized by a debit to an expense account and a credit to a related liability.

- **Deferred performance liabilities** Obligations that will be satisfied, not by paying cash, but instead, by providing products or services to customers. Examples of deferred performance liabilities include customer deposits, unearned gift card revenues for retail companies, and liabilities for frequent flier programs offered by airlines.

2. Current nonoperating liabilities

- **Short-term interest-bearing debt** Short-term bank borrowings and notes expected to mature in whole or in part during the upcoming year; including any accrued interest payable on these obligations.

- **Current maturities of long-term debt** Long-term borrowings that are scheduled to mature in whole or in part during the upcoming year including any accrued interest for the period on these obligations.

The remainder of this section describes current liabilities.

Accounts Payable

LO1 Identify and account for current operating liabilities.

Accounts payable, which are part of current operating liabilities, arise from the purchase of goods and services from others. Accounts payable are normally non-interest-bearing and, thus, are an inexpensive financing source. Verizon reports $13,814 million in accounts payable and accrued liabilities as of December 31, 2008. Its accounts payable represent $3,856 million, or 28%, of this total amount.

Accounting for a typical purchase of goods on account costing $100, which results in accounts payable, and the ultimate sale of those goods for $140, collection of the receivable, and payment to the supplier follows:

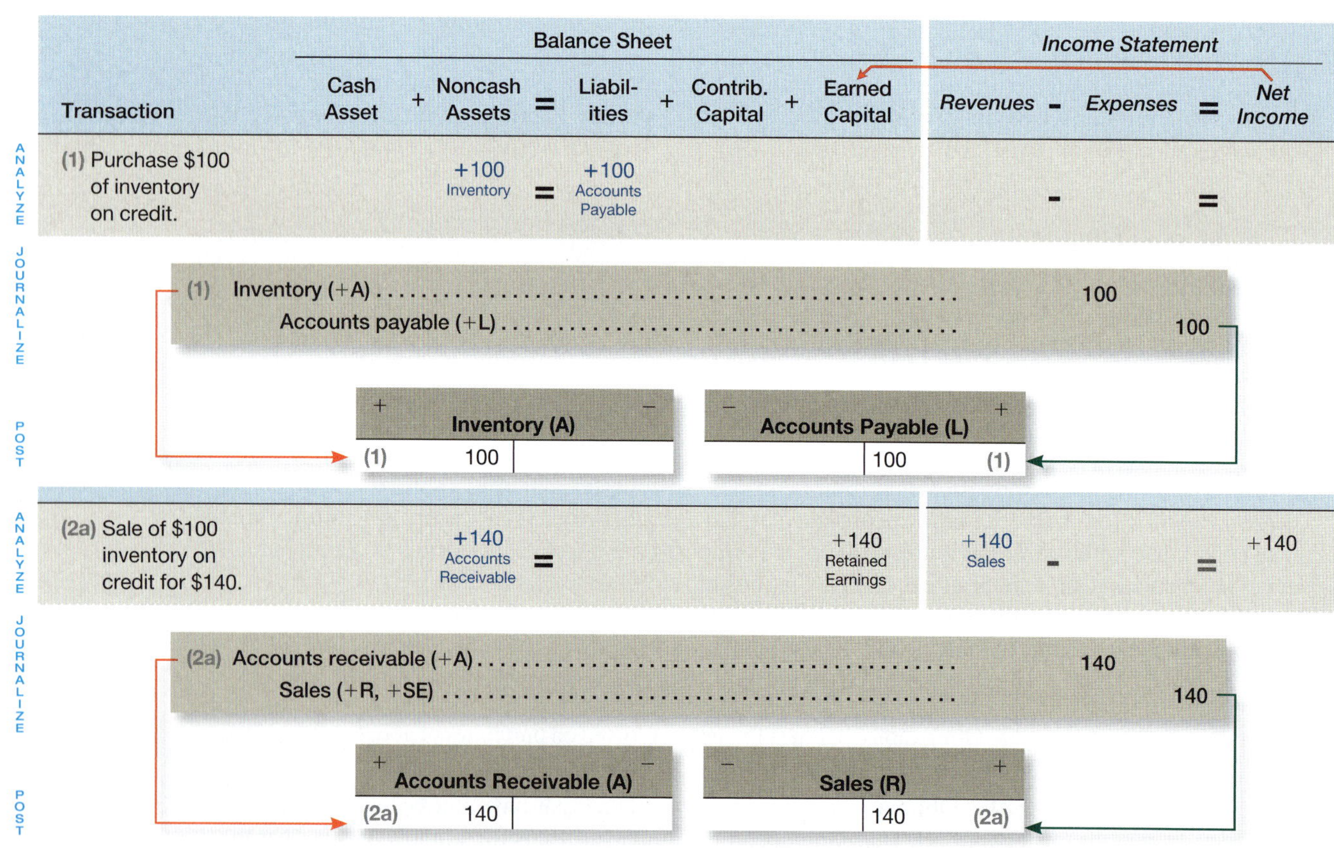

continued

continued from previous page

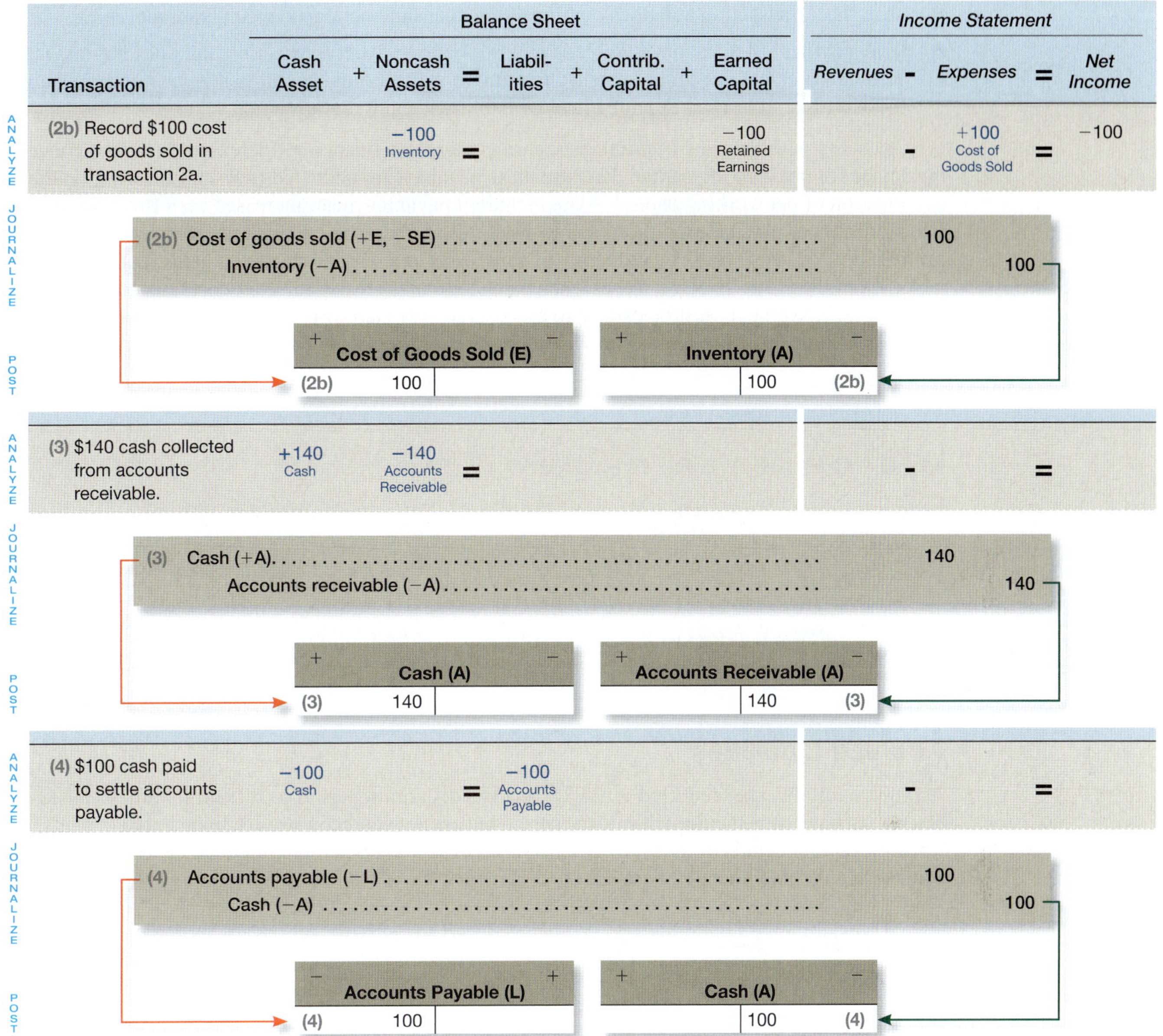

The journal entries, T-accounts, and financial statement effects template highlight the effects of each transaction related to the usual purchase of goods on account and their ultimate sale:

- Purchase of inventory is reflected on the balance sheet as an increase in inventory and an increase in accounts payable. (Transaction 1)

- Sale of inventory involves two components—revenue and expense. The revenue part reflects the increase in sales revenue and the increase in accounts receivable (revenue is recognized when earned, even though cash is not yet received). (Transaction 2a)

- The expense part of the sales transaction reflects the decrease in inventory and the increase in cost of goods sold (COGS). COGS is reported in the income statement and matched against the revenues reported (this expense is recognized because the inventory asset is sold, even if the inventory-related payables have not yet been paid). (Transaction 2b)

- Collection of the receivable reduces accounts receivable and increases cash. It is solely a balance sheet transaction and does not impact income statement accounts. (Transaction 3)

- Cash payment of accounts payable is solely a balance sheet transaction and does not impact income statement accounts (expense relating to purchase of inventories is recognized when the asset is sold or used up, not when the liability is paid). (Transaction 4)

Accounts payable are a non-interest-bearing source of financing. Increased payables reduce the amount of net working capital, because these payables are deducted from current assets in the computation of net working capital. Also, increased payables mean increased cash flow (because inventories were purchased without using cash). An increase in accounts payable also increases profitability because it causes a reduction in the level of interest-bearing debt that is required to finance operating assets. ROE increases when companies make use of this low-cost financing source. However, management must be careful to avoid excessive "**leaning on the trade**" because short-term income and cash flow gains can yield long-term costs such as damaged supply channels.[1,2]

MID-CHAPTER REVIEW 1

Verizon's accounts payable decreased from $4,491 million in 2007 to $3,856 million in 2008.

a. What effect does a decrease in accounts payable have on Verizon's net cash flows from operating activities?
b. How might management view the change in accounts payable?

The solution to this review problem can be found on page 430.

Accrued Liabilities

Accrued liabilities are identified at the end of an accounting period to reflect liabilities and expenses that have been incurred during the period but are not yet recognized in financial statements.[3] **Verizon** reports details of its $13,814 million accrued liabilities including its $3,856 million accounts payable in footnote 19 to its 2008 10-K report:

December 31 ($ millions)	2008	2007
Accounts payable	$ 3,856	$ 4,491
Accrued expenses	2,299	2,400
Accrued vacation pay, salaries and wages	4,871	4,828
Interest payable	652	473
Accrued taxes	2,136	2,270
Total	$13,814	$14,462

Verizon accrues liabilities for the following expenses: miscellaneous accrued expenses, accrued vacation pay, accrued salaries and wages, interest payable, and accrued taxes. These accruals are

---

[1] We must be careful, because excessive delays the in payment of payables can result in suppliers charging a higher price for their goods or, ultimately, refusing to sell to certain buyers. This situation is a hidden "financing" cost that, even though it is not interest, is a real cost.

[2] Accounts payable often carry credit terms such as 2/10, net 30. These terms give the buyer 2% off the invoice price of goods purchased if paid within 10 days. Otherwise the entire invoice is payable within 30 days. By its failure to take a discount, the buyer is effectively paying a 2% interest charge to use its funds for an additional 20 days. Because there are approximately 18 such 20-day periods in a year (365/20), this equates to an annual rate of interest of about 36%. Thus, borrowing funds at less than 36% to pay this liability within the discount period would be cost effective and good management.

[3] Accruals can also be made for recognition of revenue and a corresponding receivable. An example of this situation would be revenue recognition on a long-term contract that has reached a particular milestone, or for interest earned but not received on an investment in bonds that is still outstanding at period-end.

typical of most companies. The accruals are recognized with a liability on the balance sheet and a corresponding expense on the income statement. This reporting means that liabilities increase, current income decreases, and reported equity decreases. When an accrued liability is ultimately paid, both cash and the liability are decreased (but no expense is recorded because it was recognized previously).

Accounting for Accrued Liabilities　The following entries illustrate the accounting for a typical accrued liability, accrued wages:

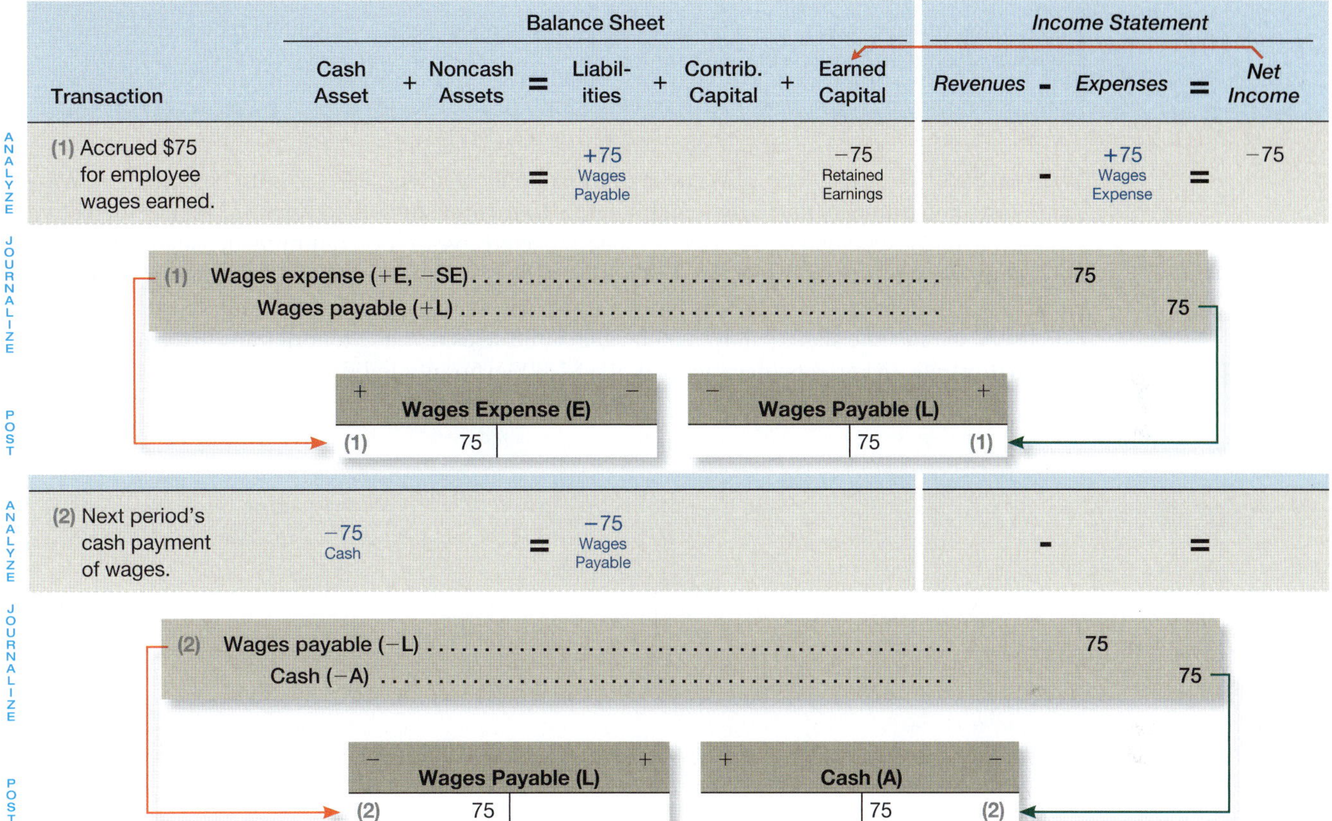

The following financial statement effects result from this accrual of employee wages:

- Employees have worked during a period and have not yet been paid. The effect of this accrual is to increase wages payable on the balance sheet and to recognize wages expense on the income statement. Failure to recognize this liability and associated expense would understate liabilities on the balance sheet and overstate income.

- Employees are paid in the following period, resulting in a cash decrease and a reduction in wages payable. This payment does not result in expense because the expense was recognized in the prior period when incurred.

Contingent Liabilities　The accrued wages illustration relates to events that are fairly certain. We know, for example, when wages are incurred but not paid. Other examples of such accruals are rental costs, insurance premiums due but not yet paid, and taxes owed.

Some accrued liabilities, however, are less certain than others. Consider a company facing a lawsuit. Should it record the possible liability and related expense? The answer depends on the likelihood of occurrence and the ability to estimate the obligation. Specifically, if the obligation is *probable* **and** the amount *estimable,* then a company will recognize this obligation, called a **contingent liability**. If an obligation is only *reasonably possible,* regardless of the company's ability to estimate the amount, the contingent liability is not reported on the balance sheet and is merely disclosed in the footnotes. All other contingent liabilities that are less than reasonably possible are not accrued although disclosure in a note is permitted but not required.

IFRS INSIGHT

Reporting Contingent Liabilities   U.S. GAAP and IFRS are similar with respect to reporting accrued liabilities. The one exception is contingencies. Under IFRS, the criteria for recognizing a contingent liability are much more stringent than under U.S. GAAP. In particular, before a liability is recorded, IFRS requires that (1) a present obligation exists, (2) the sacrifice of resources is probable, and (3) the amount can be estimated. Contingent assets may be recognized only if the recovery is virtually certain. In contrast, under U.S. GAAP, a contingent liability should be recognized whenever a probable future sacrifice can be estimated.

Warranties   Warranty liabilities are another example of an accrual that must be estimated. Warranties are commitments made by manufacturers to their customers to repair or replace defective products within a specified period of time. The expected cost of this commitment usually is reasonably estimated at the time of sale based on past experience. As a result, GAAP requires manufacturers to record the expected cost of warranties as a liability, and to record the related expected warranty expense in the income statement to match against the sales revenue reported for that period.

To illustrate, the effects of an accrual of a $1,000 warranty liability are:

	Balance Sheet						Income Statement		
Transaction	Cash Asset	+ Noncash Assets	= Liabil- ities	+ Contrib. Capital	+ Earned Capital		Revenues −	Expenses	= Net Income
(1) Accrued $1,000 of expected warranty costs on goods sold this period.		=	+1,000 Warranty Payable		−1,000 Retained Earnings		−	+1,000 Warranty Expense	= −1,000

(1)	Warranty expense (+E, −SE)	1,000	
	Warranty payable (+L)		1,000

+	Warranty Expense (E)	−		−	Warranty Payable (L)	+
(1)	1,000				1,000	(1)

	Balance Sheet						Income Statement		
(2) Next period's costs (sent $950 in replacement products) to cover failures under warranty.		−950 Inventory	= −950 Warranty Payable				−		=

(2)	Warranty payable (−L)	950	
	Inventory (−A)		950

−	Warranty Payable (L)	+		+	Inventory (A)	−
(2)	950				950	(2)

Reporting of warranty liabilities has the same effect on financial statements as does the accrual of wages expense in the previous section. That is, a liability is recorded on the balance sheet and an expense is reported in the income statement, reducing income by the warranty accrual. When the defective product is later replaced (or repaired), the liability is reduced together with the cost of the inventory (or other assets) spent to satisfy the claim. (Only a portion of the products estimated to fail does so in the current period; we expect other product failures in future periods. Management monitors this estimate and adjusts it if failure is higher or lower than expected.) As in the accrual of wages, the expense is reported when it is incurred and the liability is estimated at that time, not when payments are made.

Ford Motor Company reports $3,840 million of warranty liability in footnote 29 to its 2008 balance sheet. The footnotes reveal the following additional information:

Product Performance, Warranty—Estimated warranty costs and additional service actions are accrued for at the time the vehicle is sold to a dealer. Included in the warranty cost accruals are costs for basic warranty coverages on vehicles sold. Additional service actions, such as product recalls and other customer service actions are not included in the warranty reconciliation below, but are also accrued at the time of sale. Estimates for warranty costs are made based primarily on historical warranty claim experience. The following is a tabular reconciliation of the product warranty accrual (in millions):

Product Warranty Liability	2008	2007
Beginning balance.	$4,862	$5,235
Payments made during the period.	(3,076)	(3,287)
Changes in accrual related to warranties issued during the period.	2,242	2,894
Changes in accrual related to pre-existing warranties.	109	(232)
Foreign currency translation and other	(297)	252
Ending balance	$3,840	$4,862

Of the $4,862 million balance at the beginning of 2008, $3,076 million in cost was incurred to replace or repair defective products during the year, reducing the liability by this amount. This cost can be in the form of cash paid to customers or to employees as wages, and in the form of parts used for repairs. Ford accrued an additional $2,242 million in new warranty liabilities in 2008 and recorded additional minor adjustments. It is important to realize that only the increase in the liability resulting from additional accruals affects the income statement, reducing income through the additional warranty expense. Warranty payments reduce the warranty liability but have no impact on the income statement.

U.S. GAAP requires that the warranty liability reflect the estimated amount of cost that the company expects to incur as a result of warranty claims. This amount is often difficult to estimate and is prone to error. There is also the possibility that a company might intentionally underestimate its warranty liability to report higher current income, or overestimate it so as to depress current income and create an additional liability on the balance sheet that can be used to absorb future warranty costs without the need to record additional expense. Doing so would shift income from the current period to one or more future periods. Warranty liabilities should be compared with sales levels. Any deviations from the historical relation of the warranty liability to sales may indicate a product quality issue or, alternatively, it may reveal earnings management.

All accrued liabilities result in a liability on the balance sheet and an expense on the income statement. Management has some latitude in determining the amount and timing for accruals. This latitude can lead to misreporting of income and liabilities (unintentional or otherwise). For example, if accruals are underestimated, then liabilities are underestimated, income is overestimated, and retained earnings are overestimated. In subsequent periods when an understated accrued liability is reversed (it is recognized in the account), reported income is lower than it should be; this is because prior period income was higher than it should have been. (The reverse holds for overestimated accruals.) The over- and underreporting of accruals, therefore, results in the shifting of income from one period into another.

Experience tells us that some accrued liabilities are more prone to misstatement than others. Estimated accruals that are linked with restructuring programs, including severance accruals and accruals for asset write-downs, are often overstated, as are estimated environmental liabilities. Companies sometimes overestimate these "one-time" accruals, resulting in early recognition of expenses and a corresponding reduction in current period income. This choice, in turn, boosts income in future years when management decides that the accrual can be reversed because it was initially too large. This may suggest that management is conservative and wants to avoid understating liabilities. It can also reflect a desire by management to show earnings growth in the future by shifting current income to future periods. Accrued liabilities set up to smooth income over future periods are called "**cookie jar reserves**." The terms "clearing the decks" and "taking a big bath" have also been applied to such accounting practices.

YOU MAKE THE CALL

You are the Analyst   **Black & Decker Corporation** recognized accrued environmental liabilities in excess of $100 million in 2008. What conditions needed to be met before these liabilities could be reported? The company also indicated in a footnote that, if only the range could be estimated but with no single value in the range being more likely, only the lower bound on the range would be reported. Why would the firm report this way? Would you consider Black & Decker's reporting to be conservative? Explain.

Merck & Co., Inc. currently faces potential lawsuits related to its arthritis drug Vioxx that analysts estimate could potentially amount to $50 billion. The firm has already lost several cases and won several others. Consistent with the reporting practice of other firms, Merck is unlikely to accrue a liability for unresolved claims while they are still being litigated. Why is this reporting used? How would you as an analyst compensate for this reporting? [Answers on page 415]

MID-CHAPTER REVIEW 2

Pratt Company's employees worked during the current month and earned $10,000 in wages, which are not paid until the first of next month. Must Pratt recognize any wages liability and expense for the current month? Explain using journal entries, T-accounts, and the financial statement effects template.

The solution to this review problem can be found on page 430.

Current Nonoperating (Financial) Liabilities

LO2 Describe and account for current nonoperating (financial) liabilities.

Current nonoperating (financial) liabilities include short-term bank loans, the accrual of interest on those loans, and the current maturities of long-term debt. Companies generally try to structure their financing so that debt service requirements (payments) of those financing obligations coincide with the cash inflows from the assets financed. This strategy means that current assets are usually financed with current liabilities, and that long-term assets are financed with long-term liability (and equity) sources.

To illustrate, a seasonal company's investment in current assets tends to fluctuate during the year as depicted in the graphic below:

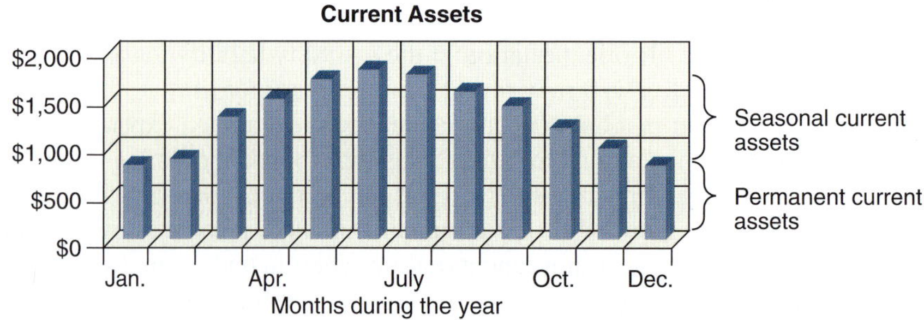

This particular company does most of its selling in the summer months. More inventory is purchased and manufactured in the early spring than at any other time of the year. Sales of the company's manufactured goods are also greater during the summer months, giving rise to accounts receivable that are higher than normal during the fall. The peak working capital level is reached at the height of the selling season and is lowest when the business slows in the off-season. There is a permanent level of working capital required for this business (about $750), and a seasonal component (maximum of about $1,000). Businesses differ in their working capital requirements, but many have permanent and seasonal components.

If a company's working capital needs fluctuate from one season to the next, then the financing needs of the company will also be seasonal. Some assets can be financed with short-term operating liabilities. For example, seasonal increases in inventory balances are typically financed with increased levels of accounts payable. However, operating liabilities are unlikely to meet all of the financing needs of a company. Additional financing is provided by short-term interest-bearing debt.

This section focuses on short-term nonoperating liabilities. These include short-term debt and interest as well as current maturities of long-term liabilities

Short-Term Interest-Bearing Debt
Seasonal swings in working capital are often financed with a bank line of credit (short-term debt). In this case the bank provides a commitment to lend up to a given level with the understanding that the amounts borrowed are repaid in full sometime during the year. An interest-bearing note is evidence of such borrowing.

When these short-term funds are borrowed, the cash received is reported on the balance sheet together with an increase in liabilities (notes payable). The note is reported as a current liability because the expectation is that it will be paid within a year. This borrowing has no effect on income or equity. The borrower incurs (and the lender earns) interest on the note as time passes. U.S. GAAP requires the borrower to accrue the interest liability and the related interest expense each time financial statements are issued.

To illustrate, assume that Verizon borrows $1,000 cash from 1st Bank on January 1. The note bears interest at a 12% annual (3% quarterly) rate, and the interest is payable on the first of each subsequent quarter (April 1, July 1, October 1, January 1). Assuming that Verizon issues calendar-quarter financial statements, this borrowing results in the following financial statement effects for the period January 1 through April 1:

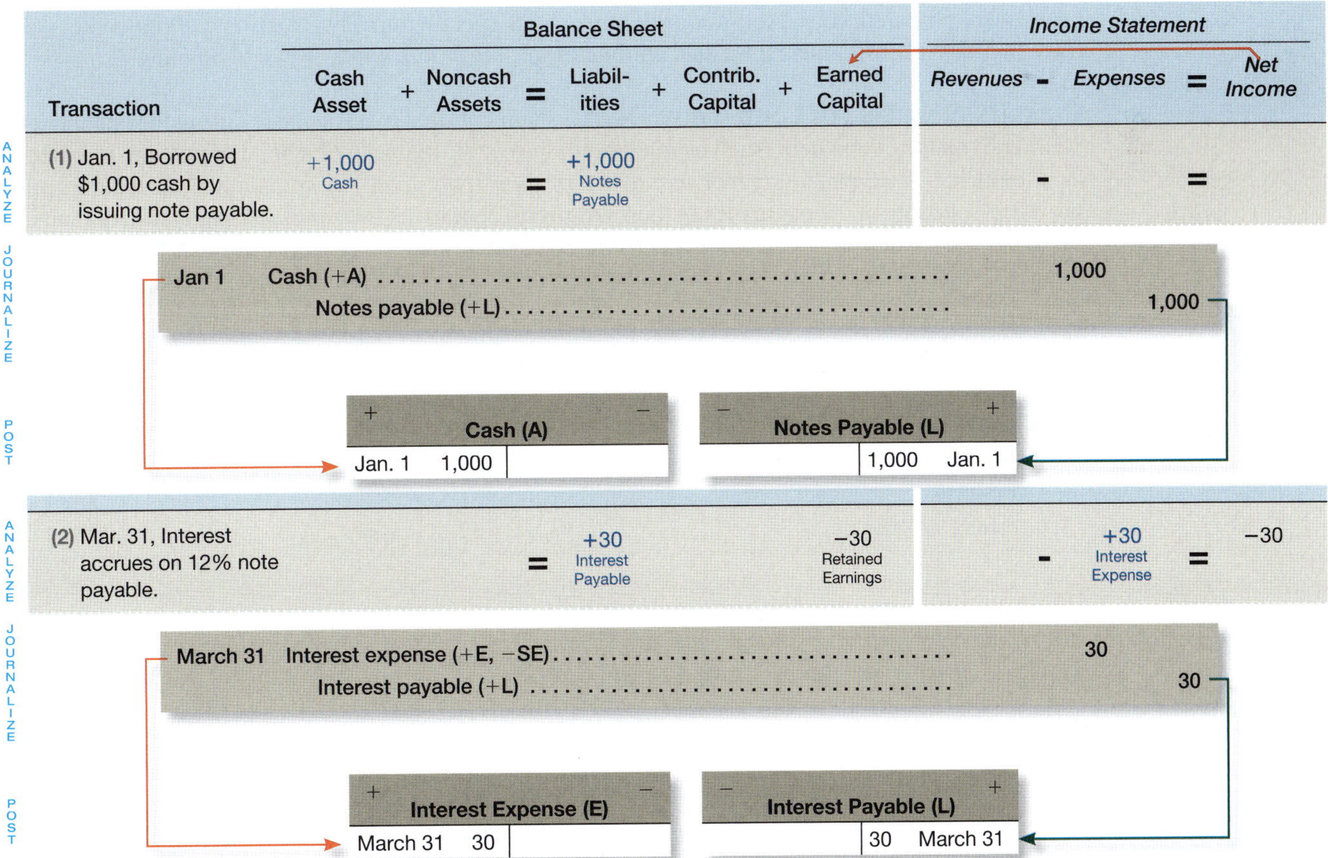

continued

continued from previous page

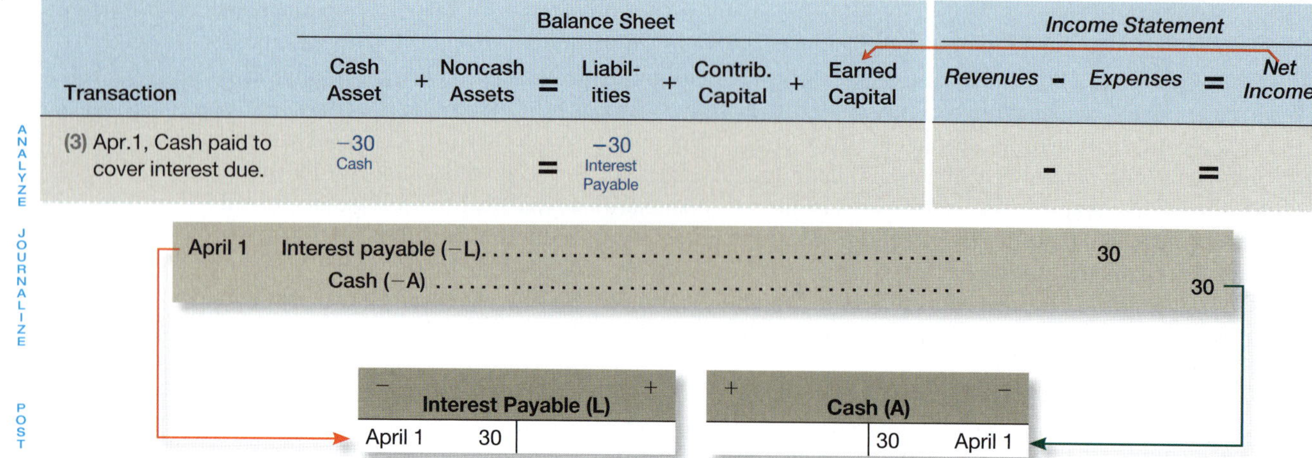

The January 1 borrowing is reflected by an increase in cash and in notes payable. On March 31, this company issues its quarterly financial statements. Although interest is not paid until April 1, the company has incurred three months' interest obligation as of March 31. Failure to recognize this liability and the expense incurred would not fairly present the financial condition of the company. Accordingly, the quarterly accrued interest is computed as follows:

$$\textbf{Interest Expense} \; = \; \textbf{Principal} \; \times \; \textbf{Annual Rate} \; \times \; \textbf{Portion of Year Outstanding}$$
$$\$30 \; = \; \$1{,}000 \; \times \; 12\% \; \times \; 3/12$$

The subsequent interest payment on April 1 is reflected in the financial statements as a reduction of cash and a reduction of the interest payable liability accrued on March 31. There is no expense reported on April 1, because it was recorded the previous day (March 31) when the financial statements were prepared. (For fixed-maturity borrowings specified in days, such as a 90-day note, we use a 365-day year for interest accrual computations, see Mid-Chapter Review 3 below.)

Current Maturities of Long-Term Debt

Payments that must be made during the upcoming 12 months on long-term debt (such as for a mortgage) or the maturity of a bond or note are reported as current liabilities called *current maturities of long-term debt*. All companies are required to provide a schedule of the maturities of their long-term debt in the footnotes to financial statements. To illustrate, the current liability section from the balance sheet of **Verizon** shows $4,993 million in long-term debt due within one year of the December 31, 2008, balance sheet date.

December 31 ($ millions)	2008
Current liabilities	
Debt maturing within one year	$ 4,993
Accounts payable and accrued liabilities	13,814
Other	7,099
Total current liabilities	$25,906

MID-CHAPTER REVIEW 3

Gigler Company borrowed $10,000 on a 90-day, 6% note payable dated January 15. The bank accrues interest daily based on a 365-day year. Use journal entries, T-accounts, and the financial statement effects template to show the implications (amounts and accounts) of the January 31 month-end interest accrual.

The solution to this review problem can be found on page 430.

LONG-TERM LIABILITIES

Companies generally try to fund long-term investments in assets with long-term financing. Long-term financing consists of long-term liabilities and stockholders' equity. The remainder of this chapter focuses on long-term debt liabilities. Other long-term liabilities are discussed in Chapter 10 and stockholders' equity is the focus of Chapter 11.

Companies can borrow small amounts of long-term debt from banks, insurance companies, or other financial institutions. These liabilities are often designed as installment loans and may be secured by specific assets called **collateral**. Installment loans are loans that require a fixed periodic payment for a fixed duration of time. For example, a company may finance an office building with a 15-year mortgage requiring 180 equal monthly payments (180 payments = 15 years $\times$ 12 months). The fixed payment on an installment loan includes a portion of the principal (i.e., the amount borrowed) plus any interest that has accrued on the loan.

Sometimes the amount of financing required by a company is greater than the amount that a bank or insurance company can provide. Companies can borrow larger amounts of money by issuing bonds (or notes) in the capital markets. Bonds and notes are debt securities issued by companies and traded in the bond markets. When a company issues bonds, it is borrowing money. The investors who buy the bonds are lending money to the issuing company. That is, the bondholders are the company's creditors. Because the bond markets provide companies with access to large amounts of capital, bonds represent a very common, cost-effective source of long-term debt financing.

Bonds and notes are structured like any other borrowing. The borrower receives cash and agrees to pay it back with interest. Generally, the entire **face amount** (principal) of the bond or note is repaid at maturity and interest payments are made (usually semiannually) in the interim.

Companies wishing to raise funds in the bond market normally work with an underwriter (e.g., **Merrill Lynch**) to set the terms of the bond issue. The underwriter sells individual bonds (usually in $1,000 denominations) from this general bond issue to its retail clients and professional portfolio managers (e.g., **The Vanguard Group**), and it receives a fee for underwriting the bond issue.

Once issued, the bonds can be traded in the secondary market between investors just like stocks. Market prices of bonds fluctuate daily despite the fact that the company's obligation for payment of principal and interest remains fixed throughout the life of the bond. This occurs because of fluctuations in the general level of interest rates and changes in the financial condition of the borrowing company.

The following sections analyze and interpret the reporting for bonds. We first examine the mechanics of bond pricing. In a subsequent section, we address the accounting for and reporting of bonds.

Pricing of Bonds

Two different interest rates are crucial for understanding how a bond is priced.

- **Coupon (contract** or **stated) rate** The coupon rate of interest is stated in the bond contract. It is used to compute the dollar amount of (semiannual) interest payments that are paid to bondholders during the life of the bond issue.

- **Market (yield) rate** The market rate is the interest rate that investors expect to earn on the investment for this debt security. This rate is used to price the bond issue.

The coupon (contract) rate is used to compute interest payments and the market (yield) rate is used to price the bond. The coupon rate and the market rate are nearly always different. The coupon rate is fixed prior to issuance of the bond and remains so throughout its life. Market rates of interest, on the other hand, fluctuate continually with the supply and demand for bonds in the marketplace, general macroeconomic conditions, and the financial condition of borrowers.

The bond price equals the **present value** of the expected cash flows to the bondholder. Specifically, bondholders normally expect to receive two different cash flows:

1. **Periodic interest payments** (usually semiannual) during the bond's life. These cash flows are typically in the form of equal payments at periodic intervals, called an **annuity**.

2. **Single payment** of the face (principal) amount of the bond at maturity.

LO3 Explain and illustrate the pricing of long-term nonoperating liabilities.

The bond price equals the present value of the periodic interest payments plus the present value of the principal payment at maturity. We next illustrate the purchase of bonds at three different prices: at par, at a discount, and at a premium.

Bonds Issued at Par   When a bond is issued at par, its coupon rate is identical to the market rate. Under this condition, a $1,000 bond sells for $1,000 in the market. To illustrate bond pricing, assume that investors wish to value a bond issue with a face amount of $100,000, a 6% annual coupon rate with interest payable semiannually (3% semiannual rate), and a maturity of 4 years.[4] Investors purchasing this issue receive the following cash flows:

	Number of Payments	Dollars per Payment	Total Cash Flows
Semiannual interest payments...............	4 years × 2 = 8	$100,000 × 3% = $ 3,000	$ 24,000
Principal payment at maturity	1	$100,000	100,000
			$124,000

Specifically, the bond agreement dictates that the borrower makes 8 semiannual payments of $3,000 each, computed as $100,000 × (6%/2), plus the $100,000 face amount at maturity, for a total of $124,000 in cash flows. Each of the 100 bonds in this bond issue provides the bondholder with an annuity of 8 payments of $30 and a principal payment of $1,000 at maturity. For an individual bond, the cash flows total $1,240 ($30 × 8 + $1,000).

When pricing bonds, the number of periods used for computing the present value is the number of interest (coupon) payments required by the bond. In this case, there are 8 semiannual interest payments required, so we use 8, six-month periods to value the bond. The market interest rate (yield) is 6% per year, which is 3% per six-month period.

The bond price is the present value of the interest annuity plus the present value of the principal payment. Assuming that investors desire a 6% annual market rate (yield), the bond sells for exactly $100,000, which is computed as follows:

	Payment	Present Value Factor[a]	Present Value
Interest......................................	$ 3,000	7.01969[b]	$ 21,059
Principal.....................................	$100,000	0.78941[c]	78,941
			$100,000

[a] Mechanics of using tables to compute present values are explained in Appendix A at the end of the text. Present value factors are taken from tables provided in Appendix A.

[b] Present value of ordinary annuity for 8 periods discounted at 3% per period.

[c] Present value of single payment in 8 periods hence discounted at 3% per period.

Because the bond contract pays investors a 6% annual rate when investors demand a 6% market rate, investors purchase these bonds at the **par (face) value** of $1,000 per bond, or $100,000 in total.

Discount Bonds   As a second illustration, assume that market conditions are such that investors demand an 8% annual yield (4% semiannual) for the 6% coupon bond, while all other details remain the same. The bond now sells for $93,267, computed as follows:

	Payment	Present Value Factor	Present Value
Interest......................................	$ 3,000	6.73274[a]	$20,198
Principal.....................................	$100,000	0.73069[b]	73,069
			$93,267

[a] Present value of ordinary annuity for 8 periods discounted at 4% per period.

[b] Present value of single payment in 8 periods hence discounted at 4% per period.

---

[4] Semiannual interest payments are typical for bonds. With semiannual interest payments, the issuer pays bondholders two interest payments per year. The semiannual interest rate is the annual rate divided by two.

Using a financial calculator, the bond is priced as follows: N = 8; I/Yr = 4; PMT = 3,000; FV = 100,000:

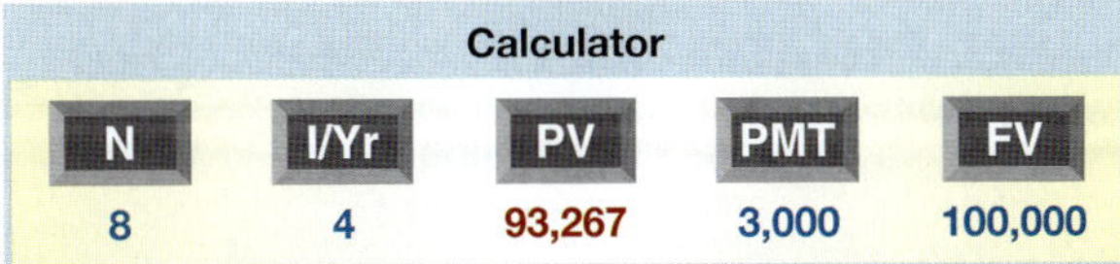

The market price of the bond issue is, therefore, $93,267. The price of each bond in the bond issue is $932.67 (= $93,267/100).

Because the bond carries a coupon rate *lower* than that which investors demand, the bond is less desirable and sells at a **discount**. In general, bonds sell at a discount whenever the coupon rate is less than the market rate.[5]

Premium Bonds   As a third illustration, assume that investors in the bond market demand a 4% annual yield (2% semiannual) for the 6% coupon bonds, while all other details remain the same. The bond now sells for $107,325, computed as follows:

	Payment	Present Value Factor	Present Value
Interest.....................................	$ 3,000	7.32548[a]	$ 21,976
Principal.....................................	$100,000	0.85349[b]	85,349
			$107,325

[a]Present value of ordinary annuity for 8 periods discounted at 2% per period.
[b]Present value of single payment in 8 periods hence discounted at 2% per period.

Using a financial calculator, the bond is priced as follows: N = 8; I/Yr = 2; PMT = 3,000; FV = 100,000:

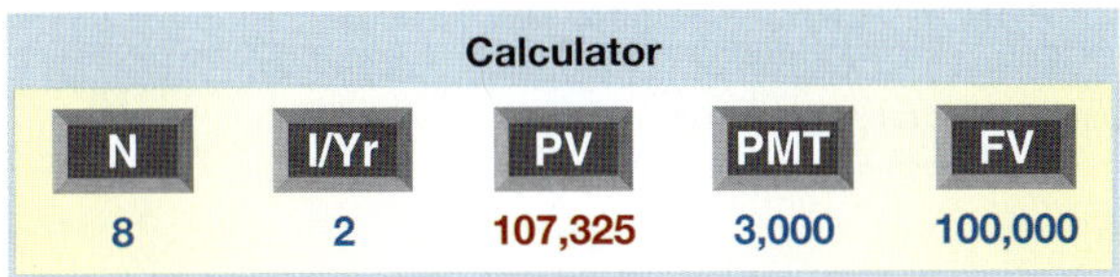

The market price of the bond issue is, therefore, $107,325. The price of each bond in the bond issue is $1,073.25 (= $107,325/100).

Because the bond carries a coupon rate higher than that which investors demand, the bond is more desirable and sells at a **premium**. In general, bonds sell at a premium whenever the coupon rate is greater than the market rate. Exhibit 9.1 summarizes this relation for bond pricing.

EXHIBIT 9.1	**Coupon Rate, Market Rate, and Bond Pricing**
Coupon rate > market rate →	Bond sells at a **premium** (above face amount)
Coupon rate = market rate →	Bond sells at **par** (at face amount)
Coupon rate < market rate →	Bond sells at a **discount** (below face amount)

Exhibit 9.2 shows an announcement (called a *tombstone*) of a recent **General Electric Company** $5 billion debt issuance. It is 5% debt, paying 2.5% semiannual interest, maturing in 2013, with an issue price of 99.626 (valued at a discount). GE's underwriters took 0.425% in fees (more than $21 million) for underwriting and selling this debt issue.[6]

---

[5] Bond prices are often stated in percent form. For example, a bond sold at par is said to be sold at 100 (that is, 100% of its face value, par). The bond sold at $932.67 is said to be sold at 93.267 (93.267% of par, computed as $932.67/$1,000).

[6] The tombstone makes clear that if we purchase any of these notes (in denominations of $1,000) after the semiannual interest date, we must pay accrued interest in addition to the purchase price. This interest is returned to us in the regular interest payment. (This procedure makes the bookkeeping easier for the issuer/underwriter.)

EXHIBIT 9.2 Announcement (Tombstone) of Debt Offering to Public

General Electric Company

$5,000,000,000
5% Notes due 2013

Issue price: 99.626%

We will pay interest on the notes semiannually on February 1 and August 1 of each year, beginning August 1, 2003. The notes will mature on February 1, 2013. We may not redeem the notes prior to maturity.

The notes will be unsecured obligations and rank equally with our other unsecured debt securities that are not subordinated obligations. The notes will be issued in registered form in denominations of $1,000.

Neither the Securities and Exchange Commission nor any state securities commission has approved or disapproved of the notes or determined if this prospectus supplement or the accompanying prospectus is truthful or complete. Any representation to the contrary is a criminal offense.

	Per Note	Total
Public Offering Price(1)	99.626%	$4,981,300,000
Underwriting Discounts	.425%	$ 21,250,000
Proceeds to General Electric Company (before expenses)	99.201%	$4,960,050,000

(1)   Plus accrued interest from January 28, 2003, if settlement occurs after that date.

The underwriters expect to deliver the notes in book-entry form only through the facilities of The Depository Trust Company, Clearstream, Luxembourg or the Euroclear System, as the case may be, on or about January 28, 2003.

Joint Bookrunners

Lehman Brothers   **Morgan Stanley**   **Salomon Smith Barney**

Senior Co-Managers

Banc of America Securities LLC	**Credit Suisse First Boston**	**Deutsche Bank Securities**
Goldman. Sachs & Co.	**JPMorgan**	**Merrill Lynch & Co.**
	UBS Warburg	

Co-Managers

Banc One Capital Markets, Inc.	**Barclays Capital**	**Blaylock & Partners, L.P.**
BNP PARIBAN	**Dresdner Kleinwort Wasserstein**	**Guzman & Company**
HSBC	**Loop Capital Markets**	**Ormes Capital Markets, Inc.**
Utendahl Capital Partners, L.P.	**The Williams Capital Group, L.P.**	

Effective Cost of Debt

When a bond sells for par, the cost to the issuing company is the cash interest paid. In our first illustration where the bond is issued at par, the *effective cost* of the bond is the 6% interest paid by the issuer.

When a bond sells at a discount, the issuer's effective cost consists of two parts: (1) the cash interest paid and (2) the discount incurred. The discount, which is the difference between par and the lower issue price, is a cost that must eventually be reflected in the issuer's income statement as an expense. This fact means that the effective cost of a discount bond is greater than if the bond had sold at par. A discount is a cost and, like any other cost, must eventually be transferred from the balance sheet to the income statement as an expense.

When a bond sells at a premium, the issuer's effective cost consists of (1) the cash interest paid and (2) a cost reduction due to the premium received. The premium is a benefit that must eventually find its way from the balance sheet to the income statement as a *reduction* of interest expense. As a result of the premium, the effective cost of a premium bond is less than if the bond had sold at par.

Bonds are priced to yield the return (market rate) demanded by investors in the bond market, which results in the effective interest rate of a bond *always* equaling the yield (market) rate, regardless of the coupon (stated) rate of the bond. Bond prices are set by the market so as to always yield the rate required by investors based on the terms and qualities of the bond. Companies cannot influence the effective cost of debt by raising or lowering the coupon rate. We discuss the factors affecting the market yield later in the chapter.

The effective cost of debt is ultimately reflected in the amount reported in the issuer's income statement as interest expense. This amount can be, and usually is, different from the cash interest paid. The two are the same only for a bond issued at par. The next section discusses how management reports bonds on the balance sheet and interest expense on the income statement.

Reporting of Bond Financing

This section identifies and describes the financial statement effects of bond transactions.

Bonds Issued at Par   When a bond sells at par, the issuing company receives the cash proceeds and accepts an obligation to make payments per the bond contract. Specifically, cash is increased and a liability (bonds payable) is increased by the same amount. Using the facts from our earlier illustration, the issuance of bonds at par has the following financial statement effects (there is no revenue or expense at the date the bond is issued):

LO4 Analyze and account for financial statement effects of long-term nonoperating liabilities.

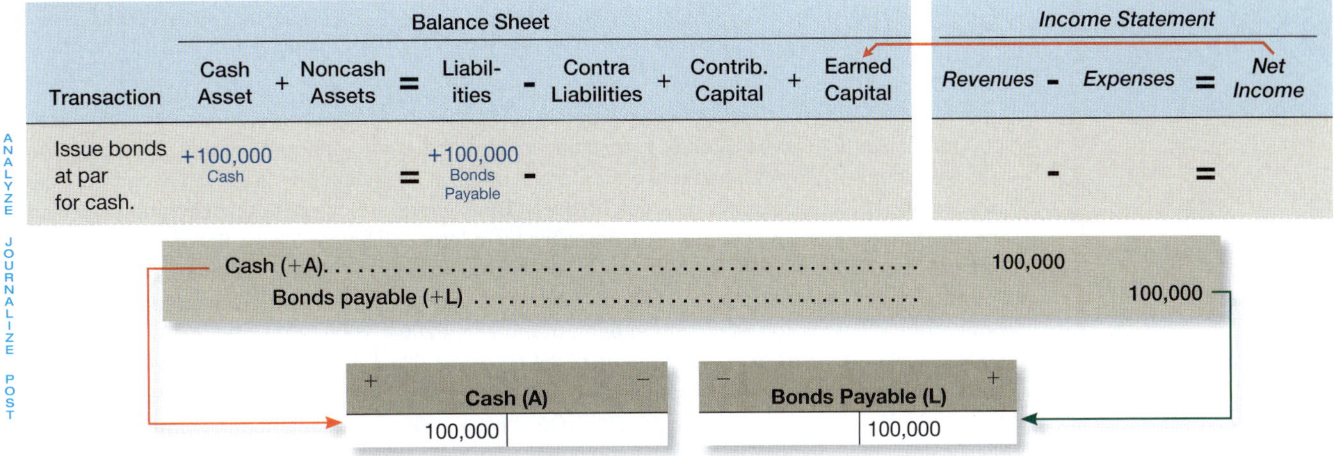

Discount Bonds   When a bond is sold at a discount, the cash proceeds and net bond liability are recorded at the amount of the proceeds received (not the face amount of the bond). Again, using the facts above from our bond discount illustration, the financial statement effects follow:

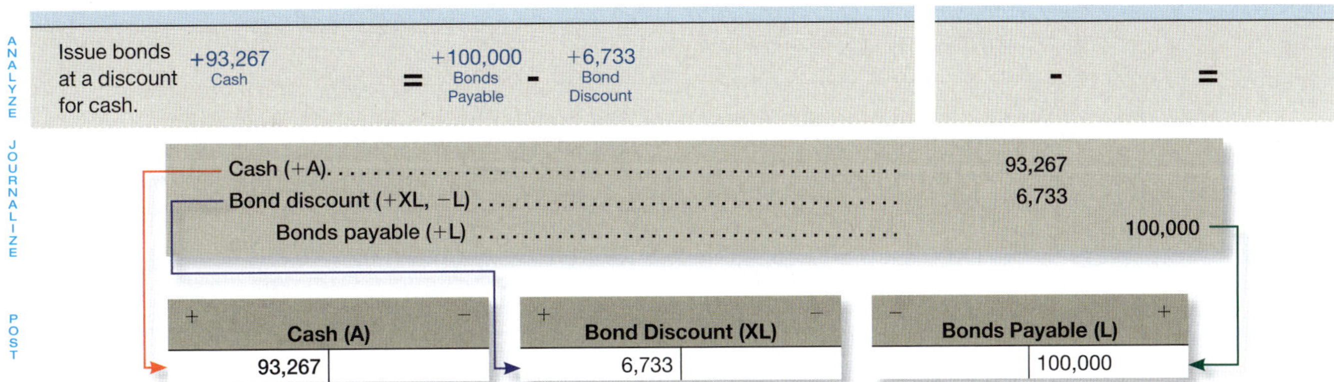

For the discount bond case, cash is increased by the proceeds from the sale of the bonds, and the liability increases by the same amount. However, the net liability consisting of the two components shown below is reported on the balance sheet.

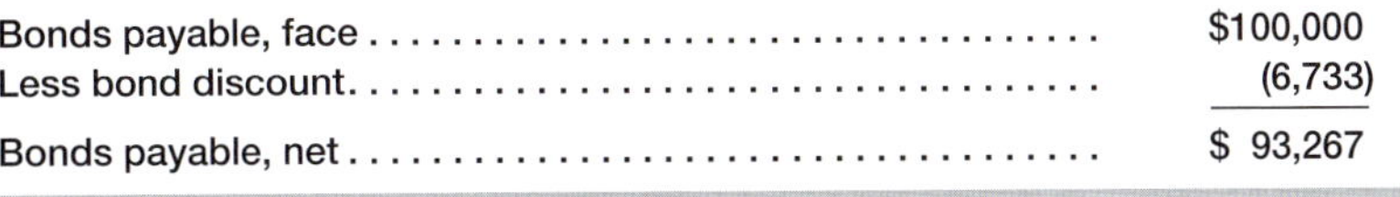

Bonds payable, face	$100,000
Less bond discount	(6,733)
Bonds payable, net	$ 93,267

FYI "Bonds Payable, Net" is a common title reflecting the face value of the bond less the unamortized discount.

Bonds are reported on the balance sheet net of any discount (or plus any premium). When the bond matures, however, the company is obligated to repay $100,000. Accordingly, at maturity, the bond liability must read $100,000, the amount that is owed. Therefore, between the bond issuance and its maturity, the discount must decline to zero. This reduction of the discount over the life of the bond is called **amortization**. This amortization causes the effective interest expense to be greater than the periodic cash interest payments based on the coupon rate.

BUSINESS INSIGHT

Verizon's Zero Coupon Debt Zero coupon bonds and notes, called *zeros,* do not carry a coupon rate. However, the pricing of these bonds and notes is done in the same manner as those with coupon rates—the exception is the absence of an interest annuity. This means that the price is the present value of just the principal payment at maturity; hence the bond is sold at a *deep discount.* (For example, in the case of the 6% bond, suppose there is no coupon rate, and hence no interest payments. The only payment would be the return of principal 4 years away. We already know that the present value of this single payment is $73,069. The bond would be a "zero" and sell for $73,069 resulting in a substantial discount of $26,931.) Following is an example from Note 10 of **Verizon's** 2006 10-K report:

> *Zero-Coupon Convertible Notes*
>
> In May 2001, Verizon . . . issued approximately $5.4 billion in principal amount at maturity of zero-coupon convertible notes due 2021, resulting in gross proceeds of approximately $3 billion. The notes are convertible into shares of our common stock at an initial price of $69.50 per share if the closing price of Verizon common stock on the NYSE exceeds specified levels or in other specified circumstances. The conversion price increases by at least 3% a year. The initial conversion price represents a 25% premium over the May 8, 2001, closing price of $55.60 per share. (There are no scheduled cash interest payments associated with the notes.) The notes were redeemable at the option of the holders on May 15th in each of the years 2004, 2006, 2011 and 2016. On May 15, 2004, $3,292 million of principal amount of the notes ($1,984 million after unamortized discount) were redeemed by Verizon Global Funding. In addition, the zero-coupon convertible notes were callable by Verizon on or after May 15, 2006. On May 16, 2006, they redeemed the remaining $1,375 million accreted principal of the remaining outstanding zero-coupon convertible principal. The total payment on the date of redemption was $1,377 million.

Verizon's zero-coupon convertible notes had a maturity value of $5.4 billion and mature in 2021. No interest was paid on the notes. The notes were sold for $3 billion. The difference between the $3 billion sales proceeds and the $5.4 billion maturity value represents Verizon's interest cost, which is the return to the investor. The effective cost of the debt is the interest rate that equates the issue price and maturity value, or approximately 3%. These notes are also convertible—an increasingly popular form of debt discussed in Chapter 11.

Premium Bonds When a bond is sold at a premium, the cash proceeds and net bond liability are recorded at the amount of the proceeds received (not the face amount of the bond). Again, using the facts above from our premium bond illustration, the financial statement effects are:

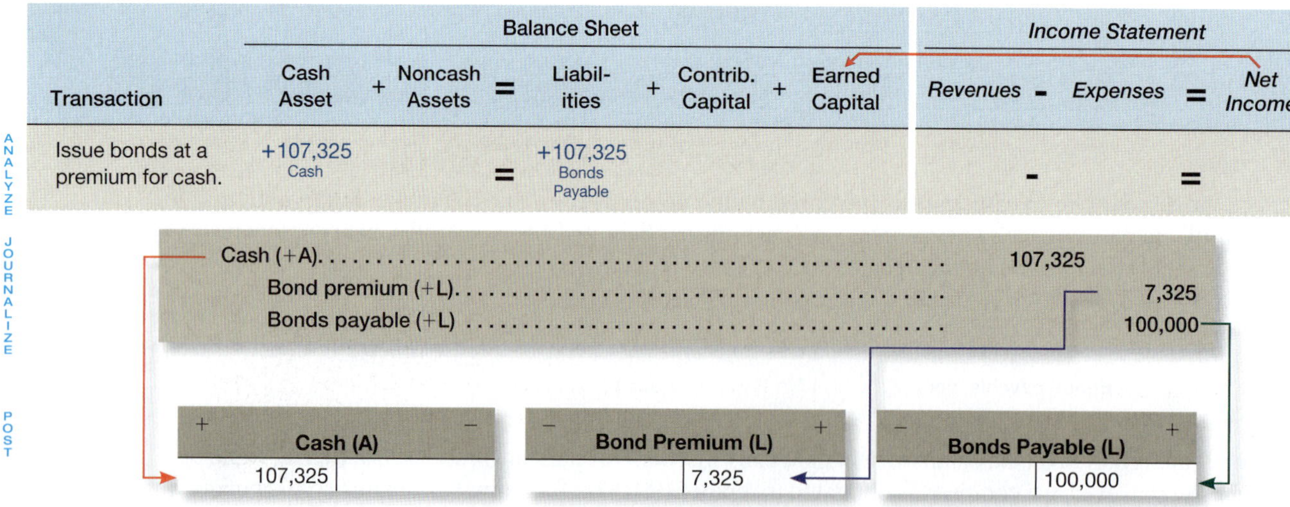

The net bond liability amount reported on the balance sheet, again, consists of two parts:

Bonds payable, face	$100,000
Add bond premium	7,325
Bonds payable, net	$107,325

The $100,000 must be repaid at maturity, and the premium is amortized to zero over the life of the bond. The premium represents a *benefit,* which yields a *reduction* in interest expense on the income statement.

Effects of Discount and Premium Amortization

For bonds issued at par, interest expense reported on the income statement equals the cash interest payment. However, for bonds issued at a discount or premium, interest expense reported on the income statement consists of one of the following two components:

+	Cash interest paid Amortization of discount	or	Cash interest paid − Amortization of premium
	Interest expense		Interest expense

Specifically, periodic amortization of a discount is added to the cash interest paid to get interest expense for a discount bond. Amortization of the discount reflects the additional cost the issuer incurs from issuance of the bonds at a discount and its recognition, via amortization, as an increase to interest expense. For a premium bond, the premium is a benefit the issuer receives at issuance. Amortization of the premium reduces interest expense over the debt term. In both cases, interest expense on the income statement represents the *effective cost* of debt (the *nominal cost* of debt is the cash interest paid).

Companies amortize discounts and premiums using the effective interest method. To illustrate, recall the assumptions of the discount bond above—face amount of $100,000, a 6% annual coupon rate payable semiannually (3% semiannual rate), a maturity of 4 years, and a market (yield) rate of 8% annual (4% semiannual). These facts resulted in a bond issue price of $932.67 per bond or $93,267 for the entire bond issue. Exhibit 9.3 illustrates a bond discount amortization table for this bond.

EXHIBIT 9.3	Bond Discount Amortization Table				
	[A]	**[B]**	**[C]**	**[D]**	**[E]**
Semi- Annual Period	**([E] × market%) Interest Expense**	**(Face × coupon%) Cash Interest Paid**	**([A] − [B]) Discount Amortization**	**(Prior bal − [C]) Discount Balance**	**(Face − [D]) Bond Payable Net**
0				$6,733	$ 93,267
1	$3,731	$3,000	$731	6,002	93,998
2	3,760	3,000	760	5,242	94,758
3	3,790	3,000	790	4,452	95,548
4	3,822	3,000	822	3,630	96,370
5	3,855	3,000	855	2,775	97,225
6	3,889	3,000	889	1,886	98,114
7	3,925	3,000	925	962	99,038
8	3,962	3,000	962	0	100,000

The interest period is denoted in the left-most column. Period 0 is the point in time at which the bond is issued. Periods 1–8 are successive six-month interest periods (recall, interest is paid semiannually). Column [A] is interest expense, which is reported in the income statement. This column is computed as the carrying amount of the bond at the beginning of the period (column [E] of the previous row) multiplied by the 8% yield rate (4% semiannual) used to compute the bond issue price. Column [B] is cash interest paid, which is a constant $3,000 per period (face amount × coupon rate). Column [C] is discount amortization, which is the difference between interest expense and cash interest paid. Column [D] is the discount balance, which is the previous balance of the discount less the discount amortization in column [C]. Column [E] is the net bond payable, which is the $100,000 face amount less the unamortized discount from column [D].

The amortization process continues until period 8, at which time the discount balance is 0 and the net bond payable is $100,000 (the maturity value). An amortization table reveals the financial statement effects of the bond for its duration. Specifically, we see the income statement effects in column [A], the cash effects in column [B], and the balance sheet effects in columns [C], [D] and [E].

To record the interest payment at the end of period 1, we use the values in row 1 of the amortization table. The resulting entry is recorded as follows:

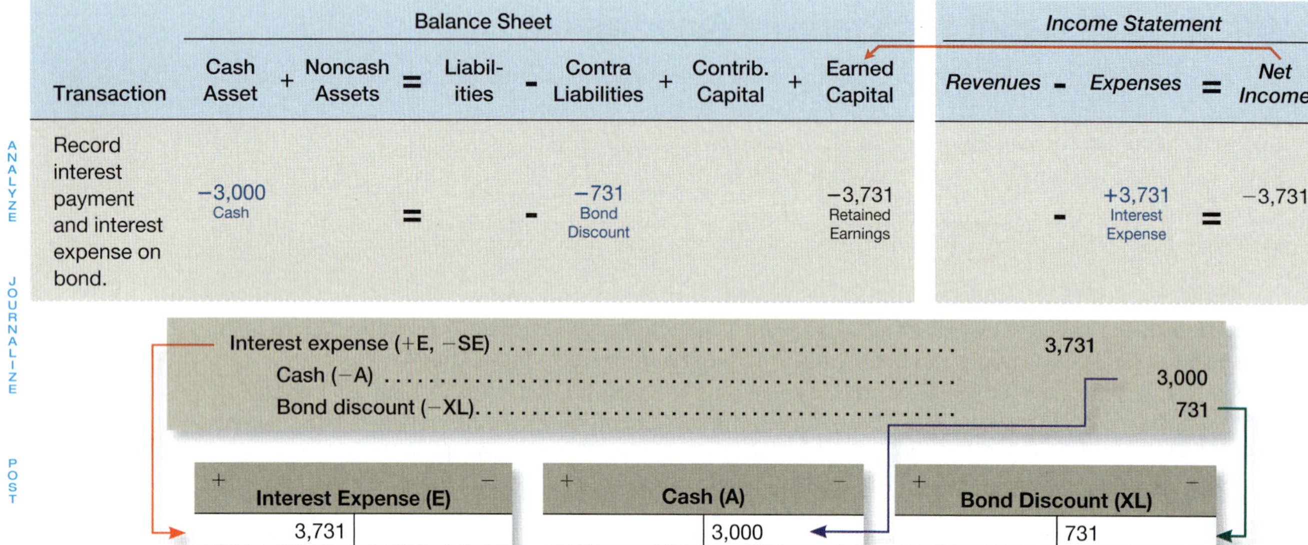

To illustrate amortization of a premium bond, we use the assumptions of the premium bond above—$100,000 face value, a 6% annual coupon rate payable semiannually (3% semiannual rate), a maturity of 4 years, and a 4% annual market (yield) rate (2% semiannual). These parameters resulted in a bond issue price of $1,073.25 per bond or $107,325 for the entire bond issue. Exhibit 9.4 shows the bond premium amortization table for this bond.

EXHIBIT 9.4	Bond Premium Amortization Table				
Semi-Annual Period	[A] ([E] × market%) Interest Expense	[B] (Face × coupon%) Cash Interest Paid	[C] ([A] − [B]) Premium Amortization	[D] (Prior bal − [C]) Premium Balance	[E] (Face + [D]) Bond Payable Net
0				$7,325	$107,325
1	$2,147	$3,000	$853	6,472	106,472
2	2,129	3,000	871	5,601	105,601
3	2,112	3,000	888	4,713	104,713
4	2,094	3,000	906	3,807	103,807
5	2,076	3,000	924	2,883	102,883
6	2,058	3,000	942	1,941	101,941
7	2,039	3,000	961	980	100,980
8	2,020	3,000	980	0	100,000

Interest expense is computed using the same process that we used for discount bonds. The difference is that the yield rate is 4% (2% semiannual) in the premium case. Also, cash interest paid follows from the bond contract (face amount × coupon rate), and the other columns' computations reflect the premium amortization. After period 8, the premium is fully amortized (equals zero) and the net bond payable balance is $100,000, the amount owed at maturity. Again, an amortization table reveals the financial statement effects of the bond—the income statement effects in column [A], the cash effects in column [B], and the balance sheet effects in columns [C], [D], and [E].

To record the interest payment at the end of period 1, we, again, use the values in row 1 of the amortization table. The resulting entry is recorded as follows:

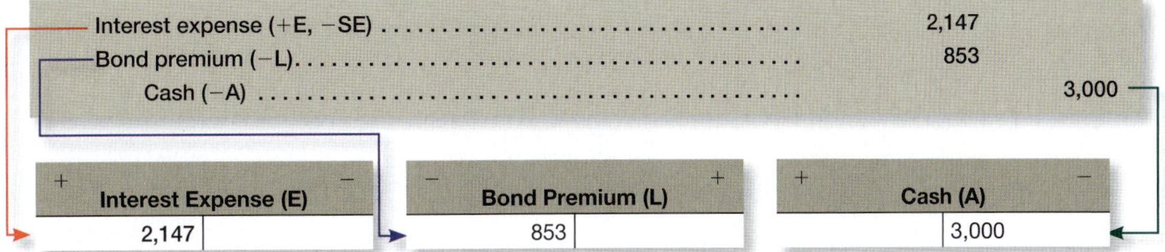

BUSINESS INSIGHT

A Simpler Approach   General Accepted Accounting Principles allow a simpler amortization approach when the difference in the resulting interest cost is not material. The approach allows the discount or premium to be amortized using the straight-line method over the life of the bond. In the case of the 6% percent bond that we have been discussing, the discount amortized each six-month period would be $842 ($6,733/8 periods). Interest expense would be a constant amount each period—$3,842 (rounded). In the premium case, the amortization each interest period, would be $916 ($7,325/8), resulting in interest expense of $2,084 each six-month period. The straight-line method should not be used in the case of deep discount bonds, such as a zero-coupon bond.

Effects of Bond Repurchase

Most companies report bonds payable at *historical (adjusted) cost*. Specifically, net bonds payable amounts follow from the amortization table, as do the related cash flows and income statement numbers. All financial statement relations are established at the time the bonds are issued and do not subsequently change.

Once issued, however, bonds are free to trade in secondary markets between bondholders. The yield rate, used in these transactions to compute bond prices, changes based on the level of interest rates in the economy and the perceived creditworthiness of the bond issuer.

Companies can and sometimes do repurchase (also called *redeem*) their bonds prior to maturity. The bond indenture (contract agreement) often includes a **call provision** giving the company the right to repurchase its bond. (This situation was true for the Verizon zero coupon bond discussed earlier in this chapter.) Alternatively, the company can repurchase bonds in the open market. When a bond repurchase occurs, a gain or loss usually results, and is computed as follows:

Gain or loss on bond repurchase = Bonds payable, net − Repurchase payment

The net bonds payable, also referred to as the *book (carrying) value of the bond,* is the net amount reported on the balance sheet. If the issuer pays more to retire the bonds than the amount carried on its balance sheet, a loss is reported on its income statement, usually called *loss on bond retirement.* The issuer reports a *gain on bond retirement* if the repurchase price is less than the net bonds payable.

GAAP dictates that any gains or losses on bond repurchases are reported as part of ordinary income unless they meet the criteria for treatment as an extraordinary item. Relatively few debt retirements meet these criteria and, hence, most gains and losses on bond repurchases are reported as part of income from continuing operations.

The question arises as to how gains and losses on the redemption of bonds should affect our analysis of a company's profitability. Because bonds and notes payable represent nonoperating items, activities including the refunding of bonds and any gain or loss resulting from such activity should be omitted from our computation of net operating profit.

Financial Statement Footnotes

Companies are required to disclose details about their long-term liabilities, including the amounts borrowed under each debt issuance, the interest rates, maturity dates, and other key provisions. Following is **Verizon's** disclosure in note 10 to its 2008 10-K for its long-term debt ($ millions):

Long-Term Debt

Outstanding long-term obligations are:

At December 31	Interest Rates %	Maturities	2008	2007
Notes payable	4.35–8.95	2009–2039	$25,441	$14,923
Verizon Wireless—notes payable and other	7.38–8.88	2011–2018	5,983	—
	LIBOR + 1%	2009–2011	4,440	—
Telephone subsidiaries—debentures	4.63–8.75	2009–2033	12,183	13,109
Other subsidiaries—debentures and other	6.84–8.75	2009–2028	2,200	2,450
ESOP loans—NYNEX debentures	9.55	2010	47	70
Capital lease obligations (average rate 6.2% and 6.8%)			390	312
Unamortized discount, net of premium			(219)	(97)
Total long-term debt, including current maturities			50,465	30,767
Less debt maturing within one year			(3,506)	(2,564)
Total long-term debt			$46,959	$28,203

Verizon reports a book value for long-term debt of $50,465 million at year-end 2008. Of this amount, $3,506 million matures in the next year, hence its classification as a current liability (current maturities of long-term debt) and the remainder matures after 2009. Verizon also reports $219 million in unamortized discount (net of unamortized premium) on this debt.

In addition to amounts, rates, and due dates on its long-term debt, Verizon also reports aggregate maturities for the 5 years subsequent to its balance sheet date:

Maturities of Long-Term Debt

Maturities of long-term debt outstanding at December 31, 2008, are as follows ($ millions):

2009	$ 3,506
2010	5,018
2011	5,647
2012	4,306
2013	5,638
Thereafter	26,350

This reporting reveals that Verizon is required to make principal payments of $24.1 billion between 2009 and 2013 and $26.35 billion thereafter. Such maturities are important as a company must meet its required payments, negotiate a rescheduling of the indebtedness, or refinance the debt to avoid default. The latter (default) usually has severe consequences as debt holders have legal remedies available to them, which can result in bankruptcy of the company.

Verizon's disclosure on the market value of its total debt follows:

> The fair value of our short-term and long-term debt, excluding capital leases, is determined based on market quotes for similar terms and maturities or future cash flows discounted at current rates. The fair value of our long-term and short-term debt, excluding capital leases, was $53,174 million and $32,380 million at December 31, 2008 and 2007, respectively, as compared to the carrying value of $51,562 million and $30,845 million, respectively at December 31, 2008 and 2007.

As of December 31, 2008, indebtedness with a book value of $51,562 million had a market value of $53,174 million, resulting in an unrecognized liability (and loss if the debt is redeemed) of $1,612 million (due mainly to a decline in interest rates subsequent to bond issuance). The justification for not recognizing unrealized gains and losses on the balance sheet and income statement is that such amounts can reverse with future fluctuations in interest rates. Further, because only the face amount of debt is repaid at maturity, unrealized gains and losses that arise during intervening years are not necessarily relevant. (This same logic is used to justify the nonrecognition of gains and losses on held-to-maturity investments in debt securities, a topic covered in Chapter 12.) However, a company is permitted to report its liabilities at fair market value if it elects the *fair value option*. The fair value option gives companies the option of reporting financial assets and liabilities at fair market value. At this time, most U.S. companies have elected to report liabilities at historical cost in the financial statements and disclose fair market values in the footnotes. We discuss the fair value option further in Chapter 12.

Interest and the Cash Flows Statement

Interest income and interest expense are typically related to nonoperating assets (security investments) and nonoperating liabilities (interest-bearing bonds and notes) respectively. As such they should be excluded from the operating activities section of the cash flows statement when we do a financial analysis. Sometimes it requires some digging in the financial statements to determine the magnitude of these items. Interest income and expense should also be omitted from all computations of net operating profit.

ANALYZING FINANCIAL STATEMENTS

Debt-to-Equity (D/E)

A major concern of managers and of analysts is the solvency of the corporation. The most common measure of solvency is the ratio of debt to equity (D/E), which measures the corporation's *financial leverage*. The **debt-to-equity ratio** is calculated using the following equation.

LO5 Explain how solvency ratios and debt ratings are determined and how they impact the cost of debt.

$$\text{Debt-to-equity} = \frac{\text{Total liabilities}}{\text{Total stockholders' equity}}$$

This ratio was introduced in the Financial Statement Analysis section of Chapter 1. A higher value for this ratio indicates a greater proportion of debt in a company's capital structure. After trending downward for the previous 6 years, Verizon's debt-to-equity ratio increased significantly by December 31, 2008, to 3.85, up from 2.70 at year-end 2007. The 3.85 ratio indicates that more than 79% of the company's financing comes from debt, which is quite high. The increase in 2008 largely stems from the acquisition of Alltel. In that acquisition, Verizon assumed approximately $17 billion of Alltel's outstanding debt (net of repurchased debt). The increase in financial leverage could limit Verizon's ability to borrow additional funds, if needed, in the future.

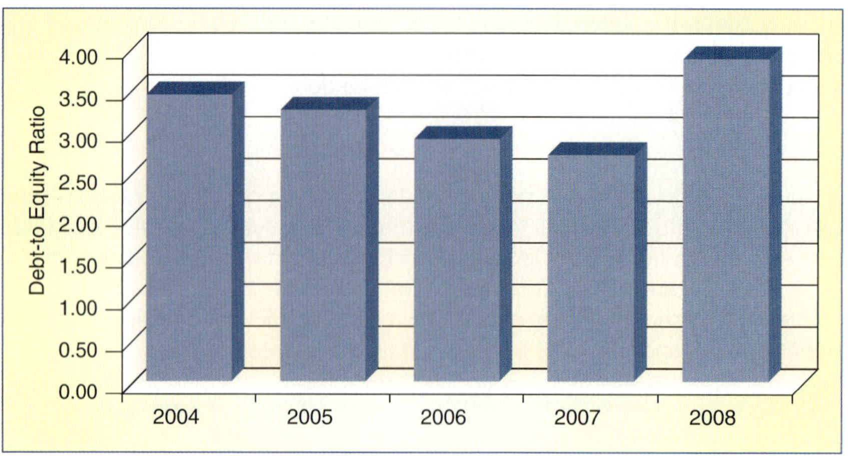

Times Interest Earned (TIE)

When a company relies on debt financing, it assumes an additional burden created by the require-ment to pay interest on its debt. Because interest is deducted from earnings, the burden typically is calculated by dividing **earnings before interest and taxes (EBIT)** by interest expense.

$$\text{TIE} = \frac{\textbf{EBIT}}{\textbf{Interest expense}}$$

The **times interest earned (TIE)** ratio measures how many times interest expense is covered by the profit generating activities of the firm.

Verizon's times interest earned ratio was 6.4 in 2008 and 6.2 in 2007. While this ratio is not high, it represents a significant improvement relative to its 4.5 ratio in 2006. The improvement can be explained by steady growth in revenues and operating income.

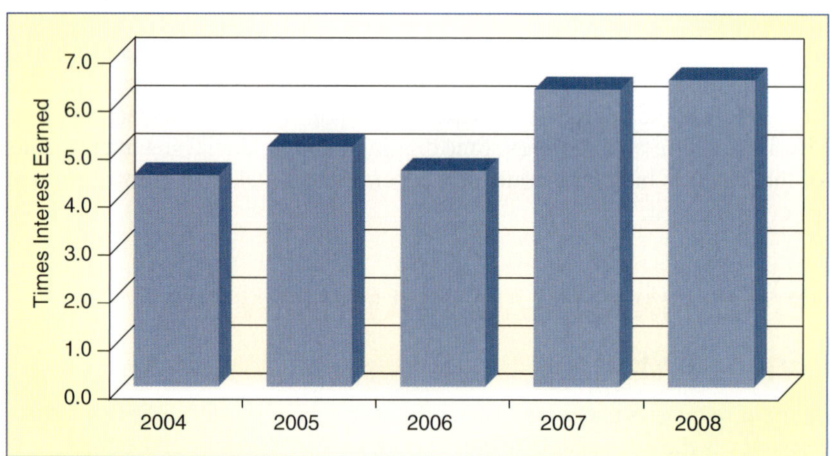

In most circumstances, the times interest earned ratio is a good indicator of a company's ability to meet its interest obligations. However, interest must be paid with cash. In order to fully assess a company's interest burden, we should also compare cash flow metrics, such as operating cash flow and free cash flow, with interest paid. Verizon's cash flow from operations totaled $26,620 million in 2008 and its free cash flow was $4,388 million. When compared with interest payments of $1,664 million, Verizon's cash flow appears adequate to cover its interest costs.[7]

There are several additional variations of leverage ratios. However, the basic idea is to construct multiple measures that best reflect a company's credit risk exposure. There is no single best mea-sure. As with all ratios, we are compelled to draw on definitions that usually need clarification and

---

[7] Interest expense ($1,819 million) is greater than the amount of interest payments ($1,664 million). This difference is due to the increase in accrued interest payable and the amortization of bond discounts.

which can be impacted by uncertain, inappropriate or even inaccurate data. There is no substitute for being skeptical.

Debt Ratings and the Cost of Debt

Earlier in the chapter we learned that the effective cost of debt to the issuing company is the market (yield) rate of interest used to price the bond, regardless of the bond coupon rate. The rate of interest that a company must pay on its debt is a function of the maturity of that debt and the creditworthiness of the issuing company.

RESEARCH INSIGHT

Accounting Conservatism and Cost of Debt   Research indicates that companies applying more conservative accounting methods incur a lower cost of debt. Research also suggests that while accounting conservatism can lead to lower-quality accounting income (because such income does not fully reflect economic reality), creditors are more confident in the numbers and view them as more credible. Evidence also implies that companies can lower the required return demanded by creditors (the risk premium) by issuing high-quality financial reports that include enhanced footnote disclosures and detailed supplemental reports.

A company's debt rating, also referred to as credit quality and creditworthiness, is related to default risk. **Default** refers to the nonpayment of interest and principal or the failure to adhere to the various terms and conditions (covenants) of the bond indenture. Companies seeking to obtain bond financing from the capital markets, normally first seek a rating on their proposed debt issuance from one of several rating agencies such as **Standard & Poor's**, **Moody's Investors Service**, or **Fitch**. The aim of rating agencies is to rate debt so that its default risk is more accurately determined and priced by the market. Such debt issuances carry debt ratings from one or more of the three large rating agencies as shown in Exhibit 9.5. This exhibit includes the general description attached to the debt for each rating class—for example, AAA is assigned to debt of prime maximum safety (maximum creditworthiness).

EXHIBIT 9.5	Corporate Debt Ratings and Descriptions		
Moody's	**S&P**	**Fitch**	**Description**
Aaa	AAA	AAA	Prime Maximum Safety
Aa	AA	AA	High Grade, High Quality
A	A	A	Upper-Medium Grade
Baa	BBB	BBB	Lower-Medium Grade
Ba	BB	BB	Non-Investment Grade
B	B	B	Speculative
Caa	CCC	CCC	Substantial Risk
Ca			Extremely Speculative
C			May be in Default
		DDD	Default
		DD	
	D	D	

YOU MAKE THE CALL

You are the Vice President of Finance   Your company is currently rated B by credit rating agencies. You are considering possible financial and other restructurings of the company to increase your credit rating. What types of restructurings might you consider? What benefits will your company receive from those restructurings? What costs will your company incur to implement such restructurings? [Answers on pages 415–416]

Verizon bonds are rated A as of 2008. It is this rating that, in conjunction with the maturity of its bonds, establishes the market interest rate and consequent selling price. There are a number of considerations that affect the rating of a bond. **Standard & Poor's** list the following factors among its credit rating criteria:

Business Risk
    Industry characteristics
    Competitive position (e.g., marketing, technology, efficiency, regulation)
    Management
Financial Risk
    Financial characteristics
    Financial policy
    Profitability
    Capital structure
    Cash flow protection
    Financial flexibility

Rating agencies use a number of accounting ratios to help establish creditworthiness, including measures of liquidity, solvency and profitability. These ratios are variants of the ratios we describe in Chapter 12, especially those used to assess solvency.

There are other relevant factors in setting debt ratings including the following:

- **Collateral** Companies can provide security for debt in the form of mortgages on assets. To the extent debt is secured, the debt holder is in a preferred position vis-à-vis other creditors.

- **Covenants** Debt agreements (indentures) can contain restrictions on the issuing company to protect debt holders. Examples are restrictions on excessive dividend payment, on other company acquisitions, on further borrowing, and on maintaining minimum levels for key liquidity and solvency ratios. These covenants provide debt holders some means of control over the issuer's operations because, unlike equity investors, they do not have voting rights.

- **Options** Debt obligations involve contracts between the borrowing company and debt holders. Options are sometimes written into debt contracts. Examples are options to convert debt into stock (so that debt holders have a stake in value creation) and options allowing the issuing company to repurchase its debt before maturity (usually at a premium).

CHAPTER-END REVIEW

On January 1, 2010, Givoly Company issues $300,000 of 15-year, 10% bonds payable for $351,876, yielding an effective interest rate of 8%. Interest is payable semiannually on June 30 and December 31. (1) Show computations to confirm the issue price of $351,876, and (2) provide Givoly's journal entries, T-accounts, and complete financial statement effects template for (a) bond issuance, (b) semiannual interest payment and premium amortization on June 30, 2010, and (c) semiannual interest payment and premium amortization on December 31, 2010.

The solution to this review problem can be found on pages 431–432.

SUMMARY

LO1 **Identify and account for current operating liabilities. (p. 392)**
- Current liabilities are short-term and generally non-interest-bearing; accordingly, firms try to maximize the financing of their assets using these sources of funds.
- ROE increases when firms make use of accounts payable increases to finance operating assets; a firm must avoid excessive "leaning on the trade" for short-term gains that can damage long-term supplier relationships.

- Accrued liabilities reflect liabilities and expenses that have been incurred during the period, but which have not yet been recognized in financial statements.
- While all accruals result in a liability on the balance sheet and an expense on the income statement, management has latitude in determining (in some cases, estimating) their amount and timing; this discretion offers the opportunity for managing earnings.

Describe and account for current nonoperating (financial) liabilities. (p. 398)   LO2

- Management will generally try to assure that the debt service on financial (nonoperating) liabilities coincides with the cash flows from the assets financed.
- When large amounts of financing are required for, say, plant and equipment, firms find that bonds, notes, and other forms of long-term financing provide a cost-efficient means of raising capital.

Explain and illustrate the pricing of long-term nonoperating liabilities. (p. 401)   LO3

- The coupon rate indicated on a bond contract determines the periodic interest payment. The required return on any bond called the market (yield or effective) rate is determined by market conditions and rarely equals the coupon (contract) rate. The market rate is used to price the bond and determines the effective cost of the debt to the issuer.
- If the market rate is below the coupon rate, the bond will sell at a premium to its face value, assuring that the owner of the bond earns only the market rate of interest. If the market rate exceeds the coupon rate, the bond will sell at a discount so that the bond is issued at less than its face value.

Analyze and account for financial statement effects of long-term nonoperating liabilities. (p. 405)   LO4

- A discount for a bond selling below its face value represents additional interest expense over time to the issuer because the issuer received less than face value upon issuance, but must pay the holder the face value at the bond's maturity; this discount represents additional interest beyond the coupon payment to the holder. The premium on a bond selling above its face value lowers the interest cost to the issuer and the interest revenue received by the holder.
- Gains and losses on bonds repurchased, equal to the difference between the book value and the cash paid, must be reported in operating income, unless extraordinary; they do not represent operating activities and should be removed from operating cash flows in our analysis.

Explain how solvency ratios and debt ratings are determined and how they affect the cost of debt. (p. 411)   LO5

- Two debt-related ratios that are particularly useful in evaluating a company's solvency include the debt-to-equity ratio (page 000) and the times interest earned ratio (page 000).
- The market rate of interest to a firm reflects the creditworthiness of the particular issuer. Credit agencies play an important role in this process by issuing debt ratings.
- Borrowing is typically secured by covenants that place the issuer in a superior position to other creditors and covenants that put restrictions on the borrower's activities; bonds can also contain options including those for conversion or repurchase.

GUIDANCE ANSWERS . . . YOU MAKE THE CALL

You are the Analyst Accrued liabilities must be probable and estimable before they can be reported in the balance sheet. Black & Decker's reporting is not conservative, because in using the lower bound of a range of values, it may be understating its liabilities (and overstating equity).

As the defendant in the Vioxx lawsuits, Merck's management would argue that these claims are not probable, because they expect to win in court. As an analyst, you might believe otherwise and add an estimated liability to Merck's balance sheet.

You are the Vice President of Finance The types of restructurings you might consider are those yielding a strengthening of the financial ratios typically used to assess liquidity and solvency by the rating agencies. Such restructurings typically include inventory reduction to generate cash, the reallocation of cash outflows from investing activities (PPE) to debt reduction, and issuing stock for cash used to reduce debt (an equity-for-debt recapitalization). These actions increase liquidity or reduce financial leverage and, thus, should yield an improved debt rating. An improved debt rating gives your company access to more debt holders, as your current debt rating is below investment grade and is not a suitable investment for many professionally managed portfolios. An improved debt rating also yields a lower interest rate on your debt. Offsetting these benefits are costs such as the following: (1) potential loss of sales from inventory stock-outs; (2) potential future cash flow reductions and loss of market power from reduced investing in PPE; and (3) costs of equity issuances (which is more than debt since investors demand a higher return to compensate for added risk and the lack of tax deductibility of dividends vis-à-vis interest payments), which can yield a net increase in the total cost of capital. All cost and benefits must be assessed before you pursue any restructurings.

KEY RATIOS

$$\text{Debt-to-equity} = \frac{\text{Total liabilities}}{\text{Total stockholders' equity}} \qquad \text{Times interest earned} = \frac{\text{Earnings before interest and taxes}}{\text{Interest}}$$

KEY TERMS

Accounts payable (p. 391)

Accrued liabilities (p. 391)

Amortization (p. 406)

Annuity (p. 401)

Call provision (p. 409)

Collateral (pp. 401, 414)

Contingent liability (p. 395)

Cookie jar reserves (p. 398)

Coupon (contract or stated) rate (p. 401)

Covenants (p. 414)

Current maturities of long-term debt (p. 392)

Debt-to-equity ratio (D/E) (p. 411)

Default (p. 413)

Deferred performance liabilities (p. 392)

Discount (p. 403)

Earnings before interest and taxes (EBIT) (p. 412)

Face amount (p. 401)

Financial leverage (p. 391)

Leaning on the trade (p. 394)

Market (yield) rate (p. 401)

Options (p. 414)

Par (face) value (p. 402)

Periodic interest payments (p. 401)

Premium (p. 403)

Present value (p. 401)

Short-term interest-bearing debt (p. 392)

Single payment (p. 401)

Times interest earned (TIE) (p. 412)

MULTIPLE CHOICE

1. Which of the following statements is correct? A decrease in accrued wages liability:
   a. decreases cash flows from operations.
   b. decreases working capital.
   c. increases net income.
   d. increases net nonoperating (financial) assets.

2. On April 1, 2010, a firm borrows $12,000 at an annual interest rate of 10% with payments required semiannually on September 30 and March 31. How much interest payable and how much interest expense should appear on the firm's books at the end of the firm's fiscal year, December 31, 2011?
   a. $900 payable and $300 expense.
   b. $300 payable and $900 expense.
   c. $600 payable and $600 expense.
   d. $900 payable and $600 expense.

3. A firm issues $30,000,000 of 10-year bonds and receives $29.5 million in cash. Which of the following statements is correct?
   a. The bonds do not have a coupon rate because they are zeros.
   b. The market rate exceeds the coupon rate.
   c. The contract rate exceeds the market rate.
   d. The bonds were issued at par.

4. A firm issues $5 million of 10-year 6% notes with interest paid semiannually. At issuance the firm received $5,817,565 cash reflecting a 4% yield. What is the amount of premium written off against interest expense in the first year the notes are outstanding?
   a. $48,318
   b. $24,527
   c. $67,971
   d. $33,649

5. On June 1, 2010, Wild Inc. repays long-term debt due maturing on June 1, 2010. Which of the following ratios for the year 2010 is (are) decreased by this repayment?
    a. Current Ratio
    b. Quick Ratio
    c. Times Interest Earned
    d. Debt-to-Equity

Superscript [A]denotes assignments based on Appendix.

DISCUSSION QUESTIONS

Q9-1. What does the term *current liabilities* mean? What assets are usually used to settle current liabilities?

Q9-2. What is an accrual? How do accruals impact the balance sheet and the income statement?

Q9-3. What is the difference between a bond coupon rate and its market interest rate (yield)?

Q9-4. How does issuing a bond at a premium or discount affect the bond's *effective* interest rate vis-à-vis the coupon (stated) rate?

Q9-5. Why do companies report a gain or loss on the repurchase of their bonds (assuming the repurchase price is different from bond book value)?

Q9-6. How do debt ratings affect the cost of borrowing for a company?

Q9-7. How would you interpret a company's reported gain or loss on the repurchase of its bonds?

Q9-8. What do the following terms mean? (a) term loan, (b) bonds payable, (c) serial bonds, (d) call provision, (e) convertible bonds, (f) face value, (g) nominal rate, (h) bond discount, (i) bond premium, and (j) amortization of bond premium or discount.

Q9-9. What are the advantages and disadvantages of issuing bonds rather than common stock?

Q9-10. A $3,000,000 issue of 10-year, 9% bonds was sold at 98 plus accrued interest three months after the bonds were dated. What net amount of cash is received?

Q9-11. How does issuing bonds at a premium or discount "adjust the contract rate to the applicable market rate of interest"?

Q9-12. Regardless of whether premium or discount is involved, what generalization can be made about the change in the book value of bonds payable during the period in which they are outstanding?

Q9-13. If the effective interest amortization method is used for bonds payable, how does the periodic interest expense change over the life of the bonds when they are issued (a) at a discount and (b) at a premium?

Q9-14. How should premium and discount on bonds payable be presented in the balance sheet?

Q9-15. On April 30, 2010, one year before maturity, Weber Company retired $200,000 of 9% bonds payable at 101. The book value of the bonds on April 30 was $197,600. Bond interest was last paid on April 30, 2010. What is the gain or loss on the retirement of the bonds?

Q9-16. Brownlee Company borrowed money by issuing a 20-year mortgage note payable. The note will be repaid in equal monthly installments. The interest expense component of each payment decreases with each payment. Why?

Assignments with the Web Assign**. logo in the margin are available in WebAssign.**
See the Preface of the book for details.

MINI EXERCISES

M9-17. **Analyzing and Computing Financial Statement Effects of Bond Interest**   **LO4**
Huddart Company gave a creditor a 90-day, 8% note payable for $7,200 on December 16.

    a. Prepare the journal entry to record the year-end December 31st accounting adjustment Hubbart must make.
    b. Post the journal entries from part *a* to their respective T-accounts.
    c. Record the transaction from part *a* in the financial statement effects template.

	Balance Sheet					Income Statement		
Transaction	Cash Asset	+ Noncash Assets	= Liabil- ities	+ Contrib. Capital	+ Earned Capital	Revenues	– Expenses	= Net Income

LO1, LO2 — **M9-18. Analyzing and Determining the Amount of a Liability**

For each of the following situations, indicate the liability amount, if any, which is reported on the balance sheet of Hirst, Inc., at December 31, 2010.

a. Hirst owes $110,000 at year-end 2010 for its inventory purchases.

b. Hirst agreed to purchase a $28,000 drill press in January 2011.

c. During November and December of 2010, Hirst sold products to a firm with a 90-day warranty against product failure. Estimated 2011 costs of honoring this warranty are $2,200.

d. Hirst provides a profit-sharing bonus for its executives equal to 5% of its reported pretax annual income. The estimated pretax income for 2010 is $600,000. Bonuses are not paid until January of the following year.

LO3 — **M9-19. Interpreting Relations between Bond Price, Coupon, Yield, and Rating**

BOSTON SCIENTIFIC CORPORATION
NYSE :: BSX

The following notice appeared in *The Wall Street Journal* regarding a bond issuance by **Boston Scientific Corporation (BSX)**:

Boston Scientific Corp.—$500 million of notes was priced with the following terms in two parts via joint lead managers Merrill Lynch & Co., UBS Securities and Wachovia:

Amount: $250 million; Maturity: Jan. 12, 2011; Coupon: 4.25%; Price: 99.476;
Yield: 4.349%; Ratings: Baa (Moody's), A (S&P).

Amount: $250 million; Maturity: Jan. 12, 2017; Coupon: 5.125%; Price: 99.926;
Yield: 5.134%; Ratings: Baa (Moody's), A (S&P).

a. Discuss the relation between the coupon rate, issuance price, and yield for the 2011 issue.

b. Compare the yields on the two bond issues. Why are the yields different when the bond ratings are the same?

LO4, LO5 — **M9-20. Determining Gain or Loss on Bond Redemption**

WebAssign.

On April 30, 2011, one year before maturity, Easton Company retires $200,000 of its 9% bonds payable at the current market price of 101 (101% of the bond face amount, or $200,000 × 1.01 = $202,000). The bond book value on April 30, 2011, is $197,600 reflecting an unamortized discount of $2,400. Bond interest is presently fully paid and recorded up to the date of retirement. What is the gain or loss on retirement of these bonds?

LO4 — **M9-21. Interpreting Bond Footnote**

BRISTOL-MYERS SQUIBB COMPANY
NYSE :: BMY

Bristol-Myers Squibb Company (BMY) reports the following maturities schedule for its long-term debt in its 2009 10-K report:

The Company's principal value of long-term debt obligations was $5,737 million at December 31, 2008, of which $45 million is due in 2010, $647 million is due in 2013, and the remaining $5,045 million is due later than 2013.

a. What does the $45 million indicate for 2010?

b. What implications does this payment schedule have for your evaluation of BMY's liquidity and solvency?

LO1 — **M9-22. Classifying Debt Accounts into the Balance Sheet or Income Statement**

WebAssign.

Indicate the proper financial statement classification (balance sheet or income statement) for each of the following accounts:

a. Gain on Bond Retirement

b. Discount on Bonds Payable

c. Mortgage Notes Payable

d. Bonds Payable

e. Bond Interest Expense

f. Bond Interest Payable (due next period)

g. Premium on Bonds Payable

h. Loss on Bond Retirement

LO4 — **M9-23. Interpreting Bond Footnote Disclosures**

COMCAST
NASDAQ :: CMCSA

Comcast Corporation reports the following footnote to the long-term debt section of its 2008 10-K report:

Debt Covenants

Some of our loan agreements require that we maintain financial ratios based on debt, interest and operating income before depreciation and amortization, as defined in the agreements. In addition, certain of our subsidiary loan agreements contain restrictions on dividend payments and advances. We were in compliance with all financial covenants for all periods presented.

a. The financial ratios to which Comcast refers are similar to those discussed in this chapter. What effects might these ratios have on the degree of freedom that management has in running Comcast?

b. Violation of debt covenants is a serious event that typically triggers an "immediately due and payable" provision in the debt contract. What pressures might you envision for management if the company's ratios are near their covenant limits?

c. Certain of its assets are often restricted by a firm's bond covenants. What implications do these restrictions have on an analysis of the company and its liquidity and solvency position?

M9-24. Analyzing Financial Statement Effects of Bond Redemption   LO4

Holthausen Corporation issued $400,000 of 11%, 20-year bonds at 108 on January 1, 2004. Interest is payable semiannually on June 30 and December 31. Through January 1, 2010, Holthausen amortized $4,191 of the bond premium. On January 1, 2010, Holthausen retires the bonds at 103.

a. Prepare journal entries to record the transactions.
b. Post the journal entries from part *a* to their respective T-accounts.
c. Record each of the transactions from part *a* in the financial statement effects template.

M9-25. Analyzing Financial Statement Effects of Bond Redemption   LO4

Dechow, Inc., issued $250,000 of 8%, 15-year bonds at 96 on July 1, 2003. Interest is payable semiannually on December 31 and June 30. Through June 30, 2010, Dechow amortized $3,186 of the bond discount. On July 1, 2010, Dechow retired the bonds at 101.

a. Prepare journal entries to record the issue and retirement of these bonds. (Assume the June interest expense has already been recorded.)
b. Post the journal entries from part *a* to their respective T-accounts.
c. Record each of the transactions from part *a* in the financial statement effects template.

M9-26. Analyzing and Computing Accrued Interest on Notes   LO4

Compute any interest accrued for each of the following notes payable owed by Penman, Inc., as of December 31, 2010 (use a 365-day year):

Lender	Issuance Date	Principal	Coupon Rate (%)	Term
Nissim	11/21/10	$18,000	10%	120 days
Klein	12/13/10	14,000	9	90 days
Bildersee	12/19/10	16,000	12	60 days

M9-27. Debt Ratings and Capital Structure   LO5

General Mills, Inc. reports the following information in the Management Discussion & Analysis section of its 2008 10-K report:

GENERAL MILLS, INC.
NYSE :: GIS

Cash Flows from Financing Activities ($ millions)	2008
Change in notes payable	$ 946.6
Issuance of long-term debt	1,450.0
Repayment of long-term debt	(1,623.4)
Proceeds from stock issuances	1,089.4
Stock repurchases	(2,425.9)
Dividends paid	(529.7)
Total cash used for financing activities	($1,093.0)

a. General Mills reported net income of $1,294.7 million in 2008. What effect did these financing cash flows have on General Mills solvency measures in 2008? Explain.

b. Would the changes in financing tend to lower or increase the firm's debt rating? (Currently General Mills long-term debt is rated at lower medium grade.)

LO3 **M9-28. Computing Bond Issue Price**

WebAssign.

Bushman, Inc., issues $500,000 of 9% bonds that pay interest semiannually and mature in 10 years. Compute the bond issue price assuming that the bonds' market rate is:

a.   8% per year compounded semiannually.

b.   10% per year compounded semiannually.

LO3 **M9-29. Computing Issue Price for Zero-Coupon Bonds**

Baiman, Inc., issues $500,000 of zero-coupon bonds that mature in 10 years. Compute the bond issue price assuming that the bonds' market rate is:

a.   8% per year compounded semiannually.

b.   10% per year compounded semiannually.

c.   If prior to the debt issue at 10%, the firm had total assets of $3 million and total equity of $1 million, what would be the effect of the new borrowing on the financial leverage of the firm?

LO1 **M9-30. Financial Statement Effects of Accounts Payable Transactions**

WebAssign.

Petroni Company had the following transactions relating to its accounts payable:

1.   Purchases $300 of inventory on credit.
2.   Sells $300 of inventory for $420 on credit (cost side recorded in part 3).
3.   Records $300 cost of sales with transaction 2.
4. $300 cash paid to settle accounts payable from 1.
5. $420 cash received from accounts receivable in 2.

a.   Prepare journal entries to record the transactions.

b.   Post the journal entries from part *a* to their respective T-accounts.

c.   Record each of the transactions from part *a* in the financial statement effects template.

LO3, LO4 **M9-31. Computing Bond Issue Price and Preparing an Amortization Table in Excel**

On January 1, 2009, Kaplan, Inc., issues $500,000 of 9% bonds that pay interest semiannually and mature in 10 years (December 31, 2009).

a.   Using the Excel PRICE worksheet function, compute the issue price assuming that the bonds' market rate is 8% per year compounded semiannually. (Use 100 for the redemption value to get a price as a percentage of the face amount, and use 1 for the basis.)

b.   Prepare an amortization table in Excel to demonstrate the amortization of the book (carrying) value to the $500,000 maturity value at the end of the 20th semiannual period.

LO5 **M9-32. Assessing the Effects of Financial Leverage**

VERIZON
NYSE :: VZ

The following data relate to three of **Verizon**'s major competitors in the telecommunications industry based on data from the firms' 10-K reports:

Firm	D/E	TIE
Comcast Corporation	1.79	2.66
Qwest Communications	**	2.08
Sprint/Nextel Corporation	1.97	*

COMCAST
NASDAQ :: CMCSA

QWEST
NYSE :: Q

SPRINT NEXTEL
NYSE :: S

*Not meaningful because income is negative. ** Not meaningful because equity is negative.

Using Verizon's ratios calculated in this chapter, comment on Verizon's solvency as compared to three of its largest competitors.

LO4 **M9-33. Classifying Bond-Related Accounts**

Indicate the proper financial statement classification for each of the following accounts:

Gain on Bond Retirement (material amount)
Discount on Bonds Payable
Mortgage Notes Payable
Bonds Payable
Bond Interest Expense
Bond Interest Payable
Premium on Bonds Payable

M9-34. **Recording and Assessing the Effects of Installment Loans**   **LO3, LO4**
On December 31, 2010, Thomas, Inc., borrowed $700,000 on a 12%, 15-year mortgage note payable. The note is to be repaid in equal semiannual installments of $50,854 (payable on June 30 and December 31).

    a. Prepare journal entries to record (1) the issuance of the mortgage note payable, (2) the payment of the first installment on June 30, 2011, and (3) the payment of the second installment on December 31, 2011. Round amounts to the nearest dollar.

    b. Post the journal entries from part *a* to their respective T-accounts.

    c. Record each of the transactions from part *a* in the financial statement effects template.

M9-35. **Determining Bond Prices**   **LO3**
Lunar, Inc., plans to issue $900,000 of 10% bonds that will pay interest semiannually and mature in 5 years. Assume that the effective interest rate is 12% per year compounded semiannually. Compute the selling price of the bonds. Use Tables 2 and 3 in Appendix A near the end of the book.

EXERCISES

E9-36. **Analyzing and Computing Accrued Warranty Liability and Expense**   **LO1**
Waymire Company sells a motor that carries a 60-day unconditional warranty against product failure. Waymire estimates that between the sale and lapse of the product warranty, 2% of the 69,000 units sold this period will require repair at an average cost of $50 per unit. A warranty liability of $10,000 is currently on the balance sheet.

    a. How much warranty expense must Waymire report in its income statement and what amount of *additional* warranty liability must it report on its balance sheet for this year?

    b. What analysis issues do we need to consider with respect to the amount of reported warranty liability?

    c. What solvency ratios are increased if warranty liabilities rise?

E9-37. **Analyzing Contingencies and Assessing Liabilities**   **LO1**
The following independent situations represent various types of liabilities. Analyze each situation and indicate which of the following is the proper accounting treatment for each company: (1) record in accounts, (2) disclose in a financial statement footnote, or (3) neither record nor disclose.

    a. A stockholder has filed a lawsuit against Clinch Corporation. Clinch's attorneys have reviewed the facts of the case. Their review revealed that similar lawsuits have never resulted in a cash award and it is highly unlikely that this lawsuit will either.

    b. Foster Company signed a 60-day, 10% note when it purchased items from another company.

    c. The Department of Environment Protection notifies Shevlin Company that a state where it has a plant is filing a lawsuit for groundwater pollution against Shevlin and another company that has a plant adjacent to Shevlin's plant. Test results have not identified the exact source of the pollution. Shevlin's manufacturing process often produces by-products that can pollute groundwater.

    d. Sloan Company manufactured and sold products to a retailer that sold the products to consumers. The Sloan Company warranty offers replacement of the product if it is found to be defective within 90 days of the sale to the consumer. Historically, 1.2% of the products are returned for replacement.

E9-38. **Analyzing and Computing Accrued Wages Liability and Expense**   **LO1**
Demski Company pays its employees on the 1st and 15th of each month. It is March 31 and Demski is preparing financial statements for this quarter. Its employees have earned $25,000 since the 15th of this month and have not yet been paid. How will Demski's balance sheet and income statement change to reflect the accrual of wages that must be made at March 31? What balance sheet and income statement accounts would be incorrectly reported if Demski failed to make this accrual (for each account indicate whether it would be overstated or understated)?

E9-39. **Analyzing and Reporting Financial Statement Effects of Bond Transactions**   **LO4**
On January 1, 2010, Hutton Corp. issued $300,000 of 15-year, 11% bonds payable for $377,814, yielding an effective interest rate of 8%. Interest is payable semiannually on June 30 and December 31.

    a. Show computations to confirm the issue price of $377,814.

    b. Prepare journal entries to record the bond issuance, semiannual interest payment and premium amortization on June 30, 2010, and semiannual interest payment and premium amortization on December 31, 2010. Use the effective interest rate.

    c. Post the journal entries from part *b* to their respective T-accounts.

    d. Record each of the transactions from part *b* in the financial statement effects template.

LO3   E9-40.   Computing the Bond Issue Price

D'Souza, Inc., issues $900,000 of 11% bonds that pay interest semiannually and mature in seven years. Assume that the market interest (yield) rate is 12% per year compounded semiannually. Compute the bond issue price.

LO5   E9-41.   Interpreting Warranty Liability Disclosures

THE BLACK & DECKER CORPORATION
NYSE :: BDK

The following disclosure was provided by **The Black & Decker Corporation** in its 2008 10-K report:

Product Warranties: Most of the Corporation's products in the Power Tools and Accessories segment and Hardware and Home Improvement segment carry a product warranty. That product warranty, in the United States, generally provides that customers can return a defective product during the specified warranty period following purchase in exchange for a replacement product or repair at no cost to the consumer.

    The following provides information with respect to the Corporation's warranty accrual ($ millions):

	2008	2007
Warranty reserve at January 1	$ 60.5	$ 60.2
Accruals for warranties issued during the period and changes in estimates related to pre-existing warranties	123.0	118.8
Settlements made	(125.1)	(120.9)
Currency translation adjustments	(3.2)	2.4
Warranty reserve at December 31	$ 55.2	$ 60.5

    a. Prepare a journal entry to record warranty expense for Black & Decker in 2008.

    b. Post the entry from part *a* in the T-accounts.

    c. Black & Decker reported sales of $6,086.1 million in 2008 and $6,563.2 million in 2007. Calculate the ratio of warranty expense to sales for each year.

LO4   E9-42.   Reporting Financial Statement Effects of Bond Transactions

Lundholm, Inc., which reports financial statements each December 31, is authorized to issue $500,000 of 9%, 15-year bonds dated May 1, 2010, with interest payments on October 31 and April 30. Assume the bonds are issued at par on May 1, 2010.

    a. Prepare journal entries to record the bond issuance, payment of the first semiannual period's interest, and retirement of $300,000 of the bonds at 101 on November 1, 2011.

    b. Post the journal entries from part *a* to their respective T-accounts.

    c. Record each of the transactions from part *a* in the financial statement effects template.

LO3, LO4   E9-43.   Reporting Financial Statement Effects of Bond Transactions

WebAssign.

On January 1, 2010, McKeown, Inc., issued $250,000 of 8%, 9-year bonds for $220,776, yielding a market (yield) rate of 10%. Semiannual interest is payable on June 30 and December 31 of each year.

    a. Show computations to confirm the bond issue price.

    b. Prepare journal entries to record the bond issuance, semiannual interest payment and discount amortization on June 30, 2010, and semiannual interest payment and discount amortization on December 31, 2010. Use the effective interest rate.

    c. Post the journal entries from part *b* to their respective T-accounts.

    d. Record each of the transactions from part *b* in the financial statement effects template.

LO3, LO4   E9-44.   Reporting Financial Statement Effects of Bond Transactions

On January 1, 2010, Shields, Inc., issued $800,000 of 9%, 20-year bonds for $879,172, yielding a market (yield) rate of 8%. Semiannual interest is payable on June 30 and December 31 of each year.

    a. Show computations to confirm the bond issue price.

    b. Prepare journal entries to record the bond issuance, semiannual interest payment and premium amortization on June 30, 2010, and semiannual interest payment and premium amortization on December 31, 2010. Use the effective interest rate.

   c. Post the journal entries from part *b* to their respective T-accounts.

   d. Record each of the transactions from part *b* in the financial statement effects template.

E9-45. Analyzing Bond Pricing, Interest Rates, and Financial Statement Effect of a Bond Issue **LO3, LO4**
Following is a price quote for $200 million of 6.55% coupon bonds issued by **Deere & Company**
that mature in October 2028 (from www.bondpage.com):

DEERE & COMPANY
NYSE :: DE

Ratings Industry	Issue Call Information	Coupon/Maturity	Price/YTM
A1/AA........................	**Deere & Company**	6.550	108.104
Industrial	Non Callable, NYBE, DE	10-01-2028	5.890

This quote indicates that Deere's bonds have a market price of 108.104 (108.104% of face value),
resulting in a yield of 5.89%.

   a. Assuming that these bonds were originally issued at or close to par value, what does the above
market price reveal about the direction that interest rates have changed since Deere issued its
bonds? (Assume that Deere's debt rating has remained the same.)

   b. Does the change in interest rates since the issuance of these bonds affect the amount of interest expense that Deere is reporting in its income statement? Explain.

   c. If Deere was to repurchase its bonds at the above market price of 108.104, how would the
repurchase affect its current income?

   d. Assuming that the bonds remain outstanding until their maturity, at what market price will the
bonds sell on their due date of October 1, 2028?

E9-46.[A] **Computing Present Values of Single Amounts and Annuities** **LO3**
Refer to Tables 2 and 3 in Appendix A near the end of the book to compute the present value for
each of the following amounts:

   a. $90,000 received 10 years hence if the annual interest rate is
      1. 8% compounded annually.
      2. 8% compounded semiannually.

   b. $1,000 received at the end of each year for the next 8 years if money is worth 10% per year
compounded annually.

   c. $600 received at the end of each six months for the next 15 years if the interest rate is 8% per
year compounded semiannually.

   d. $500,000 inheritance 10 years hence if money is worth 10% per year compounded annually.

E9-47. Analyzing and Reporting Financial Statement Effects of Bond Transactions **LO3, LO4**
On January 1, 2010, Trueman Corp. issued $600,000 of 20-year, 11% bonds for $554,860, yielding
a market (yield) rate of 12%. Interest is payable semiannually on June 30 and December 31.

   a. Confirm the bond issue price.

   b. Prepare journal entries to record the bond issuance, semiannual interest payment and discount
amortization on June 30, 2010, and semiannual interest payment and discount amortization on
December 31, 2010. Use the effective interest rate.

   c. Post the journal entries from part *b* to their respective T-accounts.

   d. Record each of the transactions from part *b* in the financial statement effects template.

E9-48. Analyzing and Reporting Financial Statement Effects of Bond Transactions **LO3, LO4**
On January 1, 2010, Verrecchia Company issued $400,000 of 5-year, 13% bonds for $446,329, yielding a market (yield) rate of 10%. Interest is payable semiannually on June 30 and December 31.

   a. Show computations to confirm the bond issue price.

   b. Prepare journal entries to record the bond issuance, semiannual interest payment and premium
amortization on June 30, 2010, and semiannual interest payment and premium amortization
on December 31, 2010. Use the effective interest rate.

   c. Post the journal entries from part *b* to their respective T-accounts.

   d. Record each of the transactions from part *b* in the financial statement effects template.

LO1, LO2, LO4   **E9-49.**   **Reporting and Interpreting Bond Disclosures**

The adjusted trial balance for the Hass Corporation at the end of 2010 contains the following accounts:

$ 25,000	Bond Interest Payable
600,000	9% Bonds Payable due 2012
500,000	10% Bonds Payable due 2011
19,000	Discount on 9% Bonds Payable
15,000	Premium on 10% Bonds Payable
170,500	Zero-Coupon Bonds Payable due 2013
100,000	8% Bonds Payable due 2015

Prepare the long-term liabilities section of the balance sheet. Indicate the proper balance sheet classification for accounts listed above that do not belong in the long-term liabilities section.

LO3, LO4   **E9-50.**   **Recording and Assessing the Effects of Installment Loans**

On December 31, 2010, Dehning, Inc., borrowed $500,000 on an 8%, 10-year mortgage note payable. The note is to be repaid in equal quarterly installments of $18,278 (beginning March 31, 2011).

a.   Prepare journal entries to reflect (1) the issuance of the mortgage note payable, (2) the payment of the first installment on March 31, 2011, and (3) the payment of the second installment on June 30, 2011. Round amounts to the nearest dollar.

b.   Post the journal entries from part *a* to their respective T-accounts.

c.   Record each of the transactions from part *a* in the financial statement effects template.

PROBLEMS

LO3, LO4, LO5   **P9-51.**   **Interpreting Warranty Liability Disclosures**

HEWLETT-PACKARD
NYSE :: HPQ

DELL, INC.
NASDAQ :: DELL

The following information was extracted from the 2008 10-K reports of **Hewlett-Packard Company** and **Dell Inc.**

($ millions)	Hewlett-Packard		Dell, Inc.	
	2008	2007	2008	2007
Sales revenue	$91,697	$84,229	$61,101	$61,133
Warranty expense	3,244	2,604	1,180	1,176
Accrued warranty liability	2,614	2,376	1,035	929

Required

a.   Compute the amount of warranty costs incurred in 2008 for each company. (That is, what amount was spent for warranty repairs and settlements in 2008?)

b.   Compare these two companies on the basis of the ratio of warranty expense to sales. What factors might explain any difference that you observe?

LO3, LO4   **P9-52.**   **Recording and Assessing the Effects of Bond Financing (with Accrued Interest)**

Eskew, Inc., which closes its books on December 31, is authorized to issue $500,000 of 9%, 15-year bonds dated May 1, 2010, with interest payments on November 1 and May 1.

Required

Assuming that the bonds were sold at 100 plus accrued interest on October 1, 2010, prepare the necessary journal entries, post the journal entries to their respective T-accounts, and record each transaction in the financial statement effects template.

a.   The bond issuance.

b.   Payment of the first semiannual period's interest on November 1, 2010.

c.   Accrual of bond interest expense at December 31, 2010.

d.   Payment of the semiannual interest on May 1, 2011. (The firm does not make reversing entries.)

e.   Retirement of $300,000 of the bonds at 101 on May 1, 2015 (immediately after the interest payment on that date).

LO3, LO4   **P9-53.**   **Interpreting Debt Footnotes on Interest Rates and Expense**

CVS CAREMARK
CORPORATION
NYSE :: CVS

CVS Caremark Corporation discloses the following footnote in its 10-K relating to its debt:

BORROWING AND CREDIT AGREEMENTS

Following is a summary of the Company's borrowings as reported in note 4 to the firm's 10-K.

(in millions)	Dec. 31, 2008	Dec. 29, 2007
Commercial paper.	$ 2,544.1	$ 2,085.0
Bridge credit facility	500.0	—
4.0% senior notes due 2009	650.0	650.0
Floating rate notes due 2010	2,100.0	1,750.0
5.75% senior notes due 2011	800.0	800.0
4.875% senior notes due 2014	550.0	550.0
6.125% senior notes due 2016	700.0	700.0
5.75% senior notes due 2017	1,750.0	1,750.0
6.25% senior notes due 2027	1,000.0	1,000.0
8.52% ESOP notes due 2008	—	44.5
6.302% Enhanced Capital Advantage Preferred Securities	1,000.0	1,000.0
Mortgage notes payable	7.1	7.3
Capital lease obligations.	153.4	145.1
	11,754.6	10,481.9
Less:		
Short-term debt	(3,044.1)	(2,085.0)
Current portion of long-term debt.	(653.3)	(47.2)
	$ 8,057.2	$ 8,349.7

CVS also discloses that its gross interest expense was $529.8 million, but that it paid interest of $573.7 million.

Required

a. What is the average interest rate that CVS paid on its debt in 2008?

b. Does your computation in part *a* seem reasonable given the disclosure relating to specific bond issues? Explain.

c. Why can the amount of interest paid be different from the amount of interest expense recorded in the income statement?

P9-54. Recording and Assessing the Effects of Bond Financing (with Accrued Interest)   LO3, LO4

Petroni, Inc., which closes its books on December 31, is authorized to issue $800,000 of 9%, 20-year bonds dated March 1, 2010, with interest payments on September 1 and March 1.

Required

Assuming that the bonds were sold at 100 plus accrued interest on July 1, 2010, prepare the necessary journal entries, post the journal entries to their respective T-accounts, and record each transaction in the financial statement effects template.

a. The bond issuance.

b. Payment of the semiannual interest on September 1, 2010.

c. Accrual of bond interest expense at December 31, 2010.

d. Payment of the semiannual interest on March 1, 2011. (The firm does not make reversing entries.)

e. Retirement of $200,000 of the bonds at 101 on March 1, 2011 (immediately after the interest payment on that date).

P9-55. Preparing an Amortization Schedule and Recording the Effects of Bonds   LO3, LO4

On December 31, 2010, Kasznik, Inc., issued $720,000 of 11%, 10-year bonds for $678,708, yielding an effective interest rate of 12%. Semiannual interest is payable on June 30 and December 31 each year. The firm uses the effective interest method to amortize the discount.

Required

a. Prepare an amortization schedule showing the necessary information for the first two interest periods. Round amounts to the nearest dollar.

b. Prepare the journal entries for (1) the bond issuance on December 31, 2010, (2) to record bond interest expense and discount amortization at June 30, 2011, and (3) to record bond interest expense and discount amortization at December 31, 2011.

c. Post the journal entries from part *b* to their respective T-accounts.

d. Record each of the transactions from part *b* in the financial statement effects template.

LO3, LO4 **P9-56.** **Preparing an Amortization Schedule and Recording the Effects of Bonds**

On April 30, 2010, Cheng, Inc., issued $250,000 of 6%, 15-year bonds for $206,770, yielding an effective interest rate of 8%. Semiannual interest is payable on October 31 and April 30 each year. The firm uses the effective interest method to amortize the discount.

Required

a. Prepare an amortization schedule showing the necessary information for the first two interest periods. Round amounts to the nearest dollar.

b. Prepare the journal entries (1) for the bond issuance on April 30, 2010, (2) to record the bond interest payment and discount amortization at October 31, 2010, (3) the adjusting entry to record bond interest expense and discount amortization at December 31, 2010, the close of the firm's accounting year, and (4) to record the bond interest payment and discount amortization at April 30, 2011.

c. Post the journal entries from part *b* to their respective T-accounts.

d. Record each of the transactions from part *b* in the financial statement effects template.

LO3, LO4 **P9-57.** **Recording and Assessing the Effects of Installment Loans: Semiannual Installments**

On December 31, 2010, Wasley Corporation borrowed $500,000 on a 10%, 10-year mortgage note payable. The note is to be repaid with equal semiannual installments, beginning June 30, 2011.

Required

a. Compute the amount of the semiannual installment payment. Use the appropriate table (in Appendix A near the end of the book) or a financial calculator, and round amount to the nearest dollar.

b. Prepare the journal entry (1) to record Wasley's borrowing of funds on December 31, 2010, (2) to record Wasley's installment payment on June 30, 2011, and (3) to record Wasley's installment payment on December 31, 2011. (Round amounts to the nearest dollar.)

c. Post the journal entries from part *b* to their respective T-accounts.

d. Record each of the transactions from part *b* in the financial statement effects template.

LO3, LO4 **P9-58.** **Recording and Assessing the Effects of Installment Loans: Quarterly Installments**

On December 31, 2010, Watts Corporation borrowed $950,000 on an 8%, 5-year mortgage note payable. The note is to be repaid with equal quarterly installments, beginning March 31, 2011.

Required

a. Compute the amount of the quarterly installment payment. Use the appropriate table (in Appendix A near the end of the book) or a financial calculator, and round amount to the nearest dollar.

b. Prepare the journal entries (1) to record the borrowing of funds by Watts Corporation on December 31, 2010, (2) to record the installment payment by Watts Corporation on March 31, 2011, and (3) to record the installment payment by Watts Corporation on June 30, 2011.

c. Post the journal entries from part *b* to their respective T-accounts.

d. Record each of the transactions from part *b* in the financial statement effects template.

LO3 **P9-59.**[A] **Computing Present Values**

Use the interest tables in Appendix A near the end of the book (or a calculator) to answer the following.

Compute the present value of each of the following items.

Required

a. $90,000 seven years hence if the annual interest rate is
  1. 9% compounded annually.
  2. 9% compounded semiannually.
  3. 9% compounded quarterly.

b. $1,000 received at the end of each year for the next 5 years if money is worth 6% per year compounded annually.

c. $2,400 received at the end of each period of six months for the next 12 years if the interest rate is 8% per year compounded semiannually.

d. $500,000 inheritance 10 years hence if money is worth 10% per year compounded annually.

e. $2,500 received each half-year for the next 10 years, plus a single sum of $85,000 at the end of 10 years if the interest rate is 12% per year compounded semiannually.

P9-60. ^A Determining Present and Future Values

Use the interest tables in Appendix A near the end of the book (or a calculator) to compute the following amounts requested.

Required

a. Calculate the future value of a single amount of $7,000 invested for 15 years at 10% compounded annually.

b. Calculate the future value of a single amount of $7,000 invested for 15 years at 10% compounded semiannually.

c. Calculate the present value of $29,241 received 15 years from today, assuming a discount rate of 10% compounded annually.

d. Calculate the present value of an annuity of 2 annual payments of $6,000 discounted at 12% per year (compounded annually).

e. Calculate the present value of 24 monthly payments of $500 discounted at 12% per year (1% per month).

CASES AND PROJECTS

C9-61. Interpreting Debt Disclosures

The Pepsi Bottling Group Inc. reports $4,784 million of long-term debt in Note 9 of its 2008 10-K report.

Note 9 – Short-Term Borrowings and Long-Term Debt

	2008	2007
Short-term borrowings		
Current maturities of long-term debt	$1,305	$ 7
Other short-term borrowings	103	240
	$1,408	$ 247
Long-term debt		
5.63% (5.2% effective rate) senior notes due 2009	$1,300	$1,300
4.63% (4.6% effective rate) senior notes due 2012	1,000	1,000
5.00% (5.2% effective rate) senior notes due 2013	400	400
6.95% (7.4% effective rate) senior notes due 2014	1,300	–
4.13% (4.4% effective rate) senior notes due 2015	250	250
5.50% (5.3% effective rate) senior notes due 2016	800	800
7.00% (7.1% effective rate) senior notes due 2029	1,000	1,000
Capital lease obligations	8	9
Other (average rate 14.43%)	37	29
	6,095	4,788
SFAS 133 adjustment (adjustment for the fair value of interest rate hedges)	6	–
Unamortized discount, net	(12)	(11)
Current maturities of long-term debt	(1,305)	(7)
	$4,784	$4,770

On October 24, 2008, we issued $1.3 billion of 6.95% senior notes due 2014 (the "Notes"). The Notes were guaranteed by PepsiCo on February 17, 2009. A portion of this debt was used to repay our senior notes due in 2009 at their maturity on February 17, 2009. In the interim, these proceeds were placed in short-term investments.

Debt Covenants—Certain of our senior notes have redemption features and non-financial covenants that will, among other things, limit our ability to create or assume liens, enter into sale and lease-back transactions, engage in mergers or consolidations and transfer or lease all or substantially all of our assets. Additionally, certain of our credit facilities and senior notes have financial covenants consisting of the following:

- Our debt to capitalization ratio should not be greater than 0.75 on the last day of a fiscal quarter when PepsiCo's ratings are A- by S&P and A3 by Moody's or higher. Debt is defined as total long-term and short-term debt plus accrued interest plus total standby letters of credit and other guarantees less cash and cash equivalents not in excess of $500 million. Capitalization is defined as debt plus shareholders' equity plus minority interest, excluding the impact of the cumulative translation adjustment.

- Our debt to EBITDA ratio should not be greater than five on the last day of a fiscal quarter when PepsiCo's ratings are less than A- by S&P or A3 by Moody's. EBITDA is defined as the last four quarters of earnings before depreciation, amortization, net interest expense, income taxes, minority interest, net other non-operating expenses and extraordinary items.

- New secured debt should not be greater than 15% of our net tangible assets. Net tangible assets are defined as total assets less current liabilities and net intangible assets.

As of December 27, 2008, we were in compliance with all debt covenants.

Interest Payments and Expense—Amounts paid to third parties for interest, net of settlements from our interest rate swaps, were $293 million, $305 million and $289 million in 2008, 2007 and 2006, respectively. Total interest expense incurred during 2008, 2007 and 2006 was $316 million, $305 million and $298 million, respectively.

Required

a. PBG reports $1,305 million as current maturities of long-term debt at December 31, 2008. Explain this reporting. Why is this relevant to any analysis of PBG's creditworthiness?

b. At December 31, 2008, the $1,000 million of 7% senior notes maturing in 2029 were priced at 98.919. Assuming that these notes were originally issued at par, and also assuming that PBG's bond rating has not changed, what has happened to interest rates since 1999 when these bonds were issued?

c. Explain how the restrictive covenants reported in PBG's 10-K might affect our analysis of the company.

d. PBG reports unamortized discount of $12 million. What is this? What effect does unamortized discount have on PBG's interest expense?

C9-62. **Analyzing Bond Rates, Yields, Prices, and Credit Ratings**

Reproduced below is footnote 7 covering long-term debt from the 10-K report of **Southwest Airlines Co.**:

Long-Term Debt

(in millions)	2007	2006
Pass Through Certificates.	$ 480	—
7 7/8% Notes due 2007.	—	100
French Credit Agreements due 2012	32	37
6 1/2% Notes due 2012.	386	369
5 1/4% Notes due 2014.	352	336
5 3/4% Notes due 2016.	300	300
5 1/4% Notes due 2017.	311	300
French Credit Agreements due 2017	94	100
7 3/8% Debentures due 2027	103	100
Capital leases	52	63
	2,110	1,705
Less current maturities	41	122
Less debt discount and issue costs.	19	16
	$2,050	$1,567

As of December 31, 2007, aggregate annual principal maturities of debt and capital leases for the 5-year period ending December 31, 2012, were $40 million in 2008, $42 million in 2009, $50 million in 2010, $44 million in 2011, $418 million in 2012, and $1.5 billion thereafter.

Reproduced below is a rating of Southwest Airlines's $385 million, 6.5% note issuance, due in 2012. The rating is from Fitch Ratings, Ltd.:

				Ratings			
Maturity Date	Currency	Total Amount	Coupon Rate	Long Term	Short Term	CUSIP	ISIN
01-MAR-2012	USD	$385,000,000	6.5%	A	—	844741AV0	US844741AV08

Following is a price quote on those same Southwest Airlines's $385 million notes at the date of issue:

Ratings	Ticker	Description	Coupon	Maturity	YTC/YTM	Price
Baa/A	LUV	Southwest Airls Co	6.500	03-01-2012	7.450	97.29

This quote indicates that the Southwest Airlines notes with a 6.5% coupon rate trades at 97.29% of par resulting in a yield to the investor of 7.45%.

Required

a. Why is information relating to a company's scheduled maturities of debt useful in an analysis of its financial condition?

b. Southwest reported $119 million in interest expense in its 2007 income statement. In the note to its statement of cash flows, Southwest indicates that the cash portion of this expense is $63 million. What could account for the difference between interest expense and interest paid? Explain.

c. What factors would be important to consider in attempting to quantify the relative riskiness of Southwest compared with other borrowers? Explain.

d. What is the concurrent dollar value of Southwest's $385 million 6.5% notes? How would the difference between this value and the $385 million face amount of the issue be reflected in Southwest's financial statements if they originally sold at par? What effect would the repurchase of this entire note issue at the market price have on Southwest's financial statements? What does the 97.29 price tell you about the general trend in interest rates since Southwest sold this bond issue? Explain.

e. Give the entry for the issue of the $300 million senior unsecured Notes due 2016 assuming that the notes were issued at a price of 99.

C9-63. Assessing Debt Financing, Company Interests, and Managerial Ethics **LO3, LO4, LO5**

Foster Corporation is in the third quarter of the current year, and projections are that net income will be down about $600,000 from the previous year. Foster's return on assets is also projected to decline from its usual 15% to approximately 13%. If earnings do decline, this year will be the second consecutive year of decline. Foster's president is quite concerned about these projections (and his job) and has called a meeting of the firm's officers for next week to consider ways to "turn things around—and fast."

Margot Barth, treasurer of Foster Corporation, has received a memorandum from her assistant, Lorie McNichols. Barth had asked McNichols if she had any suggestions as to how Foster might improve its earnings performance for the current year. McNichols' memo reads as follows:

> As you know, we have $3,000,000 of 8%, 20-year bonds payable outstanding. We issued these bonds 10 years ago at face value. When they mature, we would probably replace them with other bonds. The economy right now is in a phase of high inflation, and interest rates for bonds have soared to about 16%. My proposal is to replace these bonds right now. More specifically, I propose:
>
> 1. Immediately issue $3,000,000 of 20-year, 16% bonds payable. These bonds will be issued at face value.
> 2. Use the proceeds from the new bonds to buy back and retire our outstanding 8% bonds. Because of the current high rates of interest, these bonds are trading in the market at $1,900,000.
> 3. The benefits to Foster are that (a) the retirement of the old bonds will generate a $1,100,000 gain for the income statement and (b) there will be an extra $1,100,000 of cash available for other uses.

Barth is intrigued by the possibility of generating a $1,100,000 gain for the income statement. However, she is not sure this proposal is in the best long-run interests of the firm and its stockholders.

Required

a. How is the $1,100,000 gain calculated from the retirement of the old bonds? Where would this gain be reported in Foster's income statement?

b. Why might this proposal not be in the best long-run interests of the firm and its stockholders?

c. What possible ethical conflict is present in this proposal?

SOLUTIONS TO REVIEW PROBLEMS

Mid-Chapter Review 1

Solution

a. A decrease in accounts payable results in a decrease in net cash flows from operating activities. This is the opposite of *leaning on the trade*.

b. A decrease in accounts payable (and accrued liabilities) increases net operating working capital, with consequent decline in reported cash flow. As a result, the reduction in payables can be costly, because it may force the company to seek alternative financing at a higher interest cost. On the other hand, if payables were previously too high, the reduction in payables may have been a necessary step to maintaining good terms with suppliers. Management must always be aware of the potentially damaging consequences of leaning on the trade to a much greater extent than is customary.

Mid-Chapter Review 2

Solution

Yes. Liabilities and expenses must be recognized when incurred, regardless of when payment is made, and matched with the revenues they helped generate. Failure to recognize the wages owed and wages expense to employees for the period would understate liabilities and overstate income. Pratt must reflect the wages earned and the related expense in its financial statements as follows:

The appropriate journal entry would be:

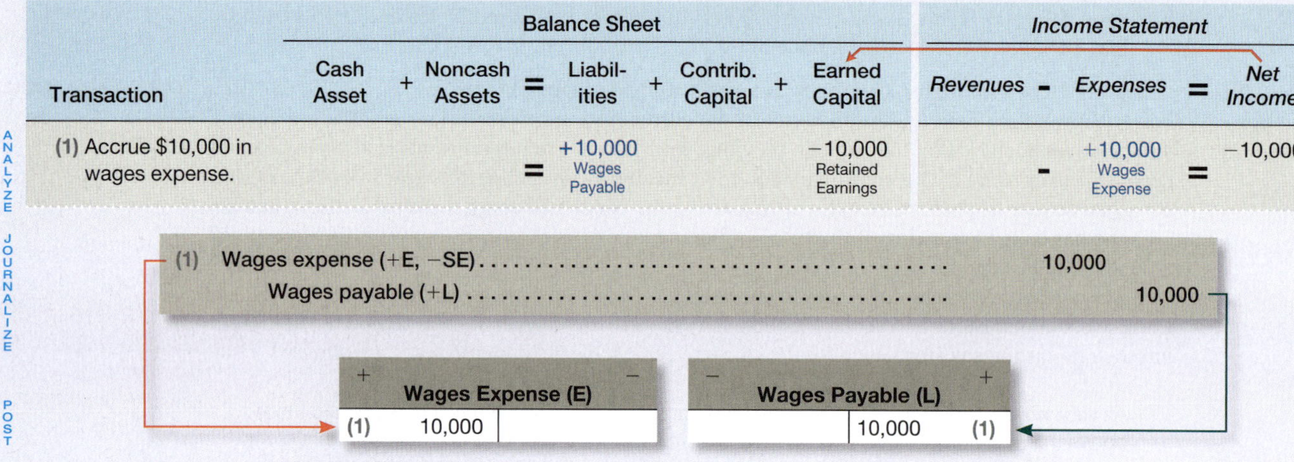

Mid-Chapter Review 3

Solution

The related journal entry to recognize the accrual of interest is:

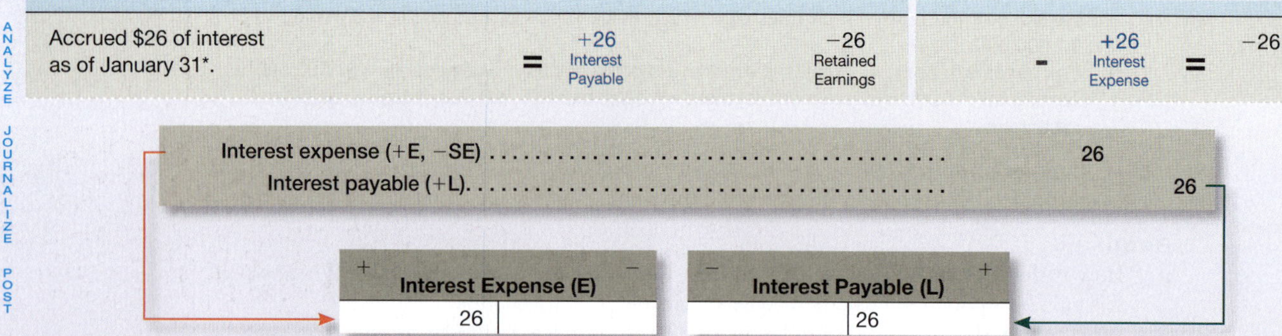

*Accrued interest for a 16-day period at January 31 = $10,000 × 0.06 × 16/365 = $26.

Chapter-End Review

Solution

1. Issue price for $300,000, 15-year, 10% semiannual bonds discounted at 8%:

Present value of principal payment ($300,000 × 0.30832)	$ 92,496
Present value of semiannual interest payments ($15,000 × 17.29203) . . .	259,380
Issue price of bonds	$351,876

2.

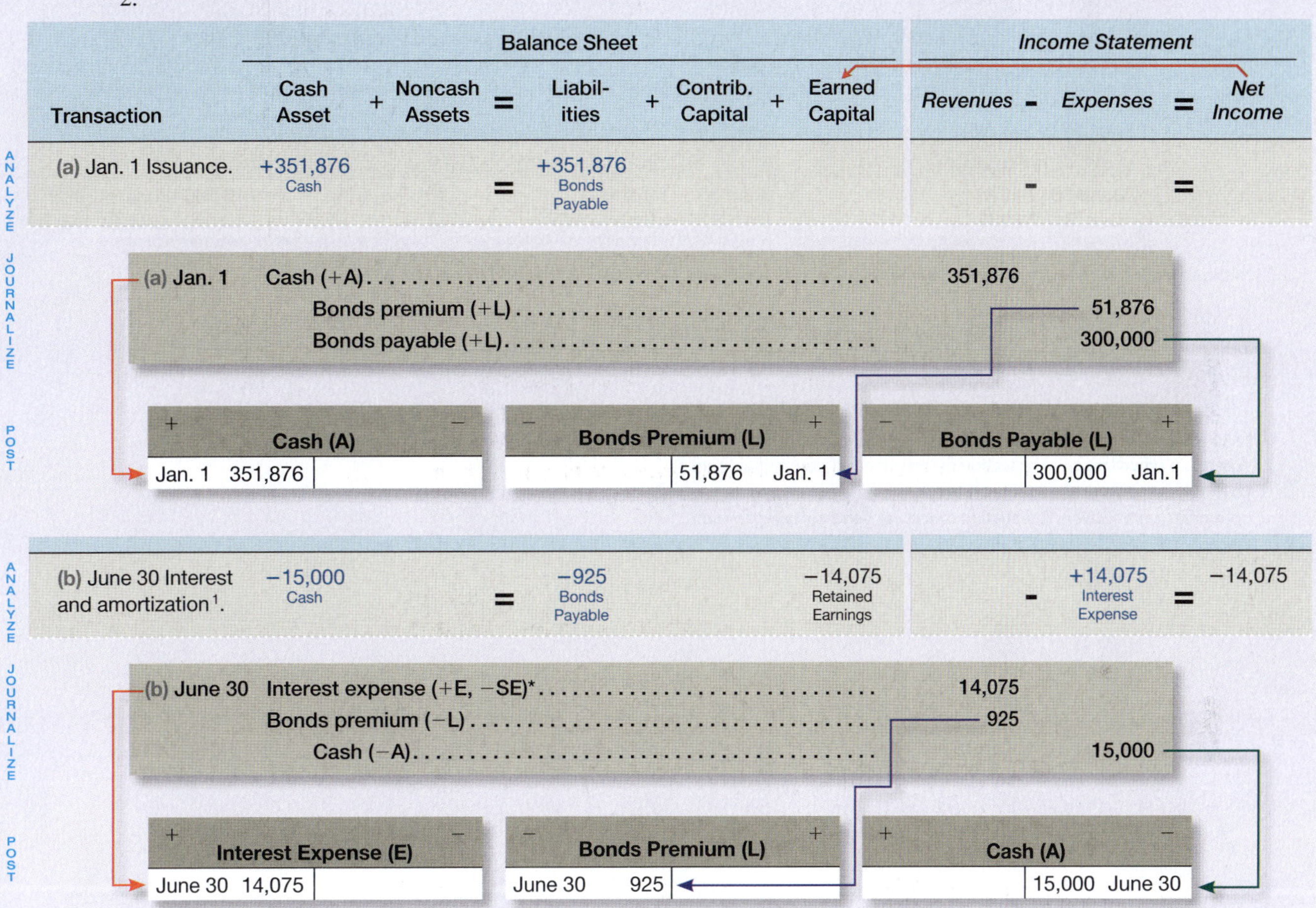

continued

continued from previous page

	Balance Sheet						Income Statement		
Transaction	Cash Asset	+ Noncash Assets	= Liabil-ities	+ Contrib. Capital	+ Earned Capital		Revenues −	Expenses	= Net Income
(c) Dec. 31 Interest and amortization².	−15,000 Cash		= −962 Bonds Payable		−14,038 Retained Earnings		−	+14,038 Interest Expense	= −14,038

(c) Dec. 31	Interest expense (+E, −SE)	14,038	
	Bonds premium (−L)	962	
	Cash (−A)...		15,000

+	Interest Expense (E)	−		−	Bonds Premium (L)	+		+	Cash (A)	−
June 30	14,075				June 30	925			15,000	June 30
Dec. 31	14,038				Dec. 31	962			15,000	Dec. 31

*If the straight-line method of amortizing the discount had been used, each six-month period's entry would have been:

Interest expense (+E, −SE) amount plugged................................	13,270.80	
Bonds premium (−L) [$51,876 ÷ 30]......................................	1,729.20	
Cash (−A)		15,000

¹ $300,000 × 0.10 × 6/12 = $15,000 cash payment; 0.04 × $351,876 = $14,075 interest expense; the difference is the bond premium amortization, a reduction of the net bond carrying amount.

² 0.04 × ($351,876 − $925) = $14,038 interest expense. The difference between this amount and the $15,000 cash payment is the premium amortization, a reduction of the net bond carrying amount.

© Getty Images

Reporting and Analyzing Leases, Pensions, and Income Taxes

American Airlines, Inc. (a subsidiary of **AMR Corporation**) confronts competing demands for its available cash flow as a result of a heavy debt load that includes borrowed money, aircraft leases, and pension and other postemployment obligations. The magnitude of obligations arising from aircraft leases often surprises those outside the industry. Many airlines do not own the planes that they fly. To a large extent, those planes are owned by commercial leasing companies like **General Electric Capital Corporation** (**General Electric Company**'s financial subsidiary), and are leased by the airlines.

If structured in a specific way, neither the leased planes (the assets) nor the lease obligations (the liabilities) would be on American Airlines' balance sheet. That nondisclosure can alter investors' perceptions of the capital investment American Airlines needs to operate its business as well as the level of debt it carries. Methods that companies apply to avoid reporting potential liabilities (and expenses), are commonly referred to as *off-balance-sheet financing*. In this chapter, we describe an analytical procedure that provides an alternative view of the company's investing and financing activities.

The analytical adjustment increases the liability on American Airlines' balance sheet: lease payment obligations on aircraft total $5 billion in 2008, which is a significant amount when compared to the company's total liabilities of $28 billion. This chapter discusses the accounting for leases and explains this analytical adjustment and how to apply it.

Pensions and deferred income taxes are major liabilities reported in many firm's financial statements, including American Airlines. These liabilities represent a substantial obligation for most companies. In this chapter, we will explore the reporting of leases, pensions, and income taxes, along with the various assumptions that underlie the reported figures. We also examine the impact that these obligations have on reported earnings and cash flows. Our task will be to explain how these obligations arise, and how they affect the company's financial position and performance. Understanding this information is essential if we are to assess the future potential of American Airlines and other companies.

(continued on next page)

CHAPTER ORGANIZATION

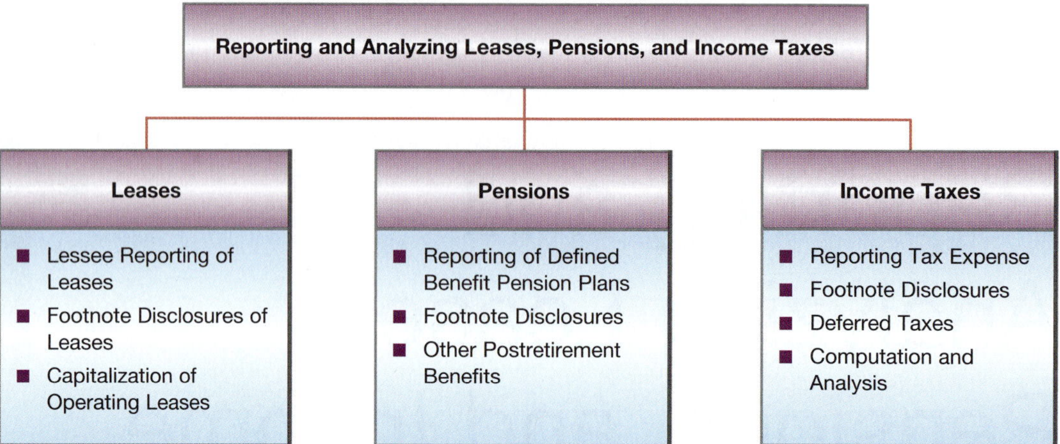

INTRODUCTION

LO1 Define off-balance-sheet financing and explain its effects on financial analysis.

Investors, creditors, and other users of financial statements assess the composition of a company's balance sheet and its relation to the income statement. Chapter 6 introduced the concept of earnings quality to refer to the extent to which reported income reflects the underlying economic performance of a company. Similarly, the quality of the balance sheet refers to the extent to which the assets and liabilities of a company are reported in a manner that accurately reflects its economic resources and obligations. For example, in previous chapters, we highlighted the reporting of LIFO inventories and noncapitalized intangible assets to illustrate how some assets can be undervalued or even excluded from the balance sheet. This chapter focuses on the reporting of liabilities that can often only be found in the notes to the financial statements.

Financial managers are keenly aware of the importance that financial markets place on the quality of balance sheets. This importance creates pressure on companies to *window dress* their financial statements in order to report their financial condition and performance in the best possible light. One means of improving the perceived financial condition of the company is by keeping debt off the balance sheet. **Off-balance-sheet financing** refers to financial obligations of a company that are not reported as liabilities in the balance sheet.

FYI Off-balance-sheet financing usually requires off-balance-sheet assets—this means the off-balance-sheet remains balanced!

Off-balance-sheet financing reduces the amount of debt reported in the balance sheet, thereby lowering financial leverage ratios. Additionally, many off-balance-sheet financing techniques remove assets from the balance sheet, along with the liabilities, without reducing revenues or markedly affecting net income. Such techniques cause operation ratios to appear stronger than they are.

This chapter focuses on three common financial obligations that companies report in their financial statements—leases, pensions, and income taxes. Some of these obligations are off-balance-sheet obligations. Others are reported as balance sheet liabilities, but management enjoys considerable discretion in the valuation of these liabilities. U.S. GAAP requires detailed footnote disclosures of these obligations. Understanding the information in these disclosures enables us to analyze the impact of these obligations on the financial condition of the company.

LEASES

LO2 Account for leases using the operating lease method and the capital lease method.

We begin the discussion of off-balance-sheet financing with leasing. The following graphic shows (in red) that leasing affects both the balance sheet (liabilities and assets) and the income statement (expenses).

Income Statement		Balance Sheet	
Sales		Cash	**Current liabilities**
Cost of goods sold		Accounts receivable	**Long-term liabilities**
Selling, general & administrative		Inventory	
Income taxes		**Long-term operating assets**	Shareholders' equity
Net income		Investments	

BUSINESS INSIGHT

Nike's Off-Balance-Sheet Obligations Michael Jordan, Tiger Woods, Tom Brady, and Lance Armstrong are just some of the marquee athletes who endorse Nike, Inc. products. These athletes sign long-term, multimillion dollar contracts to use and promote Nike shoes, apparel, and accessories. These long-term endorsement contracts are just one of Nike's off-balance-sheet obligations. Consider the following note from Nike's 10-K report.

Contractual Obligations

Our significant long-term contractual obligations as of May 31, 2008, and significant endorsement contracts entered into through the date of this report are as follows ($ millions):

Description of Commitment	Cash Payments Due During the Year Ended May 31,						
	2009	2010	2011	2012	2013	Thereafter	Total
Operating Leases	$ 312.4	$264.4	$228.9	$192.1	$163.9	$ 692.3	$1,854.0
Long-term Debt	6.3	31.3	6.3	153.4	46.3	197.5	441.1
Endorsement Contracts	700.4	599.3	518.3	480.3	407.2	1,122.0	3,827.5
Product Purchase Obligations	2,272.0	1.9	—	—	—	—	2,273.9
Other	250.7	76.4	62.6	55.1	50.7	1.2	496.7
Total	$3,541.8	$973.3	$816.1	$880.9	$668.1	$2,013.0	$8,893.2

Of these obligations disclosed, only its long-term debt is included in the balance sheet. If the other obligations were presented in the balance sheet at their present values, Nike's debt-to-equity ratio would increase in 2008 by 77% from 0.59 to 1.042.

A lease is a contract between the owner of an asset (the **lessor**) and the party desiring to use that asset (the **lessee**). Because this is a private contract between two willing parties, it is governed only by applicable commercial law, and can include whatever provisions are negotiated between the parties. The lessor and lessee can be any legal form of organization, including private individuals, corporations, partnerships, and joint ventures.

Leases generally contain the following terms:

- The lessor allows the lessee the unrestricted right to use the asset during the lease term.

- The lessee agrees to make periodic payments to the lessor and to maintain the asset.

- The asset title remains with the lessor. At the end of the lease, either the lessor takes physical possession of the asset, or the lessee purchases the asset from the lessor at a price specified in the lease contract.

From the lessor's standpoint, lease payments are set at an amount that yields an acceptable return on investment, commensurate with the credit standing of the lessee. The lessor, thus, obtains a quality investment, and the lessee gains use of the asset.

The lease serves as a financing vehicle, similar to an intermediate-term secured bank loan. However, there are several advantages to leasing over bank financing:

- Leases often require less equity investment than bank financing. That is, banks often only lend a portion of the asset's cost and require the borrower to make up the difference from its available cash.

- Leases often require payments to be made at the beginning of the period (e.g., the first of the month). However, because leases are contracts between two parties, their terms can be structured in any way to meet their respective needs. For example, a lease can allow variable payments to match seasonal cash inflows of the lessee, or have graduated payments for companies in their start-up phase.

- If the lessee requires the use of the asset for only a part of its useful life, leasing avoids the need to sell a used asset.

- Because the lessor retains ownership of the asset, leases provide the lessor with tax benefits such as accelerated depreciation deductions. This fact can lead to lower payments for lessees.

■ If the lease is properly structured, neither the leased asset nor the lease liability is reported on the lessee's balance sheet. Accordingly, leasing can be a form of off-balance-sheet financing.

Lessee Reporting of Leases

GAAP identifies two different approaches for the reporting of leases by the lessee:

■ **Capital lease method.** This method requires that both the lease asset and the lease liability be reported on the balance sheet. The lease asset is depreciated like any other long-term asset. The lease liability is amortized like debt, where lease payments are separated into interest expense and principal repayment.

■ **Operating lease method.** Under this method, neither the lease asset nor the lease liability is on the balance sheet. Lease payments are recorded as rent expense by the lessee when paid.

To illustrate the two approaches to lease accounting, assume that Richardson Electronics agrees to lease retail store space in a shopping center. The lease is a 5-year lease with annual payments of $10,000 due at each year-end. (Most leases require payments at the beginning of each period; we use year-end payments here for simplification.) Using a 7% interest rate, the present value of the five annual lease payments equals $41,002, computed as $10,000 × 4.10020 (Appendix A, Table A.3). This amount is used for valuing the lease under the capital lease method.

Using a calculator, the present value of the annual lease payments is computed as follows:

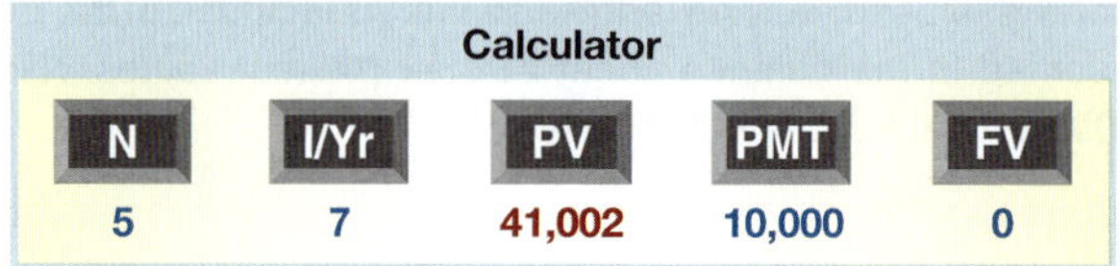

Operating Leases   When the operating lease method is used, lease assets and lease liabilities are not recorded in the balance sheet. No accounting entry is recorded when the lease agreement is signed. At each year-end, Richardson would record the rent payment as rent expense as follows.

(1)	Rent expense (+E, −SE)	10,000
	Cash (−A)	10,000

Because no asset or liability is reported, the only time an operating lease affects the balance sheet is if rent is prepaid (resulting in prepaid rent in current assets) or if unpaid rent is accrued (resulting in accrued rent payable, a current liability). The income statement reports the lease payment as rent expense. The existence and key details of the lease agreement are disclosed in a footnote.

Capital Leases   When the capital lease method is applied, the lessee records an asset and a liability at the time that the lease agreement is signed. Both the asset and the liability are valued using the present value of the lease payments. The entry that would be recorded when Richardson Electronics signs its lease is:

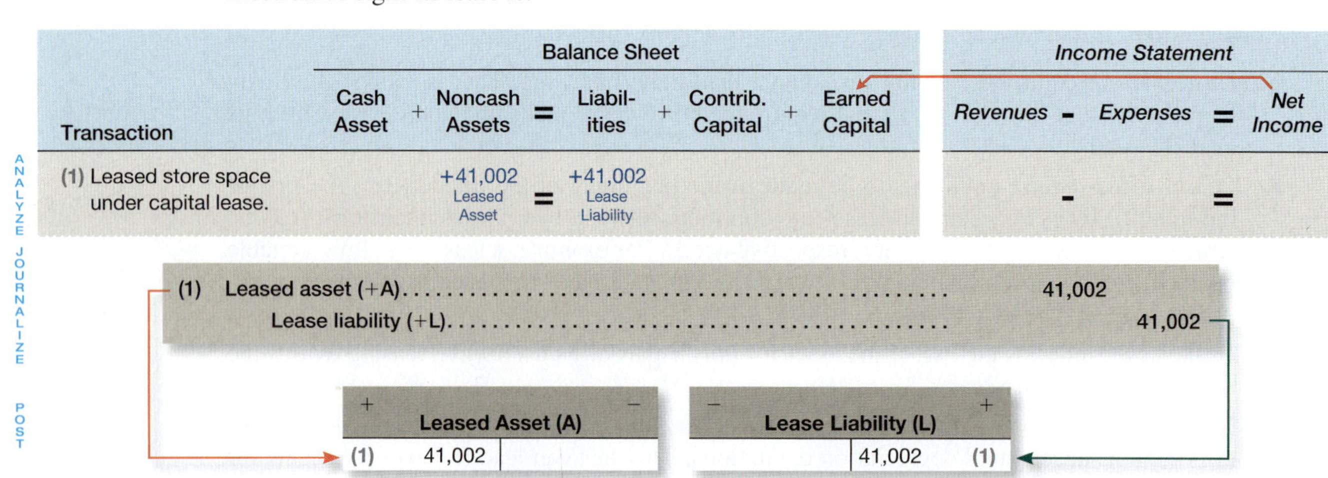

	Balance Sheet						Income Statement		
Transaction	Cash Asset	+ Noncash Assets	= Liabil-ities	+ Contrib. Capital	+ Earned Capital		Revenues −	Expenses =	Net Income
(1) Leased store space under capital lease.		+41,002 Leased Asset	= +41,002 Lease Liability					−	=

(1)	Leased asset (+A)	41,002	
	Lease liability (+L)		41,002

+	Leased Asset (A)	−		−	Lease Liability (L)	+
(1)	41,002				41,002	(1)

ANALYZE   JOURNALIZE   POST

The asset is reported among long-term (PPE) assets in the balance sheet and the liability is reported in long-term debt.

At the end of the first year, two entries are required, one to account for the asset and the other to account for the lease payment. Like other long-term assets, the leased asset must be depreciated. The entry to depreciate Richardson's leased asset (assuming straight-line depreciation and zero residual value) is:

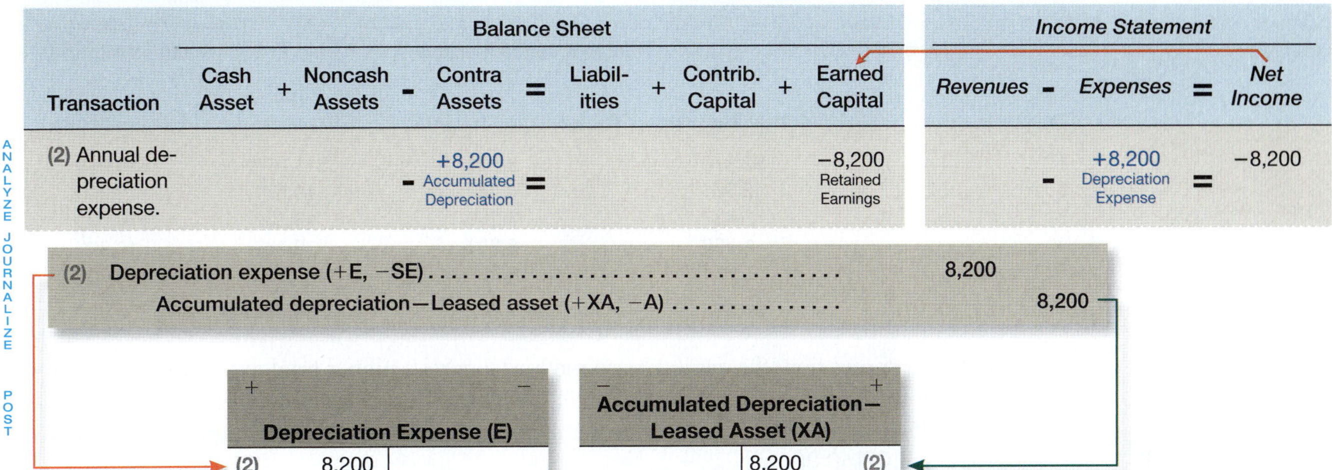

The financial statement effects and related entry to record the annual lease payment are:

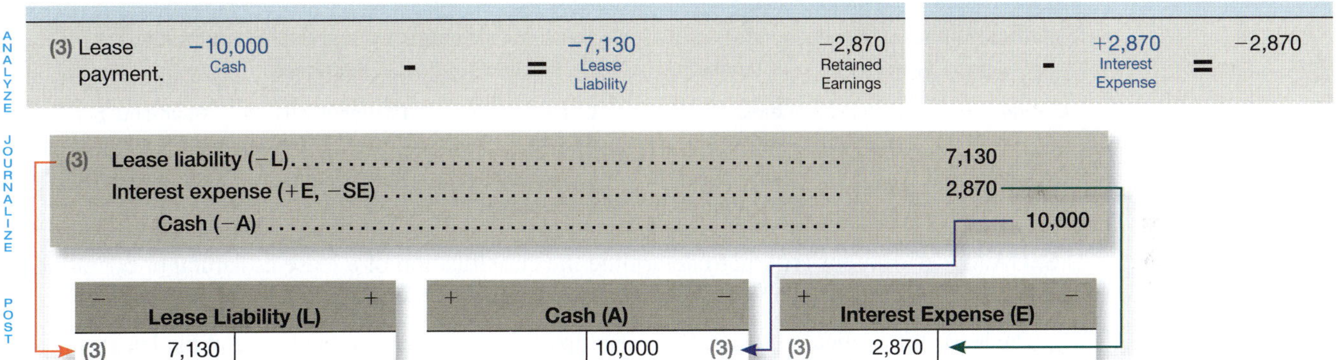

The $10,000 cash payment is split between interest expense and principal repayment. The $2,870 interest expense is computed by multiplying the unpaid balance in the lease liability by the interest rate ($41,002 × 7%). The $7,130 debit to lease liability (principal repayment) is the difference between the lease payment and interest expense ($10,000 − $2,870). The year-end balance in the lease liability account is $33,872, calculated as ($41,002 − $7,130).

Exhibit 10.1 presents the amortization table for Richardson's lease liability under the capital lease method.

EXHIBIT 10.1	Amortization Table for a Capital Lease Liability				
A	B	C	D	E	F
		Interest		Principal	Ending-year
	Beginning-year	Expense		Repayment	Lease Liability
Year	Lease Liability	(B × 7%)	Payment	(D − C)	(B − E)
1	$41,002	$2,870	$10,000	$7,130	$33,872
2	33,872	2,371	10,000	7,629	26,243
3	26,243	1,837	10,000	8,163	18,080
4	18,080	1,266	10,000	8,734	9,346
5	9,346	654	10,000	9,346	0

Comparing Operating Lease and Capital Lease Methods   In Exhibit 10.1, the interest expense decreases each year as the lease liability decreases. Exhibit 10.2 compares total expenses for the operating lease and the capital lease methods over the 5-year life of the Richardson Electronics lease.

EXHIBIT 10.2	Comparison of Expenses under Alternative Lease Accounting Methods			
	Capital Lease Method			**Operating Lease Method**
Year	**Interest Expense**	**Depreciation Expense**	**Total Expense**	**Rent Expense**
1.................	$2,870	$ 8,200	$11,070	$10,000
2.................	2,371	8,200	10,571	10,000
3.................	1,837	8,200	10,037	10,000
4.................	1,266	8,201	9,467	10,000
5.................	654	8,201	8,855	10,000
Total.............	$8,998	$41,002	$50,000	$50,000

Exhibit 10.2 shows how the capital lease method reports a higher total expense (depreciation plus interest) in the early years of the lease and a lower total expense in the later years. Total expense over the 5-year life of the lease is the same under both methods and is equal to the total of the lease payments ($50,000).

The effects of these two accounting methods on the lessee's financial statements are summarized in Exhibit 10.3.

EXHIBIT 10.3	Financial Statement Effects of Lease Methods for the Lessee			
Lease Type	**Assets**	**Liabilities**	**Expenses**	**Cash Flows**
Capital	Lease asset reported	Lease liability reported	Depreciation and interest expense	Payments per lease contract
Operating..............	Lease asset not reported	Lease liability not reported	Rent expense	Same as above

U.S. GAAP defines four criteria to determine the classification of a lease as capital or operating. The lessee *must* capitalize the lease *if one or more* of these criteria are met:

1. The lease automatically transfers ownership of the lease asset to the lessee at the lease-end.
2. The lease agreement allows the lessee to purchase the asset at a discounted price (say $1) at the lease-end; this is called a bargain purchase option.
3. The lease term is at least 75% of the economic useful life of the asset.
4. The present value of the lease payments is at least 90% of the asset's fair market value.

Accounting for leases using the operating lease method offers several reporting benefits to the lessee:

1. The lease asset is not reported on the balance sheet. This reporting means that asset turnover ratios are higher because reported operating assets are lower and revenues are unaffected.
2. The lease liability is not reported on the balance sheet. This means that common balance sheet measures of leverage (such as liabilities divided by equity) are improved. Consequently, many managers believe the company would then command a better debt rating and a lower interest rate on borrowed funds.
3. For the early years of the lease term, rent expense reported for an operating lease is less than the sum of depreciation and interest expense reported for a capital lease. This reporting means that net income is higher in those early years with an operating lease. (However, the corporation's net *operating* profit after taxes is *lower* for an operating lease because rent expense is an operating expense whereas only depreciation expense [not interest expense] is considered an operating expense for a capital lease.)

The benefits of using the operating method to account for leases are quite clear to managers, leading them to avoid lease capitalization if possible. Furthermore, the lease accounting standard is structured around rigid requirements relating to capitalization. Whenever accounting standards are rigidly defined, clever managers that are so inclined can structure lease contracts to meet the letter of the standard to achieve a desired accounting result even though the essence of the transaction would suggest a different accounting treatment.

IFRS REPORTING INSIGHT

U.S. GAAP and IFRS both require that leases be capitalized if the lease asset's risks and rewards are transferred to the lessee. The main difference between the two reporting systems is that IFRS are more principles based and GAAP is more rules based. Given the broader application of principles, IFRS classify more leases as *finance leases* (termed "capital leases" under GAAP). Other small differences exist in the accounting for leases but these will not lead to materially different reporting outcomes in most cases.

Footnote Disclosures of Leases

Disclosures of expected payments for leases are required under both operating and capital lease methods. American Airlines provides a typical disclosure from its 2008 annual report:

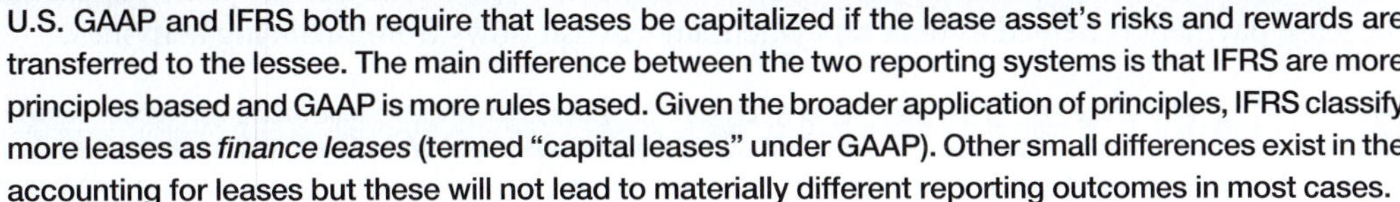

Leases AMR's subsidiaries lease various types of equipment and property, primarily aircraft and airport facilities. The future minimum lease payments required under capital leases, together with the present value of such payments, and future minimum lease payments required under operating leases that have initial or remaining noncancelable lease terms in excess of one year as of December 31, 2008, were (in millions):

Year Ending December 31	Capital Leases	Operating Leases
2009	$ 182	$ 998
2010	143	932
2011	146	922
2012	97	739
2013	83	652
2014 and thereafter	476	4,944
	$1,127	$9,187
Less amount representing interest	438	
Present value of net minimum lease payments	$ 689	

At December 31, 2008, the Company was operating 181 jet aircraft and 39 turboprop aircraft under operating leases and 84 jet aircraft under capital leases. The aircraft leases can generally be renewed at rates based on fair market value at the end of the lease term for one to five years. Some aircraft leases have purchase options at or near the end of the lease term at fair market value, but generally not to exceed a stated percentage of the defined lessor's cost of the aircraft or a predetermined fixed amount. Rent expense, excluding landing fees, was $1.3 billion, $1.4 billion, and $1.4 billion in 2008, 2007, and 2006, respectively.

American Airlines' footnote disclosure reports minimum (base) contractual lease payment obligations for each of the next five years and the total lease payment obligations that come due in year six and beyond. This is similar to disclosures of future maturities for long-term debt. The company also must provide separate disclosures for operating leases and capital leases (American Airlines has both operating and capital leases outstanding).

The purpose of this lease disclosure is to provide information concerning current and future payment obligations. These contractual obligations are similar to debt payments. While the obligations under capital leases are reported in long-term debt, the operating lease obligations are not reported in the balance sheet. However, the operating lease obligations must be considered in our evaluation of the company's financial condition.

Capital Leases and the Cash Flow Statement   A capital lease results in an increase to long-term operating assets and an increase in long-term liabilities. However, in many cases, there is no effect on cash flows at the inception of the lease—see entry (1) on page 438. As a consequence, the initial inception of the lease must be reported as a material noncash transaction and is not presented in the cash flow statement under either investing or financing cash flows. Subsequently, the depreciation of the leased asset is added to cash flow from operations and the principal portion of the lease payment is treated as debt repayment under cash flows from financing activities.

Capitalization of Operating Leases

LO3 Convert off-balance-sheet operating leases to the capital lease method.

When a company uses the operating lease method to report its leases, it can have significant resources that are not recognized as assets and significant obligations that are not recognized as liabilities on its balance sheet. As a result, there are distortions in many important measures of financial condition and performance.

- Return on assets (ROA) and asset turnover ratios are overstated due to nonreporting of lease assets.

- Financial leverage ratios are understated by the nonreporting of lease liabilities.

- Net operating profit margin (NOPM) is understated. Although, over the life of the lease, rent expense under operating leases equals depreciation plus interest expense under capital leases, only depreciation expense is included in net operating profit after tax (NOPAT)—interest is a nonoperating expense.

- While cash payments are the same whether the lease is classified as operating or capital, cash flow from operations is higher for capital leases because part of the lease payment (the principal) is treated as a financing cash outflow.

When operating leases are not capitalized, the balance sheet neither reflects all of the assets that are used in the business, nor the nonoperating obligations for which the company is liable. Such noncapitalization of leases makes ROE appear to be of higher quality. This result is, of course, an important reason why managers want to exclude leases from the balance sheet.

Despite structuring leases to achieve off-balance-sheet financing, required lease disclosures allow us to capitalize operating leases for analysis purposes. This capitalization process involves three steps (this is the process that would have been used if the leases had been classified as capital leases):

1. Determine the discount rate.

2. Compute the present value of future operating lease payments.

3. Adjust statements to include the present value from Step 2 as both a lease asset and a lease liability.

Step 1. There are at least two approaches to determine the appropriate discount rate for our analysis: (1) If the company discloses capital leases, we can impute (infer) an implicit rate of return: a rate that yields the present value computed by the company given the future capital lease payments (see Business Insight box later in this section). (2) Use the rate that corresponds to the company's credit rating or the rate from any recent borrowings involving intermediate-term secured obligations. Companies typically disclose these details in their long-term debt footnote. To illustrate the capitalization of operating leases, we use the American Airlines lease footnote. Step 1 estimates the implicit rate for American's capital leases to be 11.5% (see the following Business Insight box on computing the imputed discount rate for leases).

BUSINESS INSIGHT

Imputed Discount Rate Computation for Leases   When companies report both operating and capital leases, the average rate used to discount capital leases can be imputed (inferred) from disclosures in the leasing footnote. American Airlines reports total undiscounted minimum capital lease payments of $1,127 million and a discounted value for those lease payments of $689 million. Using Excel, we estimate the discount rate that American used for its capital lease computations with the IRR function (=**IRR(values)**) as shown in the following spreadsheet. The entries in cells B2 through G2 are taken from American's reported schedule of lease maturities in the footnote shown earlier in this section, and those in cells H2 through M2 assume a continuation of the $83 million in capital lease payments in Year 5 until the $476 million of estimated payments after Year 5 is accounted for. The spreadsheet method yields an estimate of 11.5% for the discount rate that American implicitly used for capitalization of its capital leases in its 2008 balance sheet.

	A	B	C	D	E	F	G	H	I	J	K	L	M
1	N	0	1	2	3	4	5	6	7	8	9	10	11
2	Amount	-689	182	143	146	97	83	83	83	83	83	83	61
3	IRR	11.5% *											
4										= 476			
5	*Formula for cell B3 is =IRR(B2:M2)												

Step 2. Compute the present value of future operating lease payments using the 11.5% discount rate that we estimated in Step 1. We demonstrate this computation using a financial calculator, as illustrated in Appendix A. The present value of the operating lease payments equals the sum of the present values of each of the annual lease payments due over the next five years, plus the present value of the lease payments occurring after the fifth year. This two-step computation follows:

2a. *Present values for Years 1 through 5.* Because the lease payments vary from year to year, we cannot compute the present value of the first five lease payments as an ordinary annuity. Instead, we compute the present value of each payment and then total them. The present value of each lease payment for Years 1 through 5 can be computed using a financial calculator. To illustrate using American Airlines (for years 2009 through 2013), we set the payment number (1, 2, 3, 4 or 5) as N, enter 11.5% as the discount rate (I/YR), and the payment amount as the future value (FV). For the first payment (2009), the present value is computed as follows:

Calculator				
N	I/Yr	PV	PMT	FV
1	11.5	895	0	998

The present value of the second payment (2010) is computed as:

Calculator				
N	I/Yr	PV	PMT	FV
2	11.5	750	0	932

This procedure is repeated for each of the remaining payments for 2011 (Year 3) through 2013 (Year 5). The resulting present values are listed in the first five rows of the right-hand column of Exhibit 10.4.[1]

---

[1] The present value of the payments for Year 1 through Year 5 (2009 – 2013) can also be computed using the NPV function in an Excel spreadsheet. The function is entered as =NPV(.115,998,932,922,739,652). This computation results in a present value of $3,166 million for the first five payments.

EXHIBIT 10.4	Present Value of Operating Lease Payments ($ millions)		
Year	**Payment**	**Operating Lease Payment**	**Present Value**
2009	1	$ 998	$ 895
2010	2	932	750
2011	3	922	665
2012	4	739	478
2013	5	652	378
2014 and later	6+	4,944	1,849
			$5,015
Remaining life		$4,944/$652 = 7.583 years	

2b. *Present value for Year 6 and thereafter.* To compute the present value of the lease payments remaining after 2013, we make an assumption that the company continues to make lease payments at the 2013 (or Year 5) level for the remainder of the lease term. The remaining lease term is estimated by dividing the total scheduled payments for years after Year 5 by the lease payment for Year 5 (millions):

$$\text{Estimated lease term beyond Year 5} = \frac{\text{Total payments after Year 5}}{\text{Year 5 payment}} = \frac{\$4{,}944}{\$652} = 7.583 \text{ years}$$

Therefore, the payments after 2013 (Year 5) are assumed to be an annuity of equal payments beginning in 2014 (which is Year 6) and extending for 7.583 years. We can calculate the present value of this annuity using a calculator. We use 11.5% for the discount rate (I/YR), 7.583 for the number of payments (N), and $652 million for the annual payment (PMT):

Calculator				
N	**I/Yr**	**PV**	**PMT**	**FV**
7.583	11.5	3,186	652	0

This calculation results in the present value of the remaining payments *as of the end of 2013 (Year 5).* Next we must compute the present value of this amount as of the beginning of 2009 (Year 1):

Calculator				
N	**I/Yr**	**PV**	**PMT**	**FV**
5	11.5	1,849	0	3,186

Thus, the present value of the lease payments for 2014 and thereafter is $1,849 million. This amount is entered in the sixth row of the right-hand column of Exhibit 10.4.

We sum the present values from steps 2a and 2b above to obtain the present value of future operating lease payments; for American, this totals $5,015 ($ millions), computed as $895 + $750 + $665 + $478 + $378 + $1,849.

Step 3. Use the computed present value of future operating lease payments to adjust the balance sheet and income statement as we illustrate in Exhibit 10.5.

EXHIBIT 10.5	Analytical Adjustments from Capitalization of Operating Leases ($ millions)			
	Reported	**Adjustments**	**Adjusted**	**Percent Increase**
Net assets	$25,175	$5,015	$30,190	19.9%
Net liabilities	28,110	5,015	33,125	17.8%
Equity.	(2,935)		(2,935)	—

By adding the present value of the operating lease payments to both the assets and the liabilities in the balance sheet, we are, in effect, treating these leases as capital leases. If these operating leases had been recorded as capital leases all along, the initial entry to record the leases would have been as shown in the following financial statement effects template.

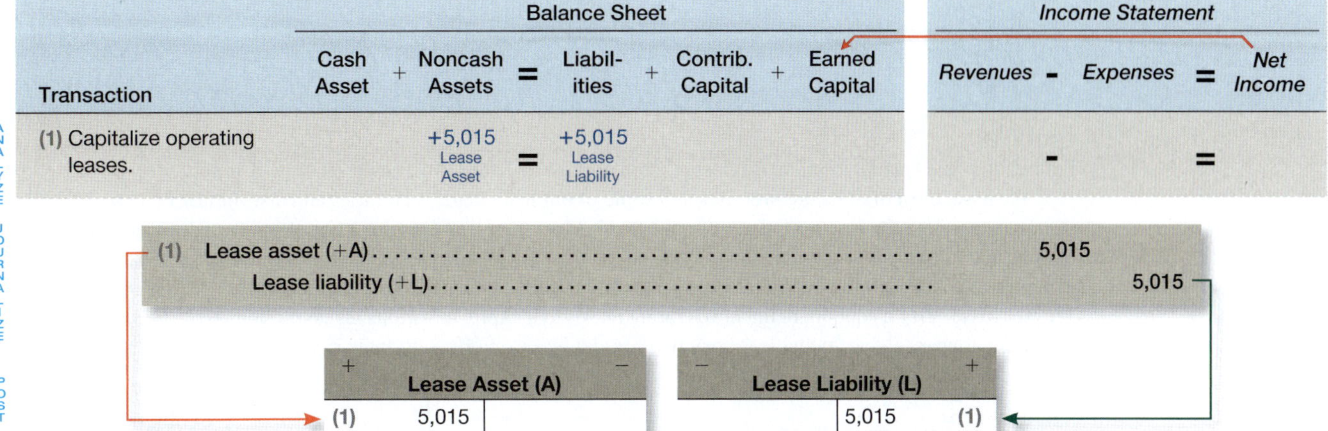

Operating Leases and Financial Ratios   An asset acquired under an operating lease will not appear in the company balance sheet and the related liability will not appear among the liabilities. The omission also impacts the income statement, although to a lesser extent. Depreciation is understated but the rent expense offsets the understatement. However, as we have seen, it is possible to estimate the capitalized value of the assets and the size of the associated obligation, which can then be considered in an analysis of the firm using the ratios we have previously introduced.

The capitalization of operating leases has a marked impact on American's balance sheet. For the airline and retailing industries, in particular, lease assets (airplanes and real estate) comprise a large portion of net operating assets and these leases are usually classified as operating.

Using the year-end data presented in Exhibit 10.5 and given revenues of $23,766 million, asset turnover (using year-end figures) decreases from .94 ($23,766/$25,175) to .79 ($23,766/$30,190). In general for firms with operating leases, leverage (liabilities to equity) would be higher than we would infer from reported financial statements. The adjusted assets and liabilities arguably present a more realistic picture of the invested capital required to operate American as well as other firms with significant operating lease commitments.

It is important to consider operating lease commitments that do not appear on the balance sheet as payments that must be satisfied with cash, just as is the case with the other fixed commitments such as interest on outstanding debt. (Other off-balance-sheet commitment items, such as purchase commitments, should also be included.) The impact of these commitments can be indicated using the ratio of operating cash flow to fixed commitments.

$$\text{Fixed commitments ratio} = \frac{\text{Operating cash flow}}{\text{Fixed commitments}}$$

American had a negative operating cash flow of $1,394 million in 2008, so this ratio is not meaningful for American. However it is clear that American will need to find additional sources of cash, perhaps through additional borrowing, to continue operations.

MID-CHAPTER REVIEW 1

PART A
Assume that **The Gap Inc.** leased a vacant retail space with the intention of opening another store. The lease calls for annual lease payments of $32,000, due at the end of each of the next ten years. The appropriate discount rate is 7%.

1. If the lease is treated as a capital lease, what journal entry(ies) would Gap make to record the initial signing of the lease agreement?
2. How would Gap record the first lease payment and depreciation expense at the end of the first year of the lease?
3. If this lease is accounted for as an operating lease, what entry(ies) would be necessary during the first year?

PART B

Following is the leasing footnote disclosure from note 11 in **The Gap Inc.**'s 2008 10-K report.

We lease most of our store premises and some of our headquarters facilities and distribution centers. These operating leases expire at various dates through 2033. Most store leases are for a five-year base period and include options that allow us to extend the lease term beyond the initial base period, subject to terms agreed to at lease inception. Some leases also include early termination options, which can be exercised under specific conditions. We also lease certain equipment under operating leases that expire at various dates through 2012. The aggregate minimum noncancelable annual lease payments under leases in effect on January 31, 2009, are:

Fiscal Year	(In millions)
2009	$1,069
2010	927
2011	712
2012	520
2013	386
Thereafter	1,080
Total minimum lease commitment	$4,694

The total minimum lease commitment amount above does not include minimum sublease rental income of $24 million receivable in the future under non-cancelable sublease agreements.

1. Does Gap classify these leases as operating or capital leases? How do you know?
2. Assuming its leases are operating leases, compute the adjustments that are necessary for analysis of Gap's balance sheet? (Use Gap's recent intermediate term borrowing rate of 7%.)
3. Assuming the same facts as determined in part 2, what income statement adjustments should an analyst consider, if any?

The solution to this review problem can be found on pages 486–487.

PENSIONS

Companies frequently offer retirement or pension plans as a benefit for their employees. There are two general types of pension plans:

1. **Defined contribution plan**. This plan requires the company to make periodic contributions to an employee's account (usually with a third-party trustee like a bank), and many plans require an employee matching contribution. Following retirement, the employee makes periodic withdrawals from that account. A tax-advantaged 401(k) account is a typical example. Under a 401(k) plan, the employee makes contributions that are exempt from federal taxes until they are withdrawn after retirement.

2. **Defined benefit plan**. This plan also requires the company to make periodic payments to a third party, which then makes payments to an employee after retirement. Payments are usually based on years of service and the employee's salary. The company may or may not set aside sufficient funds to cover these obligations (federal law does set minimum funding requirements). As a result, defined benefit plans can be overfunded or underfunded. All pension investments are retained by the third party until paid to the employee. In the event of bankruptcy, employees have the standing of a general creditor, but usually have additional protection in the form of government pension benefit insurance.

For a defined contribution plan, the company contribution is recorded as an expense in the income statement when the cash is paid or the liability accrued. A defined benefit plan is more complex. Although the company contributes cash or securities to the pension investment account, the pension obligation is not satisfied until the employee receives pension benefits, which may be many years into the future. This section focuses on how a defined benefit plan is reported in the financial statements, and how we assess company performance and financial condition when such a plan exists.

Reporting of Defined Benefit Pension Plans

There are two accounting issues concerning the reporting of defined benefit pension plans.

1. How are pension plans (assets and liabilities) reported in the balance sheet (if at all)?
2. How are pension costs and returns from pension plan assets reported in the income statement?

The following graphic shows where pensions appear on the balance sheet (liabilities and assets) and the income statement (pension expense is usually reported in SG&A).

Income Statement	Balance Sheet	
Sales	Cash	Current liabilities
Cost of goods sold	Accounts receivable	**Long-term liabilities**
Selling, general & administrative	Inventory	Shareholders' equity
Income taxes	**Long-term operating assets**	
Net income	Investments	

Balance Sheet Effects

Pension plan assets are primarily investments in stocks and bonds (mostly of other companies, but it is not uncommon for companies to invest pension funds in their own stock). Pension liabilities (called the **projected benefit obligation** or **PBO**) are the company's obligations to pay current and former employees. The difference between the market value of the pension plan assets and the projected benefit obligation is called the **funded status** of the pension plan. If the PBO exceeds the pension plan assets, the pension is **underfunded**. Conversely, if pension plan assets exceed the PBO, the pension plan is **overfunded**. Under current U.S. GAAP, companies are required to record only the funded status on their balance sheets (namely, the *net* amount, not the pension plan assets and PBO separately), either as an asset if the plan is overfunded, or as a liability if it is underfunded.

Pension plan assets consist of stocks and bonds whose value changes each period in three ways. First, the value of the investments increases or decreases as a result of interest, dividends, and gains or losses on the stocks and bonds held. Second, the pension plan assets increase when the company contributes additional cash or stock to the investment account. Third, the pension plan assets decrease by the amount of benefits paid to retirees during the period. These three changes in the pension plan assets are articulated below.

Pension Plan Assets
Pension plan assets, beginning balance
+ Actual returns on investments (interest, dividends, gains and losses)
+ Company contributions to pension plan
− Benefits paid to retirees
= Pension plan assets, ending balance

The pension liability, or PBO (projected benefit obligation), is computed as the present value of the expected future benefit payments to employees. The present value of these future payments depends on the number of years the employee is expected to work (years of service) and the employee's salary level at retirement. Consequently, companies must estimate future wage increases, as well as the number of employees expected to reach retirement age with the company and how long they are likely to receive pension benefits following retirement. Once the future retiree pool is determined, the expected future payments under the plan are discounted to arrive at the present value of the pension obligation. This is the PBO. A reconciliation of the PBO from beginning balance to year-end balance follows.

Pension Obligation
Projected benefit obligation, beginning balance
+ Service cost
+ Interest cost
+/− Actuarial losses (gains)
− Benefits paid to retirees
= Projected benefit obligation, ending balance

As this reconciliation shows, the balance in the PBO changes during the period for four reasons.

- First, as employees continue to work for the company, their pension benefits increase. The annual **service cost** represents the additional (future) pension benefits earned by employees during the current year.

- Second, **interest cost** accrues on the outstanding pension liability, just as it would with any other long-term liability (see the accounting for bond liabilities in Chapter 9). Because there are no scheduled interest payments on the PBO, the interest cost accrues each year, that is, interest is added to the existing liability.

- Third, the PBO can increase (or decrease) due to actuarial losses (and gains), which arise when companies make changes in their pension plans or make *changes in actuarial assumptions* (including assumptions that are used to estimate the PBO, such as the rate of wage inflation, termination and mortality rates, and the discount rate used to compute the present value of future obligations). For example, if a company increases the discount rate used to compute the present value of future pension plan payments from, say, 8% to 9%, the present value of future benefit payments declines (just like bond prices). Conversely, if the discount rate is reduced to 7%, the present value of the PBO increases. Other assumptions used to estimate the pension liability (such as the expected wage inflation rate or the expected life span of current and former employees) can create similar actuarial losses or gains.

- Fourth, pension benefit payments to retirees reduce the PBO (just as the payments reduce the pension plan assets).

Finally, the net pension liability (or asset) that is reported in a company's balance sheet, then, is computed as follows:

Net Pension Asset (or Liability)
Pension plan assets (at market value)
− Projected benefit obligation (PBO)
Funded status

If the funded status is positive (assets exceed liabilities), the overfunded pension plan is reported on the balance sheet as an asset, typically called prepaid pension cost. If the funded status is negative (liabilities exceed assets), it is reported as a liability.[2] During the early 2000s, long-term interest rates declined drastically and many companies lowered their discount rate for computing the present value of future pension payments. Lower discount rates meant higher PBO values. This period also witnessed a bear market and pension plan assets declined in value. The combined effect of the

---

[2] Companies typically maintain many pension plans. Some are overfunded and others are underfunded. Current U.S. GAAP requires companies to group all of the overfunded and underfunded plans together, and to present a net asset for the overfunded plans and a net liability for the underfunded plans.

increase in PBO and the decrease in asset values caused many pension funds to become severely underfunded. Of the 1,912 U.S. publicly traded companies reporting pension plans in 2005, a total of 1,721 (90%) were underfunded. (American Airlines, for example, reports an underfunded pension plan of $4.95 billion in 2009.)

Income Statement Effects

A company's net pension expense is computed as follows.

<table>
<tr><td colspan="2" align="center">**Net Pension Expense**</td></tr>
<tr><td></td><td>Service cost</td></tr>
<tr><td>+</td><td>Interest cost</td></tr>
<tr><td>−</td><td>*Expected* return on pension plan assets</td></tr>
<tr><td>±</td><td>Amortization of deferred amounts</td></tr>
<tr><td></td><td>Net pension expense</td></tr>
</table>

The net pension expense is rarely reported separately on the income statement. Instead, it is included with other forms of compensation expense in selling, general and administrative (SG&A) expenses. However, pension expense is disclosed separately in footnotes.

The net pension expense has four components. The previous PBO section described the first two components: service costs and interest costs. The third component of pension expense relates to the return on pension plan assets, which *reduces* total pension expense. To compute this component, companies use the long-term *expected* rate of return on the pension plan assets, rather than the *actual* return, and multiply that expected rate by the balance in the pension plan assets account. Use of the expected return rather than actual return is an important distinction. Company CEOs and CFOs dislike income variability because they believe that stockholders react negatively to it, and so company executives intensely (and successfully) lobbied the FASB to use the more stable expected long-term investment return, rather than the actual return, in computing pension expense. Thus, the pension plan assets' expected return is deducted to compute net pension expense.[3]

Any difference between the expected and the actual return is accumulated, together with other deferred amounts, off-balance-sheet and reported in the footnotes. Other deferred amounts include changes in PBO resulting from changes in estimates used to compute the PBO and from amendments to the pension plans made by the company. However, if the deferred amounts exceed certain limits, the excess is recognized on-balance-sheet with a corresponding amount recognized as amortization in the income statement.[4] This amortization is the fourth component of pension expense and can be either a positive or negative amount depending on the sign of the difference between expected and actual return on plan assets.

Most analysts consider the service cost portion of pension expense to be an operating expense, similar to salaries and other benefits. However, the interest cost component is generally viewed as a financing cost. Similarly, the expected return on plan assets is not considered operating.

---

[3] The FASB has issued an exposure draft containing a proposal to further amend the pension accounting standard to eliminate the use of the expected return. If passed, this amendment will result in increased earnings volatility as changes in the market value of the pension investments will impact net pension expense (and operating profits before tax) directly.

[4] To avoid amortization, the deferred amounts must be less than 10% of the PBO or pension investments, whichever is less. The excess, if any, is amortized until no further excess remains. When the excess is eliminated (by investment returns or company contributions, for example), the amortization ceases.

Footnote Disclosures—Components of Plan Assets and PBO

GAAP requires extensive footnote disclosures for pensions (and other postretirement benefits that we discuss later). These notes provide details relating to the net pension liability reported in the balance sheet and the components of pension expense reported as part of SG&A expense in the income statement.

American Airlines indicates in footnote 10 to its 2008 10K that the funded status of its pension plan is $(4,170) million on December 31, 2008. This means American's plan is underfunded. Following are the disclosures American Airlines makes in its pension footnote, $ millions.

Pension Benefits		
	2008	**2007**
Reconciliation of benefit obligation		
Obligation at January 1	$10,451	$11,048
Service cost	324	370
Interest cost	684	672
Actuarial (gain) loss	254	(1,021)
Plan amendments	(14)	—
Benefit payments	(815)	(618)
Obligation at December 31	$10,884	$10,451
Reconciliation of fair value of plan assets		
Fair value of plan assets at January 1	$ 9,099	$ 8,565
Actual return on plan assets	(1,659)	766
Employer contributions	89	386
Benefit payments	(815)	(618)
Fair value of plan assets at December 31	$ 6,714	$ 9,099
Funded status at December 31	$ (4,170)	$ (1,352)

American Airlines' PBO began 2008 with a balance of $10,451 million. It increased by the accrual of $324 million in service cost and $684 million in interest cost. During the year, American also realized an actuarial loss of $254 million, which increased the pension liability. The PBO decreased as a result of $815 million in benefits paid to retirees and plan amendment costs of $14 million, leaving a balance of $10,884 million at year-end.

Pension plan assets began the year with at a fair market value of $9,099 million, which decreased by $1,659 million from investment returns (losses) and increased by $89 million from company contributions. The company drew down its investments to make pension payments of $815 million to retirees. The $815 million payment reduced the PBO by the same amount, as discussed above, leaving the pension plan assets with a year-end balance of $6,714 million. The funded status of American Airlines' pension plan at year-end is $(4,170) million ($10,884 million − $6,714 million at year-end). The negative balance indicates that its pension plan is underfunded. The PBO and pension plan assets accounts cannot be separated into operating and nonoperating components; thus, most analysts treat the entire funded status as an operating item (either asset or liability).

American Airlines incurred $341 million of pension expense in 2008. This is not broken out separately in its income statement. Instead, it is included in SG&A expense. Details of this expense are found in its pension footnote, which follows ($ millions):

Service cost	$324
Interest cost	684
Expected return on assets	(789)
Amortizations	122
Net periodic benefit cost for defined benefit plans	$341

Using the information in American Airlines' footnote, we can parse the pension expense into operating and nonoperating components. Most analysts treat service cost as operating, and interest costs and expected return as nonoperating. The amortization expense of $122 million indicates that the deferred amounts have exceeded the maximum limit prescribed under U.S. GAAP, and the excess is now amortized gradually to expense so long as the deferred amount still exceeds those limits.

RESEARCH INSIGHT

Valuation of Pension Footnote Disclosures   The FASB requires footnote disclosure of the major components of pension cost presumably because it is useful for investors. Pension-related research has examined whether investors assign different valuation multiples to the components of pension cost when assessing company market value. Research finds that the market does, indeed, attach different interpretation to pension components, reflecting differences in information about recurring vs. nonrecurring expenses.

Footnote Disclosures and Future Cash Flows

Companies use their pension plan assets to pay pension benefits to retirees. When markets are booming, as was true during the 1990s, pension plan assets can grow rapidly. However, when markets reverse, as in the bear market of the early 2000s and in 2008–2009, the value of pension plan assets can decline. The company's annual pension plan contribution is an investment decision influenced, in part, by market conditions and minimum required contributions specified by law.[5] Companies' cash contributions come from borrowed funds or operating cash flows.

RESEARCH INSIGHT

Why Do Companies Offer Pensions?   Research examines why companies choose to offer pension benefits. It finds that deferred compensation plans and pensions help align the long-term interests of owners and employees. Research also examines the composition of pension investments. It finds that a large portion of pension fund assets are invested in fixed-income securities, which are of lower risk than other investment securities. This implies that pension assets are less risky than nonpension assets. However, in severe economic downturns, the case in the 2008–2009 period, some corporations will curtail their pension plan contributions.

American Airlines paid $815 million in pension benefits to retirees in 2008, yet it contributed only $89 million to pension assets that year. The remaining amount was paid out of available funds

---

[5] The Pension Protection Act of 2006 mandates that companies fully fund pension obligations by 2013. The bipartisan act also shields taxpayers from assuming airline pension plan obligations, tightens funding requirements so employers make greater cash contributions to pension funds, closes loopholes that allow companies with underfunded plans to skip cash pension payments, prohibits employers and union leaders from promising extra benefits if pension plans are markedly underfunded, and strengthens disclosure rules to give workers and retirees more information about the status of their pension plan.

in the investment account. Cash contributions to the pension plan assets are the relevant amounts for an analysis of projected cash flows. Benefits paid in relation to the pension liability balance can provide a clue about the need for *future* cash contributions. Companies are required to disclose the expected benefit payments for five years after the statement date and the remaining obligations thereafter. Following is American Airlines' benefit disclosure statement:

The following benefit payments, which reflect expected future service as appropriate, are expected to be paid:

	Pension	Retiree Medical and Other
2009	$ 514	$ 163
2010	565	168
2011	587	176
2012	617	175
2013	728	181
2014–2018	4,372	1,007

As of 2008, American Airlines pension plan assets account reports a balance of $6,714 million, as discussed above, and during the year, the plan assets actually suffered a loss of $1,659 million. Hence, the pension plan asset account is currently failing to generate investment returns sufficient to cover the $514 million to $728 million in projected benefit payments outlined in the schedule above. Because investment returns are not sufficient, the company will have to use operating cash flow or borrow money to fund the deficit.

One application of the pension footnote is to assess the likelihood that the company will be required to increase its cash contributions to the pension plan. This estimate is made by examining the funded status of the pension plan and the projected payments to retirees. For severely underfunded plans, the projected payments to retirees ($514 to $728 million per year in American's footnote disclosure) will not be covered by existing pension assets and current negative investment returns. In this case, the company will need to divert operating cash flow from other prospective projects to cover its pension plan. Alternatively, if operating cash flows will not be sufficient, it will likely need to borrow to fund those payments. This decision can be especially troublesome as the debt service payments include interest, thus, effectively increasing the required pension contribution. General Motors Corporation's situation illustrates the problems associated with underfunded plans, as shown in the following Business Insight.

Footnote Disclosures and Profit Implications

The following breakdown for pension expense is repeated from page 449:

Net Pension Expense
Service cost
+ Interest cost
− *Expected* return on pension plan assets
± Amortization of deferred amounts
Net pension expense

Interest cost is the product of the PBO and the discount rate. This discount rate is set by the company. The expected dollar return on pension assets is the product of the pension plan asset balance and the expected long-run rate of return on the investment portfolio. This rate is also set by the company.

Further, PBO is affected by the expected rate of wage inflation, termination and mortality rates, all of which are estimated by the company.

U.S. GAAP requires disclosure of several rates used by the company in its estimation of PBO and the related pension expense. American Airlines discloses the following table in its pension footnote:

Pension Benefits	2008	2007	2006
Weighted-average assumptions used to determine net periodic benefit cost for the years ended December 31			
Discount rate	6.50%	6.00%	5.75%
Salary scale (ultimate)	3.78	3.78	3.78
Expected return on plan assets	8.75	8.75	8.75

During 2007 and 2008, American Airlines increased its discount rate (used to compute the present value of its pension obligations, or PBO), while leaving unchanged its estimates of the rate of wage inflation and the expected return on plan assets.

Changes in these assumptions have the following general effects on pension expense and, thus, profitability. This table summarizes the effects of increases in the various rates. Decreases have the exact opposite effects of increases.

Estimate change	Probable effect on pension expense	Reason for effect
Discount rate increase	Increases	While the higher discount rate reduces the PBO, the lower PBO is multiplied by a higher interest rate. The rate effect is generally larger than the discount effect, resulting in increased pension expense.
Investment return increase	Decreases	The dollar amount of expected return on plan assets is the product of the plan assets balance and the expected long-term rate of return. Increasing the return increases the expected return on plan assets, thus reducing pension expense.
Wage inflation increase	Increases	The expected rate of wage inflation affects future wage levels that determine expected pension payments. An increase, thus, increases PBO, which increases both the service and interest cost components of pension expense.

In the case of American Airlines, for example, an increased discount rate, coupled with no change in the expected rate of wage inflation and return on investments, served to increase pension expense and decrease profitability in that year. It is often the case that companies reduce

BUSINESS INSIGHT

How Pensions Confound Income Analysis   Overfunded pension plans and boom markets can inflate income. Specifically, when the stock market is booming, pension investments realize large gains that flow to income (via reduced pension expense). Although pension plan assets do not belong to shareholders (as they are the legal entitlement of current and future retirees), the gains and losses from those plan assets are reported in income. The following graph plots the funded status of **General Electric Company**'s pension plan together with pension expense (revenue) that GE reported from 1998 to 2008.

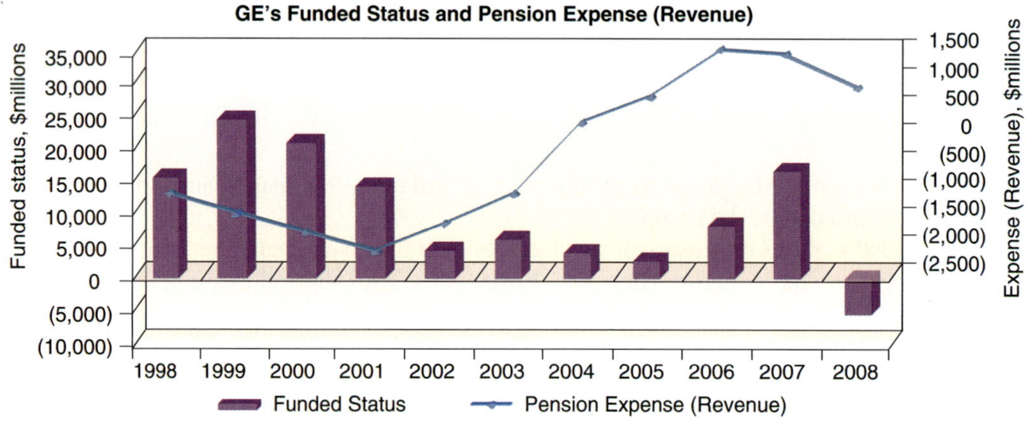

GE's funded status has consistently been positive (indicating an overfunded plan until 2009). The degree of overfunding peaked in 1999 at the height of the stock market, and began to decline during the bear market of the early 2000s. GE reported pension *revenue* (not expense) during this period. In 2001, GE's reported pension *revenue* was $2,095 million (10.6% of its pretax income). Because of the plan's overfunded status, the expected return and amortization of deferred gains components of pension expense amounted to $5,288 million, far in excess of the service and interest costs of $3,193 million. Since 2004, GE has recorded pension expense (rather than revenue) as the pension plan's overfunding and expected long-term rates of return declined, and in 2009 the funded status turned negative.

the expected investment returns with a lag, but increase them without a lag, to favorably impact profitability. We must be aware of the impact of these changes in assumptions in our evaluation of company profitability.

Other Post-Employment Benefits

In addition to pension benefits, many companies provide health care and insurance benefits to retired employees. These benefits are referred to as **other post-employment benefits (OPEB)**. These benefits present reporting challenges similar to pension accounting. However, companies most often provide these benefits on a "pay-as-you-go" basis and it is rare for companies to make contributions in advance for OPEB. As a result, this liability, known as the **accumulated post-employment benefit obligation (APBO)**, is largely, if not totally, unfunded. GAAP requires that the unfunded APBO liability, net of any unrecognized amounts, be reported in the balance sheet and the annual service costs and interest costs be accrued as expenses each year. This requirement is controversial for two reasons. First, future health care costs are especially difficult to estimate, so the value of the resulting APBO (the present value of the future benefits) is fraught with error. Second, these benefits are provided at the discretion of the employer and can be altered or terminated at any time. Consequently, employers argue that without a legal obligation to pay these benefits, the liability should not be reported in the balance sheet.

Other post-employment benefits can produce large liabilities. For example, American Airlines' footnotes report a funded status for the company's health care obligation of $2,618 million, consisting of an APBO liability of $2,779 million less health care plan investments with a market value of $161 million. General Motors provides an extreme OPEB example (as described in the Business Insight box above). Our analysis of cash flows related to pension obligations can be extended to other post-employment benefit obligations. For example, in addition to its pension payments, American Airlines also discloses that it is obligated to make health care payments to retirees totaling almost $1,870 million over the next 10 years. Because health care obligations are rarely funded until payment is required (federal minimum funding standards do not apply to OPEB and there is no tax benefit to pre-funding), there are no investment returns to fund the payments. Our analysis of projected cash flows must consider this potential cash outflow.

MID-CHAPTER REVIEW 2

The following pension data is taken from footnote 11 of **Continental Airlines, Inc.**, 10-K report.

($ millions)	2008	2007
Change in Benefit Obligation		
Benefit obligation at beginning of year	$2,353	$2,697
Service cost	59	61
Interest cost	149	158
Plan amendments	—	—
Actuarial (gains) losses	168	(347)
Participant contributions	—	—
Benefits paid	(118)	(59)
Settlements	(129)	(157)
Benefit obligation at end of year	$2,482	$2,353
Change in Plan Assets		
Fair value of plan assets at beginning of year	$1,817	$1,545
Actual gains (losses) on plan assets	(618)	150
Employer contributions, including benefits paid under unfunded plans	105	338
Benefits paid	(118)	(59)
Lump sum settlements	(129)	(157)
Fair value of plan assets at end of year	$1,057	$1,817
Funded status of the plans—net underfunded	$1,425	$ 536

Following is Continental Airlines' footnote for its pension cost as reported in its income statement.

	Defined Benefit Pension		
Components of Net Periodic Benefit Cost	2008	2007	2006
Service cost	$ 59	$ 61	$ 59
Interest cost	149	158	146
Expected return on plan assets	(157)	(137)	(122)
Amortization of unrecognized net actuarial (gain) loss	34	68	68
Amortization of prior service cost	10	10	9
Net periodic benefit expense	95	160	160
Settlement charges (included in special charges)	52	31	59
Net benefit expense	$147	$191	$219

Required

1. In general, what factors impact a company's pension benefit obligation during a period?
2. In general, what factors impact a company's pension plan investments during a period?
3. What amount is reported on the balance sheet relating to the Continental Airlines pension plan?
4. How does the expected return on plan assets affect pension cost?
5. How does Continental Airlines' expected return on plan assets compare with its actual return (in $s) for 2008?
6. How much net pension cost is reflected in Continental Airlines' 2008 income statement?
7. Assess Continental Airlines' ability to meet payment obligations to retirees.

The solution to this review problem can be found on page 487.

INCOME TAXES: TAX EXPENSE AND DEFERRED TAXES

Income Tax Expense

LO6 Describe and interpret accounting for income taxes.

While income tax expense appears in the income statement after operating income has been determined, it is an operating expense. Items included in the income statement below income from continuing operations, such as extraordinary items, are therefore reported net of their associated tax effects. This reporting allows us to compute a corporation's effective tax rate by dividing the tax expense by net income. However, determining a corporation's income tax expense is not a simple matter as we shall now see.

Companies maintain two sets of books, one for reporting to their shareholders and another for reporting to tax authorities. This practice is neither illegal nor unethical. In fact, it is expected. Financial accounting is concerned with presenting information in the financial statements that is useful to investors and creditors. These statements are prepared in accordance with GAAP. Tax returns, on the other hand, are prepared to report to tax authorities such as the Internal Revenue Service (IRS) and must comply with whatever tax regulations are established by these agencies. Because tax authorities have different objectives than shareholders, it is not surprising that income tax regulations differ from U.S. GAAP.

The difference between U.S. GAAP and tax regulations means that income before income taxes, as presented in the income statement, will differ from taxable income in the tax return. Taxable income is used to calculate the company's tax obligation for that period. Usually this involves multiplying taxable income by the tax rate. However, in the income statement prepared for shareholders, the calculation of income tax expense is less straightforward. Below, we summarize two of the more important types of differences between GAAP and the tax code, temporary differences and permanent differences.

FYI We use the term book income to refer to income before income taxes, as reported in financial statements. Taxable income refers to income reported in the income tax return.

A. Temporary Differences:

 1. Created by using accrual accounting for books and cash accounting for the IRS, or

 2. Created by using different rules for determining the book accrual from the rules for determining the tax deduction.

B. Permanent Difference:

 Created by events that create revenues or expenses under accrual accounting but which create no revenue or expense recognized by the IRS.

To illustrate the challenge of measuring tax expense, we use a revenue recognition example (item A1 above). Consider the Built-Rite Construction Company, which uses the cash basis of reporting to the IRS. Built-Rite signed a two-year $10 million contract to construct a building estimated to cost $7.5 million. The $10 million is received by Built-Rite when the contract is completed. The company incurs $4.5 million of construction costs in the first year, and the remaining $3 million in the second year. For financial reporting, Built-Rite uses the percentage-of-completion method to determine income. The percentage completion for year one is 60% ($4.5/$7.5) and 40% ($3/$7.5) in year two. Built-Rite would show a gross profit before tax of $1.5 million in year one and $1.0 million in year two calculated as follows:

Built-Rite's Income Tax Calculation Under Percentage-of Completion

Year	Revenue Recognized	Expenses	Gross Profit
1........	0.6($10 m) = $6 m	$4.5 m	$6 m − $4.5 m = $1.5 m
2.......	0.4($10 m) = $4 m	$3.0 m	$4 m − $3.0 m = $1.0 m

Because Built-Rite reports to the IRS under a cash basis, taxes need not be paid until the cash is received at the end of the second year. Thus under IRS reporting, because no revenues are received in the first year, no tax is due. But in year two the entire contract price is received by Built-Rite and therefore, the entire $10 m is received yielding taxes payable to the IRS of $0.875 m = 0.35[$10 m − ($4.5 m + $3.0 m)]. The question at hand is what should be the tax expense reported for this contract on Built-Rite's income statement?

In year 1, income before income taxes ($1,500,000) is higher than taxable income ($0). In year 2, the difference *reverses*. Income before income taxes ($1,000,000) is lower than taxable income ($2,500,000). Because this difference between the two statements reverses, the difference is called a **temporary difference**. Most differences between financial and tax reporting are temporary differences. Differences that do not reverse are called **permanent differences**. (An example of a permanent difference is municipal bond interest, which is a revenue to the company but is not subject to tax under IRS rules.)

How much should Built-Rite report as a provision for income taxes (income tax expense) in year 1? In year 2? One possible answer is to expense the same amount that is calculated on the tax return. It is easy to see how this approach can distort net income. In the Built-Rite example, all of the tax expense would be reported in year 2, even though most of the pretax income is reported in year 1.

A more reasonable approach (and the one that is acceptable for U.S. GAAP) is to recognize tax expense based on the *temporary difference* between the tax return and the income statement. Following this approach, the income statements appear as follows.

<table>
<tr><td colspan="3">BUILT-RITE CONSTRUCTION
Income Statements</td></tr>
<tr><td></td><td>Year 1</td><td>Year 2</td></tr>
<tr><td>Revenues...</td><td>$6,000,000</td><td>$4,000,000</td></tr>
<tr><td>Expenses..</td><td>4,500,000</td><td>3,000,000</td></tr>
<tr><td>Gross profit (income before income taxes).....................</td><td>1,500,000</td><td>1,000,000</td></tr>
<tr><td>Provision for income taxes...................................</td><td>525,000</td><td>350,000</td></tr>
<tr><td>Net income..</td><td>$ 975,000</td><td>$ 650,000</td></tr>
</table>

The tax expense of $525,000 ($1,500,000 × 35%) that is recognized in year 1 will be paid in cash in year 2 when the temporary difference reverses. As a consequence, the entry to record income tax expense in year 1 appears as follows using the financial statement effects template and in journal entry form.

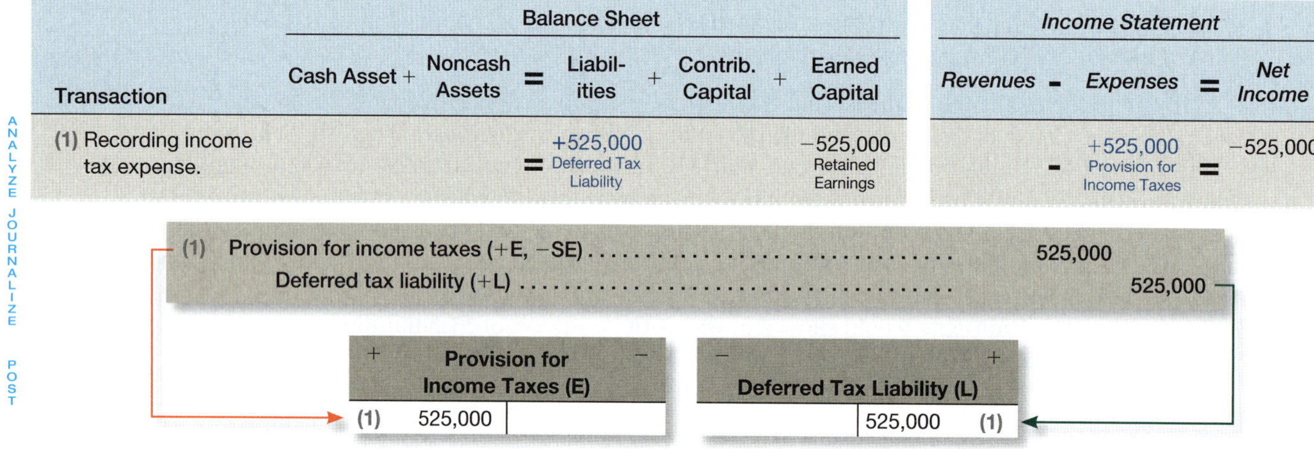

The account called **Deferred Tax Liability** (also called *Deferred Taxes*) is reported on the balance sheet as a liability. When reported as a liability, deferred taxes represent taxes to be paid in the future when taxable income is higher than financial reporting income. In year 2, when the temporary difference reverses, the entry to record tax expense and tax payments would be:

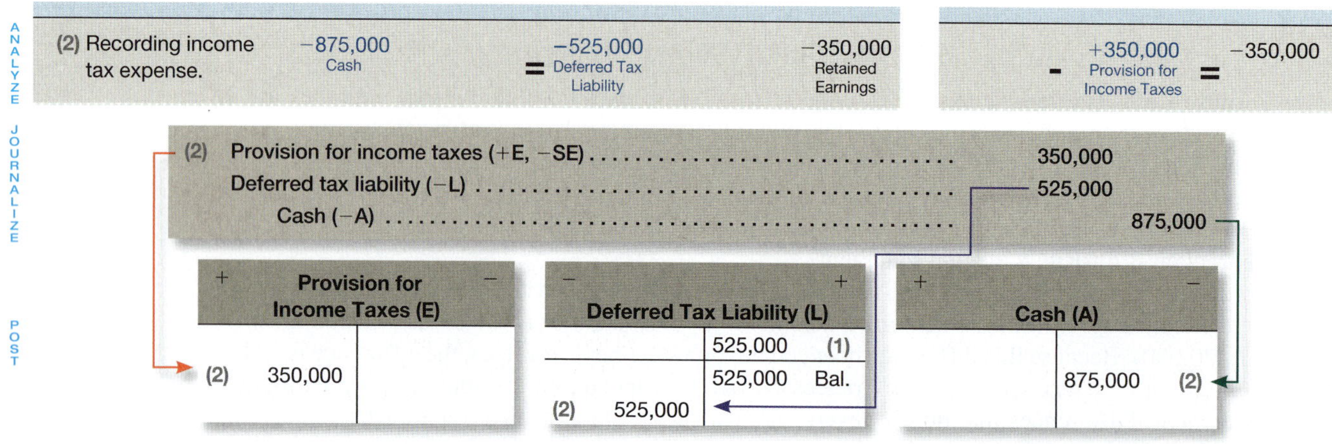

Deferred Taxes

A *Deferred Tax Liability* arises when tax reporting income is *less than* financial reporting income. When this occurs, the tax expense reported on the income statement is greater than the current tax due from the tax return. This result implies that the taxes will be paid when the temporary differences reverse. In the Built-Rite example, the deferred tax liability results from the difference between financial reporting and tax reporting of revenue from long-term contracts. The most common cause of a deferred tax liability, however, is a difference in the reporting of depreciation. While most companies use straight-line depreciation for financial reporting, the IRS mandates the use of MACRS (Modified Accelerated Cost Recovery Schedule) for tax reporting of most assets. This method fixes the useful life for various classes of assets, assumes no salvage value, and generally produces depreciation amounts consistent with the double-declining balance method. The result is that, in the early years of an asset's useful life, the company reports lower depreciation expense and higher pretax income in the income statement than it reports on its tax return. This difference reverses in the later years of the asset's useful life.

A **Deferred Tax Asset** arises when tax reporting income is *higher than* financial reporting income. In this situation, the deferred tax asset expires when the temporary difference reverses. Examples of temporary differences that lead to deferred tax assets include costs of uncollectible accounts receivable, warranty costs, and some pension expenses. For example, estimated warranty costs reduce reported pretax income and thereby tax expense on the income statement. These costs, however, cannot be deducted on the company's tax return until they are paid in cash. Thus, the recognized tax expense is less than the tax liability due currently (the debit is less than the credit) creating a deferred tax asset.[6]

It is reasonable to ask why we go to all this trouble. There are several reasons.

1. Income taxes are expenses and should be matched to revenues on an accrual basis.

2. Income tax expense on the income statement is based on financial, or pretax, income.

3. The difference between pretax income, as reported on the income statement, and taxable income arises from either permanent or temporary differences, the latter of which reverses over time.

    a. Permanent differences do not cause a matching problem. They have the same effect on tax expense (books) and on taxes owed (IRS).

    b. Temporary differences do cause a matching problem because they will eventually be included in taxable income and hence in reported income.

4. Tax expense is matched to income in the period by basing it on financial income adjusted for any permanent differences. Deferred tax accounts on the balance sheet make up the difference between the accrual based tax expense and the taxes actually paid.

5. The resulting asset or liability needs to be recognized to reflect the financial health of the company.

We conclude this subsection with an example based on depreciation accounting. Under IRS rules, accelerated depreciation is normally used, which moves the depreciation forward in time. Under GAAP, however, straight-line depreciation is normally used. The example below is based on the timing difference created by the different rules used by the IRS and the rules allowed under GAAP to determine the periodic depreciation expense.

Example:

Equipment costing $200,000 with a useful life of 4 years and no net salvage value is purchased in year 1. The firm uses straight-line depreciation for book calculations and tax depreciation schedules for tax purposes. The depreciation schedules reveal the following information:

---

[6] When a company has both deferred tax assets and deferred tax liabilities, the assets and liabilities are first separated into current and long-term amounts. The current deferred tax assets and current deferred tax liabilities are then reported *net* in the balance sheet under current assets or current liabilities, whichever is greater. Long-term amounts are treated similarly. It is not uncommon, therefore to see a company report deferred tax assets under current assets in the balance sheet, while reporting deferred tax liabilities under long-term liabilities.

	IRS		GAAP		
Year	Rate(%)	Depreciation	Depreciation	IRS vs. GAAP Difference	Cumulative Difference
1	50	$100,000*	$50,000**	$50,000	$50,000
2	25	50,000	50,000	0	50,000
3	12.5	25,000	50,000	(25,000)	25,000
4	12.5	25,000	50,000	(25,000)	0

*$200,000 × .5 = $100,000; IRS rates are obtained from IRS publications
**$200,000/4 = $50,000

Now assume for illustration that financial earnings each year before depreciation and taxes are $100,000.Assume also for ease of calculation the statutory tax rate is 40%. Tax expense and the taxes owed for each year are calculated next.

	Tax				Book			
Year	1	2	3	4	1	2	3	4
Earnings before depreciation and taxes	$100,000	$100,000	$100,000	$100,000	$100,000	$100,000	$100,000	$100,000
Depreciation	100,000	50,000	25,000	25,000	50,000	50,000	50,000	50,000
Earnings before taxes.	0	50,000	75,000	75,000	50,000	50,000	50,000	50,000
Taxes*	0	20,000	30,000	30,000	20,000	20,000	20,000	20,000

* Taxes = Earnings before taxes × 40% tax rate

The deferred tax liability at the end of each year would, in the absence of any other factors, be:

Year	Cumulative Depreciation Expense Difference	Tax Rate	Deferred Tax Liability, End of Year	Adjustment to Deferred Tax Liability, End of Year
1	$(50,000)	40%	$20,000	$20,000
2	(50,000)	40%	20,000	0
3	(25,000)	40%	10,000	(10,000)
4	0	40%	0	(10,000)

The analysis highlights several facts:

1. The second table shows that over the 4 years, tax payments to the IRS total $80,000 = ($0 + $20,000 + 30,000 + $30,000), which is also 40% of the total income after depreciation allowed by the IRS. Total tax expense on the books for the 4 years also equals $80,000 = 4($20,000).

2. The timing of the tax payments differs from the tax expense recognized on the books.

3. The deferred tax liability created in the first year because the tax code allows a larger deduction for depreciation, is reduced to zero in the 4th year when the timing of the depreciation deduction reverses.

4. The cash flow takes place consistent with the tax code. The deferred tax liability acknowledges the fact that the cash saving in taxes in year one represents cash outflows in future years.

Both the Built-Rite example and the depreciation example created *deferred tax liabilities*. Both are due to temporary differences. The Built-Rite deferred tax liability was due to income being recognized before the government taxed it (A1). The depreciation liability occurred because a deduction was allowed by the tax code before it was taken for books (A2).

Deferred tax assets are also encountered. They arise when income is recognized by the *tax code* before being recognized for *books* and when an expense is recognized for *book purposes* before it is recognized under the *tax code*. Both differences are also due to timing differences created by using accrual accounting for books and a cash-flow approach to calculating taxes under the IRS. For example, a customer may pay in advance for a bundled purchase of software. For book income, the company recognizes revenue as it delivers the components of the bundle, but tax accounting recognizes all the revenue when the software bundle is sold. Or, a company could recognize a restructuring charge for the future cost of employee severance, but it does not receive a tax deduction until the cash outflows are made. In each case, tax income is higher than book income thus creating a temporary difference. These temporary differences give rise to deferred tax assets.

As another example, suppose a warehouse rental company receives prepaid rent of $100,000 on January 1 for two years rent. Assume the tax rate is 34% and the company computes income taxes on a cash basis. The IRS will levy a tax of $34,000 for the year ($100,000 × 0.34). However, the warehouse company will only record $50,000 as income under GAAP. Thus, it will recognize $17,000 of income tax expense for the current year and $17,000 will be recorded as a deferred tax asset.

Income Tax Disclosures

Southwest Airlines, Co.'s provision for income taxes has fluctuated dramatically over the years as is illustrated in the graph below.

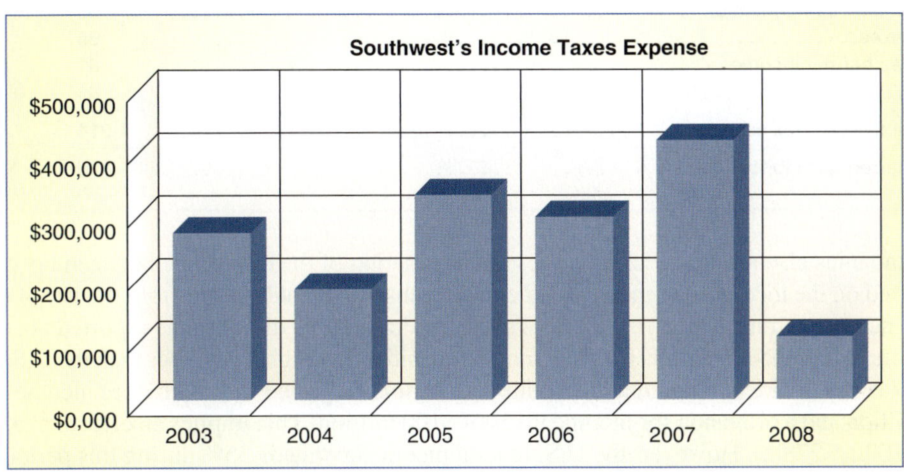

To see how income tax expense is disclosed, Southwest's tax footnote 16 to its 2008 income statement is shown in Exhibit 10.6. Southwest's $100 million tax expense reported in its income statement consists of the following two components:

1. *Current tax expense.* Amount currently payable (in cash) to tax authorities.
2. *Deferred tax expense.* Effect on tax expense from changes in deferred tax liabilities and deferred tax assets.

EXHIBIT 10.6	Income Tax Expense Footnote for Southwest Airlines		
Year Ended ($ millions)		**2008**	**2007**
Current			
Federal.		$ 23	$108
State		10	9
Total current		33	117
Deferred			
Federal.		80	246
State		(13)	50
Total deferred		67	296
Total		$100	$413

Companies must disclose the components of deferred tax liabilities and assets. Southwest's deferred tax footnote to its balance sheet (shown in Exhibit 10.7) reports deferred tax liabilities of

$2,789 million and deferred tax assets of $1,214 million. This results in a net deferred tax liability of $1,575 million. The largest source of deferred tax liabilities, as listed in the footnote, is the use of accelerated depreciation (MACRS) for tax purposes.

EXHIBIT 10.7	Income Tax Expense Footnote for Southwest Airlines		
($ millions)		**2008**	**2007**
Deferred Tax Liabilities:			
Accelerated depreciation		$2,760	$2,612
Fuel derivative instruments		—	884
Other		29	19
Total deferred tax liabilities		2,789	3,515
Deferred Tax Assets:			
Fuel derivative instruments		567	—
Deferred gains from sale and leaseback of aircraft		60	65
Capital and operating leases		47	58
Accrued employee benefits		211	187
Stock-based compensation		93	110
State taxes		69	75
Business partner income		81	78
Other		86	37
Total deferred tax assets		1,214	610
Net deferred tax liability		$1,575	$2,905

Companies also report in the footnotes an explanation of the difference between tax expense, as reported on the income statement, and the tax expense that would result from the use of the U.S. federal income tax rate. The **effective tax rate** is determined by dividing the reported tax expense by income before income taxes. This rate may be considerably higher or lower than the U.S. federal income tax rate. For example, in 2008 Southwest Airlines reported income before income taxes of $278 million and a provision for income taxes of $100 million. This implies an effective tax rate of 36% ($100m/$278m). However, the U.S. federal income tax rate is 35% during this period. Using this rate would have produced a tax provision of $97.3 million ($278 million × 0.35). Exhibit 10.8 shows the reconciliation of these two amounts from Southwest's income tax footnote. In the case of Southwest, the difference between the effective tax rate and the federal rate is primarily due to permanent differences between financial and tax reporting. Some of that difference is offset by state income taxes and other differences.

EXHIBIT 10.8	Income Tax Expense Footnote for Southwest Airlines	
($ millions)		**2008**
Tax at statutory U.S. tax rate		$97
Nondeductible items		10
State income taxes, net of federal benefit		(2)
Other, net		(5)
Total income tax provision		$100

Deferred taxes affect the operating section of the cash flow statement. The net income figure should be adjusted upward for any increase in the net deferred tax liability.

Computation and Analysis of Taxes

The procedure for computing income tax expense is to first calculate the tax obligation (from the company's tax return), then compute any changes in deferred tax liabilities or assets. From these two amounts, we can then calculate tax expense as follows.

Tax expense = Tax obligation − Changes in deferred tax assets and liabilities

An analysis of deferred taxes can yield useful insights. An increase in deferred tax liabilities indicates that a company is reporting higher profits in its income statement than in its tax return. The difference between reported corporate profits and taxable income increased substantially in the late 1990s, just prior to the stock market decline. The following quote from *CFO Magazine* (November 2002) implies that such differences should be carefully monitored.

> Fueling the sense that something [was] amiss [was] the growing gap between the two sets of numbers. In 1992, there was no significant difference between pretax book income and taxable net income . . . By 1996, according to IRS data, a $92.5 billion gap had appeared. By 1998 [prior to the market decline], the gap was $159 billion—a fourth of the total taxable income reported . . . If people had seen numbers showing very significant differences between book numbers for trading and tax numbers, they would have wondered if those [income] numbers were completely real.

Although an increase in deferred tax liabilities can legitimately result, we must be aware of the possibility that such differences can also be the result of improper revenue recognition or other questionable accounting practices. More advanced courses cover the reporting of deferred taxes when a company is not sure it will be able to realize all its available tax credits, and the effects of changes in the tax law.

CHAPTER-END REVIEW

The following footnote is from the 2010 annual report of Adler Corporation.

Note 9: Income Taxes
The provision for income taxes includes the following

($ thousands)	2010
Current provision	
Domestic	$1,342
Foreign	146
Deferred provision (credit)	
Domestic	960
Foreign	(58)
Total	$2,390

Required

1. (a) What is the amount of income tax expense reported on its income statement? (b) How much of its income tax expense is payable in cash? (c) Assuming that its deferred tax liability increased, identify an example that could account for such a change.
2. Prepare the entry, using both the financial statement effects template and in journal entry form, to record its income tax expense for 2010.

The solution to this review problem can be found on page 487.

SUMMARY

Define off-balance-sheet financing and explain its effects on financial analysis. (p. 436)   LO1

- Off-balance-sheet financing refers to financial obligations of the company that are not recognized as liabilities in the balance sheet. Recognizing these obligations often requires recognizing off-balance-sheet assets.

- Off-balance-sheet financing improves financial leverage ratios and its corresponding unrecognized assets improve performance measures.

LO2 **Account for leases using the operating lease method and the capital lease method. (p. 436)**
- Operating lease payments are treated as ordinary rent expense. No asset or liability is recorded.
- A capital lease records an asset and a liability equal to the present value of the minimum lease payments. The income statement reports interest expense on the liability and depreciation on the asset.

LO3 **Convert off-balance-sheet operating leases to the capital lease method. (p. 442)**
- Compute the present value of future cash payments required under operating leases. These cash obligations are disclosed in footnotes.
- Add a lease asset and a lease liability to the balance sheet equal to the present value of the future cash payments.

LO4 **Explain and interpret the reporting for pension plans. (p. 446)**
- Pension and other postretirement obligations represent one of the largest obligations for most companies.
- The projected benefit obligation is the present value of the estimated future benefits that a company expects to pay retired employees.
- The net liability that a company reports on the balance sheet is the projected benefit obligation offset by the plan assets.

LO5 **Analyze and interpret pension footnote disclosures. (p. 450)**
- Pension footnotes provide detailed information about changes in pension obligations, changes in plan assets, and the determinants of pension expense.
- Pension footnotes provide information allowing us to interpret pension expenses and cash flows.

LO6 **Describe and interpret accounting for income taxes. (p. 456)**
- While income tax expense is reported below income from operations, it is an operating expense. The initial item in an indirect cash flow statement is net income, which reflects the deduction of the tax expense.
- Income tax expense is determined as the sum of the tax computed as due to the government and the net change in deferred taxes.
- Deferred taxes occur because of differences between U.S. GAAP reporting and the tax due based on the rules of the tax authority. The former are based on accrual accounting while the latter are often based on a cash-based accounting system.

<h2>GUIDANCE ANSWERS . . . YOU MAKE THE CALL</h2>

You are the Division President   You must take care in accepting lease terms that are not advantageous to your company merely to achieve off-balance-sheet financing. Long-term shareholder value is created by managing your operation well, including negotiating leases with acceptable terms. Lease footnote disclosures also provide sufficient information for skilled analysts to undo the operating lease treatment. This means that you can end up with effective capitalization of a lease with lease terms that are not in the best interests of your company and with few benefits from off-balance-sheet financing. There is also the potential for lost credibility with stakeholders.

You are a Consultant to the FASB   This issue is one of the questions confronting the FASB. Normally accountants do not favor offsetting liabilities against the related assets as is currently the reporting practice required under GAAP. Alternatively there is a problem with reporting the pension plan assets among the firm's assets. A company does not have unilateral control over a pension trust. It can put assets into the trust but can not easily get them out of the trust. For this reason, the pension assets do not possess the flexibility we normally require for recognition. While we do not know how the FASB will resolve this matter, we suspect the reporting of the net asset or liability will continue to be the required reporting.

<h2>KEY RATIOS</h2>

$$\text{Fixed commitments ratio} = \frac{\text{Operating cash flow}}{\text{Fixed commitments}} \qquad \text{Effective tax rate} = \frac{\text{Provision for income taxes (expense)}}{\text{Income before income taxes}}$$

KEY TERMS

Accumulated post-employment benefit obligation (APBO) (p. 455)

Capital lease method (p. 438)

Deferred Tax Asset (p. 459)

Deferred Tax Liability (p. 458)

Defined benefit plan (p. 446)

Defined contribution plan (p. 446)

Effective tax rate (p. 462)

Fixed commitments ratio (FCR) (p. 445)

Funded status (p. 447)

Interest cost (p. 448)

Lessee (p. 437)

Lessor (p. 437)

Off-balance-sheet financing (p. 436)

Operating lease method (p. 438)

Other post-employment benefits (OPEB) (p. 455)

Overfunded (p. 447)

Pension plan assets (p. 447)

Permanent differences (p. 457)

Projected benefit obligation (PBO) (p. 447)

Provision for income tax (p. 458)

Service cost (p. 448)

Temporary difference (p. 457)

Underfunded (p. 447)

MULTIPLE CHOICE

1. U.S. GAAP requires that certain leases be accounted for as *capital leases*. The reason for this treatment is that this type of lease
    a.   conveys all of the benefits and risks of ownership of the asset.
    b.   is an example of form over substance.
    c.   provides the use of the lease asset to the lessee for a limited period of time.
    d.   is an example of off-balance-sheet financing.

2. For a lease that is accounted for as an operating lease by the lessee, the monthly rental payments should be
    a.   allocated between interest expense and depreciation expense.
    b.   allocated between a reduction in the liability for lease assets and interest expense.
    c.   recorded as a reduction in the liability for lease assets.
    d.   recorded as rent expense.

3. The balance sheet liability for a capital lease would be reduced each period by the
    a.   lease payment.
    b.   lease payment plus the amortization of the related asset.
    c.   lease payment less the amortization of the related asset.
    d.   lease payment less the periodic interest expense.

4. Which of the following statements characterizes defined benefit pension plans?
    a.   The employer's obligation is satisfied by making the necessary periodic contribution.
    b.   Retirement benefits are based on the plan's benefit formula.
    c.   Retirement benefits depend on how well pension fund assets have been managed.
    d.   Contributions are made in equal amounts by employer and employees.

5. When the value of pension plan assets is greater than the projected benefit obligation,
    a.   the difference is added to pension expense.
    b.   the difference is reported as deferred pension cost.
    c.   the difference is reported as a contra equity adjustment.
    d.   the pension plan is overfunded.

6. Which of the following is *not* a component of net pension expense?
    a.   Interest cost
    b.   Return on plan assets
    c.   Benefits paid to retirees
    d.   Amortization of prior service cost

DISCUSSION QUESTIONS

Q10-1.   What are the financial reporting differences between an operating lease and a capital lease? Explain.

Q10-2.   Are footnote disclosures sufficient to overcome nonrecognition on the balance sheet of assets and related liabilities for operating leases? Explain.

Q10-3. Is the expense of a lease over its entire life the same whether or not it is capitalized? Explain.

Q10-4. What are the economic and accounting differences between a defined contribution plan and a defined benefit plan?

Q10-5. Under what circumstances will a company report a net pension asset? A net pension liability?

Q10-6. What are the components of pension expense that is reported in the income statement?

Q10-7. What effect does the use of expected returns on pension investments and the deferral of unexpected gains and losses on those investments have on income?

Q10-8. How is the initial valuation determined for the asset and the liability with a capital lease?

Q10-9. Over what time period should the cost of providing retirement benefits to employees be expensed?

Q10-10. What accounting analysis is required when the accumulated retirement benefits under a firm's pension plan exceed the assets in its pension fund?

Q10-11. Under what circumstances should a tax payment be recorded as deferred taxes?

**Assignments with the WebAssign. logo in the margin are available in WebAssign.
See the Preface of the book for details.**

MINI EXERCISES

LO2   M10-12. Accounting for Leases

On January 3, 2010, Hanna Corporation signed a lease on a machine for its manufacturing operation. The lease requires Hanna to make six annual lease payments of $12,000 with the first payment due December 31, 2010. Hanna could have financed the machine by borrowing the purchase price at an interest rate of 7%.

   a. Prepare the journal entries that Hanna Corporation would make on January 3 and December 31, 2010, to record this lease assuming
      i.   the lease is reported as an operating lease.
      ii. the lease is reported as a capital lease.
   b. Assuming that the lease is treated as a capital lease, post the journal entries of part *a* to the appropriate T-accounts.
   c. Show how the entries posted in part *b* would affect the financial statements using the financial statement effects template.

LO2   M10-13. Accounting for Leases

On July 1, 2010, Stokes Company leased a warehouse building under a 10-year lease agreement. The lease requires quarterly lease payments of $4,500. The first lease payment is due on September 30, 2010. The lease was reported as a capital lease using an 8% annual interest rate.

   a. Prepare the journal entry to record the initial signing of the lease on July 1, 2010.
   b. Prepare the journal entries that would be necessary on September 30 and December 31, 2010.
   c. Post the entries from parts *a* and *b* in their appropriate T-accounts.
   d. Prepare a financial statement effects template to show the effects of the entries from parts *a* and *b* on the balance sheet and income statement.
   e. Redo parts *a* and *b* assuming that the lease is reported as an operating lease. Is the expense recognized in 2010 under the operating lease method higher or lower than under the capital lease method? Explain.

LO2   M10-14. Analyzing and Interpreting Leasing Footnote Disclosures

YUM! Brands, Inc., reports the following information related to non-cancelable leases in Note 13 of its 2008 10K.

At December 27, 2008, we operated more than 7,300 restaurants, leasing the underlying land and/or building in more than 5,800 of those restaurants with the vast majority of our commitments expiring within 20 years from the inception of the lease. Our longest lease expires in 2151. We also lease office space for headquarters and support functions, as well as certain office and restaurant equipment. We do not consider any of these individual leases material to our operations. Most leases require us to pay related executory costs, which include property taxes, maintenance, and insurance.

a. Yum has both capital and operating leases. In general, what effects does each of these lease types have on Yum's balance sheet and its income statement?

b. What types of adjustments might you consider to Yum's balance sheet for analysis purposes?

M10-15. Analyzing and Capitalizing Operating Lease Payments Disclosed in Footnotes

LO3

SOUTHWEST AIRLINES
NYSE :: LUV

Southwest Airlines Co. discloses the following in footnote 8 to its 2007 10-K report relating to its leasing activities:

(In millions)	Capital leases	Operating leases
2008	$16	$ 400
2009	17	335
2010	15	298
2011	12	235
2012	—	195
After 2012	—	876
Total minimum lease payments	60	$2,339
Less amount representing interest	8	
Present value of minimum lease payments	52	
Less current portion	13	
Long-term portion	$39	

Operating leases are not reflected on-balance-sheet. In our analysis of a company, we often desire to capitalize these operating leases, that is, add the present value of these lease payments to both the reported assets and liabilities.

a. Compute the present value of Southwest's operating lease payments assuming a 7% discount rate.

b. What effect does capitalization of Southwest's operating leases have on its total liabilities (it reported total liabilities of $9,831 million for 2007).

M10-16. Analyzing and Interpreting Pension Disclosures—Expenses and Returns

LO4, LO5

AMERICAN EXPRESS
NYSE :: AXP

American Express Company discloses the following information in footnote 20 in its 10-K report:

(In millions)	2008
Service cost	$ 23
Interest cost	136
Expected return on plan assets	(169)
Amortization of prior service cost	—
Recognized net actuarial loss (gain)	17
Settlement/curtailment loss (gain)	6
Net periodic pension benefit cost	$13

a. How much pension expense does American Express report in its 2008 income statement?

b. What effect does its "expected return on plan assets" have on its reported pension expense? Explain.

c. Explain use of the word *expected* as it relates to results of pension plan investments.

M10-17. Analyzing and Interpreting Pension Disclosures—Expenses and Returns

LO4, LO5

YUM! BRANDS
NYSE :: YUM

YUM! Brands, Inc., discloses the following pension footnote in its 10-K report:

	Pension Benefits	
(In millions)	2008	2007
Service cost	$30	$33
Interest cost	53	50
Amortization of prior service cost	—	1
Expected return on plan assets	(53)	(51)
Recognized actuarial loss	6	23
Net periodic benefit cost	$36	$56

a. How much pension expense does Yum report in its 2008 income statement?

b. What effect does its "expected return on plan assets" have on its reported pension expense? Explain.

c. Explain use of the word *expected* as it relates to results of pension plan investments.

LO4, LO5

ABERCROMBIE & FITCH
NYSE :: ANF

M10-18. Analyzing and Interpreting Retirement Benefit Footnote

Abercrombie & Fitch Co. discloses the following footnote relating to its retirement plans in its 2008 10-K report:

15. RETIREMENT BENEFITS The Company maintains the Abercombie & Fitch Co. Savings & Retirement Plan, a qualified plan. All U.S. associates are eligible to participate in this plan if they are at least 21 years of age and have completed a year of employment with 1,000 or more hours of service. In addition, the Company maintains the Abercrombie & Fitch Nonqualified Savings and Supplemental Retirement Plan. Participation in this plan is based on service and compensation. The Company's contributions are based on a percentage of associates' eligible annual compensation. The cost of the Company's contributions to these plans was $24.7 million in Fiscal 2008, $21.0 million in Fiscal 2007, and $15.0 million in Fiscal 2006.

a. Does Abercrombie have a defined contribution or defined benefit pension plan? Explain.

b. How does Abercrombie account for its contributions to its retirement plan?

c. How is Abercrombie's obligation to its retirement plan reported on its balance sheet?

LO4, LO5

TARGET
NYSE :: TGT

M10-19. Analyzing and Interpreting Pension Plan Benefit Footnote

Target Corporation provides the following footnote relating to its retirement plans in its 2008 10-K report:

Defined Contribution Plans Team members who meet certain eligibility requirements can participate in a defined contribution 401(k) plan by investing up to 80 percent of their compensation, as limited by statute or regulation. Generally, we match 100 percent of each team member's contribution up to 5 percent of total compensation. Our contribution to the plan is initially invested in Target common stock. These amounts are free to be diversified by the team member immediately. Benefits expense related to these matching contributions was $178 million, $172 million, and $141 million in 2008, 2007, and 2006, respectively.

a. Does Target have a defined contribution or defined benefit pension plan? Explain.

b. How would Target account for its contributions to its retirement plan?

c. How is Target's obligation to its retirement plan reported on its balance sheet?

d. Do you see any problems for employees in Target's plan?

LO1

TARGET
NYSE :: TGT

M10-20. Analyzing and Interpreting Leasing Footnote

The 2008 10-K report of **Target Corporation**, provides the following footnote ($ thousands).

21. Leases We lease certain retail locations, warehouses, distribution centers, office space, equipment, and land. Assets held under capital lease are included in property and equipment. Operating lease rentals are expensed on a straight-line basis over the life of the lease. At lease inception, we determine the lease term by assuming the exercise of those renewal options that are reasonably assured because of the significant economic penalty that exists for not exercising those options. The exercise of lease renewal options is at our sole discretion. The expected lease term is used to determine whether a lease is capital or operating and is used to calculate straight-line rent expense. Additionally, the depreciable life of buildings and leasehold improvements is limited by the expected lease term.

Rent expense on buildings, which is included in SG&A, includes rental payments based on a percentage of retail sales over contractual levels for certain stores. Total rent expense was $169 million in 2008, $165 million in 2007, and $158 million in 2006, including percentage rent expense of $4 million in 2008 and $5 million in 2007 and 2006. Certain leases require us to pay real estate taxes, insurance, maintenance, and other operating expenses associated with the leased premises. These expenses are classified in SG&A consistent with similar costs for owned locations. Most long-term leases include one or more options to renew, with renewal terms that can extend the lease term from one to more than fifty years. Certain leases also include options to purchase the leased property.

Future Minimum Lease Payments (millions)	Operating Leases	Capital Leases
2009	$ 245	$ 30
2010	216	20
2011	157	21
2012	146	22
2013	143	22
After 2013.	2,950	138
Total future minimum lease payments (a)	$3,857	253
Less: Interest (b)		(129)
Present value of future minimum capital lease payments (c) . . .		$124

a. Compute the present value of Target's operating leases. Assume a 6% discount rate.
b. If the operating leases are classified as capial leases, indicate how the amount in part *a* would be reported in Target's balance sheet using the financial statement effects template.
c. Would recognition of the operating leases affect the current ratio? Explain.
d. Prepare journal entries to record the capitalization of Target's operating leases at the end of fiscal 2008. Enter them in the appropriate T-accounts.
e. Do these leases represent a substantial fixed commitment to Target given Target's operating cash flow of $4,430 million in 2008?

M10-21. Analyzing and Interpreting Footnote on Contract Manufacturers LO1

NIKE
NYSE :: NKE

Nike, Inc. reports the following information relating to its manufacturing activities in the footnotes to its 2008 10-K report:

MANUFACTURING   Virtually all of our footwear is produced outside of the United States. In fiscal 2006, contract suppliers in China, Vietnam, Indonesia, and Thailand manufactured 36 percent, 23 percent, 21 percent, and 9 percent of total NIKE brand footwear, respectively. We also have manufacturing agreements with independent factories in Argentina, Brazil, India, Italy, and South Africa to manufacture footwear for sale primarily within those countries. Our largest single footwear factory accounted for approximately 6 percent of total fiscal 2008 footwear production.

a. What effect does the use of contract manufacturers have on Nike's balance sheet?
b. Nike executes purchase contracts with its contract manufacturers to purchase their output. How are executory contracts reported under GAAP? Does your answer suggest a possible motivation for the use of contract manufacturing?

M10-22. Computing and Reporting Deferred Income Taxes LO6

Web**Assign**.

Fisk, Inc., purchased $600,000 of construction equipment on January 1, 2008. The equipment is being depreciated on a straight-line basis over six years with no expected salvage value. MACRS depreciation is being used on the firm's tax returns. At December 31, 2010, the equipment's book value is $300,000 and its tax basis is $173,000 (this is Fisk's only temporary difference). Over the next three years, straight-line depreciation will exceed MACRS depreciation by $31,000 in 2011, $31,000 in 2012, and $65,000 in 2013. Assume that the income tax rate in effect for all years is 40%.

a. What amount of deferred tax liability should appear in Fisk's December 31, 2010, balance sheet?
b. What amount of deferred tax liability should appear in Fisk's December 31, 2011, balance sheet?
c. What amount of deferred tax liability should appear in Fisk's December 31, 2012, balance sheet?
d. Where should the deferred tax liability accounts be classified in Fisk's 2010, 2011, and 2012 year-end balance sheets?

EXERCISES

E10-23. Analyzing and Interpreting Leasing Footnote LO2

FORTUNE BRANDS
NYSE :: FO

Fortune Brands, Inc., reports the following footnote relating to its leased facilities in its 2008 10-K report. Future minimum rental payments under noncancelable operating leases as of December 31, 2008, are as follows:

(In millions)	
2009	$ 57.8
2010	45.4
2011	35.1
2012	26.3
2013	22.4
Remainder	18.0
Total minimum rental payments	205.0
Less minimum rentals to be received under noncancelable subleases	5.7
	$199.3

Fortune Brands reports stockholders' equity of $4,672 million and total assets of $12,092 million.

a. Assuming that this is the only information available about its leasing activities, does Fortune Brands classify its leases as operating or capital? Explain.

b. What effect has its lease classification had on Fortune Brands' balance sheet? Over the life of the lease, what effect does this classification have on net income?

c. Calculate the effect on Fortune Brands total liabilities and its debt-to-equity ratio. (Use a 7% discount rate.)

LO2 **E10-24. Analyzing and Interpreting Footnote on Both Operating and Capital Leases**

VERIZON
NYSE :: VZ

Verizon Communications Inc. provides the following footnote relating to its leasing activities in its 10-K report.

The aggregate minimum rental commitments under noncancelable leases for the periods shown at December 31, 2008, are:

Years (dollars in millions)	Capital Leases	Operating Leases
2009	$ 90	$1,620
2010	81	1,339
2011	76	1,039
2012	56	770
2013	51	539
Thereafter	126	1,995
Total minimum rental commitments	480	$7,302
Less interest and executory costs	(90)	
Present value of minimum lease payments	390	
Less current installments	(63)	
Long-term obligation at December 31, 2008	$327	

a. Assuming that this is the only available information relating to its leasing activities, what amount does Verizon report on its balance sheet for its lease obligations? Does this amount represent its total obligation to lessors? How do you know?

b. What effect has its lease classification as capital or operating had on Verizon's balance sheet? Over the life of its leases, what effect does this lease classification have on its net income?

LO2, LO3 **E10-25. Analyzing, Interpreting, and Capitalizing Operating Leases**

STAPLES, INC.
NASDAQ :: SPLS

Staples, Inc., reports the following footnote relating to its capital and operating leases in its 2008 10-K report ($ thousands).

Other long-term obligations at January 31, 2009, include $135.0 million relating to future rent escalation clauses and lease incentives under certain existing store operating lease arrangements. These rent expenses are recognized on a straight-line basis over the respective terms of the leases. Future minimum lease commitments due for retail and support facilities (including lease commitments for 74 retail stores not yet opened at January 31, 2009) and equipment leases under noncancellable operating leases are as follows (in thousands):

Fiscal Year	Total
2009	$ 851,412
2010	803,071
2011	731,808
2012	645,215
2013	556,031
Thereafter	2,132,053
	$5,719,590

Future minimum lease commitments do not include $47.6 million of minimum rentals due under noncancelable subleases.

Rent expense was approximately $744.6 million, $646.2 million, and $612.8 million for 2008, 2007, and 2006, respectively.

a. What dollar adjustment(s) might you consider to Staples' balance sheet given this information and assuming that Staples intermediate-term borrowing rate is 7%? Explain. (Staples reported total liabilities of $7.442 billion for 2008.) Round the average life to the nearest year.

b. Show how the amount computed in part *a* would be reported in the balance sheet using the financial statement effects template.

c. Prepare journal entries to record the capitalization of these operating leases at the end of fiscal 2008. What journal entries would be required to record lease payments and lease related expenses in 2009 if these leases were accounted for as capital leases? Assume leased assets are depreciated over a 10-year life using the straight-line method.

d. Post the journal entries from part *c* to the appropriate T-accounts.

E10-26. Analyzing, Interpreting, and Capitalizing Operating Leases   **LO3**

YUM! Brands, Inc., reports the following footnote relating to its capital and operating leases in Note 13 to its 2008 10-K report ($ millions).   **YUM! BRANDS**
NYSE :: YUM

Future minimum commitments and amounts to be received as lessor or sublessor under noncancelable leases are set forth below:

(In millions)	Commitments		Lease Receivables	
	Capital	Operating	Direct Financing	Operating
2009	$ 26	$ 491	$ 13	$ 41
2010	64	451	13	37
2011	23	409	14	34
2012	22	368	14	30
2013	21	333	14	27
Thereafter	228	2,524	79	103
	$384	$4,576	$147	$272

What adjustment(s), assuming a discount rate of 7%, might you consider making to Yum's balance sheet given this information? Explain. Yum reported total liabilities of $6,635 million for 2008. (Hint: Net the respective operating commitments and lease receivables columns.)

E10-27. Analyzing, Interpreting, and Capitalizing Operating Leases   **LO2, LO3**

Nike, Inc. reports the following data concerning leases in its 2008 10-K.   **NIKE**
NYSE :: NKE

Note 14—Commitments and Contingencies
The Company leases space for certain of its offices, warehouses and retail stores under leases expiring from one to twenty-six years after May 31, 2008. Rent expense was $344.2 million, $285.2 million and $252.0 million for the years ended May 31, 2008, 2007 and 2006, respectively. Amounts of minimum future annual rental commitments under noncancelable operating leases in each of the five years ending May 31, 2009 through 2013 are $312.4 million, $264.4 million, $228.9 million, $192.1 million, $163.9 million, respectively, and $692.3 million in later years.

a. What adjustment(s) might you consider to Nike's balance sheet given this information and assuming that Nike's discount rate is 7%? Explain.

b. Show how the amount computed in part *a* would be reported in the balance sheet using the financial statement effects template.

c. Prepare journal entries to record the capitalization of these operating leases at the end of fiscal 2008. What journal entries would be required to record lease payments and lease related expenses in 2009 if these leases were accounted for as capital leases? Assume straight-line depreciation and a ten-year life.

d. Post the journal entries from part *c* to the appropriate T-accounts.

LO5 **E10-28. Analyzing and Interpreting Pension Footnote—Funded and Reported Amounts**

Web**Assign**.

YUM! BRANDS
NYSE :: YUM

YUM! Brands, Inc., reports the following pension footnote in Note 15 of its 10-K report.

	U.S. Pension Plans	
September 30 (In millions)	**2008**	**2007**
Change in benefit obligation		
Benefit obligation at beginning of year	$ 842	$864
SFAS 158 measurement date adjustment	21	—
Service cost	30	33
Interest cost	53	50
Participant contributions	—	—
Plan amendments	1	4
Acquisitions	—	—
Curtailment gain	(6)	(4)
Settlement loss	1	—
Special termination benefits	13	—
Exchange rate changes	—	—
Benefits paid	(48)	(34)
Settlement payments	(9)	—
Actuarial (gain) loss	25	(71)
Benefit obligation at end of year	$ 923	$842
Change in plan assets		
Fair value of plan assets at beginning of year	$ 732	$673
Actual return on plan assets	(213)	93
Employer contributions	54	2
Settlement payments	—	—
Participant contributions	(9)	—
Benefits paid	(48)	(33)
Exchange rate changes	—	—
Administrative expenses	(3)	(3)
Fair value of plan assets at end of year	$ 513	$ 732
Funded status	$(410)	$(110)

a. Describe what is meant by *service cost* and *interest cost*.

b. What is the source of funds to make payments to retirees?

c. Show the computation of the 2008 funded status for Yum.

d. What net pension amount is reported on its 2008 balance sheet?

LO4, LO5 **E10-29. Analyzing and Interpreting Pension Footnote—Funded and Reported Amounts**

XEROX CORPORATION
NYSE :: XRX

Xerox Corporation reports the following pension footnote as part of its 2008 10-K report.

	Pension Benefits	
(In millions)	**2008**	**2007**
Change in Benefit Obligation		
Benefit obligation, January 1	$10,458	$10,467
Service cost	209	237
Interest cost	(5)	578
Plan participants' contributions	13	12
Plan amendments	1	11
Actuarial (gain) loss	(550)	(508)
Acquisitions	20	–
Currency exchange rate changes	(1,090)	331
Curtailments	3	(1)
Benefits paid/settlements	(657)	(669)
Other*	93	–
Benefit obligation, December 31	$ 8,495	$10,458
Change in Plan Assets		
Fair value of plan assets, January 1	$ 9,805	$ 9,217
Actual return on plan assets	(1,527)	667
Employer contribution	299	298
Plan participants' contributions	13	12
Acquisitions	20	–
Currency exchange rate changes	(1,049)	280
Benefits paid/settlements	(657)	(669)
Other*	19	–
Fair value of plan assets, December 31	$ 6,923	$ 9,805
Funded status (including under-funded and non-funded plans)	$ (1,572)	$ (653)

	Pension Benefits			Retiree Health		
(In millions)	**2008**	**2007**	**2006**	**2008**	**2007**	**2006**
Components of Net Periodic Benefit Cost						
Service cost	$209	$237	$244	$14	$ 17	$ 19
Interest cost	(5)	578	732	84	87	92
Expected return on plan assets	(80)	(668)	(802)	–	–	–
Recognized net actuarial loss	36	75	104	–	10	19
Amortization of prior service credit	(20)	(20)	(16)	(21)	(12)	(13)
Recognized curtailment/settlement loss	34	33	93	–	–	–
Net periodic benefit cost	174	235	355	77	102	117
Defined contribution plans	80	80	70	–	–	–
Total net periodic benefit costs	$254	$315	$425	$ 77	$ 102	$ 117

a. Describe what is meant by *service cost* and *interest cost* (the service and interest costs appear both in the reconciliation of the PBO and in the computation of pension expense).

b. What is the actual return on pension investments in 2008?

c. Provide an example under which an "actuarial gain," such as the $550 million gain that Xerox reports in 2008, might arise.

d. What is the source of funds to make payments to retirees?

e. How much cash did Xerox contribute to its pension plans in 2008?

f. How much cash did the company pay to retirees in 2008?

g. Show the computation of its 2008 funded status.

h. What net pension amount is reported on its 2008 balance sheet?

LO4, LO5

E10-30. Analyzing and Interpreting Pension Footnote—Funded and Reported Amounts

Verizon Communications Inc. reports the following pension data in Note 15 to its 2008 10-K report.

	Pension	
At December 31 ($ millions)	**2008**	**2007**
Change in Benefit Obligations		
Beginning of year	$32,495	$34,159
Service cost	382	442
Interest cost	1,966	1,975
Plan amendments	300	—
Actuarial loss (gain), net	(154)	123
Benefits paid	(2,577)	(4,204)
Termination benefits	32	—
Acquisitions and divestitures, net	(183)	—
Settlements	(1,867)	—
End of year	30,394	32,495
Change in Plan Assets		
Beginning of year	42,659	41,509
Actual return on plan assets	(10,680)	4,591
Company contributions	487	737
Benefits paid	(2,577)	(4,204)
Settlements	(1,867)	—
Acquisitions and divestitures, net	(231)	26
End of year	27,791	42,659
Funded Status		
End of year	$ (2,603)	$10,164

a. Describe what is meant by service cost and interest cost.

b. What is the source of funds to make payments to retirees?

c. Show the computation of Verizon's 2008 funded status.

d. What net pension amount is reported on its 2008 balance sheet?

LO6

E10-31. Recording Income Tax Expense

Nike, Inc., reports the the following tax information in Note 8 to its 2008 financial report. Income before income taxes is as follows:

Year Ended May 31 (In millions)	**2008**	**2007**	**2006**
Income before income taxes:			
United States	$ 713.0	$ 805.1	$ 838.6
Foreign	1,789.9	1,394.8	1,303.0
	$2,502.9	$2,199.9	$2,141.6

The provision for income taxes is as follows:

Year Ended May 31 (In millions)	**2008**	**2007**	**2006**
Current:			
United States			
Federal	$469.9	$ 352.6	$359.0
State	58.4	59.6	60.6
Foreign	391.8	261.9	356.0
	920.1	674.1	775.6

continued

continued from previous page

Year Ended May 31 (In millions)	2008	2007	2006
Deferred:			
United States			
Federal	(273.0)	38.7	(4.2)
State	(5.0)	(4.8)	(6.8)
Foreign	(22.6)	0.4	(15.0)
	(300.6)	34.3	(26.0)
	$619.5	$708.4	$749.6

   a.   Record Nike's provision for income taxes for 2008 using the FSET.

   b.   Record Nike's provision for income taxes for 2008 using journal entries.

   c.   Explain how the provision for income taxes affects Nike's financial statements.

E10-32. Recording Income Tax Expense

The Boeing Company reports the following tax information in Note 4 to its 2008 financial report.

Year ended December 31,	2008	2007	2006
Current tax expense			
U.S. federal	$ 44	$1,260	$193
Non-U.S.	29	139	35
U.S. state	20	164	(58)
	93	1,563	170
Deferred tax expense			
U.S. federal	1,151	487	750
Non-U.S.	26	(6)	(6)
U.S. state	71	16	74
	1,248	497	818
Total income tax expense	$1,341	$2,060	$988

   a.   Record Boeing's provision for income taxes for 2008 using the FSET.

   b.   Record Boeing's provision for income taxes for 2008 using journal entries.

   c.   Explain how the provision for income affects Boeing's financial statements.

   d.   In 2004 Boeing received a cash refund of $896 million from the IRS. What factor(s) might explain the refund?

PROBLEMS

P10-33. Capitalizing Operating Leases

The 2008 10-K report of OSI Restaurant Partners, LLC (**Outback Steakhouse, Inc.**), included the following footnote.

OPERATING LEASES The Company leases restaurant and office facilities and certain equipment under operating leases having initial terms expiring between 2009 and 2021. Certain of these leases require the payment of contingent rentals based on a percentage of gross revenues, as defined by the terms of the applicable lease agreement. Total rental expense for the year ended December 31, 2008, the period from January 1 to June 14, 2007, the period from June 15 to December 31, 2007, and the year ended December 31, 2006, was approximately $208,085,000, $54,806,000, $113,914,000 and $111,987,000, respectively, and included contingent rent of approximately $2,934,000, $3,761,000, $3,512,000 and $7,361,000, respectively. Future minimum rental payments on operating leases (including leases for restaurants scheduled to open in 2009) are as follows (in thousands):

2009	$ 175,367
2010	167,613
2011	156,382
2012	148,186
2013	139,902
Thereafter	831,160
Total minimum lease payments	$1,618,610

Required

a.   Prepare the journal entry to record Outback's rent expense under operating leases on December 31, 2008. Assume that this expense was paid in cash and none of this expense was prepaid or accrued in other years.

b.   Assume that Outback reclassified its operating leases as capital leases and that the appropriate discount rate is 8%. What amount would Outback report as a lease liability in its December 31, 2008, balance sheet?

c.   If these leases are treated as capital leases instead of operating leases, what would be the effect on Outback's 2008 income statement? Its 2009 income statement? The assets are depreciated on a straight-line basis over 10 years.

d.   Show the results of capitalization using the Financial Statement Effects Template.

e.   If these leases had been treated as capital leases instead of operating leases, what would be the effect on Outback's 2008 statement of cash flows?

LO3   P10-34.   Analyzing, Interpreting, and Capitalizing Leasing Disclosures

ABERCROMBIE &
FITCH
NYSE :: ANF

The **Abercrombie & Fitch Co.** 2008 10-K report contains the following footnote relating to its leasing activities. This is the only information it discloses relating to its leasing activity.

At January 31, 2009, the Company was committed to noncancelable leases with remaining terms of one to 20 years. A summary of operating lease commitments under noncancelable leases follows (thousands):

2009	$ 314,587
2010	318,845
2011	305,830
2012	287,772
2013	267,951
Thereafter	1,302,139

Required

a.   Describe in words, how the balance of its lease assets and lease liabilities are reported on Abercrombie's balance sheet.

b.   Assuming that all of A&F's leases are classified as operating, what general effect has this classification had on A&F's balance sheet? Over the life of the lease, what effect does this classification have on its net income? Explain in words. Calculations are not required.

c.   Using a 10% discount rate (the rate used by Moody's), estimate the assets and liabilities that A&F fails to report as a result of its off-balance-sheet lease financing. Assume the lease assets are depreciated by the straight-line method over 10 years.

d.   Using the financial statement effects template, show how capitalizing these operating leases would affect the balance sheet and income statement.

e.   Prepare journal entries to record the capitalization of these operating leases at the end of fiscal year 2008. What journal entries would be required to record lease payments and lease related expenses in fiscal year 2009 if these leases were accounted for as capital leases?

f.   Post the journal entries from part *e* to the appropriate T-accounts.

g.   What are the effects of capitalization on A&F's gross margin, turnover, leverage, fixed commitments, the D/E ratio, and ROE? Describe in words only.

P10-35. Analyzing, Interpreting, and Capitalizing Leasing Disclosures   **LO3**

The **Best Buy Co., Inc.**, 10-K report has the following footnote (8) related to its leasing activities. **BEST BUY** NYSE :: BBY
This is the only information it discloses relating to its leasing activity.

The future minimum lease payments under our capital, financing, and operating leases by fiscal year (not including contingent rentals) at February 28, 2009, were as follows ($ millions):

Fiscal Year	Capital Leases	Financing Leases	Operating Leases
2010	$28	$ 31	$1,097
2011	19	31	1,045
2012	8	31	964
2013	3	31	900
2014	2	29	846
Thereafter	24	107	3,748
Subtotal	84	260	$8,600
Less: imputed interest.	(19)	(60)	
Present value of lease obligations	$65	$200	

Required

a. What does Best Buy report on its balance sheet in regard to its leases?

b. What is the general effect that capitalization of Best Buy's operating leases would have on its balance sheet? Over the life of the lease, what effect does this classification have on its net income?

c. Using a 10% discount rate, estimate the assets and liabilities that it fails to report as a result of its off-balance-sheet lease financing.

d. Using the financial statement effects template, show how capitalizing these operating leases would affect the balance sheet and income statement. Assume straight-line depreciation over a 10-year life.

e. Prepare journal entries to record the capitalization of these operating leases at the end of fiscal year 2009. What journal entries would be required to record the operating lease and lease related expenses in fiscal year 2010 if these leases were accounted for as capital leases?

f. Post the journal entries from part *e* to the appropriate T-accounts.

g. What impact would capitalization of the company's operating leases have on analyzing Best Buy? What ratios might be affected?

P10-36. Accounting for Operating and Capital Leases   **LO2, LO3**

On January 1, 2010, Springer, Inc., entered into two lease contracts. The first lease contract was a six-year lease for computer equipment with $15,000 annual lease payments due at the end of each year. Springer took possession of the equipment on January 1, 2010. The second lease contract was a six-month lease, beginning January 1, 2010, for warehouse storage space with $1,000 monthly lease payments due the first of each month. Springer made the first month's payment on January 1, 2010. The present value of the lease payments under the first contract is $74,520. The present value of the lease payments under the second contract is $5,853.

Required

a. Assume that the first lease contract is a capital lease. Prepare the appropriate journal entry for this lease on January 1, 2010.

b. Assume the second lease contract is an operating lease. Prepare the proper journal entry for this lease on January 1, 2010.

P10-37. Analyzing and Interpreting Pension Disclosures   **LO4, LO5**

FedEx Corp.'s May 31, 2009, 10-K report has the following disclosures related to its retirement plans. **FEDEX** NYSE :: FDX

The following table provides a reconciliation of the changes in the pension and postretirement health-care plans' benefit obligations and fair value of assets over the two-year period ended May 31, 2009, and a statement of the funded status as of May 31, 2009 and 2008 (in millions):

(In millions)	Pension Plans [1]	
	2009	2008
Accumulated Benefit Obligation ("ABO")	$10,745	$11,212
Changes in Projected Benefit Obligation ("PBO")		
PBO at the beginning of year	$11,617	$12,209
Adjustments due to change in measurement date		
Service cost plus interest cost during gap period	309	—
Additional experience during gap period	(302)	—
Changes due to gap period cash flow	(83)	—
Service cost	499	518
Interest cost	798	720
Actuarial (gain) loss	(1,420)	(1,531)
Benefits paid	(351)	(318)
Amendments	(1)	1
Other	(16)	18
PBO at end of year	$11,050	$11,617
Change in Plan Assets		
Fair value of plan assets at beginning of year	$11,879	$11,506
Adjustments due to change in measurement date		
Additional experience during gap period	522	—
Changes due to gap period cash flow	(76)	—
Actual return on plan assets	(2,306)	141
Company contributions	1,146	548
Benefits paid	(351)	(318)
Other	(2)	2
Fair value of plan assets at end of year	$10,812	$11,879
Funded Status of the Plans	$ (238)	$ 262
Employer contributions after measurement date	—	15
Net amount recognized	$ (238)	$ 277

Net periodic benefit cost for the three years ended May 31 were as follows:

In millions	Pension Plans		
	2009	2008	2007
Service cost	$ 499	$518	$540
Interest cost	798	720	707
Expected return on plan assets	(1,059)	(985)	(930)
Recognized actuarial (gains) losses and other	(61)	70	150
Net periodic benefit cost	$ 177	$323	$467

Weighted-average actuarial assumptions for our primary U.S. pension plans, which represent substantially all of our PBO, are as follows:

In millions	Pension Plans		
	2009	2008	2007
Discount rate used to determine benefit obligation [1]	7.68%	6.96%	6.01%
Discount rate used to determine net periodic benefit cost	7.15	6.01	5.91
Rate of increase in future compensation levels used to determine benefit obligation	4.42	4.51	4.47
Rate of increase in future compensation levels used to determine net periodic benefit cost [2]	4.49	4.47	3.46
Expected long-term rate of return on assets	8.50	8.50	9.10

Required

a. How much pension expense (revenue) does FedEx report in its 2009 income statement?

b. FedEx reports a $1,059 million expected return on plan assets as an offset to 2009 pension expense. Approximately, how is this amount computed? What is the actual gain or loss realized on its 2009 plan assets? What is the purpose of using this estimated amount instead of the actual gain or loss?

c. What factors affected its 2009 pension liability? What factors affected its 2009 plan assets?

d. What does the term *funded status* mean? What is the funded status of the 2009 FedEx retirement plans? What amount of asset or liability does FedEx report on its 2009 balance sheet relating to its retirement plans?

e. FedEx increased its discount rate from 6.96% to 7.68% in 2009. What effect(s) does this have on its balance sheet and its income statement?

f. FedEx decreased its estimate of expected annual wage increases used to determine its defined benefit obligation in 2009. What effect(s) does this increase have on its financial statements? In general, how does such an increase affect income?

P10-38. Accounting for Pension Benefits **LO4**

Bartov Corporation has a defined contribution pension plan for its employees. Each year, Bartov contributes to the plan an amount equal to 4% of the employee payroll for the year. Bartov's 2010 payroll was $400,000. Bartov also provides a life insurance benefit that pays a $50,000 death benefit to the beneficiaries of retired employees. At the end of 2010, Bartov estimates that its liability under the life insurance program is $625,000. Bartov has assets with a fair value of $175,000 in a trust fund that are available to meet the death benefit payments.

Required

a. Prepare the journal entry at December 31, 2010, to record Bartov's 2010 defined contribution to a pension trustee who will manage the pension funds for the firm's employees.

b. What amount of liability for death benefit payments must Bartov report in its December 31, 2010, balance sheet? Explain.

P10-39. Interpreting the Income Tax Expense Footnote (Difficult) **LO6**

Ethan Allen Interiors Inc. reports the following tax information in Note 12 to its 2008 financial report.

ETHAN ALLEN INTERIORS INC.
NYSE :: ETH

In thousands	2008	2007	2006
Current:			
Federal.	$32,431	$34,768	$43,844
State	4,151	5,125	9,371
Foreign	(112)	406	—
Total current	36,470	40,299	53,215
Deferred:			
Federal.	(2,172)	190	(610)
State	(192)	10	(182)
Total deferred	(2,364)	200	(792)
Income tax expense	$34,106	$40,499	$52,423

Required

a. What amount of tax expense is reported in Ethan Allen's 2008 income statement?

b. How much of the 2008 income tax expense is payable in cash?

c. Assume that Ethan Allen's deferred tax expense of $200,000 in 2007 is due to a decrease in deferred tax liabilities. Provide an example that would be consistent with this situation.

d. Assume that Ethan Allen's deferred tax expense of $200,000 in 2007 is due to a decrease in a deferred tax asset. Explain how restructuring charges would create a deferred tax asset. What would cause this asset to decrease in value?

P10-40. Computing and Reporting Deferred Income Taxes **LO6**

Early in January 2009, Oler, Inc., purchased equipment costing $16,000. The equipment had a 2-year useful life and was depreciated in the amount of $8,000 in 2009 and 2010. Oler deducted the entire $16,000 on its tax return in 2009. This difference was the only one between its tax return and its financial statements. Oler's income before depreciation expense and income taxes was $236,000 in 2009 and $245,000 in 2010. The tax rate in each year was 40%.

Required

a. What amount of deferred tax liability should Oler report in 2009 and 2010?

b. Give the journal entries to record income taxes for 2009 and 2010.

c. Repeat requirement *b* if the tax rate in 2009 was only 35%.

LO6   **P10-41. Calculating and Reporting Income Tax Expense**

Lynch Company began operations in 2009. The company reported $24,000 of depreciation expense on its income statement in 2009 and $26,000 in 2010. On its tax returns, Lynch deducted $32,000 for depreciation in 2009 and $37,000 in 2010. The 2010 tax return shows a tax obligation (liability) of $19,200 based on a 40% tax rate.

Required

a. Determine the temporary difference between the book value of depreciable assets and the tax basis of these assets at the end of 2009 and 2010.

b. Calculate the deferred tax liability for each year.

c. Calculate the income tax expense for 2010.

d. Prepare a journal entry to record income tax expense and post the entry to the appropriate T-accounts for 2010.

LO6   **P10-42. Calculating and Reporting Income Tax Expense**

Carter Inc. began operations in 2009. The company reported $130,000 of depreciation expense on its 2009 income statement and $128,000 in 2010. Carter Inc. deducted $140,000 for depreciation on its tax return in 2009 and $122,000 in 2010. The company reports a tax obligation of $45,150 for 2010 based on a tax rate of 35%.

Required

a. Determine the temporary difference between the book value of depreciable assets and the tax basis of these assets at the end of 2009 and 2010.

b. Calculate the deferred tax liability at the end of each year.

c. Calculate the income tax expense for 2010.

d. Prepare a journal entry to record income tax for 2010 and post the entry to the appropriate T-accounts.

LO6   **P10-43. Calculating and Reporting Deferred Income Taxes**

Bens' Corporation paid $12,000 on December 31, 2009, for equipment with a three-year useful life. The equipment will be depreciated in the amount of $4,000 each year. Bens' took the entire $12,000 as an expense in its tax return in 2009. Assume this is the only timing difference between the firm's books and its tax return. Bens' tax rate is 40%.

Required

a. What amount of deferred tax liability should appear in Bens' 12/31/2009 balance sheet?

b. Where in the balance sheet should the deferred tax liability appear?

c. What amount of deferred tax liability should appear in Bens' 12/31/2010 balance sheet?

LO6   **P10-44. Computing and Reporting Deferred Income Taxes**

Robinson Inc. paid $12,000 on December 31, 2009, for equipment with a two-year useful life. The equipment was depreciated for book purposes at $6,000 in 2010 and 2011. Robinson deducted the entire amount on its 2009 tax return. Assume this was the firm's only depreciable asset and that the firm's tax rate was 35% for 2009 and 2010 and 40% for 2011. Assume, further, that Robinson's income before depreciation and taxes was $320,000 in 2009, $400,000 in 2010, and $420,000 in 2011.

Required

a. Calculate the book value of the asset on 12/31 for 2009, 2010, and 2011.

b. Calculate the tax basis of the asset on 12/31 for 2009, 2010, and 2011.

c. What deferred tax liability should be reported for 2009, 2010, and 2011?

d. Prepare journal entries to record income taxes for 2009, 2010, and 2011.

LO3   **P10-45. Analyzing, Interpreting, and Capitalizing Leasing Disclosures**

FedEx Corp. reports total assets of $24,244 and total liabilities of $10,618 and operating cash flow of $2,753 for 2009 ($ millions). Its 2009 10-K report has the following footnote related to its leasing activities.

Contingent rentals are based on equipment usage.

A summary of future minimum lease payments under capital leases and noncancelable operating leases with an initial or remaining term in excess of one year at May 31, 2009, is as follows (in millions):

		Operating Leases		
In millions	**Capital Leases**	**Aircraft and Related Equipment**	**Facilities and Other**	**Total Operating Leases**
2010	$164	$ 512	$1,247	$ 1,759
2011	20	526	1,086	1,612
2012	8	504	947	1,451
2013	119	499	817	1,316
2014	2	472	694	1,166
Thereafter	15	2,458	4,894	7,352
Total	328	$4,971	$9,685	$14,656
Less amount representing interest	34			
Present value of net minimum lease payments	$294			

Required

a. What is the balance of its lease liabilities as reported on its balance sheet? Explain.

b. Show calculations to indicate that the discount rate implicit to the capital leases slightly exceeds 3%. (See American Airlines Business Insight box in the chapter for a description of the mechanics).

c. Using a 4% discount rate, estimate the amount of assets and liabilities that FedEx fails to report as a result of its off-balance-sheet lease financing.

d. Which financial ratios would be affected, and in what direction (increased or decreased), by including its off-balance-sheet lease financing?

e. Based on your analysis, do you believe that FedEx's balance sheet adequately reports its aircraft and facilities assets and related obligations? Explain.

f. FedEx has facilities in Paris, France. How does lease reporting in France differ from that in the United States?

CASES AND PROJECTS

C10-46. Analyzing and Interpreting Pension Disclosures

LO4, LO5

DOW CHEMICAL
NYSE :: DOW

The Dow Chemical Company provides the following footnote disclosures in its 10-K report relating to its pension plans.

	Defined Benefit Pension Plans	
(In millions)	**2008**	**2007**
Service cost	$ 264	$ 289
Interest cost	961	881
Expected return on plan assets	(1,232)	(1,179)
Amortization of prior service cost	32	23
Amortization of unrecognized loss (gain)	43	191
Termination/curtailment cost	54	11
Net periodic cost	$ 122	$ 216

continued

continued from previous page

(In millions)	Defined Benefit Pension Plans	
	2008	2007
Change in projected benefit obligation		
Benefit obligation at beginning of year	$15,604	$15,850
Service cost	264	289
Interest cost	961	881
Plan participants' contributions	21	23
Amendments	15	143
Actuarial changes in assumptions and experience	72	(1,354)
Acquisition/divestiture/other activity	(8)	140
Benefits paid	(980)	(918)
Currency impact	(420)	553
Termination/curtailment cost (credit)	44	(3)
Benefit obligation at end of year	$15,573	$15,604
Change in plan assets		
Fair value of plan assets at beginning of year	$16,130	$14,958
Actual return on plan assets	(3,442)	1,424
Currency impact	(341)	437
Employer contributions	185	183
Plan participants' contributions	21	19
Acquisition/divestiture/other activity	—	27
Benefits paid	(980)	(918)
Fair value of plan assets at end of year	$11,573	$16,130

Weighted Average Assumptions for All Pension Plans	Benefit Obligations at December 31	
	2008	2007
Discount rate	6.35%	6.30%
Rate of increase in future compensation levels	4.14%	4.13%
Expected long-term rate of return on plan assets	—	—

Required

a. How much pension expense (revenue) does Dow Chemical report in its 2008 income statement?

b. Dow reports a $1,232 million expected return on plan assets as an offset to 2008 pension expense. Estimate the rate of return Dow expects to earn on its 2008 plan assets.

c. What factors affected its 2008 pension liability? What factors affected its 2008 plan assets?

d. What does the term *funded status* mean? What is the funded status of the 2008 Dow retirement plans? What amount of asset or liability should Dow report on its 2008 balance sheet relating to its retirement plans?

e. Dow increased its discount rate from 6.30% to 6.35% in 2008. What effect(s) does this increase have on its balance sheet and its income statement?

f. Suppose Dow increased its estimate of expected returns on plan assets in 2009. What effect(s) would this increase have on its income statement? Explain.

g. Dow provides us with its weighted-average discount rate. The company operates with manufacturing facilities in over 150 sites in 35 countries. Would you expect that the discount rate differed in the United States from the average rate outside the United States? Explain. What would you expect for future compensation levels?

C10-47. Interpreting Capital and Operating Leases

Delta Air Lines, Inc. reports the following leasing information in its 2008 10-K.

Note 7. Lease Obligations

We lease aircraft, airport terminals, and maintenance facilities, ticket offices and other property and equipment from third parties. Rental expense for operating leases, which is recorded on a straight-line basis over the life of the lease term, totaled $850 million for the year ended December 31, 2008, $470 million for the eight months ended December 31, 2007, $261 million for the four months ended April 30, 2007, and $961 million for the year ended December 31, 2006. Amounts due under capital leases are recorded as liabilities on our Consolidated Balance Sheets. Our interest in assets acquired under capital leases is recorded as property and equipment on our Consolidated Balance Sheets. Amortization of assets recorded under capital leases is included in depreciation and amortization expense on our Consolidated Statements of Operations. Our leases do not include residual value guarantees.

The following tables summarize, as of December 31, 2008, our minimum rental commitments under capital leases and noncancelable operating leases (including certain aircraft under contract carrier agreements) with initial or remaining terms in excess of one year:

Capital Leases

Years Ending December 31, (in millions)	Not Subject to Compromise
2009	$135
2010	134
2011	129
2012	98
2013	64
After 2013	264
Total minimum lease payments	824
Less: amount of lease payments representing interest	(323)
Present value of future minimum capital lease payments	501
Plus: unamortized premium, net	64
Less: current obligations under capital leases	(92)
Long-term capital lease obligations	$473

Operating Leases

Years Ending December 31, (in millions)	Delta Lease Payments	Contract Carrier Aircraft Lease Payments	Total
2009	$1,104	$ 542	$ 1,646
2010	1,040	519	1,559
2011	822	504	1,326
2012	703	501	1,204
2013	592	467	1,059
After 2013	3,641	2,023	5,664
	7,902	4,556	12,458
Less: sublease rental income	(29)	—	(29)
Total minimum lease payments	$7,873	$4,556	$12,429

At December 31, 2008, we operated 258 aircraft under operating leases and 81 aircraft under capital leases. Our contract carriers operated 443 aircraft under operating leases. Leases for aircraft operated by us and our contract carriers have expiration dates ranging from 2009 to 2025. During the four months ended April 30, 2007, and the year ended December 31, 2006, we recorded estimated claims relating to the restructuring of the financing arrangements for many of our aircraft and the rejection of certain of our leases in connection with our bankruptcy proceedings.

Note 8. Purchase Commitments and Contingencies

Aircraft Order Commitments

Future commitments for aircraft on firm order as of December 31, 2008, are estimated to be $2.9 billion. The following table shows the timing of these commitments:

Years Ending December 31, (in millions)	
2009	$1,520
2010	990
2011	60
2012	110
2013	90
After 2013	130
Total	$2,900

Our aircraft order commitments as of December 31, 2008, consist of firm orders to purchase eight B-777-200LR aircraft, five B-737-700 aircraft, 33 B-737-800 aircraft, two A320-200 aircraft, five A3110-100 aircraft and 10 CRJ-900 aircraft. We have excluded from the table above our order for 18 B-787-8 aircraft. The Boeing Company ("Boeing") has informed us that Boeing will be unable to meet the contractual delivery schedule for these aircraft. We are in discussions with Boeing regarding this situation.

Our firm orders to purchase 33 B-737-800 aircraft include 31 B-737-800 aircraft, which we have entered into definitive agreements to sell to two third parties immediately following delivery of these aircraft to us by the manufacturer. We have not received any notice that these parties have defaulted on their purchase obligations. These sales will reduce our future commitments by approximately $1.3 billion during the period from 2009 through 2011 ($490 million, $730 million, and $40 million for 2009, 2010, and 2011, respectively).

We have financing commitments from third parties, cancellation rights or, with respect to the 31 B-737-800 aircraft referred to above, definitive agreements to sell, all Mainline and CRJ-900 aircraft on firm order as of December 31, 2008. Under these financing commitments, third parties have agreed to finance, on a long-term secured basis, a substantial portion of the purchase price of the covered aircraft,

Our firm orders to purchase 10 CRJ-900 aircraft include two CRJ-900 aircraft, which we have assigned to a Contract Carrier. We are required to cure any default by the Contract Carrier of its purchase obligation, and have certain indemnification rights against the Contract Carrier for costs incurred in effecting such a cure.

Required

a. In footnote 8, Delta indicates firm purchase commitments for $1,520 million for new aircraft in 2009. Will this commitment appear on the firm's balance sheet? Why or why not? What entry, if any will be made by Delta when the aircraft are received? What accounts would be affected and would they be increased or decreased?

b. What entry will Delta make at the end of the 2008 fiscal year to recognize rent expense on its operating leases?

c. At the beginning of Delta's 2009 fiscal year, what amount, if any, would the company show as a liability for leases in its current liabilities?

d. What expense would Delta recognize at the end of the year related to its operating leases? What entry would the lessor make?

e. Using a rate of 10%, as Moody's does, estimate the asset and liability that Delta would have if it capitalized its operating leases. Delta reports $44.140 billion in total liabilities. Is the firm's liability level affected substantially if the operating leases are capitalized?

C10-48. Interpreting Income Tax Footnotes

The following information is taken from Footnote D from **Williams-Sonoma, Inc.**'s February 1, 2009, 10-K.

Significant components of our deferred tax accounts are as follows:

Dollars in thousands	February 1, 2009 (52 Weeks)	February 3, 2008 (53 Weeks)
Deferred tax asset (liability)		
Current:		
Compensation	$ 12,436	$ 11,392
Inventory	19,538	22,117
Accrued liabilities	11,868	17,585
Customer deposits	58,197	61,215
Deferred catalog costs	(14,589)	(21,184)
Other	2,899	718
Total current	90,349	91,843
Non-current:		
Depreciation	13,392	14,616
Deferred rent	15,672	12,390
Stock-based compensation	20,828	17,757
Deferred lease incentives	(27,548)	(23,046)
Executive deferral plan	4,527	6,214
State taxes	8,260	15,985
Other	1,424	1,081
Total non-current	36,555	44,997
Total deferred tax assets, net	$126,904	$136,840

Required

a. For the year ended February 1, 2009, Williams-Sonoma reported a current tax obligation (based on its tax return) of $6,822 thousand. What amount of income tax expense did it report in its income statement?

b. Prepare a journal entry to record income tax expense for the year ended February 1, 2009.

c. The company reported a net book value of property, plant and equipment of $942,219 thousand on February 1, 2009. Given a tax rate of 35%, what was the tax basis of these assets?

d. The company reported prepaid catalog expense of $36,424 thousand as a current asset in its February 1, 2009, balance sheet. The company provided the following explanation of this asset in footnote A to its 10-K:

Prepaid Catalog Expenses
Prepaid catalog expenses consist primarily of third-party incremental direct costs, including creative design, paper, printing, postage and mailing costs for all of our direct response catalogs. Such costs are capitalized as prepaid catalog expenses and are amortized over their expected period of future benefit. . . . Each catalog is generally fully amortized over a six to nine month period, with the majority of the amortization occurring within the first four to five months.

Explain how this expense results in a temporary difference between tax and financial reporting. Did the item create a current or long-term deferred tax asset or a liability and in what amount?

SOLUTIONS TO REVIEW PROBLEMS

Mid-Chapter Review 1

Solution to Part A

1.   The present value of the lease payments is $224,755, computed as $32,000 × 7.02358.

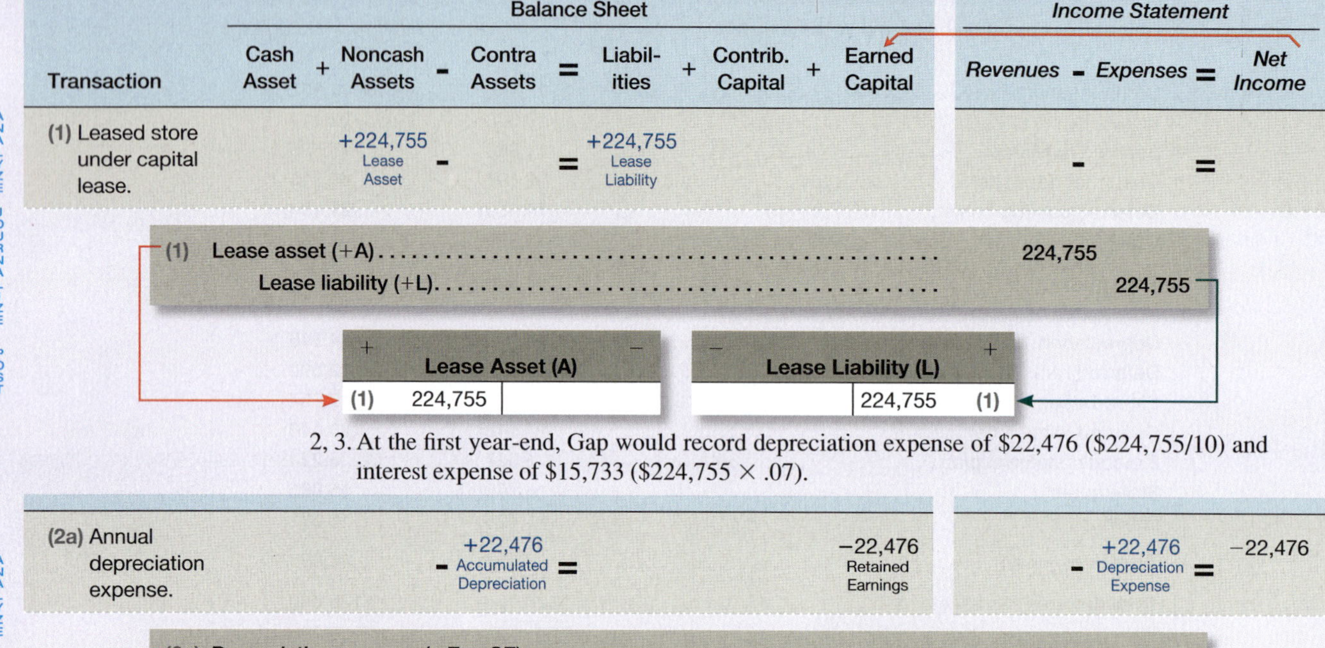

2, 3. At the first year-end, Gap would record depreciation expense of $22,476 ($224,755/10) and interest expense of $15,733 ($224,755 × .07).

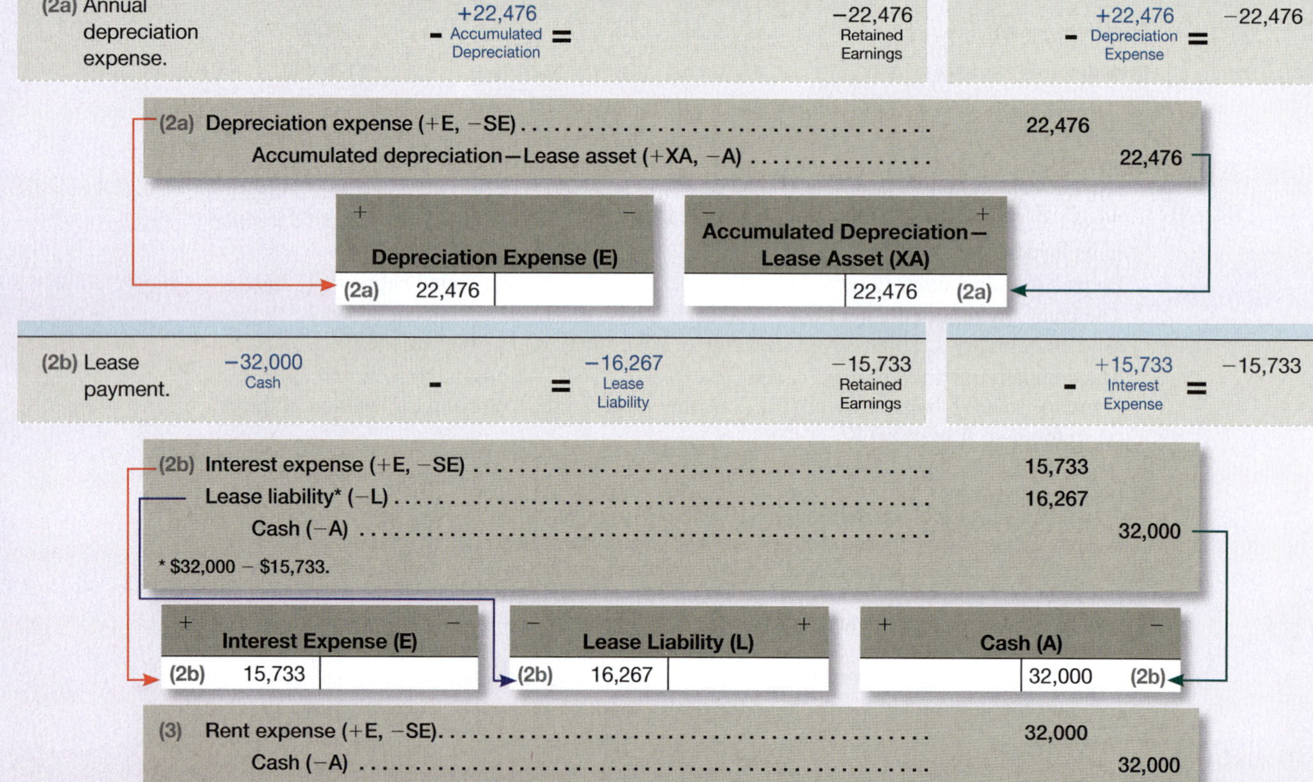

No journal entry is required at lease signing. At the end of the first year, Gap would record the lease payment as rent expense.

Solution to Part B

1.   Gap's leases are classified as operating leases—see footnote. Also, since there are no disclosures in the leasing footnote related to capital leases, we know that all of the leases are classified as operating.

2.   Using a 7% discount rate, the present value of its operating leases follows ($ millions):

Year	Operating Lease Payment	Present Value ($i = 0.07$)
1.................	$1,069	$ 999
2.................	927	810
3.................	712	581
4.................	520	397
5.................	386	275
>5.................	1,080	678
		$3,740
Average life	$1,080/$386 = 2.7979 years	

Gap's operating leases represent $3,740 million of unreported operating assets and unreported non-operating liabilities. These amounts should be added to the balance sheet for analysis purposes.

3. Potential income statement adjustments would include elimination of the rent expense currently reported in Gap's SG&A expenses and replacing it with the depreciation of the capitalized lease asset and the interest on the capitalized lease liability. Whereas rent expense is considered as an operating expense, only the depreciation expense is similarly classified. The interest is, of course, a nonoperating expense. NOPAT, as a result, is increased following the financial statement adjustment for operating lease capitalization.

Mid-Chaper Review 2

Solution

1. A pension benefit obligation increases primarily by service cost, interest cost, and actuarial losses. The latter are increases in the pension liability as a result of changes in actuarial assumptions. It is decreased by the payment of benefits to retirees and by actuarial gains.

2. Pension investments increase through positive investment returns for the period and by cash contributions made by the company. Investments decrease by payments made to retirees and investment losses.

3. Continental Airlines' funded status is $(1,425) million ($2,482 million PBO − $1,057 million pension assets) as of 2008. The negative amount indicates that the plan is underfunded. Therefore, this amount is reported as a liability on the company's balance sheet.

4. Expected return on plan assets acts as an offset to service cost and interest cost in computing the net pension cost. As the expected return increases (decreases), net pension cost decreases (increases).

5. Continental Airlines' expected return of $157 million exceeded its actual return of $(618) million in 2008.

6. Continental Airlines reports net pension expense of $147 million in 2008.

7. Continental's funded status is negative, indicating an underfunded plan. The company contributed $105 million to the pension plan in 2008, a decline from $338 contributed in 2007. It is likely that the company will need to increase its future funding levels to cover the plan's requirements. This action is likely to have negative consequences for its ability to fund other operating needs, and could damage its competitive position in the future.

Chapter-End Review

Solution

1. a. $2,390.
   b. $1,488 = $1,342 + $146 is currently payable or has already been paid in 2010
   c. The most obvious example would be depreciation allowed in 2010 by the tax code exceeded that calculated by the straight-line method.

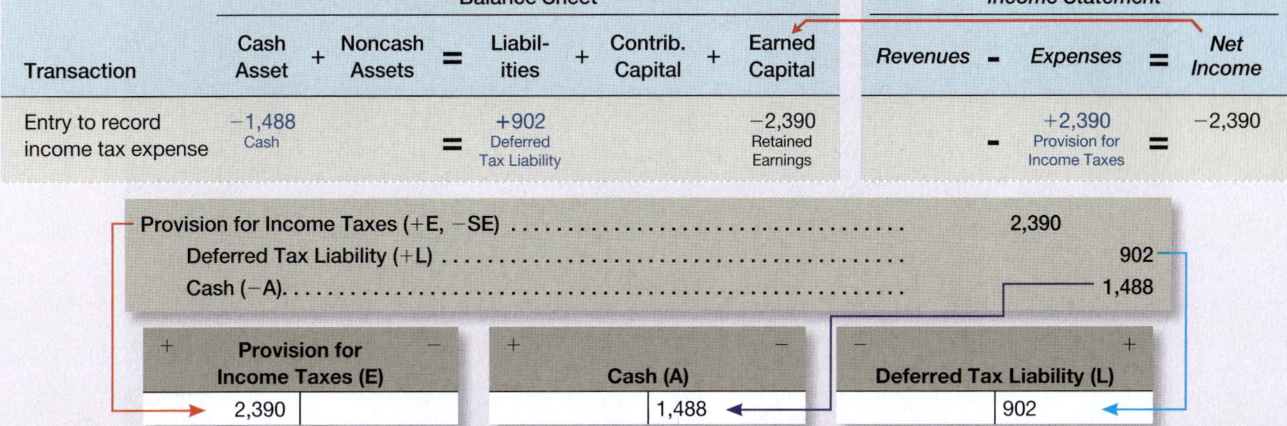

1. Describe business financing through stock issuances. (p. 490)

2. Explain and account for the issuance and repurchase of stock. (p. 494)

3. Describe how operations increase the equity of a business. (p. 498)

4. Explain and account for dividends and stock splits. (p. 498)

5. Define and illustrate comprehensive income. (p. 503)

6. Describe and illustrate the basic and diluted earnings per share computations. (p. 505)

7. Appendix 11A: Analyze the accounting for convertible securities, stock rights, and stock options. (p. 508)

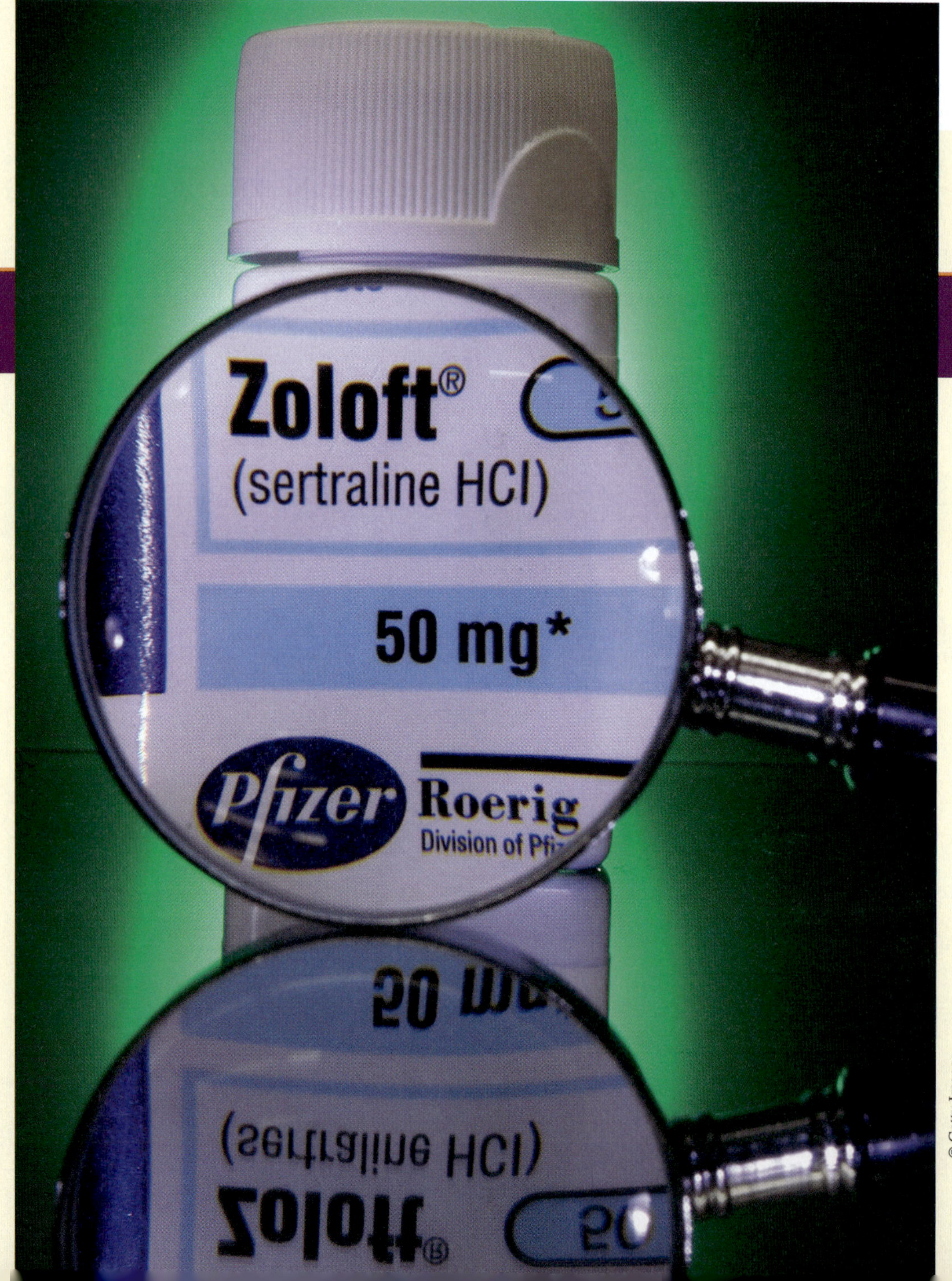

© Getty Images

Reporting and Analyzing Stockholders' Equity

Pfizer Inc. is a research-based, global pharmaceutical company that discovers, develops, manufactures, and markets leading prescription medicines for humans and animals.

PFIZER
www.pfizer.com

Pfizer's business is divided into two segments, pharmaceutical and animal health. Pfizer's 2008 revenues exceeded $48 billion with the pharmaceutical division contributing 92% of the firm's revenues. Although Lipitor led the division with 28% of pharmaceutical sales, Viagra, Lyrica, and Celebrex also contributed substantially to Pfizer's bottom line.

Unfortunately, many of Pfizer's pharmaceutical patents are due to expire in the near future. Lipitor's patent expires in 2010. Of immediate concern is the loss of patent protection for Viagra in 2012 and Celebrex in 2014. Pfizer's primary business activities include discovering and marketing new, patentable drugs. To discover new drugs, Pfizer spends sizeable amounts each year on research and development: $8 billion in each of the last two years. Furthermore, Pfizer faces increased competition from its major rivals, **Merck & Co., Inc.**, **Abbott Laboratories**, and **GlaxoSmithKline PLC**.

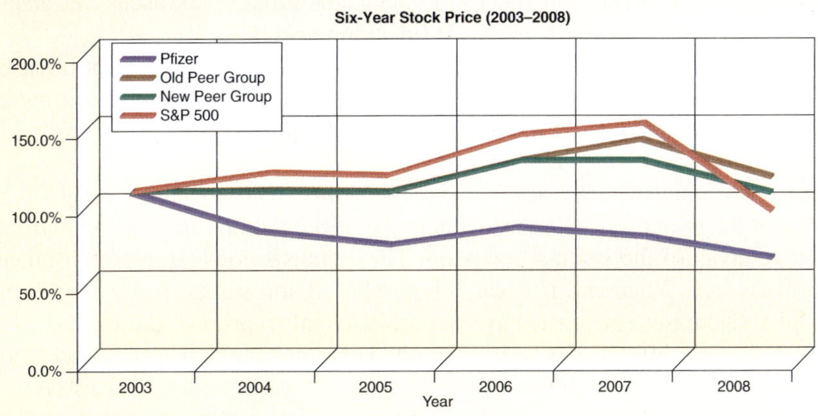

One critical component of Pfizer's recent strategy has been to increase its size in order to spread its high overhead costs across a broader sales base. In 2000, Pfizer merged with **Warner-Lambert Company**, and in 2003 it acquired **Pharmacia**. The merger with Warner-Lambert and acquisition of Pharmacia made Pfizer the largest pharmaceutical company in the world. Since 2003, Pfizer has con- *(continued on next page)*

(continued from previous page)

tinued to acquire other companies, including **Esperion Therapeutics, Inc.** (2004), **Vicuron Pharmaceuticals, Inc.** (2005), **BioRexis Pharmaceuticals Corporation** (2007), and **Coley Pharmaceutical Group** (2008). In its most recent deal, **Pfizer** acquired **Wyeth** for $68 billion to obtain new pharmaceuticals to offset Lipitor's patent expiration in 2010. This acquisition is also designed to improve the company's research capability in biologics—research on large molecules that are difficult and expensive to create—critical in the face of increasing competition from generic alternatives.

The capital needed to support Pfizer's acquisition strategy and its heavy commitment to research and development exceeds the funds generated directly from operating activities. The acquisition of Wyeth, for example, required Pfizer to borrow $22.5 billion. The company also raises additional capital, in part, from equity investors through the issuance of stock. Many companies also engage in equity transactions for other reasons, including stock option plans and stock repurchase programs. This chapter describes the reporting and analysis of equity transactions, including sales and repurchases of stock, dividends, comprehensive income, and convertible securities.

Sources: *The Wall Street Journal* (January 27, 2009; May 21, 2009), *New York Times* (January 27, 2009), *Business Week* (April and June, 2009), *Fortune* (August, 2009), and Pfizer 2005, 2006, 2007 and 2008 10-K Reports.

CHAPTER ORGANIZATION

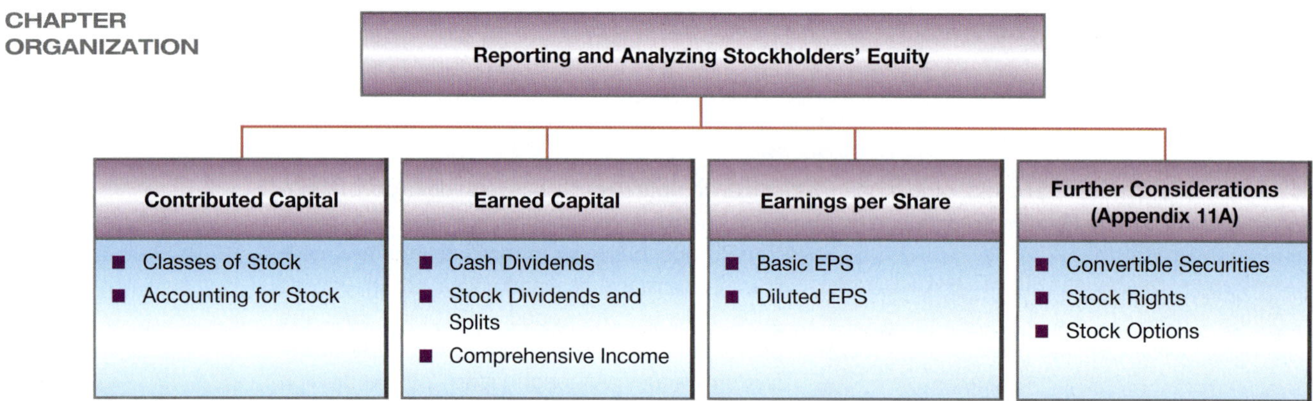

INTRODUCTION

LO1 Describe business financing through stock issuances.

A company finances its assets (other than through operating cash flows) from one of two sources: either it borrows funds from creditors or it obtains funds from shareholders. On average, companies obtain about half of their external financing from borrowed sources and the other half from shareholder investment. This chapter describes the issues relating to stockholders' equity, including the accounting for stock transactions (sales and repurchases of stock, and dividends), the accounting for stock options, and the computation of earnings per share. Finally, we discuss the accounting for convertible securities, an increasingly prevalent financing vehicle.

When a company issues stock to the investing public, it records the receipt of cash (or other assets) and an increase in contributed capital, a part of stockholders' equity, representing investment in the company by shareholders. The increase in cash and equity is equal to the issue of the stock on the issue date multiplied by the number of shares sold.

Like bonds, contributed capital is accounted for at *historical cost*. Consequently, fluctuations in the market price of the issuer's stock subsequent to the initial public offering do not directly affect the financial statements of the issuing company. These transactions are between outside parties not involving the issuer. When and if stock is repurchased and subsequently resold, the issuer's contributed capital decreases (increases) by the purchase (sales) price of the shares.

There is an important difference between accounting for stockholders' equity and accounting for transactions involving assets and liabilities: *there is never any gain or loss reported on the purchase and sale of stock or the payment of dividends*. Instead, these "gains and losses" are reflected as increases and decreases in the contributed capital component of the issuing company's stockholders' equity.

This chapter focuses on the two broad categories of shareholder investment: contributed capital and earned capital. Exhibit 11.1 provides an illustration of this breakdown using **Pfizer**'s stockholders' equity as of December 31, 2008.

EXHIBIT 11.1	Stockholders' Equity from Pfizer's Balance Sheet	
	Shareholders' Equity (millions, except preferred shares issued)	**Dec. 31, 2008**
Contributed capital	Preferred stock, without par value, at stated value; 27 shares authorized; 1,804 issued in 2008	$ 73
	Common stock, $.05 par value; 12,000 shares authorized; issued: 2008—8,863	443
	Additional paid-in capital	70,283
	Employee benefit trust	(425)
	Treasury stock, shares at cost; issued: 2008—2,117	(57,391)
Earned capital	Retained earnings	49,142
	Accumulated other comprehensive income (expense)	(4,569)
	Total shareholders' equity	$57,556

Pfizer, like other companies, has two broad categories of stockholders' equity:

1. **Contributed capital**   This section reports the proceeds received by the issuing company from original stock issuances. Contributed capital often includes common stock, preferred stock, and additional paid-in capital. Netted against these capital accounts is treasury stock, the amounts paid to repurchase shares of the issuer's stock from its investors less the proceeds from the resale of such shares. Collectively, these accounts are generically referred to as contributed capital (or *paid-in capital*).

2. **Earned capital**   This section consists of (a) retained earnings, which represent the cumulative income and losses of the company less any dividends to shareholders, and (b) accumulated other comprehensive income (AOCI), which includes changes to equity that are not included in income and are, therefore, not reflected in retained earnings. For Pfizer, AOCI includes foreign currency translation adjustments, changes in market values of derivatives, unrecognized gains and losses on available-for-sale securities, and pension adjustments.

We discuss each of these two categories in turn. For each section, a graphic is provided that displays the part of stockholders' equity in the balance sheet impacted by the discussion of that section.

CONTRIBUTED CAPITAL

We begin our discussion with contributed capital. Contributed capital represents the cumulative cash inflow that the company has received from the sale of various classes of stock, less the net cash that it has paid out to repurchase its stock from the market.

Pfizer's contributed capital consists of preferred and common stock, additional paid-in capital, less costs of treasury stock (repurchased shares) and the reduction of stockholders' equity arising from its employee benefit trust.[1]

Classes of Stock

There are two general classes of stock: preferred and common. The difference between the two lies in the respective legal rights conferred upon each class.

Common Stock   Shares of **common stock** represent the primary ownership unit in a corporation. Common stockholders have voting rights which allow them to participate in the governance of the corporation. The total number of common shares is usually presented on the face of the balance sheet. There are three numbers of shares to be aware of:

■ The number of **shares authorized** represents the upper limit on the number of shares that the corporation can issue. This number is established in the *articles of incorporation* and can only be increased by an affirmative shareholder vote.

---

[1] Its employee benefit trust (also called *employee stock ownership plan*, or *ESOP*) purchases company stock for the benefit of its employees with borrowed funds. Common stock increases from those purchases of shares; but until the debt is paid, the company reports an offset (reduction) in stockholders' equity equal to the unpaid debt. This item explains the negative amount reported in its employee benefit trust account. As of December 31, 2008, Pfizer reports an unpaid balance of $425 million.

- The number of **shares issued** is the actual number of shares that have been sold to stockholders by the corporation.
- The number of **shares outstanding** is the number of issued shares less the number of shares repurchased as treasury stock.

Pfizer's common stock is described as follows in its 2008 balance sheet (shares in millions):

> Common stock, $.05 par value; 12,000 shares authorized; issued: 2008—8,863

The Pfizer common stock has the following important characteristics:

- Pfizer common stock has a par value of $0.05 per share. The **par value** is an arbitrary amount set by company organizers at the time of formation. Generally, par value has no substance from a financial reporting or statement analysis perspective (there are some legal implications, which are usually minor). Its main impact is in specifying the allocation of proceeds from stock issuances between the two contributed capital accounts on the balance sheet: common stock and additional paid-in capital.
- Pfizer has authorized the issuance of 12,000 million shares. As of December 31, 2008, 8,863 million shares are issued yielding a value of $443.15 million = $0.05 \times 8,863$. When shares are first issued, the number of shares outstanding equals those issued. Any shares subsequently repurchased as treasury stock are subtracted from issued shares to derive outstanding shares.

Preferred Stock **Preferred stock** generally has some preference, or priority, with respect to common stock. Two typical preferences are:

1. **Dividend preference** Preferred shareholders receive dividends on their shares before common shareholders do. If dividends are not paid in a given year, those dividends are normally forgone. However, some preferred stock contracts include a *cumulative provision* stipulating that any forgone dividends must first be paid to preferred shareholders, together with the current year's dividends, before any dividends are paid to common shareholders.

2. **Liquidation preference** If a company fails, its assets are sold (liquidated) and the proceeds are paid to the creditors and shareholders, in that order. Shareholders, therefore, have a greater risk of loss than do creditors. Among shareholders, the preferred shareholders receive payment in full before any proceeds are paid to common shareholders. This liquidation preference makes preferred shares less risky than common shares. Any liquidation payment to preferred shares is normally at its par value, although it is sometimes specified in excess of par, called a *liquidating value*.

The preferred stock of Pfizer is described in Note 14 to its 2008 10-K:

> The Series A convertible perpetual preferred stock is held by an Employee Stock Ownership Plan ("Preferred ESOP") Trust and provides dividends at the rate of 6.25%, which are accumulated and paid quarterly. The per-share stated value is $40,300 and the preferred stock ranks senior to our common stock as to dividends and liquidation rights. Each share is convertible, at the holder's option, into 2,574.87 shares of our common stock with equal voting rights. The conversion option is indexed to our common stock and requires share settlement, and therefore, is reported at the fair value at the date of issuance. We may redeem the preferred stock at any time or upon termination of the Preferred ESOP, at our option, in cash, in shares of common stock or a combination of both at a price of $40,300 per share.

Following are several important features of the Pfizer preferred stock:

- There are 27 million preferred shares authorized, of which 1,804 shares are issued as of December 31, 2008. The articles of incorporation set the number of shares authorized for issuance. Once that limit is reached, shareholders must approve any increase in authorized shares.

- Pfizer preferred stock is convertible into common stock at the option of the holder and at a predetermined exchange rate. A preferred share is convertible, at the holder's option, into 2,574.87 common shares.

- Pfizer preferred stock pays a dividend of 6.25% of its par (stated) value of $40,300. This feature means that each preferred share is entitled to annual dividends of $2,518.75 ($40,300 × 6.25%), payable quarterly.

- Pfizer preferred stock is *cumulative*. This feature provides preferred shareholders with protection that unpaid dividends (called *dividends in arrears*) must be paid to them before any dividends are paid to common shareholders.

- Pfizer preferred stock has a preference with respect to dividends and liquidation; meaning that preferred shareholders are paid before common shareholders.

- Pfizer can redeem (repurchase) its preferred stock at any time in cash, common stock, or both.

Pfizer's cumulative preferred shares carry a dividend yield of 6.25%. This dividend yield compares favorably with the $0.32 per share (1.8% yield on an $18 share price) paid to its common shareholders. Generally, preferred stock can be an attractive investment for shareholders seeking higher dividend yields, especially when tax laws wholly or partially exempt such dividends from taxation.

There are three additional features sometimes seen in preferred stock agreements:

1. **Call feature**   The call feature provides the issuer with the right, but not the obligation, to repurchase the preferred shares at a specified price. This price can vary according to a specified time. A decline in the market rate of interest is one event that can lead to the firm exercising the call provision. While of value to the issuer of the preferred stock, the call provision makes the issue less attractive to potential investors. The result is a lower offering price per share.

2. **Conversion feature**   The yield on preferred stock, especially when coupled with a cumulative feature, is similar to the interest rate on a bond or note. Further limited protection is offered because preferred shareholders receive the par value at liquidation like debtholders receive face value. The fixed yield and liquidation value for the preferred stock limit the upside potential return of preferred shareholders. This constraint can be overcome by inclusion of a *conversion feature* that allows preferred stockholders to convert their shares into common shares at their option at a predetermined conversion ratio. Some preferred contracts give the company an option to force conversion.

   The conversion feature causes the shares to be more attractive to potential investors because the preferred stockholders now have the opportunity to share in the fruits of a successful company with the common stockholders. Indeed, the market price of the preferred tends to reflect the value of the conversion feature.

3. **Participation feature**   Preferred shares sometimes carry a *participation feature* that allows preferred shareholders to share ratably with common stockholders in dividends. The dividend preference over common shares can be a benefit when dividend payments are meager, but a fixed dividend yield limits upside potential if the company performs exceptionally well. This limitation can be overcome with a participation feature.

IFRS REPORTING INSIGHT

Under IFRS, convertible securities are termed compound financial instruments because the conversion feature has a value even if it is not legally detachable for sale. IFRS (but not GAAP) splits the convertible bonds' value into the separate debt and equity values for reporting purposes.

Accounting for Stock Transactions

We cover the accounting for stock transactions in this section, including the accounting for stock issuances and for stock repurchases.

Stock Issuance   Stock issuances, whether common or preferred, yield an increase in both assets and stockholders' equity. Companies use stock issuances to obtain cash and other assets for use in their business.

Stock issuances increase assets (cash) by the number of shares sold multiplied by the issuance price of the stock on the issue date. Equity increases by the same amount, which is reflected in contributed capital accounts. Specifically, assuming the issuance of common stock, the common stock account increases by the number of shares sold multiplied by its par value and the additional paid-in capital account is increased for the remainder of the purchase price.[2]

BUSINESS INSIGHT

Google's Common Stock   Google has a rather unusual common stock situation. The firm has outstanding two classes of common stock: series A Common and a series B Common. Usually, voting rights, for example, on the membership of the company's board of directors, are restricted to the common stock. Where multiple series of common exist, voting is restricted typically to only one class. In Google's case, both series have the same rights except in voting (e.g., for the board of directors) where each share of the B Common has 10 votes per share while each A Common share has only one vote. Further, the class B stock is convertible into A shares, but not vice versa, and B shares convert automatically to Class A common stock upon sale or transfer. We suspect this feature exists to retain voting control in a limited and select group.

To illustrate, assume that Pfizer issues 10,000 shares at a market price of $43 cash per share. The financial statement effects and entries for this stock issuance follow.

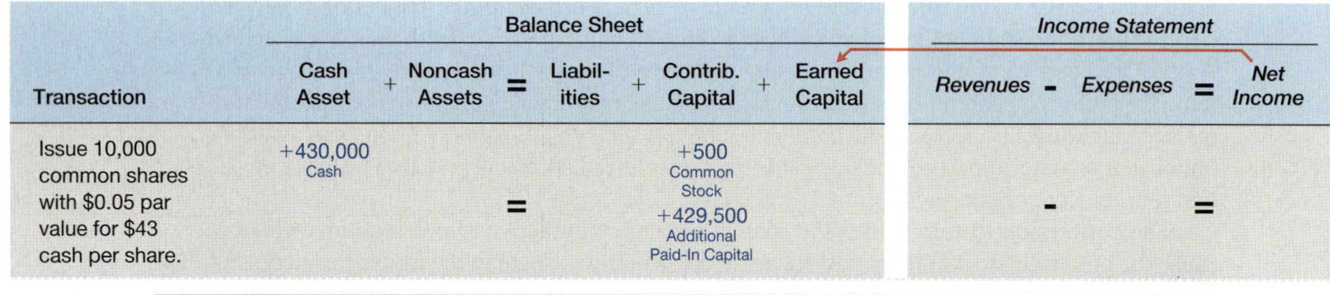

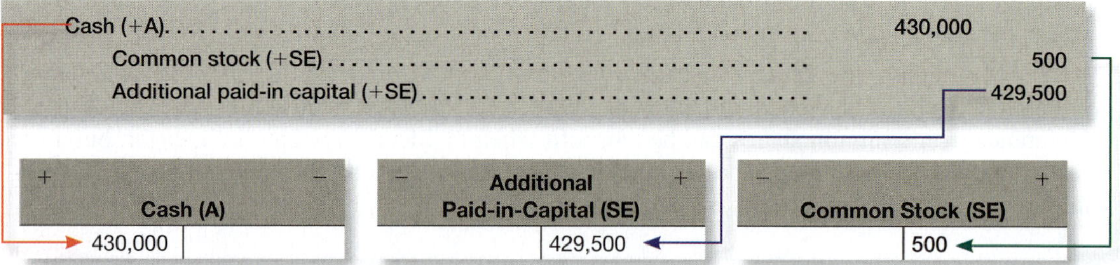

Specifically, the following financial statement effects of the stock issuance are:

1. Cash increases by $430,000 (10,000 shares × $43 per share).

---

[2] The first public sale of common stock by a corporation is called an initial public offering, or IPO for short. After the IPO, any public offering of stock for sale is called a seasoned equity offering.

2. Common stock increases by the $500 par value of shares sold (10,000 shares $\times$ $0.05 par value).[3]

3. Additional paid-in capital increases by the $429,500 difference between the issue price and par value ($430,000 − $500).

Once shares are issued, they are freely traded in the market among investors. The proceeds of those sales and their associated gains and losses on sales do not affect the issuing company and are not recorded in its accounting records. Further, fluctuations in the issuing company's stock price subsequent to issuance do not directly affect its financial statements. Hence, the equity section of the balance sheet cannot be used to obtain the current market value of the company. The market value is given by the product of the number of common shares outstanding times the per-share price of the stock.

Pfizer's outstanding common shares, repeated from Exhibit 11.1 are (in millions):

Common stock, $.05 par value; 12,000 shares authorized; issued: 2008—8,863	$ 443
Additional paid-in capital	70,283

Pfizer's common stock, in the amount of $443 million, equals the number of shares issued multiplied by the common stock's par value: 8,863 million $\times$ $0.05 = $443 million.[4] Total proceeds from stock issuances are $70,726 million, or $7.98 per share ($70,726 million/8,863 million shares). The balance of the proceeds from stock issuances ($70,283 million) is included in the additional paid-in capital account.

RESEARCH INSIGHT

Stock Issuance and Stock Returns   Research shows that, historically, companies issuing equity securities experience unusually low stock returns for several years following those offerings. Evidence suggests that this poor performance is partly due to overly optimistic estimates of long-term growth for these companies by equity analysts that impact the offering price. This over-optimism is most pronounced when the analyst is employed by the brokerage firm that underwrites the issue. There is also evidence that companies manage earnings upward prior to an equity offering. This evidence means the observed decrease in returns following an issuance likely reflects the market's negative reaction, on average, to earnings management. The result is a classic "chicken or egg" dilemma: do stock returns decline following issuance because analysts or managers are skewing performance measures upward, or do managers skew performance measures upward because they anticipate that investors rationally adjust those measures downward?

Stock Repurchase   **Pfizer** provides the following description of its stock repurchase program in notes to its 10-K report.

In June 2005, we announced a $5 billion share-purchase program. In June 2006, the Board of Directors increased our share-purchase authorization from $5 billion to $18 billion, which is primarily being funded by operating cash flows and a portion of the proceeds from the sale of our Consumer Healthcare business. In total, under the June 2005 program, through December 31, 2008, we purchased approximately 710 million shares for approximately $18.0 billion.

continued

---

[3] Common stock can also be issued as "no par" or as "no par with a stated value." For no par stock, the common stock account is increased by the entire proceeds of the sale and no amount is assigned to additional paid-in capital. For no par stock with a stated value, the stated value is treated just like par value; that is, common stock is increased by the number of shares multiplied by the stated value, and the remainder is assigned to the additional paid-in capital account.

[4] The par value of the shares issued is rounded to the nearest million dollars.

---

continued from previous page

> In January 2008, we announced a new $5 billion share-purchase program, to be funded by operating cash flows, that may be utilized from time to time. On January 26, 2009, we announced that we have entered into a definitive merger agreement under which we will acquire Wyeth in a cash-and-stock transaction. The merger agreement limits our stock purchases to a maximum of $500 million prior to the completion of the transaction without Wyeth's consent.
>
> A summary of common stock purchases follows:

For the Year Ended December 31, (Millions of Shares and Dollars, Except Per-Share Data)	Shares of Common Stock Purchased	Average Per-Share Price Paid	Total Cost of Common Stock Purchased
2008:			
June 2005 program	26	$18.96	$500
Total	26		$500
2007:			
June 2005 program	395	$25.27	$9,994
Total	395		$9,994

Pfizer initiated several stock buyback programs in the past six years. One reason a company will repurchase shares is if it feels that the market undervalues them. They reason that the repurchase sends a positive signal to the market about the company's financial condition that favorably affects its share price and, thus, allows the company to resell those shares for a "gain." Recent research provides evidence that share prices generally increase following the announcement of a share repurchase program. Any such gain on resale is *never* reflected in the income statement. Instead, the excess of the resale price over the repurchase price is added to additional paid-in capital. GAAP prohibits companies from reporting gains via stock transactions with their own shareholders.

Another reason shares are repurchased is to offset the dilutive effects of an employee stock option program. When an employee exercises stock options, the number of shares outstanding increases. These additional shares reduce earnings per share and are, therefore, viewed as *dilutive*. In response, many companies repurchase an equivalent number of shares in a desire to keep outstanding shares constant. Corporations also buy back their own shares in order to concentrate ownership to avoid an unwelcome takeover action.

IFRS REPORTING INSIGHT

The accounting for share repurchases under IFRS is similar to GAAP. IFRS allows the repurchase also to be recorded as a decrease to the common equity, additional paid-in capital, and retained earnings or some combination.

A stock repurchase has the opposite financial statement effects from a stock issuance. That is, cash is reduced by the price of the shares repurchased (number of shares repurchased multiplied by the purchase price per share) and stockholders' equity is reduced by the same amount. The reduction in equity is achieved by increasing a contra equity account called **treasury stock**. *A contra equity account is a negative equity account,* which reduces stockholders' equity. Thus, when a contra equity account increases, total equity decreases.

Any subsequent reissuance of treasury stock does not yield a gain or loss. Instead, the difference between the proceeds received and the repurchase price of the treasury stock is reflected as an increase or decease to additional paid-in capital.

To illustrate, assume that 3,000 common shares of Pfizer previously issued for $43 are later repurchased for $40. The financial statement effects and entries for this stock repurchase follow.

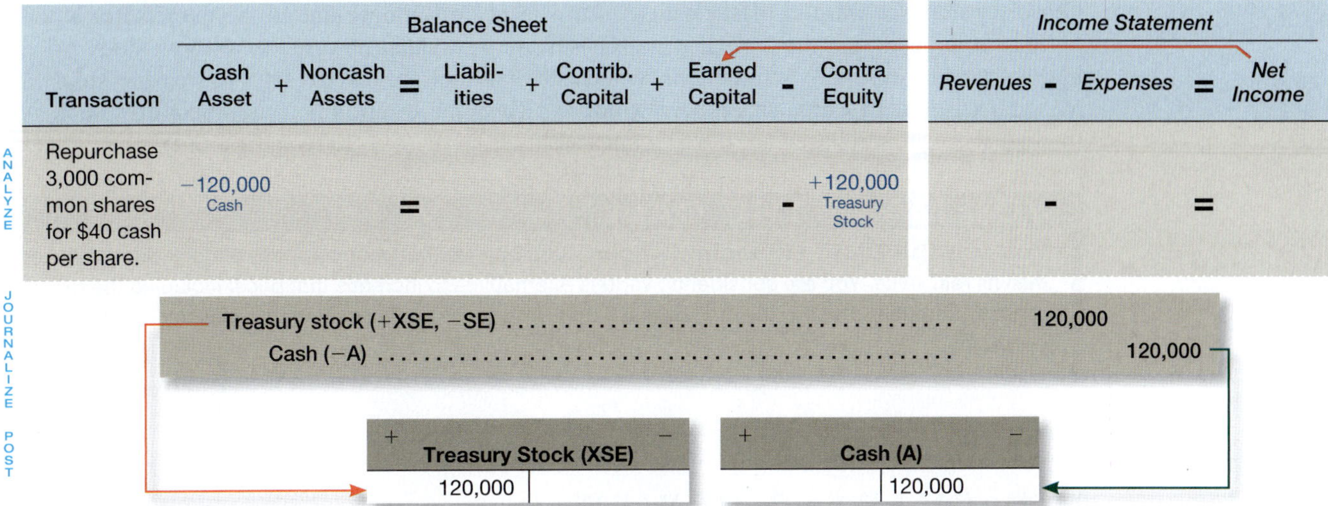

Assets (cash) and equity both decrease. Treasury stock (a contra equity account) increases by $120,000, which reduces stockholders' equity by that same amount.

Assume that these 3,000 shares are then subsequently resold for $42 cash per share. The financial statement effects and entries for this treasury stock sale follow.

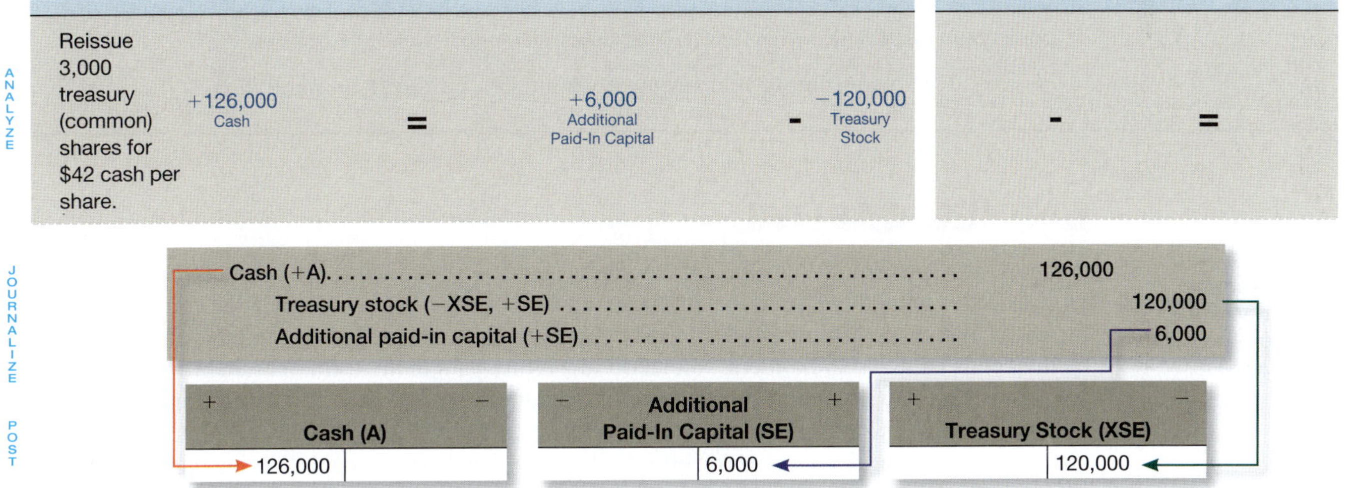

If the reissue price is below the repurchase price, then additional paid-in capital is reduced until it reaches a zero balance, after which retained earnings is reduced.

Cash assets increase by $126,000 (3,000 shares × $42 per share), the treasury stock account is reduced by the $120,000 cost of the treasury shares issued, and the $6,000 excess (3,000 shares × $2 per share) is reported as an increase in additional paid-in capital. Again, there is no effect on the income statement—companies are prohibited from reporting gains and losses from repurchases and reissuances of their own stock.

The treasury stock section of Pfizer's 2008 balance sheet is reproduced below.

At December 31 (millions)	2008
Treasury stock, shares at cost; issued: 2008—2,117	$(57,391)

Pfizer has repurchased a cumulative total of 2,117 million shares of its common stock for $57,391 million, an average repurchase price of $27.11 per share. This compares with total contributed capital of $70,374 million ($73 million + $443 million + $70,283 million −$425 million). Thus, over 80% of its original contributed capital has been repurchased. Although some of Pfizer's treasury purchases were to offset increases in shares outstanding due to the exercise of stock options, it appears that most of these purchases are motivated by a perceived low stock price by Pfizer management. When there have been several repurchases and sales of treasury stock, a question arises as to which shares were sold. Typically the solution is to assume a flow such as the first shares repurchased are the first ones assumed to be sold (first-in, first-out).

YOU MAKE THE CALL

You are the Chief Financial Officer   You believe that your company's stock price is lower than its real value. You are considering various alternatives to increase that price, including the repurchase of company stock in the market. What are some considerations relating to this decision? [Answer on page 513]

MID-CHAPTER REVIEW 1

Plesko Corporation reported the following transactions relating to its stock accounts in 2010.

Jan. 15	Issued 10,000 shares of $5 par value common stock at $17 cash per share.
Mar. 31	Purchased 2,000 shares of its own common stock at $15 cash per share.
June 25	Reissued 1,000 shares of its treasury stock at $20 cash per share.

Show the financial impact of each transaction using the financial statement effects template, provide the appropriate journal entry for each transaction, and post the journal entries to the related T-accounts.

The solution to this review problem can be found on page 531.

EARNED CAPITAL

LO3 Describe how operations increase the equity of a business.

We now turn our attention to the earned capital portion of stockholders' equity. Earned capital represents the cumulative profit that has been retained by the company. Recall that earned capital is increased by income earned and decreased by any losses incurred. Earned capital is also decreased by dividends paid to shareholders. Not all dividends are paid in the form of cash, however. In fact, companies can pay dividends in many forms, including property (such as land, for example) or additional shares of stock. We cover both cash and stock dividends in this section. Earned capital also includes the positive or negative effects of accumulated other comprehensive income (AOCI). The earned capital of Pfizer is highlighted in the following graphic:

Shareholders' Equity (millions, except preferred shares issued)	Dec. 31, 2008
Preferred stock, without par value, at stated value;	
27 shares authorized; 1,804 issued in 2008	$ 73
Common stock, $.05 par value; 12,000 shares authorized; issued: 2008—8,863	443
Additional paid-in capital	70,283
Employee benefit trust	(425)
Treasury stock, shares at cost; issued: 2008—2,117	(57,391)
Retained earnings	49,142
Accumulated other comprehensive income (expense)	(4,569)
Total shareholders' equity	$57,556

Cash Dividends

LO4 Explain and account for dividends and stock splits.

Many companies, but not all, pay dividends. Their reasons for dividend payments are varied. Most dividends are paid in cash on a quarterly basis. The following is a description of Pfizer's dividend policy from its 2008 10-K.

Dividends on Common Stock
Our current dividend provides a return to shareholders while maintaining sufficient capital to invest in growing our businesses and increasing shareholder value, including through the proposed acquisition of Wyeth. Our dividends are funded from operating cash flows, our financial asset portfolio, and short-term commercial paper borrowings and are not restricted by debt covenants. We believe that our profitability and access to financial markets provide sufficient capability for us to pay current and future dividends.

Outsiders closely monitor dividend payments. It is generally perceived that the level of dividend payments is related to the expected long-term core income. Accordingly, dividend increases are usually accompanied by stock price increases, and companies rarely reduce their dividends unless absolutely necessary. Dividend reductions are, therefore, met with substantial stock-price declines.

Pfizer's short-run dividend payment history, as reported in its 2008 10-K, is:

We declared dividends of $8.6 billion in 2008 and $8.2 billion in 2007 on our common stock. In December 2008, our Board of Directors declared a first-quarter 2009 dividend of $0.32 per share. The first-quarter 2009 cash dividend will be our 281st consecutive quarterly dividend. In January 2009, in connection with the proposed merger between Pfizer and Wyeth, the Board of Directors determined that, effective with the dividend to be paid in the second quarter of 2009, it will reduce our quarterly dividend per share to $0.16. The merger agreement prohibits us from declaring a quarterly dividend on our common stock in excess of $0.16 per share without Wyeth's consent prior to the completion of the transaction.

Financial Effects of Cash Dividends   Cash dividends reduce both cash and retained earnings by the amount of the cash dividends paid. To illustrate, Pfizer paid $8.5 billion in 2008 cash dividends on its common and preferred shares. The financial statement effects of this cash dividend payment are reflected as a reduction in assets (cash) and a reduction in retained earnings as follows.

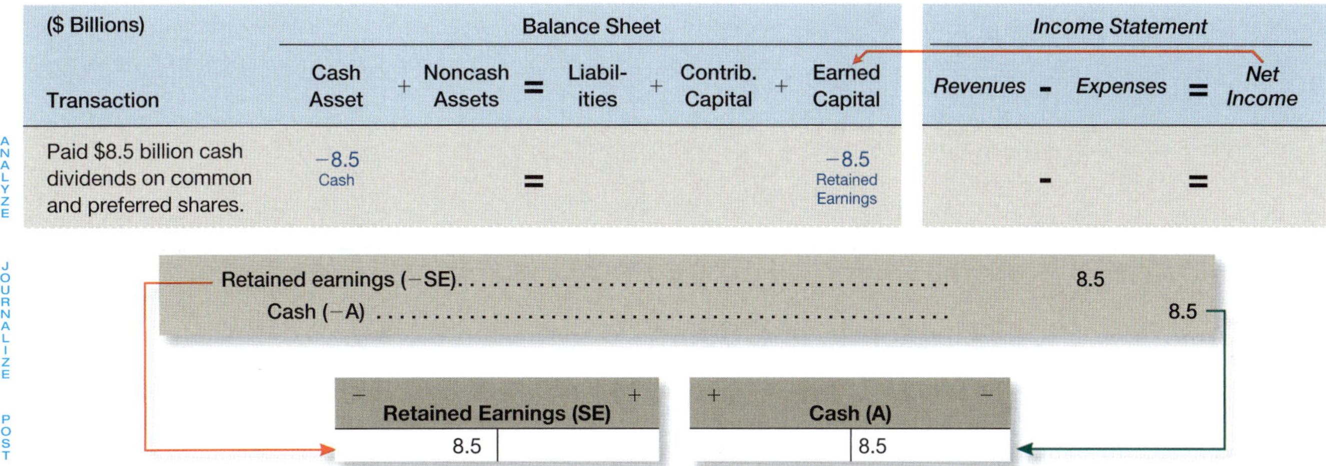

Dividend payments have no effect on profitability. They are a direct reduction to retained earnings and bypass the income statement.

BUSINESS INSIGHT

Importance of Dividends   Dividends are traditionally viewed as an indicator of the health of the paying corporation. Dividend-paying companies are typically reluctant to reduce dividends, let alone eliminate their periodic dividend payment. But as Anne Mulcahy, the former CEO of Xerox, has pointed out (*WSJ*. 11/28/2007), such behavior can be shortsighted if not downright foolish. Mulcahy suggests, "Heed outsiders' key warnings of a looming cash squeeze. Prioritize spending needs and accept that dividends might not top the list. Get ready for a new set of shareholders once the [dividend] payout goes. And don't rush to reinstate the dividend payout until . . . recovery is rock solid." She goes on to advise not to dispense with essential activities or to sell subsidiaries at bargain prices to assure the dividend payment.

Preferred stock dividends have priority over those for common shares, including unpaid prior years' preferred dividends (dividends in arrears) when preferred stock is cumulative. To illustrate, assume that Hanna Company has 15,000 shares of $50 par value, 8% preferred stock outstanding and 50,000 shares of $5 par value common stock outstanding. During its first three years in business, assume that Hanna declares $20,000 dividends in the first year, $260,000 of dividends in the second year, and $60,000 of dividends in the third year. If the preferred stock is cumulative, the total amount of dividends paid to each class of stock in each of the three years would be:

	Preferred Stock	Common Stock
Year 1		
Current-year dividend ($750,000 × 8%;	$20,000	
but only $20,000 is paid, leaving $40,000 in arrears)		
Balance to common		$ 0
Year 2		
Arrearage from Year 1 [($750,000 × 8%) − $20,000]	40,000	
Current-year dividend ($750,000 × 8%)	60,000	
Balance to common [$260,000 − ($40,000 + $60,000)]		160,000
Year 3		
Current-year dividend ($750,000 × 8%)	60,000	
Balance to common		0

MID-CHAPTER REVIEW 2

Finn Corporation has outstanding 10,000 shares of $100 par value, 5% preferred stock and 50,000 shares of $5 par value common stock. During its first three years in business, Finn declared no dividends in the first year, $300,000 of cash dividends in the second year, and $80,000 of cash dividends in the third year.

a. If the preferred stock is cumulative, determine the total amount of dividends paid to each class of stock for each of the three years.

b. If the preferred stock is not cumulative, determine the total amount of dividends paid to each class of stock for each of the three years.

The solution to this review problem can be found on page 532.

Stock Dividends and Splits

Dividends need not be paid in cash. Many companies pay **stock dividends**, that is dividends in the form of additional shares of stock. Companies can also distribute additional shares to their stockholders with a stock split. We cover both of these distributions in this section.

Stock Dividends   When dividends are paid in the form of the company's stock, retained earnings are reduced and contributed capital is increased. However, the amount by which retained earnings are reduced depends on the proportion of the outstanding shares distributed to the total outstanding shares on the issue date. Exhibit 11.2 illustrates two possibilities depending on whether stock dividends are classified as either small stock dividends or large stock dividends. When the additional number of shares issued as a stock dividend is so great that it is likely to negatively impact the market price per share of the stock, the dividend must be treated as a large stock dividend. Dividends of less than 20%–25% of the outstanding shares are considered to be small stock dividends, while dividends of more than 20%–25% are classified as large stock dividends.

EXHIBIT 11.2	Analysis of Stock Dividend Effects	
Percentage of Outstanding Shares Distributed	**Retained Earnings**	**Contributed Capital**
Less than 20%–25% *(small stock dividend)*	Reduce by **market value** of shares distributed	Common stock increased by par value of shares distributed; additional paid-in capital increased for the balance
More than 20%–25% *(large stock dividend)*	Reduce by **par value** of shares distributed	Common stock increased by par value of shares distributed

For *small stock dividends,* retained earnings are reduced by the *market* value of the shares distributed (dividend shares × market price per share) and contributed capital is increased by the same amount. For the contributed capital increase, the common stock is increased by the par value of the shares distributed and the remainder [dividend shares × (market value per share − par value per share)] increases additional paid-in capital. For *large stock dividends,* retained earnings are reduced by the *par* value of the shares distributed (dividend shares × par value per share), and common stock is increased by the same amount (no change to additional paid-in capital).

To illustrate the financial statement effects of dividends, assume that a company has 1 million shares of $5 par common stock outstanding. It then declares a small stock dividend of 15% of the outstanding shares (1,000,000 shares × 15% = 150,000 shares) when the market price of the stock is $30 per share. This small stock dividend has the following financial statement effects:

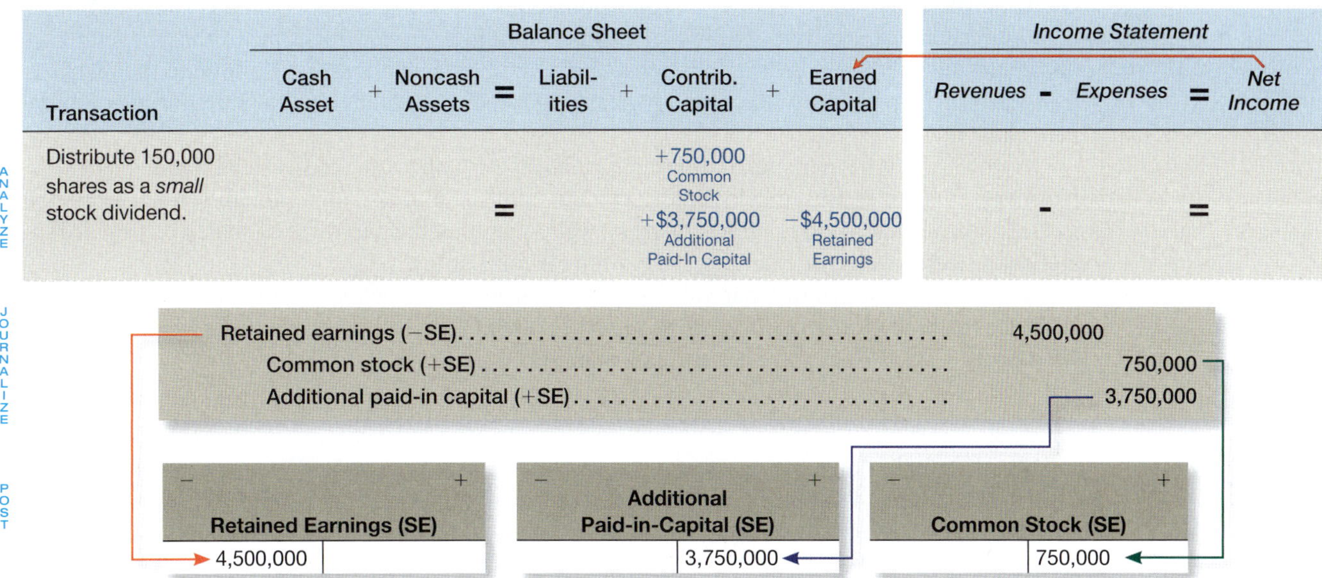

Retained earnings are reduced by $4,500,000, which equals the market value of the small stock dividend (150,000 shares × $30 market price per share). The increase in contributed capital is treated as follows: common stock is increased by the par value of $750,000 (150,000 shares × $5 par value), and the remainder of $3,750,000 increases additional paid-in capital. Similar to cash dividend payments, the stock dividends, whether large or small, never impact income.

Next, assume instead that a company declares a large stock dividend of 70% of the 1 million outstanding common ($5 par) shares when the market price of the stock is $30 per share. This large stock dividend has the following financial statement effects and related entries:

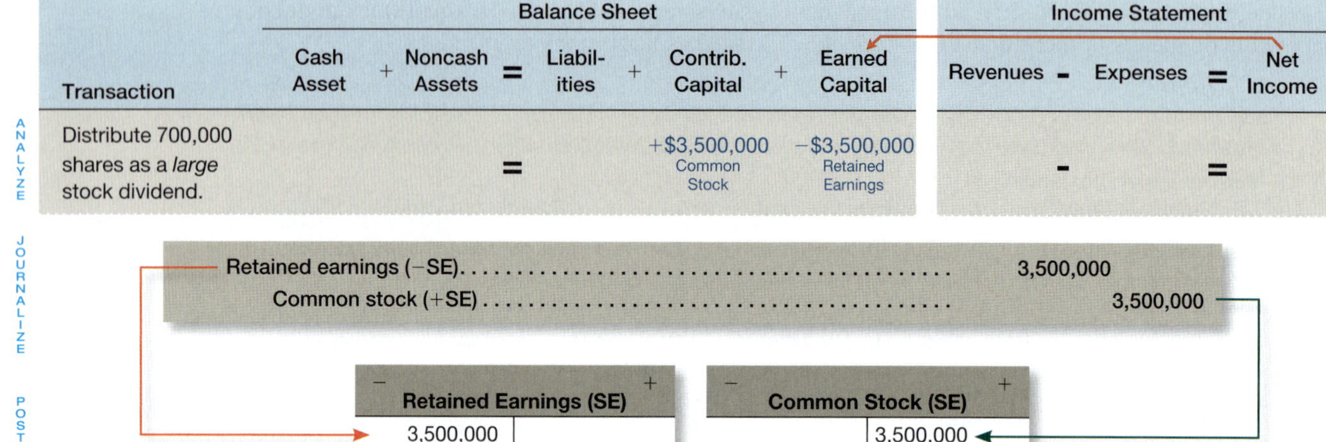

Retained earnings are reduced by $3,500,000, which equals the par value of the large stock dividend (700,000 shares × $5 par value per share). Common stock is increased by the par value of $3,500,000. There is no effect on additional paid-in capital because the dividend is reported at par value.

For both large and small stock dividends, companies are required to show comparable shares outstanding for all prior periods for which earnings per share (EPS) is reported in the statements. The reasoning is that a stock dividend has no effect on the ownership percentage of each common stockholder. As such, to show a dilution in reported EPS would erroneously suggest a decline in profitability when it is simply due to an increase in shares outstanding.

Stock Splits   A **stock split** is a proportionate distribution of shares and, as such, is similar in substance to a stock dividend. A typical stock split is 2-for-1, which means that the company distributes one additional share for each share owned by a shareholder. Following the distribution, each investor owns twice as many shares, yet their percentage ownership in the company is unchanged.

A stock split is not a monetary transaction and, as such, there are no financial statement effects. However, companies must disclose the new number of shares outstanding for all periods presented in the financial statements. Further, many states require that the par value of shares be proportionately adjusted as well (for example, halved for a 2-for-1 split).

If state law requires that par value not be reduced for a stock split, this event should be described as a *stock split effected in the form of a dividend*. The following disclosure from **Deere & Company**'s 2008 10-K provides such an example:

Stock Split in Form of Dividend

On November 14, 2007, a special meeting of stockholders was held authorizing a two-for-one stock split effected in the form of a 100 percent stock dividend to holders of record on November 26, 2007, distributed on December 3, 2007. All share and per share data (except par value) have been adjusted to reflect the effect of the stock split for all periods presented. The number of shares of common stock issuable upon exercise of outstanding stock options, vesting of other stock awards, and the number of shares reserved for issuance under various employee benefit plans were proportionately increased in accordance with terms of the respective plans.

Stock Transactions and the Cash Flows Statement

The issuance of common stock, the acquisition of treasury stock, and cash (but not stock) dividends affect the financing section of the cash flow statement as follows:

Transaction	Effect on Cash Flow
Issuance of Common Stock	Increase
Acquisition of Treasury Stock	Decrease
Sale of Treasury Stock	Increase
Cash Dividends Paid	Decrease

Stock splits and stock dividends do not influence the cash flows statement and are often used when cash is short but the continuation of a dividend is considered necessary.

MID-CHAPTER REVIEW 3

The stockholders' equity of Zhang Corporation at December 31, 2010, follows.

5% preferred stock, $100 par value, 10,000 shares authorized; 4,000 shares issued and outstanding	$ 400,000
Common stock, $5 par value, 200,000 shares authorized; 50,000 shares issued and outstanding	250,000
Paid-in capital in excess of par value—Preferred stock	40,000
Paid-in capital in excess of par value—Common stock	300,000
Retained earnings	656,000
Total stockholders' equity	$1,646,000

The following transactions occurred during 2011. Show the financial impact of each transaction using the financial statement effects template, provide the appropriate journal entry for each transaction, and post the journal entries to the related T-accounts.

Apr. 1   Declared and issued a 100% stock dividend on all outstanding shares of common stock when the market value of the stock was $11 per share.

Dec. 7   Declared and issued a 3% stock dividend on all outstanding shares of common stock when the market value of the stock was $7 per share.

Dec 31   Declared and paid a cash dividend of $1.20 per share on all outstanding common shares.

The solution to this review problem can be found on pages 532–533.

Comprehensive Income

Comprehensive income is a more inclusive notion of company performance than net income. It includes all recognized changes in equity that occur during a period except those resulting from contributions by and distributions to owners.

LO5 Define and illustrate comprehensive income.

Specifically, comprehensive income includes net income *plus* additional gains and losses not included in the income statement. These additional gains and losses are called *other comprehensive income* and include, for example, foreign currency adjustments, unrealized gains or losses on available-for-sale securities and derivatives, and adjustments to pension and other benefit plans. Comprehensive income includes the effects on a company of some economic events that are often outside of management's control. Accordingly, some observers assert that net income is a measure of management's performance, while comprehensive income is a measure of company performance.

Unlike net income, other comprehensive income is not closed to retained earnings at the end of each accounting period. Instead, other comprehensive income is closed to a separate earned capital account called **accumulated other comprehensive income** (abbreviated AOCI).

Pfizer reports an AOCI balance of negative $4,569 million in the equity section of its 2008 balance sheet. The 2007 balance was negative $2,299 million. Thus, in 2008, Pfizer reported other comprehensive expense of $6,868 million and net income of $8,104 million. A detailed breakdown of comprehensive income from the footnotes is presented below:

($ millions)		Comprehensive Income (Expense)
Net income		$8,104
Other comprehensive income, net of tax:		
Foreign currency translation adjustment	$(5,898)	
Unrealized gains (losses)	(146)	
Benefit plans	(2,486)	
Income taxes	1,662	
Total other comprehensive income		(6,868)
Comprehensive income		$1,236

IFRS REPORTING INSIGHT

Comprehensive income is disclosed on the Statement of Recognized Income and Expenses under IFRS (SoRIE). It includes all changes to equity, except transactions with owners.

Summary of Stockholders' Equity

A summary of transactions that affect stockholders' equity is included in the statement of shareholders' equity. This statement reports a reconciliation of the beginning and ending balances of important stockholders' equity accounts. Pfizer's statement of stockholders' equity is shown in Exhibit 11.3:

EXHIBIT 11.3 — Pfizer's Stockholders' Equity (December 31, 2008)

(Millions, Except Preferred Shares)	Preferred Stock Shares	Preferred Stock Stated Value	Common Stock Shares	Common Stock Par Value	Additional Paid-In Capital	Employee Benefit Trust Shares	Employee Benefit Trust Fair Value	Treasury Stock Shares	Treasury Stock Cost	Retained Earnings	Accum. Other Comprehensive Inc./(Exp.)	Total
Balance December 31, 2007	2,302	$93	8,850	$442	$69,913	(24)	$(550)	(2,089)	$56,847	$49,660	$2,229	$65,010
Comprehensive income:												
Net income										8,104		8,104
Total other comprehensive expense—net of tax:											6,868	6,868
Total comprehensive income												1,236
Cash dividends declared—												
common stock										(8,617)		(8,617)
preferred stock										(5)		(5)
Stock option transactions					207	1	32					239
Purchases of common stock								(26)	(500)			(500)
Employee benefit trust transactions—net					(113)	(1)	93					(20)
Preferred stock—conversions and redemptions	(498)	(20)			(7)				2			(25)
Other			13	1	283			(2)	(46)			238
Balance December 31, 2008	1,804	$73	8,863	$443	$70,283	(24)	$(425)	(2,117)	$(57,391)	$49,142	$(4,569)	$57,556

Pfizer's statement of shareholders' equity reveals the following key transactions for 2008:

- Net income plus other comprehensive income increased shareholders' equity by $1,236 million.

- Dividend payments to preferred and common shareholders decreased stockholders' equity by $8,622 million ($8,617 million + $5 million).

- Issuance of shares as a result of the exercise of employee stock options increased equity by $239 million.

- Stock repurchases decreased equity by $500 million.

- Employee benefit trust transactions decreased stockholders' equity by $20 million.

- Conversion of preferred stock into common stock and redemptions decreased the preferred stock account, for a net decrease in stockholders' equity of $25 million.

- Other transactions increased stockholders' equity by $238 million.

One final point: the financial press sometimes refers to a measure called **book value per share**. This amount is the net book value of the company that is available to common shareholders, defined as: stockholders' equity less preferred stock divided by the number of common shares outstanding (issued common shares less treasury shares). Pfizer's book value per share is computed as: ($57,556 million − $73 million)/(8,863 million shares − 2,117 million shares) = $8.52 book value per common share.

MID-CHAPTER REVIEW 4

The stockholders' equity of Sloan Corporation at December 31, 2010, follows.

Common stock, $5 par value, 400,000 shares authorized; 160,000 shares issued and outstanding	$800,000
Paid-in capital in excess of par value	920,000
Retained earnings	513,000

During 2011, the following transactions occurred:

June 28	Declared and issued a 10% common stock dividend when the market value is $11 per share.
Dec. 5	Declared and paid a cash dividend of $1.25 per share.
Dec. 31	Updated retained earnings for net income of $412,000

Compute the year-ending balance of retained earnings for 2011.

The solution to this review problem can be found on page 533.

EARNINGS PER SHARE

The income statement reports at least one, and potentially two, earnings per share (EPS) numbers: basic and diluted. The difference between the two measures is illustrated as follows:

LO6 Describe and illustrate the basic and diluted earnings per share computations.

Basic EPS

$$\text{EPS} = \frac{\text{Net income less Preferred dividends}}{\text{Weighted average common shares}} - \text{EPS impact of dilutive options and warrants} - \text{EPS impact of dilutive convertibles}$$

Diluted EPS

All public companies are required to report basic EPS. If the company has a complex capital structure, it is also required to report diluted EPS. A company is said to have a **complex capital structure** if it has certain *dilutive securities* outstanding. **Dilutive securities** are securities that can be converted into shares of common stock and would therefore reduce (or dilute) the earnings per share upon conversion. The three primary types of dilutive securities are:

- Stock options
- Convertible debt
- Convertible preferred stock

The Appendix at the end of this chapter details the accounting for these securities. A company with none of these dilutive securities outstanding is said to have a **simple capital structure**.

Basic EPS (BEPS) is computed as earnings available for common shareholders (net income less preferred dividends) divided by the weighted average number of common shares outstanding for the year. The subtraction of preferred stock dividends yields the income per common share available for dividend payments to common shareholders. The preferred dividends are subtracted because this portion of net income does not accrue to the common stockholders.

Computation of **Diluted EPS (DEPS)** reflects the added shares that would have been issued if all stock options and other convertible securities had been exercised at the beginning of the year. When DEPS is calculated, the corporation needs to consider the maximum potential reduction (dilution) of its BEPS that could occur if the conversion of these securities took place. To do so means that any of these securities that do not reduce BEPS upon conversion are not to be considered converted. The result must be a figure that is lower than BEPS. The actual calculation can be quite complex. This does not detract from the importance of the DEPS value. The diluted earnings per share figure is favored by analysts as a better indicator of performance compared to basic earnings per share. Because reported DEPS never exceeds reported BEPS, the calculation is considered conservative.

Computation and Analysis of EPS

The computation of basic EPS is relatively straightforward, particularly when the firm neither issues nor buys any of its shares during the year. The formula is:

$$\text{Basic EPS} = \frac{\text{Net income} - \text{Preferred dividends}}{\text{Weighted average number of common shares outstanding}}$$

To illustrate this calculation, assume that United Bridge Corporation reported net income of $200,000 in 2008 and paid $24,000 in preferred dividends. At the beginning of the year, the company had 44,000 shares of common stock outstanding. On June 30 (exactly the midpoint of the year) United Bridge purchased 8,000 shares of stock as treasury stock. Thus, the number of shares outstanding for the first six months of 2008 was 44,000 and, for the second half of the year, the company had 36,000 shares outstanding. The weighted average number of shares outstanding was, therefore, 40,000 [(44,000 + 36,000)/2]. Basic EPS would be calculated as follows:

$$\text{Basic EPS} = \frac{\$200,000 - \$24,000}{40,000 \text{ shares}} = \$4.40 \text{ per share}$$

The computation of diluted EPS is more complex in that it requires adjusting the basic EPS calculation for the effect of dilutive securities. This will typically require adjusting both the numerator and denominator of the calculation.

To illustrate, assume that United Bridge Corporation's preferred stock is convertible into 8,000 shares of common stock. To calculate diluted EPS, we must assume that the convertible preferred shares were converted at the beginning of the year. If this had occurred, two things would have been different for United Bridge. First, the weighted average number of shares outstanding would be higher by 8,000 shares. Second, the company would not have paid preferred dividends of $24,000. The resulting calculation would be:

$$\text{Diluted EPS} = \frac{\$200,000}{48,000 \text{ shares}} = \$4.17 \text{ per share}$$

A full description of the procedures for calculating diluted EPS is beyond the scope of this text. However, as the calculation above illustrates, diluted EPS adjusts basic EPS for the effect of dilutive securities. Reported DEPS must be no larger than BEPS to reflect its conservative message.

Pfizer reports both basic and diluted EPS. The table below, drawn from Pfizer's 2008 consolidated income statement, presents its basic and diluted EPS figures.

Year Ended December 31 ($ millions, except earnings per share)	2008	2007
Earnings per common share—basic		
Income from continuing operations	$1.19	$1.19
Discontinued operations	0.01	(0.01)
Net income	$1.20	$1.18
Earnings per common share—diluted		
Income from continuing operations before cumulative effect		
of a change in accounting principles	$1.19	$1.18
Discontinued operations	0.01	(0.01)
Net income	$1.20	$1.17

Several observations should be made regarding Pfizer's EPS disclosures:

1. Pfizer reports basic and diluted EPS of $1.20 for 2008. In 2007, Pfizer reports basic EPS of $1.18 and diluted EPS of $1.17 per share. The difference in 2007 is caused by the effect of dilutive securities. Specifically, Pfizer has outstanding stock options and convertible preferred stock. Most publicly traded companies have at least one type of dilutive security outstanding. However, the dilutive effect of these securities on Pfizer's EPS is negligible.

2. The income statement further separates these EPS figures into EPS from continuing operations and EPS from discontinued operations. In 2007, the latter reduced Pfizer's EPS by $0.01 per share while in 2008 it increased EPS by the same amount. GAAP requires separate reporting of the effects of nonrecurring items on EPS, including discontinued operations and extraordinary items (see Chapter 6).

3. Footnote 16 from the company's 2008 10-K reveals that Pfizer used weighted average shares outstanding of 6,727 million shares to calculate basic EPS. This number is not the same as the number of shares outstanding in its December 31, 2008, balance sheet. Nor is it the simple average of the beginning and ending numbers of shares outstanding. The precise number of shares used in the EPS calculations requires knowing exactly when common stock and treasury stock transactions occurred during the year so that the weighted average number of shares outstanding can be calculated. This information is not always available in a company's 10-K report.

EPS figures are often used as a method of comparing operating results for companies of different sizes under the assumption that the number of shares outstanding is proportional to the income level (that is, a company twice the size of another will report double the income and will have double the common shares outstanding, leaving EPS approximately equal for the two companies). This assumption is erroneous. Management controls the number of common shares outstanding. Different companies also have different philosophies regarding share issuance and repurchase. For example, consider that most companies report annual EPS of less than $5, while **Berkshire Hathaway Inc.** reported EPS of $3,224 for 2008! The large amount occurs because Berkshire Hathaway has so few common shares outstanding, not necessarily because it has stellar profits.

Most analysts prefer to concentrate their attention on diluted EPS versus basic EPS as the more important measure, but the value of the EPS number is influenced by a number of factors including the number of common shares outstanding. For this reason, comparisons are more useful over time than across firms, but a careful reader should differentiate between EPS growth that comes from increases in the numerator and EPS growth that comes from decreases in the denominator. For these reasons, EPS may be of limited use in evaluating a firm's operational performance.

CHAPTER-END REVIEW

Petroni Corporation reported net income of $1,750 million in 2011. The weighted average number of common shares outstanding during 2011 was 760 million shares. Petroni paid $40 million in dividends on preferred stock, which was convertible into 10 million shares of common stock.

1. Calculate Petroni's basic earnings per share for 2011.
2. Calculate Petroni's diluted earnings per share for 2011.
3. What EPS numbers should Petroni report on its 2011 income statement?

The solution to this review problem can be found on page 534.

APPENDIX 11A: Dilutive Securities: Further Considerations
Convertible Securities

L07 Analyze the accounting for convertible securities, stock rights, and stock options.

Convertible securities are debt and equity securities that provide the holder with an option to convert those securities into other securities. Convertible debentures, for example, are debt securities that give the holder the option to convert the debt into common stock at a predetermined conversion price. Preferred stock can also contain a conversion privilege. Pfizer provides an example of the latter in Note 14 to its 2008 10-K.

The Series A convertible perpetual preferred stock is held by an Employee Stock Ownership Plan ("Preferred ESOP") Trust and provides dividends at the rate of 6.25%, which are accumulated and paid quarterly. The per share stated value is $40,300 and the preferred stock ranks senior to our common stock as to dividends and liquidation rights. Each share is convertible, at the holder's option, into 2,574.87 shares of our common stock with equal voting rights. The conversion option is indexed to our common stock and requires share settlement, and therefore, is reported at the fair value at the date of issuance. We may redeem the preferred stock at any time or upon termination of the Preferred ESOP, at our option, in cash, in shares of common stock or a combination of both at a price of $40,300 per share.

Assume 5,000 shares of the preferred stock were issued at the stated value. The appropriate journal entry would be ($ thousands):

Cash (+A).	201,500	
Preferred stock (stated value) (+SE)		201,500

Now assume that 2,000 shares are converted to 2,000(2,574.87) = 5,149,740 shares of common stock. The appropriate journal entry is ($ thousands, rounded):

Preferred stock (stated value) (−SE)	80,600	
Common stock (par $0.05) (+SE).		257
Contributed capital (+SE).		80,343

Conversion privileges offer an additional benefit to the holder of a security. That is, debtholders and preferred stockholders carry senior positions as claimants in bankruptcy, and carry a fixed-interest or dividend yield. With a conversion privilege, they can enjoy the residual benefits of common shareholders should the company perform well.

A conversion option is valuable and yields a higher price for the securities than they would otherwise command. However, conversion privileges impose a cost on common shareholders. That is, the higher market price received for convertible securities is offset by the cost imposed on the subordinate (common) securities. In addition, conversion into common shares dilutes the ownership percentage of existing holders of the firm's common stock.

Accounting for the issuance of a convertible security is straightforward: the conversion option is *not* valued on the balance sheet unless it is detachable from the security (and, thus, separately saleable). Instead, the convertible preferred stock or convertible debt is recorded just like preferred stock or debt that does not have a conversion feature.

When securities are converted, the book value of the converted security is removed from the balance sheet and a corresponding increase is made to contributed capital. To illustrate further, assume that Pfizer has convertible bonds with a face value of $1,000 and an unamortized premium of $100. Its holders convert them into 20 shares of $10 par value common stock. The financial statement effects and related entries of this conversion would be:

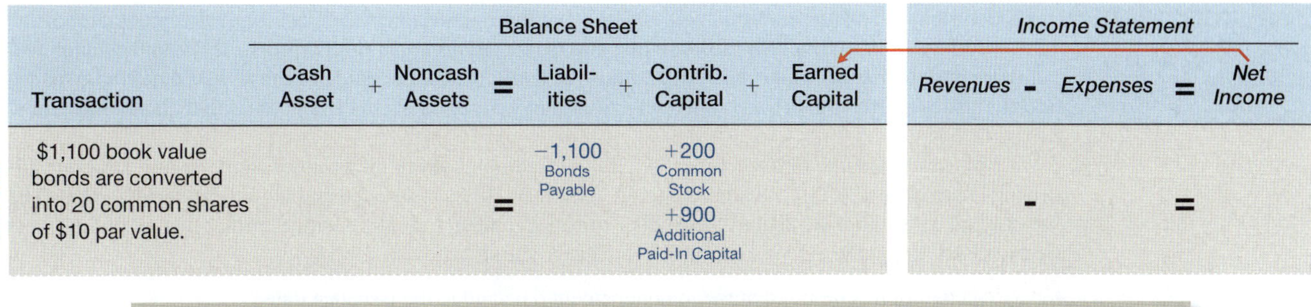

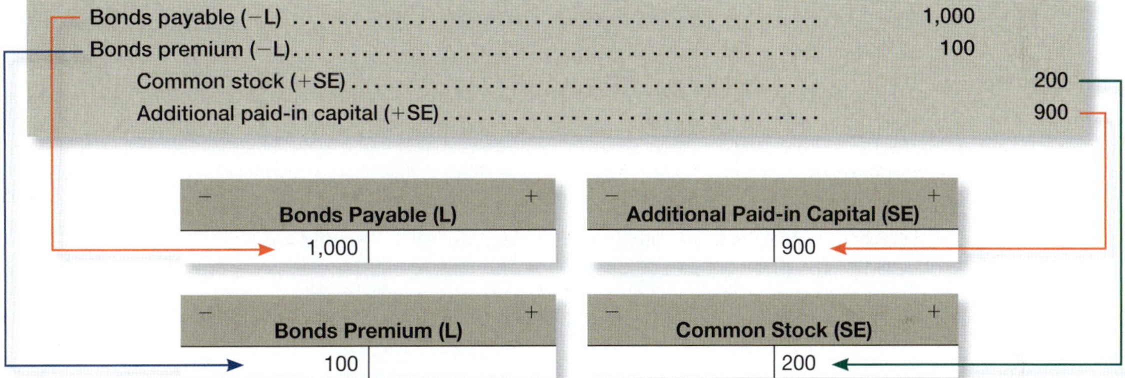

The key financial statement effects of this transaction are:

- The bond's face value ($1,000) and unamortized premium ($100) of the bonds are removed from the balance sheet.
- Common stock increases by the par value of the shares issued (20 shares $\times$ $10 par = $200) and additional paid-in capital increases for the balance ($900).
- There is no effect on income from this conversion unless an interest accrual is required.

One final note: the potentially dilutive effect of convertible securities is taken into account in the computation of diluted earnings per share (EPS). Specifically, the diluted EPS computation assumes conversion at the beginning of the year (or when the security is issued if during the year). The earnings available to common shares in the numerator are increased by any forgone after-tax interest expense or preferred dividends, and the additional shares to be issued in the conversion increase the shares outstanding in the denominator.

Stock Rights

Corporations often issue **stock rights** that give the holder an option to acquire a specified number of shares of capital stock under prescribed conditions and within a stated period. The evidence of stock rights is a certificate called a **stock warrant**. Stock rights are issued for several reasons that include the following:

- To compensate outside parties (such as underwriters, promoters, board members, and other professionals) for services provided to the company;
- As a preemptive right that gives existing stockholders the first chance to buy additional shares when the corporation decides to raise additional equity capital through share issuances;
- To compensate officers and other employees of the corporation (rights in this form are referred to as **stock options**);

- To enhance the marketability of other securities issued by the company (an example is issuing rights to purchase common stock with convertible bonds).

Stock rights or warrants specify the:

- Number of rights represented by the warrant
- Option price per share (which can be zero)
- Number of rights needed to obtain a share of the stock
- Expiration date of the rights
- Instructions for the exercise of rights

Accounting for stock rights is complex. The goals of this discussion are to understand the essence of (1) stock rights issued to current stockholders and (2) stock options issued to employees and others.

Stock rights issued to current stockholders have three important dates: (1) Announcement date of the rights offering; (2) Issuance date of the rights; and (3) Expiration date of the rights. Between the announcement date and the issuance date, the price of the stock will reflect the value of the rights. After the issuance date, the shares and the rights trade separately. Shareholders can exercise their rights, sell their stock, or allow the rights to lapse.

To illustrate, assume on December 10, 2009, Pfizer announces the issue of rights to purchase one additional share of its $0.05 par value common for every 10 shares currently held on January 1, 2010. The exercise price per share is $20 and the rights expire September 1, 2010. Assume further that all of the rights are exercised. Using the data in Exhibit 11.1, the accounting follows:

- No recognition is required at the announcement date and at the issuance date.
- The first entry is made when the first stock right is exercised. We give only the summary entry that would be appropriate after September 1, 2010.

Sept 1: To record the issuance of 674.6 million shares of common stock on exercise of all of the stock rights: The financial statement effects and related entries would be (amounts in millions):

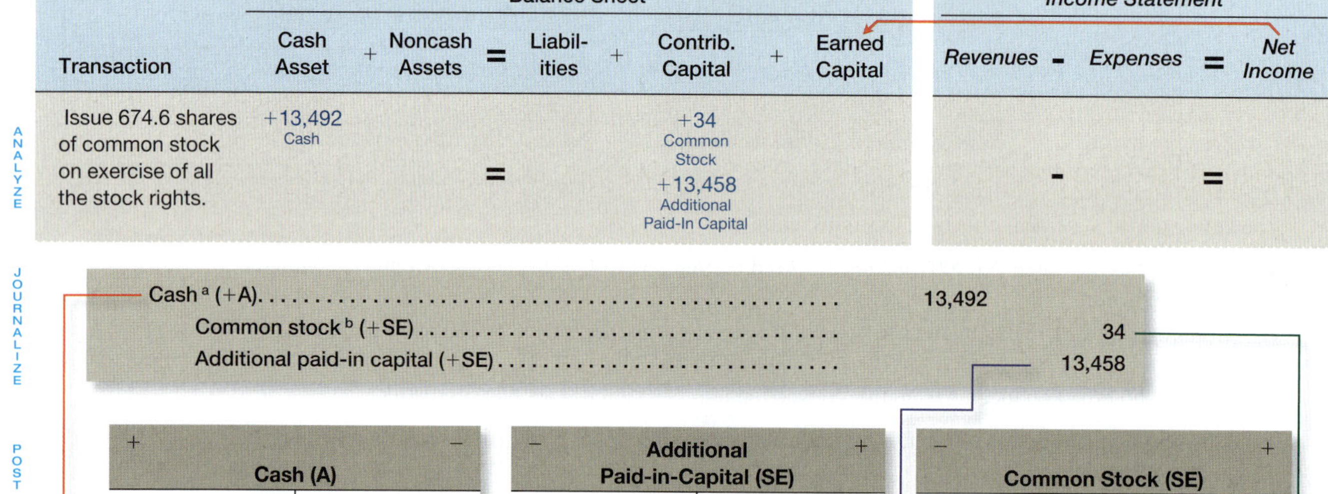

[a] [(8,863 − 2,117)/ 10] × $20 = $13,492 (See Exhibit 11.1. The 2,117 figure represents the treasury shares that were issued but were repurchased and are no longer outstanding.)

[b] [(8,863 − 2,117)/ 10] × $0.05 = $33.730 rounded to $34 for this example

Stock Options

Accounting for stock options has been a contentious issue for a number of years. Accounting standard setters, on the one hand, argue that the options to purchase a corporation's stock at a discount (or even without a discount) are valuable. They point to the willingness of senior management and others to accept stock options instead of cash in payment for services rendered as evidence of their value. Thus the FASB concluded that the fair value of each stock option award must be recognized as an expense on the firm's income statement.

However, senior managements of start-up firms typically argue that it is necessary in the face of cash shortages to compensate those providing service at least partly using stock options. If these option grants are treated as an expense, it will cause their firms to appear less profitable, thereby stifling investment and business growth. Those arguing against recognizing an expense also point to the difficulties in obtaining precise values for these options. In Note 15 to its 2008 10-K, Pfizer estimates that its stock-option expense will amount to $270 million, net of tax.

These difficulties are real, but methods of valuing options do exist that provide reasonable estimates of option values. The FASB decided that such awards are expenses and most publicly traded firms are required to report the associated expense for fiscal years beginning after December 15, 2005. The expense must be reported at the fair value of the option grant.

Stock option grants normally require a vesting period. The **vesting period** is a period of time during which the employee is not allowed to exercise the stock option. For example, a stock option may expire in 5 years and vest over a period of 3 years. Such an option would be exercisable in the fourth or fifth year of its life. Rather than recognizing the entire option value as compensation expense at the time that the option grant is awarded, GAAP requires that the fair value of the option be recorded ratably over the vesting period.

To illustrate stock option accounting, suppose that on January 1, 2010, Pfizer grants options to purchase 200,000 shares to senior management as part of its 2008 performance bonus plan. The options are granted with an exercise price of $30 (the current price), and can be exercised after vesting in 2 years. The firm uses an accepted valuation method (not discussed here) to obtain a value of $10 per share. The accounting and financial statement effects and related entries for 2008 would be:

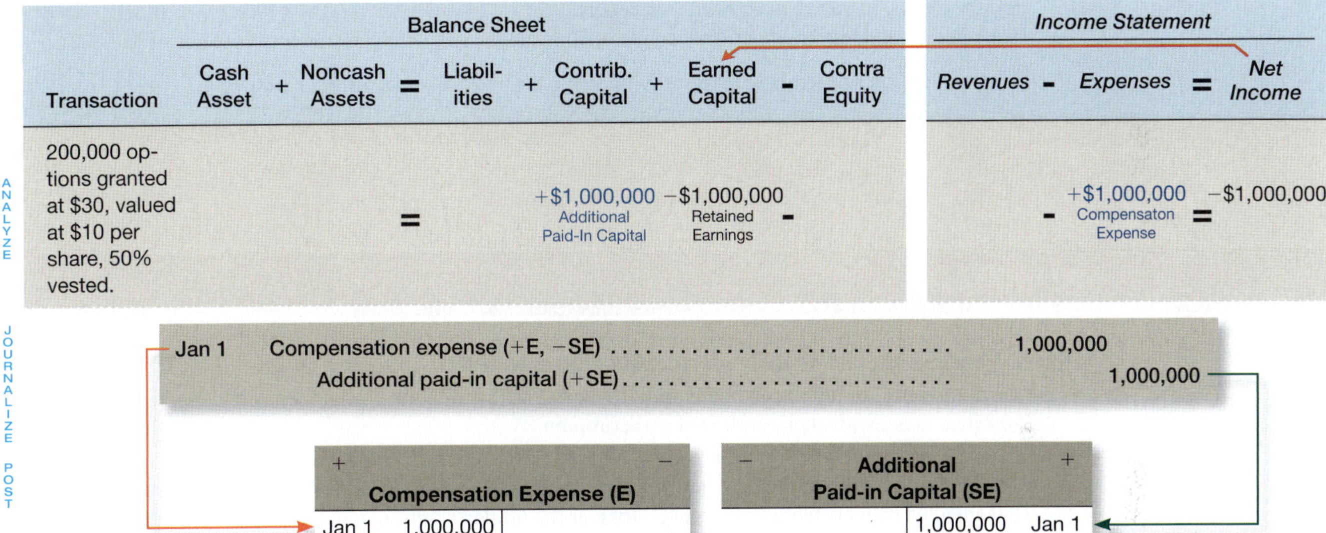

A similar entry is required in 2011, bringing the total stock-based compensation expense to $2 million. Next, suppose that its stock price rises and all options are exercised on November 15, 2012, with the stock being issued from treasury shares purchased previously at $25. The accounting and financial statement effects follow. In effect, senior management has purchased these shares by contributing $2 million in employment services and $6 million in cash.

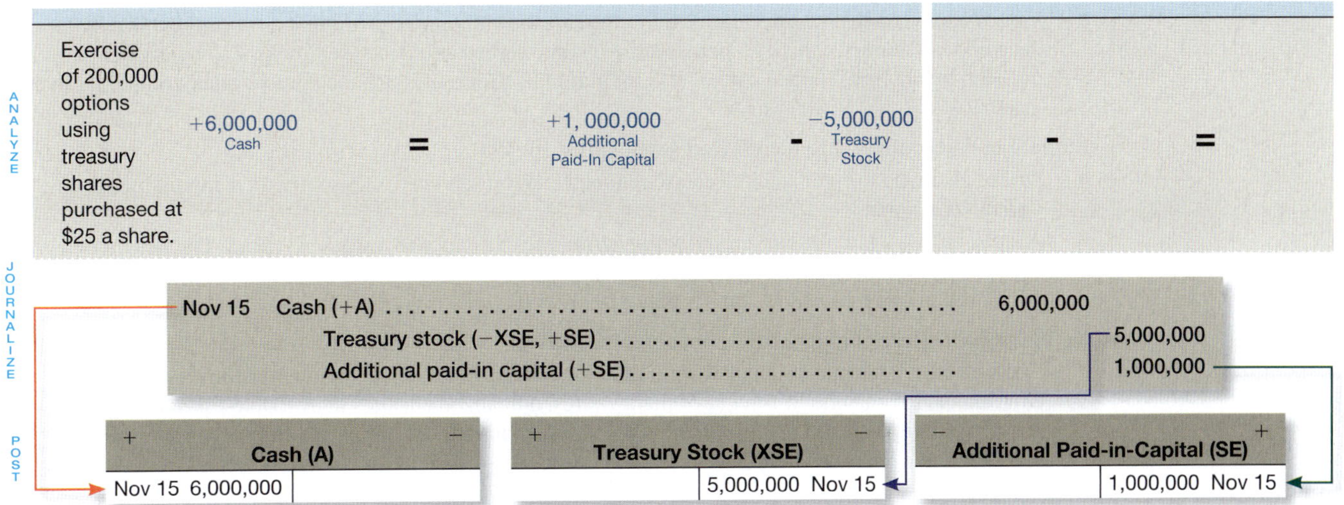

YOU MAKE THE CALL

You are the CEO   Your Board of Directors indicates that it intends to recommend that your company stop granting employee stock options because of the FASB's decision to require their expensing at fair value. What is likely to be the Board's reasoning and how would you respond? [Answer on page 513]

APPENDIX 11A REVIEW

Kallapur, Inc. has issued convertible debentures: each $1,000 bond is convertible into 200 shares of $1 par common. Assume that the bonds were sold at a discount, and that each bond has a current unamortized discount equal to $150.

Required

1. Prepare journal entries for the transaction assuming conversion of one bond.
2. Post the journal entries to the related T-accounts.
3. Using the financial statement effects template, illustrate the effects of the conversion of one of its bonds.

The solution to this review problem can be found on page 534.

SUMMARY

LO1 Describe business financing through stock issuances. (p. 490)

- Contributed capital represents the cumulative cash inflow that the company has received from the sale of various classes of stock, preferred and common.
- Preferred stock receives preference in terms of dividends before common and if cumulative receives all dividends not paid in the past before common dividends can be paid. Preferred stock can also be designated as convertible into common stock at the holder's option and at a predetermined conversion ratio. Voting privileges reside only with the common stock.

LO2 Explain and account for the issuance and repurchase of stock. (p. 494)

- Common stock is often repurchased by the firm for use in stock award programs or to signal management confidence in the company. Repurchased stock is either cancelled or held for reissue. The repurchase is debited to a contra equity account titled treasury stock.

LO3 Describe how operations increase the equity of a business. (p. 498)

- Earned capital, called retained earnings, represents the cumulative profit that has been retained by the company. Earned capital is increased by income earned and decreased by losses and dividends declared by the firm. Earned capital also includes the effects of items included in other comprehensive income.

LO4 Explain and account for dividends and stock splits. (p. 498)

- Dividends in the form of stock decrease retained earnings and increase contributed capital by an equivalent amount.
- A stock split is a proportionate distribution similar in substance to a stock dividend. The new number of shares outstanding must be disclosed. Otherwise, no further accounting is required unless the state of incorporation requires that the par value be proportionally adjusted.

LO5 Define and illustrate comprehensive income. (p. 503)

- Comprehensive income includes several additional items not recognized in net income including: adjustments for changes in foreign exchange rates, unrealized changes in available-for-sale securities, pension liability adjustments. The concept is designed to highlight impacts on equity that are beyond management's control.

Describe and illustrate the basic and diluted earnings per share computations. (p. 505)   **LO6**

- Earnings per share is a closely watched number reported for all publicly traded firms. Basic EPS is computed as the ratio of net income (less preferred dividends) to the average number of outstanding shares for the period. The value of this performance metric is subject to all the difficulties in measuring net income including the fact that net income can increase due to an acquisition that can have no impact on the number of outstanding shares.
- Most analysts are more interested in what is termed diluted earnings per share. This conservative calculation, which, if reported, never exceeds basic EPS, reflects the maximum reduction in basic EPS possible assuming conversion of the convertible securities.
- Stock options that are "in the money" are always dilutive.
- Convertible securities that would be antidilutive are treated as if they were not converted.

Appendix 11A: Analyze the accounting for convertible securities, stock rights, and stock options.   **LO7**
(p. 508)

- Convertible securities are debt and equity instruments, including stock rights, that allow these securities to be exchanged for other securities, typically common stock. The convertible feature adds value to the security to which it is attached.
- Stock options, one form of stock right, allow the holders to exchange them at a specified (strike) price for common stock. This right is valuable and should create an expense when granted to an employee or other individual. Expense recognition is appropriate, using the value obtained by applying an options-pricing model, even though the calculation is not precise. The option will not be exercised unless the market price of the common stock exceeds the strike price.
- Convertible preferred stock and convertible debt securities need to be considered in the calculation of DEPS to the extent conversion reduces reported BEPS.

GUIDANCE ANSWERS . . . YOU MAKE THE CALL

You are the Chief Financial Officer   Several points must be considered. (1) Treasury shares are likely to prop up earnings per share (EPS). While the numerator (earnings) is likely dampened by the use of cash for the stock repurchase, EPS is likely to increase because of the reduced shares in the denominator. (2) If the shares are sufficiently undervalued (in management's opinion), the stock repurchase and subsequent resale can provide a better return than some alternative investments. (3) Stock repurchases send a strong signal to the market that management feels its stock is undervalued. This is more credible than merely making that argument with analysts. On the other hand, company cash is diverted from other investments. This is bothersome if such investments are mutually exclusive either now or in the future.

You are the CEO   The Board is likely to be concerned primarily that the additional expense will lower net income from operations. In addition, the Board will indicate that the expense will be aggregated into other expenses and not subject to separate evaluation. Finally, the Board will argue that the amounts are disclosed in the footnotes, require no cash outlay, and hence, mislead investors as to the profitability of the corporation.

  While you could respond that granted options are an expense because they represent compensation to the receiving employee, you should also observe that reporting the estimated cost of stock options is proper full disclosure and gives a conservative bias to the firm's reporting that could increase the perceived quality of its reporting thereby lowering the firm's cost of capital.

KEY RATIOS

$$\text{Basic earnings per share (BEPS)} = \frac{(\text{Net income} - \text{Preferred dividends})}{\text{Weighted average number of common shares outstanding}}$$

Diluted earnings per share (DEPS) =

$$\frac{(\text{Net income} - \text{Preferred dividends} + \text{Add-backs})}{\text{Average number of common shares} + \text{Shares of convertible securities and stock options assumed to be converted}}$$

KEY TERMS

Accumulated other comprehensive income (p. 503)

Basic EPS (p. 506)

Book value per share (p. 505)

Call feature (p. 493)

Common stock (p. 491)

Complex capital structure (p. 505)

Contributed capital (p. 491)

Conversion feature (p. 493)

Convertible securities (p. 508)

Diluted EPS (p. 506)

Dilutive securities (p. 505)

Dividend preference (p. 492)

Earned capital (p. 491)

Liquidation preference (p. 492)

Participation feature (p. 493)

Par value (p. 492)

Preferred stock (p. 492)

Shares authorized (p. 491)

Shares issued (p. 492)

Shares outstanding (p. 492)

Simple capital structure (p. 506)

Stock dividends (p. 500)

Stock options (p. 509)

Stock rights (p. 509)

Stock split (p. 502)

Stock warrant (p. 509)

Treasury stock (p. 496)

Vesting period (p. 511)

MULTIPLE CHOICE

1. Suppose Pfizer issues 100,000 shares of its common stock, $0.05 par value, to obtain a warehouse and the accompanying land when the price of the stock is $22.00. Which one of the following statements is **not** true?
    a. The newly acquired assets will increase total assets by $2.2 million.
    b. Retained earnings are unaffected.
    c. The common stock account increases by $5,000.
    d. Total shareholders' equity increases by $2,195,000.

2. Assume Pfizer resells 10,000 shares of its stock that were purchased when the market price of the stock was $25. If the shares are resold for $22, which one of the following statements holds?
    a. Additional paid-in capital decreases by $30,000.
    b. The treasury stock account increases by $30,000.
    c. Additional paid-in capital increases by $30,000.
    d. The treasury stock account decreases by $30,000.

3. Suppose Pfizer declares a 200,000 common stock dividend (par $0.05) when the market value of a share is $20.00. Which one of the following statements is true?
    a. The common stock account increases by $10,000.
    b. Additional paid-in capital decreases by $3.99 million.
    c. Retained earnings increases by $4 million.
    d. Additional paid-in capital increases by $4 million.

4. Which of the following statements is true?
    a. When a *large stock dividend* is paid, retained earnings are reduced by the market value of the shares distributed.
    b. Neither stock dividends nor stock splits affect basic earnings per share calculations.
    c. A three-for-one stock split increases the total outstanding shares by 300%.
    d. A stock split has no financial statement effects because it is not a monetary transaction.

5. Which of the following statements is **not** true in relation to diluted EPS (DEPS)?
    a. Stock options that are in the money will always cause DEPS to be less than basic EPS.
    b. Convertible bonds, if dilutive, will cause changes in both the numerator and the denominator of DEPS.
    c. Stock analysts tend to concentrate their attention on DEPS instead of basic EPS.
    d. Pfizer's only equity contract that can lead to dilution is stock options.

DISCUSSION QUESTIONS

Q11-1. Define *par value stock*. What is the significance of a stock's par value from an accounting and analysis perspective?

Q11-2. What are the basic differences between preferred stock and common stock? What are the typical features of preferred stock?

Q11-3. What features make preferred stock similar to debt? Similar to common stock?

Q11-4. What is meant by dividend arrearage on preferred stock? If dividends are two years in arrears on $500,000 of 6% preferred stock, and dividends are declared at the end of this year, what amount of total dividends must preferred shareholders receive before any distributions are made to common shareholders?

Q11-5. Distinguish between authorized stock and issued stock. Why might the number of shares issued be more than the number of shares outstanding?

Q11-6. Describe the difference between contributed capital and earned capital. Specifically, how can earned capital be considered as an investment by the company's shareholders?

Q11-7. How does the account "additional paid-in capital" (APIC) arise? What inferences, if any, can you draw from the amount of APIC as reported on the balance sheet relative to the common stock amount in relation to the financial condition of the company?

Q11-8. Define *stock split*. What are the major reasons for a stock split?

Q11-9. Define *treasury stock*. Why might a corporation acquire treasury stock? How is treasury stock reported in the balance sheet?

Q11-10. If a corporation purchases 600 shares of its own common stock at $10 per share and resells them at $14 per share, where would the $2,400 increase in capital be reported in the financial statements? Why is no gain reported?

Q11-11. A corporation has total stockholders' equity of $4,628,000 and one class of $2 par value common stock. The corporation has 500,000 shares authorized; 300,000 shares issued; 260,000 shares outstanding; and 40,000 shares as treasury stock. What is its book value per share?

Q11-12. What is a stock dividend? How does a common stock dividend distributed to common shareholders affect their respective ownership interests?

Q11-13. What is the difference between the accounting for a small stock dividend and the accounting for a large stock dividend?

Q11-14. Employee stock options have a potentially dilutive effect on earnings per share (EPS) that is recognized in the diluted EPS computation. What can companies do to offset these dilutive effects and how might this action affect the balance sheet?

Q11-15. What information is reported in a statement of stockholders' equity?

Q11-16. What items are typically reported under the stockholders' equity category of other comprehensive income (OCI)?

Q11-17. What is a stock option vesting period? How does the vesting period affect the recognition of compensation expense for stock options?

Q11-18. Describe the accounting for a convertible bond. Can the conversion ever result in the recognition of a gain in the income statement?

Assignments with the WebAssign. **logo in the margin are available in WebAssign.**
See the Preface of the book for details.

MINI EXERCISES

M11-19. Analyzing and Identifying Financial Statement Effects of Stock Issuances   **LO2**
On June 1, 2010, Beatty Corp. issues (*a*) 8,000 shares of $50 par value preferred stock at $68 cash per share and it issues (*b*) 12,000 shares of $1 par value common stock at $10 cash per share. Indicate the financial statement effects of these two issuances using the financial statement effects template.

M11-20. Analyzing and Identifying Financial Statement Effects of Stock Issuances   **LO2**
On September 1, 2010, Magliolo, Inc., (*a*) issues 18,000 shares of $10 par value preferred stock at $48 cash per share and (*b*) issues 120,000 shares of $2 par value common stock at $37 cash per share.

WebAssign.

    a.   Prepare the journal entries for the two issuances.
    b.   Post the journal entries from *a* to the related T-accounts.
    c.   Using the financial statement effects template, illustrate the effects of these two issuances.

LO2   **M11-21. Distinguishing between Common Stock and Additional Paid-in Capital**

Following is the 2008 stockholders' equity section from the **Cisco Systems, Inc.,** balance sheet (in millions, except par value).

Shareholders' equity	July 26, 2008
Preferred stock, no par value: 5 shares authorized; none issued and outstanding.	$ —
Common stock and additional paid-in capital, $0.001 par value: 20,000 shares authorized: 6,100 shares issued and outstanding	33,505
Retained earnings	120
Accumulated other comprehensive income	728
Total shareholders' equity	$34,353

For the $33,505 million reported as "common stock and additional paid-in capital," what portion is common stock and what portion is additional paid-in capital? Explain.

LO2   **M11-22. Identifying and Analyzing Financial Statement Effects of Stock Issuance and Repurchase**

On January 1, 2010, Bartov Company issues 5,000 shares of $100 par value preferred stock at $250 cash per share. On March 1, the company repurchases 5,000 shares of previously issued $1 par value common stock at $83 cash per share.

    a.   Prepare the journal entries for the two transactions.
    b.   Post the journal entries from *a* to the related T-accounts.
    c.   Using the financial statement effects template, illustrate the effects of these two transactions.

LO4, LO6   **M11-23. Assessing the Financial Statement Effects of a Stock Split**

Cigna Corporation

On April 25, 2007, the Company's Board of Directors approved a three-for-one stock split (in the form of a stock dividend) of the Company's common shares. The stock split was effective on June 4, 2007, for shareholders of record on May 21, 2007. All weighted average shares, per share amounts, and references to stock compensation data for all periods have been adjusted to reflect the effect of the stock split

This note to its 2007 balance sheet further indicates that amounts have been "restated for three-for-one stock split effective June 4, 2007." What restatements has Cigna made to its balance sheet as a result of this action?

LO6   **M11-24. Computing Basic and Diluted Earnings per Share**

Zeller Corporation began 2010 with 120,000 shares of common stock and 16,000 shares of convertible preferred stock outstanding. On March 1 an additional 10,000 shares of common stock were issued. On August 1, another 16,000 shares of common stock were issued. On November 1, 6,000 shares of common stock were acquired for the treasury. The preferred stock has a $2 per-share dividend rate, and each share may be converted into one share of common stock. Zeller Corporation's 2010 net income is $501,000.

    a.   Compute basic earnings per share for 2010,
    b.   Compute diluted earnings per share for 2010.
    c.   If the preferred stock were not convertible, Zeller Corporation would have a simple capital structure. How would this change Zeller's earnings per share presentation?

LO2, LO6   **M11-25. Assessing Common Stock and Treasury Stock Balances**

Following is the stockholders' equity section from the **Abercrombie & Fitch Co.** balance sheet ($ thousands).

Shareholders' Equity	January 31, 2009
Common stock—$.01 par value: 150,000,000 shares authorized,	
103,300,000 shares issued.	$ 1,033
Paid-in capital	328,488
Retained earnings	2,244,936
Accumulated other comprehensive (loss) income, net of tax.	(22,681)
Treasury stock, at average cost 15,664,385 shares	(706,198)
Total shareholders' equity	$1,845,578

   a.   A&F has repurchased 15,664,385 shares that comprise its January 31, 2009, treasury stock account. Compute the number of outstanding shares as of January 31, 2009.

   b.   If this repurchase took place March 31, 2008, what would have been the effect on the denominator of the basic EPS calculation?

M11-26. Identifying and Analyzing Financial Statement Effects of Cash Dividends   **LO4**

Freid Corp. has outstanding 6,000 shares of $50 par value, 6% preferred stock, and 40,000 shares of $1 par value common stock. The company has $328,000 of retained earnings. At year-end, the company declares and pays the regular $3 per share cash dividend on preferred stock and a $2.20 per share cash dividend on common stock.

   a.   Prepare the journal entries for the two dividend payments.

   b.   Post the journal entries from *a* to the related T-accounts.

   c.   Using the financial statement effects template, illustrate the effects of these two dividend payments.

M11-27. Analyzing and Identifying Financial Statement Effects of Stock Dividends   **LO4**

Dutta Corp. has outstanding 70,000 shares of $5 par value common stock. At year-end, the company declares and issues a 4% common stock dividend when the market price of the stock is $21 per share.

   a.   Prepare the journal entries for the stock dividend declaration and payment.

   b.   Post the journal entries from *a* to the related T-accounts.

   c.   Using the financial statement effects template, illustrate the effects of this dividend declaration and payment.

M11-28. Analyzing, Identifying, and Explaining the Effects of a Stock Split   **LO4**

On September 1, 2010, Weiss Company has 250,000 shares of $15 par value ($165 market value) common stock that are issued and outstanding. Its balance sheet on that date shows the following account balances relating to the common stock.

Common stock	$3,750,000
Paid-in capital in excess of par value	2,250,000

On September 2, Weiss splits its stock 3-for-2 and reduces the par value to $10 per share.

   a.   How many shares of common stock are issued and outstanding immediately after the stock split?

   b.   What is the dollar balance of the common stock account immediately after the stock split?

   c.   What is the likely reason that Weiss Company split its stock?

M11-29. Distributing Cash Dividends to Preferred and Common Shareholders   **LO4**

Dechow Company has outstanding 20,000 shares of $50 par value, 6% cumulative preferred stock, and 80,000 shares of $10 par value common stock. The company declares and pays cash dividends amounting to $160,000.

   a.   If no arrearage on the preferred stock exists, how much in total dividends, and in dividends per share, is paid to each class of stock?

   b.   If one year's dividend arrearage on the preferred stock exists, how much in total dividends, and in dividends per share, is paid to each class of stock?

LO3, LO4   **M11-30. Analyzing and Preparing a Retained Earnings Reconciliation**

WebAssign.

Use the following data to prepare the 2011 retained earnings reconciliation for Bamber Company.

Total retained earnings, December 31, 2010	$347,000
Stock dividends declared and paid in 2011	28,000
Cash dividends declared and paid in 2011	35,000
Net income for 2011	94,000

LO4   **M11-31. Accounting for Large Stock Dividend and Stock Split**

Watts Corporation has 40,000 shares of $10 par value common stock outstanding and retained earnings of $820,000. The company declares a 100% stock dividend. The market price at the declaration is $17 per share.

a. Prepare the general journal entry for the stock dividend.

b. Assume that the company splits its stock two shares for one share and reduces the par value from $10 to $5 rather than declaring a 100% stock dividend. How does the accounting for the stock split differ from the accounting for the 100% stock dividend?

LO6   **M11-32. Computing Basic and Diluted Earnings per Share**

WebAssign.

During 2010, Park Corporation had 50,000 shares of $10 par value common stock and 10,000 shares of 8%, $50 par value convertible preferred stock outstanding. Each share of preferred stock may be converted into three shares of common stock. Park Corporation's 2010 net income was $440,000.

a. Compute the basic earnings per share for 2010.

b. Compute the diluted earnings per share for 2010.

LO6   **M11-33. Computing Earnings per Share**

Kingery Corporation began the year with a simple structure consisting of 38,000 shares of common stock outstanding. On May 1, 10,000 additional shares were issued, and another 1,000 shares were issued on September 1. The company had a net income for the year of $234,000.

a. Compute the earnings per share of common stock.

b. Assume that the company also had 6,000 shares of 6%, $50 par value cumulative preferred stock outstanding throughout the year. Compute the earnings per share of common stock.

LO6   **M11-34. Defining and Computing Earnings per Share**

3M COMPANY
NYSE :: MMM

3M Company reports the following basic and diluted earnings per share in its 2008 10-K report (shares in million).

a. Describe the accounting definitions for basic and diluted earnings per share.

b. Identify the 3M numbers that make up both EPS computations.

c. What calculation limits the reported value of diluted EPS?

Weighted average common shares outstanding—basic	699.2
Earnings per share—basic	$4.95
Weighted average common shares outstanding—diluted	707.2
Earnings per share—diluted	$4.89

LO7   **M11-35. Analyzing Stock Option Expense for Income**

MERCK & CO.
NYSE :: MRK

Merck & Co., Inc., reported net income of $4,631.3 million for the 2005 fiscal year. That amount included $214 million of employee stock-option compensation. In 2006, Merck adopted FAS 126 (R), which requires companies to recognize the implicit cost to shareholders of issuing options to its employees. FAS 126 (R) requires the use of a method called the fair value approach in place of the intrinsic value approach used before 2006.

Years Ended December 31 ($ millions)	2005	2004
Net income, as reported	$4,631.3	$5,813.4
Compensation expense, net of tax		
Reported	31.2	16.7
Fair value method	(357.1)	(491.8)
Pro forma net income	$4,305.4	$5,338.3

a. Why did Merck include the above table in its 10-K report?

b. What impact on Merck's 2004 and 2005 cash flows, net income and retained earnings would have been caused by the change in accounting for stock options?

c. Would the change have caused EPS to increase or decline over the period? Explain.

M11-36. Examining the Effect of Stock Transactions

LO2, LO4, LO6

Year 1: Noreen Company sells 10,000 shares of its no-par common stock for $30/share. Year 2: Noreen Company buys 1,000 shares of its no-par common stock for $28/share. Year 3: Noreen Company declares but has not yet paid a dividend on its no-par common stock of $2 per share. The company's basic earnings per share were $10 in the third year.

Indicate the effect (increase, decrease, no effect) of each of these stock decisions for each year on the items listed.

Year	Total Assets	Total Liabilities	Total S.E.	EPS	Operating Income
1					
2					
3					

M11-37. Reporting Stockholders' Equity

LO1, LO2, LO6

Bonner Company began business this year and immediately sold 600,000 common shares for $18,000,000 and paid $1,000,000 in common dividends. In midyear, the firm bought back some of its own shares. The company reports the following additional information at year-end:

Net income.	$5,000,000
Common stock	$6,000,000
Retained earnings beginning of year	$ 0
Common shares authorized:	1,000,000
Outstanding at year's end:	550,000

a. What was the average sales price of a common share?

b. What is the par value of the common?

c. How much is in the Paid-in Capital account at the end of the year?

d. Determine the retained earnings amount at the end of the year.

e. How many shares of stock are in the treasury at the end of the year?

f. Compute BEPS.

M11-38. Analyzing Earnings Per Share Effects of Convertible Securities

LO1, LO2, LO4
JETBLUE
NASDAQ :: JBLU

JetBlue Airways Corporation reports the following data in footnote 6 to its 2008 10-K. The data relate to the corporation's computation of its earnings per share calculations. Convertible debt has the same effect, if converted, as convertible preferred.

For 2008, JetBlue reports Basic EPS and Diluted EPS of $0.34.

A total of 38.3 million shares for the year ended December 31, 2008, and a total of 20.8 million shares for each of the years ended December 31, 2007 and 2006, which are issuable upon conversion of our convertible debt were excluded from the diluted earnings per share calculation since the assumed conversions would be anti-dilutive.

Required

a. What is the objective behind the calculation of diluted EPS?

b. For 2008, JetBlue excludes 38.3 million shares from its calculation of diluted EPS that would be issued upon conversion because the result would be "anti-dilutive." This action reflects the fact that inclusion of these shares in the calculation of reported diluted EPS would cause the result to exceed what value?

c. Describe, in general, the effects conversion of the debt would have on the denominator of basic EPS.

d. (Difficult) Can you think of any reason as to why JetBlue omitted these shares in the computation of diluted EPS, given that the additional shares would be added to the denominator of the ratio calculation, which alone decreases earnings per share?

EXERCISES

LO2 **E11-39. Identifying and Analyzing Financial Statement Effects of Stock Transactions**
Lipe Company reports the following 2010 transactions relating to its stock accounts.

Feb 20	Issued 10,000 shares of $1 par value common stock at $25 cash per share.
Feb 21	Issued 15,000 shares of $100 par value, 8% preferred stock at $275 cash per share.
Jun 30	Purchased 2,000 shares of its own common stock at $15 cash per share.
Sep 25	Sold 1,000 shares of the treasury stock at $21 cash per share.

a. Prepare the journal entries for these transactions.
b. Post the journal entries from *a* to the related T-accounts.
c. Using the financial statement effects template, illustrate the effects of these transactions.

LO2 **E11-40. Analyzing and Identifying Financial Statement Effects of Stock Transactions**
Web**Assign**. McNichols Corp. reports the following transactions relating to its stock accounts in 2010.

Jan 15	Issued 25,000 shares of $5 par value common stock at $17 cash per share.
Jan 20	Issued 6,000 shares of $50 par value, 8% preferred stock at $78 cash per share.
Mar 31	Purchased 3,000 shares of its own common stock at $20 cash per share.
June 25	Sold 2,000 shares of the treasury stock at $26 cash per share.
July 15	Sold the remaining 1,000 shares of treasury stock at $19 cash per share.

a. Prepare the journal entries for these transactions.
b. Post the journal entries from *a* to the related T-accounts.
c. Using the financial statement effects template, illustrate the effects of these transactions.

LO1, LO2, LO3, LO6

ABERCROMBIE & FITCH
NYSE :: ANF

E11-41. Analyzing and Computing Average Issue Price and Treasury Stock Cost
Following is the stockholders' equity section from the **Abercrombie & Fitch Co.** balance sheet.

Shareholders' Equity ($ thousands)	January 31, 2009	February 2, 2008
Class A Common stock—$.01 par value: 150,000,000 shares authorized and 103,300,000 shares issued at January 31, 2009 and February 2, 2008, respectively	$ 1,033	$ 1,033
Paid-In Capital	328,488	319,451
Retained Earnings	2,244,936	2,051,463
Accumulated Other Comprehensive Income	(22,681)	7,118
Treasury Stock, at Average Cost 14,999,945 and 15,573,789 shares at January 31, 2009 and February 2, 2008, respectively	(706,198)	(760,752)
Total Shareholders' Equity	$1,845,578	$1,618,313

a. Compute the number of shares outstanding.
b. At what average issue price were the A&F shares issued?
c. At what average cost were the A&F treasury stock shares purchased?
d. How should Treasury Stock be treated in calculating EPS?

LO4 **E11-42. Analyzing and Distributing Cash Dividends to Preferred and Common Stocks**
WebAssign. Moser Company began business on March 1, 2010. At that time, it issued 20,000 shares of $60 par value, 7% cumulative preferred stock and 100,000 shares of $5 par value common stock. Through the end of 2012, there has been no change in the number of preferred and common shares outstanding.

a. Assume that Moser declared and paid cash dividends of $0 in 2010, $183,000 in 2011, and $200,000 in 2012. Compute the total cash dividends and the dividends per share paid to each class of stock in 2010, 2011, and 2012.
b. Assume that Moser declared and paid cash dividends of $0 in 2010, $84,000 in 2011, and $150,000 in 2012. Compute the total cash dividends and the dividends per share paid to each class of stock in 2010, 2011, and 2012.

E11-43. **Computing Basic and Diluted Earnings per Share**

LO6

Nichols Corporation began the year 2010 with 25,000 shares of common stock and 5,000 shares of convertible preferred stock outstanding. On May 1, an additional 9,000 shares of common stock were issued. On July 1, 6,000 shares of common stock were acquired for the treasury. On September 1, the 6,000 treasury shares of common stock were reissued. The preferred stock has a $4 per-share dividend rate, and each share may be converted into two shares of common stock. Nichols Corporation's 2010 net income is $230,000.

   a.   Compute earnings per share for 2010.

   b.   Compute diluted earnings per share for 2010.

   c.   If the preferred stock were not convertible, Nichols Corporation would have a simple capital structure. How would this change Nichols's earnings per share presentation?

E11-44. **Analyzing and Distributing Cash Dividends to Preferred and Common Stocks**

LO4, LO6

Potter Company has outstanding 15,000 shares of $50 par value, 8% preferred stock and 50,000 shares of $5 par value common stock. During its first three years in business, it declared and paid no cash dividends in the first year, $280,000 in the second year, and $60,000 in the third year.

   a.   If the preferred stock is cumulative, determine the total amount of cash dividends paid to each class of stock in each of the three years.

   b.   If the preferred stock is noncumulative, determine the total amount of cash dividends paid to each class of stock in each of the three years.

   c.   How should each type of preferred dividends be treated in calculating EPS?

E11-45. **Analyzing and Computing Issue Price, Treasury Stock Cost, and Shares Outstanding**

LO2

Following is the stockholders' equity section from **Altria Group, Inc.**'s balance sheet ($ million).

ALTRIA
NYSE :: MO

December 31 ($ millions)	2008	2007
Stockholders' Equity		
Common stock, par value $0.33 1/3 per share		
(2,805,961,317 shares issued).	$ 935	$ 935
Additional paid-in capital	6,350	6,884
Earnings reinvested in the business	22,131	34,426
Accumulated other comprehensive (losses) earnings	(2,181)	111
Cost of repurchased stock (744,589,733 shares in 2008 and	(24,407)	(23,454)
698,284,555 shares in 2007)		
Total stockholders' equity	$ 2,828	$18,902

   a.   Show the computation to derive the $935 million for common stock.

   b.   At what average price has Altria issued its common stock?

   c.   How many shares of Altria common stock are outstanding as of December 31, 2008?

   d.   At what average cost has Altria repurchased its treasury stock as of December 31, 2008?

   e.   Give 3 reasons why a company such as Altria would want to repurchase more than $24 billion of its common stock.

E11-46. **Analyzing and Distributing Cash Dividends to Preferred and Common Stocks**

LO4

Skinner Company began business on June 30, 2009. At that time, it issued 18,000 shares of $50 par value, 6% cumulative preferred stock and 90,000 shares of $10 par value common stock. Through the end of 2011, there has been no change in the number of preferred and common shares outstanding.

   a.   Assume that Skinner declared and paid cash dividends of $63,000 in 2009, $0 in 2010, and $378,000 in 2011. Compute the total cash dividends and the dividends per share paid to each class of stock in 2009, 2010, and 2011.

   b.   Assume that Skinner declared and paid cash dividends of $0 in 2009, $108,000 in 2010, and $189,000 in 2011. Compute the total cash dividends and the dividends per share paid to each class of stock in 2009, 2010, and 2011.

E11-47. **Analyzing and Identifying Financial Statement Effects of Dividends**

LO4

Chaney Company has outstanding 25,000 shares of $10 par value common stock. It also has $405,000 of retained earnings. Near the current year-end, the company declares and pays a cash dividend of $1.90 per share and declares and issues a 4% stock dividend. The market price of the stock at the declaration date is $35 per share.

a. Prepare the journal entries for these two separate dividend transactions.

b. Post the journal entries from *a* to the related T-accounts.

c. Using the financial statement effects template, illustrate the effects of these two separate dividends.

LO4 **E11-48.** **Identifying and Analyzing Financial Statement Effects of Dividends**

Web**Assign**.

The stockholders' equity of Palepu Company at December 31, 2010, appears below.

Common stock, $10 par value, 200,000 shares authorized;	
80,000 shares issued and outstanding	$800,000
Paid-in capital in excess of par value	480,000
Retained earnings	305,000

During 2011, the following transactions occurred:

May 12   Declared and issued a 7% stock dividend; the common stock market value was $18 per share.

Dec. 31   Declared and paid a cash dividend of 75 cents per share.

a. Prepare the journal entries for these transactions.

b. Post the journal entries from *a* to the related T-accounts.

c. Using the financial statement effects template, illustrate the effects of these transactions.

d. Prepare a retained earnings reconciliation for 2011 assuming that the company reports 2011 net income of $283,000.

LO4 **E11-49.** **Analyzing and Identifying Financial Statement Effects of Dividends**

The stockholders' equity of Kinney Company at December 31, 2010, is shown below:

5% preferred stock, $100 par value, 10,000 shares authorized;	
4,000 shares issued and outstanding	$ 400,000
Common stock, $5 par value, 200,000 shares authorized;	
50,000 shares issued and outstanding	250,000
Paid-in capital in excess of par value—preferred stock	40,000
Paid-in capital in excess of par value—common stock	300,000
Retained earnings	656,000
Total stockholders' equity	$1,646,000

The following transactions, among others, occurred during 2011.

Apr. 1   Declared and issued a 100% stock dividend on all outstanding shares of common stock. The market value of the stock was $11 per share.

Dec. 7   Declared and issued a 3% stock dividend on all outstanding shares of common stock. The market value of the stock was $14 per share.

Dec. 20   Declared and paid (1) the annual cash dividend on the preferred stock and (2) a cash dividend of 80 cents per common share.

a. Prepare the journal entries for these transactions.

b. Post the journal entries from *a* to the related T-accounts.

c. Using the financial statement effects template, illustrate the effects of these transactions.

d. Prepare a 2011 retained earnings reconciliation assuming that the company reports 2011 net income of $253,000.

LO4, LO6 **E11-50.** **Analyzing, Identifying, and Explaining the Effects of a Stock Split**

WebStudies**Assign**.

On March 1 of the current year, Xie Company has 400,000 shares of $20 par value common stock that are issued and outstanding. Its balance sheet shows the following account balances relating to common stock.

Common stock	$8,000,000
Paid-in capital in excess of par value	3,400,000

On March 2, Xie Company splits its common stock 2-for-1 and reduces the par value to $10 per share.

a. How many shares of common stock are issued and outstanding immediately after the stock split?

b. What is the dollar balance in its common stock account immediately after the stock split?

c. What is the dollar balance in its paid-in capital in excess of par value account immediately after the stock split?

d. What is the effect of a stock split on the calculation of EPS?

E11-51. Analyzing and Computing Issue Price, Treasury Stock Cost, and Shares Outstanding
Following is the stockholders' equity section of the **Caterpillar Inc.** balance sheet.

LO4
CATERPILLAR INC.
NYSE :: CAT

Stockholders' equity ($ millions)	2008	2007	2006
Common stock of $1.00 par value			
Authorized shares: 900,000,000			
Issued shares (2008, 2007 and 2006—814,894,624)			
at paid-in amount	$ 3,057	$ 2,744	$2,465
Treasury stock (2008—213,367,983 shares; 2007—190,908,490			
shares and 2006—169,086,448 shares) at cost	(11,217)	(9,451)	(7,352)
Profit employed in the business	19,826	17,398	14,593
Accumulated other comprehensive income	(5,579)	(1,808)	(2,847)
Total stockholders' equity	**$ 6,087**	**$ 8,883**	**$6,859**

a. How many shares of Caterpillar common stock are outstanding at year-end 2008?

b. What does the phrase "at paid-in amount" mean?

c. At what average cost has Caterpillar repurchased its stock as of year-end 2008?

d. Why would a company such as Caterpillar want to repurchase its common stock?

e. Explain how the repurchase affects the computation of EPS.

E11-52. Analyzing and Computing Issue Price, Treasury Stock Cost, and Shares Outstanding
Following is the stockholders' equity section of the **Merck & Co., Inc.**, balance sheet.

LO2
MERCK & CO.
NYSE :: MRK

($ millions)	Dec. 31, 2008	Dec. 31, 2007
Stockholders' equity		
Common stock, one cent par value		
Authorized—5,400,000,000 shares		
Issued—2,983,508,675 shares—2008 and 2007	$ 29.8	$ 29.8
Other paid-in capital	8,319.1	8,014.9
Retained earnings	43,698.8	39,140.8
Accumulated other comprehensive income	(2,553.9)	(826.1)
	49,493.8	46,359.4
Less treasury stock, at cost		
875,818,333 shares—2008, 811,005,791 shares—2007	30,735.5	28,174.7
Total stockholders' equity	$18,758.3	$18,184.7

a. Explain the derivation of the $29.8 million in the common stock account.

b. Using December 31, 2008, balances, at what average issue price were the Merck common shares issued?

c. At what average cost was the Merck treasury stock purchased in 2008?

d. How many common shares are outstanding as of December 31, 2008?

E11-53. Assessing Effects of Employee Stock Options for Income and EPS
The following data is taken from the December 31, 2008, income statement of **Viacom, Inc.**, ($ in millions, except per share). Viacom has neither preferred stock nor convertible securities outstanding.

LO7
VIACOM, INC.
NYSE :: VIA

Year Ended December 31	2008	2007	2006
Net earnings	$1,251	$1,838	$1,592
Basic earnings per common share amounts:			
Earnings per share, continuing operations	$ 1.97	$ 2.42	$ 2.19
Earnings per share, discontinued operations	$ 0.03	$ 0.31	$ 0.04
Net earnings per share	$ 2.00	$ 2.73	$ 2.23
Diluted earnings per common share amounts:			
Earnings per share, continuing operations	$ 1.97	$ 2.41	$ 2.19
Earnings per share, discontinued operations	$ 0.03	$ 0.31	$ 0.03
Net earnings per share	$ 2.00	$ 2.72	$ 2.22
Weighted average number of common shares outstanding:			
Basic	624.7	674.1	715.2
Diluted	625.4	675.6	716.2

a. Did Viacom have either gains or losses from *extraordinary* items in 2008? Did Viacom experience a change in accounting principle in 2008? How do you know?

b. Estimate Viacom's 2008 gain (loss) from discontinued operations in 2008. Was it a gain or loss? Is the amount you calculated before or after tax?

c. Estimate Viacom's net earnings from continuing operations in 2008.

d. Viacom reports diluted earnings per share of $2.72 in 2007. What might have caused the dilution?

LO2, LO4, LO6

PROCTER & GAMBLE
NYSE :: PG

E11-54. Determining the Items Missing from an Annual Report

The Procter & Gamble Company reports the following information for the year ended in June 30, 2009 ($ millions):

Operating income:	$16,123	Net earnings:	$13,436
Common dividends/share:	$ 1.64	Preferred dividends:	$ 192
Basic EPS:	$4.49/share	Diluted EPS:	$4.26/share
Share price 6/30/2009:	$ 54.77	Par value of common:	$ 1.00
Common stock (in $ millions) 6/30/2009:			$4,007 and $4,002 at 6/30/2008
Treasury shares (in shares) 6/30/2009:			1,090.3 and 969.1 at 6/30/2008

a. Estimate the average number of common shares outstanding for the year.

b. Calculate the dividend yield ratio (Common dividend per share/Price per share) for the year. Would investors requiring cash find this stock an attractive investment?

c. P & G has no convertible debt. What could explain the reported DEPS?

d. How many additional shares of common stock are outstanding in June 2009 versus June 30, 2008?

PROBLEMS

LO2, LO6

WebAssign.

P11-55. Analyzing and Identifying Financial Statement Effects of Stock Transactions

The stockholders' equity section of Gupta Company at December 31, 2010, follows.

8% preferred stock, $25 par value, 50,000 shares authorized;	
6,800 shares issued and outstanding	$170,000
Common stock, $10 par value, 200,000 shares authorized;	
50,000 shares issued and outstanding	500,000
Paid-in capital in excess of par value—preferred stock	68,000
Paid-in capital in excess of par value—common stock	200,000
Retained earnings	270,000

During 2010, the following transactions occurred:

Jan. 10   Issued 28,000 shares of common stock for $17 cash per share.

Jan. 23   Purchased 8,000 shares of common stock for the treasury at $19 cash per share.

Mar. 14   Sold one-half of the treasury shares acquired January 23 for $21 cash per share.

July 15   Issued 3,200 shares of preferred stock for $128,000 cash.

Nov. 15   Sold 1,000 of the treasury shares acquired January 23 for $24 cash per share.

Required

a.   Prepare the journal entries for these transactions.

b.   Post the journal entries from *a* to the related T-accounts.

c.   Using the financial statement effects template, illustrate the effects of each transaction.

d.   Indicate the impact of each transaction on the calculation of basic EPS.

e.   Prepare the December 31, 2011, stockholders' equity section of the balance sheet assuming the company reports 2011 net income of $59,000.

P11-56.   Analyzing and Identifying Financial Statement Effects of Stock Transactions   LO2, LO6

The stockholders' equity of Sougiannis Company at December 31, 2010, follows.

7% Preferred stock, $100 par value, 20,000 shares authorized; 5,000 shares issued and outstanding	$ 500,000
Common stock, $15 par value, 100,000 shares authorized; 40,000 shares issued and outstanding	600,000
Paid-in capital in excess of par value—preferred stock	24,000
Paid-in capital in excess of par value—common stock	360,000
Retained earnings	325,000
Total stockholders' equity	$1,809,000

The following transactions, among others, occurred during the year.

Jan. 12   Announced a 3-for-1 common stock split, reducing the par value of the common stock to $5 per share. The authorized shares were increased to 300,000 shares.

Sept. 1   Acquired 10,000 shares of common stock for the treasury at $10 cash per share.

Oct. 12   Sold 1,500 treasury shares acquired September 1 at $12 cash per share.

Nov. 21   Issued 5,000 shares of common stock at $11 cash per share.

Dec. 28   Sold 1,200 treasury shares acquired September 1 at $9 cash per share.

Required

a.   Prepare the journal entries for these transactions.

b.   Post the journal entries from *a* to the related T-accounts.

c.   Using the financial statement effects template, illustrate the effects of each transaction.

d.   Indicate the impact of each transaction on the calculation of basic EPS.

e.   Prepare the December 31, 2011, stockholders' equity section of the balance sheet assuming that the company reports 2011 net income of $83,000.

P11-57.   Identifying and Analyzing Financial Statement Effects of Stock Transactions   LO2, LO6

The stockholders' equity of Verrecchia Company at December 31, 2010, follows.

Web**Assign**.

Common stock, $5 par value, 350,000 shares authorized; 150,000 shares issued and outstanding	$750,000
Paid-in capital in excess of par value	600,000
Retained earnings	346,000

During 2011, the following transactions occurred.

Jan. 5   Issued 10,000 shares of common stock for $12 cash per share.

Jan. 18   Purchased 4,000 shares of common stock for the treasury at $14 cash per share.

Mar 12   Sold one-fourth of the treasury shares acquired January 18 for $17 cash per share.

July 17   Sold 500 shares of the remaining treasury stock for $13 cash per share.

Oct. 1   Issued 5,000 shares of 8%, $25 par value preferred stock for $35 cash per share. This is the first issuance of preferred shares from 50,000 authorized shares.

Required

a.   Prepare the journal entries for these transactions.

b.   Post the journal entries from *a* to the related T-accounts.

c.   Using the financial statement effects template, illustrate the effects of each transaction.

   d. Prepare the December 31, 2011, stockholders' equity section of the balance sheet assuming that the company reports net income of $72,500 for the year.

   e. How will each transaction affect the calculation of basic EPS?

LO2, LO4 **P11-58. Identifying and Analyzing Financial Statement Effects of Stock Transactions**

Following is the stockholders' equity of Dennis Corporation at December 31, 2010.

8% preferred stock, $50 par value, 10,000 shares authorized; 7,000 shares issued and outstanding	$ 350,000
Common stock, $20 par value, 50,000 shares authorized; 25,000 shares issued and outstanding	500,000
Paid-in capital in excess of par value—preferred stock	70,000
Paid-in capital in excess of par value—common stock	385,000
Retained earnings	238,000
Total stockholders' equity	$1,543,000

The following transactions, among others, occurred during the year.

Jan. 15	Issued 1,000 shares of preferred stock for $62 cash per share.
Jan. 20	Issued 4,000 shares of common stock at $36 cash per share.
May 18	Announced a 2-for-1 common stock split, reducing the par value of the common stock to $10 per share. The authorization was increased to 100,000 shares.
June 1	Issued 2,000 shares of common stock for $60,000 cash.
Sept. 1	Purchased 2,500 shares of common stock for the treasury at $18 cash per share.
Oct. 12	Sold 900 treasury shares at $21 cash per share.
Dec. 22	Issued 500 shares of preferred stock for $59 cash per share.

Required

   a. Prepare the journal entries for these transactions.

   b. Post the journal entries from *a* to the related T-accounts.

   c. Using the financial statement effects template, illustrate the effects of each transaction.

LO2, LO5, LO7 **P11-59. Analyzing and Interpreting Equity Accounts and Comprehensive Income**

PROCTER & GAMBLE
NYSE :: PG

Following is the stockholders' equity section of the balance sheet for **The Procter & Gamble Company** and its statement of stockholders' equity.

Shareholders' Equity ($ millions)	2009	2008
Convertible Class A preferred stock, stated value $1 per share (600 shares authorized)	$ 1,324	$ 1,366
Non-voting Class B preferred stock, stated value $1 per share (200 shares authorized)	—	—
Common stock, stated value $1 per share (10,000 shares authorized; issued: 2009—4,007.3, 2008—4,001.8)	4,007	4,002
Additional paid-in capital	61,118	60,307
Reserve for ESOP debt retirement	(1,340)	(1,325)
Accumulated other comprehensive income (loss)	(3,358)	3,746
Treasury stock, at cost (shares held: 2009—1,090.3, 2008—969.1)	(55,961)	(47,588)
Retained earnings	57,309	48,986
Total shareholders' equity	63,099	69,494

Consolidated Statements of Shareholders' Equity

Dollars in millions/ Shares in thousands	Common Shares Outstanding	Common Stock	Preferred Stock	Additional Paid-In Capital	Reserve for ESOP Debt Retirement	Accumulated Other Comprehensive Income	Treasury Stock	Retained Earnings	Total
Balance June 30, 2008	3,032,717	$4,002	$1,366	$60,307	$(1,325)	$ 3,746	$(47,588)	$48,986	$69,494
Net earnings								13,436	13,436
Other comprehensive income:									
Financial statement translation						(6,151)			(6,151)
Hedges and investment securities, net of $452 tax. .						748			748
Defined benefit retirement plans, net of $879 tax						(1,701)			(1,701)
Total comprehensive income									$ 6,332
Cumulative impact for adoption of new accounting guidance.								(84)	(84)
Dividends to shareholders:									
Common.								(4,852)	(4,852)
Preferred, net of tax benefit								(192)	(192)
Treasury purchases.	(98,862)						(6,730)		(6,370)
Employee plan issuances	16,841	5		804			428		1,237
Preferred stock conversions.	4,992		(42)	7			35		—
Shares tendered for Folgers coffee subsidiary	(38,653)						(2,466)		(2,466)
ESOP debt impacts.					(15)			15	
Balance June 30, 2009	2,917,035	$4,007	$1,324	$61,118	$(1,340)	$(3,358)	$(55,961)	$57,309	$63,099

Required

a. How many shares of convertible Class A preferred stock are issued at fiscal year-end 2009?

b. What does the term *convertible* mean?

c. Show (confirm) the computation yielding the $4,007 million for common stock at year-end 2009.

d. Assuming that the convertible Class A preferred stock was sold at par value, at what average price were the common shares issued as of year-end 2009?

e. What is the Accumulated Other Comprehensive Income account? Explain.

f. What items are included in the $6,332 million "total comprehensive income" at year-end 2009? How do these items affect stockholders' equity?

g. What amount of cash dividends was paid in 2009 for each of P & G's classes of stock?

h. In which statement is comprehensive income reported under IFRS.

P11-60. Analyzing and Interpreting Equity Accounts and Comprehensive Income

LO5, LO7

FORTUNE BRANDS
NYSE :: FO

Following is the stockholders' equity section of **Fortune Brands, Inc.**, balance sheet and its statement of stockholders' equity.

Stockholders' equity ($ millions except per share amounts)	2008	2007
$2.67 Convertible preferred stock	$ 5.5	$ 5.7
Common stock, par value $3.125 per share, 234.9 shares issued.	734.0	734.0
Paid-in capital.	716.4	684.3
Accumulated other comprehensive income (loss)	478.4	349.1
Retained earnings.	7,046.2	6,999.3
Treasury stock, at cost.	(3,337.7)	(3,086.9)
Total stockholders' equity	$4,686.0	$5,685.5

Consolidated Statement of Stockholders' Equity
Fortune Brands, Inc. and Subsidiaries

(In millions except per share amounts)	$2.67 Convertible Preferred Stock	Common Stock	Paid-In Capital	Accumulated Other Comprehensive Income (Loss)	Retained Earnings	Treasury Stock, At Cost	Total
Balance at December 31, 2007..............	$5.7	$734.0	$684.3	$349.1	$6,999.3	$(3,086.9)	$5,685.5
Comprehensive income							
Net income	—	—	—	—	311.1	—	311.1
Translation adjustments, net of effect of hedging activities (net of tax benefit of $27.5 million)........................	—	—	—	(659.7)	—	—	(659.7)
Pension and postretirement benefit adjustments (net of tax benefit of $105.0 million).......................	—	—	—	(167.8)	—	—	(167.8)
Total comprehensive income (loss)	—	—	—	(827.5)	311.1	—	(516.4)
Dividends ($1.72 per Common share and $2.67 per Preferred share)	—	—	—	—	(261.2)	—	(261.2)
Treasury stock purchases.................	—	—	—	—	—	(278.6)	(278.6)
Stock-based compensation	—	—	30.3	—	(3.0)	25.6	52.9
Tax benefit on exercise of stock options.....	—	—	3.8	—	—	—	3.8
Conversion of preferred stock	(0.2)	—	(2.0)	—	—	2.2	—
Balance at December 31, 2008.............	$5.5	$734.0	$716.4	$478.4	$7,046.2	$(3,337.7)	$4,686.0

Required

a.   Explain the "$2.67" as reported in the convertible preferred stock account title.

b.   Show (confirm) the computation that yields the $734 million common stock in 2008.

c.   Assuming that the convertible preferred stock was sold at par value, at what average price were the common shares issued as of year-end 2008?

d.   What accounts typically comprise the Accumulated Other Comprehensive Income (or loss) account? What accounts are included in Fortune Brands' accumulated comprehensive income and loss adjustments for 2008?

e.   Estimate the average amount Fortune Brands paid for its treasury shares. The company reports 84,775,617 shares of treasury stock at December 31, 2008. What effect did the dividend payment of $1.72 per common share have on the stockholders' equity of Fortune Brands?

CASES AND PROJECTS

LO7   **C11-61. Interpreting Disclosure on Convertible Preferred Securities**

NORTHROP GRUMMAN
NYSE :: NOC

Northrop Grumman Corporation reports the following in footnote 4 to its 2008 10-K related to its convertible preferred stock.

Conversion of Preferred Stock – On February 20, 2008, the company's board of directors approved the redemption of the 3.5 million shares of mandatorily redeemable convertible preferred stock on April 4, 2008. Prior to the redemption date, substantially all of the preferred shares were converted into common stock at the election of shareholders. All remaining unconverted preferred shares were redeemed by the company on the redemption date. As a result of the conversion and redemption, the company issued approximately 6.4 million shares of common stock.

Required

a.   What do you believe is meant by the terms "mandatorily redeemable" prior to the words "preferred stock"?

b.   Northrop's balance sheet at December 31, 2007, shows preferred stock of $350 million and $0 million on December 31, 2008. Northrop originally sold the preferred shares at par. What was the preferred par value per share?

c.   The fair market value of a preferred share, as reported by Northrop on December 31, 2008, was $146. What could account for the substantial increase in the value per share?

d.   How should preferred stock be treated in an analysis of a company?

e.   Discuss the general effects of the April 4th conversion on Northrop Grumman's balance sheet.

C11-62.   Identifying Corporate Takeover, Stock Ownership, and Managerial Ethics   LO1, LO2, LO3

Ron King, chairperson of the board of directors and chief executive officer of Image, Inc., is pondering a recommendation to make to the firm's board of directors in response to actions taken by Jack Hatcher. Hatcher recently informed King and other board members that he (Hatcher) had purchased 15% of the voting stock of Image at $12 per share and is considering an attempt to take control of the company. His effort to take control would include offering $16 per share to stockholders to induce them to sell shares to him. Hatcher also indicated that he would abandon his takeover plans if the company would buy back his stock at a price 50% over its current market price of $13 per share.

King views the proposed takeover by Hatcher as a hostile maneuver. Hatcher has a reputation of identifying companies that are undervalued (that is, their underlying net assets are worth more than the price of the outstanding stock), buying enough stock to take control of such a company, replacing top management, and, on occasion, breaking up the company (that is, selling off the various divisions to the highest bidder). The process has proven profitable to Hatcher and his financial backers. Stockholders of the companies taken over also benefited because Hatcher paid them attractive prices to buy their stock.

King recognizes that Image is currently undervalued by the stock market but believes that eventually the company will significantly improve its financial performance to the long-run benefit of its stockholders.

Required

What are the ethical issues that King should consider in arriving at a recommendation to make to the board of directors regarding Hatcher's offer to be "bought out" of his takeover plans?

C11-63.   Understanding Shareholders' Meeting, Managerial Communications, and Financial   LO1, LO2, LO3
Interpretations

The stockholders' equity section of Pillar Corporation's comparative balance sheet at the end of 2010 and 2011 is presented below. It is part of the financial data just reviewed at a stockholders' meeting.

	December 31, 2011	December 31, 2010
Common Stock, $10 Par Value, 600,000 shares authorized; issued at December 31, 2011, 275,000 shares; 2010, 250,000 shares	$ 2,750,000	$2,500,000
Paid-in Capital in Excess of Par	4,575,000	4,125,000
Retained Earnings (see Note)	2,960,000	2,825,000
Total Stockholders' Equity	$10,285,000	$9,450,000

Note: Availability of retained earnings for cash dividends is restricted by $2,000,000 due to a planned plant expansion.

The following items were also disclosed at the stockholders' meeting: net income for 2011 was $1,220,000; a 10% stock dividend was issued December 14, 2011; when the stock dividend was declared, the market value was $28 per share; the market value per share at December 31, 2011, was $26; management plans to borrow $500,000 to help finance a new plant addition, which is expected to cost a total of $2,300,000; and the customary $1.54 per share cash dividend had been revised to $1.40 when declared and issued the last week of December 2011. As part of its investor relations program, during the stockholders' meeting management asked stockholders to write any questions they might have concerning the firm's operations or finances. As assistant controller, you are given the stockholders' questions.

Required

Prepare brief but reasonably complete answers to the following questions:

a. What did Pillar do with the cash proceeds from the stock dividend issued in December?

b. What was my book value per share at the end of 2010 and 2011?

c. I owned 7,500 shares of Pillar in 2010 and have not sold any shares. How much more or less of the corporation do I own at December 31, 2011, and what happened to the market value of my interest in the company?

d. I heard someone say that stock dividends don't give me anything I didn't already have. Why did you issue one? Are you trying to fool us?

e. Instead of a stock dividend, why didn't you declare a cash dividend and let us buy the new shares that were issued?

f. Why are you cutting back on the dividends I receive?

g. If you have $2,000,000 put aside in retained earnings for the new plant addition, which will cost $2,300,000, why are you borrowing $500,000 instead of just the $300,000 needed?

LO2, LO3 **C11-64.** **Assessing Stock Buybacks, Corporate Accountability, and Managerial Ethics**

Liz Plummer, vice president and general counsel, chairs the Executive Compensation Committee for Sunlight Corporation. Four and one-half years ago, the compensation committee designed a performance bonus plan for top management that was approved by the board of directors. The plan provides an attractive bonus for top management if the firm's earnings per share grows each year over a five-year period. The plan is now in its fifth year; for the past four years, earnings per share has grown each year. Last year, earnings per share was $1.95 (net income was $7,800,000 and the weighted average common shares outstanding was 4,000,000). Sunlight Corporation has no preferred stock and has had 4,000,000 common shares outstanding for several years. Plummer has recently seen an estimate that Sunlight's net income this year will decrease about 5% from last year because of a slight recession in the economy.

Plummer is disturbed by an item on the agenda for the board of directors meeting on June 20 and an accompanying note from Rob Lundy. Lundy is vice president and chief financial officer for Sunlight. Lundy is proposing to the board that Sunlight buy back 600,000 shares of its own common stock on July 1. Lundy's explanation is that the firm's stock is undervalued now and that Sunlight has excess cash available. When the stock subsequently recovers in value, Lundy notes, Sunlight will reissue the shares and generate a nice increase in contributed captal.

Lundy's note to Plummer merely states, "Look forward to your support of my proposal at the board meeting."

Required

Why is Plummer disturbed by Lundy's proposal and note? What possible ethical problem does Plummer face when Lundy's proposal is up for a vote at the board meeting?

SOLUTIONS TO REVIEW PROBLEMS

Mid-Chapter Review 1

Solution

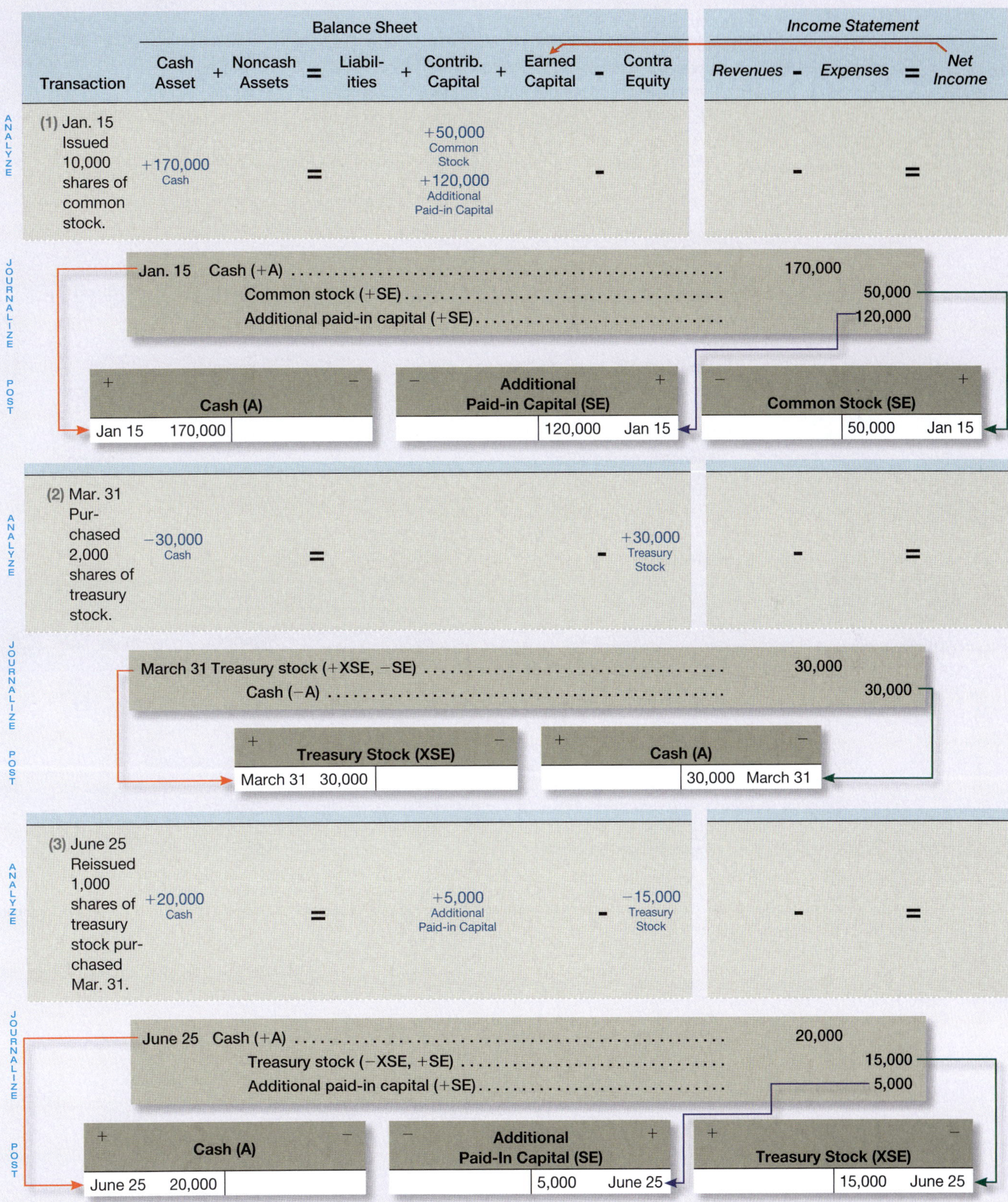

Mid-Chapter Review 2

Solution

a.

	Preferred Stock	Common Stock
Year 1.	$ 0	$ 0
Year 2		
Arrearage from Year 1 ($1,000,000 × 5%).	50,000	
Current-year dividend ($1,000,000 × 5%).	50,000	
Balance to common		200,000
Year 3		
Current-year dividend ($1,000,000 × 5%).	50,000	
Balance to common		30,000

b.

	Preferred Stock	Common Stock
Year 1.	$ 0	$ 0
Year 2		
Current-year dividend ($1,000,000 × 5%).	50,000	
Balance to common		250,000
Year 3		
Current-year dividend ($1,000,000 × 5%).	50,000	
Balance to common		30,000

Mid-Chapter Review 3

Solution

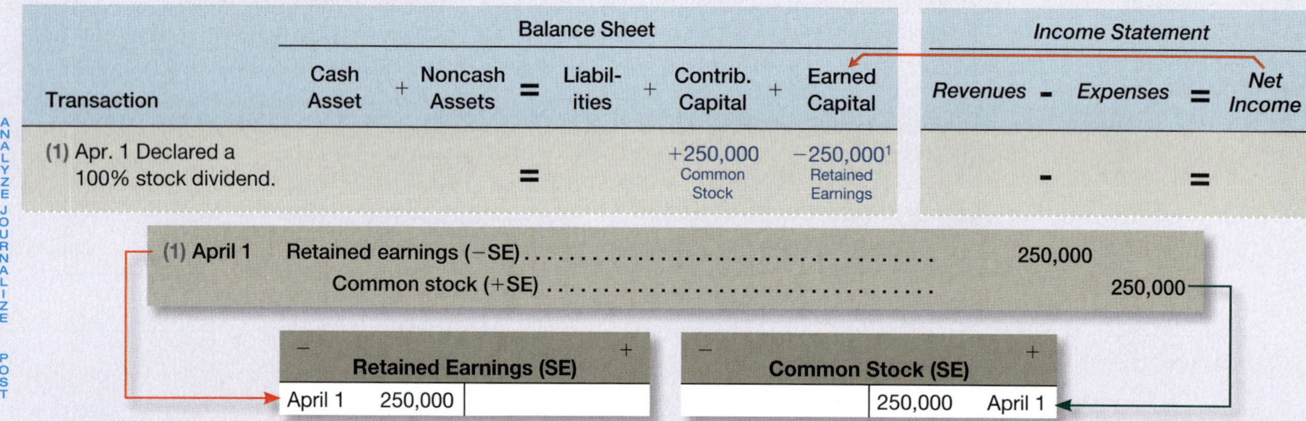

¹ This large stock dividend reduces retained earnings at the par value of shares distributed (50,000 shares × 100% × $5 par value = $250,000). Contributed capital (common stock) increases by the same amount.

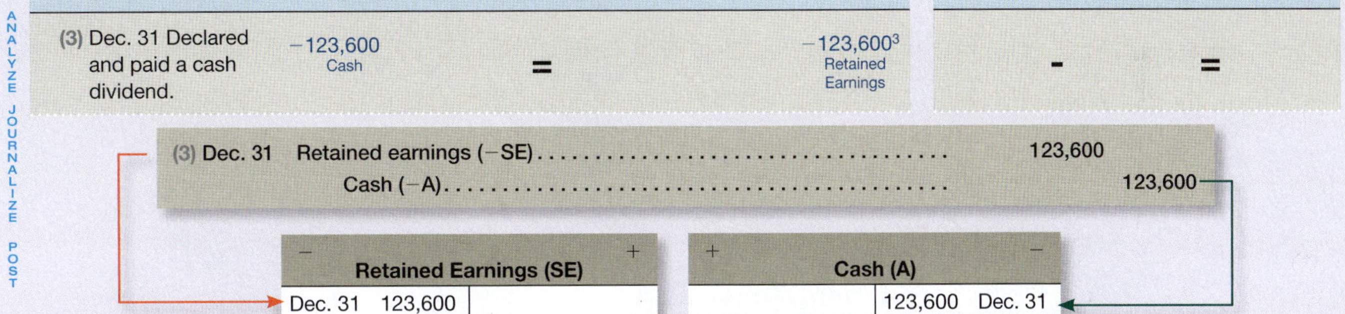

[2] This small stock dividend reduces retained earnings at the market value of shares distributed (3% × 100,000 shares × $7 per share = $21,000). Contributed capital increases by the same amount ($15,000 to common stock and $6,000 to paid-in capital).

[3] At the time of the cash dividend, there are 103,000 shares outstanding. The cash paid is, therefore, 103,000 shares × $1.20 per share = $123,600.

Mid-Chapter Review 4

Solution

Retained Earnings Reconciliation For Year Ended December 31, 2011		
Retained earnings, December 31, 2010		$513,000
Add: Net income		412,000
		925,000
Less: Cash dividends declared [160,000 + .10(160,000)][$1.25]	$220,000	
Stock dividends declared (160,000)(.10)($11)	176,000	396,000
Retained earnings, December 31, 2011		$529,000

Chapter-End Review

Solution

1. Basic EPS would be calculated as follows (millions, except per share amount):

$$\text{Basic EPS} = \frac{\$1{,}750 - \$40}{760 \text{ shares}} = \$2.25 \text{ per share}$$

2. Diluted EPS is calculated as follows (millions, except per share amounts):

$$\text{Diluted EPS} = \frac{\$1{,}750}{770 \text{ shares}} = \$2.27 \text{ per share}$$

3. Petroni would only report basic EPS on its income statement. Diluted EPS, as calculated in requirement 2, is actually higher than basic EPS because the convertible preferred stock is anti-dilutive. GAAP requires that reported diluted EPS must be lower than basic EPS. Consequently, Petroni would not report the diluted EPS number.

Apendix 11A Review

Solution

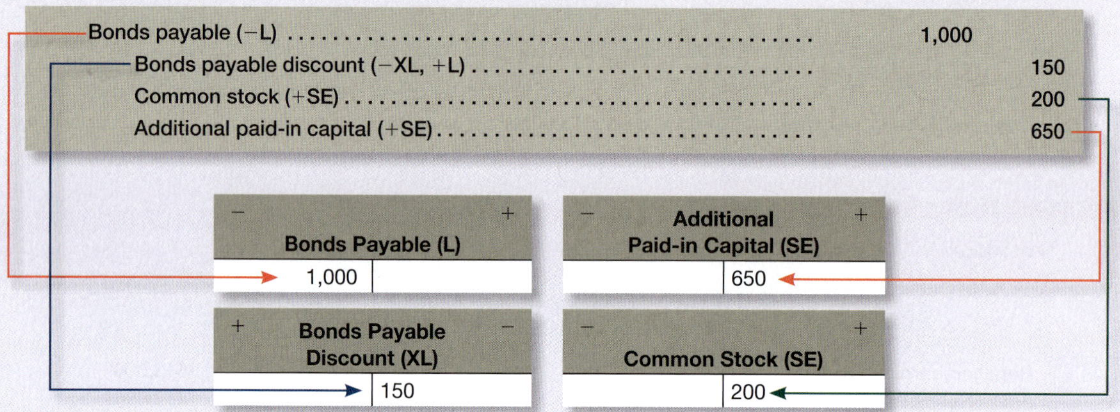

Google

Reporting and Analyzing Intercorporate Investments

When Sergey Brin and Larry Page, Stanford computer science students, started **Google, Inc.**, in September, 1998, they were probably unaware that their fortune would be made in the advertising field that now generates nearly all its revenue.

GOOGLE
www.google.com

Google went public in August, 2004, with an offering price below $100 a share. By November 1, 2007, the share price exceeded $700! Google "has created more investor wealth in less time than any other company in history." Even with the 2008–2009 economic downturn, Google currently is up over 500% since its IPO. Only **General Electric Company**, **Exxon Mobil Corporation**, and **Microsoft Corporation** surpass Google in wealth creation, and each has a longer history. Recent acquisitions of **YouTube, Inc.** in 2006 for $1.36 billion and **DoubleClick, Inc.** in 2008 for $3.2 billion have contributed to the company's value increase. Google's market success up to November 2007, is clearly indicated on the accompanying chart along with the recent decline in value of over 50% by the end of 2008. Recently the firm's fortunes have improved and the company's stock has doubled from its 53-week low in November 2008. However, Google expects revenue growth in 2009 to be only 4% compared to 31% in 2008. As we write this chapter, Google, using its DoubleClick subsidiary, is embarking on a campaign to wrestle away display advertising from **Yahoo, Inc.**, which has dominated this field historically.

Comparison of 52 Month Cumulative Total Return*
Among Google Inc., The S & P 500 Index, The NASDAQ Composite Index
And The RDG Internet Composite Index

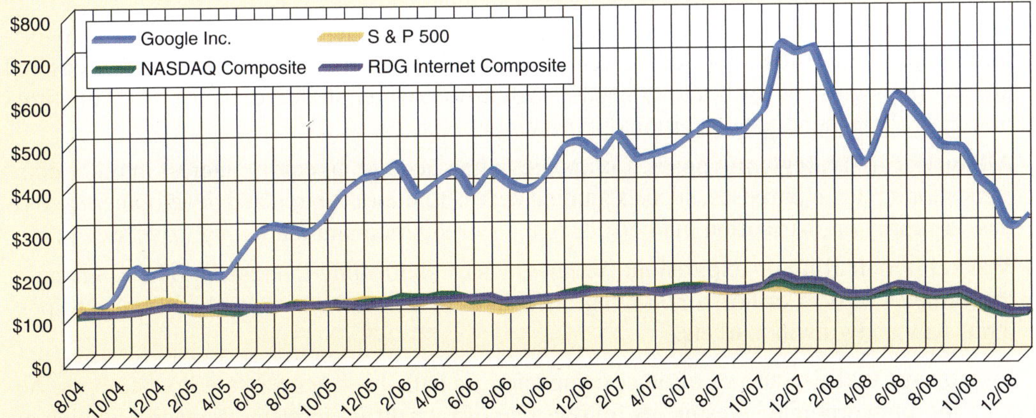

*$100 invested on 8/19/04 in stock & 7/31/04 in index-including reinvestment of dividends.
Fiscal year ending December 31.

(continued on next page)

Despite all its success, Google is not without problems. Google is faced with substantial competition as it attempts to build its presence in the second largest Internet market, China. Further, analysts point to the substantial challenge faced by the company to find investments that will allow Google to match its past returns of over 50 percent. Google continues to face negotiations with the Justice Department in regard to its concern about Google's settlement with authors and publishers to post out-of-copyright and out-of-print books on-line. In addition, the firm faces new challenges to its 70% domination of the search-engine market from Microsoft's Bing, Twitter, Inc., OneRiot, Inc., Aardvark, and Wolfram Research, Inc.

We will discover that Google addresses growth in several ways. As we noted previously, the firm invests money in other companies. As we will discover in this chapter, the accounting method used to report investments depends on the degree of influence or control that the investor company can exert over the investee company (the company whose securities are being purchased).

Sources: Google 2008 10-K report; *The Wall Street Journal*, July 2007, September 2008, and November 2009; *BusinessWeek*, July, August, and September 2009; *Fortune*, October 2009.

CHAPTER ORGANIZATION

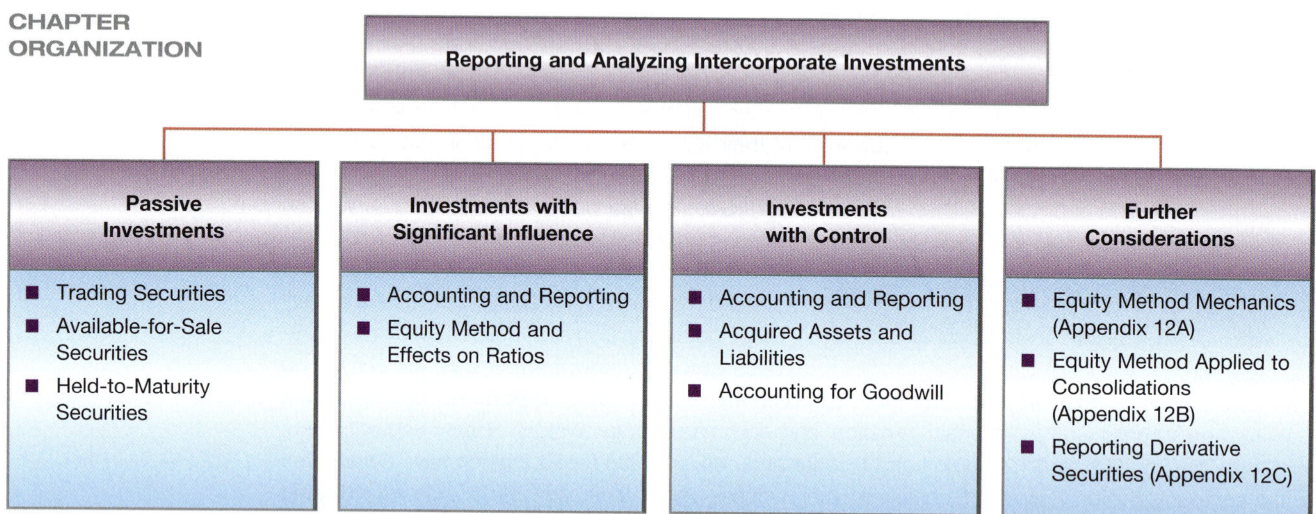

INTRODUCTION

LO1 Explain and interpret the three levels of investor influence over an investee—passive, significant, and controlling.

Most companies invest in government securities or the securities of other companies. These investments often have the following strategic goals:

■ **Short-term investment of excess cash.** Companies often generate excess cash for investment either during slow times of the year (after receivables are collected and before seasonal production begins) or for liquidity needs (such as to counter strategic moves by competitors or to quickly respond to acquisition opportunities).

■ **Alliances for strategic purposes.** Companies often acquire an equity interest in other companies for strategic purposes, such as gaining access to their research and development activities, to supply or distribution markets, or to their production and marketing expertise.

■ **Market penetration or expansion.** Acquisitions of controlling interests in other companies can achieve vertical or horizontal integration in existing markets or can be avenues to penetrate new and growth markets.

Investments in the securities of other companies are called **intercorporate investments**. Accounting for intercorporate investments follows one of four different methods, each of which affects the balance sheet and the income statement differently. To help assimilate the materials in this chapter, Exhibit 12.1 provides a graphical depiction of accounting for intercorporate investments.

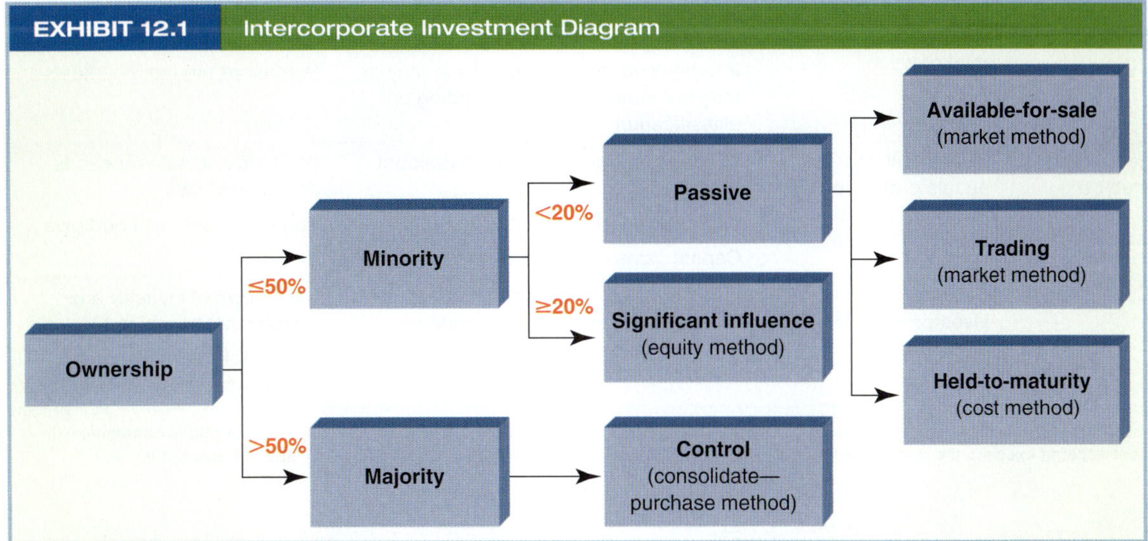

The degree of influence or control that the investor company (purchaser) can exert over the investee company (the company whose securities are being purchased) determines the accounting method. U.S. GAAP identifies three levels of influence/control:

1. **Passive influence**. In this case, the purchasing company is merely an investor and cannot exert influence over the investee company. The purchaser's goal for this investment is to realize dividends and capital gains. Generally, passive investor status is presumed if the investor company owns less than 20% of the outstanding voting stock of the investee. Investments in debt securities, such as bonds or notes of other companies, are also classified as passive investments.

2. **Significant influence**. An investor company can sometimes exert significant influence over, but not control, the activities of the investee company. This level of influence can result from the percentage of voting stock owned. It also can result from legal agreements, such as a license to use technology, a formula, or a trade secret like production know-how. It also can occur when the investor company is the sole supplier or customer of the investee. Generally, significant influence is presumed if the investor company owns 20% to 50% of the voting stock of the investee.

3. **Controlling influence**. When a company has control over another, it has the ability to elect a majority of the board of directors and, as a result, the ability to affect its strategic direction and hiring of executive management. Control is generally presumed if the investor company owns more than 50% of the outstanding voting stock of the investee company. Control can sometimes occur at less than 50% stock ownership by virtue of legal agreements, technology licensing, or other contractual means.

IFRS INSIGHT

GAAP uses the term "equity" to describe an investment involving significant influence, (usually between 20% and 50%). IFRS uses the term "associate" to describe such an investment.

Once the level of influence/control is determined, the appropriate accounting method is applied as outlined in Exhibit 12.2.

EXHIBIT 12.2	Investment Type, Accounting Treatment, and Financial Statement Effects			
	Accounting	**Balance Sheet Effects**	**Income Statement Effects**	**Cash Flow Effects**
Passive	Market method	Investment account is reported at current market value	Dividends and capital gains affect income Interim changes in market value may or may not affect income depending on classification	Dividend and sale proceeds are cash inflows Purchases are cash outflows
Significant influence	Equity method	Investment account equals proportion owned of investee company's equity*	Dividends reduce investment account Investor reports income equal to percent owned of investee income Capital gains are income	Dividend and sale proceeds are cash inflows Purchases are cash outflows
Control	Consolidation	Balance sheets of investor and investee are combined	Income statements of investor and investee are combined (and sale of investee yields capital gain or loss)	Cash flows of investor and investee are combined Sale/purchase of investee yields cash inflow/outflow

*Investments are often acquired at purchase prices in excess of book value (on average, market prices are 1.5 times book value for public companies). In this case the investment account exceeds the proportionate ownership of the investee's equity. We discuss this situation later in the chapter.

There are two basic reporting issues with investments: (1) how investment income should be recognized and (2) at what amount (cost or fair market value) the investment should be reported on the balance sheet. We next discuss both of these issues under each of the three investment types.

PASSIVE INVESTMENTS

Short-term investments of excess cash are typically passive investments. Passive investments can involve equity or debt securities. Equity securities involve an ownership interest such as common stock or preferred stock, whereas debt securities have no ownership interest. A voting stock investment is passive when the investor does not possess sufficient ownership to either influence or control the investee company. The *market method* is used to account for most passive investments.

Acquisition and Sale

When an investment is acquired, regardless of the amount of shares purchased or the percentage of outstanding shares acquired, the investment is initially recorded on the balance sheet at its fair market value, that is, its price on the date of purchase. This accounting is the same as that for the acquisition of other assets such as inventories or plant assets. Subsequent to acquisition, investments are carried on the balance sheet as current or long-term assets, depending on management's expectations about their ultimate holding period (the assets are reported as current assets if management expects to dispose of them within one year).

When investments are sold, any recognized gain or loss on sale is equal to the difference between the proceeds received and the book (carrying) value of the investment on the balance sheet.

Gain or loss on sale = Proceeds from sale − Book value of investment sold

To illustrate the acquisition and sale of a passive investment, assume that Pownall Company purchases an investment in King Company consisting of 1,000 shares for $20 cash per share (the acquisition price includes transaction costs such as brokerage fees). Near year-end, Pownall sells 400 of the 1,000 shares for $30 cash per share. The financial statement effects of these transactions and their related entries for Pownall follow:

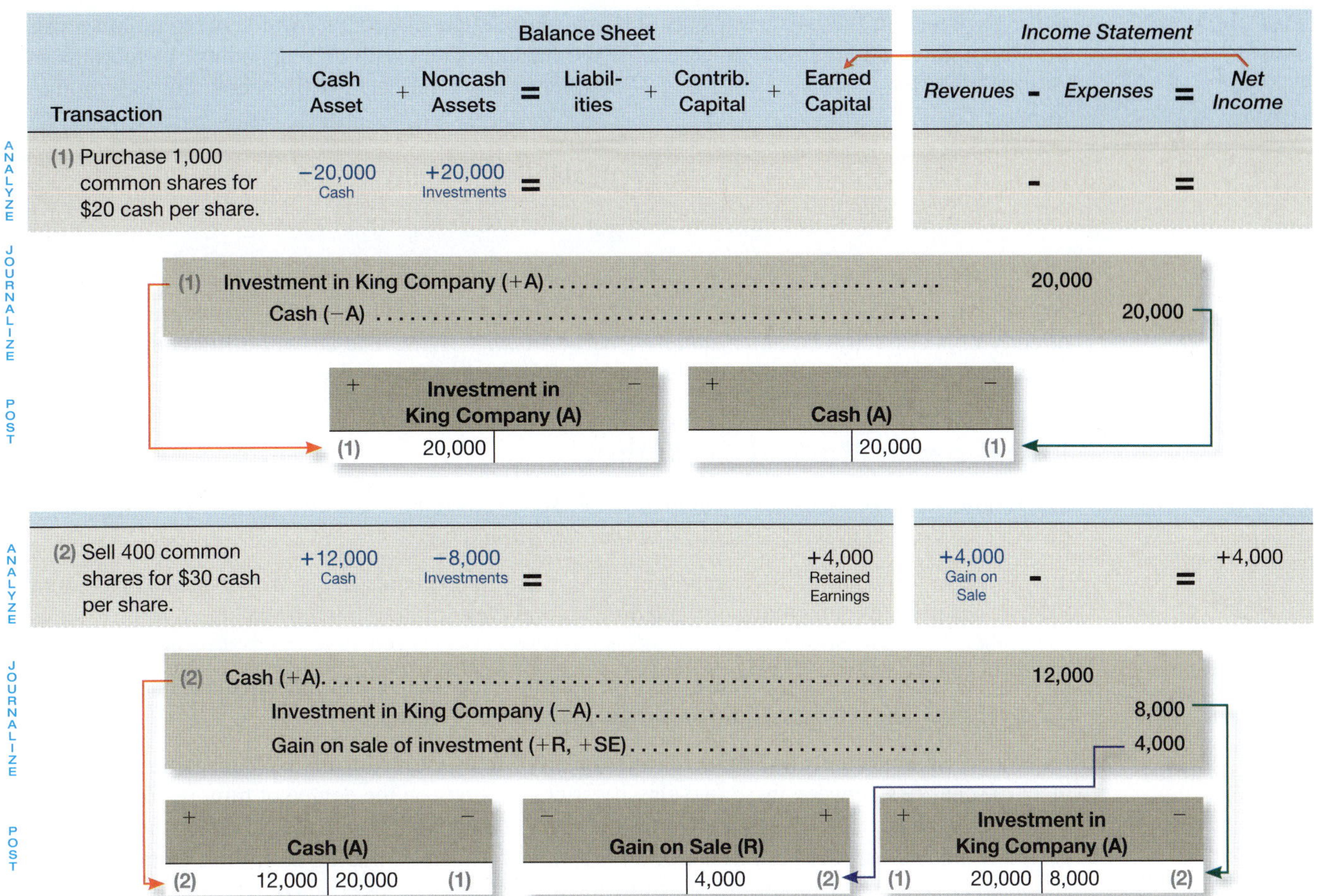

The gain or loss on sale is reported as a component of *other income,* which is commonly commingled with interest and dividend revenue in the income statement.

Accounting for the purchase and sale of investments is the same as with any other asset. Further, there is no difference in accounting for purchases and sales across the different types of passive investments discussed in this section. However, there are differences in accounting for the different passive investments *between* their purchase and their sale. We next address this issue.

Mark-to-Market Versus Cost

If a passive investment in marketable securities has an active market with published prices, that investment is reported on the balance sheet at its fair market value as of the balance sheet date. If such a market does not exist, that investment is reported at its historical cost. **Fair market value** is the published price (as listed on a stock exchange) multiplied by the number of shares owned. This is one of only a few assets that are reported at market value instead of historical cost.[1]

There is a trade-off between the *objectivity* of historical cost and the *relevance* of market value. All things equal, we prefer to know current market values of assets as these are more relevant in determining the market value of the company. However, for most assets, market values cannot be reliably determined. Their use would introduce excessive subjectivity into the financial reporting process.

In the case of marketable securities, market prices result from numerous transactions between willing buyers and sellers. Market prices in this case provide an unbiased (objective) estimate of

---

[1] Other assets that *must* be reported at fair market value include (1) derivative securities, such as options, futures and forward contracts, that are purchased to hedge price, interest rate, or foreign exchange rate fluctuations, (2) long-term assets that are impaired, and (3) inventories that have been written down to market based on the lower-of-cost-or-market rule. In addition, U.S. GAAP provides companies with the *option* of using fair market value to measure the value of most financial assets and liabilities. (See the Business Insight on page 547.)

value to report on the balance sheet. This market method of accounting for marketable securities yields fluctuations in the asset side of the balance sheet with corresponding fluctuations in equity (liabilities are unaffected). This valuation process is reflected in the accounting equation as follows:

$$\text{Assets} \uparrow = \text{Liabilities} + \text{Equity} \uparrow$$
$$\text{or Assets} \downarrow = \text{Liabilities} + \text{Equity} \downarrow$$

An important issue is whether such changes in equity should be reported as income (with a consequent change in retained earnings), or whether they should bypass the income statement and directly impact equity via *other comprehensive income (OCI)*. The answer differs depending on the classification of the securities, which we explain in the next section.

Investments Marked to Market

The following two classifications of marketable securities require the investment to be reported on the balance sheet at current market value (*marked-to-market*):

1. **Available-for-sale (AFS) securities.** These are investments in securities that management intends to hold for capital gains and dividend revenue; although it may sell them if the price is right.

2. **Trading (T) securities.** These are investments in securities that management intends to actively buy and sell for trading profits as market prices fluctuate.

Investments in both equity and debt securities qualify for these classifications. Management's assignment of securities between these two classifications depends on the degree of turnover (transaction volume) it expects in the investment portfolio, which reflects its intent to actively trade the securities or not. Available-for-sale portfolios exhibit less turnover than do trading portfolios. Once that classification is established, reporting for a portfolio follows procedures detailed in Exhibit 12.3.

EXHIBIT 12.3	Accounting Treatment for Available-for-Sale and for Trading Investments	
Investment Classification	**Reporting of Market Value Changes**	**Reporting Dividends Received and Gains and Losses on Sale**
Available-for-Sale (AFS)	Market value changes bypass the income statement and are reported directly in accumulated other comprehensive income (AOCI) ; these changes are reported in the statement of stockholders' equity.	Reported as investment income in income statement
Trading (T)	Market value changes are reported in the income statement as unrealized gains or losses; affects equity via retained earnings	Same as above

Both available-for-sale (AFS) and trading (T) investments are reported at fair market values (marked-to-market) on the statement date. Whether the change in market value affects current income depends on the investment classification: available-for-sale securities have no income effect; trading securities have an income effect. The impact on equity is similar for both classifications, with the only difference being whether the change is reflected in retained earnings or in accumulated other comprehensive income (AOCI) in equity. Dividends and any gains or losses on security sales are reported in the investment income section of the income statement for both classifications.

Market Adjustments   To illustrate the accounting for changes in market value subsequent to purchase (and before sale), assume that Pownall's investment in King Co. (600 remaining shares purchased for $20 per share) increases in value to $25 per share at year-end. The investment must be marked to market in an adjusting entry to reflect the $3,000 unrealized gain ($5 per share increase for 600 shares). If the securities are classified as available-for-sale (AFS), the financial statements and their related entries are as follows.

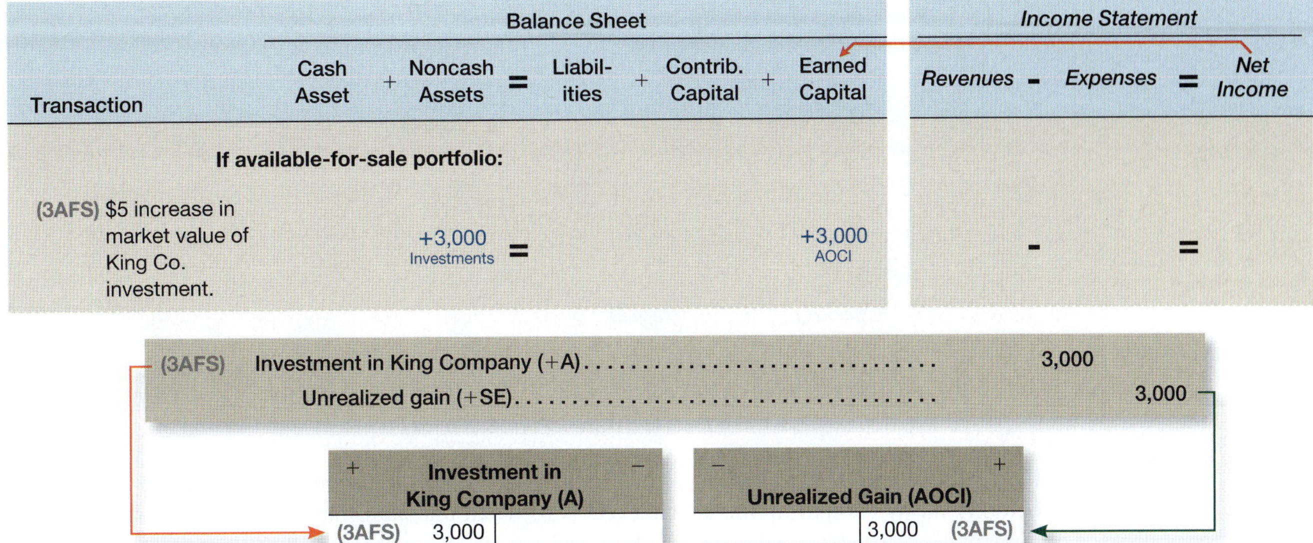

If the investment is classified as trading securities (T) the entry would be:

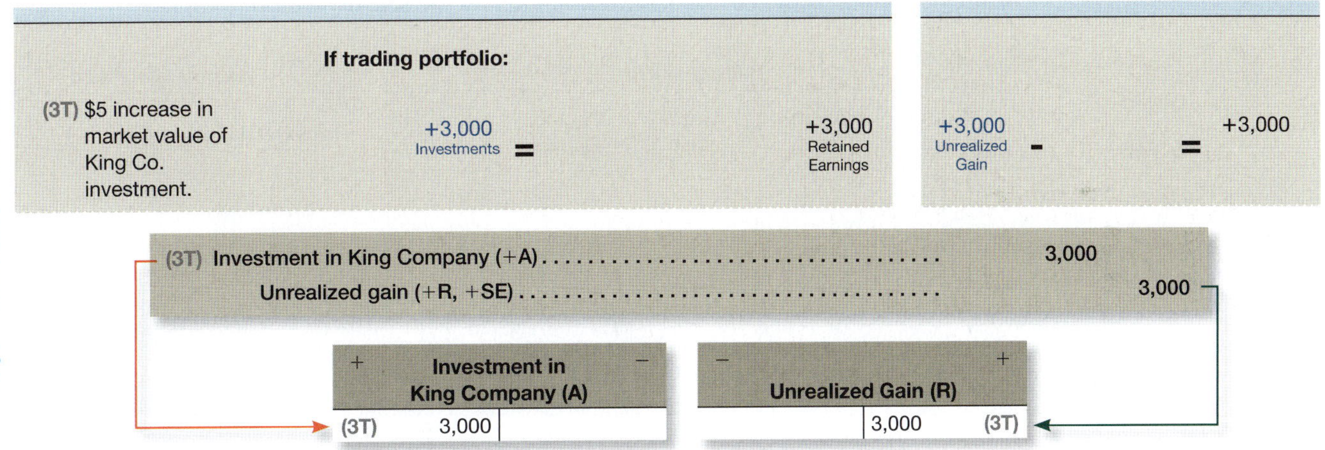

Under both classifications, the investment account is increased by $3,000 to reflect the increase in market value of the shares owned. When accounted for as available-for-sale, the unrealized gain is reflected as an increase in accumulated other comprehensive income (AOCI). However, when accounted for as trading, the unrealized gain is recorded as income, thus increasing both reported income and retained earnings for that period. Our illustration uses a portfolio with only one security for simplicity. Portfolios usually consist of multiple securities, and the unrealized gain or loss is computed for the entire portfolio.

These market adjustments are only applied to publicly traded securities. Companies sometimes purchase securities for which current market values are unavailable. Examples are investments in start-up companies, privately held corporations, and in local bond offerings. Investments in non-publicly traded companies are usually valued at cost as we discuss later in this section.

What happens when the securities are subsequently sold? Assume that Pownall Company sells its 600 shares of King Company for $23 per share shortly after the end of the last reporting period. Pownall receives $13,800 in cash, and it no longer owns the shares of King Company. Under the available-for-sale method, the following entries would be made:

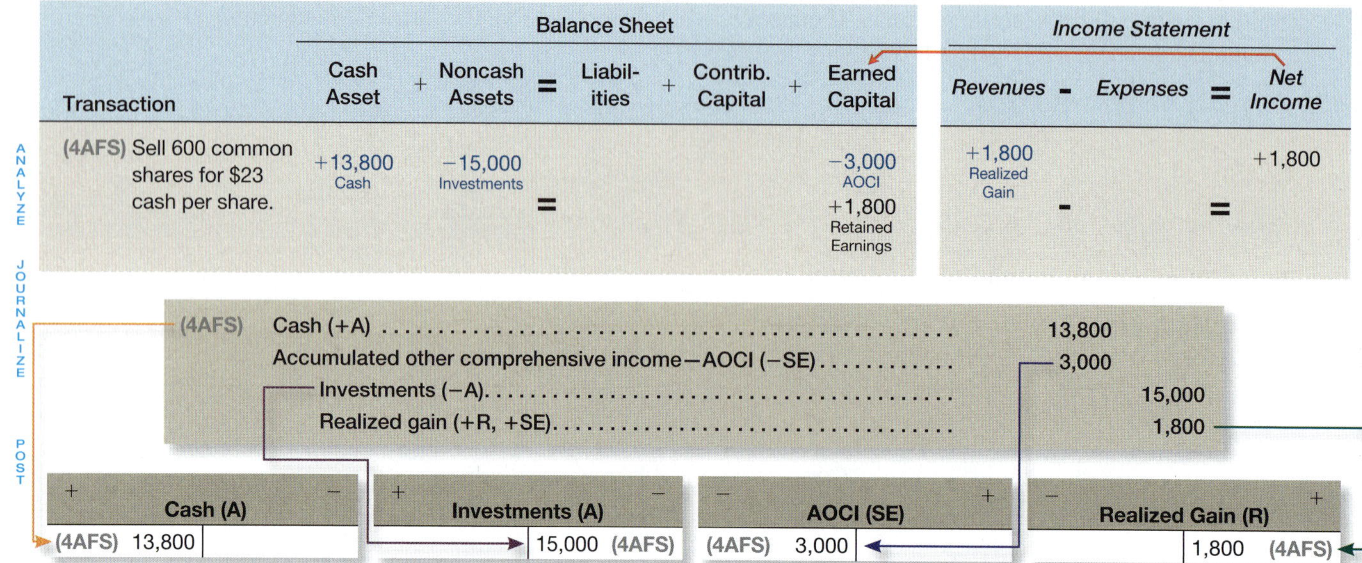

Under AFS, the realized gain (loss) goes into income when the security is sold, and the amount is determined by comparing the amount received when the shares are sold ($23 per share) to the amount paid for the shares when originally purchased ($20 per share). When the investment is sold, the entry must delete the investment (which was valued at $25 per share at the end of last period) *and* the unrealized holding gain ($5 per share) that was put into accumulated other comprehensive income when those shares were revalued.

When the trading method is used, the accounting for the sale of shares is simpler.

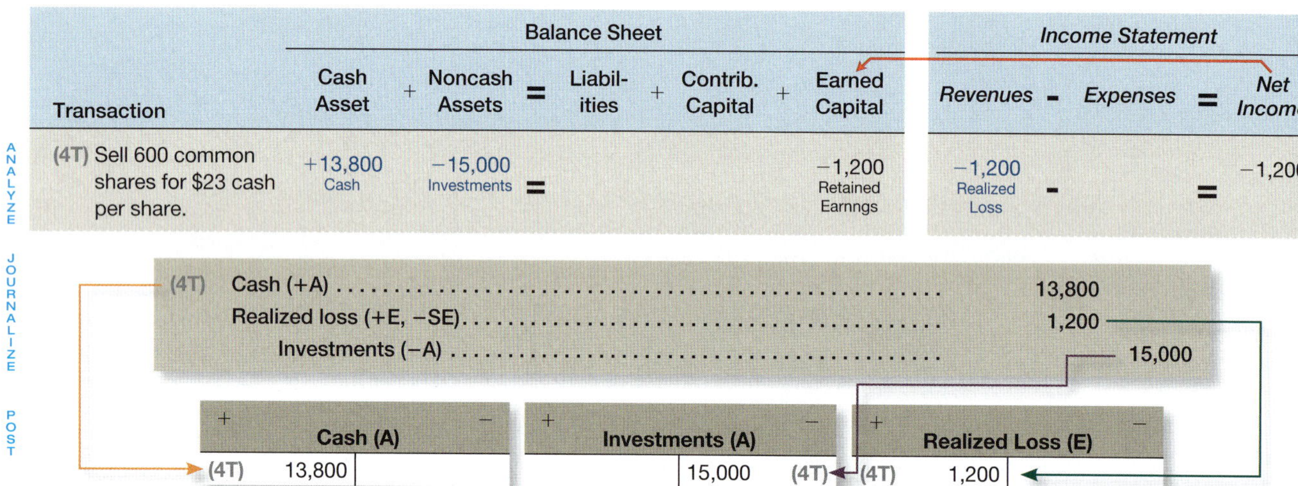

Under the trading securities method, holding gains and losses are recognized in income in the period in which they occur. Holding these 600 shares caused a gain of $3,000 in the prior period and a loss of $1,200 in the current period. In contrast, AFS shows no income statement effect in the prior period on these 600 shares and a gain of $1,800 in the current period when the shares are sold. In this way, AFS delays the income statement news about investment performance until management decides to sell the securities.

Financial Statement Disclosures

Companies are required to disclose cost and market value information on their investment portfolios in footnotes to financial statements. **Google** reports its accounting policies for its investments in footnote 1 to its 2008 10-K report:

Cash and Cash Equivalents and Marketable Securities

We invest our excess cash in money market funds and in highly liquid debt instruments of the U.S. government and its agencies , municipalities in the United States, time deposits, money market mutual funds, and corporate securities. All highly liquid investments with stated maturities of three months or less from date of purchase are classified as cash equivalents; all highly liquid investments with stated maturities of greater than three months are classified as marketable securities.

We determine the appropriate classification of our investments in marketable debt and equity securities at the time of purchase and reevaluate such designation at each balance sheet date. Our marketable securities have been classified and accounted for as available-for-sale. We may or may not hold securities with stated maturities greater than 12 months until maturity. After consideration of our risk versus reward objectives, as well as our liquidity requirements, we may sell these securities prior to their stated maturities. As these securities are viewed by us as available to support current operations, based on the provisions of Accounting Research Bulletin No. 43, Chapter 3A, *Working Capital*—Current Assets and Liabilities, securities with maturities beyond 12 months are classified as current assets under the caption marketable securities in the accompanying Consolidated Balance Sheets. These securities are carried at fair value, with the unrealized gains and losses, net of taxes, reported as a component of stockholders' equity, except for unrealized losses determined to be other than temporary which are recorded as interest income and other, net, in accordance with our policy and FASB Staff Position (FSP) Nos. FAS 115-1 (FSP 115-1) and FAS 124-1, *The Meaning of Other-Than-Temporary Impairment and Its Application to Certain Investments*. Any realized gains or losses on the sale of marketable securities are determined on a specific identification method, and such gains and losses are reflected as a component of interest income and other, net.

Non-Marketable Equity Securities

We have accounted for non-marketable equity security investments at historical cost because we do not have significant influence over the underlying investees. These investments are subject to a periodic impairment review. To the extent any impairment is considered other-than-temporary, the investment is written down to its fair value and the loss is recorded as interest income and other, net.

This footnote reveals that Google generally accounts for its investments as available-for-sale. Consistent with this classification, it reports that unrealized gains and losses are "reported as a component of stockholders' equity." Google also reports that these investments are reported on its balance sheet at fair market value. Following is the investments line item from the asset section of Google's balance sheet ($ thousands):

December 31 ($ thousands)	2008
Marketable securities	$7,189,099

Google's investment portfolio is carried as an asset with a current market value of $7,189.099 million. Unrealized gains and losses on its available-for-sale investments bypass its income statement (they do not affect current income), and are reported as a component of equity called accumulated other comprehensive income (AOCI). Gains and losses on the *sale* of investments, however, are reported in current income. Also, as Google reports in its footnote, if investments suffer a decline in value prior to sale that is deemed "other-than-temporary," they are written down to current market value and that loss is reported in current income.

Footnotes to Google's 10-K provide further information about the composition of its investment portfolio ($ millions):

Note 3. Cash and Investments

Cash, cash equivalents and marketable securities consists of the following (in thousands):

As of December 31 ($ thousands)	2007	2008
Marketable securities:		
U.S. government notes	$ 475,781	$ —
U.S. government agencies	2,120,972	3,342,406
Municipal securities	4,991,564	2,721,603
Time deposits	500,000	—
Money market mutual funds	—	73,034
Corporate debt securities	—	907,056
Auction rate preferred securities	48,703	—
Marketable equity security	—	145,000
Total marketable securities	$8,137,020	$7,189,099

The majority of Google's investments are in government debt securities (including municipal securities), such as bonds and T-bills. Google accounts for all of these investments as available-for-sale and reports them in the current asset section of the balance sheet because they can be readily sold, if necessary and they are not subject to significant risk due to changes in interest rates.

Google provides additional (required) disclosures on the costs, market values, and unrealized gains and losses for its available-for-sale investments as follows:

As of December 31, 2008 ($ thousands)	Adjusted Cost	Gross Unrealized Gains	Gross Unrealized Losses	Fair Value
U.S. government agencies	$3,324,750	$17,747	$ (91)	$3,342,406
Municipal securities	2,690,270	34,685	(3,352	2,721,603
Money market mutual funds	73,034	—	—	73,034
Corporate debt securities	903,963	3,265	(172)	907,056
Total marketable securities	$6,992,017	$55,697	$(3,615)	$7,044,099

For each type of investment, Google reports its cost, fair market value, and gross unrealized gains and losses; the latter reflect differences between cost and market. Google reports that the cost of its available-for-sale investment portfolio is $6,992,017, and that there are unrealized gains (losses) of $55,697 ($3,615) as of December 31, 2008. Google's balance sheet reports the total market value of $7,044,099 at December 31, 2008 ($ thousands).

Google's net unrealized gain of $52,082 = $55,697 − $3,615 is reported net of tax in accumulated other comprehensive income (AOCI), which is included in the stockholders' section of the balance sheet.

Google reports accumulated other comprehensive income (AOCI) of $226.579 million in its 2008 balance sheet. Unrealized gains on investments in AFS securities represent only one component of AOCI. AOCI also includes accumulated foreign currency translation adjustments and gains on cash hedges.

Potential for Earnings Management

The difference between available-for-sale investments and trading securities—as far as the way changes in fair market value are reported—creates the potential for earnings management. For example, if management wishes to report higher net income, investments that have increased in value could be classified as trading securities while investments that have declined in value could be classified as available-for-sale securities. This would mean that the unrealized gains on the trading securities would be reported on the income statement, while the unrealized losses on available-for-sale securities would bypass the income statement and be subtracted from AOCI. In addition, management is free to reclassify investments it sees fit to do so.

Because of the potential for earnings management, the FASB requires that investments be measured at fair market value at the time that a security is reclassified from one category to another. If trading securities are reclassified as available-for-sale securities, for example, any unrealized gain or loss must be recognized as income at the time of the reclassification. This prevents management from moving investments between categories to hide a loss in AOCI.

Nevertheless, available-for-sale securities offer the opportunity for earnings management, because management can decide when to recognize the unrealized gain (or loss) in the income statement. When investments are classified as available-for-sale securities, any unrealized gain or loss is recorded directly in stockholders' equity as AOCI until one of two things happens: (1) management decides to sell the securities, or (2) management decides to reclassify the investment as trading securities. In either case, the unrealized gain or loss is immediately recognized in the income statement and thus transferred from AOCI to retained earnings.

Google's footnote allows us to observe how a firm might use its investments in marketable securities to manage its net income for the year. Suppose, for example, that Google wanted to increase net income for the 2008 reporting year. Google's available-for-sale securities show gross unrealized gains of $55.697 million. These gains have not been reported previously in Google's income statement. So, if Google decided to reclassify these available-for-sale securities as trading securities, it could immediately recognize the $55.697 million unrealized gain and report it on its 2008 income statement.

Instead of reclassifying the investments, Google could sell the securities and recognize the gain. (The unrealized gain would now be realized.) In fact, Google could sell the investment to record the gain and then immediately buy back the securities at the same price (or very near to it). The

BUSINESS INSIGHT

Determining Fair Market Value   In 2007, the FASB issued two standards that provide guidance on how and when to use fair value in the financial statements. The first standard (SFAS 157) defined fair value and detailed what information about fair value must be disclosed in the footnotes. This standard applies to all assets and liabilities that are measured at fair market value. The standard also established a hierarchy of evidence for determining fair market value:

- Level 1—quoted market prices for identical assets or liabilities in active markets.
- Level 2—inputs, other than quoted prices, that are observable either directly or through corroboration with observable data.
- Level 3—unobservable inputs, such as management estimates or assumptions.

Level 1 evidence is considered the most reliable, while level 3 evidence is considered the least reliable and, thus, requires greater explanation in the footnotes.

The second standard (SFAS 159)—called the **fair value option**—provides companies with the *option* of using fair market value to measure the value of most financial assets and liabilities. This option extends the use of fair market value to a wide range of financial assets and liabilities, including accounts and notes receivable, accounts and notes payable, and bonds payable. This standard is optional, however, and thus far its application has been limited mostly to financial institutions such as banks and insurance companies. However, the use of fair values in financial reporting is expanding internationally. As U.S. GAAP and international accounting standards begin to converge, the use of fair value to measure asset and liability values will grow, along with questions about how unrealized gains and losses should be presented in the income statement.

company would incur some transaction costs, but it would be able to increase its income without changing its portfolio or reclassifying its investments.

One way to determine whether a company is selling and buying available-for-sale securities to manage earnings is to examine the cash flow statement. Under the heading of investing activities, companies are required to report cash flows from buying and selling investments separately. During 2008, Google reported that cash proceeds from the sale or maturity of available-for-sale investments totaled $15,762.796 million, while cash spent to buy available-for-sale investments totaled $15,356.304 million. These two cash flow numbers were, by far, the largest cash flows reported in Google's cash flow statement. Of course, we cannot automatically conclude that these transactions were the result of earnings management. Realized gains and losses on available-for-sale investments should be disclosed in a company's footnotes. In addition, we could look at the adjustments to net income in the indirect method cash from operations to identify gains and losses from investing activities.

Investments Reported at Cost

Investments for which no current market values exist must be accounted for using the cost method. Under the **cost method**, the investment is continually reported at its historical cost, and any cash dividends and interest received are recognized in current income.

Debt securities that management intends to hold to maturity are also reported using the cost method. These debt securities are classified as **held-to-maturity (HTM)**. Exhibit 12.4 identifies the reporting of these securities.

EXHIBIT 12.4	Accounting Treatment for Held-to-Maturity Investments	
Investment Classification	**Reporting of Market Value Changes**	**Reporting Interest Received and Gains and Losses on Sale**
Held-to-Maturity (HTM)	Market value changes are not reported in either the balance sheet or income statement	Reported as other income in income statement

Changes in market value are not reflected on either the balance sheet or the income statement. The presumption is that these investments are held to maturity, at which time they are settled at their face value. Fluctuations in market value, as a result, are less relevant for this investment classification. Any interest received, and gains and losses on the sale of these investments, are recorded in current income.

IFRS INSIGHT

Under proposed International Financial Reporting Standards (IFRS), trading, available for sale, and held-to-maturity portfolios are accounted for similar to GAAP.

MID-CHAPTER REVIEW 1

Part 1: Available-for-sale securities

Show the effects (amount and account) of the following four transactions involving investments in marketable securities classified as available-for-sale in the financial statement effects template, prepare the journal entries, and post the journal entries to the appropriate T-accounts.

1. Purchased 1,000 shares of Pincus common stock for $15 cash per share.
2. Received cash dividend of $2 per share on Pincus common stock.
3. Year-end market price of Pincus common stock is $18 per share.
4. Sold all 1,000 shares of Pincus common stock for $19,000 cash.

INVESTMENTS WITH SIGNIFICANT INFLUENCE

Many companies make investments in other companies that yield them significant influence over those other companies. These intercorporate investments are usually made for strategic reasons including:

LO3 Explain and analyze accounting for investments with significant influence.

- **Prelude to acquisition.** Significant ownership can allow the investor company to gain a seat on the board of directors from which it can learn much about the investee company, its products, and its industry.

- **Strategic alliance.** One example of a strategic alliance is an investment in a company that provides inputs for the investor's production process. This relationship is closer than the usual supplier-buyer relationship, often because the investor company provides trade secrets or technical know-how of its production process.

- **Pursuit of research and development.** Many research activities in the pharmaceutical, software, and oil and gas industries are conducted jointly. The common motivation is to reduce risk or the amount of capital invested by the investor. The investor company's equity investment often carries an option to purchase additional shares or the entire company, which it can exercise if the research activities are fruitful.

A crucial feature in each of these investments is that the investor company has ownership sufficient to exert *significant influence* over the investee company. GAAP requires that such investments be accounted for using the *equity method*.

Significant influence is the ability of the investor to affect the financing or operating policies of the investee. Ownership levels of 20% to 50% of the outstanding common stock of the investee presume significant influence. Significant influence can also exist when ownership is less than 20%. Evidence of such influence can be that the investor company is able to gain a seat on the board of directors of the investee by virtue of its equity investment, or the investor controls technical know-how or patents that are used by the investee, or the investor is able to exert significant influence by virtue of legal contracts between it and the investee. There is growing pressure for determining significant influence by the facts and circumstances of the investment instead of the strict ownership percentage rule reflected in current corporate reporting.

Accounting for Investments with Significant Influence

Investments with significant influence must be accounted for using the **equity method**. The equity method of accounting for investments reports the investment on the balance sheet at an amount equal to the proportion of the investee's equity owned by the investor; hence the name equity method. (This accounting assumes acquisition at book value. Acquisition at an amount greater than book value is covered in Appendix 12A.) Contrary to passive investments that are reported at market value, equity method investments increase (decrease) with increases (decreases) in the equity of the investee.

Equity method accounting is summarized as follows:

- Investments are initially recorded at their purchase cost.

- Dividends received are treated as a recovery of the investment and, thus, reduce the investment balance (dividends are *not* reported as income as is the case with passive investments).

- The investor reports income equal to its proportionate share of the reported income of the investee; the investment account is increased by that income or decreased by its share of any loss. ·

- The investment is *not* reported at market value as are passive market investments.

To illustrate the accounting for investments using the equity method, consider the following scenario: Assume that Google acquires a 30% interest in Mitel Networks, a company seeking to develop a new technology in a strategic alliance with Google. At acquisition, Mitel reports $1,000 of stockholders' equity, and Google purchases its 30% stake for $300. At the first year-end, Mitel reports profits of $100 and pays $20 in cash dividends to its shareholders ($6 to Google). Following are the financial statement effects for Google (the investor company) for this investment using the equity method:

Transaction	Cash Asset +	Noncash Assets	=	Liabil- ities	+	Contrib. Capital	+	Earned Capital	Revenues -	Expenses	=	Net Income
(1) Purchased 30% investment in Mitel for $300 cash.	−300 Cash	+300 Investment in Mitel =								-	=	
(2) Mitel reports $100 income.		+30 Investment in Mitel =						+30 Retained Earnings	+30 Investment Income -		=	+30
(3) Mitel pays $20 cash dividends, $6 to Google.	+6 Cash	−6 Investment in Mitel =								-	=	
Ending balance of Google's investment account.		324										

The related journal entries and T-accounts are:

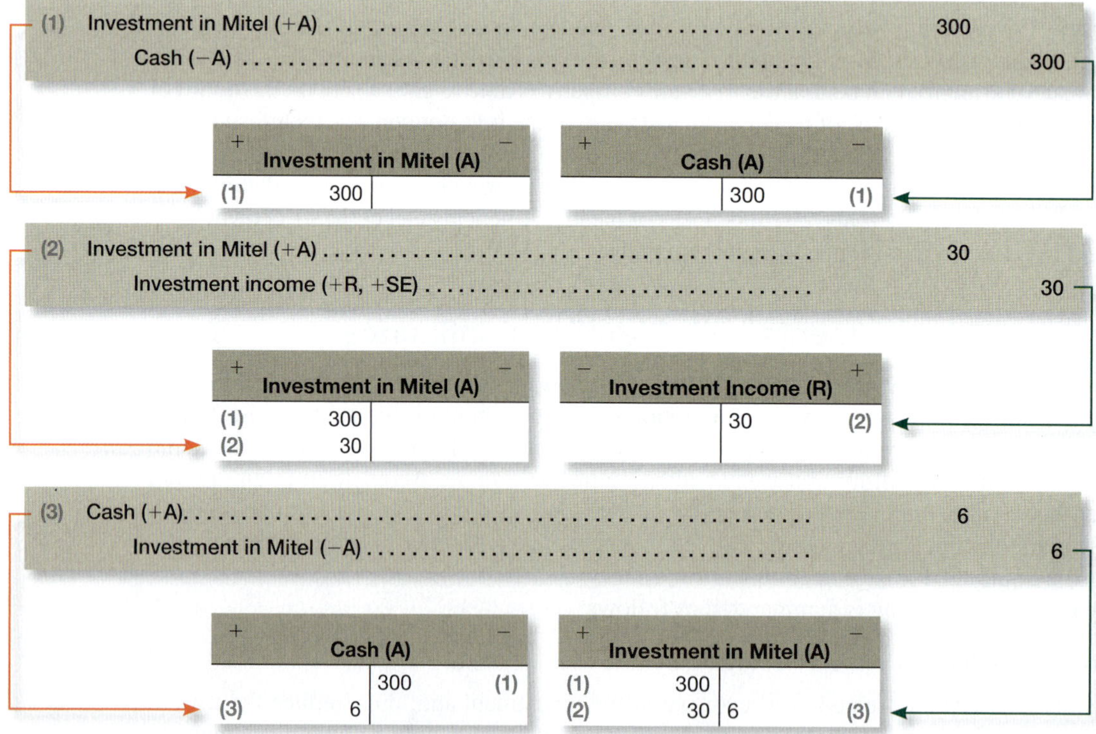

The investment is initially reported on Google's balance sheet at its purchase price of $300, representing a 30% interest in Mitel's equity of $1,000. During the year, Mitel's equity increases to $1,080 ($1,000 plus $100 income and less $20 dividends). Likewise, Google's investment increases by $30 to reflect its 30% share of Mitel's $100 income and decreases by $6 from Mitel's $20 of dividends (30% × $20). After these transactions, Google's investment in Mitel is reported on Google's balance sheet at 30% of $1,080, or $324.

Two final points about equity method accounting: First, just as the equity of a company is different from its market value, so is the balance of the equity investment account different from its market value. Indeed, there can be a substantial difference between the book value of an investment and its market value. Second, if the investee company reports income, the investor company also reports income. Recognition of equity income by the investor, however, does not mean that it has received that income in cash. Cash is only received if the investee's directors declare a dividend payment. In the statement of cash flows, there is an adjustment for the difference between reported equity income and dividends received in the operating section of the statement. The net amount remaining in operating cash flows is equal to the *cash* income received.

> **FYI** Investee dividend-paying ability can be (a) restricted by regulatory agencies or foreign governments, (b) prohibited under debt agreements for highly leveraged borrowers, and/or (c) influenced by directors that the investor does not control.

RESEARCH INSIGHT

Equity Income and Stock Prices   The equity method of accounting for investments does not recognize any dividends received from the investee or any market value changes for the investee in the investor's income until the investment is sold. However, research has found a positive relation between investors' and investees' stock prices at the time of investees' earnings and dividend announcements. This relation suggests that the market includes information regarding investees' earnings and dividends when assessing the stock prices of investor companies. This finding implies the market looks beyond the book value of the investment account in determining stock prices of investor companies. The finding also reflects the fact that the earnings from the operations of subsidiaries are considered earnings of the parent corporation.

Equity Method Accounting and Effects on Ratios

The balance sheet amount for an equity method investment is equal to the proportion owned of the equity of the investee company when the investment is acquired at book value. Consider **DuPont de Nemours & Co. (DD)**, which reports consolidated subsidiaries using the equity method as indicated in notes 1 and 12 to its 2008 10-K report. Pertinent portions of the footnotes are summarized next.

For those consolidated subsidiaries in which the company's ownership is less than 100 percent, the outside stockholders' interests are shown as minority interests. Investments in affiliates over which the company has significant influence but not a controlling interest are carried on the equity basis. This includes majority-owned entities for which the company does not consolidate because a minority investor holds substantive participating rights. Investments in affiliates over which the company does not have significant influence are accounted for by the cost method or as available-for-sale securities.

12. Summarized Financial Information for Affiliated Companies
Summarized combined financial information for affiliated companies for which the equity method of accounting is used (see paragraph above) is shown on a 100 percent basis. The most significant of these affiliates at December 31, 2008, are DuPont Teijin Films, DuPont-Toray Company Ltd. and DuPont-Mitsui, all of which are owned 50 percent by the company. Dividends received from equity affiliates were $87 in 2008, $88 in 2007.

continued

continued from previous page

Results of operations	2008	2007
Net sales[1]	$3,064	$3,414
Earnings before income taxes	281	171
Net income	190	66
DuPont's equity in (losses) earnings of affiliates:		
Partnerships-pretax	(4)	(19)
Corporate joint ventures—after tax	85	54
Write-down of investment	—	(165)
	$ 81	$ (130)

[1] Includes sales to DuPont of $390 in 2008, $496 in 2007, and $624 in 2006.

Financial position at December 31,	2008	2007
Current assets	$1,638	$1,345
Noncurrent assets	1,304	1,325
Total assets	2,942	2,670
Short-term borrowings	496	420
Other current liabilities	797	689
Long-term borrowings	93	82
Other long-term liabilities	143	118
Total liabilities	1,529	1,309
DuPont's investment in affiliates (includes advances)	$ 844	$ 818

At the end of fiscal 2008, DuPont reports an investment balance of $844 million (including advances made by DuPont to its equity-reported subsidiaries). As is indicated in footnote 12, this represents DuPont's 50% ownership in these subsidiaries. DuPont also reports net subsidiary sales of $3,064 million and net income from these sales of $190 million (about 6%).

The footnote also reveals that DuPont's equity-reported subsidiaries assets total $2,942 at the end of fiscal 2008 and liabilities of $1,529 million. DuPont owns only 50% of these assets and liabilities and therefore reports only the net amount (50%) of the equity subsidiaries as an equity investment.

Under equity method accounting, only the net equity owned is reported on the balance sheet (not the assets and liabilities to which the investment relates), and only the net equity in earnings is reported in the income statement (not the investee's sales and expenses). Both the balance sheet and income statements are, therefore, markedly affected. Further, because the assets and liabilities are left off the balance sheet, and because the sales and expenses are omitted from the income statement, several financial ratios are also affected.

■ **Net operating profit margin (NOPM = NOPAT/Sales revenue).** Most analysts include equity income (sales less expenses) in NOPAT because it relates to operating investments. (These subsidiaries are performing operating activities, for example, producing processed materials, for DuPont.) However, the investee's sales are omitted from the investor's sales. The reported NOPM is, thus, *overstated*.

■ **Asset turnover ratios (Sales revenue/Average assets).** Because the investee's sales and its assets are omitted from the investor's financial statements, asset turnover ratios such as inventory turnover, receivables turnover, and PPE turnover are misstated. The direction of the effect is, however, *indeterminable*.

■ **Financial leverage (Debt-to-equity = Total liabilities/Total stockholders' equity).** Financial leverage is *understated* because the liabilities of the investee are omitted from the numerator of the debt-to-equity ratio.

Although ROE components are affected, ROE is unaffected by use of equity method accounting. Still, the evaluation of the quality of ROE is affected. Analysts frequently adjust reported financial statements for equity investments before conducting their analysis. One approach to adjusting the reported financial statements would be to consolidate the equity method investee with the investor company.

YOU MAKE THE CALL

You are the Chief Financial Officer   You are receiving capital expenditure requests for long-term operating asset purchases from various managers. You are concerned that capacity utilization is too low. What potential courses of action can you consider? Explain. [Answer on page 568]

MID-CHAPTER REVIEW 2

Show the effects (amount and account) relating to the following four transactions involving investments in marketable securities accounted for using the equity method in the financial statement effects template, prepare the journal entries, and post the journal entries to the related T-accounts.

1. Purchased 5,000 shares of Hribar common stock at $10 cash per share. These shares reflect 30% ownership of Hribar.
2. Received a $2 per share cash dividend on Hribar common stock.
3. Made an adjustment to reflect $100,000 income reported by Hribar.
4. Sold all 5,000 shares of Hribar common stock for $90,000.

The solution to this review problem can be found on pages 589–590.

INVESTMENTS WITH CONTROL

If the investor company owns enough of the voting stock of the investee company such that it can exercise control over the investee, it must report **consolidated financial statements**. For example, in footnote 1 to its 2008 10-K describing its accounting policies, Google reports:

LO4 Describe and analyze accounting for investments with control.

Basis of Consolidation   The Consolidated Financial Statements include the accounts of Google and our wholly-owned subsidiaries. All intercompany balances and transactions have been eliminated.

This statement means that Google's financial statements are an aggregation (an adding up) of those of the parent company and all its subsidiary companies, less any intercompany activities.

Accounting for Investments with Control

Accounting for business combinations (acquisitions) involves one additional step to equity method accounting. Under the equity method, the investment balance represents the proportion of the investee's equity owned by the investor, and the investor company income statement includes its proportionate share of the investee's income. Consolidation accounting (1) replaces the investment balance with the investee's assets and liabilities to which it relates, and (2) replaces the equity income reported by the investor with the investee's sales and expenses to which it relates. Specifically, the consolidated balance sheet includes the gross assets and liabilities of the investee company, and the income statement includes the gross sales and expenses of the investee.

To illustrate, consider the following scenario. Penman Company acquires all of the common stock of Nissim Company by exchanging newly issued shares for all of Nissim's common stock.

The purchase price is equal to the $3,000 book value of Nissim's stockholders' equity (contributed capital of $2,000 and retained earnings of $1,000). The investment in Nissim Co. on Penman's balance sheet is accounted for using the equity method (GAAP only requires consolidation for financial statements issued to the public, not for the internal financial records of the separate companies). Penman records an initial balance in the investment account of $3,000, which equals the purchase price. The balance sheets for Penman and Nissim immediately after the acquisition, together with the required consolidating adjustments (or eliminations), and the consolidated balance sheet that the two companies report are shown in Exhibit 12.5.

EXHIBIT 12.5	Mechanics of Consolidation Accounting (Purchased at Book Value)			
	Penman Company	**Nissim Company**	**Consolidating Adjustments***	**Consolidated**
Current assets	$ 5,000	$1,000		$ 6,000
Investment in Nissim	3,000	0	(3,000)	0
PPE, net	10,000	4,000		14,000
Total assets	$18,000	$5,000		$20,000
Liabilities	$ 5,000	$2,000		$ 7,000
Contributed capital	10,000	2,000	(2,000)	10,000
Retained earnings	3,000	1,000	(1,000)	3,000
Total liabilities and equity	$18,000	$5,000		$20,000

*The accounting equation remains in balance with these adjustments.

Because Penman "controls" the activities of Nissim, GAAP requires consolidation of the two balance sheets. This process involves summing the individual lines for each balance sheet less the elimination of any intercompany transactions (investments and loans, or sales and purchases, within the consolidated group). The consolidated balances for current assets, PPE, and liabilities are, for example, the sum of those accounts on each balance sheet. The equity investment, however, represents an intercompany transaction that must be eliminated prior to consolidation. This elimination is accomplished by removing the equity investment of $3,000, and removing Nissim's equity to which that investment relates.[2]

The consolidated balance sheet is shown in the far right column of Exhibit 12.5. It shows total assets of $20,000, total liabilities of $7,000, and stockholders' equity of $13,000. Consolidated equity equals that of the parent company—this is always the case when the parent owns 100% of the subsidiary's shares.[3]

---

[2] In the event that Penman acquires less than 100% of the stock of Nissim, Penman's equity must increase to maintain the accounting equation. This equity account is titled noncontrolling interest. For example, assume that Penman acquired 80% of Nissim for $2,400 (80% of $3,000). The consolidation worksheet is presented below:

Mechanics of Consolidation Accounting (Less than 100% Acquisition)				
	Penman Company	**Nissim Company**	**Consolidating Adjustments**	**Consolidated**
Current assets	$ 5,600	$1,000		$ 6,600
Investment in Nissim	2,400	0	(2,400)	0
PPE, net	10,000	4,000		14,000
Total assets	$18,000	$5,000		$20,600
Liabilities	$ 5,000	$2,000		$ 7,000
Noncontrolling interest in Nissim	0	0	600	600
Contributed capital	10,000	2,000	(2,000)	10,000
Retained earnings	3,000	1,000	(1,000)	3,000
Total liabilities and equity	$18,000	$5,000		$20,600

Accounting for ownership of less than 100% introduces complexities that are beyond the scope of this text, so we will assume 100% ownership in the material that follows.

[3] Also, consolidated net income always equals the parent company's net income as the wholly-owned subsidiary's net income is already reflected in the parent's income statement as equity income from its investment.

The illustration above assumes that the purchase price of the acquisition equals book value. What changes, if any, occur when the purchase price and book value are different? To explore this case, consider an acquisition where purchase price exceeds book value (the typical scenario). This situation might arise, for example, if an investor company believes it is acquiring something of value that is not reported on the investee's balance sheet—such as tangible assets whose market values have risen above book value, or unrecorded intangible assets like patents or corporate synergies. If an acquisition is made at a price in excess of book value, all net assets acquired (both tangible and intangible) must be recognized on the consolidated balance sheet.

To illustrate an acquisition where purchase price exceeds book value, assume that Penman Company acquires Nissim Company for $4,000 instead of the $3,000 purchase price we used in the previous illustration. Also assume that in determining its purchase price, Penman feels that the additional $1,000 ($4,000 vs. $3,000) is justified because (1) Nissim's PPE is worth $300 more than its book value, and (2) Penman expects to realize $700 in additional value from corporate synergies.

The $4,000 investment account reflects two components: the book value acquired of $3,000 (as before) and an additional $1,000 of newly acquired assets. The post-acquisition balance sheets of the two companies, together with the consolidating adjustments and the consolidated balance sheet, are shown in Exhibit 12.6.

EXHIBIT 12.6	Mechanics of Consolidation Accounting (Purchased above Book Value)			
	Penman Company	Nissim Company	Consolidating Adjustments	Consolidated
Current assets	$ 5,000	$1,000		$ 6,000
Investment in Nissim	4,000	0	(4,000)	0
PPE, net	10,000	4,000	300	14,300
Goodwill			700	700
Total assets	$19,000	$5,000		$21,000
Liabilities	$ 5,000	$2,000		$ 7,000
Contributed capital	11,000	2,000	(2,000)	11,000
Retained earnings	3,000	1,000	(1,000)	3,000
Total liabilities and equity	$19,000	$5,000		$21,000

The consolidated balances for current assets, PPE, and liabilities are the sum of those accounts on each company's balance sheet. The investment account, however, includes newly acquired assets that must be reported on the consolidated balance sheet. The consolidation process in this case has two steps. First, the $3,000 equity of Nissim Company is eliminated against the investment account as before. Then, the remaining $1,000 of the investment account is eliminated through the adjustments for newly acquired assets ($300 of PPE and $700 of goodwill not reported on Nissim's balance sheet) on the consolidated balance sheet. Thus, the consolidated balance sheet reflects the book value of Penman and the *fair market value* (book value plus the excess of Nissim's market value over book value) for Nissim Company at the acquisition date.

To illustrate consolidation mechanics with an actual case, consider the consolidated balance sheet (parent company, subsidiary and consolidated balance sheet) that **General Electric Company** reports in a supplemental schedule to its 10-K report as shown in Exhibit 12.7.

General Electric Company (GE) owns 100% of its financial products subsidiary, General Electric Capital Services (GECS), whose stockholders' equity is $53,279 million as of 2008. The Investment in GECS account is also reported at $53,279 million on GE's (parent company) balance sheet. This investment account is subsequently removed (eliminated) in the consolidation process, together with the equity of GECS to which it relates.

GECS was founded by GE, so there are no revaluations or goodwill recognized in the consolidation process. As shown above, the general process of consolidation is an adding up of the resources

EXHIBIT 12.7	General Electric's Consolidated Balance Sheet		
At December 31, 2008 (In millions, except share amounts)	**General Electric Company and Consolidated Affiliates**	**GE (Parent)**	**GECS (Subsidiary)**
Assets			
Cash and equivalents	$ 48,187	$ 12,090	$ 37,486
Investment securities	41,446	213	41,236
Current receivables	21,411	15,064	—
Inventories	13,674	13,597	77
Financing receivables—net	365,168	—	372,456
Other GECS receivables	13,439	—	18,636
Property, plant and equipment—net	78,530	14,433	64,097
Investment in GECS	—	53,279	—
Goodwill	81,759	56,394	25,365
Other intangible assets—net	14,977	11,364	3,613
All other assets	106,899	22,435	85,721
Assets of businesses held for sale	10,556	—	10,556
Assets of discontinued operations	1,723	64	1,659
Total assets	**$797,769**	**$198,933**	**$660,902**
Liabilities and equity			
Short-term borrowings	$193,695	$ 2,375	$193,533
Accounts payable, principally trade accounts	20,819	11,699	13,882
Progress collections and price adjustments accrued	12,536	13,058	—
Dividends payable	3,340	3,340	—
Other GE current liabilities	18,220	18,284	—
Long-term borrowings	330,067	9,827	321,068
Investment contracts, insurance liabilities and insurance annuity benefits	34,032	—	34,369
All other liabilities	64,796	32,767	32,090
Deferred income taxes	4,584	(3,949)	8,533
Liabilities of businesses held for sale	636	—	636
Liabilities of discontinued operations	1,432	189	1,243
Total liabilities	**684,157**	**87,590**	**605,354**
Minority interest in equity of consolidated affiliates	8,947	6,678	2,269
Preferred stock (30,000 and 0 shares outstanding at year-end 2008 and 2007, respectively)	—	—	—
Common stock (10,536,897,000 and 9,987,599,000 shares outstanding at year-end 2008 and 2007, respectively)	702	702	1
Accumulated gains/(losses)—net			
Investment securities	(3,094)	(3,094)	(3,097)
Currency translation adjustments	(299)	(299)	(1,258)
Cash flow hedges	(3,332)	(3,332)	(3,134)
Benefit plans	(15,128)	(15,128)	(367)
Other capital	40,390	40,390	18,079
Retained earnings	122,123	122,123	43,055
Less common stock held in treasury	(36,697)	(36,697)	—
Total shareowners' equity	**104,665**	**104,665**	**53,279**
Total liabilities and equity	**$797,769**	**$198,933**	**$660,902**

and obligations of the various entities. In Exhibit 12.7, the consolidated PPE – net of $78,530 million is equal to the sum of PPE – net at GE ($14,433 million) and at GECS ($64,097 million).

However, comparing the three columns also provides a glimpse into the intercompany relationships between parent and subsidiary. For instance, accounts payable is $11,699 million at GE and $13,882 million at GECS, which total $25,581 million. But the consolidated accounts payable is $20,819 million, implying that some of the accounts payable by the parent and subsidiary are payable to each other.

Reporting of Acquired Assets and Liabilities

Acquisitions are often made at a purchase price in excess of the book value of the investee company's equity. The excess purchase price must be allocated to all of the assets and liabilities acquired, including those that do not currently appear on the balance sheet of the investee. This allocation can be done in three steps:

Step 1: Adjust the book value of all tangible assets and all liabilities to fair market value. This adjustment addresses the issue of undervalued assets on the investee firm's balance sheet.

Step 2: Assign a fair value to any identifiable intangible assets. Recall from Chapter 8 that intangible assets are only reported on the balance sheet if they are purchased; internally created intangible assets are not capitalized. This step allows the acquiring firm to assign a value to the investee's intangible assets, even if those assets are not reported on the investee firm's balance sheet.

Step 3: Assign the residual amount to goodwill. Goodwill is the excess of the acquisition price over the value of identifiable net assets acquired. That is, whatever value cannot be assigned to identifiable tangible and intangible assets is considered goodwill.

The acquiring company is required to disclose relevant information about the allocation of the purchase price in its footnotes.

For example, consider Google's reported allocation of its total $3,193.403 million purchase price in March, 2008, for DoubleClick as reported in Note 7 to its 2008 10-K:

The following table summarizes the allocation of the initial purchase price for DoubleClick as of December 31, 2008 (in thousands):

($ thousands)	
Goodwill	$2,353,503
Customer relationships	629,600
Patents and developed technology	143,400
Tradenames and other	27,800
Net assets assumed	83,276
Deferred tax assets	257,003
Deferred tax liabilities	(301,179)
Total	$3,193,403

Goodwill is not deductible for tax purposes.

Customer relationships have a weighted average useful life of 6.7 years. Patents and developed technology have a weighted average useful life of 5.0 years. Trade names and other have a weighted average useful life of 5.5 years. The majority of these assets are not deductible for tax purposes.

The first four listed items listed in Google's footnote constitute intangible long-term assets. The total amount paid for the acquisitions listed is established by first valuing all the identifiable tangible and intangible assets; including the patents, trade names, customer lists, and net assets acquired. Second, net deferred taxes assumed are subtracted. The established value is ($629,600 + $143,400 + $27,800 + $83,276) − ($301,179 − $257,003) = $839,900 thousand. Google, however, actually paid $3,193,403 thousand for DoubleClick, which exceeds this value by $2,353,503 thousand. This remaining amount is recorded as goodwill. Google reports its aggregated goodwill separately on its balance sheet but combines its other intangibles assets in its balance sheet under the title "Other intangible assets, net." Goodwill can only be recognized as an asset in an acquisition and only then in the amount by which the purchase price exceeds the fair market value of the net assets acquired, including all identifiable intangible assets.

Google estimates customer relationships have a weighted average useful life of 6.7 years. Patents and developed technology have a weighted average useful life of 5.0 years. Tradenames and other have a weighted average useful life of 5.5 years. The majority of these assets are not deductible for tax purposes. These estimated lives determine the annual amortization expense associated with these assets on the firm's financial books. Goodwill is not amortized under GAAP although it is subject to impairment write-down. The effect of this accounting treatment is to relieve the income statement of the annual amortization expense. The SEC is sufficiently concerned with the impact on the income statement that it scrutinizes acquisition accounting for excessive goodwill capitalization.

Reporting of Goodwill   GAAP requires companies to test goodwill annually for impairment just like any other asset. The impairment test is a two-step process:

1. The market value of the investee company is compared with the book value of the investor's equity investment account.[4]

2. If the market value is less than the investment balance, the investment is deemed impaired. The company must then estimate the goodwill value as if the subsidiary were acquired for its current market value, and the imputed balance for goodwill becomes the amount at which it is recorded. If this imputed amount is less than its book value, goodwill must be written down, resulting in an impairment loss that is reported in the consolidated income statement.

To illustrate the impairment computation, assume that an investment, currently reported at $1 million on the investor's balance sheet, has a current fair market value of $900,000. The consolidated balance sheet reports net assets (absent goodwill) at $700,000 and goodwill at $300,000. Analysis reveals that the current fair market value of the net assets of the investee company (absent goodwill) is $700,000. This analysis indicates goodwill is impaired by $100,000, which is computed as follows.

Fair market value of investee company	$ 900,000
Fair market value of net assets (absent goodwill)	(700,000)
Implied goodwill	200,000
Current goodwill balance	(300,000)
Impairment loss	$(100,000)

The financial statement effects and related journal entry and T-accounts are:

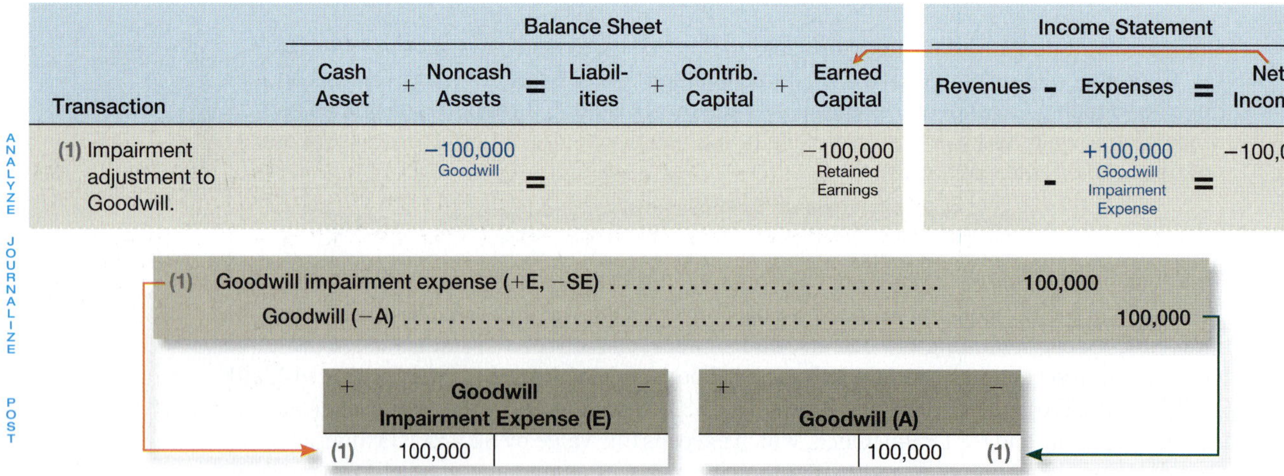

4 The fair market value of the investee company can be determined using market comparables or another valuation method (such as the discounted cash flow model, residual operating income model, or P/E multiples).

This analysis of investee company implies that goodwill must be written down by $100,000. The impairment loss is reported as a separate line item in the consolidated income statement. The related footnote disclosure describes the reasons for the write-down.

Nike reports the following goodwill impairmant in note 5 to its 2008 10-K:

NIKE, INC.
Notes to Consolidated Financial Statements — (Continued)

Umbro Impairment

In accordance with FAS 142 "Goodwill and Other Intangible Assets," the Company performs annual impairment tests on goodwill and intangible assets with indefinite lives in the fourth quarter of each fiscal year, or when events occur or circumstances change that would, more likely than not, reduce the fair value of a reporting unit or intangible assets with an indefinite life below its carrying value. As a result of a significant decline in global consumer demand and continued weakness in the macroeconomic environment, as well as decisions by Company management to adjust planned investment in the Umbro brand, the Company concluded that sufficient indicators of impairment existed to require the performance of an interim assessment of Umbro's goodwill and indefinite lived intangible assets as of February 1, 2009. Accordingly, the Company performed the first step of the goodwill impairment assessment for Umbro by comparing the estimated fair value of Umbro to its carrying amount, and determined there was a potential impairment of goodwill as the carrying amount exceeded the estimated fair value. Therefore, the Company performed the second step of the assessment which compared the implied fair value of Umbro's goodwill to the book value of goodwill. The implied fair value of goodwill is determined by allocating the estimated fair value of Umbro to all of its assets and liabilities, including both recognized and unrecognized intangibles, in the same manner as goodwill was determined in the original business combination.

The Company measured the fair value of Umbro by using an equal weighting of the fair value implied by a discounted cash flow analysis and by comparisons with the market values of similar publicly traded companies. The Company believes the blended use of both models compensates for the inherent risk associated with either model if used on a stand-alone basis, and this combination is indicative of the factors a market participant would consider when performing a similar valuation. The fair value of Umbro's indefinite-lived trademark was estimated using the relief from royalty method, which assumes that the trademark has value to the extent that Umbro is relieved of the obligation to pay royalties for the benefits received from the trademark. The assessments of the Company resulted in the recognition of impairment charges of $199.3 million and $181.3 million related to Umbro's goodwill and trademark, respectively, during the third quarter ended February 28, 2009. A deferred tax benefit of $54.5 million was recognized as a result of the trademark impairment charge. In addition to the above impairment analysis, the Company determined an equity investment held by Umbro was impaired, and recognized a charge of $20.7 million related to the impairment of this investment. These charges are included in the Company's "Other" category for segment reporting purposes.

The discounted cash flow analysis calculated the fair value of Umbro using management's business plans and projections as the basis for expected cash flows for the next twelve years and a 3% residual growth rate thereafter. The Company used a weighted average discount rate of 14% in its analysis, which was derived primarily from published sources as well as our adjustment for increased market risk given current market conditions. Other significant estimates used in the discounted cash flow analysis include the rates of projected growth and profitability of Umbro's business and working capital effects. The market valuation approach indicates the fair value of Umbro based on a comparison of Umbro to publicly traded companies in similar lines of business. Significant estimates in the market valuation approach include identifying similar companies with comparable

continued

continued from previous page

business factors such as size, growth, profitability, mix of revenue generated from licensed and direct distribution, and risk of return on investment.

Holding all other assumptions constant at the test date, a 100 basis point increase in the discount rate would reduce the adjusted carrying value of Umbro's net assets by 12%.

Identified Intangible Assets and Goodwill

All goodwill balances are included in the Company's "Other" category for segment reporting purposes. The following table summarizes the Company's goodwill balance as of May 31, 2009 and 2008 (in millions):

Goodwill, May 31, 2007	$130.8
Acquisition of Umbro Plc	319.2
Other	(1.2)
Goodwill, May 31, 2008	448.8
Purchase price adjustments	23.6
Impairment charge	(199.3)
Other	(79.6)
Goodwill, May 31, 2009	$193.5

Nike determined that the goodwill recognized when Umbro was acquired in the amount of $319.2 million was impaired to a current estimated value of $119.9 ($319.2 − $199.3) million. Impairment recognition resulted in a charge to income of $199.3 million. Nike's computations described in the note above are complex and illustrate the difficulties in determining impairment charges.

Reported goodwill across companies differs widely in total and as a percentage of company assets as the following 2008 figures indicate ($ millions).

Company	Total Assets	Reported Goodwill	Goodwill Percentage
Corning, Inc.	$ 19,256	$ 277	1.44
Google, Inc.	25,336	2,299	9.07
Nike, Inc.	13,250	194	1.46
The Procter & Gamble Company	134,833	56,512	41.91
Yahoo, Inc.	12,230	4,002	32.72

Reported goodwill is not always a useful measure of the asset's value, particularly when the actual value exceeds the reported value. For example, the value of the Coca Cola brand name alone exceeds the reported total asset value of the firm.

BUSINESS INSIGHT

Pitfalls of Acquired Growth   It may be the greatest destruction of shareholder value in history, and it happened in the bull market between 1995 and 2001. That is, the subsequent year's returns of most shareholders of purchasing companies that were hit with merger and acquisition fever fell below those of their peers. The winners were shareholders of target companies who sold their stock within the first week of takeover. What went wrong? The short answer is that companies overpaid as a result of overestimating the cost-cuttings and synergies such takeovers would bring. Then, they failed to quickly integrate operations. The results? Fully 61% of corporate buyers of intercorporate investments decreased their shareholders' wealth.

Limitations of Consolidation Reporting   Consolidation of financial statements is meant to present a financial picture of the entire set of companies under control of the parent. Because investors typically purchase stock in the parent company and not in the subsidiaries, the view is more relevant than would be one of the parent company's own balance sheet with subsidiaries reported as equity investments. Still, we must be aware of certain limitations that the consolidation process entails:

1. Consolidated income does not imply that cash is received by the parent company and is available for subsidiaries. The parent can only receive cash via dividend payments. It is quite possible, therefore, for an individual subsidiary to experience cash flow problems even though the consolidated group has strong cash flows. Likewise, debts of a subsidiary are not obligations of the consolidated group. Thus, even if the consolidated balance sheet is strong, creditors of a failing subsidiary are often unable to sue the parent or other subsidiaries to recoup losses.

2. Consolidated balance sheets and income statements are a mix of the subsidiaries, often from different industries. Comparisons across companies, even if in similar industries, are often complicated by the different mix of subsidiary companies.

3. Segment disclosures on individual subsidiaries are affected by intercorporate transfer-pricing policies that can artificially inflate the profitability of one segment at the expense of another. Companies also have considerable discretion in the allocation of corporate overhead to subsidiaries, which can markedly affect segment and subsidiary profitability.

Reporting Consolidations under Pooling-of-Interest   Prior to 2001, companies had a choice in their accounting for business combinations. They could use the **purchase method** as described in this chapter (now required for all acquisitions), or they could use the **pooling-of-interest (pooling) method**. A large number of acquisitions were accounted for under pooling-of-interest, and its impact on financial statements will linger for many years.

The main difference between the pooling-of-interest and the purchase method of accounting for acquisitions is this: under the purchase method, the investment account is initially recorded at the *fair market value* of the acquired company at acquisition. Under the pooling-of-interest method, the investment account is initially recorded at the *book value* of equity for the acquired company, regardless of the amount of purchase price. As a result, no goodwill is created. Further, because goodwill amortization was required under previous GAAP, subsequent income was larger under pooling in part because no goodwill amortization was recorded. This feature spawned widespread use of pooling-of-interest, especially for high-tech companies.

Acquisitions previously accounted for under pooling-of-interest remain unaffected under current GAAP. Therefore, we must be aware of at least two points for analysis purposes:

1. Assets were usually understated when using pooling-of-interest because investee companies were recorded at book rather than market value. This implies that consolidated asset turnover ratios are overstated.

2. Income of companies using pooling-of-interest was nearly always overstated due to elimination of additional depreciation and amortization. This continues to create difficulties for comparative analysis when looking at companies that previously applied pooling-of-interest accounting.

CHAPTER-END REVIEW

On January 1 of the current year, Bradshaw Company purchased all of the common shares of Dukes Company for $600,000 cash—this is $200,000 in excess of Dukes's book value of its equity. The balance sheets of the two firms immediately after the acquisition follow:

	Bradshaw (Parent)	Dukes (Subsidiary)	Consolidating Adjustments	Consolidated
Current assets	$1,000,000	$100,000		
Investment in Dukes	600,000	–		
PPE, net	3,000,000	400,000		
Goodwill	–	–		
Total assets	$4,600,000	$500,000		
Liabilities	$1,000,000	$100,000		
Contributed capital	2,000,000	200,000		
Retained earnings	1,600,000	200,000		
Total liabilities and equity	$4,600,000	$500,000		

During purchase negotiations, Dukes's PPE was appraised at $500,000, and all of Dukes's remaining assets and liabilities were appraised at values approximating their book values. Also, Bradshaw concluded that payment of an additional $100,000 was warranted because of anticipated corporate synergies. Show the impact of the transaction in the financial statement effects template, prepare the appropriate journal entry, post the journal entry to the related T-accounts, and prepare the consolidated balance sheet at acquisition.

The solution to this review problem can be found on page 591.

APPENDIX 12A: Equity Method Mechanics

LO5 Illustrate and analyze accounting mechanics for equity method investments.

The appendix provides a comprehensive example of accounting for an equity method investment. Assume that Petroni Company acquires a 30% interest in the outstanding voting shares of Wahlen Company on January 1, 2010, for $234,000 in cash. On that date, Wahlen's book value of equity is $560,000. Petroni agrees to pay $234,000 for a company with a book value of equity equivalent to $168,000 ($560,000 × 30%) because it feels that (1) Wahlen's balance sheet is undervalued by $140,000 (Petroni estimates PPE is undervalued by $50,000 and that Wahlen has unrecorded patents valued at $90,000) and (2) the investment is expected to yield intangible benefits valued at $24,000. (The $140,000 by which the balance sheet is undervalued translates into an investment equivalent of $42,000 [$140,000 × 30%]. This, plus the intangible benefits valued at $24,000, comprises the $66,000 difference between the purchase price [$234,000] and the book value equivalent [$168,000].)

The effect of the investment on Petroni's books is to reduce cash by $234,000 and to report the investment in Wahlen for $234,000. The investment is reported at its fair market value at acquisition, just like all other asset acquisitions, and it is reported as a noncurrent asset since the expected holding period of equity method investments is in excess of one year. Subsequent to this purchase there are three main aspects of equity method accounting:

1. Dividends received from the investee are treated as a return *of* the investment rather than a return *on* the investment (investor company records an increase in cash received and a decrease in the investment account).

2. When the investee company reports net income for a period, the investor company reports its proportionate ownership of that income. This is usually reported in the investment income section of its income statement. Thus, both equity and the investment account increase from equity method income. If the investee company reports a net *loss* for the period, income of the investor company is reduced as well as its investment account by its proportionate share.

3. The investment balance is not marked-to-market as with passive investments. Instead, it is recorded at its historical cost and is increased (decreased) by the investor company's proportionate share of investee income (loss) and decreased by any cash dividends received. Unrecognized gains (losses) can, therefore, occur if the market value of the investment differs from this adjusted cost.

To illustrate these mechanics, let's return to our illustration and assume that subsequent to acquisition, Wahlen reports net income of $50,000 and pays $10,000 cash dividends. Petroni's balance sheet and income statement are affected as follows:

Transaction	Change in Investment Account on Petroni's Balance Sheet	Equity Income on Petroni's Income Statement
Acquisition balance.............................	$234,000	
Wahlen reports income of $50,000 (30% for Petroni)	15,000	$15,000
Wahlen pays a $10,000 cash dividend ($3,000 to Petroni)	(3,000)	
Updated balance..................................	$246,000	

Petroni's ending investment balance is $246,000 and its cash balance increased by the $3,000 dividend received (note, the market value of the investment [$234,000] differs from its book value [$168,000]). Corresponding to the $15,000 increase in assets from Wahlen's income is a $15,000 increase in retained earnings (following the reporting of income to retained earnings). Petroni reports this $15,000 as investment income. Dividends received are treated as a return of the capital invested in Wahlen and, thus, the investment account is reduced.

There is symmetry between Petroni's investment account and Wahlen's stockholders' equity as follows:

Investment Account on Petroni's Balance Sheet		Wahlen's Stockholders' Equity	
Acquisition balance....................	$234,000	Acquisition balance.........	$560,000
Income..............................	15,000	Income....................	50,000
Dividends...........................	(3,000)	Dividends.................	(10,000)
Ending balance	$246,000	Ending balance	$600,000

Petroni's ending investment balance of $246,000 is 30% of Wahlen's $600,000 stockholders' equity plus the original $66,000 excess. This explains why the equity investment balance we see reported on a balance sheet does not always equal the percentage owned of the investee company.

To the extent that the excess is attributed to depreciable (amortizable) assets of the investee, the excess is depreciated (amortized) and that amount is reflected in the investor's income statement as expense. Eventually, the excess is entirely depreciated (amortized) and the investment balance equals the percentage owned (30%) of the investee's stockholders' equity with no excess. Any portion of the excess attributed to goodwill is not amortized, resulting in a permanent difference unless and until the goodwill is deemed to be impaired and written down.

APPENDIX 12B: Consolidation Accounting Mechanics

This appendix is a continuation of the example we introduced in Appendix 12A, extended to the consolidation of a parent company and one wholly owned subsidiary. Assume that Petroni Company acquires 100% (rather than 30% as in Appendix 12A) of the outstanding voting shares of Wahlen Company on January 1, 2010. To obtain these shares, Petroni pays $420,000 cash and issues 20,000 shares of its $10 par value common stock. On this date, Petroni's stock has a fair market value of $18 per share, and Wahlen's book value of equity is $560,000. Petroni is willing to pay $780,000 ($420,000 plus 20,000 shares at $18 per share) for this company with a book value of equity of $560,000 because it believes Wahlen's balance sheet is understated by $140,000 (its PPE is undervalued by $50,000 and it has unrecorded patents valued at $90,000). The remaining $80,000 of the purchase price excess over book value is ascribed to corporate synergies and other unidentifiable intangible assets (goodwill). Thus, the purchase price consists of the following three components:

LO6 Apply equity method accounting mechanics to consolidations.

$$\text{Investment (\$780,000)} \begin{cases} \text{Book value of Wahlen (\$560,000)} \\ \text{Excess fair market value over book (\$140,000)} \\ \text{Goodwill (\$80,000)} \end{cases}$$

The investment in Wahlen on Petroni's books is accounted for using the equity method of accounting.[5] This means that at acquisition, Petroni's assets increase by $360,000 (cash decreases by $420,000 and the investments account increases by $780,000) and its equity (contributed capital) increases by the same amount.

---

[5] The equity method is used for all investments other than passive investments. Once "control" is achieved, the investor company is required to consolidate its financial statements with those of other entities in the control set. The investment account remains unchanged on the parent's books; it is merely replaced with the assets and liabilities of the subsidiaries to which it relates for the consolidation process.

The balance sheets of Petroni and Wahlen at acquisition follow, including the adjustments that occur in the consolidation process and the ultimate consolidated balance sheet.

Transaction	Balance Sheet					Income Statement		
	Cash Asset +	Noncash Assets	= Liabil-ities	+ Contrib. Capital	+ Earned Capital	Revenues -	Expenses	= Net Income
Entry S		−560,000 Investment in Wahlen =		−80,000 Wahlen Common	−480,000 Wahlen Retained Earnings	-		=
Entry A		+50,000 PPE, net +80,000 Goodwill +90,000 = Patent −220,000 Investment in Wahlen				-		=

Accounts	Petroni Company	Wahlen Company	Consolidation Adjustments*		Consolidated Balance Sheet
Cash..............................	$ 168,000	$ 80,000			$ 248,000
Receivables, net	320,000	180,000			500,000
Inventory	440,000	260,000			700,000
Investment in Wahlen	780,000	0	[S] [A]	(560,000) (220,000)	0
Land..............................	200,000	120,000			320,000
PPE, net..........................	1,040,000	320,000	[A]	50,000	1,410,000
Patent............................	0	0	[A]	90,000	90,000
Goodwill..........................	0	0	[A]	80,000	80,000
Totals............................	$2,948,000	$960,000			$3,348,000
Accounts payable	$ 320,000	$ 60,000			$ 380,000
Long-term liabilities.................	760,000	340,000			1,100,000
Contributed capital	1,148,000	80,000	[S]	(80,000)	1,148,000
Retained earnings...................	720,000	480,000	[S]	(480,000)	720,000
Totals............................	$2,948,000	$960,000			$3,348,000

*[S] refers to elimination of stockholders' equity and [A] refers to recognition of assets acquired.

The initial balance of the investment account at acquisition ($780,000) reflects the $700,000 market value of Wahlen's net tangible assets ($560,000 book value + $140,000 undervaluation of assets) plus the goodwill ($80,000) acquired. Goodwill is the excess of the purchase price over the fair market of the net assets acquired. It does not appear on Petroni's balance sheet as an explicit asset at this point. It is, however, included in the investment balance and will emerge as a separate asset during consolidation.

The process of completing the initial consolidated balance sheet involves eliminating the investment account and replacing it with the assets and liabilities of Wahlen Company to which it relates. Recall the investment account consists of three items: the book value of Wahlen ($560,000), the excess of market price over book value ($140,000), and goodwill ($80,000). The consolidation process eliminates each item as follows:

[S] Elimination of Wahlen's book value of equity: Investment account is reduced by the $560,000 book value of Wahlen, and each of the components of Wahlen's equity ($80,000 common stock and $480,000 retained earnings) are eliminated.

[A] Elimination of the excess of purchase price over book value: Investment account is reduced by $220,000. The remaining adjustments increase assets (A) by the additional purchase price paid. PPE is written up by $50,000, and a $90,000 patent asset and an $80,000 goodwill asset are reported.

Stepping back from the consolidation process, we can see its effects by comparing the Petroni Company (parent) balance sheet to the consolidated balance sheet. The Petroni Company balance sheet shows a financial asset valued at $780,000. Consolidation gives us a different perspective. Rather than viewing this as a financial investment, consolidation views the financial investment as the *means* by which Petroni Company acquired a bundle of assets and liabilities. That is, the financial asset of $780,000 has been replaced by Cash ($80,000), Receivables ($180,000), Inventory ($260,000), Land ($120,000), PPE – net ($370,000), Patent ($90,000), Goodwill ($80,000), Payables ($60,000) and Long-term liabilities ($340,000). This bundle has a net value equal to the $780,000, but it provides much more detail about the transaction that Petroni engaged in.

The one part of the balance sheet that is not changed by the consolidation is the shareholders' equity section. The consolidated shareholders' equity accounts are the same as the parent company shareholders' equity accounts when the parent owns 100% of the subsidiary.

Consolidation is similar in successive periods. To the extent that the excess purchase price has been assigned to depreciable assets, or identifiable intangible assets that are amortized over their useful lives, the new assets recognized initially are depreciated. For example, if the PPE has an estimated life of 20 years with no salvage value, we must depreciate 1/20 of the $50,000 each year. Likewise, the $90,000 patent is amortized over its remaining life. Depreciation and amortization are reflected in Petroni's income statement (depreciation of the book value portion is on Wahlen's income statement). Finally, because goodwill is not amortized under GAAP, it remains at its carrying amount of $80,000 on the consolidated balance sheet unless and until it is impaired and written down.

As the excess of the purchase price over book value acquired is depreciated/amortized, the investment account gradually declines. Assuming goodwill is not impaired, the investment reaches a balance equal to the percentage of the investee's equity owned (100% in this case) plus the balance of goodwill. Generally, the investment account equals the percentage of the equity owned plus any remaining undepreciated/unamortized excess over purchase price.

APPENDIX 12C: Accounting for Investments in Derivatives

Derivatives refer to financial instruments that are utilized by companies to reduce various kinds of risks. Some examples follow:

LO7 Discuss the reporting of derivative securities

- A company expects to purchase raw materials for its production process and wants to reduce the risk that the purchase price increases prior to the purchase.

- A company has an accounts receivable on its books that is payable in a foreign currency and wants to reduce the risk that exchange rates move unfavorably prior to collection.

- A company borrows funds on a floating rate of interest (such as linked to the prime rate) and wants to convert the loan to a fixed rate of interest.

Companies are commonly exposed to these and many similar types of risk. Although companies are generally willing to assume the normal market risks that are inherent in their business, many of these financial-type risks can add variability to income and are uncontrollable. Fortunately, commodities, currencies, and interest rates are all traded on various markets and, further, securities have been developed to manage all of these risks. These securities fall under the label of derivatives. They include forward contracts, futures contracts, option contracts, and swap agreements.

Companies use derivatives to manage many of these financial risks. The reduction of risk comes at a price: the fee that another party (called the counterparty) is charging to assume that risk. Most counterparties are financial institutions, and managing financial risk is their business and a source of their profits. Although derivatives can be used effectively to manage financial risk, they can also be used for speculation with potentially disastrous results. It is for this reason that regulators passed standards regarding their disclosure in financial statements.

Reporting of Derivatives

Derivatives work by offsetting the gain or loss for the asset or liability to which they relate. Derivatives thus shelter the company from such fluctuations. For example, if a hedged receivable denominated in a foreign currency declines in value (due to a strengthening of the $US), the derivative security will increase in value by an offsetting amount, at least in theory. As a result, net equity remains unaffected and no gain or loss arises, nor is a loss reported in income.[6]

Although accounting for derivatives is complex, it essentially boils down to this: the derivative contract, and the asset or liability to which it relates, are both reported on the balance sheet at market value. The asset

---

[6] Unrealized gains and losses on derivatives classified as *cash flow hedges* (such as those relating to planned purchases of commodities) are accumulated in other comprehensive income (OCI) and are not recognized in current income until the transaction is complete (such as when both the purchase and sale of inventory occurs). Unrealized gains and losses on derivatives classified as *fair value hedges* (such as those relating to interest rate hedges and swaps, and the hedging of asset values such as relating to securities) as well as the changes in value of the hedged asset (liability) are recorded in current income.

and liability are offsetting *if* the hedge is effective and, thus, net equity is unaffected. Likewise, the related gains and losses are largely offsetting, leaving income unaffected. Income is impacted only to the extent that the hedging activities are ineffective or result from speculative activities. It is this latter activity, in particular, that regulators were concerned about in formulating accounting standards for derivatives.

Disclosure of Derivatives

Companies are required to disclose both qualitative and quantitative information about derivatives in notes to their financial statements and elsewhere (usually in Management's Discussion and Analysis section). The aim of these disclosures is to inform outsiders about potential risks underlying derivative securities.

Following is **Southwest Airlines Co.**'s disclosures from note 1 to its 2008 10-K report relating to its use of derivatives.

Financial derivative instruments

The Company accounts for financial derivative instruments utilizing Statement of Financial Accounting Standards No. 133 (SFAS 133), "Accounting for Derivative Instruments and Hedging Activities," as amended. The Company utilizes various derivative instruments, including crude oil, unleaded gasoline, and heating oil-based derivatives, to attempt to reduce the risk of its exposure to jet fuel price increases. These instruments primarily consist of purchased call options, collar structures, and fixed-price swap agreements, and upon proper qualification are accounted for as cash-flow hedges, as defined by SFAS 133. The Company has also entered into interest rate swap agreements to convert a portion of its fixed-rate debt to floating rates and one floating-rate debt issuance to a fixed-rate. These interest rate hedges are accounted for as fair value hedges or as cash flow hedges, as defined by SFAS 133.

Since the majority of the Company's financial derivative instruments are not traded on a market exchange, the Company estimates their fair values. Depending on the type of instrument, the values are determined by the use of present value methods or standard option value models with assumptions about commodity prices based on those observed in underlying markets. Also, since there is not a reliable forward market for jet fuel, the Company must estimate the future prices of jet fuel in order to measure the effectiveness of the hedging instruments in offsetting changes to those prices, as required by SFAS 133. Forward jet fuel prices are estimated through utilization of a statistical-based regression equation with data from market forward prices of like commodities. This equation is then adjusted for certain items, such as transportation costs, that are stated in the Company's fuel purchasing contracts with its vendors.

For the effective portion of settled hedges, as defined in SFAS 133, the Company records the associated gains or losses as a component of "Fuel and oil" expense in the Consolidated Statement of Income. For amounts representing ineffectiveness, as defined, or changes in fair value of derivative instruments for which hedge accounting is not applied, the Company records any gains or losses as a component of "Other (gains) losses, net", in the Consolidated Statement of Income. Amounts that are paid or received associated with the purchase or sale of financial derivative instruments (i.e., premium costs of option contracts) are classified as a component of "Other (gains) losses, net," in the Consolidated Statement of Income in the period in which the instrument settles or expires. All cash flows associated with purchasing and selling derivatives are classified as operating cash flows in the Consolidated Statement of Cash Flows, within "Changes in certain assets and liabilities."

Southwest Air's derivative use is mainly to hedge against fuel cost. Those hedges act to place a ceiling on fuel cost. For 2008, these instruments covered 78% of the company's fuel and oil requirements.

From a reporting standpoint, unrealized gains and losses on these option contracts are accumulated in the Other Comprehensive Income (OCI) portion of its stockholders' equity until the fuel is purchased. Once that fuel is purchased, those unrealized gains and losses are removed from OCI and the gain (loss) on the option is used to offset the loss (gain) on fuel. In 2008, financial instruments saved the company $1.3 billion.

Although the market value of derivatives and their related assets or liabilities can be substantial, as is the case for Southwest in 2008, the net effect on earnings and stockholders' equity is usually minor. This is because companies are mainly using them as hedges and not as speculative securities. SFAS 133, "Accounting for Derivative Instruments and Hedging Activities," was enacted in response to a concern that speculative activities were not adequately disclosed. However, subsequent to its passage the financial effects have been minimal. Either these companies were not speculating to the extent expected, or they have since reduced their level of speculation in response to increased scrutiny from better disclosures.

SUMMARY

Explain and interpret the three levels of investor influence over an investee—passive, significant, and controlling. (p. 538)   LO1

- Ownership of 20% or less in another corporation is treated as a passive investment by the investor.
- Significant influence is assumed to be available to the investor corporation if it owns more than 20% but not over 50% of the outstanding voting stock of the investee corporation.
- Control is generally presumed if the investing firm owns more than 50% of the outstanding voting stock of the investee corporation.

Describe and analyze accounting for passive investments. (p. 540)   LO2

- Ownership of 20% or less in another corporation is treated as a passive investment by the investor. Investing for returns is the objective rather than influencing another corporation's decisions. The investment is reported as a long-term asset only if the intention is to retain the asset for longer than a year. Passive investments are segregated into two types, called trading securities or securities available for sale.
- Trading securities are securities that will be converted into cash in a very short period of time. Any trading securities held at the end of an accounting period are marked to their market value. The value change is recognized as an unrealized gain (or loss) in the income statement.
- Available-for-sale securities are held for long-term capital gains or dividends. Any securities held at the end of an accounting period are also marked to their market value. However, the value change bypasses the income statement to become part of retained earnings called other comprehensive income.
- Gains, losses realized on sale, and dividends on passive investments are reported as other income in the income statement.
- Debt securities that management intends to hold to maturity are carried at cost unless their value is considered impaired in which case the security is written down. Otherwise changes in market value are not recognized on the balance sheet or the income statement.

Explain and analyze accounting for investments with significant influence. (p. 549)   LO3

- Significant influence is assumed to be available to the investor corporation if it owns more than 20% but not over 50% of the outstanding voting stock of the investee corporation. Typically, the investment is initially recorded as a long-term asset at the purchase price.
- In the case of significant influence, the equity method of reporting is followed.
- Under the equity method, the investor corporation reports the investment as a, typically, long-term asset. The investor recognizes its proportionate share of the investee's net income as income and an increase in the investment account. Any dividends received by the investor are treated as a recovery of the investment and reduce the investment balance.

Describe and analyze accounting for investments with control. (p. 553)   LO4

- If a corporation is considered to have control of another corporation, the financial statements of both firms are consolidated and reported as though they were a single entity.
- Control is generally presumed if the investing firm owns more than 50% of the outstanding voting stock of the investee corporation.
- Control can exist in special cases with less than 50% of the outstanding voting stock of the investee. Control means that the investor has the ability to affect the strategic direction of the investee.

Appendix 12A: Illustrate and analyze accounting mechanics for equity method investments. (p. 562)   LO5

- Under the equity method of accounting, neither the investee's assets nor its liabilities are reported on the investor's balance sheet. Only the proportionate investment is reported. Further, only the investor's net equity is reported in income; and the investee's sales and expenses are omitted.
- The result is that revenues and expenses, but not NOPAT, are understated; NOPM (NOPAT/Sales) is overstated; and net operating assets (NOA) are understated. Also, financial leverage is understated. ROE remains unaffected.

Appendix 12B: Apply equity method accounting mechanics to consolidations. (p. 563)   LO6

- Identifiable intangible assets (such as patents, trademarks, customer lists) often result from the acquisition of one corporation by another. This is a situation in which the acquirer will have control and consolidation accounting is required.
- Intangibles are valued at the purchase date and then amortized over their economic life. Any remaining purchase price not allocated to tangible or identifiable intangible assets is treated as goodwill.
- Goodwill is not amortized but is written down when and if considered impaired. The write-down is an expense of the period.

- Reports of consolidated corporations are often difficult to understand because they commingle the assets, liabilities, revenues, expenses, and cash flows of several businesses that can be very different. General Electric and its subsidiary provide an example.

LO7 **Appendix 12C: Discuss the reporting of derivative securities. (p. 565)**

- Derivatives refer to financial instruments that are utilized by companies to reduce various kinds of risks.
- Derivatives work by offsetting the gain or loss for the asset or liability to which they relate.
- The accounting for derivatives boils down to this: the derivative contract and the asset or liability to which it relates are both reported on the balance sheet at market value. The asset and liability are offsetting if the hedge is effective. Likewise, the related gains and losses are largely offsetting, leaving income unaffected.

GUIDANCE ANSWERS . . . YOU MAKE THE CALL

You are the Chief Financial Officer   Capacity utilization is important. If long-term operating assets are not sufficiently utilized, cost per unit produced is too high. Cost per unit does not relate solely to manufacturing products, but also applies to the cost of providing services and many other operating activities. However, if we purchase assets with little productive slack, our costs of production at peak levels can be excessive. Further, the company may be unable to service peak demand and risk losing customers. In response, many companies have explored alliances. These take many forms. Some require a simple contract to use another company's manufacturing, service, or administrative capability for a fee (note: these executory contracts are not recorded under GAAP). Another type of alliance is that of a joint venture to share ownership of manufacturing or IT facilities. In this case, if demand can be coordinated with that of a partner, perhaps operating assets can be more effectively used. Finally, a variable interest entity (VIE) can be formed to acquire the asset for use by the company and its partner.

KEY TERMS

Asset turnover ratios (Sales revenue/Average assets) (p. 552)

Available-for-sale (AFS) securities (p. 542)

Consolidated financial statements (p. 553)

Controlling influence (p. 539)

Cost method (p. 548)

Derivatives (p. 565)

Equity method (p. 549)

Fair market value (p. 541)

Fair value option (p. 547)

Financial leverage (Debt-to-equity = Total liabilities/Total stockholders' equity) (p. 552)

Held-to-maturity (HTM) (p. 548)

Intercorporate investments (p. 538)

Net operating profit margin (NOPM = NOPAT/Sales revenue) (p. 552)

Passive influence (p. 539)

Pooling-of-interest method (p. 561)

Purchase method (p. 561)

Significant influence (p. 539)

Trading (T) securities (p. 542)

MULTIPLE CHOICE

1. Corporation A owns 50% of corporation B. This is a case where:
   a. Corporation A controls corporation B.
   b. Corporation A does not control corporation B.
   c. Corporation A has significant influence on corporation B.
   d. Corporation A does not have a significant influence on corporation B.
   e. Both *a* and *c* are correct.

2. In accounting for available-for-sale securities, the
   a. securities are reported at their market value, along with their market adjustment from cost.
   b. securities are reported at cost.
   c. increases in market value are reported in income.
   d. increases in market value are not reported in income.
   e. Both *a* and *d* are correct.

3. Which of the following statements is true of investments accounted for under the equity method?
   a. Investor reports its percentage share of the investee's income in its operating income.
   b. Investor reports dividends received from the investee in its operating income.
   c. Investment is reported at its market value.
   d. Investment is reported at cost plus any dividends received from the investee.
   e. Investment is reported at market value less any dividends received from the investee.

4. Which of the following statements is true about goodwill?
   a. Current reporting standards require that goodwill be amortized over its economic life.
   b. Goodwill is written down when the market value of the investee implies a goodwill value below the investor's goodwill account.
   c. Goodwill can be recognized only when the acquisition price does not exceed the value of the tangible and identifiable intangible assets acquired.
   d. The recording of goodwill can be based on the acquisition of assets such as patents and trademarks.
   e. Goodwill equals retained earnings.

Superscript A (B, C) denotes assignments based on Appendix 12A (12B, 12C).

DISCUSSION QUESTIONS

Q12-1. What measure (fair market value or amortized cost) is used for the balance sheet to report (a) trading securities, (b) available-for-sale securities, and (c) held-to-maturity securities?

Q12-2. What is an unrealized holding gain (loss)? Explain.

Q12-3. Where are unrealized holding gains and losses related to trading securities reported in the financial statements? Where are unrealized holding gains and losses related to available-for-sale securities reported in the financial statements?

Q12-4. What does *significant influence* imply regarding intercorporate investments? Describe the accounting procedures used for such investments.

Q12-5. On January 1 of the current year, Yetman Company purchases 40% of the common stock of Livnat Company for $250,000 cash. During the year, Livnat reports $80,000 of net income and pays $60,000 in cash dividends. At year-end, what amount should appear in Yetman's balance sheet for its investment in Livnat?

Q12-6. What accounting method is used when a stock investment represents more than 50% of the investee company's voting stock? Explain.

Q12-7. What is the underlying objective of consolidated financial statements?

Q12-8. Finn Company purchases all of the common stock of Murray Company for $750,000 when Murray Company has $300,000 of common stock and $450,000 of retained earnings. If a consolidated balance sheet is prepared immediately after the acquisition, what amounts are eliminated in preparing it? Explain.

Q12-9.[B] Bradshaw Company owns 100% of Dee Company. At year-end, Dee owes Bradshaw $75,000. If a consolidated balance sheet is prepared at year-end, how is the $75,000 handled? Explain.

Q12-10. What are some limitations of consolidated financial statements?

Assignments with the WebAssign. logo in the margin are available in WebAssign.
See the Preface of the book for details.

MINI EXERCISES

M12-11. Interpreting Disclosures of Available-for-Sale Securities

LO1, LO2

PFIZER, INC.
NYSE :: PFE

Use the following year-end footnote disclosure from **Pfizer Inc.**'s 10-K report to answer parts *a* and *b*.

($ millions)	2008
Cost of available-for-sale equity securities	$341
Gross unrealized gains	17
Gross unrealized losses	(39)
Fair value of available-for-sale equity securities	$319

a. At what amount is its available-for-sale equity securities reported on Pfizer's 2008 balance sheet? Explain.

b. How is its net unrealized loss of $22 million ($39 million − $17 million) reported by Pfizer in its financial statements?

LO2

M12-12. Accounting for Available-for-Sale and Trading Securities

Assume that Wasley Company purchases 6,000 common shares of Pincus Company for $12 cash per share. During the year, Wasley receives a cash dividend of $1.10 per common share from Pincus, and the year-end market price of Pincus common stock is $13 per share. How much income does Wasley report relating to this investment for the year if it accounts for the investment as:

a. Available-for-sale investment?

b. Trading investment?

LO1, LO2, LO3, LO4

ABBOTT LABORATORIES
NYSE :: ABT

M12-13. Analyzing Disclosures of Investment Securities

Abbott Laboratories reports the following disclosure in Note 1 to its 2008 10-K relating to its December 31 after-tax comprehensive income. How is Abbott accounting for its investment in securities? How do you know?

Comprehensive Income, net of tax ($ millions)	2008
Foreign currency (loss) gain translation adjustments	$(2,208)
Net actuarial (losses) gains and prior service cost and credits and amortization of net actuarial losses and prior service cost and credits, net of taxes of $638 in 2008	5,361
Unrealized (losses) gains on marketable equity securities, net of taxes of $28 in 2008	(987)
Net adjustments for derivative instruments designated as cash flow hedges	(49)
Reclassification adjustments for realized (gains)	(2)
Other comprehensive (loss) income	(3,246)
Net earnings	4,881
Comprehensive income	$1,635

LO1, LO3

M12-14. Analyzing and Interpreting Equity Method Investments

Stober Company purchases an investment in Lang Company at a purchase price of $1 million cash, representing 30% of the book value of Lang. During the year, Lang reports net income of $100,000 and pays cash dividends of $40,000. At the end of the year, the market value of Stober's investment is $1.2 million.

a. At what amount is the investment reported on Stober's balance sheet at year-end?

b. What amount of income from investments does Stober report? Explain.

c. Stober's $200,000 unrealized gain in investment market value (choose one and explain):

  (1) Is not reflected on either its income statement or balance sheet.

  (2) Is reported in its current income.

  (3) Is reported on its balance sheet only.

  (4) Is reported in its other comprehensive income.

d. Prepare journal entries to record the transactions and events above.

e. Post the journal entries from d to their respective T-accounts.

f. Record each of the transactions from d in the financial statement effects template.

LO1, LO3

M12-15. Calculating Income for Equity Method Investments

Kross Company purchases an equity investment in Penno Company at a purchase price of $5 million, representing 40% of the book value of Penno. During the current year, Penno reports net income of $600,000 and pays cash dividends of $200,000. At the end of the year, the market value of Kross's investment is $5.3 million. What amount of income does Kross report relating to this investment in Penno for the year? Explain.

LO1, LO3

MERCK & CO.
NYSE :: MRK

M12-16. Interpreting Disclosures on Investments in Affiliates

Merck & Co., Inc.'s 10-K report included the following footnote disclosure.

Joint Ventures and Other Equity Method Affiliates Equity income from affiliates reflects the performance of the Company's joint ventures and other equity method affiliates and was comprised of the following:

Years Ended December 31 ($ millions)	2008	2007
Merck/Schering-Plough	$1,536.3	$1,830.8
AstraZeneca LP	598.4	820.1
Other*	425.9	325.6
	$2,560.6	$2,976.5

*Primarily reflects results from Merial Limited, Sanofi Pasteur MSD and Johnson & Johnson°Merck Consumer Pharmaceuticals Company.

a. How will the amount reported in the table for 2008 affect Merck's financial statements.

b. How will Merck account for the dividends received on these investments?

M12-17. Computing Consolidating Adjustments and Minority Interest

LO1, LO4

Philipich Company purchases 80% of Hirst Company's common stock for $600,000 cash when Hirst Company has $300,000 of common stock and $450,000 of retained earnings. If a consolidated balance sheet is prepared immediately after the acquisition, what amounts are eliminated when preparing that statement? What amount of minority interest appears in the consolidated balance sheet?

M12-18. Computing Consolidated Net Income

LO1, LO4

Benartzi Company purchased a 90% interest in Liang Company on January 1 of the current year. Benartzi Company had $600,000 net income for the current year *before* recognizing its share of Liang Company's net income. If Liang Company had net income of $150,000 for the year, what is the consolidated net income for the year?

M12-19. Understanding Earnings under Pooling-of-Interest Method

LO1, LO4

DeFond Company acquired 100% of Verduzco Company on September 1 of the current year. Why might the consolidated earnings of the two companies for the current year be higher if the transaction had been treated as a pooling-of-interest (which is no longer accepted under GAAP) rather than as a purchase?

M12-20. Reporting of and Analyzing Financial Effects of Trading (Debt) Securities

LO1, LO2

Hartgraves Company had the following transactions and adjustments related to a bond investment.

2010

Oct. 1   Purchased $500,000 face value of Skyline, Inc.'s 7% bonds at 97 plus a brokerage commission of $1,000. The bonds pay interest on September 30 and March 31 and mature in 20 years. Hartgraves Company expects to sell the bonds in the near future.

Dec. 31   Made the adjusting entry to record interest earned on investment in the Skyline bonds.

31   Made the adjusting entry to record the current fair value of the Skyline bonds. At December 31, 2010, the market value of the Skyline bonds was $490,000.

2011

Mar. 31   Received the semiannual interest payment on investment in the Skyline bonds.

Apr. 1   Sold the Skyline bond investment for $492,300 cash.

a. Prepare journal entries to record these transactions.

b. Post the journal entries from *a* to their respective T-accounts.

c. Record each of the transactions in the financial statement effects template.

M12-21. Reporting of and Analyzing Financial Effects of Trading (Equity) Securities

LO1, LO2

Blouin Company had the following transactions and adjustment related to a stock investment.

2010

Nov. 15   Purchased 6,000 shares of Lane, Inc.'s common stock at $12 per share plus a brokerage commission of $750. Blouin expects to sell the stock in the near future.

Dec. 22   Received a cash dividend of $1.10 per share of common stock from Lane.

31   Made the adjusting entry to reflect year-end fair value of the stock investment in Lane. The year-end market price of the Lane common stock is $11.25 per share.

2011

Jan. 20   Sold all 6,000 shares of the Lane common stock for $66,900.

a. Prepare journal entries to record these transactions.

b. Post the journal entries from *a* to their respective T-accounts.

c. Record each of the transactions in the financial statement effects template.

LO1, LO2 M12-22. Reporting of and Analyzing Financial Effects of Available-for-Sale (Equity) Securities

Refer to the data for Blouin Company in Mini Exercise 12-21. Assume that when the shares were purchased, management did not intend to sell the stock in the near future. Record the transactions and adjustments for Blouin Company under this assumption.

LO1, LO4 M12-23. Computing Stockholders' Equity in Consolidation

On January 1 of the current year, Halen Company purchased all of the common shares of Jolson Company for $575,000 cash. On this date, the stockholders' equity of Halen Company consisted of $600,000 in common stock and $310,000 in retained earnings. Jolson Company had $350,000 in common stock and $225,000 in retained earnings. What amount of total stockholders' equity appears on the consolidated balance sheet?

EXERCISES

LO1, LO2 E12-24. Assessing Financial Statement Effects of Trading and Available-for-Sale Securities

Four transactions involving investments in marketable securities classified as trading follow.

(1) Purchased 6,000 common shares of Liu, Inc., for $12 cash per share.
(2) Received a cash dividend of $1.10 per common share from Liu.
(3) Year-end market price of Liu common stock is $11.25 per share.
(4) Sold all 6,000 common shares of Liu for $66,900.

a. Prepare journal entries to record the four transactions.
b. Post the journal entries from *a* to their respective T-accounts.
c. Record each of the transactions from *a* in the financial statement effects template.
d. Using the same transaction information as above and assuming the investments in marketable securities are classified as available-for-sale, (i) prepare journal entries to record the transactions, (ii) post the journal entries to their respective T-accounts, and (iii) record each of the transactions in the financial statement effects template.

LO1, LO2 E12-25. Assessing Financial Statement Effects of Trading and Available-for-Sale Securities

WebAssign.

For the following transactions involving investments in marketable securities, assume that:

a. Investments are classified as trading.

(1) Ohlson Co. purchases 5,000 common shares of Freeman Co. at $16 cash per share.
(2) Ohlson Co. receives a cash dividend of $1.25 per common share from Freeman.
(3) Year-end market price of Freeman common stock is $17.50 per share.
(4) Ohlson Co. sells all 5,000 common shares of Freeman for $86,400 cash.
(i) prepare journal entries to record the four transactions, (ii) post the journal entries to their respective T-accounts, and (iii) record each of the transactions in the financial statement effects template.

b. Investments are classified as available-for-sale (for same four transactions from *a*).
(i) prepare journal entries to record the transactions, (ii) post the journal entries to their respective T-accounts, and (iii) record each of the transactions in the financial statement effects template.

LO1, LO3 E12-26. Interpreting Footnotes on Security Investments

DEVRY INC.
NYSE :: DV

DeVry Inc. reports the following in Note 2 to its 2008 10-K.

Marketable Securities

Marketable securities consist of auction-rate certificates and investments in mutual funds all of which are classified as available-for-sale securities. The following is a summary of our short-term and long-term available-for-sale marketable securities at June 30, 2008:

($ thousands)	Cost	Gross Unrealized (Loss)	Gross Unrealized Gain	Fair Value
Short-term Investments:				
Bond Mutual Fund	$ 746	$ —	$12	$ 758
Stock Mutual Funds	1,939	(389)	—	1,550
Total Short-term Investments	$ 2,685	$ (389)	$12	$ 2,308
Long-term Investments:				
Auction Rate Certificates	$59,475	$(2,304)	$—	$57,171
Total Long-term Investments	$59,475	$(2,304)	$—	$57,171

a. At what amount is its equity securities investment portfolio reported on its balance sheet? Does that amount include any unrealized gains or losses? Explain.

b. What amount related to DeVry's AFS securities appears in DeVry's 2008 income statement?

c. Assuming an effective tax rate of 38.2%, what amount related to DeVry's AFS securities should appear in DeVry's Accumulated Other Comprehensive Income footnote?

E12-27. **Reporting of and Analyzing Financial Effects of Trading (Debt) Securities**   LO1, LO2

Barclay, Inc., had the following transactions and adjustments related to a bond investment.

2010

Nov. 1 Purchased $300,000 face value of Joos, Inc.'s 9% bonds at 102 plus a brokerage commission of $900. The bonds pay interest on October 31 and April 30 and mature in 15 years. Barclay expects to sell the bonds in the near future.

Dec. 31 Made the adjusting entry to record interest earned on investment in the Joos bonds.

     31 Made the adjusting entry to record the current fair value of the Joos bonds. At December 31, 2010, the market value of the Joos bonds was $301,500.

2011

Apr. 30 Received the semiannual interest payment on investment in the Joos bonds.

May 1 Sold the Joos bond investment for $300,900 cash.

a. Prepare journal entries to record these transactions.

b. Post the journal entries from a to their respective T-accounts.

c. Record each of the transactions in the financial statement effects template.

E12-28. **Reporting of Stockholders' Equity in Consolidation**   LO1, LO4

Baylor Company purchased 75% of the common stock of Reed Company for $600,000 in cash when the stockholders' equity of Reed Company consisted of $500,000 in common stock and $300,000 in retained earnings. On the acquisition date, the stockholders' equity of Baylor Company consisted of $900,000 in common stock and $440,000 in retained earnings. Prepare the stockholders' equity section in the consolidated balance sheet as of the acquisition date.

E12-29. **Interpreting Footnote Disclosures for Investments**   LO1, LO2

CNA Financial Corporation provides the following information in Note A to its 2008 10-K report:

CNA FINANCIAL CORPORATION
NYSE :: CNA

Valuation of investments: CNA classifies its fixed maturity securities and its equity securities as either available-for-sale or trading, and as such, they are carried at fair value. Changes in fair value of trading securities are reported within Net investment income on the Consolidated Statement of Operations. The amortized cost of fixed maturity securities classified as available-for-sale is adjusted for amortization of premiums and accretion of discounts to maturity, which are included in Net investment income on the Consolidated Statement of Operations. Changes in fair value related to available-for-sale securities are reported as a component of other comprehensive income. Investments are written down to fair value and losses are recognized in Realized investment gains (losses) on the Consolidated Statements of Operations when a decline in value is determined to be other-than-temporary.

Summary of Fixed Maturity and Equity Securities

December 31, 2008 ($ millions)	Cost or Amortized Cost	Gross Unrealized Gains	Gross Unrealized Losses Less than 12 Months	12 Months or Greater	Estimated Fair Value
Fixed maturity securities available-for-sale:					
U.S. Treasury securities and obligations of government agencies	$ 2,862	$ 69	$ 1	$ —	$ 2,930
Asset-backed securities	9,670	24	961	969	7,764
States, municipalities and political subdivisions—tax-exempt securities	8,557	90	609	623	7,415
Corporate and other taxable bonds	12,993	275	1,164	1,374	10,730
Redeemable preferred stock	72	1	23	3	47
Total fixed maturity securities available-for-sale:	34,154	459	2,758	2,969	28,886
Total fixed maturity securities trading	1	—	—	—	1

continued on next page

continued from previous page

December 31, 2008 ($ millions)	Cost or Amortized Cost	Gross Unrealized Gains	Gross Unrealized Losses		Estimated Fair Value
			Less than 12 Months	12 Months or Greater	
Equity securities available-for-sale:					
Common stock	134	190	1	3	320
Preferred stock	882	5	15	321	551
Total equity securities available-for-sale	1,016	195	16	324	871
Total	$35,171	$654	$2,774	$3,293	$29,758

   a. At what amount is its investment portfolio reflected on its balance sheet? In your answer identify its market value, cost, and any unrealized gains and losses.

   b. How are its unrealized gains and/or losses reflected in CNA's balance sheet and income statement?

   c. How are any impairment losses and the gains and losses realized from the sale of securities reflected in CNA's balance sheet and income statement?

LO1, LO3

E12-30. Assessing Financial Statement Effects of Equity Method Securities

The following transactions involve investments in marketable securities and are accounted for using the equity method.

   (1) Purchased 12,000 common shares of Barth Co. at $9 cash per share; the shares represent 30% ownership in Barth.

   (2) Received a cash dividend of $1.25 per common share from Barth.

   (3) Recorded income from Barth stock investment when Barth's net income is $80,000.

   (4) Sold all 12,000 common shares of Barth for $120,500.

   a. Prepare journal entries to record these four transactions.

   b. Post the journal entries from *a* to their respective T-accounts.

   c. Record each of the transactions in the financial statement effects template.

LO1, LO3

E12-31. Assessing Financial Statement Effects of Equity Method Securities

The following transactions involve investments in marketable securities and are accounted for using the equity method.

   (1) Healy Co. purchases 15,000 common shares of Palepu Co. at $8 cash per share; the shares represent 25% ownership of Palepu.

   (2) Healy receives a cash dividend of $0.80 per common share from Palepu.

   (3) Palepu reports annual net income of $120,000.

   (4) Healy sells all 15,000 common shares of Palepu for $140,000 cash.

   a. Prepare journal entries to record these four transactions.

   b. Post the journal entries from *a* to their respective T-accounts.

   c. Record each of the transactions in the financial statement effects template.

LO1, LO2, LO3

E12-32. Assessing Financial Statement Effects of Passive and Equity Method Investments

On January 1, 2010, Ball Corporation purchased, as a stock investment, 10,000 shares of Leftwich Company common stock for $15 cash per share. On December 31, 2010, Leftwich announced net income of $80,000 for the year and paid a cash dividend of $1.10 per share. At December 31, 2010, the market value of Leftwich's stock was $19 per share.

   a. Assume that the stock acquired by Ball represents 15% of Leftwich's voting stock and that Ball classifies it as available-for-sale. For the following transactions, (1) prepare journal entries, (2) post those journal entries to their respective T-accounts, and (3) record each of the transactions in the financial statement effects template.

      (1) Ball purchased 10,000 common shares of Leftwich at $15 cash per share; the shares represent a 15% ownership in Leftwich.

      (2) Leftwich reported annual net income of $80,000.

      (3) Received a cash dividend of $1.10 per common share from Leftwich.

      (4) Year-end market price of Leftwich common stock is $19 per share.

b. Assume that the stock acquired by Ball represents 30% of Leftwich's voting stock and that Ball accounts for this investment using the equity method since it is able to exert significant influence. For the following transactions, (1) prepare journal entries, (2) post those journal entries to their respective T-accounts, and (3) record each of the transactions in the financial statement effects template.

(1) Ball purchased 10,000 common shares of Leftwich at $15 cash per share; the shares represent a 30% ownership in Leftwich.

(2) Leftwich reported annual net income of $80,000.

(3) Received a cash dividend of $1.10 per common share from Leftwich.

(4) Year-end market price of Leftwich common stock is $19 per share.

E12-33. Interpreting Equity Method Investment Footnotes

DuPont reports the following in footnote 12 to its 2008 10-K report relating to its equity method investments ($ millions).

LO1, LO3

DUPONT
NYSE :: DD

Financial Position at December 31	2008	2007
Current assets	$1,638	$1,345
Noncurrent assets	1,304	1,325
Total assets	$2,942	$2,670
Short-term borrowings[1]	$ 496	$ 420
Other current liabilities	797	689
Long-term borrowings[1]	93	82
Other long-term liabilities	143	118
Total liabilities	$1,529	$1,309
DuPont's investment in affiliates (includes advances)	$ 844	$ 818

[1] The company's pro rata interest in total borrowings was $288 in 2008 and $246 in 2007, of which $25 in 2008 and $48 in 2007 were guaranteed by the company. These amounts are included in the guarantees disclosed in Note 19.

a. DuPont reports its investment in equity method affiliates on its balance sheet at $844 million. Does this reflect the adjusted cost or market value of its interest in these companies?

b. Approximate what percentage DuPont owns, on average, of these affiliates. Explain.

c. DuPont reports that its equity interest in reported gains of these affiliates is approximately $81 million in 2008, and that it received $87 million in dividends from these affiliates in 2008. Using this information, and the above footnote, can we explain much of the change in the investment balance from $818 million in 2007 to $844 million in 2008?

d. In general, how does use of the equity method impact DuPont's ROE and its components (asset turnover and profit margin)?

E12-34. Analyzing and Interpreting Disclosures on Equity Method Investments

Caterpillar Inc. (CAT) owned 50% of Shin Caterpillar Mitsubishi, Ltd. prior to August 2008. It reported the investment on its balance sheet at $582 million on December 31, 2007, and provides the following information in footnote 11 to its 2008 10-K report.

LO1, LO3

CATERPILLAR, INC.
NYSE :: CAT

Our investments in affiliated companies accounted for by the equity method have historically consisted primarily of a 50 percent interest in Shin Caterpillar Mitsubishi Ltd. (SCM) located in Japan. On August 1, 2008, SCM redeemed half of Mitsubishi Heavy Industries Ltd.'s (MHI's) shares in SCM. As a result, Caterpillar now owns 67 percent of the renamed entity, Caterpillar Japan Ltd. (Cat Japan). Because Cat Japan is accounted for on a lag, Cat Japan's August 1, 2008, financial position was consolidated on September 30, 2008. Cat Japan's results of operations were consolidated in the fourth quarter. See Note 25 for details on this share redemption. In February 2008, we sold our 23 percent equity investment in A.S.V. Inc. (ASV) resulting in a $60 million pretax gain. Accordingly, the December 31, 2008, financial position and equity investment amounts noted below do not include ASV or Cat Japan.

Combined financial information of the unconsolidated affiliated companies accounted for by the equity method (generally on a lag of 3 months or less) was as follows:

Years Ended December 31 ($ millions)	2008	2007	2006
Results of operations			
Sales	$3,727	$4,007	$4,420
Cost of sales	3,082	3,210	3,526
Gross profit	$ 645	$ 797	$ 894
Profit (loss)	$ 55	$ 157	$ 187
Caterpillar's profit (loss)	$ 37	$ 73	$ 81

Sales from SCM, while an unconsolidated affiliate, to Caterpillar of approximately $1.67 billion, $1.67 billion, and $1.81 billion in 2008, 2007, and 2006, respectively, are included in the affiliated company sales. In addition, SCM purchases of Caterpillar product, while an unconsolidated affiliate, were $353 million, $268 million, and $273 million in 2008, 2007, and 2006, respectively.

Financial Position of unconsolidated affiliated companies: ($ millions)	2008	2007	2006
Financial position			
Assets			
Current assets	$209	$2,062	$1,807
Property, plant and equipment—net	227	1,286	1,119
Other assets	26	173	176
	462	3,521	3,102
Liabilities			
Current liabilities	173	1,546	1,394
Long-term debt due after one year	110	269	309
Other liabilities	35	393	145
	318	2,208	1,848
Ownership	$144	$1,313	$1,254

Caterpillar's Investment in unconsolidated affiliated companies:

($ millions)	2008	2007	2006
Investment in equity method companies	$66	$582	$542
Plus: Investment in cost method companies	28	16	20
Investment in unconsolidated affiliated companies	$94	$598	$562

At December 31, 2008, consolidated "Profit employed in the business" in Statement 2 included $10 million representing undistributed profit of the unconsolidated affiliated companies.

a. Did CAT acquire its investment in Shin Caterpillar Mitsubishi, Ltd at book value (with no goodwill)? Show computations supporting your response.

b. What assets and liabilities of SCM are omitted at December 31, 2007 and 2008, respectively, from CAT's balance sheet as a result of the equity method of accounting for this investment?

c. Do the liabilities of the investee company affect CAT? Explain.

d. How, in general, does the use of the equity method impact CAT's ROE and its components (asset turnover and profit margin)?

LO1, LO2 E12-35. Reporting of and Analyzing Financial Effects of Trading (Equity) Securities

WebAssign.

Guay Company had the following transactions and adjustment related to a stock investment.

2010

Nov. 15 Purchased 5,000 shares of Core, Inc.'s common stock at $16 per share plus a brokerage commission of $900. Guay Company expects to sell the stock in the near future.

Dec. 22 Received a cash dividend of $1.25 per share of common stock from Core.

31 Made the adjusting entry to reflect year-end fair value of the stock investment in Core. The year-end market price of the Core common stock is $17.50 per share.

2011

Jan. 20 Sold all 5,000 shares of the Core common stock for $86,400.

a. Prepare journal entries to record these transactions.

b. Post the journal entries from *a* to their respective T-accounts.

c. Record each of the transactions in the financial statement effects template.

E12-36. **Reporting of and Analyzing Financial Effects of Available-for-Sale (Equity) Securities**   **LO1, LO2**
Refer to the data for Guay Company in Exercise 12-35. Assume that when the shares were purchased, management did not intend to sell the stock in the near future. Record the transactions and adjustments for Guay Company under this assumption.

E12-37. **Reporting and Interpreting Stock Investment Performance**   **LO1, LO2, LO3**
Kasznik Company began operations in 2010 and, by year-end (December 31), had made six stock investments. Year-end information on these stock investments follows.

Company	Cost or Equity Basis (as appropriate)	Year-End Market Value	Market Classification
Barth, Inc.	$ 68,000	$ 65,300	Trading
Foster, Inc.	162,500	160,000	Trading
McNichols, Inc.	197,000	192,000	Available-for-sale
Patell, Inc.	157,000	154,700	Available-for-sale
Ertimur, Inc.	100,000	102,400	Equity method
Soliman, Inc.	136,000	133,200	Equity method

a. At what total amount are the trading stock investments reported at in the December 31, 2010, balance sheet?

b. At what total amount are the available-for-sale stock investments reported at in the December 31, 2010, balance sheet?

c. At what total amount are the equity method stock investments reported at in the December 31, 2010, balance sheet?

d. What total amount of unrealized holding gains or unrealized holding losses related to stock investments appears in the 2010 income statement?

e. What total amount of unrealized holding gains or unrealized holding losses related to stock investments appears in the stockholders' equity section of the December 31, 2010, balance sheet?

f. What total amount of market value adjustment to stock investments appears in the December 31, 2010, balance sheet? Which category of stock investments does the market value adjustment relate to? Does the market value adjustment increase or decrease the financial statement presentation of these stock investments?

E12-38. **Analyzing Equity Method Investment Footnotes**   **LO1, LO3**
Abbott Laboratories reports the following in Note 12 to its 2007 10-K report: **ABBOTT LABORATORIES** NYSE :: ABT

Note 12 — Equity Method Investments (dollars in millions)
Abbott's 50 percent-owned joint venture, TAP Pharmaceutical Products Inc. (TAP), is accounted for under the equity method of accounting. The investment in TAP was $152, $159, and $167 at December 31, 2007, 2006, and 2005, respectively, and dividends received from TAP were $502, $487, and $343 in 2007, 2006, and 2005, respectively. Abbott performs certain administrative and manufacturing services for TAP at negotiated rates that approximate fair market value. Summarized financial information for TAP is as follows:

Year Ended December 31	2007	2006	2005
Net sales	$3,002	$3,363	$3,260
Cost of sales	720	836	883
Income before taxes	1,564	1,524	1,379
Net income.	996	952	883

December 31	2007	2006	2005
Current assets	$1,101	$1,181	$1,339
Total assets	1,354	1,333	1,470
Current liabilities	914	955	1,082
Total liabilities	1,037	1,009	1,136

Undistributed earnings of investments accounted for under the equity method amounted to approximately $136 as of December 31, 2007.

a. At what amount is Abbott's equity investment in TAP reported on Abbott's December, 2007 balance sheet?

b. In 2007, TAP paid $502 million in dividends to Abbott. How did the receipt of $502 in dividends from TAP affect Abbott's balance sheet and income statement in 2007?

c. How much income did Abbott report in 2007 relating to this investment in TAP?

d. Interpret the Abbott statement that "undistributed earnings of investments accounted for under the equity method amounted to $136 as of December 31, 2007."

e. How, in general, does use of the equity method impact Abbott's ROE and its components (asset turnover and profit margin)?

LO1, LO4 E12-39. Constructing the Consolidated Balance Sheet at Acquisition

On January 1 of the current year, Healy Company purchased all of the common shares of Miller Company for $500,000 cash. Balance sheets of the two firms at acquisition follow.

	Healy Company	Miller Company	Consolidating Adjustments	Consolidated
Current assets	$1,700,000	$120,000		
Investment in Miller	500,000	—		
Plant assets, net	3,000,000	410,000		
Goodwill	—	—		
Total assets	$5,200,000	$530,000		
Liabilities	$ 700,000	$ 90,000		
Contributed capital	3,500,000	400,000		
Retained earnings	1,000,000	40,000		
Total liabilities and equity	$5,200,000	$530,000		

During purchase negotiations, Miller's plant assets were appraised at $425,000; and, all of its remaining assets and liabilities were appraised at values approximating their book values. Healy also concluded that an additional $45,000 (in goodwill) demanded by Miller's shareholders was warranted because Miller's earning power was better than the industry average. (1) Prepare the consolidating adjustments, (2) Prepare the consolidated balance sheet at acquisition, (3) Prepare journal entries to record the transactions, (4) Post the journal entries to their respective T-accounts, and (5) Record each of the transactions in the financial statement effects template.

LO1, LO4 E12-40. Constructing the Consolidated Balance Sheet at Acquisition

Rayburn Company purchased all of Kanodia Company's common stock for cash on January 1, at which time the separate balance sheets of the two corporations appeared as follows:

	Rayburn Company	Kanodia Company	Consolidating Adjustments	Consolidated
Investment in Kanodia	$ 600,000	—		
Other assets	2,300,000	$700,000		
Goodwill	—	—		
Total assets	$2,900,000	$700,000		
Liabilities	$ 900,000	$160,000		
Contributed capital	1,400,000	300,000		
Retained earnings	600,000	240,000		
Total liabilities and equity	$2,900,000	$700,000		

During purchase negotiations, Rayburn determined that the appraised value of Kanodia's Other Assets was $720,000; and, all of its remaining assets and liabilities were appraised at values approximating their book values. The remaining $40,000 of the purchase price was ascribed to goodwill. (1) Prepare the consolidating adjustments, (2) Prepare the consolidated balance sheet at acquisition, (3) Prepare journal entries to record the transactions, (4) Post the journal entries to their respective T-accounts, and (5) Record each of the transactions in the financial statement effects template.

LO1, LO4 E12-41. Assessing Goodwill Impairment

On January 1, 2010, Engel Company purchases 100% of Ball Company for $16.8 million. At the time of acquisition, Ball's stockholders' equity is reported at $16.2 million. Engel ascribes the excess of

$600,000 to goodwill. Assume that the market value of Ball declines to $12.5 million and that the fair market value of Ball's tangible net assets is estimated at $12.3 million as of December 31, 2010.

- a. Provide computations to determine if the goodwill has become impaired and, if so, the amount of the impairment.
- b. What impact does the impairment of goodwill have on Engel's financial statements?

E12-42.[B] **Constructing the Consolidated Balance Sheet at Acquisition**   LO1, LO4, LO6

Easton Company acquires 100 percent of the outstanding voting shares of Harris Company on January 1, 2010. To obtain these shares, Easton pays $210,000 in cash and issues 5,000 of its $10 par value common stock. On this date, Easton's stock has a fair market value of $36 per share, and Harris's book value of stockholders' equity is $280,000. Easton is willing to pay $390,000 for a company with a book value for equity of $280,000 because it believes that (1) Harris's buildings are undervalued by $40,000, and (2) Harris has an unrecorded patent that Easton values at $30,000. Easton considers the remaining balance sheet items to be fairly valued (no book-to-market difference). The remaining $40,000 of the purchase price excess over book value is ascribed to corporate synergies and other general unidentifiable intangible assets (goodwill). The January 1, 2010, balance sheets at the acquisition date follow:

	Easton Company	Harris Company	Consolidating Adjustments	Consolidated
Cash..........................	$ 84,000	$ 40,000		
Receivables..................	160,000	90,000		
Inventory	220,000	130,000		
Investment in Harris	390,000	—		
Land........................	100,000	60,000		
Buildings, net...............	400,000	110,000		
Equipment, net	120,000	50,000		
Total assets.................	$1,474,000	$480,000		
Accounts payable	$ 160,000	$ 30,000		
Long-term liabilities...........	380,000	170,000		
Common stock	500,000	40,000		
Additional paid-in capital	74,000	—		
Retained earnings.............	360,000	240,000		
Total liabilities & equity.........	$1,474,000	$480,000		

- a. Show the breakdown of the investment into the book value acquired, the excess of fair value over book value, and the portion of the investment representing goodwill.
- b. Prepare the consolidating adjustments and the consolidated balance sheet. Identify the adjustments by whether they relate to the elimination of stockholders' equity [S] or the excess of purchase price over book value [A].
- c. How will the excess of the purchase price over book value acquired be treated in years subsequent to the acquisition?

E12-43.[C] **Reporting and Analyzing Derivatives**   LO7

Hewlett-Packard Company reports the following information on its cash-flow hedges (derivatives) in comprehensive income (net income plus other comprehensive income) in Note 14 to its 2008 10-K report:

HEWLETT-PACKARD COMPANY
NYSE :: HPQ

($ millions)	Accumulated Other Comprehensive Income (Loss)	Total
Net earnings		$8,329
(Decrease) in net unrealized gain on available-for-sale securities	$ (16)	(16)
Increase in net unrealized gain on cash flow hedges	866	866
(Decrease) in cumulative translation adjustment..............	(936)	(936)
(Decrease) in unrealized components of defined benefit pension plans.......................................	(538)	(538)
Comprehensive income		$7,705

- a. Identify and describe the usual applications for derivatives.

b. How are derivatives and their related assets (and/or liabilities) reported on the balance sheet?

c. By what amount has the unrealized gain or loss on the HP derivatives affected its current income? What are the analysis implications?

PROBLEMS

LO2, LO3, LO4

METLIFE INC.
NYSE :: MET

P12-44. Analyzing and Interpreting Available-for-Sale Securities Disclosures

Following is a portion of the investments footnote 3 from **MetLife Inc.**'s 2008 10-K report. Investment earnings are a crucial component of the financial performance of insurance companies such as MetLife, and investments comprise a large part of its assets. MetLife accounts for its bond investments as available-for-sale securities.

The following tables present the cost or amortized cost, gross unrealized gain and loss, estimated fair value of the Company's fixed maturity and equity securities, and the percentage that each sector represents by the respective total holdings at:

December 31, 2008 ($ millions)	Cost or Amortized Cost	Gross Unrealized Gain	Gross Unrealized Loss	Estimated Fair Value	% of Total
U.S. corporate securities	$ 72,211	$ 994	$ 9,902	$ 63,303	33.6%
Residential mortgage-backed securities	39,995	753	4,720	36,028	19.2
Foreign corporate securities	34,798	565	5,684	29,679	15.8
U.S. Treasury/agency securities	17,229	4,082	1	21,310	11.3
Commercial mortgage-backed securities	16,079	18	3,453	12,644	6.7
Asset-backed securities	14,246	16	3,739	10,523	5.6
Foreign government securities	9,474	1,056	377	10,153	5.4
State and political subdivision securities	5,419	80	942	4,557	2.4
Other fixed maturity securities	57	—	3	54	—
Total fixed maturity securities	$209,508	$7,564	$28,821	$188,251	100.0%

December 31, 2007 ($ millions)	Cost or Amortized Cost	Gross Unrealized Gain	Gross Unrealized Loss	Estimated Fair Value	% of Total
U.S. corporate securities	$ 74,310	$1,685	$ 2,076	$ 73,919	31.8%
Residential mortgage-backed securities	54,773	598	376	54,995	23.7
Foreign corporate securities	36,232	1,701	767	37,166	16.0
U.S. Treasury/agency securities	19,723	1,482	13	21,192	9.1
Commercial mortgage-backed securities	16,946	241	194	16,993	7.3
Asset-backed securities	11,048	40	516	10,572	4.6
Foreign government securities	11,645	1,350	182	12,813	5.5
State and political subdivision securities	4,342	140	114	4,368	1.9
Other fixed maturity securities	335	13	30	318	0.1
Total fixed maturity securities	$229,354	$7,250	$4,268	$232,336	100.0%

Required

a. At what amount does MetLife report its bond investments on its balance sheets for 2008 and 2007?

b. What are its net unrealized gains (losses) for 2008 and 2007? By what amount did these unrealized gains (losses) affect its reported income in 2008 and 2007?

c. What is the difference between *realized* and *unrealized* gains and losses? Are realized gains and losses treated differently in the income statement than unrealized gains and losses?

d. Many analysts compute a *mark-to-market investment return* as follows: Net investment income + Realized gains and losses + Change in unrealized gains and losses. Do you think that this metric provides insights into the performance of MetLife's investment portfolio beyond that which is included in GAAP income statements? Explain.

P12-45. **Preparing the Consolidated Balance Sheet** LO1, LO4, LO6

On January 1, 2010, Gem Company purchased for $450,000 cash a 70% stock interest in Alpine, Inc., which then had common stock of $420,000 and retained earnings of $140,000. Balance sheets of the two companies immediately after the acquisition were as follows:

	Gem	Alpine
Current assets	$200,000	$160,000
Stock investment—Controlling (Alpine)	450,000	—
Plant and equipment (net)	265,000	460,000
Total assets	$915,000	$620,000
Liabilities	$ 50,000	$ 60,000
Common stock	700,000	420,000
Retained earnings	165,000	140,000
Total liabilities and stockholders' equity	$915,000	$620,000

Sixty percent of the amount paid by Gem in excess of the equity acquired is attributed to undervalued plant and equipment; the other 40% is based on Alpine's potential for future superior earning power.

Required

Prepare the consolidated balance sheet on the acquisition date; include a column for consolidating adjustments (see Exhibits 12.5 and 12.6 for guidance).

P12-46. **Analyzing Price Allocation Including In-Process R&D** LO1, LO4, LO6

Amgen Inc., reports the following in footnote 8 to its 2008 10-K report.

AMGEN INC.
NASDAQ :: AMGN

Abgenix, Inc.

On April 1, 2006, we acquired all of the outstanding common stock of Abgenix, a company with expertise in the discovery and development of monoclonal antibodies. We paid cash consideration of $22.50 per share in this transaction that was accounted for as a business combination. Additionally, we issued 1.9 million stock options in exchange for Abgenix stock options assumed in the acquisition, 1.4 million of which were vested at the date of acquisition. The purchase price was as follows (in millions):

Cash paid for shares	$2,103
Other, principally fair value of vested options assumed	96
Total	$2,199

The purchase price was allocated to all of the tangible and amortizable intangible assets acquired, including acquired IPR&D, and liabilities assumed based on their estimated fair values at the acquisition date. The excess of the purchase price over the fair values of assets and liabilities acquired was assigned to goodwill. The following table summarizes the allocation of the purchase price (in millions):

Acquired IPR&D	$1,101
Identifiable intangible asset	320
Cash	252
Deferred tax assets, net	290
Property, plant and equipment	220
Other assets	75
Liabilities, principally debt	(743)
Goodwill	684
Net assets acquired	$2,199

The estimated fair values of the acquired IPR&D and the identifiable intangible asset were determined based upon discounted after-tax cash flows adjusted for the probabilities of successful development and commercialization. The identifiable intangible asset consists of certain technology that has alternative future uses in our R&D activities and will be amortized over its five-year estimated useful life. The amount allocated to acquired IPR&D was immediately expensed in the Consolidated Statement of Income (see Note 1, "Summary of significant accounting policies — Acquired in-process research and development"). The results of Abgenix's operations have been included in the consolidated financial statements commencing April 1, 2006. Pro forma results of operations for the year ended December 31, 2006, assuming the acquisition of Abgenix had taken place at the beginning of 2006 would not differ significantly from actual reported results.

Required

a. Of the total assets acquired, what portion is allocated to tangible assets and what portion to intangible assets?

b. Are the assets (both tangible and intangible) of the acquired company reported on the consolidated balance sheet at the book value as reported on the acquired company's balance sheet immediately prior to the acquisition, or at the fair market value on the date of the acquisition? Explain.

c. How are the tangible and intangible assets accounted for subsequent to the acquisition?

d. Comment on the valuation of the in-process R&D and the accounting for this portion of the purchase price.

e. If the amount allocated to in-process R&D was decreased, what effect would this have on the allocation of the purchase price to the remaining acquired assets? What effect would this have on current and future earnings?

LO1, LO2, LO3, LO5   **P12-47. Analyzing and Reporting Debt Investment Performance**

Columbia Company began operations in 2010 and by year-end (December 31) had made six bond investments. Year-end information on these bond investments follows.

Company	Face Value	Cost or Amortized Cost	Year-End Market Value	Classification
Ling, Inc.	$100,000	$102,400	$105,300	Trading
Wren, Inc......................	$250,000	$262,500	$270,000	Trading
Olanamic, Inc.	$200,000	$197,000	$199,000	Available for sale
Fossil, Inc.	$150,000	$154,000	$160,000	Available for sale
Meander, Inc....................	$100,000	$101,200	$102,400	Held to maturity
Resin, Inc.	$140,000	$136,000	$137,000	Held to maturity

Required

a. At what total amount will the trading bond investments be reported in the December 31, 2010, balance sheet?

b. At what total amount will the available-for-sale bond investments be reported in the December 31, 2010, balance sheet?

c. At what total amount will the held-to-maturity bond investments be reported in the December 31, 2010, balance sheet?

d. What total amount of unrealized holding gains or unrealized holding losses related to bond investments will appear in the 2010 income statement?

e. What total amount of unrealized holding gains or unrealized holding losses related to bond investments will appear in the stockholders' equity section of the December 31, 2010, balance sheet?

f. What total amount of fair value adjustment to bond investments will appear in the December 31, 2010, balance sheet? Which category of bond investments does the fair value adjustment relate to? Does the fair value adjustment increase or decrease the financial statement presentation of these bond investments?

LO1, LO4, LO6   **P12-48. Analyzing and Interpreting Disclosures on Consolidations**

CATERPILLAR INC.
NYSE :: CAT

Caterpillar Inc. consists of two business units: the manufacturing company (parent corporation) and a wholly owned finance subsidiary. These two units are consolidated in Caterpillar's 2008 10-K report. Following is a supplemental disclosure that Caterpillar includes in its 10-K report that shows the separate balance sheets of the parent and its subsidiary, as well as consolidating adjustments and the consolidated balance sheet presented to shareholders. This supplemental disclosure is not mandated under GAAP, but is voluntarily reported by Caterpillar as useful information for investors and creditors. Using this disclosure, answer the following requirements:

Required

a. Does each individual company (unit) maintain its own financial statements? Explain. Why does GAAP require consolidation instead of providing the financial statements of individual companies (units)?

b. What is the balance of Investments in Financial Products Subsidiaries as of December 31, 2008, on the parent's balance sheet (Machinery and Engines)? What is the equity balance of the financial products subsidiary to which this relates as of December 31, 2008? Do you see a relation? Will this relation always exist? Explain the consolidating adjustment shown on the line labeled Investments in unconsolidated affiliated companies?

c. Refer to your answer for *a*. How does the equity method of accounting for the investment in the subsidiary company obscure the actual financial condition of the parent company that is revealed in the consolidated financial statements?

d. Refer to the Consolidating Adjustments column reported—it is used to prepare the consolidated balance sheet. Generally, what do these adjustments accomplish?

e. Compare the consolidated balance of stockholders' equity with the stockholders' equity of the parent company (Machinery and Engines). Will the relation that is evident always hold? Explain.

f. Recall that the parent company uses the equity method of accounting for its investment in the subsidiary, and that this account is eliminated in the consolidation process. What is the relation between consolidated net income and the net income of the parent company? Explain.

g. What do you believe is the implication for the consolidated balance sheet if the market value of the Financial Products subsidiary is greater than the book value of its stockholders' equity?

| | | Supplemental Consolidating Data | | |
December 31, 2008 ($ millions)	Consolidated	Machinery and Engines	Financial Products	Consolidating Adjustments
Assets				
Current assets				
Cash and short-term investments	$ 2,736	$ 1,517	$ 1,219	$ —
Receivables—trade and other	9,397	6,032	545	2,820
Receivables—finance	8,731	—	12,137	(3,406)
Deferred and refundable income taxes	1,223	1,014	209	—
Prepaid expenses and other current assets	765	510	280	(25)
Inventories	8,781	8,781	—	—
Total current assets	31,633	17,854	14,390	(611)
Property, plant and equipment—net	12,524	9,380	3,144	—
Long-term receivables—trade and other	1,479	357	549	573
Long-term receivables—finance	14,264	—	14,867	(603)
Investments in unconsolidated affiliated companies	94	137	—	(43)
Investments in Financial Products subsidiaries	—	3,727	—	(3,727)
Noncurrent deferred and refundable income taxes	3,311	3,725	35	(449)
Intangible assets	511	510	1	—
Goodwill	2,261	2,261	—	—
Other assets	1,705	310	1,395	—
Total assets	**$67,782**	**$38,261**	**$34,381**	**$(4,860)**
Liabilities				
Current liabilities				
Short-term borrowings	$ 7,209	$ 1,632	$ 6,012	$ (435)
Accounts payable	4,827	4,654	323	(150)
Accrued expenses	4,121	2,621	1,526	(26)
Accrued wages, salaries and employee benefits	1,242	1,228	14	—
Customer advances	1,898	1,898	—	—
Dividends payable	253	253	—	—
Other current liabilities	1,027	1,002	29	(4)
Long-term debt due within one year	5,492	456	5,036	—
Total current liabilities	26,069	13,744	12,940	(615)
Long-term debt due after one year	22,834	5,766	17,098	(30)
Liability for postemployment benefits	9,975	9,975	—	—
Other liabilities	2,293	2,165	616	(488)
Total liabilities	**61,171**	**31,650**	**30,654**	**(1,133)**
Commitments and contingencies				
Redeemable noncontrolling interest	524	524	—	—
Stockholders' equity				
Common stock	3,057	3,057	860	(860)
Treasury stock	(11,217)	(11,217)	—	—
Profit employed in the business	19,826	19,826	2,975	(2,975)
Accumulated other comprehensive income	(5,579)	(5,579)	(108)	108
Total stockholders' equity	**6,087**	**6,087**	**3,727**	**(3,727)**
Total liabilities, redeemable noncontrolling interest and stockholders' equity	**$67,782**	**$38,261**	**$34,381**	**$(4,860)**

CASES AND PROJECTS

LO1, LO3, LO4, LO5

GENERAL MILLS INC.
NYSE :: GIS

C12-49. **Analyzing and Interpreting Disclosures on Equity Method Investments**

General Mills Inc. invests in a number of joint ventures to manufacture and distribute its food products as discussed in the following footnote to its fiscal year 2008 10-K report.

INVESTMENTS IN JOINT VENTURES

We have a 50 percent equity interest in CPW that manufactures and markets ready-to-eat cereal products in more than 130 countries and republics outside the United States and Canada. CPW also markets cereal bars in several European countries and manufactures private label cereals for customers in the United Kingdom. We have guaranteed a portion of CPW's debt and its pension obligation in the United Kingdom. Results from our CPW joint venture are reported as of and for the 12 months ended March 31.

We have 50 percent equity interests in Häagen-Dazs Japan, Inc. and Häagen-Dazs Korea Company Limited. These joint ventures manufacture, distribute, and market Häagen-Dazs ice cream products and frozen novelties. In fiscal 2007, we changed this reporting period to include results through March 31. In previous years, we included results for the twelve months ended April 30. Accordingly, fiscal 2007 results include only 11 months of results from these joint ventures compared to 12 months in fiscal 2008 and 2006. The impact of this change was not material to our consolidated results of operations, so we did not restate prior periods for comparability.

During the third quarter of fiscal 2008, the 8th Continent soymilk business was sold. Our 50 percent share of the after-tax gain on the sale was $2.2 million, of which we recognized $1.7 million in after-tax earnings from joint ventures in fiscal 2008. We will record an additional after-tax gain of up to $0.5 million in the first quarter of fiscal 2010 if certain conditions are satisfied.

In February 2006, CPW announced a restructuring of its manufacturing plants in the United Kingdom. Our after-tax share of CPW restructuring, impairment, and other exit costs pursuant to approved plans during fiscal 2008 and prior years was as follows:

	Fiscal Year		
Expense (Income), ($ millions)	2008	2007	2006
Gain on sale of property	$(15.9)	$ —	$ —
Accelerated depreciation charges and severance associated with previously announced restructuring actions	4.5	8.2	8.0
Other charges resulting from fiscal 2008 restructuring actions	3.2	—	—
Total	$ (8.2)	$8.2	$8.0

During the first quarter of fiscal 2007, CPW acquired the Uncle Tobys cereal business in Australia for $385.6 million. We funded advances and an equity contribution to CPW from cash generated from our international operations, including our international joint ventures.

Our cumulative investment in these joint ventures was $278.6 million at the end of fiscal 2008 and $294.6 million at the end of fiscal 2007. We also have goodwill of $577.0 million associated with our joint ventures. Our investments in these joint ventures include aggregate advances of $124.4 million as of May 25, 2008, and $157.1 million as of May 27, 2007. Our sales to these joint ventures were $12.8 million in fiscal 2008, $31.8 million in fiscal 2007, and $34.8 million in fiscal 2006. We had a net return of capital from the joint ventures of $75.2 million in fiscal 2008 and made net investments of $103.4 million in fiscal 2007 and $7.0 million in fiscal 2006. We received dividends from the joint ventures of $108.7 million in fiscal 2008, $45.2 million in fiscal 2007, and $77.4 million in fiscal 2006.

Summary combined financial information for the joint ventures on a 100 percent basis follows:

	Fiscal Year		
($ millions)	2008	2007	2006
Net sales	$2,404.2	$2,016.3	$1,795.2
Gross margin	1,008.4	835.4	770.3
Earnings before income taxes	231.7	167.3	157.4
Earnings after income taxes	190.4	132.0	120.9

($ millions)	May 25, 2008	May 27, 2007
Current assets	$1,021.5	$ 815.3
Noncurrent assets	1,002.0	898.1
Current liabilities	1,592.6	1,227.8
Noncurrent liabilities	75.9	81.7

Required

a. How does General Mills account for its investments in joint ventures? How are these investments reflected on its balance sheet, and how generally is income recognized on these investments?

b. General Mills reports the total of all of these investments on its May 25, 2008, balance sheet at $278.6 million. Approximately what percent of these joint ventures does it own, on average? Given this percent, approximately how much income would you expect that General Mills reports relating to these investments?

c. Does the $278.6 million investment reported on General Mills' balance sheet sufficiently reflect the assets and liabilities required to conduct these operations? Explain.

d. Do you believe that the liabilities of these joint venture entities represent actual obligations of General Mills? Explain.

e. What potential problem(s) does equity method accounting present for analysis purposes?

C12-50. Analyzing Financial Statement Effects of Passive and Equity Investments   LO1, LO2, LO3

On January 2, 2010, Magee, Inc., purchased, as a stock investment, 20,000 shares of Dye, Inc.'s common stock for $21 per share, including commissions and taxes. On December 31, 2010, Dye announced a net income of $280,000 for the year and declared a dividend of 80 cents per share, payable January 15, 2011, to stockholders of record on January 5, 2011. At December 31, 2010, the market value of Dye's stock was $18 per share. Magee received its dividend on January 18, 2011.

Required

a. Assume that the stock acquired by Magee represents 10% of Dye's voting stock and is classified in the trading category. Prepare all journal entries appropriate for this investment, beginning with the purchase on January 2, 2010, and ending with the receipt of the dividend on January 18, 2011. (Magee recognizes dividend income when received.)

b. Post the journal entries from part a to their respective T-accounts.

c. Record each of the transactions from part a in the financial statement effects template.

d. Assume that the stock acquired by Magee represents 40% of Dye's voting stock. Prepare all journal entries appropriate for this investment, beginning with the purchase on January 2, 2010, and ending with the receipt of the dividend on January 18, 2011.

e. Post the journal entries from part d to their respective T-accounts.

f. Record each of the transactions from part d in the financial statement effects template.

C12-51. Assessing Management Interpretation of Consolidated Financial Statements   LO1, LO2, LO3, LO4

Demski, Inc., manufactures heating and cooling systems. It has a 75% interest in Asare Company, which manufactures thermostats, switches, and other controls for heating and cooling products. It also has a 100% interest in Demski Finance Company, created by the parent company to finance sales of its products to contractors and other consumers. The parent company's only other investment is a 25% interest in the common stock of Knechel, Inc., which produces certain circuits used by Demski, Inc. A condensed consolidated balance sheet of the entity for the current year follows.

DEMSKI, INC., AND SUBSIDIARIES
Consolidated Balance Sheet
December 31, 2010

Assets		
Current assets		$19,300,000
Stock investment—Influential (Knechel).		2,600,000
Other assets		71,400,000
Excess of cost over equity acquired in net assets of Asare Company		1,700,000
Total assets		$95,000,000
Liabilities and stockholders' equity		
Current liabilities		$10,300,000
Long-term liabilities.		14,200,000
Stockholders' equity		
Minority interest	$ 3,800,000	
Common stock	50,000,000	
Retained earnings.	16,700,000	70,500,000
Total liabilities and stockholders' equity		$95,000,000

This balance sheet, along with other financial statements, was furnished to shareholders before their annual meeting, and all shareholders were invited to submit questions to be answered at the meeting. As chief financial officer of Demski, you have been appointed to respond to the questions at the meeting.

Required

Answer the following stockholder questions.

a.　What is meant by *consolidated* financial statements?

b.　Why is the investment in Knechel shown on the consolidated balance sheet, but the investments in Asare and Demski Finance are omitted?

c.　Explain the meaning of the asset Excess of Cost over Equity Acquired in Net Assets of Asare Company.

d.　What is meant by *minority interest* and to what company is this account related?

e.　How is the value ($3,800,000) of the minority interest reported on Demski's balance sheet determined under GAAP? How would it be determined if Demski were reporting under IFRS?

LO1, LO2, LO3　**C12-52.**　**Understanding Intercorporate Investments, Accounting Practices, and Managerial Ethics**

Doug Stevens, controller of Nexgen, Inc., has asked his assistant, Gayle Sayres, for suggestions as to how the company can improve its financial performance for the year. The company is in the last quarter of the year and projections to the end of the year show the company will have a net loss of about $400,000.

"My suggestion," said Sayres, "is that we sell 1,000 of the 200,000 common shares of Heflin Company that we own. The 200,000 shares gives us a 20% ownership of Heflin, and we have been using the equity method to account for this investment. We have owned this stock a long time and the current market value of the 200,000 shares is about $750,000 above our book value for the stock."

"That sale will only generate a gain of about $3,750," replied Stevens.

"The rest of the story," continued Sayres, "is that once we sell the 1,000 shares, we will own less than 20% of Heflin. We can then reclassify the remaining 199,000 shares from the influential category to the trading category. Once in the trading category, we value the stocks at their current fair value, include the rest of the $750,000 gain in this year's income statement, and finish the year with a healthy net income."

"But," responded Stevens, "we aren't going to sell all the Heflin stock; 1,000 shares maybe, but certainly not any more. We own that stock because they are a long-term supplier of ours. Indeed, we even have representation on their board of directors. The 199,000 shares do not belong in the trading category."

Sayres rolled her eyes and continued, "The classification of an investment as trading or not depends on management's intent. This year-end we claim it was our intent to sell the stock. Next year we change our minds and take the stock out of the trading category. Generally accepted accounting principles can't legislate management intent, nor can our outside auditors read our minds. Besides, why shouldn't we take advantage of the flexibility in GAAP to avoid reporting a net loss for this year?"

Required

a.　Should generally accepted accounting principles permit management's intent to influence accounting classifications and measurements?

b.　Is it ethical for Doug Stevens to implement the recommendation of Gayle Sayres?

SOLUTIONS TO REVIEW PROBLEMS

Mid-Chapter Review 1

Solution for Part 1

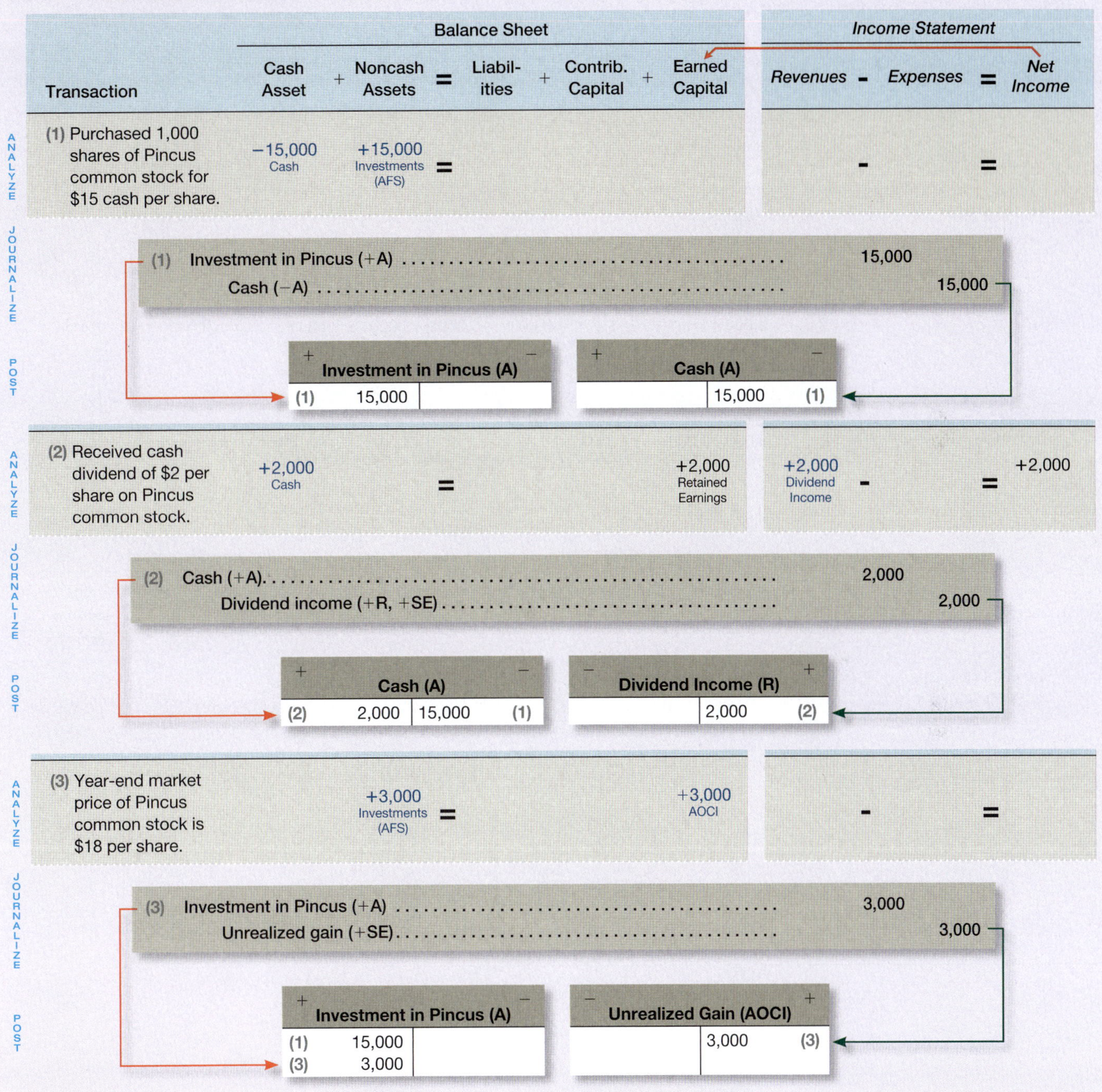

continued

continued from previous page

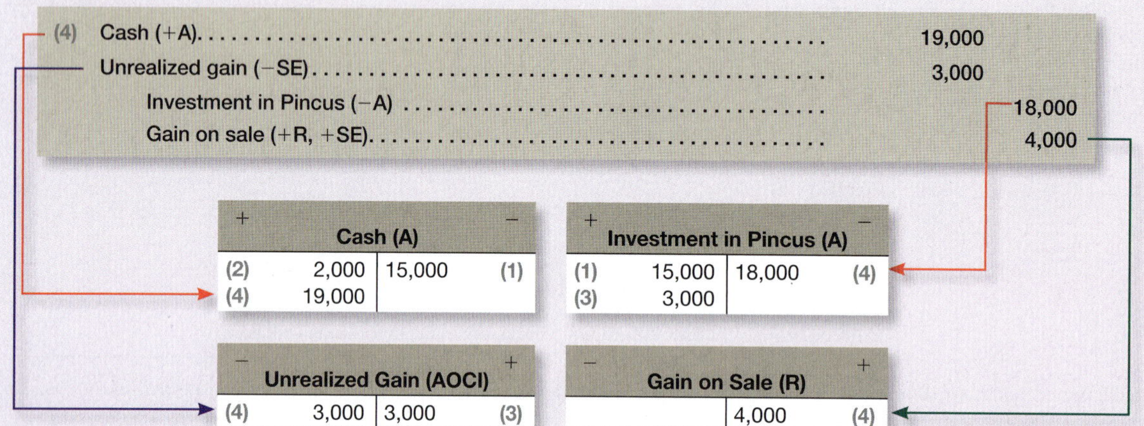

Solution for Part 2

Transaction	Balance Sheet								Income Statement			
	Cash Asset	+	Noncash Assets	=	Liabil-ities	+	Contrib. Capital	+	Earned Capital	Revenues	− Expenses =	Net Income
(1) Purchased 1,000 shares of Pincus common stock for $15 cash per share.	−15,000 Cash		+15,000 Investments (Trading)	=							−	=

(1)	Investment in Pincus (+A)	15,000	
	Cash (−A)		15,000

+ Investment in Pincus (A) −			+ Cash (A) −	
(1)	15,000			15,000 (1)

Transaction	Balance Sheet								Income Statement			
(2) Received cash dividend of $2 per share on Pincus common stock.	+2,000 Cash			=					+2,000 Retained Earnings	+2,000 Dividend Income	−	= +2,000

(2)	Cash (+A)..	2,000	
	Dividend income (+R, +SE)		2,000

+ Cash (A) −			− Dividend Income (R) +	
(2)	2,000	15,000 (1)		2,000 (2)

continued

continued from previous page

	Balance Sheet					Income Statement		
Transaction	Cash Asset +	Noncash Assets =	Liabil-ities +	Contrib. Capital +	Earned Capital	Revenues −	Expenses =	Net Income
(3) Year-end market price of Pincus common stock is $18 per share.		+3,000 Investments (Trading) =			+3,000 Retained Earnings	+3,000 Unrealized Gain −		=	+3,000

ANALYZE

JOURNALIZE

(3) Investment in Pincus (+A)	3,000	
Unrealized gain (+R, +SE)		3,000

POST

+ Investment in Pincus (A) −	
(1) 15,000	
(3) 3,000	

− Unrealized Gain (R) +	
	3,000 (3)

ANALYZE

	Balance Sheet					Income Statement		
(4) Sold all 1,000 shares of Pincus common stock for $19,000 cash.	+19,000 Cash	−18,000 Investments (Trading) =			+1,000 Retained Earnings	+1,000 Gain on Sale −		=	+1,000

JOURNALIZE

(4) Cash (+A)...	19,000		
Investment in Pincus (−A)		18,000	
Gain on sale (+R, +SE)..			1,000

POST

+ Cash (A) −	
(2) 2,000	15,000 (1)
(4) 19,000	

− Gain on Sale (R) +	
	1,000 (4)

+ Investment in Pincus (A) −	
(1) 15,000	18,000 (4)
(3) 3,000	

Mid-Chapter Review 2

Solution

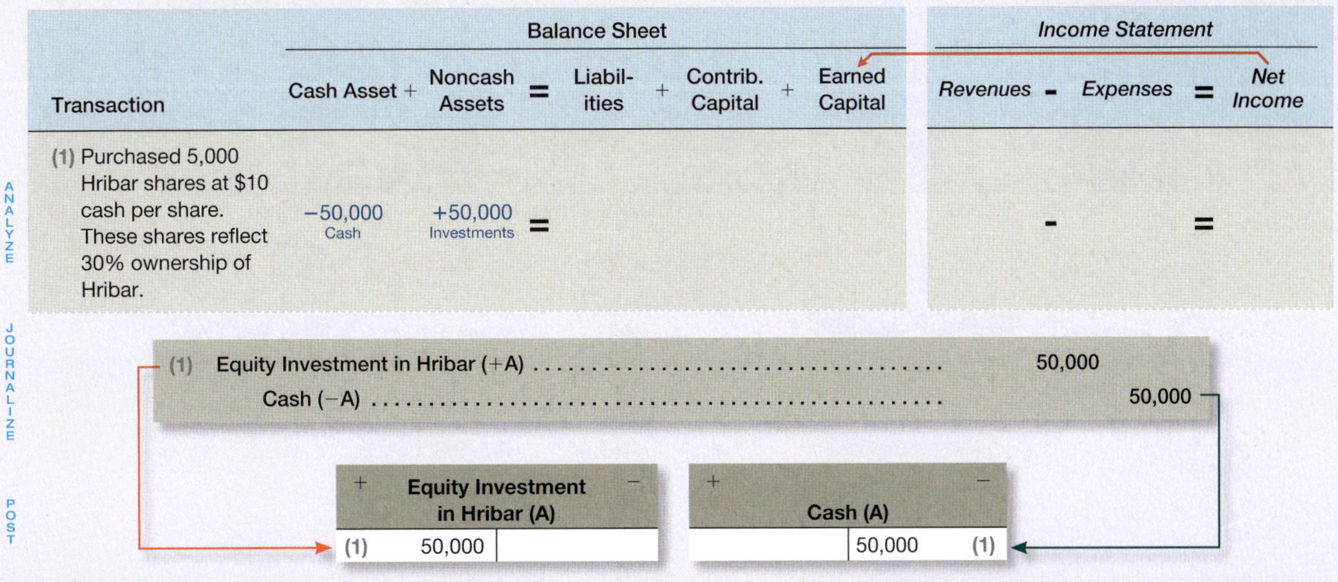

	Balance Sheet					Income Statement		
Transaction	Cash Asset +	Noncash Assets =	Liabil-ities +	Contrib. Capital +	Earned Capital	Revenues −	Expenses =	Net Income
(1) Purchased 5,000 Hribar shares at $10 cash per share. These shares reflect 30% ownership of Hribar.	−50,000 Cash	+50,000 Investments =				−		=

ANALYZE

JOURNALIZE

(1) Equity Investment in Hribar (+A)	50,000	
Cash (−A)		50,000

POST

+ Equity Investment in Hribar (A) −	
(1) 50,000	

+ Cash (A) −	
	50,000 (1)

continued

continued from previous page

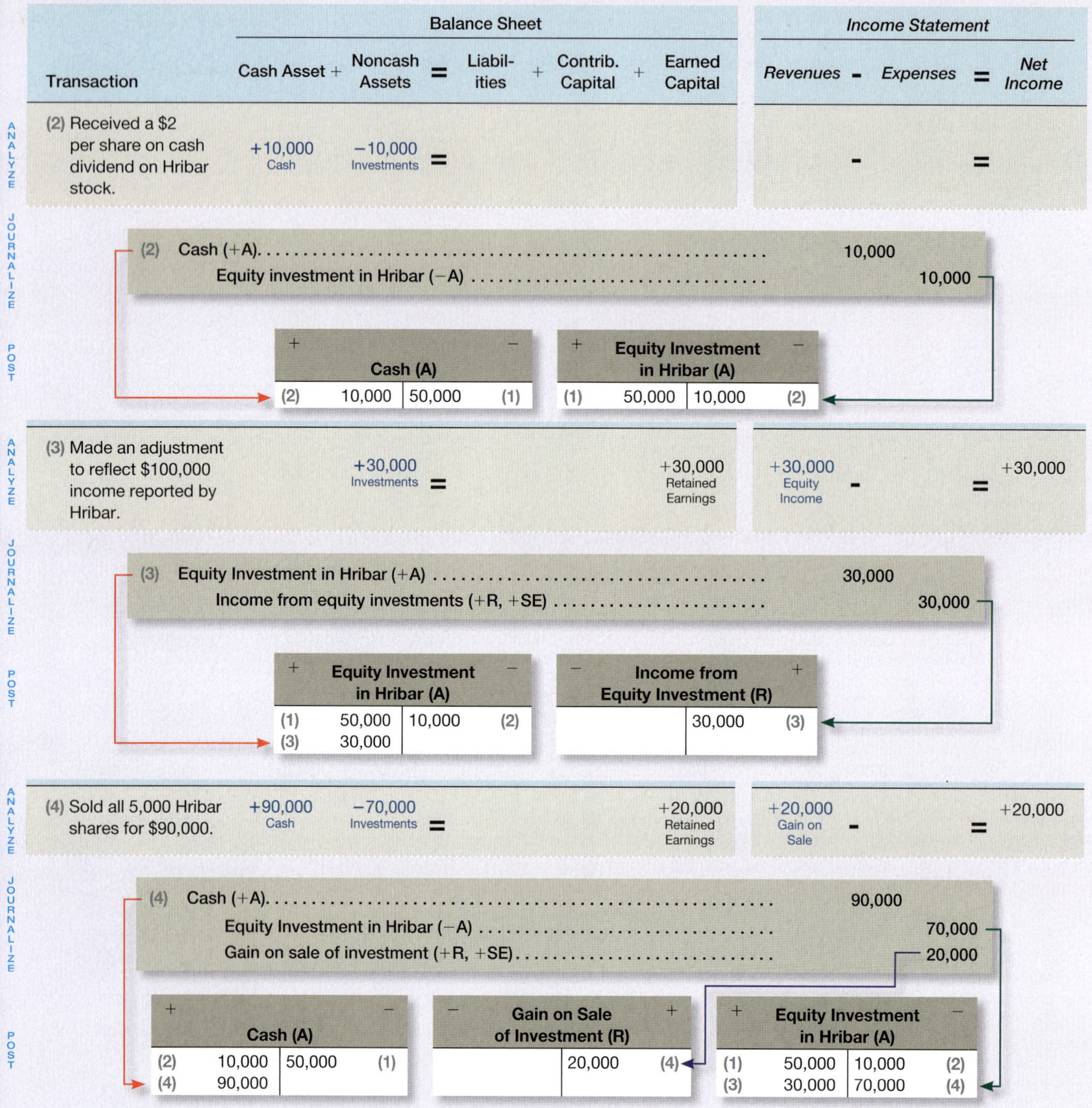

Chapter-End Review

Solution

	Balance Sheet						Income Statement		
Transaction	Cash Asset +	Noncash Assets	=	Liabil- ities	+	Contrib. Capital	+	Earned Capital	Revenues − Expenses = Net Income
(1) Consolidation adjustment for Bradshaw.		+100,000 PPE, net +100,000 Goodwill −600,000 Investment in Dukes	=			−200,000 Dukes Common Stock		−200,000 Dukes Retained Earnings	− =

(1)

PPE, net (+A)	100,000	
Goodwill (+A)	100,000	
Dukes common stock (−SE)	200,000	
Dukes retained earnings (−SE)	200,000	
Investment in Dukes (−A)		600,000

+ PPE (A) −	− Goodwill (A) −	− Dukes Common Stock (SE) +
(1) 100,000	(1) 100,000	(1) 200,000

− Retained Earnings (SE) +	+ Investment Dukes (A) −
(1) 200,000	600,000 (1)

	Bradshaw (Parent)	Dukes (Subsidiary)	Consolidating Adjustments	Consolidated
Current assets	$1,000,000	$100,000		$1,100,000
Investment in Dukes	600,000	—	$(600,000)	
PPE, net	3,000,000	400,000	100,000	3,500,000
Goodwill	—	—	100,000	100,000
Total assets	$4,600,000	$500,000		$4,700,000
Liabilities	$1,000,000	$100,000		$1,100,000
Contributed capital	2,000,000	200,000	(200,000)	2,000,000
Retained earnings	1,600,000	200,000	(200,000)	1,600,000
Total liabilities and equity	$4,600,000	$500,000		$4,700,000

Notes: The $600,000 investment account is eliminated together with the $400,000 book value of Dukes's equity to which it mainly relates. The remaining $200,000 consists of the additional $100,000 in PPE assets and the $100,000 in goodwill from expected corporate synergies. Following these adjustments, the balance sheet items are summed to yield the consolidated balance sheet.

A Compound Interest and the Time-Value of Money

Suppose you were lucky enough to hold a winning lottery ticket that allowed you to choose when you would receive your prize. Most of us would answer: Now! But let's say this ticket gave you the option of receiving $20,000 now, or $24,000 two years from now. Which would you choose?

Of course, $24,000 is better than $20,000. But the choice is not that simple. If you take the $20,000 today, you can buy a new car, pay next semester's tuition, or invest the money in the stock market. If you wait, you'll receive the larger prize, but you may have to take the bus for the next two years, postpone your college studies, or pass up on a great investment opportunity.

This is the essence of what is called the **time-value of money**. A dollar received today is worth more than a dollar received two years in the future. Having cash in our possession, gives us the opportunity to spend or invest that cash today. Cash received in the future cannot be spent or invested today.[1]

The easiest way to illustrate the time-value of money is to assume that we collect the $20,000 cash prize today and invest it in a money-market account that guarantees a 10% return on your investment. In one year, the investment would be worth $22,000—which is the original $20,000 investment plus $2,000 interest ($20,000 × 10%). At the end of two years, the investment would be worth $24,200 [= $22,000 + ($22,000 × 10%) = $22,000 × 1.10].

In the second year, the investment earns a return of $2,200, which is $22,000 × 10%. The interest earned in the second year is greater than the interest earned in year one because the interest earned in the first year earns interest in year two. This interest earned on interest is called **compound interest**. As interest accumulates on an investment, both the original investment and the accumulated interest will earn a return in subsequent periods.

This Appendix explains and illustrates the concepts of time-value of money and compound interest. It is divided into two sections: future value concepts and present value concepts.

Future Value Concepts

As illustrated above, $20,000 invested today to earn a return of 10% per year will accumulate interest and be worth $24,200 in two years. The $24,200 is referred to as the *future value* of $20,000 because it represents what $20,000 invested today at 10% would be worth two years in the future. The **future value** of any amount is the amount that an investment is worth at a future date if invested at a given rate of compound interest.

Assume that we allow our $20,000 investment to continue to earn interest for three years. The interest will continue to compound and the future value will continue to grow. This is illustrated in Exhibit A.1.

---

[1] The time value of money is primarily due to lost opportunities. However, the risk associated with some future cash flows will influence our assessment of their time value. That is, there may be some uncertainty associated with a future payment. For instance, in our lottery ticket example, there may be a possibility that the payer could default on the $24,000 payment. Risk is reflected in time value calculations by using higher interest rates for risky cash flows.

EXHIBIT A.1	Future Value of $20,000

Initial investment	$20,000
Interest earned in year 1 (initial investment × 10%)	2,000
Investment plus accumulated interest (future value) in 1 year	22,000
Interest earned in year 2 (year 1 amount × 10%)	2,200
Investment plus accumulated interest (future value) in 2 years	24,200
Interest earned in year 3 (year 2 amount × 10%)	2,420
Investment plus accumulated interest (future value) in 3 years	$26,620

As Exhibit A.1 illustrates, the future value of $20,000 invested for three years at 10% per year is $26,620. This can be calculated as $26,620 = \$20,000 \times 1.10 \times 1.10 \times 1.10 = \$20,000 \times (1.10)^3$. Similarly, if the interest rate is 8%, the future value is $25,194 = \$20,000 \times (1.08)^3$. That is, to determine the future value of an amount n periods in the future, we multiply the present value by one plus the interest rate, raised to the nth power:

$$\textbf{Future Value} = \textbf{Present Value} \times \textbf{(1 + interest rate)}^{\textbf{n}}$$

The future value of any amount depends on two factors: time and rate. That is, how many periods (e.g., years) into the future do we want to project the future value and what rate of return (or interest rate) do we use? There are two simple methods that we can use to obtain future values. The first method uses tables presented at the end of this Appendix. Table 1 presents the future value of a single amount. To use the table, move across the top of the table to choose the appropriate interest rate and then move down the column to choose the number of periods in the future.

For example, if we move across the top to the 10% column and the down to period 3, Table 1 provides a value of 1.33100. This is the future value of $1 in three periods at 10% interest per period and is called the **future value factor**. If we want to calculate the future value of $20,000, we multiply the *future value factor* from Table 1 by $20,000:

$$\textbf{Initial Amount} \quad \times \quad \textbf{Future Value Factor} \quad = \quad \textbf{Future Value}$$
$$\textbf{\$20,000} \qquad \times \qquad \textbf{1.33100} \qquad = \qquad \textbf{\$26,620}$$

The future value can also be calculated using a financial calculator. Financial calculators require four inputs to calculate a fifth value, which is the solution. We illustrate the use of a calculator with the following graphic:

Calculator				
N	**I/Yr**	**PV**	**PMT**	**FV**
3	10	20,000	0	26,620

On the financial calculator, N is the number of periods (3), I/Yr is the interest rate per period (10), PV is the current, or present, value ($20,000), PMT refers to a periodic payment (0 in our example) and FV is the future value. Because we are calculating the future value in this illustration, that value is highlighted in red as the solution.[2]

Whether we use the tables at the end of the Appendix or a financial calculator, it is important to recognize that these computations are based on an interest rate *per period*. Most interest rates are stated on an annual, or *per year*, basis. However, for compound interest calculations, a period need not be equal to a year. Therefore, we must always be careful to adjust our interest rate *per year* to the appropriate interest rate *per period* and use the corresponding number of time periods in our calculations.

To illustrate, assume that our $20,000 investment paid 8% annual interest, *compounded quarterly*. Although the interest rate is quoted as 8% *per year*, the rate is actually 2% every three-month *period* (=8%/4). Hence, in three years, we would have twelve periods. To determine the future value, we would go down the 2% column in Table 1 to the 12-period row to get a future value factor of 1.26824.

---

[2] Actually, most calculators return a solution of $-26,620$. The calculator interprets the PV as an investment (cash out) and FV as the return (cash in). So, if PV is entered as a positive amount, then FV will come back negative, and vice versa.

$$\begin{array}{ccccc}
\textbf{Initial Amount} & \times & \textbf{Future Value Factor} & = & \textbf{Future Value} \\
\$20{,}000 & \times & 1.26824 & = & \$25{,}365
\end{array}$$

Alternatively, using the financial calculator:

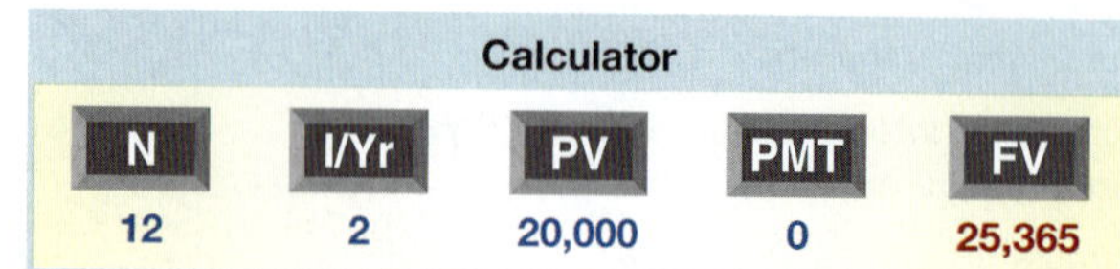

That is, the future value of $20,000 invested for three years at 8%, compounded quarterly, is $25,365.

Present Value Concepts

The concept of *present value* is the inverse of future value. Rather than determining how much an amount today is worth in the future, present value determines how much a future amount is worth today. The present value of an amount is the value *today* of a cash flow occurring at a future date given a rate of compound interest. As was the case with future value, present values depend on two factors: time and rate.

Present value is a particularly useful concept because it allows us to compare cash flows occurring at different times in the future. We can do this because we can calculate the value of each cash flow at a common point in time—today. For example, let's say we want to compare two investments. Investment A pays $15,000 in two years. Investment B pays $16,000 in three years. We cannot compare these two investments directly, because the payoffs occur at different times in the future.[3] However, we can determine how much each payoff is worth today. If the appropriate interest rate is 8%, the present value of Investment A is $12,860 and the present value of Investment B is $12,701. (We demonstrate how to compute these amounts below.) Hence, Investment A is worth more today than investment B. By determining the value of each cash payoff at the same point in time (today) we can easily compare the alternatives.

Present Value of a Single Amount   To determine the present value of a single cash payment occurring one period in the future, we simply divide the future cash flow by one plus the interest rate (the interest rate is also called the **discount rate**):[4]

$$\text{Present Value} = \frac{\text{Future Value}}{(1 + \text{discount rate})}$$

If the cash flow occurs *n* periods in the future, we divide by one plus the discount rate raised to the *n*th power:

$$\text{Present Value} = \frac{\text{Future Value}}{(1 + \text{discount rate})^n}$$

There are two simple methods for obtaining the present value of a single cash flow occurring at any date in the future. The first method relies on Table 2 at the end of this Appendix. We use Table 2 in the same way we used Table 1 to calculate future values. First, we choose the column representing the appropriate discount rate, and then we move down the column to select the number of periods in the future. The value in the table is the **present value factor**. We then multiply the future amount by the *present value factor* to get the present value.

For example, consider Investment A. From Table 2, the present value factor for 8% and two periods is 0.85734. The present value of $15,000 received in two years, discounted at 8% per year is calculated as follows:

---

[3] The reason that this comparison is difficult is that Investment A pays a return in two years while Investment B doesn't pay a return until year 3. One way to understand this complexity is to ask: What will happen to the cash earned on Investment A during the third year? Or, alternatively, if we invest the return on Investment A for an additional year, how much would we earn after three years? By comparing present values, we are implicitly assuming that any cash payoffs from either investment could be reinvested at the rate of return used to calculate the present value.

[4] The term "discount rate" is often used when referring to present values. This is because when future cash flows are valued using present value calculations, the present value is always less than the future cash amount. Hence, we say that the future value is "discounted" to the present value using the "discount rate."

$$
\begin{array}{ccccc}
\textbf{Future Amount} & \times & \textbf{Present Value Factor} & = & \textbf{Present Value} \\
\$15,000 & \times & 0.85734 & = & \$12,860
\end{array}
$$

The present value can also be computed using a financial calculator. In this case, N=2; I/Yr = 8; PMT = 0; FV = 15,000 and PV is our answer (highlighted in red).

	Calculator			
N	**I/Yr**	**PV**	**PMT**	**FV**
2	8	12,860	0	15,000

By similar means we can compute the present value of Investment B. The present value factor for 8%, and three periods is 0.79383. The present value of $16,000 received in three years, discounted at 8% per year is:

$$
\begin{array}{ccccc}
\textbf{Future Amount} & \times & \textbf{Present Value Factor} & = & \textbf{Present Value} \\
\$16,000 & \times & 0.79383 & = & \$12,701
\end{array}
$$

Or, using the financial calculator, we get the same answer as follows:

	Calculator			
N	**I/Yr**	**PV**	**PMT**	**FV**
3	8	12,701	0	16,000

Present Value of an Annuity Sometimes, we are faced with determining the present value of a series of regular, equal payments, called an **annuity**. For example, let's say we have an investment that pays $7,000 each year for the next three years. We can calculate the present value of each payment and then sum the results to get the present value of the entire annuity. Assume the appropriate discount rate is 6% per year. From Table 2, the present value factors for a 6% discount rate are 0.94340 for one period, 0.89000 for two periods, and 0.83962 for three periods. The calculation of the present value is presented in Exhibit A.2 (rounded to the nearest whole dollar):

EXHIBIT A.2	Present Value of an Annuity of 3 Payments of $7,000 Discounted at 6%		
Future Payment ×	**Present Value Factor**	=	**Present Value**
1 $7,000	0.94340		6,604
2 7,000	0.89000		6,230
3 7,000	0.83962		5,877
			$18,711

While this method of computing the present value of an annuity is accurate, it can be tedious for annuities with many cash payments. Table 3 at the end of this Appendix presents present value factors for annuities of various lengths. This table is used in the same way as Table 2: first we choose the column reflecting our discount rate, and then we choose the row representing the number of payments. From Table 3, the present value factor for an annuity of three payments discounted at 6% is 2.67301. To calculate the present value of an annuity, we multiply the periodic payment by the present value factor:

$$
\begin{array}{ccccc}
\textbf{Payment} & \times & \textbf{Present Value Factor} & = & \textbf{Present Value} \\
\$7,000 & \times & 2.67301 & = & \$18,711
\end{array}
$$

Or alternatively, using a financial calculator, we enter N=3, I/Yr=6, PMT=7,000, FV=0, and the solution is the PV, highlighted in red:

Calculator

N	I/Yr	PV	PMT	FV
3	6	18,711	7,000	0

Installment Loans One useful application of the present value of an annuity is to value an *installment loan*. An **installment loan** is a loan that requires a series of equal payments, or installments, each of which includes interest and some of the original principal. Assume that we take out a bank loan requiring 12 quarterly payments of $2,000 and an annual interest rate of 8%. When working with annuities, a period is the time between payments and the number of payments is the number of periods we use in our calculations. Because the payments are made quarterly, the 8% annual rate is compounded quarterly. That is, the effective interest rate is 2% per quarter. To calculate the loan amount, we use Table 3 to get the present value factor for 12 payments discounted at 2%, and then multiply the factor by our $2,000 payment, as follows:

Payment	×	**Present Value Factor**	=	**Present Value**
$2,000	×	**10.57534**	=	**$21,151**

Calculator

N	I/Yr	PV	PMT	FV
12	2	21,151	2,000	0

That is, if we agreed to make 12 quarterly payments of $2,000, including an interest charge of 2% per quarter, we could borrow $21,151.

A more common calculation would be to determine the loan payment given the amount borrowed. For example, if we borrow $30,000 and agree to repay the loan in 24 equal monthly payments at a 12% annual interest rate (1% per month), what monthly payment would we need to make to repay the loan plus interest? To compute the payment, we divide the present value (the loan amount) by the present value factor from Table 3 (1%, 24 periods) as follows:

Present Value	÷	**Present Value Factor**	=	**Payment**
$30,000	÷	**21.24339**	=	**$1,412.20**

Using a financial calculator, we can calculate the payment (PMT) directly, given the other inputs:

Calculator

N	I/Yr	PV	PMT	FV
24	1	30,000	1,412.20	0

Bond Valuation From Chapter 9, we know that a typical corporate bond has a face value of $1,000 and pays periodic interest payments every six months based on the stated (or coupon) interest rate. That is, the face value and the stated rate of a bond allow us to lay out the cash flows that will be paid to the bondholder. We also know that bonds are valued using the market interest rate, which may be different from the stated rate.

Bonds represent a combination of an annuity of the periodic interest payments and a single future payment of the face value, or principal payment, sometimes called a **balloon payment**. In order to value a bond, we must calculate the present value of each of these two components. Let's assume that we wish to value a $1,000, 5-year, 7% bond that pays a semi-annual coupon payment. The face value is $1,000 and the semi-annual payment is $35 (= $1,000 × 7%/2). Let's assume a market interest rate (yield) of 8% (which is 4% every six months). The bond is valued as the sum of two parts:

1. Use Table 2 to compute the value of the principal (balloon) payment.
2. Use Table 3 to compute the value of the annuity of interest (coupon) payments.

This calculation is illustrated in Exhibit A.3:

EXHIBIT A.3	Calculating a Bond Value Using Present Value Tables (4%, 10 periods)			
	Cash Flow	× Present Value Factor	=	Present Value
Face value: 1 payment of $1,000 at the end of 5 years (Table 2—4%, 10 periods)	$1,000 ×	0.67556	=	675.56
Semi-annual coupon payments: 10-payment annuity of $35 every six months (Table 3—4%, 10 periods)	$35 ×	8.11090	=	283.88
				$959.44

The bond value can also be calculated using a financial calculator, with the following inputs: N=10; I/Yr=4; PMT=35; FV=1,000. The solution is the PV:

Calculator				
N	I/Yr	PV	PMT	FV
10	4	959.45	35	1,000

The calculator automatically adds the present value of the annuity (10 payments of $35) to the present value of the single amount ($1,000 principal value) to get the bond value.

Calculating Bond Yields Sometimes we know the future cash payments and the present value of those payments, but not the discount rate used to compute the present value. This would be useful, for example, if we knew the price of a bond but wanted to determine the yield.

To illustrate the calculation of a bond yield, assume that we have a $1,000, 8-year, 5% bond that is currently priced at 104 (104% of par value or $1,040). The semiannual interest payment is $25 (= $1,000 × 5%/2) and the principal amount of $1,000 is due in 8 years (16 semiannual periods). We input the following values: N=16; PV=1,040; PMT=25; FV=1,000. The solution is returned by pressing the I/Yr button:

Calculator				
N	I/Yr	PV	PMT	FV
16	2.20	1,040	25	1,000

In this case, the calculator returns a solution of 2.20%. This is the interest rate *per period* that discounts the future payments on the bond to the present value of $1,040. Because each period is six months, we must double this rate to get the bond yield (or market rate of interest), which is always quoted on an annual basis. Thus the yield on this bond is 4.4% (= 2.2% × 2).[5]

---

[5] Technically, in order to obtain the result illustrated here, the amounts for PMT and FV must be entered with the same sign, but the PV amount must be entered with the opposite sign. For example, if we enter PV = −1,040, PMT = 25 and FV = 1,000, we would get the result above.

KEY TERMS

TABLE A.1	Future Value of Single Amount											$f = (1 + i)^t$
						Interest Rate						
Period	0.01	0.02	0.03	0.04	0.05	0.06	0.07	0.08	0.09	0.10	0.11	0.12
1	1.01000	1.02000	1.03000	1.04000	1.05000	1.06000	1.07000	1.08000	1.09000	1.10000	1.11000	1.12000
2	1.02010	1.04040	1.06090	1.08160	1.10250	1.12360	1.14490	1.16640	1.18810	1.21000	1.23210	1.25440
3	1.03030	1.06121	1.09273	1.12486	1.15763	1.19102	1.22504	1.25971	1.29503	1.33100	1.36763	1.40493
4	1.04060	1.08243	1.12551	1.16986	1.21551	1.26248	1.31080	1.36049	1.41158	1.46410	1.51807	1.57352
5	1.05101	1.10408	1.15927	1.21665	1.27628	1.33823	1.40255	1.46933	1.53862	1.61051	1.68506	1.76234
6	1.06152	1.12616	1.19405	1.26532	1.34010	1.41852	1.50073	1.58687	1.67710	1.77156	1.87041	1.97382
7	1.07214	1.14869	1.22987	1.31593	1.40710	1.50363	1.60578	1.71382	1.82804	1.94872	2.07616	2.21068
8	1.08286	1.17166	1.26677	1.36857	1.47746	1.59385	1.71819	1.85093	1.99256	2.14359	2.30454	2.47596
9	1.09369	1.19509	1.30477	1.42331	1.55133	1.68948	1.83846	1.99900	2.17189	2.35795	2.55804	2.77308
10	1.10462	1.21899	1.34392	1.48024	1.62889	1.79085	1.96715	2.15892	2.36736	2.59374	2.83942	3.10585
11	1.11567	1.24337	1.38423	1.53945	1.71034	1.89830	2.10485	2.33164	2.58043	2.85312	3.15176	3.47855
12	1.12683	1.26824	1.42576	1.60103	1.79586	2.01220	2.25219	2.51817	2.81266	3.13843	3.49845	3.89598
13	1.13809	1.29361	1.46853	1.66507	1.88565	2.13293	2.40985	2.71962	3.06580	3.45227	3.88328	4.36349
14	1.14947	1.31948	1.51259	1.73168	1.97993	2.26090	2.57853	2.93719	3.34173	3.79750	4.31044	4.88711
15	1.16097	1.34587	1.55797	1.80094	2.07893	2.39656	2.75903	3.17217	3.64248	4.17725	4.78459	5.47357
16	1.17258	1.37279	1.60471	1.87298	2.18287	2.54035	2.95216	3.42594	3.97031	4.59497	5.31089	6.13039
17	1.18430	1.40024	1.65285	1.94790	2.29202	2.69277	3.15882	3.70002	4.32763	5.05447	5.89509	6.86604
18	1.19615	1.42825	1.70243	2.02582	2.40662	2.85434	3.37993	3.99602	4.71712	5.55992	6.54355	7.68997
19	1.20811	1.45681	1.75351	2.10685	2.52695	3.02560	3.61653	4.31570	5.14166	6.11591	7.26334	8.61276
20	1.22019	1.48595	1.80611	2.19112	2.65330	3.20714	3.86968	4.66096	5.60441	6.72750	8.06231	9.64629
21	1.23239	1.51567	1.86029	2.27877	2.78596	3.39956	4.14056	5.03383	6.10881	7.40025	8.94917	10.80385
22	1.24472	1.54598	1.91610	2.36992	2.92526	3.60354	4.43040	5.43654	6.65860	8.14027	9.93357	12.10031
23	1.25716	1.57690	1.97359	2.46472	3.07152	3.81975	4.74053	5.87146	7.25787	8.95430	11.02627	13.55235
24	1.26973	1.60844	2.03279	2.56330	3.22510	4.04893	5.07237	6.34118	7.91108	9.84973	12.23916	15.17863
25	1.28243	1.64061	2.09378	2.66584	3.38635	4.29187	5.42743	6.84848	8.62308	10.83471	13.58546	17.00006
30	1.34785	1.81136	2.42726	3.24340	4.32194	5.74349	7.61226	10.06266	13.26768	17.44940	22.89230	29.95992
35	1.41660	1.99989	2.81386	3.94609	5.51602	7.68609	10.67658	14.78534	20.41397	28.10244	38.57485	52.79962
40	1.48886	2.20804	3.26204	4.80102	7.03999	10.28572	14.97446	21.72452	31.40942	45.25926	65.00087	93.05097

TABLE A.2	Present Value of Single Amount											$p = 1/(1 + i)^t$
	Interest Rate											
Period	**0.01**	**0.02**	**0.03**	**0.04**	**0.05**	**0.06**	**0.07**	**0.08**	**0.09**	**0.10**	**0.11**	**0.12**
1	0.99010	0.98039	0.97087	0.96154	0.95238	0.94340	0.93458	0.92593	0.91743	0.90909	0.90090	0.89286
2	0.98030	0.96117	0.94260	0.92456	0.90703	0.89000	0.87344	0.85734	0.84168	0.82645	0.81162	0.79719
3	0.97059	0.94232	0.91514	0.88900	0.86384	0.83962	0.81630	0.79383	0.77218	0.75131	0.73119	0.71178
4	0.96098	0.92385	0.88849	0.85480	0.82270	0.79209	0.76290	0.73503	0.70843	0.68301	0.65873	0.63552
5	0.95147	0.90573	0.86261	0.82193	0.78353	0.74726	0.71299	0.68058	0.64993	0.62092	0.59345	0.56743
6	0.94205	0.88797	0.83748	0.79031	0.74622	0.70496	0.66634	0.63017	0.59627	0.56447	0.53464	0.50663
7	0.93272	0.87056	0.81309	0.75992	0.71068	0.66506	0.62275	0.58349	0.54703	0.51316	0.48166	0.45235
8	0.92348	0.85349	0.78941	0.73069	0.67684	0.62741	0.58201	0.54027	0.50187	0.46651	0.43393	0.40388
9	0.91434	0.83676	0.76642	0.70259	0.64461	0.59190	0.54393	0.50025	0.46043	0.42410	0.39092	0.36061
10	0.90529	0.82035	0.74409	0.67556	0.61391	0.55839	0.50835	0.46319	0.42241	0.38554	0.35218	0.32197
11	0.89632	0.80426	0.72242	0.64958	0.58468	0.52679	0.47509	0.42888	0.38753	0.35049	0.31728	0.28748
12	0.88745	0.78849	0.70138	0.62460	0.55684	0.49697	0.44401	0.39711	0.35553	0.31863	0.28584	0.25668
13	0.87866	0.77303	0.68095	0.60057	0.53032	0.46884	0.41496	0.36770	0.32618	0.28966	0.25751	0.22917
14	0.86996	0.75788	0.66112	0.57748	0.50507	0.44230	0.38782	0.34046	0.29925	0.26333	0.23199	0.20462
15	0.86135	0.74301	0.64186	0.55526	0.48102	0.41727	0.36245	0.31524	0.27454	0.23939	0.20900	0.18270
16	0.85282	0.72845	0.62317	0.53391	0.45811	0.39365	0.33873	0.29189	0.25187	0.21763	0.18829	0.16312
17	0.84438	0.71416	0.60502	0.51337	0.43630	0.37136	0.31657	0.27027	0.23107	0.19784	0.16963	0.14564
18	0.83602	0.70016	0.58739	0.49363	0.41552	0.35034	0.29586	0.25025	0.21199	0.17986	0.15282	0.13004
19	0.82774	0.68643	0.57029	0.47464	0.39573	0.33051	0.27651	0.23171	0.19449	0.16351	0.13768	0.11611
20	0.81954	0.67297	0.55368	0.45639	0.37689	0.31180	0.25842	0.21455	0.17843	0.14864	0.12403	0.10367
21	0.81143	0.65978	0.53755	0.43883	0.35894	0.29416	0.24151	0.19866	0.16370	0.13513	0.11174	0.09256
22	0.80340	0.64684	0.52189	0.42196	0.34185	0.27751	0.22571	0.18394	0.15018	0.12285	0.10067	0.08264
23	0.79544	0.63416	0.50669	0.40573	0.32557	0.26180	0.21095	0.17032	0.13778	0.11168	0.09069	0.07379
24	0.78757	0.62172	0.49193	0.39012	0.31007	0.24698	0.19715	0.15770	0.12640	0.10153	0.08170	0.06588
25	0.77977	0.60953	0.47761	0.37512	0.29530	0.23300	0.18425	0.14602	0.11597	0.09230	0.07361	0.05882
30	0.74192	0.55207	0.41199	0.30832	0.23138	0.17411	0.13137	0.09938	0.07537	0.05731	0.04368	0.03338
35	0.70591	0.50003	0.35538	0.25342	0.18129	0.13011	0.09366	0.06763	0.04899	0.03558	0.02592	0.01894
40	0.67165	0.45289	0.30656	0.20829	0.14205	0.09722	0.06678	0.04603	0.03184	0.02209	0.01538	0.01075

TABLE A.3	Present Value of Ordinary Annuity											$p = \{1 - [1/(1 + i)^t]\}/i$
					Interest Rate							
Period	0.01	0.02	0.03	0.04	0.05	0.06	0.07	0.08	0.09	0.10	0.11	0.12
1	0.99010	0.98039	0.97087	0.96154	0.95238	0.94340	0.93458	0.92593	0.91743	0.90909	0.90090	0.89286
2	1.97040	1.94156	1.91347	1.88609	1.85941	1.83339	1.80802	1.78326	1.75911	1.73554	1.71252	1.69005
3	2.94099	2.88388	2.82861	2.77509	2.72325	2.67301	2.62432	2.57710	2.53129	2.48685	2.44371	2.40183
4	3.90197	3.80773	3.71710	3.62990	3.54595	3.46511	3.38721	3.31213	3.23972	3.16987	3.10245	3.03735
5	4.85343	4.71346	4.57971	4.45182	4.32948	4.21236	4.10020	3.99271	3.88965	3.79079	3.69590	3.60478
6	5.79548	5.60143	5.41719	5.24214	5.07569	4.91732	4.76654	4.62288	4.48592	4.35526	4.23054	4.11141
7	6.72819	6.47199	6.23028	6.00205	5.78637	5.58238	5.38929	5.20637	5.03295	4.86842	4.71220	4.56376
8	7.65168	7.32548	7.01969	6.73274	6.46321	6.20979	5.97130	5.74664	5.53482	5.33493	5.14612	4.96764
9	8.56602	8.16224	7.78611	7.43533	7.10782	6.80169	6.51523	6.24689	5.99525	5.75902	5.53705	5.32825
10	9.47130	8.98259	8.53020	8.11090	7.72173	7.36009	7.02358	6.71008	6.41766	6.14457	5.88923	5.65022
11	10.36763	9.78685	9.25262	8.76048	8.30641	7.88687	7.49867	7.13896	6.80519	6.49506	6.20652	5.93770
12	11.25508	10.57534	9.95400	9.38507	8.86325	8.38384	7.94269	7.53608	7.16073	6.81369	6.49236	6.19437
13	12.13374	11.34837	10.63496	9.98565	9.39357	8.85268	8.35765	7.90378	7.48690	7.10336	6.74987	6.42355
14	13.00370	12.10625	11.29607	10.56312	9.89864	9.29498	8.74547	8.24424	7.78615	7.36669	6.98187	6.62817
15	13.86505	12.84926	11.93794	11.11839	10.37966	9.71225	9.10791	8.55948	8.06069	7.60608	7.19087	6.81086
16	14.71787	13.57771	12.56110	11.65230	10.83777	10.10590	9.44665	8.85137	8.31256	7.82371	7.37916	6.97399
17	15.56225	14.29187	13.16612	12.16567	11.27407	10.47726	9.76322	9.12164	8.54363	8.02155	7.54879	7.11963
18	16.39827	14.99203	13.75351	12.65930	11.68959	10.82760	10.05909	9.37189	8.75563	8.20141	7.70162	7.24967
19	17.22601	15.67846	14.32380	13.13394	12.08532	11.15812	10.33560	9.60360	8.95011	8.36492	7.83929	7.36578
20	18.04555	16.35143	14.87747	13.59033	12.46221	11.46992	10.59401	9.81815	9.12855	8.51356	7.96333	7.46944
21	18.85698	17.01121	15.41502	14.02916	12.82115	11.76408	10.83553	10.01680	9.29224	8.64869	8.07507	7.56200
22	19.66038	17.65805	15.93692	14.45112	13.16300	12.04158	11.06124	10.20074	9.44243	8.77154	8.17574	7.64465
23	20.45582	18.29220	16.44361	14.85684	13.48857	12.30338	11.27219	10.37106	9.58021	8.88322	8.26643	7.71843
24	21.24339	18.91393	16.93554	15.24696	13.79864	12.55036	11.46933	10.52876	9.70661	8.98474	8.34814	7.78432
25	22.02316	19.52346	17.41315	15.62208	14.09394	12.78336	11.65358	10.67478	9.82258	9.07704	8.42174	7.84314
30	25.80771	22.39646	19.60044	17.29203	15.37245	13.76483	12.40904	11.25778	10.27365	9.42691	8.69379	8.05518
35	29.40858	24.99862	21.48722	18.66461	16.37419	14.49825	12.94767	11.65457	10.56682	9.64416	8.85524	8.17550
40	32.83469	27.35548	23.11477	19.79277	17.15909	15.04630	13.33171	11.92461	10.75736	9.77905	8.95105	8.24378

Glossary

accelerated depreciation Depreciation method in which more depreciation expense is recorded early in an asset's useful life and less in its later life

account An individual record of increases and decreases for an item in the accounting system

accounting The process of identifying, measuring, and communicating financial information to help people make economic decisions

accounting cycle The sequence of activities used to accumulate and report financial statements during a fiscal year

accounting equation The basic financial relationship that investing equals financing, commonly expressed as assets = liabilities + equity

accounts payable Amounts owed to suppliers for goods and services purchased on credit

accounts payable turnover Ratio defined as cost of goods sold divided by average accounts payable

accounts receivable Amounts due to a company from customers arising from the sale of products on credit

accounts receivable turnover (ART) Annual net sales divided by average accounts receivable (net)

accrual accounting The recognition of revenue when earned and the matching of expenses when incurred

accruals Adjustments that reflect revenues earned but not received or recorded and expenses incurred but not paid or recorded

accrued expense An expense incurred before payment is made, such as wages, utilities, and taxes; recognized with an adjusting entry

accrued income Any revenues or income for an accounting period that have been earned and realized, but are not received or billed

accrued liabilities Obligations for expenses that have been recognized and recorded but not yet paid

accrued revenue The value of services provided that have not as yet been billed or paid for by a client

accumulated depreciation A contra asset reported in the balance sheet; reflects the total depreciation recorded for an asset up to the balance sheet date

accumulated other comprehensive income or loss Accumulated changes in equity that are not reported in the income statement

accumulated postretirement obligation (APBO) A liability for benefits, such as health care benefits, to be paid after an employee retires

additional paid-in capital Amounts received from the primary owners of a company in addition to the par or stated value of common stock

adjusting entries Journal entries made at the end of an accounting period to reflect accrual accounting; rarely involve cash; usually affect a balance sheet account (an asset or liability account) and an income statement account (an expense or revenue account)

adjusted trial balance A listing of all general ledger account balances prepared after adjustments are recorded and posted

aging analysis Estimate of expected uncollectible accounts based on the number of days past invoices are outstanding

allowance for uncollectible accounts An estimate of the receivables that a company will be unable to collect; reported as a contra-asset

American Institute of Certified Public Accountants (AICPA) Professional organization of CPAs in the United States

amortization The systematic allocation of an account balance to expense; usually refers to the periodic writing off of an intangible asset

annuity A pattern of cash flows in which equal amounts are spaced equally over a number of periods

arm's length Any transaction between two unrelated parties

articulation The linkage of financial statements within and across accounting periods

asset a resource owned by the company that is expected to provide the company future economic benefits

asset turnover The sales to average assets ratio, which reflects effectiveness in generating sales from assets; also called *total asset turnover*

asset utilization The efficiency a company has in turning over assets

asset write-downs Restructuring activity where long-term assets or unsalable inventory is reduced in value in the company financial reports; also called *write-offs* or *charge-offs*

audited Financial statements that have been reviewed by an *independent party (such as an audit firm); financial statements that present fairly* and *in all material respects* the company's financial condition and the results of its operations

available-for-sale (AFS) Investments in securities that management intends to hold for capital gains and dividend revenue

average cash cycle (ACC) The average period of time from when cash is invested in inventories until they are sold; the addition of the average collection period and modified average inventory days outstanding less the modified average payable days outstanding

average collection period (ACP) A measure related to accounts receivable turnover, which is defined as average accounts receivable divided by average daily sales

average cost (AC) Inventory costing method that views cost of goods sold as an average of the cost to purchase all inventories available for sale during a particular period

average inventory days outstanding (AIDO) A companion measure to inventory turnover computed as average inventory divided by average daily cost of goods sold; also called *days inventory outstanding*

average payable days outstanding A ratio defined as average accounts payable divided by average daily cost of goods sold

B

bad debt expense The cost of uncollectible accounts; also called *provision for uncollectible accounts*

balance sheet A financial report based on the accounting equation that lists a company's assets, liabilities, and equity at a certain point in time

balloon payment A lump sum payment due when a bond or other loan matures

bank reconciliation A schedule that accounts for all differences between the ending balance on the bank statement and the ending balance of the general ledger's cash account, as well as determining the reconciled cash balance at the end of the month

basic EPS Earnings per share, defined as net income less dividends on preferred stock divided by weighted average of common shares outstanding for the year

big bath Situation where a company recognizes large write-offs in a period of already depressed income

board of directors Governing body of a corporation; elected by the shareholders to represent shareholder interests and oversee management

book value The dollar amount carried in the accounts of a particular item; the value of an item less its accumulated depreciation; also called *net book value* or *carrying value*

book value per share The net book value of a company available to common shareholders, defined as stockholders' equity less preferred stock divided by the number of common shares outstanding

bundled sales Two or more products sold together under one lump-sum price

C

calendar year A fiscal year that runs from January 1 to December 31

call provision A company's right to repurchase its own bond

capacity costs Operating expenses related to providing the ability to produce and sell products and provide services to customers; includes costs such as depreciation, rent, utilities, insurance and other related costs

capital The assets that provide value to the company

capital expenditures Financial outlays to acquire property, plant, and equipment

capital lease method Method of reporting leases that requires both the lease asset and lease liability to be reported on the balance sheet

capital markets Financing sources that often involve a company's issuance of securities (stocks, bonds, and notes)

capitalization The recording of an asset's cost as an asset on the balance sheet rather than as an expense on the income statement; these costs are transferred to expense as the asset is used up

capitalized To include a portion of an asset's cost on the balance sheet

capitalized interest Interest incurred during construction that is recorded as a part of the cost of a self-constructed (rather than purchased) asset

cash Currency, bank deposits, certificates of deposit, and other cash equivalents

cash accounting Accounting method where revenues are only recognized when received in cash and expenses are only recognized when paid in cash

cash and cash equivalents A balance sheet account that combines cash with certain short-term, highly liquid investments

cash discounts A price reduction offered by suppliers to buyers if payment is made within a specified time period; usually established as part of the credit terms and stated as a percentage of the purchase price

cash equivalents Short-term, highly liquid investments that are easily convertible into a known cash amount and are relatively unaffected by interest rate changes

cash flow from operations divided by net income An objective performance measure; the higher this ratio, the higher the quality of income

change in accounting estimate Adjustment in a generally accepted accounting principle, such as varying the time period an item is depreciated, that is applied prospectively from the date of change

change in accounting principle Adoption of a generally accepted accounting principle that differs from one previously used for reporting purposes

channel stuffing When a company uses its market power over customers or distributors to induce them to purchase more goods than necessary to meet their normal needs

chart of accounts Form that facilitates transaction analysis and the preparation of general ledger entries

check A written order directing a particular bank to pay a specified amount of money to a person named on the check

closing procedures Part of the accounting cycle in which the balances of temporary accounts are transferred into permanent accounts

collateral Mortgages on assets a company owns as security for debt financing

collectibility risk The chance that items sold on credit will not be paid in full

common-size comparative financial statement A financial statement in which each item is presented as a percentage of a key figure such as sales or total assets

common stock The basic ownership class of corporate capital stock, carrying the rights to vote, share in earnings, participate in future stock issues, and share in any liquidation proceeds after prior claims have been settled

comparative balance sheet Financial statement that compares the assets, liabilities, and equity of a company over several distinct periods

comparative financial statements A frequently encountered form of horizontal analysis that compares dollar and percentage changes for important items and classification totals

comparative income statement Financial statement that compares the revenues and expenses of a company over several distinct periods

compensating balance A minimum amount that a bank requires a firm to maintain in a bank account as part of a borrowing arrangement

completed contract method Revenue recognition method in which revenue is deferred until the contract is complete

complex capital structure Stockholders' equity that includes *dilutive securities* outstanding; required to report diluted EPS (earnings per share)

compound interest Interest that accrues on outstanding interest

compound journal entry A journal entry that involves more than two accounts

conceptual framework Guidelines developed by the FASB to provide a structure for considering future standards, as well as to guide accountants in areas where standards do not currently exist

consignment A type of sale in which a *consignor* delivers product to a *consignee*, but retains ownership until the consignee sells the product to the ultimate customer

consolidated financial statements An aggregation (an adding up) of financial statements of the parent company and all its subsidiary companies, less any intercompany activities

contingent liability A potential obligation, the eventual occurrence of which usually depends on some future event beyond the control of the firm; contingent liabilities may originate with such events as lawsuits, credit guarantees, and environmental damages

contra accounts Accounts used to record reductions in or offsets to a related account

contra-asset account A means to offset an asset account without directly reducing that account

contributed capital The net funding that a company receives from issuing and reacquiring its equity shares; the difference between what the company receives from issuing shares and the cost it takes to buy them back

controlling influence When a company owns a majority of another company's voting stock, such that it has the ability to elect a majority of the board of directors and, as a result, the ability to affect its strategic direction and hiring of executive management

conversion feature Contract provision that allows bondholders or preferred shareholders to convert their shares into common stock at a predetermined conversion ratio

convertible securities Debt and equity securities that provide the holder with an option to convert those securities into other securities

cookie jar reserve Accounting method in which income is shifted from the current period to a future period

core (persistent) components Elements of income that are most likely to persist and are most relevant for projecting future financial performance

corporation A form of business organization that is a separate legal entity from its owners; characterized by a large number of owners who own shares of equity and who are not involved in managing the day-to-day operations of the company

cost flow assumption One of several alternative methods used to account for inventory and cost of goods sold when input prices change

cost method Accounting method in which investment is continually reported at its historical cost, and cash dividends and interest are recognized in current income

cost of goods sold An expense reflecting the cost of merchandise or manufactured products sold to customers

coupon (contract or stated) rate The interest rate stated in the bond contract; used to compute interest payments during the bond's life

covenants Contractual requirements that the loan recipient maintain minimum levels of capital to safeguard lenders

credit entry An entry on the right-hand side of an account; used to record decreases in assets and increases in liabilities and stockholders' equity

credit sales A business transaction between companies where no cash immediately changes hands; also called *sales on account*

creditors Those to whom a company owes money; those who provide debt financing

currency translation adjustment The unrecognized gain or loss on assets and liabilities denominated in foreign currencies

current assets The most liquid assets, which can be converted into cash within one year or one operating cycle

current liabilities Obligations such as accounts payable, accrued liabilities, unearned revenues, short-term notes payable, and current maturities of long-term debt that are due within one year

current maturities of long-term debt Long-term borrowings that are scheduled to mature in whole or in part during the upcoming year, including accrued interest

current ratio Measure of liquidity defined as current assets divided by current liabilities; a ratio greater than 1.0 implies positive net working capital

D

debit entry An entry on the left-hand side of an account; used to record increases in assets and decreases in liabilities and stockholders' equity

debt-to-equity (DE) A common measure of financial leverage, defined as total liabilities divided by stockholder's equity

default The nonpayment of interest and principal or the failure to adhere to various terms and conditions of an investment

deferral An accounting adjustment in which assets and revenues received in advance of a certain accounting period are allocated as expenses and revenues during that period

deferred income taxes The difference between income tax expense as reported in the income statement and income taxes due to taxing authorities; reported in the balance sheet as either an asset or liability

deferred performance liabilities Obligations that will be satisfied, not by paying cash, but instead, by providing products or services to customers

deferred revenue See *unearned revenue*

deferred tax asset Situation when tax reporting income is less than financial reporting income; the deferred tax asset expires when the temporary difference reverses

deferred tax liability Taxes to be paid in the future when taxable income is higher than financial reporting income; also called *deferred taxes*

defined benefit plan Pension plan in which the company makes periodic payments to an employee after retirement, generally based on years of service and employee's age

defined contribution plan Pension plan in which a company makes periodic contributions to a current employee's account, which the employee may drawn upon following retirement; many plans require an employee matching contribution

definite life A determinable period of time that an intangible asset, such as a patent or franchise right, exists

depletion The process of transferring costs from the resource account into inventory as resources are used up

deposits in transit Deposits not yet recorded by the bank

depreciation The decline in value of equipment and assets due to wear, deterioration, and obsolescence; process of allocating costs of equipment, vehicles, and buildings to the periods benefiting from their use

depreciation and amortization expenses Write-offs of previously recorded assets added to net income as it is converted to net operating cash flow

depreciation base The capitalized cost of an asset less the estimated residual value

depreciation method Means of calculating the reduction in an asset's value over its useful life

depreciation rate Method of depreciation equal to one divided by the item's useful life

derivatives Financial instruments that are utilized by companies to reduce various kinds of risk

detection control An internal control a company adopts to discover problems soon after they arise

diluted EPS Earnings per share that includes stock options and convertible securities in the calculations

dilutive securities Securities that can be converted into shares of common stock and would therefore reduce (or dilute) the earnings per share upon conversion

direct association Recognizing a cost directly associated with a specific source of revenue at the same time the related revenue is recognized

direct method Accounting method that presents net cash flow from operating activities by showing the major categories of operating cash receipts and payments

disclosure The act of providing financial and nonfinancial information to external users

discontinued operations Any separately identifiable component of a company that management abandons, sells or intends to sell

discount Situation where a bond's coupon rate is less than market rate

discount rate The interest rate used in present value calculations

dividend payout ratio Dividend payments divided by net income

dividend preference The order in which shareholders receive dividends; preferred shareholders take precedence over common shareholders

double declining balance (DDB) method An accelerated depreciation method that computes the depreciation rate as twice the straight-line rate times the remaining balance of the asset

double entry accounting system The dual effects where, in order to maintain the equality of the accounting equation, each transaction must affect at least two accounts

E

earned capital The cumulative net income (losses) retained by the company; income not paid to shareholders as dividends

earned income Income in which the seller has executed its duties under the terms of the sales agreement and the title has passed to the buyer

earnings before interest (EBI) Measures the income generated by a firm before taking into account any of its financing costs; computed as Net income + [Interest expense $\times$ (1 $-$ Statutory tax rate)]

earnings before interest and taxes (EBIT) Measures the income generated by a firm before interest expense and income taxes

earnings management Discretionary choices management makes that mask the underlying economic performance of a company

earnings quality A measure of earnings in terms of sustainability, the ability for income to persist in future periods

economic consequences Issues resulting from accounting changes

economic value added (EVA) Net operating profits after tax less a charge for the use of capital equal to beginning capital utilized in the business multiplied by the weighted average cost of capital

EDGAR Database maintained by the SEC where financial statements are available for download

effective cost The cost to a bond's issuing company for offering the bond, generally as cash interest paid plus the discount or premium incurred

effective tax rate The average tax rate applied to pretax earnings; computed by dividing reported income tax expense by reported pretax earnings

employee severance costs Accrued (estimated) costs for termination of employees as part of a restructuring program

equity Capital provided by the company's owners, including stock, retained earnings, and additional paid-in capital; the owners' claim in the company

equity carve outs Corporate divestitures that are generally motivated by the belief that consolidated financial statements obscure the performance of individual business units

equity method Accounting method that reports investment on the balance sheet at an amount equal to the percentage of the investee's equity owned by the investor

equity valuation model A means of defining the value of an equity security in terms of the present value of future forecasted amounts

executory contract Situation such as a purchase order where a future sacrifice is probable and the amount of the sacrifice can be reasonably estimated, but the transaction that caused the obligation has not yet occurred

expense Outflow or use of assets, including costs of products and services sold, operating costs, and interest on debt, to generate revenue

expense to sales (ETS) A ratio measuring the percentage of each sales dollar that goes to cover a specific expense item; computed by dividing the expense by sales revenue

expensed Situation when a cost is recorded in the income statement and labeled as an expense

extraordinary items Material gains or losses that are not related to normal business operations; must be both unusual in nature and infrequent in occurrence

F

face amount The principal amount of a bond, which is repaid at maturity

fair market value The value of an asset based on current rates in the general public

fair value option Provides companies with the option of using fair market value to measure the value of most financial assets and liabilities

feedback value A characteristic of information that enables users to confirm or correct prior expectations

financial accounting The process of recording, summarizing, and analyzing financial transactions designed primarily for decision makers outside of the company

Financial Accounting Standards Board (FASB) Standard-setting organization which publishes accounting standards governing the preparation of financial reports

financial leverage The proportionate use of borrowed funds in the capital structure

financial statement analysis Identifying and examining relationships between numbers within the financial statements and trends in these relationships from one period to the next

financial statement effects template Form that captures each transaction and its financial statement effects on the balance sheet and income statement

financing activities Methods companies use to fund investment resources

finished goods Inventory account that records completed manufactured items waiting to be sold

first-in first-out (FIFO) Inventory costing method that transfers costs from inventory in the order they were initially recorded

fiscal year The annual (one year) accounting period adopted by a company for its financial activities

fixed commitments ratio The ratio of operating cash flow to fixed commitments; computed as operating cash flow divided by fixed commitments

fixed costs Expenses that do not change with changes in sales volume (over a reasonable range)

forecast error Differences between amounts reported in the financial statements and amounts forecasted in pro forma financial statements

franchise A contractual agreement that gives a company the right to operate a particular business in an area for a particular period of time

free cash flow The net cash flow from operations less capital expenditures and dividends

fundamental analysis Method of using a company's financial information to estimate its value, which is used in buy-sell strategies

funded status The difference between a company's pension plan assets and the projected benefit obligation

future benefits Revenues or some other compensation a company expects to receive in a later period

future value The amount that a specific investment is worth at a future date if invested at a given rate of compound interest

future value factor A value that is multiplied by a current amount to obtain its equivalent value at a future date; the value of $1 invested for a number of periods at a specified interest rate

G

gain on bond retirement Situation where the repurchase price of a bond is less than the net bonds payable

general journal A flexible journal that allows any type of business transaction to be included

generally accepted accounting principles (GAAP) An overall set of standards and procedures accountants have developed that apply to the preparation of financial statements

goodwill An intangible asset recorded when a company acquires another company, consisting of the value of a company above and beyond the fair value of its specific assets

gross profit The difference between revenues (at selling prices) and cost of goods sold (at purchasing price or manufacturing cost)

gross profit margin (GPM) A measure that reflects the net impact of sales on profitability, defined as gross profit divided by net sales

H

held-to-maturity (HTM) Debt securities that management holds on to for their full term

historical cost The original acquisition cost, less the portion that that has expired or been transferred to the income statement

horizontal analysis An examination of data across two or more consecutive time periods, which assists in analyzing company performance and predicting future performance

I

immediate recognition Costs recognized as expenses in a period when they were incurred, even though they cannot be directly linked to specific revenues

impairment Loss of property, plant, and equipment value determined by comparing the sum of expected future cash flows to the asset's net book value

income Also called *net income*, equals revenue minus expense, and is the increase in net assets (equity) resulting from the company's operations

income smoothing The discretionary management practice of choosing the timing of transactions in order to minimize fluctuations and maintain steady improvements in net income

income statement A financial report on operating activities that lists revenues less expenses over a period of time, yielding a company's net income

indefinite lives Situation where an intangible asset's expected useful life extends far enough into the future that it is practically impossible to accurately determine

indirect method Accounting method for preparing the statement of cash flows in which the operating section begins with net income and converts it to cash flows from operations

in-process research and development An intangible asset whose cost must be written off immediately upon purchase

installment loan Loan that requires a fixed periodic payment for a fixed duration of time

installment method Revenue recognition method which recognizes revenue when cash is collected, and records costs and gross profit in proportion to the amount of cash collected

insufficient write-down Impairment of assets to a larger degree than is recognized

intangible assets Assets such as trademarks and patents that supply the owner rights rather than physical objects

intercorporate investments Investments in the securities of other companies

interest cost Interest accrued on outstanding pension liability, which is added to the liability each year

internal auditing A company function that provides independent appraisals of the company's financial statements, its internal controls, and its operations

internal controls Policies and procedures used to protect assets, ensure reliable accounting, promote efficient operations, and urge adherence to company policies

International Accounting Standards Board (IASB) The governing body established to develop acceptable accounting standards on a worldwide basis

International Financial Reporting Standards (IFRS) Guidelines developed by the IASB with the intention of unifying all public companies under one global set of reporting standards

inventory Goods purchased or produced for sale to customers

inventory quality The rate at which inventory is turned over; the faster the turnover, the higher the quality

inventory turnover (INVT) Measure of inventory management computed as cost of goods sold divided by average inventory

investing activities Methods companies use to acquire and dispose of assets in the course of production and sales

J

journal A tabular record in which business activities are analyzed in terms of debits and credits and recorded in chronological order before they are entered in the general ledger; also called *book of original entry*

journal entries An accounting entry in a company's financial records that accountants use to represent individual transactions

L

last-in, first-out (LIFO) Inventory costing method that transfers the most recent costs from inventory first

leaning on the trade An increase in accounts payable, which results in an increase in net cash flows from operating activities

lease asset The value of a leased item

lease liability The payments required to lease an item

lessee A party to a lease who wishes to use the asset

lessor The owner of an asset

liability A probable future economic sacrifice resulting from a past or current event

licenses See *operating rights*

LIFO layer New layer added to inventory at an updated price each time inventory is purchased in companies using LIFO inventory costing; the most recent costs are transferred to cost of goods sold

LIFO liquidation Situation when, in companies using LIFO inventory costing, quantity of inventory sold exceeds that purchased, in which case the costs of older inventory is transferred to cost of good sold

LIFO reserve The difference between the cost of inventories using FIFO and the cost using LIFO

liquidation preference In the event of a company's failure, preferred shareholders are reimbursed in full before common shareholders are paid

liquidity The ease of converting noncash assets into cash

long-term debt Amounts borrowed from creditors that are scheduled to be repaid more than one year into the future

long-term debt-to-equity A common measure of leverage that focuses on long-term financing, defined as long-term debt divided by stockholders' equity

long-term investments Investments that the company does not intend to sell in the near future

long-term operating asset turnover The rate that reflects capital intensity relative to sales, defined as net sales divided by average long-term operating assets

loss on bond retirement Situation if a bond's issuer pays more to retire the bonds than the amount carried on its balance sheet

lower of cost or market (LCM) Process of reporting inventories at the lower of its cost or its current market value

M

maker Owner of a checking account

managerial accounting The process of recording, summarizing, and analyzing financial transactions designed primarily for decision makers within the company

manufacturing costs Expenses associated with product production, including materials, labor, and overhead

marginal tax rate The tax rate that applies to the marginal dollar of income; the tax rate generally applied to nonoperating revenues and expenses

mark-to-market Method of valuing assets that results in an adjustment of an asset's carrying amount to its fair market value

market rate The interest rate that investors expect to earn on their debt security investment; used to price the bond; also called *yield rate*

market value Company value computed by multiplying the number of outstanding shares of common stock by the market price per share

marketable securities Short-term investments that can be quickly sold to raise cash

markup The difference between an item's selling price and the cost incurred to produce it

matching Recognizing expenses in the same period that the associated revenue is recognized

minority interest An ownership in a company that is less than a majority or controlling interest

N

net assets Assets minus liabilities

net financial expense Net operating profit after tax less net income

net financial obligations (NFO) The difference between financial (nonoperating) obligations and financial (nonoperating) assets; positive if obligations exceed assets

net financial rate Net financial expense divided by average net financial obligations

net income The difference between revenues and expenses when revenues exceed expenses

net interest rate (NIR) The average interest rate after taxes on total liabilities; calculated as [Interest expense $\times$ (1 $-$ Statutory tax rate)]/Average total liabilities

net loss The difference between revenues and expenses when expenses exceed revenues

net-of-discount method Inventory capitalized at the net cost, assuming that a cash discount will be taken by the buyer

net operating assets (NOA) Current and long-term operating assets less current and long-term operating liabilities

net operating assets turnover (NOAT) A measure of turnover defined as sales divided by average net operating assets

net operating profit margin (NOPM) The amount of operating profit produced as a percentage of each sales dollar; excludes all nonoperating revenues and expenses; calculated as Net operating profit after tax (NOPAT) divided by Sales revenue

net operating profit after tax (NOPAT) Sales less operating expenses (including taxes)

net operating working capital (NOWC) Operating current assets less operating current liabilities

net operating working capital turnover (NOWCT) Management's effectiveness in using operating working capital, defined as net sales divided by average net operating working capital

net profit margin The income to sales ratio, which reflects the profitability of sales; also called simply *profit margin*

net realizable value The value of a company's receivables, less an allowance for uncollectible accounts

net working capital The difference between current assets and current liabilities; also called *working capital*

neutrality A characteristic of information that is free of any bias intended to attain a predetermined result or to induce a particular mode of behavior

nominal cost Cash interest paid on a debt

non pro rata distribution A case where stockholders can accept or reject the distribution of shares

noncash investing and financing activities Significant financial events that do not affect current cash flows, such as issuance of stocks and bonds in exchange for property, plant, and equipment

noncurrent assets Assets not used up or converted to cash in one year; include Long-term financial investments, Property, plant, and equipment (PPE), and Intangible and other assets

noncurrent liabilities Obligations such as long-term debt and other long-term liabilities that are to be paid after one year

non-operating revenues and expenses Costs related to the company's financing and investing activities, including interest revenue and interest expense

nonrecurring Revenues and expenses that are unlikely to arise in the future and are largely irrelevant to predictions of future performance

notes payable Account assigned to a company's financial borrowings

notes receivable Receivables that are based on a formal written promise to pay a specified amount and a predetermined date

O

off-balance-sheet financing A company's financial obligations that are not reported as liabilities in the balance sheet

on-balance-sheet financing The reporting of financing effects, namely current and noncurrent liabilities, on the balance sheet

operating activities Methods companies use to produce, promote, and sell its products and services

operating cash flow to capital expenditures ratio A measure that helps assess a firm's ability to replace its property, plant, and equipment, or expand as needed; calculated as operating cash flows from operating activities divided by annual capital expenditures

operating cash flow to current liabilities ratio A measure of the ability to liquidate current liabilities, calculated as net cash flow from operating activities divided by average current liabilities

operating cash flow to liabilities (OCFL) A method to compare operating flows to liabilities, defined as net cash flow from operations divided by total liabilities

operating cycle The time between paying cash for goods or employee services and receiving cash from customers

operating expense The usual and customary costs a company incurs to support its main business activities, including cost of goods sold, selling expenses, depreciation expenses, amortization expenses, and research and development expenses

operating expense margin (OEM) The ratio obtained by dividing any operating expense category by sales

operating lease method Method of reporting leases where neither the lease asset nor the lease liability is on the balance sheet

operating rights A contractual agreement similar to franchise rights, but typically granted by government agencies

options See stock options

ordinary annuity A series of fixed payments made at the end of each period over a specified time period

other long-term liabilities Various obligations, such as pension liabilities and long-term tax liabilities, that will be satisfied at least one year in the future

other post-employment benefits (OPEB) Benefits, other than pension benefits, such as health care and insurance benefits, provided by a company to retired employees

other postretirement benefits Items such as health care and insurance benefits offered to retired employees

outstanding checks Checks not yet recorded by the bank

overfunded Situation where pension plan assets exceed pension liabilities

P

par value Face value of a bond; in stocks, an arbitrary amount set by company organizers at the time of formation

participation feature Contract provision that allows preferred shareholders to share ratably with common shareholders in dividends

partnership A form of business entity characterized by two or more owners who are also usually involved in managing the business

passive influence Indicating lack of control of, or active participation in, the affairs of an investee company.

patent An exclusive right to produce a product or use a technology

payee The person named on a check who will receive compensation

payer The bank that will compensate the recipient of a check

percent change Financial statement adjustment computed by dollar change (analysis period amount less base period amount) divided by base period amount, with the result multiplied by 100

percentage-of-completion method Revenue recognition method which recognizes revenue by determining the costs incurred under the contract relative to its total expected costs

percentage of sales A means to estimate uncollectible accounts that computes bad debts expense as a percentage of total sales

periodic interest payment Interest payments made in the form of equal cash flows at periodic intervals

permanent account An account used to prepare the balance sheet; that is, asset, liability, and equity capital (capital stock and retained earnings) accounts; any balance in a permanent account at the end of an accounting period is carried forward to the next period

permanent difference A difference in amount between two financial statements that does not reverse in time

persistent An amount that is expected to be maintained in future periods; see also recurring

plan assets The assets of a pension plan that involve investments in stocks and bonds

planning activities The process of identifying a company's goals, and the strategies adopted to reach those goals

pooling of interests method A method of accounting for business combinations under which the acquired company is recorded on the acquirer's balance sheet at its book value, rather than market value; this method is no longer acceptable under GAAP for acquisitions occurring after 2001

post-closing trial balance Accounting balance prepared after closing entries are recorded and posted to verify the equality between debits and credits in the general ledger after the adjusting and closing process

posting The transfer of debit and credit entries from the journal to their related general ledger accounts

predictive value A characteristic of information referring to its ability to increase the accuracy of a forecast

preferred stock Stock that possesses priority over common stock, such as first right to dividends or liquidation payout

premium When a bond's coupon rate is greater than the market rate

prepaid expenses Costs paid in advance for rent, insurance, or other services

present value The amount of money a stock or bond is worth at the current time

present value factor A value that is multiplied by a future amount to obtain its equivalent value at the current date; the value of $1 received in the future discounted for a number of periods at a specified discount rate

prevention control An internal control companies adopt to deter problems before they arise

profit margin (PM) A ratio measuring profit, before interest expense, that is generated from each dollar of sales revenue; calculated as Earnings before interest (EBI) divided by Sales revenue

profitability The ability of a company to generate net income

pro forma financial statements Hypothetical statements prepared to reflect specific assumptions about a company and its transactions; often referring to forecasted financial statements

pro forma income GAAP income from continuing operations (excluding discontinued operations and extraordinary items), less transitory items

pro rata distribution Shares distributed to stockholders on a pro rata basis

projected benefit obligation (PBO) Pension liabilities that represent future obligations to current and former employees

property, plant, and equipment (PPE) Tangible assets recorded on a balance sheet, including land, factory buildings, warehouses, office buildings, office equipment, and other items used in the operation of a business

provision for income tax Income tax expense

Public Company Accounting Oversight Board (PCAOB) Board established by the Sarbanes-Oxley Act to approve auditing standards and monitor the quality of financial statements and audits

purchase method The prescribed method of accounting for business combinations; under the purchase method, assets and liabilities of the acquired company are recorded at fair market value, together with identifiable intangible assets; the balance is ascribed to goodwill

Q

quality of earnings The extent to which reported income reflects the underlying economic performance of a company

quick ratio (QR) A ratio that reflects a company's ability to meet its current liabilities without liquidating inventories

R

raw materials and supplies Inventory account that records items used in production processes

realized or realizable income Income in which the company's net assets increase

receivables quality The likelihood of collecting on a receivables account, which a company can change by extending credit terms, taking on longer-paying customers, and increasing the allowance provision

reconciled cash balance A company's cash balance after accounting for deposits in transit and outstanding checks

recurring An amount that is expected to be reported again in future periods; see also persistent

redeem Company repurchasing their bonds prior to maturity

relevance The usefulness of information to those who use financial statements in decision making

reliability The ability to objectively determine and accurately measure a value, such as historical cost

representational faithfulness A characteristic of accounting information referring to the degree with which it reflects the underlying economic events it purports to measure

residual (or salvage) value The expected realizable value of an asset at the end of its useful life

restructuring costs Expenses typically associated with activities such as consolidating production facilities, reorganizing sales operations, outsourcing activities, or discontinuing product lines

retained earnings Earned capital, the cumulative net income and loss, of the company (from its inception) that has not been paid to shareholders as dividends

return The amount of money earned on an investment, often expressed as investment income divided by the amount invested; also called *yield*

return on assets (ROA) A computation of net income divided by average total assets; also called *return on invested capital*

return on equity (ROE) The ultimate measure of performance from the shareholders' perspective, computed as net income divided by average equity

return on financial leverage (ROFL) A measure of the effect that financial leverage has on Return on equity (ROE); calculated as Return on equity (ROE) minus Return on assets (ROA)

return on net operating assets (RNOA) A measure of operating returns; calculated as Net operating profit after taxes (NOPAT) divided by Average net operating assets (NOA)

return on sales An overall test of operating efficiency defined as net income divided by net sales revenue; Increase in net assets (assets less liabilities) as a result of business activities

revenue The increase in equity resulting from the sale of goods and services to customers

revenue recognition The timing and amount of revenue reported by a company

revenue recognition criteria Requirements that must be met for income to be recognized on the income statement; according to GAAP, revenue must be realized/realizable and earned

revenue recognition principle Accounting rule that requires revenue to be recognized (recorded) only when earned

right of return The allowance for a customer to return a product within a specified period of time

risk The uncertainty of expected return, which is an intrinsic part of each investment

risk-free rate The market rate of interest defined as the yield on U.S. Government borrowings, computed as yield rate less spread

S

Sarbanes-Oxley Act Act passed in 2002 which requires a company's CEO and CFO to personally sign a statement attesting to the accuracy and completeness of financial statements

Securities and Exchange Commision (SEC) Commision created by the 1934 Securities Act to regulate the issuance and trading of securities

security valuation A determination of the value of equity securities

sell-off The outright sale of a business unit

sensitivity analysis The process of examining the effect of alternative assumptions on the pro forma statements; helps to identify these effects before a decision is made so that costly mistakes can be avoided

service cost The additional pension benefits earned by employees each year

shareholders' equity See *equity*

shares authorized The number of shares that a corporation can issue without amending its corporate charter

shares issued The actual number of shares that have been sold to stockholders by a corporation

shares outstanding The number of issued shares less the number of shares repurchased as treasury stock

short term borrowings Debt payable to banks or other creditors that is due within one year or within one operating cycle

short-term interest-bearing debt Short-term bank borrowings and notes expected to mature in whole or in part during the upcoming year

short-term notes payable Short-term debt payable to banks or other creditors

significant influence The ability of an investor to affect an investee's financing or operating policies

simple capital structure Stockholders' equity with no *dilutive securities* outstanding

sole proprietorship A form of business characterized by a single owner who typically manages the daily operations

solvency A company's ability to meet its obligations, mainly to creditors

solvency analysis A review of a company's ability to meet its financial obligations, which is aided by financial leverage ratios

spin-off A form of equity carve out in which a company distributes subsidiary shares it owns as dividends to its shareholders, making shareholders owners of the subsidiary

spread The difference between the net financial return (NFR) and the return on net operating activities (RNOA); also called *risk premium*

statement of cash flows A financial report that identifies net cash flows into and out of a company from operating, investing, and financing activities over a period of time

statement of responsibility Form included with each financial statement of a publicly traded company assuring management is responsible for the statements, they have been prepared using GAAP, and they are audited by an outside organization

statement of stockholders' equity A financial statement that reports on changes in key equity accounts over a period of time; also called a *statement of equity*

stock option A stock right giving the holder the right to acquire a share of stock at a preset price within a specified period of time; used to compensate officers and other employees

stock rights A stockholder's option to acquire a specified number of shares of capital stock under prescribed conditions and within a stated period

stock split A distribution (or increase in the number) of shares of common stock accompanied by a proportionate decrease in the par value

stock warrant A certificate that provides the holder with stock rights

stockholders Owners of a corporation; holders of shares of stock in a corporation

stockholders' equity See *equity*

straight-line depreciation Determination of annual depreciation expense by dividing the asset's cost by its estimated useful life

suppliers Providers of merchandise for resale or materials needed for operating activities

systematic allocation Costs that benefit more than one accounting period and cannot be associated with specific revenues

T

T-account A graphic representation of an account, shaped like a large T, which uses one side to record increases to the account and the other side to record decreases

tangible assets Assets that have physical substance, such as property, plant, and equipment

temporary account An account used to gather information for an accounting period; at the end of the period, the balance is transferred to a permanent owners' equity account; revenue, expense, and dividends accounts are temporary accounts

temporary difference A difference in amount between two financial statements that reverses in time

timeliness A characteristic of information that is received by decision makers before it loses its capacity to influence decisions

times interest earned (TIE) A determination of how much income is available to service debt, defined as earnings before interest and taxes divided by interest expense

time value of money The recognition that the value of an amount of money depends on when the money is received;

tombstone An announcement of debt offered to the public

trade credit The financing used to purchase inventories on credit from other companies

trademark A registered name, logo, package design, image, jingle, or slogan associated with a product

trading securities Investments in securities that management intends to actively buy and sell for trading profits as market prices fluctuate

transitory components Elements of income that are not recurring; financial projections are improved if these are excluded from them

treasury stock Shares of outstanding stock that have been acquired by the issuing corporation; a contra equity account

trend analysis A type of horizontal analysis in which a base period is chosen and all subsequent period amounts are defined relative to the base

trend percentages A comparison of the same financial item over two or more years, stated as a percentage of a base-year amount

U

unadjusted trial balance Account balances before any adjustments are made

underfunded Situation where pension liabilities exceed pension plan assets

unearned revenue Cash received for products or services to be provided at a later time

units-of-production method A common depreciation method in which the useful life of the asset is defined in terms of the number of units of service provided by the asset

unrealized holding gain A gain resulting from holding an asset such as inventory as prices are rising

unrecognized prior service cost An accounting adjustment to a pension that represents the portion of the liability earned by employees prior to the plan's inception or a plan amendment

useful life The period of time over which the asset in expected to provide economic benefits to the company

V

variable costs Expenses that change in proportion to changes in sales volume

verifiability A characteristic of accounting information referring to the ability of an independent auditor to reproduce the accounting information by examining the underlying economic events and transactions

vertical analysis A means of overcoming size differences among companies by expressing income statement items as a percentage of net sales and all balance sheet items as a percentage of total assets

vesting period A period of time during which the employee is not allowed to exercise a stock option; also refers to a period after which an employee retains his or her pension benefits even if employment is terminated

W

wasting assets Assets consumed as they are used, including natural resources such as oil reserves, mineral deposits, or timberland

weighted average cost of capital (WACC) The discount rate where the weights are the relative percentages of debt and equity in the capital structure and are applied to the expected returns on debt and equity, respectively

work in process Inventory account that tracks the value of items currently being produced

working capital Current assets less current liabilities

INDEX